Donated by
Dr. Archie Wortham

John Willis
Theatre World
1989–1990 SEASON

VOLUME 46

CROWN PUBLISHERS, INC.

201 EAST 50TH STREET
NEW YORK, NEW YORK 10022

T O
M A R T I N E . S E G A L
with gratitude for his encouragement of new talent, and for his many contributions
to the performing arts in New York City, including the New York International Festival of the Arts.

CONTENTS

Dedication: Martin E. Segal 2

The Season in Review 5

Broadway Calendar:
    Productions that opened June 1, 1989 through May 31, 1990 6
    Productions from past seasons that played through this season 40
    Productions from previous seasons that closed this season 49

Off-Broadway Calendar:
    Productions from previous seasons that played through this season 47
    Productions that opened June 1, 1989 through May 31, 1990 50
    Off-Broadway Companies Series 74

National Touring Companies 102

Professional Regional Companies 118

Annual Shakespeare Festivals 171

Previous Theatre World Award recipients 178

Theatre World Award recipients of 1990 179

Theatre World Awards presentations June 4, 1990 182

Award-winning Productions: Pulitzer, New York Drama Critics Circle, Antoinette Perry "Tony"
Awards 184

Biographical Data on This Season's Casts 185

Obituaries from June 1, 1987 through May 31, 1988 229

Index 233

EDITOR: JOHN WILLIS
Assistant Editor: Tom Lynch
Assistants: Herbert Hayward, Jr., Barry Monush, Stanley Reeves, John Sala
Staff Photographers: Bert Andrews, Michael Riordan, Michael Viade, Van Williams
Designer: Peggy Goddard

Entire cast of "City of Angels" with James Naughton, Kay McClelland and Gregg Edelman in lift. Honored as Best Musical of the season by NY Drama Critics Circle, Outer Critics Circle, Drama Desk, and Antoinette Perry ("Tony") voters. "Tonys" were also awarded James Naughton (Best Actor), Randy Graff (Best Featured Actress), Best Book, Best Score, Best Set Design. See page 24. *Martha Swope Photo*

4

THE SEASON IN REVIEW
June 1, 1989–May 31, 1990

After a bleak two years, New York experienced a diversified and optimistic theatre season; not completely satisfying, but encouraging, nevertheless. A survery by the League of American Theatres and Producers showed that theatre as a pastime ranks second only to baseball. Although the number of Broadway productions during the past few decades has decreased appreciably, Off-Broadway and regional theatres have provided an enormous choice of productions, and are helping "the fabulous invalid" to stay alive and active. This season seemed to indicate a move from the doldrums into a period of rejuvenation. Statistics show a third consecutive year with attendance and receipts on the rise, as well as the price of tickets. The average admission rose to $35.25 with "Jerome Robbins' Broadway" collecting $60 for orchestra seats. It was also a record high for the price of tickets to touring companies. There were more quality productions than in the past season, and it was a strong year for straight plays: 15 new plays and 6 revivals. There were 8 new musicals and 4 musical revivals. The two special productions were "Oba Oba '90" and "Mandy Patinkin: Dress Casual." At the end of the season, 16 new productions were still playing, in addition to those held over from past seasons. It is interesting to note that from December to March there was no Broadway opening.

Fortunately, this season's list of "Tony" nominees was not as embarrassing as in the preceding two years. The "Tony" for Best Play went to "The Grapes of Wrath," but its recognition did not increase ticket sales, nor prevent its early demise. Best Musical was awarded "City of Angels," as were Best Book, Best Score, Leading Actor in a Musical (James Naughton), Featured Actress in a Musical (Randy Graff), and Scenic Design. "Grand Hotel" received 5 "Tonys": for Best Featured Actor in a Musical (Michael Jeter), Musical Direction, Costumes, Lighting, and Choreography. Best revival went to "Gypsy," and its leading lady, Tyne Daly, received the "Tony" for Best Actress in a Musical. Best Actor in a Play was Robert Morse for his solo performance in "Tru," and from the play "Lettice and Lovage" Maggie Smith and Margaret Tyzack were voted Best Actress and Best Featured Actress, respectively. Charles Durning was voted Best Featured Actor in a Play for his "Big Daddy" in "Cat on a Hot Tin Roof." Alfred Drake received an honorary "Tony" for Excellence in the Theatre, and the Seattle Repertory Theatre received recognition for outstanding regional productions. The televised presentation ceremony in the Lunt-Fontanne Theatre was produced by Joseph Cates, and Kathleen Turner served as hostess. The Pulitzer Prize, and the New York Drama Critics Circle citation went to August Wilson's "The Piano Lesson.".

Other outstanding plays were "A Few Good Men" with award-worthy performances by Stephen Lang and Tom Hulce, "Prelude to a Kiss" with Barnard Hughes, Mary-Louise Parker and Timothy Hutton, "The Circle" with Glynis Johns, Stewart Granger and the late Rex Harrison in his last performance, "Love Letters" with two new artists every week, and "The Merchant of Venice" with Dustin Hoffman in a sold-out limited run. "Orpheus Descending" with Vanessa Redgrave again proved that a superstar does not always guarantee a long and profitable run. The curtain fell for the last time on Broadway's two longest running productions: "A Chorus Line" after 6137 performances, and "Oh! Calcutta!" after 5959 performances. "Cats" began its 8th year, and "The Phantom of the Opera" celebrated its 1000th performance.

In addition to the performers mentioned above, the following Broadway actors should be noted for their admirable efforts: Rene Auberjonois, Blair Brown, Georgia Brown, David Carroll, Rocky Carroll, Kevin Colson, Frances Conroy, John Cullum, Charles S. Dutton, Gregg Edelman, SuEllen Estey, Beth Fowler, Elizabeth Franz, Megan Gallagher, Betty Garrett, Tammy Grimes, Laurence Guittard, Bob Gunton, Jonathan Hadary, Linda Hart, Eileen Heckart, Tommy Hollis, Geraldine James, Donna Kane, Jane Krakowski, Terry Kinney, Eddie Korbich, Robert Lambert, Larry Marshall, Kathleen Rowe McAllen, Michael McKean, S. Epatha Merkerson, Debra Monk, Lilianne Montevecchi, Crista Moore, Milo O'Shea, Estelle Parsons, Sloane Shelton, Gary Sinise, Lois Smith, Christen Tassin, Marianne Tatum, Linda Thorson, Anne Twomey, Daniel von Bargen, Lee Wallace, Paxton Whitehead and Jason Workman.

Off Broadway continued its usual busy season with such enjoyable productions as "Forbidden Broadway '90," "A Bronx Tale" (Chazz Palminteri in a memorable performance), "The Widow's Blind Date," "Carbondale Dreams," "Closer than Ever," "American Bagpipes," "Adam and the Experts," "Juan Darien," "The Strike," "By and For Havel," Alec McCowen's incredible solo reading of "St. Mark's Gospel," "Hamlet," "Mountain," "Further Mo'," "Forever Plaid," "Smoke on the Mountain," "A Quiet End," "Elliot Loves," "The Rothschilds," "Ground People," "Beside Herself," "The Birthday Party," "Oh, Hell," "The Art of Success," "Bad Habits," "My Children! My Africa ," "The Waves," "When She Danced," "Bovver Boys" and "Spunk." "The Fantasticks" and "Nunsense" continued on their record-breaking runs.

Lincoln Center Theater had a less successful season than the past four, but continued to prove its theatres viable and worthy of any production. Its hit was "Six Degrees of Separation" that is apparently set for a long run. At the end of May, Joseph Papp announced a re-organization of his New York Shakespeare Festival staff, and released some of his authority and creativity after 35 years in a solo performance. He named Joanne Akalaitis (veteran of Mabou Mines) as his "Artistic Associate," and as resident directors he appointed George C. Wolfe, Michael Greif and David Greenspan. His Shakespeare Marathon has received mixed notices, but continues. Two new musicals, conceived hopefully to approximate the success of "A Chorus Line," and to help subsidize his complex, were not the anticipated hits.

Off-Broadway performances that deserve being remembered, were given by Jace Alexander, Elizabeth Ashley, Eileen Atkins, Alec Baldwin, Brent Barrett, Simon Brooking, Vernel Bagneris, Christine Baranski, Suzanne Bertish, Trazana Beverley, Fran Brill, Ivar Brogger, Graham Brown, Denise Burse-Mickelbury, Mike Burstyn, Kate Burton, Charles Busch, Joanne Camp, Erma Campbell, Len Cariou, Philip Casnoff, Stockard Channing, Topsy Chapman, Stephen Collins, Joan Copeland, Tim Curry, Ralph DeMatthews, Christine Estabrook, Patrick Fitzgerald, Peter Frechette, Lisa Fugard, David Marshall Grant, Anthony Heald, Gregory Hines, Dana Ivey, John Kani, Kevin Kline, Nathan Lane, Robert Sean Leonard, James Lish, Cleavon Little, Jeff Lyons, W. HL Macy, Lizbeth Mackay, Sally Mayes, James McDaniel, Rita McKenzie, Reggie Montgomery, Richard Muenz, Kate Nelligan, Kevin O'Connor, John O'Hara, John Pankow, Michelle Pfeiffer, David Pierce, Lonny Price, Faith Prince, Eric Riley, Peter Riegert, John Sala, Jean Stapleton, Colin Stinton, Eric Stoltz, David Strathairn, Sam Tsoutsouvas, Courtney B. Vance, Danita Vance, Elizabeth Van Dyke, Amelia White, Margaret Whitton, Kathleen Widdoes, Treat Williams, and Charlaine Woodard.

5

BROADWAY PRODUCTIONS

(June 1, 1989 through May 31, 1990)

SHENANDOAH

Book, James Lee Barrett, Peter Udell, Philip Rose; Based on screenplay by James Lee Barrett; Music, Gary Geld; Lyrics, Peter Udell; Director, Philip Rose; Choreographer, Robert Tucker; Set, Kert Lundell; Adapted by Reginald Bronskill; Costumes, Guy Geoly; Lighting, Stephen Ross; Musical Director, David Warrack; Casting, Karen Hazzard; Presented by Howard Hurst, Sophie Hurst, Peter Ingster; General Manager, Charlotte Wilcox; Props, Tom Ciacco, Jeff Wondsel; Assistant Conductor, Charles Homewood; Technical Direction, Jeremiah J. Harris Associates; Company Manager, Leo K. Cohen; Stage Managers, Mortimor Halpern, Jim Roe, Amelia Linden; Press: Joshua Ellis, Adrian Bryan-Brown, Jackie Green, Susanne Tighe, Tim Ray, Chris Boneau, Shannon Barr. Opened at the Virginia Theatre on Tuesday, Aug. 8, 1989*

CAST

Charlie Anderson	John Cullum
Jacob	Burke Lawrence
James	Christopher Martin
Nathan	Nigel Hamer
John	Stephen McIntyre
Jenny	Tracey Moore
Henry	Robin Blake
Robert (The Boy)	Jason Zimbler
Anne	Camilla Scott
Gabriel	Roy McKay
Rev. Byrd, Engineer	Donald Saunders
Sam	Thomas Cavanagh
Sgt. Johnson	Jim Selman
Lieutenant	Casper Roos
Tinkham	Richard Liss
Carol	Jim Bearden
Corporal	Stephen Simms
Marauder	Sam Mancuso
Confederate Snipers	David Connolly, Gerhard Kruschke

ENSEMBLE: Henry Alessan, Jim Bearden, Mark Bernkoff, David Connolly, Lesley Corne, Mark Ferguson, Brian Gow, Jennifer Griffin, Gerhard Kruschke, Richard Liss, Robert Longo, Sam Mancuso, Casper Roos, Fernando Santos, Jim Selman, Stephen Simms, Paul Mulloy (Swing)

UNDERSTUDIES/STANDBYS: Casper Roos (Charlie), Lesley Corne (Anne), Jennifer Griffin (Jenny), Fernando Santos (Jacob), Mark Bernkoff (John), Brian Gow (James), David Connolly (Robert), Z. Wright (Gabriel), Robert Longo (Sam), Richard Liss (Rev.), David Connolly (Corporal)

MUSICAL NUMBERS: Raise the Flag of Dixie, I've Heard It All Before, Pass the Cross to Me, Why Am I Me?, Next to Lovin' I Like Fightin', Over the Hill, The Pickers Are Coming, Meditation, We Make a Beautiful Pair, Violets and Silverbells, It's a Boy, Freedom, Papa's Gonna Make It Alright, The Only Home I Know

A musical in two acts with a prologue. The action takes place in the Shenandoah Valley of Virginia during the Civil War.

*Closed Sept. 2, 1989 after limited engagement of 31 performances and 17 previews. Original production opened Jan. 7, 1975 in the Alvin Theatre and played 1,050 performances. See *Theatre World* Vol. 31.

Martha Swope/Carol Rosegg Photos

(front) Tracey Moore, Tom Cavanagh, John Cullum, (back) Robin Blake, Burke Lawrence, Nigel Hamer, Stephen McIntyre, Christopher Martin, Camilla Scott Above: Moore, Cullum Top: Cullum

MANDY PATINKIN IN CONCERT: DRESS CASUAL

Paul Ford on Piano; Lighting, Richard Nelson; General Management, David Strong Warner; Stage Manager, Brian A. Kaufman; Press, PMK: Jim Baldassare, Lois Smith, Wendy Morris; Presented by Ron Delsener; Originally presented by Joseph Papp at the New York Shakespeare Festival's Public Theater; Opened in the Helen Hayes Theatre on Tuesday, July 25, 1989 and closed Sept. 16, 1989 after 62 performances.

Performed without intermission.

Peter Cunningham Photos

Mandy Patinkin

Mandy Patinkin

7

SWEENEY TODD

Music and Lyrics, Stephen Sondheim; Book, Hugh Wheeler; From an adaptation by Christopher Bond; Director, Susan H. Schulman; Choreography, Michael Lichtefeld; Music Direction/Design, David Krane; Scenic Design, James Morgan; Costumes, Beba Shamash; Lighting, Mary Jo Dondlinger; A York Theatre Production (Janet Hayes Walker, Producing Director); Presented by Circle in the Square Theatre (Theodore Mann, Artistic Director; Paul Libin, Producing Director); Assistant Musical Director, Jan Rosenberg; Casting, Julie Hughes, Barry Moss; Production Manager, William Hare; Wardrobe, Claire Libin; Props, Frank Hauser; Company Manager, Susan Elrod; Wigs, Paul Huntley; Stage Managers, Perry Cline, Trey Hunt; Press, Merle DeBuskey, Leo Stern. Opened in the Circle in the Square Theatre on Thursday, Sept. 14, 1989*

CAST

Jonas Fogg	Tony Gilbert
Policeman	David E. Mallard
Bird Seller	Ted Keegan
Dora	Sylvia Rhyne
Mrs. Mooney	Mary Phillips
Anthony Hope	Jim Walton
Sweeney Todd	Bob Gunton
Beggar Woman	SuEllen Estey
Mrs. Lovett	Beth Fowler
Judge Turpin	David Barron
The Beadle	Michael McCarty
Johanna	Gretchen Kingsley
Tobias Ragg	Eddie Korbich
Pirelli	Bill Nabel

STANDBYS: David Chaney (Sweeney), R. F. Daley (Sweeney/Jonas/Bird Seller), Annie McGreevey (Mrs. Lovett/Beggar Woman), Tony Gilbert (Judge), Rebecca Judd/Sylvia Rhyne (Beggar Woman), Carol Logen/Sylvia Rhyne (Johanna), Franc D'Ambrosio/David E. Mallard (Tobias), Bill Nabel/David Vosburgh (Beadle), Franc D'Ambrosio/David Vosburgh (Pirelli), Ted Keegan/Franc D'Ambrosio (Anthony), Carol Logan (Dora)

MUSICAL NUMBERS: The Ballad of Sweeney Todd, No Place Like London, The Worst Pies in London, Poor Thing, My Friends, Green Finch and Linnet Bird, Ah Miss, Johanna, Pirelli's Miracle Elixir, The Contest, Wait, Kiss Me, Ladies in Their Sensitivities, Pretty Women, Epiphany, A Little Priest, God That's Good, By the Sea, Wigmaker Sequence, Not While I'm Around, Parlour Songs, City on Fire, The Judge's Return, Finale

A musical in two acts. The action takes place during the 19th Century in London's Fleet Street and environs.

*Closed Feb. 25, 1990 after 189 performances and 46 previews. Original production opened Thursday, March 1, 1979 in the Uris Theatre (Now the Gershwin) where it played 557 performances. See *Theatre World* Vol. 35. This production played 24 performances last season for the York Theatre Company.

Martha Swope Photos

Top Right: Eddie Korbick, Beth Fowler, Sylvia Rhyne (seated), Ted Keegan, David E. Mallard (top, with cup), Tony Gilbert, Mary Phillips, Bill Nabel Below: Bob Gunton, David Barron, Jim Walton

Bob Gunton, Beth Fowler

Beth Fowler, Eddie Korbich

ORPHEUS DESCENDING

By Tennessee Williams; Director, Peter Hall; Design, Alison Chitty; American Costumes in association with Richard Schurkamp; Lighting, Paul Pyant, Neil Peter Jampolis; Electronic Score, Stephen Edwards; Sound, Paul Arditti; Casting, Johnson-Liff & Zerman; Management, Barbara Darwall; Presented by James M. Nederlander, Elizabeth Ireland McCann, by arrangement with Duncan C. Weldon & Jerome Minskoff; Associate Producer, Nicki Frei; Wardrobe, E. Kevin Woodworth; Assistant to Producers, Thom Schilling; Assistant Director, John Cagan; Executive Producer for Peter Hall Company, Thelma Holt; Stage Managers, William Dodds, Steven Shaw, Fred Tyson; Press, Joshua Ellis, Adrian Bryan-Brown, Jackie Green, Susanne Tighe, Tim Ray, Chris Boneau. Opened in the Neil Simon Theatre Sunday, Sept. 24, 1989*

CAST

Dolly Hamma	Patti Allison
Beulah Binnings	Sloane Shelton
Pee Wee Binnings	Pat McNamara
Dog Hamma	Mitch Webb
Carol Cutrere	Anne Twomey
Eva Temple	Bette Henritze
Sister Temple	Peg Small
Uncle Pleasant	Doyle Richmond
Val Xavier	Kevin Anderson
Vee Talbott	Tammy Grimes
Lady Torrance	Vanessa Redgrave
Jabe Torrance	Brad Sullivan
Sheriff Talbott	Manning Redwood
Mr. Dubinsky	Thomas Kopache
Woman	Constance Crawford
David Cutrere	Lewis Arlt
Nurse Porter	Marcia Lewis
Clown	Stephen Mendillo
1st Man	Thomas Kopache
2nd Man	Stephen Mendillo
Townspeople	Lynn Cohen, Richard McWilliams

UNDERSTUDIES: Joan MacIntosh (Lady Torrance/Carol Cutrere), Richard McWilliams (Val/Dubinsky/1st Man/Clown), Constance Crawford (Vee/Beulah/Dolly), Thomas Kopache (Jabe), Mitch Webb (Sheriff), Stephen Mendillo (Dog/Pee Wee/David), Lynn Cohen (Eva/Sister/Nurse), Fred Tyson (Uncle Pleasant/Delivery Man), Peg Small (Woman)

A drama in two acts. The action takes place in a general dry-goods store and part of the connecting "confectionary" in a small Southern town, during the rainy season, from January to Easter Sunday.

*Closed Dec. 17, 1989 after limited engagement of 96 performances and 14 previews. Original production with Maureen Stapleton and Cliff Robertson opened Mar. 21, 1957 in the Martin Beck Theatre where it gave 68 performances. See *Theatre World* Vol. 13.

Martha Swope Photos

Top Right: Vanessa Redgrave, Kevin Anderson

Vanessa Redgrave, Bette Henritze, Peg Small, Sloane Shelton, Patti Allison

Vanessa Redgrave

MASTERGATE

By Larry Gelbart; Director, Michael Engler; Scenery, Philipp Jung; Costumes, Candice Donnelly; Lighting, Stephen Strawbridge; Sound, Marc Salzberg; Video, Dennis Diamond; Video Music, Glen Roven; Casting, Meg Simon/Fran Kumin; General Manager, Steven Suskin; Wardrobe, Melanie Hansen; Assistant Director, Michael Sexton; Production Assistant, Jessica Murrow; Stage Managers, Cathy B. Blaser, Pat Sosnow; Press, Merle Debuskey, Bruce Campbell. Opened in Criterion Center Stage Right on Thursday, Oct. 12, 1989*

CAST

The Committee:
Senator Bowman, Chairman .... Jerome Kilty
Representative Proctor ....Tom McDermott
Shepherd Hunter, Chief Counsel ....John Dossett
Representative Byers .... Wayne Knight
Senator Bunting .... Jeff Weiss
Representative Sellers .... Jeff Weiss
Senator Knight .... Wayne Knight
The Witnesses:
Steward Butler .... Wayne Knight
Abel Lamb .... Steve Hofvendahl
Major Manley Battle ....Daniel von Bargen
Secretary of State Bishop .... Tom McDermott
Vice President Burden .... Joseph Daly
Wylie Slaughter .... Jeff Weiss
The Lawyers:
Mr. Child, Mr. Picker, Mr. Boyle, Mr. Carver .... Zach Grenier
For Total Network News:
Merry Chase ....Melinda Mullins
Clay Fielder .... Joseph Daly
TNN Director .... Katrina Stevens
TNN Cameramen .... Merrill Holtzman, Harold Dean James
Senior Staffer .... William Cain
The Wives ....Ann McDonough
Pages .... Charles Geyer, Isiah Whitlock, Jr.,
Priscilla C. Shanks

UNDERSTUDIES: Charles Geyer, Isiah Whitlock, Jr., Priscilla C. Shanks, William Cain, Zach Grenier, Katrina Stevens

The action takes place in Washington, DC, "the morning after" and is performed without intermission.

*Closed Dec. 10, 1989 after 68 performances and 24 previews.

Top Left: Daniel von Bargen (center) Below: Jerome Kilty, Tom McDermott

Jeff Weiss, John Dossett Above: Daniel von Bargen, Melinda Mullins

Melinda Mullins, Daniel von Bargen, Zach Grenier

DANGEROUS GAMES

Music, Astor Piazzolla; Lyrics, William Finn; Book, Jim Lewis, Graciela Daniele; Conceived, Choreographed, Directed by Graciela Daniele; Co-Choreographer, Tina Paul; Scenery, Tony Straiges; Costumes, Patricia Zipprodt; Lighting, Peggy Eisenhouer; Sound, Otts Munderloh; Musical Direction/Arrangements, James Kowal; Musical Consultant/Arrangements, Rodolfo Alchourron; Fight Direction, B. H. Barry, Luis Perez; Music Coordinator, John Monaco; Casting, Brian Chavanne, Julie Mossberg; General Management, Marvin A. Krauss, Joey Parnes; Presented by Jules Fisher, James M. Nederlander, Arthur Rubin in association with Mary Kantor; Company Manager, Beth Fremgen; Props, Charlie Zuckerman; Wardrobe, Linda Lee; Dance Captain, John Mineo; Stage Managers, Robert Mark Kalfin, Paula Gray; Press, Shirley Herz Associates/Robert Larkin, Sam Rudy, Glenna Freedman, Pete Sanders. Opened in the Nederlander Theatre on Thursday, Oct. 19, 1989*

CAST

TANGO:
Delia, the Madam .... Dana Moore
The Men: Felipe .... Philip Jerry
      Ricardo .... Richard Amaro
      Carlos .... Ken Ard
The Women: Renata .... Rene Ceballos
      Diana .... Diana Laurenson
      Maria .... Malinda Shaffer
      Adriana .... Adrienne Hurd-Sharlein
The Brothers: Juan .... John Mineo
      Gregorio .... Gregory Mitchell or Luis Perez
Cristina, the new whore .... Tina Paul or Elizabeth Mozer
ORFEO:
Orfeo .... Gregory Mitchell or Luis Perez
Dicha .... Rene Ceballos
Aurora, a child .... Danyelle Weaver
Pluton .... Ken Ard
Nora/Lascivia .... Tina Paul or Elizabeth Mozer
Antares/Altivo .... John Mineo
Mira/Codicia .... Dana Moore
Lyrae/LaGula .... Malinda Shaffer
Cleo/Envidia .... Diana Laurenson
Alberio/Ira .... Marc Villa
Ursula/Malicia .... Adrienne Hurd-Sharlein
Leon/Mentira .... Philip Jerry
Arturo/Charon/Perez .... Richard Amaro
Bambo Player .... Adrian Brito
THE QUINTET:
Guitar .... Rodolfo Alchourron
Bass/Bamboo Flute .... Jorge Alfano
Bandoneon .... Miguel Arrabal
Violin .... Jon Kass
Piano/Conductor .... James Kowal
Offstage Vocals .... Rene Ceballos

Performed with one intermission.

*Closed Oct. 21, 1989 after 4 performances and 12 previews.

Martha Swope Photos

Top Left: Rene Ceballos, Gregory Mitchell Below: Tango

John Mineo, Gregory Mitchell Above: Rene Ceballos, Mitchell

Gregory Mitchell, Rene Ceballos

TAKARAZUKA

Producer, Kohei Kobayashi; President, Haruhiko Saka; Artistic Directors, Shinju Ueda, Hirotoshi Ohara; Composers/Arrangers, Takio Terada, Kenji Yoshizaki, Kaoru Irie, Kazuakira Hashimoto, Toshiko Yonekawa; Conductor, Kazuakira Hashimoto; Choreographers, Yoshijiro Hanayagi, Mayumi Nishizaki, Eiken Fujima, Hagi Hanayagi, Kiyomi Hayama, Taku Yamada, Roger Minami; Sets, Hideo Ishihama, Toshiaki Sekiya; Costumes, Harumi Tokoro, Kikue Nakagawa, Ikuei Touda; Lighting, Naoji Imai, Ken Billington; Assistant Directors, Masazumi Tani, Masaya Ishida; Management, ICM Artists in cooperation with Toho International; General Manager, Kenichi Takano; Manager, Ken IIjima; Props, Magoichi Macoka; Wardrobe, Tacko Chiyoda; Press, Jeffrey Richards Associates/Irene Gandy, Susan Chicoine, Jillana Devine. Opened in Radio City Music Hall on Wednesday, Oct. 25, 1989*

PROGRAM

PART I: Prologue/Takarazuka March, Snow Moon and Flower, Icy Moon, Swirling Snow, The Cherry Flower,
PART II: Prologue, Takarazuka Forever, A Pretty Girl Is Like a Melody, Flower Fantasy, I'll String Along with You, I Only Have Eyes for You, Arabian Dream, Keep Young and Beautiful, Piano Fantasy, Finale

A revue in two acts.

*Closed Oct. 29, 1989 after limited engagement of 6 performances.

Right and Top: Takarazuka

John Rubinstein, Stockard Channing

LOVE LETTERS

By A. R. Gurney; Director, John Tillinger; Lighting, Dennis Parichy; Casting, Linda Wright; General Management, Richard Frankel, Marc Routh; Company Manager, Kim Sellon; Press, Joshua Ellis, Adrian Bryan-Brown, Jackie Green, Susanne Tighe, Tim Ray, Chris Boneau. Opened in the Edison Theatre on Tuesday, Oct. 31, 1989*

CAST

Colleen Dewhurst and Jason Robards (10/31/89–11/5/89), Stockard Channing and John Rubinstein (11/7/89–11/12/89), Swoosie Kurtz and Richard Thomas (11/14–19/89), David Dukes and Kate Nelligan, Timothy Hutton and Elizabeth McGovern, John Clark and Lynn Redgrave, Polly Bergen and Robert Vaughn, Kate Nelligan and Treat Williams, Cliff Robertson and Elaine Stritch, Ken Howard and Donna Mills, Dick Cavett and Carrie Nye.

A two character play in two acts. It relates the lifelong relationship between Andrew Makepeace Ladd III and Melissa Gardner entirely from their correspondence.

*Closed Jan. 21, 1990 after 96 performances. It had previously played 64 performances Off-Broadway in the Promenade Theatre.

Left Center: Swoosie Kurtz Right Center: Edward Herrmann

THE SECRET RAPTURE

By David Hare; Director, Mr. Hare; Scenery, Santo Loquasto; Costumes, Jane Greenwood; Lighting, Richard Nelson; Music, Nick Bicat; Casting, Rosemarie Tichler/Nancy Piccione; Presented by Joseph Papp and the Shubert Organization; Associate Producer, Jason Steven Cohen; General Managers, Bob MacDonald, Susan Sampliner; Company Manager, Steven H. David; Props, Patricia Avery; Wardrobe, W. Tony Powell; Hair Design, Aaron F. Quarles; Stage Managers, Karen Armstrong, Buzz Cohen; Press, Richard Kornberg, Barbara Carroll, Reva Cooper, Carol Fineman, Steve Krementz. Opened in the Ethel Barrymore Theatre on Thursday, Oct. 26, 1989*

CAST

Isobel Glass	Blair Brown
Marion French	Frances Conroy
Tom French	Stephen Vinovich
Katherine Glass	Mary Beth Hurt
Irwin Posner	Michael Wincott
Rhonda Milne	Jennifer Van Dyck

UNDERSTUDIES: Alma Cuervo (Isobel/Marion), Joyce O'Connor (Katherine/Rhonda), Armand Schultz (Irwin/Tom)

A drama in two acts and eight scenes. The action takes place at the present time in England.

*Closed Nov. 4, 1989 after 12 performances and 19 previews. It had played 22 performances in the Public Theater (Sept. 8–27, 1989) prior to its Broadway opening.

Martha Swope Photos

Top Right: Mary Beth Hurt, Blair Brown

Frances Conroy, Mary Beth Hurt, Stephen Vinovich Center: Blair Brown, Michael Wincott

SID CAESAR & COMPANY
Does Anybody Know What I'm Talking About?

Director, Martin Charnin; Scenery/Lighting, Neil Peter Jampolis; Costumes, Karen Roston; Sound, Bruce Cameron; Musical Director, Elliot Finkel; Original Songs, Martin Charnin; General Management, Darwall von Mayrhauser; Presented by Ivan Bloch and Harold Thau in association with Larry Spellman; Associate Producers, J. Scott Broder, Sonny Bloch, Robert Courson; Company Manager, Marcia Goldberg; Technical Director, Peter Fulbright; Props, Sal Sciafani; Production Associate, Jolie Gabler; Stage Managers, Frank Hartenstein, Jonathan Secor; Press, Solters/Roskin/ Friedman, Keith Sherman, Robert Pini, Bonnie Benstar, Scott Gorenstein. Opened in the John Golden Theatre on Wednesday, Nov. 1, 1989*
COMPANY: Lee Delano, Linda Hart, Lubitza Gregus, Peter Shawn, Laura Turnbull, Erick Devine, Carolyn Michel, and starring Sid Caesar
PROGRAM: Sleep, A Boy at His First Dance, A Man Walking Down the Aisle, Zero Hour, A Man with His Wife Arguing to the First Movement of Beethoven's Fifth Symphony, The Last Angry Bull, At the Movies, We Aren't Fooling Anyone, The World through the Eyes of a Baby, The Penny Candy Machine, The Greig Piano Concerto, The Professor, Make a New Now, Now!

Performed with one intermission.

*Closed Nov. 5, 1989 after 5 performances and 6 previews.

Peter Cunningham Photos

Top: Erick Devine, Lee Delano, Carolyn Michel, Sid Caesar, Lubitza Gregus, Peter Shawn, Linda Hart, Laura Turnbull

Carolyn Michel, Peter Shawn, Linda Hart, Sid Caesar, Lee Delano, Laura Turnbull, Erick Devine, Lubitza Gregus
Center: Caesar

MEET ME IN ST. LOUIS

Songs, Hugh Martin & Ralph Blane; Book, Hugh Wheeler; Based on "The Kensington Stories" by Sally Benson and the MGM film "Meet Me in St. Louis"; Director, Louis Burke; Choreographer, Joan Brickhill; Assistant Director, Lonnie Chase; Associate Choreographer, Herman-Jay Muller; Production Design, Keith Anderson; Lighting, Ken Billington; Musical Supervisor, Milton Rosenstock; Musical Director, Bruce Pomahac; Orchestrations, Michael Gibson; Dance Arranger, James Raitt; Sound, Alan Stieb, James Brousseau; Vocal Arrangers, Hugh Martin, Bruce Pomahac; Ice Choreographer, Michael Tokar; Casting, Jay Binder; Hairstylist, Jean Block; General Management, Weiler/Miller/Carrellas; Presented by Brickhill-Burke Productions, Christopher Seabrooke and EPI Products; Associate Producers, Loren Krok, P. K. Sloman, L. Everett Chase; Props, Michael Durnin, Will Sweeney; Original Cast Recording on DRG; Wardrobe, Nancy Schaefer, James Nadeau; Stage Managers, Robert Bennett, Jay Adler, Robin Rumpf, Jim Semmelman; Press, Joshua Ellis Office/Adrian Bryan-Brown, Jackie Green, Susanne Tighe, Tim Ray, Chris Boneau, Aaron Deutchman. Opened in the Gershwin Theatre on Thursday, Nov. 2, 1989*

CAST

Lon Smith	Michael O'Steen†1
Randy Travis	Brian Jay
Katie	Betty Garrett
Motorman	Jim Semmelman
Tootie Smith	Courtney Peldon
Mrs. Smith	Charlotte Moore
Grandpa Prophater	Milo O'Shea
Esther Smith	Donna Kane
Rose Smith	Juliet Lambert'
John Truitt	Jason Workman
Agnes Smith	Rachael Graham
Mr. Alonzo Smith	George Hearn
Warren Sheffield	Peter Reardon†2
Ida Boothby	Naomi Reddin
Douglas Moore	Gregg Whitney
Eve Finley	Shauna Hicks
Dr. Bond	Gordon Stanley†3
Lucille Ballard	Karen Culliver†4
Clinton A. Badger	Craig A. Meyer

ENSEMBLE: Kevin Backstrom, Dan Buelow, Victoria Lynn Burton, Karen Culliver, Deanna Dys, H. David Gunderman, Shauna Hicks, K. Craig Innes, Brian Jay, Rachel Jones, Nancy Lemenager, Joanne McHugh, Frank Maio, Carol Lee Meadows, Craig A. Meyer, Christopher Lee Michaels, Ron Morgan, Georga L. Osborne, Rachelle Ottley, Christina Pawl, Naomi Reddin, Carol Schuberg, Jim Semmelman, Ken Shepski, Gordon Stanley, Sean Frank Sullivan, Cynthia Thole, Gregg Whitney, Kyle Whyte, Lee Wilson
UNDERSTUDIES: Gordon Stanley (Father/Grandpa), Cynthia Thole (Mrs. Smith), Georga L. Osborne (Katie), Shauna Hicks (Esther), Victoria Lynn Burton (Tootie/Agnes), Christopher Lee Michaels (John Truitt), Rachelle Ottley (Rose Lucille), H. David Gunderman (Lon), Sean Frank Sullivan (Warren), Ken Shepski (Douglas), Christopher Lee Michaels (Motorman), Dance Captains: Carol Schulberg, K. Craig Innes
MUSICAL NUMBERS: Meet Me in St. Louis, The Boy Next Door, Be Anything But a Girl, Skip to My Lou, Under the Bamboo Tree, Banjos, Ghosties and Ghoulies and Things That Go Bump in the Night, Halloween Ballet, Wasn't It Fun?, The Trolley Song, Ice, Raving Beauty, A Touch of the Irish, You Are for Loving, A Day in New York, The Ball, Diamonds in the Starlight, Have Yourself a Merry Little Christmas, Paging Mr. Sousa, Finale

A musical in 2 acts and 14 scenes. The action takes place in and around the Smith family home (5135 Kensington Avenue, St. Louis) from summer 1903 to the spring of 1904 and the opening of the Louisiana Purchase Exposition.

*Closed June 10, 1990 after 253 performances and 16 previews.

†Succeeded by: 1. Christopher Scott, 2. Kevin Blair, 3. Jess Richards, 4. Rebecca Baxter

Martha Swope Photos

Top Right: Betty Garrett, Juliet Lambert, Michael O'Steen, Donna Kane, Milo O'Shea, George Hearn, Charlotte Moore, (front) Rachael Graham, Courtney Peldon Below: Kane, Jason Workman

Donna Kane, Courtney Peldon, Juliet Lambert, Michael O'Steen Above: The Cast

Teresa De Zarn, Sting, Nancy Ringham Above: Suzzanne
Douglas, Ethyl Eichelberger

3 PENNY OPERA

Book/Lyrics, Bertolt Brecht; Translation, Michael Feingold; Music, Kurt Weill; Director, John Dexter; Musical Staging, Peter Gennaro; Musical Director, Julius Rudel; Scenery & Costumes, Jocelyn Herbert; Associate Scenic Design, Duke Durfee; Lighting, Andy Phillips, Brian Nason; Hairstylist, Phyllis Della; Sound, Peter Fitzgerald; General Management, Joseph Harris, Peter T. Kulok; Casting, Johnson-Liff & Zerman; Presented by Jerome Hellman in association with Haruki Kadokawa and James M. Nederlander; Associate Producers, Margo Lion, Hiroshi Sugawara, Lloyd Phillips, Kiki Miyake, Nancy Ellison; Company Manager, Kathleen Lowe; Technical Supervision, Jeremiah J. Harris; Props, Joseph Harris, Jr., Ted Wondsei; Wardrobe, Jennifer Bryan, Roberta Christy; Associate Conductor, Robert Fisher; Make-up, Michael Laudati; Stage Managers, Bob Borod, Joe Cappelli, Artie Gaffin; Press, Shirley Herz/Pete Sanders, Glenna Freedman, Sam Rudy, Robert W. Larkin, Miller Wright. Opened Sunday, Nov. 5, 1989 in the Lunt-Fontanne Theatre*

CAST

A Ballad Singer	Ethyl Eichelberger
Jenny Diver	Suzzanne Douglas
Jonathan Jeremiah Peachum	Alvin Epstein
Filch	Jeff Blumenkrantz
Mrs. Peachum	Georgia Brown
Macheath	Sting
Matt of the Mint	Josh Mostel
Crook-Finger Jack	Mitchell Greenberg
Sawtooth Bob	David Schechter
Ed	Philip Carroll
Walter Dreary	Tom Robbins
Jimmy	Alex Santoriello
Tiger Brown, Chief of Police	Larry Marshall
Dolly	Anne Kerry Ford
Betty	Jan Horvath
Vixen	Teresa De Zarn
Molly	Nancy Ringham†1
Suky Tawdry	K. T. Sullivan
Old Whore	Fiddle Viracola
Polly Peachum	Maureen McGovern†2
Constable Smith	David Pursley
Policemen	MacIntyre Dixon, Michael Piontek
Lucy Brown	Kim Criswell
Beggars, Bystanders	Philip Carroll, MacIntyre Dixon, Michael Piontek, David Schechter, Steven Major West

UNDERSTUDIES: Alex Santoriello (Macheath), Fiddle Viracola (Mrs. Peachum), Nancy Ringham (Polly), David Pursley (Mr. Peachum), Teresa DeZarn (Lucy), Jan Horvath (Jenny), Steven Major West (Tiger Brown), Robert Ousley (Matt/Ballad Singer/Smith/Ed/Walter/Jimmy/Bob/Policemen), Leslie Castay (Molly/Dolly/Betty/Vixen/Suky)

MUSICAL NUMBERS: Ballad of Mack the Knife (Moritat), Peachum's Morning Hymn, Why-Can't-They Song, Wedding Song, Pirate Jenny, Soldiers Song, Love Song, Barbara Song, Melodrama and Polly's Song, Ballad of the Prisoner of Sex, Pimp's Ballad (Tango), Ballad of Living in Style, Jealousy Duet, Song of Futility, Lucy's Aria, Solomon Song, Call from the Grave, Epitaph, March to the Gallows, Finale.

A musical in 3 acts and 9 scenes with a prologue and two intermissions. The action takes place in London during the nineteenth century.

*Closed Dec. 31, 1989 after 65 performances and 20 previews.

†Succeeded by: 1. Leslie Castay, 2. Nancy Ringham

Nancy Ellison Photos

Top Left: Sting, Kim Criswell Below: Georgia Brown, Maureen McGovern, Alvin Epstein

PRINCE OF CENTRAL PARK

Book, Evan H. Rhodes; Music, Don Sebesky; Lyrics, Gloria Nissenson; Based on novel by Evan H. Rhodes; Director-Choreographer, Tony Tanner; Musical Direction/ Vocal Arrangements, Joel Silberman; Scenery/Costumes, Michael Bottari/Ronald Case; Lighting, Norman Coates; Sound, Daryl Bornstein; Associate Choreographer, Stephen Bourneuf; Supervisor/Orchestrator, Don Sebesky; Dance Arrangements, Henry Aronson; General Management, George Elmer, Patricia Berry; Company Manager, Richard Berg; Technical Supervision, Arthur Siccardi, Pete Feller; Props, Gregory Tassinaro; Wardrobe, Robert Strong Miller; Wigs and Hair, Scott Mortimer, Alan Francis; Presented by Abe Hirschfeld and Jan McArt; Executive Producer, Karen Poindexter; Associate Producer, Belle M. Deitch; Stage Managers, Steven Ehrenberg, Susan Whelan, Michael A. Clarke; Press, Shirley Herz Associates/ Glenna Freedman, Pete Sanders, Sam Rudy, Robert Larkin, Miller Wright. Opened in the Belasco Theatre on Thursday, Nov. 9, 1989*

CAST

Jay-Jay	Richard H. Blake
School Guard/Park Ranger/Waiter	Sel Vitella
Street People/Stock Broker/Young Richard	John Hoshko
Street People/Officer/Student	Adrian Bailey
Agnes/Anna	Bonnie Perlman
Officer Washinski/Young Margie/Student	Ruth Gottschall
Bag Lady/Floor Walker	Marilyn Hudgins
May Berg/Twitchy/Student	Anne-Marie Gerard
Aerobics Instructor	Stephen Bourneuf
Margie Miller	Jo Anne Worley
Sally	Chris Callen
Fist	Sean Grant
Bird Brain	Jason Ma
Feather/Ballet Dancer	Alice Yearsley
Elmo	Anthony Galde
Carpenter/Maitre'd/Student	Terry Eno
Tap Dancers	Adrian Bailey, Stephen Bourneuf, Ruth Gottschall, John Hoshko, Bonnie Perlman

STANDBYS & UNDERSTUDIES: Jan McArt (Margie), David Burdick (Jay-Jay), Sean Grant (Elmo), Anne-Marie Gerard (Feather), Terry Iten (Sally/Agnes), Swings: Terry Iten, Jody Keith Barrie

A musical in two acts. The action takes place at the present time at various locations in and around New York's Central Park.

*Closed Nov. 11, 1989 after 4 performances and 19 previews.

Top Left: Richard H. Blake, Jasmine Below: Blake, Sean Grant, Alice Yearsley, Jason Ma, Anthony Galde Top Right: Blake, Jo Ann Worley

Alice Yearsley, (background) John Hoshko, Ruth Gottschall, Sel Vitella, Jo Ann Worley, Richard H. Blake, Stephen Bourneuf, Adrian Bailey, Bonnie Perlman, Anne-Marie Gerard Above: Yearsley, Jason Ma, Anthony Galde, Sean Grant, Gerard

GRAND HOTEL

Book, Luther Davis; Songs, Robert Wright and George Forrest; Based on Vicki Baum's novel "Grand Hotel" by arrangement with Turner Entertainment Co., owner of the motion picture of the same title; Additional Music & Lyrics, Maury Yeston; Direction/Choreography, Tommy Tune; Setting, Tony Walton; Costumes, Santo Loquasto; Lighting, Jules Fisher; Sound, Otts Munderloh; Orchestrations, Peter Matz; Musical and Vocal Direction, Jack Lee; Music Supervision/Additional Music, Wally Harper; Associate Director, Bruce Lumpkin; Musical Conductor, John Monaco; Casting, Julie Hughes, Barry Moss; Hairstylist, Werner Sherer; Production Associate, Kathleen Raitt; General Manager, Joey Parnes; Presented by Martin Richards, Mary Lea Johnson, Sam Crothers, Sander Jacobs, Kenneth D. Greenblatt, Paramount Pictures, Jujamcyn Theaters in association with Patty Grubman and Marvin A. Krauss; Associate Producers, Sandra Greenblatt, Martin R. Kaufman, Kim Poster; Company Managers, Nina Skriloff, Jeff Capitola; Props, Charlie Zuckerman, Joe Schwarz; Wardrobe, Alyce Gilbert, Daniel Eaton; Stage Managers, Bruce Lumpkin, Robert Kellogg, Rob Babbitt; Original Cast Recording on Elektra; Press, Judy Jacksina/Julianne Waldheim, Brig Berney. Opened in the Martin Beck Theatre on Sunday, Nov. 12, 1989*

CAST

The Doorman	Charles Mandracchia
Colonel Dr. Otternschlag	John Wylie
The Countess & The Gigolo	Yvonne Marceau, Pierre Dulaine
Rohna, the Grand Concierge	Rex D. Hays
Erik, Front Desk	Bob Stillman

Bellboys:

Georg Strunk	Ken Jennings
Kurt Kronenberg	Keith Crowningshield
Hanns Bittner	Gerrit deBeer
Willibald, captain	J. J. Jepson

Telephone Operators:

Hildegarde Bratts	Jennifer Lee Andrews†1
Sigfriede Holzheim	Suzanne Henderson
Wolffe Bratts	Lynnette Perry†2
The Jimmys	David Jackson, Danny Strayhorn
The Chauffeur	Ben George
Zinnowitz, the lawyer	Hal Robinson
Sandor, Impresario	Mitchell Jason
Victor Witt, Company Manager	Michel Moinot
Madame Peepee	Kathi Moss
General Director Preysing	Timothy Jerome†3
Flaemmchen, the typist	Jane Krakowski
Otto Kringelein, the bookkeeper	Michael Jeter†4
Baron Felix Von Gaigern	David Carroll†5
Raffaela, the confidante	Karen Akers
Elizaveta Grushinskaya, ballerina	Liliane Montevecchi

Scullery Workers:

Gunther Gustafsson	Walter Willison
Werner Holst	David Elledge
Franz Kohl	William Ryall
Ernst Schmidt	Henry Grossman
Hotel Courtesan	Suzanne Henderson
Tootsie	Lynette Perry†2
Trude the maid	Jennifer Lee Andrews†1
The Detective	William Ryall

STANDBYS & UNDERSTUDIES: Gerrit deBeer (Sandor), Michael DeVries (Zinnowitz/Erik), Niki Harris (Countess), Ken Jennings (Witt), J. J. Jepson (Otto/Gigolo), Lynnette Perry (Flaemmchen), William Ryall (Rohna/Chauffeur), Glenn Turner (the Jimmys), Rex D. Hays (the doctor), Hal Robinson (Preysing), Keith Crowningshield (Erik), Penny Worth (Grushinskaya/Raffaela/Mme. Peepee). Mark Jacoby†6 (Baron/Preysing/Doctor), Chip Zien (Kringelein), Swings: Michael DeVries, Niki Harris, Glenn Turner, Eivind Harum.

MUSICAL NUMBERS: The Grand Parade, As It Should Be, Some Have Some Have Not, At the Grand Hotel, Table with a View, Maybe My Baby Loves Me, Fire and Ice, Twenty-two Years, Villa on a Hill, I Want to Go to Hollywood, Everybody's Doing It, The Crooked Path, Who Couldn't Dance with You, The Boston Merger, No Encore, Love Can't Happen, What She Needs, Bonjour Amour, Happy, We'll Take a Glass Together, I Waltz Alone, Roses at the Station, How Can I Tell Her?, The Grand Waltz

A musical in 20 scenes performed without intermission. The action takes place in Berlin's Grand Hotel in 1928.

†Succeeded by: 1. Lisa Merrill McCord during illness, 2. DeLee Lively Mekka, 3. Michael DeVries during illness, 4. Chip Zien during illness, 5. Mark Jacoby, Brent Barrett, Rex Smith, 6. Brent Barrett

Martha Swope Photos

Top Right: Walter Willison, J. J. Jepson, David Elledge, Ken Jennings, William Ryall, Gerrit de Beer, Henry Grossman, Keith Crowningshield, Rex D. Hays **Below Left:** Liliane Montevecchi **Right:** Jane Krakowski

Rex Smith, Liliane Montevecchi Above: David Carroll, Michael Jeter

A FEW GOOD MEN

By Aaron Sorkin; Director, Don Scardino; Set, Ben Edwards; Costumes, David C. Woolard; Lighting, Thomas R. Skelton; Casting, Pat McCorkle; Sound Score/ Design, John Gromada; Presented by David Brown, Lewis Allen, Robert Whitehead, Roger L. Stevens, Kathy Levin, Suntory International Corp., The Shubert Organization in association with John F. Kennedy Center for the Performing Arts; General Manager, Stuart Thompson; Company Manager, Bruce Klinger; Technical Supervision, Neal Mazzella, Gene O'Donovan; Wardrobe, Elonzo Dann; Hairstylist, Robert Cybula; Stage Managers, Dianne Trulock, John Handy; Press, David Powers, David Roggensack. Opened in the Music Box on Wednesday, Nov. 15, 1989*

CAST

Sentry	Ron Ostrow
Lance Cpl. Harold W. Dawson	Victor Love†1
Pfc. Louden Downey	Michael Dolan†2
Lt. j. g. Sam Weinberg	Mark Nelson†3
Lt. j. g. Daniel A. Kaffee	Tom Hulce†4
Lt. Cmdr. Joanne Galloway	Megan Gallagher†5
Capt. Isaac Whitaker	Edmond Genest
Capt. Matthew A. Markinson	Robert Hogan†6
Pfc. William T. Santiago	Arnold Molina
Lt. Col. Nathan Jessep	Stephen Lang†7
Lt. Jonathan James Kendrick	Ted Marcoux†8
Lt. Jack Ross	Clark Gregg†9
Cpl. Jeffrey Owen Howard	Geoffrey Nauffts†10
Capt. Julius Alexander Randolph	Paul Butler†11
Cmdr. Walter Stone	Fritz Sperberg†12

Marines, Sailors, Etc. ....Stephen Bradbury, Michael Genet, Jon Ehrlich, Jeffrey Dreisbach, George Gerdes, Bryan Hicks, Joshua Malina, Conan McCarty, Michael O'Hare

UNDERSTUDIES: Clark Gregg (Kaffee), Joshua Malina (Weinberg/Downey/ Howard), Michael Genet (Dawson/Santiago), Stephen Bradbury (Whitaker/ Markinson/Randolph), George Gerdes (Jessep/Ross), Jeffrey Dreisbach (Kendrick/ Stone), Ron Ostrow (Marines/Sailors/Lawyers), Annette Helde†13 (Standby for Galloway)

A drama in two acts. The action takes place in various locations in Washington, DC, and on the U.S. Naval Base in Guantanamo Bay, Cuba, during the summer of 1986. The play is fictional, but inspired by an occurrence which served as a point of departure for the playwright.

*Still playing May 31, 1990

†Succeeded by: 1. Michael Genet, 2. Joshua Malina, 3. Michael Countryman, 4. Timothy Busfield, Bradley Whitford, 5. Pamela Blair, 6. Stephen Bradbury, 7. Ron Perlman, 8. Jeffrey Dreisbach, 9. Bradley Whitford, 10. Kurt Deutsch, 11. Mike Hodge, 12. Keith Langsdale, 13. Beth McDonald

Top Right: Megan Gallagher, Mark Nelson, Tom Hulce
Below: Hulce, Michael Dolan, Victor Love

Tom Hulce, Megan Gallagher

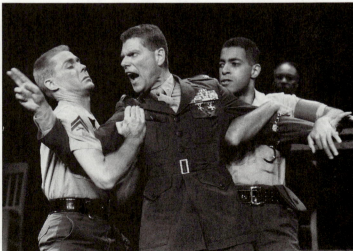

Jeffrey Dreisbach, Stephen Lang, Michael Genet, (back) Paul Butler Above: Geoffrey Nauffts, Tom Hulce, (back) Butler

GYPSY

Book, Arthur Laurents; Suggested by memoirs of Gypsy Rose Lee; Music, Jule Styne; Lyrics, Stephen Sondheim; Director, Arthur Laurents; Original choreography of Jerome Robbins reproduced by Bonnie Walker; Scenery, Kenneth Foy; Costumes, Theoni V. Aldredge; Lighting, Natasha Katz; Sound, Peter Fitzgerald; Hairstyling-Make-up, Robert DiNiro, Alan E. Schubert; Automation & Showdeck, Feller Precision; Musical Director, Eric Stern; Orchestrations, Sid Ramin, Robert Ginzler; Dance Music Arrangements, John Kander; General Manager, Alecia Parker; Production Supervisor, James Pentecost; Technical Supervisor, Arthur Siccardi; Assistant to Director, Richard Sabellico; Casting, Stuart Howard, Amy Specter; Musical Coordinator, John Monaco; Presented by Barry and Fran Weissler, Kathy Levin and Barry Brown; Produced in association with Tokyo Broadcasting System Intl. and Pace Theatrical Group; Company Managers, Nancy Nagel Gibbs, Jim Brandeberry; Props, Jim Wilchinski; Wardrobe, Larch Miller, Karen Eifert; Hairstylists, Geordie Sheffer, Rosie Shore; Assistant Conductor, Michael Rafter; Stage Managers, Craig Jacobs, Tom Capps, James Bernardi; Press, Shirley Herz Associates/Robert W. Larkin, Glenna Freedman, Sam Rudy, Pete Sanders, Miller Wright. Opened in the St. James Theatre on Thursday, Nov. 16, 1989*

CAST

Uncle Jocko/Kringelein	Tony Hoty
George/Mr. Goldstone	John Remme
Clarence	Bobby John Carter
Balloon Girl	Jeana Haege
Baby Louise	Kristen Mahon
Baby June	Christen Tassin
Rose	Tyne Daly†
Pop/Cigar	Ronn Carroll
Newsboys	Demetri Callas, Bobby John Carter, Danny Cistone, Jason Minor
Herbie	Jonathan Hadary
Louise	Crista Moore
June	Tracy Venner
Tulsa	Robert Lambert
Yonkers	Bruce Moore
L. A.	Craig Waletzko
Kansas	Ned Hannah
Flagstaff	Paul Geraci
St. Paul	Alec Timerman
Miss Cratchitt	Barbara Erwin
Hollywood Blondes:	Barbara Folts, Teri Furr, Nancy Melius, Michele Pigliavento, Robin Robinson
Agnes	Lori Ann Mahl
Tessie Tura	Barbara Erwin
Mazeppa	Jana Robbins
Electra	Anna McNeely
Maid	Ginger Prince
Phil	Mace Barrett
Bougeron-Cochon/Weber/Pastey	Jim Bracchitta
Swings	Julie Graves, Eric H. Kaufman

UNDERSTUDIES & STANDBYS: Jana Robbins (Rose), Michele Pigliavento (Louise), Mace Barrett (Herbie), Ginger Prince (Mazeppa/Tessie/Electra/Miss Cratchitt), Jim Bracchitta (George/Goldstone), John Remme (Pop/Pastey), Tony Hoty (Weber/Cigar/Phil), Alec Timerman (Tulsa), Teri Furr (Agnes/June), Jeana Haege (Baby June/Baby Louise)
MUSICAL NUMBERS: Let Me Entertain You, Some People, Small World, Baby June & Her Newsboys, Mr. Goldstone, Little Lamb, You'll Never Get Away from Me, Dainty June and Her Farmboys, If Momma Was Married, All I Need Is the Girl, Everything's Coming Up Roses, Toreadorables, Together, You Gotta Have a Gimmick, The Strip, Rose's Turn

A musical in two acts. The action takes place in various cities in the U.S.A. from the 1920's to the 1930's.

*Still playing May 31, 1990. For original production with Ethel Merman, see *Theatre World* Vol. 15, and revival with Angela Lansbury Vol. 31.

†Succeeded by Jana Robbins during Miss Daly's absence, then Linda Lavin.

Robert C. Ragsdale, Martha Swope Photos

Top Left: Jonathan Hadary, Tyne Daly Below: Crista Moore, Robert Lambert

Crista Moore, Tyne Daly Above: Anna McNeely, Barbara Erwin, Jana Robbins

THE CIRCLE

By W. Somerset Maugham; Director, Brian Murray; Set, Desmond Heeley; Costumes, Jane Greenwood; Lighting, John Michael Deegan; Casting, Marjorie Martin; Presented by Elliot Martin, The Shubert Organization and Suntory International Corp.; General Manager, Ralph Roseman; Props, Roger Snyder, Sal Sciafani; Wardrobe, James M. Kabel; Wigs, David H. Lawrence; Stage Managers, Mitchell Erickson, Wally Peterson, Hugh A. Rose; Press, Jeffrey Richards Associates/Irene Gandy, David LeShay, Jillana Devine. Opened in the Ambassador Theatre on Monday, Nov. 20, 1989*

CAST

Arnold Champion-Cheney, M.P.	Robin Chadwick
Mrs. Shenstone	Patricia Conolly
Footman	Robertson Dean
Elizabeth	Roma Downey
Edward Luton	Harley Venton
Clive Champion-Cheney	Stewart Granger
Butler	Louis Turenne
Lady Catherine Champion-Cheney	Glynis Johns
Lord Porteous	Rex Harrison†

UNDERSTUDIES: Louis Turenne (Porteous/Clive), Robertson Dean (Arnold/Edward), Ellen Maguire (Elizabeth/Mrs. Shenstone), Hugh A. Rose (Butler/Footman)

A romantic comedy in three acts. The action takes place in the drawing-room at Aston-Adey, Arnold Champion-Cheney's house in Dorset, England.

*Closed May 20, 1990 after 208 performances. Original New York production opened in the Selwyn Theatre on Sept. 12, 1921 with Mrs. Leslie Carter, John Drew and Estelle Winwood in the leading roles.

†Succeeded by Louis Turenne when Mr. Harrison became ill.

Peter Cunningham Photos

Left: Robin Chadwick, Stewart Granger, Glynis Johns, Roma Downey Top: Rex Harrison, Glynis Johns, Stewart Granger

Harley Venton, Roma Downey, Glynis Johns, Rex Harrison

Rex Harrison, Glynis Johns

ARTIST DESCENDING A STAIRCASE

By Tom Stoppard; Director, Tim Luscombe; Set, Tony Straiges; Costumes, Joseph G. Aulisi; Lighting, Tharon Musser; Sound, Tom Morse; Music/Sound Effects, Kevin Malpass; Casting, Meg Simon/Fran Kumin; Production Manager, Peter Lawrence; General Manager, Leonard Soloway; Presented by The Staircase Company: Emanuel Azenberg, Roger Berlind, Dick Button, Dennis Grimaldi, Robert Whitehead, Roger Stevens, Kathy Levin; Associate Producer, Michael Brandman; By arrangement with Bill Kenwright and Dan Crawford; Manager, Abby Evans; Technical Supervisors, Theatrical Services (Arthur Siccardi/Peter Feller); Props, Jan Marasek; Wardrobe, Penny Davis, Pat White, Anne-Marie Wright; Hairstylist, David Brown; Production Assistant, Suzanne Turner; Stage Managers, Peter Lawrence, Don Judge; Press, Bill Evans Associates/Becky Flora/Jim Randolph. Opened in the Helen Hayes Theatre on Thursday, Nov. 30, 1989*

CAST

Beauchamp	Harold Gould
Martello	Paxton Whitehead
Donner	John McMartin
Young Beauchamp	Michael Cumpsty
Young Martello	Jim Fyfe
Young Donner	Michael Winther
Sophie	Stephanie Roth

UNDERSTUDIES/STANDBYS: Edmund Lyndeck (Beauchamp/Martello/Donner), Brian Cousins (Younger Men), Marcia Cross (Sophie)

A drama in eleven scenes performed without intermission. The action takes place from 1914 to 1972.

*Closed Dec. 31, 1989 after 36 performances and 10 previews.

Sheldon Secunda Photos

Right Center: Michael Winther, Michael Cumpsty, Stephanie Roth, Jim Fyfe Top Right: Harold Gould, Paxton Whitehead

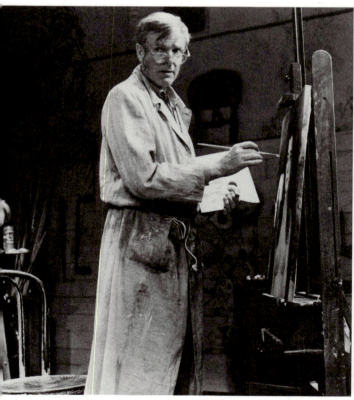

John McMartin

Paxton Whitehead

THE VICTOR BORGE HOLIDAY SHOW
on Broadway

A Musical Entertainment by Victor Borge; Assistant to Mr. Borge, Jim Colias; Presented by Music Fair Productions; Stage Managers, Ronald Borge, Kevin Hickson; Company Manager, Dana F. X. Amendola; Press, Daniel J. P. Kellachan, Kevin P. McAnarney. Opened in the Brooks Atkinson Theatre on Tuesday, Dec. 5, 1989 and closed Dec. 10, 1989 after limited engagement of 8 performances.

Right: Victor Borge

PETER, PAUL & MARY
A Holiday Celebration

Presented by Music Fair Productions in association with Ken Fritz; Production Manager, Martha Hertzberg; Co-Production Manager, Shelley Belusar; Choral and Orchestral Arrangements/Conductor, Robert DeCormier; Sound, Dave Tkachuk; Lighting, Marc B. Weiss; Ms. Travers' Wardrobe, Ouida Tharpe; Graphics, Milton Glaser, George Leavitt; Company Manager, Dana F. X. Amendola; Stage Manager, Kevin Hickson; Press, Daniel J. P. Kellachan, Kevin McAnarney. Opened in the Brooks Atkinson Theatre on Tuesday, Dec. 12, 1989*

CAST

Peter Yarrow
Noel Paul Stookey
Mary Travers

New York Choral Society
and Orchestra

*Closed Dec. 17, 1989 after a limited engagement of 6 performances.

**Right Center: Noel Paul Stookey, Mary Travers,
Peter Yarrow**

TRU

Written and Directed by Jay Presson Allen; From the words and works of Truman Capote; Set, David Mitchell; Lighting, Ken Billington, Jason Kantrowitz; Costumes, Sarah Edwards; Sound, Otts Munderloh; Make-up, Kevin Haney; Wig, Paul Huntley; Casting Consultant, Pat McCorkle; Presented by Lewis Allen and David Brown with Suntory International Corp. and the Shubert Organization in association with Landmark Entertainment Group; By arrangement with the Truman Capote estate, Alan U. Schwartz, Executor; General Management, Stuart Thompson Associates/Thomas P. Santopietro, Douglas C. Baker; Technical Supervisor, Neil Mazzella; Wardrobe, Kate Edwards; Stage Manager, Jane Grey; Press, Bill Evans & Associates/Becky Flora, Jim Randolph. Opened in the Booth Theatre on Thursday, Dec. 14, 1989*

CAST

Truman Capote .... Robert Morse

Performed with one intermission. The action takes place in Truman Capote's New York apartment at 870 United Nations Plaza during the week before Christmas of 1975.

*Closed Sept. 1, 1990 after 295 performances and 11 previews. Mr. Morse received a 1990 "Tony" for Best Performance by an Actor in a Play, the Drama Desk, Outer Critics Circle, and Drama League Awards.

Martha Swope Photos

Robert Morse

CITY OF ANGELS

Book, Larry Gelbart; Music, Cy Coleman; Lyrics, David Zippel; Director, Michael Blakemore; Musical Staging, Walter Painter; Scenery, Robin Wagner; Costumes, Florence Klotz; Lighting, Paul Gallo; Sound, Peter Fitzgerald, Bernard Fox; Orchestrations, Billy Byers; Vocal Arrangements, Cy Coleman, Varon Gershovsky; Musical Direction, Gordon Lowry Harrell; Fight Staging, B. H. Barry; Casting, Johnson-Liff & Zerman; Hairstylist, Steve Atha; General Manager, Ralph Roseman; Presented by Nick Vanoff, Roger Berlind, Jujamcyn Theaters, Suntory International Corp., The Shubert Organization; Company Manager, Susan Gustafson; Assistant Choreographer, Sandy Roveta; Dance Captain, Jacquey Maltby; Props, George Wagner, Pat Cheeseman; Wardrobe, Joseph Busheme, Mary Eno; Associate Conductor, Kathy Sommer; Stage Managers, Steven Zweigbaum, Brian Meister, Matthew Mundinger; Original Cast Recording by Columbia; Press, Bill Evans & Associates/Becky Flora, Jim Randolph. Opened in the Virginia Theatre on Monday, Dec. 12, 1989*

CAST

MOVIE CAST:
Stone .... James Naughton
Orderlies .... James Hindman, Tom Galantich
Oolie .... Randy Graff
Alaura Kingsley .... Dee Hoty
Big Six .... Herschel Sparber
Sonny .... Raymond Xifo
Jimmy Powers .... Scott Waara
Angel City Four .... Peter Davis, Amy Jane London,
                                                            Gary Kahn, Jackie Presti
Munoz .... Shawn Elliott
Officer Pasco .... Tom Galantich
Bobbi .... Kay McClelland
Irwin S. Irving .... Rene Auberjonois
Peter Kingsley .... Doug Tompos
Margaret .... Carolee Carmello
Luther Kingsley .... Keith Perry
Dr. Mandril .... James Cahill
Mallory Kingsley .... Rachel York
Mahoney .... James Hindman
Yamato .... Alvin Lum
Commissioner Gaines .... Evan Thompson
Margie .... Eleanor Glockner
Bootsie .... Jacquey Maltby
HOLLYWOOD CAST:
Stine .... Gregg Edelman
Buddy Fidler .... Rene Auberjonois
Shoeshine .... Evan Thompson
Gabby .... Kay McClelland
Barber .... James Cahill
Donna .... Randy Graff
Anna .... Eleanor Glockner
Jimmy Powers .... Scott Waara
Angel City Four .... Peter Davis, Amy Jane London,
                                                            Gary Kahn, Jackie Presti
Carla Haywood .... Dee Hoty
Del Dacosta .... James Hindman
Pancho Vargas .... Shawn Elliott
Werner Kriegler .... Keith Perry
Gerlad Pierce .... Doug Tompos
Avril Raines .... Rachel York
Gene .... Tom Galantich
Cinematographer .... Alvin Lum
Stand-In .... Carolee Carmello
Hairdresser .... Eleanor Glockner
Studio Cops .... Herschel Sparber, Raymond Xifo

UNDERSTUDIES: Tom Galantich (Stone/Powers), James Hindman (Stine/Buddy/Irving/Munoz/Sonny), Carolee Carmello (Alaura/Carla/Gabby/Bobbi), Jacquey Maltby (Oolie/Donna/Mallory/Ann/Margie), Evan Thompson (Luther/Werner/Mandril/Big 6), Alvin Lum (Barber), Marcus Neville (Orderly/Mahoney/Dacosta/Pasco/Gene/Commissioner/Angel City 4), Chrissy Faith (Margaret/Bootsie/Angel City 4), Swings: Marcus Neville, Chrissy Faith
MUSICAL NUMBERS: City of Angels, Double Talk, What You Don't Know about Women, Ya Gotta Look Out for Yourself, The Buddy System, With Every Breath I Take, Tennis Song, Ev'rybody's Gotta Be Somewhere, Lost and Found, All Ya Have to Do Is Wait, You're Nothing without Me, Stay with Me, You Can Always Count on Me, It Needs Work, Funny

A musical in 2 acts and 37 scenes. The action takes place in Los Angeles during the late 1940's.

*Still playing May 31, 1990. Voted Best Musical by NY Drama Critics Circle, Outer Critics Circle, Drama Desk, and "Tony" voters. "Tonys" were also awarded James Naughton (Best Actor), Randy Graff (Best Featured Actress), Best Book, Best Score, Best Set Design.

Martha Swope Photos

Top Right: James Naughton, Doug Tompos, Dee Hoty
Below: Rene Auberjonois, Gregg Edelman

Randy Graff, James Naughton Above: Gary Kahn, Jackie Presti, Scott Waara, Amy Jane London, Peter Davis

THE MERCHANT OF VENICE

By William Shakespeare; Director, Peter Hall; Design, Chris Dyer; Lighting, Neil Peter Jampolis; Costumes Supervised by Barbara Forbes; Associate Director, Giles Block; Casting Consultants, Johnson-Liff & Zerman; Music, Robert Lockhart; Sound, Paul Arditti; Executive Producer, Thelma Holt; Presented by Duncan C. Weldon & Jerome Minskoff in association with Punch Productions; General Management, Joseph Harris/Peter T. Kulok; Technical Supervisor, Jeremiah J. Harris Inc./ Nancy Simmons; Props, Joseph Harris, Jr.; Wardrobe, Kathleen Gallagher; Wigs, Jonhenry Gordon; Hairstylist, Shontae Olivia Johnson; Stage Managers, Thomas A. Kelly, Charles Kindl, James Dawson, Donna A. Drake; Press, Joshua Ellis Office/ Adrian Bryan-Brown, Jackie Green, Susanne Tighe, Tim Ray, Chris Boneau. Opened in the 46th Street Theatre on Tuesday, Dec. 19, 1989*

CAST

Antonio	Leigh Lawson
Bassanio	Nathaniel Parker
Lorenzo	Richard Garnett
Gratiano	Michael Siberry
Salerio	Donald Burton
Solanio	Gordon Gould
Leonardo	Ben Browder
Shylock	Dustin Hoffman
Jessica	Francesca Buller
Tubal	Leon Lissek
Lancelot Gobbo	Peter-Hugo Daly
Old Gobbo	Leo Leyden
Portia	Geraldine James
Nerissa	Julia Swift
Balthasar	Neal Ben-Ari
Stefano	John Wojda
Prince of Morocco	Herb Downer
Prince of Aragon	Michael Carter
Duke of Venice	Basil Henson

and William Beckwith, Neal Ben-Ari, Margery Daley, Dale Dickey, Elisabeth Engan, Denis Holmes, Wilbur Pauley, Margaret Poyner, Gary Rayppy, John Norman Thomas, Isiah Whitlock, Jr., John Wojda, Taylor Young.

UNDERSTUDIES: Ben Browder (Lorenzo/Stefano), Michael Carter (Antonio), Neal Ben-Ari (Shylock/Prince of Aragon), Denis Holmes (Old Gobbo/Tubal/Duke), William Beckwith (Salerio/Balthasar), John Wojda (Bassanio), Isiah Whitlock, Jr. (Prince of Morocco/Leonardo/Antonio's Man), Gary Rayppy (Solanio/Gratiano), Taylor Young (Portia), Dale Dickey (Jessica/Nerissa), Margaret Poyner (Soprano), John Norman Thomas (Lancelot/Bass).

Performed with one intermission.

*Closed March 10, 1990 after a limited run of 81 performances and 19 previews.

John Haynes Photos

Top Right: Geraldine James, Dustin Hoffman
Below: Hoffman, Leigh Lawson

Dustin Hoffman

Geraldine James, Leigh Lawson, Dustin Hoffman

DON COSSACKS

State Academic Ensemble of Rostov, USSR; Artistic Director, Anatoly Kvasov; Choirmaster, Ludmila Melnichenko; Principal Folklorist, Raisa Kvasova; Balletmaster, Viktor Alekseyenko; Conductor, Boris Ogurtsov; Costume Designer, Paulina Korotkova; Administrative Director, Vladimir Kravchenko; Presented by James M. Nederlander and I.C.M. Artists; General Manager, Leonard Stein; Stage Managers, Kristina Kinet; Wardrobe, Stephanie Cheretun; Press, Lillian Libman. Opened in the Neil Simon Theatre on Tuesday, Jan. 23, 1990*

PROGRAM

ACT I: Bylina, White Fish, The Long Journey, Cossack Lament, Horsemen and Friends, Sing in the Garden oh Nightingale, The Beehive in the Garden, Oh You Berry!
ACT II: Razin's Revolt, Twixt Forest and Mountain, For a Lady Who Cannot Stand Still!, Beyond the Forest the Sun Shines, I'll Go for a Walk, Don Festive Suite, Finale

*Closed Feb. 4, 1990 after a limited engagement of 16 performances.

Above and Top Right: Members of the Dance Corps

Estelle Parsons, also above

MISS MARGARIDA'S WAY

Written and Directed by Roberto Athayde; Costumes, Santo Loquasto; Lighting, Jason Sturm; Presented by Bernard and Toby Nussbaum; Executive Producer, Laurel Ann Wilson; General Management, L. A. Wilson Management; Company Manager, Daniel Kearns; Wardrobe, Kia Heath; Stage Managers, Lisa Ledwich, Koji Okamura; Press, Fred Nathan Company/Marc P. Thibodeau, Merle Frimark, William Schelble, Maria Somma, Ian Rand. Opened in the Helen Hayes Theatre on Thursday, Feb. 15, 1990*

CAST

Miss Margarida ....Estelle Parsons
One of her students ....Koji Okamura
The Rest of her students .... The Audience

A play in two acts. The action takes place at the present time in Miss Margarida's classroom.

*Closed Feb. 25, 1990 after 11 performances and 8 previews.

Martha Swope Photos

THE SOUND OF MUSIC

Music, Richard Rodgers; Lyrics, Oscar Hammerstein II; Book, Howard Lindsay, Russell Crouse; Suggested by "The Trapp Family Singers" by Maria Augusta Trapp; Orchestrations, Robert Russell Bennett; Director, James Hammerstein; Conductor, Richard Parrinello; Set/Lighting, Neil Peter Jampolis; Costumes, Suzanne Mess; Presented by New York City Opera Company; Sound, Abe Jacob; Musical Staging, Joel Bishoff; Stage Managers, Stephen Chaiken, Joseph Gasperec, John Knudsen; Press, Susan Woelzl, Dale Zeidman, Shirley Herz Associates/Glenna Freedman. Opened in the New York State Theater on Thursday, March 8, 1990*

CAST

Maria Rainer	Debby Boone
Sister Berthe	Jill Bosworth
Sister Margaretta	Michele McBride
Mother Abbess	Claudia Cummings
Sister Sophia	Robin Tabachnik
Capt. Georg von Trapp	Laurence Guittard
Franz	David Rae Smith
Frau Schmidt	Ellen Tovatt

Children of Captain von Trapp:

Liesl	Emily Loesser
Friedrich	Richard H. Blake
Louisa	Kelly Karbacz
Kurt	Ted Huffman
Brigitta	Kia Graves
Marta	Lauren Gaffney
Gretl	Mary Mazzello
Rolf Gruber	Marc Heller
Elsa Schraeder	Marianne Tatum
Ursula	Bridget Ramos
Max Detweiler	Werner Klemperer
Herr Zeller	Louis Perry
Baron Elberfeld	William Ledbetter
Postulant	Barbara Shirvis
Admiral von Schreiber	Glenn Rowen

STANDBYS: Kathleen Williams (Maria), Hal Davis (Capt. von Trapp), Jill Bosworth (Mother Abbess), Paula Hostetter (Elsa), David Rae Smith (Max), Kirsten Gamble (Liesl), Andrew Denler (Rolf), The Children: Michelle Aravena, Kirsten Gamble, Elizabeth Hart, Sam Riegel
MUSICAL NUMBERS: Preludium, The Sound of Music, Maria, My Favorite Things, Do-Re-Mi, 16 going on 17, The Lonely Goatherd, How Can Love Survive, Grand Waltz, Laendler, So Long Farewell, Climb Every Mountain, No Way to Stop It, An Ordinary Couple, Processional, Edelweiss

A musical in 2 acts and 19 scenes. The action takes place in Austria early in 1938.

*Closed April 22, 1990 after 60 performances. The original production with Mary Martin and Theodore Bikel opened in the Lunt-Fontanne Theatre on Monday, Nov. 16, 1959 and played 1443 performances.

Top Right: Laurence Guittard, Debby Boone Below: Boone, Lauren Gaffney, Mary Mazzello

The Company

OBA OBA '90

Producer, Franco Fontana; Musical Director, Wilson Mauro; Choreographer, Roberto Abrahao; Lighting Consultant, Giancarlo Campora; Technical Director, Mario Ruffo; Production Supervisor, Leda Moraes; Coordinator, Vera Lima; General Manager, Charlotte Wilcox; Production Coordinator, Jay B. Jacobson; Props, Sal Sciafani; Company Manager, Wilmar Bosaipo; Cast Manager, Claudio Carneiro; Stage Manager, Monica Goncalves; Press, Peter Cromarty & Co./Kevin Brockman, Patrick Paris, Joanne Giorgio, Opened in the Marquis Theatre on Thursday, March 15, 1990*

PROGRAM

ACT I: Liberation from Slavery, Homage to Chorinho, Samba de Roda-Lambada, Homage to the Northeast, Homage to the Bossanova and the '70's, Tribute to the "Brazilian Bombshell" Carmen Miranda
ACT II: Macumba, Afro-Brazilian Folk Songs and Dances, Berimbau Medley, Rhythm Beaters, Show of Samba Dancers, Grand Carnival

A "Brazilian Extravaganza" revue in two acts.

*Closed April 22, 1990 after 45 performances and 11 previews. Resumed tour.

Chris Fessler Photos

CAT ON A HOT TIN ROOF

By Tennessee Williams; Director, Howard Davies; Scenery, William Dudley; Costumes, Patricia Zipprodt; Lighting, Mark Henderson; Sound, T. Richard Fitzgerald; Hairstylist, Robert DiNiro; Music, Ilona Sekacz; Technical Supervisor, Arthur Siccardi; Associate Lighting Designer, Beverly Emmons; Casting, Stuart Howard/ Amy Schecter; Presented by Barry and Fran Weissler; In association with Jujamcyn Theatres and James and Maureen O'Sullivan Cushing; General Manager, Charlotte Wilcox; Associate Producer, Alecia Parker; Company Manager, Robert H. Wallner; Props, Andrew Acabbo; Wardrobe, Frank Green; Hairstylist, Scott A. Mortimer; Stage Managers, Patrick Horrigan, Betsy Nicholson, Ron Brice; Press, Shirley Herz Associates/Pete Sanders, Glenna Freedman, Sam Rudy, Robert W. Larkin. Opened in the Eugene O'Neill Theatre on Wednesday, March 21, 1990*

CAST

Maggie	Kathleen Turner
Brick	Daniel Hugh Kelly
Mae	Debra Jo Rupp
Big Mama	Polly Holliday
Sookey	Edwina Lewis
Dixie	Amy Gross
Big Daddy	Charles Durning
Gooper	Kevin O'Rourke†1
Rev. Tooker	Nesbitt Blaisdell
Dr. Baugh	Jerome Dempsey†2
Trixie	Erin Torpey
Polly	Suzy Bouffard
Buster	Seth Jerome Walker
Sonny	Billy L. Sullivan
Brightie	Ron Brice
Lacey	Marcial Howard

UNDERSTUDIES: Mary Layne (Maggie/Mae), Jerome Dempsey (Big Daddy), Tom Stechschulte (Brick/Gooper), John Newton (Tooker/Baugh), Suzy Bouffard (Dixie)

A drama in three acts. The action takes place in a bed-sitting room and section of the gallery of a plantation home in the Mississippi Delta, during an evening in summer.

*Closed Aug. 1, 1990 after a limited engagement of 149 performances and 7 previews. Charles Durning received a "Tony" Award for Best Featured Actor in a Play. Original production with Ben Gazzara and Barbara Bel Geddes opened in the Morosco Theatre on Mar. 24, 1955 and played 694 performances (see *Theatre World* Vol. 11). The 1974 revival with Elizabeth Ashley and Keir Dullea played 160 performances in the ANTA Theatre (see *Theatre World* Vol. 31).

†Succeeded by: 1. Ray Gill, 2. Thomas Hill

Michael Tighe Photos

Top Left: Kathleen Turner, Daniel Hugh Kelly Below: Charles Durning, Kelly

Daniel Hugh Kelly, Kathleen Turner Above: Turner, Polly Holliday

Kathleen Turner

THE GRAPES OF WRATH

Based on the novel by John Steinbeck; Adaptation & Direction, Frank Galati; Sets/Lighting, Kevin Rigdon; Costumes, Erin Quigley; Sound, Rob Milburn; Original Music Composed & Directed by Michael Smith; Production Stage Manager, Malcolm Ewen; Stage Managers, Janet Friedman, Robyn Karen Taylor; Company Manager, Mitchell A. Weiss; Associate Lighting, Howard Werner; Dance Consultant, Peter Amster; Fights, Michael Sokoloff; Wardrobe, Helen Toth, Sheri Maher; Asst. Costumes, Mindy Wolfe; Asst. Sets, Tim Oien; Asst. Sound, Jennifer Carr, Valerie Spradling; A Steppenwolf Theatre Co. Production; Presented by The Shubert Organization, Suntory International Corp., Jujamcyn Theatres and Steppenwolf; Press, Fred Nathan/Merle Frimark, William Schelble, Marc P. Thibodeau. Opened in the Cort Theatre on Thursday, March 22, 1990.*

CAST

1st Narrator/Car Salesman/Man Going Back/ Weedpatch Camp Director/Mr. Wainwright	Francis Guinan
Jim Casy	Terry Kinney
Tom Joad	Gary Sinise
Muley Graves/Floyd Knowles	Rick Snyder
Willy/Mayor of Hooverville	Ron Crawford
Car Salesman	Keith Byron-Kirk
Pa Joad	Robert Breuler
Ma Joad	Lois Smith
Granma	Lucina Paquet
Grampa	Nathan Davis
Noah	Jeff Perry
Ruthie Joad	Zoe Taleporos
Uncle John	James Noah
Winfield Joad	Calvin Lennon Armitage
Rose of Sharon	Sally Murphy
Connie Rivers	Mark Deakins
Al Joad	Jim True
Camp Proprietor/Salesman	Terrance MacNamara
Gas Station Attendant	Steve Ramsey
3rd Narrator/Gas Station Owner/Contractor/ Hooper Ranch Guard	Michael Hartman
2nd Narrator/Elizabeth Sandry	Cheryl Lynn Bruce
Agricultural Officers	Theodore Schulz, P. J. Brown
Car Salesman/Deputy Sheriff/4th Narrator	Skipp Sudduth
Camp Nurse	Nicola Sheara
Al's Girl	Jessica Wilder
Car Salesman/Hooper Ranch Bookkeeper	Eric Simonson
Mrs. Wainwright	Rondi Reed
Aggie Wainwright	Kathryn Erbe
Man in the Barn	Lex Monson
Son of Man in the Barn	Jeremiah Birkett
Guitar	Michael Smith
Fiddle	Miriam Sturm
Harmonica/Saw/Jaw Harp/Banjo	L. J. Slavin
Accordian/Bass	William Schwarz

UNDERSTUDIES: Keith Byron-Kirk (1st Narrator/Camp Director/Wainwright/Man in Barn/His Son/Salesman), Rick Snyder (Jim Casey/Man Going Back), Jeff Perry (Tom Joad), Theodore Schulz (Muley/Knowles/Noah/Willy/Mayor), Michael Hartman (Pa), Rondi Reed (Ma/Fiddle), Nicola Sheara (Granma/Elizabeth/2nd Narrator/Mrs. Wainwright), Ron Crawford (Grampa/Contactor/Station Owner/3rd Narrator/Guard/Proprietor/Salesman), Terrance MacNamara (Uncle John), Tommy J. Michaels (Winfield), Kathryn Erbe (Rose of Sharon/Al's Girl/Nurse), Eric Simonson (Connie), Steve Ramsey (Al/Harmonica/Salesman), William Schwarz (Guitar), Jeremiah Birkett (Accordian/Bass/Attendant), P. J. Brown (4th Narrator/Salesman/Deputy), Jessica Wilder (Aggie), Skipp Sudduth (Bookkeeper/Officers/Salesman)

A drama in two acts. The action takes place in Oklahoma and then California in 1938.

*Closed Sept. 2, 1990 after 188 performances and 11 previews. 1990 "Tonys" were awarded for Best Play and Best Direction of a Play (Frank Galati).

Peter Cunningham Photos

Top Left: The Company Below: Gary Sinise, Lois Smith

Terry Kinney, Gary Sinise Above: The Cast

LETTICE & LOVAGE

By Peter Shaffer; Director, Michael Blakemore; Design, Alan Tagg; Costumes, Frank Krenz; Miss Smith's Costumes, Anthony Powell; Lighting, Ken Billington; Casting, Johnson-Liff & Zerman; General Management, Gatchell & Neufeld, Ltd.; Production Stage Manager, Mitchell Erickson; Stage Manager, John Handy; Technical Supervisor, Arthur Siccardi; Company Manager, Mitzi Harder; Asst. Stage Manager, Tyrone Wilson; Asst. Company Manager, Stephen W. Nebgen; Wardrobe, David Hemenway, Jeane Argast, Margie Marchionni; Hair, Leon Gagliardi; Cat Handler, Alice Merton; Presented by The Shubert Organization, Robert Fox Ltd. & Roger Berlind; Press, Fred Nathan/William Schelble. Opened in the Ethel Barrymore Theatre on Sunday, March 25, 1990.*

CAST

Lettice Douffet	Maggie Smith
Surly Man	Dane Knell
Lotte Schoen	Margaret Tyzack
Miss Framer	Bette Henritze
Mr. Bardolph	Paxton Whitehead
Visitors to Fustian House	Herb Foster, Prudence Wright Holmes, Patricia Kilgarriff, Dane Knell, Barbara Lester, Sybil Lines, Laurine Towler, Tyrone Wilson, Ronald Yamamoto and Felina, Queen of Sorrows

STANDBYS: Margaret Hall (Lettice), Barbara Lester (Lotte), Herb Foster (Bardolph/Man), Prudence Wright Holmes (Miss Framer)

A comedy in three acts and 4 scenes. The action takes place in Fustian House, Wiltshire, England, the office of the Preservation Trust, London and a basement flat, Earls Court, London. The time is the present.

*Still Playing May 31, 1990.

Winner of 1990 "Tonys" for Best Actress in a Play (Maggie Smith) and Best Featured Actress in a Play (Margaret Tyzack).

Zoe Dominic Photos

Right Center: Maggie Smith, Margaret Tyzack Above: Smith, Tyzack

Maggie Smith

Paxton Whitehead, Maggie Smith

ASPECTS OF LOVE

Music, Andrew Lloyd Webber; Lyrics, Don Black & Charles Hart; Based on the novel by David Garnett; Adaptation, Lloyd Webber; Director, Trevor Nunn; Choreography, Gillian Lynne; Production Design, Maria Björnson; Lighting, Andrew Bridge; Sound, Martin Levan; Production Musical Director, Paul Bogaev; Orchestrations, David Cullen, Lloyd Webber; General Manager, Gatchell & Neufeld Ltd.; Casting, Johnson-Liff & Zerman; Production Stage Manager, Perry Cline; Stage Managers, Elisabeth Farwell, Michael J. Passaro; Production Manager, Peter Fulbright; Company Manager, Mary Miller; Dance Captain, Gregory Mitchell; Technical Coordinator, Alexander Fraser; Asst. Director, Andrew MacBean; Asst. Choreographer, Richard Stafford; Presented by The Really Useful Theatre Company, Inc. (Bridget Hayward, Producer; Edward Windsor, Assistant); London Cast Recording on Polydor; Press, Fred Nathan/Merle Frimark. Opened in the Broadhurst Theatre on Sunday, April 8, 1990.*

CAST

Rose Vibert	Ann Crumb
Alex Dillingham	Michael Ball
George Dillingham	Kevin Colson
Giulietta Trapani	Kathleen Rowe McAllen
Marcel Richard	Walter Charles
Jenny Dillingham	
age 12	Deanna Du Clos
age 14	Danielle Du Clos
Elizabeth/Date/Veteran's Wife/Friend	Suzanne Briar
Hugo Le Muenier/Stage Manager	Don Goodspeed
Jerome Actor/Alex's Friend/Rose's Friend/Clown	Philip Clayton
Actor/War Veteran/Dr./Asst. Registrar/Rose's Friend/Clown	John Dewar
Actor/Local Man/Rose's Friend/Clown	Marcus Lovett
Actor/2nd Barker/Gondolier/Rose's Friend/Knife Thrower	Kurt Johns
Actress/Nun/Rose's Friend/Girlfriend	Elinore O'Connell
Actress/Girlfriend/Hotel Cashier/Rose's Friend	Lisa Vroman
Actress/Local Woman/Pharmacist/Rose's Friend	Wysandria Woolsey
Asst. Stage Manager/Alex's Date/Rose's Friend	Jane Todd Baird
Waiter/Local Man/Rose's Friend/Clown/Young Peasant	Gregory Mitchell
Man on Date/1st Barker/Hotelier/Registrar/Rose's Friend	Eric Johnson

UNDERSTUDIES: Elinore O'Connell (Rose), Wysandria Woolsey (Rose/Giulietta), Don Goodspeed (Alex), Walter Charles (George), Lisa Vroman (Giulietta), Eric Johnson (Marcel), Jane Todd Baird (Jenny, 14), Brooke Sunny Moriber (Jenny, 12), Marcus Lovett (Hugo), Wiley Kidd, Brad Oscar, Anne Marie Runolfsson (Swings)

MUSICAL NUMBERS: Love Changes Everything, Parlez-vous francais?/The Cafe, Seeing is Believing, A Memory of a Happy Moment, Chanson d'enfance, Everybody Loves a Hero, She'd Be Far Better Off with You, Stop. Wait. Please., Leading Lady, Other Pleasures, There Is More to Love, Mermaid Song, The First Man You Remember, Journey of a Lifetime, Falling, Hand Me the Wine and the Dice, Anything But Lonely

A musical in two acts and 35 scenes. The action takes place on the continent between 1947–64.

*Still Playing May 31, 1990.

Bob Marshak/Joan Marcus Photos

Ann Crumb, Danielle DuClos, Kevin Colson
Top Right: Crumb, Michael Ball

Michael Ball, Kathleen Rowe McAllen Above: Deanna
DuClos, Kevin Colson

THE PIANO LESSON

By August Wilson; Director, Lloyd Richards; Sets, E. David Cosier, Jr.; Lighting, Christopher Akerlind; Costumes, Constanza Romero; Musical Director/Composer, Dwight D. Andrews; Sound, G. Thomas Clark; General Manager, Laurel Ann Wilson; Casting, Meg Simon/Fran Kumin; Production Stage Manager, Karen L. Carpenter; Stage Manager, Russell W. Johnson; Company Manager, Sally Campbell; Wardrobe, Linda Lee; Production Asst., James Mountcastle; Associate Producer, Stephen J. Albert; Presented by Lloyd Richards, Yale Repertory Theatre; Center Theatre Group/Ahmanson Theatre; Gordon Davidson and Jujamcyn Theatres with Benjamin Mordecai, Executive Producer in association with Eugene O'Neill Theatre Center, Huntington Theatre Co., Goodman Theatre and Old Globe Theatre; Press, Jeffrey Richards/Irene Gandy, David LeShay, Jillana Devine. Opened in the Walter Kerr Theatre on Monday, April 16, 1990.*

CAST

Doaker	Carl Gordon
Boy Willie	Charles S. Dutton
Lymon	Rocky Carroll
Berniece	S. Epatha Merkerson
Maretha	Apryl R. Foster
Avery	Tommy Hollis
Wining Boy	Lou Myers†
Grace	Lisa Gay Hamilton

UNDERSTUDIES: Kim Staunton (Berniece/Grace), Danny Robinson Clark (Wining Boy)

A drama in two acts. The action takes place in Pittsburgh, 1936.

*Still playing May 31, 1990. Winner of the 1990 Pulitzer Prize and NY Drama Critic's Circle awards for Best Play. This production inaugurated the refurbished Ritz Theatre newly christened The Walter Kerr Theatre.

†Succeeded by Ernie Scott

Gerry Goodstein Photos

Top Left: Charles S. Dutton, Rocky Carroll Below: Carroll, S. Epatha Merkerson

Charles S. Dutton

Charles S. Dutton, Tommy Hollis, S. Epatha Merkerson
Above: Lou Myers, Rocky Carroll, Dutton, Carl Gordon

TRULY BLESSED
A MUSICAL CELEBRATION OF MAHALIA JACKSON

Written, Conceived and Original Music & Lyrics by Queen Esther Marrow; Additional Music/Lyrics, Reginald Royal; Direction, Robert Kalfin; Choreography, Larry Vickers; Music Supervision/Orchestrations, Joseph Joubert; Sets/Lighting, Fred Kolo; Costumes, Andrew B. Marlay; Sound, Peter Fitzgerald; General Manager, Charlotte Wilcox; Production Supervisor, Mortimer Halpern; Production Stage Manager, Kenneth Hanson; Stage Managers, Janice C. Lane, Tina Fabrique; Wardrobe, Breelund Daniels; Hair, Jheri Terrell; Production Asst., Michael Troublefield, Makeup/Hair Design, Michael Robinson; Conductor, Aaron Graves; Executive Producers, Philip Rose, Howard Hurst; Technical, Jeremiah J. Harris Associates; Presented by Howard Hurst, Philip Rose, Sophie Hurst in association with Frankie Hewitt; Originally Produced by Ford's Theatre, Washington, D.C.; Press, Joshua Ellis/Jackie Green, Adrian Bryan-Brown, Susanne Tighe, Tim Ray. Opened in the Longacre Theatre on Sunday, April 22, 1990.*

CAST

Mahalia Jackson .... Queen Esther Marrow
Ensemble
Carl Hall   Lynette G. DuPré
Doug Eskew   Gwen Stewart

UNDERSTUDIES: Lynette G. DuPré (Mahalia), Tina Fabrique (other women)
MUSICAL NUMBERS: I Found the Answer, St. Louis Blues, It's Amazing What God Can Do, On the Battlefield for My Lord/Glory Hallelujah, He May Not Come When You Want Him, Lord I'm Determined, Happy Days Are Here Again, Precious Lord, Jesus Remembers When Others Forget, Thank You for the Change in My Life, Come on Children Let's Sing, Even Me, Didn't It Rain, Wade in the Water/Old Ship of Zion/Battle Hymn of the Republic/I've Been Buked, Soon I Will Be Done, His Gift to Me, Move on up a Little Higher, Rusty Bell, Truly Blessed, He's Got the Whole World in His Hand

A musical in two acts and 14 scenes.

*Closed May 20, 1990 after 33 performances and 12 previews.

Martha Swope/Eric Stephen Jacobs Photos

**Top: Queen Esther Marrow, Gwen Stewart, Lynette G.
DuPré, Carl Hall, Doug Eskew**

**Gwen Stewart, Doug Eskew, Queen Esther Marrow, Lynette
G. DuPré, Carl Hall Above: DuPré, Stewart, Marrow**

33

ACCOMPLICE

By Rupert Holmes; Director, Art Wolff; Sets, David Jenkins; Costumes, Alvin Colt; Lighting, Martin Aronstein; Special Effects, Gregory Meeh; Incidental Music, Rupert Holmes; Music Performed by Deborah Grunfeld; Sound, Peter J. Fitzgerald; Casting Consultant, Pat McCorkle; Production Stage Manager, Thomas A. Kelly; Stage Manager, Glen Gardali; Company Manager, Gerri Higgins; Production Associate, Seymour Herscher; Pyrotechnist, Tony De Paulo; Wardrobe, Kathleen Gallagher; Hair, Michael Heller; Sound Effects, Dan Tramon; Associate Producer, Steve Harris; Dialect, Robert Easton; Makeup, Joe Cranzano; Presented by Alexander H. Cohen and Hildy Parks, Max Cooper and Normand Kurtz; Press, John Springer/Gary Springer. Opened in the Richard Rodgers Theatre on Thursday, April 26, 1990.*

CAST

Michael McKean	Natalia Nogulich
Jason Alexander	Pamela Brüll

A thriller in two acts and 4 scenes. The action takes place in an English moorland cottage and a Claridge's suite in the mid-1970s.

*Closed June 10, 1990 after 52 performances and 23 previews. The Forty-sixth St. Theatre was re-named the Richard Rodgers Theatre with this production.

Martha Swope Photos

Right Center: Pamela Brull, Jason Alexander Top Right: Natalia Nogulich, Michael McKean

Pamela Brull, Jason Alexander, Natalia Nogulich, Michael McKean

A CHANGE IN THE HEIR

Music, Dan Sticco; Lyrics, George H. Gorham; Book, Gorham & Sticco; Director/Choreographer, David H. Bell; Sets, Michael Anania, Ron Kadri; Musical Director/Dance Arrangements, Rob Bowman; Orchestrations, Robby Merkin; Costumes, David Murin; Lighting, Jeff Davis; General Management, Gindi Theatrical; Casting, Joseph Abaldo; Production Stage Manager, Terrence J. Witter; Stage Manager, Cheryl Mintz; Dance Captain, David Serko; Company Manager, Barbara Seinfeld; Assistant Director, Greg Schaffert; Assistant Set Design, Tim Saternow; Assistant Costumes, Ellen Ryba; Assistant Lights, John Heretz; Wardrobe, Rachael Scheib, Tommy Bourgeois; Props, David T. Fletcher, Michael Stein; Produced by Stewart F. Lane; Press, Shirley Herz Associates/Shirley Herz, Sam Rudy. Opened in the Edison Theatre on Sunday, April 29, 1990.*

CAST

Aunt Julia	Brooks Almy
Giles	Brian Sutherland
Edwin	J. K. Simmons
Nicholas	David Gunderman
Countess	Connie Day
Lady Enid	Mary Stout
Prince Conrad	Judy Blazer
Princess Agnes	Jeffrey Herbst
Martha	Jan Neuberger
Lady Elizabeth	Jennifer Smith

UNDERSTUDIES: Connie Day (Julia), David Gunderman (Agnes), Kathy Morath (Conrad/Elizabeth/Martha/Countess/Enid), David Serko (Edwin/Nicholas/Giles)
MUSICAL NUMBERS: Prologue, Here I Am, The Weekend, Look at Me, Take a Look at That, Quintet, Can't I, When, A Fairy Tale, An Ordinary Family, Happily Ever After, After All, Duet, Hold That Crown, By Myself, Finale

A musical comedy in two acts. The action takes place in a castle far, far away once upon a time.

*Closed May 13, 1990 after 17 performances and 23 previews.

Gerry Goodstein Photos

Judy Blazer (center) and Cast Top Right: Brooks Almy, Jan Neuberger

Barnard Hughes, Timothy Hutton Left: Hutton, Mary-Louise Parker (also top)

PRELUDE TO A KISS

By Craig Lucas; Director, Norman René; Sets, Loy Arcenas; Costumes, Walker Hicklin; Lighting, Debra J. Kletter; Sound, Scott Lehrer; Hair/Wigs, Bobby H. Grayson; Production Stage Manager, James Harker; Stage Manager, M. A. Howard; Company Manager, Douglas C. Baker; General Management, David Strong Warner, Inc.; Production Supervisor, Neil Mazzella; Wardrobe, Dawn Walnut; Associate Producer, Lawrence J. Wilker; Presented by Christopher Gould, Suzanne Golden, Dodger Productions; Originally Produced by South Coast Repertory with support from the National Endowment for the Arts; Produced Off-Broadway by Circle Repertory Co.; Press, Joshua Ellis/Adrian Bryan-Brown, Jackie Green, Susanne Tighe, Tim Ray. Opened in the Helen Hayes Theatre on Tuesday, May 1, 1990.*

CAST

Peter	Timothy Hutton
Rita	Mary-Louise Parker
Taylor	John Dossett
Tom/Jamaican Waiter	L. Peter Callender
Mrs. Boyle	Debra Monk
Dr. Boyle	Larry Bryggman
Minister/Guest/Barfly/Vacationer	Craig Bockhorn
Aunt Dorothy/Leah	Joyce Reehling
Uncle Fred/Guest/Barfly/Vacationer	Michael Warren Powell
Old Man	Barnard Hughes
Party-Wedding Guests/Barflies/Vacationers	Brian Cousins, Kimberly Dudwitt

A contemporary fairy tale in two acts. The action takes place in NYC, New Jersey and Jamaica.

UNDERSTUDIES: John Dossett (Peter), Susan Gabriel (Rita/Dorothy/Leah), Brian Cousins (Taylor/Peter), Monté Russell (Tom/Waiter/Minister), Cynthia Darlow (Mrs. Boyle/Leah/Dorothy), Ron Parady (Dr. Boyle/Minister/Fred/Old Man), Wyman Pendleton (Old Man/Fred/Minister), Kimberly Dudwitt (Rita), Joyce Reehling (Mrs. Boyle), Michael Warren Powell (Dr. Boyle).

*Still playing May 31, 1990. It had previously played 57 performances in the Circle Repertory Theatre with Alec Baldwin in the lead.

Bob Marshak/Gerry Goodstein Photos

Barnard Hughes, Mary-Louise Parker, Debra Monk

Left Center: Timothy Hutton, Mary-Louise Parker

ZOYA'S APARTMENT

By Mikhail Bulgakov; Translation, Nicholas Saunders, Frank Dwyer; Director, Boris A. Morozov; Sets, James Morgan; Original Designs, Josef Sumbatsivily; Lighting, Mary Jo Dondlinger; Costumes, Cynthia Doty; Original Designs, Tatiana Gleboya; Music, Gregory Gobernik; Movement, Mina Yakim; Hair, Linda Rice; Production Stage Manager, Wm. Hare; Asst. Stage Manager, Zoya Wyeth; Casting, Julie Hughes, Barry Moss, Jessica Gilburne, Arnold Mungioli; Asst. to Director/ Translator, Nina Gutenberg; Wardrobe, Claire Libin; Asst. Scenic Design, Steven Perry, John Shimrock; Asst. Lighting, Farid Kebour; Wigs, Linda Rice; Hair, Anita-Ali Davis; Presented by Circle in the Square Theatre (Theodore Mann, Artistic Director; Paul Libin, Producing Director); Press, Merle Debuskey/Leo Stern; Company Manager, Susan Elrod. Opened in the Circle in the Square Uptown Theatre on Thursday, May 10, 1990.*

CAST

Zoya Denisova Peltz	Linda Thorson
Manyushka	Chandra Lee
Anisism Zotikovich Aliluya	Ray DeMattis
Pavel Fyodorovich Abolyaninov	Robert LuPone
Gandzalin	Akira Takayama
Cherubim	Ernest Abuba
Aleksander Tarasovich Ametistov	Bronson Pinchot
Agnes Nikolaevna	Florence Rowe
Tailor/3rd Stranger	Kevin Crawford
Sepoorakhina	Fiona Davis
Shopping Lady	Talia Paul
Alla Vadimovna	Lauri Landry
Marya Nikiforovna	Colleen Gallagher
Lizanka	Holly Chant
Madame Ivanova	Careayre Rambeau
Boris Semyonovich Goose	Robert Stattel
First Stranger	Dana Mills
2nd Stranger	David Silber
Dead Body of Ivan Vasilyevich	Joe Palmieri
Robert	Robertson Carricart

A Russian comedy in two acts and 8 scenes. The action takes place in Moscow in 1926.

*Closed June 17, 1990 after 45 performances and 13 previews.

Right: Bronson Pinchot, Linda Thorson Top: Robert LuPone, Linda Thorson, Bronson Pinchot

Bronson Pinchot, Linda Thorson, Chandra Lee, Robert LuPone

THE CEMETERY CLUB

By Ivan Menchell; Director, Pamela Berlin; Sets, John Lee Beatty; Costumes, Lindsay W. Davis; Lighting, Natasha Katz; Sound, Scott T. Anderson; Music, Robert Dennis; Production Supervisor, Mortimer Halpern; General Manager, Charlotte Wilcox; Technical Supervisor, Jeremiah J. Harris Associates; Production Stage Manager, Barbara-Mae Phillips; Stage Manager, Charles Kindl; Company Manager, Robb Lady; Wardrobe, Sharon A. Lewis; Executive Producers, Philip Rose, Howard Hurst; Presented by Mr. Hurst, Mr. Rose, David Brown and Sophie Hurst; Press, Joshua Ellis/Adrian Bryan-Brown, Jackie Green, Susanne Tighe, Tim Ray; Produced originally at Yale Repertory and subsequently at Cleveland Play House. Opened in the Brooks Atkinson Theatre on Tuesday, May 15, 1990.*

CAST

Ida	Elizabeth Franz
Lucille	Eileen Heckart
Doris	Doris Belack
Sam	Lee Wallace
Mildred	Judith Granite

UNDERSTUDIES/STANDBYS: Lucille Patton (Lucille/Mildred), Catherine Wolf, Judith Granite (Ida/Doris), Roger Serbagi (Sam).

A comedy in two acts. The action takes place in the living room of Ida's house and at a cemetery in Forest Hills, Queens, at present.

*Closed June 1, 1990 after 56 performances and 10 previews.

Joan Marcus Photos

Right: Doris Belack, Elizabeth Franz, Eileen Heckart

Doris Belack, Eileen Heckart, Lee Wallace, Elizabeth Franz

NIGHT OF 100 STARS III

Presented by Alexander H. Cohen for the Actors' Fund of America; A Brentwood Television Corp. Production; Director, Jeff Margolis; Written by Hildy Parks; Produced by Hildy Parks, Jeff Margolis, Co-Producer, Vern T. Calhoun; Musical Direction, Glen Roven; Musical Numbers Staged and Choreographed by Albert Stephenson; Designer, Ray Klausen; Costumes, Alvin Colt; Lighting, Jeff Engel; Associate Producer, Glen Roven; Executive in charge of Production, Robin C. Mathiesen; Talent Executive, Laurie Kaufman; Production Stage Manager, Robert L. Borod; Film Segment, John Springer; Sports Segment, Joe Goldstein and David Herscher; Piano Segment, Karen Sherry; Fashion Segment, Alvin Colt; Production Supervisor, Paula Shugart; Assistant to Mr. Cohen, Jennifer Ober; Script Supervisor, Betsy Krouner; Talent Consultant, Gus Schirmer; Associate Directors, Terri McCoy, Steve Santos; Additional Arrangements, Ted Sperling; Orchestrations, Larry Schwartz, Joe Curiale, Peter Cannarozzi, Danny Troob, Bruce Miller, Ned Ginsberg; Orchestra Contractor, John Miller; Hair Supervisor, Robert DiNiro; Make-up Supervisor, Joe Cranzano; Wardrobe Supervisor, Kate Gaudio; Press, Merle Debuskey, Susan Chicoine. Presented in Radio City Music Hall on Saturday, May 5, 1990, and on television Monday, May 21, 1990.

PARTICIPATING ARTISTS

Hank Aaron, Danny Aiello, Col. "Buzz" Aldrin, Jane Alexander, Kim Alexis, Muhammad Ali, Eddie Arcaro, Beatrice Arthur, Ed Asner, Mark Linn Baker, Carl Banks, Alan & Marilyn Bergman, Debby Boone, Riddick Bowe, Garth Brooks, Joe Brooks, Leslie Browne, Don Budge, Raymond Burr, Michael Caine, Maria Calegari, Cab Calloway, Dick Cavett, Carol Channing, Dick Clark, Howard Cosell, Bob Cousy, Walter Cronkite, Hume Cronyn, Cathy Lee Crosby, Randall Cunningham, Tyne Daly, Stanley Dancer, Hal David, Clifton Davis, Felicity de Jager, Carmen de Lavallade, Don Diamont, Harrison Dillard, Joe DiMaggio, Mayor David Dinkins, E. L. Doctorow, James "Buster" Douglas, Keir Dullea, Christine Dunham, Greg Evigan, Douglas Fairbanks, Jr., Morgan Fairchild, John Farrar, Michael Feinstein, Jane Fonda, Faith Ford, Aretha Franklin, Joe Frazier, Willie Gault, Crystal Gayle, Richard Gere, Estelle Getty, Mickey Gilley, Jose Greco, Cynthia Gregory, Joel Grey, Mother Hale, Gregory Harrison, Kitty Carlisle Hart, Helen Hayes, Katharine Hepburn, Edward Herrmann, Geoffrey Holder, Thelma Hopkins, Freddie Jackson, Beverly Johnson, Denton Johnson, Virginia Johnson, Jackie Joyner-Kersee, Stacy Keach, Kid 'n' Play, Robert Klein, Gladys Knight, Valentina Kozlova, Dr. Mathilde Krim, Swoosie Kurtz, Patti LaBelle, Sean Landeta, Linda Lavin, Jean LeClerc, Peggy Lee, Jerry Leiber, Richard Leigh, Hal Linden, John Lithgow, Rich Little, Robert Loggia, Priscilla Lopez, Greg Louganis, Chad Lowe, Susan Lucci, Sidney Lumet, Loretta Lynn, Marty Lyons, Galt MacDermot, Larkin Malloy, Joseph Mankiewicz, Rue McClanahan, Marilyn McCoo, Donna McKechnie, Julianne McNamara, Audrey Meadows, Jayne Meadows, Ray Mercer, Dina Merrill, Robert Merrill, George Mikan, Liliane Montevecchi, Robert Morse, Joe Namath, Diane Nelson, Barry Newman, Olivia Newton-John, Sandi Patti, Minnie Pearl, Joseph Phillips, Stefanie Powers, Eddie Rabbitt, Tony Randall, Rex Reed, Christopher Reeve, Ann Reinking, Jerry Rice, Chita Rivera, Geraldo Rivera, Jason Robards, Eric Roberts, Oscar Robertson, The Rockettes, Jerry Seinfeld, Brooke Shields, Martin Short, Sylvia Sidney, Ron Silver, Liz Smith, Toukie Smith, Paul Sorvino, Dr. Benjamin Spock, Sylvester Stallone, James Stewart, Michael Stoller, Charles Strouse, Jule Styne, Raven-Symone, Jessica Tandy, Judy Tenuta, Alan Thicke, B. J. Thomas, Marian Tompson, Mel Torme, Conway Twitty, Bonnie Tyler, Liv Ullmann, Joan Van Ark, John Vanbiesbrouck, Luther Vandross, Dick Van Dyke, Ricky Van Shelton, Abe Vigoda, Christopher Walken, Mike Wallace, Barbara Walters, Diane Warren, Sam Waterston, Raquel Welch, Betty White, Jesse White, Elie Wiesel, Wild Rose, Mary Wilson, Connie Paraskevin Young, Henny Youngman, Pia Zadora

LENINGRAD STATE MUSIC HALL

Producer/Art Director, Ilya Rakhlin; Chief Choreographer, Igor Belsky; Producer, Kyuf Kaufman; Costume Designer, Yadviga Kuptsova; Company Manager, Valentin Tkachenko; Stage Manager, Kristina Kinet; Coordinator, V. Mustafin; Art Director, Neal Krause; Press, Susan Bloch & Co./Kevin P. McAnarney, Ellen Zeisler, Tara McBride. Opened in City Center Theater on Saturday, May 26, 1990*

SOLOISTS

Olga Vardasheva, Evgeniya Vlasova, Evgeny Shpitko, Anatoly Tukish, Olga & Irina Lobanov, Galina Kuznetsova, Nina & Alexandr Balmont, Mikhail Gubanov, Oleg Zheltkov, Ballet Dancers of Leningrad Music Hall

PROGRAM

Fair, Russian Songs, Butterfly and Flower, Girls' Gathering, Gypsy Romances, Gypsy Dance, Comic Tricks, Oriental Legend, Hussar's Ballad, Airy Fantasy, Barynya, Gzhel, Songs of Peoples of the World, Acrobatic Etude, Cossack's Souvenir, Girls, All the Stars, Kreschendo, Two under the Umbrella, Bolero, Songs of Peoples of the World, Russian Souvenir, Finale. Performed in two acts.

*Closed Sunday, June 3, 1990 after a limited engagement of 16 performances.

CATS

Based on "Old Possum's Book of Practical Cats" by T. S. Eliot; Additional Lyrics, Trevor Nunn, Richard Stilgoe; Music, Andrew Lloyd Webber; Director, Trevor Nunn; Associate Director/Choreographer, Gillian Lynne; Presented by Cameron Mackintosh, The Really Useful Company, David Geffen, The Shubert Organization; Executive Producers, R. Tyler Gatchell, Jr., Peter Neufeld; Casting, Johnson-Liff & Zerman; Orchestrations, David Cullen, Andrew Lloyd Webber; Production Musical Director, David Caddick; Musical Directors, Ethyl Will, Sue Anderson; Sound, Martin Levan; Lighting, David Hersey; Production Design, John Napier; Original Cast Album on Geffen Records & Tapes; Production Supervisor, Jeff Lee; Company Manager, James G. Mennen; Dance Supervisor, Richard Stafford; Assistant Choreographer, Jo-Anne Robinson; Dance Captain, Suzanne Viverito; Associate Conductor, Bill Grossman; Production Assistant, Nancy Hall; Technical Supervisors, Arthur Siccardi, Peter Feller; Props, George Green, Jr., George Green III, Robert Bostwick; Wardrobe, Adelaide Laurino, Rachele Bussanich; Hair Stylists, Leon Gagliardi, Frank Paul; Scenic Design Associate, Raymond Huessy; Wigs, Paul Huntley; Makeup, Candace Carell; Stage Managers, Sally J. Jacobs, Dan Hild, Peggy Peterson; Press, Fred Nathan Co./Merle Frimark, Marc P. Thibodeau, William Schelble, Ian Rand, Colleen Brown. Opened in the Winter Garden on Thursday, Oct. 7, 1982*

CAST

Alonzo	Scott Taylor
Gus/Growltiger/Bustopher	Paul Harman/Dale Hensley
Bombalurina	Marlene Danielle
Mungojerrie	Ray Roderick
Cassandra	Leigh Webster
Coricopat	Johnny Anzalone
Demeter	Beth Swearingnen/Brenda Braxton
Rumpleteazer	Kristi Lynes
Grizabella	Loni Ackerman
Jellylorum/Griddlebone	Bonnie Simmons
Jennyanydots	Cindy Benson
Mistoffelees	Michael Barriskill/Michael Arnold
Munkustrap	Robert Amirante, Greg Minahan
Old Deuteronomy	Larry Small
Plato/Macavity/Rumpus Cat	Jamie/Randy Wojcik
Pouncival	John Joseph Festa
Rum Tum Tugger	Frank Mastracola
Sillabub	Dana Walker, Michelle Schumacher
Skimbleshanks	Richard Stafford, Eric Scott Kincaid
Tantomile	Lisa Dawn Cave
Tumblebrutus	Jay Poindexter
Victoria	Claudia Shell
Cats Chorus	Jay Aubrey Jones, Bryan Landrine, Susan Powers, Heidi Stallings, Lee Lobenhoffer

STANDBYS/UNDERSTUDIES: John Aller (Alonzo/Coricopat/Munkustrap/Plato/Macavity/Rumpus Cat/Rum Tum Tugger), Brian Andrews (Alonzo/Mungojerrie/Plato/Macavity/Rumpus Cat/Pouncival/Tumblebrutus), Jack Magradey (Alonzo/Coricopat/Mungojerrie/Munkustrap/Rum Tum Tugger/Skimbleshanks), Lee Lobenhofer (Bustopher/Asparagus/Growltiger/Old Deuteronomy), Rebecca Timms (Cassandra/Bombalurina/Demeter/Sillabub/Tantomile), Darlene Wilson (Bombalurina/Demeter/Tantomile), Lily-Lee Wong (Cassandra/Sillabub/Tantomile/Victoria), Wade Laboissonniere (Coricopat/Mungojerrie/Pouncival/Skimbleshanks/Tumblebrutus), John Vincent Leggio (Coricopat/Mistoffelees/Mungojerrie/Pouncival/Tumblebrutus), Lisa Dawn Cave (Demeter/Victoria), Marcy DeGonge (Jennyanydots/Jellylorum/Griddlebone), Heidi Stallings (Grizabella), Susan Powers (Jellylorum/Griddlebone/Jennyanydots), Suzanne Viverito (Jennyanydots/Rumpleteazer/Sillabub/Tantomile/Victoria), Scott Taylor (Rum Tum Tugger/Munkustrap/Plato/Macavity/Rumpus Cat), Johnny Anzalone (Mistoffelees), Jay Aubrey Jones (Old Deuteronomy), Michelle Schomacher (Rumpleteazer).

MUSICAL NUMBERS: The Naming of Cats, Invitation to the Jellicle Ball, The Old Gumbie Cat, The Rum Tum Tugger, Grizabella the Glamour Cat, Bustopher Jones, Mungojerrie and Rumpleteazer, Old Deuteronomy, The Awefull Battle of the Pekes and Pollicles, The Marching Songs of the Pollice Dogs, The Jellicle Ball, Memory, Moments of Happiness, Gus the Theatre Cat, Growltiger's Last Stand, Skimbleshanks, Macavity, Mr. Mistoffelees, The Journey to the Heaviside Layer, The Ad-Dressing of Cats.

A musical in 2 acts and 20 scenes.

*Still playing May 31, 1990. Winner of 1983 "Tonys" for Best Musical, Book, Score, Direction, Supporting Musical Actress (Betty Buckley as Grizabella), Costumes, and Lighting. For original production, see *Theatre World* Vol. 39.

Martha Swope Photos

Loni Ackerman (right)

A CHORUS LINE

Conceived, Choreographed and Directed by Michael Bennett; Book, James Kirkwood, Nicholas Dante; Music, Marvin Hamlisch; Lyrics, Edward Kleban; Co-Choreographer, Bob Avian; A New York Shakespeare Festival Production presented by Joseph Papp in association with Plum Productions; Musical Direction/Vocal Arrangements, Don Pippin; Orchestrations, Bill Byers, Hershy Kay, Jonathan Tunick; Setting, Robin Wagner; Costumes, Theoni V. Aldredge; Lighting, Tharon Musser; Sound, Abe Jacob; Music Director, Jerry Goldberg; Music Coordinator, Robert Thomas; Associate Producer, Bernard Gerston; Assistant to Choreographers, Baayork Lee; Associate Producer, Jason Steven Cohen; Company Manager, Robert Reilly; Dance Captain, Troy Garza; Wardrobe, Alyce Gilbert; Stage Managers, Tom Porter, Ronald Stafford, Fraser Ellis; Press, Merle Debuskey, Richard Kornberg, Susan Chicoine. Opened in the Shubert Theatre on Friday, July 25, 1975*

FINAL CAST

Don	Keith Bernardo
Diana	Roxann Biggs
Sheila	Susan Danielle
Herman	Fraser Ellis
Kristine	Cynthia Fleming
Greg	Doug Friedman
Cassie	Laurie Gamache
Jarad	Troy Garza
Paul	Drew Geraci
Mike	Michael Gruber
Zach	Eivind Harum
Judy	Angelique Ilo
Val	Diana Kavilis
Douglas	Frank Kliegel
Bobby	Ron Kurowski
Ed	Joe Langworth
Vicki	Paula Leggett
Tom	Carlos Lopez
Tricia	Robin Lyon
Bebe	Christine Maglione
Larry	Kevin Neil McCready
Frank	William Mead
Linda	Dana Moore
Butch	Kevyn Morrow
Mark	Jack Noseworthy
Richie	Gordon Owens
Roy	Matt Pedersen
Hilary	Donna M. Pompei
Al	Tommy Re
Maggie	Susan Santoro
Connie	Sachi Shimizu
Lois	Julie Tussey

UNDERSTUDIES: Fraser Ellis (Mark/Bobby/Don), Troy Garza (Mike/Greg/Paul/Larry/Al), Angelique Ilo (Cassie), Diana Kavilis (Cassie/Diana), Frank Kliegel (Don/Zach/Bobby), Joe Langworth (Mark/Larry), Paula Leggett (Sheila/Judy/Kristine), Carlos Lopez (Paul/Mark/Mike/Al), Robin Lyon (Bebe/Diana/Val/Maggie), Kevin Neil McCready (Zach), William Mead (Al/Greg/Mike), Dana Moore (Judy/Sheila), Kevyn Morrow (Richie), Matt Pedersen (Larry/Don/Al/Mike), Donna M. Pompei (Diana/Connie/Bebe/Maggie/Val), Julie Tussey (Val/Kristine).
MUSICAL NUMBERS: I Hope I Get It, I Can Do That, "And . . .", At the Ballet, Sing!, Hello 12 Hello 13 Hello Love, Nothing, Dance: 10 Looks: 3, The Music and the Mirror, One, The Tap Combination, What I Did for Love

A musical performed without intermission. The action takes place in 1975 during an audition in this theatre.

*Closed April 28, 1990 after 6137 performances, the longest running show in Broadway history. Cited as Best Musical of 1975 by NY Drama Critics Circle, winner of 1976 Pulitzer Prize, 1976 "Tonys" for Best Musical, Book, Score, Direction, Lighting, Choreography, Best Actress in a Musical (Donna McKechnie), Best Featured Actor and Actress in a Musical (Sammy Williams, Kelly Bishop), and a Special Theatre World Award was presented to each member of the creative staff and original cast. See *Theatre World,* Vol. 31.

Martha Swope Photos

Top Right: Entire Cast
Below: Laurie Gamache

Current Company

Boyd Gaines, Joan Allen, Peter Friedman, Joanne Camp
Right: Anne Lange, Marita Geraghty, Deborah Hedwall,
Christine Lahti, Amy Aquino

THE HEIDI CHRONICLES

By Wendy Wasserstein; Director, Daniel Sullivan; Set, Thomas Lynch; Costumes, Jennifer von Mayrhauser; Lighting, Pat Collins; Sound, Scott Lehrer; Projection Design, Wendall Harrington; Casting, Daniel Swee; Presented by The Shubert Organization, Suntory International Corp., and James Walsh in association with Playwrights Horizons; General Manager, James Walsh; Company Manager, Florie Seery; Production Coordinator, Carl Mulert; Technical Supervisors, Theatre Services; Props, Karen Caton; Wardrobe, Barbara Hladsky; Hairstylist, David H. Lawrence; Wigs, Paul Huntley; Stage Managers, Roy Harris, Mary Fran Loftus; Press, Fred Nathan Co./Marc P. Thibodeau, Philip Rinaldi, Merle Frimark, William Schelble, Maria Somma, Ian Rand; Opened in the Plymouth Theatre on Thursday, March 9, 1989*

CAST

Heidi Holland .... Joan Allen†1
Susan Johnston .... Ellen Parker†2
Chris Boxer/Mark/TV Attendant/Waiter/Ray .... Drew McVey†3
Peter Patrone .... Boyd Gaines†4
Scoop Rosenbaum .... Peter Friedman†5
Jill/Debbie/Lisa .... Anne Lange†6
Becky/Clara/Denise .... Cynthia Nixon†7
Fran/Molly/Betsy/April .... Joanne Camp†8

UNDERSTUDIES: Laura Hicks (Heidi/Susan), Stephen Stout (Scoop/Peter/Chris, etc), Amanda Carlin (Jill/Fran/Becky)

A play in 2 acts and 11 scenes. The action takes place from 1965 to 1989 at various locations.

*Closed Sept. 1, 1990 after 621 performances. Recipient of 1989 Pulitzer Prize, New York Drama Critics Circle Citation, Drama Desk, Outer Critics Circle, and "Tonys" for Best New Play, and Best Featured Actor in a Play (Boyd Gaines).

†Succeeded by: 1. Christine Lahti, Brooke Adams, Mary McDonnell, 2. Amy Aquino, 3. Tony Carlin, 4. David Pierce, David Lansbury, 5. Tony Shalhoub, 6. Julie White, 7. Marita Geraghty, 8. Deborah Hedwall, Alma Cuervo

Peter Cunningham Photos

Right Center: Christine Lahti, David Pierce

Tony Shalhoub, Brooke Adams

JEROME ROBBINS' BROADWAY

By James M. Barrie, Irving Berlin, Leonard Bernstein, Jerry Bock, Sammy Cahn, Moose Charlop, Betty Comden, Larry Gelbart, Morton Gould, Adolph Green, Oscar Hammerstein II, Sheldon Harnick, Arthur Laurents, Carolyn Leigh, Stephen Longstreet, Hugh Martin, Jerome Robbins, Richard Rodgers, Burt Shevelove, Stephen Sondheim, Joseph Stein, Jule Styne; Entire production Choreographed and Directed by Jerome Robbins; Co-Director, Grover Dale; Assistants to Choreographer, Cynthia Onrubia, Victor Castelli, Jerry Mitchell; Musical Director, Paul Gemignani; Sound, Otts Munderloh; Hair/Makeup, J. Roy Helland; Casting, Jay Binder; Orchestrations, Sid Ramin, William D. Brohn; Musical Continuity, Scott Frankel; Scenic Design, Robin Wagner; Supervising Costume Designer, Joseph G. Ausili; Lighting, Jennifer Tipton; Scenery, Boris Aronson, Jo Mielziner, Oliver Smith, Robin Wagner, Tony Walton; Costumes, Joseph Ausili, Alvin Colt, Raoul Pene du Bois, Irene Sharaff, Tony Walton, Miles White, Patricia Zipprodt; General Manager, Leonard Soloway; Production Supervisor, Charles Blackwell; Company Manager, Brian Dunbar; Technical Supervision, Theatrical Services/Pete Feller, Arthur Sicardi; Props, Tommy Thomson; Wardrobe, Joe Busheme; Hair Supervisor, David Brian Brown; Stage Managers, Beverly Randolph, Pamela Singer, Dale Kaufman, Joe Konicki; Press, Fred Nathan Co./William Schelble, Merle Frimark, Ellen Levene, Marc P. Thibodeau, Ian Rand, Colleen Brown. Opened in the Imperial Theatre Sunday, Feb. 26, 1989*

CAST

Jason Alexander (succeeded by Terrence Mann, Tony Roberts), Richard Amaro, Dorothy Benham, Jim Rorstelmann, Jeffrey Lee Broadhurst, Bill Burns, Christophe Caballero, Mindy Cartwright, Irene Cho (succeeded by JoAnn M. Hunter, Ellen Troy), Jamie Cohen, Charlotte d'Amboise (Nancy Ticotin, Leslie Trayer), Camille de Ganon, Donna Di Meo, Donna Marie Elio, Mark Esposito, Scott Fowler (succeeded by John MacInnis), Angelo H. Fraboni, Ramon Galindo, Nicholas Garr, Gregorey Garrison, Michael Scott Gregory (succeeded by Marc Villa, Cleve Asbury, Jack Noseworthy, Ned Hannah), Andrew Grose, Carolyn Goor, Sean Grant, (succeeded by Bill Brassea), Alexia Hess, Nancy Hess, Louise Hickey, Mark Hoebec, Eric A. Hoisington, Barbara Hoon (succeeded by Linda Talcott, Mindy Cartwright), JoAnn M. Hunter (succeeded by Lyd-Lyd Gaston, Andi Tyler), Scott Jovovich (succeeded by Scott Spahr), Pamela Khoury, Susan Kikuchi (succeeded by Lyd-Lyd Gaston), Joe Konicki, Michael Kubala, Robert La Fosse (succeeded by Scott Fowler, Cleve Asbury, Kipling Houston, Angelo H. Fraboni, Troy Myers), Mary Ann Lamb (succeeded by Lisa Leguillou, Lori Werner, Maria Neenan), Jane Lanier (succeeded by Lori Werner, Alexia Hess, Maria Neenan), David Lanier, Andrea Leigh-Smith, David Lowenstein, Michael Lynch (succeeded by K. Craig Innes, Alan Arino, Steve Ochoa, Harrison Beal), Greta Martin, Joey McKneely (succeeded by Steve Ochoa), Julio Monge (succeeded by Sergio Trujillo, Tony Caligagan), Troy Myers, Maria Neenan (succeeded by Erin Robbins), Jack Noseworthy, Steve Ochoa (succeeded by Christophe Caballero), Kelly Patterson (succeeded by Cleve Asbury, John MacInnis), Luis Perez (succeeded by Angelo H. Fraboni), Faith Prince (succeeded by Dorothy Stanley), Stephen Reed, James Rivera, Tom Robbins (succeeded by Jeff Gardner, Greg Schanuel), George Russell, Greg Schanuel, Debbie Shapiro (succeeded by Karen Mason, Donna Marie Elio, Dorothy Stanley), Renee Stork, Mary Ellen Stuart (succeeded by Deanna Wells, Maureen Moore, Colleen Fitzpatrick), Linda Talcott (succeeded by Christine DeVito, Mindy Cartwright), Leslie Trayer, Ellen Troy, Andi Tyler, Sergio Trujillo, Scott Wise, Elaine Wright, Barbara Yeager (succeeded by Nancy Ticotin), Alice Yearsley.

MUSICAL NUMBERS

ACT I: Overture, New York New York, Sailors on the Town, Ya Got Me, Charleston, Comedy Tonight, I Still Get Jealous, Suite of dances from "West Side Story"
ACT II: The Small House of Uncle Thomas, You Gotta Have a Gimmick, I'm Flying, On a Sunday by the Sea, Mr. Monotony, Fiddler on the Roof, Some Other Time, Finale

*Closed Sept. 1, 1990 after 634 performances and 55 previews. Recipient of 1989 "Tonys" for Best Musical, Best Performance by Leading Actor in a Musical (Jason Alexander), Best Performance by a Featured Actor and Actress in a Musical (Scott Wise, Debbie Shapiro), Best Direction, Best Lighting.

Martha Swope Photos

Top Right: Terrence Mann, Michael Kubala, Joey McKneely, Scott Wise in "Comedy Tonight" Below: Entire Cast

Tony Roberts, Cleve Asbury, Angelo H. Fraboni, Gregorey Garrison in scene from "High Button Shoes"

LEND ME A TENOR

By Ken Ludwig; Director, Jerry Zaks; Setting, Tony Walton; Costumes, William Ivey Long; Lighting, Paul Gallo; Sound, Aural Fixation; Hair, Angela Gari; Casting, Johnson-Liff & Zerman; Music Coordinator, Edward Strauss; Presented by Martin Starger and The Really Useful Theatre Co. (Bridget Hayward, Andrew Lloyd Webber, Keith Turner); General Manager, Robert Kamlot; Company Manager, Lisa M. Poyer; Technical Supervision, Theatrical Services (Arthur Siccardi, Peter Feller, Sr.); Props, George Wagner; Wardrobe, Karen Lloyd; Production Assistant, Richard Hester; Stage Managers, Steven Beckler, Clifford Schwartz; Press, Joshua Ellis/ Adrian Bryan-Brown, Jackie Green, Susanne Tighe, Tim Ray, Chris Boneau, Shannon Barr, John Barlow. Opened in the Royale Theatre on Thursday, March 2, 1989*

CAST

Maggie	J. Smith-Cameron†1
Max	Victor Garber†2
Saunders	Philip Bosco
Tito Merelli	Ron Holgate
Maria Merelli	Tovah Feldshuh†3
Bellhop	Jeff Brooks
Diana	Caroline Lagerfelt†4
Julia	Jane Connell

UNDERSTUDIES & STANDBYS: David Cryer (Saunders/Merelli), Michael Waldron (Max/Bellhop), Jane Cronin (Maria/Julia), Eileen Dunn (Diana/Maggie)

A farce in 2 acts and 4 scenes. The action takes place in a hotel suite in Cleveland, Ohio, in 1934.

*Closed April 22, 1990 after 468 performances. Recipient of 1989 "Tonys" for Best Performance by a Leading Actor in a Play (Philip Bosco), and Best Director of a Play (Jerry Zaks)

†Succeeded by: 1. Wendy Makkena, 2. Patrick Quinn, 3. Chris Callen, 4. Jane Summerhays

Martha Swope Photos

Top Right: Philip Bosco, Jane Connell, Tovah Feldshuh

Wendy Makkena, Philip Bosco, Jeff Brooks, Jane Connell, Jane Summerhays, Patrick Quinn, Chris Callen, Ron Holgate

LES MISÉRABLES

By Alain Boublil, Claude-Michel Schonberg; Based on novel of same title by Victor Hugo; Music, Claude-Michel Schonberg; Lyrics, Herbert Kretzmer; Original French text, Alain Boublil, Jean-Marc Natel; Additional Material, James Fenton; Orchestral Score, John Cameron; Musical Supervision/Direction, Robert Billig; Sound, Andrew Bruce/Autograph; Associate Director/Executive Producer, Richard Jay-Alexander; Executive Producer, Martin McCallum; Casting, Johnson-Liff & Zerman; General Management, Alan Wasser; Presented by Cameron Macintosh; Direction/ Adaptation, Trevor Nunn, John Caird; Design, John Napier; Lighting, David Hersey; Costumes, Andreane Neofitou; Produced in association with JFK Center for the Performing Arts (Roger L. Stevens, Chairman); Original Cast Recording by Geffen; Production Supervisor, Sam Stickler; Associate General Manager, Allan Williams; Technical Manager, John H. Paull III; Props, Timothy Abel, Larry Palazzo; Wardrobe, Adelaide Laurino, Kelly Supple, John Laurino; Wigs, Jody Thomas, Carmel Vargyas; Company Managers, Mark S. Andrews, Harriett Kittner; Stage Managers, Marybeth Abel, Thom Schilling, Deborah Clelland; Press, Fred Nathan Co./Marc Thibodeau, Merle Frimark, William Schelble, Maria Somma, Ian Rand. Opened in the Broadway Theatre on Thursday, March 12, 1987*

CAST

PROLOGUE: William Solo†1 (Jean Valjean), Herndon Lackey†2 (Javert), Chain Gang: J. C. Sheets, Joel Robertson, Tom Zemon, Rohn Seykell, Ed Dixon, Joe Locarro, Hugh Panaro, Bruce Kuhn, Jeffrey Clonts (Farmer), Bruce Kuhn (Labourer), Deborah Bradshaw (Innkeeper's Wife), Merwin Foard (Innkeeper), Adam Heller (Bishop of Digne), Willy Falk, Paul Avedisian (Constables).
MONTREUIL-SUR-MER 1823: Susan Dawn Carson†3 (Fantine), Joel Robertson (Foreman), Workers: Jeffrey Clonts, Rohn Seykell, Jessica Molaskey, Olga Merediz, Cissy Rebich, Jean Fitzgibbons, Mary Gutzi (Factory Girl), Jordan Leeds, J. C. Sheets, Rohn Seykell (Sailors), Mary Gutzi, Jean Fitzgibbons, Cissy Rebich, Natalie Toro, Lisa Ann Grant, Tracy Shayne, Betsy True, Deborah Bradshaw (Whores), Jessica Molaskey (Old Woman), Adam Heller (Pimp), Tom Zemon (Bamatabois), Adam Heller (Fauchelevent).
MONTFERMEIL 1823: Marlo Landry, Eden Riegel or Tamara Robin Spiewak (Young Cosette), Jennifer Butt†4 (Mme. Thenardier), Leo Burmeister†5 (Thenardier), Eden Riegel or Tamara Robin Spiewak (Young Eponine), Jeffrey Clonts (Drinker), Bruce Kuhn, Betsy True (Young Couple), Merwin Foard (Drunk), Paul Avedisian, Jean Fitzgibbons (Diners), Jordan Leeds (Young Man), Cissy Rebich, Lisa Ann Grant (Young Girls), Olga Merediz, Rohn Seykell (Old Couple), Joel Robertson, Willy Falk (Travelers), Others: Adam Heller, Tom Zemon, J. C. Sheets, Jessica Molaskey, Deborah Bradshaw, Mary Gutzi
PARIS 1832: Alex Dezen or Joey Rigol (Gavroche), Deborah Bradshaw (Old Beggar Woman), Mary Gutzi (Young Prostitute), Merwin Foard (Pimp), Natalie Toro (Eponine), Bruce Kuhn (Montparnasse), Willy Falk (Babet), J. C. Sheets (Brujon), Adam Heller (Claqueous), Joel Robertson (Combeferre), Jordan Leeds (Feuilly), Jeffrey Clonts (Courfeyrac), Rohn Seykell (Joly), Paul Avedisian (Lesgles), Merwin Foard (Jean Prouvaire), Joe Locarro†6 (Enjolras), Ray Walker†7 (Marius), Tracy Shayne†8 (Cosette)

MUSICAL NUMBERS: Prologue, Soliloquy, At the End of the Day, I Dreamed a Dream, Lovely Ladies, Who Am I?, Come to Me, Castle on a Cloud, Master of the House, Thenardier Waltz, Look Down, Stars, Red and Black, Do You Hear the People Sing?, In My Life, A Heart Full of Love, One Day More, On My Own, A Little Fall of Rain, Drink with Me to Days Gone By, Bring Him Home, Dog Eats Dog, Javert's Soliloquy, Turning, Empty Chairs at Empty Tables, Wedding Chorale, Beggars at the Feast, Finale

A dramatic musical in 2 acts and 4 scenes with a prologue.

*Still playing May 31, 1990. Winner of 1987 "Tonys" for Best Musical, Book, Score, Featured Actor and Actress in a Musical (Michael Maguire, Frances Ruffelle), Direction, Scenic Design, Lighting.

†Succeeded by: 1. Craig Schulman, 2. Peter Samuel, Robert Westenberg, 3. Laurie Beechman, Christy Baron, 4. Evalyn Baron, 5. Ed Dixon, 6. Joseph Kolinski, 7. Hugh Panaro, 8. Jacquelyn Piro

Joan Marcus Photos

Top Right: Craig Schulman, Peter Samuel Below: Laurie Beechman

Evalyn Baron

45

THE PHANTOM OF THE OPERA

Music, Andrew Lloyd Webber; Lyrics, Charles Hart; Additional Lyrics, Richard Stilgoe; Book, Richard Stilgoe, Andrew Lloyd Webber; Based on novel of same title by Gaston Leroux; Director, Harold Prince; Musical Staging/Choreography, Gillian Lynne; Production Design, Maria Bjornson; Lighting, Andrew Bridge; Sound, Martin Levan; Musical Supervision/Direction, David Caddick; Orchestrations, David Cullen, Andrew Lloyd Webber; Casting, Johnson-Liff & Zerman; General Management, Alan Wasser; Presented by Cameron Mackintosh and The Really Useful Theatre Company; Assistant to Director, Ruth Mitchell; Production Supervisor, Mitchell Lemsky; Dance Supervisor, Denny Berry; Associate General Manager, Allan Williams; Technical Production Manager, John H. Paull III; Company Manager, Michael Gill; Assistant to Miss Lynne, Naomi Sorkin; Props, Timothy Abel, Victor Amerling; Wardrobe, Adelaide Laurino, Alan Eskolsky; Stage Managers, Fred Hanson, Bethe Ward, Frank Marino; Press, Fred Nathan Co./Merle Frimark, William Schelble, Marc P. Thibodeau, Ian Rand, Colleen Brown. Opened in the Majestic Theatre on Tuesday, Jan. 26, 1988*

CAST

The Phantom of the Opera	Cris Groenendaal†1
Christine Daae	Rebecca Luker or Katharine Buffaloe
Raoul, Vicomte de Chagny	Steve Barton†2
Carlotta Giudicelli	Marilyn Caskey
Monsieur Andre	Jeff Keller
Monsieur Firmin	Nicholas Wyman†3
Madame Giry	Leila Martin
Ubaldo Piangi	David Romano†4
Meg Giry	Elisa Heinsohn
Monsieur Reyer	Frank Mastrone†5
Auctioneer	Richard Warren Pugh
Porter/Marksman	David Cleveland†6
Monsieur Lefevre	Kenneth Waller
Joseph Buquet	Philip Steele
Don Attilio/Passarino	George Lee Andrews†7
Slave Master	David Loring
Flunky/Stagehand	Barry McNabb†8
Policeman	Charles Rule
Page	Olga Talyn†9
Porter/Fireman	William Scott Brown
Page	Rhonda Dillon†10
Wardrobe Mistress/Confidante	Mary Leigh Stahl
Princess	Raissa Katona
Madame Firmin	Dawn Leigh Stone
Innkeeper's Wife	Jan Horvath†11
Ballet Chorus of Opera	Tener Brown, Nicole Fosse†12, Alina Hernandez, Lisa Lockwood†13, Dodie Pettit, Catherine Ulissey
Ballet Swing	Lori MacPherson
Swings	Keith Buterbaugh†14, Paul Laureano, Alba Quezada†15

MUSICAL NUMBERS: Think of Me, Angel of Music, Little Lotte, The Mirror, The Phantom of the Opera, The Music of the Night, I Remember, Stranger Than You Dreamt It, Magical Lasso, Notes, Prima Donna, Poor Fool He Makes Me Laugh, Why Have You Brought Me Here?, I've Been There, All I Ask of You, Masquerade, Why So Silent, Twisted Every Way, Wishing You Were Somehow Here Again, Wandering Child, Bravo Bravo, The Point of No Return, Down Once More, Track Down the Murderer

UNDERSTUDIES: Jeff Keller (Phantom), Raissa Katona (Christine), James Romick, Gary Lindemann (Raoul), Paul Laureano, Richard Warren Pugh (Firmin), George Lee Andrews, Gary Barker (Andre), Suzanne Ishee, Dawn Leigh Stone (Carlotta), Suzanne Ishee, Patrice Pickering, Mary Leigh Stahl (Mme. Giry), William Scott Brown, Richard Pugh (Piangi), Dodie Pettit, Catherine Ulissev (Meg Giry), Jeff Siebert (Slave Master/Solo Dancer)

A musical in 2 acts and 19 scenes with a prologue. The action takes place in the Paris Opera House.

*Still playing May 31, 1990. 1988 "Tonys" were awarded for Best Musical, Leading Actor in a Musical (Michael Crawford), Featured Actress in a Musical (Judy Kaye), Scenic Design, Lighting, Direction of a Musical.

†Succeeded by: 1. Steve Barton, 2. Kevin Gray, Davis Gaines, 3. George Lee Andrews, 4. John Horton Murray, 5. Gary Barker, 6. David Cleveland, 7. Thomas Sandri, 8. Jeff Siebert, 9. Patrice Pickering, 10. Elena Jeanne Batman, 11. Lorian Stein, 12. Natasha MacAller, 13. Tania Philip, 14. James Romick, 15. Suzanne Ishee

Clive Barda, Joan Marcus, Bob Marshak Photos

Top Left: Steve Barton, Rebecca Luker Below: George Lee Andrews, Jeff Keller

Kevin Gray, Rebecca Luker

THE FANTASTICKS

Book & Lyrics, Tom Jones; Music, Harvey Schmidt; Suggested by Edmund Rostand's play "Les Romanesques"; Director, Word Baker; Presented by Lore Noto; Original Musical Direction/Arrangements, Julian Stein; Production Design, Ed Wittstein; Co-Producer, Don Thompson; Associate Producers, Sheldon Baron, Dorothy Olim, Jules Field; Assistant Producer, Michael Yarborough; Current Musical Director, Dorothy Martin; Original Stage Manager, Geoffrey Brown; Current Stage Managers, James Cook, Steven Michael Daley; Production Consultant, Tony Noto; Press, Ginnie Weidmann. Opened in the Sullivan Street Playhouse on Tuesday, May 3, 1960, and still playing May 31, 1990.

CAST

The Narrator/El Gallo	Robert Vincent Smith*
The Girl	Glory Crampton†1
The Boy	Neil Nash†2
Girl's Father	William Tost*
Boy's Father	Dale O'Brien†3
Old Actor	Bryan Hull*
Man Who Dies/Indian	John Thomas Waite†4
The Mute	Matthew Eaton Bennett†5
At the piano	Dorothy Martin*
At the harp	Joy Plaisted*

UNDERSTUDIES: Anne Fisher (The Girl), Steven Michael Daley (The Boy), William Tost (Boy's Father), Neil Nash (Narrator) succeeded by Matthew Eaton Bennett

MUSICAL NUMBERS: Overture, Try to Remember, Much More, Metaphor, Never Say No, It Depends on What You Pay, Soon It's Gonna Rain, Rape Ballet, Happy Ending, This Plum Is Too Ripe, I Can See It, Plant a Radish, Round and Round, They Were You

The world's longest-running musical is performed with one intermission.

*30th anniversary cast

†Succeeded by: 1. Kate Suber*, 2. Howard Lawrence, Neil Nash, Mathew Eaton Bennett*, 3. Ron Kidd*, 4. Earl Aaron Levine*, 5. Steven Michael Daley*

Steve Young Photos

Right: Kate Suber, Mathew Eaton Bennett

Earl Aaron Levine, Bryan Hull

Bill Tost

Steven Michael Daley

VAMPIRE LESBIANS OF SODOM

By Charles Busch; Director, Kenneth Elliott; Presented by Theatre in Limbo, Kenneth Elliott, Gerald A. Davis; Choreography, Jeff Veazey; Casting, Stuart Howard; Wigs, Elizabeth Katherine Carr; Company Manager, Richard Biederman; Wardrobe, Alee Ralph; Production Assistant, Loretta Grande; Stage Managers, Jim Griffith, Jeff Barneson; Press, Shirley Herz/Sam Rudy, Pete Sanders, Glenna Freedman, Miller Wright. Opened in the Provincetown Playhouse on Wednesday, June 19, 1985*

CAST

"Sleeping Beauty" or "Coma":
Miss Thick	Charles Kelly
Enid Wetwhistle	Dea Lawrence
Sebastian Lore	Roy Cockrum
Fauna Alexander	Howard Samuelsohn
Ian McKenzie	Laurence Overmire
Anthea Arlo	Theresa McElwee
Barry Posner	Robert Carey
Craig Prince	Matt McLanahan

The action takes place in and around London in the 1960's.

"Vampire Lesbians of Sodom":
Ali/P. J.	Robert Carey
Hujar/Zack	Matt McLanahan
Virgin Sacrifice/Madeleine Astarte	Howard Samuelsohn
The Succubus/LaCondessa	Dea Lawrence
King Carlisle	Roy Cockrum
Butler Etienne/Danny	Laurence Overmire
Renee Vain/Tracy	Theresa McElwee
Oatsie Carewe	Roy Cockrum

Performed in 3 scenes: Sodom in days of old, Hollywood in 1920 and a Las Vegas rehearsal hall today.

*Closed May 27, 1990 after 2024 performances and 14 previews.

Dea Lawrence, Theresa McElwee, Howard Samuelsohn in
"Vampire Lesbians of Sodom"
T. L. Boston Photo

TONY 'N' TINA'S WEDDING

By Artificial Intelligence (Nancy Cassaro, Artistic Director); Conceived by Nancy Cassaro; Director, Larry Pellegrini; Supervisory Director, Julie Cesari; Musical Director, Debra Barsha; Choreography, Hal Simons; Design/Decor, Randall Thropp; Costumes/Hair/Make-up Design, Juan DeArmas; Producers, Joseph Corcoran, Daniel Corcoran; General Manager, Leonard A. Mulhern; Company Manager, James Hannah; Wardrobe/Hair Supervision, Rosemary Keough, Billy Hipkins, Kathryn Abbott; Catering, Gus' Place; Stage Managers, Teresa Hagar, Douglas Gettel; Press, David Rothenberg Associates/Terence Womble. Opened in the Washington Square Church & Carmelita's on Saturday, Feb. 6, 1988*

CAST

Valentina Lynne Nunzio, the bride	Nancy Cassaro/Kelly Cinnante
Anthony Angelo Nunzio, the groom	David Dundara/Robert Cea
Connie Mocogni, maid of honor	Dina Losito
Barry Wheeler, best man	Bruce Kronenberg
Donna Marsala, bridesmaid	Lisa Casillo
Dominick Fabrizzi, usher	George Schifini
Marina Gulino, Bridesmaid	Aida Turturro
Johnny Nunzio, usher and brother	James Georgiades
Josephine Vitale, bride's mother	Louise Drevers
Joseph Vitale, bride's brother	Billy Joe Young
Luigi Domenico, great uncle of bride	Kirk Duncan
Rose Domenico, aunt of the bride	Kelly Ebsary
Sister Albert Maria, bride's cousin	Jean Synodinos
Anthony Nunzio, Sr., groom's father	Dan Grimaldi
Madeline Monroe, his girlfriend	Liliane DuRae
Grandma Nunzio, groom's grandmother	Bonnie Rose Marcus
Michael Just, Tina's ex-boyfriend	Eric Cadora
Father Mark, parish priest	David Carr
Vinnie Black, caterer	Tom Karlya
Loretta Black, his wife	Victoria Constan
Mick Black, caterer's brother	Gary Schneider
Nikki Black, caterer's daughter	Sharon Angela
Mikie Black, caterer's son	Paul Maisano
Pat Black, caterer's sister	Donna Villella
Timmy Sullivan, video man	Patrick Smith
Sal Antonucci, photographer	Lou Martini, Jr.
Donny Dulce, band leader	Ken Phillips

Fusion, combo: Debra Barsha, Scott Rosette, Robert Kent

An environmental theatre production. The action takes place at the present time at Tony and Tina's wedding, and subsequently at the reception.

*Still playing May 31, 1990, after moving to St. John's Church and Vinnie Black's Coliseum.

Kelly Cinnante, Robert Cea

OTHER PEOPLE'S MONEY

By Jerry Sterner; Director, Gloria Muzio; Set, David Jenkins; Costumes, Jess Goldstein; Lighting, F. Mitchell Dana; Sound, David Budries; Casting, Judy Henderson; Presented by Jeffrey Ash and Susan Quint Gallin in association with Dennis Grimaldi; The Hartford Stage Company production (Mark Lamos, Artistic Director), General Management, George Elmer, Patricia Berry; Props, Kirk Lawrence; Wardrobe, Joanna Viverta; Technical Director, Jim Keller; Stage Managers, Stacey Fleischer, Peter Jack Tkatch; Production Manager, Steven Ehrenberg; Management Associate, Sheila Mathews; Press, Shirley Herz Associates/Sam Rudy, Glenna Freedman, Pete Sanders, Miller Wright. Opened in the Minetta Lane Theatre on Tuesday, Feb. 7, 1989*

Priscilla Lopez, Arch Johnson, James Murtaugh, Scotty Bloch, Jon Polito

CAST

William Coles .... James Murtaugh
Andrew Jorgenson .... Arch Johnson
Lawrence Garfinkle .... Kevin Conway†1
Bea Sullivan .... Scotty Bloch†2
Kate Sullivan .... Mercedes Ruehl†3

A play in two acts. The action takes place at the present time in New York City and in Rhode Island.

*Still playing May 31, 1990.

†Succeeded by: 1. Jon Polito, Steven Keats, 2. Lenka Peterson, 3. Janet Zarish, Priscilla Lopez

PRODUCTIONS FROM PAST SEASONS THAT CLOSED DURING THIS SEASON

Title	Opened	Closed	Performances
Anything Goes	9/11/87	9/3/89	848 (804 + 44)
Aristocrats	4/11/89	9/24/89	186
Arms and the Man	5/17/89	7/9/89	62
A Chorus Line	7/25/75	4/28/90	6137
Driving Miss Daisy	7/24/87	6/3/90	1195
Florida Crackers	5/17/87	6/25/90	46
Into the Woods	11/7/87	9/3/89	764 + 43 previews
The Kathy & Mo Show: Parallel Lives	1/28/89	4/29/90	466 + 16 previews
Largely/New York	5/1/89	9/2/89	152 + 11 previews
Lend Me a Tenor	3/2/89	4/22/90	468
M. Butterfly	3/20/88	1/27/90	777 + 9 previews
Me and My Girl	8/10/86	12/31/89	1420 + 11 previews
Metamorphosis	3/6/89	7/1/89	97 + 5 previews
Oh! Calcutta!	9/24/76	8/6/89	5959
Only Kidding	4/14/89	12/31/89	300
A Quiet End	5/21/90	6/15/90	18 + 8 previews
Rumors	11/17/88	2/24/90	531 + 12 previews
S. J. Perelman in Person	5/15/89	6/18/89	38 + 8 previews
Sarafina!	1/19/88	7/2/89	597 + 11 previews
Shirley Valentine	2/16/89	11/25/89	324 + 8 previews
Showing Off	5/9/89	10/15/89	172 + 11 previews
Starmites	4/27/89	6/18/89	60 + 35 previews
Steel Magnolias	6/19/87	2/25/90	1126
Tamara	11/9/87	7/15/90	1036
Vampire Lesbians of Sodom	6/19/85	5/27/90	2024 + 17 previews
Yankee Dawg You Die	4/28/89	6/11/89	52

OFF BROADWAY PRODUCTIONS
(June 1, 1989 through May 31, 1990)

(Mann Theatre) Thursday June 1–1, 1989 (7 performances) Naked Angels and The Sticking Place (Adrienne Weiss, Joan Cusack, Nicholas Gottlieb, Franco Carbone) present:
THE MYTH PROJECT: A FESTIVAL OF COMPETENCY; CAST: Lili Taylor, Joan Cusack, Laura Ekstrand, Merrill Holtzman, Cynthia Kane, Michael Mastrototaro, Lisa Beth Miller, Cam Sanders, Jeff Williams.
A play with music exploring the creation of modern myth, utilizing ancient poetry and divergent theatrical techniques.

(Steve McGraws) Friday June 2–17, 1989 (6 performances)
THE BEST OF SEIMA HAZOURI & PALS by Art Murray with music by Selma Hazouri, Lenny Babbish, Sean Hartley, Art Murray; Press, Patt Dale. CAST: Selma Hazouri, Lenny Babbish (musical director), Michael Davis.
A cabaret performance.

(South St. Theatre) Friday June 2–18, 1989 (16 performances) Red Earth Tours in association with One World Arts Foundation presents:
REAL FAMILY by Harvey Huddleston; Director, Richard Lichte; Sets, Wilber Ball; Lighting, Jed Stiles; Technical, Richard Schaefer; Production Consultant, Seth Hamilton; Stage Manager, Larry Sowa CAST: Ellen Adamson (Em), Sandy Dirk (Janet), Tom Dybek (Bill), William Hill (Gar)
A drama in two acts. The action takes place during the present in Chicago.

(The Real Garage) Friday, June 3–26, 1988 (20 performances).
WHEEL AND DEAL by Phil Bosakowski; Director, Joshua Astrachan; Press, Shirley Herz Associates/David Roggensack, Sam Rudy CAST: George Emilio Sanchez (Melendez), Glenn Kubota (Lop), Michael French (Mickey)
The action takes place at the present time in the garage of a San Francisco Police Department precinct station.

(Steve McGraws) Monday June 5–July 31, 1989 (9 Monday performances)
BREAKS by Diana Canova & Colleen Dodson; Director, John Monteith; Press, Patt Dale. CAST: Diana Canova, Colleen Dodson, Larry Esposito, Jeffrey Griglak, Lee Raines.
A comic duet with special assistance.

Colleen Dodson, Diana Canova in "Breaks" *(Martha Swope Photo)*
Top: Selma Hazouri

(Lincoln Center/Avery Fisher Hall) June 5, 1989 (1 night only) Evans Haile presents:
BABES IN ARMS; with Music by Richard Rodgers; Lyrics, Lorenz Hart; Script Adaptation, Tommy Krasker based on Rodgers/Hart original; Director, Sara Louise Lazarus; Conductor, Evans Haile; Choreography, Charles Repole; General Manager, David Cash. CAST: Judy Blazer, Gregg Edelman, Jason Graae, Donna Kane, Judy Kaye, Anita Morris, Philip Bosco, Jean LeClerc, JQ and the Bandits (Michael Taranto, Christopher May, David Montgomery, Steven Katz), Adam Grupper.
A concert performance of the musical to benefit the Starlight Foundation. This program was repeated Feb. 17, 1990 at State Theatre, New Brunswick, NJ with Jim Walton replacing Edelman and Olympia Dukakis as host replacing Morris/Bosco.

(Intar Theatre) Tuesday June 6–24, 1989 (21 performances and 3 previews) New Arts Theatre (Joshua Astrachan, Artistic Director) presents:
APOCALYPTIC BUTTERFLIES by Wendy Macleod; Director, Marcus Stern; Sets, Nephelie Andonyadis; Lighting, Scott Zielinski; Costumes, Melina Root; Sound, John Huntington; Production Manager, Phineas Perkins; Music, Marcus Stern; Stage Manager, James Mountcastle; Press, Cromarty & Co. CAST: Marylouise Burke (Francine), Greg Germann (Hank), Colette Kilroy (Muriel), Susan Knight (Trudi), Matthew Lewis (Dick)
A comedy in two acts. The action takes place at Christmas time in and around Fryeburg, Maine.

(Beacon Theatre) Tuesday June 6–30, 1989 (31 performances) Jules Fisher, Rodger Hess, Magic Promotions Inc., Pace Theatrical Group Inc., Concert Productions Int'l., Marvin A. Krauss, Act III Communications Inc., Joseph Rascoff, Mark Levy, Julian and Jean Aberbach, the Estate of Elvis Presley present:
ELVIS: A ROCKIN' REMEMBRANCE by Robert Rabinowitz; Music, Lyrics, Various; Director & Choreographer, Patricia Birch; Sets, Douglas W. Schmidt; Costumes, Jeanne Button; Lighting, Jules Fisher, Peggy Eisenhauer; Sound, Otts Munderloh; Music Supervision, Phil Ramone, Robby Merkin; Orchestrations & Vocal Arrangements, Robby Merkin; Musical Director, Terry Mike Jeffrey; Music Coordinator, John Monaco; Film Production, Chrisann Verges; Film Design & Direction, Robert Rabinowitz; Projection, Bran Ferren; Hair, Robert Diniro; Assistant Director, John Mineo; Stage Manager, Mark Krause; General Manager, Gary Gunas, Joey Parnes; Casting, Alan Amtzis, Joan Fishman; Presented by Madison Square Garden Enterprises; Press, Smyth/Katzen. CAST: Terry Mike Jeffrey (Young Elvis), Johnny Seaton (Heyday Elvis), Julian Whitaker (Older Elvis), Helena Andreyko, Dannul Dailey, Darren Dollar, James Ellis, Tina Gutrick, Collette Hill, Debbie Jeffrey, Leonard Joseph, Paul Mahos, Pat Moya, David Mullen, Kaye Pryor, Carol Denise Smith, Trish Vevera, Patrick Weathers.
A musical biography of Elvis Presley in two acts. The action takes place between 1935 and 1977 in Mississippi, Graceland, Hollywood, Las Vegas etc . . .

Terry Mike Jeffrey, Johnny Seaton, Julian Whitaker in "Elvis" Above: MaryLouise Burke, Colette Kilroy, Matthew Lewis, Greg Germann in "Apocalyptic Butterflies" *(Martha Swope/Rebecca Lesher)*

(Apple Corps Theatre) Wednesday June 7–July 8, 1989 (32 performances and 7 previews) Samuel Gesser presents:
THE PASSION OF NARCISSE MONDOUX by Gratien Gelinas; Director, Peter Moss; English version adapted by Linda Garboriau; Sets, Michael Egan; Costumes, Francois Barbeau; Lighting, Susan Chute; Sound, Wayne Teplay; Technical, Andy Calamates; Stage Manager, Brian A Kaufman; Press, Joshua Ellis, Adrian Bryan-Brown. CAST: Huguette Oligny (Laurentienne Robinchaud), Gratien Gelinas (Narcisse Mondoux)

A comedy in two acts. The action takes place in a village, Saint-Espirit-En-Bas, Quebec. The play was performed in both English and French at alternating performances.

(Henry St. Settlement) Wednesday, June 7–July 1, 1989 (15 performances and 4 previews) The Working Theatre (Bill Mitchelson, Artistic Director; Laurie Grossman, General Manager) presents:
WORKING ONE ACTS '89; Sets/Costumes, Anne C. Patterson; Stage Managers, Mihaly Kerenyi, Christine Schanda; Lighting, Spencer Mosse; Sound, Mark Bennett; John Gromada, Tom Gould, Mark Bennett; Press Bruce Cohen/Victoria Lynch
THE CLOSER by Will Holtzman; Director, R. J. Cutler CAST: Murray Rubinstein (Howard), Earl Hagan, Jr. (Al)

The action takes place in a city apartment at present.
FLOOR ABOVE THE ROOF by Daniel Therriault; Director, John Pynchon Holms CAST: Mark Kenneth Smaltz (Cantor), David Wolos-Fonteno (Jay), Richard Fiske (Swifty), Randy Frazier (Elroy)

The action takes place in the service elevator lobby of a NYC building at present.
FREEZE TAG by Jackie Reingold; Director, Evan Handler CAST: Lyn Greene (Aldrich), Julie Boyd (Andrea)

The action takes place outside an old fashioned candy store in the East Village at present.
SAND MOUNTAIN MATCHMAKING; Written & Directed by Romulus Linney CAST: Adrienne Thompson (Rebecca Tull), Earl Hagen, Jr. (Clink Williams), Paul O'Brien (Slate Foley), Robert Arcaro (Radley Nollins), Mary Foskett (Lottie Stiles), John Karol (Vester Stiles), Scott Sowers (Sam Bean)

The setting is Sand Mountain, a while ago.

Mark Kenneth Smaltz, Richard Fiske, Randy Frazier, David Wolos-Fonteno *(Carol Rosegg Photo)* Top: Huguette Oligny, Gratien Gelinas in "Passion of Narcisse . . ."

Marcus Naylor, Denise Burse-Mickelbury, Gwendolyn Roberts-Frost in "Boochie" *(Jessica Katz Photo)* Above: Sid Caesar

(Central Park) Wednesday June 7–July 2, 1989 (20 performances) En Garde Arts presents:
PLAYS IN THE PARK; Producer, Anne Hamburger; Costumes, Claudia Brown; Sets, Props, Sound, Kyle Chepulis; Site Coordinator, William H. Lang.
Babel On Babylon; Written and Directed by Matthew Maguire; Assistant Director, Jeff Sichel; Stage Manager, Jennifer McDowall; A presentation of Creation Company. Press, Ted Killmer. CAST: Kevin Davis (Jacob), Tessie Hogan (Ruth), Gregory Phillip Berry, Kim Carlucci, Sarah Davis, Monique Holt, Clayton Nemrow, Chuck Streeper
Bad Penny by Mac Wellman; Director, Jim Simpson; Composer, Michael Roth; Assistant Director, Jeff Sichel; Stage Manager, Dan M. Weir. CAST: Reg E. Cathey (Man 2), Zivia Flomenhaft (Woman 2), Jan Leslie Harding (Woman 1), Jeffrey M. Jones (Man 3), Stephen Mellor (Man 1), Mitch Markowitz (Boatman of Bow Bridge), Sari Allyn, Robert Canaan, Laura Cox, Dennis Davis, Lori Alan Denniberg, Katherine Gooch, Johannes Oppusunggu, Fia Perera, Jessica Porter, Danielle Reddick, Ken Schatz, Matt Scott
Minny And The James Boys by Anna Theresa Cascio; Director, Kevin Kelley; Stage Manager, Eddie Phillips. CAST: Augusta Allen-Jones (Minny), Thomas Gibson (Jesse James), Bill Kux (Henry James)

(Village Gate Downstairs) Tuesday June 13–September 3, 1989 (72 performances and 9 previews) Art D'Lugoff and Larry Spellman present:
SID CAESAR & COMPANY: THE LEGENDARY GENIUS OF COMEDY; Production Supervisor, Duane Mazey; Stage Manager, Neil Hayes; Wardrobe, Bobby Pearce; Musical Director, Elliot Finkel; Press, Philip Leshin. CAST: Sid Caesar, Marilyn Sokol, Lee Delano, Gerianne Raphael, Carolyn Michel PROGRAM: Overture, Man Walking Down The Aisle, Boy at his First Dance, World Through the Eyes of a Baby, Man & Wife Arguing to First Movement of Beethoven's Fifth, Wicked Man, At the Movies, Entre'act, "Little Me" medley, Penny Candy Gum Machine, Grieg Piano Concerto, Gershwin medley, The Professor, Finale

A revue in two acts. Transferred to Broadway. See Broadway section

(Billie Holiday Theatre) Thursday June 15–July 9, 1989 (20 performances and 6 previews) Billie Holiday Theatre (Marjorie Moon, Producer) presents:
AN EVENING OF TWO ONE ACT PLAYS: Director, Mikell Pinkney; Sets, Costumes, Felix E. Cochren; Lighting, Christian Epps; Stage Manager, Avan; Press, Howard Atlee.
BOOCHIE by Mari Evans; CAST: Denise Burse-Mickelbury (Joy)
EVERY GOODBYE AIN'T GONE by Bill Harris; CAST: Marcus Naylor (Frank Dandridge), Gwendolyn Roberts-Frost (Rula Payton)

Toni DiBuono, Dorothy Kiara, Jeff Lyons, Phillip George (on knees) in "Forbidden Broadway" *(Henry Grossman Photo)*

Kenny Lund, Donald Faison, Dedre Guevara, Shawn Benjamin in "Red Sneaks" *(Gerry Goodstein Photo)*

Charles Busch, Arnie Kolodner in "Lady in Question" *(T. L. Boston Photo)* Above: Frank Muller, Susan Pellegrino in "Cyrano" *(Marc Bryan-Brown)*

(Theatre East) Tuesday June 20, 1989 Jonathan Scharer presents:
FORBIDDEN BROADWAY 1989: SUMMER SHOCK EDITION; parodies written and Directed by Gerard Alessandrini; Press, Shirley Herz/Glenna Freedman. CAST: Toni DiBuono, Phillip Fortenberry, Dorothy Kiara, Jeff Lyons, David B. McDonald
    Summer edition of the long running revue.

(Bouwerie Lane Theatre) Thursday June 22–July 30, 1989 (40 performances) then re-opened at Choices Theatre Project Wednesday August 16–Sept. 24, 1989 (42 performances) Dramatic Risks, Inc. presents:
. . . MEXICO by Mark Waren; Director, Stanley A. Waren; Sound, Peter Gingerich; Sets, Edmond Ramage; Lighting, Craig Kennedy; Press, Mark G. Waren. CAST: Richard Masotti (Peter), Troy Ruptash (Michael)
    A romantic vaudeville set in Mexico.

(Perry St. Theatre) Sunday June 24–July 16, 1989 (23 performances and 4 previews) Theatre For a New Audience (Jeffrey Horowitz, Artistic/Producing Director) presents:
THE RED SNEAKS with Music, Lyrics & Book by Elizabeth Swados; Based on "*The Red Shoes;* Inspired by improvisations with the cast; Director, Ms. Swados; Sets & Costumes, G. W. Mercier; Lighting, M. L. Geiger; Choreography, Arthur Fredric; Stage Manager, Frank Dalrymple; Music Performance, Paul O'Keefe, Lewis Robinson; Press, Shirley Herz Associates/Miller Wright. CAST: Shawn Benjamin, Valerie Monique Evering, Donald "Shun"Faison, Dedre Guevara, Kenny Lund, Raquel Richard, James Sheffield-Dewees, Teresina Sullo
    The action takes place at the present time in NYC.

(Riverside Shakespeare Co. in NYC Parks) Friday June 30–July 23, 1989 (20 performances) Riverside Shakespeare Co. and Ben & Jerry's present:
CYRANO DE BERGERAC by Edmond Rostand; Translation, Brian Hooker; Director, Robert Mooney, Timothy W. Oman; Producer, Gus Kaikkonen; Sets, David P. Gordon; Costumes Martha Hally; Music & Lyrics, Shoukoufeh-Azari; Fights, Ian Rose; Technical, James E. Fuller, Jr. Stage Manager, Matthew G. Marholin; Press, Chris Boneau. CAST: Frank Muller (Cyrano), Robert Sedgwick (Christian), Susan Pellegrino (Roxanne), Weston Blakesley (DeGuiche), Daniel Timothy Johnson (Ragueneau), James Maxson (Le Bret), William Michie (Ligniere), Jared Hammond (Valvert), Edward Henzel (Cuigy), Christopher Mixon (D'Artagnan), Maggie McClellan (Duenna/Marguerite), Gregory Lamont Allen, Russ Cusick, Brian Dykstra, Fred Fahmie, Belynda Hardin, Jane Macfie, Matt McLain, Carine Monthertrand, Herbert Mark Parker, Ian Rose, Melinda Wade, Gregory Linus Weiss, Grover Zucker

(Schreiber Studio) Thursday, July 6–30, 1989 (16 performances and 1 preview) Theta Theater Co. and Anthony Spina present:
ORIENT BEACH by Donald Kvares; Director & Designer, Anthony Spina; Lighting, Neil Victor; Stage Manager, Ben Jacobs; Photography, Bert Andrews; Press, Howard & Barbara Atlee CAST: Deborah Alexander (Maggie), Lory Marcosson (Jill), Paul Dommermuth (Peter), Michael Philip Del Rio (Ned), Gisela Bruckner (Nikki)
    A drama in two acts. The action takes place at the Denham home at Orient Point, L.I., near the shore, in May, 1982.

(Bottom Line) Thursday, July 6–August 31, 1989 (28 performances) Bottom Line Repertory presents:
A HOT MINUTE; Conceived and written by Melanie Mintz; Director, Wayne Cilento; Producers, Allan Pepper, Stanley Snadowsky; Music Supervision, Jimmy Vivino; Music Director, Bette Sussman; Music Consultant, Leo Adamian; New Songs, Desmond Child, Franne Gold, David Lasley, John Hall, Jeff Franzel, Marilyn Berglass, Gordon Grody; Press, Joshua Ellis/Adrian Bryan-Brown, Chris Boneau. CAST: Vivian Cherry, Pattie Darcy, Jon Fiore, Annie Golden, John Martin Green
    A musical about background singers dreaming of their "hot minute" in the spotlight.

(Orpheum Theatre) Friday July 14–December 3, 1989 (151 performances and 14 preview) Kyle Renick and Kenneth Elliot in association with Theatre-In-Limbo present:
THE LADY IN QUESTION by Charles Busch; Director, Kenneth Elliott; Sets, B. T. Whitehill; Costumes, Robert Locke, Jennifer Arnold; Lighting, Vivien Leone; Wigs, Elizabeth Katherine Carr; Stage Manager, Robert Vandergriff; Original Producers, WPA Theatre; Press, Shirley Herz Assoc./Sam Rudy CAST: Charles Busch (Gertrude Garnet), Robert Carey (Karel), Kenneth Elliott (Baron Von Elsner), Andy Halliday (Hugo/Lotte), Julie Halston (Kitty), Mark Hamilton (Mittelhoffer/Maximilian), Arnie Kolodner (Erik), Theresa Marlowe (Heidi), Meghan Robinson (Augusta/Raina)
    The action takes place in a schloss and train station in the Bavarian Alps in 1940.

Richard Masotti, Troy Ruptash in "Mexico"
(Cheung Ching Ming)

John Wylie, Amanda Boxer, Steven Crossley in "The Pixie Led" *(Carol Rosegg)*

Charles Major, Monica Parks, Christine Jones in "Black Hat Karma" *(Adena Burger)*

Chris Kelly, David Conaway in "Best Friends"
(Carol Rosegg)

(Lincoln Center/Alice Tully Hall) Friday, July 14–August 3, 1989 (17 performances) Lincoln Center presents:
SERIOUS FUN!: THIRD SEASON; a contemporary performing arts festival; Offerings for the season include: *The Fall of the House of Usher* by Philip Glass; *The Terrors of Pleasure-The Uncut Version,* written and performed by Spalding Gray; Molissa Fenley and Bill T. Jones/Arnie Zane & Co.; Zvuki Mu and the Residents; *Masque of the Red Death* by Diamanda Galas; Scott Johnson, Lucia Hwong and Anthony Davis; Dancenoise, Danny Mydlack, Stuart Sherman, Paul Zaloom; Tom Cayler, John O'Keefe, Michael Peppe; Reno: Eric Bogosian; Ann Carlson, Blondell Cummings, Doug Elkins, Marguerite Guergue, Ohad Naharin, Stephen Petronio, Marta Renzi, Second Hand Dance, Stephanie Skura, Christian Swenson, Tina Barney & Dennis Diamond (Visuals)

(Courtyard Playhouse) Friday July 14–Nov. 12, 1989 (106 performances). The Glines Presents:
THE QUINTESSENTIAL IMAGE by Jane Chambers
IN HER OWN WORDS: A PORTRAIT OF JANE by John Glines; Director, Peg Murray; Lighting, Tracy Dedrickson; Costumes, Charles Catanese; Stage Managers, Kathleen Mary, Courtney Flanagan; Technical, William Castleman; Associate Producers, Jim Lorigo, Jonathan Slaff; Press, Jonathan Slaff. CAST: Mary Kay Adams, Shelly Conger, Rochelle DuBoff, Ruth Kulerman, Judy Tate
   An evening of work by the lesbian writer.

(Educational Alliance) Monday, July 17–August 3, 1989 (11 performances and 5 previews) SoupStone Project presents:
BLACK HAT KARMA by Don Rifkin; Director, Neile Weissman; Lights, Clark Middleton; Sound, Ken Dovel; Press, Francine L. Trevens; LeaAnn Johnson CAST: Maria Cellario, Robert Jimenez, Christine Jones, Charles Major, Monica Parks, Linda Powell, Charles Turner
   A drama concerning the after-effects of divorce in a multi racial family.

(Judith Anderson Theatre) Tuesday July 18–Aug. 12, 1989 (30 performances). Union 212 and Cole Theatrical Enterprises, Inc. in association with Krystyna & David Winn and Susan & Richard Madris present:
THE PIXIE LED by Christopher Harris; Director, Julian Richards; Sets, Michael T. Roberts, John Pope; Costumes, Tim Heywood; Lighting, Clifton Taylor; Stage Manager, John Handy; Asst. Director, Kate Chate; Producers, Geoffrey M. Freeman, Jonathan Willis, Beatie Edney, Julian Richards, Darren Lee Cole; Press, Max Eisen; Madelon Rosen Solomon CAST: Amanda Boxer (Concubine), Steven Crossley (Clerk), John Wylie (King), Kovolyov (Himself)
   An absurdist comedy loosely based on Nikolai Gogol's *"Diary of a Madman"* and *"The Nose."* The setting is London in the Victorian era.

(Dance Theatre Workshop/Shoenberg Theatre) Wednesday, July 26–August 1, 1989 El Hakawati presents:
THE STORY OF KUFUR SHAMMA by Jackie Lubeck and Francois Abu Salem; Director, Abu Salem; Sets, Costumes & Masks, Francine Gaspar; Music, Sheikh Imam; Lighting, Philipe Andrieux CAST: Jackie Lubeck, Francois Abu Salem, Amer Khalil
   A presentation of the Palestinian Arab Theatre Co. El Hakawati ("The Storytellers").

(South Street Theatre) Thursday, July 27–September 3, 1989 (41 performances and 6 previews) Eric Krebs in association with South St. Theatre and The Warp and Woof Theatre Co. present:
THE PEOPLE WHO COULD FLY, Conceived and Directed by Joe Hart; Sets, Ron Kadri; Costumes, Vicki Esposito; Lights, Chris Gorzelnik; Asst. Director, Jackie Gill; Management, Paul Morer, Gail Bell; Press, Shirley Herz Assoc./Miller Wright CAST: Rich Bianco, Heide Brehm, Michael Calderone, Caprice Cosgrove, John Di Maggio, Jacqueline Gregg, Jennifer Krasnansky, Christopher Petit, Anne Shapiro, Steve Sieger, Kristina Swedlund, Scott Wasser
   An evening in two acts of storytales from around the globe.

(Actors Outlet) Wednesday August 9–Sept. 10, 1989 (16 performances) Psychic Comic Productions present:
STEPHEN REHBERG: CYNNRCTFCTLDGLLLLLHW OR THE SECRET OF TRUE HAPPINESS by Stephen Rehberg; Director, Marck A. Fedor; Stage Manager, Rich Kiamco. CAST: Stephen Rehberg, M. R. Meadow
   A comic evening set "here and there" during "now and then."

(Actors Playhouse) Thursday August 10–20, 1989 (12 performances and 9 previews) Paul Carlton Productions in association with T.O.T.A.L. present:
BEST FRIENDS by John Voulgaris; Director, Donald L. Brooks; Music, Mark Barkan, David Conaway; Stage Manager, Bill Maloney; Press, Robert Ganshaw. CAST: David Conaway (Andrew Turner), Chris A. Kelly (Greg Meadows)
   A play in two acts. The action takes place in a loft in SoHo.

(Home For Contemporary Theatre And Art) Friday August 11–26, 1989 (10 performances) Home For Contemporary Theatre and Art and Joumana Rizk present:
THE YEAR OF THE BABY by Quincy Long; Director, Joumana Rizk; Sets, Jeff Makstutis; Lighting, Clay Shirkey; Videos, Marina Abs; Costumes, Pamela Korp; Music, Jeffrey Taylor; Press, Francine L. Trevens, Lea Ann Johnson. CAST: Quincy Long (Kenny), Kathleen Dimmick (Donna), Viki Boyle (Cashier/Storekeeper), Patrick Kerr (Bartender/Mechanic), Edward Baran (Luther), Verna Hampton (Martha).

A surrealistic drama about one couple's quest for parenthood.

(Gotham Cabaret) Wednesday August 16–Gotham City Improv Co. presents:
YOU DIE AT RECESS: Director, Hilaury Stern; Music, Connie Meng; Press, Peter Cromarty, Kevin Brockman. CAST: Melinda Buckley, Eric DeLancey, Bob Hebert, Austin Murphy, Steve Reyvler, Andrew Winters, Jody Wood, Pamela Woodruff, Pat Barker, Amy Scribner, Nancy Johnston, Tom Chalmers, Bart Sumner, Nick Davis, Mark Kwinn, Jennifer Smith

An evening of comedy sketches and improvisations.

(Riverwest Theatre) Friday, August 25–September 16, 1989 (16 performances and 4 previews) Dina and Alexander E. Racolin and CHS Productions presents:
THE ACHING HEART OF SAMUEL KLEINERMAN by Marion Andre; *(American Premiere);* Director, Donald Hampton; Sets & Costumes, Romy Phillips; Lighting, Matt Ehlert; Sound, David Lawson CAST: Michael Collier, J. D. Daniels, Kristin Norton, J. T. Phillips; Jeff Reade, James Terpis

The action takes place in pre-Kristal Nacht Berlin.

(Theatre 808) Friday August 25–September 17, 1989 (18 performances and 3 previews) Quaigh Theatre (Will Lieberson, Artistic Director; Patricia Kearney, Managing Director; Judith Rubin, Producer) presents:
BEFORE DAWN by Terence Rattigan; Director, Will Lieberson; Sets, Adrienne Brockway; Costumes, Christine Vlasak; Lighting, Deborah Matlack; Sound, George Jacobs; Stage Manager, Winifred H. Powers; Press, Francine L. Trevens. CAST: Elizabeth Karr (Tosca), Eddie Lane (Cpt. Scharrone), Lee Moore (Baron Scarpia), Stephen Colantti (Mario)

A comedy performed without intermission. The action takes place in Rome on June 17, 1800.

Kim Merrill, Bernie Barrow, Elizabeth Lawrence, Colleen Quinn in "Beauty Marks" *(Martha Swope)* Above: Gary Mink, Everett Quinton in "Big Hotel" *(Anita & Steve Shevett)*

Viki Boyle, Kathleen Dimmick in "Year of the Baby" *(Marc Bryan-Brown)*

Elizabeth Karr, Lee Moore in "Before Dawn" *(Scott Humbert)*

(Metropolitan Opera House) Wednesday, September 6–12, 1989 (8 performances) Metropolitan Opera presents:
ENNOSUKE'S KABUKI: Director, Ichikawa Ennosuke III; Sets, Shunichiro Kanai; Lighting, Sumio Yoshii; Press, Susan Bloch & Co/Ellen Zeisler. CAST: Ichikawa Ennosuke III, Ichikawa Danshiro, Nakamura Karoku, Bando Yajuro and company.

An evening of Japanese Kabuki theatre.

(West Bank Cafe, Theatre) Tuesday, September 12–14, 1989 (5 performances) Act Four presents:
BOX OFFICE OF THE DAMNED, PART II Book, Music and Lyrics by Michael James Ogborn; Director, James Ireland; Choreography, James V. Flynn; Set, Will Klein; Musical Direction, James Lopardo; Technical Manager, Brian Klinger; Poster Design, Loyce Arthur; Stage Manager, Carol Van Keuren. CAST: Matthew Cloran, Bethanne Collins, Jim Flynn, Susan Kurowski, Robert MacCallum, Tracie Normoyle, John O'Hara, Anne Robinson. MUSICAL NUMBERS: A Season You'll Never Forget, Festival Fever/Gala Galore, Please Hold, Go Away, Mrs. Levittown, Just Say NO, Viva La Matinee, Metropolitan Midge, I'm In The Show, We See It All, Our Exchange Policy, Remember Me, The New Non-Union Usher Polka, One Ticket, Stragger, 8:00 Auto-Pilot, T.M.I., This Job Is For The Birds, Clerk, Curtain Speech, Subscribe!, LATE, Finale. A musical revue in two acts.

(City Center) Tuesday, September 12–17, 1989 (8 performances) City Center presents:
THE ALEXANDROV RED ARMY SONG AND DANCE ENSEMBLE; Director, Anatoly Maltsev; Artistic Director/Conductor, Igor Agafonnikov; Assistant Director, Yevgeni Zakharenko; Choir Masters, Yuri Petrov, Viktor Fyodorov; Choreography, Usher Khmelnitsi, Viktor Nikitushkin; Conductor, Vyacheslav Korobko; Concert Masters, Vladimir Brodski, Vladimir Ogarkov, Pytor Khmelnitski; Tour Management, USSR Artists' Touring Co., Great World Artists Ltd., SAI Entertainment; Press, Susan Bloch/Ellen Zeisler, Kevin P. McAnarney CAST: Soloists: Valeri Gavva, Vadim Korshunov, Eduard Labkovski, Leonid Pshenichny, Vasili Shtefutsa, Barseg Tumanyan, Boris Zhaivoronok

The U.S. debut of this "Red Army Chorus" featuring over 200 singers, dancers and musicians.

(Astor Place Theatre) Tuesday, September 12–Oct. 1, 1989 (24 performances)
William De Dilva in association with Claridge Productions, Inc. presents:
THE MAN WHO SHOT LINCOLN by Luigi Creatore; Director, Crandall Diehl; Sets/Costumes, Michael Bottari, Ronald Case; Lighting, Craig Miller; Stage Manager, Renee F. Lutz; Management, Marshall B. Purdy; Casting, Alan Coleridge; Company Manager, Jean Rocco; Press, Cromarty & Co./Kevin Brockman CAST: Sam Tsoutsouvas (Edwin Booth), Marcia Gay Harden (Mary Devlin), Conan McCarty (John Wilkes Booth), Eric Tull (Player)

A drama on events leading up to the Lincoln assassination from Edwin Booth's viewpoint. The setting is a theatre in 1865.

(Charles Ludlam Theatre) Wednesday, Sept. 13–Oct. 28, 1989 (40 performances)
The Ridiculous Theatrical Co. presents:
BIG HOTEL by Charles Ludlam; Director, Everett Quinton; Sets, Mark Beard; Costumes, Susan Young; Lighting, Richard Currie; Music/Sound, James S. Badrak, Alan Gregorie, Jan Bell; Properties, Daphne Groos, James Eckerle; Hair, Joe Anthony; Production Coordinator, James Eckerle; Stage Manager, Pedro Rosado, Jr.; Press, Jacksina Co./David Musselman CAST: Eureka (Drago Rubles, Martok), H. M. Koutoukas (Svengali, Gypsy), James Robert Lamb (Bellhop, Lupe Velez), Sophie Maletsky (Birdshitskaya), Therese McIntyre (Bride, Assorted Guests), Gary Mink (Elwynn Chamberpot, Waiter), Terence Mintern (Chocha Caliente, Devil), Stephen Pell (Mr. X, God), Everett Quinton (Norma Desmond, Mafonga, Director), Bobby Reed (Cramwell, Masie Madigan, Santa), Bryan Webster (Magic Mandarin, Mati Hari) Christine Weiss (Trilby, Blondine Blondell)

The first New York revival of Charles Ludlam's first play (1967). A study of "lust, intrigue and mayhem set in and about the rooms of a really big hotel."

(Intar Theatre) Thursday, Sept. 14–Nov. 5, 1989 (47 performances and 7 previews)
Alley Cat Productions presents:
BEAUTY MARKS by Kim Merrill; Director, Peter Askin; Producer, Melanie Webber; Sets, Roy Hine; Lighting, Greg MacPherson; Costumes, Laura Drawbaugh; Sound, Bruce Ellman; Stage Manager, Ken Simmons; Press, FLT/Francine L. Trevens CAST: Bernie Barrow (Henry), Elizabeth Lawrence (Margaret), Kim Merrill (Daphne), Colleen Quinn (June)

A comedy in two acts. The action takes place in Wichitalla, NE at the present.

(47th St. Theatre) Friday, September 15, 1989. Ervin Litkei, in association with Ethel Gabriel and Larry Lipp, presents:
THE AUNTS by Gary Bonasorte; Director, Charles Maryan; Sets, Atkin Pace; Lighting, John Gleason; Costumes, Lana Fritz; Stage Manager, Bill McComb; Sound, Brian Ronan; Dances, Bertram Ross; Press, Shirley Herz/Miller Wright CAST: Bethel Leslie (Meg), Ann Wedgeworth (Nan), Mia Dillon (Pita), Christopher Wynkoop (Chuck)

A drama in two acts. The action takes place in Pittsburgh in 1979.

Conan McCarty, Sam Tsoutsouvas in "Man Who Shot Lincoln" *(Martha Swope)*

Carmen de Lavallade in "Dreams of Clytemnestra"
(Kenn Duncan)

(Judith Anderson Theatre) Sunday, September 17–October 1, 1989 (12 performances) The City Troupe presents:
THE DREAMS OF CLYTEMNESTRA by Dacia Maraini; Translation, Timothy Vode; Director, Greg Johnson; Artistic Director, Michael Smit; Managing Director, John Oliver; Lighting, John Malinowski; Costumes, Barbara Wolf; Score, Michael Sottile; Casting, Olivia Harris; Sets, Marian Kolsby; Stage Manager, Mark Waggenhurst; Assist. Director, Julia Nasvytis; Production Manager, Michael J. Kondrat; Press, Francine L. Trevens/Lea Ann Johnson CAST: Brenda Daly (Moria), Carmen De Lavallade (Clytemnestra), Taylor Howard (Pilot), Marko Maglich (Orestes), Aurelia Mills (Fury #1), Julia Nasvytis (Fury #2), Maggie Rush (Electra), Christopher Scotellano (Aegisthus), Stephen Singer (Agamemnon, Psychoanalyst), Wendy Way (Cassandra), Joan Saporta (Fury #3)

A retelling in modern perspective of an ancient Greek Tale. The action takes place in Prato, a small town near Florence at the present time.

(Brooklyn Academy of Music) Tuesday, September 19–24, 1989 (7 performances)
Polam Entertainment Inc. presents:
SLASK: THE NATIONAL FOLK BALLET OF POLAND: Artistic Director, Stanislaw Tokarski; Choreography, Michal Jarczyk; Musical Director, Marek Witkowski; Lighting, Beverly Emmons; Sound, Gary Harris; General Manager, Malcolm Allen; Stage Manager, Robert LoBianco; Producers, Jan & Zofia Sklepinski, Gabriel Berde, Saxon/Blume Productions; Press, Max Eisen SOLOISTS: Marek Wojtzysiak, Benedykt Bykowski, Jerzy Rubiecki, Ryszard Kisciolek, Kam Czechlewski, Iwana Kosak, Żofia Czecklewska, Krystyna Lecyk, Elzbieta Kosciolek LEAD SINGERS: Ewa Gromkowska, Ewa Staniak

A program of 25 dances and songs performed by a company of 100.

(Radio City Music Hall) Friday, September 22–October 15, 1989 (32 performances)
Radio City Music Hall presents:
SIEGFRIED & ROY; Producer, Kenneth Feld CAST: Siegfried & Roy
An evening of illusion and variety featuring a cast of 55.

National Folk Ballet of Poland/SLASK

(Home for Contemporary Theatre and Art) Wednesday, September 27–October 15, 1989 (14 performances and 2 previews) returned Wednesday, May 2–June 10, 1990 (30 performances) Home for Contemporary Theatre and Art presents:
2 SAMUEL 11, ETC. by David Greenspan; Director, Mr. Greenspan; Lighting, David Bergstein; Sets, William Kennon; Production Manager, David Markowitz; Stage Manager/Sound, Clare Blackmer; Technical, David Rising CAST: Ron Bagden (Character 1), Mary Shultz (Character 2)

An upside down version of the David and Bathsheba story in two acts. The action takes place in Character 1's workroom and bathroom.

(Equity Library Theatre) Thursday, September 28–October 22, 1989 (30 performances and 2 previews) Equity Library Theatre (Jeffrey R. Costello, Producing Director) presents:
WONDERFUL TOWN; Music, Leonard Bernstein; Lyrics, Betty Comden, Adolph Green; Book, Joseph Fields, Jerome Chodorov; Based on play "My Sister Eileen" by Fields & Chodorov and stories by Ruth McKenney; Musical Director, Barbara Irvine; Choreography, Jonathan Cerullo; Director, Adrienne Weiss; Sets, Wendy Ponte; Costumes, Claudia Stephens; Lighting, Brian MacDevitt; Sound, Hector Milia; Coordinator, Helyn Taylor; Stage Managers, Bernita Robinson, Jill Cordle; Press, Ellen Jacobs & Co. CAST: Robert Bianca (Guide/Ensemble), Eric Brooks (Wreck), Christine Campbell (Lonigan), Lucio Fernandez (Cadet/Ensemble), Allen Fitzpatrick (Robert Baker), Margaret Fung (Shore patrol/Ensemble) replaced by Rebecca Downing, Deborah Geneviere (Violet), Walker Jones (Frank Lippencott), Colette Kilroy (Ruth), Nancy Leach (Longshoreman/Ensemble), Stacey Logan (Eileen), Bill Martel (Irish Tenor/Ensemble), Michael Metzel (Chick Clark), Terry Reamer (Mrs. Wade), Roger Rifkin (Appopolous), Mason Roberts (Editor/Ensemble), Blair Ross (Helen), Greg Templeton (Editor/Ensemble), Ovidio Vargas (Valenti)

A revival of the 1953 musical. For original production see *Theatre World* Vol. 9.
MUSICAL NUMBERS: Overture, Christopher St., Ohio, Conquering the City, 100 Easy Ways to Lose a Man, What a Waste, Ruth's Story Vignettes, A Little Bit in Love, Pass That Football, Nice People, A Quiet Girl, Conga, My Darlin' Eileen, Swing, It's Love, Let it Come Down/Village Vortex Ballet, Wrong Note Rag, Finale
A lack of funds forced ELT to close its 47th season and off-Broadway's longest running showcase.

(South St. Theatre) Wednesday, Oct. 4–Nov. 5, 1989 (28 performances) The Vietnam Veterans Ensemble Theatre Co. (Thomas Bird, Artistic Director) presents:
THE AMBASSADOR by Slawomir Mrozek; Translation, Ralph Manheim, Slawomir Mrozek; Director, Mac Ewing; Lighting, Terry Wuthrich; Sets, George Allison; Costumes, Deborah Rooney; Sound, Ben Adam; Stage Manager, Anne Marie Hobson; Press, Merle Debuskey & Associates/Bruce Campbell CAST: David Adamson (Ambassador), Anthony Chisholm (Othello), Sharon Ernster (Amelia), James Gleason (Deputy), Michael Manetta (Man)

A political comedy-drama in two acts. The action takes place in a democratic embassy in a totalitarian country at the present.

(Apple Corps. Theatre) Tuesday, October 10–29, 1989 (20 performances) The Women's Project and Productions (Julia Miles, Artistic Director) presents:
MILL FIRE by Sally Nemeth; Director, David Petrarca; Sets, Linda Buchanan; Costumes, Laura Cunningham; Lighting, Robert Christen; Sound, Rob Milburn; Stage Manager, Nancy Harrington; Press, Fred Nathan/Merle Frimark CAST: Martha Lavey, Mary Ann Thebus, Jacqueline Williams (Widows), Kelly Coffield (Marlene), James Krag (Champ), Kate Buddeke (Sunny), B. J. Jones (Bo), Joseph Phillip, Paul Mabon (Jemison), Timothy Grimm (Minister/Investigator)

A drama in two acts. The action takes place in Birmingham, Alabama in July 1978.

(Playhouse 91) Tuesday, October 10–December 24, 1989 (76 performances and 8 previews) Peter Gatien and Dan Lauria present:
A BRONX TALE by Chazz Palminteri; Director, Mark X. Travis; Sets, James Noone; Lighting, Jeffrey Schissler; Music, Glenn Mehrbach; Executive Producer, Arthur Cantor; Company Manager, Steven M. Levy; Stage Manager, Bill McComb; Press, Arthur Cantor/Deborah Navins, Max Reynal CAST: Chazz Palminteri

A solo performance. The action takes place at 187th St. and Belmont Ave. in the Bronx in 1960.

(The Producers Club) Saturday, Oct. 10–28, 1989. (9 performances and 3 previews) Bondrov/Mayhem Productions presents:
LIARS by Elliot Meyers; Director, Shellen Lubin; Sets/Lighting, Kevin S. West; Press, Francine L. Trevens. CAST: James Wlcek, Peter Sprague, Annie Hughes, Joyce West.

A comedy in two acts.

(Lamb's Theatre) Friday, October 13–November 26, 1989 John Cullen, Jennifer Hadley & Michael Hadley present:
ALL GOD'S DANGERS by Theodore Rosengarten, Michael Hadley, Jennifer Hadley; Based on "All God's Dangers: The Life Of Nate Shaw" by Rosengarten; Director, William Partlan; Scenery/Costumes, G. W. Mercier; Lighting, Tina Charney; Sound, Greg Sutton; Stage Manager, Tom Aberger, Steven Loehle; Gener-

Stacy Logan, Colette Kilroy in "Wonderful Town" (*Ned Snyder*)

Chazz Palminteri in "A Bronx Tale"   Ron Bagden in "2 Samuel 11" (*Adrienne Urbanski*)

David Adamson, Sharon Ernster in "The Ambassador" (*Susan Cook*)

Martha Lavey, Kelly Coffield, Jacqueline Williams, Mary Ann Thebus in "Mill Fire" (*Lisa Ebright*)

al Management, Marshall B. Purdy; Associate Producer, Rick Azar; Company Manager, Mary Miller; Press, Callaghan & Co./Edward Callaghan, Brigette Devine, Jill Larkin CAST: Cleavon Little (Nate Shaw)

A drama in two acts. The action takes place in rural Alabama.

Cleavon Little in "All God's Dangers" *(Scarsbrook)*

(Actors Outlet) Friday, Oct. 13–Nov. 1, 1989 (12 performances and 4 previews) Broadway Tomorrow (Elyse Curtis) presents:
SLAY IT WITH MUSIC with Music by Paul Katz; Book/Lyrics, Michael Colby; Director, Charles Repole; Scenery, James Wolk; Costumes, Michele Reisch; Lighting, Dan Kotlowitz; Musical Director, Phil Reno; Hair/Makeup, Joseph LaPenna; Music Coordinator, Kenneth Faulkner-Alexander; Choreography, Dennis Dennehy; Stage Managers, Paul J. Smith, Carol Tomlinson; Assistant to Producers, Bobby Harcum; Press, Francine L. Trevens CAST: Janet Metz (Rosemarie Clinger/Young Edna/Rhonda Carlisle/Lenore Hooper), Susan Bernstein (Jill Little/Young Marcy), J. P. Dougherty (Zachary Von Zell), Virginia Sandifur (Edna Beaucoup), Louisa Flaningam (Marcy Beaumont), Barry Williams (Chad Walker/Marcel Beaucoup/Grant Foster/Melvin Grundy/t.v. announcer) MUSICAL NUMBERS: Whatever Happened to . . .?, Second Chance/Slasher Movie, My Darling, My Dearest, I Gotta Get Her Back, Sisters, Anything, In Love, You're There When I Need You, Got It All, Two Actresses Practicing Their Art, I Know a Secret, Slay It With Music, Trapped, More Than Just a Movie Fan, That's a Wrap!/Second Chance, Now We Can't Miss, Finale.

A musical chiller in two acts. The action takes place in Hollywood in 1968, the era of "Grand Dame Guignol".

Virginia Sandifur, J. P. Dougherty, Louisa Flanigam in "Slay It with Music" *(Elizabeth Wolynski)*

(All Souls Fellowship Hall) Friday, Oct. 13–28, 1989. (15 performances) All Souls Players Productions presents:
THE LION IN WINTER by James Goldman; Director, Roslyn Davis; Sets, David McNitt; Costumes, John Michel; Lighting, Jay Johnson; Producer, Tran Wm. Rhodes; Stage Manager/Props, Foster Rhalse. CAST: Nancy Arrigo, Lynette Bennett, Brent Erdy, Michael Graves, George Millenbach, Daniel J. Sherman, Owen Thompson.

A play in two acts. The action takes place in King Henry II's castle at Chinon, France on Christmas in 1183.

(ChoreoSpace) Friday, October 13–29 (11 performances) Pro Arts and Stefan Fitterman present:
THE OPENING by Stephen Magowan; Director, Steven Samuels; Sets/Costumes, Marina Draghici, Kim Jennings; Puppet Design, Bart P. Roccoberton, Jr.; Lighting, Peter Koletzke; Original Music/Sound, Christopher Thall; Stage Managers, Jill Merzon, Kevin Hardwick; Press, Dolph Browning Enterprises CAST: Sam Goodyear (Father), Paula DeCaro (Mother), Irma St. Paule (Miss Humphries), Gregory Pekar (Dudley), Patty O'Brien (Jayne), Charles Wisnet (Cook), David Amarel (Cass), Charmaine Cruz (Maria), Preston Foerder (Puppeteer), Isabelle Dufour (Puppeteer), Amy Casale (Puppeteer).

A comedy in rhyme in two acts.

Sally Mayes, Brent Barrett, Lynne Wintersteller, Richard Muenz in "Closer Than Ever"

(Cherry Lane Theatre) Tuesday, Oct. 17–July 1, 1990 (288 performances and 24 previews) Janet Brenner, Michael Gill and Daryl Roth present:
CLOSER THAN EVER with Music by David Shire; Lyrics by Richard Maltby, Jr.; Conceived & Co-Directed by Steven Scott Smith; Director, Richard Maltby, Jr.; Musical Director/Additional Vocal Arrangements, Patrick Scott Brady; Set, Philipp Jung; Costumes, Jess Goldstein; Lighting, Natasha Katz; Press, Shirley Herz Associates/Pete Sanders, Cromarty & Co./Kevin Brockman. CAST: Brent Barrett succeeded by Jim Walton, Scott Hayward Eck, Sally Mayes, Richard Muenz succeeded by Craig Wells, Lynne Wintersteller; Patrick Scott Brady (piano), Robert D. Renino (bass). MUSICAL NUMBERS: Doors, She Loves Me Not, You Want to Be My Friend?, What Am I Doin'?, The Bear the Tiger the Hamster and the Mole, Like a Baby, Miss Byrd, The Sound of Muzak, One of the Good Guys, There's Nothing Like It, Life Story, Next Time, I Wouldn't Go Back, Three Friends, Fandango, There, Patterns, Another Wedding Song, If I Sing, Back on Base, The March of Time, Fathers of Fathers, It's Never That Easy/I've Been Here Before, Closer Than Ever.

A musical revue in two acts.

(Perry Street Theatre) Wednesday, Oct. 18, 1989–May 20, 1990 (216 performances). Moved to Judith Anderson Theatre, and subsequently to the Kaufman Theatre where it closed. Lion King Productions in association with the Writers Theatre present:
CARBONDALE DREAMS: BRADLEY & BETH by Steven Sater; Director, Byam Stevens; Sets, Jeff Freund; Lights, Stan Pressner; Costumes, Rosi Zingales; Music, Patricia Lee Strotter; Stage Manager, Jennifer Gilbert; Press, Max Eisen, Madelon Rosen Solomon. CAST: *"Bradley"* with Jeff Bender (Bradley), James Lish (David), Cheryl Thornton (Candi), J. R. Nutt (Brian); *"Beth"*: Navida Stein (Beth), James Lish (David), James Maxson (Barry), Heather Coleman (Betty), Anita Keal (Barone), Robert Trumbull (Arnold), Jeff Bender (Bradley), Cheryl Thornton (Candi); *"Arnold"*: (added to production on Wed. Jan. 31, 1990) Richard Thomsen (Arnold), Anita Keal (Barone). The action takes place at the present time in the living room of Barone and Arnold's home, in the kitchen of Beth's home on a lake, and in the last empty room in Bradley and Candi's new home, all in Carbondale, Illinois, just before Thanksgiving. Performed with two intermissions.

James Lish, Anita Keal, Navida Stein in "Bradley and Beth" *(Martha Swope)*

(Theatre for the New City) Thursday, Oct. 19–Nov. 18, 1989 (12 performances)
MONSTER TIME by Stephen DiLauro; Director, Willem Brugman; Costumes/Makeup, Natasha von Rosenchilde; Lighting, Zdenek Kriz; Press, David Rothenberg Assocs. CAST: Eric Douglas, Don Hannah, Sara Jackson.

A drama in two acts.

(Promenade Theatre) Friday, Oct. 20, 1989–Jan. 28, 1990. (104 performances and 12 previews) Manhattan Theatre Club (Artistic Director, Lynne Meadow; Managing Director, Barry Grove) presents:
THE LISBON TRAVIATA by Terrence McNally; Director, John Tillinger; Sets, Philipp Jung; Costumes, Jane Greenwood; Lighting, Ken Billington; Sound, Gary & Timmy Harris; Fight Staging, B. H. Barry; Stage Manager, Pamela Singer; Casting, Lyons/Isaacson; Press, Helene Davis, Clay Martin. CAST: Anthony Heald (Stephen), Nathan Lane (Mendy), Dan Butler (Mike), John Slattery (Paul). Understudy: James E. Reynolds (Mike/Paul).

A play in two acts. This is a transfer of the production from last season at Manhattan Theatre Club with a new ending.

(Circle in the Square Downtown) Wednesday, Oct. 25, 1989 David Bulasky, Barbara Darwall and Peter von Mayrhauser present:
THE WIDOW'S BLIND DATE by Israel Horowitz; Director, Israel Horowitz; Sets, Edward Gianfrancesco; Lighting, Craig Evans; Costumes, Janet Irving; Fight Sequences, B. H. Barry; Stage Manager, Crystal Huntington; Press, Jeffrey Richards, Jillana Devine. CAST: Tom Bloom (George Ferguson), Paul O'Brien (Archie Crisp), Christine Estabrook (Margy Burke).

A play in two acts. The action takes place in the present time at the baling-press room, waste paper company, Wakefield, Massachusetts on an October evening.

(Theatre 603) Friday, Oct. 27–Nov. 12, 1989. (9 performances) Spuyten Duyvil Theatre Co., Inc. presents:
THEM by Tom Coffey; Director, Dennis Delaney; Sets, Charles Golden; Lighting, Chris Gorzelnik; Press, Carol Brooks. CAST: Isabel Glasser (Eileen), Clarke Gordon (Sean), Maureen MacDougall (Ann), Casey McDonald (Johnsie), Leslie McMahon (Kitty), Rusty Owen (Seamus), Joan Penn (Brid), Robert Poletick (Padraig), Janelle Sperow (Maeve), Robert Verlaque.

A drama in two acts.

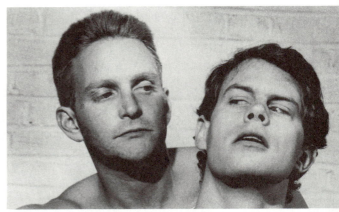

Eric Douglas, Don Hannah in "Monster Time"

Nathan Lane, Anthony Heald in "Lisbon Traviata" *(Gerry Goodstein)*

(AMAS Musical Theatre); Formerly AMAS Repertory Theatre; Founder/Artistic Director, Rosetta Lenoire; Administrator, Carla Mele; Managing Director, Jeffrey Solis; Press, Fred Nathan Co./Merle Frimark, William Schelble; Twenty-first Season Thursday, Nov. 2–26, 1989 (22 performances)
PARIS '31, with Music & Lyrics by Cole Porter; Book/Director, John Fearnley; Stage Managers, J. Andrew Burgreen, Janice Lee; Choreographer, Robert Longbottom; Musical Supervisor, William Roy; Lighting, Beau Kennedy; Costumes, Kathryn Wagner; Sets, Jane Sablow. CAST: Thelma Carpenter (Toni), Zelie Daniels (Tracy), Kevin John Gee (Torquil), Nancy Groff (Princess), Randy Hills (Peter), Sebastian Hobart (Jeff), Michael McAssey (Cliff), Debbie Petrino (Vivienne), Brian Quinn (Michael), Monte Ralstin (Nick), Pamela Shaddock (Lucky), Jeffrey Solis (Dmitri), Betty Winsett (Helen), Ellen Zachos (Peggy). MUSICAL NUMBERS: Dizzy Baby, Bad Girl in Paree, Quelque Chose, Find Me a Primitive Man, You Don't Know Paree, Paree, What Did You Do to Me, I'm in Love, Let's Do It, You Do Something to Me, Bull Dog, Why Shouldn't I Have You, The Queen of Terre Haute, After You, Let's Fly Away, The Heaven Hop, Don't Look at Me That Way, They All Fall in Love, I Worship You, You Can Do No Wrong, I'm Unlucky at Gambling, Vivienne, Why Don't We Try Staying Home, Let's Step Out

A musical revue in two acts.

(Astor Place Theatre) Friday, November 3–December 10, 1989 Ray Greenwald & Jack Levitt Productions, Inc. in association with Ben Sprecher and the Joseph Papp Yiddish Theatre present:
SONGS OF PARADISE; with Music by Rosalie Gerut; Book, Miriam Hoffman, Rena Berkowicz Borow; Director, Avi Hoffman; Choreography, Eleanor Reissa; Sets, Steven Perry; Lighting, Anne Militello; Musical Director, Jonny Bowden; Arrangements, Bevan Manson; Stage Manager, Donald Christy; Press, Jeffrey Richards CAST: Adrienne Cooper, Rosalie Gerut, Avi Hoffman, Eleanor Reissa, David Kener succeeded by Harry Peerce
MUSICAL NUMBERS: Di Demerung, Khave and the Apple Tree, Odem and Khave Duet, Avrum and Sore's Duet, Hoger and the Turks, Shir Hamaylesn, Hoger's Lament/Sore's Lullaby, Yankev and Rokhl Duet, Yosef's Tango, The Farewell Song

A Yiddish/English musical in two acts.

Paul O'Brien, Christine Estabrook, Tom Bloom in "The Widow's Blind Date"

David Kener (standing), Avi Hoffman, Eleanor Rissa in "Songs of Paradise" *(Martha Swope)*

(Walker St. Theatre) Friday, November 3–26, 1989 (16 performances) Salamander Repertory Theatre presents:
THE STRAW by Eugene O'Neill; Director, Toni Dorfman; Sets/Lighting, Robert Klingelhoefer; Stage Manager, M. Leah Schneider; Costumes, Neville Bean; Press, Chris Boneau/Shannon Barr CAST: Caitlin Hart (Miss Gilpin), Warren Kelley (Fred Nicholls, Sloan, Peters), Karen Kennedy (Miss Howard), Joel Leffert (Stephen Murray), Cecile Mann (Mrs. Abner, Mrs. Brennan), Nancy Nichols (Eileen Carmody), Bud Thorpe (Bill Carmody, Dr. Stanton)

A drama in two acts and 4 scenes. The action takes place in Hill Farm Sanitarium. The first NYC staging of this play since the 1921 original at the Greenwich Village Theatre.

(Soho Rep./Greenwich House) Friday, Nov. 3–Dec. 3, 1989 (22 performances and 8 previews) Soho Repertory presents:
AMERICAN BAGPIPES by Iain Heggie; Director, Julian Webber; Sets, Julian Webber; Costumes, Patricia Adshead; Lighting, Donald Holder; Sound, Phil Lee; Stage Manager, Nina L. Adshead; Production Manager, David Wagget; Press, Cromarty & Co./Peter Cromarty, Richard Brandt CAST: Amelia White (Sandra Michigan), Darcy Pulliam (Rena Nauldie), Peter McRobbie (Willie Nauldie), Simon Brooking (Patrick Nauldie)

The American premiere of a vicious comedy in two acts. The action takes place in Glasgow, Scotland at present.

(Apple Corps Theatre) Wednesday, November 8–December 31, 1989 (52 performances) 3-Dollar Bill Theatre presents:
ADAM AND THE EXPERTS by Victor Bumbalo; Director, Nicholas Deutsch; Sets, Campbell Baird; Costumes, Paul Tazewell; Lighting, Paul Palazzo; Music, Chris DeBlasio; Sound, Timothy Pritchard; Stage Manager, James Latus; Press, David Rothenberg CAST: John Finch (Adam), Althea Lewis (Sarah), John-Michael Lander (Jim), Benjamin Evett (Eddie), Susan Kaslow (Melissa/Mama Mata/Mom), Joseph DiRocco (Man), John Seidman (William/Baba Mata/Dr. Alp/Priest/Ralph/Dad)

A drama in two acts. The action takes place in NYC today.

(Theatre-Off-Park) Thursday, November 9–19, 1989 (12 performances) De Nova Repertory Theatre presents:
LA RONDE by Arthur Schnitzler; Adaptation, John Barton; Translation, Sue Davies; Director, Ada Brown Mather; Sets, Sharon Sprague; Costumes, Lori S. Catlin; Lighting, Rick Murray; Music, Paul Jensen; Movement, Marie Elena Scioscia; Stage Manager, Philip Lenger; Press, Michael Dalby CAST: Sharon Fogarty (the Prostitute), Patrick Falls (the Soldier), Suzanne Shubart (the Parlourmaid), Harry Blackman (the Young Gentleman), Kaethleen Cullen (the Young Wife), Michael Dalby (the Husband), Janet Roitz (the Sweet Girl), David Scott (the Poet), Linda Donald (the Actress), John Fistos (the Count)

The American premiere of a new adaptation of the 1903 drama. The action takes place in Vienna in the 1890's.

David Rogow, Zypora Spaisman in "Land of Dreams"

Everett Quinton in "Dr. Jekyll & Mr. Hyde" *(Anita & Steve Shevett)*

Darcy Pulliam, Amelia White, Peter McRobbie, Simon Brooking in "American Bagpipes" *(Gerry Goodstein)*

Ralph Carter, John Amos in "The Past Is the Past" *(Martha Swope)*

(Billie Holiday Theatre) Saturday, November 9–28, 1989 (15 performances) and returned Thursday, December 28, 1989–January 14, 1990 (11 performances) Billie Holiday Theatre (Marjorie Moon, Producer) presents:
THE PAST IS THE PAST by Richard Wesley; Director, Woodie King, Jr.; Sets/Costumes, Felix E. Cochren; Lighting, Christian Epps; Stage Manager, Avan; Press, Howard Atlee CAST: John Amos (Earl Davis), Ralph Carter (Eddie Green)

A drama in one act. The action takes place in a pool hall at the present. and **YESTERDAYS: BILLIE HOLIDAY REMEMBERED** by Reenie Upchurch CAST: Reenie Upchurch (Billie Holiday), Herb Lovelle, Weldon (Musicians)

(Charles Ludlam Theatre) Friday, Nov. 10, 1989–Mar. 11, 1990 (103 performances) The Ridiculous Theatrical Company (Everett Quinton, Artistic Director; David Musselman, Managing Director) presents:
DR. JEKYLL & MR. HYDE by Georg Osterman; Director, Kate Stafford; Sets, Mark Beard; Costumes, Susan Young; Lighting, Richard Currie; Music/Sound, James S. Badrak, Alan Gregorie, Jan Bell; Stage Manager, James Eckerle; Press, David Musselman CAST: Terence Mintern (Minerva), Eureka (Mary Jekyll), Everett Quinton (Henry Jekyll), Mary Neufeld (Bernice Braintwain), Georg Osterman (Lily Gay), Minnette Coleman (Aculine)

A new adaptation of Robert Louis Stevenson's classic tale of good vs. evil. This version takes place in Coxsackie, NY.

(Folksbiene Theatre) Saturday, Nov. 11–Mar. 18, 1990 (45 performances) The Folksbiene Theatre (Ben Schechter, Executive Director) presents:
THE LAND OF DREAMS by Nahum Stutchkoff; Adaptation, Miriam Kressyn; Translation, Simcha Kruger; Director, Bryna Wortman; Music, Raphael Crystal; Lyrics, Ms. Kressyn; Sets, Brian P. Kelly; Costumes, Mimi Maxman; Lighting, Jason Sturm; Stage Manager, Judith Scher; Press, Max Eisen CAST: David Rogow (Reb Aaren Ziskind), Rachel Black (Helen Ziskind), Zypora Spaisman (Baile Ziskind), Yosi Sokolsky (Sam Goldwasser), Mark Ethan Toporek (Sidney Ziskind), Molly Stark (Mrs. Katzenelenbogen), I. W. Firestone (Cantor Katz), Norman Golden (Hymie Ziskind), Richard Carlow (Milton Ziskind), Shira Flam (Natalie Katzenelenbogen), Lee Ann Levinson (Cookie)

A play with music. The action takes place in NYC in the 1930's.

Michael Santoro, Jamie Martin, Amy Stiller, Frank Smith in "There's an Angel in Las Vegas" *(Martha Swope)*

John Leguizamo, Ilka Tanya Payan in "Parting Gestures" *(Carol Rosegg)*

William Ragsdale, Elizabeth Berridge in "Briar Patch" *(Carol Rosegg)*

Bronagh Murphy, Michael Healy in "Away Alone" *(Martha Swope)*

(Courtyard Playhouse) Wednesday, November 15–December 10, 1989 The Glines (John Glines, Artistic Director) presents:
MY BLUE HEAVEN by Jane Chambers; Director, Kathleen Mary; Sets, Raymond J. S. Ruybe; Costumes, Charles Catanese; Lighting, Tracy Dedrickson; Stage Managers, Larry Courtney, Courtney Flanagan CAST: Dawn Evans (Molly), Richard Roy (Ralph/Dr. John), Judy Tate (Josie)
   A revival of a 1981 comedy in two acts. The action takes place on a dilapidated farmhouse in upstate New York at the present.

(Riverside Shakespeare Center) Thursday, November 16–December 10, 1989 (29 performances) The Riverside Shakespeare Co. presents:
RICHARD III by William Shakespeare; Director, Gus Kaikkonen CAST: Austin Pendleton (Richard), Penny Allen (Elizabeth), Brian Cousins (Hastings), Libby George (Margaret), Timothy W. Oman (Buckingham), Cary Spear (Lady Anne), Tom Tammi (Clarence), Grover Zucker (Stanley)

(Village Theatre) Wednesday, November 22–December 10, 1989 (18 performances) The Village Theatre Company presents:
CLOUD NINE by Caryl Churchill; Director, Linda Atkinson; Sets, Wendy Feldstein; Music, Jimmy Flynn; Lighting, Susan Kelleher; Stage Managers, Michelle Berke, Sherian Xavier CAST: Barbara Bercu, Milton Elliot, Susan Farwell, Marj Feenan, Randy Kelly, David McConnell, Howard Thoresen

(Mazur Theatre/Playwrights' Preview) Friday, November 24–December 16, 1989 (13 performances and 4 previews) Playwrights' Preview Productions (Frances Hill, Artistic Director) presents:
THERE IS AN ANGEL IN LAS VEGAS by Sean O'Connor; Director, Paul Dervis; Sets, Al Doyle; Costumes, Traci Di Gesu; Lighting, John Harrison; Technical, Joseph McGranaghan; Stage Managers, Scot A. Parish, Leslie Wint; Press, David Lipsky, Avivah Simon CAST: Michael Santoro (Dean), Tara Dolan (Glenda), Scott J. Weir (Chip), F. R. Smith (Eddie), Amy Stiller (Wilma), Jamie Martin (Betty), Paul Doherty (Dale)
   A black comedy in two acts. The action takes place in Las Vegas in a residential motel during August.

(Church of the Holy Trinity) Saturday, November 25–December 17, 1989 (18 performances) The Triangle Theatre Company presents:
IN PURSUIT OF THE SONG OF HYDROGEN by Tom Dunn; Director, Michael Ramach; Lighting, Nancy Collings; Sets, Bob Phillips; Costumes, Joan V. Evans; Sound, Miles Ray; Stage Manager, Robert Cartwright; Assistant Lighting, Anne E. Mitchell; Scenic Artist, Jeff Freund; Technical, Edmond Ramage; Press, Chris Boneau/Sharon Barr CAST: Fred Burrell (Mark Milton), Abby Dylan (Robin Till), Peter Guttmacher (Dr. William Wells), Cynthia Hayden (Margaret Wells), Woody Sempliner (Dr. Jack Wells)
   A drama in two acts. The action takes place in California, Washington, D.C. and London between 1968–1985.

(Intar Theatre) Sunday, November 26–December 23, 1989 (28 performances) Intar Hispanic American Arts Center (Max Ferra, Founder & Artistic Director) presents:
PARTING GESTURES by Rafael Lima; Director, John Ferraro; Sets, Loren Sherman; Lighting, Jackie Manassee; Costumes, Jennifer Von Mayrhauser; Production Manager, Darren Lee Cole; Press, Cromarty & Co./Peter Cromarty, Richard Brandt CAST: John Leguizamo (Marc), Ilka Tanya Payan (Carmen)
   A drama in one act. The action takes place in Miami at present.

(Ensemble Studio Theatre) Monday, November 27–December 16, 1989 (15 performances and 6 previews) The Ensemble Studio Theatre (Curt Dempster, Artistic Director; Peter Shavitz, Managing Director) presents:
BRIAR PATCH by Deborah Pryor; Director, Lisa Peterson; Producer, Kate Baggot; Sets, David Birn; Costumes, Michael Krass; Lighting, Greg MacPherson; Music/Sound, Michael Keck; Fights, Ron Piretti; Supervisor, Kevin Causey; Stage Manager, Greta Minsky; Press, Cromarty & Co./Peter Cromarty, Richard Brandt CAST: Elizabeth Berridge (Inez), Victor Slezak (Edgar), Paul McCrane (Flowers), Connie Ray (Butcher Lee), William Ragsdale (Druden), Nancy Franklin (Avon)
   A drama in two acts. The action takes place in a small town in Virginia at the present.

(Irish Arts Center) Friday, Dec. 1–May 20, 1990 (98 performances and 18 previews) Irish Arts Center (Jim Sheridan, Artistic Director; Nye Heron, Executive Director) presents:
AWAY ALONE by Janet Noble; Director, Terence Lamude; Music, Larry Kirwan; performed by Black 47; Sets, David Raphel; Lighting, Harry Feiner, Jon Terry; Sound, Tom Gould; Costumes, C. Jane Epperson; Press, Francine L. Trevens/Lea Ann Johnson CAST: Michael Healy (Liam), Paul Pillitteri (Mario), Anto Nolan (Owen), Barry O'Rourke (Paddy), Don Creedon (Desmond), Cora Murray (Mary), Bronagh Murphy (Breda), Joelle Martel (Girl)
   A comedy-drama concerning Irish immigrants. The action takes place in the Bronx at the present time.

Ric Ryder in "Gifts of the Magi" *(Martha Swope)*

"Juan Darien" *(Kenneth Van Sickle)*

Stephen Miller, David Baird in "Wind Beneath My Wings"
(Joanne Giganti)

Alexander Abdulov, Yelena Shanina, Nikolai Karachentsev in
"Junon and Avos"

(Playwrights Horizon Studio) Tuesday, December 5–10, 1989 (7 performances) The Basic Theatre presents:

PERICLES, PRINCE OF TYRE by William Shakespeare; Director, Jared Hammond; Sets/Lighting, Marc D. Malamud; Costumes, Mr. Hammond; Sound, Joe Gallant; Stage Manager, Mary Connally; Press, Sheri Delaine, Mr. Hammond CAST: Arlene Sterne (Gower), Weston Blakesley (Antiochus/Cleon/Knight), Eric Brandenburg (Pericles), Jenny Martel (Antiochus's Daughter/Lychorida/Diana), Neil Tadken (Thaliard/Fisherman/Knight/Gentleman/Lysimachus), Katherine Mayfield (Messenger/Thaisa), David Goldman (Escanes/Boult), Margaret Burnham (Lord/Servant/Marina), Robert Martini (Helicanus/Fisherman/Gentleman/Pirate), Sheri Delaine (Dionyza/Lord), Elizabeth Ann Townsend (Servant/Philemon/Bawd), Spruce Henry (Fisherman/Knight/Cerimon/Leonine/Gentleman), William Charlton (Simonides/Pander)

Shakespeare's comedy in two acts.

(Lamb's Theatre) Thursday, December 7–31, 1990 (32 performances) The Lamb's Theatre Company (Carolyn Rossi Copeland, Producing Director) presents:

THE GIFTS OF THE MAGI with Music & Lyrics by Randy Courts; Book & Lyrics by Mark St. Germain; Director, Sonya Baehr; Sets, Michael C. Smith; Costumes, Hope Hanafin; Lighting, Heather Carson; Musical Director, Mr. Courts; Incidental Music, Steven M. Alper; Choreography, Terpsie Toon; Production Manager, Denise Nations; Costumes, Kathryn Wagner; Stage Manager, Robin Anne Joseph; Original Staging, Christopher Catt CAST: Michael Calkins (Him), Rebecca Renfroe (Her), Ric Ryder (Willy), Paul Jackel (Jim), Lyn Vaux (Della), Ron Lee Savin (Soapy) MUSICAL NUMBERS: Star of the Night, Gifts of the Magi, Jim and Della, Christmas to Blame, How Much to Buy My Dream, The Restaurant, Once More, Bum Luck, Greed, Pockets, The Same Girl, Gift of Christmas, Finale

This season's production of the annual (since 1984) Christmas musical. Performed without intermission.

(St. Clement's Theatre) Tuesday, December 26, 1989–February 3, 1990 (48 performances) Music-Theatre Group (Lyn Austin, Producing Director; Diane Wondisford, Managing Director) presents:

JUAN DARIEN; Conceived & written by Julie Taymor & Elliot Goldenthal; Music/Text, Mr. Goldenthal; Direction/Puppetry/Masks, Ms. Taymor; Music Director, Richard Cordova; Sets/Costumes, G. W. Mercier/Ms. Taymor; Lighting, Debra Dumas; Sound, Bob Bielecki; Production Manager, Steven Ehrenberg; Stage Manager, Anne Marie Hobson; Press, Peter Cromarty/Kevin Brockman CAST: Ariel Ashwell, Kristofer Batho, Jamie Blachly, Thuli Dumakude, Geoffrey Gordon, Philip Johnson, Andrea Kane, Stephen Kaplin, Matthew Kimbrough, Richard Martinez, Nancy Mayans, Valerie Naranjo, Lawrence A. Neals, Jr., Lenard Petit, Susan Rawcliffe, Ray Stewart, John C. Thomas, Irene Wiley, Mimi Wyche

A musical carnival Mass based on a short story by Horacio Quiroga.

(Courtyard Playhouse) Wednesday, December 27, 1989–February 25, 1990 (53 performances) The Glines Mainstage Project presents:

THE WIND BENEATH MY WINGS by Sydney Morris; Director, John Wall; Sets, Leon Munier; Lighting, Clifton Taylor; Costumes, Charles Catanese; Stage Manager, Courtney Flanagan; Associate Producer, Steve Carpenter; CAST: David Baird (Casey), Stephen Miller (Jay)

A play in one act. The action takes place in NYC at present.

(City Center) Friday, January 5–February 4, 1990 (35 performances) Pierre Cardin presents:

JUNON AND AVOS-THE HOPE with Music by Alexis Ribnikov; Book/Lyrics, Andrey Voznesensky; Director, Mark Zakharov; Choreography, Vladimir Vassiliev; Sets, Oleg Sheintsiss; Costumes, Valentina Komolova; Sound, Abe Jacob; Technical, Steve Cochrane; General Manager, Robert V. Straus; American Producer, Lucy Jarvis; Stage Manager, Paul Moore; Press, Philip Rinaldi CAST: Philip Casnoff (Storyteller), Nikolai Karachentzov (Count Rezanov), Yelena Shanina (Conchita), Alexander Abdulov (Narrator/Lopez/Heretic), Yury Naumkin, Gennady Trofimov, Ludmilla Porgina, Vladimir Shiryayev, Vladimir Belousov, Boris Chunayev, Vladimir Kuznetsov, Rady Ovchinnikov, Villor Kuznetsov, Irena Alfiorova, Tatiana Derbeneva, Alexandra Zakharova, Ludmilla Artemieva, Yury Zelenin, Alexander Sado, Vladislav Bykov, Victor Rakov, Alexander Sririn, Nikolai Shusharin, Alexander Karnaushkin, Igor Fokin, Andrey Leonov, Andrey Druzhkin, Gennady Kozlov, Sergey Chonishvilli, Oleg Ruduk, Leonid Luvinsky, Leonid Gromov, Denis Karasiov

A Soviet rock musical in two acts. The action takes place in Russia and San Francisco in the 1800's.

(Triplex) Tuesday, January 9–February 18, 1990 (36 performances) The Mabou Mines presents:
LEAR by William Shakespeare; Direction & Adaptation, Lee Breuer; Score, Pauline Oliveros; Lighting, Arden Fingerhut, Lenore Doxsee; Costumes, Ghretta Hynd; Sound, L. B. Dallas, Eric Liljestrand; Fights, B. H. Barry; Dramaturg, Alisa Solomon, Stage Manager, Elizabeth Valsing; Managing Director, Anthony Vasconcellos; Company Manager, Joel Bassin, Production Manager, Monica Bowin; Press, Ellen Jacobs CAST: Ruth Maleczech (Lear), Greg Mehrten (Fool), Isabell Monk (Gloucester), Kimberly Scott (Wilda), Lola Pashalinski (Kent), Ellen McElduff (Elva), Karen Evans-Kandel (Edna), Bill Raymond (Goneril), Ron Vawter (Regan), Black-Eyed Susan (Albany), Honora Fergusson (Cornwall), Lute Ramblin' (Cordelion), Clove Galilee (France), Maya O'Relly (Burgundy), Joanna Adler (Henchwoman), Allison Dubin (Henchwoman), Frier McCollister, Pedro Rosado, Duncan Raymond, Lane Savadove, Alex Klimovitsky

A gender-reversed adaptation of Shakespeare. The action takes place in Smyrna, Georgia in the late 1950's.

(Ohio Theatre) Wednesday, January 10–February 4, 1990 (21 performances) The Barrow Group presents:
THE WEATHER OUTSIDE by Tom Donaghy; Director, Leonard Foglia; Sets, Jim Noone; Costumes, Nina Canter; Lighting, Wendall S. Hinkle; Stage Manager, Paul F. Hewitt; Resident Producer, Gillian Schreiber; Press, Peter Cromarty CAST: Seth Barrish (Sidewalk Artist/Skinny Man), Lee Brock (Kate/Holly), Marcia Debonis (Girl/Blabs), Tom Farrell (Jarrad/Saxman/Joey), Martha French (Holly/Old Woman/Orderly), Lance Guest (James), Nate Harvey (Waiter/Nichols' Asst.), Robert Jimenez (Man 2/Policeman/Boy), Michael Warren Powell (Genealogist/Ken), Raymond Anthony Thomas (Man 1/Priest/Doctor)

A play about an advertising man who loses his job, girlfriend, wallet and identity on one New Year's Eve in NYC.

(South St. Theatre) Wednesday, January 10–February 11, 1990 (35 performances) Vietnam Veterans Ensemble Theatre Co. presents:
THE STRIKE by Rod Serling; Director, Thomas Bird; Sets, George A. Allison; Costumes, Jim Buff; Lighting, Terry Wuthrich; Sound, Scott Sanders; Stage Manager, Jerry Bihm; Press, Bruce Campbell CAST: Russ Ericson (Fox), Tucker Smallwood (Gaylord), Jim Tracy (Franks), Matt Tomasino (Peters), Ray Robertson (Chick), Brian Markinson (Hannify), Ralph DeMatthews (Grace), Stephen Lee (Kim), Brian Markinson (Golden), Sean Michael Rice (Sloane), Michael Manetta (Jones), David Adamson (Chaxfield), Anthony Chisholm (Walker)

A stage premiere of a television drama from 1954. The action takes place in Japan and the Pacific from June to December, 1950.

(Theatre East) Tuesday, January 16– still playing May 31, 1990. Jonathan Scharer presents:
FORBIDDEN BROADWAY 1990; Concept, Parody Lyrics & Direction by Gerard Alessandrini; Costumes, Erika Dyson; Wigs, Bobby Pearce; Consultant, Pete Blue; Stage Manager, Jerry James; Associate Producer, Chip Quigley; Management, Kevin Dowling; Executive Director, Arthur B. Brown; Press, Shirley Herz/Glenna Freedman CAST: Suzanne Blakeslee, Jeff Lyons, Marilyn Pasekoff, Bob Rogerson, Philip Fortenberry

The newest edition of the long running revue spoofing other shows.

(Actor's Outlet) Thursday, January 18–February 18, 1990 (25 performances)
DEEP TO CENTER by James O'Connor; Director, Ken Lowstetter; Set, Randall Etheredge; Lighting, Amy A. C. Coombs; Assistant Director, Eve Martinez; Stage Manager, Alan Hemingway; Costumes, Mary Marsicano; Press, Max Eisen CAST: John J. Barilla (George Banks), Jacqueline DeCosmo (Doris), Larry Filiaci (Joey/Kevin), Les Forshey (Ben), Michael Gilpin (Paulie/Rudy), Larry Maxwell (Rip/Rex), Betty McKinley (Rita Banks), Phil Miller (Vendor/Outfielder/Eddie Lomax), Howie Muir (Mitch/Ken)

A play in three acts. The action takes place in early October in the near future at Shea Stadium, New York City.

(Cubiculo Theatre) Thursday, January 25–February 4, 1990 (16 performances and 4 previews) ClassicWorks, in association with Cubiculo Producing Group, presents:
VENUS AND ADONIS by William Shakespeare; Adapted & Directed by Anthony Naylor; Lighting, Tammy Richardson; Producer, Russ Billingsly; Coordinator, Meredith Luce; Press, Shirley Herz/Miller Wright CAST: Sandra Laub, Leila Boyd, Anne Lilly, Susan Thompson (Venus), Russ Billingsly, David Comstock, Robert Johnson (Adonis)

Shakespeare's epic poem performed without intermission.

Ruth Maleczech as Lear *(Beatriz Schiller)*

Russ Ericson, Brian Markinson, Sean Michael Rice, Mike Manetta, Stephen Lee, Ralph DeMatthews, Jim Tracy, Matt Tomasino in "The Strike" *(Susan Cook)*

Suzanne Blakeslee, Jeff Lyons, Marilyn Pasekoff, Bob Rogerson (kneeling) in "Forbidden Broadway 1990" *(Carol Rosegg)*

David Comstock, Sandra Laub, Russ Billingsley, Leila Boyd in "Venus and Adonis" *(Martha Swope)*

(Judith Anderson Theatre) Saturday, January 20–March 4, 1990 (52 performances and 10 previews) Manhattan Punch Line Theatre (Steve Kaplan, Artistic Director) presents:

MANHATTAN PUNCH LINE'S 6th ANNUAL FESTIVAL OF ONE ACT COMEDIES: Sets, David K. Gallo; Lighting, Danianne Mizzy; Costumes, Sharon Lynch (A), Julie Doyle (B); Sound, John Bowen; Stage Managers, Cathy Tomlin, Robert L. Young, Fiona Brady, Gar Chiang, J. Chris Henry, Karl Johnson, Cathy Leonard, Shawn O'Toole, Linda Wielkotz; Production Manager, Chris A. Kelly; Press, Shirley Herz/Miller Wright
EVENING A: PHILIP GLASS BUYS A LOAF OF BREAD by David Ives; Director, Jason McConnell Buzas CAST: Liz Larsen (Woman #1), Randy Danson (Woman #2), Chris Wells (Philip Glass), Ryan Hilliard (Baker) The action takes place in a bakery at present.
PORTFOLIO by Tom Donaghy; Director, Chris Ashley CAST: Gary Yudman (Tim), Michael Aschner (Voice), Theresa McElwee (Nicoise) The action takes place in a photo studio at present.
THE SHOW MUST GO ON by Laurence Klavan; Director, Stephen Hollis CAST: Kathrin King Segal (Rita Binder), Dan Hagen (Ed Binder), Gus Rogerson (Pip), Nick Sadler (Soupy), Kitty Crooks (Helda Rose), Bill Cohen (Phil Gramble) The action takes place in a suburban home at present.
HOW ARE THINGS IN COSTA DEL FUEGO? by Rick Louis; Director, Steve Kaplan; Music, Chris Hajian; Choreography, William Fleet Lively CAST: Don Lowe (Pacoguitar), Deryl Caitlyn (Major Domo), Robert Montano (Gustavo), Paul O'Brien (Nick), Howard Samuelsohn (Etienne), Caryn Rosenthal (Pola), Dea Lawrence (Candace St. Jill), Rhonda Hayter (Maria), David Konig, Theresa McElwee (The People) The action takes place in a bar in Costa Del Fuego, whenever.
EVENING B: THE FERTILIZATION OPERA with Music & Lyrics by Peter Tolan; Director, Jason McConnell Buzas; Musical Director, Albert Ahromheim CAST: Christopher Wells (Sperm #1), Mark Chmiel (Sperm #2), Michael Kelly Boone (Sperm #3), Linda Wallem (Egg)
GRUNIONS by Barbara Lindsay; Director, Kay Matschulat CAST: Arthur Hanket (Augie), Robin Groves (Carla) The action takes place on a Southern California beach late one night.
BRUNCH AT TRUDY AND PAUL'S by Michael Aschner; Director, Louis Scheeder CAST: Cheryl Hulteen (Trudy), Janine Robbins (Ronnie), Ken Martin (Bob) The action takes place in an apartment in Woodside, Queens during the fall.
FELLOW TRAVELLERS by Jeffrey Hatcher; Director, Jonathon Mintz CAST: Charles Gerber (Martin Vekony), Patricia Hodges (Fran Imbrey), Robert Burke (Robbertson Ellis), Daniel Hagen (Official) The action takes place at the W.R.I.T.E.S. conference in an East Berlin hotel at present.
THE ARTISTIC DIRECTION by Roger Hedden; Director, Greg Johnson CAST: Warren Burton (Art), Peter Basch (George), Anita Rogerson (Ellen), Chris A. Kelly (Cpt. Cannon) The action takes place in NYC at present.

(Greenwich House) Friday, January 26–Sunday, February 25, 1990 (24 performances)
LIMBO TALES by Len Jenkin; Director, Thomas Babe; Sets, Stephan Olson; Costumes, Claudia Brown; Lighting, Greg MacPherson; Sound, Tom Gould; Stage Manager, Jess Lynn; Technical Director, Brian McDaniel; Press, Michael Sexton CAST: Leslie Lyles (Master of Ceremonies), Steve Hofvendahl, followed by Steve Mellor (Man in Highway), Scott Renderer (Man in Hotel); Voices: Walter Bobbie, Reg E. Cathey, Crystal Field, Steve Hofvendahl, Jess Lynn, Jodie Markell and Bill Raymond
Revival of an American play in three parts (Highway, Intermezzo and Hotel), performed in two parts.

(Orpheum Theatre) Tuesday, January 30–May 20, 1990 (103 performances and 9 previews) Frederick Zollo and Robert Cole in association with 126 Second Ave. Corp. and Sine/D'addario Ltd. present:
SEX, DRUGS, ROCK & ROLL: Written & Performed by Eric Bogosian; Director, Jo Bonney; Sets, John Arnone; Lighting, Jan Kroeze; Sound, Jan Nebozenko; Stage Manager, Pat Sosnow; Associate Producers, Ethel Bayer & William Suter; Press, Philip Rinaldi CAST: Eric Bogosian
Performance art exploring three major American obsessions.

(Henry St. Settlement Theatre) Wednesday, January 31–February 25, 1990 (15 performances and 5 previews) The Working Theatre (Bill Mitchelson, Artistic Director) presents:
SPECIAL INTERESTS by Joe Sutton; Director, Mark Lutwak; Sets/Costumes, Anne C. Patterson; Lighting, Spencer Mosse; Photographic Consultant, Tom Chargin; Music, "Happy" New Yorkers; Production/Stage Manager, Nina Heller; General Manager, Denise Laffer; Press, Bruce Cohen/Victoria Lynch CAST: William Wise (Vin), Judith Granite (Edna), Lynn Anderson (Deb), James DuMont (Wes), Robert Arcaro (Fallaci), Lorey Hayes (Dot), Jude Ciccolella (Yates), Fracaswell Hyman (Nuckles)
A comedy revolving around a bus strike.

Michael Aschner, Theresa McElwee, Gary Yudman in "Portfolio" *(Martha Swope)*

Janine Robbins, Cheryl Hulteen, Ken Martin in "Brunch at Trudy & Paul's" *(Martha Swope)*

Eric Bogosian in "Sex, Drugs, etc" *(Paula Court)*

Jude Ciccolella, Fracaswell Hyman in "Special Interests" *(Tom Charsin)*

63

Susan Pellegrino, Donald Symington, Jane Welch, Mark Hofmeier in "Come As You Are" *(Martha Swope)*

Cast of "Mama, I Want to Sing Part II" *(Martha Swope)*

Michael Moriarty in "A Special Providence"

Mark Shannon, Seth Barrish in "K2"
(Cathy Blaivas)

(Riverwest) Friday, February 2–24, 1990 (21 performances)
THE FABULOUS LA FONTAINE with Conception, Book & Lyrics by Owen S. Rackleff; Music adapted from "The Carnival of the Animals" by Camille Saint-Saens; Direction/Musical Arrangements, Dennis Deal; Stage Managers, John R. Stattel, Paul J. Smith; Sets, Kaem Coughlin; Lighting, David Finley; Costumes, Traci Di Gesu; House Manager, Sally Halbert; Press, Howard Atlee CAST: Earl Aaron Levine (Louis XIV), Thomas Hetmanek (Royal Chamberlain), Maurice Edwards (Jean de La Fontaine), Colby Thomas (Claudine), Evan Matthews (Brunon), Patti Perkins (La Sabliere), Michael Shelle (Nicholas), Michael Babin (Roger), Carolyn Marlow (Marie)
MUSICAL NUMBERS: Overture, King of Beasts, Gossip, Elephant Duo, Modern and Progressive, Practice! Practice!, Jackass pantomine, Flea pantomine, There Was a Bird, Funny Moment, Paths of Glory, Fable of the Fossil, Chickens! Chickens!, Frog and the Rat, I'm a Pisces, Wife and Mistress, Age Has Its Hour, Lion in Love, Grand Finale
A musical in two acts. The action takes place in France in the 17th century.

(Actors' Playhouse) Friday, February 2–18, 1990 (7 performances and 14 previews) Roger Bowen Inc. presents:
COME AS YOU ARE; Written & Directed by N. Richard Nash; Sets, James Morgan; Lighting, Kenneth Posner; Costumes, Steven Perry; Executive Producer, Maria Di Dia; Music, Steven Aprahamian; Stage Manager, Alan Fox; Press, Peter Cromarty/Richard Brandt CAST: Susan Pellegrino (Becky McAlister), Mark Hofmaier (John McAlister), Jane Welch (Cora Briggs), Donald Symington (Lowell Briggs)
A drama in two acts. The action takes place in a country cottage in Northwestern Connecticut, at present.

(Heckscher Theatre) Friday, February 2—Still playing May 31, 1990. Reach Entertainment and Sports in association with Vy Higginsen and Ken Wydro present:
MAMA, I WANT TO SING-PART II: *The Story Continues* . . . with Music by Wesley Naylor; Book/Lyrics, Vy Higginsen, Ken Wydro; Director, Mr. Wydro; Sets, Charles McClennahan; Choreography, Cisco Drayton; Lighting, Marshall Williams; Stage Manager, Kevin P. Lewis; Press, Keith Sherman CAST: D'Atra Hicks, Victoria Hamilton (Doris Winter), Norwood, Richard Hartley, Pierre Cook (Rev. Julian Simmons), Doris Troy, Lorraine Moore (Mama Winter), Kathleen Murphy-Palmer (Sister Carrie), Charles Stewart, Stewart Hartley, Boysie White (Minster of Music), Anaysha Figueroa, Knoelle Higginsen-Wydro (Little Doris), Vy Higginsen, Hazel Smith (Narrator/D.J.)
MUSICAL NUMBERS: Joy, Joy, Joy/Great is Thy Faithfulness, Spirit of Your Father, The Lord Is Blessing Me, Sanctify Me Holy, Sermon Song, You'll Never Walk Alone, Something Pretty, Something To Remember Me By, When We All Get To Heaven, We Belong Together, Bless You, My Children, Stay Close To the Music, Long Distance Love, New Life on the Planet, Glad to be in the Service, Promise of the Future, To Love Is to Serve, Please Understand, Where Is My Mommy, Please?, Alone on the Road, Coming Back Home, Finale
A musical sequel in two acts and 18 scenes. Original "Mama" opened March 25, 1983 in the same theatre, and is still playing in repertory with Part II.

(John Houseman Theatre) Monday, Feb. 5–Mar. 25, 1990 (8 performances) East Coast Arts Theatre (Joe Cacaci, Artistic Director) in association with Eric Krebs and the John Houseman Theatre present:
A SPECIAL PROVIDENCE: *Tale To Be Told By An Actor* by Earnest Hart (Michael Moriarty); Director, Peter Von Berg; Sets, Richard Meyer, Amy Younger; Costumes, Anne-Marie Wright; Stage Manager, Ruth Moe; Press, David Rothenberg CAST: Michael Moriarty
A solo performance on Mondays in February and Sundays in March.

(Ohio Theatre) Thursday, February 8–March 4, 1990 (20 performances) The Barrow Group presents:
K2 by Patrick Meyers; Director, James Lish; Set, Charles Golden; Costumes, Deborah Bays; Lighting, Debra Dumas; Sound, David Schnirman; Stage Manager, Jennifer Gilbert; Technical Climbing Advisor, James Munson; Press, Cromarty & Co.; Resident Producer, Gillian Schreiber. CAST: Mark Shannon (Taylor), Seth Barrish (Harold).
A drama in which the action takes place on September 4, 1977 on K2, the world's second highest mountain, on a ledge located on a six hundred foot ice wall just below the summit at 27,000 feet.

(Westside Arts Theatre Upstairs) Feb. 9, 1990—Raymond L. Gaspard, Charles H. Duggan and Drew Dennett by arrangement with Randall Kline present:
FEAST OF FOOLS by Geoff Hoyle; Directorial Consultant, Anthony Taccone; Sets, Scott Weldin; Lighting, Neil Peter Jampolis; Sound, Michael Holten; Choreography, Kimi Okada; Score, Keith Terry; Production Advisor, Randall Kline CAST: Geoff Hoyle
A new vaudeville solo clown show in two acts.

"A Voice in the Well" Ensemble

Mollie O'Mara, Omar Shapli in
"Crowbar" *(Tom Brazil)*

Colette Kilroy, Ching Valdez/Aran, Allison Stair Neet, Kate
Fuglei, Regina Taylor in "New Anatomies" (Martha Swope)

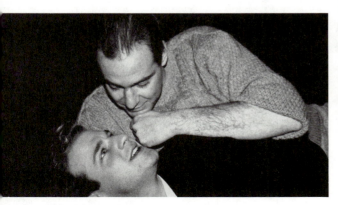

Michael Curran, Randy Kelly in "The Norman Heart"

(Producers Club Theatre) Sunday, February 11, 1990 (1 performance) Yaffa Productions II presents:

SPIRIT, BLACK & FEMALE: A Tribute To Black Womanhood by Margaret Walker, Samm Art-Williams, Douglas Turner Ward, Nikki Giovanni, Ntozake Shange CAST: Linda H. Humes, Abiodun Oyewole (host)

A choreopoem.

(Conservatory Theatre) Tuesday, February 13–24, 1990 (12 performances) A Voice in the Well Ensemble (Gayle Finer, Artistic Director) presents:

ELLISON & EDEN by Paul Mullin; Director, Jordan Merkur; Sets, Jeff Freund; Costumes, Rosemary Ponzo; Lighting, Anne Mitchell; Sound, Wayne Laakko; Stage Manager, Joshua Sherer; Press, Rick Draughon CAST: Lionel Chute (Ellison), Gayle Finer (Eden), Andy Buckley (Puma/Tomas/Pallidin), Ennis Smith (Alligator/Merc/Cop), Eve Annenberg (Jack Rabbit/Night-mare Nun/Lady/Hat), Susan Jirovec (Buffalo/Joan), Ken Sawyer (Condor/Toad/Yuppie), Kimberly Westcott (Bear/Dana), Tom Williams (Popper/Whale)

A play in two acts.

(Victory Theatre) Tuesday, February 13–April 22, 1990 (57 performances and 5 previews) En Garde Arts presents:

CROWBAR by Mac Wellman; Director, Richard Caliban; Producer, Anne Hamburger; Music, David Van Tieghem; Dramaturgy/Slides, James Sanders; Sets/Props, Kyle Chepulis; Costumes, Claudia Brown; Lighting, Brian Aldous; Sound, Eric Liljestrand; Stage Manager, Dan Weir; Production Manager, SallyAnne Santos; Press, Ted Killmer CAST: Yusef Bulos (Ghost of David Belasco), Reg E. Cathey succeeded by Ascanio Sharpe (Mr. Rioso), Elzbieta Czyzewska (First Woman), Nora Dunfee (Second Woman), Mollie O'Mara succeeded by Jan Leslie Harding (Second Girl), Cordelia Richards (First Girl), Glen Santiago succeeded by Steve Coats (Young Man/J. Henry Fruitnight/Strane Man/Ghost of Oscar Hammerstein/Worried Man), Omar Shapli (First Man), David Van Tieghem (Ghost of William Gorman) CHORUS: Julia Mengers (Opera Singer), Sara Bladen, Charles Bolan, Karen Casteel, Susanne Columbia, Pat Crawford, Anita Durst, Suzanne Farkas, Michael Garces, Lori Johnson, Llewellyn Jones, Kati Kormendi, Kelly Anne Megara, Kevin O'Connor, Joy Pincus, Sharon Port, Catherine Porter, Yvette Sharon, Liz Sherman, Suzanne Steele, K. C. Ligon, Ken Schatz

The first play in the Victory Theatre in 60 years. The theatre was built in 1899 as the Theatre Republic, and was later known as the Belasco, Republic and since 1942, the Victory. This production is "site-specific" theatre, examining the glorius past of the building.

(Home For Contemporary Theatre and Art) Wednesday, February 14–March 4, 1990 (18 performances) Home for Contemporary Theatre and Art in association with Compass Theatre Co. presents:

NEW ANATOMIES by Timberlake Wertenbaker; Dramaturg, Victoria Abrash; Director, Melia Bensussen; Lighting, David Bergstein; Sets/Costumes, Connie Singer; Music, Michele Navazio; Stage Manager, Tamara Holt CAST: Colette Kilroy (Isabelle Eberhardt), Alison Stair Neet (Severine/Antoine/Bou Saadi), Kate Fuglei (Verda Miles/Anna/Si Lachmi/Yasmina/Capt. Soubiel), Ching Valdes/Aran (Natalie/Eugenie/Murderer/Judge), Regina Taylor (Jenny/Saleh/Lydia/Col. Lyautey)

A drama based on the real life of Isabelle Eberhardt, an adventurer who explored Africa posing as a man.

(Village Theatre) Wednesday, Feb. 14–Mar. 18, 1990 (31 performances) The Village Theatre Company presents:

THE NORMAL HEART by Larry Kramer; Director, Henry Fonte; Assistant Director, Gigi Rivkin; Sets, Henry Fonte; Lighting, Douglas O'Flaherty; Assistant Lighting, Susan Kelleher; Costumes, Ismael Hernandez; Sound, Jimmy Flynn; Technical, Zeke Zaccaro; Stage Manager, Elizabeth Brady Davis CAST: Peter Michael Marino (Craig Donner/Grady), Howard Thoresen (Mickey Marcus), Randy Kelly (Ned Weeks), Wally Dunn (David/Hiram Keebler/Doctor), Julia McLaughlin (Dr. Emma Brookner), Terrence Martin (Bruce Niles), Michael Curran (Felix Turner), Dugg Smith (Ben Weeks), David McConnell (Tommy Boatwright)

The first NYC revival of a drama in two acts and 16 scenes. The action takes place in NYC between 1981–84. For original production, see Theatre World Vol. 41.

(Pulse Ensemble Theatre) Wednesday, February 14–March 4, 1990 (12 performances) Pulse Ensemble Theatre presents:

BACHELOR FLATS by Jan Buttram; Director, Alexa Kelly; Sets, Michael Kay; Lighting/Sound, Donovan; Associate Producer, Marc Raphael; Production Assistant, Jeff P. Weiss; Graphic, Paula Ng CAST: Stephen Bittrich (Joe Bob Bachelor), Kelly Champion (Betty Sue), C. K. Harris (Sly Rubins), Margaret Massman (Little Sister)

A play in two acts and 3 scenes. The action takes place in East Texas in 1987.

(Duo Theatre) Thursday, February 15–March 17, 1990 (15 performances) Duo Theatre (Michael Alasa, Executive/Artistic Director) presents:
THE L.A. SCENE with Music by Jorge Mirkin, Browen Jones, Elias Miguel Munoz; Book/Lyrics, Elias Miguel Munoz; Director, Mary Lisa Kinney; Sets/Lighting, Design Associates; Costumes, Alyson Hui CAST: Humberto Alabado (Julian), Laura E. Delano (Geneia), Agustin Rodriguez (Johnny), Sara Weaver (Erica), Pamela Scott (Interviewer)
MUSICAL NUMBERS: Once Upon a Time in the City of Angels, Song for Little Sister, Sugar Cane Drinks, Returning, Always See the Light, L.A. Boulevard, Spring
   A musical performed without intermission.

(Duo Theatre) Monday, February 19–29, 1990 (6 performances) Duo Theatre (Michael Alasa, Executive/Artistic Director) presents:
DANNY AND THE DEEP BLUE SEA by John Patrick Shanley; Director, William Electric Black; Design, Design Associates CAST: Blanca Camacho (Roberta), Anthony Ruiz (Danny)
   A presentation of Shanley's play featuring an Hispanic cast.

(Apple Corps Theatre) Tuesday, February 20–March 11, 1990 (20 performances) The Women's Project and Productions (Julia Miles, Artistic Director) presents:
VIOLENT PEACE by Lavonne Mueller; Director, Bryna Wortman; Sets, James Noone; Lighting, Victor En Yu Tan; Costumes, Mimi Maxmen; Sound, Bruce Ellman; Stage Manager, Linda Carol Young; Press, Fred Nathan, Merle Frimark CAST: Jenny Robertson (Kim Denton), Dennis Parlato (Mark Feeny)

(The New Theatre of Brooklyn) Wednesday, February 21—(performances) The New Theatre of Brooklyn (Deborah J. Pope/Steve Stettler, Artistic Directors) present:
ROUGH CROSSINGS by Tom Stoppard; Adapted from a play by Ferenc Molnar; Director, Steve Stettler; Music, André Previn; Music Director, Michael John La Chiusa; Dramaturge, Ulla Backlund; Sets, James D. Sandefur; Lighting, Pat Dignan; Costumes, Toni-Leslie James; Sound, Tom Gould; Stage Manager, Jana Lynn CAST: David Manis (Dvornichek), Lowry Miller (Turai), Simon Brooking (Adam), Robert Blumenfeld (Gal), Patricia Norcia (Natasha), Graeme Malcolm (Ivor)

Lou Brockway, Kevin O'Connor in
"By and For Havel"
(Suzanne Karp Krebs)

Georgia Bennett, Paul Doherty in "Homesick" (Martha Swope)

Jenny Robertson, Dennis Parlato in "Violent Peace" (Martha Holmes)

Kimberly Jones, Tena Wilson, Minnette Coleman, Adrian Bailey (top) in "Capitol Cakewalk" (Linda Alinz)

(Dimson Theatre) Wednesday, February 21–March 18, 1990 (16 performances and 7 previews)
CAPITOL CAKEWALK with Music, Terry Waldo; Lyrics, Lou Carter; Book, Elmer Kline with Perry Arthur Kroeger; Director, Tom O'Horgan; Choreography, Wesley Fata; Sets, Mr. Kroeger; Costumes, Kathryn Wagner; Lighting, Howard Thies; Stage Manager, Michael Schaefer; Productions Manager, Christopher Pierre; Press, Peter Cromarty, Kevin Brockman CAST: Adrian Bailey (Big Jim/Warren G.), Minnette Coleman (Dutchess/Annie), Kimberly Jones (Lil/Mabel), Jack Landron (Chancellor/H.P.), Miron Lockett (Elihue/Gaston B. Means), Janice Lee (Shack Girl/Ambassador's Wife), Yoko Matsumura (Lucy/Adelaide), Aaron Mendelson (A-1/Secretary Hall), Leonard Parker (Dickens/St. Peter), Jeffrey Smith (Jefferson/Jesse), Marc D. Summers (George/Forbes), Jack Waddell (Harry), Tena Wilson (Sally/Nan), Philip Gilmore (Norman Thomas/Hoover), Sharon Hope (Aima)
MUSICAL NUMBERS: Overture, The Only Crime, Merry Roll Round Waltz, American Dream, My Ohio, Harry and Jesse Soft Shoe, The One in My Dear Mother's Heart, Sartorial Splendor Cakewalk, Nan, Pink Pinkie, Gaston D. Means, The Deal, Nomination, Normalcy, Warren Harding March, Shack Stomp, Inaugural Dance, The Red, White and Blue U.S.A., A Louse in the White House, Washington Ragtime Dirt, Too Late to Love, Summer of '23, Hoi-Ya, You're the Prez, Finale
   A musical scandal in ragtime in two acts. The action takes place in Harlem in 1924 as a theatre company tells the story of President Warren G. Harding.

(John Houseman Theatre) Wednesday, February 21, 1990 and still running May 31, 1990. 150th performance on July 21, 1990. Eric Krebs in association with Raft Theatre presents:
BY AND FOR HAVEL; Two one-act plays; Director, Vasek Simek; Sets, Ed Morrill; Costumes, Iris Bazan; Lighting/Sound, Marc D. Malamud; Press, David Rothenberg
AUDIENCE by Vaclav Havel CAST: Kevin O'Connor (Brew Master), Lou Brockway (Vanek)
CATASTROPHE by Samuel Beckett CAST: Evelyn Tuths (Assistant Director), Kevin O'Connor (Director), Lou Brockway (Protagonist)
   One Havel piece and another dedicated to him by Beckett.

(Mazur Theatre) Friday, February 23–March 17, 1990 (12 performances) Playwrights' Preview Productions (Frances Hill, Artistic Director; Adelle Sardi, Producer) presents:
HOMESICK by Danny Cahill; Director, Bruce Lumpkin; Sets, Al Doyle; Costumes, Traci DiGesu; Lighting, Bill Simmons; Stage Manager, Lesli Wint CAST: Georgia Bennett, Marcia DeBonis, Paul Doherty, Claudia Gold, Michael Santoro, David Dawson

(Beacon Theatre) Wednesday, February 28—(performances and previews) Shelly Garrett presents:
BEAUTY SHOP; Written, Directed and Produced by Shelly Garrett; Producers, Suzanne Meyers, Evans Johnson, Shelly Garrett II, Lawrence McNeal III: Company Manager, Retha Jones; Stage Manager, Vincent Newton; Costumes, Joi Reeder; Press, Jeffrey Richards/Irene Gandy CAST: Teal Marchande (Terry), Mirage Micheaux (Sylvia), Steven Gamage (Chris), Judy Hardy (Margaret), Aurora L. Threats (Rachel), Patricia Forte (Mrs. Henderson), Shenea Starr Garrett (Priscilla), Lamont R. Bonmon (Tom), Sylvia Bronson (Cybil), Robert A. Johnson (Herman), Kym Whitley (Rosemary), Paula Stevenson (Loretta), Kimberly Ann Brooks (Naomi), Alan Flagg (Robber), Rhonda Freya English (Lorainne), Matt Gibson (Francois), Virginia Dubose (Chauffeur/Manicurist)

A soul food comedy. The action takes place in the Pamper Me beauty shop over two days.

(Intar Stage II) Wednesday, February 28–March 18, 1990 (20 performances) Intar Hispanic Arts Center (Max Ferra, Artistic Director; Eva Brune, Acting Executive Director) presents:
GOING TO NEW ENGLAND by Ana Maria Simo; Director, Maria Irene Fornes; Stage Manager, Abigail Koreto; Sets/Costumes, Ms. Fornes; Lighting, Stephen Quandt; Production Manager, Peter J. Davis; General Manager, Michael Palma; Press, Peter Cromarty/Kevin Brockman CAST: Elizabeth Clemens (Tati), Divina Cook (Delia), Rene Rivera (Willy), Martin Treat (Manolito)

(Circle In The Square Downtown) Wednesday, February 28–April 8, 1990 (32 performances and 15 previews) Pamela Kantor in association with Douglas L. Feldman and Paul A. Kaplan present:
SPARE PARTS by Elizabeth Page; Director, Susan Einhorn; Sets, Ursula Belden; Costumes, Elsa Ward; Lighting, Norman Coates; Sound, One Dream; Stage Manager, Crystal Huntington; Press, Penny Landau CAST: Stephen Hamilton (Henry), Robin Groves (Lois), Donna Haley (Jax), Margo Skinner (Selma), Reed Birney (Perry)

A drama in two acts and 12 scenes. The action takes place in Hartford and New Haven, Connecticut, at present.

Robin Groves, Reed Birney in "Spare Parts"
(Ken Howard)

Kathryn Meisle, Katherine Leask in "Cahoots"
(Gerry Goodstein)

Renee Rivera, Elizabeth Clemens in "Going to New England" *(Martha Swope)*

David Marshall Grant, Kurt Deutsch in "Making Movies" *(Martha Swope)*

(Promenade Theatre) Thursday, March 1–April 1, 1990 (8 performances and 30 previews) John A. McQuiggan in association with Lucille Lortel, Promenade Partners, Inc. and Pace Theatrical Group, Inc. presents:
MAKING MOVIES by Aaron Sorkin; Director, Don Scardino; Sets, David Potts; Costumes, Laura Crow; Lighting, Dennis Parichy; General Management, New Roads Prods.; Company Manager, Laura Heller; Consultant, George Darveris; Stage Manager, Fred Reinglas; Sound, Aural Fixation; Associate Producers, Graconn Ltd., David H. Peipers; Press, Joshua Ellis/Adrian Bryan-Brown, Jackie Green, John Barlow CAST: David Marshall Grant (Jeff), Michael Countryman (Robert), Kurt Deutsch (Craig), Christopher Murney (Reuben), Sharon Schlarth (Marty)

A comedy in two acts. The action takes place at an Astoria soundstage and a farm in Schenectady. The time is the present. Developed from a Sorkin one act called "Hidden in This Picture."

(South St. Theatre) Thursday, Mar. 1–Apr. 1, 1990 (45 performances) G.G. Productions, The Lerner Rechnitz and S.D.K. Productions present:
CAHOOTS by Rick Johnston; Director, David Taylor; Sets, Scott Bradley; Lighting, Malcolm Sturchio; Costumes, Susan Young; Stage Manager, Jessica Murrow; Sound, J. Bloomrosen; Press, Philip Rinaldi CAST: Kathryn Meisle (Jan), Katherine Leask (Lois), Malachy Cleary (Al), James DeMarse (Ken), John Hickey (Grant)

A comedy. The action takes place at an East Side dinner party at present.

(St. Genesius Guild) Friday, March 2–3, 1990 (2 performances) The St. Genesius Guild of Christ and St. Stephen's Church present:
BRUSH ARBOR REVIVAL with Music & Lyrics by Anne Phillips; Book, Frances Scott; Director, Neal Kenyon; Music Director, Anne Phillips; Stage Manager, Jodi Katzman CAST: Beauris Whitehead (Narrator), Rafael Torres, Jr. (Sweet William), Craig Pomranz (Josh), Carol McCann (Carrie), Tim Shea (Mike Meadows), Carol Hall (Sister Ellen), Chelli Jackson (Jenny), Dennis Perren (Deacon Jones), Ingrid Saxon (Sister Celia), Miriam Burton (Miranda), Craig Chambers (Arnie), Page Johnson (Billy Ludlow)
MUSICAL NUMBERS: See the Lilies of the Field, How They Bloom, Do This in Remembrance of Me, Deacon Jones' Magic Song, Just You and Me, Jesus, Hello, My Name is Jesus, Old Oak Tree, Back To Where We Started From, I Know the Way, Come Follow Me, Psalm 47, Use Me Lord, In His Works He Shall Appear, Bless Ye the Lord, So Close I Never Saw You, I Will Rise, A Spark of Faith

A Staged reading of a new musical in two acts.

(Actor's Outlet) Saturday, March 3–24, 1990 (20 performances)
BLACK MEDEA by Ernest Ferlita; Director, Ken Lowstetter; Set, Randall Etheredge; Choreographer, Mari Nobles Da Silva; Composer, Bonnie Devlin; Stage Manager, Juliann Flynn; Women's Costumes, Ellen Ryba; Press, Max Eisen. CAST: Kilian Ganly, Mari Nobles Da Silva, Simon Jutras, Essene R, Lola Loui, John Steber, Marie McKinney

Alec McCowen of "St. Mark's Gospel"

William Broderick, Kyle Waters in "Dorian" *(T. L. Boston)*

(Lambs Theatre) Tuesday, March 20–April 15, 1990 (32 performances) Arthur Cantor presents:
ST. MARK'S GOSPEL; A solo performance by Alec McCowen; Lighting by Lloyd Sobel; Company Manager, Nancy Nagel Gibbs; Stage Manager, Fred Hahn; Press, Arthur Cantor/Deborah Navins, Mark McKinney, Terry Ashe-Croft
    Alec McCowen first performed this show in 1978 (see Theatre World Vol. 35).

(Lucille Lortel Theatre) Friday, March 23–May 20, 1990 (54 performances and 16 previews) K & D Productions, Margery Klain and Robert G. Donnalley, Jr., in association with Lucille Lortel present:
MOUNTAIN by Douglass Scott; Director, John Henry Davis; Sets, Philipp Jung; Costumes, David C. Woolard; Lighting, Dennis Parichy; Score/Sound, John Gromada; Stage Manager, James Fitzsimmons; Associate Producer, Susan Urban Horsey; General Management, Darwall or Mayrhauser; Press, David Rothenberg CAST: Len Cariou (William O. Douglas), John C. Vennema (FDR/Gordon Hirabayashi/Jasper Crisbody/Richard Nixon/Amir Ahmadi/Louis Brandeis/Other Memories), Heather Summerhayes (Julia Fisk Douglas/Mildred Riddle Douglas/Mercedes Davidson Douglas/Catherine Heffernan Douglas/Other Memories)
    A drama in two acts on the life of Justice William O. Douglas. The action spans 1898–1980.

(Symphony Space) Thursday, March 29–April 15, 1990 (16 performances) New York Gilbert & Sullivan Players (Albert Bergeret, Artistic Director) presents:
OF THEE I SING with Music by George Gershwin; Lyrics, Ira Gershwin; Book, George S. Kaufman & Morrie Ryskind; Director, Kristen Garver; Choreography, Bill Fabris; Sets, Jack Garver; Lighting, Robert Bessoir; Costumes, Jan Holland; Assistant Director, R. Scott Kenison; Assistant Music Director, Richard Holmes; Conductor, Albert Bergeret; Assistant Choreographer, Mary Lou Barber; Stage Manager, Bill Fabris CAST: Steven Ungar (Louis Lippman), Shawn Churchman (Francis X. Gilhooley), Mary Lou Barber (Chambermaid), Del-Bourree Bach (Matthew Arnold Fulton), Philip Reilly (Sen. Carver Crockett Jones), Michael Collins (Sen. Robert E. Lyons), Alan Hill (Alexander Throttlebottom), Joel Stevenor (Waiter), Keith Jurosko (John P. Wintergreen), Jayne Ackley Lynch (Diana Devereaux), Michael Kumor (Sam Jenkins), Kate Egan (Mary Turner), Sally Ann Swarm (Miss Benson), Benjamin Zooda (Announcer), Bobby Smith (Vladimir Vidovitch/Doctor), Ovidio Vargas (Yussef Yussevitch), Daniel Adamian (Referee), Mary Lou Barber (Twirler), David Jones (Chief Justice/Senator), Jane Hamilton (Guide/Scrubwoman), Melissa Jane Boher (1st Sightseer), Stephen M. Quint (French Ambassador), Wills Newman (Senate Clerk)
MUSICAL NUMBERS: Wintergreen For President, Who Is the Lucky Girl to Be?, Because Because, Never Was There A Girl So Fair, Some Girls Can Bake a Pie, Love Is Sweeping the Country, Of Thee I Sing, Entrance of the Supreme Court, Here's a Kiss for Cinderella, I Was the Most Beautiful Blossom, Hello Good Morning, Who Cares?, The Illegitimate Daughter, We Are All in This Together, The Senator from Minnesota, Jilted, I'm About to Be a Mother, Posterity Is Just Around the Corner, Trumpeter Blow Your Golden Horn, Finale
    The Gershwins' 1931 musical satire in two acts and 11 scenes. The show was the first musical to win a Pulitzer prize.

(Perry St. Theatre) Wednesday, March 7–April 7, 1990 (28 performances)
THE NATURE OF THINGS by David Cale in collaboration with Roy Nathanson, Marc Ribot, E. J. Rodriguez; Director, Bill Barnes; Lighting, Anne Militello; Sound, Richard Kirschner; Stage Manager, Elise-Ann Konstantin; Production Manager, George Xenos CAST: David Cale
    A solo performance in one act. The monologue concerns sex, relationships, childhood and letting go of it, power-dressing and birds.

(Theater at St. Mark's Church) Thursday, Mar. 8,–Mar. 25, 1990 (12 performances). Merry Enterprises Theatre and Alexander E. Racolin (Lily Turner, Artistic Director) present:
ALL THAT FALL by Samuel Beckett; Director, Phillip Price; Design, Michael Sharp; Stage Manager, Karen Kalriess; Press, David Rothenberg.
CAST: Virginia Downing (Mrs. Maddy Rooney), Malcolm Gray (Christy), John Hagan (Mr. Tyler), Jeff Reade (Mr. Slocum), Jim Ricketts (Tommy), Malcolm Gray (Mr. Barrell), Diane Barry (Miss Fitt), Thomas Carson (Mr. Rooney), Annie Simon (Jerry).
    Performed without an intermission.

(Saval Theatre) Saturday, March 10—(performances and previews) The American Ensemble Company (Robert Petito, Artistic Director) present:
DORIAN with Music by Michael Rubell; Lyrics, Mr. Rubell, Nan Barcan; Book, Ms. Barcan; Director, Robert Petito; Music Director/Arranger, Marc Abel; Choreography, Irene Rubell; Sets, Joseph A. Varga; Lighting, Jonathan Terry; Costumes, Judy Kahn; Stage Manager, Christopher Parenti; Technical, Bob Lyons; Press, Shirley Herz/Bob Larkin, Sam Rudy CAST: Joel Briel (Basil Hallward), Hank Schob (Lord Wotten), William Broderick (Dorian Gray), Robert Schwarz (Lord Peck), Paula Newman (Lady Wotten), Elaine Terriss (Lady Peck), Gemma DeBiase (Lady Olivia), Jamie Stern (Adrian), Sarah Downs (Gladys), May Ellis (Mrs. Erskine), Ian Fleet (Peters/Mr. Erskine/Lord Charles), Kyle Waters (Sibyl Vane), Dan Frank (James Vane), Kurt Elftman (Victor/Lord Burdon), Lorraine Serabian (Kate)
MUSICAL NUMBERS: Art Is Forever, Creation, Temptation, Men on My Mind, American Girls, You Are the Magic, I Love Him, You Must Remember, Night at the Theatre, My Perfection, The Lady Can't Act, Till I Met You, A Perfect Tragedy, The Picture of Dorian Gray, Dissipation, Marriage, For Old Time's Sake, Jim's Song, Prince Charming, We Knew How to Live, Chatter, Confession, Finale
    A musical adaptation of Wilde's *"The Picture of Dorian Gray"* in two acts and 10 scenes. The action takes place in London 1882–1900.

"Of Thee I Sing" *(Lee Snider)* Above: Len Cariou, Heather Summerhayes in **"Mountain"**
(Martha Swope)

(Brooklyn Academy of Music) Sunday, April 2–8, 1990 (6 performances)
KING LEAR by William Shakespeare; Director, Robert Sturua; Translated into Georgian by C. Tcharkviani, R. Sturua and L. Popkhadze; Assistant Directors, Revaz Tchkhaidze, Lily Burbutashvili; Designer, Mirian Mshvelidze; Composer, Ghia Kancheli; Choreography, Giorgi Aleksidze CAST: Ramaz Tchkhikvadze (Lear), Tatuli Dolidze (Goneril), Daredjan Kharshiladze (Regan), Marina Kakhiani (Cordelia), Avtandil Makharadze (Gloucester), Akaki Khidasheli (Edmund), Ghia Dzneladze (Edgar), Djemal Ghaghanidze (Albany), Ivan Ghoghitidze (Cornwall), Mourman Djinoria (Kent), Zhanri Lolashvili (Fool), Guram Sagharadze (Duke of Burgundy), Soso Laghidze (King of France), David Papuashvili (Oswald), Revaz Tchkhaidze (Doctor).
   The Rustaveli Theatre Company of the USSR in Shakespeare's play.

Ramaz Tchkhikvadze as "King Lear" *(Alma Law)*

(St. Clement's Theatre) Tuesday, April 3–27, 1990 (36 performances)
PARADISE FOR THE WORRIED; Conceived by Kinematic, Tamar Kotoske, Maria Lakis, Mary Richter with Holly Anderson; Director, Diane Wondisford; Music Adaptation, Jill Jaffe; Score, Stanley Silverman; Text/Lyrics, Ms. Anderson; Choreography, Kinematic, Eric Barsness; Created in collaboration with Mr. Barsness, Laura Innes and Campbell Scott; Music Director, Ms. Jaffe; Dance Director, Pam Critelli; Sets, Victoria Petrovich; Costumes, Donna Zakowska; Lighting, Debra Dumas; Production Manager, Steven Ehrenberg; Stage Manager, Barbara Ann O'Leary CAST: Campbell Scott (Dr. Fellowes), Eric Barsness (Hugo Fellowes), Laura Innes (Daisy), Mary Richter (Phoebe), Maria Lakis (Opal), Tamar Kotoske (Delphine), Jill Jafe (Violin/Viola), Ted Sperling (Piano), Alfredo Pedernera
   A Dance Theatre piece exploring the conflicting forces of romance and reason on Manhattan's Upper West Side upon the 1910 apparition of Halley's Comet.

**H. M. Koutoukas, Everett Quinton in
"Der Ring Gott Farblonjett"**
(Anita & Steve Shevett)

(Charles Ludlam Theatre) Sunday, April 8–May 20, 1990 (56 performances) The Ridiculous Theatrical Company presents:
DER RING GOTT FABLONJET by Charles Ludlam; Director, Everett Quinton; Sets, Mark Beard; Costumes, Susan Young; Lighting, Richard Currie; Props, Daphne Groos, Sophie Maletsky; Hair, Joe Anthony; Music/Sound, Mark Bennett; Stage Manager, Ron Murphy; Press, Judy Jacksina/Robin Monchek, Brig Berney CAST: Adam MacAdam (Twoton), H. M. Koutoukas (Eartha), Jim Lamb (Siegmund/Siegfried), Sophie Maletsky (Brunnhilda/Fasdolt), Stephen Pell (Ninny/Rossweisse), Bryan Webster (Loge/Grimgerda), Mary Neufeld (Hunding/Gutruna), Eureka (Fricka/Gunther), Everett Quinton (Alverruck and Valtruata), Ivory (Froh/Gerhilda), Robert Lanier (Flosshilde/Ortlinda/Norn), Gary Mink (Dunderhead/Hagen/Siegruna), Therese McIntyre (Freia/Sieglinda), Bobby Reed (Welgunde/Schwertleita), Jean-Claude Vasseux (Fafner/Helmvige/Norn/Bear), Christine Weiss (Woglinde/Forest Bird)
   Freely adapted from Wagner's Ring Cycle; the story of a giant, a lecher, seven virgins, a nasty dwarf, a dragon, some slain heroes and a group of Rheinmaidens, among others, in pursuit of a magical ring.

Mark Dold, Saul Stein in "Body Builder's Book of Love"
(Martha Swope)

(Intar Theatre) Wednesday, April 11–May 13, 1990 (21 performances and 14 previews) Intar Hispanic American Arts Center (Max Ferra, Founder & Artistic Director, Eva Brune, Acting Executive Director) presents:
THE BODY BUILDER'S BOOK OF LOVE by Arrabal; Translation, Lorenzo Mans; Direction/Music, Tom O'Horgan; Sets, Christina Weppner; Lighting, Debra Dumas; Costumes, Deborah Shaw; Sound, Bernard Fox, Gene Perla; Special Effects, Steve Dunnington; General Manager, Michael Palma; Production Manager, Peter J. Davis; Stage Managers, Robert V. Thurber, Michael Garces; Press, Peter Cromarty/Patrick Paris CAST: Mark Dold (Tao), Saul Stein (Job)
   An absurdist comedy performed without intermission.

(Judith Anderson Theatre) Wednesday, April 11–May 5, 1990 (30 performances and 3 previews) Manhattan Punch Line (Steve Kaplan, Artistic Director) presents The London Small Theater Co. in:
BEYOND BELIEF; Written, Directed and Arranged by Fiona Laird; Costumes, Julie Speechley; Lighting, Cliff Vic, Ms. Laird
   A musical using 1930's tunes to trace adventures of a comic and a doctor trapped in an alien dimension.
THE CLOUDS by Aristophanes; Adaption, Direction, Music and Arrangements, Fiona Laird; Producer, Peter Meineck; Lighting, Jacqui Leigh, Mr. Meineck; Costumes, Julie Speechley; Press, Shirley Herz/Miller Wright CAST: Anthony James, Nicholas Smith, Rachel Spriggs, Adrian Schiller, Jonathan Williams, Fiona Laird

Rosemary Prinz, Edward Seamon, Lizbeth Mackay in "Tales of the Lost Formicans" *(Martha Holmes)*

(Apple Corps Theatre) Tuesday, April 17–May 6, 1990 (21 performances) The Women's Project & Productions (Julia Miles, Artistic Director) presents:
TALES OF THE LOST FORMICANS by Constance Congdon; Director, Gordon Edelstein; Sets, James Youmans; Lighting, Anne Militello; Costumes, Danielle Hollywood; Sound, John Gromada; Composer, Melissa Shiflett; Stage Manager, Susie Gordon; Press, Fred Nathan/Merle Frimark CAST: Michael Countryman (Jerry), Lizbeth Mackay (Cathy), Edward Seamon (Jim), Deirdre O'Connell (Judy), Noel Derecki (Eric), Rosemary Prinz (Evelyn), Fred Sanders (Actor 7/Hank/Trucker/B-Movie Alien/Jack)
   A serio-comic look at life in the Colorado suburbs through the eyes of Alien observers.

(Village Gate) Tuesday, Apr. 17, still playing May 31, 1990. Nozar Productions, Inc. & Michael Frazier present:

FURTHER MO', written and directed by Vernel Bagneris; Set, Charles McClennahan; Costumes, Joann Clevenger; Lighting, John McKernon; Songs by various artists; Sound, Peter Fitzgerald; Musical Director, Orange Kellin; Musical Arrangements, Lars Edegran, Orange Kellin; Vocal Arrangements, Topsy Chapman, Lars Edegran; General Management, Frank Scardino Associates, Inc.; Press, The Jacksina Company, Inc.; Stage Manager, K. R. Williams; Choreographer, Pepsi Bethel. CAST: James "Red" Wilcher (Theatre Owner), Topsy Chapman (Thelma), Vernel Bagneris (Papa Du), Frozine Thomas (Ma Reed), Sandra Reaves-Phillips (Big Bertha), Joseph Daley, Bill Dillard, Orange Kellin, Emme Kemp, Kenneth Sara (The New Orleans Blue Serenaders), Ronald Wyche, Ron Woodall, Barbara Shorts, Wanda Rouzan (Understudies). MUSICAL NUMBERS: Shake It and Break It, Messing Around, Sweetie Dear, Salty Dog, One Hour Mama, Mississippi Mud, Wild Women, Sweet Man, Positively No (Construction Gang), Had to Give Up Gym, Pretty Doll, Trouble in Mind, Here Comes the Hot Tamale Man, Boogie Woogie, Come On In, My Man, Don't Advertise Your Man, Baby Won't You Please Come Home, Funny Feathers, Clarinet Marmalade, West Indies Blues, Boot-It Boy, Alabamy Bound, Home Sweet Home, Hot Times in the Ole Town Tonight.

A musical revue in two acts. The action takes place at the Lyric Theatre in New Orleans in 1927.

Sandra Reaves-Phillips, Vernel Bagneris in "Further Mo' " *(Martha Swope)*

(Carnegie/Weill Hall) Wednesday, April 18–22, 1990 (6 performances) Carnegie Hall presents:

THE CAT AND THE FIDDLE with Music by Jerome Kern; Lyrics/Book, Otto Harbach; Music Director, John McGlinn; Orchestrations, Robert Russell Bennett CAST: Jeff Mattsey (Vendor), Lydia Mila (Madeline), Brian Gow (Pierre), Burr Cochran Phillips (Old Roué), Olga Talyn (Mme. Abajour), Christine Abraham (Mme. Grandjean), Kip Wilborn (Policeman/Adrien), Jason Graae (Alexander Sheridan), Judy Kaye (Shirley Sheridan), Cris Groenendaal (Pompineau), Davis Gaines (Victor Florescu), Paige O'Hara (Angie Sheridan), Maureen Brennan (Maizie Gripps), Angelina Réaux (Odette), Ruth Golden (Constance Carrington), Paul V. Ames (Chester Biddlesby), Leo Leyden (Major Sir George Wilfred Chatterly), Richard Woods (Clement Daudet), Kurt Ollmann (Jean Colbert), Jeff Mattsey (Colbert-matinee), Julia Parks (Claudine), Olaf Lauder (Paul)
MUSICAL NUMBERS: The Night Was Made for Love, The Love Parade, The Breeze Kissed Your Hair, Try to Forget, Poor Pierrot, Passionate Pilgrim, Finaletto, She Didn't Say Yes, A New Love Is Old, One Moment Alone, Don't Ask Me Not to Sing, Street Scene, Oh! Cha Cha, Finale Ultimo

A concert version of the 1931 musical in two acts and 15 scenes. The Princess Theatre Orchestra played the original orchestrations.

Richard Woods, Judy Kaye, John McGlinn, Davis Gaines, Cris Groenendaal, Paige O'Hara in "Cat & Fiddle" *(Steve Sherman)*

(45th Street Theatre) Thursday, Apr., 19,–May 5, 1990 (12 performances) The Sackett Group presents:

MAGIC TIME by James Sherman; Director/Lighting, Robert J. Weinstein; Set, Chris Morreale; Stage Manager, Malik; Press, Gertrude Brooks. CAST: John Haggerty (Larry Mandell), Diane Sykes (Joan Douglas), Adrian Williams (Alan Kenmore), Ronald Lew Harris (Scott Porterfield), Paul Motondo (Chris), Dawn Marie Hale (Laurie Black), Jane B. Harris (Ann Porterfield), Dan Haft (David Singer).

A comedy in one act. The action takes place in a dressing room in Chicago on a Sunday night, the day before Labor Day, 1974.

Nate Harvey, Lee Brock in "Split"

(Ohio Theatre) Sunday, April 22–May 13, 1990 The Barrow Group presents:
SPLIT by Michael Weller; Director, Seth Barrish; Costumes, Nina Canter; Lighting, Debra Dumas; Sound, David Schirman; Stage Manager, Haley Alpiar; Resident Producer, Gillian Schreiber; Press, Robert Shampain. CAST: Nate Harvey (Paul), Lee Brock (Carol), Seth Barrish, Sean Blackman, Marcia DeBonis, Tom Farrell, Colleen Gallagher.

(Actors' Playhouse) Wednesday, May 2–July 1, 1990 (80 performances) Bill Repicci presents:
TALKING THINGS OVER WITH CHEKHOV by John Ford Noonan; Director, Marjorie Mahle; Sets, Ron Kron; Lighting, Tracy Dedrickson; Costumes, Gene Lauze; Stage Manager, Joe McGuire; Associate Producers, M. D. Minichiello, Albert Repicci; Publicity, Robert Ganshaw; Press, Pat Dale/Joel V. Dein, Philip Thurston CAST: John Ford Noonan (Jeremy M.), Diane Salinger (Marlene D.)

A comedy/drama in two acts and six scenes. The action revolves around a playwright who feels the phantom of Chekhov visits him daily. The setting is Riverside Park, NYC at the present time.

(The Village Theatre) Thursday, May 3–20, 1990 (18 performances) The Village Theatre Company presents:
THE WINTER'S TALE by William Shakespeare; Director, Bob Verini; Set, Deborah Scott; Lighting, David Edwardson; Costumes, Kate M. Sherman, Rita Russo; Composer/Sound, Jimmy Flynn; Choreographer, Dona Lee Kelly; Technical Director, Zeke Zaccaro; Fight Choreographer, Jamie Cheatham. CAST: Park Brochert, Barbara Bercu, Susan Farwell, Marj Feenan, Andrea Gallo, Jill Jason, David McConnell, Julia McLaughlin, Randolph Messersmith, David Sennett, Kenneth Talberth, Howard Thoresen, Patrick Turner, Tom Williams

John Ford Noonan, Diane Salinger in "Talking Things Over . . ."

(The Pearl Theatre) Thursday, May 3–13, 1990. HOLA presents:
PICTURE PERFECT by Pablo Salinas; English translation, Raul Moncada; Director, Susana Tubert; Set, Bob Harper; Lighting, Ron Selke; Sound, Sergio Garcia Marruz; Wardrobe, Miriam Colyn; Stage Manager, David Sanchez; Press, Chris Boneau, Eva Patton, Bob Fennell. CAST: Elisa Loti (Evelia), Robert Montano (Rene)

Robert Montano, Elisa Loti in "Picture Perfect" *(Anita & Steve Shevett)*

(Steve McGraw's) Friday, May 4, 1990. Still playing as of May 31, 1990. Gene Wolsk in association with Steven Suskin presents:
FOREVER PLAID; Written, Directed and Staged by Stuart Ross; Scenery, Neil Peter Jampolis; Lighting, Jane Reisman; Costumes, Debra Stein; Casting, Judy Henderson; Assistant Director, Larry Raben; Musical Continuity/Arrangements/Musical Direction, James Raitt; Stage Manager, John Rainwater; Producer, Gene Wolsk; Associate Producer, Steven Suskin; Press, Shirley Herz Associates, Shirley Herz, Miller Wright. CAST: Stan Chandler (Jinx), David Engel (Smudge), Jason Graae (Sparky), Guy Stroman (Francis). Understudies: Larry Raben, Drew Geraci.
   A musical in two acts. The action takes place on a night in 1964.

David Engel, Guy Stroman, Stan Chandler, Jason Graae in "Forever Plaid" *(Martha Swope)*

(45th Street Theatre) Thursday, May 10,–May 26, 1990 (14 performances and 4 previews) Hazel Productions presents:
INFIDELITIES, adapted by William Gaskill from Marivaux; Director, William Foeller; Set, Ray Kluga; Costumes, Deb Rooney; Lighting, Dave Feldman; Stage Manager, Kim Russell; Press, Cromarty & Company. CAST: Sandra La Vallee (Silvia), Jonathan Bustle (Trivelin), Warren Keith (Prince/Lord), Margaret Dulaney (Flaminia), Christine Dunford (Lisette), John Gould Rubin (Harlequin)
   A play in three acts.

(Lambs Theatre) Thursday, May 10, 1990. Still playing May 31, 1990. Carolyn Rossi Copeland (Producing Director) presents:
SMOKE ON THE MOUNTAIN; Written by Connie Ray; Conceived/Directed by Alan Bailey; Set, Peter Harrison; Costumes, Pamela Scofield; Lighting, Don Ehman; Stage Manager, Tom Clewell; Musical Director, John Foley, Mike Craver; Production Manager, Clark Cameron; Musical Arrangements, Mike Craver, Mark Hardwick; General Manager, Nancy Nagel Gibbs; Press, Cromarty & Co. CAST: Reathel Bean (Burl Sanders), Kevin Chamberlin (Mervin Oglethorpe), Linda Kerns (Vera Sanders), Dan Manning (Stanley), Robert Olsen (Dennis Sanders), Jane Potter (Denise Sanders), Connie Ray (June Sanders). MUSICAL NUMBERS: The Church in the Wildwood, A Wonderful Time Up There, Build on the Rock, Meet Mother in the Skies, No Tears in Heaven, Christian Cowboy, The Filling Station, I'll Never Die (I'll Just Change My Address), Jesus is Mine, Blood Medley: Nothing But the Blood/There is Power in the Blood/Are You Washed in the Blood/There is a Fountain Filled with Blood. I'll Live a Million Years, Everyone Home But Me, I Wouldn't Take Nothing For My Journey Now, Angel Band, Bringing in the Sheaves, Whispering Hope, Inching Along, Transportational Medley: I'm Using My Bible for a Roadmap/I'll Walk Every Step of the Way/Life's Railway to Heaven, Smoke on the Mountain, I'll Fly Away, When the Roll is Called Up Yonder.
   A musical in two acts. The action takes place on a Saturday Night, June, 1938 at Mount Pleasant Baptist Church, Mount Pleasant, North Carolina.

(Billie Holiday Theatre) Thursday, May 10–June 3, 1990 (26 performances) The Billie Holiday Theatre (Marjorie Moon, Producer) presents:
HALLEY'S COMET; A One-Man Play Written & Performed by John Amos
   An invented life of a 75 yr. old man spanning the time between two appearances of Halley's Comet.

(front) Robert Olsen, Jane Potter, Linda Kerns, (back) Dan Manning, Connie Ray, Kevin Chamberlin, Reathel Bean in "Smoke on the Mountain" *(Martha Swope)*

(Apple Corps Theatre) Thursday, May 17–June 17, 1990 (40 performances)
A PERFECT DIAMOND by Don Rifkin; Director, Philip D. Giberson; Sets, Robert Klingelhoefer; Lighting, William J. Plachy; Costumes, Jo-Dee Mercurio; Sound, Neal Arluck; Stage Manager, Michael Perreca CAST: Dennis Sook (Buck Beauregard), Daryl Edwards (Gentleman Jim Wilson), Michael Cullen (Legs Lannigan), Milton Elliot (Mark Haftel), Iona Morris (Tess Gallagher), Earl Whitted (The Kid), Paul O'Brien (Buster Ziltz), Josh Mostel (Dollar Bill Brunowski)
   A baseball comedy in two acts.

(Pearl Theatre) Thursday, May 17–27, 1990 (8 performances)
SHE FIRST MET HER PARENTS ON THE SUBWAY by Sergio Castilla; Director, Mr. Castilla; Sets, Elizabeth Lipton; Lighting, Tomasz Magierski; Sound, James Lopicolo; Costumes, Miriam Colyn; Stage Manager, Margaret Bodriguian; CAST: Frank Algarin (Keith), Michael Baez (Phil), Peter Byrnes (Joe), Roxxane Laham (Martha), John Leguizamo (Pito), Patricia Montoya (Monica), Selena Nelson (Jane), Manuel Rivera (Bum), Lucille Rivin (Rebecca), Alba Sanchez (Teresa), Sharon Shah (Mirna), Pilar Uribe (Sharon)

Josh Mostel, Dennis Sook, Michael Cullen in "Perfect Diamond" *(Martha Holmes)*

(Riverwest Theatre) Friday, May 18–June 10, 1990 (16 performances and 3 previews)
TROUBADOUR with Music by Bert Draesel; Lyrics, John Martin; Book, Martin & Draesel; Director, John Margulis; Musical Director/Arrangements, Howard Kilik; Sets, Ralph Castaldo; Lighting, Jeff Glovsky; Costumes, Debbie Hall; Choreography, Paul Nunes; Stage Managers, Jillian M. Ramirez, Elizabeth M. Ebel CAST: Christopher Mellon (Francesco), Paul Romanello (Elias), Evan Matthews (Bernardo), Keith Clark (Leo), Drew Kelly (Juniper), Sibel Ergener (Clare), Daniel Timothy Johnson (Pietro/Cardinal Ugolino/Pope Innocent III/Syltan), Tom Tomasovic (Signor Faverone/Merchant/Friar/Papal Secretary/Saracen/Crusader), Elizabeth M. Ebel (Leper)

MUSICAL NUMBERS: Assisi, The Troubador, Dance, Who Can Benefit You Most?, Change, How Strange, Troubador of the Lord, There Must Be Something More, You Can't Have Me, The Earth is the Lord's, Organize, The Rule/Called to the Simple Life, Listen to the Voice, An Unusual Normal, There Is a Mystery, Brother Mountain, There Is a Time, This Is the Man, Every Day, Jerusalem, Soon, I Wonder I Wonder, And We Were One, It Was Magnificent, Listen to the Voice, The Order, Let's Go to Tuscany, It's Glorious, Let There Be Books, Once I Had a Vision, A Great Cathedral, Praised Be My Lord

A musical about the life of Francis of Assisi in two acts and 15 scenes. The action takes place in and around Assisi between the years 1205–1225.

(Riverwest Theatre) Friday, May 18–June 10, 1990 (16 performances and 3 previews) Alexander E. Racolin, Annette Moskowitz and CHS Productions in association with Riverwest Theatre and the Independent Theatre Co. present:
RIVERMAN by Sam Dowling; Director, Anne De Mare; Stage Manager, Cheryl Z. Allera; Sets, Thomas Rupich, Alexandra Limpet; Lighting, Jeff Glovsky; Costumes, Cathy Small; Sound, Patricia Burgess, Bruce Ditmas; Press, Howard Atlee CAST: David Burland (Walter Greaves), Nina F. Minton (Jenny), Barbara Schofield (Tinnie Greaves), Frederick Zimmer (Augustus John), Christine Zito (Elizabeth Pennell), Nina F. Minton (Sarah Spencer), Paul Todaro (Joseph Pennell), Timothy Lane (William Marchant)

A play on the life of painter Walter Greaves. Performed in two acts. The action takes place in 1911.

Lonny Price, Rob Gomes (standing), Jordan Mott, Philip Coccioletti in "Quiet End" (*Martha Swope*) **Above: Christopher Mellon in "Troubadour"**

David Burland, Timothy Lane in "Riverman"

Cathy Reinheimer, Jay Patterson in "A Doll House" (*Paul Germaine-Brown*)

(Playhouse 91) Friday, May 18–May 31, 1990 Aboutface and Sean Burke present:
THE GRAND GUIGNOL: Sets, Vicki R. Davis; Lighting, Ken Davis; Costumes, Mary Myers; Music, Robert Montgomery CAST: Robert Alexander, Dina Corsetti, Gary Evans, Leslie R. Hollander, Kelleigh McKenzie, Ellen McQueeney, Gina Menza, Chuck Pooler, J. J. Reap, J. Kelly Salvadore, Nomi Tichman, David D. Yezzi
EXPERIMENT AT THE ASYLUM by Annie G & Mitch Hogue; Director, Richard Galgano
THE TREATMENT OF DR. LOVE by William Squier; Director, Linda Feinberg, Martin Fluger
ORGY IN THE AIR-TRAFFIC CONTROL TOWER by Sean Burke & Steve Nelson; Director, Michael Hillyer
Three tales of terror.

(Actor's Outlet) Friday, May 18–June 9, 1990 (16 performances) The Doll Company Inc. presents:
A DOLL HOUSE by Henrik Ibsen; Translation, Gerry Bamman & Irene B. Berman; Director, Brian Delate; Sets, Charles H. McClennahan; Lighting, Karl Haas; Costumes, Sarah Lederberg; Choreography, Deborah Hanna; General Manager, Whitbell Productions, Inc; Stage Manager, Debora E. Kingston CAST: Cathy Reinheimer (Nora Helmer), Stephen Day (Messenger), Lauri Grace Langone (Helene), Stuart Rider (Torvald Helmer), Susan Keith (Kristine Linde), Brian Mallon (Nils Krogstad), Jay Patterson (Dr. Rank), Joan Mattheissen (Anne Marie), Frank Rosati, Jr. (Ivar), Jared Hillman (Bob), Meagan Smith (Emmy)
A new translation in three acts. The action takes place in Norway on Christmas of 1879.

(Courtyard Theatre) Friday, May 18–June 10, 1990 (15 performances) Kindred Productions presents:
OTHELLO by William Shakespeare; Director, Scott Noflet Carr; Costumes, Jackie Alexander; Lighting, Kendall A. Smith; Fights, Robert Ruffin; Sets, Scott N. Carr; Stage Manager, Dawn Hunter CAST: Rex Slate (Roderigo), Lawrence Preston (Iago), Ronald Durling (Brabantio), Tony Evans (Othello), David Gutmann (Cassio), Bob O'Melia (Duke), Frank Sawyer (Gratiano), Andrea Lauren Herz (Desdemona), Gary Cowling (Sailor/Clown), Robert Ruffin (Montano), Nancy Shaheen (Emilia), Marilyn Majeski (Bianca), Herschel Kruger (Lodovico)

(Theatre Off Park) Monday, May 21–June 15, 1990 (18 performances and 8 previews) Theatre Off Park (Albert Harris, Artistic Director) presents:
A QUIET END by Robin Swados; Director, Tony Giordano; Sets, Philipp Jung; Costumes, David Murin; Lighting, Dennis Parichy; Sound, Tony Meola; Stage Manager, Alan Fox; General Manager, Joseph Piazza; Music, Mr. Swados; Press, Jim Randolph CAST: Lonny Price (Max), Philip Coccioletti (Tony), Jordan Mott (Billy), Paul Milikin (Dr.), Rob Gomes (Jason)
A drama in two acts. The action takes place in Manhattan's Upper West Side during the winter.

(House of Candles Theatre) Wednesday, May 23, 1990– The Irondale Ensemble Project presents:
HAPPY END with Music by Kurt Weill; Lyrics, Bertold Brecht; Original German play by Dorothy Lane; Translation/Adaptation, Michael Feingold; Director, James Niesen CAST: Montana Latin (Fly), Paul Lazar (Governor), Steve Cross (Bill Cracker), Molly Hickok (Lillian Holiday), James Niesen, Josh Broder, Annie B. Parson, Steve Osgood, Terry Greiss, Hilarie Blumenthal, Ken Rothchild, Barbara Mackenzie-Wood, Jody Reiss, Nicole Potter, Gerry Goodstein, Elena Pellicciaro, Michael Cain, Ann Delaney

(Producers Club) Thursday, May 24–June 17, 1990 (15 performances and 5 previews) The Denby Production Company (Gerry Nay, Artistic Director) presents:
EVERYBODY KNOWS YOUR NAME by Ed Cachianes; Director, John Albano; Sets, Mark Tambella; Costumes, Gabriel Berry; Lighting, Bruce Rubin; Sound, Chuck London; Stage Manager, Deborah A. Fowlkes; Associate Producer, Christopher Cade; Press, Francine Trevens/Roger Lane CAST: John Finch (Andrew), Robert Zukerman (Carl), Joe Pichette (Ellison), Barbara Gruen (Nurse), Mark Irish (Ray), Barbara Harner (Mother)
The action takes place in a hospital at present.

(Studio 603) Thursday, May 24–June 10, 1990 (16 performances) Aronica Productions presents:
SAVAGE IN LIMBO by John Patrick Shanley; Director, Tim Phillips; Producer, Gwen Cassel; Lighting, Tim Hunter; Design, H. G. Arrott; Make Up/Hair, Jacques Cellier; Dialect, Gordon Jacoby; Stage Managers, Nathalie Ferrier, Laura Murphy; Production Assistants, Tim Runion, Stacey Wyman CAST: Maggie Low (April White), Arnie Mazer (Murk), Kim Haroche (Denise Savage), Gloria Crist (Linda Rotunda), Michael Krauss (Tony Aronica)
The action takes place in a dilapidated bar in the Bronx, NYC

(Promenade Theatre) Friday, May 25–July 15, 1990 (44 performances and 16 previews) Roger Berlind presents:
ELLIOT LOVES by Jules Feiffer; Director, Mike Nichols; Sets, Tony Walton; Costumes, Ann Roth; Lighting, Paul Gallo; Sound, Tom Sorce; Production Supervisor, Peter Lawrence; Associate Producer, Susan MacNair; Stage Managers, John Brigleb, Jim Wooley; Company Manager, Leslie Butler; Assistant General Manager, Abby Evans; Press, Bill Evans CAST: Anthony Heald (Elliot), Christine Baranski (Joanna), Latanya Richardson (Vera), David Pierce (Phil), Oliver Platt (Larry), Bruce A. Young (Bobby)
A comedy in two acts. The action takes place in Chicago in the mid '80s.

(Joyce Theatre) Wednesday, May 30–June 24, 1990 Joyce Theatre Foundation Inc. in association with Jomandi Productions presents:
SISTERS by Marsha A. Jackson; Based on short story by Barbara Neely; Director, Thomas W. Jones 2d; Sets/Lighting, John Harris; Costumes, Debi Frye Barber; Sound, Craig Cousins; Stage Manager, Kimberly Harding; Press, Ellen Jacobs CAST: Marsha A. Jackson (Olivia), Andrea Frye (Cassie)
A comedy in two acts. The action takes place in a high rise in Atlanta, Ga., on New Year's Eve.

(Cubiculo) Thursday, May 31–June 10, 1990 (12 performances) Echo Repertory presents:
THE LOST ART; Director, Melia Bensussen; Stage Manager, Julie Swenson; Technical Design, Scot A. Newell CAST: Leila Boyd, Amelia David, Julie Lloyd, Cherry Madole, Janice Orlandi, Lisa Randall, Sandra Waugh
A piece woven from letters penned by some of the 20th Century's foremost women.

(Theatre 808) Thursday, May 31–June 10 (7 performances and 3 previews) The Quaigh Theatre Co. and Acorn Productions present:
THE BENCH; Director, Jeffrey Wolf *NEW LISTINGS* by Jane Stanton Hitchcock CAST: Karen Valentine, Pamela Moller *ON THE BENCH* by Carole Schweid CAST: Karen Valentine, Kristin Griffith, Robin Moseley
Two one act comedies about parenting in NYC.

(Mazur Theatre) Thursday, May 31–June 23, 1990 (20 performances) Playwrights' Preview Productions (Frances Hill, Artistic Director; Adelle Sardi, Managing Director) presents:
ONE ACT PLAY FESTIVAL Sets, Al Doyle; Costumes, Traci Di Gesu; Lighting, Jeffrey S. Koger; Stage Manager, Dwayne B. Perryman III
PROGRAM I: CORNISH GAME by Danny Cahill; Director, Paul Dervis; Assistant Director, Tara Dolan CAST: Arthur Anderson (Owen James), Youssif Kamal (Sidney), Joe Hillyer (Raymond)
The action takes place in Cornish, New Hampshire in late fall.
FLIGHT by Terry Dodd; Director, Margaret Mancinelli; Composer/Sound, Steve Stevens CAST: Fred Burrell (Dale), Paul Doherty (Mark)
The action takes place in a void, somewhere near 20,000 feet
SOMEWHERE FOREIGN by Dennis Clontz; Director, Penny Allen CAST: Michael Santoro (Rick Lansberry), Christi Minarovich (Mayauel)
The action takes place in a two room hut amid a barren landscape.
PROGRAM II: A MATCH MADE IN HEAVEN by Dennis Clontz; Director, Andrew Burgreen CAST: Scott Weir (Willard S. Wayson), Jennifer Johnson (Elaine Swan)
The action takes place in Elaine's apartment at present.
MATINEE by Hal Corley; Director, Anne Meara CAST: Joanna Merlin (Jewell), Grace Roberts (Celia), Frances Foster (Betty)
The action takes place in the ladies room of an old movie house at present.

Top Right: Christine Baranski, David Pierce, Anthony Heald in "Elliot Loves" (*Martha Swope*) Below: Karen Valentine, Pamela Moller in "The Bench" (*Tim Lewis*)

Joan See, Frances Foster, Gracie Roberts in "Matinee" (*Martha Swope*)

73

OFF-BROADWAY COMPANY SERIES

AMERICAN JEWISH THEATRE

Sixteenth Season

Artistic Director, Stanley Brechner; Creative Consultant, Anna Basoli; Associate Artistic Director, Lonny Price; Technical Director, Ed Fisher; Props, Stephen Weihs; Press, Peter Cromarty & Co./Kevin Brockman

(Susan Bloch Theatre) Thursday, June 8–Oct. 8, 1989 (67 performances)
CALL ME ETHEL! by Christopher Powich & Rita McKenzie; Music, Lyrics, Various; Director, Christopher Powich; Musical Director, Peter Blue; Sets, Russell Pyle; Lighting, Robert Bessoir; Costumes, Dale Wibbin; Sound, Phillip Allen; Special Costumes, Georgia Reese; Assistant Lighting, Stefan Jacobs; CAST: Rita McKenzie
A musical evening built around the life and times of Ethel Merman.

Saturday, Oct. 21, 1989–Nov. 19, 1989 (22 performances and 9 previews)
THE PRISONER OF SECOND AVENUE by Neil Simon; Sets, Madelyn Cates; Lighting, Susan A. White; Costumes, Victoria Lee; Sound, J. Wise; Stage Manager, Patrick Ward; Production Coordinator, Mark York; CAST: Mike Burstyn (Mel Edison), Lyn Greene (Edna Edison), Ronald Hunter (Harry Edison), Madelyn Cates (Jessie), Sylvia Kaunders (Pearl), Estelle Harris (Pauline).
A play in two acts. The action takes place in apartment #14A at 385 E. 88th St., a 6 year old hi-rise off 2nd Avenue in New York City. The time is 1971.

Tuesday, December 16, 1989–January 14, 1990 (23 performances and 10 previews)
THE PUPPETMASTER OF LODZ by Giles Segal; Translation, Sara o'Conner; Director, John Driver; Sets, James Wolk; Lighting, Susan A. White; Costumes, Victoria Lee; Sound, J. Wise; Stage Manager, Jon Roger Clark; CAST: Ann Hillary (Concierge), Sam Tsoutsouvas (Finkelbaum), Jay Rubenstein (Popov), Leo Rovain (Spencer), Ron Hunter (Schwartzkopf)

Saturday, February 10–April 8, 1990 (performances) and re-opened on Friday, April 27, 1990 at Circle-in-the-Square Downtown where it was still playing May 31, 1990.
THE ROTHSCHILDS with Music by Jerry Bock; Lyrics, Sheldon Harnick; Book, Sherman Yellen; Director, Lonny Price; Music Director, Grant Sturiale; Choreographer, Michael Arnold; Sets, E. David Cosier, Jr.; Costumes, Gail Brassard; Lighting, Betsy Adams; Assistant Music Director, Connie Meng; Assistant Director, Daisy Prince; Stage Manager, Rachel S. Levine; Sheriff, Julie Wilde; CAST: Mike Burstyn (Mayer), David Cantor (Amshel), Nick Corley (Jacob), Bob Cucciolo (Nathan), Leslie Ellis (Hannah), Evan Ferrante (Young Nathan), Allen Fitzpatrick (William/Herries/Fouche/Metternich), Ted Forlow (Budurus), Sue Anne Gershenson (Gutele), Hal Goldberg (Young Solomon), Joel Malina (Kalman), Etan & Josh (Young Jacob), Adam Paul Plotch (Young Amshel), Judith Thiergaard (Mrs. Segal), Ray Willis (Solomon)
MUSICAL NUMBERS: Pleasure and Privilege, One Room, He Tossed a Coin, Sons, Everything, Rothschilds and Sons., Allons, The British Free Enterprise Auction, This Amazing London Town, They Say, I'm in Love! I'm in Love!, In My Own Lifetime, Have You Ever Seen A Prettier Little Congress?, Bonds
A revival in two acts. For original production see Theatre World Vol. 27.

Saturday, April 21–May 20, 1990 (performances)
MADE IN HEAVEN by Edward Belling; Director, Stanley Brechner; Sets, James Wolk; Costumes, Victoria Lee; Lighting, Susan A. White; Stage Manager, Benjamin Gutkin; Sound, John Wise CAST: Grace Roberts (Rose Rothenberg), Herbert Rubens (Jack Rothenberg), Jack Aaron (Milton Gross), Anita Keal (Bunny Gross), Bruce Nozick (Richard Rothenberg), Alexandra Gersten (Ellen Rothenberg), Stuart Zagnit (Harvey Zagnit)
A comedy in two acts and four scenes. The action takes place in Israel and NYC at present.

Estelle Harris, Madelyn Cates, Sylvia Kauders, Mike Burstyn in "Prisoner of 2nd Ave." (Swope)

Bob Cucciolo, Leslie Ellis, Mike Burstyn, Sue Anne Gershenson, Allen Fitzpatrick, in "The Rothschilds" (Martha Swope)

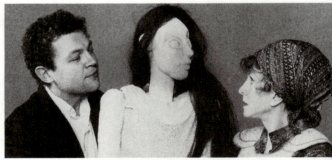

Right: Sam Tsoutsouvas, Ann Hillary in "Puppetmaster . . ." (Martha Swope)

Rita McKenzie in "Call Me Ethel"

Grace Roberts, Herbert Rubens in "Made in Heaven"

AMERICAN PLACE THEATRE

Twenty-sixth Season

Director, Wynn Handman; General Manager, Stephen Lisner; Production Management, Tom McDermott, Jr., Christopher Engel; Technical Director, Andrew Meyer; Dramaturg, Cynthia Jenner; Press, David Rothenberg Associates

Saturday, Jan. 20–Mar. 4, 1990 (33 performances and 17 previews)
ZORA NEALE HURSTON by Laurence Holder; Director, Wynn Handman; Sets, Terry Chandler; Lighting, Shirley Prendergast; Stage Manager, Lloyd Davis, Jr.; CAST: Elizabeth Van Dyke (Zora Neale Hurston), Tim Johnson (Herbert Sheen/Langston Hughes/Alain Locke/Richard Wright)
  A theatrical biography in one act. The action takes place in a bus station in NYC on Christmas Eve, 1949.

Saturday, March 17,–April 1, 1990 (9 performances and 9 previews)
NEDDY by Jeffrey Hatcher; Director, Amy Saltz; Sets/Costumes, G. W. Mercier; Lighting, Frances Aronson; Sound, Rob Gorton; Production Assistant, Sandra C. Mintz; Stage Manager, Richard Hester CAST: Kristine Nielsen (Elizabeth), Colette Kilroy (Fayle), Kevin Chamberlin (Raymond), John Michael Higgins (Allan), Don R. McManus (David), Michael Heintzman (Ned)
  A comedy set in faculty homes of an elite New England boarding school.

Saturday, April 21–May 20, 1990 (19 performances and 20 previews)
GROUND PEOPLE by Leslie Lee; Director, Walter Dallas; Sets, Charles McClennahan; Costumes, Beth A. Ribblett; Lighting, Shirley Prendergast; Sound, David Lawson; Movement Consultant, Bernard J. Marsh; Musical Consultant, Robert LaPierre; Music Coordinator, Don Meissner; Stage Manager, Lloyd Davis, Jr.; CAST: Bahni Turpin (Berlinda), Ron Richardson (Singin' Willie Ford), Denise Burse-Mickelbury (Holly Day), Raymond Anthony Thomas (Reggie), Frances Foster (Viola), Erma Campbell (Bertha), Kim Sullivan (Johnny Hopper), Tajj AsSwaudi, Arthur Harper (Musicians)
  A drama with music in two acts. The action takes place in the Mississippi Delta in the summer of 1920.

Monday Apr. 4–May 11, 1990 (6 performances)
BOBO'S BIRTHDAY written and performed by Catherine Butterfield; Director, Stephen Stout; joined in repertory on Monday, Apr. 30, 1990 by
THE CONSUMING PASSIONS OF LYDIA PINKHAM & REV. SYLVESTER GRAHAM conceived by Margery Cohen; performed by Margery Cohen and Eric Johnson; Director, Wynn Handman; Musical Director, Paul Greenwood; Musical Staging, Maris Heller.

Right: Kim Sullivan, Denise Burse-Mickelbury, Ron Richardson, Erma Campbell in "Ground People" Top: Michael Heintzman, John Michael Higgins in "Neddy"

Tim Johnson, Elizabeth Van Dyke in "Zora Neale Hurston"

Eric Johnson, Margery Cohen in "Consuming Passions of . . ."
Gerry Goodstein Photos

75

CIRCLE REPERTORY THEATRE

Artistic Director, Tanya Berezin; Managing Director, Connie L. Alexis; Associate Artistic Director, Mark Ramont; Literary Manager, Adrienne Hiegel; Company Manager, Harold E. Wolpert; Production Manager, Jody Boese; Technical Director, Tim Hamilton; Props, Kimberly Dudwitt, Kevin Wittmaack; Sound, Elizabeth Frank; Wardrobe, Madeleine Arthurs; Press, Gary Murphy, Belinda Miller

(Circle Rep.) Wednesday, Oct. 4–Nov. 19, 1989 (54 performances)
BESIDE HERSELF by Joe Pintauro; Director, John Bishop; Sets, John Lee Beatty; Costumes, Ann Emonts; Lights, Dennis Parichy; Music, Jonathan Brielle; Sound, Chuck London, Stewart Werner; Hair, Bobby H. Grayson; Stage Manager, Denise Yaney; CAST: Susan Bruce (Violet), Calista Flockhart (Skidie), Melissa Joan Hart (Alexandra), William Hurt (Augie-Jake), Edward Seamon (Harry/Bear), Lois Smith (Mary)

A comic fairy tale in two acts. The action takes place at a house in the woods on an island during September-October.

Wednesday, December 6, 1989–January 14, 1990 (45 performances)
SUNSHINE by William Mastrosimone; Director, Marshall W. Mason; Sets, David Potts; Costumes, Susan Lyall; Lights, Dennis Parichy; Music, Peter Kater; Sound, Stewart Werner, Chuck London; Stage Manager, Fred Reinglas; CAST: Jennifer Jason Leigh (Sunshine), Jordan Mott (Robby), John Dossett (Nelson), Bruno Alberti (Jerry)

A drama performed without intermission. The action takes place at the Jersey shore during November.

(Players Theatre) Wednesday, Jan. 24–Feb. 25, 1990 (38 performances)
IMAGINING BRAD by Peter Hedges; Director, Joe Mantello; Sets, Loy Arcenas; Costumes, Laura Cunningham; Lights, Dennis Parichy; Sound, Stewart Werner, Chuck London; Stage Manager, Denise Yaney CAST: Melissa Joan Hart (Valerie), Sharon Ernster (Dana Sue Kaye), Erin Cressida Wilson (Brad's Wife)

A comedy without intermission. The action takes place in Valerie's living room and Nashville, Tennessee. The time spans 1977 to the present.

Tuesday, February 20–April 19, 1990 (57 performances)
PRELUDE TO A KISS by Craig Lucas; Director, Norman Rene; Sets, Loy Arcenas; Costumes, Walker Hicklin; Lighting, Debra J. Kletter; Sound, Scott Lehrer; Hair/Wigs, Bobby H. Grayson; Stage Manager, M. A. Howard CAST: Alec Baldwin (Peter), Mary-Louise Parker (Rita), John Dossett (Taylor), L. Peter Callender (Tom/Jamaican Waiter), Debra Monk (Mrs. Boyle), Larry Bryggman (Dr. Boyle), Craig Bockhorn (Minister), Joyce Reehling (Aunt Dorothy/Leah), Michael Warren Powell (Uncle Fred), Barnard Hughes (Old Man), Kimberly Dudwitt, Pete Tyler (Guests, etc . . .)

A comic fairy tale in two acts. See Broadway calender for Broadway transfer.

Friday, May 4,–June 10, 1990 (44 performances)
EACH DAY DIES WITH SLEEP by Jose Rivera; Director, Roberta Levitow; Sets, Tom Kamm; Costumes, Tina Cantu Navarro; Lighting, Robert Wierzel; New York Sound Design, Janet Kalas; Scenic Projections Design, Charles Rose; Stage Manager, Fred Reinglas; Presented in association with Berkeley Repertory Theatre and AT&T On Stage. CAST: Randy Vasquez (Johnny), Erica Gimpel (Nelly), Alex Colon (Augie)

A drama in two acts

Left: Randy Vasquez, Erica Gimpel in "Each Day Dies . . ."
Above: Jennifer Jason Leigh, John Dossett in "Sunshine"
Top: Lois Smith, William Hurt in "Beside Herself"

Mary-Louise Parker, Alec Baldwin in "Prelude to a Kiss"

Erin Cressida Wilson, Sharon Ernster in "Imagining Brad"

Olivia Birkelund, Michael Rogers in "Othello"
Paula Court Photos

Bill Raymond, Anthony Fusco, Jace Alexander in
"Heart of a Dog"

CLASSIC STAGE COMPANY/CSC

Artistic Director, Carey Perloff; Managing Director, Ellen Novack; General Manager, Dara Hershman; Production Manager, Jeffrey Barzon; Artistic Associate, Lenora Champagne; Wardrobe, Christine Verleny; Press, Peter Cromarty & Co./ Kevin Brockman, Richard Brandt, Shirley Herz Co./Miller Wright

(CSC Theatre) Tuesday, Oct. 31–Dec. 23, 1989 (45 performances and 8 previews)
MOUNTAIN LANGUAGE and **THE BIRTHDAY PARTY** by Harold Pinter; Director, Carey Perloff; Sets, Loy Arcenas; Costumes, Gabriel Berry; Lighting, Beverly Emmons; Music, Wayne Horvitz; Sound, Daniel Moss Schreier; Stage Manager, Richard Hester; Casting, Ellen Novack; Dialect Coach, Nancy Lane; CAST ("Mountain Language"): Jean Stapleton (Elderly Woman), Wendy Makkena (Young Woman), Richard Riehle (Sergeant), David Strathairn (Officer/Hooded Man), Peter Riegert (Prisoner), Miguel Perez (Guard), Thomas Delling (Second Guard), Katie Cohen, Ellie Hannibal, Mary Beth Kilkelly, Gwynne Rivers (Women in Line); CAST ("The Birthday Party"): Bill Moor (Petey), Jean Stapleton (Meg), David Strathairn (Stanley), Wendy Makkena (Lulu), Peter Riegert (Goldberg), Richard Riehle (McCann). "Mountain Language" is performed without intermission; "The Birthday Party" is a play in three acts, performed with one intermission. The action takes place in the living room of a house in an English seaside town.

(CSC Theatre) Thursday, January 11–February 17, 1990 (47 performances and 2 previews) Theatre For A New Audience (Jeffrey Horowitz, Artistic/Producing Director) presents:
OTHELLO by William Shakespeare; Director, William Gaskill; Music, Jeff Langley; Sets/Costumes, Annie Smart; Lighting, Frances Aronson; Fights, David S. Leong; Voice/Text Consultant, Robert N. Williams; Associate Director, Patrick Kelly; Stage Manager, Steven H. Wildern; Press, Shirley Herz/Miller Wright CAST: Dan Cordle (Roderigo), Jessica Hecht (Bianca), Bryan Hicks (Understudy), Max Jacobs (Brabantio), Becky London (Emilia), Jonathan Nichols (Officer/Messenger), Brian Reddy (Iago), Michael Rogers (Othello), Craig Wroe (Cassio), Robert Zukerman (Duke/Gratiano), Roger Bechtel (Montano/Senator), Olivia Birkelund (Desdemona), P. J. Brown (Lodovico/Sailor/Gentleman)
The action takes place in Venice and Cyprus.

Wednesday, March 7–April 8, 1989 (30 performances and 8 previews)
HEART OF A DOG by Deloss Brown; From novella by Mikhail Bulgakov; Director, Robert Lanchester; Sets, Tom Kamm; Costumes, Jane Eliot; Lighting, Mary Louise Geiger; Sound, Daniel Schreier; Stage Manager, Debora Kingston CAST: Jace Alexander (Pooch/Poochkov), Josh Pais (Shvonder), Leslie Geraci (Svetlana), Gwynne Rivers (Natasha), Bill Raymond (Preobrazhensky), William Newman (Josef Lobohenkov), Anna Levine Thomson (Zina), Anthony Fusco (Bormenthal), Mary Beth Kilkelly (Sonia)
A satire in two acts. The action takes place in Moscow from 1925 to 1926.

Monday, May 7,–June 10, 1990 (43 performances and 9 previews)
THE TOWER OF EVIL by Alexandre Dumas, translated by Michael Feingold; Director, Carey Perloff; Sets, Donald Eastman; Costumes, Gabriel Berry; Lighting, Frances Aronson; Composer, Elizabeth Swados; Stage Manager, Richard Jakiel; Casting, Ellen Novack. CAST: Thomas Delling (Richard/De Pierrefonds), Michael Reilly (Simon/Sir Raoul), Ethan Mintz (John/Halberdier), Katharine Cohen (Gypsy), Olek Krupa (Orsini), David Bishins (Philippe Dolnay), Armand Schultz (Landry/Sir Guilbert de Marigny), Patrick O'Connell (Capt. Buridan), Ellie Hannibal (Courtier/A Veiled Woman), Bradley Whitford (Gaultier Dolnay), Kathleen Widdoes (Margaret Burgundy), Mary Beth Kilkelly (Charlotte), Frank Raiter (Savoisy/King Louis X), Gwynne Rivers (Courtier)
A drama in two acts. The action takes place in Paris during the reign of Louis X.

David Bishins, Kathleen Widdoes in "The Tower of Evil"

Top: (L) David Strathairn, Jean Stapleton in "Mountain Language" (R) Peter Riegert, David Strathairn in "The Birthday Party" *(Michael Tighe)*

77

HUDSON GUILD THEATRE

Producing Artistic Director, Geoffrey Sherman; Associate Director, Steven Ramay; General Manager, Paul Hutchison; Artistic Associate, John Daines; Production Manager, Patrick J. Scully; Stage Manager, Melissa L. Burdick; Press, Jeffrey Richards Associates/Irene Gandy, Susan Chicoine, Diane Judge, Maria Somma, Kathryn Frawley, Jillana Devine, Tony Armento, Robert Thurber, David LeShay

(Hudson Guild Theatre) Wednesday, September 27–October 22, 1989 (28 performances) Hudson Guild Theatre with permission of Raymond J. Greenwald & Feste Inc. present:
HOME GAMES by Tom Ziegler; Director, Roderick Cook; Sets, Paul Wonsek; Lighting, Stuart Duke; Costumes, Barbara Forbes; Sound, Aural Fixation; CAST: John Braden (Anton Tucker), Kymberly Dakin (Mertle Mae Tucker), Michael E. Knight (Frank Whitfield)
A romantic comedy in two acts. The action takes place in the Washington Heights section of Manhattan in the fall of 1985.

Wednesday, November 29–December 23, 1989 (28 performances)
PROGRESS by Doug Lucie; Director, Geoffrey Sherman; Sets, Paul Wonsek; Lighting, Phil Monat; Costumes, Pamela Scofield; Stage Manager, Melissa L. Burdick; CAST: Diana Van Fossen (Ronee), Ivar Brogger (Will), John Curless (Mark), Anne Bobby (Ange), Joe Mantello (Lenny), Nelson Avidon (Bruce), Edmund Lewis (Oliver), Ray Virta (Martin)
A comedy in two acts. The action takes place in Kilburn, North London at the present.

Monday, February 19–March 18, 1990 (32 performances)
DYLAN THOMAS: RETURN JOURNEY; based on the works of Dylan Thomas; Director, Anthony Hopkins; Stage Manager, Peter Baird; Lights, Rosalynn J. Evans CAST: Bob Kingdom
A solo recreation of Dylan Thomas in two parts.

Wednesday, March 28–April 22, 1990 (28 performances)
THE BALCONY by Jean Genet; Translation, Bernard Frechtman; Director, Geoffrey Sherman; Sets/Lighting, Paul Wonsek; Sound, Richard Rose; Stage Manager, Gary M. Zabinski CAST: Charles E. Gerber (Bishop), Matt Penn (Arthur/Photographer/Revolutionary/Slave), Valarie Pettiford (Penitent/Chantal/Photographer), Mimi Quillin (Horse/Revolutionary/Photographer), John Henry Redwood (General), Will Rhys (Chief of Police), Angela Sargeant (Mme. Irma), David Schechter (Beggar/Roger), Freda Foh Shen (Carmen), Albert Sinkys (Judge), Lynne Faljian Taylor (Thief/Revolutionary/photographer), Sharon Washington (Envoy)
A 30th anniversary production of Genet's play. For original production see *Theatre World* Vol. 16

Gerry Goodstein Photos
Top: Bob Kingdom in "Dylan Thomas" Right: John Braden in "Home Games"
Center: Anne Bobby, Diana Van Fossen in "Progress"

Edmund Lewis, Anne Bobby, Ray Virta, Nelson Avidon, Ivar Brogger in "Progress"

IRISH REPERTORY THEATRE

Second Season

Producing Director, Ciaran O'Reilly; Artistic Director, Charlotte Moore; Company Manager, Chris A. Kelly; Press, Chris Boneau/Eva Patton, Bob Fennell

(TADA Theatre) Tuesday, September 26–October 22, 1989 (18 performances) **SEA MARKS** by Gardner McKay; Director, Paul Weidner; Sets/Lighting, Kent Hoffman; Sound, Richard Clausen; Costumes, Natalie Walker; Stage Manager, Kathe Mull; CAST: Madeline Potter (Timothea Stiles), Patrick Fitzgerald (Colm Primrose).
  The action takes place in Cliffhorn Heads, west of Ireland and Liverpool at present.

(Irish Rep./TADA Theatre) Sunday, October 1–18 (12 performances) **ENGLISH THAT FOR ME!;** Devised and performed by Eamon Kelly; Sets & Lighting, Kent Hoffman; Stage Manager, Marcie Lowy; Press, Chris Boneau
  An evening of Irish yarn-spinning.

(South Street Theatre) Thursday, Nov. 9–Dec. 3, 1989 (26 performances) **A WHISTLE IN THE DARK** by Thomas Murphy; Director, Charlotte Moore; Sets, Patricia Heitman; Sound/Lighting, Richard Clausen; Costumes, Natalie Walker; Stage Manager, Kathe Mull; Press, James Brady. CAST: Chris A. Kelly (Iggy Carney), Ciaran O'Reilly (Harry Carney), Ron Bottitta (Hugo Carney), Jean Parker (Betty), Denis O'Neill (Mush O'Reilly), Maurice Sheehan (Michael Carney), W. B. Brydon (Dada), Patrick Fitzgerald (Des Carney). A play in two acts. The action takes place in the present time at Michael Carney's home in Coventry, England.

Wednesday, May 9–June 3, 1990 (17 performances) **PHILADELPHIA, HERE I COME!** by Brian Friel; Director, Paul Weidner; Sets, David Raphel; Costumes, Natalie Walker; Sound/Lighting, Richard Clausen; Hair, Gary Brennan; Stage Manager, Margaret Ritchie; Properties, Athena Baer CAST: Pauline Flanagan (Madge), Patrick Fitzgerald (Gareth O'Donnell-Public), Ciaran O'Reilly (Gareth O'Donnell-Private), W. B. Brydon (S. B. O'Donnell), Deidre Moore (Kate Doogan), Chris Carrick (Sen. Doogan), Frank McCourt (Master Boyle), Paddy Croft (Lizzy Sweeney), Bernard Frawley (Con Sweeney), John Short (Ben Burton), Colin Lane (Ned), Brian F. O'Byrne (Tom), Denis O'Neill (Joe), Dermot McNamara (Canon Mick O'Byrne)
  A play in two acts. The action takes place in the small village of Ballybeg, Ireland in 1962.

Monday, May 14–30, 1990 (16 performances) **ENDWORDS:** An evening of Samuel Beckett; Director, Vincent O'Neill CAST: Chris O'Neil
  An evening drawn from the writings and plays of Beckett.

Martha Swope, Len Tavares Photos

Top Right: Patrick Fitzgerald, Madeleine Potter in "Sea Marks"

Jean Parker, Patrick Fitzgerald in "A Whistle in the Dark"

Eamon Kelly in "English That for Me!"

79

JEWISH REPERTORY THEATRE

Sixteenth Season

Artistic Director, Ran Avni; Associate Director, Edward M. Cohen; Casting, Stephanie Klapper; Press, Shirley Herz Associates/Pete Sanders, Glenna Freedman, Sam Rudy, Miller Wright

(Jewish Repertory Theatre) Saturday, Oct. 28–Dec. 3, 1989. (20 performances) **THE WITCH** based on Abraham Goldfaden's musical; Director/Choreographer, Benjamin Zemach; Book Adaptation/English Lyrics, Amielle Zemach; Additional Lyrics, Itzik Manger, Dennis Perman; Additional Music, Max Helfman, Lori McKelvey, Henoch Cohn; Musical Director/Arranger, Lori McKelvey; Set Designer, Ray Recht; Costumes, Frances Blau; Lighting, Kevin Connaughton; Associate Director, Amielle Zemach; Stage Manager, Ellen-Stuart Plotnick. CAST: Elizabeth McDonough (Witch #1/Miriam (shoes)/Little Girl), Giulietta Lavezzo (Witch #2/Leah (dress)/Horse Dancer/Belly Dancer), Lori Wilner (Witch #3/Rachel (husband)/Babkelah Boy), Priscilla Quinby (Bobbe Yachne), Emily Loesser (Mirele), Joseph Travers (Abraham), Anna Bess Lank (Batya/Baile), Samuel D. Cohen (Elyakum), Daniel Neiden (Hotzmach #1), Avery Saltzman (Hotzmach #2/Leo, the Gypsy), Bruce Connelly (Hotzmach #3). MUSICAL NUMBERS: Once There Was a Little Town, Faster Faster, To Your Birthday, Of What Use to Me is Joy, Magic Song, The Curse, White Feathers, Potatoes, Hotzmach Is a Blind Man, Father Go, Lonely, How I Suffer, Three Hotzmachs' Song, Buy, Hot Little Breads, Household Goods, Fresh, Oh Kind Jews, Come With Me, In the Temple, Dream Fly Fly, Onward Horse Onward, Oh How Beautiful, Turkish Chant, Is That Your Daughter Gypsy?, Something Turns Up, Storm, Into the Cauldron. A musical in two acts. The action takes place in the Shtetl and on the road at the turn of the century.

Saturday, December 16, 1989—
THE RETURN by Frederic Glover; Director, Michael Bloom; Sets, Scott Bradley; Costumes, Edi Giguere; Lighting, Donald Holder; Sound, Gary & Timmy Harris; Stage Manager, D. C. Rosenberg; Press, Shirley Herz/Pete Sanders CAST: Dominic Chianese (Dr. Chaim Weizmann), Bruce Nozick (Benjamin Weizmann), Joseph Ragno (David Ben-Gurion), Annie Korzen (Paula Ben-Gurion), Jennifer Sternberg (Vera Weizmann), Graeme Malcolm (Halifax/Wingate/Lloyd), Jon Krupp (Michael Weizmann)
A drama in two acts. The action takes place in Europe, Palestine and NYC in the early 1940's.

Saturday, February 17, 1990—
DIVIDENDS by Gary Richards; Director, Tony Giordano; Sets, Ray Recht; Costumes, Barbara Bush; Lighting, Jeremy Kumin; Music, Elliot Finkel; Sound, Garry & Timmy Harris; Stage Manager, D. C. Rosenberg; Paintings, Robert Kalaidjian CAST: James Rutigliano (Neal), Reizl Bozyk (Bessie), Fyvush Finkel (Bernie)

Thursday, Apr. 24, 1990—
NEW YORK 1937 by Jose Yglesias; Director, Charles Maryan; Set, Atkin Pace; Costumes, Lana Fritz; Lighting, Brian Nason; Sound, Gary and Timmy Harris; Stage Manager, Nina Heller. CAST: Antonia Rey (Sophia), Joseph Palmas (Abelardo), Teresa Parente (Emma), Abigael Sanders (Clara), Al Rodrigo (Miguel), Tim Perez (Julian), Michael Egan (Mr. Schlein), Ann Dowd (Elsie), Gerald Orange (Uncle Raul), Royce Rich (Mr. Levin).
A comedy set in the Washington Heights section of New York in 1937.

Carol Rosegg/Martha Swope Photos

Top Left: Emily Loesser, Daniel Neiden in "The Witch"

Domenic Chianese, Joseph Ragno in "The Return"

Joseph Ragno, Domenic Chianese in "The Return"

LINCOLN CENTER THEATER COMPANY

Fifth Season

Director, Gregory Mosher; Executive Producer, Bernard Gersten; General Manager, Steven C. Callahan; Company Manager, Lynn Landis; Production Manager, Jeff Hamlin; Resident Director, Jerry Zaks; Dramaturg, Anne Cattaneo; Casting, Risa Bramon/Billy Hopkins; Press, Merle Debuskey, Bruce Campbell, Susan Chicoine, Leo Stern

(Mitzi E. Newhouse Theatre) Tuesday, November 7–December 31, 1989 (32 performances and 32 previews)
OH, HELL; a double bill with Direction by Gregory Mosher; Sets, John Lee Beatty; Costumes, Jane Greenwood; Lighting, Kevin Rigdon; Sound, Bill Dreisbach; Illusionist Consultant, George Schindler; General Manager, Steven C. Callahan; Production Manager, Jeff Hamlin; Stage Managers, Michael F. Ritchie, Sarah Manley
THE DEVIL AND BILLY MARKHAM by Shel Silverstein; CAST: Dennis Locorriere
BOBBY GOULD IN HELL by David Mamet; CAST: Treat Williams (Bobby Gould), Steven Goldstein (Interrogator's Assistant), W. H. Macy (Interrogator), Felicity Huffman (Glenna)
Two one act plays that deal with modern interpretations of the devil. Mamet's Bobby Gould character also appears in "Disappearance of the Jews" and "Speed-the-Plow".

SOME AMERICANS ABROAD

By Richard Nelson; Director, Roger Michell; Sets/Costumes, Alexandra Byrne; Lighting, Rick Fisher; Original Music, Jeremy Sams; Poster Art, Edward Sorel; Production Stage Manager, Michael F. Ritchie; Stage Manager, Mark Baltazar; Assistant Director, Sydney Sidner, Rear Projections, Greg Meeh; Presented by arrangement with Royal Shakespeare Theatre, Stratford-upon-Avon, England. Opened in the Vivian Beaumont Theatre on Wednesday, May 2, 1990.*

CAST

Joe Taylor	Colin Stinton
Philip Brown	John Bedford Lloyd
Henry McNeil	Nathan Lane†
Betty McNeil	Kate Burton
Frankie Lewis	Frances Conroy
Katie Taylor	Cara Buono
Harriet Baldwin	Jane Hoffman
Orson Baldwin	Henderson Forsythe
Joanne Smith	Ann Talman
An American	John Rothman
Donna Silliman	Elisabeth Shue
Musicians	Michelle Johnson (Singer)

Michael Goetz (Bass), Joshua Rosenblum (Piano)

UNDERSTUDIES: Stephen Rowe (Joe/Philip/American), Carol Schneider (Katie/Donna/Joanna), Robert Hock (Orson), Rebecca Nelson (Frankie/Betty), Jennie Ventriss (Harriet)

A comedy in two acts. The action takes place in various English locations at the present time.

*Closed June 17, 1990 after 55 Broadway performances and 8 previews. Opened Off-Broadway in the Mitzi E. Newhouse where it played 81 performances. Beaumont previews began Wednesday, April 25, 1990.
†Played by Bob Balaban in the Newhouse run.

Brigitte Lacombe Photos

Top Right: Dennis Locorriere in "The Devil and Billy Markham" Below: Treat Williams, Felicity Huffman, Steven Goldstein, W. H. Macy in "Bobby Gould in Hell" Center: Colin Stinton, Cara Buono, Ann Talman, Frances Conroy, Henderson Forsythe, Kate Burton, Nathan Lane, Jane Hoffman, John Bedford Lloyd in "Some Americans Abroad" (*Martha Swope*)

Kate Burton, John Bedford Lloyd, Colin Stinton, Frances Conroy, Bob Balaban in "Some Americans Abroad"

LINCOLN CENTER THEATER COMPANY
(continued)

THE TENTH MAN

By Paddy Chayefsky; Director, Ulu Grosbard; Set, Santo Loquasto; Costumes, Jane Greenwood; Lighting, Dennis Parichy; Sound, Daniel Schreier; General Manager, Steven C. Callahan; Production Manager, Jeff Hamlin; Company Manager, Lynn Landis; Assistant to Director, Judy Goldman; Wardrobe, Don Brassington; Hairstylist, Linda Rice; Stage Managers, Maureen F. Gibson, Fredric H. Orner, David Pittu. Opened Sunday, Dec. 10, 1989 in the Lincoln Center Vivian Beaumont Theater*

CAST

Hirschman/Cabalist	Joseph Wiseman
Schlissel	Bob Dishy
Zitorsky	Jack Weston
Sexton	Sidney Armus
Alper	Ron Rifkin
Foreman	Alan Manson
Evelyn Foreman	Phoebe Cates
Arthur Brooks	Peter Friedman
Harris	Carl Don
Elder Kessler	David Berman
Younger Kessler	Kenny Morris
Rabbi	Michael Mantell
Policeman	Dan Daily

STANDBYS: Ben Kapen (Cabalist/Hirschman/Zitorsky), Stan Lachow (Schlissel/Alper/Sexton), David Berman (Arthur Brooks), Kenny Morris (Rabbi), Cara Buono (Evelyn), Carl Don (Foreman), David Pittu (Elder Kessler/Younger Kessler/Policeman)

A drama in three acts and four scenes. The action takes place in an orthodox synagogue in Mineola, Long Island, NY, in 1959.

*Closed Jan. 14, 1990 after 41 performances and 35 previews. Original production opened in the Booth Theatre on Nov. 5, 1959 and played 623 performances.

Brigitte Lacombe Photos

Top Right: Phoebe Cates, Alan Manson, Michael Mantell, Ron Rifkin, Dan Daily, Peter Friedman Center: Joseph Wiseman, Peter Friedman, Phoebe Cates in "The Tenth Man"

(Mitzi E. Newhouse) Wednesday, May 16–Oct. 28, 1990 (185 performances)
SIX DEGREES OF SEPARATION by John Guare; Director, Jerry Zaks; Sets, Tony Walton; Costumes, William Ivey Long; Lighting, Paul Gallo; Sound, Aural Fixation; Hair, Robert DiNiro; Poster, James McMullan; Stage Managers, Steve Beckler, Sarah Manley; Assistant Director, Lori Steinberg; Wardrobe, Florence Aubert; CAST: Stockard Channing succeeded by Kelly Bishop, Swoosie Kurtz (Ouisa), John Cunningham (Flan), James McDaniel succeeded by Gregory Simmons, Courtney B. Vance (Paul), Paul McCrane (Rick), Sam Stoneburner (Geoffrey), Evan Handler (Doug), Anthony Rapp (Ben), Robin Morse (Tess), David Eigenberg (Hustler), Kelly Bishop (Kitty), Peter Maloney (Larkin), Brian Evers (Detective), Gus Rogerson (Woody), Stephen Pearlman (Dr. Fine), John Cameron Mitchell (Trent), Mari Nelson (Elizabeth), Philip LeStrange (Police/Doorman)
The action takes place in N.Y.C. today. A comedic drama performed without intermission. Transferred to Vivian Beaumont Theatre Oct. 30, 1990.

John Cunningham, Stockard Channing, Philip LeStrange, James McDaniel, Sam Stoneburner in "Six Degrees of Separation"

MANHATTAN THEATRE CLUB

Artistic Director, Lynne Meadow; Managing Director, Barry Grove; General Manager, Victoria Bailey; Artistic Associates, Jonathan Alper, Michael Bush; Design Associate, John Lee Beatty; Literary Manager, Tom Szentgyorgyi; Casting, Lyons/Isaacson; Company Managers, Denise Cooper, Michael Stotts; Production Manager, Michael R. Moody; Technical Director, Betsy Tanner; Press, Helene Davis, Linda Feinberg, Clay Martin

(Stage I) Monday, October 9–November 22, 1989 (52 performances)
THE TALENTED TENTH by Richard Wesley; Director, M. Neema Barnette; Sets, Charles McClennahan; Costumes, Alvin B. Perry; Lighting, Anne Militello; Sound, James Mtume; Stage Manager, Diane Ward CAST: Graham Brown (Father/Sam Griggs), Richard Lawson (Bernard), Marie Thomas (Pam), Richard Gant (Marvin), LaTanya Richardson (Rowena), Elain Graham (Irene), Rony Clanton (Ron), Lorraine Toussaint (Tanya)
A drama in two acts. The action takes place in the 1980's.

(Manhattan Theatre Club Stage II) Tuesday, Oct. 31–Nov. 26, 1989 (32 performances)
WOLF-MAN by Elizabeth Egloff; Director, Thomas Allan Bullard; Sets, James Youmans; Costumes, Jess Goldstein; Lighting, Phil Monat; Sound, Bruce Ellman; CAST: Dylan Baker (Oskar Mendelssohn), Patricia Clarkson (Dido Mendelssohn). A drama in two acts. The action takes place in 1938 Vienna.

Tuesday, December 5, 1989–February 4, 1990 (71 performances)
THE ART OF SUCCESS by Nick Dear; Director, Adrian Noble; Sets/Costumes, Ultz; Lighting, Beverly Emmons; Music/Sound, John Gromada; Stage Managers, Ed Fitzgerald, Ara Marx; Dialects, Howard Samuelson; CAST: Mary-Louise Parker (Jane Hogarth), Tim Curry (William Hogarth), Nicholas Woodeson (Harry Fielding), Patrick Tull (Frank), Don R. McManus (Oliver), Patricia Kilgarriff (Mrs. Needham), Suzanne Bertish (Louisa), Jayne Atkinson (Sarah Sprackling), Daniel Benzali (Robert Walpole), Jodie Lynne McClintock (Queen Caroline)
A play in two acts. The action revolves around artist William Hogarth and takes place in England. The play condenses the years 1727–1737 into a single night.

(Stage II) Tuesday, January 23–February 18, 1990 (32 performances)
THE AMERICAN PLAN by Richard Greenberg; Director, Evan Yionoulis; Sets, James Youmans; Costumes, Jess Goldstein; Lighting, Donald Holder; Music/Sound, Thomas Cabaniss; Stage Manager, Richard Hester CAST: Tate Donovan (Nick Lockridge), Eric Stoltz (Gil Harbison), Rebecca Miller (Lili Adler), Joan Copeland (Eva Adler), Beatrice Winde (Olivia Shaw)
A drama in two acts. The play concerns an all-American golden boy with secrets of his own and a troubled young jewish woman. The action takes place in the Catskills and NYC and spans the early 60's to the early 70's

(Stage I) Tuesday February 27–April 13, 1990 (64 performances)
BAD HABITS by Terrence McNally; Director, Paul Benedict; Sets, John Lee Beatty; Costumes, Jane Greenwood; Lighting, Peter Kaczorowski; Sound, John Gromada; Stage Manager, Tom Aberger CAST: ACT I/DUNELAWN-Ralph Marrero (Otto), Nathan Lane (Jason Pepper, M.D.), Faith Prince (Dolly Scupp), Kate Nelligan (April Pitt), Robert Clohessy (Roy Pitt), David Cromwell (Hiram Spane), Bill Buell (Francis Tear), Michael Mantell (Harry Scupp) ACT II/RAVENSWOOD-Kate Nelligan (Ruth Benson, R.N.), Faith Prince (Becky Hedges, R.N.), Robert Clohessy (Bruno), Bill Buell (Mr. Ponce), David Cromwell (Dr. Toynbee), Michael Mantell (Mr. Blum), Ralph Marrero (Mr. Yamadoro), Nathan Lane (Hugh Gumbs)
A revival of McNally's related one-act comedies.

(City Center Stage II) Tuesday, May 8–June 3, 1990 (32 performances)
MI VIDA LOCA by Eric Overmyer; Director, David Warren; Sets, James Noone; Costumes, David Woolard; Lighting, Donald Holder; Music/Sound, Mark Bennett; Stage Manager, Richard Hester; CAST: Robert Lansing (Ajay), Caris Corfman (Lulu), John Slattery (Paco), J. Smith-Cameron (Diana), Barbara Barrie (Maggie), Lou Milione (Bubba)
A drama in two acts. The action takes place on the Washington coast, the Olympic Peninsula, in the early spring of 1985.

(Stage I) Tuesday, May 22–July 6, 1990 (52 performances)
PRIN by Andrew Davies; Director, John Tillinger; Sets, John Lee Beatty; Costumes, Jane Greenwood; Lighting, Richard Nelson; Sound, Bruce Ellman; Stage Manager, Travis Decastro CAST: Eileen Atkins (Prin), Amy Wright (Dibs), John Curless (Boyle), John Christopher Jones (Walker), Remak Ramsay (Kite), Wendy Makkena (Melanie)
A drama in two acts. The action takes place at a British teacher's college.

Gerry Goodstein Photos

Right Center: Eric Stoltz (standing), Tate Donovan in "American Plan"; Kate Nelligan, Faith Prince in "Bad Habits"
Above: Tim Curry, Suzanne Bertish in "The Art of Success"
Top: Elain Graham, LaTanya Richardson, Marie Thomas in "The Talented Tenth"

Eileen Atkins, Amy Wright in "Prin"

Ethel Beatty Barnes, Jeree Palmer Wade, Cheryl
Freeman in "Sugar Hill"

MUSICAL THEATRE WORKS

Sixth Season

Artistic Director, Anthony J. Stimac; General Manager, Denys Sebastian; Literary Manager, Brook Garrett; Production Manager, Randy Lee Hartwig; Wardrobe, Gwenna Perry; Props, Jill Cordle; Press, Cromarty & Co./Joe Wolhandler, Kevin Brockman

(St. Peter's Church) Wednesday, September 13–October 1, 1989 (13 performances and 8 previews) Musical Theatre Works (Anthony J. Stimac, Artistic Director) and Midtown Arts Common at St. Peter's Church (Edmund Anderson, Executive Director) present:
MIDSUMMER NIGHTS; Music, Kevin Kuhn; Lyrics/Book, Bryan D. Leys; Director, David Saint; Musical Director, Seth Rudetsky; Set, James Noone; Lighting, Mark London; Costumes, Amanda J. Klein; Choreography, Jonathan Cerullo; Casting, Brook Garrett; Stage Manager, Ira Mont; Press, Cromarty & Co./Kevin Brockman CAST: Tracey Berg (Titania), Brenda Braxton (Helena), Wally Dunn (Theseus), Joyce P. King (Cobweb), Eric Kornfeld (Oberon), Peter Marc (Lysander) Jamie Martin (Blossom), George Merritt (Bottom), Judith Moore (Penelope), Stacy Morze (Moth), Kristine Nevins (Hippolyta), Harold Perrineau, Jr. (Puck), Howard Samuelsohn (Demetrius), Traci Lyn Thomas (Hermia)
MUSICAL NUMBERS: Get It Right, Bikinis, Surfboards & Sand, Hopeless Love, He's Gonna Be My Boyfriend, Community Theatre, A Small Affair, Magic Midsummer Nights, I'm Square, Something There Between Us, You've Changed, Hold On Tight, Bright and New, Good For You, Guys Will Be Guys, Wake Up, What Good is Being a Beatnick?, Her Her Hermia, Finale/Midsummer Nights
A musical in two acts. A 1960's Laguna Beach party musical version of Shakespeare's "Midsummer Night's Dream."

Sunday, Jan. 28–Feb. 18, 1990 (21 performances)
GOOSE! BEYOND THE NURSERY . . . with Music by Mark Frawley; Lyrics, Scott Evans; Book, Mr. Evans, Austin Tichenor; Direction & Choreography, Peter Gennaro; Musical Director, Joe Baker; Sets, Allen Moyer; Costumes, Gregg Barnes; Lighting, Mary Louise Geiger; Musical Supervisor, Michael Rafter; Stage Manager, Ira Mont; Hair, Bobby H. Grayson; CAST: Jan Neuberger (Mary), Jeff Blumenkrantz (Simon), David Schechter (Peter), Jennifer Leigh Warren (Jill), Mark Lotito (Jack), Adinah Alexander (Joan)
MUSICAL NUMBERS: I Don't Want to Talk About It, Rhyme Figure, Rub-a-Dub, I've Lost It, Little Boy Blue, Garden Grow, Wee Willie Winkie, I Met a Girl, Stop! Don't Squash Our Love, Man in the Moon, Humpty-The Pop Opera, Mulbery Bush, Jumping Joan, I Follow the Parade, Lullaby, Wishes
A musical treatment of nursery rhymes and relating them to the 1990's.

(St. Peter's Church Theatre) Wednesday, April 18–May 6, 1990 (19 performances and 8 previews)
SUGAR HILL with Music by Louis St. Louis; Lyrics, St. Louis, Roberto Fernandez, Tony Walsh; Book, St. Louis, Fernandez; Based on an original story by Mr. Fernandez; Director, Hattie Winston; Musical Staging, Carmen de Lavallade; Sets, James Noone; Costumes, Carrie Robbins; Lighting, Ken Smith; Musical Director, Pookie Johnson; Logo, Carrie Robbins; Stage Manager, Michael Schmalz; Production Manager, Randy Lee Hartwig; Press, Peter Cromarty/Kevin Brockman CAST: Ethel Beatty Barnes (Beatrice DuBois), Cheryl Freeman (Cassandra DuBois), Tatyana Ali (Baby Bea), Jeree Palmer Wade (Nettie DuBois), Edwin Battle (Jaxon DuBois/Boo), Carol Jean Lewis (Cookie Allen), James Stovall (Malcolm McDaniels), Marcella Lowery (Blanca Stromberg-Carlson), Tony Hoylen (Eddie Van Der Vere)
MUSICAL NUMBERS: Up on Sugar Hill, My Man Jaxon, Who's Gonna Take Care of Me, A Woman Alone, Dignity Is the Key, The Grown Up Me, Sippin', Cinnamon Lady, All on My Own, If I Had the 2nd Chance, When You Lose Your Heart to Harlem, What Color Is Love?, Harlem at It's Best, Another Sunday Morning without Love, Where Were You? This Human Race
A musical in two acts and 13 scenes. The action takes place in the Sugar Hill area of Harlem from 1927–1970.

Martha Swope/Carol Rosegg Photos

Top Left: Brenda Braxton, Traci Lyn Thomas, Peter Marc, Stacy Morze in "Midsummer Nights" Below: (front) Jennifer Leigh Warren, David Schechter, Jan Neuberger, (back) Mark Lotito, Adinah Alexander, Jeff Blumenkrantz in "Goose! Beyond the Nursery"

NEGRO ENSEMBLE COMPANY

Twenty-third Season

Artistic Director/President, Douglas Turner Ward; General Manager, Susan Watson Turner; Company Manager, Lauren P. Yates; Technical Director, Lisa Watson; Sound, Eric King; Wardrobe, Gregory Glenn; Stage Managers, Ed De Shae; Costumes, Judy Dearing; Sets, Charles McClennahan; Press, Howard Atlee

(Theatre Four) Wednesday, September 20–November 26, 1989 (72 performances) **HERE IN MY FATHER'S HOUSE** by Jewel Brimage, Ellen Cleghorne, Cheryle Lane, Toni Ann Johnson, Zelda Patterson and Leslie Lee; Director, Douglas Turner Ward; Costumes, Ali Turns; Lighting, Sandra Ross; Sound, Carmen Griffin; Stage Manager, Lisa L. Watson; Press, Howard Atlee. CAST: O. L. Duke (Father I), Samuel Jackson (Father II), Ellen Cleghorne (Daughter I), Cheryl Lane (Daughter II), Jewel Brimage (Daughter III), Toni Ann Johnson (Daughter IV), Zelda Patterson (Daughter V)

Performed without intermission. The action takes place in various locales. The time is Father's Day and beyond.

(Theatre Four) Saturday, December 16, 1989–February 4, 1990 (60 performances) **JONQUIL** by Charles Fuller; Director, Douglas Turner Ward; Sets, Charles McClennahan; Lighting, Sylvester A. Weaver, Jr.; CAST: Cynthia Bond (Jonquil), O. L. Duke (Klux #2/Isaiah), Samuel L. Jackson (Klux #3/Daniel), Iris Little (Sally), Charles Weldon (Calvin), Tacy Griswold (Cable), William Mooney (Judge Bridges), Rebecca Nelson (Hannah), Peggy Alston (Aunt Bessie), Graham Brown (Silas), Ed Wheeler (George Turner), William Jay (Bobby Williams), Amanda Jobe (Woman/Hallie), Curt Williams (Colson), Kenshaka, Ali, Tiffany McClinn, Leonard Thomas (Farmers)

A drama in two acts. The action takes place in Neal County, South Carolina in the fall of 1886. This is the third play in the "WE" cycle following "SALLY" and "PRINCE".

Wednesday, Feb. 21–May 18, 1990 (40 performances) **BURNER'S FROLIC** by Charles Fuller; Director, Douglas Turner Ward; Lighting, Sylvester A. Weaver Jr.; Supervisor, Lisa L. Watson; CAST: Adam Wade (Burner), Ed Wheeler (Albert Tunes), Charles Weldon (Ralph Buford), Graham Brown (Rev. Quash), Sandra Nutt (Tiche), Cynthia Bond (Charlotte), Iris Little (Mabel Buford), O. L. Duke (Wade Harris), Samuel L. Jackson (Jim Paine), William Mooney (Kimble), Peggy Alston (Aunt Becky), Wayne Elbert (Reed), William Jay (Vaughn), Leonard Thomas (Tommy), Mitchell Marchand (Jasper), Gregory Glenn (Curtis)

Part IV in the "WE" cycle, following "SALLY", "PRINCE" and "JONQUIL". The action takes place in Virginia in 1876.

(Theatre Four) Friday, Mar. 28–May 27, 1990 (56 performances and 16 previews) **LIFETIMES ON THE STREETS** by Gus Edwards; Director, Douglas Turner Ward; Set, Lisa L. Watson; Lighting, Sandra Ross; Sound/Composer, Richard V. Turner; Company Manager, J. Heather Wiley. CAST: Peggy Alston (Marvis/Mavis), Douglas Turner Ward (New Ice Age), Iris Little (Hooker/Marvin Gaye Died for Your Sins), O. L. Duke (Sorry to Disturb You/Bag Lady), Charles Weldon (Ain't No Other City Like It), Cynthia Brown (Stop Me If You've Heard This), Leonard Thomas (Collector), Adam Wade (Lifetimes on the Streets), Sandra Nutt (How I Lost Religion), Graham Brown (A Garden in the City/War Story), Charles Brown (Streetwalker).

A collection of monologues on black life presented in two acts. The action takes place in Harlem in the present day.

Bert Andrews Photos

Left Center: Charles Brown, Iris Little, Adam Wade, Cynthia Bond, Charles Weldon, O. L. Duke in "Lifetimes" Above: Adam Wade, Sandra Nutt in "Burner's Frolic" Top: Iris Little, Charles Weldon, Curt Williams, William Mooney in "Jonquil"

Cynthia Bond, Douglas Turner Ward in "Lifetimes"

NEW FEDERAL THEATRE

Twentieth Season

Producer, Woodie King, Jr.; Production Manager, Dwayne B. Perryman III; Company Manager, Linda Herring; Business Manager, Gloria Mitchell; Lighting, William H. Grant III; Sets, Llewellyn Harrison; Costumes, Judy Dearing; Press, Max Eisen, Madelon Rosen Solomon

(New Federal Theatre at Riverside Church) Thursday, September 14–24, 1989 (12 performances) New Federal Theatre Workshop and Soyikwa Institute of African Theatre present:
GOREE by Matsemela Manaka; Music conceived, composed and arranged by Motsumi Makhene; Director, John Kani; Choreography, Nomsa Manaka; Lighting, Siphiwe Khumalo; Sets, Matsemela Manaka; Press, Max Eisen CAST: Nomsa Manaka, Sibongile Khumalo

(New Federal Theatre at Riverside Church) Wednesday, October 4–November 5, 1989 (30 performances) New Federal Theatre, Inc. at Theatre of the Riverside Church (Woodie King, Jr., Producer) presents:
GOD'S TROMBONES: a gospel musical adaptation of James Weldon Johnson's writings; Director, Woodie King, Jr.; Music Director, Grenoldo Frazier; Sets, Llewellyn Harrison; Lighting, William H. Grant, III; Costumes, Judy Dearing; Movement, Dianne McIntyre; Stage Manager, Dwayne B. Perryman, III; Press, Max Eisen CAST: Lex Monson (Rev. Bradford Parham), Theresa Merritt (Rev. Sister Rena Pinkston), Rhetta Hughes (Sister Odessa Jackson), Trazana Beverley (Rev. Sister Marion Alexander), Cliff Frazier (Rev. Ridgley Washington), Deborah Blackwell-Cook, Sabrynaah Pope, Don Corey Washington (Jackson Family)
MUSICAL NUMBERS: Prelude, So Glad I'm Here, Twelve Gates, Sweet Hour of Prayer, Amen, Lord Don't Move This Mountain, Trombones Ensemble, In Shady Green Pastures, How Great Thou Art, Didn't It Rain, Just A Little Talk With Jesus, I'm Coming Home Dear Lord, Hush, He'll Understand, Were You There, Swing Low Sweet Chariot, How I Got Over, Finale
A revival of the 1969 musical in two acts. Sermons on the telling of the Creation form the action.

(New Federal Theatre/Riverside Church) Friday, February 2–March 4, 1990 (30 performances) Woodie King, Jr. (producer) presents:
SURVIVAL; written and performed by Fana Kekana, Selaelo Maredi, Mshengu THemba Ntinga, Seth Sibanda; Director, Jerry Mofokeng; Stage Manager, Jacqui Casto; Set, Craig Kennedy; Costumes, Ali Turns; Lighting, Richard Harmon; Dramaturg, Cathy Madison; Press, Max Eisen. CAST: Fana Kekana (Vusi Mabandla), Selaelo Maredi (Slasksa Mphahlele/Judge/Highway Patrol/Pass Office Official/Store Owner), THemba Ntinga (Leroi Williams/Prosecutor/Interpreter/Third Official), Seth Sibanda (Habakuk Ngwenya/Edwards Nkosi)
A play with music. The action takes place inside and outside of a South African Jail, John Vorster Square, at the present time.

Right: Sabrynaah Pope, Rhetta Hughes, Debbie Blackwell Cook, Cory Washington in "God's Trombones" Top: Nomsa Manaka, Sibongile Khumalo in "Goree"

Selaelo Maredi, Themba Ntinga, Fana Kekana, Seth Sibanda in "Survival"

Theresa Merritt, Lex Monson, Trazana Beverley in "God's Trombones"

NEW YORK SHAKESPEARE FESTIVAL

Twenty-third season

Producer, Joseph Papp; Associate Producer, Jason Steven Cohen; General Manager, Bob MacDonald; Associate, Susan Sampliner; Plays and Musical Development, Gail Merrifield; Casting, Rosemarie Tichler; Executive Assistant to Mr. Papp, Barbara Carroll; Production Manager, Andrew Mihok; Technical Director, Mervyn Haines, Jr., Audio Master, Gene Ricciardi; Props, James Gill; Art Director, Paul Davis; Press, Richard Kornberg, Barbara Carroll, Reva Cooper, Carol Fineman, Steven J. Krementz, Christopher M. Montpetit, Amy Reiter.

(Delacorte Theatre/Central Park) Friday June 23–July 23, 1989 (24 performances) **TWELFTH NIGHT, Or What You Will** by William Shakespeare; Director, Harold Guskin; Sets, John Lee Beatty; Costumes, Jeanne Button; Lighting, Richard Nelson; Music, Peter Golub; Fights, B. H. Barry; Clown/Movement, Bob Berky; Stage Managers, James Harker, Allison Sommers; Production Assistants, Jenny Peek, Alison Rabenau. CAST: John Amos (Sir Toby Belch), Dan Berkey (Officer), Gigi Bermingham (Ensemble), David Borror (Ensemble), Andre Braugher (Antonia), James Cahill (Priest), L. Peter Callender (Curio), Bill Camp (Waiter), Stephen Collins (Orsino), Jeff Goldblum (Malvolio), Lisa Gay Hamilton (Ensemble), John Hickey (Officer), Gregory Hines (Feste), Mary Mara (Servant to Olivia), Mary Elizabeth Mastrantonio (Viola), Stephen Mendillo (Sea Capt.), Mari Nelson (Ensemble), Michelle Pfeiffer (Olivia), Frank Raiter (Valentine), Patrick Rameau (Ensemble), Fisher Stevens (Sir Andrew Aguecheek), Jake Weber (Officer), Rainn Wilson (Ensemble), Graham Winton (Sebastian), Charlaine Woodard (Maria).

Performed with one intermission. This production set around the turn of the century somewhere on the Mediterranean. Shakespeare Marathon #10.

(Delacorte Theatre/Central Park) Friday August 4–September 2, 1989 (24 performances) Joseph Papp presents:
TITUS ANDRONICUS by William Shakespeare; Director, Michael Maggio; Sets, John Lee Beatty; Costumes, Lewis D. Rampino; Lighting, Jennifer Tipton; Music, Louis Rosen; Fights, B. H. Barry CAST: Peter Appel (Clown), N. Richard Arif (Ensemble/Patrician I), Daniel Berkley (Ensemble), Deryl Caitlyn (Quintus, Goth 2), Bill Camp (Chiron), Joseph M. Costa (Aemilius), Robert Curtis-Brown (Bassianus/Goth 3), Keith David (Aaron), Jon DeVries (Marcus), Pamela Gien (Lavina), Don Harvey (Demetrius), Bryan Hicks (Young Lucius), Susan Knight (Ensemble), William Langan (Ensemble), James McCauley (Attendant/Soldier), Tanny McDonald (Nurse), Don R. McManus (Saturninus), Cameron Miller (Soldier/Ensemble), Donald Moffat (Titus Andronicus), Kate Mulgrew (Tamora), Erik Onate (Ensemble), Joshua Perl (Ensemble), Steve Pickering (Mutius/Publius), Andrew Prosky (Soldier/Ensemble), David Purdham (Lucius), Armand Schultz (Alarbus, Messenger, Goth 1), Guy S. Wagner (Soldier), William Wheeler (Ensemble), Rainn Wilson (Martius)

Shakespeare's play in two acts. The action takes place in Rome in ancient days. Number 11 of the Shakespeare Marathon.

Martha Swope Photos

Right: David Purdham, Donald Moffat, Pamela Gien, Jon De-Vries in "Titus Andronicus" Above: Michelle Pfeiffer, Mary Elizabeth Mastrantonio in "Twelfth Night" Top: John Amos, Gregory Hines, Fisher Stevens in "Twelfth Night"

Jeff Goldblum, Michelle Pfeiffer, Charlaine Woodard

Stephen Collins, Mary Elizabeth Mastrantonio in "Twelfth Night"

Kate Mulgrew, Keith David in "Titus Andronicus"

NEW YORK SHAKESPEARE FESTIVAL
(continued)

(Public Theatres) Tuesday, August 1–31, 1989
FESTIVAL LATINO; The thirteenth annual celebration of Latin music, theatre and dance; Directors, Carlos Giménez, Myrna Casas, Michael Alasa, Mark Pennington, Raul Osorio, Ramon Pareja, Santiago García; Plays: *El Coronel No Tiene Quien Le Escriba (No One Writes To the Colonel)* by Gabriel García Márquez; Adaptation, Mr. Giménez; Translation, Nina Miller; *El Gran Circo E. U. Craniano (The Great U.S. Kranial Circus)* by Myrna Casas; *Peggy and Jackson* by David Welch & Michael Alasa; *Adios, Tropicana* by Mark Pennington & Chuck Gomez; *No+ (No More)* by Raul Osorio; *Sueño de Una Noche de Verano (Midsummer Night's Dream)* by Shakespeare; Adaptation, Manuel Rueda; Translation, Melia Bensussen; *El Paso o Parábola del Camino (El Paso or Parable of the Path)* by La Candelaria

(Public/Susan Stein Shiva Theatre) Tuesday August 15–19, 1989 (6 performances) Joseph Papp, Vladimir I. Nemirovich-Danchenko School and M. Gorky Moscow Art Theatre, USSR present:
MY BIG LAND (SAILORS' SILENCE) by Alexander Galich; Director, Oleg P. Tabakov; Translation, Alexander Gelman; Pedagogue, A. Seliverstov; Scenography, S. Kutsevalov; Costumes, E. Pechenkina; Lighting, N. Kurdyumova; Sound, N. Koloskov; CAST: Filip Yankovsky (David), Vladimir Mashkov (Abram), Roman Kuznechenko (Meyer), Alyona Khovanskaya (Tanya), Irina Apeksemova (Hanna), Liya Yelshevskaya (Roza), Dmitry Stolbtsov (Mitya), Yuri Yekimov (Slavka), Igor Kozlov (Chernyshov), Irina Gordina (Lyudmila/Arisha), Nina Muzhikova (Lyudmila/Arisha), Sergei Shentalinsky (Lapshin), Dmitry Stolbtsov (Odintsov), Yevgeny Mironov (Zhenka).

A drama in three acts. The action takes place in the Ukraine in the 1920's. The play was written in 1957 but banned in the USSR until this year. Performed in Russian with English translation.

(Public/Susan Stein) Friday, September 8–October 8, 1989 (37 performances) Joseph Papp and The Actors' Gang present:
CARNAGE, A COMEDY by Adam Simon and Tim Robbins; Director, Tim Robbins; Sets, Catherine Hardwicke, Mason Rader; Costumes, Neil Spisak; Lighting, Robert Wierzel, Chris Akerlind; Backdrops, Ethan Johnson; Original Music/Arrangements, Anarchestra; Musical Director, David Robbins; Actors' Gang Producer, Patti McGuire; CAST: Lee "Beef" Arenberg (Cotton Slocum), Ned "Corn Dancer" Bellamy (Deacon Tack), Jack "Flesh" Black (Opie, A-Company Comando, Photographer, Donner child), Cynthia "Mojave" Ettinger (Pristeena, Dana Donner, Reporter), Jeff "V. J." Foster (Jerry, Butcher, Sycophant, Homeless Reject), Kyle "Gassman" Gass (Chip Donner, Henry Henderson, Bob, A-Company Commando, Photographer), Brent "Hink" Hinkley (Ralph), Shannon "Bunny" Holt (Dot), Lisa "Sparrow" Moncure (Tipper Slocum, TV Anchorman, Donner child, Homeless reject, Sycophant), Dean "D-No" Robinson (Phil the War Vet, A-Company Commando, Huckleman, God's Happy Acre Guard), Cari Dean "Miss Clary G." Whittemore (Clare the Cripple, Magpie, Pocahontas)

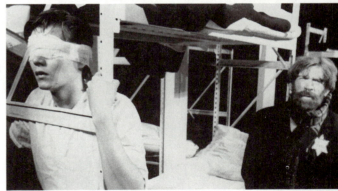

A comedy in two acts. The action takes place in the world of TV evangelism at the present time.

Right Center: Moscow Studio-Theatre's "My Big Land" with Filip Yankovsky, Vladimir Mashkov Above: Cynthia Ettinger, Kyle Gass, Lee Arenberg in "Carnage, A Comedy" Top: Cari Dean Whittemore (c) in "Carnage, A Comedy"

Martha Swope Photos

William R. Morales, Josie Perez, Angel Domenech in "The Great US Kranial Circus" (Festival Latino)

Vladimir Mashkov, Dmitri Stolbtsov in "My Big Land" (Moscow Studio-Theatre)

(Public/Newman Theatre) Tuesday, November 14–December 17, 1989 (6 performances and 46 previews)

ROMANCE IN HARD TIMES with Music, Lyrics & Book by William Finn; Director, David Warren; Choreography, Marcia Milgrom Dodge; Musical Direction/Vocal Arrangements, Ted Sperling; Sets, James Youmans; Costumes, David C. Woolard; Orchestrations, Bruce Coughlin; Lighting, Peter Kaczorowski; Sound, John Kilgore; Projections, Wendall K. Harrington; CAST: Rufus Bonds, Jr. (Harmonizing Fool), Stacey Lynn Brass (Younger Handcuffed Sister), Lawrence Clayton (Harvey), Victor Trent Cook (Kid, Harmonizing Fool), Cleavant Derricks (Boris), Ray Gill (Polly), Peggy Hewett (Eleanor Roosevelt), Alix Korey (Zoe), Michael Mandell (Gus) Amanda Naughton (Older Handcuffed Sister), Melodee Savage (Harmonizing Fool), John Sloman (Babe Ruth/Harmonizing Fool), James Stovall (FDR/Radio Announcer/Harmonizing Fool), Lillias White (Hennie)

MUSICAL NUMBERS: Harvey, Standing in Line, I'll Get out of Here, Harvey Promised to Change the World, Supreme Court Saved from Fire, Red Faces at the Kremlin, Charity Quartet, Lovesong, Eleanor Roosevelt: A Discussion of Soup, I Never Said I Didn't Love You, You Got Me Crazy, That's Enough for Me, Places I Fainted from Hunger/Time Passes, All Fall Down, The Good Times Are Here, Feeling Rich, Hold My Baby Back, Hennie Soup, Thinking About You, I Don't Want to Feel What I Feel, Prosperity Song, A Gaggle of Celebrities, I'll Get You Out of My Life, How Could You Do This to Someone Who Robbed for You?, Blame It on These Times, You Can't Let Romance Die, Gus' Triumph, The Last Can of Hennie Soup, That's Enough For Me Duet, Finale

A musical in two acts. The action takes place in a NYC soup Kitchen during the great depression.

(Public/LuEsther) Tuesday, November 14–December 17, 1989 (16 performances and 41 previews)

UP AGAINST IT with Music & Lyrics by Todd Rundgren; Based on screenplay by Joe Orton; Adapted by Tom Ross; Director, Kenneth Elliott; Orchestrations, Doug Katsaros; Choreography, Jennifer Muller; Musical Director, Tom Fay; Sets, B. T. Whitehill; Costumes, John Glaser; Lighting, Vivien Leone; Sound, John Kilgore; Vocal Arrangements, Mr. Rundgren CAST: Philip Casnoff (Ian McTurk), Alison Fraser (Miss Drumgoole), Roger Bart (Christopher Low), Toni DiBuono (Connie Boon), Judith Cohen (Lilly Corbett/Man in the Hole), Dan Tubb (Ramsay), Tom Aulino (Bernard Coates), Marnie Carmichael (Georgina), Joel McKinnon Miller (Mayor), Mari Nelson (Rowena), Stephen Temperley (Father Brodie/Old Man), Brian Arsenault (Guard), Scott Carollo, Mindy Cooper, Dorothy R. Earle, Julia C. Hughes, Gary Mendelson, Jim Newman

MUSICAL NUMBERS: When Worlds Collide, Parallel Lines, Free, Male and Twenty-One, Smell of Money, If I Have to Be Alone, Up Against It, Life is a Drag, Lilly's Address, You'll Thank Me in the End, Maybe I'm Better Off, From Hunger, Entropy, Finale

A musical in two acts from an unproduced script for the Beatles. The action takes place in a mythical place not unlike England in the 1960's.

(Public/Susan Stein Shiva Theatre) Tuesday, November 21–December 17, 1989 (31 performances)

KATE'S DIARY by Kathleen Tolan; Director, David Greenspan; Sets, William Kennon; Costumes, Elsa Ward; Lighting, David Bergstein; Stage Managers, Diane Hartdagen, Mark McMahon; CAST: Lizbeth Mackay (Kate), Michael Bryan French (Tim/Frank), Laura Hughes (Ellen/Angie/Trish), John Griesemer (Father Hernandez/Walter), Rafael Baez (Pablo)

A drama performed without intermission. The action takes place in NYC in Kate's bedroom and Kate's imagination. The time is the recent past.

Right Center: Lizbeth Mackay, Michael Bryan French in "Kate's Diary" Above: Alison Fraser, Stephen Temperley, Joel McKinnon Miller, Toni DiBuono, Marnie Carmichael, Philip Casnoff, Roger Bart in "Up Against It" Top: Michael Mandell, Peggy Hewett, Victor Trent Cook, Amanda Naughton, Stacey Lynn Brass in "Romance in Hard Times"

Cleavant Derricks, Lillias White in "Romance in Hard Times"

Lizbeth Mackay, Laura Hughes in "Kate's Diary"

NEW YORK SHAKESPEARE FESTIVAL
(continued)

(Public/Martinson Hall) Tuesday, December 5–31, 1989 (13 performances and 18 previews)
KINGFISH by Marlane Meyer; Director, David Schweizer; Sets, Rosario Provenza; Costumes, Susan Nininger; Lighting, Robert Wierzel; Music, Steven Moshier; Projections, Perry Hoberman; Stage Managers, David S. Franklin, J. Michael Stein; CAST: Buch Henry (Wylie), Barry Sherman (Hal), Kevin O'Rourke (Finney), Jacque Lynn Colton (Wanda), Tony Abatemarco (Edward/Mack), Arthur Hanket (Kingfish)

A drama in two acts.

(Public/Anspacher) Tuesday, December 19, 1989–February 4, 1990 (55 performances)
MACBETH by William Shakespeare; Director, Richard Jordan; Sets, John Conklin; Costumes, Jeanne Button; Lighting, Brian Gale; Music, Daniel Schreier; Fights, Peter Nels; Stage Manager, Michael Chambers CAST: Scott Allegrucci (Donalbain/Murderer/Messenger), Daniel Berkey (Soldier), Jesse Bernstein (Macduff's son), Larry Bryggman (Banquo), Reg E. Cathey (Lord/Gentleman), William Converse-Roberts (Captain/Macduff), Joseph Costa (Old Siward/Old Man/Messenger), Peter Jay Fernandez (Lennox), Thomas Gibson (Malcolm), Mark Hammer (Duncan/Doctor), Harriet Harris (Lady Macduff), Katherine Hiller (Witch #3/Messenger), Raul Julia (Macbeth), Rob LaBelle (Soldier), Christopher McHale (Murderer #2/Caithness), Melinda Mullins (Lady Macbeth), Harry S. Murphy (Porter/Menteith), Gabriel Olds (Fleance), Rene Rivera (Murderer #1/Seyton), Stephen Rowe (Angus), Jeanne Sakata (Witch #2), Laura Sametz (Gentlewoman), Matt Bradford Sullivan (Young Siward/Murderer/Servant), Daniel von Bargen (Ross), Mary Louise Wilson (Witch #1/Gentlewoman)

Shakespeare's play in two acts and 22 scenes. The action takes place in Scotland in the Middle Ages. The 12th production in the NYSF Marathon.

(Public/Newman) Tuesday, January 30–February 18, 1990 (24 previews)
ONE OF THE GUYS by Marilyn Suzanne Miller; Director, Arthur Penn; Sets, Loren Sherman; Costumes, Ruth Morley; Lighting, Richard Nelson; Stage Manager, Susie Cordon; Fights, B. H. Barry CAST: Stephen Collins (Joe), Wayne Knight (Art), Bruce MacVittie (Des), Vyto Ruginis (Alan), Ben Siegler (Denny), Don R. McManus (Will), Paul J. Q. Lee (Delivery Man), Kathleen McNenny (Chrissie)

A drama performed without intermission. The action takes place in NYC in the recent past.

(Public/Martinson Hall) Tuesday, Feb. 13–Mar. 25, 1990 (48 performances)
JONAH; Adapted, Composed and Directed by Elizabeth Swados; Choreography/Musical Staging, Bill Castellino; Sets, Michael E. Downs; Costumes, Judy Dearing; Lighting, Beverly Emmons; Whale Design, Tobi Kahn; Musical Director, Michael S. Sottile CAST: Jake Ehrenreich (Jonah), Cathy Porter (Jonettes/Phyllis/Others), Ann Marie Milazzo (Marguarita Jonette), Paul O'Keefe, Michael S. Sottile (Musicians)

A musical adaptation of "Jonah and the Whale" by Robert Nathan. This is the fifth biblical cantata Ms. Swados has written.

(Public/Shiva) Wednesday, Feb. 28–Apr. 22, 1990 (63 performances)
A MOM'S LIFE by Kathryn Grody; Director, Timothy Near; Sets, James Youmans; Costumes, Holland Vose; Lighting, Phil Monat CAST: Kathryn Grody

A solo performance detailing one day in the life of a Manhattan mother.

Top Right: Raul Julia, Melinda Mullins in "Macbeth" Below: Stephen Collins, Bruce MacVittie, Wayne Knight in "One of the Guys"

Kathryn Grody in "A Mom's Life"

(Public/Anspacher Theater) Tuesday, April 10–June 3, 1990 (63 performances)
HAMLET by William Shakespeare; Director, Kevin Kline; Sets, Robin Wagner; Costumes, Martin Pakledinaz; Lighting, Jules Fisher; Music, Bob James; Fights, B. H. Barry CAST: Rene Rivera (Bernardo/Lucianus), MacIntyre Dixon (Francisco/Gravedigger/Prologue), Peter Francis James (Horatio), Bill Camp (Marcellus/Lord/Sailor), Brian Murray (Claudius), Miguel Perez (Voltemand/Messenger), Michael Cumpsty (Laertes), Kevin Kline (Hamlet), Dana Ivey (Gertrude), Diane Venora (Ophelia), Josef Sommer (Polonius), Robert Murch (Ghost of Hamlet's Father/Priest), Leo Burmester (Osric/Lord), Philip Goodwin (Rosencrantz), Reg E. Cathey (Guildenstern), Clement Fowler (Player King), Susan Gabriel (Player Queen/Lady-in-Waiting), Don Reilly (Fortinbras), Larry Green (Norwegian Captain/Guard/Servant), Erik Knutsen (Messenger/Servant/Lord), Claire Beckman (Player/Lady-in-Waiting), Curt Hostetter (Lord/Pallbearer)

The 13th production in the Shakespeare Marathon. Presented with one intermission and one pause. Mr. Kline played Hamlet in the 1985 NYSF production (Theatre World Vol. 42).

(Public/Martinsen Hall) Tuesday, April 10–September 2, 1990 (165 performances)
SPUNK: THREE TALES BY ZORA NEALE HURSTON; Adapted & Directed by George C. Wolfe; Music, Chic Street Man; Choreography, Hope Clarke; Sets, Loy Arcenas; Costumes, Toni-Leslie James; Lighting, Don Holder; Masks/Puppets, Barbara Pollitt; Stage Manager, Jacqui Casto; Produced in association with Crossroads Theatre CAST: Ann Duquesnay (Blues Speak Woman/Voice Two/Voice Joe Clark/Mother), K. Todd Freeman (Man Two/Jelly/Voice Three/Clerk), Kevin Jackson (Joe/Slang Talk Man/Man One), Reggie Montgomery (Sykes/Sweetback/Voice One), Chic Street Man (Guitar Man), Danitra Vance (Delia/Girl/Missy May)

Three short stories in two acts. The action takes place Way down nearby round about long 'go.

(Public/Newman) Tuesday, April 17–June 3, 1990 (56 performances)
ICE CREAM with HOT FUDGE by Caryl Churchill; Director, Les Waters; Sets/Costumes, Annie Smart; Lighting, Stephen Strawbridge; Fights, B. H. Barry HOT FUDGE CAST: Margaret Whitton (Ruby), John Pankow (Colin), Jane Kaczmarek (June/Grace), James Rebhorn (Charlie/Jerry), Julianne Moore (Sonia/Lena), Robert Knepper (Matt/Hugh) ICE CREAM CAST: James Rebhorn (Lance), Jane Kaczmarek (Vera), Robert Knepper (Phil), Julianne Moore (Jaq), John Pankow (Man in Devon/Shrink/Colleague/Fellow Guest/Hitcher/Professor), Margaret Whitton (Drunk Woman/Hitcher's Mother/South American Woman Passenger)

Two one-act social comedies. HOT FUDGE is a series of vignettes during one evening in a pub and winebar. ICE CREAM looks at American tourists in the U.K. during summertime in the late eighties.

NEW YORK THEATRE WORKSHOP

Seventh Season

Artistic Director, James C. Nicola; Managing Director, Nancy Kassak Diekmann; Associate Artistic Director, Morgan Jenness; Dramaturg, Nina Mankin; Production Manager, George Xenos; Technical Director, Patrick Hydenburg; Wardrobe, Alison Foley; Press, Gary Murphy, Belinda Miller

(Perry Street Theatre) Saturday, December 2, 1989–January 14, 1990 (45 performances)
MY CHILDREN! MY AFRICA!; Written & Directed by Athol Fugard; Sets/Costumes, Susan Hilferty; Lighting, Dennis Parichy; Sound, Mark Bennett; Associate Director, Susan Hilferty; Stage Manager, Mary Michele Miner; CAST: John Kani (Mr. M), Lisa Fugard (Isabel Dyson), Courtney B. Vance (Thami Mbikwana)
A drama in two acts. The action takes place in a small Eastern Cape Karoo town in the fall of 1984.

Friday, January 26–February 24, 1990 (30 performances)
A FOREST IN ARDEN by Christopher Grabowski; Adapted from Shakespeare's "As You Like It"; Director, Mr. Grabowski; Sets, Tom Kamm; Costumes, Claudia Brown; Lighting, Pat Dignan; Composer/Sound, Scott Killian; Stage Manager, Liz Small; CAST: Fanni Green (Fool/Oliver), Michael James-Reed (Orlando), Susan Knight (Celia/Aliena), Michael Liani (Rosalind/Ganymede)
An adaptation of "As You Like It" focusing on gender and sexual identity.

Friday, Apr. 27–June 2, 1990 (37 performances)
THE WAVES by David Bucknam and Lisa Peterson, adapted from the novel by Virginia Woolf; Music/Additional Lyrics, David Bucknam; Musical Director/Orchestrations, Helen Gregory; Set, Randy Benjamin; Costumes, Michael Krass; Lighting, Brian MacDevitt; Sound, Bruce A. Kraemer; Director, Lisa Peterson; Choreographer, Marcia Milgrom Dodge; Text and Dialect Coach, Robert Neff Williams; Casting, Simon/Kumin Casting; Stage Manager, Liz Small; CAST: Catherine Cox (Rhoda), Diane Fratantoni (Jinny), Aloysius Gigl (Neville), John Jellison (Louis), Sarah Rice (Susan), John Sloman (Bernard)
A musical in two acts. The action takes place in Edwardian England.

Gerry Goodstein Photos

Top: Kevin Kline, Dana Ivey in "Hamlet"
Below: Peter Francis James, Kevin Kline in "Hamlet"

Below: John Kani, Courtney Vance in "My Africa"

Reggie Montgomery, Ann Duquesnay, K. Todd Freeman, Kevin Jackson, Danitra Vance in "Spunk" Above: Kevin Kline, Dana Ivey, Brian Murray, Michael Cumpsty in "Hamlet"

(front) Michael James-Reed, Michael Liani, (back) Fanni Green, Susan Knight in "A Forest in Arden"

91

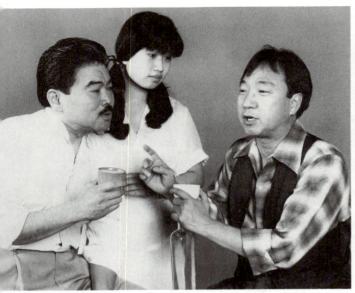

Norris Shimabuku, Yuko Komiyama in "And the Soul Shall Dance" Right: Dennis Dun, Anne M. Tauji, Stan Egi in "F.O.B."

PAN ASIAN REPERTORY THEATRE

Thirteenth Season

Artistic/Producing Director, Tisa Chang; Producing Associate, Dominick Balletta; Artistic Associates, Ernest Abuba, Raul Aranas, Ron Nakahara; Audience Development, John Q. Jiang; Business Associate, Gladys Lai; House Manager, Don Wong, Jonathan Lee; Administrative Assistant, Diana Namkoong; Community Liason, Chia Lin Chien; Graphic Designer, Sokie Lee; Press, Peter Cromarty/Cromarty & Co.

(Playhouse 46) Tuesday, November 7–December 2, 1989 (18 performances and 6 previews)
THE SONG OF SHIM CHUNG by Terence Cranendonk in collaboration with Du-Yee Chang; Conceived & Directed by Du-Yee Chang; Music, Du-Yee Chang; Costumes, James Livingston; Lighting, Victor En Yu Tan; Set/Masks/Puppets, Atsushi Moriyasu; Stage Manager, Sue Jane Stoker CAST: Ernest Abuba (Village Bum), June Angela (Shim Chung), Mia Katigbak (Mama Setong), Mary Lee (Shim's Wife), Donald Li (Bird), William Lucas (Young Man), Norris M. Shimabuku (Blind Shim), Steve Park, Shigeko, Tsuyu Shimizu, Christen Villamor (Villagers & Fishermen)
A world premiere music-theatre version of a Korean folktale. The action takes place in Korea during ancient times.

(Apple Corps Theatre) Tuesday, March 20–April 7, 1990 (18 performances)
AND THE SOUL SHALL DANCE by Wakako Yamauchi; Director, Kati Kuroda; Lighting, Tina Charney; Costumes, Toni-Leslie James; Sets, Robert Klingelhoefer; Stage Manager, David H. Bosboom CAST: Carol A. Honda (Hana Murata), Ron Nakahara (Murata), Roxanne Chang (Masako), Norris M. Shimabuku (Oka), Dawn A. Saito (Emiko Oka), Yuko Komiyama (Kiyoko)
A drama in two acts. The action takes place in California in the depression era.

(Playhouse 46) Tuesday, May 8–June 2, 1990 (16 performances and 7 previews)
F.O.B.; Director/Playwright, David Henry Hwang; Set, Alex Poiner; Lighting, Victor En Yu Tan; Costumes, Eiko Yamaguchi; Choreographer, Jamie H. J. Guan; Composer/Musician, Lucia Hwong; Sound, Robert Barnes; Arranger/Musician, Yukio Tsuji; Stage Manager, Sue Jane Stoker. CAST: Stan Egi (Dale), Ann M. Tsuji (Grace), Dennis Dun (Steve).
A play in two acts. The action takes place in the back room of a small Chinese restaurant in Torrance, California.

Martha Swope Photos

William Lucas, June Angela, Donald Li in "The Song of Shim Chung"

THE PEARL THEATRE COMPANY

Sixth Season

Artistic Director, Shepard Sobel; General Manager, Mary L. Hurd, Artistic Associate, Joanne Camp; Dramaturge, Dale Ramsey; Development, Steven Somkin, James van Maanen; Assistant Production Manager, Jennifer E. Boggs; Editor, Art Mortensen; Galas, Jay Philip Klampert; Press, Mary-Stewart Lawson, Elizabeth L. Henry, Fluffy Abry
RESIDENT COMPANY: Robin Leslie Brown, Joanne Camp, Frank Geraci, Stuart Lerch, Michael John McGuinness, Anna Minot, James Nugent, Laura Rathgeb, Joseph Warren, Donnah Welby

Saturday, October 7–November 4, 1989 (24 performances)
A MIDSUMMER NIGHT'S DREAM by William Shakespeare; Director, Shepard Sobel; Sets, Robert Joel Schwartz; Lighting, Douglas O'Flaherty; Costumes, Phillip Contic; Sound, Richard L. Sirois; Choreography, Alice Teirstein; Music, Thom Tilney; Stage Manager, Judith Sostek CAST: Frank Geraci (Theseus/Oberon), Robin Leslie Brown (Hippolyta/Titania), Dugg Smith (Egeus/Quince), Donnah Welby (Hermia), Michael John McGuinness (Lysander), Stuart Lerch (Demetrius), Joanne Camp (Helena), James Nugent (Bottom), Richard Hart (Flute/Peaseblossom), Eric Walstedt (Starveling/Mustardseed), John Will (Snout/Moth), Andrew W. Sellon (Snug/Cobweb), Laura Rathgeb (Puck/Philostrate)

Saturday, November 11–December 9, 1989 (24 performances)
THE THREE SISTERS by Anton Chekhov; Translation, Earle Edgerton; Director, Allan Carlsen; Sets, Robert Joel Schwartz; Lighting, Douglas O'Flaherty; Costumes, Barbara A. Bell; CAST: Michael John McGuinness (Andrei), Robin Leslie Brown (Natalya), Donnah Welby (Olga), Joanne Camp (Masha), Laura Rathgeb (Irina), James Nugent (Kulygin), Stuart Lerch (Vershinin), Kurt Ziskie (Tuzenbach), Kevin Hogan (Solyony), Frank Geraci (Chebutykin), Sylvia Davis, James Gene Di Zazzo 2d, Paul Lima, Joseph Warren

Saturday, December 16, 1989–January 13, 1990 (24 performances)
THE SCHOOL FOR WIVES by Moliere; Translation, Earle Edgerton; Director, Joel Bernstein; Sets, Robert Joel Schwartz; Lighting, Douglas O'Flaherty; Costumes, Barbara A. Bell CAST: Stuart Lerch (Chrysalde), James Nugent (Arnolphe), Richard Hart (Alain), Joanne Camp (Georgette), Robin Leslie Brown (Agnes), Kevin Hogan (Horace), Miller Lide (Notary/Oronte)

Saturday, Jan. 20–Feb. 17, 1990 (24 performances)
MEDEA by Euripides; Translation, E. P. Coleridge; Director, Shepard Sobel; Stage Manager, William Ellis; Sets, Robert Joel Schwartz; Lighting, Stephen Petrilli; Costumes, Barbara A. Bell; Choreography, Alice Teirstein; Technical, Richard A. Kendrick; CAST: Sylvia Davis (Nurse), Frank Geraci (Tutor/Creon/Aegeus/Messenger), Joanne Camp (Medea), Erin Martin (Choragos), Michael John McGuinness (Jason), Lisa Goodman, Laura Rathgeb (Corinthian Women/Sons)

Saturday, February 24–March 24, 1990 (24 performances)
THE IMPORTANCE OF BEING EARNEST by Oscar Wilde; Director, Anthony Cornish; Sets, Robert Joel Schwartz; Lighting, Stephen Petrilli; Costumes, Barbara A. Bell; Technical, Richard A. Kendrick; Stage Managers, Jennifer E. Boggs, Jillian Ramirez; Props, David Johnson; Sound, Arthur C. Mortensen; Pianist, Stephen J. Schaffer CAST: Michael John McGuinness (Algernon), K. Bruce Harpster (Lane), Stuart Lerch (John Worthing), Margaret Hilton (Lady Bracknell), Donnah Welby (Gwendolen), Laura Rathgeb (Cecily), Joanne Camp (Miss Prism), Frank Geraci (Chasuble), K. Bruce Harpster (Merriman)
Wilde's comedy in three acts. The action takes place in London and Hertfordshire in the late 1890's.

Saturday, March 31–April 15, 1990 (16 performances) E. James Mahanna presents:
DANCE WITH ME by Stephen Temperley; Director, Vivan Matalon; Sets, David Potts; Lighting, Richard Nelson; Costumes, David Loveless; Stage Manager, Harold Goldfaden; Press, Chris Boneau/Eva Patton CAST: David Bulasky (Talbot), Gregory Salata (Jack), Didi Sinclair (Daisy), Amy Van Nostrand (Sally), Carl Wallnau (Waiter)
A comedy in two acts. The action takes place in NYC one year ago and now.

Martha Swope/Carol Rosegg Photos

Right Center: Laura Rethgeb, Donnah Welby, Joanne Camp in "The Three Sisters" Above: Joanne Camp, Frank Geraci in "Medea" Top: James Nugent, Robin Leslie Brown in "A Midsummer Night's Dream"

David Bulasky, Didi Sinclair, Gregory Salata, Amy van Nostrand in "Dance with Me"

PLAYWRIGHTS HORIZONS

Eighteenth Season

Artistic Director, Andre Bishop; Executive Director, Paul S. Daniels; Production Manager, Carl Mulert; Development, Ruth Cohen; Casting, Daniel Swee; Literary Manager, Tim Sanford; Technical Director, Joshua Alemany; Props, Denise Grille; Press, Philip Rinaldi, Dennis Crowley

(Playwrights Horizons) Wednesday, June 6–18, 1989 (14 performances) Playwrights Horizons New Theatre Wing presents:
KATE'S DIARY by Kathleen Tolan; Director, David Greenspan; Sets, William Kennon; Costumes, Elsa Ward; Lighting, David Bergstein; Sound, John Gromada; Stage Manager, Diane Hartdagen; CAST: Rafael Baez, Michael French, John Griesemer, Laura Hughes, Lizbeth Mackay.

A dark comedy.

(Playwrights Horizons/Studio) Wednesday July 17–29, 1989 (14 performances) Playwrights Horizons' New Theatre Wing, in association with Portland Opera presents:
LUCY'S LAPSES with Music by Christopher Drobny, Libretto, Laura Harrington; Direction, David Warren; Choreography, John Carrafa; Musical Direction, Paulette Haupt; Sets, James Youmans; Costumes, David C. Woolard; Lighting, Debra Dumas; Sound, John Kilgore; Program Director, Ira Weitzman; Stage Manager, Eric Osbun; CAST: Rita Gardner, Robert Duncan McNeill, Lynette Perry, Jamie Ross

An Absurdist musical on the onset of Alzheimer's disease in a vibrant mother and the effects on her family.

(Playwrights Horizons) Tuesday, September 12–October 8 (30 performances) The Foundation of the Dramatists Guild presents:
THE 1989 YOUNG PLAYWRIGHTS FESTIVAL: Producing Director, Nancy Quinn; Managing Director, Sheri M. Goldhirsch; Sets, Allen Moyer; Costumes, Jess Goldstein; Lighting, Karl E. Haas; Sound, Janet Kalas; Manager, Carl Mulert; Stage Manager, Mimi Apfel, James Fitz-Simmons, Jeanne Fornadel; Press, Shirley Herz/Sam Rudy

Painted Rain by Janet Allard; Director, Mary B. Robinson; Advisor, Morgan Jenness CAST: Kimble Joyner (Teddy), Christopher Shaw (Dustin), Debra Monk (Barbara)
Finnegan's Funeral Parlor and Ice Cream Shoppe by Robert Kerr; Director, Thomas Babe; Advisor, Christopher Durang CAST: David Barry Gray (Kevin), James McDonnell (Arthur), David Eigenberg (Anvil), Debra Monk (Mona), Jill Tasker (Pamela), Allison Dean (Carol), Mary Testa (Mrs. Dewey)
Twice Shy by Debra Neff; Director, Mark Brokaw; Advisor, Morgan Jenness CAST: Ray Cochran (Jonathan), Katherine Hiler (Louise), David Lansbury (Desmond), Mark W. Conklin (Steven), Lauren Klein (Cookie)
Peter Breaks Through by Alejandro Membreno; Director, Thomas Babe; Advisor, Albert Innaurato CAST: Mary Testa (Mona), James McDonnell (Guido), Ray Cochran (Peter)
Readings: A Night With Doris by Stephanie Brown; Director, Thomas Babe
And One Bell Shattered by Karen Hartman; Director, Lisa Peterson
Hat by Gilbert David Feke; Director, R. J. Cutler

The annual series, initiated by Stephen Sondheim, featuring plays by writers under the age of nineteen.

(American Place Theatre) Tuesday, October 24–December 10, 1989 (54 performances) Playwrights Horizons and American Playhouse Theatre Productions present:
HYDE IN HOLLYWOOD by Peter Parnell; Director, Gerald Gutierrez; Sets, Douglas Stein; Costumes, Ann Hould-Ward; Lighting, Frances Aronson; Sound, Scott Lehrer; Projections, Wendall K. Harrington; Fights, David Leong; Music, Robert Waldman; Stage Managers, Peter B. Mumford, Kate Riddle; CAST: Robert Joy (Julian Hyde), Keith Szarabajka (Hollywood Confidential), Stephen Pearlman (Charles Hock), Peter Frechette (Jake Singer), Robert Curtis-Brown (David Hogarth), Fran Brill (Betty Armstrong), Julie Boyd (Lida Todd/Susan), Derek D. Smith (Reynaldo Romero), Kurt Deutsch (Bookie/Andrew/Florist), Matthew Locricchio (Buddy/Art Director/Audio Man), Herbert Rubens (Harry Slezak/Rex Markum/Sugie Sugerman/Senator), Theresa McElwee (Movie Star/Costume Designer/Faye Norris/Film Actress/Studio Secretary), Kenneth L. Marks (Ricardo/Ensemble), Richard Topol (Martin/Ensemble), Ed Mahler (Lead Film Crew), Thomas Eldon, Thia Gartner, Rob Richards (Reporters/Film Crew/Extras)

A drama in two acts. The action takes place in and around the lot of Hock International Pictures and neighboring Hollywood. The time runs from 1932–1957.

Tuesday, January 30–March 24, 1990 (62 performances)
WHEN SHE DANCED by Martin Sherman; Director, Tim Luscombe; Sets, Steven Rubin; Costumes, Jess Goldstein; Lighting, Nancy Schertler; Music/Sound, John Gromada; Choreography, Peter Anastos; Stage Manager, Roy Harris; CAST: Elizabeth Ashley (Isadora), Robert Sean Leonard (Alexandros), Jonathan Walker (Sergei), Jacqueline Bertrand (Jeanne), Marcia Lewis (Mary), Marcia Jean Kurtz (Miss Belzer), Robert Dorfman (Luciano), Clea Montville (Christine)

A drama in two acts exploring one day in the life of Isadora Duncan. The action takes place in a house on the Rue de la Pompe, Paris in 1923.

Top Right: Keith Szarabajka, Robert Joy in "Hyde in Hollywood," Below: Robert Sean Leonard, Elizabeth Ashley

Wednesday, March 14–25, 1990 (14 performances)
SUBFERTILE by Tom Mardirosian; Director, John Ferraro; Sets, Rick Dennis; Costumes, Abigail Murray; Lighting, Brian MacDevitt; Sound, Frederick Wessler; Stage Manager, Karen Armstrong CAST: Richard Council, Kitty Crooks, Susan Knight, Tom Mardirosian, Fredrica Meister

A comedy taking place in the Museum of Natural History.

Friday, April 6–May 27, 1990 (60 performances)
ONCE ON THIS ISLAND with Music by Stephen Flaherty; Book/Lyrics, Lynn Ahrens; Based on the novel "My Love, My Love" by Rosa Guy; Director/Choreographer, Graciela Daniele; Orchestrations, Michael Starobin; Musical Director, Steve Marzullo; Sets, Loy Arcenas; Costumes, Judy Dearing; Lighting, Allen Lee Hughes; Sound, Scott Lehrer; Musical Theatre Director, Ira Weitzman; Stage Manager, Leslie Loeb; Produced in association with AT&T Onstage CAST: Jerry Dixon (Daniel), Andrea Frierson (Erzulie, Goddess of Love), Sheila Gibbs (Mama Euralie), La Chanze (Ti Moune), Kecia Lewis-Evans (Asaka, Mother of Earth), Afi McClendon (Little Ti Moune), Gerry McIntyre (Armand), Milton Craig Nealy (Agwe, God of Water), Nikki Rene (Andrea), Eric Riley (Papa Ge, Demon of Death), Ellis E. Williams (Tonton Julian)
MUSICAL NUMBERS: We Dance, One Small Girl, Waiting for Life, And the Gods Heard Her Prayer, Rain, Pray, Forever Yours, Sad Tale of the Beauxhommes, Ti Moune, Mama Will Provide, Some Say, The Human Heart, Some Girls, The Ball, A Part of Us, Why We Tell the Story

A musical performed without intermission. The action takes place on an island in the French Antilles at night, during a storm.

"Once on This Island"
Martha Swope Photos

PRIMARY STAGES

Fifth Season

Artistic Director, Casey Childs; Associate Artistic Director, Janet Reed; Associate Producer, Herbert H. O'Dell; Public Relations, Anne Einhorn; General Manager, Gordon Farrell; Press, Literary Manager, Seth Gordon; Press, Shirley Herz Associates/Miller Wright

(Primary Stages 45th St. Theatre) Friday, September 15–October 7, 1989 (17 performances and 8 previews)
HOLLYWOOD SCHEHERAZADE by Charlie Peters; Director, Gregory Lehane; Sets, Herbert H. O'Dell; Lighting, Deborah Constantine; Costumes, Claudia Stephens; Composer/Sound Design, Michael Keck; Stage Managers, Greg Weiss, Tony Luna; Casting, Cindy Storm Segal; Associate Producer, Herbert H. O'Dell; General Manager, Gordon Farrell; Public Relations, Anne Einhorn; CAST: Daniel Ahearn (Peter Fortune), Herbert Rubens (Morley Waxman), Tom McBride (Boyd), Robert Verlaque (Jurgen Sallow), Jennifer Ashe (Darla Freehandle), Christopher Randolph (Prole), Cynthia Mace (Telia)
A comedy set in 1940's Hollywood.

Tuesday, November 21–Dec 9, 1989 (16 performances and 4 previews)
BLACK MARKET by Joe Sutton; Director, Scott Rubsam; Design, Sally Plass, Deborah Scott; Lighting, Bill Simmons; Assistant Director, Angela Foster; Stage Manager, Tony Luna; CAST: Elaine Rinehart (JoAnn), Bruce McCarty (Hatch), Charlotte Colavin (Rosie), Christopher McCann (Bijan)
A drama in two acts. The action takes place in and around the Hell's Kitchen area of Manhattan at the present.

Friday, February 16–March 17, 1990 (24 performances)
BOVVER BOYS by Willy Holtzman; Director, John Pynchon Holms; Sets, Philipp Jung; Lighting, Mary Louise Geiger; Costumes, Ellen McCartney; Sound, Tom Gould; Combat, Jake Turner; Associate Producer, Herbert H. O'Dell; General Manager, Gordon Farrell; Public Relations, Anne Einhorn; CAST: Jack Gwaltney (Allie), John Plumpis (Jack), Robert Kerbeck (Gene), Leigh Dillon (Joyce), Keith Lansdale (John), Holt McCallany (Ennis), Michael Lewis (Chick), Calista Flockhart (Christine)
A drama in two acts. The action takes place in a tenement development in Dundee, Scotland during the summer of 1970.

Martha Swope/Carol Rosegg Photos

Jack Gwaltney, Calista Flockhart, Holt McCallany, Robert Kerbeck Top: McCallany, Gwaltney, Keith Langsdale in "Bovver Boys"

Christopher McCann, Bruce McCarty, Elaine Rinehart Above: Bruce McCarty, Charlotte Colavin in "Black Market"

Daniel Ahearn, Jennifer Ashe in "Hollywood Scheherazade"

Jack Landron, Marta Vidal in "I Am a Winner!" Right: Jimmy Borbon, Edouard DeSoto in "Spanish Eyes" Below: Denia Brache, Candace Brecker, Machiste in "Ariano"

PUERTO RICAN TRAVELING THEATRE

Twenty-third Season

Artistic Director/Founder, Miriam Colon Valle; Managing Director, Nicki Genovese; Development, Vera Ryan; Technical Director, Ed Bartosik; Press, Max Eisen, Madelon Rosen Solomon

(Puerto Rican Traveling Theatre/Lincoln Center Outdoors) Wednesday August 9–31, 1959 (23 performances)
THE CHINESE CHARADE; Music, Sergio Garcia Marruz, Saul Spangenberg; Lyrics, Emilia Conde, Anita Velez; Book, Manuel Pereiras; Director, Susana Tubert; Choreography, Poli Rogers; Sets, Robert Klingelhoefer; Costumes, Steve Pardee; Sound, Gary Harris; CAST: Cinta Cruz, Eileen Galindo, Bonnie Diaz, Jack Landron, Jorge Oliver.
A musical about the American dream and a lottery, set in present day NYC.

Friday, Jan. 19–Feb. 25, 1990 (36 performances)
ARIANO by Richard V. Irizarry; Director, Vicente Castro; Producer, Miriam Colon Valle; Translation, Margarita Lopez Chiclana; Sets, James Sandefur; Costumes, Toni-Leslie James; Lighting, Spencer S. Brown; Sound, Garry & Timmy Harris; Design, Rachel Budin; Stage Manager, Sandra M. Bloom; CAST: Machiste (Ariano/English performances), Jose Rey (Ariano/Spanish performances), Graciela Lecube (Dona Aida), Angel Salazar (Soldier), Denia Brache (Dolores), Jimmy Borbon (Serafin), Eileen Galindo (Clara), Candace Brecker (Crystal)
A drama in 2 acts and seven scenes. The action takes place in NYC at present. Performances given in English and Spanish.

Wednesday, March 14–April 22, 1990 (36 performances)
I AM A WINNER by Fred Valle; Director, Melia Bensussen; Sets, Carl Baldasso; Lighting, Bill Simmons; Costumes, Mary Marsicano; Sound, Hector Melia; Stage Manager, Roger Franklin CAST: Jose Rey (Arturo), Marta Vidal (Carmela), Jorge Luis Abreu (Hector), Jack Landron (Tony), Joseph Jamrog, James Hunt (Cops)
A comedy performed on rotating nights in English and Spanish.

Wednesday, May 9–June 17, 1990 (36 performances)
SPANISH EYES by Eduardo Iván López; Translation, Graciela Lecube; Director, Roger Franklin; Sets, Robert Klingelhoefer; Lighting, Bill Simmons; Costumes, Mary Marsicano; Sound, Héctor Milia; CAST: Eddie Andino (Esteban Salazar), Jimmy Borbón (Young Esteban), Edouard de Soto (Abuelo), Alexandra Reichler (Myra), Christofer de Oni (Francisco/Foreman/Priest/Sleazak/Dr./Andre Ramirez)

Peter Krupenye Photos

Jose Rey, Marta Vidal in "I Am a Winner!"

ROUNDABOUT THEATRE

Twenty-fourth Season

Artistic Director, Gene Feist; Producing Director, Todd Haimes; General Manager, Ellen Richard; Business Manager, Ellen Scrimger Gordon; Literary Manager, Mark A. Michaels; Technical Director, John A. Kincaid; Props, Janet E. Smith; Wardrobe, Julie Alderfer; Stage Managers, Kathy J. Faul, Roy W. Backes; Press, Joshua Ellis Office/Adrian Bryan-Brown, Jackie Green, Susanne Tighe, Tim Ray, Chris Boneau

(Roundabout Theatre) Wednesday, July 26–September 30, 1989 (94 performances)
PRIVATES ON PARADE with Book & Lyrics by Peter Nichols; Music, Denis King; Director, Larry Carpenter; Musical Director, Philip Campanella; Choreography, Daniel Pelzig; Sets, Loren Sherman; Costumes, Lindsay W. Davis; Lighting, Marcia Madeira; Sound, Robert E. Casey, Eric Santaniello; Dialects, Howard Samuelsohn; CAST: Jim Dale (Terri Dennis), Simon Jones (Giles Flack), Ross Bickell (Len Bonny), Donald Burton (Reg Drummond), John Curry (Charles Bishop), Jim Fyfe (Steven Flowers), Edward Hibbert (Eric Young-Love), Gregory Jbara (Kevin Cartwright), Stephen Lee (Cheng), Tom Matsusaka (Lee), Donna Murphy (Sylvia Morgan)
MUSICAL NUMBERS: S.A.D.U.S.E.A., Les Girls, Danke Schon, Western Approaches Ballet, Little Things We Used To Do, Black Velvet, Prince of Peace, Could You Please Inform Us, Privates On Parade, Latin American Way, Sunnyside Lane
A musical play in two acts. The action takes place in Singapore and Malaya in 1948.

Wednesday, Oct. 25, 1989–Dec. 10, 1989. (64 performances)
THE TEMPEST by William Shakespeare; Director, Jude Kelly; Sets, Franco Colavecchia; Costumes, Lindsay W. Davis; Lighting, Dennis Parichy; Music, Michael Ward; Sound, Eric Santaniello; Casting, Pat McCorkle; Stage Manager, Roy W. Backes; Assistant Director, Michael Birch; CAST: Evan O'Meara (A Boatswain), Craig Wroe (Master of a Ship), Jack Ryland (Alonso, King of Naples), Rocco Sisto (Antonio, the usurping Duke of Milan), Gabriel Barre (Sebastian, Alonso's Brother), Robert Stattel (Gonzalo, a counsellor), John Wittenbauer (Ferdinand, Alonso's son), Erik Knutsen (Adrian, a Lord), Angela Sherrill (Miranda, Prospero's Daughter), Frank Langella (Prospero, the rightful Duke of Milan), B. D. Wong (Ariel, a spirit), Jay Patterson (Caliban, a half-monster), Michael Countryman (Trinculo, a jester), Michaeljohn McGann (Stephano, a butler), Vincent Dopulos, Ed Hart, Jason MacDonald, Jack Smith, Dave Spaulding, Buddy Stoccardo (Sailors, spirits, goddesses).
A play presented in two acts

Wednesday, January 3–February 18, 1990 (53 performances)
THE DOCTOR'S DILEMMA by George Bernard Shaw; Director, Larry Carpenter; Sets, Campbell Baird; Costumes, John Falabella; Lighting, Jason Kantrowitz; Sound, Philip Campanella; CAST: Adam Redfield (Redpenny/Mr. Danby), Avril Gentiles (Emmy), Charles Keating (Sir Colenso Ridgeon), Victor Raider-Wexler (Leo Schutzmacher), George Hall (Sir Patrick Cullen), Ian Stuart (Cutler Walpole), Jerome Kilty (Sir Ralph Bloomfield Bonington B.B.), Gregg Almquist (Dr. Blenkinsop), Anne Newhall (Jennifer Dubedat), Graham Winton (Louis Dubedat), Cate McNider (Minnie Tinwell), Adam LeFevre (Newpaper Man)
Shaw's comedy in two acts and 5 scenes. The action takes place in and around London in 1903.

Wednesday, March 14–May 13, 1990 (70 performances)
THE CRUCIBLE by Arthur Miller; Director, Gerald Freedman; Sets, Christopher H. Barreca; Costumes, Jeanne Button; Lighting, Mary Jo Dondlinger; Sound, Philip Campanella; CAST: Noble Shropshire (Parris), Julia Gibson (Betty Parris), Hazel J. Medina (Tituba), Justine Bateman (Abagail Williams), Maria Deasy (Susanna Walcott), Kathleen Chalfant (Mrs. Ann Putnam), Joseph Costa (Thomas Putnam), Valorie Hubbard (Mercy Lewis), Vicki Lewis (Mary Warren), Randle Mell (John Proctor), Ruth Nelson (Rebecca Nurse), William Leach (Rev. Hale), Harriet Harris (Elizabeth Proctor), George Hall (Francis Nurse), Frank Muller (Ezekiel Cheever), Scott Cohen (Marshal Herrick), Robert Donley (Judge Hathorne), Neil Vipond (Deputy Gov. Danforth), Deedy Lederer (Sarah Good), Joe Ambrose (Hopkin's)
Miller's drama in two acts and 4 scenes. The action takes place in Salem Village, Massachusetts in 1692. For original production see Theatre World Vol. 9.

Wednesday, May 23–July 8, 1990 (31 performances)
PRICE OF FAME by Charles Grodin; Director, Gloria Muzio; Sets, David Jenkins; Costumes, Jess Goldstein; Lighting, Tharon Musser; Sound, Philip Campanella; Stage Manager, Kathy J. Faul CAST: Charles Grodin (Roger), W. J. Paterson (Pete), Jace Alexander (Matt), Joseph R. Sicari (Mario), Lizbeth Mackay (Karen), Jeannie Berlin (Evelyn), Michael Ingram (Cappy), Sam Groom (Bob)
A comedy in two acts. The action takes place in a movie star's motor home dressing room in Hollywood, at present.

Carol Rosegg/Martha Swope Photos

Right Center: Justine Bateman and cast of "The Crucible" Above: (center) B. D. Wong, Frank Langella in "The Tempest" Top: Jim Dale (c) and cast of "Privates on Parade"

Lizbeth Mackay, Charles Grodin, Sam Groom in "Price of Fame"
Susan Cook Photos

SECOND STAGE

Eleventh Season

Artistic Directors, Robyn Goodman, Carole Rothman; Managing Director, Dorothy J. Maffel; Dramaturg, Jim Lewis; Casting, Simon & Kumin; Sound, Gary Harris; Production Manager, Carol Fishman; Development, Robin L. Drummond; Press, Richard Kornberg

Monday July 10–August 13, 1989 (19 performances and 17 previews)
SHIMMER by John O'Keefe; Lighting, James Cave; Stage Manager, Edward Phillips; CAST: John O'Keefe
A 1 man play in one act telling the story of the flight of two adolescent boys from a Midwestern reformatory.

Tuesday, October 31–December 10, 1989 (44 performances)
BABA GOYA by Steve Tesich; Director, Harris Yulin; Sets, Tom Kamm; Lighting, Mal Sturchio; Costumes, Candice Donnelly; Sound, Gary and Timmy Harris; Hair, Antonio Soddu; Stage Managers, Camille Calman, Edward Phillips; Press, Richard Kornberg CAST: Estelle Parsons (Goya), Jack Wallace (Mario), David Clarke (Old Man), Patrick Breen (Bruno), Martha Gehman (Sylvia), Ron Faber (Adolf), Thom Sesma (Criminal), Irving Metzman (Client)
A comedy in two acts. The action takes place in Queens in the Nixon era.

Thursday, January 25–March 18, 1990 (54 performances)
SQUARE ONE by Steve Tesich; Director, Jerry Zaks; Sets, Tony Walton; Lighting, Paul Gallo; Costumes, Ann Roth; Sound, Aural Fixation; Hair, Antonio Soddu; Musical Director, Norman Weiss; Stage Managers, Leslie Loeb, Scott Rodabaugh; Produced in association with AT&T; Press, Richard Kornberg CAST: Dianne Wiest (Dianne), Richard Thomas (Adam)
A world premiere of a new play in two acts. The action takes place in a repressive society in the future.

Wednesday, Apr. 25–June 3, 1990 (44 performances)
WHAT A MAN WEIGHS by Sherry Kramer; Director, Carole Rothman; Set, Andrew Jackness; Lighting, Dennis Parichy; Costumes, Susan Hilferty; Sound, Gary and Timmy Harris; Hair, Antonio Soddu; Stage Managers, Pamela Edington, Lori Lundquist; Casting, Simon and Kumin Casting. CAST: Christine Estabrook (Joan), Harriet Harris (Ruth), Katherine Hiler (The Debbie), Richard Cox (Haseltine)
A play in two acts. The action takes place in the present time in and around a book conservation lab at a large university.

Left Center: Christine Estabrook, Catherine Hiler, Harriet Harris in "What a Man Weighs" Above: Dianne Wiest, Richard Thomas in "Square One" Top: Jack Wallace, David Clarke, Estelle Parsons, Martha Gehman, Patrick Breen in "Baba Goya"

Christine Estabrook, Richard Cox in "What a Man Weighs"

John O'Keefe in "Shimmer"

Paul Zaloom in "House of Horror"

VINEYARD THEATRE

Ninth Season

Executive Director, Barbara Zinn Krieger; Managing Director, Jon Nakagawa; Production Manager, Kate Mennone; Technical Director, Mark Lorenzen; Artistic Director, Douglas Aibel; Casting, Donna Jacobson; Press, Shirley Herz Associates/Sam Rudy

(Vineyard Theatre) Wednesday June 14–30, 1989 (12 performances) and returned Nov. 22–Dec. 17, 1989 (30 performances)
FEAST HERE TONIGHT with Music & Lyrics by Daniel Jenkins; Book, Ken Jenkins; Director, Gloria Muzio; Sets, William Barclay; Costumes, Jess Goldstein; Lighting, Phil Monat; Musical Supervision, Jeff Waxman; Stage Manager, Jana Llynn; CAST: Daniel Jenkins (Jesse), Susan Glaze (Sissy), Patrick Tovatt (Tolbert), Cass Morgan (Louise), Kenny Kosek, Don Brooks, Tom Hanway, Larry Cohen (Musicians)
MUSICAL NUMBERS: My Soul Was Born To This Land, Where You Been, This World, December Light, Back Way Home, David, Pumpkin Pie, Hound Dog, Little Rabbit, Home on the Hill, If You Knew Eula Well, Mason Boys, Breath of an Angel, Finale
 A bluegrass musical in two acts. The action takes place in a small Kentucky town.

(26th St. Location) Thursday, January 25–February 18, 1990 (33 performances)
MOVING TARGETS by Joe Pintauro; Director, Andre Ernotte; Sets, William Barclay; Costumes, Juliet Polcsa; Lighting, Phil Monat; Sound, Bruce Ellman; Associate Designer, Caty Maxey; Stage Manager, Edward Phillips; Press, Shirley Herz/Sam Rudy CAST: Reed Birney, Ned Eisenberg, Ron Faber, Anita Gillette, Mary Mara
PLAYS: Rex, Seymour in the Very Heart of Winter, Dirty Talk, Lenten Pudding, Rosen's Son, Five Dollar Drinks, Soft Dude, Men Without Wives, Fiat
 An evening of short plays. Some of the plays were performed previously under the title "WILD BLUE" (See Theatre World Vol. 44)

(Vineyard Downtown) Thursday, May 17–June 17, 1990 (39 performances)
HANNAH . . . 1939 with Music, Lyrics & Book by Bob Merrill; Director, Douglas Aibel; Musical Director/Arrangements, Stephen Milbank; Choreography, Tina Paul; Sets, G. W. Mercier; Costumes, James Scott; Lighting, Phil Monat; Orchestrations, Bob Goldstone; Stage Manager, Ira Mont; Sound, Bruce Ellman; CAST: Julie Wilson (Hannah Schuler), Tony Carlin (Lt. Kurt Wald), Richard Thomsen (Commandant Baumann), Yusef Bulos (Janos), Patti Perkins (Luba), Lori Wilner (Toby), Deirdre Lovejoy (Mina), Leah Hocking (Vera), Allan Heinberg (Reuben), Mary Setrakian (Paulina), Mark Ankeny (Jules), Neva Small (Esther), Nicolette Salas (Leah), Kathleen Mahony-Bennett (Young Hannah), Leigh Beery (Gerte Baumann), Paul Klementowicz, Kirk Lombard (German Soldiers)
MUSICAL NUMBERS: Opening, Ah Our Germans, Pearl We Called Prague, Martina, Wear a Little Grin, Kissed on the Eyes, Things Will Be Different, We Dance, Hannah Will Take Care of You, Learn About Life, Someday, Gentle Afternoon, So Good to See You, Who is Hannah?
 A musical in two acts. The action takes place in a dress factory in Nazi-occupied Prague in 1939.

(Vineyard Theatre) Wednesday, October 11, 1989–
THE HOUSE OF HORRORS by Paul Zaloom. Directed by and starring Paul Zaloom.
 A solo performance piece examining our contemporary world.

Carol Rosegg/Martha Swope Photos

Left Center: Julie Wilson (C) and company in "Hannah"
Above: Anita Gillette, Ron Faber in "Moving Targets" Top:
Mary Mara, Ron Faber, Reed Birney in "Moving Targets"

Ellen Greene, Pamela Wiggins in "Starting Monday"

WPA THEATRE
(Workshop of the Players Art)

Twelfth Season

Artistic Director, Kyle Renick; Managing Director, Donna Lieberman; Casting, Brian Chavanne; Production Manager, Stephen Jones; Sets, Edward T. Gianfrancesco; Costumes, Don Newcomb; Sound, Aural Fixation; Lighting, Craig Evans; General Manager, Lori Sherman; Press, Jeffrey Richards Associates/Susan Chicoine, Diane Judge, Maria Somma, Irene Gandy, Jillana Devine, Ian Rand

(WPA Theatre) Tuesday, August 1–27, 1989 (8 performances and 19 previews) **BUZZSAW BERKELEY** with Music & Lyrics by Michael John LaChiusa; Book, Doug Wright; Conception, Christopher Ashley, Doug Wright; Director, Christopher Ashley; Sets, Edward T. Gianfrancesco; Lighting, Craig Evans; Costumes, Don Newcomb; Sound, Aural Fixation; Choreography, Joe Lanteri; Props, Regina B. Santore; Stage Manager, Greta Minsky; Press, Jeffrey Richards CAST: Peter Bartlett (Mr. Krupps/James Looney/Zack Fleece/Ace Hammerstein), Ethyl Eichelberger (Old Miss Soames/Mary Looney/Buzzsaw Berkeley), Becky Gelke (Voice of Ima Payne, Mona Starch), John Hickok (Edgore Soames/Howie Stubbs), Shauna Hicks (Judy Gorgon), Vicki Lewis (Prudy Doody), Keith Reddin (Mickey Looney)
A WPA Silly Series presentation. A musical in two acts. The action takes place in Grave Hollow, U.S.A. in 1939.

Thursday, Nov. 2–19, 1989 (28 performances)
HEAVEN ON EARTH by Robert Schenkkan; Director, Mark Brokaw; Costumes, Ellen McCartney; Props, Catherine Policella; Stage Manager, Liz Small. CAST: Jay O. Sanders (Bobby, Jr.), Helen Stenborg (Martha), Bob Lewis (Jessie), Steven Rodriguez (Miguel), Arthur Hanket (John Morrow), Raynor Scheine (Tom Dooley).
A play in two acts. The action takes place in Waylon, Texas, at the present time.

Tuesday, Dec. 19, 1989–Jan. 21, 1990 (35 performances)
TWENTY FINGERS, TWENTY TOES with Music & Lyrics by Michael Dansicker; Book, Mr. Dansicker, Bob Nigro; Director, Mr. Nigro; Sets, Edward T. Gianfrancesco; Lighting, Craig Evans; Costumes, Gregg Barnes; Sound, Aural Fixation; Choreography, Ken Prescott; Musical Director, Dick Gallagher; Stage Manager, K. R. Williams; Press, Jeffrey Richards/Jillana Devine CAST: Jonathan Courie (Quick Change Artist), Ann Brown (Hanna/Daisy Hilton), Maura Hanlon (Helen/Violet Hilton), Roxie Lucas (Auntie Verna Hilton), Paul Kandel (Myer Myers), Ken Prymus (Bert the Baffling)
MUSICAL NUMBERS: We Don't Have a Mother, Bluebirds, Sign on the Dotted Line, Feet, Doubletalk, Twenty Fingers, Twenty Toes, Natural Harmony, We'll Always Be Together, Nothin's Gonna Stay the Same Forever, Abracadabra, Cooperation, Two Different People, Bad, The Clock is Ticking
A musical biography of Siamese twins, the Hilton sisters, in two acts. The action takes place in carnival sideshows and vaudeville theatres across America from 1925–29.

Tuesday, March 20–April 22, 1990 (35 performances)
STARTING MONDAY by Anne Commire; Director, Zina Jasper; Costumes, Mimi Maxmen; Sound, Aural Fixation; Stage Manager, Jana Llynn CAST: Pamela Wiggins (Lynne), David Manis (Man/1rst German/Doctor/Dr. Benberg/Cop/Technician), Ellen Greene (Ellis), Ilo Orleans (Jim/2nd German/Patient/Farmer/Nurse), Patricia O'Connell (Helen), Paddy Croft (Nurse Eaton), Susan Brenner (Patient/Farmer's Wife/Blood Nurse), Pamela Tucker-White (Trish)
A drama in two acts.

Martha Swope Photos

Left Center: Ann Brown, Maura Hanlon in "20 Fingers, 20 Toes" Above: Jay O. Sanders, Helen Stenborg in "Heaven on Earth" Top: Ethyl Eichelberger, Shauna Hicks in "Buzzsaw Berkeley"

YORK THEATRE COMPANY

Twenty-first Season

Producing Director, Janet Hayes Walker; Managing Director, Molly Pickering Grose; Production Stage Manager, Bob Forman; Sets, James Morgan; Lighting, Mary Jo Dondlinger; Technical Director, James E. Fuller, Jr.; Costumes, Maryanne Powell-Parker; Press, Keith Sherman & Associates

(York Theatre) Friday, October 6–29, 1989 (24 performances)
FRANKIE with Music by Joseph Turrin; Lyrics, Gloria Nissenson; Book, George Abbott; Based on "Frankenstein" by Mary Shelley; Co-Directors, George Abbott & Donald Saddler; Music Director, Arthur M. Greene; Sets, James Morgan; Costumes, Beba Shamash; Lighting, Stuart Duke; Stage Manager, William J. Buckley III; CAST: Richard White (Victor Stanford), Elizabeth Walsh (Elizabeth Blake), Ellia English (Flora), Mark Zimmerman (Henry Green), Kim Moore (Jake/Nurse), Howard Pinhasik (Fred/Nurse), Ron Wisniski (Joe/Sheriff), Gil Rogers (Frankie), Casper Roos (Burton Stabford), Colleen Fitzpatrick (Tracy)
   A world premiere musical in two acts. The action takes place in NYC and the Catskills at the present.

Friday, January 12–28, 1990 (20 performances)
TRAVELER IN THE DARK by Marsha Norman; Director, D. Lynn Meyers; Sets, Joe Tilford; Costumes, Becky Senske; Lighting, Mary Jo Dondlinger; Stage Manager, Victor Lukas; Technical, Norman Frith; Assistant Director, Patricia Piggot; Assistant Sets, Deborah Scott; Press, Keith Sherman CAST: Dennis Parlato (Sam), Lynn Ritchie (Glory), Jeffrey Landman (Stephen), Jim Oyster (Everett)
   A drama in two acts. The setting is the backyard of Everett's house one afternoon and night.

Friday, March 23–April 22, 1990 (23 performances)
THE GOLDEN APPLE with Music by Jerome Moross; Lyrics/Book, John Latouche; Director, Charles Kondek; Musical Director, Lawrence W. Hill; Choreography/Musical Staging, David Holdgrive; CAST: Ann Brown (Helen), Mimi Wyche (Lovely Mars/Siren), Mary Stout (Mrs. Juniper/Calypso), Cynthia Sophiea (Minerva Oliver/Scientist), Muriel Costa-Greenspon (Mother Hare), Sylvia Rhyne (Penelope/Circe), Gordon Stanley (Meneleus/Scylla), Tim Warmen (Ajax), Alan Souza (Nestor), Glen Pannell (Diomede), John Kozeluh (Achilles), Bryan Batt (Petroclus), Tim Salce (Doc MacCahan), Robert R. McCormick (Ulysses), Kelly Patterson (Paris), Kip Niven (Hector Charybdis), Mary Phillips (Figurehead), Mary Lee Marson, Gina Todd, Jim Athens, Mitchell Kantor, Brent Winborn
MUSICAL NUMBERS: Nothing Ever Happens in Angel's Roost, Mother Hare's Seance, My Love is On the Way, The Heroes Come Home, It Was a Glad Adventure, Come Along Boys, It's the Going Home Together, Mother Hare's Prophecy, Helen is Always Willing, Church Social, Introducin' Mr. Paris, Lazy Afternoon, Departure for Rhododendron, My Picture in the Papers, Taking of Rhododendron, Hector's Song, Windflowers, Store-bought Suit, Calypso, Scylla and Charybdis, Goona-Goona, Doomed Doomed Doomed, Circe Circe, Ulysses' Soliloquy, The Sewing Bee, Tirade, Finale
   A musical based on "Ulysses" in two acts and 10 scenes. The action takes place in Washington State between 1900 and 1910. This is the second York revival of this work. For original NYC production see Theatre World Vol. 10

Thursday, May 11–June 3, 1990 (22 performances)
THE CHERRY ORCHARD by Anton Chekhov; Revised English Translation, Jean-Claude Van Itallie; Director, Luke Yankee; Costumes, Kerri Lea Robbins; Lighting, A. C. Hickox; Original Music, Dennis Holly; Choreography, Hal Simons; Stage Manager, Kim Vernace; CAST: Paul Hecht (Lopakhin), Corliss Preston (Dunyasha), Michael Nostrand (Yepikhodov), Cynthia Nixon (Anya), Penny Fuller (Ranevskaya), Louise Roberts (Varya), David Canary (Gayev), Merle Louise (Charlotta), Victor Raider-Wexler (Simeonov-Pischik), Paul Schoeffler (Yasha), Phillip Pruneau (Firs), Tim Loughrin (Trofimov), Scott Barton (Vagrant), Robert Warren (Station Master)
   Chekhov's play in two acts and 4 scenes.

Right Center: Penny Fuller, David Canary in "The Cherry Orchard" Above: Jim Oyster, Dennis Parlato, Jeffrey Landman in "Traveler in the Dark" Top: Gil Rogers, Elizabeth Walsh in "Frankie" *Carol Rosegg/Martha Swope Photos*

Robert McCormick, Sylvia Rhyne, Muriel Costa Greenspan in "The Golden Apple"

101

CATS

For this production: Orchestrations, Stanley Lebowsky; Lighting reproduced by Rick Belzer; Scenic Design reproduced by Rick Belzer; Scenic reproduction by Raymond Huessy; Choreography reproduced by T. Michael Reed and Richard Stafford; Direction reproduced by David Taylor; For other original credits, see Broadway Productions from other seasons. Production Supervisor, Jeff Lee; Dance Supervisor, Richard Stafford; Associate Musical Director, Jack Gaughan; Company Managers, Mitzi Harder, Frank Lott; Wardrobe, Adelaide Laurino, Kathleen Melcher, Sandra Hanlon-Cressler; Props, George Green, Jr., John Selig, Joseph Colyott; Hairstylists, Leon Gagliardi, Elaine Jarzabski; Wigs, Paul Huntley; Stage Managers, B. J. Allen, Peter Wolf, Judy Grothe; Press, Fred Nathan Co./Jim Kerber.

CAST

Alonzo/Rumpus Cat	General McArthur Hambrick
Bustopher Jones/Asparagus/Growltiger	Lee Lobenhofer
Bombalurina	Helen Frank
Cassandra	Linda May
Demeter	Sylvia Dohi
Grizabella	Rosemary Loar
Jellylorum/Griddlebone	Alice Lynn
Jennyanydots	Linda Leonard
Mistoffelees	Joey Pizzi
Mungojerrie	Enrique Segura
Munkustrap	Frank Cruz
Old Deuteronomy	Francis Ruivivar
Plato/Macavity	Randy Wojcik
Pouncival	Daniel Wright
Rumpleteazer	Karen Webster
Rum Tum Tugger	Bradford Minkoff
Sillabub	Holly Cruz
Skimbleshanks	Danny Rounds
Tumblebrutus	Randy Bettis
Victoria	Natasha Davison
Cats Chorus	Austin Jetton, Marjorie McGovern, Jacqueline Reilly, Steve Watkins

STANDBYS & UNDERSTUDIES: Dan O'Grady, Michael Koetting, Charles H. Lubeck, Philip Masterton, Danny Rounds, Steve Watkins, Roxane Barlow, Kathleen Marshall, Roger Kachel, Michelle Kelly, Marjorie McGovern, Terry Mason, Austin Jetton, General McArthur Hambrick

For Musical Numbers, see Broadway Calendar.

Jan Horvath as Grizabella

Carol Rosegg/Martha Swope Photos
Top: "Jellicle Cats"

CHESS

Music, Benny Andersson, Bjorn Ulvaeus; Lyrics, Tim Rice; Based on idea by Tim Rice; Book for Broadway Production, Richard Nelson; Revised Book, Robert Coe; Director, Des McAnuff; Choreography, Wayne Cilento; Original Choreography, Peter Anastos; Scenery, David Mitchell; Costumes, Susan Hilferty; Lighting, Ken Billington; Sound, Gary Stocker; Musical Supervision/Additional Orchestrations, Steven Margoshes, Danny Troob; Musical Director, Jonny Bowden; Musical Consultant, Paul Bogaev; Orchestrations/Arrangements, Anders Eljas; Presented by Tom Mallow, Willian H. Kessler, Jr., Michael M. Weatherly, Robert R. Larsen; Executive Producer, George McPherson; Tour Direction, American Theatre Productions; General Management, George MacPherson; Company Manager, Alan Ross Kosher; Assistant Director, Ross Wasserman; Dance Captain, Steve Ochoa; Props, Robert Adams, K. Aurora Adney; Wardrobe, Jean C. Smolens, Lucy Martinov; Hairstylist, Brent Dillon, Cathy Podlozny; Assistant Conductor, Larry Goldberg; Stage Managers, Mark S. Krause, John Actman, Femi Sarah Heggie; Press, Patt Dale Associates/ Joel W. Dein, Diane Judge, Philip Thurston. Opened Jan. 9, 1990 at the Jackie Gleason Theatre, Miami, Florida.

CAST

Arbiter .... Ken Ard
Freddie .... Stephen Bogardus
Walter .... Gregory Jbara
Florence .... Carolee Carmello
Molokov .... David Hurst
Anatoly .... John Herrera
Svetlana .... Barbara Walsh

ENSEMBLE: Edward Conery, Dina Dailey, Valerie Depena, Justine DiCostanzo, Tom Flynn, Timm Fujii, Philip Hernandez, Kim Lindsay, Pat Moya, Brenda O'Brien, Steve Ochoa, Thomas James O'Leary, Tom Rocco, Carol Denise Smith, Larry Solowitz, Vernon Spencer, Nephi Jay Wimmer, Susan Wood, Swings: Michael Gerhart, Malinda Shaffer
UNDERSTUDIES: Vernon Spencer (Arbiter/Walter), Thomas James O'Leary (Freddie), Kim Lindsay (Florence), Tom Flynn (Molokov), Larry Solowitz (Anatoly), Brenda O'Brien (Svetlana)
MUSICAL NUMBERS: The Story of Chess, What a Scene What a Joy, The Russian and the Molokov, Where I Want to Be, Arbiter's Song, U.S. vs U.S.S.R., A Model of Decorum and Tranquility, You Wanna Lose Your Only Friend, Nobody's on Nobody's Side, Terrace Duet, Who'd Ever Think It, No Contest, So You Got What You Want, Pity the Child, Heaven Help My Heart, The Reporters, Anthem, One Night in Bangkok, You and I, Let's Work Together, I Know Him So Well, Engame, You and I, Finale, Someone Else's Story

A musical in 2 acts and 22 scenes. The action takes place at the present time in Bangkok, Thailand.

*For original Broadway production, see *Theatre World* Vol. 44.

Martha Swope Photos

Right Center: Carolee Carmello, John Herrera, Gregory Jbara, Stephen Bogardus Top: Bogardus, Herrera

Carolee Carmello, Pat Moya, John Herrera, Barbara Walsh

Susan Wood, Justine DiCostanzo, Ken Ard, Pat Moya, Denise Smith

Rosemary Prinz, Ted Lange

DRIVING MISS DAISY

By Alfred Uhry; Director, Charles Nelson Reilly; Set, Thomas Lynch; Costumes, Michael Krass; Lighting, Arden Fingerhut; Sound, Tony Meola; Incidental Music, Robert Waldman; Casting, Pat McCorkle; Press, David Powers. For original New York production, see *Theatre World* Vol. 44. Recipient of 1988 Pulitzer Prize.

CAST

Daisy Werthan .... Rosemary Prinz
Hoke Coleburn .... Ted Lange
Boolie Werthan .... Fred Sanders

Performed without intermission. The action takes place in Atlanta, Ga., from 1948 to 1973.

Martha Swope/Carol Rosegg Photos

Rosemary Prinz, Fred Sanders

DURANTE

Book, Frank Peppiatt, John Aylesworth; Additional Dialogue, Caroline Peppiatt; Based on life and times of Jimmy Durante; Music, favorite compositions of Mr. Durante; Director, Ernest O. Flatt; Musical Numbers Staging/Choreography, Toni Kaye; Design, Cameron Porteus; Costumes, Christina Poddubiuk; Lighting, Sholem Dolgoy; Sound, John Hazen; Musical Director, Grant Sturiale; Dance/Vocal Arrangements, David Krane, Grant Sturiale; Orchestrations, James E. Dale; Special Consultant, Mrs. Margie Durante; Technical Producer, John Wilbur; Technical Director, John Tiggeloven; Original Concept/Producer, Nicky Fylan; Co-Producer, Mary Murphy; Executive Producer, John MacNamara; General Management, Frank Scardino Associates; Company Managers, Ron Francis, Ray Chandler; Props, Michael Kennedy, Tim Anderson, Doug Fraser, Yvette Drumgold; Wardrobe, Woody Millholland, Lisa Sheaves, Jenny Fraser; Wigs, Sherri Neeb; Stage Managers, Roman Humeniuk, Aileen Wilson, Susan Konynenburg; Assistant Conductor, Andrew McKenna; Press, Patt Dale Associates/Joel W. Dein, Philip Thurston. Opened Saturday, Aug. 12, 1989 in Toronto's Blum Appel Theatre, and closed Nov. 19, 1989 in the Shubert Theatre in Los Angeles. Its run in San Francisco was interrupted and cancelled by an earthquake.

CAST

Jimmy Durante	Lonny Price
Coney Tony/Irving Thalberg	Ralph Small
Eddie Jackson	Evan Pappas
Moe the Gimp	B. Alan Geddes
Lou Clayton	Joel Blum
Moe's Girl 1	Risa Waldman
Moe's Girl 2	Terrie Turai
Jeanne	Jane Johanson
David	Brian Hill
Waiters	David Gibb, Bob Riddell
Major Domo (Courtship Ballet)	Michel LaFleche
Chorus Girl	Melodee Finlay
Mike the Cop	Ira Denmark
Radio Announcer	Ralph Small
Sound Effects Man	David Gibb

ENSEMBLE: Michael Arnold, Dale Azzard, Stephen Beamish, Patric A. Creelman, Ira Denmark, Melodee Finlay, Lili Francks, Susan Gattoni, B. Alan Geddes, David Gibb, Jacqueline Haigh, Brian Hill, Michel LaFleche, Bob Riddell, Kim Scarcella, Kent Sheridan, Bernadette Taylor, Terri Turai, Risa Waldman, Kerri Lynn Wasylik, Michael Whitehead
UNDERSTUDIES: Stephen Beamish (Coney/Thalberg/Announcer/Moe), Patric A. Creelman (Jackson), Ira Denmark, Melodee Finlay (Jeanne), Michel Gervais (Swing), David Gibb (Clayton), Darcia Kember (Swing), Michel LaFleche (David), Bob Riddell (Mike), Michael Whitehead (Sound Effects Man)
MUSICAL NUMBERS: Grandpa's Spells, People Would Laugh, Who Will Be with You When I'm Far Away, What a Day, Put Your Arms Around Me Honey, I'll Do the Strutaway, Courtship Ballet, Hello Hello Hello, Jimmy the Well-Dressed Man, Whispering, Challenge, I Know Darn Well I Can Do without Broadway, Llamas in the Bahamas, Don't Lose Your Sense of Humor, You Gotta Start Off Each Day with a Song, I Love Ya, Bill Bailey, Goodnight, Toot Toot Tootsie, Did You Ever Have the Feeling? What Do I Have to Do, One Room Home, Partners, Inka Dinka Doo, We're the Men, A Razz a Ma Tazz, September Song, Goodnight.

A musical in 2 acts and 21 scenes.

Michael & David Cooper Photos

Right Center: Evan Pappas, Lonny Price, Joel Blum Top: Lonny Price (center) and chorus

Lonny Price as Jimmy Durante

FIDDLER ON THE ROOF

Book, Joseph Stein; Music, Jerry Bock; Lyrics, Sheldon Harnick; Based on Sholom Aleichem's stories by special permission of Arnold Perl; Direction of Jerome Robbins reproduced by Ruth Mitchell; Choeography of Mr. Robbins reproduced by Sammy Dallas Bayes; Musical Supervisor/Conductor, Kevin Farrell; Scenery, Boris Aronson; Costumes based on originals by Patricia Zipprodt; Lighting, Ken Billington; Sound, Christopher Bond; Orchestrations, Don Walker; Casting, Stuart Howard/ Amy Schecter; General Manager, Richard Martini/Connie Weinstein; Produced in association with A. Deshe (Pashanel); Presented by Barry and Fran Weissler and Pace Theatrical Group; Tour Direction, Namco Booking; Opened Tuesday, June 26, 1989 in San Francisco, Ca.*

CAST

Tevye	Topol
Golde	Marcia Rodd
Tzeitel	Sharon Lawrence
Hodel	Tia Riebling
Chava	Jennifer Prescott
Bielke	Judy Dodd
Sprintze/Grandma Tzeitel	Kathy St. George
Motel	Jack Kenny
Perchik	Gary Schwartz
Fyedka	Mark Damon
Lazar Wolf	Joel Kramer
Mordcha	Bob Carroll
Nachum	James F. Brandt
Yente	Ruth Jaroslow
Rabbi	Jerry Matz
Avram	David Masters
Constable	Paul Hart
Mendel	David Pevsner
The Fiddler	Stephen Wright
Russian Tenor	Brad Little
Fruma-Sarah	Jeri Sager

VILLAGERS: Jennifer Rae Beck, Michael Berresse, Joanne Borts, Kenneth M. Daigle, David Enriquez, Craig Gahnz, Brian Henry, Todd Heughens, Keith Keen, Brad Little, A. Michael McKee, Panchali Null, Irma Rogers, Jeri Sager, Beth Thompson, Julie Waldman
UNDERSTUDIES: Bob Carroll (Tevye), Irma Rogers (Golde), Julie Waldman (Tzeitel), Beth Thompson (Hodel), Jennifer Rae Beck (Chava), David Pevsner (Motel), Paul Hart (Perchik/Lazar), A. Michael McKee (Fyedka), Panchali Null (Yente), David Masters (Rabbi/Mordcha), Brad Little (Constable), Todd Heughens (Mendel), David Enriquez (Fiddler), Swings: Chris Jamison, John Nicoletti
MUSICAL NUMBERS: Tradition, Matchmaker, If I Were a Rich Man, Sabbath Prayer, To Life, Miracle of Miracles, The Dream, Sunrise Sunset, Wedding Dance, Now I Have Everything, Do You Love Me, The Rumor, Far from the Home I Love, Chavaleh, Anatevka, Epilogue

A musical in 2 acts and 17 scenes with prologue and epilogue. The action takes place on the eve of the Russian Revolution in 1905 in Anatevka, a small village in Russia.

*Still touring May 31, 1990. For original Broadway production starring Zero Mostel, see *Theatre World* Vol. 21. "Tonys" were awarded Zero Mostel (Best Actor), Maria Karnilova (Best Actress), Best Musical, Best Book, Producer, Director, Composer/ Lyricist, Choreographer.

Right Center: Jennifer Prescott, Sharon Lawrence, Tia Riebling Top: Topol

Carol Rosegg/Martha Swope Photos

Topol, Mark Zeller

INTO THE WOODS

Music and Lyrics, Stephen Sondheim; Book, James Lapine; Director, Mr. Lapine; Settings, Tony Straiges; Lighting, Richard Nelson; Costumes, Ann Hould-Ward; Based on original concepts by Patricia Zipprodt and Ann Hould-Ward; Sound, Alan Stieb, James Brousseau; Hairstylist, Phyllis Della Illien; Orchestrations, Jonathan Tunick; Musical Director, Randy Booth; Musical Staging, Lar Lubovitch; Casting, Joanna Merlin; Presented by Tom Mallow and Pace Theatrical Group in association with Heidi Landesman, Rocco Landesman, Rick Steiner, M. Anthony Fisher, Frederick H. Mayerson, Jujamcyn Theatres; Executive Producer, George MacPherson; Company Manager, Alan Ross Kosher; Production Supervisor, Peter Feller, Sr.; Props, Edward "Buddy" Horton, Leon B. Chenier, Jr.; Wardrobe, Bobbi Langhofer, Lucy Martinov; Assistant Conductor, Peter Prosser; Stage Managers, Dan W. Langhofer, David Lober, Jill B. Gounder; Press, Patt Dale Associates, Joshua Ellis Office/Adrian Bryan-Brown. Tour began Nov. 22, 1988 in the Parker Playhouse, Ft. Lauderdale, Fl., and closed May 13, 1990 in Baltimore's Mechanic Theatre.

CAST

Narrator/Mysterious Man	Rex Robbins
Cinderella	Jill Geddes
Jack	Kevin R. Wright
Baker	Marcus Olson
Baker's Wife	Mary Gordon Murray
Cinderella's Stepmother	Jo Ann Cunningham
Florinda	Judy McLane
Lucinda	Danette Cuming
Jack's Mother	Nora Mae Lyng
Little Red Ridinghood	Tracy Katz
Witch	Betsy Joslyn
Cinderella's Father	Don Crosby
Cinderella's Mother	Anne Rickenbacher
Wolf/Cinderella's Prince	Chuck Wagner
Rapunzel	Marguerite Lowell
Rapunzel's Prince	Douglas Sills
Grandmother/Giant	Barbara Marineau
Steward	Stuart Zagnit

STANDBYS & UNDERSTUDIES: Don Crosby (Narrator/Mysterious Man), Stuart Zagnit (Narrator/Mysterious Man/Baker/Cinderella's Father), Jonathan Hadley (Jack/Prince), James Weatherstone (Jack/Baker/Prince/Wolf/Steward), Paul Jackel (Cinderella's Father/Prince/Wolf/Steward), Douglas Sills (Prince), Barbara Marineau (Stepmother/Witch/Jack's Mother), Danette Cuming (Baker's Wife), Judy McLane (Baker's Wife), Anne Rickenbacher (Stepmother/Lucinda/Florinda), Marguerite Lowell (Cinderella), Gay Willis (Cinderella/Rapunzel/Little Red Ridinghood/Cinderella's Mother), Jody Walker-Lichtig (Rapunzel/Little Red Ridinghood/Cinderella's Mother), Jo Ann Cunningham (Witch/Jack's Mother), Jill B. Gounder (Grandmother/Giant)

MUSICAL NUMBERS: Into the Woods, Hello Little Girl, I Guess This Is Goodbye, Maybe They're Magic, I Know Things Now, A Very Nice Prince, Giants in the Sky, Agony, It Takes Two, Stay with Me, On the Steps of the Palace, Ever After, So Happy, Agony, Lament, Any Moment, Moments in the Woods, Your Fault, Last Midnight, No More, No One Is Alone, Children Will Listen

A musical in two acts.

*For original Broadway production, see *Theatre World* Vol. 44.

Martha Swope Photos

Top Right: Betsy Joslyn with cast

Betsy Joslyn

107

THE KING AND I

Music, Richard Rodgers; Book/Lyrics, Oscar Hammerstein II; Based on book *Anna and the King of Siam* by Margaret Landon; Director, Arthur Storch; Choreography, Jerome Robbins, reproduced by Patricia Weber; Sets, John Jay Moore; Costumes, Stanley Simmons based on originals by Irene Sharaff; Lighting, Jason Kantrowitz; Musical Supervisor, Don Pippin; Sound, Gary Stocker; Hairstylist, Vidal Sassoon; Musical Director, Michael D. Biagi; Casting, Stuart Howard/Amy Schecter; General Management, Niko Associates/Abbie M. Strassler; Associate Director, Conwell S. Worthington II; Presented by Manny Kladitis, Columbia Artists Management, Concert Productions Intl., and Pace Theatrical Group; Associate Conductor, Ben Whiteley; Props, Ron Korker, Russell Korker; Wardrobe, Sydney Smith, R. J. Malkmus II; Company Managers, Scott Moore, Erich Hammer; Stage Managers, John M. Galo, Matthew G. Marholin, Mark Tynan; Press, Joshua Ellis Office/Adrian Bryan-Brown, Jackie Green, Susanne Tighe, Tim Ray, Chris Boneau, John Barlow, Jennifer Friedman. Opened Friday, Aug. 18, 1989 in the Civic Center of Syracuse, NY, and closed in San Francisco's Orpheum Theatre on March 4, 1990. For original Broadway production, see *Theatre World* Vol. 7.

CAST

Captain Orton	Kenneth Garner
Louis Leonowens	Kenny Lund
Anna Leonowens	Liz Robertson
The Interpreter	Kaipo Daniels
The Kralahome	Michael Kermoyan
The King	Rudolf Nureyev
Tuptim	Suzan Postel
Lady Thiang	Irma-Estel LaGuerre
Prince Chulalongkorn	Jason (J.J.) Brown
Princess Ying Yaowalak	Shana Sueoka-Matos
Lun Tha	Patrick A'Hearn
Sir Edward Ramsey	Kenneth Garner
Princess	John Babcock, Jeffrey Rosato

PRIESTS & SLAVES: Alberto Guzman, Michael Hayward-Jones, Stanley Earl Harrison, Stuart Marland, Kenji Nakao, Sal Mistretta, Harold Yi
ROYAL DANCERS & WIVES: Lori Lynn Bauer, Nancy Latuja, Deborah Harada, Jayne Ackley Lynch, Grace Napier, Ryoko Sawaishi, Sandy Sueoka-Matos, Marie Takazawa, Kyoko Takita, Chiaki Toda, Kym Weber, Sylvia Yamada
STANDBYS & UNDERSTUDIES: Michael Kermoyan (King), Sal Mistretta (King/Kralahome), Elizabeth Hansen (Anna), Michael Hayward-Jones (Captain Ramsey), John Babcock (Louis), Lori Lynn Bauer (Tuptim), Jane Ackley Lynch (Lady Thiang), Stuart Marland (Lu Tha), Deborah Harada (Angel/Fan Dancer), Sylvia Yamada (Eliza), Ryoko Sawaishi (Topsy), Chiaki Toda (Uncle Thomas), Kym Weber (Little Eva), Charlie Selzt (Simon), Swings: Marjorie Anita Mann, Charlie Seltz
MUSICAL NUMBERS: I Whistle a Happy Tune, My Lord and Master, Hello Young Lovers, March of the Siamese Children, A Puzzlement, Royal Bangkok Academy, Getting to Know You, We Kiss in a Shadow, Shall I Tell You What I Think of You? Something Wonderful, Western People Funny, I Have Dreamed, The Small House of Uncle Thomas, Song of King, Shall We Dance, Finale.

Roy Round Photos

Top Left: Rudolf Nureyev

Rudolf Nureyev, Liz Robertson

J. Mark McVey

LES MISÉRABLES

For original creative credits and musical numbers, see Broadway Production. First National Company opened Tuesday, Dec. 15, 1987 in Boston's Shubert Theatre, and still touring May 31, 1990. For original Broadway production, see *Theatre World* Vol. 43.

CAST

Craig Schulman/J. Mark McVey (Jean Valjean), Charles Pistone/Robert DuSold (Javert), J. Mark McVey, Michael McCormick, Al DeCristo, Scott Elliot, Andy Gale, Tom Robbins, Hugh Panaro, Bjorn Johnson, Joseph Locarro (Chain Gang), Michael Babin (Farmer), Bjorn Johnson (Labourer), Deborah Bradshaw (Innkeeper's Wife), Willy Falk (Innkeeper), Kevin McGuire (Bishop), Rick Sparks, Gary Harger (Constables), Hollis Resnick/Kathy Taylor/Susan Dawn Carson (Fantine), Robert DuSold (Foreman), Michael Babin, Scot Elliot (Workers), Rosalyn Rahn, Olga Merediz, Carolee Carmello, Bertilla Baker (Women), Kirsti Carnahan (Factory Girl), J. Mark McVey, Andy Gale, Gary Harger (Sailors), Deborah Bradshaw, Bertilla Baker, Carolee Carmello, Jennifer Naimo, Kirsti Carnahan, Renee Veneziale, Tamara Jenkins, Betsy True (Whores), Rosalyn Rahn (Old Woman), Olga Merediz (Crone), Scott Elliott (Pimp), Sal DeCristo (Bamataboi), Scott Elliott (Fauchelevant), Christina Marie DeAngelis, Christa Larson, Sara Nelson (Young Cosette), Victoria Clark/Rosalyn Rahn (Mme. Thenardier), Michael McCormick/ Drew Eschelman (Thenardier), Christina Marie DeAngelis, Christa Larson, Sara Nelson (Young Eponine), Michael Babin (Drinker), Bjorn Johnson, Betsy True (Young Couple), Willy Falk (Drunk), Kevin McGuire, Bertilla Baker (Diners), Gary Harger, Michael McCormick, Al Decristo, J. Mark McVey, Kirsti Carnahan, Deborah Bradshaw, Rosalyn Rahn (Drinkers), Andy Gale (Young Man), Carolee Carmello, Jennifer Naimo (Young Girls), Olga Merediz, Scott Elliott (Old Couple), Robert DuSold, Rick Sparks (Travelers), Lantz Landry, Sam Brent Riegel (Gavroche), Rosalyn Rahn (Old Beggar Woman), Kirsti Carnahan (Young Prostitute), Willy Falk (Pimp), Jennifer Naimo (Eponine), Bjorn Johnson, Rick Sparks, J. Mark McVey, Gary Harger (Thenardier's Gang), Joseph Locarro/Kurt Johns/Pete Herber (Enjolras), John Ruess/Peter Gunther (Marius), Tamara Jenkins/Melissa Errico (Cosette), Robert DuSold (Combeferre), Andy Gale (Feuilly), Michael Babin (Courfeyrac), Scott Elliott (Joly), Al DeCristo (Grantaire), Kevin McGuire (Lesgles), Willy Falk (Jean Prouvaire)

J. Mark McVey, Robert DuSold

Top Right: Susan Dawn Carson Below: Cast

LES MISÉRABLES

For original creative credits and musical numbers, see Broadway Productions from past seasons. For this company: Music Director, John David Scott; Company Manager, Michael Sanfilippo; Dance Captain, Kevin McGuire; Associate Production Manager, Jake Bell; Stage Managers, Pamela J. Young, John Kirman, Ray Gin; Press, Fred Nathan Co./Marc Thibodeau, Gail Browne, Anne Abrams.

CAST

Rich Hebert (Jean Valjean), Richard Kinsey (Javert), Ravil Atlas, Bruce Winant, Jim Zubiena, Michael Vodde, Gary Beach, Dann Fink, Matthew Porretta, Martin Croft, Craig Oldfather (Chain Gang), John DeLuise (Farmer), Martin Croft (Laborer), Anne Buelteman (Innkeeper's Wife), John Powell (Innkeeper), Kevin McGuire (Bishop of Digne), Brian Beacock, Liam O'Brien (Constables), Kelly Ground (Fantine), Bruce Winant (Foreman), Jeanne Smith, Maggie Bilder, Jennifer Kruskamp, Michelle Murlin-Gardner (Women Workers), Richel Kompst (Factory Girl), John DeLuise, Michael Vodde (Workers), Ravil Atlas, Dann Fink, Michael Vodde (Sailors), Anne Buelteman, Michelle Murlin-Gardner, Jennifer Kruskamp, Michele Maika, Richel Kompst, Misty Cotton, Jacquelyn Piro, Lynn Donahoe (Whores), Jeanne Smith (Old Woman), Maggie Bilder (Crone), Liam O'Brien (Pimp), Jim Zubiena (Bamatabois), Liam O'Brien (Fauchelevent), Sabrina Harris/Larisa Oleynik (Young Cosette), Gina Ferrall (Mme. Thenardier), Gary Beach (Thenardier), Sabrina Harris/Larisa Oleynik (Young Eponine), John DeLuise, Liam O'Brien, Jim Zubiena, Ravil Atlas, Richel Kompst, Anne Buelteman, Jeanne Smith (Drinkers), Martin Croft, Lynn Donahoe (Young Couple), John Powell (Drunk), Michelle Murlin-Gardner, Kevin McGuire (Diners), Dann Fink (Young Man), Jennifer Kruskamp, Misty Cotton (Young Girls), Maggie Bilder/Michael Vodde (Old Couple), Bruce Winant, Brian Beacock (Travelers), Rider Strong/Ian Werkheiser (Gavroche), Anne Buelteman (Old Beggar Woman), Richel Kompst (Young Prostitute), John Powell (Pimp), Michele Maika (Eponine), Martin Croft (Montparnasse), Brian Beacock (Babet), Ravil Atlas (Brujon), Liam O'Brien (Claquesous), Craig Oldfather (Enjolras), Matthew Porretta (Marius), Jacquelyn Piro, Ellen Rockne (Cosette), Bruce Winant (Combeferre), Dann Fink (Feuilly), John DeLuise (Courfeyrac), Michael Vodde (Joly), Jim Zubiena (Grantaire), Kevin McGuire (Lesgles), John Powell (Jean Prouvaire), Eydie Alyson, Jeff Barnett, Mara Finerty, Clark Sterling (Swings)

Joan Marcus Photos

Christy Baron as Fantine   **Dana Lynn Caruso as Eponine**

LES MISÉRABLES

For original creative credits, see Broadway Productions; General Managers, Alan Wasser, Allan P. Williams; Production Supervisor, Sam Stickler; Production Manager, John H. Paull III; Company Managers, Daryl T. Dodson, Terry L. Smiley; Dance Captain, Brian Lynch; Props, Timothy Abel, Glenn Belfer; Wardrobe, Adelaide Laurino, Jerry Wolf; Hair/Makeup Supervisor, Michael Moore; Stage Managers, Alice Dewey, Karl Lengel, K. Lee Harvey; Press, Fred Nathan Co./Bill Miller, Marc Thibodeau, Merle Frimark, William Schelble, Ian Rand. Opened in Jones Hall, Houston, Tx., on Tuesday, May 30, 1989 and still touring May 31, 1990.

CAST

Gary Barker[1] (Jean Valjean), Peter Samuel[2] (Javert), Richard Poole, Jeff Gardner, Craig Wells, Rohn Seykell, Paul Ainsley, Greg Zerkle, Matthew Porretta, Clay Guthrie, Brian Lynch (Chain Gang), Jerry Christakos (Farmer), Clay Guthrie (Labourer), Beth Williams[3] (Innkeeper's Wife), Reed Armstrong (Innkeeper), Claude R. Tessier[4] (Bishop of Digne), Christopher Pecaro, Adam Heller (Constables), Christy Baron (Fantine), Jeff Gardner[5] (Foreman), Jerry Christakos, Rohn Seykell, Jeanne Smith[6], Merri Sugarman, Elizabeth Ward, Anne L. Nathan (Workers), Lisa Vroman[7] (Factory Girl), Brian Lynch, Richard Poole, Rohn Seykell (Sailors), Beth Williams, Anne L. Nathan, Elizabeth Ward, Michele Maika, Lisa Vroman, Dana Lynn Caruso[8], Jacquelyn Piro, Cindi Page (Whores), Jeanne Smith (Old Woman), Merri Sugarman (Crone), Adam Heller (Pimp), Craig Wells (Bambatabois), Adam Heller (Fauchelevent), Eden Riegel[9]/Tracy Ward[10] (Young Cosette), Linda Kerns[11] (Mme. Thenardier), Paul Ainsley (Thenardier), Eden Riegel/Tracy Ward (Young Eponine), Jerry Christakos, Adam Heller, Richard Poole, Craig Wells, Lisa Vroman, Beth Williams, Jeanne Smith (Drinkers), Reed Armstrong (Drunk), Brian Lynch (Young Man), Dana Lynn Caruso, Elizabeth Ward (Young Girls), Merri Sugarman, Rohn Seykell (Old Couple), Jeff Gardner, Christopher Pecaro (Travelers), Andrew Harrison Leeds/Sam Brent Riegel[12] (Gavroche), Beth Williams (Old Beggar), Lisa Vroman (Young Prostitute), Reed Armstrong (Pimp), Michele Maika[13] (Eponine), Clay Guthrie[14] (Montparnasse), Christopher Pecaro[15] (Babet), Richard Poole[16] (Brujon), Adam Heller[17] (Claquesous), Greg Zerkle[18] (Enjolras), Matthew Porretta[19] (Marius), Jacquelyn Piro[20] (Cosette), Jeff Gardner (Combeferre), Brian Lynch[21] (Feuilly), Jerry Christakos[22] (Courfeyrac), Rohn Seykell[23] (Joly), Craig Wells[24] (Grantaire), Claude R. Tessier (Lesgles), Reed Armstrong (Jean Prouvaire)

For musical Numbers, See Broadway Productions.

†Succeeded by: 1. Richard Poole, Brian Lynch, 2. Paul Schoeffler, David Jordan, 3. Mary Chesterman, 4. Dario Coletta, Kelly Briggs, 5. Paul Schoeffler, Craig Bennett, 6. Lorraine Dale, 7. Robin Skye, Jeanne Bennett, 8. Maureen Duffey, 9. Jessica Ann Lightburn, 10. Samantha Jordan, 11. Diana Rogers, 12. Brian Fessenden, 13. Dana Lynn Caruso, 14. David Jordan, Geoffrey Blaisdell, 15. Joshua Finkel, 16. Douglas Webster, Richard Nickol, 17. Kirk Mouser, 18. Jerry Christakos, 19. Christopher Pecaro, 20. Lisa Vroman, Tamra Hayden, 21. Peter Lind Harris, 22. Douglas Webster, 23. Amick Byram, Gilles Chiasson, 24. Alan Osburn

Joan Marcus Photos

Brian Lynch, David Jordan Above: Diana Rogers, Samantha Jordan

LOVE LETTERS

By A. R. Gurney; Director, Kenneth Frankel; Lighting, Dennis Parichy; Casting, Steven Fertig; Scenic Consultant, John Lee Beatty; General Management, Theatre-pop/Joan Stein; Company Management, Andrea Ladik, Mark Richard; Management Associate, Sharon Klein; Production Supervisor, Tom Ware; Production Assistant, Justin Harvey; Presented by Susan Dietz and Joan Stein in association with Elizabeth Williams and the Pasadena Playhouse; Press, Anne Abrams, Eileen McMahon, Ellen Schachter. Opened in Los Angeles in the Canon Theatre on Tuesday, April 17, 1990*

CAST

(a different couple each week) Christine Lahti and Treat Williams, Ned Beatty and Michael Learned, Meredith Baxter-Birney and Richard Thomas, Julie Hagerty and Christopher Reeve, Matthew Broderick and Helen Hunt, Ed Begley, Jr. and Swoosie Kurtz, Carol Burnett and Leslie Nielsen, Polly Draper and Gregory Harrison, Beau Bridges and Lesley Ann Warren, Ben Gazzara and Gena Rowlands, Patrick O'Neal and Gwen Verdon

*Still playing May 31, 1990. It had been preceded by runs in Boston, San Francisco and Pasadena.

Treat Williams   Christine Lahti

MY FAIR LADY

Book and Lyrics, Alan Jay Lerner; Music, Frederick Loewe; Director, James Hammerstein; Choreography, Michael Shawn; Adapted from George Bernard Shaw's play and Gabriel Pascal's film *Pygmalion;* Musical Director, Richard Parrinello; Sound, Abe Jacob; Costumes, Michael Bottari, Ronald Case; Lighting, Steve Cochrane; Casting, Jeffrey Dunn; Associate Director, Joel Bishoff; Assistant Choreographer, Mary Rotella; Presented by AMPAC Enterprises and Robert Young Associates; General Manager, Ronald Stokes; Company Manager, Stephen Arnold; Dance Captain, Mary T. Rotella; Associate Conductor, Jeff Conrad; Props, Michael Smanko; Wardrobe, Judith Marsh; Production Coordinator; Stage Managers, Robert Vandergriff, John W. Calder III; Press, N. Patricia Story. Opened in Providence, RI, on March 10, 1989*

CAST

Busker/Flower Girl	Julia Gregory
Busker/Ensemble	Bill Brassea
Mrs. Eynsford-Hill/Queen of Transylvania	Marilyn Hudgins
Freddy Eynsford-Hill	Michael DeVries
Eliza Doolittle	Katharine Buffaloe
Colonel Pickering	Richard Neilson
Henry Higgins	Noel Harrison
1st Cockney/Ensemble/Footman	Robert Randle
2nd Cockney/Butler/Ensemble	Russ Jones
3rd Cockney/Ensemble	James Gerth
4th Cockney/Ensemble	Steven Edward Moore
Bartender/Zoltan Karpathy	Tom Souhrada
Harry/Lord Boxington/Ensemble	Alan Gilbert
Jamie/Ensemble	Jonathan Brody
Alfred P. Doolittle	Ben Wrigley
Mrs. Pearce	Darcy Pulliam
Mrs. Hopkins/Servant/Ensemble	Eileen McNamara
Servant/Ensemble	Ruth Bormann
Servant/Ensemble	Kate Egan
Mrs. Higgins	Marie Paxton
Chauffeur/Ensemble	Michael Koetting
Lady Boxington/Ensemble	Anne Gunderson
Constable/Ensemble	Robert Randle
Bartender/Ensemble	D. J. Salisbury
Mrs. Higgins' Maid/Ensemble	Jennifer Rymer
Swings	Mary T. Rotella, Russell Giesenschlag

A musical in 2 acts and 18 scenes.

*Closed in June of 1989 in Tokyo, Japan. For original Broadway production, see *Theatre World* Vol. 12. It opened March 15, 1956 with Julie Andrews and Rex Harrison, and closed after 2715 performances.

Noel Harrison, Katharine Buffaloe, Marie Paxton in "My Fair Lady"

PETER PAN

Based on play by James M. Barrie; Lyrics, Carolyn Leigh; Music, Moose Charlap; Additional Lyrics, Betty Comden, Adolph Green; Additional Music, Jule Styne; Director, Fran Soeder; Original production conceived, directed and choreographed by Jerome Robbins; Musical Supervision/Direction, Kevin Farrell; Choreography, Marilyn Magness; Flying by Foy; Sets, Michael J. Hotopp, Paul de Pass; Additional Scenery, James Leonard Joy; Costumes, Mariann Verheyan; Lighting, Natasha Katz; Sound, Peter J. Fitzgerald; Wigs, Rick Geyer; Fight/Additional Arrangements, M. Michael Fauss; General Management, Lonn Entertainment; Tour Directors, Marvin A. Krauss, Irving Siders; Company Manager, Stephen Arnold; Stage Manager, John M. Galo; Press, Patt Dale Associates. Opened Tuesday, Dec. 19, 1989 in Boston's Colonial Theatre and still touring May 31, 1990.

CAST

Mrs. Darling/Wendy Grown	Lauren Thompson
Wendy Darling/Jane	Cindy Robinson
John Darling	Britt West
Michael Darling	Jeremy Cooper
Liza	Anne McVey
Nana	Bill Bateman
Mr. Darling/Capt. Hook	Stephen Hanan
Peter Pan	Cathy Rigby
The Never Bear	Courtney Wyn
Curly	Alon Williams
Twins	Janet Kay Higgins, Kevin Mangold
Slightly	Christopher Ayers
Tootles	Julian Brightman
Mr. Smee	Don Potter
Cecco	Calvin Smith
Gentleman Starkey	Carl Packard
Tiger Lily	Holly Irwin

MUSICAL NUMBERS: Tender Shepherd, I've Got to Crow, Neverland, I'm Flying, Pirate March, A Princely Scheme, Indians!, Wendy, Tarantella, I Won't Grow Up, Ugg-a-Wugg, Distant Melody, Hook's Waltz

Carol Rosegg/Martha Swope Photos

Cathy Rigby, and Top with Cindy Robinson, Jeremy Cooper, Britt West

THE PHANTOM OF THE OPERA

For original creative credits and Musical Numbers, see Broadway Productions; Musical Director, Roger Cantrell; Production Supervisor, Mitchell Lemsky; Dance Supervisor, Denny Berry; General Manager, Alan Wasser; Company Manager, Martin Cohen; Props, Doug Krantz; Wardrobe, Mario Brera; Assistant Conductor, Larry Blank; Stage Managers, David Rubinstein, Sherry Cohen, Noel Stern, Kevin Larkin; Press, Fred Nathan Co./Merle Frimark, Marc Thibodeau, Ellen Schachter. Opened in Los Angeles' Ahmanson Theatre on Wednesday, May 31, 1989, and still playing May 31, 1990.

CAST

Phantom of the Opera	Michael Crawford, Robert Guillaume
Christine Daae	Dale Kristien/Mary D'Arcy
Raoul	Reece Holland
Carlotta Giudicelli	Leigh Munro
M. Andre	Norman Large
M. Firmin	Calvin Remsberg
Mme. Giry	Barbara Lang
Ubaldo Piangi	Gualtiero Negrini
Meg Giry	Elisabeth Stringer
M. Reyer	D. C. Anderson
Auctioneer	Richard Gould
Porter/Marksman	Sean Smith
M. Lefevre/Don Attilio/Passarino	Gary Marshal
Joseph Buquet	Gene Brundage
Firechief	Kris Pruet
Slave Master	Jeffrey Amsden
Flunky/Stagehand	James Hogan
Policeman	Carlo Thomas
Page	Patrice Pickering, Rhonda Dillon
Porter/Fireman	Maurizio Corbino, William Scott Brown
Page	Candace Rogers-Adler
Wardrobe Mistress/Confidante	Gail Land Hart
Princess	Jani Neuman
M. Firmin	Rio Hibler-Kerr
Innkeeper's Wife	Rebecca Eichenberger, Catherine Caccavallo

Ballet Chorus: Elkin Antoniou, Leslie-Noriko Beadles, Madelyn Berdes, Rebeca Gorostiza, Mary Alyce Laubacher, Sylvia Rico, Swings: Irene Cho, Karen Benjamin, Joseph Dellger, Brad Scott

Robert Guillaume, Dale Kristien

Calvin Remsberg, Leigh Munro, Norman
Large Above: Entire Cast
Robert Millard Photos

THE PHANTOM OF THE OPERA

For original creative credits and Musical Numbers see Broadway Calendar; Presented by Cineplex Odeon in association with Tina VanderHeyden and the Really Useful Theatre Co. of Canada; Musical Director, Jeffrey Hubbard; Casting, Johnson-Liff & Zerman; General Management, Allan Wasser; Opened in Toronto's Pantages Theatre on Wednesday, Sept. 20, 1989, and still playing May 31, 1990

CAST

Phantom of the Opera	Colm Wilkinson†
Christine Daae	Rebecca Cain
Raoul	Byron Nease
Carlotta Giudicelli	Lyse Guerin
M. Firmin	Gregory Cross
M. Andre	Paul Massel
Mme. Giry	Kristina Marie Guiguet
Ubaldo Piangi	Peter Cormican
Meg Giry	Donna Rubin
M. Reyer	Blaine Parker
Auctioneer	Barry Stilwell
Porter/Marksman	Paul Gatchell
M. Lefevre	Michael Fawkes
Joseph Buquet	Steven Henrikson
Don Attilio Passarino	Timothy Anderson
Slave Master	Mark Dovey
Flunky/Stagehand	Glen Kerr
Policeman	Norman Roberts
Page	Glenda Balkan
Porter/Fireman	J. P. Michaels
Page	Rhonda Liss
Wardrobe Mistress/Confidante	Elizabeth Mabee
Princess	Caroline Schiller
Mme. Firmin	Mary Anne Barcellona
Innkeeper's Wife	Gretchen Helrig

Ballet Chorus: Suzanne Brown, Susan Burk, Neve Campbell, Holly Frances Farmer, Donna Kelly, Marie-Claude Sabourin, Julie Whittaker (Dance Captain), Swings: Devin Dalton, David Rogers, Susan Sereda, Julie Whittaker

†Standby: Chris Groenendaal

THE PHANTOM OF THE OPERA

For original creative credits and musical numbers, see Broadway Productions. Musical Director, Jacl Gaughan; General Managers, Alan Wasser, Allan Williams, Michael Gill, Thom Mitchell; Technical Production Managers, Jake Bell, Laura Eichholz; Props, Joe Feikis, Gary Moreland; Wardrobe, Michael Hannah, Geoffrey Polischuk; Associate Musical Supervisor, Kristin Blodgette; Assistant Conductor, Kevin Stites; Wigs/Makeup Supervisor, Christine Cantrell; Stage Managers, Steve McCorkle, Susan Green, David Lober; Company Managers, Barbara Nunn, Joey Loggia; Press, Fred Nathan Co./Merle Frimark, Marc Thibodeau, William Schelble, Ian Rand, Colleen Brown/Chicago: Margie Korshak/Nancy Henig. Opened in Chicago's Auditorium Theatre on Thursday, May 24, 1990, and still playing at press time.

CAST

Phantom of the Opera	Mark Jacoby
Christine Daae	Karen Culliver/Teri Bibb
Raoul	Keith Buterbaugh
Monsieur Andre	Rick Hilsabeck
Monsieur Firmin	David Huneryager
Carlotta Giudicelli	Patricia Hurd
Madame Giry	Olga Talyn
Ubaldo Piangi	Donn Cook
Meg Giry	Patricia Ward
Porter/Marksman	Charles Bergell
Wardrobe Mistress/Confidante	Dorothy Byrne
Innkeeper's Wife	Virginia Croskery
Pages	Patti Davidson-Gorbea, Valerie DeBartolo
Policeman	William Lynn Dixon
Madame Firmin	Lisa Faletto
Porter/Stagehand	Stephen Gould
Slave Master	Douglas Graham
Lion Man	James R. Guthrie
M. LeFevre/Fireman	Robert Hildreth
Joseph Buquet	Brad Keating
Princess	Sarah Pfisterer
Monsieur Reyer	Richard L. Reardon
Auctioneer/Don Attilio/Passarino	Lawson Skala
Flunky/Stagehand	Travis L. Wright
Ballet Chorus	Diane Anastasio, Jennifer Carney, Nicole Chelini, Candice Peterson, Tait Runnfeldt, Susan Zaguirre
Swings	Teresa DeRose, Steven Douglas Blair, Randal Keith, Lisa Kristina

Marc Jacoby, Teri Bibb

Keith Buterbaugh, Karen Culliver

THE PHANTOM OF THE OPERA

Music and Lyrics, Lawrence Rosen, Paul Schierhorn; Adapted from the Gaston Leroux novel by Bruce Falstein; Staging/Choreography, Darwin Knight; Presented by Abraham Hirschfeld; Settings, Ken Kurtz; Costumes, Susan Tsu; Lighting, Norman Coates; Sound, Jeff Curtis; Musical Director, Sand Lawn; Orchestrations, Curtis J. McKonly, Joe Gianono; Producer, Karen Poindexter; Associate Producers, Linda Bryant, Darwin Knight; Stage Manager, Todd Taylor. Opened Monday, Feb. 5, 1990 in the Al Hirschfeld Theatre in Miami Beach, FL*

CAST

The Phantom	David Staller
Christine Daae	Elizabeth Walsh
Raoul De Chagny	Grant Norman
The Persian	Harsh Nayyar
Carlotta	Beth McVey
Moncharmin	Darin De Paul
Richard	Richard Kinter
Madame Giry	Kim Ostrenko
Joseph Buquet	James Baldwin
Mifroid	Garrett States
Old Man Daae	Erick Walck
Young Christine	Alexandra Kinter
Young Raoul	Joey Leone
Ballet Chorus	Peter Anthony, Sylvia Casas, Brian Chenoweth, Cynthia Khoury, Angela Lattanzio, Joey Leone, Margaret Martinez

MUSICAL NUMBERS: Spirit of Music, Shadows in the House, Running the Show, Jewel Song (from "Faust"), Light and Darkness, An Able Woman, Perfect Music Perfect Love, Danse Macabre, Oh Hellish Wrath, Something Out There, excerpt from "Otello," Back into the Darkness

A serio-comic musical in 2 acts and 12 scenes.

*No photos submitted. Another version of "The Phantom of the Opera" by Ken Hill and Kenley/Noll was also touring, but failed to supply material for this volume.

RENAISSANCE THEATRE COMPANY

Artistic Director, Kenneth Branagh; Managing Director, David Parfitt; Executive Director, Stephen Evans; Associate Directors, Marilyn Eardley, Iona Price; Technical Director, Nicholas Ferguson; Designer, Jenny Tiramani; Lighting, Jon Linstrum; Music, Patrick Doyle; Assistant Director, Colin Wakefield; Fights, Nicholas Hall; Choreography, Gillian Gregory; Production Manager, Nicholas Ferguson; Text Adviser, Russell Jackson; Production Consultant, Hugh Cruttwell; Costume Supervisors, Susan Coates, Stephanie Collie; Company Manager, Marilyn Eardley; Stage Managers, Christine Hathway, Sally Hoskins; Press, Peter Thompson. Opened in the Mark Taper Forum, Los Angeles, on Sunday, Jan. 7, 1990, and still touring May 31, 1990.

A MIDSUMMER NIGHT'S DREAM

CAST

Moth	Christopher Armstrong
Peter Quince	Kenneth Branagh
Nick Bottom	Richard Briers
Peaseblossom	Ann Davies
Demetrius	Max Gold
Francis Flute	Gerard Horan
Snug	Karl James
Robin Starveling	Edward Jewesbury
Tom Snout	Bryan Kennedy
Lysander	James Larkin
Cobweb	Sue Long
Hermia	Francine Morgan
Hippolyta/Titania	Siobhan Redmond
Oberon/Theseus	Simon Roberts
Puck	Ethna Roddy
Helena	Emma Thompson
Egeus/Mustarseed/Philostrate	Jimmy Yuill

KING LEAR

CAST

Servant/Messenger/Officer	Christopher Armstrong
Edgar	Kenneth Branagh
King Lear	Richard Briers
Maid to Regan	Ann Davies
France/Curan/Herald	Max Gold
Cornwall	Gerard Horan
Albany	Karl James
Gloucester	Edward Jewesbury
Burgundy/Gentleman	Bryan Kennedy
Oswald	James Larkin
Maid to Goneril	Sue Long
Regan	Francine Morgan
Goneril	Siobhan Redmond
Edmund	Simon Roberts
Cordelia	Ethna Roddy
Fool	Emma Thompson
Kent	Jimmy Yuill

Performed in repertory with one intermission each performance of each play.

Jay Thompson Photos

Top Right: Gerard Horan, Bryan Kennedy, Edward Jewesbury, Kenneth Branagh, Karl James, Richard Briers in "A Midsummer Night's Dream" and below: James Larkin, Francine Morgan, Emma Thompson Right Center: Jimmy Yuill, Emma Thompson in "King Lear"

Richard Briars, Ethna Roddy, Kenneth Branagh in
"King Lear"

SARAFINA!

Conceived, Directed and Choreographed by Mbongeni Ngema; Music/Lyrics, Ngema with additional songs by Hugh Masekela; Musical Arrangements, Ngema/Masekela; Setting/Costumes, Sarah Roberts; Lighting, Mannie Manim; Set supervised by Ray Recht; Conductor, Ray Molefe; Sound, Tom Sorce; General Manager, Leonard Soloway; Production Manager, Peter Lawrence; Presented by Lincoln Center Theater/Committed Artists in association with Irene Gandy and Alma Viator; Associate Producers, Voza Rivers, Duma Ndlovu; Stage Manager, Bruce A. Hoover. Opened in New Haven's (Ct.) Shubert Theatre on Monday, March 19, 1990 and still touring May 31, 1990.

CAST

Leleti Khumalo, Pat Mlaba, Lindiwe Dtamini, Dumisani Diamini, Congo Hadeba, Nhlanhia Ngema, Baby Cele, Mhlathi Khuzwayo, Leleti Khumalo, Thandekile Nhlanhla, Thandi Zulu, Lindiwe Hlegwa, Thamsanga Hlatywayo, Siboniso Kumalo, Ntob'khona Diamini, Kipizane Skweyiya, Linda Mchunu, Kumbuzile Diamini, Thandani Mavimbela, Mubi Mokokeng, Harrison White, Nandi Ndlovu, Tim Hunter

MUSICAL NUMBERS: Overture, Zibuyile Emasisweni, Sarafina, The Lord's Prayer, Yes Mistress It's a Pity, Give Us Power, Afunani Amphoyisae Soweto, Nkosi Sikeleli, Afrika, Freedom Is Toming Tomorrow, Excuse Me Baby, Meeting Tonight, Stand and Fight, Uyamemeza Umgoma, Voster Sisolilwela, Wawungalelani, Mama, Sechaba, Isizwe, Goodbye, Kilimanjaro, Africa Burning in the Sun, Stimela Sasezola, Olayithi, Bring Back Nelson Mandela

A musical in two acts. The action takes place at the present time in South Africa.

Brigitte Lacombe Photos

STARLIGHT EXPRESS

Based on the original London and Broadway productions directed by Trevor Nunn; Choreography, Arlene Phillips; Music, Andrew Lloyd Webber; Lyrics, Richard Stilgoe; Orchestrations, David Cullen, Andrew Lloyd Webber; Sound, Martin Levan; Lighting, David Hersey; Design, John Napier; Executive Producer, Gatchell & Neufeld; Production Supervisor, Perry Cline; Technical Supervisor, Jeremiah J. Harris Associates; Casting, Johnson-Liff & Zerman; Musical Director, Paul Bogaev; Conductor, Jan Rosenberg; Automated Lighting, Aland Henderson; Film, Kevin Biles; Tour Lighting, Rick Belzer, Ted Mather; Costumes, John Napier; Associate Scenic Designer, Raymond Hussey; Direction/Choreography, Arlene Phillips; Props, Jack Montgomery; Wardrobe, Adelaide Laurino, David Hemenway, Deborah Cheretun; Hair Supervisors, Mundi Lawrey, Karen Dickenson; Make-up, Nanci Powell; Tour Direction, Columbia Artists; Company Managers, Robert Nolan, Joseph Traina; Stage Managers, Randall Whitescarver, Bonnie Panson, Dean Greer, Michal Fraley; Press, Solters/Roskin/Friedman. Opened Tuesday, Nov. 7, 1989*

CAST

Greaseball	Ron DeVito
Rusty	Sean McDermott
Pearl	Reva Rice
Dinah	Dawn Marie Church
Buffy	Nicole Picard
Ashley	Rachelle Rak
Rocky I	Ronald Garza
Rocky II	Dwight Toppin
Rocky III	Angel Vargas
Flat-Top	Dennis Courtney
Dustin	Anthony Marciona
Red Caboose	Todd Lester
Bobo	Peter Liciaga
Espresso	Steven Cates
Weltschaft	Fred Tallaksen
Turnov	Steven K. Dry
Hashamoto	Glenn Shiroma
Krupp	Nelson Yee
Wrench	Renee Lynette Chambers
Volta	Kimberly A. Gladman
Joule	Angela Pupello
Purse	Michael-Demby Cain
Electra	Eric Clausell
Poppa	Jimmy Lockett
Voice of the boy	Bori Flynn

Greaseball Gang: Michael-Demby Cain, Steven Cates, Dennis Courtney, Steven K. Dry, Ronald Garza, Peter Liciaga, Anthony Marciona, Glenn Shiroma, Fred Tallaksen, Dwight Toppin, Angel Vargas, Nelson Yee
Starlight Chorus: Mary Denise Bentley, Paul Binotto, Lori Flynn, Lon Hoyt
Swings: Matthew V. Daugherty, Steve Kadel, Bobby Love, Rick Mujica, Meera Popkin, Steven M. Schultz, Brett Stone, Matt Terry
MUSICAL NUMBERS: Rolling Stock, Engine of Love, Taunting Rusty, Lotta Locomotion, Freight, AC/DC, Pumping Iron, Make Up My Heart, Race One, There's Me, Poppa's Blues, Race Two, Laughing Stock, Starlight Express, The Rap, U.N.C.O.U.P.L.E.D., Wide Smile High Style, First Final, Right Place Right Time, I Am the Starlight, Final Selection, One Rock and Roll Too Many, Only You, Light at the End of the Tunnel.

A musical in two acts.

*Still touring May 31, 1990. For original Broadway production, see *Theatre World* Vol. 44.

Ken Howard Photos

Top Right: Reva Rice, Ron DeVito, Dawn Marie Church

PROFESSIONAL REGIONAL COMPANIES

(Failure to submit material necessitated omission of several companies)

ACT/A CONTEMPORARY THEATRE

Seattle, Washington
Twenty-fifth Season

Founding Director, Gregory A. Falls; Artistic Director, Jeff Steitzer; Producing Director, Phil Schermer; Managing Director, Susan Trapnell Moritz; Associate Artistic Director, David Ira Goldstein; Press, Michael Sande; Choreographer, Steve Tomkins; Sets, Scott Weldin, Karen Gjelsteen, Bill Forrester, Shelley Henze Schermer; Costumes, Rose Pederson, Sally Richardson, Susan Haas, Michael Sommers, Francis Kenny; Lighting, Rick Paulsen, Jody Briggs; Music Director, Daniel Barry; Sound, David Hunter Koch, Steven M. Klein, Jim Ragland; Stage Managers, Mary K. Sigvardt, Ten Eyck Swackhamer, Craig Weindling, Suzanne Fry.

PRODUCTIONS & CASTS

THE DOWNSIDE by Richard Dresser; Director, Jeff Steitzer; CAST: Jayne Muirhead, Cheri Sorenson, Mark Chamberlin, David Mong, Clyde Lund, David Drummond, Paul Redford, Rex McDowell
BREAKING THE SILENCE by Stephen Poliakoff; Director, David Ira Goldstein. CAST: Jane Jones, Jonas Basom, Mary Machala, Peter Silbert, Frank Corrado, D. Scott Glasser, Ben Prager
A WALK IN THE WOODS by Lee Blessing; Director, Jeff Steitzer. CAST: Laurence Ballard, Tony Mockus
RED NOSES by Peter Barnes; Director, Jeff Steitzer; Co-Directors, David Ira Goldstein, Judith Shahn. CAST: Geoffrey Alm, Eric Ray Anderson, Laurence Ballard, Kurt Beattie, Tom Francis, Eric Jensen, Jeff Klein, Jerry McGarity, David Mong, David Pichette, Michael Santo, Lizanne Schader, Judith Shahn, Peter Silbert, Tom Spiller, G. Valmont Thomas, Steve Tomkins, David White, David P. Whitehead, Michael Winters, R. Hamilton Wright
HAPPENSTANCE by Steven Dietz; Music/Lyrics, Eric Bain Peltoniemi; Director, Steven Dietz. CAST: Carole Jean Anderson, Mary Ewald, Richard Farrell, Chuck McQuary, Victor Morris, Jayne Muirhead, Robert Nadir, Cynthena Sanders, Claudine Wallace, Michael Winters
WOMAN IN MIND by Alan Ayckbourn; Director, David Ira Goldstein. CAST: Patricia Hodges, Michael Winters, Laurence Ballard, Lori Larsen, David P. Whitehead, Robert Nadir, Mark Chamberlin, Mar'ia Lodahl
A CHRISTMAS CAROL adapted by Gregory A. Falls; Director, Jeff Steitzer; CAST: Laurence Ballard, Peter Silbert, Larry Paulsen, J. Christopher O'Connor, Craig Huisenga, Frankie Trevino, Mark Drusch, Jeanne Paulsen, David Drummond, Rex McDowell, Ryan O'Connor, Michael Tuttle, Karen Meyer, Lori Larsen, Michael Tompkins, Shana Bestock, Gretchen O'Connell, Claudine Wallace

Chris Bennion Photos

Right Center: Laurence Ballard in "A Christmas Carol" Top: David Pichette, R. Hamilton Wright, G. Valmont Thomas in "Red Roses"

Laurence Ballard, Tony Mockus in "A Walk in the Woods"

ALLIANCE THEATRE COMPANY

Atlanta, Georgia
Twenty-first Season

Artistic Director, Robert J. Farley; Managing Director, Edith H. Love; Associate Artistic Director, Kenneth Leon; Literary Manager, Sandra Deer; Production Manager, Rixon Hammond; Technical Director, Bob Hoffman; Production Stage Manager, Pat A. Flora; Stage Managers, Julie A. Richardson, Dale C. Lawrence, Hazel Youngs, Kathy E. Richardson, John Kirman; General Manager, T. Jane Bishop; Press, Janece Shaffer; Marketing, Mark Arnold

PRODUCTIONS & CASTS

COTTON PATCH GOSPEL; Book, Tom Key, Russell Treyz; Music/Lyrics, Harry Chapin; Based on "The Cotton Patch Version of Matthew and John" by Clarence Jordan; Director, Russell M. Treyz; Musical Director, Scott Ainslie; Set, John Falabella; Lighting, P. Hamilton Shinn. CAST: Scott Ainslie, Dan Fox, Tom Key, Jim Lauderdale, Steven J. Riddle.

SOUTHERN CROSS by Jon Klein; Director, Robert J. Farley; Set, Victor Becker; Costumes, Pamela Scofield; Lighting, Jim Sale. CAST: Bruce Evers, Sam Hensley Jr., William Jay, Tom Key, Gerald Brown, Lynn Brown, John Clark, Stuart Culpepper, Brad Davidorf, Mark Kincaid, Larry Larson, Carol Mitchell-Leon, Jack Mason, James Mayberry, Janet Metzger, Margo Moorer, Joanna Neel, Rosemary Newcott, Afemo Omilami, Elizabeth Omilami, Sam Peabody, Jamal Peoples, John Purcell, Brian Reddy, Leon Ross, Lawrence E. Snead, Tom Stechschulte, Eric Stenson, Ken Strong, Peter Thomasson, Regina Tucker.

ANNIE GET YOUR GUN; Book, Herbert & Dorothy Fields; Music/Lyrics, Irving Berlin; Director, Fran Soeder; Musical Director, M. Michael Fauss; Choreographer, Janet Watson; Set, James Leonard Joy; Costumes, Mariann Verheyen; Lighting, Marcia Madeira. CAST: Mitch Andrews, Jonica Asters, Wade Benson, Robin Blitch, Kim Bowers-Rheay, Barry Bruce, Bill Buell, Lulu Downs, Donna Frotscher, Jeffrey Goodson, Lainie Gulliksen, Marguerite Hannah, Joanna Hayes, Thomas Ikeda, Roberta Illg, Joel Imbody, Doug Johnson, Bryan C. Jones, Tom Key, Kim Kilby, Doug Lothes, Judge Luckey, Thomas Jay Miller, Pamela Myers, Brian Parks, Angela Pridgen, Robin Robinson, Jay Scovill, Steven Shawn, Kathryn Skatual, Jane Smithwick, Thaddeus Valdez, Brad Wages, Robert Yacko.

FENCES by August Wilson; Director, Kenny Leon; Set, Michael Olich; Costumes, Susan E. Mickey; Lighting, Ann G. Wrightson. CAST: Frederick Charles Canada, Lauren Johnson, Tramekia Mangham, Carol Mitchell-Leon, Bill Nunn, Afemo Omilami, John Henry Redwood, Tico Wells, Bruce Beatty.

GAL BABY by Sandra Deer; Director, Kenny Leon; Set, Michael Olich; Costumes, Susan E. Mickey; Lighting, Ann G. Wrightson. CAST: Brenda Bynum, Sylvia Cardwell, Mr. Kim Chan, Raphael Nash, Peter Thomasson, Jeffrey Watkins.

THE COCKTAIL HOUR by A. R. Gurney; Director, Dan Bonnell; Set, David Potts; Costumes, Jeff Cone; Lighting, Liz Lee. CAST: Richard Bekins, Laurie Kennedy, Rex Robbins, Eve Roberts.

DRIVING MISS DAISY by Alfred Uhry; Director, Robert J. Farley; Set/Costume/Lighting, Michael Stauffer. CAST: Al Hamacher, William Hall Jr., DeAnn Mears, Mary Nell Santacroce.

MEASURE FOR MEASURE by William Shakespeare, adapted and directed by Skip Foster; Set, Victor Becker; Costume, Susan E. Mickey; Lighting, Liz Lee. CAST: Peter Bradbury, Jonathan Davis, Scott MacDonald, Rosemary Newcott, Kee Strong, Ken Strong.

THE VOICE OF THE PRAIRIE by John Olive; Director, Fontaine Syer; Set, Dex Edwards; Costumes, Jeff Cone; Lighting, P. Hamilton Shinn. CAST: Howard Brunner, Scott Depoy, Rosemary Newcott, Jeff Woodman.

COBB by Lee Blessing; Director, Lloyd Richards; Set, Rob Greenberg; Costumes, Joel O. Thayer; Lighting, Ashley York Kennedy. CAST: George Gerdes, Dan Martin, William Newman, James E. Reynolds.

THE ADVENTURES OF MARCO POLO written and directed by Skip Foster; Set, Victor Becker; Costumes, Susan E. Mickey; Lighting, Liz Lee. CAST: Jonathan Davis, Vicki Ellis, Donald Griffin, Elisa Hurt, Nancy Ann Lowery, Buck Newman, Allen O'Reilly, Brad Sherrill, Kee Strong, K. Edward Vickery.

MERLIN! by Larry Larson, Levi Lee; Director, Larry Larson; Set, Dex Edwards; Costumes, Jeff Cone; Lighting, Liz Lee. CAST: Ann Marie Akin, Teresa DeBerry, Elisa Hurt, Judge Luckey, Jack Mason, Allen O'Reilly, Sam Peabody, Clark Taylor.

Jonathan Burnette Photos

Top Right: Rosemary Newcott, Peter Bradbury in "Measure for Measure" Below: Bill Buell, Robert Yacko, Pamela Myers, Tom Key in "Annie Get Your Gun"

John Henry Redwood, Carol Mitchell-Leon in
"Fences"

ACTORS THEATRE OF LOUISVILLE

Louisville, Kentucky
Twenty-sixth Season

Producing Director, Jon Jory; Administrative Director, Alexander Speer; Associate Director, Marilee Hebert-Slater; Development, J. Christopher Wineman; Press, Elizabeth W. Clarke; Sets, Paul Owen; Costumes, Lewis D. Rampino; Lighting, Ralph Dressler; Sound, Mark Hendren; Props, Mark J. Bissonnette; Production Manager, Frazier W. Marsh; Stage Manager, Lori M. Doyle; Technical Director, Steve Goodin

RESIDENT COMPANY: Bob Burrus, Ray Fry, V Craig Heidenreich, Fred Major, Adale O'Brien, Mark Sawyer-Dailey

INTERN COMPANY: Steve Bova, Diane Box, Gillian Darlow, Rob Dillard, Chris Eigeman, Kara Flannery, Jeremy Gold, Arthur Halpern, Elizabeth Hayward, Margaret Howard, Marta Johnson, Matt Kozlowski, Rob Lanier, Josh Liveright, Carrie Luft, Jennifer Marshall, Amanda McElya, Belinda Morgan, Connan Morrissey, Melissa Pepper, Sarah E. Peters, Karen Price, Paul Rogers, Bruce Marshall Romans, Mary Samson, Kate Splaine, Hannah Vesenka

GUEST ARTISTS: Joan Ackermann-Blount, Jack Aranson, Dennis Bailey, Gail Benedict, Curtis Blake, Selena Carey-Jones, David Chandler, Catherine Christianson, Glory Crampton, Mike Craver, Kymberly Dakin, Randy Danson, Beth Dixon, William Duff-Griffin, Barbara eda-Young, Rebecca Ellens, Christine Elliot, Patricia Ann Everson, Christopher Fields, William Frankfather, Margaret Gibson, Peter Michael Goetz, Tom Greenfield, Barbara Gulan, Mark Hardwick, Helen Harrelson, Annette Helde, Michelle Horman, Sakina Jaffrey, Hubert Baron Kelly, David A. Kimball, Diane Kinerk, Bob Krakower, Tom Luce, Neil Maffin, David Manis, Gregory Manukov, Vaughn McBride, Tom McGowan, Ellen McLaughlin, Peter Messaline, Percy Metcalf, Kim Moore, Ann Bennett Nesby, Anne O'Sullivan, Richard Odom, Patricia Ben Peterson, John Pielmeier, Andrew Polk, Greg Porreta, Alan Pottinger, Peggity Price, Janet Sarno, Priscilla Shanks, Lori Shearer, Madeleine Sherwood, Clarence Snow, Scott Sowers, Don Spalding, Susan Riley Stevens, Pamela Stewart, Robert Stoeckle, Lanitta Swanson, Myra Taylor, Hal Tenny, Michael Terry, Christopher Wells, Steve Wise, William Youmans, Mark Zeisler, Sergei Zemisov, Igor Zolotovitski

PRODUCTIONS: *The Seagull* by Anton Chekhov, translated by Michael Frayn, *Children of the Sun* by Maxim Gorky, translated by Zirka Derlycia, *Cinzano* by Liudmila Petrushevskaya, *Rock 'n' Roles from William Shakespeare* by Jim Luigs, *Sing Hallelujah!* by Worth Gardner and Donald Lawrence, *The Immigrant* by Mark Harelik, *Frankie & Johnny in the Clair de Lune* by Terrence McNally, *A Christmas Carol* by Charles Dickens, *The Gift of the Magi* by Peter Ekstrom, *Oil City Symphony* by Mike Craver, Debra Monk, Mark Hardwick, Mary Murfitt, The Humana Festival of New American Plays, *The Boys Next Door* by Tom Griffin, *As You Like It* by William Shakespeare

PREMIERES: *Anton Himself* by Karen Sunde, *The Pink Studio* by Jane Anderson, *2 Plays* by Romulus Linney, *Vital Signs* by Jane Martin, *In Darkest America* by Joyce Carol Oates (2 one-act plays: *Tone Clusters/The Eclipse*), *Zara Spook and Other Lures* by Joan Ackermann-Blount, *The Swan* by Elizabeth Egloff, *Infinity's House* by Ellen McLaughlin

David Talbott Photos

Right: Madeleine Sherwood, Beth Dixon in "In Darkest Africa" **Above:** Anne O'Sullivan, Joan Ackermann-Blount in "Zara Spook . . ." **(R)** Pamela Stewart, Paul Rogers in "Vital Signs" **Top:** Mike Craver, Michelle Horman, Christine Elliott, Mark Hardwick in "Oil City Symphony"

Peter Michael Goetz, William McNulty in "The Pink Studio"

Dennis Bailey, Bob Burrus in "The Immigrant"

120

AMERICAN CONSERVATORY THEATRE

San Francisco, California
Twenty-fourth Season

Artistic Director, Edward Hastings; Managing Director, John Sullivan; Conservatory Co-Directors, Sabin Epstein, Susan Stauter; General Manager, Dianne M. Prichard; Company Manager, Mary Garrett; Associate Artistic Directors, Joy Carlin, Dennis Powers; Resident Director, Albert Takazauckas; Directors, Paul Blake, Joy Carlin, George Coates, Sabin Epstein, John C. Fletcher, Edward Hastings, Albert Takazauckas, Laird Williamson; Sets, Robert Blackman, Joel Fontaine, Ralph Funicello, Rick Goodwin, Gerard Howland; Costumes, Beaver Bauer, David F. Draper, Robert Fletcher, Robert Morgan, Terence Tam Soon, Warren Travis, Sandra Woodall; Lighting, Derek Duarte; Production Stage Manager, Karen Van Zandt; Stage Managers, Eugene Barcone, Bruce Elsperger, Alice Eliott Smith.
COMPANY: Wilma Bonet, Velina Brown, Richard Butterfield, Joy Carlin, Nancy Carlin, Keene Curtis, Andrew Dolan, Peter Donat, Sam Fontana, Scott Freeman, Rick Hamilton, Stephen Hanan, Lawrence Hecht, Leslie Hicks, Ed Hodson, Leslie Ishii, Steven Anthony Jones, Richard Johnston, Robert Keefe, Ruth Kobart, Barry Kraft, Lauren Lane, Anne Lawder, Michael Learned, Frances Lee McCain, Michael McFall, Michael McShane, Michael Maguire, David Maier, Wesley Mann, Andrea Marcovicci, Nadine Mozon, Fredi Olster, Luis Oropeza, Frank Ottiwell, William Paterson, Martino N. Pistone, Daniel Reichert, Ken Ruta, Michael Scott Ryan, Shari Simpson, Marlynn Smith, Patrick Stretch, Harold Surratt, Deborah Sussel, Howard Swain, Cathy Thomas-Grant, Jeanie Tracy, Sydney Walker, Bruce Williams, Pippa Winslow, Michael Winters, Gretchen Wyler, Kelvin Han Yee.
PRODUCTIONS: *Right Mind* by George Coates Performance Works (*World Premiere*), *Two Acts of Passion: Dutchman* by Amiri Baraka and *Clara* by Arthur Miller (*West Coast Premiere*), *A Tale of Two Cities,* adapted by Nagle Jackson (*World Premiere*), *A Christmas Carol,* adapted by Dennis Powers and Laird Williamson, *Almost Like Being in Love: The Magic of Alan Jay Lerner,* adapted by Paul Blake (*World Premiere*), *Judevine* by David Budbill (*Professional Premiere*), *Twelfth Night* by William Shakespeare, *Hapgood* by Tom Stoppard, *The Imaginary Invalid* by Moliere, *Burn This* by Lanford Wilson, *Plays in Progress* series: *Pick Up Ax* by Anthony Clarvoe, *Inside Technocult* by David Michael Erickson, *Them That's Got* by Robyn Hatcher, *Food and Shelter* by Jane Anderson, *Utterances* by Susan Yankowitz

Morty Sohl Photos

Right: Howard Swain, Cathy Thomas-Grant, Lauren Lane, Anne Lawder, David Maier, Scott Freeman in "Judevine"
Top: Barry Kraft, Michael Learned in "Hapgood"

Ruth Kobart, Peter Donat in "Imaginary Invalid" Above: Rick Hamilton, Daniel Reichert, Wesley Mann, Andrea Marcovicci in "Burn This"

Michael McShane, Nadine Mozon, Leslie Ishii, Wesley Mann in "Twelfth Night" Above: Harold Surratt holds Nicholas Bicardo in "A Christmas Carol"

AMERICAN REPERTORY THEATRE

Cambridge, Massachusetts
Eleventh Season

Artistic Director, Robert Brustein; Managing Director, Robert J. Orchard; Associate Director, Richard Riddell; Artistic Administrator, Jan Geidt; Literary Directors, Michael Bloom/Robert Scanlan; General Manager, Jonathan Seth Miller; Director of Development and Long-Range Planning, Charles Marz; Director of Marketing, Henry Lussier; Press, Katalin Mitchell; Technical Production Director, Max Leventhal; Stage Managers, Abbie H. Katz/Anne S. King.

PRODUCTIONS & CASTS

TRU; written and directed by Jay Presson Allen; Produced by Lewis Allen & David Brown; From the words and works of Truman Capote; Sets, David Mitchell; Costumes, Sarah Edwards; Lighting, Ken Billington/Jason Kantrowitz; Sound, Otts Munderloh; Make-up, Kevin Haney; Wig, Paul Huntley. CAST: Robert Morse
1000 AIRPLANES ON THE ROOF; Composed and directed by Philip Glass; Written by David Henry Hwang; Set Design/Projections by Jerome Sirlin; Presented in association with Emerson College; Produced by Jedediah Wheeler for the Real Events Company; Sound, Kurt Munkacsi; Music direction, Martin Goldray; Lighting, Robert Wierzel; Performed by the Philip Glass Ensemble. CAST: Betsy Aidem
MORE SEX DRUGS ROCK & ROLL; Written and performed by Eric Bogosian, directed by Jo Bonney. CAST: Eric Bogosian.
THE BALD SOPRANO/THE CHAIRS by Eugene Ionesco; Translated by Donald Watson; Directed by Andrei Belgrader; Sets, Anita Stewart; Costumes, Candice Donnelly; Lighting, Stephen Strawbridge; Sound, Maribeth Back. CAST: Lynn Chausow, Thomas Derrah, Deborah Lewin, Jeremy Geidt, Tresa Hughes, Rodney Scott Hudson, Roberts Blossom.
TWELFTH NIGHT by William Shakespeare; Directed by Andrei Serban; Music composed by Mel Marvin; Sets, Derek McLane; Costumes, Catherine Zuber; Lighting, Howell Binkley; Sound, Maribeth Back; Fight Choreography, William Finlay. CAST: Kario Salem, Ross Salinger, Christopher Colt, Cherry Jones, Kevin Costin, Jeremy Geidt, Lynn Chausow, Robert Stanton, Thomas Derrah, Diane Lane, James Lally, Steven Skybell, Rodney Scott Hudson, Dan Nutu, Deborah Lewin.
MAJOR BARBARA by George Bernard Shaw; Directed by Michael Engler; Sets, Philipp Jung; Costumes, Catherine Zuber; Lighting, James Ingalls; Sound, Maribeth Back. CAST: Steven Skybell, Kate Wilkinson, Cherry Jones, Ellen Kohrman, Kario Salem, Robert Stanton, William Young, Jeremy Geidt, Bronia Stefan Wheeler, Thomas Derrah, Rodney Scott Hudson, Fran Harrison, Mark Zeisler, Julia Pearlstein, Dean Harrison.
THE FATHER by August Strindberg; Adapted and directed by Robert Brustein; Sets, Derek McLane; Costumes, Dunya Ramicova; Lighting, Richard Riddell; Sound, Maribeth Back. CAST: Christopher Lloyd, Rodney Scott Hudson, Dean Harrison, Christopher Colt, Candy Buckley, Dan Nutu, Bronia Stefan Wheeler, Daria Martel.
THE CAUCASIAN CHALK CIRCLE by Bertolt Brecht; Translated by Ralph Manheim; Directed by Slobodan Unkovski; Music composed by Mel Marvin; Sets, Meta Hocevar; Costumes, Catherine Zuber; Lighting, Richard Riddell; Music Director/Conductor, Barry Rocklin; Sound, Maribeth Back. CAST: Thomas Derrah, Candy Buckley, Gustave Johnson, Remo Airaldi, Matthew Sheehan, Robert Stanton, Steven Zahn, Kevin Costin, Nicolette Vajtay, Donna LaBrecque, Joy Ehrlich, Deborah Lewin, Cherry Jones, Steven Skybell, Sean Runnette, Daria Martel, Ross Salinger, Christopher Colt, Cassidy Downing-Bryant/Tyler John Dorson/Gabriel Maeck.
ROAD TO NIRVANA by Arthur Kopit; Directed by Michael Bloom; Sets, Scott Bradley; Costumes, Ellen McCartney; Lighting, Peter West; Sound, Maribeth Back. Original song "Who I Am" words and music by Frank Wildhorn and Arthur Kopit. CAST: Mark Zeisler, Candy Buckley, Lynn Chausow, Thomas Derrah, Steve Hofvendahl, Ray Bokhour, Debora Jean Culpin, David Grove.
THE LOST BOYS by Allan Knee; Directed by Jerome Kilty; Set, Scott Bradley; Costumes, Karen Eister; Lighting, John Ambrosone; Sound, Maribeth Back. CAST: Jeremy Geidt, Ken Jones, Steven Skybell, Robert Stanton, Steven Zahn, Ross Salinger, Cherry Jones.

Photographer: Richard M. Feldman

Left Center: Jeremy Geidt, Cherry Jones, Julia Pearlstein, Mark Zeisler, Fran Harrison in "Major Barbara" Above: Cherry Jones, Diane Lane in "Twelfth Night" Top: Lynn Chausow, Deborah Lewin, Thomas Derrah in "The Bald Soprano"

Cherry Jones, Thomas Derrah, Steven Skybell in "The Caucasian Chalk Circle"

Joe Barrett, Sophie Hayden in "A Fine and Private Place"
Right: Maggie Rush, Adina Porter, Pamala Tyson, Jeffrey
Wright in "Bus Stop" Below: Michael Elich, Liann Pattison,
J. R. Horne in "Legal Tender"

AMERICAN STAGE COMPANY

Fairleigh Dickinson University
Teaneck, New Jersey
Fifth Season

Artistic Director, Paul Sorvino; Executive Producer, Theodore Rawlins; Executive Director, James R. Singer; Business Manager, Robert A. Lusko; Associate Artistic Director, Sheldon Epps; Artist in Residence, John Amos; Resident Director, Seret Scott; Resident Scenic Designer, James Morgan; Production Stage Manager, Mary Ellen Allison
GUEST ARTISTS: John Amos, James Pritchett, Robert Kalfin, Julianne Boyd

PRODUCTIONS & CASTS

BUS STOP by William Inge; Directed by Seret Scott. CAST: Jerome Preston Bates, Clebert Ford, Kim Sullivan, Jasper McGruder, Adina Porter, Maggie Rush, Ascanio Sharpe, Pamala Tyson, Jeffrey Wright.
THE LEAST OF THESE (World Premiere) by Martin Halpern; Directed by Alex Dmitriev. CAST: James Pritchett, Martha Thompson, Matthew Lewis, Joan Matthiessen, Jack R. Marks.
A FINE AND PRIVATE PLACE (World Premiere) Book and Lyrics by Erik Haagensen; Music by Richard Isen; Directed by Robert Kalfin. CAST: Mary Ellen Ashley, Sophie Hayden, Gabriel Barre, Joe Barrett, David Green.
LEGAL TENDER (World Premiere) by Mark St. Germain. Directed by Julianne Boyd. CAST: Liann Pattison, Michael Elich, J. R. Horne.
HALLEY'S COMET (World Premiere) by John Amos; Directed by John Harris. CAST: John Amos

Joan Matthiessen, Martha Thompson, James Pritchett in
"The Least of These"

Yaphet Kotto, Kim Hamilton, Wally Taylor in "Fences"
Right: Pamela Nyberg, Henry Strozier in "A Doll House" Below: David Galloway, Trevor Jackson, Luis Ramos, Kelly Chauncey Smith, Roumel Reaux in "Stand-Up Tragedy"

ARENA STAGE

Washington, D.C.
Thirty-ninth Season

Producing Director, Zelda Fichandler; Associate Producing Director, Douglas C. Wager; Associate Producer, Guy Berquist; Artistic Associate, Tazewell Thompson; Interim Executive Director, Bert I. Helfinstein; Producing Associate, Benita Hofstetter; Directors, Liviu Ciulei, Joe Dowling, Zelda Fichandler, Max Mayer, Tazewell Thompson, Douglas C. Wager, Paul Walker; Sets, Loy Arcenas, Liviu Ciulei, F. Hallinan Flood, David M. Glenn, Andrew Jackness, Douglas Stein; Costumes, Smaranda Branescu, Ann Hould-Ward, Betty Siegel, Marjorie Slaiman, Paul Tazewell; Lighting, Donald Holder, Allen Lee Hughes, Christopher V. Lewton, Nancy Schertler; Sound, Eric Annis, Susan R. White; Stage Managers, Maxine Kraswoski Bertone, Janet Clark, Jessica Evans, Tara M. Galvin, Martha Knight, Wendy Streeter.

RESIDENT COMPANY: Stanley Anderson, Richard Bauer, Marissa Copeland, Ralph Cosham, Terrence Currier, Margo Hall, Tom Hewitt, Tana Hicken, Clayton LeBouef, David Marks, Cary Anne Spear, Henry Strozier, John Leonard Thompson, Halo Wines

GUEST ARTISTS: Jennifer Selby Albright, George Alexander, Ricky Allen, Denis Arndt, Helen-Jean Arthur, Becky Ann Baker, Chris Bauer, Tuka Bazin, Christina Benkahala, Shawn Benkahala, Alisa Beth Bernstein, Trazana Beverley, Jacy Bird, Jeffrey Bizub, Louise Bloom, Rufus Bonds Jr., Aisha Boston, Teagle F. Bougere, Matthew Allen Bretz, Earl Buchanan, Joy Faye Burgess, David Calloway, Leo Charles, Brian Clarke, Neana Collins, Jarlath Conroy, Victoria Cosham, Quinn Cress, A. Benard Cummings, Tenille Daniels, Ruby Dee, Todd Dellinger, Erick Devine, John Deyle, Mark Douglas, Norman Fitz, Clebert Ford, Thomas Fox, Victor Garber, David Garrison, Kathleen Goldpaugh, Kim Hamilton, Dorothea Hammond, C. W. Hardy, M. E. Hart, Casey Heer, Jim Hicks, Samantha Hope, Trevor Jackson, Kathryn Ann James, Keith Johnson, Danielle T. Koch, Yaphett Kotto, Ken LaRon, Jennifer M. Lee, Abby Lynn, Neil Maffin, Narin Mazzie, Lowry Miller, Bill Mondy, Christina Moore, Mary Gordon Murray, Pamela Nyberg, Constance Ogden, Nick Olcott, LaFontaine Oliver, Petronia Paley, Jonathan Earl Peck, William Pitts, Luis Ramos, Roumel Reaux, Lawrence Redmond, Louise Reynolds, Nannette Rickert, Eddie Robinson, Wendy Robinson, Tiffany Rose, Tonia Rowe, Melodee Savage, Thom Sesma, Monti Sharp, Kelly Chauncey Smith, Alex Spencer, Wally Taylor, Jeffrey V. Thompson, Kerry Thompson, Brad Waller, Steve Washington, Amanda Waters, Deanna Wells, Bart Whiteman, Ruth Williamson, Jeffrey Wright, Dorothy Yanes, Stefanie Zadravec.

PRODUCTIONS: *A Midsummer Night's Dream* by William Shakespeare, *The Glass Menagerie* by Tennessee Williams, *The Man Who Came to Dinner* by Moss Hart and George S. Kaufman, *Stand-Up Tragedy* by Bill Cain, *Merrily We Roll Along* by Stephen Sondheim (music/lyrics), George Furth (book), *A Doll House* by Henrik Ibsen, *Fences* by August Wilson, *Juno and the Paycock* by Sean O'Casey, *Stephen Wade on the Way Home* by Stephen Wade

PREMIERE: *Conquest of the South Pole* by Manfred Karge, adapted by Silas Jones and Laurence Maslon

Joan Marcus Photos

Tonia Rowe, Ruby Dee, Jonathan Earl Peck in "The Glass Menagerie"

124

ARKANSAS REPERTORY THEATRE

Little Rock, Arkansas

Producing Artist Director, Cliff Fannin Baker; Equity Stage Managers, Carey Upton, Marcie Leek; Resident Scenic Designer and Technical Director, Mike Nichols; Production Manager, Charles Carr; Props, Marion Hampton; Costumers, Don Bolinger, Marilyn Powers; Resident Sound Designer, David Polantz; Development Director, Ruth Shepherd, Development Coordinator and Company Manager, Linda Sue Sanders; Marketing and Public Relations Director, Sherry Gavin.

INTERN/APPRENTICE COMPANY: Stage Management, Lisa Abbott, Jimmy-John Akins; Properties, Sean Michael DeVine; Sound, Brian Hemesath; Lighting, Chris Gulledge, William Young; Acting, Nathaniel Buck, Todd William Frampton, Mary Hilton, Kathleen McClaine, Jonna McElrath, Rusty Nail, Denise Odom; Public Relations and Marketing, Susan Bridges, Leann Reas; Development, Scott Hutcheson; House Management and Box Office, Brady Leet; Box Office, Libby Smith.

GUEST ARTISTS: Acting/Directing, Frank Bonner, Sally Sockwell, Mary Steenburgen, Mark DeMichele; Technical Artists, Nels Anderson, Connie Fails, Kathy C. Gray, Mark Hughes, David Neville, Sally Riggs, Jeff Thomson, Elfin Frederick Vogel.

PRODUCTIONS AND CASTS

NOISES OFF by Michael Frayn; Director, Terry Sneed; Scenic Designer, Nels Anderson; Costumes, Mark Hughes; Lighting, Robert A. Jones; Sound, Shari Bethel. CAST: Theresa Quick (Dotty Otley), James Harbour (Lloyd Dallas), Don Bolinger (Garry Lejeune), Jane McNeill (Brook Ashton), Vivian Morrison (Poppy Norton-Taylor), Peter Bradshaw (Frederick Fellowes), Caroline Pugh (Belinda Blair), Jon Meyer (Tim Allgood), Alan Hanson, (Selsdon Mowbray).

THE NERD by Larry Shue, Director, Mark DeMichele; Scenic Designer, Mike Nichols; Costumes, Don Bolinger; Lighting, Robert A. Jones; Sound, Shari Bethel. CAST: Peter Bradshaw (Willum Cubbert), Molly Posey (Tansy McGinnis), Terry Sneed (Axel Hammond), Ronald J. Aulgur (Warnock Waldgrave), Dianne Tack (Clelia Waldgrave), Jay Johnston (Thor Waldgrave), Carl Sturmer (Rick Steadman).

BROADWAY BOUND by Neil Simon; Director, Cliff Fannin Baker; Scenic Designer, Mike Nichols; Costumes, Don Bolinger; Lighting, Kathy C. Gray; Sound, David Polantz. CAST: Jean Lind (Kate), Mahlon Sharp (Ben), Steve Wilkerson (Eugene), J. Barrett Cooper (Stanley), Jo Boswell (Blanche), Ronald J. Aulgur (Jack).

LADY DAY AT EMERSON'S BAR AND GRILL by Lanie Robertson with musical arrangements by Danny Holgate; Director, Brad Mooy; Musical Director, Fred Rakestraw; Scenic Designer, Richard Grace; Costumes, Don Bolinger; Lighting, William Young; Sound, David Polantz. CAST: Mable Bealer (Billie Holiday), Fred Rakestraw (Jimmy Powers).

A MIDSUMMER NIGHT'S DREAM by William Shakespeare; Director, Elfin Frederick Vogel; Choreographer, Charles Halden; Scenic Designer, Mike Nichols; Costumes, Mark Hughes; Lighting, David Neville; Sound, David Polantz. CAST: Clive Carlin (Theseus, Oberon), Kathleen McClaine (Hippolyta, Titania), Charles Halden (Puck, Philostrate), Bob Hulsey (Egeus), Jonna McElrath (Hermia), J. Barrett Cooper (Demetrius), Steve Wilkerson (Lysander), Mary Hilton (Helena), Candyce Hinkle (Paula Quince, Prologue), Ronald J. Aulgur (Nick Bottom, Pyramus), Todd William Frampton (Francis Flute, Thisbe), Martin McGeachy (Robin Starveling, Moonshine), Kermit Medsker (Tom Snout, Wall), Richard Glover (Snug, Lion), Rusty Nail (Cobweb), Sarah Boss (Peaseblossom), Misty Rice (Spirit), Ben Lybrand (Moth), Nathaniel Buck (Mustardseed).

GUYS AND DOLLS with music and lyrics by Frank Loesser; Book by Jo Swerling and Abe Burrows; Director, Cliff Fannin Baker; Choreographer, Sally Riggs; Musical Director, Kermit Medsker; Scenic Designer, Mike Nichols; Costumes, Mark Hughes; Lighting, Kathy C. Gray; Sound, David Polantz. CAST: Ronald J. Aulgur (Arvide Abernathy), Guy Couch (Rusty Charlie), Tom Crone (Lt. Brannigan), Richard Glover (Nathan Detroit), Julianne Griffin (Sarah Brown), Candyce Hinkle (General Matilda B. Cartwright), Robert Hulsey (Big Jule), Ralph Hyman (Benny Southstreet), Mark Whitman Johnson (Sky Masterson), Dianne Tack (Agatha), Joe Thibodeau (Harry the Horse), Debbie Weber (Miss Adelaide), Steve Wilkerson (Nicely-Nicely Johnson), Peggy Kooch, Debbie Rawn, Pamela Wells-Ruhl, Jana Stodola, Mary Twedt (Hot Box Girls), Nathaniel Buck, Brandi Bunting, Sharon Carr, Larry Edwards, Joe Featherston, Todd William Frampton, Mary Hilton, Jonna McElrath, Rusty Nail, Joey Stocks, Susan Stopoulos, Mike Tidwell (Ensemble).

LITTLE LULU IN A TIGHT ORANGE DRESS by John G. Moynihan; Director, Cliff Fannin Baker; Scenic Designer, Mike Nichols; Costumes, Connie Fails; Lighting, Crickette Brendel; Sound, Brian Hemesath. CAST: Jennifer Griffin (Judy), Jean Lind (Yvonne), Sally Sockwell (Oma Lynn).

Jennifer Griffin, Jean Lind, Sally Sockwell in "Little Lulu in a Tight Orange Dress"

THE MYSTERY OF IRMA VEP by Charles Ludlam; Director, Mark DeMichele; Scenic Designer, Mike Nichols; Costumes, Rosemary E. Bengele; Lighting, Kathy Gray; Sound, David Polantz. CAST: Richard Glover (Jane Twisden, Lord Edgar Hillcrest, An Intruder), Bob Sorenson (Nicodemus Underwood, Lady Enid Hillcrest, Alcazar).

I'M NOT RAPPAPORT by Herb Gardner; Director, Frank Bonner; Scenic Designer, Jeff Thomson; Costumes, Don Bolinger; Lighting, David Neville; Sound, David Polantz. CAST: Ronald J. Aulgur (Nat), Tyress Allen (Midge), Richard Glover (Danforth), Jonna McElrath (Laurie), Todd William Frampton (Gilley), Graciela Marin (Clara), Mark Whitman Johnson (The Cowboy).

SPECIAL EVENTS: BARGAINS play reading by Jack Heifner, directed by Cliff Fannin Baker, starring Mary Steenburgen; **ROAD,** an intern showcase directed by Brad Mooy

BOYS' PLAY *(World Premiere)* by Jack Heifner; Director, Cliff Fannin Baker; Scenic Designer, Mike Nichols; Costumes, Don Bolinger; Lighting, Crickette Brendel; Sound, David Polantz. CAST: Todd William Frampton (Tom), Nathaniel Buck (Joe).

ARIZONA THEATRE COMPANY

Tucson, Arizona

Artistic Director, Gary Gisselman; Managing Director, Robert Alpaugh; Development/Phoenix, Doug Richards; Development/Tucson, Don W. Haskell; Marketing, Margo Gisselman; Press, Prindle Gorman-Oomens; Production Manager, Kent Conrad; Stage Manager, Elizabeth Lohr; Technical Director, Scott K. Haun; Props, Mark Harris, Robyn Stoutenburg

PRODUCTIONS & CASTS

QUILTERS; Director, Gary Gisselman; Musical Director, Anita Ruth; Set, Greg Lucas; Costumes, Jared Aswegan; Lighting, Don Darnutzer. CAST: Grace Keagy, Seraiah Carol, Bridget Connors, Kathy Fitzgerald, Karon Kearney, Delrae Novak, Teresa Wolf
THE COCKTAIL HOUR; Director, Richard Ramos; Set, Tom Butsch; Costumes, David Kay Mickelsen. CAST: Dalton R. Dearborn, Terrence Caza, Laurinda Barrett, Liann Pattison
THE BOYS NEXT DOOR; Director, David Ira Goldstein; Set, Greg Lucas; Costumes, David Kay Mickelsen; Lighting, Don Darnutzer. CAST: Richard Farrell, George Anthony Bell, Robert Nadir, Wayne A. Evenson, Tom Harrison, Oliver Cliff, Delrae Novak, Susan Appel, Benjamin Stewart
THE IMPORTANCE OF BEING EARNEST; Director, Gary Gisselman; Set, Greg Lucas; Costumes, David Kay Mickelsen; Lighting, Don Darnutzer. CAST: Wayne A. Evenson, Tom Harrison, Robert Nadir, Benjamin Stewart, Delrae Novak, Wendy Lehr, Francia DiMase, Oliver Cliff, Wayne A. Evenson
FENCES; Director, Claude Purdy; Set, Vicki Smith; Costumes, Constanza Romero; Lighting, Don Darnutzer. CAST: Lawrence James, Hugh Hurd, Delores Mitchell, Kelvin R. Shepard, Adolphus Ward, Jonathan Adams, Angela Johnson, Tani Rasheen Sylvester, Atchudta Halim, Jessica Arnwine Morkert
THE ROAD TO MECCA: Director, Gary Gisselman; Set, Greg Lucas; Costumes, David Kay Mickelsen; Lighting, Tracy Odishaw. CAST: Patricia Fraser, Caryn West, Benjamin Stewart

Tim Fuller Photos

Jonathan Adams, Tani Rasheen Sylvester in "Fences" Above: Robert Nadir, Oliver Cliff, Wendy Lehr in "The Importance of Being Earnest"

Meghan Cary, Kathryn Grant in "Talking Pictures" Above: Victor Griffin, Marilyn Cooper in "70, Girls, 70"

ASOLO THEATRE COMPANY

Sarasota, Florida
Thirty-first Season

Executive Director, Lee H. Warner; Artistic Director, John Ulmer; Associate Executive Director, Don Creason; Resident Directors, John Gulley, Garry Allan Breul; Lighting Director, Martin Petlock; Costume Designer, Howard Tsvi Kaplan; Managing Director, Linda DiGabriele; Stage Managers, Marian Wallace, Stephanie Moss, Juanita Munford
GUEST ARTISTS: Guest Directors, Jamie Brown, Fred Chappell, Rob Marshall; Scenic Designers, Ken Kurtz, John Ezell; Costume Designers, Sharon Sobel, Joy Breckenridge.
PREMIERES (U.S. and world): World premiere of *Talking Pictures* by Horton Foote, April 20–May 10, 1990. World premiere of *Quarry* by Ronald Bazarini, May 31–July 21, 1990. No other details submitted.

Alan Ulmer Photos

BARTER THEATRE

Abingdon, Virginia
Fifty-seventh Season

Artistic Director/Producer, Rex Partington; Directors, Ken Costigan, Geoffrey Kitch, William Van Keyser, Joe Warik; Sets, Gary Aday, Daniel Ettinger, Daniel Gray; Costumes, Karen Brewster, Pamela Hale; Lighting, Tony Partington; Stage Managers, John Atherlay, Champe Leary, Marjorie Terry, James Wood; Marketing, Lori W. Hamm
RESIDENT COMPANY: Michele Bailey, Peter Borzotta, Richard R. Bowden, John Hall Burnett, Katherine Carlson, Marc Carver, George Cavey, Jonathan Chambers, Judy Chesnutt, Karen Case Cook, Richard Dolce, Rob Donohoe, Iris Dorbian, Frank Foster, Jr., Georgeanne Franke, Stephen Gabis, Patricia Guinan, Kent Heacock, Robert Hock, Lizz Hodgin, Cleo Holladay, Robert L. Horen, Jessica Houston, Leslie Kincaid, Richard Kinter, Roddy Kinter, James A. Kroll, John R. Little, Daniel MacKenzie, Leslie Marcus, Valerie Mercurio, Kenny Morris, David Mulkey, Sean O'Sullivan, Dixie Partington, Rex Partington, Tony Partington, Lynn Paynter, Trip Plymale, Arleigh Richards, Marnice Richmond, Douglas Simes, Diane Warren, Christopher James Wright
PRODUCTIONS: *Blithe Spirit* by Noel Coward (Tour), *Tom Sawyer* by Richard Kinter, *Noises Off* by Michael Frayn, *The Voice of the Prairie* by John Oliver, *Taking Steps* by Alan Ayckbourn, *Offstage Voices* by Stephanie Correa, *The Business of Murder* by Richard Harris, *Don Juan in Hell* by George Bernard Shaw, *LaRonde* by Arthur Schnitzler, *Berlin to Broadway with Kurt Weill, Clown's Play* by Reginald F. Bain, *Robin Goodfellow* by Aurand Harris, *The Ghost of the Chinese Elm* by Adele Gordon, *Afternoons at the Playhouse*—Four One Act Plays by Tennessee Williams

John Little, Judy Chestnutt, Kent Heacock (standing), Cleo Holladay, Diane Warren, Stephen Gabis, Richard Kinter in "Noises Off"

BEEF AND BOARDS DINNER THEATRE

Indianapolis, Indiana
Seventeenth Season

Artistic Director, Douglas E. Stark; Managing Director, Robert Zehr; Stage Manager, Ed Stockman; Sets/Lighting, Michael Layton; Costumes, Livingston; Public Relations, Amy Jo Stark; Asst. to Producers, Peggy Zehr; Technical Director, Jeff Pajer; Musical Director, Richard Laughlin

PRODUCTIONS & CASTS

LA CAGE AUX FOLLES by Jerry Herman, Harvey Fierstein; Director, Douglas Stark; Choreography, Stephen W. Essner. CAST: Brian Horton (Zaza), Stephen W. Essner (Georges), Adrienne Doucette, Ray Hatch, Doug Holmes, Pam Klappas, Dan Scharbrough, Mark Traxler, Sherry Santillano, Gary Marshall Dieter, L. A. McCord, Ron Morgan, Brian K. Rardin, Tony Sapp, Reggie Valdez
AIN'T MISBEHAVIN' by Fats Waller, Richard Maltby, Jr.; Director, Stephen W. Essner; Choreography, Ray Hatch. CAST: Alvaleta Guess, Felicia Caldwell-Fields, Shirese Hursey, Myron E. El, Monroe Kent
FIDDLER ON THE ROOF by Jerry Bock, Sheldon Harnick, Stein; Director, Robert D. Zehr; Choreography, Michael Worcell. CAST: Douglas E. Stark (Tevye), Norma Crawford (Golde), Doug Holmes, Richard Pruitt, Bill Book, Linda Brinkerhoff, Jennifer Campbell, Eddie Curry, Ron Dwenger, Brian Horton, Michael Lang, Kori McOmber, Kyra McOmber, Elizabeth Anne Morgan, Karen Olson, Dan Scharbrough, Ty Stover, Jacque Workman
IT'S A WONDERFUL LIFE! THE MUSICAL *(world premiere)* with Original Book by Doug Holmes, Original Music, John Kroner; Original Lyrics, Walter Willison; Director, Douglas E. Stark; Choreography, Linda Rees. CAST: Lee Chew (George Bailey), Neva Rae Powers (Mary Hatch Bailey), Doug Holmes (Clarence), Richard Pruitt, Yvette de Botton, Jacquiline Rohrbacher, Dan Scharbrough, Bill Book, Jennifer Brozzo, Eddie Curry, Ronald Dwenger, Jana Lugar, Joel Lugar, Richard Merriman, Karen Olson, Robina Peterson, Jack L. Russell, James D. Shaw, Ty Stover, Lorraine K. M. Weimerskirch
THE BEST OF BURLESQUE; Producer, David Hanson. CAST: Sandy O'Hara, Pat Davison, Lauren, Ray Pierce
MY FAIR LADY by Lerner & Loewe; Director, Douglas E. Stark; Choreography, Paula Lynn. CAST: James Anthony (Higgins), Suzanne Stark (Eliza), Jack Sevier (Pickering), Jacque Workman, Helen Masloff, Ty Stover, Eddie Curry, Lorraine K. M. Weimerskirch, Bill Book, Ron Dwenger, Doug King, Dan Scharbrough, Michell Moye, Elizabeth Anne Morgan

Lee Chew, Yvette de Botton, Doug Holmes in "Wonderful Life" Above: (L) Jacque Workman, Douglas Stark, Norma Crawford in "Fiddler on the Roof" (R) Mark Traxler, Stephen Essner, Brian Horton in "La Cage . . ."

(L) Ginni Randall in "Shakin' the Mess . . ." (R) Mark Arnold, Juliette Kurth in "Burn This"

CAPITAL REPERTORY COMPANY

Albany, New York

Producing Director, Bruce Bouchard, Peter H. Clough; General Manager, Peter M. Kindlon; Press, Patricia Titterton; Marketing, Susan Phillips, Marybeth Hassett-Murphy; Business Manager, Susan Robert; Stage Manager, Julie A. Fife, Michele Samal; Technical Director, Patrick A. Ferlo; Costumes, Lynda L. Salsbury, Kevin Pothier, Felix E. Cochren, Rebecca Senske, Martha Hally; Sets, Charles McClennahan, James Noone, Andi Lyons, Rick Dennis, Joseph P. Tilford; Lighting, Kenneth Decker, David Wiggall, Shirley Prendergast, David Yergan, Andi Lyons, Brian MacDevitt, Spencer Mosse

SHAKIN' THE MESS OUTTA MISERY by Shay Youngblood; Director, Glenda Dickerson; with Monica Parks, Rosanna Carter, Ginni Randall, Carol Jean Lewis, Gwendolyn Roberts-Frost, Lynda Gravatt, Rosemarie Jackson, Elizabeth Van Dyke
TWELFTH NIGHT by William Shakespeare; Director, Rene Buch; with Michael J. Hume, Don Fischer, Susan J. Coon, Josie de Guzman, Wayne Maugans, Albert Owens, Edwin C. Owens, Marceline Hugot, Bill Leone, Will Rhys, Ron Baslow, Elleen Hannah, Amy J. Rapp, Steven Sunderlin
THE SEA HORSE by Edward J. Moore; Director, Bruce Bouchard; with Michael Fischetti, Janni Brenn
CROSSING DELANCEY by Susan Sandler; Director, D. Lynn Meyers; with Kathy Danzer, Elaine Grollman, Kaye Kingston, Albert Owens, Sam Guncler
BURN THIS by Lanford Wilson; Director, Bruce Bouchard; with Juliette Kurth, James Goodwin Rice, Barry Lee, Mark Arnold
PRIVATE LIVES by Noel Coward; Director, Michael J. Hume; with Meghan Rose Krank, Quentin O'Brien, Albert Owens, Kate Kelly, Tammy Smith

Joseph Schuyler Photos

CALDWELL THEATRE COMPANY

Boca Raton, Florida

Artistic and Managing Director, Michael Hall; Director of Design, Frank Bennett; Company Manager, Patricia Burdett; PR Director, Joe Gillie; Marketing Director, Kathy Walton; Publicity Director, Paul Perone; Accountant, Helen Mavromatis; Production Coordinator, Chip Latimer; Technical Director, Ken Melvin; Prop Master, George Sproul; Graphic Designer and Associate Scene Designer, James Morgan; Lighting Designer, Mary Jo Dondlinger; Costume Designer, Bridget Bartlett; Asst. House Manager, Hank Allen; Asst. Company Manager, Nick Skoulaxenos; Administrative Asst., Marcie Hall; Box Office Manager, Hollie Mueller; Stage Manager, Bob Carter; Director, Michael Hall
GUEST ARTISTS: Beth Fowler, Rick Rasmussen, r l markham

PRODUCTIONS AND CASTS

BUS STOP by William Inge. CAST: Kim Cozort, Pepper Sweeney, Barbara Bradshaw, Kenneth Kay, Andrea O'Connell, K. Lype O'Dell, Michael Hartman, Peter Haig
THE PERFECT PARTY by A. R. Gurney. CAST: Dru Dempsey, Peter Haig, Maggie Marshall, Gary Nathanson, Carolyn Hurlburt
ANGEL STREET by Patrick Hamilton. CAST: Amelia White, K. Lype O'Dell, Anthony Newfield, Joy Johnson, Andrea O'Connell
LES LIAISONS DANGEREUSES by Christopher Hampton. CAST: Kathleen Huber, Anthony Newfield, Andrea O'Connell, Barbara Bradshaw, Grace Cook, Richard Thompson, Harriet Oser, Don Spalding, Vita Lucia, Wayne Demaline, Robert Palisin, Bernadette Mackey
HAY FEVER by Noel Coward. CAST: Beth Fowler, John Gardiner, Grace Cook, Steven McCloskey, Dru Dempsey, Richard Thompson, Viki Boyle, Billie Lou Watt, Anthony Newfield
SHOWSTOPPERS (Cabaret). CAST: Kay Brady, Joe Gillie, Susan Hatfield, Kevin Wallace, Rupert Ziawinski, Jean Bolduc
All productions directed by Michael Hall

Joyce Brock Photos

K. Lype O'Dell, Anthony Newfield in "Angel Street" Above: Viki Boyle, Richard Thompson in "Hay Fever"

CENTER STAGE

Baltimore, Maryland

Artistic Director, Stan Wojewodski, Jr.; Managing Director, Peter W. Culman; Translators, Joel Agee, Brian Johnston, Leon Katz; Dramaturg, Colette Brooks; Directors, Michael Engler, Travis Preston; Playwright, Eric Overmyer; Designer, Maurice Sendak; Composer, Kim D. Sherman; Artistic Administrator, Del W. Risberg; Resident Dramaturg, Rick Davis; Production Manager, Katharyn Davies; Stage Managers, Keri Muir, Julie Thompson; Technical Director, Tom Rupp; Costumes, F. T. Brown; Properties Manager, Cheryl Riggins; Sound, James Swonger; Associate Managing Director, Patricia Egan; Business Manager, Lucia Schliessmann; Development, Mary E. Howell; Audience Development/Public Relations, Betsy Kunzelman; Young People's Theatre Playwrights, Jim Cary, Kenneth Hoke-Witherspoon, Mark Novak, Steve Schutzman, Judith Shotwell, Jim Sizemore.

PRODUCTIONS & CASTS

MAN AND SUPERMAN by George Bernard Shaw; Director, Stan Wojewodski, Jr.; Sets, Derek McLane; Costumes, Catherine Zuber; Lighting, Stephen Strawbridge; Speech, Timothy Monich. CAST: E. G. Marshall (Roebuck), Jennifer Roblin (Maid), John Patrick Rice (Octavius), William Converse-Roberts (Tanner), Megan Gallagher (Ann), Mary Fogarty (Mrs. Whitefield), Pennell Somsen (Miss Ramsden), Sharon Washington (Violet), Jon Krupp (Henry), Tom Fervoy (Hector), L. Peter Callender (Mendoza), Roland Bull (Anarchist), Chris Lamb, Matthew S. Ramsay, Edwyn Williams (Brigands), Terrence Currier (Mr. Malone), Keith Allaway, Colin Krain, Harry Susser, Lloyd Ziel (Ensemble)

MISS EVERS' BOYS *(premiere)* by David Feldshuh; Director, Irene Lewis; Sets, Douglas Stein; Costumes, Catherine Zuber, Lighting, Pat Collins; Sound, Janet Kalas; Choreography, Dianne McIntyre; Music Director, Dwight Andrews. CAST: Delroy Lindo (Caleb Humphries), Damien Leake (Hodman Bryan), K. Todd Freeman (Willie Johnson), Allie Woods, Jr. (Ben Washington), Ethan Phillips (Dr. John Douglass), David Downing (Dr. Eugene Brodus), Seret Scott (Eunice Evers)

A fictional account of the U.S. Health Service's witholding of treatment for V.D. in Alabama for poor black men from 1932–72.

THE FILM SOCIETY by Jon Robin Baitz; Director, Jackson Phippin; Sets, Derek McLane; Costumes, Catherine Zuber; Lighting, Deborah Hecht. CAST: Bill Kux (Jonathon), Caitlin O'Connell (Nan), Scott Wentworth (Terry), Mikel Sarah Lambert (Sylvia), Thomas Barbour (Neville), Casper Roos (Hamish)

AN ENEMY OF THE PEOPLE by Henrik Ibsen; Director, Stan Wojewodski, Jr.; Sets, Christopher Barreca; Costumes, Marina Draghici; Lighting, Stephen Strawbridge. CAST: William Hardy (Morten), Mark Niebuhr (Billing), Kristin Griffith (Katherine), Armand Schultz (Hovstad), Kent Broadhust (Dr. Stockman), Derek D. Smith (Peter), Mark Wilson (Corster), Katy Selverstone (Petra), Wil Love (Aslaksen)

ALL'S WELL THAT ENDS WELL by William Shakespeare; Director, Stan Wojewodski, Jr.; Sets, Derek McLane; Costumes, Catherine Zuber; Lighting, Robert Wierzel; Composers, Scott Killian, Kim D. Sherman. CAST: Rosalind Cash (Countess), Derek D. Smith (Bertram), Ben Halley, Jr. (Lafew), Lili Flanders (Helena), Robert Dorfman (Parolles), Alexander Zale (King), Peter Mackenzie, Dion Graham (Brothers Dumaine), Karl Otter (Rinaldo), Wil Love (Lavatch), Mark Niebuhr (Interpreter), Mark Wilson (Duke/Astringer), Rosemary Knower (Widow Capilet), Regina Taylor (Diana), Linda Cavell (Mariana)

THE MAKING OF AMERICANS with Music by Al Carmines; Libretto, Leon Katz; Based on the novel by Gertrude Stein; Director, Lawrence Kornfeld; Sets/Costumes, Marina Draghici; Lighting, Clay Shirky; Music Director, Charles Berigan. CAST: Al Carmines (Voice of Gertrude Stein), Scott Elliott (Grandfather David Hersland/Phillip Redfern/George Dehning), Maureen Sadusk (Grandmother Martha Hersland/Sister Bertha), Jane Moore (Sister Martha Hersland/Pauline/Miss Downer), David Pursley (David Hersland), Margaret Wright (Fanny Hissen, later Hersland), Paul Eichel (Henry Dehning), Judith Moore (Jenny Dehning), Gayton Scott (Julia Dehning, later Hersland), Ken Ward (Alfred Hersland), George Feaster (David Hersland), Allison Charney (Martha Hersland)

BECKETT: SHORT WORKS; Directors, Cheryl Faver, Jackson Phippin; Sets, Marina Draghici; Costumes, Catharine Zuber; Lighting, Clay Shirky. CASTS: *Molloy,* William Foeller (Molloy), *Stirrings Still,* Kirk Jackson (Man), *Play,* Derek Smith (Man), Cara Duff-MacCormick (Woman 1), Mikel Sarah Lambert (Woman 2), *Rockaby,* Cara Duff-MacCormick (Woman in Rocker), *Catastrophe,* William Foeller (Protagonist), Kirk Jackson (Director), Marc Honea (Luke), Mikel Sarah Lambert (Asst.)

Seret Scott (R) and clockwise: Delroy Lindo, Damien Leake, K. Todd Freeman, Allie Woods, Jr. in "Miss Evers's Boys"

(no other photos submitted)

129

CENTER THEATRE GROUP
AHMANSON THEATRE

Los Angeles, California

Producing Director, Gordon Davidson; General Manager, Veronica Claypool; Press Director, Tony Sherwood; Press Associate, Joyce Friedmann; Associate Manager, David Cipriano; Staff Liaison to Mr. Davidson, Susan Obrow; Audience Development Director, Robert Schlosser; Technical Director, Robert Routolo.

PRODUCTIONS AND CASTS
James A. Doolittle Theatre

BYRON—Mad, Bad and Dangerous to Know written and compiled by Jane McCulloch *(American Premiere);* Director, Jane McCulloch; Music, Donald Fraser, Lighting, Martin Aronstein; Company Manager, John Wilson; Production Stage Manager, Tami Toon; Stage Manager, Caryn Shick. Presented by arrangement with Harold Shaw, in association with the English Chamber Theatre. CAST: Derek Jacobi (Lord Byron); Isla Blair.

WHO'S AFRAID OF VIRGINIA WOOLF? by Edward Albee; Director, Edward Albee; Scenery, D Martyn Bookwalter (adapted from the original design by William Ritman); Lighting, Martin Aronstein; Costumes, Albert Wolsky; Production Stage Manager, Mark Wright; Stage Manager, James T. McDermott. CAST: Glenda Jackson (Martha); John Lithgow (George); Brian Kerwin (Nick); Cynthia Nixon (Honey); Cynthia Bassham, Bruce Gray, Carol Mayo Jenkins, John Ottavino.

THE PIANO LESSON by August Wilson; Director, Lloyd Richards; Scenic Design, E. David Cosier, Jr.; Lighting Design, Christopher Akerlind; Costume Design, Constanza Romero; Musical Director/Composer, Dwight D. Andrews; Sound Design, G. Thomas Clark; Executive Producer, Benjamin Mordecai; Production Stage Manager, Karen L. Carpenter; Stage Manager, Russell W. Johnson. A Yale Repertory Theatre Production. Presented in association with Huntington Theatre Company, Goodman Theatre, Old Globe Theatre and Eugene O'Neill Theatre Center. CAST: Charles S. Dutton (Boy Willie); Rocky Carroll (Lymon); Carl Gordon (Doaker); Lisa Gay Hamilton (Grace); Tommy Hollis (Avery); Melissa Bess Wright (Maretha); S. Epatha Merkerson (Berniece); Lou Myers (Wining Boy); Danny Robinson-Clark (Wining Boy alternate); Charles Champion; Nakomi Hunter; Fred Pinkard; Kim Staunton.

THE COCKTAIL HOUR by A. R. Gurney; Director, Jack O'Brien; Scenic and Costume Design, Steven Rubin; Lighting Design, Kent Dorsey; Production Supervisor, Douglas Pagliotti; Production Stage Manager, Mary Michele Miner; Stage Manager, Tami Toon. CAST: Nancy Marchand (Ann); Keene Curtis (Bradley); Bruce Davison (John); Holland Taylor (Nina); Valorie Armstrong; Gloria Cromwell; Gregory Itzin; Sandy Kenyon.

RUMORS by Neil Simon; Director, Gene Saks; Scenery, Tony Straiges; Costumes, Joseph G. Aulisi; Lighting, Tharon Musser; Sound, Tom Morse; Casting, Jay Binder; Production Supervisor, Peter Lawrence; Company Manager, Sammy Ledbetter; Production Stage Manager, Mindy Farbrother. Produced by Emanuel Azenberg. CAST: Ron Leibman (Lenny); Jessica Walter (Claire); Gibby Brand (Ken); Charles Brown (Welch); Kandis Chappell (Chris); Dan Desmond (Ernie); Lisa Emery (Cassie); Timothy Landfield (Glenn); Mary O'Brady (Pudney); Peggy Pope (Cookie); Lynnda Ferguson; Guy Paul.

Jay Thompson Photos

Right Center: Isla Blair, Derek Jacobi in "Byron . . ." *(Christian Steiner)* **Top:** Bruce Davison, Holland Taylor, Keene Curtis, Nancy Marchand in "The Cocktail Hour" *(Martha Swope)*

Brian Kerwin, Glenda Jackson, Cynthia Nixon, John Lithgow in "Who's Afraid of Virginia Woolf?"

Lou Myers in "The Piano Lesson" *(Gerry Goodstein)*

CENTER THEATRE GROUP
MARK TAPER FORUM

Los Angeles, California
Twenty-third Season

Artistic Director/Producer, Gordon Davidson; Managing Director, Stephen J. Albert; Associate Artistic Director, Robert Egan; Resident Director, Oskar Eustis; Manager, Karen S. Wood; Staff Director for ITP, Peter C. Brosius; Staff Producer, Corey Beth Madden; Literary Administrator, Jeremy Lawrence; Development, Mary K Bailey; Christine Fiedler; Audience Development Director, Robert J. Schlosser; Technical Director/CTG, Robert Routolo; Production Supervisor, Frank Bayer; Production Administrator, Jonathan Barlow Lee; Casting Director, Stanley Soble, C.S.A.; Press, Nancy Hereford, Phyllis Moberly, Evelyn Kiyomi Emi, Carol Oken, Devin M. Keudell

PRODUCTIONS & CASTS

OUR COUNTRY'S GOOD by Timberlake Wertenbaker (*American Premiere*); based on the novel *The Playmaker* by Thomas Keneally; Co-directed by Max Stafford-Clark and Les Waters; Set and Costumes, Peter Hartwell; Lighting, Kevin Rigdon; Sound, Bryan Bowen and Jon Gottlieb; Casting, Stanley Soble, C.S.A.; Dialect Coach, James Wilson; Wigs, Bill Fletcher; Hair and Make-up, Richard Arias; Fight Choreography, Mark Moses; Production Stage Manager, Mary Michele Miner; Stage Manager, Dana Axelrod; Production Assistant, Susie Walsh. CAST: Tony Amendola (Captain Phillip/Wisehammer), Caitlin Clarke (Lt. Dawes/Morden), Deborah Fallender (2nd Lt. Faddy/Bryant), Gail Grate (Lt. Johnston/Smith), Harris Laskawy (Cpt. Campbell/Midshipman Brewer/Arscott), Valerie Mahaffey (Rev. Johnson/Brenham/Long), John Cameron Mitchell (Cpt. Collins/Sideway), Michael Morgan (Cpt. Tench/Caesar/Australian), Mark Moses (2nd Lt. Clark), James Walch (Maj. Ross/Freeman). Understudies: Terry Alexander, Mark Belden, Tom Flynn, John Harnagel, Elaine Hausman, Kimberly LaMarque, Lori Michael, Andrew Myler.

MYSTERY OF THE ROSE BOUQUET by Manuel Puig (*American Premiere*); Translation, Allan Baker; American Adaptation, Jeremy Lawrence; Director, Robert Allan Ackerman; Set and Costumes, Kenny Miller; Lighting, Arden Fingerhut; Casting, Stanley Soble, C.S.A.; Assistant to the Director, Franco Zavani; Wigs, Bill Fletcher; Hairstylist, Claude Diaz; Production Stage Manager, Tami Toon; Stage Manager, Mary K Klinger; Production Assistant, Susie Walsh. CAST: Anne Bancroft (Patient), Jane Alexander (Nurse). Understudies: Sally Kemp and Barbara Sohmers.

A MIDSUMMER NIGHT'S DREAM in repertory with KING LEAR by William Shakespeare; *American Debut of the Renaissance Theatre Company;* Director, Kenneth Branagh; Producer, David Parfitt; Set and Costumes, Jenny Tiramani; Lighting, Jon Linstrum; Music Director, Patrick Doyle; Fight Director, Nicholas Hall; Choreography, Gilliam Gregory; Text Advisor, Russell Jackson; Production Consultant, Hugh Cruttwell; Assistant Director, Colin Wakefield; Stage Management, Christine Hathway and Sally Hoskins; Administrator, Iona Price; Company Manager, Marilyn Eardley; Costume Supervisors, Susan Coates and Stephanie Collie; Taper Production Stage Manager, Tami Toon; Production Manager, Susie Walsh. CAST: The Renaissance Theatre Company—Christopher Armstrong (Moth/Servant/Messenger/Officer), Kenneth Branagh (Peter Quince/Edgar), Richard Briers (Bottom/Lear), Ann Davies (Peaseblossom/Maid to Regan), Gerard Horan (Flute/Cornwall), Karl James (Snug/Albany), Edward Jewesbury (Starveling/Gloucester), Bryan Kennedy (Snout/Burgundy/Gentleman), James Larkin (Lysander/Oswald), Sue Long (Cobweb/Maid to Goneril), Francine Morgan (Hermia/Regan), Siobhán Redmond (Hippolyta/Titania/Goneril), Simon Roberts (Oberon/Theseus/Edmund), Ethna Roddy (Puck/Cordelia), Emma Thompson (Helena/Fool), Jimmy Yuill (Egeus/Mustardseed/Philostrate/Kent).

50/60 VISION—Plays and Playwrights that Changed the Theatre! Thirteen Plays in Repertory Conceived and produced by Edward Parone, with works by Edward Albee, Amiri Baraka (LeRoy Jones), Samuel Beckett, Jean Genet, Eugene Ionesco, Harold Pinter, Sam Shepard; Directors, Michael Arabian, Peter C. Brosius, Daniel O'Connor, Carey Perloff, Ethan Silverman; Sets, Yael Pardess; Costumes, Julie Weiss; Lighting, Paulie Jenkins; Sound, Jon Gottlieb; Casting, Stanley Soble, C.S.A.; Associate Producer, Karen S. Wood; Dramaturg, James Leverett; Dialect Coach, James Wilson; Wigs, Bill Fletcher; Hair Stylist, Claude Diaz; Production Stage Manager, James T. McDermott; Productions Managers, Frank Bayer, Jonathan Barlow Lee and Robert Routolo; Stage Managers, Dana Axelrod, Mary K Klinger and L. A. Lavin; Production Assistants, Kirk Brustman and Thomas Adam Brady. CAST: Phillip R. Allen, Christopher Allport, Megan Butler, Ron Campbell, Mary Carver, Teri Garr, Jihmi Kennedy, John Robert Lafleur, Gloria Mann, Bill Moor, Jan Munroe, Karmin Murcelo, John Nesci, Maria O'Brien, Randy Oglesby, Alan Oppenheimer, Angela Paton, Charlotte Rae, Michael Tulin.

Anne Bancroft, Jane Alexander in "Mystery of the Rose Bouquet" (R) John Robert LaFleur, Angela Paton, Bill Moor in "The Sandbox"

ARISTOCRATS by Brian Friel; Director, Robert Egan; Set, Mark Wendland; Costumes, Dona Granata; Lighting, Kevin Rigdon; Music and Sound, Nathan Birnbaum; Casting, Stanley Soble, C.S.A.; Production Stage Manager, Cari Norton; Stage Manager, Richard Manfredi; Production Assistant, Susie Walsh. CAST: Raye Birk (Willie Diver), Rachael Dowling (Anna's Voice), Christine Healy (Judith), John Larroquette (Casimir), Kate Mulgrew (Alice), Joycelyn O'Brien (Claire), Ford Rainey (Uncle George/Father), Andrew Robinson (Eamon), John Vickery (Tom Hoffnung). Understudies: Rachael Dowling, Dan Mason, Melinda McGraw, Joseph G. Medalis, Jan Munroe.

MISS EVERS' BOYS by David Feldshuh; Director, Irene Lewis; Set, Douglas Stein; Costumes, Catherine Zuber; Lighting, Pat Collins; Sound, Jon Gottlieb; Music Director, Olu Dara; Choreographer, Dianne McIntyre; Dramaturg, Oskar Eustis; Casting, Stanley Soble, C.S.A.; Production Stage Manager, James T. McDermott; Stage Manager, Jill Ragaway; Production Assistant, Susie Walsh. CAST: John Cothran, Jr. (Ben), Starletta DuPois (Eunice Evers), K. Todd Freeman (Willie Johnson), Bennet Guillory (Dr. Brodus), Charles Lanyer (Dr. Douglas), Carl Lumbly (Caleb Humphries), Mel Winkler (Hodman Bryan).

TAPER, TOO: THE THRILL by John Steppling; Co-directors, John Steppling and Robert Egan; Set and Costumes, Mark Wendland; Lighting, Casey Cowan; Composer and Sound, Nathan Birnbaum; Stage Manager, Hilliary Fox; Production Assistant, Laura Brown; Assistant to the Directors, Kai Ephron; Dance Sequence, Kate Crush. CAST: Robb Curtis-Brown (Nat Pink), Kate Dornan (Beverly), Diane DeFoe (Linda), Robert Hummer (Perry), Pamela Gordon (Lindsay), John Horn (Walter).

WAITING FOR GODOT by Samuel Beckett; Director, Joseph Chaikin; Producer, Corey Beth Madden; Set, Andy Stacklin; Costumes, Mary Brecht; Lighting, Margaret Anne Dunn; Vaudeville Routines Consultant, John Achom; Beckett Consultant, Ruby Cohn; Stage Manager, Cari Norton; Production Assistant, Laura Brown. CAST: Robert Machray (Pozzo), Damon Motley (Boy), Shabaka [Barry Henley] (Vladimir), Leif Tilden (Lucky), Sam Tsoutsouvas (Estragon).

ROBINSON & CRUSOE by Nino D'Introna and Giacomo Ravicchio; English Language Adaptor, Shem Bitterman; Director, Peter C. Brosius; Set, Richard Hoover; Costumes, Kathleen Waln; Lighting, Margaret Anne Dunn; Original Music Composer, Giacomo Ravicchio; Music Arranger, Claudio Mantovani; Assistant Director, John Wills Martin; Sound Consultant, Michael Silversher; Lighting Technician, Mark Svastics; Stage Manager, Chip Washabaugh; Assistant Stage Manager, Karen Maruyama; Production Assistants, David Brian Alley and Sanjay Chandani. CAST: Jerry Tondo, Valente Rodriguez. Understudies: David Brian Alley and Sanjay Chandani.

MILLENNIUM APPROACHES by Tony Kushner; Director, Oskar Eustis; Producer, Corey Beth Madden; Set, Mark Wendland; Costumes, Lydia Tanji; Lighting, Casey Cowan and Brian Gale; Music and Sound, Nathan Birnbaum; Stage Manager, Sarah Joem Bradley; Production Assistant, Laura Brown; Production Intern, Kirk Brustman. CAST: Kathleen Chalfant (Hannah Pitt), Richard Frank (Roy Cohn), Lorri Holt (Harper Pitt), Jeffrey King (Joe Pitt), Jon Matthews (Louis Ironson), Ellen McLaughlin (The Angel), Stephen Spinella (Prior Walter), Harry Waters Jr. (Belize).

THE CLEVELAND PLAY HOUSE

Cleveland, Ohio
Seventy-fourth Season

STAFF: Artistic Director, Josephine R. Abady; Managing Director, Dean R. Gladden; Associate Producer, Don Roe; Production Manager, David L. Ramsey; Literary Manager, Roger T. Danforth; Company Manager, Myron Leavell; Casting, McCorkle Casting Ltd.; Director of Marketing, Barry M. Colfelt; Press Representative, Jeffrey Richards; Production Stage Manager, Robert S. Garber; Stage Managers, Jean Bruns, Benjamin Gutkin, Diedre Fudge, Morgan Kennedy; Set Designers, Dan Conway, Ken Foy, Marjorie Bradley Kellogg, David Potts, Karen Shulz; Costume Designers, Patricia E. Doherty, Linda Fisher, C. L. Hundley, Deborah Shaw, John Carver Sullivan; Lighting Designers, John Hastings, Norbert U. Kolb, Dennis Parichy, Marc B. Weiss, Richard Winkler; Sound Designers, Jeffrey Montgomerie, Lia Vollack

GUEST DIRECTORS: Larry Arrick, Josephine R. Abady, Margaret Booker, Roger T. Danforth, David Esbjornson, Marcyanne Goldman, John David Lutz, Tazewell Thompson

GUEST ARTISTS: Jim Abele, William Keeler, Joseph Mascolo, Amy Ryan, Elizabeth Shepherd, Ben Siegler, Rohn Thomas, David Adkins, John Carpenter, Kelly Gwin, John Hickey, Susan Knight, Sonja Lanzener, Kathleen Mahoney-Bennett, Barbara eda-Young, Jody Gelb, James Hurdle, William Joseph Raymond, Richard Thomsen, Michael Cooke, Peggy Cosgrave, Tamara Daniel, Paula Duesing, David O. Frazier, Providence Hollander, Lianne Kressin, Michael Lombard, Jerry Longe, Morgan Lund, Molly Renfroe, Barnaby Spring, Kevin Sweeney, Winifred Walsh, Jerry Zafer, Peter Birkenhead, John Lagioia, Stephen T. Kay, Spike McClure, Daniel J. Travanti, Bill Cobbs, Demitri Corbin, Clebert Ford, Kim Hamilton, Keith Johnson, Jonathan Peck, Leslie Ayvazian, Donna Daley, Christine Farrell, Ann Sachs, Rita Nachtmann, Providence Hollander, Kevin McCarty, Robert Meksin, Marc Moritz, Molly Renfroe, Chuck Ritchie, Rohn Thomas, Christian Webb, Cynthia Crumlish, Burt Edwards, Tammy Grimes, Charles Shaw Robinson, Susan Browning, John Carpenter, Sean G. Griffin, Bethel Leslie, Carol Locatell

PRODUCTIONS: *Stem of a Briar* by Beddow Hatch, *New Music*—A Trilogy by Reynolds Price, *August Snow, Night Dance, Better Days* (premiere), *The Man who Came to Dinner* by George S. Kaufman and Moss Hart, *Only Kidding* by Jim Geoghan, *Fences* by August Wilson, *Mama Drama* written and Performed by Leslie Ayvazian, Donna Daley, Christine Farrell, Ann Sachs, Rita Nachtman (Premiere), *Animal Farm* by George Orwell, *The Cocktail Hour* by A. R. Gurney, *The March on Russia* by David Storey

Richard Termine, Roger Mostrioanni Photos

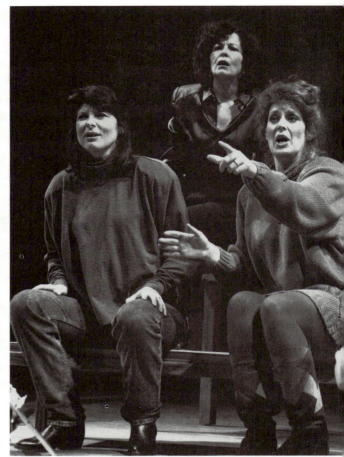

**Christine Farrell, Ann Sachs, Leslie Ayvazian in
"Mama Drama"**

**Bill Raymond, Barbara eda-Young in
"Better Days"**

Bethel Leslie, Sean G. Griffin, Carol Locatell, John Carpenter, Susan Browning in "The March on Russia"

THE COCONUT GROVE PLAYHOUSE

Miami, Florida

Producing Artistic Director, Arnold Mittelman; Associate Producer, Lynne Peyser; General Manager, Christopher Kawolsky; Production Manager, Deborah Simon; Technical Director, Dorset Noble; Resident Costume Designer/Costumier, Ellis Tillman; Property Master, Stephen Lambert; Audio Technician, Allen Zipper; Production Stage Manager, Rafael V. Blanco; Assistant Stage Managers, Heather D. MacKenzie, Colleen E. Riley, Sheila M. Sheeler; Public Relations Manager, Lee Zimmerman; Sales and Promotion Manager, Mark D. Sylvester; Development Associate, Fred Salancy; Business Manager, K. William Kerlin; Company Manager, Jane Mazzarantani

PRODUCTIONS & CASTS

MATADOR; Music by Mike Leander; Lyrics by Edward Seago; Book by Edward Seago, David H. Bell and Mike Leander; Directed and Choreographed by David H. Bell; Set Design by Thomas M. Ryan; Costume Design by Nancy Missimi; Sound Design by Randy Allen Johns; Lighting Design by Diane Ferry Williams, Laura Perlman; Orchestrations by David Siegel; Assistant Choreographer—Andrew J. Lupp; Flamenco Choreography by Rafael Aguilar, Manolo De Cordoba; Musical Direction, Vocal and Dance Arrangments by Rob Bowman. CAST: Conja Abdessalam, Robert Winn Austin, Susan Bachman, Randy Bichler, Jeanne Croft, Manolo De Cordoba, Mary Ernster, Ray Frewen, Neil Friedman, Jamie Dawn Gangi, Tracey Hodgkin-Valcy, James Javore, Ronald Keaton, Jordan Leeds, Tony Lillo, Andrew J. Lupp, K. C. Lupp, Harrison McEldowney, Susan Moniz, Dale Morgan, Seth Swoboda, Bernie Yvon, Jim Zager

THE ROAR OF THE GREASEPAINT—THE SMELL OF THE CROWD; Book, Music and Lyrics by Leslie Bricusse and Anthony Newley; Directed by Arnold Mittelman; Set and Costume Design by Alexander Okun; Lighting Design by Pat Collins; Sound Design by Jeff Curtis; Musical Direction and Revised Orchestrations by Donald Chan; Musical Staging and Choreography by Wayne Cilento; Assistant Musical Director, Frank Matosich, Jr.; Assistant Choreographer, Geneva Burke; CAST: Obba Babatunde, Larry Kert, Vivian Reed, Melinda Cartwright, Margie Norris, Kathy Robinson, Robert Weber

MOVE OVER, MRS. MARKHAM; Written by Ray Cooney and John Chapman; Directed by Ray Cooney; Set and Costume Design by Kevin Rupnik; Lighting Design by Kirk Bookman; Sound Design by Gary Harris. CAST: Steeve Arlen, Ray Cooney, Beulah Garrick, George Holmes, Katy Kurtzman, Edward Mulhare, Anne Rogers, Kay Walbye, Donna Wandrey

MIAMI LIGHTS *(Premiere)* Book and Lyrics by Jacques Levy; Music by Stanley Walden; Directed by Arnold Mittelman; Lighting Design by John Ambrosone; Set and Costume Design by Kevin Rupnik; Sound Design by Gary Harris; Choreography by Margo Sappington; Musical Director/Conductor/Orchestrator, Fernando Rivas; Additional Orchestrations by Louie Ramirez. CAST: Rafael V. Blanco, Yamil Borges, Jack Dabdoub, Anne-Marie Gerard, Allen Hidalgo, Ronald Hunter, Mark Morales, Tracey Lynn Neff, Sandra Perry, Pedro Roman, Deborah Roshe.

THE BOYS NEXT DOOR; Written by Tom Griffin; Directed By Arnold Mittelman; Scenery and Lighting Design by James Tilton; Costume Design by Ellis Tillman; Sound Design by Gary Harris. CAST: Desi Arnaz, Jr., Ward Asquith, Traber Burns, Maryann Costanza, Marceline Hugot, William Jay, Steve Liebman, David E. Ornston, David Whalen

STEEL MAGNOLIAS; Written by Robert Harling; Directed by Arnold Mittelman; Scenery and Lighting by James Tilton; Costume Design by Ellis Tillman; Sound Design by Gary Harris. CAST: Tandy Cronyn, Judith Delgado, Georgia Engel, Bobo Lewis, Marcia Lewis, Jennifer Parsons

ONE MAN BAND; Book by James Lecesne; Music by Marc Elliot and Larry Hochman; Lyrics by Marc Elliot; Musical Direction by Stephanie Gaumer; Scenery by Lyle Baskin; Lighting by Andrea Wilson. CAST: James Lecesne, Sara-Page Hall, Mandy Munnell

EMBRACEABLE YOU; Written by Richard Baer; Directed by Reva Stern; Scenery by Kevin Rupnik; Lighting by Creon Thorne; Costumes Coordinated by Ellis Tillman. CAST: Jacqueline Scott, Tom Troupe, Mitchell Carrey, Joseph Perez

Luis Castaneda, Deborah Gray Mitchell Photos

Right Center: Vivian Reed, Obba Babatunde, Larry Kert in "Roar of the Greasepaint . . ." Above: (clockwise from top left) David Whalen, David Ornston, Desi Arnaz, Jr., William Jay, Steve Liebman in "The Boys Next Door" Top: (standing) Bobo Lewis, Judith Delgado, Georgia Engel, Marcia Lewis, (seated) Jennifer Parsons, Tandy Cronyn in "Steel Magnolias"

Cast of "Matador"

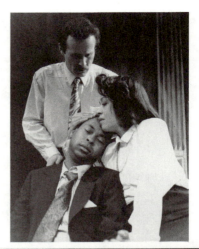

CROSSROADS THEATRE COMPANY

New Brunswick, NJ
Twelfth Season

Producing Artistic Director, Rick Khan; Associate Producer, Ken Johnson; General Manager, André Robinson, Jr.; Business Manager, Louise Smythe; Administrative Asst./House, R. C. Neal; Development Director, Judyie Al-Bilali; Audience Development, Garry Johnson; Production Manager, Gary E. Kechely; Production Coordinator, Cheri Bogdan-Kechely; Musical Consultant, Ernie Scott; Wardrobe, Cathy Clark; Costume Supervisor, Beth Ribblett; Dramaturg, Sydné Mahone

PRODUCTIONS & CASTS

SHEILA'S DAY by Duma Ndlovu; Conceived & Developed by Mr. Ndlovu in workshop with the cast; Directors, Mbongeni Ngema, Richard Grant; Sets, Lloyd Harris; Lighting, Victor En Yu Tan; Costumes, Toni-Leslie James; Stage Manager, Diane Hartdagen; Dramaturg, Sydné Mahone. CAST: Stephanie Alston, Gina Breedlove, Carla Brothers, Irene Datcher, Thuli Dumakude, Ebony Jo-Ann, Annelen Malebo, Letta Mbulu, Tu Nokwe, Valerie Jerusha Rochon, Gina Torres, Khaliq Abdul Al-Rouf
SPUNK: Three Tales by Zora Neale Hurston; Adapted/Directed by George C. Wolfe; Choreography, Hope Clarke; Composer, Chic Street Man; Sets, Loy Arcenas; Lighting, Don Holder; Costumes, Toni-Leslie James; Stage Manager, David Horton Black; Dramaturg, Sydné Mahone. CAST: Betty K. Bynum, Kevin Jackson, Chic Street Man, Reggie Montgomery, Danitra Vance, Tico Wells
AND FURTHER MO': Written & Directed by Vernel Bagneris; Co-Director, Rick Khan; Special Staging, Pepsi Bethel; Arrangements, Lars Edegran, Orange Kellin; Choreography, Thais Clark; Vocal Arrangements, Topsy Chapman, Mr. Edegran; Sets, Charles McClennahan; Lighting, Shirley Prendergast; Costumes, Joann Clevenger; Musical Director, Orange Kellin; Stage Manager, Lorna Littleway. CAST: Vernel Bagneris (Papa Du), Topsy Chapman (Thelma), Thais Clark (Ma Reed), Red Wilcher (Theatre Owner), Sandra Reaves-Phillips (Big Bertha), Yvonne Kersey (Understudy)
MUSICAL NUMBERS: Beautiful Doll, Messing Around, What's Your Price?, Salty Dog, One Hour Mama, The Mississippi, Wild Women, Positively No, Shake It and Break It, Had to Give Up Gym, Here Comes the Hot Tamale Man, Pretty Doll, Come On In, My Man, Revival Day, Baby Won't You Please Come Home, Funny Feather, Clarinet Marmelade, West Indies Blues, Boot It Boy, Baby Doll, Alabama Bound, Home Sweet Home/Hot Times in the Ole Town Tonight
BLACK EAGLES by Leslie Lee; Conceived & Directed by Rick Khan; Choreography, Hope Clarke; Sets, Charles McClennahan; Lighting, Shirley Prendergast; Costumes, Beth Ribblett; Sound, David Lawson; Fights, Rick Sordelet; Musical Consultant, Robert LaPierre; Stage Manager, Dwight R. B. Cook; Ventriloquy, Robert Aberdeen; Consultant, Roscoe C. Brown; Dramaturg, Shelby Jiggetts. CAST: William Christian (Young Clarkie), Helmar Cooper (Elder Nolan), Illeana Douglas (Pia), Denise Drayton (Cadet), Milton Elliot (Roy), Sonny Jim Gaines (Elder Leon), Larry Green (Dave), Michael Greer (Gen. Lucas), Duane Jackson (Cadet), Damien Leake (Rosco), David Rainey (Young Leon), Raymond Reeves (Cadet), W. Benson Terry (Elder Clarkie), Raymond Anthony Thomas (Buddy), Scott Whitehurst (Young Nolan)
TOD, THE BOY, TOD by Talvin Wilks; Director, Ken Johnson; Choreography, Hope Clarke; Sets, Lloyd Harris; Lighting, William H. Grant III; Costumes, Toni Leslie James; Composer/Sound, Rob Bourne; Stage Manager, Cheri Bogdan-Kechely. CAST: Jon Avner (John), Helmar Augustus Cooper (Rev. Joe), Dennis Green (Tod, the Boy, Tod), Michael Greer (Executive), Michael Haney, Spike McClure (Committee), Essene R (Mary)

Eddie Birch Photos

Top: William Christian, Ray Anthony Thomas in "Black Eagles" (R) Jon Avner (top), Essene R, Dennis Green in "Tod" Below: Reggie Montgomery, Betty K. Bynum, Tico Wells in "Spunk"

Thais Clark, Vernel Bagneris, Topsy Chapman in "And Further Mo' "

DELAWARE THEATRE COMPANY

Wilmington, Delaware

Artistic Director, Cleveland Morris; Managing Director, Robert A. Gillman; Business Manager, Donna Pody; Director of Development, Ann G. Schenck; Marketing Director, Mary H. Johnson; Administrative Assistant, Sheri M. Johnson; Box Office Manager/Student Outreach Coordinator, Charles J. Conway; Assistant to the Artistic Director, Danny Peak; Graphic Designer, Suzanne M. Green, Group Sales, Marcia B. Spivack; Artistic Associate, David Drobot; Production Stage Manager, Patricia Christian; Sets, Eric Schaeffer, Lewis Folden, Charles McClennahan; Costumes, Marla Jurglanis, Alvin Perry; Lighting, Bruce K. Morriss, Scott Pinkney; Assistant to the Director, Danny Peak; Assistant Stage Manager, Elizabeth D'Wolf, Paul Taylor; Props, Peter J. Knecht; Sound, George Stewart, David A. Strang; Costume Assistant, Melody Holton, Judith Chang; Lighting Assistant, Cynthia Curley; Master Carpenter, Charles O'Lone; Shop, Robin Brakhage, Thomas Kresten Kesling, Paul Taylor

PRODUCTIONS & CASTS

TARTUFFE by Moliere; Translated by Richard Wilbur; Director, Cleveland Morris. CAST: Joan Kendall (Madame Pernelle), Andrea Liebert (Flipote), Barbara McCulloh (Elmire), Sara M. Smarr (Mariane), Laura Brutsman (Dorine), Christopher Yohe (Damis), Leland Orser (Cleante), Warren Keith (Orgon), John Elijah Bauman (Valere), Patrick Kerr (Tartuffe), Barclay Jefferis (Monsieur Loyal), Mark Briggs (The Officer), David Drobot (Second Officer).
TOMFOOLERY The Words, Music and Lyrics of Tom Lehrer; Adapted by Cameron Mackintosh and Robin Ray; Director and Choreographer, Derek Wolshonak; Musical Director, Fred Barton. CAST: Michael Pace, Judy Bro, Robert Boles; Musicians: Piano, Fred Barton; Percussion, Harvey Price; Trombone, Neal Craver.
TOMFOOLERY was revived at the end of the theatre's regular season. The cast was as follows: Michael McGrath, Mimi Wyche, Robert Boles, Fred Barton.
BENEFACTORS by Michael Frayn; Director, Cleveland Morris. CAST: Bjorn Johnson (David), Mary Walworth (Jane), Edward Baran (Colin), Polly Pen (Sheila).
MEMOIR by John Murrell; Director, Jamie Brown; Original music composed by Leon Odenz. CAST: Mary Doyle (Sarah Bernhardt), Terry Layman (Georges Pitou).
FENCES by August Wilson; Director, Clinton Turner Davis. CAST: Ray Aranha (Troy Maxson), Allie Woods, Jr. (Jim Bono), Marjorie Johnson (Rose), Paul Garrett (Lyons), LB Williams (Gabriel), Oliver Barrero (Cory), Tiffany Brandy Trawick (Raynell).

Oliver Barrero, Ray Aranha, Marjorie Johnson in "Fences"
Top: Fred Barton, Robert Boles, Michael Pace, Judy Bro in "Tomfoolery"

DENVER CENTER THEATRE COMPANY

Denver, Colorado

Artistic Director/Conservatory Director, Donovan Marley; Executive Director, Sarah Lawless; Producing Director/New Play Development, Barbara E. Sellers; Dean National Theatre Conservatory, Tony Church; Composers, Todd Barton, Samuel Lancaster; Sound, Scott Bradford, Matthew Morgan; Sets, Richard L. Hay, Andrew V. Yelusich, Andrew Carter, Vicki Smith, John Dexter, Michael Ganio, Pavel M. Bobrusky, Carolyn Leslie Ross; Lighting, Charles Mac Leod, Daniel L. Murray, Peter Maradudin; Costumes, Mr. Yelusich, Frances Kenny, Janet Morris, Patricia Ann Whitelock, Sarah Nash Gates; Musical Directors, Henry Aronson, Larry Delinger, Bruce K. Sevy, Lee Stametz; Orchestrations, Michael Starobin; Choreography, Virginia Freeman, Riette Burdick; Directors, Laird Williamson, Randal Myler, Bruce K. Sevy, Israel Hicks, Dakin Matthews, Frank Georgianna, Gitta Honegger, Steve Stettler; Stage Managers, Christopher C. Ewing, Gary Miller, Paul Jefferson, Anthony Powell, Charlene M. White, Erik Lauch, Lyle Raper
ACTING COMPANY: Aron Accurso, Jeffrey Agnitsch, Stephen Lee Anderson, Barbara Andres, Jacqueline Antaramian, Jim Baker, W. Allen Batchelder, P. J. Benjamin, Harvy Blanks, Suzanne Bouchard, Kathleen Brady-Garvin, Brittany Nicole Bratton, William Brenner, Ben Bottoms, Michael Kelly Boone, Linda Cameron, John Edward Clark, James Michael Connor, Omar Carter, Edythe Davis, Kay Doubleday, Melinda Deane, Carole B. Elmore, Robert Eustace, Steve Elmore, John Fiedler, Louisa Flaningam, Christine Gradl, Allison Gregory, Frank Georgianna, Ann Guilbert, Suzan Hanson, Laurie Harrop, Jamie Horton, John Hancock, Stephen Henderson, Stephen Anthony Henry, Leticia Jaramillo, Byron Jennings, Diana Johnson, Christopher Keener, Eric Lorentz, James J. Lawless, Frank Lowe, Matthew Mabe, Michael X. Martin, Thomas-David McDonald, Carolyn McCormick, Ivars Mikelson, Carrie Beutler Morgan, David Morgan, Peter Messaline, Mary Jo McConnell, Trary Maddalone, Lowell V. Noel, Shannon Penrod, Anthony Powell, Laura Pulio, Timothy McCuen Piggee, Lucille Patton, Scott Quintard, Guy Raymond, Jeffery Reid, Jamey Roberts, Mick Regan, Doug Rosson, Craig Ryder, Deborah Sclar, Christopher Selbie, Archie Smith, Leslie Carroll Smith, Kate Suber, Brian Thompson, Sharon Ullrick, John Walcutt, Doug White, Steve Wilson, Tyrone Wilson, Pamela Winslow, Dane Witherspoon
PRODUCTIONS: *Saint Joan* by George Bernard Shaw, *Desire Under the Elms* by Eugene O'Neill, *A Little Night Music* by Stephen Sondheim & Wheeler, *Three Men on a Horse* by Holm & Abbott, *Henry IV* by Shakespeare, *Fences* by August Wilson, *Adventures of Huckleberry Finn* by Mark Twain, Adap. by Randal Myler, *The Road to Mecca* by Athol Fugard
PREMIERES: *Mine Alone* by Conrad Bishop & Elizabeth Fuller, *Animal Farm* with Music, Lyrics & Book by Clark Gesner, *Soundbite* by Gary Leon Hill, *Ready for the River* by Neal Bell

P. Switzer Photos

Michael Martin, Luisa Flaningam, P. J. Benjamin in "Animal Fair" Above: Allison Gregory, Alice Rorvik in "Ready for the River"

135

Les Marsden as Groucho Top: Kate Skinner, Richard McWilliams in "Streetcar Named Desire"

DETROIT REPERTORY THEATRE

Detroit, Michigan
Thirty-second Season

Artistic Director: Bruce E. Millan; Group Sales/Marketing Director: Dino A. Valdez; Outreach Director: Dee Andrus; Literary Manager: Barbara Busby; Costume: B. J. Essen; Music Director: Kelly Smith; Set Designers: Bruce E. Millan, Robert Katkowsky; Scenic Artist: John Knox; Lighting Designer: Kenneth R. Hewitt, Jr.; Sound Designers: Burr Huntington, Reuben Yabuku; Graphics: Barbara Barefield, Walden Simper; Stage Managers: Dee Andrus, William Boswell, John W. Puchalski.

PRODUCTIONS AND CASTS

BLOOD RELATIONS by Sharon Pollock: Director: Yolanda Fleischer. CAST: Dee Andrus, Barbara Busby, Henrietta Hermelin, Roosevelt T. Johnson, Anthony Lucas, Joanne McGee, Mack Palmer.
FENCES by August Wilson: Director: Reuben Yabuku. CAST: Council Cargle, Michael Jay, Jennifer Jones, Tim Rhoze, Anthony Lucas, Allen T. Sheffield, Bri Juin Warren.
BULLPEN by Steven Kluger: Director: Bruce E. Millan. CAST: Mark Bishop, Regie Carlton, Thom Galasso, Clyde T. Harper, Rod Johnson, Roosevelt T. Johnson, Gerard L. A. Smith.
DISABILITY: A COMEDY by Ron Whyte: Director: William Boswell. CAST: Barbara Busby, Annette DePetris, Jesse Newton, Harry Wetzel

GEVA THEATRE

Rochester, NY

Producing Artistic Director, Howard J. Millman; Associate Artistic Director, Anthony Zerbe; General Manager, Christopher F. Kawolsky; Literary Director, Ann Patrice Carrigan, SSJ; Production Manager, James K. Tinsley; Public Relations Director, Christine Christopher; Education Director, Vicki Duval; Production Stage Manager, Catherine Norberg; Stage Manager, Frank Cavallo.
PECCADILLO by Garson Kanin; Directed by Stephen Rothman; Set Designed by Joseph Varga; Costumes by Shigeru Yaji; Lighting by Betsy Adams. CAST: A. D. Cover (Eric), Anthony Cummings (Robert Epstein), Elizabeth Dennehy (Iris Peabody), Maeve McGuire (Rachel DeAngelis), Robert Strane (Vito DeAngelis), Bradford Wallace (Bruce)
FRANKIE AND JOHNNY IN THE CLAIR DE LUNE by Terrence McNally; Directed by Howard J. Millman; Set Designed by Bob Barnett; Lighting by Phil Monat; Sound Design by Dan Roach. CAST: Richard Ferrone (Johnny), Carol Schultz (Frankie)
A CHRISTMAS CAROL by Charles Dickens; Adapted for GeVa Theatre by Eberle Thomas; Directed by Barbara Redmond; Original music by John Franceschina; Set designed by Bob Barnett; Costumes by Pamela Scofield; Lighting by Nic Minetor; Sound design by Dan Roach; Musical Director, Corinne Aquilina; Choreography by Jim Hoskins. CAST: John Sterling Arnold (Scrooge), Thomas Carson, Ted Davis, Edmund Davys, Holly Felton, John Messenger, Patricia Oetken, Herbert Mark Parker, William Pitts, Barbara Redmond, Donna Shanahan, Robert vanLeer, Christian Zwahlen.
MA RAINEY'S BLACK BOTTOM by August Wilson; Directed by Claude Purdy; Set Design by James Sandefur; Costumes by Constanza Romero; Lighting by Phil Monat; Sound design by Dan Roach; Musical Director, Dwight Andrews. CAST: Thomas Martell Brimm (Cutler), Anthony Cozart (Sylvester), Ray Demattis (Irvin), Theresa Merritt (Ma Rainey), Natalie Oliver (Dussie Mae), Gerald Richards (Sturdyvant), David Shakes (Slow Drag), Cedric H. Turner (Levee), Mark Wenderlich (Policeman), John Wesley (Toledo)
GROUCHO: A LIFE IN REVUE by Arthur Marx and Robert Fisher; Directed by Howard J. Millman; Set and Lighting design by Michael Hotopp; Sound by Dan Roach; Musical Director, Corinne Aquilina. CAST: Jonathan Brody (Chico/Harpo), Les Marsden (Groucho), Amelia Prentice (The Girls), Robert Tekampe (Citizen of Freedonia)
A STREETCAR NAMED DESIRE by Tennessee Williams; Directed by Gus Kaikkonen; Set designed by Jim Fenhagen; Lighting Design by F. Mitchell Dana; Costumes by Constanza Romero; Sound design by Dan Roach. CAST: Pharra J. Collins (Creole/Mexican Woman), Gilbert Cruz (Pablo Gonzales), Elaine Good (Woman), Bari Hochwald (Stella Kowalski), Alfred Lakeman (Steve Hubbell), Stephanie Madden (Eunice Hubbell), Richard McWilliams (Stanley Kowalski), H. D. Midkiff (Man), Kate Skinner (Blanche DuBois), David Stone (A Young Collector), Chad Tyler (Mitch)
REFLECTIONS '90: A NEW PLAYS FESTIVAL (Premieres): FORGIVING TYPHOID MARY by Mark St. Germain; Directed by Anthony Zerbe; Set design by Marjorie B. Kellogg; Lighting design by Kirk Bookman; Costume design by Susan Mickey; Sound design by Dan Roach. CAST: Bari Hochwald (Mary Mallon), Mart Hulswit (Dr. William Mills), Cynthia Hayden (Dr. Ann Saltzer), Josh Brolin (Fr. Michael), Rebecca Lamb (Sarah), Tim DeWitt (Intern); **ADULT FICTION** by Brian Richard Mori; Directed by Allen R. Belknap; All designers same as preceding play. CAST: David S. Howard (Earl), Rick Lawless (Mikie), Rick Christopher, Tim DeWitt, Diramund McDonnell, Christopher Pitts (Patrons); **OH, THE INNOCENTS** by Ari Roth; Directed by Joe Mantello; All designers same as preceding. CAST: Peter Birkenhead (Josh), Michael Liani (Jeremy), Cordelia Richards (Betsy), Nicole Orth-Pallavicini (Alex), Josh Brolin (Zev), Jill Smithgall (Laurel), Tim DeWitt (Bartender/Waiter)

Gelfond-Piper Photos

Harry Wetzel in "Disability"   **Michael Jay, Council Cargle in "Fen**

GEORGE STREET PLAYHOUSE

New Brunswick, NJ

Producing Artistic Director, Gregory S. Hurst; General Manager, Michael P. Gennaro; Associate Artistic Director, Wendy Liscow; Marketing Director, Cynthia J. Tostevin; Director of Press/PR, Heidi W. Giovine; Director of Outreach/Affiliate Director, Susan Kerner; Resident Costume Designer, Barbara Forbes; Resident Lighting Designer, Donald Holder; Business Manager, Karen S. Price; Development Director, Marilyn Powel; Production Manager, Deborah Jasien; Technical Director, Kieran Kelly

PRODUCTIONS & CASTS

LES LIAISONS DANGEREUSES by Christopher Hampton (from the novel by Cholderlos de Laclos); Director, Gregory S. Hurst; Set Designer, Atkin Pace; Costume Designer, Barbara Forbes; Lighting Designer, Donald Holder; Fight Director, Drew Fracher; Stage Manager, Thomas L. Clewell. CAST: Ellen Tobie (La Marquise de Merteuil), Deborah Strang (Mme de Volanges), Gabrielle Carteris (Cecile Volanges), James R. Wells (Major-domo), Will Lyman (Le Vicomte de Valmont), Gary Glor (Azolan), Betty Low (Mme de Rosemonde), Laura Innes (La Presidente de Tourvel), Elizabeth Shields (Emilie), Gordon MacDonald (Le Chevalier Danceny), Kevin Draine (Footman), Richard Freda (Footman), Kacie Drury (Maid)

BRIGHTON BEACH MEMOIRS and BROADWAY BOUND by Neil Simon (performed in repertory) Directors: Susan Kerner (Brighton Beach Memoirs), Wendy Liscow (Broadway Bound); Set Designer, Deborah Jasien; Costume Designer, Barbara Forbes; Lighting Designer, Donald Holder; Choreographer, Sherry Alban; Stage Manager, Sally Ann Wood. CAST (Brighton Beach Memoirs): Andrew Polk (Eugene), Beth McDonald (Blanche), Maggie Burke (Kate), Leah Sugarman (Laurie), Nelle Stokes (Nora), Murray Rubinstein (Stanley), David S. Howard (Jack). CAST (Broadway Bound): Maggie Burke (Kate), Salem Ludwig (Ben), Andrew Polk (Eugene), Murray Rubinstein (Stanley), Beth McDonald (Blanche), David S. Howard (Jack), Peter Bradshaw (Radio Voice—Announcer & Chubby Waters), Laura MacDermott (Radio Voice—Mrs. Pitkin)

MOUNTAIN by Douglas Scott *(World Premiere);* Director, John Henry Davis; Set Designer, Philipp Jung; Costume Designer, Barbara Forbes; Lighting Designer, Donald Holder; Stage Manager, James Fitzsimmons. CAST: Len Cariou (William O. Douglas), Heather Summerhayes (Woman), John C. Vennema (Man)

JOHNNY PYE AND THE FOOLKILLER by Mark St. Germain (Book & Lyrics) and Randy Courts (Music & Lyrics); Director, Paul Lazarus; Based on a short story by Stephen Vincent Benet; Musical Director, Steven M. Alper; Orchestrations by Courts/Dellay Music; Associate Musical Director, Douglas Besterman; Set Designer, William Barclay; Costume Designer, Mary L. Hayes; Lighting Designer, Donald Holder; Sound Designer, Jim Landis; Stage Manager, Thomas L. Clewell. CAST: John Babcock (Young Johnny), Larry Cahn (Bob), Victoria Clark (Suzy Marsh), John Hickok (Johnny Pye), John Jellison (Foolkiller), Tom Robbins (Wilbur Wilberforce), Catherine Satterwhite (Young Suzy), Ron Lee Savin (Barber), Gordon Stanley (Bill), Lou Williford (Mrs. Miller)

JEKYLL AND HYDE *(world premiere musical)* by Leonora Thuna (book), Norman Sachs (music) and Mel Mandel (lyrics); Director, Gregory S. Hurst; Music Directed and Supervised by Joel Silberman; Orchestrations, Larry Hochman; Choreography, Lynne Taylor-Corbett; Set Designer, Deborah Jasien; Costume Designer, Barbara Forbes; Lighting Designer, Donald Holder; Sound Designer, Bernard Fox; Stage Manager, Sally Ann Wood. CAST: Rebecca Baxter (Lucy Turner), John Cullum (Dr. Henry Jekyll/Edward Hyde), Terrence Currier (Reverend Luster), Marianne Ferrari (Grace/Billy Bob), Anne Kerry Ford (Margaret Cavendish), Charles Goff (Sir Danvers Carew/Col. Douglas), Cady Huffman (Catherine/Alicia-Ann), James Judy (Richard Enfield), Nancy Magarill (Elizabeth/Jimmy Joe), John Rainer (Poole), Jamie Ross (Dr. Hastie Lanyon), David Sabin (Gabriel Utterson), Celia Tackaberry (Madam Goodheart), Jon Vandertholen (Inspector Elliot/Capt. Beauregard), Jane Scimeca (Flower Girl/Maid), Mary Walker (Boot Black)

HANDY DANDY by William Gibson; Director, Tony Giordano; Set Designer, Deborah Jasien; Costume Designer, Barbara Forbes; Lighting Designer, Donald Holder; Associate Set Designer, Bradley D. Kaye; Stage Manager, Sally Ann Wood. CAST: James Whitmore (Henry Pulaski), Audra Lindley (Molly Egan)

FEAST OF FOOLS by Geoff Hoyle; Directorial Consultant, Anthony Taccone; Scenic Designer, Scott Weldin; Lighting Designer, David Lincecum; Sound Designer, Michael Holten; Stage Manager, Michael Suenkel. CAST: Geoff Hoyle

Eddie Birch/Miguel Pagliere Photos

Top: (L) John Cullum in "Jekyll & Hyde" (R) Laura Innes,
Will Lyman in "Les Liaisons . . ." Below: John C. Vennema,
Len Cariou in "Mountain" (L) Audra Lindley, James Whitmore in "Handy Dandy"

Tom Robbins, John Babcock, John Jellison in
"Johnny Pye . . ."

GOODMAN THEATRE

Chicago, Illinois

Artistic Director, Robert Falls; Producing Director, Roche Schulfer; Artistic Associates, Frank Galati, Michael Maggio

PRODUCTIONS & CASTS

THE MISANTHROPE by Moliere; New Version by Neil Bartlett; Adaptation/Direction, Robert Falls; Sets, George Tsypin; Costumes, Susan Hilferty; Lighting, James F. Ingalls; Sound, Rob Milburn; Stage Manager, Lois Griffing, Jill Larmett; Dramaturgs, Walter Bilderback, Richard Pettengill. CAST: William Brown (Philinte), David Darlow (Alceste), Del Close (Oronte), Kim Cattrall (Celimene), Christina Haag (Eliante), David Alan Novak (Clitandre), John Douglas Carlile (Acaste), Peggy Roeder (Arsinoe)

A CHRISTMAS CAROL by Charles Dickens; Adaptation, Tom Creamer; Director, Steve Scott; Sets, Joseph Nieminski; Costumes, Julie Jackson; Lighting, Robert Christen; Sound, Rob Milburn, David Naunton; Choreography, Beatrix Rashid; Stage Managers, Joseph Drummond, Alden Vasquez; Music Composer/Arranger, Larry Schanker. CAST: William J. Norris (Scrooge), Robert Scogin (Cratchit), David E. Chadderdon, Paul Henry Thompson (Businessmen), Keith Byron-Kirk (Fred/Ghost Xmas to Come), Steve Pickering (Marley's Ghost/Guest/Joe), Carmen Roman (Ghost Xmas Past/Guest), John Möhrlein (Schoolmaster/Undertaker), Karl Maschek (Boy Scrooge/Turkey Boy), Rhona Bennett (Fan/Belinda), Terence Gallagher (Scrooge-Young Man/Ghost Xmas to Come), Michael Torrey (Wilkins/Man), Dennis Kennedy (Fezziwig/Businessman), Ann Whitney (Mrs. Fezziwig/Mrs. Dilber), Sally Murphy (Belle), Scott Lowell (Fiddler/Guest/Xmas to Come), Ernest Perry, Jr. (Ghost Christmas Present), Ora Jones (Mrs. Cratchit), Christa Cricket Leigh (Martha), Jack Carter Littman (Peter), Denisha V. Powell (Emily/Want), Brendon DeMay (Tiny Tim), Johanna McKay (Fred's Wife/Woman), Paula Newsome (Philomena/Charwoman), Eddie Jemison (Topper), Lewis A. Affetto (Ignorance/Urchin)

THE WINTER'S TALE by William Shakespeare; Director, Frank Galati; Sets, John Conklin; Costumes, Virgil Johnson; Lighting, Jennifer Tipton; Sound, Rob Milburn; Choreography, Peter Amster; Music, Rob Millburn, Willy Schwarz, Miriam Sturm; Dramaturg, Tom Creamer; Stage Managers, Lois Griffing, Jill Larmett. CAST: John Hutton (Leontes), Martha Lavey (Hermione), Anthony Bravo (Mamillius), Sally Murphy (Perdita), Ned Schmidtke (Camillo), Steve Pickering (Antigonus/Time), Terence Plunkett (Cleomenes), Keith Byron-Kirk (Dion), Gerry Becker (Lord), Patrick Clear (Lord), Linda Emond (Paulina), Maureen Gallagher (Emilia), Lisa Tejero (Nurse), Maurice Chasse (Jailer/Opera Performer), Edward Wilkerson (Officer/Opera Performer), Ned Mochel (Mariner), Rebecca MacLean (Opera Performer/Mopsa), Treva Tegtmeier (Opera Performer/Dorcas) Christa Cricket Leigh (Opera Performer), David Darlow (Polixenes), Bruce Norris (Archidamus), William J. Norris (Archidamus), Skipp Sudduth (Autolycus), Tom Aulino (Shepard), Ray Chapman (Clown)

'TIS PITY SHE'S A WHORE by John Ford; Director, Joanne Akalaitis; Sets, John Conklin; Costumes, Gabriel Berry; Lighting, Pat Collins; Sound, Richard Woodbury; Choreography, Timothy O'Slynne; Fights, David Leong; Music, Jan A. P. Kaczmarek; Dramaturg, Tom Creamer; Vocal Coach, Catherine Fitzmaurice; Stage Managers, Joseph Drummond, T. Paul Lynch. CAST: Steve Pickering (Bonaventure), Larry Brandenburg (Florio), Jesse Borrego (Giovanni), Lauren Tom (Annabella), Joan Cusack (Putana), Don Cheadle (Soranzo), Erick Avari (Vasques), Ernest Perry, Jr. (Donado), Ross Lehman (Bergetto), Wilson Cain III (Poggio), Daniel Oreskes (Grimaldi), Peter Aylward (Richardetto), Jenny Bacon (Philotis), Barbara E. Robertson (Hippolita), George Matthew (Cardinal), Russell Kuzuhara (Banditti/Ensemble), Matthew J. Robison (Banditti/Ensemble), Carlos Sanz (Banditti/Ensemble), Adrian Danzig, Doug VonNessen, Rengin Altay, Vikki J. Barrett, Joan Elizabeth, Peri Kaczmarek, Robert Bundy, Jan Lucas, Brian K. Spivey, Jacqueline Williams (Ensemble)

UNCLE VANYA by Anton Chekhov; Adaptation, David Mamet; Translation, Vlada Chernomirdik; Director, Michael Maggio; Sets, Linda Buchanan; Costumes, Nan Cibula; Lighting, James F. Ingalls; Sound, Rob Milburn; Dramaturg, Richard Pettengill; Stage Managers, Lois Griffing, Jill Larmett. CAST: Fern Persons (Marina), Scott Jaeck (Astrov), John Mahoney (Uncle Vanya), Howard Witt (Serebryakov), Isabella Hofmann (Yelena), Linda Emond (Sonya), William J. Norris (Waffles), Marji Bank (Mariya), Maurice Chasse (Workman)

THE MEETING by Jeff Stetson; Director, Chuck Smith; Costumes, Glenn Billings; Sets/Lighting, Tim Oien; Sound, Corbiere T. Boynes; Stage Manager, Brad White. CAST: Harry J. Lennix (Malcolm X), Edward D. Richardson (Rashid), Percy Littleton (Martin Luther King, Jr.)

MARVIN'S ROOM (*Premiere*) by Scott McPherson; Director, David Petrarca; Sets, Linda Buchanan; Costumes, Claudia Boddy; Lighting, Robert Christen; Sound/Music, Rob Milburn; Dramaturgs, Tom Creamer, Sandy Shinner; Stage Manager, Kimberly Osgood. CAST: Laura Esterman (Bessie), Tim Monison (Dr. Wally), Jane MacIver (Ruth), Peter Rybolt (Bob), Lee Guthrie (Lee), Ora Jones (Dr. Charlotte), Mark Rosenthal (Hank), Karl Maschek (Charlie), William T. Gallagher (Marvin)

Top Right: Martha Lavey, Anthony Bravo in "The Winter's Tale" Below: (L) Percy Littleton, Harry J. Lennix in "The Meeting" (R) Linda Emond, John Mahoney in "Uncle Vanya" Bottom: John Douglas Carlile, David Alan Novak, Kim Cattrall, David Darlow, Christina Haag in "The Misanthrope"

ELLIOT LOVES (*Premiere*) by Jules Feiffer; Director, Mike Nichols; Sets, Tony Walton; Costumes, Ann Roth; Lighting, Paul Gallo; Sound, Rob Milburn; Stage Manager, Kimberly Osgood; Production Supervisor, Peter Lawrence. CAST: Anthony Heald (Elliot), Christine Baranski (Joanna), Latanya Richardson (Vera), David Pierce (Phil), Oliver Platt (Larry), Bruce A. Young (Bobby)

THE GOSPEL AT COLONUS Conceived, Adapted & Directed by Lee Breuer; Music, Bob Telson; Production/Set Design, Alison Yerxa; Costumes, Ghretta Hynd; Lighting, Robert Christen; Sound, Rob Milburn; Stage Managers, Joseph Drummond, T. Paul Lynch. CAST: Rev. Earl F. Miller, Afemo Omilami, Clarence Fountain and the Five Blind Boys of Alabama: Johnny Fields, J. T. Clinkscales, Jimmy Carter, Joe Watson, Curtis Foster, Catherine Slade, Robert Earl Jones, Shari A. Seals, Roebuck Pops Staples, Terrence A. Carson, Soul Stirrers: Martin Jacox, Willie Rogers, Jackie Banks, Ben Odom, Sam Butler, Jr., Carolyn Johnson White, J. D. Steele, Calvin Bridges, Johnny Lee Davenport, Faith Tabernacle Voices, Kelvin and Co.

Steve Leonard, Lisa Ebright Photos

THE GOODSPEED OPERA HOUSE

East Haddam, Connecticut
Twenty-seventh Season

Executive Director, Michael P. Price; Associate Artistic Director, Dan Siretta; Associate Producer, Sue Frost; Casting Director/New York Representative, Warren Pincus; Press, Kay McGrath, Max Eisen; Development, Kathy Mead; Marketing, Michellee Yushkevich and Stacey Grimaldi; Company Manager, Michael Jennings; Dramaturg, Tommy Krasker; Wardrobe, John Riccucci; Props, Karen E. Ford.

PRODUCTIONS & CASTS

A CONNECTICUT YANKEE with Music by Richard Rodgers; Book, Herbert Fields; Lyrics, Lorenz Hart; Director, Thomas Gruenewald; Musical Director, Lynn Crigler; Choreography, Rodney Griffin; Sets, Clarke Dunham; Costumes, Dean Brown; Lighting, Craig Miller; Assistant Musical Director, Ted Kociolek; Technical Director, Daniel Renn; Stage Manager, Michael Brunner; Assistant Stage Manager, Donna Cooper Hilton; Dance Arrangements, Russell Warner; Additional Orchestrations, Lynn Crigler. CAST: John Almberg (Laurence Lake/Lancelot), Bill Carmichael (Martin Barrett/Martin), Kirsti Carnahan (Alice Courtleigh/Demoiselle Alisande La Carteloise [Sandy]), Gordon Connell (Arthur Pendragon/King Arthur), Teri Gibson (Gwen Wesson/Guinevere), Bryan Harris (Kenneth Kay/Sir Kay), Betsy Ann Leadbetter (Fay Merill/Morgan Le Fay), Jane Potter (Evelyn Lane/Evelyn), Christopher Scott (Gerald Lake/Galahad), Raymond Thorne (Thurston Merrill/Merlin), Libby Tomlinson (Angie Smith/Angela), Peggy Bayer, Diana Brownstone, Becky Downing, Amy Flood, G. Eugene Moose, Glen Pannell, Len Pfluger, Josef Reiter, Jeff Siebert.

MADAME SHERRY with Music by Karl Hoschna; Book and Lyrics, Otto Harbach; Director, Martin Connor; Choreography/Musical Staging, Dan Siretta; Musical Director, Ted Kociolek; Musical Supervision, Lynn Crigler; Sets, Eduardo Sicangco; Costumes, Jose Lengson; Lighting, Kirk Bookman; Technical Director, John Hugh Minor; Assistant Musical Director, John McMahon; Assistant Choreographer, Keith Savage; Stage Manager, Michael Brunner; Dance Music, G. Harrell; Assistant Stage Manager, Donna Copper Hilton. CAST: Adinah Alexander (Pepita), Teri Bibb (Yvonne), Leonard Drum (Phillippe), Douglas Fisher (Theophilus), Joanna Glushak (Lulu), Robert R. McCormick (Edward Sherry), Aurelio Padron (Leonardo Gomez), Maureen Sadusk (Catherine), Heather Berman, Molly Brown, Tim Foster, Donna Hagan, Gary Kirsch, Renee Laverdiere, David Monzione, Elizabeth Nackley, Rodney Pridgen, Kevin Weldon.

OH, KAY! with Music by George Gershwin; Book, Guy Bolton and P. G. Wodehouse; Lyrics, Ira Gershwin; Director, Martin Connor; Concept/Choreography/Musical Staging, Dan Siretta; Musical Director, David Evans; Adaptation, James Racheff; Artistic Consultant, Sheldon Epps; Sets, Kenneth Foy; Costumes, Judy Dearing; Lighting, Craig Miller; Technical Director, John Hugh Minor; Stage Manager, Michael Brunner; Assistant Choreographer, Keith Savage; Dance Arrangements/Orchestrations, Donald W. Johnston; Additional Orchestrations, Larry Moore and Danny Troob. CAST: Alexander Barton (Reverend DuGrass), Marion J. Caffey (Larry Potter), Helmar Augustus Cooper (Shorty), Pamela Isaacs (Kay Jones/Lady Katie), Stanley Wayne Mathis (Duke), Brenda Pressley (Constance DuGrass), Ron Richardson (Jimmy Winter), Mark Kenneth Smaltz (Janson), Tracey M. Bass, Keith Robert Bennett, Yvette Curtis, Denise Heard, Lynise Heard, Larry Johnson, Dexter Jones, Sara Beth Lane, Sharon Moore, Ken Leigh Rogers, Lynn Sterling, Horace Turnbull.

THE NORMA TERRIS THEATRE, GOODSPEED-AT-CHESTER

A FINE & PRIVATE PLACE with Music by Richard Isen; Book and Lyrics, Erik Haagensen; Director, Robert Kalfin; Musical Director, Henry Aronson; Sets and Lighting, Fred Kolo; Technical Director, John Hugh Minor; Stage Manager, Ruth M. Feldman. CAST: Evalyn Baron (Gertrude Klapper), Gabriel Barre (Raven), Charles Goff (Jonathan Rebeck), Maureen Silliman (Laura Durand), Brian Sutherland (Michael Morgan).

THE REAL LIFE STORY OF JOHNNY DE FACTO with Music, Book and Lyrics by Douglas Post; Director, Andre Ernotte; Musical Director, Alkiviades "Alki" Steriopoulos, Musical Supervision and Arrangements, Joseph Baker; Sets, William Barclay; Costumes, Roslyn Brunner, Lighting, Phil Monat; Technical Director, John Hugh Minor; Stage Manager, Jane Neufeld. CAST: Bertilla Baker (3rd Back-up Singer), Steve Beebe (2nd Back-up Singer), Michael Brian (Beau Pendergast), Scott Dainton (Spaz Bernstein), Paul Kandel (Leo Sobocinski), Edwina Lewis (1st Back-up Singer), Heidi Mollenhauer (Audrey Janes), Jim Morlino (Johnny de Facto).

Right Center: Bill Carmichael, Kirsti Carnahan in "A Connecticut Yankee" Above: Brenda Pressley, Ron Richardson, Pamela Isaacs in "Oh, Kay!" Top: Cast of "Madame Sherry"
Diane Sobolewski Photos

Edwina Lewis, Jim Morlino, Scott Dainton in "The Real Life Story of Johnny De Facto"

139

GREAT LAKES THEATRE FESTIVAL

Cleveland, Ohio

Artistic Director, Gerald Freedman; Managing Director, Mary Bill; Associate Directors, Bill Rudman, Victoria Bussert; Associate Artistic Director, John Enzell; Director of Development/Administration, Andrea Krist

PRODUCTIONS & CASTS

HAMLET: Peter Aylward, Judith Black, Simon Brooking, John Buck, Jr., Bernard Canepari, Brendan Corbalis, James Kall, Shirley Knight, Michael A. Krawic, Patrick Mulcahy, Anthony Powell, Ron Randell, John Patrick Rice, Tisha Roth, Steve Routman, Norman Snow, Todd Bryant Weeks
GRANDMA MOSES: AN AMERICAN PRIMITIVE: Cloris Leachman, Peter Thoemke
THE THREEPENNY OPERA: Neal Ben-Ari, Kelly Bishop, Marji Dodrill, David Drake, Colette Hawley, Michael A. Krawic, William Leach, Shari Livingston, Daniel Marcus, Don Mayo, Andre Montgomery, Carol Morley, J. K. Simmons, Lannyl Stephens, Michael Steuber, Mimi Wyche
THE SEAGULL: Brendan Corbalis, Suzanne Costallos, Anita Gillette, Jack R. Marks, Kevin McCarty, Ron Randell, Tisha Roth, Steve Routman, Lewis J. Stadlen, Isa Thomas, Neil Vipond
A CHRISTMAS CAROL: Andrew Boyer, John Buck, Jr., Julia Gibson, Sheila Heyman, James Kall, Michael A. Krawic, William Leach, Don Mayo, Kevin McCarty, Steve Routman, Ellen Jane Smith, Todd Bryant Weeks, Helene Weinberg

Roger Mastroianni Photos

Neil Vipond, Anita Gillette in "The Seagull" Above: Anthony Powell, Shirley Knight, Norman Snow in "Hamlet"

William Leach, Carol Morley in "Threepenny Opera" Above: William Leach in "A Christmas Carol"

THE GUTHRIE THEATRE

Minneapolis, Minnesota
Twenty-seventh Season

Artistic Director, Garland Wright; Executive Director, Edward A. Martenson
ACTING COMPANY: Elizabeth Acosta, Franz C. Alderfer, Anne Allgood, April Armstrong, Erick Avari, Peter Bartlett, Christopher Bayes, Terry Bellamy, Kelly Bertenshaw, Bruce Bohne, Erick Bokuniewicz, Jesse Borrego, John Bottoms, Brigid Brady, Risa Brainin, Brenda Braye, David Anthony Brinkley, Debra Cardona, Robert Cicchini, Jonathan Dokuchitz, Robert Dorfman, Tony Floyd, Gina Franz, Nathaniel Fuller, June Gibbons, Jason Graae, Marvin Grays, Fanni Green, Richard Grusin, Joseph Haj, Ben Halley, Jr., Steven Hendrickson, Emil Herrera, David Hibbard, Richard S. Iglewski, Charles Janasz, Shawn Judge, Barbara Kingsley, Hugh William Kirsch, Ken Krugman, Kati Kuroda, Lisa Lasley, T. Doyle Leverett, John Lewin, John Carroll Lynch, Ruth Maleczech, Barbara March, Cynthia Martells, Richard McKenzie, Isabell Monk, Rozz Morehead, Joseph S. Moser, David Moynihan, Ron Nakahara, Clark Niederjohn, Richard Ooms, Stephanie Park, Lola Pashalinski, Stephen Pelinski, Timothy Perez, Patricia Phillips, Peggy Pope, José Protko, David Rainey, Barbara Reid, Lia Rivamonte, Mary Lou Rosato, Cristine Rose, Mark Rosenwinkel, Daniel Southern, David J. Steinberg, Bernadette Sullivan, Andy Taylor, Michael Tezla, Peter Thoemke, Barton Tinapp, Lauren Tom, Matthew Vaky, Shirley Venard, Gregory Wallace, Margie Weaver, Brenda Wehle, Claudia Wilkens, Sally Wingert, Rob Woronoff, Stephen Yoakam
DIRECTORS: JoAnne Akalaitis, Paul Draper, David Gordon, Douglas Hughes, Michael Kahn, Richard Ooms, Stan Wojewodski, Jr., Garland Wright
DESIGNERS: John Arnone, Frances Aronson, Chris Barreca, Andrei Both, Marcus Dilliard, Jack Edwards, Linda Fisher, Eiko Ishioka, Hugh Landwehr, Derek McLane, Martin Pakledinaz, Doug Stein, Stephen Strawbridge, Jennifer Tipton, George Tsypin, David Woolard, Catherine Zuber
ASSOCIATED ARTISTS: Playwrights and Translators, Barbara Field, W. Stuart McDowell, Paul Schmidt; Composers, Philip Glass, Kim Daryl Sherman, Foday Musa Suso, Hiram Titus; Choreographers, Doug Elkins, Loyce Houlton; Movement, Maria Cheng; Vocal Coaches, Catherine Fitzmaurice, Elizabeth Smith; Musical Directors, Matt Barber, David Bishop, Eric Kodner; Musicians, James Greeney, Robert Pearson, Max Ray, Kim Salisbury, Peter Steshoel, Alexis Vaubel, Cliff Walinski; Guest Dramaturg, Colette Brooks
PRODUCTIONS: *HARVEY* by Mary Chase; Directed by Douglas Hughes; *UNCLE VANYA* by Anton Chekov; Directed by Garland Wright; *THE DUCHESS OF MALFI* by John Webster; Directed by Michael Kahn; *VOLPONE* by Ben Jonson; Directed by Stan Wojewodski; *THE SCREENS* by Jean Genet; Directed by Joanne Akalaitis; *A CHRISTMAS CAROL* by Charles Dickens; Directed by Barbara Fields; *CANDIDE* by Voltaire, Leonard Bernstein, Richard Wilbur, John LaTouche, Stephen Sondheim; Directed by Garland Wright.

Michael Daniel Photos

Richard S. Iglewski, Erick Avari in "The Screens"

June Gibbons, Brenda Wehle, Richard S. Iglewski, Cristine Rose, Richard Grusin in "Uncle Vanya"

HARTFORD STAGE COMPANY

Hartford, Connecticut
Twenty-seventh Season

Artistic Director, Mark Lamos; Managing Director, David Hawkanson; Associate Artistic Director/Dramaturg, Greg Leaming; Resident Playwright, Constance Congdon; General Manager/Marketing Director, Jeffrey Woodward; Public Relations Director, Howard Sherman; Business Manager, Michael Ross; Production Manager, Candice Chirgotis; Technical Director, Jim Keller; Costumer, Martha Christian; Properties Director/Designer, Sandy Struth; Master Electrician, Bette Regan; Audio Department Head, Frank Pavlich

PRODUCTIONS & CASTS

THE IMPORTANCE OF BEING EARNEST by Oscar Wilde; Director, Mark Lamos; Assistant Director, Rob Bundy; Set Design, Michael Yeargan; Costume Design, Jess Goldstein; Lighting Design, Peter Kaczorowski; Sound Design, David Budries; Production Stage Managers, Ruth E. Sternberg & Barbara Reo. CAST: Barbara Bryne (Lady Bracknell), Helen Carey (Miss Prism), Mark Lamos (John Worthing), Mary Layne (Gwendolen Fairfax), Mary-Louise Parker (Cecily Cardew), John Scanlan (Lane/Merriman), Victor Slezak (Algernon Moncrieff) and Benjamin Stewart (Rev. Chasuble)

STAND-UP TRAGEDY by Bill Cain; Director, Ron Link; Set Design, Yael Pardess; Costume Design, Carol Brolaski; Lighting Design, Robert W. Rosentel; Choreography, Shabba-Doo; Original Music, Shabba-Doo and Yutaka Fresh J; Sound Design, David Budries; Production Stage Manager, Ruth E. Sternberg. CAST: Anthony Barrile (Marco Ruiz), Marcus Chong (Lee Cortez), Jack Coleman (Tom Griffin), John C. Cooke (Mitchell James), Dan Gerrity (Burke Kendall), Edwin Lugo (Freddy), Ray Oriel (Henry Rodriguez), Richard Poe (Father Larkin), Sixto Ramos (Carlos) and Shabba-Doo (Luis)

THE ILLUSION by Tony Kushner; Freely adapted from a play by Pierre Corneille; Director, Mark Lamos; Set Design, John Conklin; Costume Design, Martin Pakledinaz; Lighting Design, Pat Collins; Sound Design, Mark Bennett; Production Stage Manager, Barbara Reo. CAST: J. Grant Albrecht (Calisto/Clindor/Theogenes), Andrew Colteaux (Pleribo/Adraste/The Prince), Jarlath Conroy (The Amanuensis), Ashley Gardner (Melibea/Isabelle/Hippolyta), Philip Goodwin (Matamore), Bellina Logan (Elicia/Lyse/Clarina), Frederick Neumann (Alcandre) and Marco St. John (Pridamant of Avignon)

WOYZECK by Georg Buchner; Director & Set Design, Richard Foreman; Translator, Henry J. Schmidt; Costume Design, Lindsay W. Davis; Lighting Design, Heather Carson; Production Stage Manager, Ruth E. Sternberg. CAST: Daniel Ahearn (Carnival Announcer), Hannah Bent (Child), Brian Delate (Karl the Idiot), Tracey Ellis (Margret), Kenneth Gray (Captain), Michael J. Hume (Doctor), Debbie Jarett (Child), David Patrick Kelly (Woyzeck), Peter Drew Marshall (Sergeant), Miguel Perez (Andres), Gordana Rashovich (Marie), Hayden Reed Sakow (Woyzeck's Son), Edward Seamon (Pawnbroker), Steven Stahl (Apprentice) and William Verderber (Drum Major)

DAYTRIPS by Jo Carson; Director, Michael Engler; Set Design, Loy Arcenas; Costume Design, Catherine Zuber; Lighting Design, Pat Collins; Sound Design, David Budries; Production Stage Manager, Barbara Reo. CAST: Suzanna Hay (Storyteller), Susan Pellegrino (Pat), Helen Stenborg (Rose) and Isa Thomas (Ree/Irene)

THE MISER by Moliere; Translated and Adapted by Constance Congdon; Director, Mark Lamos; Set Design, John Arnone; Costume Design, Martin Pakledinaz; Lighting Design, Pat Collins; Sound Design, David Budries; Production Stage Manager, Ruth E. Sternberg. CAST: Betsy Aidem (Elise), Gerry Bamman (Harpagon), Stephen Caffrey (Valere), Kevin Cristaldi (Brindavoine/Police Superintendant), Gabriella Diaz-Farrar (Mariane), Marcus Giamatti (La Fleche), Donna Mehle (Claudine), Pamela Payton-Wright (Frosine), Jeffery V. Thompson (Master Jacques), Ted van Griethuysen (Master Simon/Anselme) and Tom Wood (Cleante)

T. Charles Erickson Photos

Left Center: Isa Thomas, Helen Stenborg, Susan Pellegrino, Suzanna Hay in "Daytrips" Above: David Patrick Kelly, Michael J. Hume in "Woyzeck" Top: Mary-Louise Parker, Mary Layne, Barbara Bryne, Mark Lamos, Victor Slezak in "The Importance of Being Earnest"

Ashley Gardner, Bellina Logan, J. Grant Albrecht in "The Illusion"

Betsy Aidem, Donna Mehle, Gerry Bamman, Tom Wood, Stephen Caffrey in "The Miser"

HUNTINGTON THEATRE COMPANY

Boston Massachusetts
Eighth Season

Producing Director, Peter Altman; Managing Director, Michael Maso; Public Relations, William Prenevost; Press, Jennifer Maxwell

HYDE PARK *(U.S. premiere)* by James Shirley; Directed by Kyle Donnelly; Scenery Designed by Kate Edmunds; Costumes Designed by Lindsay W. Davis; Lighting Designed by Rita Pietraszek; Sound Design by Ed McDermid; Choreography by Michael Sokoloff; Production Stage Manager, Diane DiVita; Assistant Stage Manager, C. Renee Alexander. CAST: James Bodge, Ivar Brogger, Tim Buntel, Terrence Caza, Michele Farr, Monique Fowler, Matt Frederick, Munson Hicks, Todd Jamieson, Bob Knapp, Mark Lancaster, Donna Manley, Derek Meader, John Neisler, Cynthia Rider, Thomas Schall, Ellen Jane Smith, Richard Ziman.

BOESMAN AND LENA by Athol Fugard; Directed by Tazewell Thompson; Scenery Designed by James Leonard Joy; Costumes Designed by Amanda J. Klein; Lighting Designed by Roger Meeker; Sound Design by Ed McDermid; Production Stage Manager, Melinda Lamoreux; Assistant Stage Manager, Kelly Cantley. CAST: Lou Ferguson, Karen Evans-Kandel, Thomas Anderson

O PIONEERS! *(World premiere)* Adapted by Darrah Cloud; from the novel by Willa Cather; Music by Kim D. Sherman; Directed by Kevin Kuhlke; Music Director, Brian Russell; Scenery Designed by John Wulp; Costumes Designed by Ann Roth; Lighting Designed by Brian Nason; Production Stage Manager, Diane DiVita; Assistant Stage Manager, C. Renee Alexander. CAST: John Carpenter, Kate Coffman, Christopher Coucill, Robin Eldridge, Taina Elg, Tad Ingram, Douglas Krizner, Neil Maffin, Kevin McDermott, Mary McDonnell, Randle Mell, Joel Mitchell, Kate Phelan, Michelle Pinsley, Scott Rabinowitz, Jennifer Rohn, Brooke Richie, Timothy Sawyer, Thomas Schall, Eda Seasongood, Maggie Simpson, Peter Sokol-Hessner, Seth Sole-Robertson, Jessica Walling

THE MERRY WIVES OF WINDSOR by William Shakespeare; Directed by Edward Gilbert; Scenery Designed by John Falabella; Costumes Designed by Mariann Verheyen; Lighting Designed by Nicholas Cernovitch; Music Composed by Albin Konopka; Production Stage Manager, Diane DiVita; Assistant Stage Manager, C. Renee Alexander. CAST: Jack Aranson, Tony Aylward, Ross Bickell, Marie Burrage, John Henry Cox, Daniel Fierman, Tracy Griswold, Frank Groseclose, Yona Haskins-Prost, Munson Hicks, Robert Keefe, Bob Knapp, Donal Kerrigan, Pirie MacDonald, Conan McCarty, Dan McCleary, Tanny McDonald, Daniel Michaels, Robin Moseley, John Neisler, Gary Reineke, Sandra Shipley, Gary Sloan, Tara Stewart, Eric Swanson, Hayden Walling, Michael Williams

THE LADY FROM MAXIM'S by Georges Feydeau; Adapted by Larry Carpenter; from a translation by Janice Orion; Directed by Larry Carpenter; Scenery Designed by John Falabella; Costumes Designed by David Murin; Lighting Designed by Marcia Madiera; Choreography by Daniel Pelzig; Music Composed by John Clifton; Production Stage Manager, Diane DiVita; Assistant Stage Manager, C. Renee Alexander. CAST: Humbert Allen Astredo, Tony Aylward, James Bodge, John Bolger, Judy Braha, Helen Lloyd Breed, Tamara Daniel, Philip Eaton, Lynnda Ferguson, Deborah Goss, Munson Hicks, Eve Johnson, James Judy, John Kinsherf, Mary Klug, Mary Ann Lamb, Richard McElvain, James Richard Morgan, Greg Mullavey, John Neisler, Paul Niebanck, Richard Russell Ramos, Duncan M. Rogers, Jo de Winter

Richard Feldman Photos

Top Left: Randle Mell, Mary McDonnell in "O Pioneers!"

Edwin Lugo, Anthony Barrile, Shabba-Doo, Marcus Chong, Ray Oriel in "Stand-Up Tragedy" (Hartford Stage Co.)

Jack Aranson, Sandra Shipley in "Merry Wives of Windsor"

143

THE JOHN F. KENNEDY CENTER FOR THE PERFORMING ARTS

Washington, D.C.

Chairman, Ralph P. Davidson; Artistic Director, Marta Istomin

PRODUCTIONS & CASTS

(OPERA HOUSE) SOPHISTICATED LADIES by Duke Ellington; An American-Soviet Co-production; Direction/Choreography, Claudia Asbury; Sets, Yuri Kuper; Costumes, Slava Zaitsev, Willa Kim; Lighting, Richard Winkler. CAST: Hinton Battle, Gregg Burge, Donna Wood, Lonette McKee, Jackie Patterson, Christina Saffran, Cleve Asbury

INTO THE WOODS by Sondheim & Lapine; Director, Mr. Lapine; Musical Staging, Lar Lubovitch; Sets, Tony Straiges; Lighting, Richard Nelson; Costumes, Ann Hould-Ward; Musical Director, Randy Booth; Stage Manager, Dan W. Langhofer. CAST and MUSICAL NUMBERS: See touring company.

GYPSY by Styne, Sondheim & Laurents; Director, Arthur Laurents. CAST: Tyne Daly, Jonathan Hadary, Crista Moore, Robert Lambert. For full cast & credits see Broadway Calendar.

ANNIE 2: MISS HANNIGAN'S REVENGE with Music by Charles Strouse; Lyrics, Martin Charnin; Book, Thomas Meehan; Director, Martin Charnin; Choreography, Danny Daniels; Sets, David Mitchell; Costumes, Theoni V. Aldredge; Lighting, Ken Billington; Orchestrations, Michael Starobin; Musical Direction/Dance Arrangements, Peter Howard. CAST: Dorothy Louden (Miss Hannigan), Harve Presnell (Warbucks), Ronny Graham (Lionel McCoy), Danielle Findley (Annie), Lauren Mitchell (Grace Farrell), Marian Seldes (Mrs. Christmas), Raymond Thorne (FDR), Terrence P. Currier (Drake), Scott Robertson, Gerry McIntyre, Fiely Matias, Beau, Laurent Giroux, Juliana Marx, Corinne Melancon, T. J. Meyers, Barbara Moroz, Karen Murphy, Bill Nolte, Michelle O'Steen, Don Percassi, J. K. Simmons, Dorothy Stanley, Oliver Woodall, Jane Bodle, Ellyn Arons, Michael Duran, Bobby Clark, Karen L. Byers, Mary-Pat Green, Sarah Knapp, Michael Cone, Brian Evaret Chandler, Courtney Earl

MUSICAL NUMBERS: (Many Changes during engagement) 1934, You Ain't Seen the Last of Me, A Younger Man, How Could I Ever Say No, Lady of the House, Beautiful, He Doesn't Know I'm Alive, You You You!, When You Smile, Just Let Me Get Away With This One, Coney Island, All I've Got is Me, Cortez, Tenement Lullaby, I Could Get Used to This

SARAFINA by Mbongeni Ngema & Hugh Maskela; Director/Choreographer, Mr. Ngema; Sets/Costumes, Sarah Roberts; Lighting, Mannie Manim; Conductor, Ray Molefe; Sound, Tom Sorce; General Manager, Leonard Soloway; Production Manager, Peter Lawrence; Stage Manager, Bruce A. Hoover. CAST: See touring company.

(EISENHOWER THEATRE) SPEED-THE-PLOW by David Mamet; Director, Gregory Mosher; Sets, Michael Merritt; Costumes, Nan Cibula; Lighting, Kevin Rigdon; Stage Managers, Thomas A. Kelly, Lisa Buxbaum. CAST: William L. Petersen (Bobby Gould), Bob Balaban (Charlie Fox), Felicity Huffman (Karen)

THE WORLD ACCORDING TO ME; Written & Created by Jackie Mason; Sets/Lighting, Neil Peter Jampolis; Sound, Bruce D. Cameron. CAST: Jackie Mason

THE ROAD TO MECCA; Written & Directed by Athol Fugard; Sets, John Lee Beatty; Costumes, Susan Hilferty; Lighting, Dennis Parichy; Executive Producer, James B. Freydberg. CAST: Nan Martin (Helen), Kathy Bates (Elsa Barlow), Athol Fugard (Marius Byleveld)

THE COCKTAIL HOUR by A. R. Gurney; Director, Jack O'Brien; Sets/Costumes, Steven Rubin; Lighting, Kent Dorsey; Stage Manager, David Hyslop; General Manager, Ralph Roseman. CAST: Keene Curtis (Bradley), Nancy Marchand (Ann), Bruce Davison (John), Holland Taylor (Nina)

A FEW GOOD MEN by Aaron Sorkin; Director, Don Scardino; Sets, Ben Edwards; Costumes, David C. Woolard; Lighting, Thomas R. Skelton; Sound, John Gromada. CAST: Ron Ostrow (Sentry), Tom Hulce (Kaffee), Mark Nelson (Weinberg), Victor Love (Dawson), Michael Dolan (Downey), Roxanne Hart (Joanne Galloway), Edmond Genest (Whitaker), Robert Hogan (Markinson), Arnold Molina (Santiago), Stephen Lang (Jessep), Ted Marcoux (Kendrick), Clark Gregg (Ross), Geoffrey Nauffts (Howard), Paul Butler (Randolph), Fritz Sperberg (Stone), Stephen Bradbury, Jeffrey Dreisbach, Michael Genet, George Gerdes, Joshua Malina

THE PIANO LESSON by August Wilson; Director, Lloyd Richards; Sets, E. David Cosier, Jr., Lighting Design, Christopher Akerlind; Constanza Romero; Musical Director/Composer, Dwight D. Andrews; Sound, G. Thomas Clark; Stage Manager, Karen L. Carpenter. CAST: See Broadway listing.

Top Right: Ronny Graham, Dorothy Loudon in "Annie 2"
Below: Christine Andreas, Betty Buckley, Karen Ziemba in "Stardust"

STARDUST; Lyrics by Mitchell Parish; Music, Various; Conceived & Directed by Albert Harris; Sets/Costumes, Erté; Assistants, Loren Sherman, Tony Chase; Lighting, Ken Billington; Sound, Charles Bugbee; Orchestrations, Harold Wheeler; Dance Arrangements, Marvin Laird; Musical Director, Peter Howard; Wigs/Hair, Paul Huntley; Musical Coordinator, Bill Meade; Vocal Arrangements, James Raitt; Stage Manager, James Harker; Choreography, Donald McKayle. CAST: Betty Buckley, Christine Andreas, Michael Scott Gregory, Kevin Ligon, Karen Ziemba, Hinton Battle

THE CEMETERY CLUB by Ivan Menchell; Director, Pamela Berlin; See Broadway Calender for complete credits.

(TERRACE THEATRE) THE ACTING COMPANY; Founder, John Houseman; Executive Producer, Margot Harley; Artistic Director, Gerald Gutierrez; Play Repertory included BOY MEETS GIRL by Bella & Sam Spewack, LOVE'S LABOUR'S LOST by Shakespeare and THE PHANTOM TOLLBOOTH by Susan Nanus; Company includes: Larry Green, Anthony Cummings, Douglas Krizner, John Greenleaf, Martha Thompson, John Tillotson, Gayla Finer, Spencer Beckwith, Alison Stair Neet, David Rainey, Laura Perrotta, Michael MacCauley, Ken Sawyer, Gregory Wallace, Theresa McCarthy, Justine Cohen, and the voices of Kevin Kline & Robin Williams

KING OF HEARTS; adapted from the film by Philippe de Broca; Director, J Ranelli; Sets/Lighting, Chuck Baird, David Hays; Design, Peter Good; Stage Manager, Fred Noel; Presented by the National Theatre of the Deaf; Artistic Director, David Hays. CAST: Chuck Baird (Painter), Mike Lamitola (Prolouge/Archbishop), Chaz Struppmann (Shakespeare Obsessed/Actor), Willy Conley (Plumpick), Andy Vasnick (Duke), Adrian Blue (Barber), Elena Blue (Madam), Sandi Inches (Duchess), Camille L. Jeter (Acrobat), John C. Eisner (Musician), Marcia Tilchin (Child) Nat Wison, Deborah Henderson, Jayne Murphy, Fred Noel

INCOMMUNICADO by Tom Dulack; Director, Blanka Zizka; Lighting, Jerold R. Forsyth; Sets, Andrei Efremoff; Costumes, Lara Ratnikoff; Score, Adam Wernick; Stage Manager, Kathryn Bauer. CAST: David Hurst (Ezra Pound), O. L. Duke (MP), Reginald Flowers (Till), John Michael Higgins (Forbes), Edwin C. Owens (Muller)

A TUNA CHRISTMAS by Jaston Williams, Joe Sears & Ed Howard; Director, Mr. Howard; Sets, Loren Sherman; Costumes, Linda Fisher; Lighting, Judy Rasmuson; Design, Brad Braune; Stage Manager, Peter A. Still. CAST: Joe Sears, Jaston Williams

SHEAR MADNESS by Paul Portner; Director/Designer, Bruce Jordan; Continuing open end run from 8/1987. Current Cast: Tom Brooks, Andrew Clemence, Paul Hjelmervik, Naomi Jacobson, Maureen Kerrigan, Aaron Shields

ILLINOIS THEATRE CENTER

Park Forest, Illinois
Fourteenth Season

Artistic Director, Steve S. Billig; Administrative Director, Etel Billig; Directors, Steve S. Billig, Paula Markovitz, Jonathan Roark; Choreographers, Todd Hilbrich, Shole Milos, Cynthia Suarez; Set Designer, Jonathan Roark; Costumes, Stephen E. Moore, Pat Decker; Lighting, August Ziemann

PRODUCTIONS AND CASTS

LUCKY STIFF by Lynn Ahrens and Steven Flaherty. CAST: Shole Milos, Marie Michuda, Renee Aten, Bob Keefe, Steve S. Billig, August Ziemann, Shelley Crosby, Juie Volkmann, Gary Lamb, Wayne Adams
BREAKING THE CODE by Hugh Whitemore. CAST: David Perkovich, Paula Markovitz, Shole Milos, Etel Billig, Don McGrew, Steve S. Billig, Rob Langeder, Terry Dunn, Johnny Moran
KISMET by George Forrest and Robert Wright. CAST: Roy Cepero, Marie Michuda, Gary Lamb, Shelley Crosby, Bob Keefe, Steve S. Billig, Howard Hahn, Angela Friend, Cynthia Suarez, Melissa Dye, Etel Bilig, Wayne Adams, Shole Milos, Rob Langeder
SCRAPBOOKS by Larry Gray. CAST: Etel Billig, Karen Blackful, Cathy Bieber
OTHELLO by William Shakespeare. CAST: Johnny Lee Davenport, Greg Vinkler, Nancy Nickel, Cathy Bieber, Gary Lamb, Rob Langeder, Bob Keefe, John Marzullo, Wayne Adams, Jennifer Lien, Steve S. Billig, Pat Bednarczyk
ITALIAN AMERICAN RECONCILIATION by John Patrick Shanley. CAST: Anthony Cesaretti, David Barbee, Joan Schaeffer, Laura Kohler, Etel Billig
THE FANTASTICKS by Tom Jones and Harvey Schmidt. CAST: Roy Cepero, Heidi Heller, Rob Langeder, Steve S. Billig, Howard Hahn, David Six, August Ziemann, David Barbee

Peter LeGrand Photos

Anthony Cesaretti, Etel Billig in "Italian American Reconciliation" Top: Johnny Lee Davenport, Greg Vinkler in "Othello"

LONG ISLAND STAGE

Rockville Centre, NY

Artistic Director, Clinton J. Atkinson; Managing Director, Thomas M. Madden; Associate Managing Director, Jeff Ranbom; Technical Director, Chris Davis; Lighting, John Hickey, Shirley Prendergast; Scenery, Steven Perry, Philip Baldwin, Russell Parkman, Dan Conway, Dan Ettinger; Costumes, Don Newcomb, Gail Brassard, Bobbi Morse; Stage Manager, David Wahl

PRODUCTIONS & CASTS

PUMP BOYS & DINETTES conceived and written by John Foley, Mark Hardwick, Debra Monk, Cass Morgan, John Schimmel, and Jim Wann; Director, Dennis Dennehy. Musical Director Steve Liebman. CAST: Richard Eigen, John P. Griffith, Deb G. Girdler, Steve Liebman, Karyn Quackenbush, Kim Story.
NO EXIT by Jean Paul Sartre; Director Clinton J. Atkinson. CAST: Jonathan Bolt, Pamela Burrell, Trip Plymale, Phyllis Somerville.
THE BUSINESS OF MURDER by Richard Harris; Director Clinton J. Atkinson. CAST: John Corey, George Hosmer, Diane Warren.
HEDDA GABLER by Henrik Ibsen; Director Clinton J. Atkinson. CAST: Humbert Allen Astredo, Lane Binkley, Kathleen Claypool, Steven Haworth, Bjorn Johnson, Nancy Kammer, Anne Shropshire.
GETTING MARRIED by Bernard Shaw; Director David Pursley. CAST: Pamela Burrell, Catherine Byers, Jennifer Chudy, Jim Hillgartner, Bjorn Johnson, Warren Kelley, Julia Meade, Edwin Owens, Sherry Skinker, Sam Stoneburner, Ian Stuart, John Wendes Taylor.
ZOO OF TRANQUILITY by Avner Eisenberg, Mark Ross and Paul Spooner; Director Mark Ross. CAST: Avner Eisenberg, Julie Goell. (U.S. Premiere)

Brian M. Ballweg Photos

Avner Eisenberg in "Zoo of Tranquility" Above: Pamela Burrell, Ian Stuart in "Getting Married"

Caris Corfman, Kevin Geer, Mark Hammer in "Anna Christie"

LONG WHARF THEATRE

New Haven, Connecticut
Twenty-fifth season

Artistic Director, Arvin Brown; Executive Director, M. Edgar Rosenblum; Literary Consultant, John Tillinger; Associate Artistic Director, Gordon Edelstein; General Manager, John Conte; Development, Pamela Tatge; Technical Director, Ted Zuse; Props, David Fletcher; Costumes, Jean M. Routt; Press, David Mayhew

MAIN STAGE

A FLEA IN HER EAR by Georges Feydeau; Director, John Tillinger; Set Design, John Lee Beatty; Costume Design, Jane Greenwood; Lighting Design, Marc B. Weiss; Production Stage Managers, Robin Kevrick, Anne Keefe. CAST: Larry Block, Ramiro Carrillo, Veanne Cox, Donal Donnelly, Clement Fowler, A. J. Glassman, George Guidall, Harriet Harris, Ann Hutchinson, Edmund Lewis, Katlyn McNeill, David Scott Meikle, Nancy Mette, Frank Muller, Kristine Nielsen, Aideen O'Kelly, William Preston, John Rothman, Jody Rowell
THE CRUCIBLE by Arthur Miller; Directed by Arvin Brown; Set Design, Michael Yeargan; Costume Design, David Murin; Lighting Design, Ronald Wallace; Production Stage Manager, Pamela Edington. CAST: April Beth Armstrong, John Braden, Charles Cioffi, Frank Converse, Ann Dowd, Virginia Downing, Joyce Ebert, Clement Fowler, Jack Gilpin, George Guidall, John Leighton, Allen McCullough, David Scott Meikle, Novella Nelson, Pippa Pearthree, Sarah Peterson, Mary Ann Plunkett, Molly Price, Rex Robbins, Richard Spore, Magen Tracy
RE:JOYCE! *(American premiere)* by James Roose-Evans and Maureen Lipman; Music, Richard Addinsell; Director, Alan Strachan; Musical Direction by Denis King; Set Design, John Lee Beatty; Costume Design, Ben Frow; Lighting Design, Judy Rasmuson; Production Stage Manager, Anne Keefe. CAST: Denis King, Maureen Lipman
ANNA CHRISTIE by Eugene O'Neill; Director, Gordon Edelstein; Set Design, Hugh Landwehr; Costume Design, Jess Goldstein; Lighting Design, Arden Fingerhut; Original Music and Sound Design, John Gromada; Production Stage Manager, Robin Kevrick. CAST: Caris Corfman, Joyce Ebert, Ken Festa, Michael Fischetti, Kevin Geer, Mark Hammer, Karl R. Heintz, Emmet O'Sullivan-Moore, Anto Nolan, James Jaye O'Neill
IS HE STILL DEAD? *(World Premiere)* by Donald Freed; Director, Charles Nelson Reilly; Set Design, Marjorie Bradley Kellogg; Costume Design, Noel Taylor; Lighting Design, Marc B. Weiss; Music Design, David Fox; Sound Design, Brent Evans; Production Stage Manager, Anne Keefe. CAST: Julie Harris, Ronny Graham
STAGE II: A DANCE LESSON *(World Premiere)* by David Wiltse; Director, Gordon Edelstein; Set Design, Hugh Landwehr; Costume Design, David Murin; Lighting Design, Pat Collins; Production Stage Manager, Ruth M. Feldman. CAST: Josh Charles, Eric Conger, John Cunningham, Rob Kramer, Debra Mooney, Quentin O'Brien
THE RUFFIAN ON THE STAIR by Joe Orton and **THE LOVER** by Harold Pinter; Director, John Tillinger; Set Design, James Noone; Costume Design, Jess Goldstein; Lighting Design, Craig Miller; Production Stage Manager, Ruth M. Feldman. CAST: Joanne Camp, Tate Donovan, Nicholas Woodeson
STAGE II WORKSHOPS: ESTABLISHED PRICE by Dennis McIntyre; Director, Arvin Brown; Set, Hugh Landwehr; Lighting, Jay Strevey; Sound, Brent Evans; Production Stage Manager, Ruth M. Feldman. CAST: D. W. Moffett, Jason Robards, Richard Seff, William Wise
THE GHOSTMAN by Wendy Hammond; Director, John Tillinger; Set by Hugh Landwehr; Lighting, Jay Strevey; Sound, Brent Evans; Production Stage Manager, Robin Kevrick. CAST: Barbara Bradish, Kevin Cooney, George Gerdes, Paul-Felix Montez, Lois Nettleton, Sarah Peterson, Wendy Pratt, Jeanne Ruskin, Neil Vipond, John Woodson
A DARING BRIDE by Allan Havis; Directed by Bill Foeller; Set, Hugh Landwehr; Lighting, Jay Strevey; Sound, Brent Evans; Production Stage Manager, Ruth M. Feldman. CAST: Darla Cash, George Guidall, Patricia Mauceri
THE SUBSTANCE OF FIRE by Jon Robin Baitz; Directed by David Warren; Set, Hugh Landwehr; Lighting, Jay Strevey; Sound, Brent Evans; Production Stage Manager, Pamela Edington. CAST: Gina Gershon, Rose Gregorio, Merrill Holtzman, Rob Morrow, Ron Rifkin, Bradley White

T. Charles Erickson Photos

Left Center: Denis King, Maureen Lipman in "Re:Joyce!"
Top: Nancy Mette, Donal Donnelly in "A Flea in Her Ear"

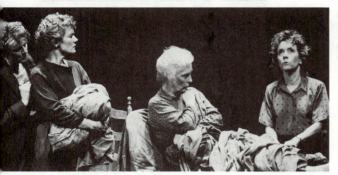

Ann Gee Byrd, Christine Murdock, Julianna McCarthy, Victoria Ann-Lewis in "Daytrips" Top: David Marshall Grant (R) and (clockwise from top: Stephen Tobolowsky, Guy Boyd, Bryan Clark, Lynn Milgrim, Lela Ivey, Stefan Gierasch, Jane Galloway, Christine Ebersole, Angela Paton in "The Marriage of Bette and Boo"

Philip Baker Hall, Gregory Wagrowski, Edith Fields, Christopher McDonald in "Death of a Salesman" Above: Marian Mercer, H. Richard Greene, Mitchell Ryan in "Dance of Death"

LOS ANGELES THEATRE CENTER

Los Angeles, California

Artistic Director, Bill Bushnell; Producing Director, Diane White; Managing Director, Robert N. Lear; Consulting Director, Alan Mandell; Head of Design, Timian Alsaker; Marketing Director, Cynthia Anderson; Development Director, Darcy Butterfield; Education Director, Keren Goldberg; Production Manager, Donald David Hill; Technical Director, David MacMurtry; Director of Press & Public Relations, Dawn Setzer; Director, Latino Theatre Lab, Jose Luis Valenzuela

PRODUCTIONS & CASTS

TEN NOVEMBER by Steven Dietz; Directed by Steven Dietz; Music and lyrics by Eric Peltoniemi; Produced by Diane White; Sets by Douglas D. Smith; Lighting by Anne Militello; Costumes by Ann Bruice; Sound by Jon Gottlieb; Stage Manager, David S. Franklin; Ensemble: E. J. Castillo, William Dick, Karole Foreman, Danny Goldring, Mark Christopher Lawrence, Marsha Mercant, Jillsyn Michaels, Jan Munroe, Markus Redmond, Valente Rodriguez, Ric Stoneback, Harold Sylvester.

BOYS' LIFE by Howard Korder; Directed by David Beaird; Produced by Diane White; Sets by Dean Tschetter; Lighting by Douglas D. Smith; Costumes by Reve Richards; Sound by Jon Gottlieb; Stage Manager, Michael F. Wolf; Ensemble: Roxanna Augeson, Jon Cryer, Greg Kean, Kari Lizer, Kate Stern, Charlie Stratton, Maria Tirabassi.

THE MARRIAGE OF BETTE AND BOO by Christopher Durang; Directed by Dennis Erdman; Sets by John Iacovelli; Lighting by Casey Cowan; Costumes by Marianna Elliott; Original music by Richard Peaslee; Sound by Jon Gottlieb; Stage Manager, Nancy Ann Adler. Ensemble: Guy Boyd, Brian Clark, Christine Ebersole, Jane Galloway, Stefan Gierasch, David Marshall Grant, Lela Ivey, Lynn Milgrim, Angela Paton, Stephen Tobolowsky.

THE GEOGRAPHY OF LUCK by Marlane Meyer; Directed by David Schweizer; Set by John Iacovelli; Lighting by Douglas D. Smith; Costumes by Gregory Poe; Sound by Jon Gottlieb; Original music by Steve Moshier; Stage Manager, Joan Toggenburger; Ensemble: Ennalls Berl, John Considine, Christine Elise, Arliss Howard, Garrett Morris, Deirdre O'Connell, Tom Rosqui, Susan Tyrrell.

DAYTRIPS by Jo Carson; *(World Premiere)* Directed by Steven Kent; Set and lighting by Douglas D. Smith; Costumes by Donna Barrier; Sound by Jon Gottlieb; Original music by Michele Brourman; Stage Manager, Danny Lewin. Ensemble: Anne Gee Byrd, Victoria Ann-Lewis, Julianna McCarthy, Christine Murdock.

ONCE IN DOUBT by Raymond J. Barry; Directed by David Saint; Set and lighting by Douglas D. Smith; Sound by Jon Gottlieb; Stage Manager, David S. Franklin. Ensemble: Raymond J. Barry, Kim O'Kelley, Howard Schechter.

DEATH OF A SALESMAN by Arthur Miller; Directed by Bill Bushnell; Sets by Mark Wendland; Lighting by Casey Cowan; Costumes by Marianna Elliott; Sound by Jon Gottlieb; Original music by Alex North; Stage Manager, Susan Slagle. Ensemble: Ron Campbell, Gina Elten, Edith Fields, Philip Baker Hall, Lynn Ann Leveridge, Christopher McDonald, Thomas Newman, Tom Rosqui, Kevin Symons, Saxon Trainor, Gregory Wagrowski, David Wohl, Holly Wolfe.

THE DANCE OF DEATH by August Strindberg; Directed by Alan Mandell; Translation by Michael Meyer; Set by John Iacovelli; Lighting by Brian Gale; Costumes by Marianna Elliott; Sound by Jon Gottlieb; Stage Manager, Nancy Ann Adler. Ensemble: Ronald Conner, Gina Elten, H. Richard Greene, Marian Mercer, Mitchell Ryan.

PIANO by Anna Deavere Smith; *(World Premiere)* Directed by Bill Bushnell; Set by Timian Alsaker; Lighting by Todd A. Jared; Costumes by Marianna Elliott; Sound by Jon Gottlieb; Stage Manager, Danny Lewin. Ensemble: L. Scott Caldwell, John Castellanos, Pamela Gien, Andrew Glazier, Benjamin Lum, Mya Risa Maury, Tony Perez, Brandi Royale Petway, Madge Sinclair.

STEVIE WANTS TO PLAY THE BLUES, a jazz play by Eduardo Machado; Music by Fredric Myrow; Lyrics by Fredric Myrow and Eduardo Machado; *(World Premiere)* Directed by Simon Callow; Produced by Diane White; Set and Costumes by Timian Alsaker; Lighting by Douglas D. Smith; Sound by Jon Gottlieb and Mark Friedman; Musical director, Fredric Myrow; Dramaturg, Morgan Jenness; Stage Manager, Susan Slagle; Ensemble: George Buck, Christie Houser, Paula Kelly, Randy Kovitz, Amy Madigan, Michael Milhoan, Louie Spears.

AND BABY MAKES SEVEN by Paula Vogel; *(World Premiere)* Directed by Peggy Shannon; Set by D. Martyn Bookwalter; Lighting by Douglas D. Smith; Costumes by Timian Alsaker and Donna Barrier; Sound by Jon Gottlieb; Original music by James MacVay; Stage Manager, Nancy Ann Adler; Ensemble: Peter Anthony Jacobs, Kim O'Kelley, Valerie Landsburg.

THE ILLUSION by Pierre Corneille; Freely adapted by Tony Kushner; Directed by David Schweizer; Set and lighting by Douglas D. Smith; Costumes by Marianna Elliott; Sound by Jon Gottlieb; Original music by Steve Moshier; Projections by Donald Krieger; Fight choreography by Randy Kovitz; Stage Manager, David S. Franklin. Ensemble: Tom Cayler, John Fleck, Karole Lynn Foreman, Mitchell Lichtenstein, Alan Mandell, Jonathan Silverman, Lea Thompson, Mary Woronov.

STRONG MAN'S WEAK CHILD by Israel Horovitz; *(World Premiere)* Directed by Israel Horovitz; Set and lighting by D. Martyn Bookwalter; Costumes by Ann Bruice; Sound by Jon Gottlieb; Stage Managers, Danny Lewin & Cheri Catherine Cary. Ensemble: Meg Foster, Sheridan Gayr, Peter Iacangelo, Sally Levi, Nick Mancuso, Don Yesso.

Craig Schwartz, R. Kaufman Photos

MARRIOTT'S LINCOLNSHIRE THEATRE

Lincolnshire, Illinois

Producer, Kary M. Walker; Artistic Director, Dyanne Earley; Marketing, Peter Grigsby; Stage Manager, Michael Hendricks; Sound, Randy Allen Johns; Sets, Thomas M. Ryan, John Paoletti; Costumes, Nancy Missimi; Lighting, Diane Ferry Williams; Props, Kathy Klaisner, Mr. Paoletti.

PRODUCTIONS & CASTS

70, GIRLS, 70 by Kander, Ebb & Martin; Director, Dyanne Earley; Choreography, Mark S. Hoebee; Musical Director, Paul Raiman. CAST: Alene Robertson (Ida), Pat Vern-Harris (Gertrude), Ann Whitney (Eunice), William Reilly (Walter), Dennis Kelly (Harry), E. Faye Butler (Melba), Renee Matthews (Fritzie), Pat Rusk (Lorraine), William Akey (Eddie), Diane Houghton (Sadie), Margaret Ingraham (Grandmother), Rob Rahn, Ron Keaton.

MATADOR; Director, David Bell; Choreography, Mr. Bell; Musical Director, Rob Bowman. CAST: Michael S. Lynch (Domingo), Jamie Dawn Gangi (Marguarita), Dale Morgan (El Puro), John Reeger (Don Ramon), William Akey, Robert Winn Austin, Susan Bachman, Randy Bichler, Jeanne Croft, Manolo De Cordoba, Tracey Hodgkin-Valcy, Tony DiFalco, Mary Ernster, Ray Frewen, Neil Friedman, Ronald Keaton, Andrew J. Lupp, Harrison McEldowney, Susan Moniz, Rob Rahn, Bernie Yvon, Jim Zager.

GREASE by Jacobs & Casey; Director, Travis Stockley; Choreography, Jim Corti; Musical Director, Paul Raiman. CAST: Rick Boynton (Eugene), Jennifer Chada (Marty), Tony DiFalco (Kineckie), Don Forston (Vince), Bob Helms (Roger), Robin Irwin (Cha-Cha), Brian d'Arcy James (Danny), James Kall (Sonny), Lori Longstreth (Patty), Renee Matthews (Miss Lynch), Susan McGhee (Sandy), Susie McMonagle (Rizzo), Robyn Peterman (Frenchy), Sharon Sachs (Jan), Sam Samuelson (Doody), Alton F. White (Teen Angel).

FUNNY GIRL by Styne, Merrill & Lennart; Director, Joe Leonardo; Choreography, Jim Corti; Musical Director, Dan Sticco. CAST: Linda Balgord (Fanny), Marilynn Bogetich (Mrs. Strakosh), Patti Davidson-Gorbea (Mrs. O'Malley), Mary Easterline (Mrs. Meeker), Don Forston (Keeney), Susie McMonagle (Emma), Rob Rahn (Eddie Ryan), Rondi Reed (Mrs. Brice), John Reeger (Nick), Lane Edwin Alexander, James Braet, Joyce Fleming, Lisa Comeaux Harloff, Susan Johnson, Randal Keith, Lori Longstreth, Andrew J. Lupp, Kelly Michaels, Kelly A. Russell, Amar, Annette Thurman, Jonathan Weir.

CHESS by Andersson, Ulvaeus & Rice; Director/Choreographer, David H. Bell; Musical Director, Kevin Stites. CAST: Neil Friedman (Molokov), Susie McMonagle (Florence), Susan Moniz (Svetlana), Dale Morgan (Walter), Kim Strauss (Freddie), David Studwell (Anatoly), Alton F. White (Arbiter), James Braet, Pattie Davidson-Gorbea, Douglas Graham, Randal Keith, Lori Longstreth, Catherine Lord, Harrison McEldowney, Rob Rahn, Russ Reneau, Larry Russo, Karyn Young-Lowe, Robert Winn-Austin.

INTO THE WOODS by Sondheim & Lapine; Director, William Pullinsi; Choreography, Rudy Hogenmiller, James Harms; Musical Director, Albert Potts. CAST: Karin Berutti (Lucinda), William Brown (Narrator/Mysterious Man), Shannon Cochran (Baker's Wife), Melissa Dye (Riding Hood), Margaret Ingraham (Cinderella's Mother), Ross Lehman (Baker), David Lewman (Rapunzel's Prince), Catherine Lord (Florinda), Darren Matthias (Steward), Susan Moniz (Rapunzel), Jennifer Nees (Cinderella), Delores Noah (Jack's Mother), Jerry O'Boyle (Cinderella's Father), Hollis Resnik (Witch), John Ruess (Cinderella's Prince), Sam Samuelson (Jack), Linda Stephens (Stepmother)

Tom Maday, Robert Carly, Edy Giles Photos

Top: (L) Michael Lynch, Dale Morgan, Mary Ernster in "Matador" (R) Kim Strauss, Susie McMonagle, David Studwell in "Chess" Below: William Brown, Shannon Cochran, Hollis Resnik, Ross Lehman in "Into the Woods"

Ann Stevenson-Whitney, Alene Robertson, Pat Vern-Harris in "70, Girls, 70"

McCARTER THEATRE

Princeton, New Jersey

Artistic Director, Nagle Jackson; Managing Director, John Herochik; Associate Artistic Director, Robert Lanchester; Development Director, Susan F. Reeves; Sales Director, James Olson; Communications Director, Kip Rosser; Publicity Manager, Daniel Y. Bauer; Administrative Director, Timothy J. Shields; Assistant to the Directors, Jeanne M. Stives; Production Manager, David York; Stage Managers, Peter C. Cook and C. Townsend Olcott II; Technical Director, Darryl S. Waskow.

PRODUCTIONS & CASTS

SMOKE ON THE MOUNTAIN by Constance Ray; Conceived and Directed by Alan Bailey; Set Designer, W. Joseph Stell; Costume Designer, Pamela Scofield; Lighting Designer, Don Ehman; Musical Directors, Mike Craver and Mark Hardwick. CAST: Kevin Chamberlin (Mervin Oglethorpe), Constance Ray (June Sanders), Reathel Bean (Burl Sanders), Rhonda Coullet (Vera Sanders), Dan Manning (Stanley Sanders), Jane Potter (Denise Sanders) and Robert Olsen (Dennis Sanders).

THE IMPORTANCE OF BEING EARNEST by Oscar Wilde; A new version edited and directed by Gavin Cameron-Webb; Set Designer, Harry Feiner; Costume Designer, Gail Brassard; Lighting Designer, F. Mitchell Dana. CAST: Samuel Maupin (John Worthing), Thomas Nahrwold (Algernon Moncrieff), George Ede (Rev. Canon Chasuble), Jay Doyle (Mr. Gribsby), Randolph Walker (Lane/Merriman), Jill Tanner (Lady Bracknell), Margery Murray (Hon. Gwendolen Fairfax), Katherine Heasley (Cecily Cardew), Jeanette Landis (Miss Prism), Rosemary Gunther (Maid) and David Savidge (Footman).

AN ENEMY OF THE PEOPLE by Henrik Ibsen; Translated by Rolf Fjelde; Directed by Kjetil Bang-Hansen; Set Designer, Stephan Olson; Costume Designer, Elizabeth Covey; Lighting Designer, F. Mitchell Dana. CAST: Barry Boys (Dr. Thomas Stockmann), Jill Tanner (Mrs. Stockmann), Katherine Heasley (Petra), Richard Leighton (Peter Stockmann), Frank Lowe (Morten Kiil), Edmund C. Davys (Hovstad), Randy Lilly (Billing), Charles Dumas (Captain Horster), Randolph Walker (Aslaksen), Justin Tecce (Eilif) and Davyd Stepper (Morten).

A TALE OF TWO CITIES; Adapted and directed by Nagle Jackson; Set Designer, Ralph Funicello; Costume Designer, Robert Fletcher; Lighting Designer, Jane Reisman; Composer, Bruce Odland. CAST: Reathel Bean (Stryver/First Judge), John A. Bukovec (Ensemble), Mark Capri (Charles Darnay), Meghan Roberts Cibulskis (French Child), Eric Conger (Sydney Carton), James Coyle (Jerry Cruncher), Edmund C. Davys (Marquis d'Evremonde), Jay Doyle (Dr. Manette), Charles Dumas (Gaspard/Coachman), George Ede (Jarvis Lorry), Elsbeth House Escher (French Child), Susan S. Garrett (Ensemble), Rufus C. Gibson (Ensemble), Katherine Heasley (Seamstress), Melissa Hill (Lucie Manette), Laurie Huntsman (Ensemble), Cassie Jones (French Child), Kimberly King (Miss Pross), Zoran Kovcic (Inn Keeper/Ensemble), Richard Leighton (Defarge), Randy Lilly (Gabelle), Frank Lowe (Tom/Attorney General/French Judge), Mary Martello (La Vengeance), Mark David Murphy (Ensemble), Scott Allen New (Ensemble), Gretchen Liddell Sword (Child Lucie), Jill Tanner (Mme. Defarge), Robin Tate (Joe/Cly/Jailer/Valet), Randolph Walker (Barsad).

WOMAN IN MIND by Alan Ayckbourn; Directed by Nagle Jackson; Set Designer, Daniel Boylen; Costume Designer, Elizabeth Covey; Lighting Designer, F. Mitchell Dana. CAST: Kimberly King (Susan), Mark Capri (Bill), William Richert (Andy), Randy Lilly (Tony), Katherine Heasley (Lucy), Robert Lanchester (Gerald), Jill Tanner (Muriel) and Mark David Murphy (Rick).

PVT. WARS by James McLure; Director, Nagle Jackson; Lighting Designer, Stephen J. Howe; Costume Coordinator, Susan Elder. CAST: Kevin Chamberlin (Gately), William Richert (Natwick) and Robin Tate (Silvio).

THE CASE OF HARRIET GRINDE by Merete Wiger; Directed by Eva Roine; English Translation by Julian Garner; Performed by the Trondelag Theatre Company of Trondehim, Norway. CAST: Janne Kokkin (Harriet Grinde), Gerdi Schjelderup (Mrs. Grinde), Johan Brun Kjeldsberg (Dr. Hermanson), Eli Doseth (Dr. Juel) and Gorli Mathiesen (Marth)

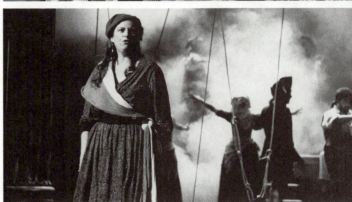

Randall Hagadorn Photos

**Top Right: Rhonda Coullet, Jane Potter, Reathel Bean,
Robert Olsen, Dan Manning in "Smoke on the Mountain"
Below: Jeanette Landis in "The Importance of Being Earnest"
Bottom: Jill Tanner in "A Tale of Two Cities"**

STAGE TWO: McCARTER'S FORUM FOR NEW PLAYS
TWO GOOD BOYS by Barry Jay Kaplan; Directed by Robert Lanchester; Set Designer, Wolfgang Hul; Costume Coordinator, Suzanne Elder; Lighting Designer, Stephen J. Howe. CAST: Peggy Cowles (Billie), Richard Topol (Tom), Stephanie Cannon (Annette) and Reathel Bean (Will).

A CHRISTMAS CAROL by Charles Dickens; Adaptation by Nagle Jackson; Directed by Robert Lanchester; Set Designer, Brian Martin; Costume Designer, Elizabeth Covey; Lighting Designer, Richard Moore; Composer, Larry Delinger; Sound Design, Rob Gorton; Choreographer, Nancy Thiel. CAST: George Ede (Scrooge), Jerome Butler (Bob Cratchit), Reathel Bean (First Narrator), Kevin Chamberlin (Second Narrator), Mark Capri (Fred), Randolph Walker (Marley), Mary Martello (Ghost of Christmas Past), Robin Tate (Young Scrooge), Katherine Heasley (Fan), Randy Lilly (Fezziwig), Robert Spain (Dick Wilkins), Penelope Reed (Mrs. Fezziwig), Alicia Rene Washington (Belle), Kyra Lanchester and Jason Bittner (Belle's Children), Charles Dumas (Ghost of Christmas Present), Penelope Reed (Mrs. Cratchit), Kinga Suto (Martha), Davyd Stepper (Ned), Megan Livingston (Dorrit), Sheandra Clark (Belinda), Teddy Beresford (Tiny Tim) Peter R. Peterson (alternate cast: Tiny Tim), Matthew Burbach (Peter), Katherine Heasley (Fred's Wife), Kari Jenson (Emily), Randolph Walker (Mr. Nutley), Randy Lilly (Topper), Jason Bittner (Ignorance), Kyra Lanchester (Want), Robert Spain (Christmas Yet To Come), Mary Martello (Caroline), Jay Doyle (Mrs. Dilber), Robin Tate (Old Joe), Rufus C. Gibson, Laurie Huntsman and Brian Lanchester (Citizens of London).

149

MEADOW BROOK THEATRE

Rochester, Michigan

Artistic & General Director, Terence Kilburn; Associate Director, James P. Spittle; Directors, Terence Kilburn, John Ulmer, Charles Nolte, Stephen Kanee, Howard Millman, Robert Spencer; Sets, Peter W. Hicks, C. Lance Brockman, Kevin Rupnick; Lighting, Reid Johnson, Jean Montgomery; Stage Managers, Terry W. Carpenter, Robert Herrle; Technical/Production Director, Daniel M. Jaffe; Assistant Technical Director, Greg Utech; Scene Shop Foreman, Douglas M. Osborne; Scenic Carpenters, Dave Haslett, George H. Sherlock, David Stanton; Scenic Artist, Elaine Sutherland; Assistant Scenic Artist, David Len; Properties Director, Mary Chmelko-Jaffe; Properties Artisans, Paula Jellis, William P. Ward; Resident Lighting Designer/Master Electrician, Reid G. Johnson; Assistant Electrician, Eric Stehl; Sound Technician, Robert Campbell; Costume Shop Coordinators, Barbara Jenks, Mary Lynn Bonnell; Costumers, Renee DiFilippo, Christa Gievers-Yntema; Shopper/Wardrobe Mistresses, Sandra Husted, Kathy Richards; Head Stage Technician, Scot B. Cleaveland; Assistant Stage Technician, Neil J. Patterson; Director of Community Relations, Jane Mosher; Public Relations Director, Sylvia Coughlin; Finance Manager, John Fischer; Box Office Manager, Suzanne Day; House Manager, Peter Spurck

PRODUCTIONS & CASTS

THE DIARY OF A SCOUNDREL: Jeanne Arnold, Anita Barone, Geoffrey Beauchamp, Mary Benson, Paul DeBoy, Richert Easley, Paul Hopper, Jillian Lindig, Phillip Locker, John Michalski, Patti Perkins, Joseph Reed, Mary Lee Richey, Thomas M. Suda, Sandra Husted, Dennis T. Kleinsmith, Dinah M. Lynch, Neil Patterson

THE BOYS NEXT DOOR: Eric Hissom, Paul Hopper, Michael James Laird, LeRoy Mitchell, Jr., Kathryn Nash, Mary Lee Richey, Parry Stewart, Eric Tavares, Bradford Wallace

A CHRISTMAS CAROL: Anita Barone, Geoffrey Beauchamp, Booth Colman, Paul Hopper, Phillip Locker, Thomas D. Mahard, Kathryn Nash, Wayne David Parker, Glen Allen Pruett, Joseph Reed, Thomas M. Suda, Liz Zweifler, Fred Buchalter, Adam Carpenter, Susan Elizabeth, Bryan Holmes, Chad Holmes, Sean Joanitis, Dennis T. Kleinsmith, Adrianne Kriewall, James Marino, Nora McGowan, Elizabeth Morrow, Mary Elizabeth Murphy, Joelle Premo, Grace Ward, Gregory Wilson

DIAL M FOR MURDER: James Anthony, John Bayliss, Geoffrey Beauchamp, Paul Hopper, Leslie Lynn Meeker, Tom Spackman

A WALK IN THE WOODS: Arthur J. Beer, Michael James Laird

THE GREAT SEBASTIANS: Tony Dobrowolski, George Gitto, Paul Hopper, Phillip Locker, Dinah Lynch, Glen Allen Pruett, Juliet Randall, Joseph Reed, David Regal, Peggy Thorp, Tyne Turner, Susan Diebolt, Tom Emmott, Dennis T. Kleinsmith, Scott Cleaveland, James C. Meli, Jr., Gregory S. Piasecki

THE IMMIGRANT: A HAMILTON COUNTY ALBUM: John Sterling Arnold, David Breitbarth, Jayne Houdyshell, Pauline Lepor, Devora Millman

DRACULA: Susan Duvall, Tony Dobrowolski, Richert Easley, Paul Hopper, Laurence Overmire, Joseph Reed, Tom Spackman, Sarah McCord Williams

Richard Hunt Photos

Left: Tony Dobrowolski, Juliet Randall, David Regal in "The Great Sebastians" Above: Tom Spackman, Leslie Lynn Meeker, James Anthony in "Dial M for Murder" Top: Mary Lee Richey, Parry Stewart in "Boys Next Door"

Michael James Laird, Arthur J. Beer in "A Walk in the Woods"

Sarah McCord Williams, Tom Spackman in "Dracula"

MISSOURI REPERTORY THEATRE

Kansas City, Missouri
Twenty-seventh Season

Artistic Director, George Keathley; Associate Artistic Director, Mary G. Guaraldi; Lighting Dir., Joseph Appelt; Scenic Design, John Ezell; Sound, Tom Mardikes, Costumes, Vincent Scassellati; Production Manager, Ron Schaeffer; Technical Director, Bruce Bacon; Dramaturg, Felicia Hardison Londre; Executive Director, James D. Costin; General Manager, Robert L. Thatch

ACTING COMPANY: Mimi Bessette, Jim Birdsall, Richard Bowden, Alan Brasington, Peter Byger, Donald Christopher, Forrest Compton, Edward Conery, Jeffrey Cookson, Liz Corrigan, Ned Coulter, Christopher Cull, Nora Denney, Milly Dupont, Kelli Edwards, Robert Elliott, Martin English, Benjamin Evett, David Fritts, C. Andrew Garrison, Allison Gendreau, Larry Greer, Michael Alan Gregory, Susan Rae Greve, Wiley Harker, Gary Holcombe, Jeannine Hutchings, Richard James-Greene, Gary Neal Johnson, Claudia Kaplan, Jay Karnes, Leonard Kelly-Young, Sara Lahey, David Lutken, Christine McCurdy, Edgar Meyer, J. F. Mitchell, Cortez Nance, Jr., Richard Alan Nichols, David Nisbet, Hannah O'Regan, Daniel Oreskes, Corliss Preston, Michael Rapport, Keith Reece, George Riddle, Bruce Roach, Mark Robbins, Janice St. John, James Shelby, K. T. Sullivan, Judith Tillman, Dean Vivian, Scott Wakefield, Stratton Walling, Eva Wilder, William Wickham, Michael Wilson, Angela Yannon

GUEST ARTISTS: Jackie Manassee, Denis Rosa, Jeff Davis, Harry Feiner, James Leonard Joy, Virgil Johnson, Philipp Jung, David Noling, Peter Glazer

PRODUCTIONS: JEKYLL! *(Premiere)* by James Costin; Director, George Keathley; ABSENT FRIENDS by Alan Ayckbourn; Director, Dennis Rosa; WOODY GUTHRIE'S AMERICAN SONG by Guthrie; Direction/Adaptation, Peter Glazer; MIDSUMMER NIGHT'S DREAM by Shakespeare; with KC Symphony playing Mendelssohn; Director, George Keathley; A CHRISTMAS CAROL by Dickens; Adapted by Barbara Field; Director, Ross Freese; BORN YESTERDAY by Garson Kanin; Director, George Keathley; OF MICE AND MEN by John Steinbeck; Director, George Keathley; AMADEUS by Peter Shaffer; Director, Dennis Rosa; THE SWEET BY AND BY *(Premiere)* by Frank Higgans; Director, Ron Schaeffer

Top: Benjamin Evett (C) in "Amadeus" Right Center: Robert Elliott, Mark Robbins, K. T. Sullivan, Gary Neal Johnson in "Born Yesterday"

Jim Birdsall in "Of Mice and Men"

NEW AMERICAN THEATER

Rockford, Illinois

Producing Director, J. R. Sullivan; Managing Director, Greg Lackner; Costume Design, Jon R. Accardo; Wardrobe Manager, Jan Bacino; Box Office Manager, Miki Bacino; Production Stage Manager, William D. Carey; Master Electrician, Nicholas R. France; Technical Director, John G. Frautschy; Marketing Director, Jacqueline M. Goetz; Group Sales Coordinator, Joan Jirak; Stage Manager, Scott Lewis; Master Carpenter, Craig Trisilla; Associate Director/Resident Actor, Stephen F. Vrtol III

PRODUCTIONS & CASTS

NOISES OFF: Suzanne Avery, Michael Krebs, Stephen F. Vrtol III, Linda Abronski, Sheila Willis, Tim Olds, Lou Ann McKinney, Daniel Scott, Stephen W. McCarty
PRECIOUS MEMORIES: James A. McCammond, Betsy Kaske, Mary MacDonald Kerr, Edgar Meyer, Pat Bauerlein, Daniel Scott, Cynthia Judge, Stephen F. Vrtol III, Rod MacDonald, G. Michael Johnson
A CHRISTMAS CAROL: James Valentine, James A. McCammond, Richard Raether, George Conde, William R. Phillip, Seth Marantz, Stephen F. Vrtol III, Jane Hannemann, Malcolm Rothman, Steven Wargo, Nick Bua, Richard Orman, Linda Abronski, Tim Maculan, Mark Ulrich, Carrie Classon Smith, Mark Lazar, Connie Willis, Sheila Willis, Michael A. McCormick, Zachery Rotello, Janet Magnuson, Amy Farrell, Rio Rigotti, Whitney Vidal, Christopher Carter, Kira Dolan, Lee Meyers, Natasha Leggero, A. Ronald Scattergood, Mark Apolloni, Lori Lynn Bauerlein, Daniel J. Bauling, Randy Bauling, Lauren Noel Boyer, Megan Erickson, Chris Farrell, Georgianna Ferguson, Mary Freeston, Stephanie Gallenz, Qiana Hardy, Todd Harris, Jennifer Hawkinson, Jared Jensen, Joe Nardiello, Dawn Renee, Jessica Phillip, Dan Schneider, Min Taber, Craig Trisilla, Ann Turner, Eryka Hope Witherby
THE BOYS NEXT DOOR: Fredric Stone, Danny Johnson, Mike Dempsey, Daniel Scott, Stephen F. Vrtol III, Cheryl Orear, Josh Burton, Leslie Nautiyal, Jamie Button
OUR TOWN: Robert Scogin, John R. Webb, Chris Farrell, Stephen W. McCarty, Linda Abronski, Pat Bauerlein, Mark Ulrich, Natasha Leggero, Steven Wargo, Catherine Lynn Davis, Bill Caisley, Rod MacDonald, Janet Wilkins, Todd C. Harris, Carol Davies, Stephen F. Vrtol III, Janet Magnuson, Richard Orman, Mary Freeston, Keith Albers, Christopher Carter, Jim Justis, Robert Hoemke, Anthony Brown, Larry Darnell Beasly, George Conde, Johnna Davenport, Shari Farrell, Laura Keith, Melinda Rayman, Min Taber, Dee Dee Walston
WENCESLAS SQUARE: Stephen F. Vrtol III, Richard Raether, Robert Koon, Mark Ulrich, Catherine Lynn Davis
BORN YESTERDAY: Catherine Lynn Davis, Kenneth Albers, Mark Ulrich, Robert Scogin, B. J. Jackson, Janet Magnuson, Malcolm Rothman, Mark Apolloni, Leslie Nautiyal, Todd Harris, Mark Coupar, Anthony Brown, Min Taber, Tracey Henderson
GUEST ARTISTS: Directors: Allan Carlsen, Fontaine Syer, Joseph Hanreddy; Scenery Design: James Wolk, E. Oliver Taylor; Les Woods; Mary Griswold, Michael S. Phillippi, Tamara Turchetta; Costume Design: Jessica Hahn, Cecelia Mason; John Paoletti, Lighting Design: Peter Gottlieb; Todd Hensley; Geoffrey Bushor, Susan McElhaney, Thomas C. Hase; Sound Design: Rob Milburn; Special Effects: Jim Janecek

McGinty Photos

Top: Daniel Scott, Tim Olds, Lou Ann McKinney, Stephen F. Vrtol III, Suzanne Avery in "Noises Off" (R) Daniel Scott, Stephen Vrtol III, Cynthia Judge, Edgar Meyer, Rod Macdonald in "Precious Memories" Below: Lee Meyers, Natasha Leggero, Malcolm Rothman in "A Christmas Carol"

Cheryl Orear, Danny Johnson, Mike Dempsey, Fredric Stone, Stephen F. Vrtol III in "The Boys Next Door"

152

OLD GLOBE THEATRE

San Diego, California
Fifty-fifth Season

Artistic Director, Jack O'Brien; Managing Director, Thomas Hall; Executive Producer, Craig Noel; Production Manager, Ken Denison; Marketing/Operations, Joe Kobryner; Development, Domenick Ietto; Publications/Media, Charlene Baldridge
(OLD GLOBE) DRIVING MISS DAISY by Alfred Uhry; Director, Jack O'Brien; Sets, Ralph Funicello; Costumes, Steven Rubin; Lighting, Peter Maradudin; Composer, Robert Waldman; Sound, Jeff Ladman; Stage Manager, Douglas Pagliotti CAST: Sada Thompson (Daisy), William Anton (Boolie), Ed Hall (Hoke)
MEASURE FOR MEASURE by William Shakespeare; Director, Adrian Hall; Sets, Ralph Funicello; Costumes, Lewis Brown; Lighting, Peter Maradudin; Composer, Conrad Susa; Sound, James LeBrecht; Dramaturge, Diana Maddox; Stage Manager, Douglas Pagliotti CAST: Richard Easton (Duke), Jonathan McMurtry (Escalus), Stephen Markle (Angelo), Nance Williamson (Isabella), Mary Kay Wulf (Francisca), Ollie Nash (Thomas/Abhorson), Allen Oliver (Peter), John Adams Morrison (Provost), Thomas S. Oleniacz (Elbow/Barnardine), Matthew Edwards (Justice), Michael Cerveris (Claudio), Hilary James (Juliet), James R. Winker (Lucio), Martha Perantoni (Mariana), Blaise Messinger, Mark Guin (Gentlemen/Soldiers), Kevin Fabian (Froth), Ellen Crawford (Overdone), Jeffrey Allan Chandler (Pompey), Richard Ortega (Varrius), Dana Pere, Robert LaPorta, Albert Valdez, Barry Mann (Servants/Officers) Laura Rearwin (Citizen)
BROTHERS AND SISTERS (*U.S. Premiere*) by L. Dodin, S. Bekhterev and A. Katsman; Based on novels by Fyodor Abramov; Translation, Mikhail Stronin & Elise Thoron; Director, Lev Dodin; Associate Directors, Roman Smirnov, Sergei Bekhterev; Costumes, Inna Gabai; Sets, Eduard Kochergin; Speech/Voice, Valeri Galendeev; Lighting, Oleg Kozlov; Sound, Boris Freidson; Stage Managers, Olga Dazidenko, Irina Lyapunova CAST: The Maly Drama Theatre of Leningrad
UNCLE VANYA by Anton Chekhov; Director, Jack O'Brien; Sets, Hugh Landwehr; Costumes, Robert Wojewodski; Lighting, Peter Maradudin; Sound, Jeff Ladman; Stage Manager, Douglas Pagliotti; Translation, Michael Henry Heim CAST: Katherine McGrath (Marina), Byron Jennings (Mikhail), Richard Easton (Ivan), Richard Kneeland (Alexandr), Carolyn McCormick (Yelena), Lynne Griffin (Sonya), Jonathan McMurtry (Waffles), Patricia Fraser (Maria), Blaise Messinger (Yefim)
JAKE'S WOMEN by Neil Simon (*World Premiere*); Director, Ron Link succeeded by Jack O'Brien; Sets, Tony Straiges; Costumes, Joseph G. Aulisi; Lighting, Tharon Musser; Sound, Jeff Ladman; Hair, Toni-Ann Walker; Stage Managers, Douglas Pagliotti, Peter Lawrence CAST: Candice Azzara (Karen), Talia Balsam (Sheila), Amelia Campbell (Mollie/21), Stockard Channing (Maggie), Peter Coyote (Jake), Sarah Michelle Gellar (Mollie/13), Felicity Huffman (Julie), Joyce Van Patten (Edith)
AND A NIGHTINGALE SANG by C. P. Taylor; Director, Craig Noel; Sets, Kent Dorsey; Costumes, Lewis Brown; Lighting, Peter Maradudin; Choreography, Bonnie Johnston; Sound, Jeff Ladman; Stage Manager, Douglas Pagliotti CAST: Alan Brooks (Norman), Kandis Chappell (Helen), Mitchell Edmonds (George), Lynne Griffin (Joyce), James Lancaster (Eric), Katherine McGrath (Mam), Jonathan McMurtry (Andie)
(CASSIUS CARTER CENTRE STAGE) WAITING FOR GODOT by Samuel Beckett; Director, Andrew J. Traister; Sets, Cliff Faulkner; Costumes, Shigeru Yaji; Lighting, John B. Forbes; Stage Manager, Peter Van Dyke CAST: Richard Easton (Estragon), Jonathan McMurtry (Vladimir), Jeffrey Allan Chandler (Pozzo), Richard Kneeland (Lucky), Kyle Wares (Boy)
BREAKING LEGS (*World Premiere*) by Tom Dulack; Director, Jack O'Brien; Sets, Cliff Faulkner; Costumes, Robert Wojewodski; Lighting, John B. Forbes; Sound, Jeff Ladman; Stage Manager, Hollie Hopson CAST: Greg Mullavey (Terence O'Keefe), T. J. Castronovo (Lou Graziano), Sue Giosa (Angie), Mike Genovese (Mike Palermo), Richard Kneeland (Tino De Felice), Eddie Zammit (Frankie Salvucci)
THE GRANNY by Roberto M. Cossa; Translation, Raúl Moncada; Director, Lillian Garrett-Groag; Sets, Robert Brill; Costumes, Robert Wojewodski; Lighting, John B. Forbes; Sound, Jeff Ladman; Dramaturg, Raúl Moncada; Stage Manager, Robert Drake CAST: John Fleck (Nonna), Rose Portillo (Maria), Myriam Tubert (Angiula), Marcelo Tubert (Chicho), Laura P. Vega (Marta), Patrick Husted (Carmelo), Julio Medina (Don Francesco)
REBEL ARMIES DEEP INTO CHAD by Mark Lee; Director, Adrian Hall; Sets, Kent Dorsey; Costumes, Christina Haatainen; Lighting, Chris Parry; Sound, Jeff Ladman; Dramaturg, Mark Hofflund; Stage Manager, Robert Drake CAST: Richard Kneeland (Charles Richardson-Dove), Jim Phipps (Neal Bateman), Rose Weaver (Mary Mungai), Cheryl Francis Harrington (Christina Kagohyera)
LADY DAY AT EMERSON'S BAR & GRILL by Lanie Robertson; Director, Will Robertson; Arrangements, Danny Holgate; Musical Director, Rahn Coleman; Sets, Robert Brill; Costumes, Lewis Brown; Lighting, David F. Segal; Sound, Jeff Ladman; Stage Manager, Robert Drake CAST: Loretta Devine (Billie Holliday), Rahn Coleman (Jimmy Powers), Charles McPherson (Sax)

Top Right: Nina Semenova, Igor Tupikin, Evgeni Sheide,
Tatyana Popova, Natalya Akimova, Pyotr Semak in "Brothers
and Sisters" **Below:** Peter Coyote, Stockard Channing in
"Jake's Women" **Bottom:** Paxton Whitehead, Lynne Griffin in
"School for Scandal"

(LOWELL DAVIES FESTIVAL THEATRE) ROMEO AND JULIET by William Shakespeare; Director, Richard E. T. White; Sets/Costumes, Steven Rubin; Lighting, Robert Peterson; Composer, Conrad Susa; Fights, Michael Caweiti; Choreography, Bonnie Johnston; Sound, Jim Ragland; Dramaturg, Mark Hofflund; Stage Manager, Robert Drake CAST: Robert Phalen (Escalus), Michael Cerveris (Mercutio), Ben Ketcham (Page), Mark Guin (Paris), Hugh McCann (Page), Mitchell Edmonds (Montague), Elizabeth Terry (Lady Montague), Jon Tenney (Romeo), Albert Farrar (Benvolio), Sterling Macer Jr. (Abram), Richard Ortega (Balthasar), Mike Genovese (Capulet), Ellen Crawford (Lady Capulet), Monique Fowler (Juliet), Henry Godinez (Tybalt), Bill Bookston (Capulet's Cousin), Dana Pere (Petruchio), Martha Perantoni (Rosaline), Hilary James, Karen Vesper (Juliet's Friends), Linda Hoy (Nurse), Blaise Messinger (Peter), Richard Soto (Sampson), Matthew Edwards (Gregory), Kevin Fabian (Anthony), Barry Mann (Potpan), M. Susan Peck (Nell), Laura Rearwin (Susan), Ken Ruta (Laurence), Matthew Edwards (John), Robert LaPorta, Deborah Pearl, Mary Kay Wulf, David Bell, Kristen Bell, Albert Jones, Olga Macias, Daniel Polese, Lekeisha Sams, Kimme Stephanson
THE SCHOOL FOR SCANDAL by Richard Brinsley Sheridan; Director, Craig Noel; Sets, Steven Rubin; Costumes, Robert Wojewodski; Lighting, Robert Peterson; Composer, Conrad Susa; Movement, Bonnie Johnston; Sound, Jim Ragland; Dramaturg, Mark Hofflund; Stage Manager, Robert Drake CAST: Paxton Whitehead (Teazle), Erica Rogers (Lady Sneerwell), Robert Phalen (Snake/Careless), William Anton (Surface), Karen Vesper (Maria), Linda Hoy (Mrs. Candour), Mitchell Edmonds (Crabtree), Nicholas Martin (Backbite), Navarre T. Perry (Rowley), Lynne Griffin (Lady Teazle), Henry J. Jordan (Oliver Surface), Ray Chambers (Charles Surface), Richard Soto, Trini Sandoval, Bill Bookston, Hugh McCann, Deborah Pearl, M. Susan Peck

Will Gullette Photos

PAPER MILL PLAYHOUSE

Millburn, New Jersey
Sixtieth Year

Executive Producer, Angelo Del Rossi; Artistic Director, Robert Johanson; General Manager, Geoffrey Cohen; Sets, Michael Anania; Press, Albertina Reilly; Stage Manager, Peggy Imbrie; Sound, David S. Paterson.

PRODUCTIONS & CASTS

42ND STREET with Music by Harry Warren; Lyrics, Al Dubin; Book, Michael Stewart & Mark Bramble; based on the novel by Bradford Ropes; Sets, Robin Wagner; Costumes, Guy Geoly; Lighting, Kirk Bookman; Associate Choreographer, Tony Parise; Director/Choreographer, Lee Roy Reams; Musical Director, Phil Hall; Wigs, Leonard Vargas. CAST: Oliver Woodall (Andy Lee), Teri Gibson (Annie), Mary Jay (Maggie Jones), Frank Root (Bert Barry), John Scherer (Billy Lawlor), Cathy Wydner (Peggy Sawyer), Aimee Turner (Lorraine), Candy Cook (Phyllis), Tom Urich (Julian Marsh), Joy Franz (Dorothy Brock), Hal Blankenship (Abner Dillon), Patrick Hamilton (Pat Denning), Jack Eldon, Franz C. Alderfer (Thugs), Michael Biondi (Doctor), Becky Lynn Adams, Elly Arons, John Clonts, Gillian Ferrigno, Leslie Guy, Lindsey Hanahan, Jennifer Jayson, Jane LeBanz, Kirsten Lind, Mia Malm, Jean Marie, Ken Nagy, Russell Ricard, Maryellen Scilla, Luke Stallins, Dean Stroop, Cindy Timms, Mary Wanamaker, Pam Wehner (Ensemble).
RHYTHM RANCH with Book & Lyrics by Hal Hackady; Music, Fred Stark; Director, Philip Wm. McKinley; Choreographer, Susan Stroman; Musical Director, Phil Hall; Costumes, Lindsay W. Davis; Lighting, Jeff Davis; Orchestrations, Steven Margoshes; Dance Arrangements, Glen Kelly. CAST: Christopher Durham (Sam Graybeal), Liz Larsen (Babe Blandish), Jason Opsahl (Conductor/Radio Show Director), Bill Rowley (Cactus Hatch), Billy Padgett (Utah Beaudeen), Ruth Williamson (Lucy Calhoun), Ella Vador (Wanda June), Chung Kee (Wa Hoo), Dorie Herndon (Ruby Sue), Teri Gibson (Opal Sue), Jessica Sheridan (Pearl), Steve Hiltebrand (Zeke), D. J. Salisbury (Russ), Steve Gray (Beau), Nora Mae Lyng (Brandy), Jimmy Changa (Natchez), Bob Cuccioli (Tulsa de Rio), Heidi Karol Johnson (Velma), Buddy Smith (Little Joey).
THE COCKTAIL HOUR by A. R. Gurney; Director, John Going; Lighting, Tim Saternow; Costumes, Jose' M. Rivera. CAST: Burt Edwards (Bradley), Ivar Brogger (John), Phyllis Thaxter (Ann), Monica Merryman (Nina).
STEEL MAGNOLIAS by Robert Harling; Director, Jane Dentinger; Lighting, Rick Butler; Costumes, Alice S. Hughes; Hair, Paul Germano; Stage Manager, Jeffry George. CAST: Pamela Lewis (Truvy), Veanne Cox (Annelle), Billie Lou Watt (Clairee), Barbara Gulan (Shelby), Barbara Andres (M'Lynn), Mary Fogarty (Ouiser).
FANNY by S. N. Behrman and Joshua Logan; Based on the Trilogy of Marcel Pagnol; Music/Lyrics, Harold Rome; Director, Robert Johanson; Musical Director, Jim Coleman; Choreographer, Sharon Halley; Costumes, Gregg Barnes; Lighting, Mark Stanley; Assistant to the Director, Larry Grey. CAST: Paul Kandel (The Admiral), John Leone (Marius), Karen Shallo (Honorine), Teri Bibb (Fanny), Debbi Fuhrman (Claudette), Peggy Bayer (Claudine), Roy Miller (Man with accordion), George S. Irving (Panisse), Jose Ferrer (Cesar), K. C. Wilson (Escartifique), Mitchell Greenberg (M. Brun), Valerie Cutko (Ayah), Larry D. French (Arab Singer), Pam Wehner (Arab Dancing Girl), Randy Charleville (1st Mate on the Malaisie), Andrew Hammond (Postman), Jonathan Gold (Cesario), Holly Newman, Joel Newman (Children), John Clonts, Deborah Collins, Keith Cromwell, Buddy Crutchfield, Robert J. Daddona, Doreen Firestone, Richard Gervais, Ralph Lewis, Linda Milani, Keith Joseph Mottola, Michael J. Novin, Wendy Piper, Andreas Royce, Kobi Shaw, Robin Taylor, Megan Thomas (Ensemble).
MIKADO INC., inspired by W. S. Gilbert & Arthur Sullivan's The Mikado; Lyrics, Albert Evans; Book, Jane Waterhouse; Musical Supervision and Adaption, Glenn Kelly; Director, Robert Johanson; Costumes, Lindsay W. Davis; Lighting, Phil Monat; Hair, Paul Germano; Costumes, Jose M. Rivera; Orchestrations, Steve Margoshes; Musical Director, Tom Helm; Assistant to the Director, Carol Calkins, Larry Grey. CAST: Jason Ma (Mr. Pish-Tush), Leslie Feagan (Mr. Obuchi/1st Brother of the Oxtail), James Rocco (Frankie Puccelli), Michael Mulhern (Mr. Pooh-Bah), Philip Wm. McKinley (Mr. Koko), Ako (Ms. Nagami/Head Teahouse Maiden), Christine Toy (Yum-Yum), Mia Korf (Peep-Bo), Ann Harada (Pitti-Sing), Zoie Lam (Mikado Spokesperson), Marsha Bagwell (Katisha), Thomas Ikeda (Mikado), John Ganun, Kevin John Gee, Cheryl Hodges, Ted Jost, Jean Mahlmann, Alan Muraoka, Paul Nakauchi, Marc Oka, Linda Poser, Monte Ralstin, Sara Wiedt, Lyd-Lyd Gaston, Grace Hyndman, Francis Jue, Alex Sharp, Joel Stevenor (Ensemble).

Gerry Goodstein Photos

Left Center: Ivar Brogger, Phyllis Thaxter, Burt Edwards in "The Cocktail Hour" Above: Christopher Durham (C) and cast of "Rhythm Ranch" Top: John Scherer, Cathy Wydner (C) in "42nd Street"

George S. Irving, John Leone, Teri Bibb, Jose Ferrer in "Fanny"

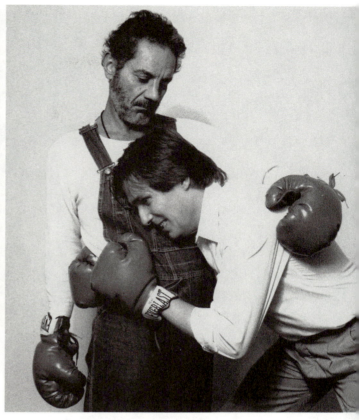

Antony Pontini, John Cygan in "The Understanding"

PENGUIN REPERTORY COMPANY

Stony Point, New York
Thirteenth Season

Artistic Director, Joe Brancato; Executive Director, Andrew M. Horn; Director, Joe Brancato.

PRODUCTIONS & CASTS

THE MAN WHO WAS PETER PAN (World Premiere) by Allan Knee; Set, Richard Cordtz, Bill Stabile; Costumes, Sally Lesser; Lighting, Dennis W. Moyes; Incidental Music, Alex Clemente; Stage Manager, April Adams. CAST: Geoffrey P. Cantor, Cara Halstead, Norman Howard, Jamie Marsh, Gus Rogerson, Judy Stadt, Geoffrey Tarson.

ITALIAN AMERICAN RECONCILIATION by John Patrick Shanley; Set, Richard Cordtz, Bill Stabile; Costumes, MaryAnn D. Smith; Lighting, Jon Terry; Stage Manager, Uriel Menson. CAST: Mary Criner, John Cygan, Deborah Laufer, Michael Mastrototaro, Angela Scorese.

THE VOICE OF THE PRAIRIE by John Olive; Set, Steven Perry; Costumes, Barbara A. Bell; Lighting, Dennis W. Moyes; Stage Manager, Sandra M. Bloom. CAST: Julia Levo, William Perley, Gus Rogerson.

ONLY THE SKY WAS BLUE! *(World Premiere)*, conceived by Joe Brancato, David Rogers, John Simon; Sketches, David Rogers; Musical Director, John Simon; Choreographer, Barry Finkel; Set, Chuck Stead; Costumes, Michael Sharp; Lighting, Jon Terry. CAST: Robert Blaney, Avi Hoffman, Susan Hull, Steve Sterner, Gail Wynters.

EPIC PROPORTIONS by Larry Cohen, David Crane; Set, Robert Klingelhoefer; Costumes, Michael Sharp; Lighting, Jon Terry; Stage Manager, Sandra M. Bloom. CAST: Jeffrey Blair Cornell, Martha Maulsby Crawford, Kurt Goldschmidt, Avi Hoffman, David Kener, Brian Sanet, Kevin Scullin, Judy Stadt.

Kerwin McCarthy Photos

Top Left: Norman Howard, and Below with Judy Stadt in "The Man Who Was Peter Pan"

Avi Hoffman, Susan Hull, Robert Blaney in "Only the Sky Was Blue!"

James Farkas, Judith Hawking in "The Glass Menagerie"

PENNSYLVANIA STAGE COMPANY

Allentown, Pennsylvania
Seventh Season

Producing Director, Peter Wrenn-Meleck; General Manager, Lisa K. Higgins; Assoc. Artistic Director/Outreach Director, Scott Edmiston; Development, Terry Stack, Amy Meleck; Director of Marketing: Janet Roth; Press, Cheri L. Guilbault; Business Manager, Beth Nelson; Stage Manager, Thomas M. Kauffman; Technical Director: William Kreider; Sets, Sarah Baptist; Costumer, Kathleen Egan; **RESIDENT ACTING COMPANY:** Steve Asciolla, Deanna Duplechain, Lisa Seacrist, Yuri Skujins.

PRODUCTIONS & CASTS

WAIT UNTIL DARK by Frederick Knott; Director, Stephen Rothman; Set, Sarah Baptist; Costumes, Kathleen Egan; Lighting, Donald Holder. CAST: Larry Attile, Deanna Duplechain, Alma Martinez, Will Osborne, Marco Rodriguez, Yuri Skujins, Courtney Thompson, Daniel Whitner
OIL CITY SYMPHONY by Mike Craver, Mary Murfitt, Mark Hardwick and Debra Monk; Director, Maureen Heffernan; Musical Director, Kathy Beaver; Set, Sarah Baptist; Costumes, Kathleen Egan; Lighting, Donald Holder; Sound, Jim Landis. CAST: Kathy Beaver, Michelle Horman, Ken Lundie, Robert Polenz.
A SHAYNA MAIDEL by Barbara Lebow; Director, Charles Richter; Set, Robert T. Odorisio; Costumes, Anna Ungar Herman; Lighting, Curtis Dretsch; Composers, Mark Golin, Mike Krisukas. CAST: David Breitbarth, Susan Cameron, Tessie Hogan, Meghan Rose Krank, Michael Marcus, Joan Rosenfels
EDUCATING RITA by Willy Russell; Director, Stephen Rothman; Set and Lighting, Bennet Averyt; Costumes, Barbara Forbes. CAST: Diana Castle, William Dennis Hunt
THE GLASS MENAGERIE by Tennessee Williams; Director, Scott Edmiston; Set and Lighting, Curtis Dretsch; Costumes, Kathleen Egan. CAST: James Farkas, Judith Hawking, Celia Howard, Peter Killy
TALLEY'S FOLLY by Lanford Wilson; Director, Charlie Hensley; Set and Lighting, Curtis Dretsch; Costumes, Kathleen Egan. CAST: Sam Guncler, Lily Knight
NOISES OFF by Michael Frayn; Director, Maureen Heffernan; Set, Ray Recht; Costume, Patricia Adshead; Lighting, Donald Holder. CAST: Steve Asciolla, Bill Bowers, A. D. Cover, W. M. Hunt, Allison Janney, Jeanette Landis, Kate Redway, Will Rhys, Lisa Seacrist

Gregory M. Fota Photos

Top: (R) William Dennis Hunt, Diana Castle in "Educating Rita" (L) Alma Martinez in "Wait until Dark" Below: Lily Knight, Sam Guncler in "Talley's Folly"

PITTSBURGH PUBLIC THEATER

Pittsburgh, Pennsylvania
Fifteenth Season

Producing Director, William T. Gardner; Managing Director, Dan Fallon; Press, Elvira DiPaolo; Technical Director, A. D. Carson; Development, Marie Mueller, David M. Bender; Company Manager, Chuck E. Gray

PRODUCTIONS & CASTS

JOE TURNER'S COME AND GONE by August Wilson; Director, Claude Purdy; Set, James D. Sandefur; Costumes, Mary Mease Warren; Lighting, Phil Monat; Stage Managers, Jane Rothman, Robert Michael Morris. CAST: John Henry Redwood, Olivia Williams, Roscoe Lee Browne, Larry John Meyers, Monte Russell, James Craven, Di Ray James, Tonya Pinkins, Eugene Stovall, Pamela Tucker-White, Leah Maddrie.

GEORGE WASHINGTON SLEPT HERE by George S. Kaufman & Moss Hart; Director, Kip Niven; Set, Ray Recht; Costumes, Martha Hally; Lighting, Jackie Manassee; Stage Managers, Robert Michael Morris, Jane Rothman. CAST: Leonard Drum, William Parry, Barbara Broughton, Amy Stoller, Jeffrey Blair Cornell, Judith Hawking, Shirl Bernheim, Randal Martin, Jeanine Morick, Matthew Woffington, Donald Christopher, Carey Cannon, Sabrina Reeves, Paul Marte, Brett Benner, W. M. Hunt.

RECKLESS by Craig Lucas; Director, Maureen Heffernan; Set, Ray Recht; Costumes, Michael J. Cesario; Lighting, Phil Monat; Stage Managers, Jane Rothman, Fred Noel. CAST: Helen Ruoti, Jim Abele, Will Osborne, Elizabeth C. Loftus, Richard Maynard, Linda Gillen, Marion McCorry.

LES LIAISONS DANGEREUSES by Christopher Hampton, from the novel by Choderlos de Laclos; Set, Cletus Anderson; Costumes, David Murin; Wigs, Paul Huntley; Lighting, Louise Giunand; Stage Managers, Fred Noel, Jane Rothman. CAST: Camille Mitchell, Funda Duyal, Barbara Broughton, Robert Austin, Jack Wetherall, John Lathen, Peg Small, Maryann Urbano, Stephanie Erb, Drew McVety, Harry Bouvy, Angela Jones, Gene Lubas, Paul Marte, Ana Munoz, Scott Schweiger, Michael Wowk.

BURN THIS by Lanford Wilson; Director, Lee Sankowich; Set, Anne Mundell; Costumes, Martha Hally; Lighting, Phil Monat; Stage Manager, Jane Rothman, Julie Pyle. CAST: Helena Ruoti, Peter Webster, Kevin Donovan, David Butler.

ELEANOR Book by Jonathan Bolt; Music, Thomas Tierney; Lyrics, John Forster; Director, Mel Shapiro; Music Director, Keith Lockhart; Sets, Karl Eigsti; Costumes, Laura Crow; Choreographer, Rob Marshall; Lighting, Roger Morgan; Orchestrations, David Siegel; Stage Managers, Jane Rothman, Paul Marte. CAST: Anthony Cummings, Mary Jay, Tamara Jenkins, Ann Kittredge, Michael McCormick, Karyn Quackenbush, Allan Stevens, Kelly Aquino, Barbara Broughton, Ted Brunetti, Catherine Campbell, Linda Gabler, Joe Joyce, James McCrum, Dale Sandish, Ty Taylor, William Thunhurst.

Ric Evans Photos

Right: David Butler, Helena Ruoti in "Burn This"; Jack Wetherall, Camille Mitchell in "Les Liaisons Dangereuses" Above: Elizabeth Loftus, Linda Gillen, Helena Ruoti, Richard Maynard, Will Osborne in "Reckless" Top: Leah Maddrie, Olivia Williams, Di Ray James, Roscoe Lee Browne, James Craven, John Henry Redwood, Larry John Meyers, Tonya Pinkins in "Joe Turner's Come and Gone"

(clockwise from top) William Parry, Jeanine Morick, Jeffrey Blair Cornell, Barbara Broughton, Amy Stoller in "George Washington Slept Here"

Mary Jay, Ann Kittredge, Anthony Cummings, Michael McCormick, Dale Sandish in "Eleanor"

157

PLAYMAKERS REPERTORY COMPANY

Chapel Hill, North Carolina

Executive Producer, Milly S. Barranger; Artistic Director, David Hammond; Managing Director, Regina F. Lickteig; Production Manager, Tom Neville, Sets and Costumes, McKay Coble; Lighting, Robert Wierzel; Stage Managers, Bonnie J. Baggesen, David Rowell; Voice Coach, Stephanie Kallos; Movement Coach, Craig Turner; Dramaturg, Adam Versenyi; Development, Justin Grimes; Press and Marketing, Sharon Broom; Business Manager, Peter S. Kernan.

RESIDENT COMPANY: Timothy Altmeyer, Patricia Barnett, Lisa Benedict, David Burke, Aaron Carlos, Dede Corvinus, Ray Dooley, Eve Eaton, Thomas Gunning, Steven Haggerty, Pilar Herrera, Aaron Knight, Daniel Krell, Emily Newman, Lynn Passarella, J'Von Pierce, Sam Potter, Steven Pounders, Joel Reider, Susanna Rinehart, Blake Robison, Matthew Ryan, Ricki Stern

GUEST ARTISTS: Tobias Andersen, Earle Edgerton, Livia Genise, William Griffis, Jim Hillgartner, Betty Leighton, Fred Summers, Sheriden Thomas, Paul Tourtillotte, Jeffery West.

PRODUCTIONS: *The Cherry Orchard* by Anton Chekhov; Director, David Hammond. *Old Times* by Harold Pinter; Director, Kathryn Long. *The Nutcracker* by David Hammond from the stories of E. T. A. Hoffmann; Director, David Hammond. *Love's Labour's Lost* by William Shakespeare; Director, Charles Newell. *True West* by Sam Shepard; Director, Martin Platt. *The Rivals* by Richard Brinsley Sheridan; Director, David Hammond.

Kevin Keisler Photos

Left: Lynn Passarella, Matthew Ryan in "The Nutcracker" Top: Susanna Rinehart, Ray Dooley, Dede Corvinus in "Old Times" Below: Ray Dooley, Lynn Passarella in "The Cherry Orchard" Left: Susanna Rinehart, Matthew Ryan in "Love's Labour's Lost"

Ray Dooley, Jeffery West in "True West"

Matthew Ryan, Betty Leighton in "The Rivals"

REPERTORY THEATRE OF ST. LOUIS

St. Louis, Missouri

Artistic Director, Steven Woolf; Managing Director, Mark D. Bernstein; Associate Artistic Director, Susan Gregg; Stage Managers, Glenn Dunn, T. R. Martin, Champe Leary, Molly Gevirtz; Development, Nancy S. Forsyth; Company Manager, Joyce Volker Ruebel; Press, Judy Andrews

PRODUCTIONS & CASTS

THE MERRY WIVES OF WINDSOR, TEXAS, conceived and adapted by John L. Haber, inspired by William Shakespeare; Music/Lyrics, Jack S. Herrick, Tommy Thompson, Bland Simpson, Jim Wann, John Foley; Director, Edward Stern; Choreographer, Marcia Milgrom Dodge; Musical Director, Jack S. Herrick; Sets, Kevin Rupnik; Costumes, Candice Donnelly; Lighting, Peter E. Sargent. CAST: Charles Antalosky, Ollie O'Shea, Paul Ukena Jr., Russ Jolly, Noble Shropshire, William Walden, William Hardy, Christopher J. Stephens, Bob Crowley, Debora Jean Culpin, Darrie Lawrence, Donna Davis, Glynis Bell, Joneal Joplin, Jennifer Brouillard, Tracy Coe, Melissa Rye, Keith Jochim, Tommy Thompson, Jack S. Herrick, Clay Buckner, Chris Frank, John Foley.

A WALK IN THE WOODS by Lee Blessing; Director, Timothy Near; Set, Joel Fontaine; Costumes, Holly Poe Durbin; Lighting, Peter Maradudin. CAST: Frank Savino, Greg Thornton.

THE MATCHMAKER by Thornton Wilder; Director, Susan Gregg; Sets, Anne Gibson; Costumes, Dorothy L. Marshall; Lighting, Max De Volder. CAST: William Newman, Paul DeBoy, Whit Reichert, Edith Taylor Hunter, John Rensenhouse, Jennifer Brouillard, Joe Palmieri, Mary Ellen Ashley, Sherry Skinker, Carol Dilley, Alan Clarey, Robert Brown, Scott Jackson Lytton, Trinity Thompson

PRECIOUS MEMORIES by Romulus Linney, from "In the Hollow" by Anton Chekov; Director, John Dillon; Musical Director, Edward Morgan; Sets, Carolyn L. Ross; Costumes, John Carver Sullivan; Lighting, Allen Lee Hughes. CAST: Gordon G. Jones, Edith Taylor Hunter, Catherine Lynn Davis, Jacqueline Knapp, Jan Leslie Harding, Robert Shampain, Tom McDermott, David Warshofsky, Michael Graves, Mark Ankeny

FENCES by August Wilson; Director, Harold Scott; Set, Peter Harrison; Costumes, Celia Bryant; Lighting, Max De Volder. CAST: Avery Brooks, Ron Bobb-Semple, Erma Campbell, Nobie Lee Lester, Rony Clanton, Monte Russell, Alana Newell, Candace Parker

HAY FEVER by Noel Coward; Director, Donald Ewer; Set, John Ezell; Costumes, Dorothy L. Marshall; Lighting, Peter E. Sargent. CAST: Shirleyann Kaladjian, John Scherer, Elizabeth Owens, Pauline Flanagan, Douglas Wing, Alexander Webb, Charlotte Maier, Carl Schurr, Susie Wall

(Studio Theatre) TOMFOOLERY; Words/Music/Lyrics, Tom Lehrer; Adapted by Cameron Mackintosh, Robin Ray; Director/Choreographer, Pamela Hunt; Musical Director, Bob McDowell; Set, John Roslevich Jr.; Costumes, Dorothy L. Marshall; Lighting, Max De Volder. CAST: Jack Cirillo, Carol Dilley, Jack Doyle, Tim Ewing, Bob McDowell

DOG LOGIC by Thomas Strelich; Director, Steven Woolf; Set, Jim Burwinkel; Costumes, Elizabeth Eisloeffel; Lighting, Mark Wilson. CAST: James Andreassi, Paul DeBoy, Susie Wall, Darrie Lawrence

RAIN. SOME FISH. NO ELEPHANTS. by Y York; Director, James Abar; Set, Richard Tollkuhn; Costumes, John Carver Sullivan; Lighting, Glenn Dunn. CAST: David Edward Jones, Lianne Kressin, Susan Bruce, Jennifer Brouillard, KellyAnn Corcoran, Mark Kenneth Smaltz

(The Lab Project) THE LAST SONG OF JOHN PROFFIT by Tommy Thompson; Director, Susan Gregg. CAST: Gordon G. Jones.

THE EDUCATION OF PAUL BUNYAN by Barbara Field; Director, Susan Gregg. CAST: Susan Bruce, Carl Schurr, Alan Clarey, David Edward Jones, Phil Coffield, John Grassilli, Whit Reichert, Chris Reilly

Judy Andrews, Rob Murphy Photos

Left Center: Jacqueline Knapp, Catherine Lynn Davis, Jan Leslie Harding, Tom McDermott, Robert Shampain in "Precious Memories" **Above:** Greg Thornton, John Honeyman in "A Walk in the Woods" **Top:** Debora Jean Culpin, William Hardy, Russ Jolly in "Merry Wives of Windsor, Texas"

Douglas Wing, John Scherer, Pauline Flanagan, Shirleyann Kaladjian in "Hay Fever"

SEATTLE REPERTORY THEATRE

Seattle, Washington

Artistic Director, Daniel Sullivan; Managing Director, Benjamin Moore; Associate Artistic Director, Douglas Hughes; Artistic Associate/Dramaturg, Mark Bly; Technical Production Director, Terry Sateren; Production Manager, Rita Calabro; Director of Marketing and Public Relations, Karen L. Robertson; Development Director, Kathleen Rasmussen; Costume Coordinator, Celeste Cleveland; Production Stage Manager, Mary Hunter.

PRODUCTIONS AND CASTS—MAINSTAGE

THE HEIDI CHRONICLES by Wendy Wasserstein (Regional Theatre Premiere); Director, Daniel Sullivan; Scenic Design, Thomas Lynch; Costume Design, Rose Pederson; Lighting Design, Pat Collins; Sound Design, Steven M. Klein & Scott Lehrer; Projection Design, Wendall K. Harrington. CAST: Sarah Brooke (Susan Johnston), Barbara Dirickson (Fran, Molly, Betsy, April); Brian Keeler (Peter Patrone); Peter Lohnes (Chris Boxer, Mark, TV Attendant, Waiter, Ray); Marianne Owen (Heidi Holland); Martha Plimpton (Becky, Clara, Denise); Julie White (Jill, Debbie, Lisa); R. Hamilton Wright (Scoop Rosenbaum).
A FLEA IN HER EAR by Georges Feydeau; Adapted by Frank Galati; Director, Michael Maggio; Scenic Design, John Lee Beatty; Costume Design, Kaye Nottbusch; Lighting Design, Craig Miller; Sound Design, Michael Holten; Fight Director, David Boushey. CAST: Beth Albrecht (Hotel Guest); John Aylward (Victor Deboshe, Goshe); Kurt Beattie (Hotel Guest); Jeannie Carson (Lucille Homenides de Histangua); Peter Crook (Perrier); Ted D'Arms (Carlos Homenides de Histangua); Woody Eney (Doctor Panache); Mitchell Hudson (Policeman); Charlotte Eve London (Olympia); Marianne Owen (Babette); David Pichette (Maher Ravvi); William Ritchie (Benedictine); Doug Rosson (Hotel Guest); Michael Santo (Maurice Blase).
FEAST OF FOOLS Conceived, Written and Performed by Geoff Hoyle; Directorial Consultant, Anthony Taccone; Scenic Design, Scott Weldin; Lighting Design, Neil Peter Jampolis; Choreographic Consultant, Kimi Okada; Folk Fool Score, Keith Terry; Production Advisor, Randall Kline. CAST: Geoff Hoyle.
THE PLAYBOY OF THE WESTERN WORLD by John Millington Synge; Director, Douglas Hughes; Scenic Design, Marjorie Bradley Kellogg; Costume Design, Michael Olich; Lighting Design, Craig Miller; Sound Design, Steven M. Klein; Dialect Coach, Gillian Lane-Plescia; Fight Director, David Boushey. CAST: Richard Anthony (Village Man); John Aylward (Old Mahon); Peter Crook (Bellman); Barbara Dirickson (Margaret Flaherty); Woody Eney (Shawn Keogh); Nancy Hume (Susan Brady); Laura MacDermott (Sara Tansey); William Biff McGuire (Michael James Flaherty); Marianne Owen (Widow Quin); William Ritchie (Village Man); Rick Tutor (Philly Cullen); Sarah Welsh (Honor Blake); R. Hamilton Wright (Christopher Mahon); Wendell Wright (Jimmy Farrell).
THE CHERRY ORCHARD by Anton Chekhov; Translation by Jean Claude van Itallie; Director, Daniel Sullivan; Scenic Design, Ralph Funicello; Costume Design, Ann Hould-Ward; Lighting Design, Pat Collins; Sound Design, Michael Holten; Music Arrangement, Todd Moeller; Production Dramaturg, Mark Bly. CAST: Richard Anthony (Guest); John Aylward (Simeonov-Pishchik); Jeannie Carson (Lyubov Andreyevna Ranevskaya); Peter Crook (Pyotr Sergeyevich Trofimov); Woody Eney (Station Master); Lou Hetler (Firs); Nancy Hume (Anya); Laura MacDermott (Varya); William Biff McGuire (Leonid Andreyevich Gayev); Marjorie Nelson (Charlotta Ivanovna); Marianne Owen (Dunyasha); William Ritchie (Vagrant, Guest); G. Valmont Thomas (Yasha); R. Hamilton Wright (Semyon Panteleyevich Yepikhodov); Wendell Wright (Yermolay Alexeyevich Lopakhin).
SUNDAY IN THE PARK WITH GEORGE Music and Lyrics by Stephen Sondheim; Book by James Lapine; Director, Laird Williamson; Musical Director, Larry Delinger; Scenic Design, Richard Seger; Costume Design, Andrew V. Yelusich; Lighting Design, Pat Collins; Sound Design, Michael Holten; Chromolume Projection Design, Charles Rose. CAST: Allan Michael Barlow (Porter, Contemporary Man, Chromolume Performer); Barbara Coffin (Mrs., Woman in the Park, Waitress); Dori Cole (The Mother, Blair Daniels); Rachel Coloff (Celeste I, Naomi Eisen); Rebecca Eichenberger (Dot, Marie); Robert Jacobs (Soldier, Follies Gentleman, Alex); Peter Kevoian (Jules, Billy Webster); John Patrick Lowrie (Mr., Man in the Park, Charles Redmond); Paula Markovitz (Frieda, Elaine); Cheryl Massey-Peters (Woman with a white Parasol, Contemporary Woman); Jeff McCarthy (George); Joseph McNally (Bather, Man with a Newspaper, Dennis); Victor Morris (Hornplayer, Chromolume Performer, Art Critic); Bob Morrisey (Franz, Chromolume Performer, Art Patron); Peggy O'Connell (Nurse, Photographer, Chromolume Performer); Tina Paradiso (Celeste II, Betty); Valerie Piacenti (Yvonne, Harriet Pawling); Catherine Gilk Robinson (Chromolume Performer); Craig Ryder (Louis, Bather, Lee Randolph); Emily Sweeney-Samuelson (Contemporary Child); Bethany Ward (Louise, Bather); Bruce Winant (Boatman, Bob Greenberg).

Top Right: Loren Dean, Lisa Zane in "Robbers" Below: (L) Nancy Hume, Wendell Wright, Peter Crook in "Measure for Measure," (R) Geoff Hoyle in "Feast of Fools" *Chris Bennion Photos*

PRODUCTIONS AND CASTS—STAGE 2

MEASURE FOR MEASURE by William Shakespeare; Director, Douglas Hughes; Scenic Design, Hugh Landwehr; Costume Design, Michael Olich; Lighting Design, Peter Maradudin; Sound Design, Steven M. Klein. CAST: Beth Albrecht (Juliet/Ensemble); Kurt Beattie (Elbow/Abhorson); Jeannie Carson (Mistress Overdone); George Catalano (Barnadine/Ensemble); Peter Crook (Angelo); Ken Droz (Choirboy); Woody Eney (Pompey/Father Thomas); Mitchell Hudson (Security Guard/Ensemble); Douglas Hughes (Claudio); Nancy Hume (Isabella); Charlotte Eve London (Mariana/Ensemble); William Biff McGuire (Duke Vincentio); Michael Meyer (Froth/Ensemble); William Ritchie (Justice/Ensemble); Michael Elting Rogers (Angelo's Aide/Ensemble); Doug Rosson (Security Guard/Ensemble); G. Valmont Thomas (Lucio); Rick Tutor (Escalus); Melanie van Betten (Ensemble); David Wright (Ensemble); Wendell Wright (Provost).
ROBBERS by Lyle Kessler *(World Premiere)*; Director, Daniel Sullivan; Scenic Design, Ralph Funicello; Costume Design, Rose Pederson; Lighting Design, Paulie Jenkins; Sound Design, Michael Holten. CAST: Paul Benvictor (Vince); Don Creery (Bartender & Others); Loren Dean (Ted); Joseph Franklin (Indian); David Margulies (Owner); William Biff McGuire (Pop); Martha Plimpton (Lucinda); Daniel Sullivan (Mr. Feathers); Lisa Zane (Cleo).
WOODY GUTHRIE'S AMERICAN SONG Songs and Writings by Woody Guthrie, Conceived and Adapted by Peter Glazer; Director, Peter Glazer; Music Director, Neil Woodward; Scenic Design, Philipp Jung; Costume Design, Deborah Shaw; Lighting Design, David Noling; Sound Design, Steven M. Klein; Choreographer, Jennifer Martin; Vocal Arrangements, Jeff Waxman and the Cast. CAST: Mimi Bessette, John Camera, Liz Corrigan, David Lutken, Scott Wakefield.
MAY DAY by Conrad Bromberg; Director, Daniel Sullivan; Scenic Design, Jeff Frkonja; Costume Design, Katherine M. Smurr; Lighting Design, Rick Paulsen; Sound Design, Steven M. Klein. CAST: Karen Evans-Kandel (Hank); Alexander Folk (Davis); Daniel Greenfield (Solly); Evan Handler (Joe); Scott MacDonald (Champ); Benjamin Prager (Keller); John Procaccino (Gene).
THE END OF THE DAY: AN ENTERTAINMENT by Jon Robin Baitz; Director, Michael Engler; Scenic Design, Jeff Frkonja; Costume Design, Katherine M. Smurr; Lighting Design, Rick Paulsen; Sound Design, Steven M. Klein. CAST: Mark Chamberlin (Jeremiah Marton); Katie Forgette (Helen Lasker-Massey/Lady Hammersmith Urbaine-Supton-Stoat); Daniel Gerroll (Graydon Massey); Meg Mundy (Carol Brackett/Joclyn Massey); Tony Soper (Jonathon Toffler); Kevin Tighe (Hilton Lasker/Swifty/Lord Kitterson).
HOME AND AWAY by Kevin Kling; Director, Kenneth Washington; Scenic Design, Jeff Frkonja; Costume Design, Rose Pederson; Lighting Design, Richard Moore; Sound Design, Steven M. Klein; Production Dramaturg, Mark Bly. CAST: Kevin Kling.
LOVE DIATRIBE by Harry Kondoleon; Director, Douglas Hughes; Scenic Design, Jeff Frkonja; Costume Design, Rose Pederson; Lighting Design, Richard Moore; Sound Design, Steven M. Klein; Production Dramaturg, Mark Bly. CAST: Jane Adams (Frieda); John Aylward (Dennis); Gordon Carpenter (Mike); Peter Crook (Orin); Katie Forgette (Sandy); Marge Kotlisky (Gerry); Peggy Pope (Mrs. Anderson).

SAN DIEGO REPERTORY THEATRE

San Diego, California

Artistic Director, Douglas Jacobs; Managing Director, Adrian Stewart; Producing Director, Sam Woodhouse; Associate Producer, Walter Schoen; General Manager, Michael Murphy; Production Manager, John Redman
GUEST ARTISTS: Directors, George Ferencz, Jorge Huerta, Michael Roth, Stephen Rothman, Roman Viktyuk; Playwrights, Lynne Alvarez, Emilio Carballido, Steve Friedman, Ron House, Alan Sherman, Mac Wellman; Designers, Brenda Berry, D Martyn Bookwalter, Vladimir Boyer, Sally Cleveland, John Gottlieb, Bob Jewett, Fred Lanuza, Gina Leishman, Jill Moon, Victoria Petrovich, Michael Roth, Nancy Jo Smith; Composers/Musical Directors, Larry Czoka, Bob Jewett, Fred Lanuza, Gina Leishman, Michael Roth, Linda Vickerman.

PRODUCTIONS & CASTS

THE MARRIAGE OF BETTE AND BOO by Christopher Durang. CAST: Rosina Widdowson-Reynolds, Bernard Baldan, Patrick Miller, Priscilla Allen, Sabrina LaRocca, Geraldine Joyce, Gale McNeeley, William Dennis Hunt, Mary Benson, Tom Oleniacz.
THE SCANDALOUS ADVENTURES OF SIR TOBY TROLLOPE by Ron House and Alan Sherman. CAST: Ron House, Alan Sherman, Anna Mathias, Melinda Peterson, Rodger Bumpass, Ron Vernan, William Dennis Hunt.
ORINOCO! by Emilio Carballido, translation by Margaret Sayers Peden. CAST: Ivonne Call, Jeannette Mirabal
THIN AIR: TALES FROM A REVOLUTION by Lynne Alvarez. CAST: Paul James Kruse, Kat Sawyer-Young, John Hertzler, Davina Dene, Regina Byrd Smith, Jaime Sanchez, Alina Denal, Mickey Hanley, Shanga Parker, John Diaquino, Damon Bryant, Rodrigo Dorfman.
ARE YOU LONESOME TONIGHT? by Alan Bleasdale. CAST: Rick Sparks, Lillian Byrd, Mindy Hull, J. Michael Ross, Duane Daniels, Drew Tombrello, William Dunnam, Tavis Ross, Luther Hanson, Jake Schmidt, Davnia Dene, Sam Woodhouse.
ALBANIAN SOFTSHOE by Mac Wellman. CAST: Darla Cash, Jan Leslie Harding, Tony Simotes, Alex Colon, Bruce McKenzie, Helen Reed Lehman, Lary Ohlson, Douglas Jacobs, Olga Macias, Damon Bryant.
SLINGSHOT by Nikolai Kolyada, translation by Susan Larsen. CAST: John David Bland, Jon Matthews, Mary Forcade.
A CHRISTMAS CAROL by Charles Dickens, adapted by Douglas Jacobs. CAST: Kory Abosada, Beth Bayless, Damon Bryant, Linda Castro, Tony de Bruno, Michael Grady, Antonio Johnson, Jason Kenny, Linda Libby, Olga Macias, Bruce Nelson, Richard Ortega, Richard Soto, Maggie Stewart, Sylvia M'Lafi Thompson, W. Francis Walters.
ANIMAL NATION by Steve Friedman. CAST: Steve Friedman, Joan Schirle, Tracy Hughes, Priscilla Allen, Regina Byrd Smith, Bernard Baldan, Joe Dieffenbacher, Donald Forrest, Bruce McKenzie.
PREMIERES: World: The Scandalous Adventures of Sir Toby Trollope, Thin Air: Tales From a Revolution, Albanian Softshoe, Slingshot, Animal Nation. U.S.: Are You Lonesome Tonight?

Ken Jacques, Douglas Jacobs Photos

Right: Sam Woodhouse in "Are You Lonesome Tonight?"
Top: "A Christmas Carol"

Jan Leslie Harding, Darla Cash in "Albanian Softshoe"

Cast of "Animal Nation"

SOUTH COAST REPERTORY

Costa Mesa, California
Twenty-sixth Season

Producing Artistic Director, David Emmes; Artistic Director, Martin Benson; Directors, Mr. Benson, Mr. Emmes, David Chambers, John-David Keller, Paul Marcus, Mary B. Robinson, Warner Shook, Simon Stokes; Designers & Composers, Chris Barreca, Linda Kostalik-Boussom, Nathan Birnbaum, Ann Bruice, David Bundries, Dennis Castellano, Michael Devine, Cliff Faulkner, Brian Gale, Susan Denison Geller, Walter Hicklin, John Iacovelli, Paulie Jenkins, Richard Jennings, Peter Maradudin, Dwight Richard Odle, Chris Parry, Dunya Ramicova, Michael Roth, Donna Ruzika, Tom Ruzika, Shigeru Yaji; Development Bonnie Brittain Hall; Dramaturg, Jerry Patch; Operations, Paul Hammond
ACTING COMPANY: Ron Boussom, Richard Doyle, John Ellington, Art Koustik, Hal Landon, Jr., Anni Long, Martha McFarland, Don Took
GUEST ARTISTS: Philip Anglim, Daniel Bright, Bridget Connors, Dante di Loreto, Peter Ellenstein, Tony Fields, Steven Flynn, Jennifer Flackett, Anthony Forkush, Marilyn Fox, Patricia Fraser, Karen Gedissman, Mark Harelik, Tom Harrison, Karen Hensel, Leslie Hope, Gregory Itzin, Dana Ivey, John-David Keller, Hubert Kelly Jr., Sally Kemp, Sybil Lines, John K. Linton, Sylvia MacCalla, Mary Anne McGarry, Elizabeth McGovern, Jonathan McMurtry, Sterling Macer Jr., Dom Magwili, Lori Michael, Ron Michaelson, Jarion Monroe, James Nardini, Bruce Norris, Jeanne Paulsen, Jim Pirri, David Poynter, Devon Raymond, Dennis Robertson, Katherine Romaine, David Schramm, Howard Shangraw, Robert Sicular, Caroline Smith, Joe Spano, Gina Spellman, Sally Spencer, Christopher Strand, Kamella Tate, Dendrie Taylor, Vic Trevino, David Chambers, Michael Devine, Craig Lucas
PRODUCTIONS: MAINSTAGE: *A Chorus of Disapproval* by Alan Ayckbourn, *Breaking the Code* by Hugh Whitemore, *Search and Destroy (Premiere)* by Howard Korder, *Midsummer Night's Dream* by Shakespeare, *Once in Arden (Premiere)* by Richard Hellesen, *Speed-the-Plow* by David Mamet SECOND STAGE: *Frankie and Johnny in the Clair de Lune* by Terrence McNally, *When I Was a Girl I Used to Scream and Shout (American Premiere)* by Sharman Macdonald, *Holy Days (American Premiere)* by Sally Nemeth, *Emerald City* by David Williamson, *Man of the Flesh (Premiere)* by Octavio Solis, *The Ramp (Premiere)* by Shem Bitterman

Ron Stone, Henry DiRocco Photos

Left Center: Patrick Roman Miller, Vic Trevino, Geoffrey Rivas in "Man of the Flesh" Above: Patrick Husted, Kay E. Kuter, Nan Martin in "Once in Arden" Top: Dendrie Taylor, Mark Harelik in "Search and Destroy" *Ron Stone, Henry DiRocco Photos*

Pamela Gien, James Winker in "The Ramp"

Elizabeth McGovern, Dana Ivey in "When I Was a Girl . . ."

THE STUDIO THEATRE

Washington, D.C.
Twelfth Season

Artistic/Managing Director, Joy Zinoman; General Manager, Keith Alan Baker; Public Relations/Marketing, Marilyn Newton; Development, Morey Epstein; Business Manager, Kelly Schoen; Dramaturg, Maynard Marshall; Sets, Russell Metheny; Lighting, Daniel MacLean Wagner; Props, Sandra Fleishman; Sound, Gil Thompson; Associates, Keith Alan Baker, Kathi Lee Redmond; Production Manager, Ms. Redmond; Production Stage Manager, Robert Daley; Technical, Chris Ellis

PRODUCTIONS & CASTS

THE COMMON PURSUIT with Scott Klavan (Stuart), Jennifer Mendenhall (Marigold), James Ream (Martin), Jon Tindle (Humphry), Jack Vernon (Nick), John Lescault (Peter)
PRINCIPIA SCRIPTORIAE with Richard Thompson (Bill), Barry Mann (Ernesto), Hugo (Man), Lawrence Redmond (Julio), Hugo Medrano (Alberto), Teman Treadway (Norton), Jim Byrnes (Hans), John Lescault (Soldier)
WEST MEMPHIS MOJO with Frederick Strother (Teddy), Aaron Caball (Elroi), Vincent Brown (Frank), Robin Baxter (Maxine)
MADE IN BANGKOK with Alan Brasington (Adrian), Marcia Churchill (Frances), Willy Corpus (Net), Liza Figueroa (Minna), Kathryn Lee (Malee), Susan Lee (Maid), Paul McCarren (Edward), Andrew Pang (Harry), Michael Russotto (Stephen), Jennifer Sackmann (Sheila), Leo Suria (Lwin), Jon Tindle (Gary)
FRANKIE AND JOHNNY IN THE CLAIR DE LUNE with Nancy Paris, Lawrence Redmond

Lise Metzger, Joan Marcus Photos

**Top: Scott Klavan, James Ream, Jennifer Mendenhall in
"The Common Pursuit" (R) Richard Thompson, Barry Mann
in "Principia Scriptoriae" Below: Aaron Cabell, Frederick
Strother in "West Memphis Mojo"**

Willy Corpus, Paul McCarren in "Made in Bangkok"

STUDIO ARENA THEATRE

Buffalo, New York
Twenty-fifth Season

Artistic Director, David Frank; Executive Director, Raymond Bonnard; Associate Artistic Directors/Dramaturgs, Kathryn Long, Ross Wassermann; Special Projects, Karen A. Rybak; Marketing, Ann Marie Sanders; Public Relations, Blossom Cohan; Publicity, Patrice Mago; Production Manager, Randy Engels; Company Manager, Christine Michael; Costumiere, Mary Ann Powell; Associate, Anne E. Gorman; Master Electrician, Lovell M. Avery, Jr.; Sound, Rick Menke; Properties, Paul N. Feinberg; Technical Director, Colin Stewart; Production Stage Manager, Glenn Bruner

PRODUCTIONS & CASTS

YOU CAN'T TAKE IT WITH YOU by George S. Kaufman & Moss Hart; Director, David Frank; Sets, Hugh Landwehr; Costumes, Mary Ann Powell; Lighting Peter Kaczorowski; Sound, Rick Menke. CAST: Marylouise Burke (Penelope), Julia Gibson (Essie), Faye M. Price (Rheba), Philip LeStrange (Paul), Carl Kowalkowski (DePinna), David Bottrell (Ed), Basil Wallace (Donald), Allen Swift (Vanderhof), Olivia Birkelund (Alice), Irv Weinstein (Henderson), Steven J. Gefroh (Tony), Bob Ari (Kolenkhov), Sheila McCarthy (Gay), David Cromwell (Mr. Kirby), Susan Blommaert (Mrs. Kirby), Stewart Roth (Man), John Kiouses (2nd Man), Art Tomczak (3rd Man), Mickey Hartnett (Olga)

JOE TURNER'S COME AND GONE by August Wilson; Director, Edward G. Smith; Sets, Charles H. McClennahan; Sound, Rick Menke; CAST: Daryl Edwards (Seth), Erma Campbell (Bertha), Stephen McKinley Henderson (Bynum), Jeffrey Ware (Rutherford), Rudy Robertson (Jeremy), Byron Utley (Harold Loomis) Rodtrice Marie Matthews, Valency Reid (Zonia), Nora Cole (Mattie), Gabriel Croom, Juba Jubulani Lomotey (Reuben), Andrea-Michelle Smith (Molly), Faye M. Price (Martha)

GALILEO (*Premiere*) with Music by Jeanine Levenson; Book/Lyrics, Keith Levenson & Alexa Junge; Director, David Frank; Associate, Mr. Levenson; Sets, David Jenkins; Costumes, Julie Weiss; Lighting, Peter Kaczorowski; Orchestrations, Daniel Troob; Musical Director, Doug Besterman; Staging, Sam Viverito; Sound, Rick Menke; Associate Musical Director, Jeffrey Buchsbaum. CAST: Susan Arundale (Duchess/Essio), Katy Clancy (Citizen), David Clemmons (Luka/Camerata), Peter Davis (Student/Citizen), Scott Elliott (Roberto), Kate Fugeli (Christina/Tucci), Joanna Glushak (Angela), Sean Greenan (Vincenzo), Paul Harman (Galileo), John Hoffman (Zabaldi/Cosimo de Medici/Pasqualigo), David Holliday (Cardinal), Walker Joyce (Landini/Inquisitor), Joanna Lange (Battaglia), Janet Metz (Mara), Dominique Plaisant (Princess/Innuncio), Amy Ryder (Fabrizzi), Carolyn Saxon (Citizen), Peter Schmitz (Firenzuola/Scheiner/Salvati), Wendy Schurr (Citizen), James J. Stein, Jr. (Barberini), Tom Treadwell (Paulo/Cruzi), Robert Zolli (Tasso), Emily Ball (Young Mara), Natalie Rosenberg (Young Mara)

SPEED-THE-PLOW by David Mamet; Director, Kathryn Long; Sets, Victor A. Becker; Costumes, Timothy Averill; Lighting, Pat Collins; Sound, Rick Menke. CAST: Jim Mezon (Bobby), James Gleason (Charlie), Melissa Weil (Karen)

A MOON FOR THE MISBEGOTTEN by Eugene O'Neill; Director, Vincent Dowling; Sets/Costumes, Wendy Shea; Lighting, Brian Nason; Sound, Rick Menke; Music, Robbie Krizan. CAST: Britta Smith (Josie), Stuart Dunne (Mike), David Kelly (Phil), Bosco Hogan (James Tyrone, Jr.), Dan Monahan (Harder)

BEYOND THERAPY and LAUGHING WILD by Christopher Durang; Director, Ross Wassermann; Sets, Philipp Jung; Costumes, Ellen V. McCartney; Lighting, Michael Chybowski; Sound, Rick Menke. CAST: Kenneth L. Marks (Bruce/Man), Tisha Roth (Prudence), Christopher McHale (Stuart), Rosemary De Angelis (Charlotte/Woman), Steven J. Gefroh (Bob), Kevin Henderson (Andrew)

LAST LOVE by Tom Cole; Original Direction, Lamont Johnson; Re-Staging, Tony Giordano; Sets/Lighting, Kent Dorsey; Costumes, Christine Dougherty. CAST: James Whitmore, Larry Block (He), Audra Lindley, Sarah Melici (She)

Irene Haupt Photos

**Right Center: Rosemary DeAngelis, Kenneth L. Marks in
"Laughing Wild" Top: Stephen McKinley Henderson, Byron
Utley in "Joe Turner's Come and Gone"**

David Kelly, Britta Smith in "A Moon for the Misbegotten"

SYRACUSE STAGE

Syracuse, New York
Seventeenth Season

Producing Artistic Director, Arthur Storch; Managing Director, James A. Clark; Business Manager, Diana Coles; Development, Shirley Lockwood; Marketing, Barbara Beckos; Press, Barbara Haas; Company Manager, Peter Sandwall; Stage Managers, Don Buschmann and Barbara Morgan; Literary Coordinator, Howard Kerner; Production Manager, Kerro Knox 3; Technical Director, William S. Tiesi; Scenic Artist, Gary May; Lighting Coordinator, Sandra Schilling; Sound Designer, James Wildman; Properties Coordinator, Susan Baker; Costumer, Maria Marrero

PRODUCTIONS AND CASTS

THE ROSE TATTOO by Tennessee Williams; Director, John Gulley; Set, Debra Booth; Costumes, Maria Marrero; Lighting, Harry Feiner. CAST: Susan Arundale (Estelle), Kathleen Baum (Miss Yorke), Laura Facciponti (Peppina), Edith Fisher (the Strega), David Gianopoulos (Alvaro), Sam Goldsman (the salesman), Aaron Harnick (Jack Hunter), Suzanne Hevner (Flora), George Hosmer (Father De Leo), Patricia Mauceri (Serafina), Jodi Lynne McClintock (Bessie), Gerard E. Moses (the doctor), Myra Stennett (Assunta), Carmen Thomas (Rosa), and Louis Fisher, Kathleen Garvey, Jane Keegan, Lisabeth Rodrigues, Chad Jared Sharp, Elizabeth Testa, and James E. Toole.

A WALK IN THE WOODS by Lee Blessing; Director, Arthur Storch; Set, David Potts; Costumes, Jennifer von Mayrhouser; Lighting, Marc B. Weiss. CAST: Ben Hammer (Andrey Botvinnik), Nicholas Hormann (John Honeyman).

THE TAMING OF THE SHREW by William Shakespeare. Director, Larry Carpenter; Sets, John Falabella; Costumes, Lowell Detweiler; Lighting, Marcia Madeira; Composer, John Clifton; Music Director, Terry Runnels. CAST: Humbert Allen Astredo (Baptista), Ross Bickell (Tranio), Kermit Brown (Grumio), Patti Cohenour (Katherine), Earle Edgerton (Vincentio), Michael Heintzman (Hortensio), Erin Hill (Bianca), Edward James Hyland (Gremio), James McDonnell (Petruchio), Kevin M. Richardson (Biondello), Maxine Taylor-Morris (widow), David Whalen (Lucentio), Richard Wright (Pedant), and David Baker, John David, David Douglas, Sean Galuszka, Sam Gordon, Dale Allen Lakes, David Ethan Levit, Karl C. Reischerl, Elizabeth Testa, Byron Tidwell, Eric Radford Weiss, Catherine Zambri.

FINDING DONIS ANNE by Hal Corley. Director, Arthur Storch; Sets, John Doepp; Costumes, Pamela Scofield; Lighting, Phil Monat, Sound, James Wildman. CAST: Cynthia Darlow (Claire), Daryl Edwards (Luther), Tom Gualtieri (Darryl), Suzanna Hay (Rachel).

SPEED-THE-PLOW by David Mamet. Director, Kathryn Long; Sets, Victor A. Becker; Costumes, Timothy Averill; Lighting, Pat Collins; Sound, Rick Menke. CAST: James Gleason (Charlie Fox), Jim Mezon (Bobby Gould), Melissa Weil (Karen).

DANGEROUS CORNER by J. B. Priestley. Director, Arthur Storch; Sets, Timothy Averill; Costumes, Nanzi Adzima; Lighting, Phil Monat, Hair and Wigs, Marcia Ann Ames. CAST: Myra Carter (Maud Mockridge), George Hosmer (Robert Chatfield), Peter Kybart (Stanton), Mary McTigue (Freda); Marjorie Ann Miller (Olwen), Angela Sherrill (Betty), Michael Winther (Gordon).

Lawrence Mason, Jr. Photos

Top Right: Marjorie Ann Miller, Peter Kybart in "Dangerous Corner"

Patti Cohenour, James McDonnell in "The Taming of the Shrew"

TACOMA ACTORS GUILD

Tacoma, Washington

Artistic Director, Bruce Sevy; Associate Artistic Director, William Becvar; Managing Director, Kate Haas; Director of Finance and Operations, Mary Bellerose; Development Director, Janice Dilworth; Director of Marketing & PR, Robert Reich; Production Manager, Hal Meng; Director's Assistant, Nancy Hoadley; Financial Assistant, Sue Headley; Development Assistant, Roxann Levesque; Box Office Manager, Kelly Gardner; Box Office Assistant, Linda Virostek; House Manager, Jamie McLeish; Maintenance, Jerry & Socorro Pinkston; Virginia Diggs; Master Carpenter, Andy Sharp; Scenic Carpenter, Jennifer Lee; Scenic Artist, Paula Swenson; Costume Shop Manager, Marienne O'Brien; Costume Shop Cutter/Stitcher, Jim Westerland

PRODUCTIONS AND CASTS

BRIGHTON BEACH MEMOIRS by Neil Simon; Director, Bruce Sevy; Set Designer, William Forrester; Costume Designer, Ron Erickson; Lighting Designer, Michael Wellborn; Sound Designer, Doug Mackey; Props Design, Greg Veatch; Stage Manager, Hal Meng; Scenic Artist, David Henderson CAST: Andrew Wilder (Eugene), Cheri Sorenson (Blanche), Sandra Ellis Lafferty (Kate), Brandy Manza (Laurie), Ann Patricio (Nora), Andrew DeRycke (Stanley), David S. Klein (Jack)
EXPECTATIONS by Dean Corrin; Director, William Becvar; Set Designer, Jeffrey Frkonja; Costume Designer, Marienne O'Brien; Lighting Designer, Robert Jones; Sound Designer, Doug Mackey; Props Design, Greg Veatch; Stage Manager, Sarah Mixson; Stage Manager, Barbara Naughton; CAST: Sheryl Schmit (Annie Sherman), Jack Poggi (Gene Schroeder), Michael James Smith (Sid Schroeder), Victoria Carver (Janine Schroeder), Wesley Rice (Roger McLean)
CORPSE! by Gerald Moon; Director, Steven Williford; Set Designer, William Forrester; Costume Designer, Ron Erickson; Lighting Designer, Phil Schermer; Fight Director, Tony Soper; Sound Designer, Doug Mackey; Props Designer, Greg Veatch; Stage Manager, Hal Meng; Stage Manager, Lisa Kelly CAST: Stuart Duckworth (Evelyn Farrant), Lyn Tyrrell (Mrs. McGee), Wayne Ballantyne (Major Powell), S. A. Duckworth (Rupert Farrant), Tony Soper (Hawkins)
FIRST NIGHT by Jack Neary; Director, Bruce Sevy; Set Designer, David Henderson; Costume Designer, Marienne O'Brien; Lighting Designer, Robert Jones; Sound Designer, Doug Mackey; Props Designer, Greg Veatch; Stage Manager, Liisa Talso; Stage Manager, Barbara Naughton CAST: Wesley Rice (Danny), Cheri Sorenson (Meredith)
THE DINING ROOM by A. R. Gurney, Jr.; Director, Bruce Sevy; Set Designer, Shelley Schermer; Costume Designer, Frances Kenny; Lighting Designer, Robert A. Jones; Sound Designer, Doug Mackey; Props Designer, Greg Veatch; Stage Manager, Hal Meng; Stage Manager, Lisa Kelly CAST: Sally Smythe, Wesley Rice, Stephen Godwin, Kathryn Mesney, Nina Wishengrad, Larry Paulsen
THE NERD by Larry Shue; Director, Bill Ontiveros; Set Director, Barbara Mesney; Costume Designer, Marienne O'Brien; Lighting Designer, Robert Jones; Sound Designer, Doug Mackey; Props Designer, Greg Veatch; Stage Manager, Liisa Talso; Stage Manager, Barbara Naughton CAST: David Mong (Willum Cubbert), Jeanette Puhich (Tansy McGinnis), Wesley Rice (Axel Hammond), Ed Caldwell (Warnock Waldgrave), Susan Ronn (Clelia Waldgrave), Elliott Miller (Thor Waldgrave), Eric Ray Anderson (Rick Steadman), Danny Baird (Understudy for Thor)

Left Center: Eric Ray Anderson in "The Nerd" *(Tami Stewart)*
Top: Andrew DeRycke, Andrew Wilder, David S. Klein in
"Brighton Beach Memoirs" *(Fred Andrews)*

Cheri Sorenson, Wesley Rice in "First Night" *(Linda Parrish)*

Marcelle Livesay, Jeffrey Ricketts, Leslie Alexander, Tamara Adams, Rosemary Baxter in "Broadway"

Connie Nelson, Esther Benson in "Road to Mecca"

Sharon Bunn, Laurence O'Dwyer in "Woman in Mind"

John Beaird, Stephen Cummins in "Nothing Sacred" Above: John Davies, Charlotte Akin, Emily Figg in "Traveling Lady"

THEATRE THREE

Dallas, Texas
Twenty-eighth Season

Founding/Artistic Director, Norma Young; Executive Producer-Director, Jac Alder; Director of Administration, Chris Harsdorff; Associate Director, Laurence O'Dwyer; Production Manager, Cheryl Denson; Production Stage Manager, Terry Tittle Holman; Technical Director, Tristan Wilson; Costumer, Christopher Kovarik; Musical Director, Terry Dobson; Assistant to the Publicist, Shannette Frazier; Publicist, Gary Yawn;
GUEST ARTISTS: Frank Ferrante, Les Marsden, Anastasia Barzee, Carlos Morton, Doug Harris

PRODUCTIONS AND CASTS

GROUCHO: A LIFE IN REVUE by Arthur Marx and Robert Fisher, with Robert Tekampe; directed by Arthur Marx; musical direction by Terry Dobson; featuring Frank Ferrante; Les Marsden; Anastasia Barzee; Robert Tekampe; set by Jac Alder; lights by Ken Hudson; costumes by Christopher Kovarik; original sound design by Tony Meola; wigs by Jacqueline M. Miller
BROADWAY by Philip Dunning and George Abbott; directed by Patrick Kelly; musical direction by Terry Dobson; choreography by Sally Soldo; sets by Cheryl Denson; lights by Ken Hudson; costumes by Christopher Kovarik; sound design by Tristan Wilson CAST: Tamara Adams, Leslie Alexander, Rosemary Baxter, Joe Conti, Jack Curry, John S. Davies, Chamblee Fergurson, Mark Hadley, Marcelle Livesay, Judy French Mahon, Shawn Patrello, Tony Ponceti, Warren Press, Russell G. Rowe, Jeffery A. Ricketts, William M. Whitehead
WOMAN IN MIND by Alan Ayckbourn; directed by Jac Alder; assistant director Mark Hadley; sets by Cheryl Denson; lights by Linda Blase; costumes by Christopher Kovarik; sound design by Tristan Wilson CAST: Sharon Bunn, Tony Brownrigg, Hugh Feagin, Kalen Hoyle, Laurence O'Dwyer, Warren Press, Midge Verhein, William M. Whitehead
NOTHING SACRED by George F. Walker; directed by Norma Young; assistant director Art Kedzierski; sets by Wade J. Giampa; lights by Linda Blase; costumes by Christopher Kovarik; sound design by Tristan Wilson CAST: John Beaird, Stephen Cummins, Hugh Feagin, Lorilyn Jenkins, Laurence O'Dwyer, Vince Phillip, Scott Pierce, Pip Newson, G. B. Riche, Douglas R. Rogers, Darrell Wofford
THE FANTASTICKS words by Tom Jones; music by Harvey Schmidt; directed by Cheryl Denson; assistant director Lori Latiolais; musical direction by Mark Miller; choreography by Jane Falcone; sets by Charles Howard; costumes by Christopher Kovarik; lights by Linda Blase CAST: Jac Alder, Nelson Coates, Terry Dobson, Greg Dulcie, Gordon Fox, Jerry Haynes, Laura Wells, Chappell Westlake
THE ROAD TO MECCA by Athol Fugard; directed by Norma Young; assistant director Mark Hadley; sets by Harland Wright and Cheryl Denson; costumes by Christopher Kovarik; lights by Linda Blase; sound design by Tristan Wilson CAST: Esther Benson, Connie Nelson, Grant James
THE TRAVELING LADY by Horton Foote; directed by Cheryl Denson; assistant director Lori Latiolais; sets by Nelson Coates; costumes by Christopher Kovarik; lights by Linda Blase; sound design by Tristan Wilson CAST: Charlotte Akin, John Clancy, John S. Davies, Dorothy Deavers, Sharon Elmore, David Figg, Emily Figg, Ann Hamilton, Gene Raye Price, Larry Randolph
A FUNNY THING HAPPENED ON THE WAY TO THE FORUM book by Burt Shevelove and Larry Gelbart; music and lyrics by Stephen Sondheim; directed by Jac Alder; assistant director Mark Hadley; musical direction by Terry Dobson; choreography by Paula Morelan; sets by Harland Wright; costumes by Christopher Kovarik; lights by Linda Blase; sound design by Tristan Wilson CAST: Mark Boyett, Greg Dulcie, Lisa Gabrielle Greene, Naomi Hatsfelt, Jerry Haynes, Maryann Keleher, Kathryn Loncar, Rita Lovett, Ronald A. Martinsen, Lynn Mathis, Laurence O'Dwyer, Tricia Osborn, Rick Prada, April Sayre, Kelly Smith, Terry Vandivort, Stacey Warner, John Willson
VOICES UNSILENCED: A MULTICULTURAL AWAKENING project coordinator Cheryle Washington; special guest moderators Doug Harris and Carlos Morton **ORIGINAL PLAYS** *At Risk* by Carlos Morton; directed by Chris Carlos; featuring Cynthia Williams, Richard Julian, Sonya Resendez, Walter Hardts, Christopher Long, Bob Coonrod. *Natural Shocks* by Neal Morton, Eddie Price and Victor Rizzo; directed by Gary Yawn; featuring Vince McGill, James Tindel, Charlotte Akin. *A Federation of Confederates* by Anne Clayton; directed by Cheryle Washington; featuring Chris Meesey, Steve Miller, Graham Brown, Anthony Ellis, Vince McGill, Libby Villari. *Homeless . . . But We Gotta Life* by Selena Donaldson; directed by Vickie Washington-Nance; featuring Len Gilliam, Walter Hardts, Lloyd W. L. Barnes, Jr., Chris Meesey, Wanda Davis. *Freedom Lies* by James T. Fields; directed by Vickie Washington-Nance; featuring Walter Hardts, Natalie King, Pam Ervin, Ulrike McIvery, Milton Killen, Russell Pierce, Graham Brown. *Untitled* by Courtney Baron, directed by Gail Cronauer; featuring Blair Sams; Cynthia Williams. *Vehicle* by Selena Donaldson; directed by Cheryle Washington; featuring Lois-Louise. *A Puddle of Hot Wax* by Patti Pollock; directed by Gail Cronauer; featuring Anthony Ellis, Bob Coonrod, Nancy Bandiera. *Profile in Faith* by Dianne Tucker; directed by Akin Babatunde; featuring Wanda Davis, Vince McGill, Lloyd W. L. Barnes, Jr., Ava Dupree, Patrick Amos. *Ain't Nobody Dead* by Diane Barber; directed by Gail Cronauer; featuring Natalie King, Barbara Brierbier, Russell Pierce, Joey Allete, Christopher Long, Ahmad Nurradin. *Agent Yellow* by Lannhi Tran; directed by Vickie Washington-Nance; featuring Lisa Schmidt. *Over by the Corner of Claredon and Hampton, on the Edge of Nowhere* by Jennifer Livingston; directed by Akin Babatunde; featuring Patrick Amos, Pam Ervin. *One Choice* by June Lissandrello; directed by Chris Carlos; featuring Bob Coonrod, Richard Julian, Joey Allete

Susan Kandell Photos

VIRGINIA STAGE COMPANY

Norfolk, Virginia
Eleventh Season

Artistic Director, Charles Towers; Interim Managing Director, Faye Bailey Timm; Associate Artistic Director, Christopher Hanna; Resident Costume Designer, Candice Cain. Controller, Pat Kenner; Development Director, Lexi Caswell; Marketing Director, Claudia Keenan; Assistant to the Directors, Marge Prendergast; Production Manager, Chuck Still; Stage Managers, Kathleen Cunneen and Lise Nyrop; Technical Director, Chris Fretts; Master Electrician, John W. Carroll; Properties Manager, Lori-Jo Brandafino.

PRODUCTIONS & CASTS

THE ROAD TO MECCA by Athol Fugard; Directed by Jody McAuliffe; Set, Andrew Jackness; Costumes, Candice Cain; Lighting, Nancy Schertler; with Cara Duff-MacCormick, Laura MacDermott, and Frank Raiter.
THE SECRET GARDEN (World Premiere); book and lyrics by Marsha Norman, Music by Lucy Simon, based on the novel by Frances Hodgson Burnett; Directed by R. J. Cutler; Choreographer, John Carrafa; Music Direction, David Loud; Set, Heidi Landesman; Lighting, Roger Morgan; Costumes, Martin Pakledinaz; with Victoria Clark, Jedidiah Cohen, Christopher Davis, Suzanne Dowaliby, Walter Hudson, Bonny Hughes, Michael McCormick, Stacey Moseley, Louis Padilla, Wade Raley, Molly Regan, Sharon Scruggs, Melanie Vaughan and William Youmans.
T BONE N WEASEL by Jon Klein; Directed by Christopher Hanna; Set, Donald Eastman; Lighting, Nancy Schertler; Costumes, Candice Cain; with LeLand Gantt, Kelly Walters, and Christopher Wynkoop.
SPEED-THE-PLOW by David Mamet; Directed by Charles Towers; Set, Bill Clarke; Lighting, Jackie Manassee; Costumes, Candice Cain; with Gloria Biegler, Ralph Buckley, and Frank Corrado.
FENCES by August Wilson; Directed by Tazewell Thompson; Set, Donald Eastman; Lighting, Anne Militello; Costumes, C. L. Hundley; with Bill Cobbs, Demitri Corbin, Clebert Ford, Kim Hamilton, Keith Johnson, Jonathan Peck, Melissa Bradby, and Adrianne Monique Edwards.
FAIRY TALES OF NEW YORK (American Premiere); by J. P. Donleavy; Directed by Charles Towers; Set, Bill Clarke; Lighting, Spencer Mosse; Costumes, Candice Cain; Sound, Dirk Kuyk; Fight Choreographer, Jim Manley; with Bob Ari, Susan Ericksen, Patrick Ryecart, and Christopher Wynkoop.

Kathy Keeney and Mark Atkinson Photos

Fred Corrado, Gloria Biegler in "Speed-the-Plow" Top: Frank Raiter, Cara Duff-MacCormick in "Road to Mecca"

WHOLE THEATRE

Montclair, New Jersey
Seventeenth Season

Producing Artistic Director, Olympia Dukakis; Co-Directors Education/Outreach, Remi Barclay Bosseau, Gerald Fierst; Associate Artistic Director, Daniel DeRaey; Production Manager, Cheryl Soper Christensen; Artistic Associate, Casey Billings; Castings, Laura Richin; Finance/Administration, Scott Clugstone; Development, Michalann Hobson

PRODUCTIONS & CASTS

TEA by Velina Hasu Houston; Director, Julianne Boyd; Sets, Daniel P. Boylen; Costumes, C. L. Hundley; Lighting, Victor EnYu Tan; Sound, Bruce Ellman; Stage Manager, William Joseph Barnes CAST: Shuko Akune, Takayo Fischer, Lily Mariye, Gerrielani Miyazaki, Marilyn Tokuda
BOESMAN AND LENA by Athol Fugard; Director, Suzanne Shepard; Sets, Roger Mooney; Costumes, Judy Dearing; Lighting, William H. Grant; Sound, Richard Sasson; Stage Manager, Douglas Gettel CAST: Tsepo Mokone, Seth Sibanda, Regina Taylor
HAPPY DAYS by Samuel Beckett; Director, William Foeller; Sets, Nancy Thun; Costumes, Donna Marie Larsen; Lighting, Rachel Budin; Stage Manager, William Joseph Barnes CAST: Olympia Dukakis, Dan Moran
KING LEAR by William Shakespeare; Director, Austin Pendleton; Dramaturg, Kenneth Cavander; Sets, Jack Chandler; Costumes, David Murin; Lighting, Rachel Budin; Fights, Ian Rose; Sound, G. Thomas Clark; Stage Managers, Douglas Bryan Bean, Sandra Lea Williams CAST: Patrick Boll, Katina Commings, Jason Duchin, Donal Egan, Stephen Engle, Phil Hoffman, Herb Lovelle, Joan Macintosh, Rocco Matone, Don Mayo, Tim Monagan, Midori Nakamura, Bill Striglos, Gregory Wallace, Ralph Williams, Louis Zorich
A STONE CARVER by William Mastrosimone; Director, Sue Lawless; Sets, Daniel Ettinger; Costumes, Donna Marie Larsen; Lighting, Rachel Budin; Fights, Jim Manley; Stage Manager, William Joseph Barnes CAST: Susan Cameron, David S. Howard, Joseph Siravo

Gerry Goodstein Photos

Olympia Dukakis in "Happy Days" Above: Joseph Siravo, Susan Cameron, David Howard in "Stone Carver"

THE WALNUT STREET THEATRE

Philadelphia, Pennsylvania

Executive Director, Bernard Havard; Facility, Bob Nimmo; Theatre School Director, Granville Burgess; Development, Donald U. Smith III; Marketing, Judy Beck; Production Manager, Al Franklin; Publicist, Cathy Welborn; Development Associates, Elizabeth A. McCoy, Jennifer Shropshire, Jill Turner; Literary Manager, Ernest Tremblay

PRODUCTIONS & CASTS

FREUD by Lynn Roth; Director, Lenore deKoven; Additional Staging, Brian Smiar; Sets, Dena Roth; Costumes, Deborah Harris, Noel Taylor; Stage Manager, James Stephen Sulanowski CAST: Harold Gould
HOW THE OTHER HALF LOVES by Alan Ayckbourn; Director, Donald Ewer; Sets, Judi Guralnick; Costumes, PattiLynne Meadows; Lighting, Paul Wonsek; Stage Managers, Frank Anzalone, Adrienne Neye CAST: Gordana Rashovich (Fiona), Celine Havard (Teresa), Douglas Wing (Frank), Connor Smith (Bob), Dudley Swetland (William), Sally Mercer (Mary)
JOSEPH AND THE AMAZING TECHNICOLOR DREAMCOAT by Lloyd Webber & Rice; Director/Choreographer, Charles Abbott; Asst. Choreography, Keith Savage; Musical Director, Robert Stecko; Costumes, Lee J. Austin; Sets/Lighting, Paul Wonsek; Stage Managers, Adrienne Neye, Frank Anzalone CAST: Laurie Beechman (Narrator), Sal Viviano (Joseph), Fred Anderson (Napthali), Robert Bartley (Levi), Tony Capone (Judah), Barry Finkel (Asher/Baker), Richard Gervais (Reuben), Patrick Hamilton (Potiphar/Ishmaelite), Marc Hunter (Simeon), Donald Ives (Issacher), Mark McGrath (Pharoh/Ismaelite), Michael Novin (Zebulun), David Olive (Gad), Stephanie Paul (Mermaid/Chorus), Mercedes Perez (Chorus), Keith Savage (Dan/Butler), Jack Sevier (Jacob), John Soroka (Ben), Eileen Tepper (Chorus), Denise Whelan (Chorus), Bernice Wood (Mermaid/Chorus), Teressa Wylie (Mrs. Potiphar/Chorus)

SHERLOCK HOLMES AND THE SPECKLED BAND by Arthur Conan Doyle; Director, Malcolm Black; Scenery/Lighting, Paul Wonsek; Costumes, Hilary Corbett; Stage Managers, Frank Anzalone, Adrienne Neye, Mary Ellen Douglass. CAST: Celine Havard (Violet), Donna Snow (Enid), David Sabin (Dr. Rylott), William Preston (Rodgers), David Medina (Ali), Geoff Garland (Dr. Watson), Joe Sigerson (Coroner), Robert Foley (Coronoer's Officer), Robert Murch (Mr. Brewer), Ian Trigger (Armitage), Ari Gould, Bruce Katlin, Bill Mitchell (Jurors), Greg Wood (Scott Wilson), Hazel Weinberg (Mrs. Staunton), Les Trade (Billy), Patrick Horgan (Sherlock Holmes), Robert Murch (Holt Loaming), Greg Wood (James Montague), Robert Foley (Milverton), Charlie Combes (Peters), Heather Hudson (Amelia)
SLY FOX by Larry Gelbart; Director, Charlie Hensley; Costumes, Lee J. Austin III; Scenery/Lighting, Paul Wonsek; Stage Manager, Adrienne Neye. CAST: David McCann (Simon Able), Stuart Zamsky (Chang), Jennifer Piech, Patrick Roe, Charlotte Wilson (Sly's Servants), Dick LaTessa (Foxwell J. Sly), William Keeler (Craven), Carl Don (Jethro) Ian Trigger (Abner), Eileen Valentino (Miss Fancy), Bernice A. Wood (Mrs. Truckle), David Fuller (Capt. Crouch), Patrick Mulcahy (Chief of Police), Peter Gallatin Beuf, Thomas Crognale, Walter McCready (Policemen), Terrence Sherman (Court Clerk), Dick Latessa (The Judge)

THE HIRED MAN with Book by Melvyn Bragg; Music/Lyrics, Howard Goodall; Director, Brian Aschinger; Musical Director, Elman R. Anderson; Associate Director, Charles Abbott; Costumes, Lee J. Austin III; Set, Judi Guralnick; Lighting, Jerold R. Forsyth; General Manager, Ken Wesler; Production Manager, Al Franklin; Stage Manager, Frank Anzalone. CAST: The Tallentire Family: James J. Mellon (John), Liz McCartney (Emily), Jennifer Piech (May), Gary Landon Wright (Harry), Michael Watson (Seth), Brent Black (Isaac), Alex Wipf (Mr. Pennington/Recruiting Officer/Vicar), Gary Jackson (Jackson), Steve Beauchamp (Mr. Stephens/Ezra/Alec), Mary Ellen Grant (Barmaid/Wench), Judy Malloy (Sally/Wench), Jennifer Piech (Landlady), Kevin Bailey (Joe Sharp/Jack/Joseph), Bob Frisch (Tom/Bill), Eric Bennyhoff (Dan/Alf), Dan Manning (Bob/Ted), Gary Landon Wright (Josh), Understudies: Walter McCready, Rob Hull, Patrick Rose, Rick Hall, Rosemary Ricci, Eric Bennyhoff, Diane Francesca, Maura Kelly, Mary Ellen Grant, Michael Watson, Cynthia Tuleja, Jean McKennan, Key Payton
LAURIE BEECHMAN IN CONCERT with David Friedman as Musical Director; Background Vocals, Stephen Bourneuf, Bruce Moore; Director, Scott Barnes; Technical Director, Randy Hansen; Wardrobe, Lee J. Austin. Performed in two acts.
STUDIO THEATRE PRODUCTIONS: *Face á Face* (Bululu Theatre from Paris), *A Man with Connections* by Alexander Gelman; Director, Granville Burgess; with Joe Aufiery (Andrei Golubev), Kathy Lichter (Natasha Golubev). *Mark Twain Revealed:* Stories by Mark Twain; Adapted and told by Conrad Bishop. *Waiting for the Parade* by John Murrell; Director, Deborah Baer Quinn; with Janis Dardaris (Catherine), Polly K. Davis (Janet), Jane Moore (Margaret), Celine Havard (Eve), Elizabeth Sanchez-Franklin (Marta). *Clear & Present Danger* by Donald C. Drake; Director, David F. Hutchman; with Richard Alliger (Rep 1), Celine Havard (Judy), Marcia Mahon (Amy), Deborah Stern (Paul). *The Petition* by Brian Clark; Director, Donald Ewer; with Donald Ewer (General Sir Edmund Milne), Jenny Turner (Lady Elizabeth Milne).

Gerry Goodstein Photos

Right Center: Kevin Bailey, James Mellon, Brent Black, Michael Watson in "The Hired Man" Above: Laurie Beechman, Sal Viviano in "Joseph . . .," Top: Douglas Wing, Dudley Swetland, Gordana Rashovich in "How the Other Half Loves"

Geoff Garland, Patrick Horgan in "Sherlock Holmes . . ."

Larry Fishburne, Ella Joyce, Sullivan Walker in "Two Trains Running"

YALE REPERTORY THEATRE

New Haven, Connecticut

Artistic Director, Lloyd Richards; Managing Director, Benjamin Mordecai; Set Design Advisor, Ming Cho Lee; Costume Design Advisor, Jane Greenwood; Lighting Design Advisor, Jennifer Tipton; Speech Advisor, Barbara Somerville; Movement Advisor, Wesley Fata; Resident Set Designer, Michael Yeargan; Lighting Director, William B. Warfel; Scene Painting Advisor, Katy Dilkes; Music Coordinator, Douglas R. Dickson; Assistant to the Artistic Director, Ellen McNally; Resident Dramaturg, Gitta Honegger; Dramaturg/Associate Director for Special Projects, Joel Schechter; General Manager, Buzz Ward; Director of Institutional Development, Robert Wildman; Audience Services Director, Thomas W. Clark; Operations Manager, William J. Reynolds; Production Supervisor, Bronislaw J. Sammler; Resident Stage Manager, Margaret Adair Quinn; Stage Managers, Karen L. Carpenter, Lori Anne Diggory, Liz Dreyer, Neal Fox, John C. McNamara, James Mountcastle, Kathleen O'Shea, Jonathan Dimock Secor, Melanie Strange; Technical Directors, Donald A. Harvey, Bob Scheeler; Costume Shop Manager, Tom McAlister; Properties Master, Brian Cookson; Resident Scenic Artist, Kim Aeby; Resident Master Electrician, Donald W. Titus; Stage Carpenter, Thomas Gordon

PRODUCTIONS AND CASTS

THE SOLID GOLD CADILLAC by Howard Teichmann and George S. Kaufman, directed by Gitta Honegger. Set Design by Ed Check; Costume Design by James A. Schuette; Lighting Design by Jennifer Tipton. CAST: Christopher Centrella, Sean Cullen, Claudia Feldstein, Joseph Fuqua, Earl Hindman, Tommy Hollis, James Lally, William Langan, Tom McGowan, Deborah Offner, Anne Pitoniak, Zoey Zimmerman. Video Cast: Diane Smith, Al Terzi, Henry Winkler.

MISS JULIE by August Strindberg, translated by Elizabeth Sprigge, directed by Dennis Scott. Set Design by Michael Yeargan; Costume Design by Nephelie Andonyadis; Lighting Design by Ashley York Kennedy; Sound Design by Patricia Bennett. CAST: Rosalyn Coleman, Cordelia González, Linda Maurel, Chris Walker.

SUMMER AND SMOKE by Tennessee Williams, directed by James Simpson. Set Design by Sarah Lambert; Costume Design by Melina Root; Lighting Design by Scott Zielinski; Sound Design by David L. Sword; Music and Sound Composed by Michael Roth. CAST: Bruce Altman, Christian Baskous, Rafeal Clements, Edouard DeSoto, Dillon Evans, Joseph Fuqua, Annette Jolles, Cindy Katz, William Langan, Dana Morosini, Meg Mundy, Kristine Nielsen, Valarie Pettiford, Laila Robins, Richard Woods.

DAYLIGHT IN EXILE by James D'Entremont, directed by Amy Saltz. Set Design by Barbra Kravitz; Costume Design by Suzanne Jackson; Lighting Design by Ashley York Kennedy. CAST: Michael Early, Kristin Flanders, Joseph Fuqua, Michel R. Gill, Tony Gillan, Tom McGowan, Deborah Offner, Jeffrey Wright.

RUST AND RUIN by William Snowden, directed by Walton Jones. Set Design by Michael Loui; Costume Design by Helen C. Ju; Lighting Design by Robert F. Campbell; Sound Design by Darren Clark. CAST: Julie Boyd, Sean Cullen, Matt Craven, Jay P. Goede, Earl Hindman, Cindy Katz.

PILL HILL by Sam Kelley, directed by Walter Dallas. Set Design by Nephelie Andonyadis; Costume Design by Chrisi Karvonides; Lighting Design by Ashley York Kennedy; Fight Choreography by Charles Conwell. CAST: Jerome Preston Bates, Robert Beatty, Jr., Shawn Brown, Rafeal Clements, A. Benard Cummings, Byron Keith Minns.

DINOSAURS by Doug Wright, directed by Rob Barron. Set Design by Ed Check; Costume Design by Tony Fanning; Lighting Design by Mark L. McCullough; Sound Design by Scott C. Robertson; Music Composed and Sung by Debra Monk. CAST: Charles Bartlett, Kate Baar-Bittman, Charlotte Booker, Marylouise Burke, Kevin Chamberlin, Arjuna Greist, Michael W. McCarty, William Mesnik, Gerry Vichi.

TROILUS AND CRESSIDA by William Shakespeare, directed by Andrei Belgrader. Set Design by Anita C. Stewart; Costume Design by Constanza Romero; Lighting Design by Christopher Akerlind; Music Composed and Performed by Serge Gubelman. CAST: Bruce Altman, Ann Bass, Shawn Brown, Bill Camp, Christopher Centrella, Lynn Chausow, Rosalyn Coleman, Sheldon Decker, Ethyl Eichelberger, Joseph Fuqua, Serge Gubelman, Edward Hibbert, Seth Jones, Cindy Katz, Phil Kaufmann, William Langan, David Little, Ron Parady, Richard Spore, Mike Starr, Saul Stein, Jill Tasker, John Turturro, Bruce H. Withey.

TWO TRAINS RUNNING by August Wilson, directed by Lloyd Richards. Set Design by Tony Fanning; Costume Design by Chrisi Karvonides; Lighting Design by Geoff Korf; Sound Design by Ann Johnson. CAST: Larry Fishburne, Samuel L. Jackson, Ella Joyce, Leonard Parker, Sullivan Walker, Al White, Samuel E. Wright.

PYGMALION by George Bernard Shaw, directed by Douglas C. Wager. Set Design by Michael Yeargan; Costume Design by Barbra Kravitz; Lighting Design by Mark L. McCullough; Sound Design by John Eustis. CAST: Jonathan Allore, Laurinda Barrett, Charles Bartlett, Richard Bauer, Sean Cullen, Terrence Currier, Malcolm Gets, Deborah Goldberg, Gail Grate, Mark Hammer, Gregory Moore, Marty New, Aideen O'Kelly, Jane White.

Gerry Goodstein Photos

Left Center: Gail Grate, Richard Bauer in "Pygmalion"
Above: Laila Robins, Christian Baskous in "Summer and Smoke" Top: Anne Pitoniak, Tommy Hollis in "Solid Gold Cadillac"

ANNUAL SHAKESPEARE FESTIVALS

ALABAMA SHAKESPEARE FESTIVAL

Montgomery, Alabama
Eighteenth Season

Artistic Director, Kent Thompson; Managing Director, Jim Volz; General Manager, Doug Perry; Development, Walter Cox; Marketing, Carol Ogus; Directors, Charles Abbott, John R. Briggs, Gavin Cameron-Webb, Bill Gregg, Robert Hall, David McClendon, William Partlan; Sets, Charles Caldwell, David M. Crank, Kent Dorsey, Harry Feiner, Charles Stanley Kading, Joseph A. Varga, G. W. Mercier; Costumes, Alan Armstrong, Mark Hughes, Kristine Kearney, Marjorie McCowan, Colleen Muscha, Stan H. Poole; Lighting, F. Mitchell Dana, Michael Rourke, Karen S. Spahn; Sound, Kristen R. Kuipers; Composers, James Conely, Christine Frezza, Faser Hardin, Dennis West; Director PAT/MFA, Will York
ACTING COMPANY: Wayne Ballantyne, Monica Bell, Laurie Birmingham, Robert Browning, Evelyn Carol Case, Ray Chambers, Kelly Douglas, Mimi Earnest, Alison Edwards, Roger Forbes, Julian Gamble, Kent Gash, David Mitchell Ghilardi, Julia Glander, Cindy Gold, Edmund J. Kearney, Martin Kildare, Willie King, Cleavon Little, Raye Lankford, Steven David Martin, Ricardo D. Martins, Cynthia Mathis, John Michalski, John Milligan, Neal Moran, Helen Mutch, Jack Parrish, Michael Patten Jr., Philip Pleasants, Clarinda Ross, Michael Rudko, Eddie Rutkowski, Melody Ryane, Lynna Schmidt, Jack Shearer, Anne Sheldon, Ed Steele, Gloria Tapley, Greg Thornton, Darrell Troutman, Joan Ulmer
PRODUCTIONS: *All God's Dangers* by Theodore Rosengarten, Michael Hadley, Jennifer Hadley, starring Cleavon Little; *Execution of Justice; Crimes of the Heart* by Beth Henley; *A Christmas Carol,* adapted by John Jakes; *You Can't Take It With You* by George S. Kaufman and Moss Hart; *Cat on a Hot Tin Roof* by Tennessee Williams; *Macbeth* by William Shakespeare; *Noises Off* by Michael Frayn; *Twelfth Night* by William Shakespeare; *Major Barbara* by George Bernard Shaw; *Tartuffe* by Moliere

Top Right: Bernadette Wilson, David Harum in "Romeo and Juliet" *(Scarsbrook)*

BERKELEY SHAKESPEARE FESTIVAL

Berkeley, California
Sixteenth Season

Artistic Director, Michael Addison; Associate Artistic Director, Julian Lopez-Morillas
THE TAMING OF THE SHREW; Director, Peggy Shannon; Sets, Joel Fontaine; Costumes, Nancy Jo Smith. CAST: Lura Dolas (Kate), Shabaka (Petruchio), Charles Shaw Robinson (Sly)
ROMEO AND JULIET; Director, Julian Lopez-Morillas; Sets, Eric Sinkonnen; Costumes, Eliza Chugg. CAST: Cindy Basco (Juliet), John Stadelman (Romeo)
MEASURE FOR MEASURE; Director, Richard E. T. White; Sets, Barbara Mesney; Costumes, Barbara Bush. CAST: Julian Lopez-Morillas (Duke), John Bellucci (Angelo), Robin Nordli (Isabella)
MUCH ADO ABOUT NOTHING; Director, Michael Addison; Sets, Jeff Struckman; Costumes, Warren Travis. CAST: Lura Dolas (Beatrice), Charles Shaw Robinson (Benedick), Julian Lopez-Morillas (Dogberry)
(No other material submitted)

Right Center: Greg Thornton, Greta Lambert in "Les Liaisons . . ." Above: Greg Thornton as "Cyrano" (R) Julian Gamble as "Macbeth" *(Scarsbrook)*

Ray Chambers, Wayne Ballantyne in "Cat on a Hot Tin Roof" *(Scarsbrook)*

FOLGER SHAKESPEARE THEATRE

Washington, D.C.
Twentieth Season

Artistic Director, Michael Kahn; Managing Director, Mary Ann de Barbieri; Production Manager, John W. Kingsbury; Business Manager, Sam Sweet; Vocal Consultant, Elizabeth Smith; Movement Consultant, Roberta Gasbarre; Development Director, Brian H. Marcus; Public Relations/Marketing, Beth Hauptle; Educational Programs, Stephen Welch; Technical Director, Ken Zommer

PRODUCTIONS & CASTS

TWELFTH NIGHT by William Shakespeare; Director, Michael Kahn; Sets, Derek McLane; Costumes, Martin Pakledinaz; Lighting, Nancy Schertler; Composer, Catherine MacDonald; Stage Manager, Scott L. Hammar. CAST: Kelly McGillis (Viola), Mark Philpot (Sebastian), Larry McMullen (Sea Captain/Priest), Raphael Nash (Antonio), Scott Blanks (Sailor/Servant/Officer), Ted McAdams (Sailor/Servant), Kate Skinner (Olivia), Philip Goodwin (Malvolio), David Sabin (Toby), Floyd King (Andrew), Franchelle Stewart Dorn (Maria), David Medina (Fabian), Yusef Bulos (Feste), Debra Port (Waiting Woman), Letha Remington (Waiting Woman), Marcus Langford-Thomas (Boy), Peter Webster (Orsino), Edward Gero (Curio), Emery Battis (Valentine), Tony Lucchi (Lord), Hunter Boyle, David Morden, Marie-Therese Lintz, Cornell Charles Womack (Servants/Musicians), Sharon Freed, Dawn Horne, Linda Pollitt, Margo L. West (Townswomen)

THE TEMPEST by William Shakespeare; Director, Richard E. T. White; Sets, Kent Dorsey; Costumes, Barbara Bush; Lighting, Peter Maradudin; Design, John Boesche; Composer/Sound, Todd Barton; Masque/Movement, Roberta Stiehm; Vocal Consultant, Ralph Zito; Stage Manager, Linda Harris. CAST: Ted van Griethuysen (Prospero), Jacqueline Kim (Miranda), Raphael Nash (Caliban), Louis A. Lotorto (Ariel), Franchelle Stewart Dorn (Spirit Voice), Sharon Freed (Spirit Voice/Island Spirit/Mariner), Linda Pollitt (Spirit Voice/Island Spirit), Dawn Horne (Island Spirit), Debra Port, Margo West (Island Spirits), Cornell Charles Womack (Island Spirit/Boatswain), Hunter Boyle (Island Spirit/Mariner), Richard M. Davidson (Alonso), Peter Webster (Sebastian), Chiron Alston (Ferdinand), Emery Battis (Gonzalo), Ted McAdams (Adrian), Morgan Duncan (Francisco), Edward Gero (Antonio), Robert Sicular (Stephano), Floyd King (Trinculo), Larry McMullen (Master), Tony Lucchi (Mariner)

MARY STUART by Friedrich von Schiller; Translation, Robert David MacDonald; Director, Sarah Pia Anderson; Sets, Donald Eastman; Costumes, Martin Pakledinaz; Lighting, Frances Aronson; Sound, Peter Scarborough Blue; Vocal Consultant, Ralph Zito; Stage Manager, Scott L. Hammar. CAST: Franchelle Stewart Dorn (Elizabeth), Monique Fowler (Mary Stuart), Edward Gero (Dudley), Clayton Corzatte (Talbot), Ted van Griethuysen (Cecil), Floyd King (Davison), Emery Battis (Paulet), Michael MacCauley (Mortimer), Jay Hillmer (Aubespine), David Downing (Melville), Susan Corzatte (Hannah), Mark Douglas, Larry McMullen (Guards)

THE MERRY WIVES OF WINDSOR by William Shakespeare; Director, Michael Kahn; Sets, Derek McLane; Costumes, Catherine Zuber; Lighting, John McLain; Composer, Steven Rydberg; Stage Manager, James Latus. CAST: Emery Battis (Justice), Matt Bradford Sullivan (Slender), John Thomas Waite (Evans), Francis Kane (Page), Pat Carroll (John Falstaff), Cornell Womack (Bardolf), Carter Jahncke (Pistol), Edward Morgan (Nym), Tonia Rowe (Anne), Franchelle Stewart Dorn (Mistress Page), Caitlin O'Connell (Mistress Ford), Jason Kravits (Peter), Richard Dix (Host), Eddie Tyclus Robinson, Baakari Askia Wilder (Robin), Marilyn Sokol (Mistress Quickly), Hunter Boyle (Rugby), Floyd King (Dr. Caius), Michael MacCauley (Fenton), Edward Gero (Master Ford), Mark Douglas (John), Conrad Feininger (Robert), Drew Kahl, Margo West (Servants), Nicole Dana, Kirstin Dorn, Kari Ginsburg, Dan Cameron Lowe, Jason Roland Reed, C. W. Hardy, Lisa Ann Miller, Areesah Mobley, Natalie Simone, Robert Zalkind (Children)

Joan Marcus, Willard Volz Photos

**Left Center: Monique Fowler, Franchelle Stewart Dorn in
"Mary Stuart" Above: Peter Webster, Kelly McGillis in
"Twelfth Night" Top: Ted Van Griethuysen in "The Tempest"**

Edward Gero, Pat Carroll in "Merry Wives of Windsor"

Houston Shakespeare Festival's "Coriolanus (*Jim Caldwell*)

HOUSTON SHAKESPEARE FESTIVAL

Houston, Texas

Producing Director, Sidney Berger; Director, Rutherford Cravens; Sets, Arch Andrus; Costumes, Ainslie Bruneau; Lighting, John Gow
ACTING COMPANY: Luis Lemus, Francis Hodges, Robert Strane, Lisa Griffith, James Gale, Charles Sanders, Wade Mylius, Rutherford Cravens, James Black, Phillip Hafer, Big Skinny Brown, Jerry Miller, Michael LaGue, Nancy Sherrard, Wayne Swallows, Gwendolyn McLarty, Carl Koch, Rene Gattica, R. Christian Tucker, Vicki Luman, Katherine Parr, Gage Tarrant
PRODUCTIONS: *Troilus and Cressida, The Tempest*
(No other material submitted.)

NEW JERSEY SHAKESPEARE FESTIVAL

Madison, New Jersey
Twenty-eighth Season

Artistic Director, Paul Barry; Producing Director, Ellen Barry; Production Stage Manager, Jan Kelik; Stage Manager/Lighting Designer, Stephen Petrilli; Scenic Designer, James A. Bazewicz; Scenic Designer, David Stern; Costume Designers, Julie Abels Chevan, Wendi L. Katzman, Nanalee Raphael-Schirmer, Janus Stefanowicz, Katherine Wagner, Ann Waugh; Musical Director, Deborah Martin; Mime Director, Craig Babcock; General Manager, Jana Mack; Public Relations/Educational Outreach Director, Mary Saarmann; Director of Marketing, Julia Averett Buteux; Staff, Oscar Archuleta, Nick Boyle, James Cantrell, Phillip Contic, Lucy Anne Dawes, Susan Deeley, Christy Dudo, Cory Fuller, Mary Godinho, Steven Graver, Susan Hammon, Constance Hoffman, Eleanor Kennedy, Christian Kraii, Mirth Lovingham, Natalie Maitre, Kevin Patrick March, Drew Martorella, Francine Matagrano, Austin Sanderson, Lydia Spooner
RESIDENT ACTING COMPANY:
Actors' Equity (professional) company: Bob Ari, Ellen Barry, Paul Barry, Jan Buttram, Thomas Carson, James Casey, David Connell, Sheridan Crist, Christopher Cull, Leland Gantt, Richard Graham, Kenneth Gray, Charles Hayman, Kevin Hogan, J. C. Hoyt, Eric Kramer, Diana LaMar, Kathleen Monteleone, Don Perkins, Phillip Pruneau, Janet Sarno, Geraldine Singer, Geddeth Smith, T. Ryder Smith, Alexander Wells, Thea Ruth White, Cheryl Williams
Supporting Company (Equity Membership Candidates/Interns): Debra Babich, Shannon Barry, Tom Biglin, John Martin Bishop, Elizabeth Bowman, Robert Branch, Shelley Brashear, Gregg W. Brevoort, Timothy T. Brown, Jeff Carley, Beth Claxon, Rachel Coburn, Cynthia Collins, Kathleen Conlon, Kelley Costigan, Kevin Elden, James Elliott, Carol Haunton, Victor Khodadad, Christopher C. Knall, Thomas Lanier, James McClure, Kara Miller, Anne Marie Morelli, Maureen Pedala, Jessica Leigh Reap, Richard M. Rose, Ryan Ross, Mark Roth, Alice Regan Stanton, Suzanne Sturn, Christopher Sullivan, Dan Teachout, Robert Toombs, Cecelia Vanti, Nicholas Viselli, Jenny Wallace, Mary Whitcomb, Maria Whitley, Russ Widdall, Andrew Zakow
GUEST ARTISTS: James Christy (Director, *As You Like It*) and Ronald Martell (Director, *Tom Jones*)
PRODUCTIONS William Shakespeare's *Titus Andronicus, As You Like It,* and *Pericles, Prince of Tyre,* and John Morrison's adaptation of Henry Fielding's *Tom Jones;* Tennessee Williams' *Night of the Iguana,* Samuel Beckett's *Waiting for Godot*

Specialized Photodesign/Jim DelGiudice Photos

Right Center: Geraldine Singer, Christopher Cull, Eric Kramer in "Titus Andronicus" Above: Cheryl Williams, Christopher Cull, Jessica Leigh Reap in "As You Like It"

Don Perkins, Geddeth Smith in "Waiting for Godot"

OREGON SHAKESPEARE FESTIVAL

Ashland & Portland, Oregon
Forty-ninth Season

Artistic Director, Jerry Turner; Associate, Pat Patton; Artistic Associate, Kirk Boyd; Producer Portland, Dennis Bigelow; Costumes, Jeannie Davidson; Designer, Richard L. Hay; Sets, William Bloodgood; Literary Manager, Cynthia White; Directors, Libby Appel, Dennis Bigelow, Bill Cain, James Edmondson, Philip Killian, Kathryn Long, Pat Patton, Warner Shook, Jeff Steitzer, Jerry Turner, Henry Woronicz; Lighting, Peter Maradudin, Rick Paulsen, Robert Peterson, James Sale; Music/Sound, Todd Barton, David de Berry; Scenery, William Bloodgood, John Dexter, Richard L. Hay, Michael Miller, Vicki M. Smith, Carey Wong; Choreography, Mary Beth Cavanaugh, JoAnn Johnson; Fights, Peter Kjenaas, Christopher Villa; Dialect, Joan Langley, Ursula Meyer

ACTING COMPANY: Roy Michael Abramsohn, Karl Backus, Marco Barricelli, Deena Burke, Bruce Burkhartsmeier, Mimi Carr, Daniel Cochren, Gregg Coffin, Nick Corley, Joseph Cronin, Philip Davidson, Matthew Davis, Tony DeBruno, Constance Doolan, Michael Edwards, Richard Elmore, James Finnegan, Brian Fraser, Bill Geisslinger, Kelly Haskell, Adam Michael Hogan, Richard Howard, Philip Hubbard, JoAnn Johnson, Jane Jones, Eric Johnson, Michael Kevin, Peter Kjenaas, Jeff Kramer, Dan Kremer, John Leistner, Dawn Lisell-Frank, Robert Lisell-Frank, Marie Livingston, Andrew Long, Louis Lotorto, Dee Maaske, Robert Machray, George F. Maguire, Sandy McCallum, Terri McMahon, Cristine McMurdo-Wallis, Matthew Meeker, Michael Meeker, Michelle Morain, Mark Murphey, Robert Nadir, Paul Nash, Allen Nause, James Newcomb, William Nielsen, Vanessa Nowitzky, Paul Vincent O'Connor, Victoria Otto, Robert Parsons, Shirley Patton, Jeanne Paulsen, Larry Paulsen, James J. Peck, J. P. Phillips, Demetra Pittman, John Pribyl, Michael A. Pocaro, Karen Pollard, Rex Rabold, Tom Ramirez, Nicholas Rempel, Robynn Rodriguez, Gretchen Rumbaugh, Remi Sandri, Stephanie Shine, Ron Snyder, Tom Spiller, David Thompson, Kathleen Turco-Lyon, Jack Vaughn, W. Francis Walters, Holly Weber, Derrick Lee Weeden, Chris Wood, Jeffrey Wooliver, Henry Woronicz, Rex Young, Grace Zandarski

PRODUCTIONS: *Much Ado About Nothing; Henry IV, Part Two; Two Gentleman of Verona; Cyrano de Bergerac; And a Nightingale Sang; All My Sons; Pericles, Prince of Tyre; Breaking the Silence; Hunting Cockroaches; Not About Heroes; Road to Mecca; The Miser; Terra Nova; Peer Gynt; House of Blue Leaves; Merry Wives of Windsor; Voice of the Prairie; The Second Man; God's Country*

Christopher Briscoe Photos

Right: John Pribyl, Mark Murphey (at table), Terri McMahon in "Voice of the Prairie" (R) Henry Woronicz, Marie Livingston in "Peer Gynt" Top: Robynn Rodriguez, JoAnn Johnson in "Merry Wives of Windsor"

Demetra Pittman, Tony DeBruno in "House of Blue Leaves"

Mark Murphey, Terri McMahon in "The Second Man"

SHAKESPEARE & COMPANY

Berkshires/Boston, Massachusetts
Eleventh Season

Artistic Director, Tina Packer; Training Director, Kristin Linklater; Managing Director, Dennis Krausnick; Education Director, Kevin Coleman; Literary Manager, Stanley Richardson; Business Manager, Martin Heffan; Development/Marketing, Kate Maguire

PRODUCTIONS & CASTS

THE TEMPEST by William Shakespeare; Director, Tina Packer; Costumes, Kiki Smith; Sets, Stephen Ball; Lighting, Richard Meyer; Dances, Susan Dibble; Text, Neil Freeman; Voice, Kristin Linklater; Coaching, Andrea Haring; Stage Managers, K. Dale White, Kate Cherry; Consultant, Jane Grey; Asst. Director, Mary Hartman. CAST: Robert Biggs (Stephano), Ken Cheeseman (Adrian), Jonathan Epstein (Antonio/Prospero), Andre Gregory (Prospero), Marina Gregory (Miranda), Mary Hartman (Ceres), Allen Leatherman (Gonzalo), Paula Langton (Iris), Midori Nakamura (Ariel), Kenny Ransom (Ferdinand), Keanu Reeves (Trinculo), Tim Saukiavicus (Alonso/Antonio), Rocco Sisto (Caliban), Brian Paul Stuart (Boatswain), Peter Wittrock (Sebastian)

RICHARD III by William Shakespeare; Director, Kristin Linklater; Costumes, Janna Kimel; Fights, Jason Kuschner; Music, Christina & Philip Bynoe; Coordinator, Claudia Park; Choreography, Susan Dibble; Asst. Director, Tim Douglas; Movement, Karen Biggs; Voice/Text, Elizabeth Ingram. CAST: Michael Lugering (Edward IV/Archbishop), Hamish Linklater (Prince Edward), Noah Abarbanel (Richard), Jonathan Frank (George), Edward Porter (Richard-Gloucester), Christopher Von Bayer (Richard-Gloucester), Michael Fanning (Henry/Cardinal), Trellis Stepter (Duke Buckingham), Scott Facher (Earl Rivers/Lord Mayor), Stacy McGovern (Marquis Dorset), Erika Johnson (Lord Grey/James Tyrrel), Emiko Tamagawa (Earl Derby), Mark Nelson (Lord Hastings), Josette Murray (Sir Brakenbury), Frederika Kesten (Ratcliffe/Jane Shore), Anne Halsey Clark (Catesby), Christina Bynoe (Elizabeth), Sarah Cathcart (Margaret), Mary Coy (Duchess of York), Yasmine Lever (Lady Anne), Elizabeth Juviler (1st Murderer), Daven Lee (2nd Murderer), Seth Rosmarin (Scrivener)

A FOLIAGE FESTIVAL OF WHARTON PLAYS; Director, Dennis Krausnick; DUET WITH VARIATIONS with Allyn Burrows (Percy Lubbock), Allen Leatherman, Dennis Krausnick (Henry James), Tina Packer (Edith Wharton) ROMAN FEVER with Tina Packer (Alida Slade), Kristin Linklater (Grace Ansley), Daniel Osman (Waiter) THE TEMPERATE ZONE; Adaptation E. E. Smith; with Corinna May (Janet), Allyn Burrows (Willis French), Kristin Linklater (Gladys Hendley), Daniel Osman (Donald Paul), Karen MacDonald (Bessie Paul) EXPIATION with Karen MacDonald (Paula Fetherel), Ms. Linklater (Bella Clinch), Ms. May (Maid), Mr. Osman (Bishop), Mr. Burrows (John Fetherel)

Richard Feldman, Jeff Greenler, Lezlie Lee Photos

**Right: Tina Packer, Allyn Burrows, Dennis Krausnick in
"Duet with Variations" Top: Yasmine Lever, Edward Porter
in "Richard III"**

**Midori Nakamura, Rocco Sisto, Andre Gregory in
"The Tempest"**

**Marina Gregory, Kenny Ransom in
"The Tempest"**

STRATFORD FESTIVAL

Stratford, Ontario, Canada
Thirty-seventh Season

Artistic Director, John Neville; Associate Directors, Bernard Hopkins, Tanya Moiseiwitsch, Richard Monette, Richard Ouzounian, David William, John Wood; Directors, Robert Beard, Jeannette Lambermont, Michael Langham, Richard Monette, John Neville, Richard Ouzounian, Donald Saddler, David William, John Wood; Designers, Susan Benson, Lewis Brown, Patrick Clark, Michael Eagan, John Ferguson, Debra Hanson, Desmond Heeley, Brian H. Jackson, Sue LePage; Composers, Louis Applebaum, Michael Conway Baker, Berthold Carrière, Alan Laing, Stanley Silverman; Lighting, Harry Frehner, Louise Guinand, John Munro, Michael J. Whitfield; Choreography/Fights, John Broome; Young Company Directors, Kelly Handerek, Bernard Hopkins; Designers, Charlotte Dean, Jacinthe Demers; Lighting, Kevin Fraser; Composer, Laura Burton

ACTING COMPANY: Brian Bedford, Andrew Binks, Mervyn Blake, James Blendick, Paul Boretski, David Brown, Sally Cahill, Douglas Chamberlain, Juan Chioran, Antoni Cimolino, Eric Coates, Peggy Coffey, Allan Craik, Richard Curnock, Nicholas de Kruyff, Keith Dinicol, Andrew Dolha, Peter Donaldson, Eric Donkin, Shirley Douglas, Deborah Drakeford, William Dunlop, Jerry Etienne, Nancy Ferguson, Patrick Galligan, Pat Galloway, Brenda Gorlick, Allan Gray, Kevin Gudahl, Michael Hanrahan, Ron Hastings, Derek Hazel, Susan Henley, Kate Hennig, Larry Herbert, Susannah Hoffmann, Roger Honeywell, Kim Horsman, Phillip Hughes, John Innes, Andrew Jackson, Melanie Janzen, Nolan Jennings, Geordie Johnson, Hubert Baron Kelly, Lorne Kennedy, Robert King, Larissa Lapchinski, Jayne Lewis, David Lloyd-Evans, Dirk Lumbard, T. Vincent MacDonald, Janet Martin, Tony Martin, Geoff McBride, Eric McCormack, Seana McKenna, Dale Mieske, Cassel H. Miles, Michèle Muzzi, William Needles, Vickie Papava, Lucy Peacock, Nicholas Pennell, David Playfair, Jeffrey Prentice, Claire Rankin, Bradley C. Rudy, Stellina Rusich, Stephen Russell, Goldie Semple, Joseph Shaw, Wenna Shaw, Christopher Shyer, Kent Staines, Dwayne Stevenson, Brian Tree, Kay Tremblay, Ian Watson, Ian White, Julia Winder, Anne Wright, Geraint Wyn Davies, Cavan Young, Victor A. Young

YOUNG COMPANY: Andrew Akman, Jacqueline Dandeneau, Chris Heyerdahl, Jeffrey Hirschfield, Camille James, David Keeley, Brian Linds, Joanne Miller, Paul Miller, David New, Jennifer Rockett, J. Craig Sandy, Julia Smith, Steve Yorke

PRODUCTIONS: *Titus Andronicus, Comedy of Errors, Merchant of Venice* by Shakespeare, *Kiss Me Kate* by Porter & Spewack, *Shoemakers' Holiday* by Thomas Dekker, *Midsummer Night's Dream* by Shakespeare, *Three Sisters* by Chekhov, *Henry V* by Shakespeare, *The Relapse* by John Vanbrugh, *Cat on a Hot Tin Roof* by Williams, *Love's Labour's Lost* by Shakespeare, *The Changeling* by Middleton & Rowley

Michael Cooper, Robert C. Ragsdale Photos

Left: Dirk Lumbard and (clockwise) Susan Henley, Jeffrey Prentice, Nancy Ferguson, Larry Herbert, Janet Martin, Victor Young, Jayne Lewis in "Kiss Me, Kate" Above: Eric Donkin, Stephen Russell, Paul Boretski, David LLoyd-Evans, Geraint Wyn Davies (front) Top: Cast of "Comedy of Errors"

Goldie Semple, Keith Dinicol, Nicholas Pennell, Geordie Johnson, Lucy Peacock in "Titus Andronicus"

Richard Curnock, Brian Bedford (front), Geraint Wyn Davies, Kim Horsman, Eric Donkin in "The Relapse"

THREE RIVERS SHAKESPEARE FESTIVAL

Pittsburgh, Pennsylvania
Tenth-Season

Producing Director, Attilio Favorini; Special Programs, Christine Frezza; Marketing/ Development, William Sharek; Public Relations, Caty DeWalt;

PRODUCTIONS & CASTS

ANTONY & CLEOPATRA by William Shakespeare; Director, Yossi Yzraely; Sets/Props/Costumes, Henry Heymann; Composer, Christine Frezza; Lighting, Stephen Petrilli; Stage Manager, Adrienne Keriotis CAST: Steven J. Anderson (Soldier/Servant), Anne Louise Bannon (Iras), James Berry (Thidias), Harry Bouvy (Silius), Alex Coleman (Lepidus/Dolabella), Michael Dowd (Scarus), Sara J. Fleming (US Charmian), Tim Hartman (Mardian), E. Bruce Hill (Varrius/Soldier/ Servant), D. E. Jukes (Ventidius/Procelius), Leonard Kelly-Young (Menas/ Decretas/Ambassador), Kelly Korzan (Charmian), David Kuhns (Maecenas), Richard McMillan (Enobarbus), Larry John Meyers (Soothsayer/Clown), Monique Morgan (Octavia), Jack Plotnick (Octavius), John Plumpis (Eros/Soldier), Kenneth Roberts (Pompeius), Marco St. John (Antony), Amy Seifried (US Iras), Mark Philip Stevenson (Alexas/Soldier), Sam Turich (Soldier/Servant), Holly Villaire (Cleopatra), Don Wadsworth (Agrippa), Dereck R. Walton (Canidius), Ron Wisniski (Diomedes)

HAMLET by William Shakespeare; Director, Gillette A. Elvgren; Sets/Props, William J. Winsor; Costumes, Lorraine Venberg; Composer, Ms. Frezza; Sound, James Capenos; Fights, W. Stephen Coleman; Lighting, Mr. Petrilli CAST: Anne Louise Bannon (Player Queen/US Ophelia), James Berry (Priest/Rinaldo), Harry Bouvy (Player), Chet Carlin (Polonius), Alex Coleman (Claudius), Michael Dowd (Bernardo/Fortinbras), Tim Hartman (Rosencrantz), Leonard Kelly-Young (Ghost/ Player King/Gravedigger), Kelly Korzan (Ophelia), David Kuhns (Guildenstern), Richard McMillan (Hamlet), Monique Morgan (Gertrude), John Plumpis (Laertes), Kenneth Roberts (Marcellus/Player), Amy Seifried (US Player Queen), Mark Philip Stevenson (Osric), Don Wadsworth (Horatio), Dereck R. Walton (Francisco/Player), Ron Wisniski (Player)

A FUNNY THING HAPPENED ON THE WAY TO THE FORUM by Sondheim, Shevelove & Gelbart; Director, W. Stephen Coleman; Music Director, Lawrence Goldberg; Sets/Props, William J. Winsor; Costumes, Bill Black; Choreography, Susan Gillis; Lighting, Mr. Petrilli CAST: Steven J. Anderson (Protean), Anne Louise Bannon (Geminae), James Berry (Senex), Chet Carlin (Erronius), Sara J. Fleming (Philia), Jane Gentry (Tintinabula), Tim Hartman (Miles Gloriosus), Kelly Korzan (Geminae), David Kuhns (Protean), Kimberly Lewis (Gymnasia), Monique Morgan (Vibrata), Myrna Paris (Domina), Jack Plotnick (Hero), John Plumpis (Protean), Mark Philip Stevenson (Hysterium), Barbara Stuart (Panacea), Don Wadsworth (Lycus), Ron Wisniski (Pseudolus)

Left: Richard McMillan, Monique Morgan in "Hamlet" Top:
Holly Villaire, Marco St. John in "Antony and Cleopatra"

Alex Coleman, Monique Morgan in "Hamlet"

Ron Wisniski, Mark Philip Stevenson in "A Funny Thing
Happened . . ."

PREVIOUS THEATRE WORLD
AWARD RECIPIENTS

1944-45: Betty Comden, Richard Davis, Richard Hart, Judy Holliday, Charles Lang, Bambi Linn, John Lund, Donald Murphy, Nancy Noland, Margaret Phillips, John Raitt

1945-46: Barbara Bel Geddes, Marlon Brando, Bill Callahan, Wendell Corey, Paul Douglas, Mary James, Burt Lancaster, Patricia Marshall, Beatrice Pearson

1946-47: Keith Andes, Marion Bell, Peter Cookson, Ann Crowley, Ellen Hanley, John Jordan, George Keane, Dorothea MacFarland, James Mitchell, Patricia Neal, David Wayne

1947-48: Valerie Bettis, Edward Bryce, Whitfield Connor, Mark Dawson, June Lockhart, Estelle Loring, Peggy Maley, Ralph Meeker, Meg Mundy, Douglass Watson, James Whitmore, Patrice Wymore

1948-49: Tod Andrews, Doe Avedon, Jean Carson, Carol Channing, Richard Derr, Julie Harris, Mary McCarty, Allyn Ann McLerie, Cameron Mitchell, Gene Nelson, Byron Palmer, Bob Scheerer

1949-50: Nancy Andrews, Phil Arthur, Barbara Brady, Lydia Clarke, Priscilla Gillette, Don Hanmer, Marcia Henderson, Charlton Heston, Rick Jason, Grace Kelly, Charles Nolte, Roger Price

1950-51: Barbara Ashley, Isabel Bigley, Martin Brooks, Richard Burton, Pat Crowley, James Daly, Cloris Leachman, Russell Nype, Jack Palance, William Smithers, Maureen Stapleton, Marcia Van Dyke, Eli Wallach

1951-52: Tony Bavaar, Patricia Benoit, Peter Conlow, Virginia de Luce, Ronny Graham, Audrey Hepburn, Diana Herbert, Conrad Janis, Dick Kallman, Charles Proctor, Eric Sinclair, Kim Stanley, Marian Winters, Helen Wood

1952-53: Edie Adams, Rosemary Harris, Eileen Heckart, Peter Kelley, John Kerr, Richard Kiley, Gloria Marlowe, Penelope Munday, Paul Newman, Sheree North, Geraldine Page, John Stewart, Ray Stricklyn, Gwen Verdon

1953-54: Orson Bean, Harry Belafonte, James Dean, Joan Diener, Ben Gazzara, Carol Haney, Jonathan Lucas, Kay Medford, Scott Merrill, Elizabeth Montgomery, Leo Penn, Eva Marie Saint

1954-55: Julie Andrews, Jacqueline Brookes, Shirl Conway, Barbara Cook, David Daniels, Mary Fickett, Page Johnson, Loretta Leversee, Jack Lord, Dennis Patrick, Anthony Perkins, Christopher Plummer

1955-56: Diane Cilento, Dick Davalos, Anthony Franciosa, Andy Griffith, Laurence Harvey, David Hedison, Earle Hyman, Susan Johnson, John Michael King, Jayne Mansfield, Sara Marshall, Gaby Rodgers, Susan Strasberg, Fritz Weaver.

1956-57: Peggy Cass, Sydney Chaplin, Sylvia Daneel, Bradford Dillman, Peter Donat, George Grizzard, Carol Lynley, Peter Palmer, Jason Robards, Cliff Robertson, Pippa Scott, Inga Swenson

1957-58: Anne Bancroft, Warren Berlinger, Colleen Dewhurst, Richard Easton, Tim Everett, Eddie Hodges, Joan Hovis, Carol Lawrence, Jacqueline McKeever, Wynne Miller, Robert Morse, George C. Scott

1958-59: Lou Antonio, Ina Balin, Richard Cross, Tammy Grimes, Larry Hagman, Dolores Hart, Roger Mollien, France Nuyen, Susan Oliver, Ben Piazza, Paul Roebling, William Shatner, Pat Suzuki, Rip Torn

1959-60: Warren Beatty, Eileen Brennan, Carol Burnett, Patty Duke, Jane Fonda, Anita Gillette, Elisa Loti, Donald Madden, George Maharis, John McMartin, Lauri Peters, Dick Van Dyke

1960-61: Joyce Bulifant, Dennis Cooney, Sandy Dennis, Nancy Dussault, Robert Goulet, Joan Hackett, June Harding, Ron Husmann, James MacArthur, Bruce Yarnell

1961-62: Elizabeth Ashley, Keith Baxter, Peter Fonda, Don Galloway, Sean Garrison, Barbara Harris, James Earl Jones, Janet Margolin, Karen Morrow, Robert Redford, John Stride, Brenda Vaccaro

1962-63: Alan Arkin, Stuart Damon, Melinda Dillon, Robert Drivas, Bob Gentry, Dorothy Loudon, Brandon Maggart, Julienne Marie, Liza Minnelli, Estelle Parsons, Diana Sands, Swen Swenson

1963-64: Alan Alda, Gloria Bleezarde, Imelda De Martin, Claude Giraud, Ketty Lester, Barbara Loden, Lawrence Pressman, Gilbert Price, Philip Proctor, John Tracy, Jennifer West.

1964-65: Carolyn Coates, Joyce Jillson, Linda Lavin, Luba Lisa, Michael O'Sullivan, Joanna Pettet, Beah Richards, Jaime Sanchez, Victor Spinetti, Nicolas Surovy, Robert Walker, Clarence Williams III

1965-66: Zoe Caldwell, David Carradine, John Cullum, John Davidson, Faye Dunaway, Gloria Foster, Robert Hooks, Jerry Lanning, Richard Mulligan, April Shawhan, Sandra Smith, Leslie Ann Warren

1966-67: Bonnie Bedelia, Richard Benjamin, Dustin Hoffman, Terry Kiser, Reva Rose, Robert Salvio, Sheila Smith, Connie Stevens, Pamela Tiffin, Leslie Uggams, Jon Voight, Christopher Walken

1967-68: David Birney, Pamela Burrell, Jordan Christopher, Jack Crowder (Thalmus Rasulala), Sandy Duncan, Julie Gregg, Stephen Joyce, Bernadette Peters, Alice Playten, Michael Rupert, Brenda Smiley, Russ Thacker

1968-69: Jane Alexander, David Cryer, Blythe Danner, Ed Evanko, Ken Howard, Lauren Jones, Ron Leibman, Marian Mercer, Jill O'Hara, Ron O'Neal, Al Pacino, Marlene Warfield

1969-70: Susan Browning, Donny Burks, Catherine Burns, Len Cariou, Bonnie Franklin, David Holliday, Katharine Houghton, Melba Moore, David Rounds, Lewis J. Stadlen, Kristoffer Tabori, Fredricka Weber

1970-71: Clifton Davis, Michael Douglas, Julie Garfield, Martha Henry, James Naughton, Tricia O'Neil, Kipp Osborne, Roger Rathburn, Ayn Ruymen, Jennifer Salt, Joan Van Ark, Walter Willison

1971-72: Jonelle Allen, Maureen Anderman, William Atherton, Richard Backus, Adrienne Barbeau, Cara Duff-MacCormick, Robert Foxworth, Elaine Joyce, Jess Richards, Ben Vereen, Beatrice Winde, James Woods

1972-73: D'Jamin Bartlett, James Farentino, Brian Farrell, Victor Garber, Kelly Garrett, Mari Gorman, Laurence Guittard, Trish Hawkins, Monte Markham, John Rubinstein, Jennifer Warren, Alexander H. Cohen (Special Award)

1973-74: Mark Baker, Maureen Brennan, Ralph Carter, Thom Christopher, John Driver, Conchata Ferrell, Ernestine Jackson, Michael Moriarty, Joe Morton, Ann Reinking, Janie Sell, Mary Woronov, Sammy Cahn (Special Award)

1974-75: Peter Burnell, Zan Charisse, Lola Falana, Peter Firth, Dorian Harewood, Joel Higgins, Marcia McClain, Linda Miller, Marti Rolph, John Sheridan, Scott Stevensen, Donna Theodore, Equity Library Theatre (Special Award)

1975-76: Danny Aiello, Christine Andreas, Dixie Carter, Tovah Feldshuh, Chip Garnett, Richard Kelton, Vivian Reed, Charles Repole, Virginia Seidel, Daniel Seltzer, John V. Shea, Meryl Streep, A Chorus Line (Special Award)

1976-77: Trazana Beverley, Michael Cristofer, Joe Fields, Joanna Gleason, Cecilia Hart, John Heard, Gloria Hodes, Juliette Koka, Andrea McArdle, Ken Page, Jonathan Pryce, Chick Vennera, Eva LeGallienne (Special Award)

1977-78: Vasili Bogazianos, Nell Carter, Carlin Glynn, Christopher Goutman, William Hurt, Judy Kaye, Florence Lacy, Armelia McQueen, Gordana Rashovich, Bo Rucker, Richard Seer, Colin Stinton, Joseph Papp (Special Award)

1978-79: Philip Anglim, Lucie Arnaz, Gregory Hines, Ken Jennings, Michael Jeter, Laurie Kennedy, Susan Kingsley, Christine Lahti, Edward James Olmos, Kathleen Quinlan, Sarah Rice, Max Wright, Marshall W. Mason (Special Award)

1979-80: Maxwell Caulfield, Leslie Denniston, Boyd Gaines, Richard Gere, Harry Groener, Stephen James, Susan Kellermann, Dinah Manoff, Lonny Price, Marianne Tatum, Anne Twomey, Dianne Wiest, Mickey Rooney (Special Award)

1980-81: Brian Backer, Lisa Banes, Meg Bussert, Michael Allen Davis, Giancarlo Esposito, Daniel Gerroll, Phyllis Hyman, Cynthia Nixon, Amanda Plummer, Adam Redfield, Wanda Richert, Rex Smith, Elizabeth Taylor (Special Award)

1981-82: Karen Akers, Laurie Beechman, Danny Glover, David Alan Grier, Jennifer Holliday, Anthony Heald, Lizbeth Mackay, Peter MacNicol, Elizabeth McGovern, Ann Morrison, Michael O'Keefe, James Widdoes, Manhatten Theatre Club (Special Award)

1982-83: Karen Allen, Suzanne Bertish, Matthew Broderick, Kate Burton, Joanne Camp, Harvey Fierstein, Peter Gallagher, John Malkovich, Anne Pitoniak, James Russo, Brian Tarantina, Linda Thorson, Natalia Makarova (Special)

1983-84: Martine Allard, Joan Allen, Kathy Whitton Baker, Mark Capri, Laura Dean, Stephen Geoffreys, Todd Graff, Glenne Headly, J. J. Johnston, Bonnie Koloc, Calvin Levels, Robert Westenberg, Ron Moody (Special)

1984-85: Kevin Anderson, Richard Chaves, Patti Cohenour, Charles S. Dutton, Nancy Giles, Whoopi Goldberg, Leilani Jones, John Mahoney, Laurie Metcalf, Barry Miller, John Turturro, Amelia White, Lucille Lortel (Special)

1985-86: Suzy Amis, Alec Baldwin, Aled Davies, Faye Grant, Julie Hagerty, Ed Harris, Mark Jacoby, Donna Kane, Cleo Laine, Howard McGillin, Marisa Tomei, Joe Urla, Ensemble Studio Theatre (Special)

1986-87: Annette Bening, Timothy Daly, Lindsay Duncan, Frank Ferrante, Robert Lindsay, Amy Madigan, Michael Maguire, Demi Moore, Molly Ringwald, Frances Ruffelle, Courtney B. Vance, Colm Wilkinson, Robert DeNiro (Special)

1987-88: Yvonne Bryceland, Philip Casnoff, Danielle Ferland, Melissa Gilbert, Linda Hart, Linzi Hateley, Brian Kerwin, Brian Mitchell, Mary Murfitt, Aidan Quinn, Eric Roberts, B. D. Wong

1988-89: Dylan Baker, Joan Cusack, Loren Dean , Peter Frechette, Sally Mayes, Sharon McNight, Jennie Moreau, Paul Provenza, Kyra Sedgwick, Howard Spiegel, Eric Stoltz, Joanne Whalley-Kilmer Special: Pauline Collins, Mikhail Baryshnikov

1990 THEATRE WORLD AWARD RECIPIENTS
(OUTSTANDING NEW TALENT)

DENISE BURSE-MICKELBURY
of "Ground People"

ROCKY CARROLL
of "The Piano Lesson"

TOMMY HOLLIS
of "The Piano Lesson"

ERMA CAMPBELL
of "Ground People"

179

MEGAN GALLAGHER
of "A Few Good Men"

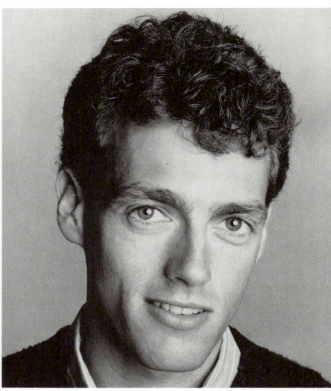

ROBERT LAMBERT
of "Gypsy"

MICHAEL McKEAN
of "Accomplice"

KATHLEEN ROWE McALLEN
of "Aspects of Love"

CRISTA MOORE
of "Gypsy"

DANIEL von BARGEN
of "Mastergate"

JASON WORKMAN
of "Meet Me in St. Louis"

MARY-LOUISE PARKER
of "Prelude to a Kiss"

THEATRE WORLD AWARDS presented Monday, June 4, 1990 on the set of "Price of Fame" in the Roundabout Theatre.
Top Left: Linda Thorson, D'Jamin Bartlett, Elizabeth McGovern; Lonny Price, Melba Moore (no show), Danny Aiello, Tammy Grimes, Robert Morse, Linda Thorson, John Willis, Bernadette Peters, James Naughton, Elizabeth McGovern, John Rubinstein, Carol Lynley, James Mitchell; Douglas Watt Below: Don Nute; Danny Aiello, Linda Thorson, Denise Burse-Mickelbury; Elliot Martin; James Naughton, Megan Gallagher; Jason Workman, Tammy Grimes; Bottom: Robert Morse, Kathleen Rowe McAllen; Michael McKean; Linda Thorson, Robert Lambert, D'Jamin Bartlett; James Mitchell; Kathleen Turner Above: Carol London accepting for Erma Campbell; Lonny Price; Carol Lynley; Rocky Carroll; Bernadette Peters

Photos by Michael Riordan, Michael Viade, Van Williams

Top: (L-R) Tommy Hollis, Crista Moore, John Rubinstein, Elizabeth McGovern, Daniel von Bargen, Mary-Louise Parker
Below: Robert Lambert, Tyne Daly, Crista Moore; Linda Thorson, James Naughton; Jason Workman, Kathleen Turner,
Robert Lambert Bottom: Louise Owens, Michael Viade, Evan Romero, Aileen Willis; Joan Bennett, John McMartin; Lucille
Lortel; Jason Workman, Crista Moore, Robert Lambert; Cristina Phillips, Evan Romero Above: Robert Morse, James
Naughton; Tony Musante, Aaron Sorkin, Anne Pitoniak, Megan Gallagher; John Sala, Bernadette Peters; James Noble,
Carolyn Coates, Rosemary Murphy, Jaime Sanchez

Photos by Michael Riordan, Michael Viade, Van Williams

PULITZER PRIZE PRODUCTIONS

1918-Why Marry? **1919**-No award, **1920**-Beyond the Horizon, **1921**-Miss Lulu Bett, **1922**-Anna Christie, **1923**-Icebound, **1924**-Hell-Bent fer Heaven, **1925**-They Knew What They Wanted, **1926**-Craig's Wife, **1927**-In Abraham's Bosom, **1928**-Strange Interlude, **1929**-Street Scene, **1930**-The Green Pastures, **1931**-Alison's House, **1932**-Of Thee I Sing, **1933**-Both Your Houses, **1934**-Men in White, **1935**-The Old Maid, **1936**-Idiot's Delight, **1937**-You Can't Take It with You, **1938**-Our Town, **1939**-Abe Lincoln in Illinois, **1940**-The Time of Your Life, **1941**-There Shall Be No Night, **1942**-No award, **1943**-The Skin of Our Teeth, **1944**-No award, **1945**-Harvey, **1946**-State of the Union, **1947**-No award, **1948**-A Streetcar Named Desire, **1949**-Death of a Salesman, **1950**-South Pacific, **1951**-No award, **1952**-The Shrike, **1953**-Picnic, **1954**-The Teahouse of the August Moon, **1955**-Cat on a Hot Tin Roof, **1956**-The Diary of Anne Frank, **1957**-Long Day's Journey into Night, **1958**-Look Homeward, Angel, **1959**-J. B., **1960**-Fiorello!, **1961**-All the Way Home, **1962**-How to Succeed in Business without Really Trying, **1963**-No award, **1964**-No award, **1965**-The Subject Was Roses, **1966**-No award, **1967**-A Delicate Balance, **1968**-No award, **1969**-The Great White Hope, **1970**-No Place to Be Somebody, **1971**-The Effect of Gamma Rays on Man-in-the-Moon Marigolds, **1972**-No award, **1973**-That Championship Season, **1974**-No award, **1975**-Seascape, **1976**-A Chorus Line, **1977**-The Shadow Box, **1978**-The Gin Game, **1979**-Buried Child, **1980**-Talley's Folly, **1981**-Crimes of the Heart, **1982**-A Soldier's Play, **1983**-'night, Mother, **1984**-Glengarry Glen Ross, **1985**-Sunday in the Park with George, **1986**-No award, **1987**-Fences, **1988**-Driving Miss Daisy, **1989**-The Heidi Chronicles, **1990**-The Piano Lesson

NEW YORK DRAMA CRITICS CIRCLE AWARDS

1936-Winterset, **1937**-High Tor, **1938**-Of Mice and Men, Shadow and Substance, **1939**-The White Steed, **1940**-The Time of Your Life, **1941**-Watch on the Rhine, The Corn is Green, **1942**-Blithe Spirit, **1943**-The Patriots, **1944**-Jacobowsky and the Colonel, **1945**-The Glass Menagerie, **1946**-Carousel, **1947**-All My Sons, No Exit, Brigadoon, **1948**-A Streetcar Named Desire, The Winslow Boy, **1949**-Death of a Salesman, The Madwoman of Chaillot, South Pacific, **1950**-The Member of the Wedding, The Cocktail Party, The Consul, **1951**-Darkness at Noon, The Lady's Not for Burning, Guys and Dolls, **1952**-I Am a Camera, Venus Observed, Pal Joey, **1953**- Picnic, The Love of Four Colonels, Wonderful Town, **1954**-Teahouse of the August Moon, Ondine, The Golden Apple, **1955**-Cat on a Hot Tin Roof, Witness for the Prosecution, The Saint of Bleecker Street, **1956**-The Diary of Anne Frank, Tiger at the Gates, My Fair Lady, **1957**-Long Day's Journey into Night, The Waltz of the Toreadors, The Most Happy Fella, **1958**-Look Homeward Angel, Look Back in Anger, The Music Man, **1959**-A Raisin in the Sun, The Visit, La Plume de Ma Tante, **1960**-Toys in the Attic, Five Finger Exercise, Fiorello! **1961**-All the Way Home, A Taste of Honey, Carnival, **1962**-Night of the Iguana, A Man for All Seasons, How to Succeed in Business without Really Trying, **1963**-Who's Afraid of Virginia Woolf?, **1964**-Luther, Hello Dolly!, **1965**-The Subject Was Roses, Fiddler on the Roof, **1966**-The Persecution and Assassination of Marat as Performed by the Inmates of the Asylum of Charenton under the Direction of the Marquis de Sade, Man of La Mancha, **1967**-The Homecoming, Cabaret, **1968**-Rosencrantz and Guildenstern Are Dead, Your Own Thing, **1969**-The Great White Hope, 1776, **1970**-The Effect of Gamma Rays on Man-in-the-Moon Marigolds, Borstal Boy, Company, **1971**-Home, Follies, The House of Blue Leaves, **1972**-That Championship Season, Two Gentlemen of Verona, **1973**-The Hot l Baltimore, The Changing Room, A Little Night Music, **1974**-The Contractor, Short Eyes, Candide, **1975**-Equus, The Taking of Miss Janie, A Chorus Line, **1976**-Travesties, Streamers, Pacific Overtures, **1977**-Otherwise Engaged, American Buffalo, Annie, **1978**-Da, Ain't Misbehavin', **1979**-The Elephant Man, Sweeney Todd, **1980**-Talley's Folly, Evita, Betrayal, **1981**-Crimes of the Heart, A Lesson from Aloes, Special Citation to Lena Horne, The Pirates of Penzance, **1982**-The Life and Adventures of Nicholas Nickleby, A Soldier's Play, (no musical honored) **1983**-Brighton Beach Memoirs, Plenty, Little Shop of Horrors, **1984**-The Real Thing, Glengarry Glen Ross, Sunday in the Park with George, **1985**-Ma Rainey's Black Bottom, no musical, **1986**-A Lie of the Mind, Benefactors, no musical, Special to Lily Tomlin and Jane Wagner, **1987**-Fences, Les Liaisons Dangereuses, Les Misérables, **1988**-Joe Turner's Come and Gone, The Road to Mecca, Into the Woods, **1989**-The Heidi Chronicles, Aristocrats, Largely New York (Special), no musical. **1990**-The Piano Lesson, City of Angels, Privates on Parade

AMERICAN THEATRE WING ANTOINETTE PERRY (TONY) AWARD PRODUCTIONS
(Play, Musical, Revival)

1948-Mister Roberts, **1949**-Death of a Salesman, Kiss Me, Kate, **1950**-The Cocktail Party, South Pacific, **1951**-The Rose Tattoo, Guys and Dolls, **1952**-The Fourposter, The King and I, **1953**-The Crucible, Wonderful Town, **1954**-The Teahouse of the August Moon, Kismet, **1955**-The Desperate Hours, The Pajama Game, **1956**-The Diary of Anne Frank, Damn Yankees, **1957**-Long Day's Journey into Night, My Fair Lady, **1958**-Sunrise at Campobello, The Music Man, **1959**-J. B., Redhead, **1960**-The Miracle Worker, Fiorello! tied with The Sound of Music, **1961**-Becket, Bye Bye Birdie, **1962**-A Man for All Seasons, How to Succeed in Business without Really Trying, **1963**-Who's Afraid of Virginia Woolf?, A Funny Thing Happened on the Way to the Forum, **1964**-Luther, Hello Dolly!, **1965**-The Subject Was Roses, Fiddler on the Roof, **1966**-The Persecution and Assassination of Marat as Performed by the Inmates of the Asylum of Charenton under the Direction of the Marquis de Sade, Man of La Mancha, **1967**-The Homecoming, Cabaret, **1968**-Rosencrantz and Guildenstern Are Dead, Hallelujah Baby!, **1969**-The Great White Hope, 1776, **1970**-Borstal Boy, Applause, **1971**-Sleuth, Company, **1972**-Sticks and Bones, Two Gentlemen of Verona, **1973**-That Championship Season, A Little Night Music, **1974**-The River Niger, Raisin, **1975**-Equus, The Wiz, **1976**-Travesties, A Chorus Line, **1977**-The Shadow Box, Annie, **1978**-Da, Ain't Misbehavin', Dracula, **1979**-The Elephant Man, Sweeney Todd, **1980**-Children of a Lesser God, Evita, Morning's at Seven, **1981**-Amadeus, 42nd Street, The Pirates of Penzance, **1982**-The Life and Adventures of Nicholas Nickleby, Nine, Othello, **1983**-Torch Song Trilogy, Cats, On Your Toes, **1984**-The Real Thing, La Cage aux Folles, **1985**-Biloxi Blues, Big River, Joe Egg, **1986**-I'm Not Rappaport, The Mystery of Edwin Drood, Sweet Charity, **1987**-Fences, Les Miserables, All My Sons, **1988**-M. Butterfly, The Phantom of the Opera, Anything Goes, **1989**-The Heidi Chronicles, Jerome Robbins' Broadway, Our Town, **1990**-The Grapes of Wrath, City of Angels, Gypsy

Ernest
Abuba

Karen
Akers

Jace
Alexander

Joan
Allen

Gregg
Almquist

Brooks
Almy

BIOGRAPHICAL DATA ON THIS SEASON'S CASTS

AARON, JACK. Born May 1, 1933 in NYC. Attended Hunter College, Actors Workshop. OB in "Swim Low Little Goldfish," "Journey of the 5th Horse," "The Nest," "One Flew over the Cuckoo's Nest," "The Birds," "The Pornographer's Daughter," "Love Death Plays," "Unlikely Heroes," "Taking Steam," "Mark VIII: xxxvi," "Made in Heaven."

ABATEMARCO, TONY. Born Mar. 15, 1952 in Brooklyn, NY. Graduate Juilliard. OB debut 1980 in "Diary of a Madman" followed by "Slow Motion", "King Fish."

ABUBA, ERNEST. Born Aug. 25, 1947 in Honolulu, HI. Attended Southwestern College. Bdwy debut 1976 in "Pacific Overtures," followed by "Loose Ends," "Zoya's Apartment," OB in "Sunrise," "Monkey Music," "Station J.," "Yellow Fever," "Pacific Overtures," "Empress of China," "The Man Who Turned into a Stick," "Shogun Macbeth," "Three Sisters," "Song of Shim Chung."

ACKERMAN, LONI. Born Apr. 10, 1949 in NYC. Attended New School. Bdwy debut 1968 in "George M!," followed by "No, No Nanette," "So Long 174th Street," "The Magic Show," "Evita," "Cats," OB in "Dames at Sea," "Starting Here Starting Now," "Roberta in Concert," "Brownstone," "Diamonds."

ADAMS, BROOKE. Born in New York City in 1949. Attended Dalton School. Debut 1974 OB in "The Petrified Forest," followed by "Split," "Key Exchange," "Linda Her," Bdwy in "The Heidi Chronicles" (1990).

ADAMSON, DAVID. Born May 30, 1940 in Orange, NJ. Graduate Bucknell, Yale. Bdwy debut 1971 in "Unlikely Heroes," followed by "Full Circle," "Hamlet," "Hide and Seek," "Children of a Lesser God," OB in "Isadora Duncan Sleeps with the Russian Navy," "Sister Aimee," "Hamlet," "Happy Birthday, Wanda June," "Henry V," "Ice Bridge," "Camp Meeting," "The Strike," "The Ambassador."

AHEARN, DANIEL. Born Aug. 7, 1948 in Washington, DC. Attended Carnegie-Mellon. Debut OB 1981 in "Woyzek," followed by "Brontosaurus Rex," "Billy Liar," "Second Prize Two Months in Leningrad," "No Time Flat," "Hollywood Scheherazade."

A'HEARN, PATRICK. Born Sept. 4, 1957 in Cortland, NY. Graduate Syracuse U. Debut 1985 OB in "Pirates of Penzance," followed by "Forbidden Broadway," followed by Bdwy in "Les Miserables" (1987).

AIDEM, BETSY. Born Oct. 28, 1957 in Eastmeadow, NY. Graduate NYU. Debut 1981 OB in "The Trading Post," followed by "A Different Moon," "Balm in Gilead," "Crossing the Bar," "Our Lady of the Tortilla," "Steel Magnolias," "Road."

AKERS, KAREN. Born Oct. 13, 1945 in NYC. Graduate Hunter College. Bdwy debut 1982 in "Nine" for which she received a Theatre World Award, followed by "Jacques Brel Is Alive and Well and Living in New York," "Grand Hotel."

ALDRICH, JANET. (formerly Aldridge). Born Oct. 16, 1956 in Hinsdale, IL. UMiami graduate. Debut 1979 OB in "A Funny Thing Happened on the Way to the Forum," followed by "American Princess," "The Men's Group," "Wanted Dead or Alive," "The Comedy of Errors," Bdwy in "Annie" (1982), "The Three Musketeers," "Broadway," "Starmites."

ALEXANDER, JACE. Born Apr. 7, 1964 in NYC. Attended NYU. Bdwy debut 1983 in "The Caine Mutiny Court Martial," OB in "I'm Not Rappaport," followed by "Wasted," "The Good Coach," "Heart of a Dog," "Price of Fame."

ALEXANDER, JASON. Born Sept. 23, 1959 in Irvington, NJ. Attended Boston U. Bdwy debut 1981 in "Merrily We Roll Along," followed by "The Rink," "Broadway Bound," "Jerome Robbins' Broadway," "Accomplice," OB in "Forbidden Broadway," "Stop the World. . . .," "D.," "Personals."

ALLEN, JOAN. Born Aug. 20, 1956 in Rochelle, IL. Attended E. Ill. U., W. Ill. U. Debut 1983 OB in "And a Nightingale Sang" for which she received a Theatre World Award, followed by "The Marriage of Bette and Boo," "Marathon '86," "Burn This," "The Heidi Chronicles," Bdwy 1987 in "Burn This," followed by "The Heidi Chronicles."

ALLESSAN, HENRY. Born May 26, 1959 in Toronto, Can. Bdwy debut 1989 in "Shenandoah."

ALLINSON, MICHAEL. Born in London, Eng. Attended RADA. Bdwy debut 1960 in "My Fair Lady," followed by "Hostile Witness," "Come Live with Me," "Coco," "Angel Street," "My Fair Lady" (1981), "Oliver!," OB in "The Importance of Being Earnest," "Staircase," "Loud Bang on June 1st," "Good and Faithful Servant," "The Nuns."

ALLISON, PATTI. Born June 26, 1942 in St. Louis, Mo. Graduate Webster Col., Ind. U. Broadway debut 1978 in "Angel," followed by "Orpheus Descending."

ALMQUIST, GREGG. Born Dec. 1, 1948 in Minneapolis, MN. Graduate UMinn. Debut 1974 OB in "Richard III," followed by "A Night at the Black Pig," "Mother Courage," "King Lear," "Algerian Romance," "Doctor's Dilemma," Bdwy in "I'm Not Rappaport" (1986)

ALMY, BROOKS. Born July 15 in Fort Belvoir, Va. Attended UHawaii. Bdwy debut 1981 in "The Little Prince and the Aviator," followed by NYCOpera's "Music Man," "Candide," "Sweeney Todd" and "Pajama Game," "A Change in the Heir," OB in "Shylock," "Nunsense."

AMOS, JOHN. Born Dec. 27, 1940 in Newark, NJ. Attended ColU. Bdwy debut 1972 in "Tough to Get Help," OB in "Split Second," "Twelfth Night," "The Past Is the Past."

ANDERSON, CHRISTINE. Born Aug. 6 in Utica, NY. Graduate UWi. Bdwy debut in "I Love My Wife" (1980), OB in "I Can't Keep Running in Place," "On the Swing Shift," "Red, Hot and Blue," "A Night at Texas Guinan's," "Nunsense."

ANDERSON, JOEL. Born Nov. 19, 1955 in San Diego, CA. Graduate UUtah. Debut 1980 OB in "A Funny Thing Happened on the Way to the Forum," followed by "Joan of Lorraine," "Last of the Knucklemen," "The Widow Claire," "The Heidi Chronicles," "Fighting Light."

ANDERSON, KEVIN. Born Jan. 13, 1960 in Illinois. Attended Goodman School. Debut 1985 OB in "Orphans," for which he received a Theatre World Award, followed by "Moonchildren," "Brilliant Traces," Bdwy in "Orpheus Descending" (1989).

ANDREWS, GEORGE LEE. Born Oct. 13, 1942 in Milwaukee, Wi. Debut OB 1970 in "Jacques Brel Is Alive and Well . . .," followed by "Starting Here Starting Now," "Vamps and Rideouts," "The Fantasticks," Bdwy in "A Little Night Music" (1973), "On the 20th Century," "Merlin," "The Phantom of the Opera."

ANDREYKO, HELENA. Born Feb. 6, 1956 in Philadelphia, Pa. Attended Hunter Col. Bdwy debut 1976 in "Music Is," followed by "Zoot Suit," "American Dance Machine," OB in "American Passion," "Elvis: A Rockin' Remembrance."

ANGELA, JUNE. Born Aug. 18, 1959 in NYC. Bdwy debut 1970 in Lovely Ladies, Kind Gentlemen," followed by "The King and I" (1977), OB in "Kitamura," "Aldersgate '88," "Song of Shim Chung."

ANKENY, MARK. Born Oct. 9, 1958 in Austin, Mn. Attended UMin. Debut 1985 OB in "She Loves Me," followed by "Murder Game," "Hannah 1939."

AQUINO, AMY. Born Mar. 20, 1957 in Teaneck, NJ. Graduate Radcliffe, Yale. Debut 1988 OB in "Cold Sweat," followed by "Right Behind the Flag," Bdwy 1989 in "The Heidi Chronicles."

ARCARO, ROBERT (a.k.a. Bob) Born Aug. 9, 1952 in Brooklyn, NY. Graduate WesleyanU. Debut 1977 OB in "New York City Street Show," followed by "Working Theatre Festival," "Man with a Raincoat," "Working One-Acts," "Henry Lumpur," "Special Interests."

ARI, BOB. Born July 1, 1949 in NYC. Graduate Carnegie-Mellon U. Debut 1976 OB in "The Boys from Syracuse," followed by "Gay Divorce," "Devour the Snow," "Carbondale Dreams."

ARLT, LEWIS. Born Dec. 5, 1949 in Kingston, NY. Graduate Carnegie Tech. Bdwy debut 1975 in "Murder among Friends," followed by "Piaf," "Orpheus Descending," OB in "War and Peace," "The Interview," "Applause," "The House across the Street," "Real Estate."

ARMITAGE, CALVIN LENNON. Born 1982. Debut 1989 OB in "Member of the Wedding," Bdwy in "The Grapes of Wrath" (1990).

ARMUS, SIDNEY. Born Dec. 19, 1924 in The Bronx, NY. Attended Brooklyn Col. Credits include "South Pacific," "Wish You Were Here," "The Flowering Peach," "A Hole in the Head,": The Cold Wind and the Warm," "Harold," "A Thousand Clowns," "Never Live over a Pretzel Factory," "The Odd Couple," "Cafe Crown," "Tenth Man."

ARRIGO, NANCY. Born Feb. 23, 1962 in Baltimore, Md. Graduate NYU. Debut 1985 OB in "Macbeth," followed by "Davy Crockett," "Othello," "The Lion in Winter."

ASHLEY, ELIZABETH. Born Aug. 30, 1939 in Ocala, FL. Attended Neighborhood Playhouse. Bdwy debut 1959 in "The Highest Tree," followed by "Take Her, She's Mine" for which she received a Theatre World Award, "Barefoot in the Park," "Ring Round the Bathtub," "Cat on a Hot Tin Roof," "The Skin of Our Teeth," "Legend," "Caesar and Cleopatra," "Hide and Seek," "Agnes of God," OB in "The Milk Train Doesn't Stop Here Anymore," "When She Danced."

ASNER, EDWARD. Born Nov. 15, 1929 in Kansas City, Ks. Graduate UChicago. OB in "Threepenny Opera," "Hamlet," "Ivanov," Bdwy in "Face of a Hero" (1960), "Born Yesterday" (1989)

ATKINS, EILEEN. Born June 16, 1934 in London, Eng. Attended Guildhall School. Bdwy debut 1966 in "The Killing of Sister George," followed by "The Promise," "Vivat! Vivat Regina!," "The Night of the Tribades," OB in "Prin."

ATKINSON, JAYNE. Born Feb. 18, 1959 in Bournemouth, Eng. Graduate Northwestern U., Yale. Debut 1986 OB in "Bloody Poetry," followed by "Terminal Bar," "Return of Pinocchio," "The Art of Success," Bdwy in "All My Sons" (1987).

AUBERJONOIS, RENE. Born June 1, 1940 in NYC. Graduate Carnegie Inst. With LCRep in "A Cry of Players," "King Lear," and "Twelfth Night," Bdwy in "Fire (1969)," "Coco," "Tricks," "The Good Doctor," "Break a Leg," "Every Good Boy Deserves Favor," "Big River," "Metamorphosis," "City of Angels," BAM Co. in "The New York Idea," "Three Sisters," "The Play's the Thing," and "Julius Caesar."

AUGUSTINE, JOHN. Born Mar. 5, 1960 in Canton, OH. Attended Baldwin-White College. Debut 1988 OB in "Young Playwrights Festival '88," followed by "Insatiable/Temporary People."

AVIDON, NELSON. Born Feb. 23, 1957 in Brooklyn, NY. Debut 1987 OB in "Second Avenue," followed by "The Green Death," "Cheapside," "Chee-Chee," "Three Sisters," "Unnatural Acts," "Progress."

AVNER, JON. Born June 24, 1953 in NYC. Graduate SyracuseU, St. John's U. Debut 1986 OB in "Murder on Broadway," followed by "Radio Roast," "Crimes of Passion," "World of Sholem Aleichem," "Penguin Blues," "Rasputin," "Sarah."

BACKUS, RICHARD. Born Mar. 28, 1945 in Goffstown, NH. Harvard graduate. Bdwy debut 1971 in "Butterflies Are Free," followed by "Promenade All," for which he received a Theatre World Award, "Ah, Wilderness!," "Camelot" (1981), OB in "Studs Edsel," "Gimme Shelter," "Sorrows of Stephen," "Missing Persons," "Henry V," "Talley and Son," "Tomorrow's Monday," "Bunker Reveries," "The Cocktail Hour."

BACON, KEVIN. Born July 8, 1958 in Philadelphia, PA. Debut OB 1978 in "Getting Out," followed by "Glad Tidings," "Album," "Flux," "Poor Little Lambs," "Slab Boys," "Men without Dates," "Loot," "The Author's Voice," "Road."

BAEZ, RAFAEL. Born Aug. 3, 1963 in NYC. Attended CCNY. Debut 1987 OB in "La Puta Vita," followed by "Enough Is Enough," "Ariano," "Kate's Diary."

BAGNERIS, VERNEL. Born July 31, 1949 in New Orleans, La. Graduate Xavier U. Debut 1979 OB in "One Mo' Time," followed by "Staggerlee," "Further Mo' " all of which he wrote and directed.

BAILEY, ADRIAN. Born Sept. 23 in Detroit, MI. Graduate UDetroit. Bdwy debut 1976 in "Your Arms Too Short to Box with God," followed by "Prince of Central Park," OB in "A Thrill a Moment."

BAKER, DYLAN. Born in Lackey, VA. Graduate Wm & Mary, Yale. Debut 1985 OB in "Not about Heroes," followed by "Two Gentlemen of Verona," "The Common Pursuit," "Much Ado about Nothing," "Eastern Standard," "Wolf-Man," Bdwy (1989) in "Eastern Standard" for which he received a Theatre World Award.

BALABAN, BOB. Born Aug. 16, 1945 in Chicago, IL. Attended Colgate, NYU. Debut 1967 OB in "You're a Good Man, Charlie Brown," followed by "Up Eden," "White House Murder Case," "Basic Training of Pavlo Hummel," "The Children," "Marie and Bruce," "Three Sisters," "Some American's Abroad," Bdwy in "Plaza Suite" (1968), "Some of My Best Friends," "Inspector General," "Speed-the-Plow."

BALDWIN, ALEC. Born Apr. 3, 1958 in Massapequa, NY. Attended George Washington U, NYU. Bdwy debut 1986 in "Loot" for which he received a Theatre World Award, followed by "Serious Money," OB in "Prelude to a Kiss."

BALL, MICHAEL. Born during July 1963 in Stratford-on-Avon, Eng. Bdwy debut 1990 in "Aspects of Love."

BALLINGER, JUNE. Born Nov. 15, 1949 in Camden, NJ. Attended Briarcliff Col. Debut 1980 OB in "Mr. Wilson's Peace of Mind," followed by "Dona Rosita," "A Man in the House," "Human Nature."

BAMMAN, GERRY. Born Sept. 18, 1941 in Independence, Ks. Graduate XavierU, NYU. Debut 1970 OB in "Alice in Wonderland," followed by "All Night Long," "Richard III," "Oedipus Rex," "A Midsummer Night's Dream," "He and She," "Johnny on the Spot," "Museum," "Henry V," "Our Late Night," "The Seagull," "Endgame," "Road," Bdwy "Accidental Death of an Anarchist" (1984), "Execution of Justice."

BANES, LISA. Born July 9, 1955 in Chagrin Falls, OH. Juilliard graduate. Debut OB 1980 in "Elizabeth I," followed by "A Call from the East," "Look Back in Anger," for which she received a Theatre World Award, "My Sister in This House," "Antigone," "Three Sisters," "The Cradle Will Rock," "Isn't It Romantic?," "Fighting International Fat," "Ten by Tennessee," "On the Verge," "Emily," Bdwy in "Rumors"

BARAN, EDWARD. Born May 18, 1950 in Minneapolis, Mn. Graduate Williams Col. Debut 1984 OB in "Fool's Errand," followed by "The Wonder Years," "The Sneaker Factory," "Cezanne Syndrome," "The Year of the Baby."

BARANSKI, CHRISTINE. Born May 2, 1952 in Buffalo, NY. Graduate Juilliard. Debut OB 1978 in "One Crack Out," followed by "Says I Says He," "The Trouble With Europe," "Coming Attractions," "Operation Midnight Climax," "Sally and Marsha," "A Midsummer Night's Dream," "It's Only a Play," "Marathon '86," "Elliot Loves," Bdwy in "Hide and Seek," (1980), "The Real Thing," "Hurlyburly," "House of Blue Leaves," "Rumors."

BARBOUR, THOMAS. Born July 25, 1921 in NYC. Graduate Princeton, Harvard. Bdwy debut 1968 in "Portrait of a Queen," followed by "The Great White Hope," "Scratch," "Lincoln Mask," "Kingdoms," OB in "Twelfth Night," "Merchant of Venice," "Admirable Bashful," "The Lady's Not for Burning," "The Enchanted," "Antony and Cleopatra," "The Saintliness of Margery Kemp," "Dr. Willy Nilly," "Under the Sycamore Tree," "Epitaph for George Dillon," "Thracian Horses," "Old Glory," "Sgt. Musgrave's Dance," "Nestless Bird," "The Seagull," "Wayside Motor Inn," "Arthur," "The Grinding Machine," "Mr. Simian," "Sorrows of Frederick," "Terrorists," "Dark Ages," "Royal Bob," "Relatively Speaking," "Aristocrats."

BARON, EVALYN. Born Apr. 21, 1948 in Atlanta, Ga. Graduate NorthwesternU, UMin. Debut 1979 OB in "Scrambled Feet," followed by "Hijinks," "I Can't Keep Running in Place," "Jerry's Girls," "Harvest of Strangers," "Quilters," Bdwy in "Fearless Frank" (1980), "Big River," "Rags," "Social Security," "Les Miserables."

BARRE, GABRIEL. Born Aug. 26, 1957 in Brattleboro, VT. Graduate AADA. Debut 1977 OB in "Jabberwock," followed by "T.N.T.," "Bodo," "The Baker's Wife," "The Time of Your Life," "Children of the Sun," "Wicked Philanthropy," "Starmites," "Mistress of the Inn," "Gifts of the Magi," "Tempest," Bdwy in "Rags" (1986), "Starmites."

BARRETT, BRENT. Born Feb. 28, 1957 in Quinter, Ks. Graduate Carnegie-MellonU. Bdwy debut 1980 in "West Side Story," followed by "Dance a Little Closer," "Grand Hotel," OB in "March of the Falsettos," "Portrait of Jenny," "The Death of Von Richthofen," "Sweethearts in Concert," "What's a Nice Country like You . . .," "Time of the Cuckoo," "Swan Song," "Closer than Ever."

BARRETT, LAURINDA. Born 1931 in NYC. Attended Wellesley Col., RADA. Bdwy debut 1956 in "Too Late the Phalatrope," followed by "The Girls in 509," "The Milk Train Doesn't Stop Here Anymore," "UTBU," "I Never Sang for My Father," "Equus," OB in "The Misanthrope," "Palm Tree in a Rose Garden," "All Is Bright," "The Carpenters," "Ah, Wilderness!," "The Other Side of Newark," "The Boys Next Door," "Phantasie."

BARRIE, BARBARA. Born May, 23, 1931 in Chicago, Il. Graduate UTx. Bdwy debut 1955 in "The Wooden Dish," followed by "Happily Never After," "Company," "Selling of the President," "Prisoner of Second Avenue," "California Suite," "Torch Song Trilogy," OB in "The Crucible," "Beaux Stratagem," "Taming of the Shrew," "Twelfth Night," "All's Well That Ends Well," "Horseman, Pass By," "Killdeer," "Big and Little," "Backer's Audition," "Isn't It Romantic," "Mi Vida Loca."

BARRON, DAVID. Born May 11, 1938 in Pilot Point, TX. Graduate Baylor U., Yale, UIll. Debut OB 1976 in "The Fantasticks," followed by "Trouble in Tahiti," "Sound of Music," "A Doll's House," "Feathertop," "Kiss Me Quick," "Sweeney Todd," Bdwy debut "Sweeney Todd" (1989).

BART, ROGER. Born Sept. 29, 1962 in Norwalk, Ct. Graduate RutgersU. Debut 1984 OB in "A Second Wind," followed by "Lessons," "Up against It," Bdwy in "Big River" (1987).

BARTENIEFF, GEORGE. Born Jan. 24, 1933 in Berlin, Ger. Bdwy debut 1947 in "The Whole World Over," followed by "Venus Is," "All's Well That Ends Well," "Quotations from Chairman Mao Tse-Tung," "The Death of Bessie Smith," "Cop-Out," "Room Service," "Unlikely Heroes," OB in "Walking to Waldheim," "Memorandum," "The Increased Difficulty of Concentration," "Trelawny of the Wells," "Charley Chestnut Rides the IRT," "Radio (Wisdom): Sophia Part I," "Images of the Dead," "Dead End Kids," "The Blonde Leading the Blonde," "The Dispossessed," "Growing Up Gothic," "Rosetti's Apologies," "On the Lam," "Samuel Beckett Trilogy," "Quartet," "Help Wanted," "A Matter of Life and Death," "The Heart That Eats Itself," "Coney Island Kid," "Cymbeline," "Better People."

BARTLETT, PETER. Born Aug. 28, 1942 in Chicago, IL. Attended LoyolaU. LAMDA. Bdwy debut 1969 in "A Patriot for Me," followed by "Gloria and Esperanza," OB in "Boom Boom Room," "I Remember the House Where I Was Born," "Crazy Locomotive," "A Thurber Carnival," "Hamlet," "Buzzsaw Berkeley."

BARTLETT, ROBIN. Born Apr. 22, 1951 in NYC. Graduate Boston U. Bdwy debut 1975 in "Yentl," followed by "The World of Sholem Aleichem," OB in "Agamemnon," "Fathers and Sons," "No End of Blame," "Living Quarters," "After the Fall," "Cheapside," "The Early Girl," "Reckless."

BARTON, STEVE. Born in Arkansas; Graduate UTexas. Bdwy debut 1988 in "Phantom of the Opera."

BATEMAN, JUSTINE. Born Feb. 19, 1966 in Rye, NY, Debut 1990 OB in "The Crucible."

BATT, BRYAN. Born March 1, 1963 in New Orleans, LA. Graduate Tulane U. Debut 1987 OB in "Too Many Girls," followed by "Golden Apple," Bdwy in "Starlight Express" (1988).

BAUM, JOANNE. Born June 30, 1960 in New Jersey. Graduate Boston Conservatory. Debut OB 1984 in "Kuni-Leml," followed by "A Flash of Lightning," "They Came from Planet Mirth."

BEAN, REATHEL. Born Aug. 24, 1942 in Missouri. Graduate Drake U. OB in "America Hurrah," "San Francisco's Burning," "Love Cure," "Henry IV," "In Circles," "Peace," "Journey of Snow White," "Wanted," "The Faggot," "Lovers," "Not Back with the Elephants," "The Art of Coarse Acting," "The Trip Back Down," "Hunting Cockroaches," "Smoke on the Mountain," Bdwy in "Doonesbury" (1983), "Big River."

BEARDEN, JIM. Born Aug. 21, 1943 in LaMesa, Tx. Graduate Little Rock U., UMis. Bdwy debut 1970 in "Chicago" (as Jim Lawrence), followed by "Shenandoah" (1989).

BECKMAN, CLAIRE. Born Apr. 16, 1961 in NYC. Graduate Carnegie-Mellon U. Debut OB in "Hamlet" (1990).

BEDFORD-LLOYD, JOHN. Born Jan. 2, 1956 in New Haven, Ct. Graduate Williams Col., Yale. Debut OB 1983 in "Vieux Carre," followed by "She Stoops to Conquer," "The Incredibly Famous Willy Rivers," "Digby," "Rum and Coke," "Trinity Site," "Richard II," "Some Americans Abroad" (also Bdwy 1990).

BEECHMAN, LAURIE. Born Apr. 4, 1954 in Philadelphia, Pa. Attended NYU. Bdwy debut 1977 in "Annie," followed by "Pirates of Penzance," "Joseph and the Amazing Technicolor Dreamcoat" for which she received a Theatre World Award, "Cats," "Les Miserables," OB in "Some Enchanted Evening," "Pal Joey in Concert."

BEERS, FRANCINE. Born Nov. 26 in NYC. Attended Hunter Col., CCNY. Debut 1962 OB in "King of the Whole Damned World," followed by "Kiss Mama," "Monopoly," "Cakes with Wine," "The Grandma Plays," Bdwy in "Cafe Crown," "6 Rms Riv Vu," "The American Clock," "Curse of an Aching Heart."

BEERY, LEIGH. Born March 20 in Minneapolis, Mn. Attended McPhail Sch. Debut 1965 OB in "Leonard Bernstein's Theatre Songs," followed by "Pic-a-Number," "Oklahoma!" (LC), "Lola," "Hannah 1939", Bdwy 1963 in "Cyrano."

BELACK, DORIS. Born Feb. 26 in NYC. Attended AADA. Debut 1956 OB in "World of Sholem Aleichem," followed by "P.S. 193," "Letters Home," "Marathon 87," "Emerald City," Bdwy in "Middle of the Night," "Owl and the Pussycat," "The Heroine," "You Know I Can't Hear You . . .," "90 Day Mistress," "Last of the Red Hot Lovers," "Bad Habits," "The Trip Back Down," "Social Security," "The Cemetery Club."

BELMONTE, VICKI. Born Jan. 20, 1947 in U.S.A. Bdwy debut 1960 in "Bye Bye Birdie," followed by "Subways Are for Sleeping," "All American," "Annie Get Your Gun" (LC), OB in "Nunsense."

BEN-ARI, NEAL. (formerly Neal Klein) Born March 20, 1952 in Brooklyn, NY, Graduate UPa. Bdwy debut 1981 in "The First" followed by "Roza," "Chess," "Merchant of Venice" (1989), OB in "La Boheme," "1-2-3-4-5."

BENDER, JEFF. Born May 20, 1962 in Oakland, CA. Attended Pacific Consv., NYU. Debut 1985 OB in "Second Hurricane," followed by "Alvrone," "Twelfth Night," "Angel City," "The Odyssey," "Bradley and Beth," "Carbondale Dreams."

BENHAM, DOROTHY. Born Dec. 11, 1955 in Minneapolis, MN. Attended Lawrence U., Macalester Col. Bdwy debut 1989 in "Jerome Robbins' Broadway."

BENNETT, LYNETTE. Born Nov. 5, 1937 in Hot Springs, AK. Attended UTulsa, UCLA. Debut OB 1960 in "Absolutely Time," followed by "Gigi," "Lion in Winter," Bdwy in "The Yearling," "Funny Girl."

BENSON, CINDY. Born Oct. 2, 1951 in Attleboro, Ma. Graduate St. Leo Col., UIll. Debut 1981 OB in "Some Like It Cole," followed by Bdwy "Les Miserables"(1987).

BERGEN, POLLY. Born July 14, 1930 in Knoxville, Tn. Bdwy debut 1953 in "John Murray Anderson's Almanac," followed by "Champagne Complex," "Love Letters."

BERGHOF, HERBERT. Born Sept. 13, 1909 in Vienna. NY debut 1942 in "Nathan the Wise," followed by "The Russian People," "Innocent Voyage," "Jacobowsky and the Colonel," "Temper the Wind," "The Whole World Over," "Miss Liberty," "Ghosts," "Hedda Gabler," "The Deep Blue Sea," "The Andersonville Trial," "Krapp's Last Tape," "The Tenth Man," "In the Matter of J. Robert Oppenheimer" (LC).

BERMAN, DAVID. Born Oct. 26, 1950 in Cleveland, Oh. Debut 1976 OB in "Marco Polo," followed by "Auto-Destruct," "Pins and Needles," "Chinchilla," "Getting Out," "Hunting Cockroaches," Bdwy in "Man and Superman" (1978), "The News," "The First," "Speed-the-Plow," "The Tenth Man."

BERNSTEIN, SUSAN. Born Dec. 13, 1965 in Manhasset, NY. Graduate Carnegie-Mellon U. Debut 1989 OB in "Slay It with Music."

BERRIDGE, ELIZABETH. Born May 2, 1962 in Westchester, NY. Attended Strasberg Inst, Debut 1984 OB in "The Vampires," followed by "The Incredibly Famous Willy Rivers," "Ground Zero Club," "Outside Waco," "Cruise Control," "Sorrows and Sons," "Crackwalker," "Coyote Ugly," "Briar Patch."

BERTISH, SUZANNE. Born Aug. 7, 1951 in London, Eng. Attended London Drama School. Bdwy debut 1981 in "Nicholas Nickleby," OB in "Skirmishes," (1982) for which she received a Theatre World Award, followed by "Rosmersholm," "Art of Success."

BERTRAND, JACQUELINE. Born June 1, 1939 in Quebec, Canada. Attended Neighborhood Playhouse, Actors Studio, LAMDA. Debut 1978 OB in "Unfinished Woman," followed by "Dancing for the Kaiser," "Lulu," "War and Peace," "Nest of the Wood Grouse," "Salon," "When She Danced."

BEVAN, ALISON. Born Nov. 20, 1959 in Cincinnati, OH. Attended NYU. Debut 1980 OB in "Trixie True Teen Detective," followed by "Brigadoon" (LC), "Little Lies."

BEVERLEY, TRAZANA. Born Aug. 9, 1945 in Baltimore, Md. Graduate NYU. Debut 1969 OB in "Rules for Running," followed by "Les Femmes Noires," "Geronimo," "Antigone," "The Brothers," "God's Trombones," Bdwy in "My Sister, My Sister," "For Colored Girls Who Have Considered Suicide" for which she received a Theatre World Award, "Death and the King's Horseman" (LC).

BICKELL, ROSS. Born Jan. 14, 1947 in Hackensack, NJ. Graduate Boston U Debut 1971 OB in "The Sweetshop Myrium," followed by "Privates on Parade," Bdwy in "A Few Good Men" (1990).

BIRKELUND, OLIVIA. Born Apr. 26, 1963 in NYC. Graduate Brown U. Debut 1990 OB in "Othello."

BIRNEY, REED. Born Sept. 11, 1954 in Alexandria, Va. Attended BostonU. Bdwy debut 1977 in "Gemini," OB in "The Master and Margarita," "Bella Figura," "Winterplay," "The Flight of the Earls," "Filthy Rich," "Lady Moonsong, Mr. Monsoon," "The Common Pursuit," "Zero Positive," "Moving Targets," "Spare Parts."

BISHOP, KELLY (formerly Carole). Born Feb. 28, 1944 in Colorado Springs, CO. Bdwy debut 1967 in "Golden Rainbow," followed by "Promises, Promises," "On the Town," "Rachel Lily Rosenbloom," "A Chorus Line," OB in "Piano Bar," "Changes," "The Blessing," "Going to New England," "Six Degrees of Separation."

BLAIR, PAMELA. Born Dec. 5, 1949 in Arlington, Vt. Attended Ntl. Acad. of Ballet. Bdwy debut 1972 in "Promises, Promises," followed by "Sugar," "Seesaw," "Of Mice and Men," "Wild and Wonderful," "A Chorus Line," "The Best Little Whorehouse in Texas," "King of Hearts," "The Nerd," "A Few Good Men," OB in "Ballad of Boris K," "Split," "Real Life Funnies," "Double Feature," "Hit Parade," "1-2-3-4-5."

BLAISDELL, NESBITT. Born Dec. 6, 1928 in NYC. Graduate Amherst, Columbia. Debut 1978 OB in "Old Man Joseph and His Family," followed by "Moliere in spite of Himself," "Guests of the Nation," "Chekhov Sketch Book," "Elba," "Ballad of Soapy Smith," "Custom of the Country," "A Cup of Coffee," "The Immigrant," Bdwy in "Cat on a Hot Tin Roof" (1990).

BLAZER, JUDITH. Born Oct. 22, 1956 in Dover, NJ. Graduate Manhattan School of Music. Debut 1979 OB in "Oh Boy!," followed by "Roberta in Concert," "A Little Night Music," "Company," "Babes in Arms," Bdwy in "Me and My Girl," "A Change in the Heir."

BLUMENFELD, ROBERT. Born Feb. 26, 1943 in NYC. Graduate Rutgers., Columbia U. Bdwy debut 1970 in "Othello," OB in "The Fall and Redemption of Man," "The Tempest," "The Dybbuk," "Count Dracula," "Nature and Purpose of the Universe," "House Music," "The Key-maker," "Epic Proportions," "Tatterdemalion," "Iolanthe," "Temple," "Friends in High Places," "Rough Crossing."

BLUMENKRANTZ, JEFF. Born June 3, 1965 in Long Branch, NJ. Graduate Northwestern U. Debut 1986 OB in "Pajama Game," Bdwy in "Into the Woods" (1987), "3 Penny Opera," "South Pacific" (LC).

BOBBIE, WALTER. Born Nov. 18, 1945 in Scranton, PA. Graduate UScranton., Catholic U. Bdwy debut 1971 in "Frank Merriwell," followed by "The Grass Harp," "Grease," "Tricks," "Going Up," "History of the American Film," "Anything Goes," OB in "Drat!," "She Loves Me," "Up from Paradise," "Goodbye Freddy," "Cafe Crown."

BOBBY, ANNE MARIE. Born Dec. 12, 1967 in Paterson, NJ. Attended Oxford U. Debut 1983 OB in "American Passion," followed by "Class 1 Acts," "Godspell," "Progress," Bdwy in "The Human Comedy," "The Real Thing," "Hurlyburly," "Precious Sons," "Smile."

BODLE, JANE. Born Nov 12 in Lawrence, KS. Attended UUtah. Bdwy debut 1983 in "Cats," followed by "Les Miserables."

BOGARDUS, STEPHEN. Born Mar. 11, 1954 in Norfolk, VA. Princeton Graduate. Bdwy debut 1980 in "West Side Story," followed by "Les Miserables," OB in "March of the Falsettos," "Feathertop," "No Way to Treat a Lady," "Look on the Bright Side."

BOGOSIAN, ERIC. Born Apr. 24, 1953 in Woburn, MA. Graduate Oberlin Col. Debut 1982 OB in "Men Inside/Voices of America," followed by "Funhouse," "Drinking in America," "Talk Radio," "Sex, Drugs, Rock & Roll."

BOOKER, CHARLOTTE. Born Dec. 21 in Illinois. Graduate Northwestern U. Debut OB 1987 in "Psycho Beach Party," Bdwy in "Born Yesterday" (1989).

BOONE, DEBBY. Born Sept. 22, 1956 in Hackensack, NJ. Bdwy debut 1982 in "Seven Brides for Seven Brothers," followed by "The Sound of Music" (LC).

BOONE, MICHAEL KELLY. Born Mar. 13, 1957 in Abingdon, Va. Graduate UTenn. Bdwy debut 1985 in "Take Me Along," OB in "The Merry Widow," "Gifts of the Magi," "The Bone Ring," "Terry by Terry," "One Act Festival."

BOSCO, PHILIP. Born Sept. 26, 1930 in Jersey City, NJ. Graduate CatholicU. Credits: "Auntie Mame," "Rape of the Belt," "Ticket of Leave Man," "Donnybrook," "Man For All Seasons," "Mrs. Warren's Profession," with LCRep in "A Great Career," "In the Matter of J. Robert Oppenheimer," "The Miser," "The Time of Your Life," "Camino Real," "Operation Sidewinder," "Amphitryon," "Enemy of the People," "Playboy of the Western World," "Good Woman of Setzuan," "Antigone," "Mary Stuart," "Narrow Road to the Deep North," "The Crucible," "Twelfth Night," "Enemies," "Plough and the Stars," "Merchant of Venice," and "A Streetcar Named Desire," "Henry V," "Threepenny Opera," "Streamers," "Stages," "St. Joan," "The Biko Inquest," "Man and Superman," "Whose Life Is It Anyway?," "Major Barbara," "A Month in the Country," "Bacchae," "Hedda Gabler," "Don Juan in Hell," "Inadmissible Evidence," "Eminent Domain," "Misalliance," "Learned Ladies," "Some Men Need Help," "Ah, Wilderness!," "The Caine Mutiny Court Martial," "Heartbreak House," "Come Back, Little Sheba," "Loves of Anatol," "Be Happy For Me," "Master Class," "You Never Can Tell," "A Man For All Seasons," "Devil's Disciple," "Lend Me a Tenor."

BOURNEUF, STEPHEN. Born Nov. 24, 1957 in St. Louis, MO. Graduate St. LouisU. Bdwy debut 1981 in "Broadway Follies," followed by "Oh, Brother!," "Dreamgirls" (1987), "A Chorus Line," "Legs Diamond," "Prince of Central Park."

BOYD, JULIE. Born Jan. 2 in Kansas City, MO. Graduate UUtah, Yale. Bdwy debut 1985 in "Noises Off," followed by OB in "Only You," "Working 1 Acts," "Hyde in Hollywood."

BOZYK, REIZL. Born May 13, 1914 in Poland. Star of many Yiddish productions before 1966 Bdwy debut in "Let's Sing Yiddish," followed by "Sing, Israel, Sing," "Mirele Efros," "The Jewish Gypsy," OB in "Light, Lively and Yiddish," "Rebecca the Rabbi's Daughter," "Wish Me Mazel-Tov," "Roumanian Wedding," "The Showgirl," "Match Made in Heaven," "Dividends."

BRACCHITTA, JIM. Born Feb. 27, 1960 in Brooklyn, NY. Graduate NYU. Bdwy debut 1989 in "Gypsy," OB in "The Tenants of 3-R," "Merchant of Venice," "Rapunzel," "Mock Doctor/ Euridice."

BRASS, STACEY LYNN. Born Aug. 31, 1968 in NYC. Attended NYU. Bdwy debut 1978 in "Annie," OB in "Romance in Hard Times."

BREEN, J. PATRICK. Born Oct. 26, 1960 in Brooklyn, NY. NYU graduate. Debut 1982 OB in "Epiphanyu," followed by "Little Murders," "Blood Sports," "Class 1 Acts," "Baba Goya," Bdwy in "Brighton Beach Memoirs" (1983).

BRENNAN, JAMES. Born Oct. 31, 1950 in Newark, NJ. Bdwy debut 1974 in "Good News," followed by "Rodgers and Hart," "So Long, 174th Street," "Little Me," "I Love My Wife," "Singin' in the Rain," "42nd Street," "Me and My Girl."

BRENNAN, MAUREEN. Born Oct. 11, 1952 in Washington, DC. Attended UCinn. Bdwy debut 1974 in "Candide" for which she received a Theatre World Award, followed by "Going Up," "Knickerbocker Holiday," "Little Johnny Jones," "Stardust," OB in "Shakespeare's Cabaret," "Candide," "Stardust," "The Cat and the Fiddle."

BRENNAN, NORA. Born Dec. 1, 1953 in East Chicago, In. Graduate PurdueU. Bdwy debut 1980 in "Camelot," followed by "Cats."

BRIAR, SUZANNE. Born Feb. 8, 1946 in Washington, DC. Graduate USyracuse. Debut 1985 OB in "Tatterdemalion," followed by "Princess Pat," "The Red Mill," "Oh, Boy!," "No, No, Nanette," "Can't Help Singing Kern," Bdwy in "Chess" (1988), "Aspects of Love."

BRILL, FRAN. Born Sept. 30 in PA. Attended Boston U. Bdwy debut 1969 in "Red, White and Maddox," OB in "What Every Woman Knows," "Scribes," "Naked," "Look Back in Anger," "Knuckle," "Skirmishes," "Baby with the Bathwater," "Holding Patterns," "Festival of One Acts," "Taking Steps," "Young Playwrights Festival," "Claptrap," "Hyde in Hollywood," "Good Grief."

BRODERICK, WILLIAM. Born Oct. 19, 1954 in Queens, NYC. Graduate Hunter Col. Debut 1986 OB in "Pere Goriot," followed by "The Real Inspector Hound," "Iolanthe," "Teasers and Tormentors," "Dorian."

BRODY, JONATHAN. Born June 16, 1963 in Englewood, NJ. Debut 1982 OB in "Shulamith," followed by "The Desk Set," Bdwy in "Me and My Girl" (1986).

BROGGER, IVAR. Born Jan. 10, in St. Paul, Mn. Graduate UMn. Debut 1979 OB in "In the Jungle of Cities," followed by "Collected Works Of Billy the Kid," "Magic Time," "Cloud 9," "Richard III," "Clarence," "Madwoman of Chaillot," "Seascapes with Sharks and Dancer," "Second Man," "Twelfth Night," "Almost Perfect," "Up 'n' Under," "Progress," Bdwy in "Macbeth" (1981), "Pygmalion" (1987).

BROOKING, SIMON. Born Dec. 23, 1960 in Edinburgh, Scot. Graduate SUNY/Fredonix, UWash. Debut 1989 OB in "American Bagpipes," followed by "The Mortality Project," "Prelude & Liebestod," "Rough Crossing."

BROOKS, ERIC. Born March 9, 1950 in NYC. Graduate UVa, Smith Col. Debut 1989 OB in "Wonderful Town."

BROOKS, JEFF. Born Apr. 7, 1950 in Vancouver, Can. Attended Portland State U. Debut 1976 OB in "Titanic," followed by "Fat Chances," "Nature and Purpose of the Universe," "Actor's Nightmare," "Sister Mary Ignatius Explains It All," "Marathon 84," "The Foreigner," "Talk Radio," "Washington Heights," Bdwy in "A History of the American Film" (1978), "Lend Me A Tenor."

BROWN, ANN. Born Dec. 1, 1960 in Westwood, NJ. Trinity Col. graduate. Debut 1987 OB in "Pacific Overtures," followed by "Side by Side by Sondheim," "Stages," "The Golden Apple," "20 Fingers, 20 Toes."

BROWN, BLAIR. Born during 1948 in Washington, DC. Attended Pine Manor Sch. Debut OB in "Comedy of Errors," followed by "The Threepenny Opera," Bdwy in "The Secret Rapture" (1989).

BROWN, GEORGIA. Born Oct. 21, 1933 in London, Eng. NYC debut 1957 OB in "Threepenny Opera," followed by "Greek," Bdwy in "Oliver!" (1962), "Side by Side by Sondheim," "Carmelina," "Roza," "3 Penny Opera."

BROWN, GRAHAM. Born Oct. 24 in NYC. Graduate Howard U. OB in "Widower's Houses" (1959), "The Emperor's Clothes," "Time of Storm," "Major Barbara," "Land Beyond the River," "The Blacks," "Firebugs," "God Is a (Guess Who?)," "Evening of 1 Acts," "Man Better Man," "Behold! Cometh the Vanderkellans," "Ride a Black Horse," "The Great MacDaddy," "Eden," "Nevis Mountain Dew," "Season Unravel," "The Devil's Tear," "Sons and Fathers of Sons," "Abercrombie Apocalypse," "Ceremonies in Dark Old Men," "Eyes of the American," "Richard II," "The Taming of the Shrew," "Winter's Tale," Bdwy in "Weekend" (1968), "Man in the Glass Booth," "River Niger," "Pericles," "Black Picture Show," "Kings," "Lifetimes," "Burners' Frolic," "Jonquil," "Talented Tenth."

BROWN, P. J. Born Nov. 5, 1956 in Staten Island, NYC. Graduate Boston Col. Debut 1990 OB in "Othello," followed by Bdwy in "Grapes of Wrath" (1990).

BROWN, ROBIN LESLIE. Born Jan. 18, in Canandaigua, NY. Graduate L.I.U. Debut 1980 OB in "The Mother of Us All," followed by "Yours Truly," "Two Gentlemen of Verona," "Taming of the Shrew," "The Mollusc," "The Contrast," "Pericles," "Andromache," "Macbeth," "Electra," "She Stoops to Conquer," "Berenice," "Hedda Gabler," "A Midsummer Night's Dream," "Three Sisters."

BROWN, RUTH. Born Jan. 31, 1928 in Portsmouth, Va. Debut 1987 OB in "Staggerlee," followed by Broadway (1988) in "Black and Blue."

BROWN, WILLIAM SCOTT. Born Mar. 27, 1959 in Seattle, WA. Attended UWash. Debut 1986 OB in "Juba," Bdwy in "Phantom of the Opera" (1988).

BRYANT, DAVID. Born May 26, 1936 in Nashville, Tn. Attended TnStateU. Bdwy debut 1972 in "Don't Play Us Cheap," followed by "Bubbling Brown Sugar," "Amadeus," "Les Miserables," OB in "Up in Central Park," "Elizabeth and Essex," "Appear and Show Cause."

BRYDON, W. B. Born Sept. 20, 1933 in Newcastle, Eng. Debut 1962 OB in "The Long, the Short and the Tall," followed by "Live Like Pigs," "Sjt. Musgrave's Dance," "The Kitchen," "Come Slowly, Eden," "The Unknown Soldier and His Wife," "Moon for the Misbegotten," "The Orphan," "Possession," "Total Abandon," "Madwoman of Chaillot," "The Circle," "Romeo and Juliet," "Philadelphia, Here I Come," Bdwy in "The Lincoln Mask," "Ulysses in Nighttown," "The Father."

BRYGGMAN, LARRY. Born Dec. 21, 1938 in Concord, Ga. Attended CCSF., Am ThWing. Debut 1962 OB in "A Pair of Pairs," followed by "Live Like Pigs," "Stop, You're Killing Me," "Mod Donna," "Waiting for Godot," "Ballymurphy," "Marco Polo Sings a Solo," "Brownsville Raid," "Two Small Bodies," "Museum," "Winter Dancers," "Resurrection of Lady Lester," "Royal Bob," "Modern Ladies of Guanabacoa," "Rum and Coke," "Bodies, Rest and Motion," "Blood Sports," "Class 1 Acts," "Spoils of War," "Coriolanus," "Prelude to a Kiss," "Macbeth," Bdwy in "Ulysses in Nighttown" (1974), "Checking Out," "Basic Training of Pavlo Hummel," "Richard III," "Prelude fo a Kiss."

BRYNE, BARBARA. Born Apr. 1, 1929 in London, Eng. Graduate RADA. NY debut 1981 OB in "Entertaining Mr. Sloane," Bdwy in "Sunday in the Park with George" (1984), "Hay Fever," "Into the Woods."

BUCKLEY, MELINDA. Born Apr. 17, 1954 in Attleboro, MA. Graduate UMa. Bdwy debut 1983 in "A Chorus Line," followed by "Raggedy Ann," OB in "Damn Yankees," "Pal Joey," "You Die at Recess," "They Came from Planet Mirth."

BUELL, BILL. Born Sept. 21, 1952 in Paipai, Taiwan. Attended Portland StateU. Debut 1972 OB in "Crazy Now," followed by "Declassee," "Lorenzaccio," "Promenade," "The Common Pursuit," "Coyote Ugly," "Alias Jimmy Valentine," "Kiss Me Quick," "Bad Habits," Bdwy in "Once a Catholic" (1979), "The First," "Welcome to the Club."

BULOS, YUSEF. Born Sept. 14, 1940 in Jerusalem. Attended Beirut Am.U, AADA. Debut 1965 OB with American Savoyards in repertory, followed by "Saints," "The Trouble With Europe," "The Penultimate Problem of Sherlock Holmes," "In the Jungle of Cities," "Hernani," "Bertrano," "Duck Variations," "Insignificance," "Panache," "Arms and the Man," "The Promise," "Crowbar," "Hannah 1939," Bdwy in "Indians" (1970), "Capt. Brassbound's Conversion."

BUONO, CARA. Born March 1, 1971 in The Bronx, NYC. Debut 1984 OB in "Spookhouse," followed by "Patience and Sarah," "Once Removed," "Hidden Parts," "Evening Star," Bdwy 1990 in "Some Americans Abroad."

BURK, TERENCE. Born Aug. 11, 1947 in Lebanon, IL. Graduate S.Ill.U. Bdwy debut 1976 in "Equus," OB in "Religion," "The Future," "Sacred and Profane Love," "Crime and Punishment."

BURKE, ROBERT. Born July 25, 1948 in Portland, Me. Graduate Boston Col. Debut 1975 OB in "Professor George," followed by "Shortchanged Review," "The Arbor," "Slab Boys," "Gardenia," "Abel & Bela/Architruc," "One Act Festival," Bdwy in "Macbeth" (1988).

BURNETT, ROBERT. Born Feb. 28, 1960 in Goshen, NY. Attended HB Studio. Bdwy debut 1985 in "Cats."

BURNHAM, MARGARET. Born May 29 in Painesville, Oh. Graduate College at Wooster. Debut 1988 OB in "A Midsummer Night's Dream," followed by "Reckonings," "The Former Mrs. Meis," "Pericles."

BURRELL, FRED. Born Sept. 18, 1936. Graduate UNC. RADA. Bdwy debut 1964 in "Never Too Late," followed by "Illya Darling," OB in "The Memorandum," "Throckmorton," "Texas," "Voices in the Head," "Chili Queen," "The Queen's Knight," "In Pursuit of the Song of Hydrogen."

BURSE-MICKELBURY, DENISE. Born Jan. 13 in Atlanta, Ga. Graduate Spellman Col., Atlanta U. Debut 1990 OB in "Ground People" for which she received a Theatre World Award.

BURSTYN, MIKE (formerly Burstein) Born July 1, 1945 in The Bronx, NY. Bdwy debut 1968 in "The Megilla of Itzak Manger," followed by "Inquest," "Barnum," OB in "Wedding in Shtetl," "Prisoner of Second Avenue," "The Rothschilds."

BURTON, DONALD. Born Feb. 10, 1934 in Norwich Norfolk, Eng. Graduate RADA. Debut 1989 OB in "Privates on Parade," Bdwy in "The Merchant of Venice" (1989).

BURTON, KATE. Born Sept. 10, 1957 in Geneva, Switz. Graduate BrownU, Yale. Bdwy debut 1982 in "Present Laughter," followed by "Alice in Wonderland," "Doonesbury," "Wild Honey," "Some Americans Abroad." OB in "Winners," for which she received a 1983 Theatre World Award, "Romeo and Juliet," "The Accrington Pals," "Playboy of the Western World," "Measure for Measure," "Some Americans Abroad."

BURTON, VICTORIA LYNN. Born Apr. 6, 1977 in Baltimore, Md. Bdwy debut 1989 in "Meet Me in St. Louis."

BURTON, WARREN. Born Oct. 23, 1944 in Chicago, IL. Attended Wright Col. Bdwy debut 1967 in "Hair," followed by "A Patriot for Me," OB in "P.S. Your Cat Is Dead," "The Truth," "One Act Festival."

BUSCH, CHARLES. Born Aug. 23, 1954 in NYC. Graduate NorthwesternU. Debut OB 1985 in "Vampire Lesbians of Sodom," followed by "Times Square Angel," "Pscyho Beach Party," "The Lady in Question," all of which he wrote.

BUSFIELD, TIMOTHY. Born June 12, 1957 in Lansing, MI. Graduate East TennStateU. OB in "Richard II," "Young Playwrights Festival," "A Tale Told," "Mass Appeal," "The Tempest," Bdwy in "A Few Good Men" (1990).

BUSSERT, MEG. Born Oct. 21, 1949 in Chicago, Il. Attended UIll. Bdwy debut 1980 in "The Music Man" for which she received a Theatre World Award, followed by "Brigadoon," "Camelot," "New Moon," "The Firefly," OB in "Lola," "Professionally Speaking," "Mexican Hayride."

BUTLER, DEAN. Born May 20, 1956 in Prince George, B.C., Canada. Graduate Uof the Pacific. Bdwy debut 1988 in "Into the Woods," OB in "Tales of the Lost Formicans."

BUTT, JENNIFER. Born May 17, 1958 in Valparaiso, In. Stephens Col. graduate. Debut 1983 OB in "The Robber Bridegroom," followed by "Into the Closet," Bdwy in "Les Miserables" (1987).

BUTTERFIELD, CATHERINE. Born Feb. 5 in New York City. Graduate SMU. Debut 1983 OB in "Marmalade Skies," followed by "Bobo's Birthday."

BYERS, CATHERINE. Born Oct. 7 in Sioux City, IA. Graduate UIa. LAMDA. Bdwy debut 1971 in "The Philanthropist," followed by "Don't Call Back," "Equus," "M. Butterfly," OB "Petrified Forest," "All My Sons," "Murder in the Cathedral," "Grace," "The Fuehrer Bunker," "Great Days."

CAESAR, SID. Born Sept. 8, 1922 in Yonkers, NY. Bdwy debut 1944 in "Tars and Spars," followed by "Make Mine Manhattan," "Little Me," "Four on a Garden," "Sid Caesar & Company," OB in "An Evening with Sid Caesar."

CAHILL, JAMES. Born May 31, 1940 in Brooklyn, NY. Bdwy debut 1967 in "Marat/deSade," followed by "Break a Leg," "The Marriage of Figaro," "City of Angels," OB in "The Hostage," "The Alchemist," "Johnny Johnson," "Peer Gynt," "Timon of Athens," "An Evening for Merlin Finch," "The Disintegration of James Cherry," "Crimes of Passion," "Rain," "Screens," "Total Eclipse," "Entertaining Mr. Sloane," "Hamlet," "Othello," "The Trouble with Europe," "Lydie Breeze," "Don Juan," "Bathroom Plays," "Wild Life," "Uncle Vanya," "Twelfth Night."

Helena Andreyko	Mark Ankeny	Amy Aquino	Lewis Arlt	Nancy Arrigo	John Augustine
Nelson Avidon	June Ballinger	Thomas Barbour	Evalyn Baron	Brent Barrett	Laurinda Barrett
Barbara Barrie	Roger Bart	Robin Bartlett	Bryan Batt	Joanne Baum	Reathel Bean
Jim Bearden	Claire Beckman	John Bedford-Lloyd	Francine Beers	Jeff Bender	Dorothy Benham
Nora Brennan	Jonathan Brody	Melinda Buckley	Terence Burk	Margaret Burnham	Dean Butler

189

Larry Cahn	Chris Callen	David Canary	Amanda Carlin	Craig Carnelia	Leslie Castay
Madelyn Cates	Kevin Chamberlin	Holley Chant	William Charlton	Thom Christopher	Lori Tan Chinn
Danny Robinson Clark	Lynn Cohen	Alex Colon	Vira Colorado	David Conaway	Jane Connell
Frances Conroy	Jarlath Conroy	Joan Copeland	Joseph Costa	Constance Crawford	Keith Crowningshiel
David Cryer	Karen Culliver	John Curless	Joan Cusack	Bill Cwikowski	Lezlie Dalton

CAHN, LARRY. Born Dec. 19, 1955 in Nassau, NY. Graduate NorthwesternU. Bdwy debut 1980 in "The Music Man," followed by "Anything Goes," OB in "Susan B!," "Jim Thorpe—All American," "Play to Win."

CAIN, WILLIAM. Born May 27, 1931 in Tuscalossa, AL. Graduate UWash., CatholicU. Debut 1962 OB in "Red Roses For Me," followed by "Jericho Jim Crow," "Henry V," "Antigone," "Relatively Speaking," "I Married an Angel in Concert," "Buddha," "Copperhead," "Forbidden City," Bdwy in "Wilson in the Promise Land" (1970), "Of the Fields Lately," "You Can't Take It with You," "Wild Honey," "Mastergate."

CAITLYN, DERYL. Born Sept. 18, 1962 in Fresno, Ca. Graduate CalStateU, UCal/San Diego. Debut 1988 OB in "King John," followed by "Coriolanus," "Measure for Measure," "Titus Andronicus," "How Are Things in Costa Del Fuego/Festival of One Acts."

CALKINS, MICHAEL. Born Apr. 27, 1948 in Chicago, IL. Graduate Webster Col. Debut 1973 OB in "Sisters of Mercy," followed by "Love! Love! Love!," "Lifesongs," "Gifts of the Magi."

CALLEN, CHRIS. Born July 14 in Fresno, CA. Graduate SanFranStateU. Bdwy debut in "Brigadoon" (1968/CC), followed by "Someone Else's Sandals," "1776," "Desert Song," "Over Here," "Rodgers and Hart," "Truckload," "Coolest Cat in Town," "Fiddler on the Roof" (1977), "Prince of Central Park," "Lend Me a Tenor."

CAMACHO, BLANCA. Born Nov. 19, 1956 in NYC. Graduate NYU. Debut 1984 OB in "Sarita," followed by "Maggie Magalita," "Salon," "You Can Come Back," "Belle Monde," "Danny and the Deep Blue Sea."

CAMP, JOANNE. Born Apr. 4, 1951 in Atlanta, GA. Graduate FlAtlanticU., GeoWashU. Debut 1981 OB in "The Dry Martini," followed by "Geniuses," for which she received a Theatre World Award, "June Moon," "Painting Churches," "Merchant of Venice," "Lady From The Sea," "The Contrast," "Coastal Disturbances," "The Rivals," "Andromache," "Electra," "Uncle Vanya," "She Stoops to Conquer," "Hedda Gabler," "The Heidi Chronicles," "Importance of Being Earnest," "Medea," "Three Sisters," "A Midsummer Night's Dream," "School for Wives." Bdwy in "The Heidi Chronicles" (1989).

CAMPBELL, ERMA. Born Aug. 14, 1940 in NYC. Attended Hunter Col. Debut 1990 OB in "Ground People" for which she received a Theatre World Award.

CANARY, DAVID. Born Aug. 25, 1938 in Elwood, In. Graduate UCin. Debut 1960 OB in "Kittyhawk Island," followed by "The Fantasticks," "The Father," "Hi, Paisano," "Summer," "Blood Moon," "Sally's Gone, She Left Her Name," "Mortally Fine," "The Cherry Orchard," Bdwy in "Great Day in the Morning," "Happiest Girl in the World," "Clothes for a Summer Hotel."

CARIOU, LEN. Born Sept. 30, 1939 in Winnipeg, Can. Bdwy debut 1968 in "House of Atreus," followed by "Henry V," and "Applause" (for which he received a Theatre World Award), "Night Watch," "A Little Night Music," "Cold Storage," "Sweeney Todd," "Dance A Little Closer," "Teddy and Alice" OB in "A Sorrow Beyond Dreams" "Up from Paradise," "Master Class," "Day Six," "Measure for Measure," "Mountain."

CARLIN, AMANDA. Born Dec. 12 in Queens, NY. Tufts U. Graduate. Bdwy debut 1980 in "Major Barbara," followed by "The Man Who Came to Dinner," "The Front Page," "The Heidi Chronicles," OB in "The Dining Room," "Twelfth Night," "The Accrington Pals," "Comedy of Errors," "Playboy of the Western World," "Waltz of the Toreadors," "The Maderati."

CARNELIA, CRAIG. Born Aug. 13, 1949 in Queens, NYC. Attended HofstraU. Debut 1969 in "The Fantasticks," followed by "Lend an Ear," "Three Postcards," "Pictures in the Hall."

CARRICART, ROBERTSON. Born Dec. 28, 1947 in Norfolk, Va. Graduate UCLA. Debut 1974 OB in "Private Ear/Public Eye," followed by "Cromwell," "Out of the Night," "Dr. Faustus," Bdwy in "Oklahoma!" (1979), "Design for Living," "Figaro," "Zoya's Apartment."

CARROLL, DAVID, (formerly David-James). Born July 30, 1950 in Rockville Centre, NY. Graduate Dartmouth Col. Debut 1975 OB in "A Matter of Time," followed by "Joseph and the Amazing Technicolor Dreamcoat," "New Tunes" "La Boheme," "Company," "Cafe Crown," Bdwy in "Rodgers and Hart" (1975), "Where's Charley," "Oh Brother!," "7 Brides for 7 Brothers," "Roberta in Concert," "Wind in the Willows," "Chess," "Cafe Crown," "Grand Hotel."

CARROLL, ROCKY. Born July 8, 1963 in Cincinnati, Oh. Graduate Webster U. Debut 1986 OB in "Macbeth," followed by "As You Like It," "Romeo and Juliet," "Henry IV," "Richard II," Bdwy in "The Piano Lesson" (1990) for which he received a Theatre World Award.

CARSON, THOMAS. Born May 27, 1939 in Iowa City, Io. Graduate UIo. Debut 1981 OB in "The Feuhrer Bunker," followed by "Breakfast Conversations in Miami," "Sullivan and Gilbert," "The Tempest," "Alive By Night," "All That Fall."

CARTER, RALPH. Born May 30, 1961 in NYC. Bdwy debut 1971 in "The Me Nobody Knows," followed by "Tough to Get Help," "Dude," "Via Galactica," "Raisin" for which he received a Theatre World Award, OB in "The Karl Marx Play," "The Past Is the Past."

CASNOFF, PHILIP. Born Aug. 3, 1953 in Philadelphia, Pa. Graduate WesleyanU. Debut 1978 OB in "Gimme Shelter," followed by "Chincilla," "King of Schnorrers," "Mary Stuart," "Henry IV," "Marathon '89," "Up Against It," Bdwy in "Grease" (1973), "Chess," for which he received a Theatre World Award, "Devil's Disciple."

CASTAY, LESLIE. Born Dec. 11, 1963 in New Orleans, La. Graduate TulaneU. Debut 1985 OB in "The Second Hurricane," followed by "Too Many Girls," Bdwy in "Threepenny Opera" (1989).

CATES, MADELYN. Born Mar. 9, 1927 in NYC. Attended Queens Col. Debut 1965 OB in "Sunset," followed by "The Kitchen," "Max," "Prisoner of Second Avenue," Bdwy in "Marat/deSade" (1966), "A Patriot for Me."

CAVETT, DICK. Born Nov. 19, 1936 in Kearny, Ne. Yale graduate. Bdwy debut 1977 in "Otherwise Engaged," followed by "Into the Woods," "Love Letters."

CAVISE, JOE ANTONY. Born Jan. 7, 1958 in Syracuse, NY. Graduate Clark U. Debut 1981 OB in "Street Scene," followed by Bdwy 1984 in "Cats."

CHALFANT, KATHLEEN. Born Jan. 14, 1945 in San Francisco, CA. Graduate StanfordU. Bdwy debut 1975 in "Dance with Me," followed by "M. Butterfly," OB in "Jules Feiffer's Hold Me," "Killings on the Last Line," "The Boor," "Blood Relations," "Signs of Life," "Sister Mary Ignatius Explains It All," "Actor's Nightmare," "Faith Healer," "All the Nice People," "Hard Times," "Investigation of the Murder in El Salvador," "3 Poets," "The Crucible."

CHAMBERLIN, KEVIN. Born Nov. 25, 1963 in Baltimore, Md. Graduate Rutgers U. Debut 1990 OB in "Neddy," followed by "Smoke on the Mountain."

CHANNING, STOCKARD. Born Feb. 13, 1944 in NYC. Attended Radcliffe Col. Debut 1970 in "Adaptation/Next," followed by "The Lady and the Clarinet," "The Golden Age," "Woman in Mind," "Six Degrees of Separation," Bdwy in "Two Gentlemen of Verona," "They're Playing Our Song," "The Rink," "Joe Egg," "House of Blue Leaves."

CHANT, HOLLEY. Born July 8, 1963 in Spartenburg, SC. Graduate NYU, RADA. Bdwy debut 1990 in "Zoya's Apartment."

CHAPPELL, KANDIS. Born July 9, 1947 in Milwaukee, WS. Graduate SanDiegoState U. Bdwy debut 1989 in "Rumors."

CHARLTON, WILLIAM. Born in Vilenza, Italy. Graduate UCol., LAMBDA. Debut 1989 OB in "Third Time Lucky," followed by "Pericles."

CHIANESE, DOMINIC. Born Feb. 24, 1932 in NYC. Graduate BrooklynCol. Debut 1952 OB with American Savoyards, followed by "Winterset," "Jacques Brel Is Alive," "Ballad for a Firing Squad," "City Scene," "End of the War," "Passione," "A Midsummer Night's Dream," "Recruiting Officer," "The Wild Duck," "Oedipus the King," "Hunting Scenes," "Operation Midnight Climax," "Rosario and the Gypsies," "Bella Figura," "House Arrest," "The Return," Bdwy in "Oliver!," "Scratch," "The Water Engine," "Richard III," "Requiem for a Heavyweight."

CHINN, LORI TAN. Born July 7 in Seattle, Wash. Bdwy debut 1970 in "Lovely Ladies, Kind Gentlemen," followed by "M. Butterfly," OB in "Coffins for Butterflies," "Hough in Blazes," "Peer Gynt," "The King and I," "Children," "The Secret Life of Walter Mitty," "Bayou Legend," "Primary English Class," "G.R. Point," "Peking Man," "Ballad of Soapy Smith."

CHRISTOPHER, THOM. Born Oct. 5, 1940 in Jackson Heights, NY. Attended Ithaca Col., Neighborhood Playhouse. Debut 1972 OB in "One Flew Over the Cuckoo's Nest," followed by "Tamara," "Investigation of the Murder in El Salvador," Bdwy in "Emperor Henry IV" (1973), "Noel Coward in Two Keys," for which he received a Theatre World Award, "Caesar and Cleopatra."

CHUTE, LIONEL. Born Oct. 18, 1962 in NYC. Attended Carnegie-Mellon. Debut OB 1988 in "Perfect Crime," followed by "Ellison and Eden."

CISTONE, DANNY. Born April 10, 1974 in Philadelphia, Pa. Bdwy debut 1989 in "Gypsy."

CLARK, DANNY ROBINSON. Born July 14, 1937 in Jonestown, Ms. Attended UMn. Bdwy debut 1990 in "The Piano Lesson."

CLARKE, DAVID. Born Aug. 30, 1908 in Chicago, Il. Attended Butler U. Bdwy debut 1930 in "Roadside," followed by "Let Freedom Ring," "Bury the Dead," "Washington Jitters," "200 Were Chosen," "Journey Man," "Abe Lincoln in Illinois," "See the Jaguar," "The Emperor's Clothes," "A View from the Bridge," "Ballad of the Sad Cafe," "Inquest," "Of Mice and Men," OB in "Madam, Will You Walk," "Rose," "Bone Garden," "Flesh, Flash and Frank Harris," "All the Nice People," "Baba Goya."

CLARKE, RICHARD. Born Jan. 31, 1933 in England. Graduate UReading. With LCRep in "St. Joan" (1968), "Tiger at the Gates," "Cyrano de Bergerac," Bdwy in "Conduct Unbecoming" (1970), "The Elephant Man," "Breaking the Code," "M. Butterfly," OB in "Old Glory," "Looking-Glass."

CLAYTON, PHILIP. Born June 4, 1954 in Billings, Mt. Attended UUtah. Bdwy debut 1987 in "Starlight Express," followed by "Aspects of Love."

COCCIOLETTI, PHILIP. Born June 26, 1953 in Greensburg, Pa. Graduate Appalachian State U. Debut 1987 OB in "The Moderati," followed by "A Quiet End."

COCHRAN, RAY. Born Sept. 4, 1964 in Lebanon, Ky. Debut 1989 OB in Young Playwrights Festival, followed by "Down the Stream," "Six Degrees of Separation" (also Bdwy).

COHEN, JAMIE. Born Apr. 20, 1959 in Peoria, IL. Bdwy debut 1989 in "Jerome Robbins' Broadway."

COHEN, LYNN. Born Aug. 10 in Kansas City, Mo. Graduate Northwestern U. Debut 1979 OB in "Don Juan Comes Back from the Wars," followed by "Getting Out," "The Arbor," "The Cat and the Canary," "Suddenly Last Summer," "Bella Figura," "The Smash," "Chinese Viewing Pavilion," "Isn't It Romantic," "Total Eclipse," "Angelo's Wedding," "Hamlet," Bdwy in "Orpheus Descending" (1989).

COHEN, MARGERY. Born June 24, 1947 in Chicago, Il. Attended UWis, UChicago. Bdwy debut 1968 in "Fiddler on the Roof," followed by "Jacques Brel Is Alive . . .," OB in "Berlin to Broadway," "By Bernstein," "Starting Here, Starting Now," "Unsung Cole," "Paris Lights," "Pere Goriot," "The Consuming Passions of Lydia Pinkham."

COHEN, SAMUEL D. Born March 10, 1963 in Memphis, Tn. Graduate Penn State. Debut 1989 OB in "The Witch."

COHENOUR, PATTI. Born Oct. 17, 1952 in Albuquerque, NMx. Attended UNMx. Bdwy debut 1982 in "A Doll's Life," followed by "Pirates of Penzance," "Big River," "The Mystery of Edwin Drood." "Phantom of the Opera," OB in "La Boheme" for which she received a Theatre World Award.

COLLINS, STEPHEN. Born Oct. 1, 1947 in Des Moines, Io. Graduate Amherst Col. Bdwy debut 1972 in "Moonchildren," followed by "No Sex, Please, We're British," "The Ritz," "Censored Scenes from King Kong," "Loves of Anatol," OB in "Twelfth Night," "More Than You Deserve," "Macbeth," "Last Days of British Honduras," BAM Co.'s "New York Idea," "Three Sisters" and "The Play's the Thing," "Beyond Therapy," "One of the Guys."

COLON, ALEX. Born Jan. 26, 1941 in Patillas, PR. Attended Hunter Col. Bdwy debut 1970 in "The Gingerbread Lady," followed by "6Rms Riv Vu," OB in "Macbeth," "Winterset," "Crossroads," "Golden Streets," "Hatful of Rain," "Each Day Dies with Sleep."

COLORADO, VIRA. Born July 6 in Blue Island, Il. Debut 1971 OB in "The Screens," followed by "Women behind Bars," "The Three Sisters," "The Petrified Forest," "Puerto Rican Obituary," "The Dispossessed," "Woman without Borders."

CONAWAY, DAVID. Born Mar. 30, 1964 in Portland, Or. Graduate SUNY/Genesco. Debut 1989 OB in "Best Friends," followed by "Scaramouche," "Daddy's Gone," "Slam."

CONNELL, JANE. Born Oct. 27, 1925 in Berkeley, CA. Attended UCal. Bdwy debut in "New Faces of 1956," followed by "Drat! The Cat!," "Mame" (1966/1983), "Dear World," "Lysistrata," "Me and My Girl," "Lend Me a Tenor," OB in "Shoestring Revue," "Threepenny Opera," "Pieces of Eight," "Demi-Dozen," "She Stoops to Conquer," "Drat!," "The Real Inspector Hound," "The Rivals," "The Rise and Rise of Daniel Rocket," "Laughing Stock," "The Singular Dorothy Parker," "No No Nanette in Concert."

CONNELLY, R. BRUCE. Born Aug. 22, 1949 in Menden, Ct. Graduate S.Ct.State Col. Debut 1973 OB in "Godspell," followed by "Macbeth," "The Witch," "A Mind of Strings."

CONNOLLY, DAVID. Born Sept. 30, 1967 in Sydney, NS, Can. Attended Sheridan Col. Bdwy debut 1989 in "Shenandoah."

CONOLLY, PATRICIA. Born Aug. 29, 1933 in Tabora, E. Africa. Attended USydney. With APA in "You Can't Take It with You," "War and Peace," "School for Scandal," "The Wild Duck," "Right You Are," "We Comrades Three," "Panagleize," "Exit the King," "The Cherry Orchard," "The Misanthrope," "The Cocktail Party," and "Cock-a-Doodle Dandy," followed by "A Streetcar Named Desire," "The Importance of Being Earnest," "The Circle," OB in "Blithe Spirit," "Woman in Mind."

CONROY, FRANCES. Born in 1953 in Monroe, GA. Attended Dickinson Col., Juilliard, Neighborhood Playhouse. Debut 1978 OB with the Acting Co. in "Mother Courage," "King Lear," and "The Other Half," followed by "All's Well That Ends Well," "Othello," "Sorrows of Stephen," "Girls Girls Girls," "Zastrozzi," "Painting Churches," "Uncle Vanya," "Romance Language," "To Gillian on Her 37th Birthday," "Man and Superman," "Zero Positive," "Secret Rapture," "Some Americans Abroad," Bdwy in "The Lady from Dubuque" (1980), "Our Town" (1989), "The Secret Rapture," "Some Americans Abroad."

CONROY, JARLATH. Born Sept. 30, 1944 in Galway, Ire. Attended RADA. Bdwy debut 1976 in "Comedians," followed by "The Elephant Man," "Macbeth," "Ghetto," OB in "Translations," "The Wind That Shook the Barley," "Gardenia," "Friends," "Playboy of the Western World," "One Act Festival," "Abel & Bela/Architruc."

CONWAY, KEVIN. Born May 29, 1942 in NYC. Debut 1968 OB in "Muzeeka," followed by "Saved," "The Plough and the Stars," "One Flew Over the Cuckoo's Nest," "When You Comin' Back, Red Ryder?," "Long Day's Journey Into Night," "Other Places," "King John," "Other People's Money," Bdwy in "Indians" (1969), "Moonchildren," "Of Mice and Men," "The Elephant Man."

COOK, VICTOR TRENT. Born Aug. 19, 1967 in NYC. Debut 1976 OB in "Joseph and the Amazing Technicolor Dreamcoat," followed by "The Haggadah," "Moby Dick," "Starmites," "Romance in Hard Times," Bdwy in "Don't Get God Started" (1988), "Starmites."

COPELAND, JOAN. Born June 1, 1922 in NYC. Attended Brooklyn Col., AADA. Debut 1945 OB in "Romeo and Juliet," followed by "Othello," "Conversation Piece," "Delightful Season," "End of Summer," "American Clock," "The Double Game," "Isn't It Romantic?," "Hunting Cockroaches," "Young Playwrights Festival," "The American Plan," Bdwy in "Sundown Beach," "Detective Story," "Not for Children," "Hatful of Fire," "Something More," "The Price," "Two by Two," "Pal Joey," "Checking Out," "The American Clock."

COREY, JILL. Born Sept. 30, 1935 in Avonmore, Pa. Attended Bergen ComCol., AADA. Debut 1979 OB in "Telecast," followed by "The First Time."

CORFMAN, CARIS. Born May 18, 1955 in Boston, MA. Graduate FlaStU. Yale. Debut 1978 OB in "Wings," followed by "Fish Riding Bikes," "Filthy Rich," "Dry Land" "All This and Moonlight," "Cezanne Syndrome," "Tea with Mommy and Jack," "Equal Wrights," "Mi Vida Loca," Bdwy in "Amadeus" (1980).

COSGRAVE, PEGGY. Born June 23, 1946 in San Mateo, CA. Graduate San Jose St, Catholic U. Debut 1980 OB in "Come Back to the Five and Dime, Jimmy Dean," Bdwy. 1987 in "The Nerd," followed by "Born Yesterday."

COSTA, JOSEPH. Born June 8, 1946 in Ithaca, NY. Graduate Gettysburg Col., Yale U. Debut 1978 OB in "The Show Off," followed by "The Tempest," "The Changeling," "A Map of the World," "Julius Caesar," "Titus Andronicus," "Love's Labour's Lost," "Macbeth," "The Crucible."

COUNCIL, RICHARD. Born Oct. 1, 1947 In Tampa, Fl. Graduate UFl. Debut 1973 OB in "Merchant of Venice," followed by "Ghost Dance," "Look, We've Come Through," "Arms and the Man," "Isadora Duncan Sleeps with the Russian Navy," "Arthur," "The Winter Dancer," "The Prevalence of Mrs. Seal," "Jane Avril," "Young Playwrights Festival 1988–89," "Sleeping Dogs," "The Good Coach," "Subfertile," Bdwy in "Royal Family" (1975), "Philadelphia Story," "I'm Not Rappaport."

COUNTRYMAN, MICHAEL. Born Sept. 15, 1955 in St. Paul, Mn. Graduate Trinity Col. AADA. Debut 1983 OB in "Changing Palettes," followed by "June Moon," "Terra Nova," "Out!," "Claptrap," "The Common Pursuit," "Woman in Mind," "Making Movies," "The Tempest," "Tales of the Lost Formicans," Bdwy in "A Few Good Men" (1990).

COURIE, JONATHAN. Born Oct. 26, 1963 in Raleigh, NC. Graduate UCin. Debut 1986 OB in "Murder in Rutherford House," followed by "The Apple Tree," "The Elephant Man," "Night Games," "A Frog in His Throat," "20 Fingers, 20 Toes."

COUSINS, BRIAN. Born May 9, 1959 in Portland, Me. Graduate Tulane, UWash. Debut 1987 OB in "Death of a Buick," followed by "Taming of the Shrew," "Enrico IV," "Richard III," "Prelude to a Kiss," Bdwy in "Artist Descending a Staircase" (1989), "Prelude to a Kiss."

COVER, FRANKLIN. Born Nov. 20, 1928 in Cleveland, Oh. Graduate Denison, Western Reserve U. OB in "Julius Caesar," "Henry IV," "She Stoops To Conquer," "The Plough and the Stars," "The Octoroon," "Hamlet," "Macbeth," "Kildeer," Bdwy in "Giants, Sons of Giants" (1962), "Calculated Risk," "Abraham Cochrane," "Any Wednesday," "The Investigation," "40 Carats," "A Warm Body," "Applause," "Wild Honey," "Born Yesterday."

COX, CATHERINE. Born Dec. 13, 1950 in Toledo, OH. Graduate Wittenberg U. Bdwy debut 1976 in "Music Is," followed by "Whoopee!," "Oklahoma!," "Shakespeare's Cabaret," "Barnum," "Baby," "Oh, Coward!," "Rumors," OB in "By Strouse," "It's Better with a Band," "In Trousers," "Crazy Arnold," "The Waves."

COX, RICHARD. Born May 6, 1948 in NYC. Yale graduate. Debut 1970 OB in "Saved," followed by "Fuga," "Moonchildren," "Alice in Concert," "Richard II," "Fishing," "What a Man Weighs," Bdwy in "The Sign in Sidney Brustein's Window," "Platinum."

CRAWFORD, CONSTANCE. Born March 5, 1959 in NYC. Graduate Vassar, Juilliard. Debut 1987 in "The Gilded Age," followed by "Much Ado about Nothing," Bdwy in "Orpheus Descending" (1989).

CRAWFORD, MICHAEL. Born Jan. 19, 1942 in Salisbury, Wiltshire, Eng. Bdwy debut 1967 in "Black Comedy," followed by "Phantom of the Opera" (1988).

CRISWELL, KIM. Born July 19, 1957 in Hampton, Va. Graduate UCin. Bdwy debut 1981 in "The First," followed by "Nine," "Baby," "Stardust," "3 Penny Opera," OB in "Sitting Pretty."

CRIVELLO, ANTHONY. Born Aug. 2, 1955 in Milwaukee, Wi. Bdwy debut 1982 in "Evita," followed by "The News," "Les Miserables," OB in "The Juniper Tree,"

CROFT, PADDY. Born in Worthing, Eng. Attended Avondale Col. Debut 1961 OB in "The Hostage," followed by "Billy Liar," "Live Like Pigs," "Hogan's Goat," "Long Day's Journey into Night," "Shadow of a Gunman," "Pygmalion," "The Plough and the Stars" (LC), "Kill," "The Plough and the Stars," "Starting Monday," "Philadelphia, Here I Come!" Bdwy in "The Killing of Sister George," "The Prime of Miss Jean Brodie," "Crown Matrimonial," "Major Barbara."

CROMWELL, DAVID. Born Feb. 16, 1946 in Cornwall, NY. Graduate Ithaca Col. Debut 1968 OB in "Up Eden," followed by "In the Boom Boom Room," "Hamlet," "Bad Habits," Bdwy in "A History of the American Film" (1978), "The Mystery of Edwin Drood."

CRONYN, TANDY. Born Nov. 27, 1945 in Los Angeles, Ca. Attended London's Central Sch. Bdwy debut 1969 in "Cabaret," followed by LC's "Playboy of the Western World," "Good Woman of Setzuan," "An Enemy of the People," and "Antigone," OB in "An Evening with the Poet Senator," "Winners" "The Killing of Sister George," "Memories of an Immortal Spirit," "A Shayna Maidel," "American Bagpipes."

CROOKS, KITTY. Born Feb. 23, 1958 in Doylestown, Pa. Yale graduate. Bdwy debut 1986 in "Wild Honey," followed by "One Act Festival," "Subfertile."

CROSBY, KIM. Born July 11, 1960 in Fort Smith, Ar. Attended SMU, ManSchMusic. Bdwy debut 1985 in "Jerry's Girls," followed by "Into the Woods."

CROSS, STEPHEN. Born Aug. 23, 1959 in Halifax, NS, Can. Attended Ryerson Poly Ins. Debut 1986 OB in "The Constant Wife," followed by "Happy End."

CROWNINGSHIELD, KEITH. Born Aug. 26, 1964 in Syracuse, NY. Graduate St. Lawrence U. Debut 1987 OB in "Starmites," Bdwy in "Grand Hotel" (1989).

CRYER, DAVID. Born Mar. 8, 1936 in Evanston, IL. Attended DePauwU. OB in "The Fantasticks," "Streets of New York," "Now Is the Time for All Good Men," "Whispers in the Wind," "The Making of Americans," "Portfolio Revue," "Paradise Lost," "The Inheritors," "Rain," "Ghosts," "Madwoman of Chaillot," "Clarence," "Mlle. Colombe," "A Little Night Music," Bdwy in "110 in the Shade," "Come Summer," for which he received a 1969 Theatre World Award, "1776," "Ari," "Leonard Bernstein's Mass," "The Desert Song," "Evita," "Chess," "Devil's Disciple."

CRYER, GRETCHEN. Born Oct. 17, 1935 in Indianapolis, IN. Graduate DePauwU. Bdwy debut 1962 in "Little Me," followed by "110 in the Shade," OB in "Now Is the Time for All Good Men," "Gallery," "Circle of Sound," "I'm Getting My Act Together . . ." "Blue Plate Special," "To Whom It May Concern," "Alterations," "Back in My Life."

CUCCIOLI, BOB. Born May 3, 1958 in Hempstead, NY. St. John's U. graduate. Debut 1982 OB in "H.M.S. Pinafore," followed by "Senor Discretion," "Gigi," "The Rothschilds."

CUERVO, ALMA. Born Aug. 13, 1951 in Tampa, FL. Graduate TulaneU, YaleU. Debut 1977 in "Uncommon Women and Others," followed by "A Foot in the Door," "Put Them All Together," "Isn't It Romantic?," "Miss Julie," "Quilters," "The Sneaker Factor," "Songs on a Shipwrecked Sofa," "Uncle Vanya," "The Grandma Plays," "The Nest," "Secret Rapture," Bdwy in "Once in a Lifetime," "Bedroom Farce," "Censored Scenes from King Kong," "Is There Life after High School?," "Ghetto," "Secret Rapture."

CULLIVER, KAREN. Born Dec. 30, 1959 in Florida. Attended StetsonU. Bdwy debut 1983 in "Show Boat," followed by "The Mystery of Edwin Drood," "Meet Me in St. Louis," OB in "The Fantasticks."

CULLUM, JOHN. Born Mar. 2, 1930 in Knoxville, Tn. Graduate UTn. Bdwy debut 1960 in "Camelot," followed by "Infidel Caesar," "The Rehearsal," "Hamlet," "On a Clear Day You Can See Forever" for which he received a Theatre World Award, "Man of La Mancha," "1776," "Vivat! Vivat Regina!," "Shenandoah" (1975/1989), "Kings," "The Trip Back Down," "On the 20th Century," "Deathtrap," "Doubles," "You Never Can Tell," "The Boys in Autumn," OB in "Three Hand Reel," "The Elizabethans," "Carousel," "In the Voodoo Parlor of Marie Leveau," "The King and I" (JB), "Whistler."

CUNNINGHAM, JOHN. Born June 22, 1932 in Auburn, NY. Graduate Yale, Dartmouth. OB in "Love Me a Little," "Pimpernel," "The Fantasticks," "Love and Let Love," "The Bone Room," "Dancing in the Dark," "Father's Day," "Snapshot," "Head over Heels," "Quartermaine's Terms," "Wednesday," "On Approval," "Miami," "Perfect Party," "Birds of Paradise," "Six Degrees of Separation." Bdwy in "Hot Spot" (1963), "Zorba," "Company," "1776," "Rose," "Devil's Disciple."

CURLESS, JOHN. Born Sept. 16 in Wigan, Eng. Attended Central School of Speech. NY debut 1982 OB in "The Entertainer," followed by "Sus," "Up 'n' Under," "Progress," "Prin."

CURRY, JOHN. Born Sept. 9, 1949 in Birmingham, AL. Bdwy debut 1980 in "Brigadoon," followed by "Ice Dancing," "John Curry's Skaters," OB in "Privates on Parade."

CURRY, TIM. Born in 1947 in Cheshire, Eng. Attended UBirmingham. Bdwy debut 1975 in "The Rocky Horror Show," followed by "Travesties," "Amadeus," "Me and My Girl" (tour), OB in "The Art of Success."

CURTIS, KEENE. Born Feb. 15, 1925 in Salt Lake City, UT. Graduate UUtah. Bdwy debut 1949 in "Shop at Sly Corner," with APA in "School for Scandal," "The Tavern," "Anatole," "Scapin," "Right You Are," "Importance of Being Earnest," "Twelfth Night," "King Lear," "Seagull," "Lower Depths," "Man and Superman," "Judith," "War and Peace," "You Can't Take It with You," "Pantaglieze," "Cherry Orchard," "Misanthrope," "Cocktail Party," "Cock-a-Doodle Dandy," and "Hamlet," "A Patriot for Me," "The Rothschilds," "Night Watch," "Via Galactica," "Annie," "Division Street," "La Cage Aux Folles," OB in "Colette," "Ride Across Lake Constance," "The Cocktail Hour."

CUSACK, JOAN. Born Oct. 11, 1962 in Evanston, IL. Graduate UWisconsin. Debut 1988 OB in "Road" for which she received a Theatre World Award, followed by "The Myth Project," "Brilliant Traces," "Cymbeline."

CWIKOWSKI, BILL. Born Aug. 4, 1945 in Newark, NJ. Graduate Smith and Monmouth Col. Debut 1972 OB in "Charlie the Chicken," followed by "Summer Brave," "Desperate Hours," "Mandrogola," "Two by Noonan," "Soft Touch," "Innocent Pleasures," "3 From the Marathon," "Two Part Harmony," "Bathroom Plays," "Little Victories," "Dolphin Position," "Cabal of Hypocrites," "Split Second," "Rose Cottages," "The Good Coach," "Marathon 88."

DAILY, DANIEL. Born July 25, 1955 in Chicago, Il. Graduate Notre Dame, UWash. Debut 1988 OB in "Love's Labours Lost," followed by Bdwy in "The Tenth Man" (1989).

DALBY, MICHAEL. Born Jan. 27, 1958 in Lafayette, In. Graduate Wabash Col., UMn. Debut 1987 OB in "Boy's Breath," followed by "LaRonde."

Michael **Dalby**	**Marlene** **Danielle**	**Michael** **Dantuono**	**Cynthia** **Darlow**	**Bruce** **Davison**	**Connie** **Day**
Jacqueline **DeCosmo**	**Lee** **Delano**	**Marcy** **DeGonge**	**Ralph** **DeMatthews**	**Leslie** **Denniston**	**Andre** **DeShields**
Kurt **Deutsch**	**Mia** **Dillon**	**MacIntyre** **Dixon**	**Rebecca** **Downing**	**Jeffrey** **Dreisbach**	**Deanna** **DuClos**
Kimberly **Dudwitt**	**Craig** **Dudley**	**Deanna** **Dys**	**Edward** **Easton**	**Keely** **Eastley**	**Michael** **Egan**
David M. **Eigenberg**	**Donna Marie** **Elio**	**Drew** **Eliot**	**Leslie** **Ellis**	**Brent** **Erdy**	**Karen** **Evans-Kandel**

DALE, JIM. Born Aug 15, 1935 in Rothwell, Eng. Debut 1974 OB with Young Vic Co. in "Taming of the Shrew," followed by "Scapino" "Privates on Parade," Bdwy in "Scapino," "Barnum," "Joe Egg," "Me and My Girl."

DALEY, R. F. Born Apr. 16, 1955 in Denver, Co. Attended NCoU. Bdwy debut 1988 in "Chess," followed by "Sweeney Todd."

DALTON, LEZLIE. Born Aug. 12, 1952 in Boston, MA. Attended Pasadena Playhouse, UCLA. Debut 1980 OB in "Annie and Arthur," followed by "After Maigret," "Blessed Event," "Times and Appetites of Toulouse-Lautrec," "Good and Faithful Servant," "Unguided Missile."

DALY, JOSEPH. Born Apr. 7, 1944 in Oakland, Ca. Debut 1959 OB in "Dance of Death," followed by "Roots," "Sjt. Musgrave's Dance," "Viet Rock," "Dark of the Moon," "Shadow of a Gunman," "Hamlet," "The Ride across Lake Constance," "A Doll's House," "Native Bird," "Yeats Trio," "Mecca," "Marching to Georgia," "Comedians," "A Country of Old Men," "Falsies," "Taming of the Shrew," "Working One Acts," Bdwy in "Mastergate" (1989).

DALY, TIMOTHY. Born Mar. 1, 1956 in NYC. Graduate Bennington Col. Debut 1984 OB in "Fables for Friends," followed by "Oliver Oliver," Bdwy in "Coastal Disturbances"(1987) for which he received a Theatre World Award.

DALY, TYNE. Born Feb. 21, 1947 in Madison, Wis. Attended Brandeis U., AMDA. Debut 1966 OB in "The Butter and Egg Man," Bdwy in "That Summer, That Fall" (1967), "Gypsy" (1989).

DANIELLE, MARLENE. Born Aug. 16 in NYC. Bdwy debut 1979 in "Sarava," followed by "West Side Story," "Marlowe," "Damn Yankees" (JB), "Cats," OB in "Little Shop of Horrors."

DANIELS, LESLIE. Born May 27, 1957 in Princeton, NJ. Graduate UPa. Debut 1985 OB in "Playboy of the Western World," followed by "Touch," "The Hairy Ape," "The Maids."

DANNER, BLYTHE. Born Feb. 3, 1944 in Philadelphia, PA. Graduate Bard Col. Debut 1966 OB in "The Infantry," followed by "Collision Course," "Summertree," "Up Eden," "Someone's Comin' Hungry," "Cyrano," "The Miser," for which she received a Theatre World Award, "Twelfth Night," "The New York Idea," "Much Ado About Nothing," "Love Letters," Bdwy in "Butterflies Are Free," "Betrayal," "The Philadelphia Story," "Blithe Spirit," "A Streetcar Named Desire."

DANNER, BRADEN. Born in 1976 in Indianapolis, IN. Bdwy debut 1984 in "Nine," followed by "Oliver!," "Starlight Express," "Les Miserables," OB in "Genesis."

DANSON, RANDY. Born Apr. 30, 1950 in Plainfield, NJ. Graduate Carnegie-Mellon U. Debut 1978 OB in "Gimme Shelter," followed by "Big and Little," "The Winter Dancers," "Time Steps," "Casualties," "Red and Blue," "The Resurrection of Lady Lester," "Jazz Poets at the Grotto," "Plenty," "Macbeth," "Blue Window," "Cave Life," "Romeo and Juliet," "One Act Festival."

DANTUONO, MICHAEL. Born July 30, 1942 in Providence, RI. Debut 1974 OB in "How To Get Rid of It," followed by "Maggie Flynn," "Charlotte Sweet," "Berlin to Broadway," Bdwy in "Caesar and Cleopatra," "Can-Can" (1981), "Zorba" (1984), "The Three Musketeers," "42nd Street."

DARLOW, CYNTHIA. Born June 13, 1949 in Detroit, MI. Attended NCSch of Arts, PaStateU. Debut 1974 OB in "This Property Is Condemned," followed by "Portrait of a Madonna," "Clytemnestra," "Unexpurgated Memoirs of Bernard Morgandigler," "Actors Nightmare," "Sister Mary Ignatius . . .," "Fables for Friends," "That's It, Folks!," "Baby with the Bathwater," "Dandy Dick," "Prelude to a Kiss," Bdwy in "Grease" (1976), "Rumors," "Prelude to a Kiss."

DAVID, AMELIA. Born Aug. 3, 1958 in NYC. Graduate NYU. Debut 1984 OB in "Couple of the Year," followed by "The Lost Art."

DAVIS, SYLVIA. Born Apr. 10, 1910 in Philadelphia, PA. Attended TempleU. AmThWing. Debut 1949 OB in "Blood Wedding," followed by "Tobacco Road," "Orpheus Descending," "Autumn Garden," "Madwoman of Chaillot," "House of Bernarda Alba," "My Old Friends," "Max," "Pahokee Beach," "Mademoiselle," "Hot l Baltimore," "Hedda Gabler," "Three Sisters," "Medea." Bdwy in "Nathan Weinstein, Mystic, Ct" (1966), "Xmas in Las Vegas."

DAVISON, BRUCE. Born June 28, 1946 in Philadelphia, PA. Graduate PennState, NYU. Debut 1969 OB in "A Home Away From," followed by "Richard III," LCRep's "Tiger at the Gates," "A Cry of Players," and "King Lear," "The Cocktail Hour," Bdwy in "The Elephant Man," "The Glass Menagerie,"

DAWSON, DAVID. Born Feb. 22, 1922 in Brooklyn, NY. Graduate CCNY. Debut 1965 OB in "Hogan's Goat," followed by "Some Rain," "About Face July Festival," "Homesick." Bdwy in "The Freaking Out of Stephanie Blake" (1967).

DAY, CONNIE. Born Dec. 26, 1940 in NYC. Debut 1971 OB in "Look Me Up," followed by "Antigone," "Walking Papers," Bdwy in "Molly"(1973), "The Magic Show," "42nd Street," "A Change in the Heir."

DEAN, ALLISON. Born in NYC. Graduate SMU Debut 1988 OB in "Young Playwright's Festival," followed by "Young Playwright's Festival '90."

DEAN, LOREN. Born July 31, 1969 in Las Vegas, NV. Debut 1989 OB in "Amulets against the Dragon Forces" for which he received a Theatre World Award.

de BEER, GERRIT. Born June 17, 1935 in Amsterdam, Neth. Bdwy debut 1965 in "Pickwick," followed by "Illya Darling," "Zorba," "Pajama Game," "All over Town," "Grand Hotel."

DeCOSMO, JACQUELINE. Born Jan. 1, 1943 in Canton, Oh. Graduate Kent State U. Debut 1973 OB in "Two Noble Kinsmen," followed by "One Flew over the Cuckoo's Nest," "In Circles," "Joe Egg," "Deep to Center."

deGANON, CAMILLE. Born in Springfield, OH. Appeared with several dance companies before making her Bdwy debut in 1986 in "The Mystery of Edwin Drood," followed by "Jerome Robbins' Broadway."

DeGONGE, MARCY. Born May 4, 1957 in Newark, NJ. Graduate Hart Col. Bdwy debut 1989 in "Cats."

DELAINE, SHERI. Born Sept. 15, 1953 in Ironwood, Mich. Graduate UWis. Debut 1988 OB in "Tartuffe," followed by "French Gray," "Pericles."

DELANO, LAURA E. Born July 10, 1958 in San Juan, PR. Graduate Goucher Col. Debut 1982 OB in "Pharaoh's Court," followed by "A Little Something to Ease the Pain," "Dona Francesquita," "Blood Wedding," "Dona Rosita," "The L.A. Scene."

DELANO, LEE. Born Jan. 19, 1931 in NYC. Attended Hunter Col., Neighborhood Playhouse. Debut 1954 OB in "Stephanie," followed by "Picture of Dorian Gray," "Wedding Breakfast," "The Gypist and the Tiger," "Hat Full of Rain," Bdwy in "Sid Caesar & Company" (1989).

DeLAURENTIS, SEMINA. Born Jan. 21 in Waterbury, Ct. Graduate Southern Ct. State Col. Debut 1985 OB in "Nunsense," followed by "Have I Got a Girl for You."

de LAVALLADE, CARMEN. Born Mar. 6, 1931 in New Orleans, La. Bdwy debut 1954 in "House of Flowers," followed by "Josephine Baker and Company," OB in "Othello," "Departures," "The Dreams of Clytemnestra."

DELLA PIAZZA, DIANE. Born Sept. 3, 1962 in Pittsburgh, Pa. Graduate Cincinnati Consv. Bdwy debut 1987 in "Les Miserables."

DeMATTHEWS, RALPH. Born Apr. 22, 1950 in Somerville, NJ. Debut 1984 OB in "Agamemnon," followed by "Bury the Dead," "A Place Called Heartbreak," "Any Corner," "The Strike."

DeMATTIS, RAY. Born June 1, 1945 in New Haven, Ct. Graduate Catholic U. Bdwy debut 1974 in "Grease," followed by "Zoya's Apartment," OB in "El Bravo!," "Talk Radio," "Flora the Red Menace," "The Balcony."

DEMPSEY, JEROME. Born Mar. 1, 1929 in St. Paul, MN. Graduate Toledo U. Bdwy debut 1959 in "West Side Story," followed by "The Deputy," "Spofford," "Room Service," "Love Suicide at Schofield Barracks," "Dracula," "Whodunit," "You Can't Take It with You," "The Mystery of Edwin Drood," "The Front Page" (LC), "Cat on a Hot Tin Roof," OB in "Cry of Players," "The Year Boston Won the Pennant," "The Crucible," "Justice Box," "Trelawny of the Wells," "Old Glory," "Six Characters in Search of an Author," "Threepenny Opera," "Johnny on the Spot," "The Barbarians," "he and she," "A Midsummer Night's Dream," "The Recruiting Officer," "Oedipus the King," "The Wild Duck," "The Fuehrer Bunker," "Entertaining Mr. Sloane," "The Clownmaker," "Two Gentlemen of Verona," "The Marry Month of May," "The Unguided Missile."

DENNISTON, LESLIE. Born May 19, 1950 in San Francisco, CA. Attended HB Studio. Bdwy debut 1976 in "Shenandoah," followed by "Happy New Year," for which she received a Theatre World Award, "To Grandmother's House We Go," "Copperfield," OB in "Class 1 Acts."

DeSHIELDS, ANDRE. Born Jan. 12, 1946 in Baltimore, Md. Graduate UWis. Bdwy debut 1973 in "Warp," followed by "Rachel Lily Rosenbloom," "The Wiz," "Ain't Misbehavin'," (1978/1988), "Haarlem Nocturne," "Just So," "Stardust," OB in "2008½," "Jazzbo Brown," "The Soldier's Tale," "The Little Prince," "Haarlem Nocturne," "Sovereign State of Boogedy Boogedy," "Kiss Me When It's Over."

DESMOND, DAN. Born July 4, 1944 in Racine, WI. Graduate UWi, Yale. Bdwy debut 1981 in "Morning's at Seven," followed by "Othello," "All My Sons," "Rumors," OB in "A Perfect Diamond," "The Bear," "Vienna Notes," "On Mt. Chimborazo," "Table Settings," "Moonchildren," "Festival of 1 Acts," "Marathon '88."

DEUTSCH, KURT. Born July 26, 1966 in St. Louis, Mo. Attended Syracuse U. Bdwy debut in "Broadway Bound" (1988), followed by "A Few Good Men," OB in "Hyde in Hollywood," "Making Movies."

DEVINE, ERICK. Born May 3, 1954 in Galveston, Tx. Graduate UTulsa, Wayne State U. Bdwy debut 1983 in "Cats," followed by "Sid Caesar & Company," OB in "Plain and Fancy," "Lucky Stiff."

DeVRIES, MICHAEL. Born Jan. 15, 1951 in Grand Rapids, Mi. Graduate UWash. Debut 1987 OB in "Ready or Not," Bdwy in "Grand Hotel" (1989).

DEWAR, JOHN. Born Jan. 24, 1953 in Evanston, Il. Graduate UMinn. Bdwy debut 1987 in "Les Miserables," followed by "Aspects of Love."

DEWHURST, COLLEEN. Born June 3, 1926 in Montreal, Can. Attended Downer Col., AADA. Bdwy debut 1952 in "Desire under the Elms," followed by "Tamburlaine the Great," "The Country Wife," "Caligula," "All the Way Home," "Great Day in the Morning," "Ballad of the Sad Cafe," "More Stately Mansions," "All Over," "Mourning Becomes Electra," "Moon for the Misbegotten," "Who's Afraid of Virginia Woolf?," "An Almost Perfect Person," "The Queen and the Rebels," "You Can't Take It with You," "Ah, Wilderness ," "Long Day's Journey into Night" (1988) OB in "The Taming of the Shrew," "The Eagle Has Two Heads," "Camille," "Macbeth," "Children of Darkness" for which she received a 1958 Theatre World Award, "Antony and Cleopatra," "Hello and Goodbye," "Good Woman of Setzuan," "Hamlet," "Are You Now or Have You Ever . . .?, "Taken in Marriage," "My Gene."

DIGIOIA, MICHAEL. Born July 26, 1962 in Niles, Il. Graduate SUNY/Purchase. Debut 1984 OB in "Cricket on the Hearth," followed by "Madwoman of Chaillot," "Vivat! Vivat Regina!," "The Time of Your Life," "Vis-a-Vis."

DILLON, MIA. Born July 9, 1955 in Colorado Springs, CO. Graduate Penn State U. Bdwy debut 1977 in "Equus," followed by "Da," "Once a Catholic," "Crimes of the Heart," "The Corn Is Green," "Hay Fever," OB in "The Crucible," "Summer," "Waiting for the Parade," "Crimes of the Heart," "Fables for Friends," "Scenes from La Vie de Boheme," "Three Sisters," "Wednesday," "Roberta in Concert," "Come Back Little Sheba," "Vienna Notes," "George White's Scandals," "Lady Moonsong, Mr. Monsoon," "Almost Perfect," "The Aunts."

DiMEO, DONNA. Born Mar. 6, 1964 in Brooklyn, NY. Bdwy debut 1989 in "Jerome Robbins' Broadway."

DISHY, BOB. Born in Brooklyn, NY. Graduate Syracuse U. Bdwy debut 1955 in "Damn Yankees," followed by "Can-Can," "Flora the Red Menace," "Something Different," "The Goodbye People," "A Way of Life," "Creation of the World and Other Business," "American Millionaire," "Sly Fox," "Murder at the Howard Johnson's," "Grownups," "Cafe Crown," "The Tenth Man," OB in "Chic," "When the Owl Screams," "Wrecking Ball," "By Jupiter," "The Unknown Soldier and His Wife," "What's Wrong with This Picture?," "Cafe Crown."

DIXON, MacINTYRE. Born Dec. 22, 1931 in Everett, MA. Graduate Emerson Col. Bdwy debut 1965 in "Xmas in Las Vegas," followed by "Cop-Out," "Story Theatre," "Metamorphosis," "Twigs," "Over Here!," "Once in a Lifetime," "Alice in Wonderland," "3 Penny Opera," OB in "Quare Fellow," "Plays for Bleecker Street," "Stewed Prunes," "Cat's Pajamas," "Three Sisters," "3×3," "Second City," "Mad Show," "Meow!," "Lotta," "Rubbers," "Conjuring an Event," "His Majesty the Devil," "Tomfoolery," "A Christmas Carol," "Times and Appetites of Toulouse-Lautrec," "Room Service," "Sills and Company," "Little Murders," "Much Ado About Nothing," "Winter's Tale," "Arms and the Man," "Hamlet."

DODSON, COLLEEN. Born May 16, 1954 in Chicago, IL. Graduate UIl. Debut 1981 OB in "The Matinee Kids," followed by "Pal Joey," "Holding Patterns," "Breaks," Bdwy 1982 in "Nine."

DOLAN, MICHAEL. Born June 21, 1965 in Oklahoma City, Ok. Debut 1984 OB in "Coming of Age in Soho," followed by Bdwy in "Breaking the Code" (1987), "A Few Good Men."

DON, CARL. Born Dec. 15, 1916 in Vitebsk, Russia. Attended Western Reserve U. Bdwy debut 1954 in "Anastasia," followed by "Romanoff and Juliet," "Dear Me, the Sky Is Falling," "The Relapse," "The Tenth Man," "Zalmen," "Wings," "The Tenth Man," OB in "Richard III," "Twelfth Night," "Winterset," "Arms and the Man," "Between Two Thieves," "He Who Gets Slapped," "Jacobowsky and the Colonel," "Carnival," "The Possessed," "Three Acts of Recognition," "The Golem," "Cafe Crown."

DONLEY, ROBERT. Born in Cumberland Township, Pa. Attended Waynesburg Col., Atlantic U. Debut 1947 on Bdwy in "Crime and Punishment," followed by "The Andersonville Trial," " 'Something about a Soldier," "The Unsinkable Molly Brown," "The Visit," "Twigs," "Anna Christie," OB in "The Crucible."

DORFMAN, ROBERT. Born Oct. 8, 1950 in Brooklyn, NY. Attended CUNY. Debut 1979 OB in "Say Goodnight, Gracie," followed by "America Kicks," "Winterplay," "The Normal Heart," "Waving Goodbye," "Richard II," "When She Died," Bdwy in "Social Security" (1987).

DOUGHERTY, J. P. Born July 25, 1953 in Lincoln, Il. Attended S. Ill. U. Debut 1982 OB in "The Frances Farmer Story," followed by "The Little Prince," "The Sound of Music," "The Trojan Woman," "Tropical Fever in Key West," "Have I Got a Girl for You," "Conrack," "Slay It with Music," Bdwy in "The Three Musketeers" (1984).

DOUGLAS, ERIC. Born June 21, 1960 in Los Angeles, Ca. Graduate Claremont Col., RADA, LAMDA. Debut 1983 OB in "The Man," followed by "Strictly Dishonorable," "The Littlest Clown," "Monster Time."

DOWNEY, ROMA. Born in Derry, N. Ireland. Graduate Brighton Polytechnic. Debut 1987 OB in "Tamara," followed by "Ghosts," "Love's Labour's Lost," "Arms and the Man," Bdwy in "The Circle."

DOWNING, REBECCA. Born Nov. 30, 1962 in Birmingham, Al. Graduate OklaCityU. Debut 1989 OB in "Wonderful Town."

DOWNING, VIRGINIA. Born March 7 in Washington, DC. Attended Bryn Mawr. Bdwy debut 1937 in "Father Malachy's Miracle," followed by "Forward the Heart," "The Cradle Will Rock," "A Gift of Time," "We Have Always Lived in a Castle," "Arsenic and Old Lace," OB in "Juno and the Paycock," "Man with the Golden Arm," "Palm Tree in a Rose Garden," "Play with a Tiger," "The Wives," "The Idiot," "Medea," "Mrs. Warren's Profession," "Mercy Street," "Thuder Rock," "Pygmalion," "First Week in Bogota," "Rimers of Eldritch," "Les Blancs," "Shadow of a Gunman," "All the Way Home," "A Winter's Tale," "Billy Liar," "Shadow and Substance," "Silent Catastrophe," "Ernest in Love," "Night Games," "A Frog in His Throat," "All That Fall."

DREISBACH, JEFFREY. Born Apr. 19, 1956 in Dowagiac, Mi. Graduate Wayne StateU. Bdwy debut 1989 in "A Few Good Men."

DuCLOS, DANIELLE. Born Sept. 29, 1974 in Warwick, NY. Debut 1988 OB in "Rimers of Eldritch," followed by "Asleep on the Wind"/Working One Acts, Bdwy in "Aspects of Love" (1990).

DuCLOS, DEANNA. Born Apr. 18, 1979 in NYC. Debut 1987 OB in "1984," followed by Bdwy in "Aspects of Love" (1990).

DUDLEY, CRAIG. Born Jan. 22, 1945 in Sheepshead Bay, NY. Graduate AADA, AmThWing. Debut 1970 OB in "Macbeth," followed by "Zou," "I Have Always Believed in Ghosts," "Othello," "War and Peace," "Dial 'M' for Murder," "Misalliance."

DUDWITT, KIMBERLY. Born Aug. 19, 1963 in Wilmington, De. Graduate UDel. Debut 1990 off and on Broadway in "Prelude to a Kiss."

DUELL, WILLIAM. Born Aug. 30, 1923 in Corinth, NY. Attended IllWesleyan, Yale. OB in "Portrait of the Artist . . .," "Barroom Monks," "A Midsummer Night's Dream," "Henry IV," "Taming of the Shrew," "The Memorandum," "Threepenny Opera," "Loves of Cass McGuire," "Romance Language," "Hamlet," Bdwy in "A Cook for Mr. General," "Ballad of the Sad Cafe," "Ilya, Darling," "1776," "Kings," "Stages," "The Inspector General," "The Marriage of Figaro," "Our Town."

DUFF-MacCORMICK, CARA. Born Dec. 12, in Woodstock, Can. Attended AADA. Debut 1969 OB in "Love Your Crooked Neighbor," followed by "The Wager," "Macbeth," "A Musical Merchant of Venice," "Ladyhouse Blues," "The Philanderer," "Bonjour, La, Bonjour," "Journey to Gdansk," "The Dining Room," "All the Nice People," "Faulkner's Bicycle," "Earthworms," "The Acting Lesson," "Craig's Wife," "Gus and Al," Bdwy in "Moonchildren" (1972) for which she received a Theatre World Award, "Out Cry," "Animals."

DUKES, DAVID. Born June 6, 1945 in San Francisco, CA. Attended Mann Col. Bdwy debut 1971 in "School for Wives," followed by "Don Juan," "The Play's the Thing," "The Visit," "Chemin de Fer," "Holiday," "Rules of the Game," "Love for Love," "Travesties," "Dracula," "Bent," "Amadeus," "M. Butterfly," "Love Letters," OB in "Rebel Women."

DULLEA, KEIR. Born May 30, 1936 in Cleveland, NJ. Attended Neighborhood Playhouse. Debut 1959 OB in "Season of Choice," followed by "Sweet Prince," "Uncle Vanya," Bdwy in "Dr. Cook's Garden," "Butterflies Are Free," "P.S. Your Cat Is Dead."

DURNING, CHARLES. Born Feb. 28, 1923 in Highland Falls, NY. Attended Columbia, NYU. Bdwy in "Poor Bitos," "Drat! The Cat!," "Pousse Cafe," "Happy Time," "Indians," "That Championship Season," "Knock Knock," "Cat on a Hot Tin Roof" (1990), OB in "Two by Saroyan," "Child Buyer," "Album of Gunther Grass," "Huui, Huui," "Invitation to a Beheading," "Lemon Sky," "Henry VI," "Happiness Cage," "Hamlet," "Boom Boom Room," "Au Pair Man."

DUSSAULT, NANCY. Born June 30, 1936 in Pensacola, FL. Graduate Northwestern U. Debut 1958 OB in "Diversions," followed by "Street Scene," "Dr. Willy Nilly," "The Cradle Will Rock," "No for an Answer," "Whispers on the Wind," "Trelawny of the Wells," "Detective Story," Bdwy in "Do Re Mi" (1960) for which she received a Theatre World Award, "Sound of Music," "Bajour," "Carousel," "Finian's Rainbow," "Side by Side by Sondheim," "Into the Woods."

DUTTON, CHARLES S. Born Jan. 30, 1951 in Baltimore, Md. Graduate YaleU. Debut 1983 OB in "Richard III," followed by "Pantomime," "Fried Chicken and Invisibility," "Splendid Mummer," Bdwy in "Ma Rainey's Black Bottom" (1984) for which he received a Theatre World Award, "The Piano Lesson."

DYS, DEANNA. Born Apr. 23, 1966 in Dearborn, Mi. Bdwy debut 1988 in "Legs Diamond," followed by "Meet Me in St. Louis."

EASTLEY, KEELY. Born Feb. 18, 1957 in New Albany, In. Attended UNev. Debut 1981 OB in "The Lesson," followed by "I Am a Camera," "Flesh, Flash and Frank Harris," "Journal of Albion Moonlight," "Split."

EASTON, EDWARD. Born Oct. 21, 1942 in Moline, IL. Graduate Lincoln Col., UIll., Neighborhood Playhouse. Debut 1967 OB in "Party on Greenwich Avenue," followed by "Middle of the Night," "Summer Brave," "Sunday Afternoon," "The Education of Miss February," "The Little Foxes," "Ghosts in the Dining Room."

EDELHART, YVETTE. Born Mar. 26, 1928 in Oak Park, IL. Attended Wright Col. Debut 1984 OB in "Office Mishegoss," followed by "Home Movies," "Night Must Fall," "The Miser," "Heart of a Dog," "Peg o My Heart," "The Dreams of Clytemnestra."

EDELMAN, GREGG. Born Sept. 12, 1958 in Chicago, IL. Graduate Northwestern U. Bdwy debut 1982 in "Evita," followed by "Oliver!," "Cats," "Cabaret," "City of Angels," OB in "Weekend," "Shop on Main Street," "Forbidden Broadway," "She Loves Me," "Babes in Arms."

EDMEAD, WENDY. Born July 6, 1956 in NYC. Graduate NYCU. Bdwy debut 1974 in "The Wiz," followed by "Stop the World . . .," "America," "Dancin'," "Encore," "Cats."

EGAN, MICHAEL. Born Aug. 24, 1926 in Washington, Pa. Graduate Rockness U. Bdwy debut 1956 in "The Great Sebastians," followed by "Luther," "A Cry of Players," "The Incomparable Max," "The Ritz," OB in "The Real Inspector Hound," "Drums in the Night," "Duck Variations," "American Buffalo," "Waiting for Godot," "The Seagull," One Act Play Festival, "New York 1937."

EICHELBERGER, ETHYL. Born July 17, 1945 in Pekins, IL. Graduate AADA. Debut 1974 OB with Charles Ludlum's Ridiculous Theatre Co., followed by "Comedy of Errors," "Measure for Measure," "Herd of Buffalo," "Buzzsaw Berkeley." Bdwy in "3 Penny Opera."

EIGENBERG, DAVID M. Born May 17, 1964 in Manhasset, NY. Graduate AADA. Debut 1989 OB in Young Playwright's Festival/"Finnagan's Funeral Parlor & Ice Cream Shop," followed by "Six Degrees of Separation," Bdwy in "Six Degrees of Separation" (1990).

EISENBERG, NED. Born Jan. 13, 1957 in NYC. Attended CalInstArts. Debut 1980 OB in "The Time of the Cuckoo," followed by "Our Lord of Lynchville," "Dream of a Blacklisted Actor," "Second Avenue," "Moving Targets."

ELDARD, RON. Born in 1964 in NYC. Attended HSPerforming Arts. Bdwy debut 1986 in "Biloxi Blues," OB in "Tony & Tina's Wedding."

ELIO, DONNA MARIE. Born Oct. 30, 1962 in Paterson, NJ. Bdwy debut 1974 in "Gypsy," followed by "Merrily We Roll Along," "Smile," "Jerome Robbins' Broadway."

ELIOT, DREW. Born in Newark, NJ. Graduate Columbia, RADA. OB in "The Fairy Garden," "Dr. Faustus," "Servant of Two Masters," "Henry V," "Stephen D," "Sjt. Musgrave's Dance," "Deadly Game," "Taming of the Shrew," "Appear and Show Cause," "The Visit," "White Collar," Bdwy in "Elizabeth the Queen," "The Physicists," "Romulus."

ELLEDGE, DAVID. Born July 27, 1957 in Omak, Wa. Graduate UUtah. Debut 1984 OB in "Clarence," followed by "Cole Cuts," Bdwy in "Grand Hotel" (1989).

ELLIOTT, KENNETH. Born June 15, 1955 in Indianapolis, IN. Graduate Northwestern U. Debut 1985 OB in "Vampire Lesbians of Sodom," followed by "Pyscho Beach Party," "Zero Positive," "Times Square Angel," "The Lady in Question."

ELLIS, LESLIE. Born July 22, 1962 in Boston, Ma. Graduate Carnegie-Mellon. Debut 1989 OB in "Up Against It," followed by "The Rothschilds."

EMERY, LISA. Born Jan. 29, in Pittsburgh, PA. Graduate Hollins Col. Debut 1981 OB in "In Connecticut," followed by "Talley & Son," "Dalton's Back," Bdwy in "Passion" (1983), "Burn This," "Rumors."

ENGEL, DAVID. Born Oct. 19, 1959 in Orange, Ca. Attended UCal/Irvine. Bdwy debut 1983 in "La Cage aux Folles," OB in "Forever Plaid."

ERDY, BRENT. Born July 29, 1962 in Hilliard, Oh. Graduate Otterbein Col. Debut 1989 OB in "The Lion in Winter."

ERWIN, BARBARA. Born June 30, 1937 in Boston, Ma. Debut 1973 OB in "The Secret Life of Walter Mitty," followed by "Broadway," "One Way to Ulan Bator," Bdwy in "Annie," "Ballroom," "Animals," "Gypsy."

ESPOSITO, GIANCARLO. Born Apr. 26, 1958 in Copenhage, Den. Bdwy debut 1968 in "Maggie Flynn," followed by "The Me Nobody Knows," "Lost in the Stars," "Seesaw," "Merrily We Roll Along," "Don't Get God Started," "3 Penny Opera," OB in "Zooman and the Sign" for which he received a Theatre World Award, "Keyboard," "Who Loves the Dancer," "House of Ramon Iglesias," "Do Lord Remember Me," "Balm in Gilead," "Anchorman."

ESTABROOK, CHRISTINE. Born Sept. 13 in Erie, Pa. OB credits include "Pastoralě," "Win/Lose/Draw," "Ladyhouse Blues," "Baby with the Bathwater," "Blue Windows," "North Shore Fish," "The Boys Next Door," "For Dear Life," "The Widow's Blind Date," "What a Man Weighs," Bdwy in "I'm Not Rappaport" (1987).

ESTEY, SUELLEN. Born Nov. 21, in Mason City, IA. Graduate Stephens Col., Northwestern U. Debut 1970 OB in "Some Other Time," followed by "June Moon," "Buy Bonds Buster," "Smile, Smile, Smile," "Carousel," "Lullaby of Broadway," "I Can't Keep Running," "The Guys in the Truck," "Stop the World . . .," "Bittersuite—One More Time," "Passionate Extremes," "Sweeney Todd," Bdwy in "The Selling of the President" (1972), "Barnum," "Sweethearts in Concert," "Sweeney Todd" (1989).

EVANS, DILLON. Born Jan. 2, 1921 in London, Eng. Attended RADA. Bdwy debut 1950 in "The Lady's Not for Burning," followed by "School for Scandal," "Streamers," "Hamlet," "Ivanov," "Vivat! Vivat Regina!," "Jockey Club Stakes," "Dracula," "Death and the King's Horseman" (LC), OB in "Druid's Rest," "Rondelay," "The Littles Foxes," "Playing with Fire," "The Film Society."

EVANS, HARVEY. Born Jan. 7, 1941 in Cincinnati, OH. Bdwy debut 1957 in "New Girl in Town," followed by "West Side Story," "Redhead," "Gypsy," "Anyone Can Whistle," "Hello, Dolly!," "George M!," "Our Town," "The Boy Friend," "Follies," "Barnum," "La Cage aux Folles," OB in "Sextet."

EVANS-KANDEL, KAREN. Born Aug. 11 in NYC. Queens Col. graduate. Debut 1977 OB in "Nightclub Cantata," followed by "1951," "The Making of Americans," "Underfire," "Alice in Concert," "Dispatches," "Human Nature," Bdwy in "Runaways" (1978).

EVERS, BRIAN. Born Feb. 14, 1942 in Miami, Fl. Graduate Capital U., UMiami. Debut 1979 OB in "How's the House?," followed by "Details of the 16th Frame," "Divine Fire," "Silent Night, Lonely Night," "Uncommon Holidays," "The Tamer Tamed," "Death of a Buick," "The Racket," "6 Degrees of Separation," Bdwy in "House of Blue Leaves," "6 Degrees . . ."

Ron
Faber

Rhonda
Farer

Lucio
Fernandez

Crystal
Field

Fyvush
Finkel

Geraldine
Fitzgerald

Louisa
Flaningam

John-Michael
Flate

Susann
Fletcher

Ted
Forlow

Gloria
Foster

Herb
Foster

Scott
Fowler

Beth
Fowler

Peter
Francis-James

Nancy
Franklin

Joel
Fredrickson

Kate
Fuglei

Janice
Fuller

Timm
Fujii

Teri
Furr

Boyd
Gaines

Susan
Gabriel

Tom
Galantich

Ramon
Galindo

Colleen
Gallagher

David
Gallegly

Rita
Gam

Victor
Garber

Barbara
Garrick

FABER, RON. Born Feb. 16, 1933 in Milwaukee, WI. Graduate Marquette U. Debut 1959 OB in "An Enemy of the People," followed by "The Exception and the Rule," "America Hurrah," "They Put Handcuffs on Flowers," "Dr. Selavy's Magic Theatre," "Troilus and Cressida," "The Beauty Part," "Woyzeck," "St. Joan of the Stockyards," "Jungle of Cities," "Scenes from Everyday Life," "Mary Stuart," "3 by Pirandello," "Times and Appetites of Toulouse-Lautrec," "Hamlet," "Johnstown Vindicator," "Don Juan of Seville," "Between the Acts," "Baba Goya," "Moving Targets." Bdwy in "Medea" (1973), "First Monday in October."

FALK, WILLY. Born July 21 in NYC. Harvard, LAMDA graduate. Debut 1982 OB in "The Robber Bridegroom," followed by "Pacific Overtures," "The House in the Woods," "Elizabeth and Essex," Bdwy in "Marilyn: An American Fable," "Starlight Express," "Les Miserables."

FARER, RHONDA (a,k,a, Ronnie) Born Oct. 19, 1951 in Colonia, NJ. Graduate Rider Col. Debut 1973 on Bdwy in "Rachel Lily Rosenbloom," followed by "They're Playing Our Song," OB in "The Dog beneath the Skin," "Sally and Marsha," "The Deep End," "Tamara."

FARINA, MARILYN J. Born Apr. 9, 1947 in NYC. Graduate Sacred Heart Col. Debut 1985 OB in "Nunsense."

FELDSHUH, TOVAH. Born Dec. 28, 1953 in NYC. Graduate Sarah Lawrence Col., UMn. Bdwy debut 1973 in "Cyrano," followed by "Dreyfus in Rehearsal," "Rodgers and Hart," "Yentl," for which she received a Theatre World Award, "Sarava," "Lend Me a Tenor," OB in "Yentl, the Yeshiva Boy," "Straws in the Wind," "Three Sisters," "She Stoops to Conquer," "Springtime for Henry," "The Time of Your Life," "Children of the Sun," "The Last of the Red Hot Lovers," "Mistress of the Inn."

FERNANDEZ, LUCIO. Born Sept. 24, 1962 in Havana, Cuba. Graduate Rutgers U. Debut 1989 OB in "Wonderful Town."

FIEDLER, JOHN. Born Feb. 3, 1925 in Plateville, Wi. Attended Neighborhood Playhouse. OB in "The Seagull," "Sing Me No Lullaby," "The Terrible Swift Sword," "The Raspberry Picker," "The Frog Prince," "Raisin in the Sun," "Marathon '88," "Human Nature," Bdwy in "One Eye Closed" (1954), "Howie," "Raisin in the Sun," "Harold," "The Odd Couple," "Our Town."

FIELD, CRYSTAL. Born Dec. 10, 1942 in NYC. Attended Juilliard. Graduate Hunter Col. Debut OB in "A Country Scandal" (1960) and most recently in "A Matter of Life and Death," "The Heart That Eats Itself," "Ruzzante Returns from the Wars," "An Evening of British Music Hall," "Ride That Never Was," "House Arrest," "Us," "Beverly's Yard Sale," "Bruno's Donuts," "Coney Island Kid," "Till the Eagle Hollers."

FINKEL, FYVUSH. Born Oct. 9, 1922 in Brooklyn, NY. Bdwy debut 1970 in "Fiddler on the Roof" (also 1981 revival) followed by "Cafe Crown" (1989), OB in "Gorky," "Little Shop of Horrors," "Cafe Crown," "Dividends."

FITZGERALD, GERALDINE. Born Nov. 24, 1914 in Dublin, Ire. Bdwy debut 1938 in "Heartbreak House," followed by "Sons and Soldiers," "Doctor's Dilemma," "King Lear," "Hide and Seek," "Ah, Wilderness," "The Shadow Box," "A Touch of the Poet," OB in "Cave Dwellers," "Pigeons," "Long Day's Journey into Night," "Everyman and Roach," "Danger: Memory!" (LC), "Streetsongs."

FITZPATRICK, ALLEN. Born Jan. 31, 1955 in Boston, Ma. Graduate UVa. Debut 1977 OB in "Come Back, Little Sheba," followed by "Wonderful Town," "The Rothschilds."

FLANAGAN, PAULINE. Born June 29, 1925 in Sligo, Ire. Debut 1958 OB in "Ulysses in Nighttown," followed by "Pictures in the Hallway," "Later," "Antigone," "The Crucible," "The Plough and the Stars," "Summer," "Close of Play," "In Celebration," "Without Apologies," "Yeats, a Celebration," "Philadelphia Here I Come!," Bdwy in "God and Kate Murphy," "The Living Room," "The Innocents," "The Father," "Medea," "Steaming," "Corpse."

FLANINGAM, LOUISA. Born May 5, 1945 in Chester, SC. Graduate UMd. Debut 1971 OB in "The Shrinking Bridge," followed by "Pigeons on the Walk," "Etiquette," "The Knife," "Slay It with Music," Bdwy in "Magic Show," "Most Happy Fella" (1979), "Play Me a Country Song."

FLATE, JOHN-MICHAEL. Born Aug. 24, 1959 in Framingham, MA. Attended Mass. Col. of Art. Bdwy debut 1989 in "Starmites."

FLEET, IAN. Born Mar. 6, 1957 in London, Eng. Graduate UBristol. Debut 1989 OB in "Equus," followed by "The Elephant Man," "Caligula," "Dorian," "Internal Affairs," "Little Lies."

FLETCHER, SUSANN. Born Sept. 7, 1955 in Wilmington, DE. Graduate Longwood Col. Bdwy debut 1980 in "The Best Little Whorehouse in Texas," followed by "Raggedy Ann," "Jerome Robbins' Broadway."

FOKINE, ISABELLE. Born Jan 9th in Paris, France. Attended OxfordU/London. Ballet dancer before OB debut 1989 in "Tamara."

FORLOW, TED. Born Apr. 29, 1931 in Independence, Mo. Attended Baker U. Bdwy debut 1957 in "New Girl in Town," followed by "Juno," "Destry Rides Again," "Subways Are for Sleeping," "Can-Can," "Wonderful Town," "A Funny Thing Happened on the Way to the Forum," "Milk and Honey," "Carnival" (CC), "Man of La Mancha" (1965/1977), "Into the Light," OB in "A Night at the Black Pig," "Glory in the Flower," "Perfect Analysis Given by a Parrot," "Cat and the Fiddle," "One Cannot Think of Everything," "Man of Destiny," "The Rothschilds."

FORSYTHE, HENDERSON. Born Sept. 11, 1917 in Macon, Mo. Attended UIowa. Debut 1956 OB in "The Iceman Cometh," followed by "The Collection," "The Room," "A Slight Ache," "Happiness Cage," "Waiting for Godot," "In Case of Accident," "Not I," "An Evening with the Poet Senator," "Museum," "How Far Is It to Babylon?," "Wild Life," "Other Places," "Cliffhanger," "Broadcast Baby," "After the Fall," "Some Americans Abroad," Bdwy in "The Cellar and the Well" (1950), "Miss Lonelyhearts," "Who's Afraid of Virginia Woolf?," "Malcolm," "Right Honourable Gentleman," "Delicate Balance," "Birthday Party," "Harvey," "Engagement Baby," "Freedom of the City," "Texas Trilogy," "Best Little Whorehouse in Texas," "Some Americans Abroad."

FOSTER, FRANCES. Born June 11 in Yonkers, NY. Bdwy debut 1955 in "The Wisteria Trees," followed by "Nobody Loves an Albatross," "Raisin in the Sun," "The River Niger," "First Breeze of Summer," "Tap Dance Kid," "Fences," OB in "Take a Giant Step," "Edge of the City," "Tammy and the Doctor," "The Crucible," "Happy Ending," "Day of Absence," "An Evening of One Acts," "Man Better Man," "Brotherhood," "Akokawe," "Rosalee Pritchett," "Sty of the Blind Pig," "Ballet Behind the Bridge," "Good Woman of Setzuan" (LC), "Behold! Cometh the Vanderkellans," "Origin," "Boesman and Lena," "Do Lord Remember Me," "Henrietta," "Welcome to Black River," "House of Shadows," "Miracle Worker," "You Have Come Back," "Ground People."

FOSTER, GLORIA. Born Nov. 15, 1936 in Chicago, IL. Attended IllStU, Goodman Th. Debut 1963 OB in "In White America," followed by "Medea" for which she received a Theatre World Award, "Yerma," "A Hand Is on the Gate," "Black Visions," "Cherry Orchard," "Agamemnon," "Coriolanus," "Mother Courage," "Long Days Journey into Night," "Trespassing," "Forbidden City," "Hamlet."

FOSTER, HERBERT. Born May 14, 1936 in Winnipeg, Can. Debut 1967 in "The Imaginary Invalid," followed by "A Touch of the Poet," "Tonight at 8:30," "Papers," "Henry V," "Playboy of the Western World," "Good Woman of Setzuan," "Scenes from American Life," "Mary Stuart," "Twelfth Night," Bdwy 1990 in "Lettice and Lovage."

FOWLER, BETH. Born Nov. 1, 1940 in NJ. Graduate Caldwell Col. Bdwy debut 1970 in "Gantry," followed by "A Little Night Music," "Over Here," "1600 Pennsylvania Avenue," "Peter Pan," "Baby," "Teddy and Alice," "Sweeney Todd" (1989), OB in "Preppies" "The Blessing," "Sweeney Todd."

FOWLER, SCOTT. Born March 22, 1967 in Medford, MA. Debut 1989 on Bdwy in "Jerome Robbins' Broadway."

FRANCIS-JAMES, PETER. Born Sept. 16, 1956 in Chicago, IL. Graduate RADA. Debut 1979 OB in "Julius Caesar," followed by "Long Day's Journey into Night," "Antigone," "Richard III," "Romeo and Juliet," "Enrico IV," "Cymbeline," "Hamlet."

FRANKLIN, NANCY. Born in NYC. Debut 1959 OB in "Buffalo Skinner," followed by "Power of Darkness," "Oh, Dad, Poor Dad . . . ," "Theatre of Peretz," "7 Days of Mourning," "Here Be Dragons," "Beach Children," "Safe Place," "Innocent Pleasures," "Loves of Cass McGuire," "After the Fall," "Bloodletters," "Briar Patch," Bdwy in "Never Live over a Pretzel Factory," (1964). "Happily Never After," "The White House," "Charlie and Algernon."

FRANZ, ELIZABETH. Born June 18, 1941 in Akron, Oh. Attended AADA. Debut 1965 OB in "In White America," followed by "One Night Stands of a Noisey Passenger," "The Real Inspector Hound," "Augusta," "Yesterday Is Over," "Actor's Nightmare," "Sister Mary Ignatius Explains It All," "The Time of Your Life," "Children of the Sun," Bdwy in "Rosencrantz and Guildenstern Are Dead," "The Cherry Orchard," "Brighton Beach Memoirs," "The Octette Bridge Club," "Broadway Bound," "The Cemetery Club."

FRANZ, JOY. Born in 1944 in Modesto, Ca. Graduate UMo. Debut 1969 OB in "Of Thee I Sing," followed by "Jacques Brel Is Alive . . . ," "Out of This World," "Curtains," "I Can't Keep Running in Place," "Tomfoolery," "Penelope," "Bittersuite," Bdwy in "Sweet Charity," "Lysistrata," "A Little Night Music," "Pippin," "Musical Chairs," "Into the Woods."

FRASER, ALISON. Born July 8, 1955 in Natick, Ma. Attended Carnegie-MellonU., Boston Consv. Debut 1979 OB in "In Trousers," followed by "March of the Falsettos," "Beehive," "Four One-Act Musicals," "Tales of Tinseltown," "Next, Please!" "Up Against It," Bdwy in "The Mystery of Edwin Drood" (1986), "Romance, Romance."

FRECHETTE, PETER. Born Oct. 3, 1956 in Warwick, RI. Graduate U RI. Debut OB 1979 in "The Hornbeam Maze," followed by "Journey's End," "In Cahoots," "Harry Ruby's Songs My Mother Never Sang," "Pontifications on Pigtails and Puberty," "Scotter Thomas Makes it to the Top of the World," "We're Home," "Flora, the Red Menace," "Eastern Standard," "Hyde in Hollywood." Bdwy in "Eastern Standard," (1989) for which he received a Theatre World Award.

FREDRICKSON, JOEL. Born May 11, 1959 in Bethesda, Md. Yale graduate. Debut 1982 OB in "Scenes Dedicated to My Brother," followed by "The Miser," "Shylock," "After the Rain."

FREEMAN, MORGAN. Born June 1, 1937 in Memphis, Tn. Attended LACC. Bdwy debut 1967 in "Hello, Dolly!," followed by "The Mighty Gents," "OB in "Ostrich Feathers," "Niggerlovers," "Exhibition," "Black Visions," "Cockfight," "White Pelicans," "Julius Caesar," "Coriolanus," "Mother Courage," "The Connection," "The World of Ben Caldwell," "Buck," "The Gospel at Colonus," (also Bdwy) "Medea and the Doll," "Driving Miss Daisy."

FRID, JONATHAN. Born Dec. 1924 in Hamilton, Ont., Can. Graduate McMaster U., Yale, RADA. Debut 1959 OB in "The Golem," followed by "Henry IV, Parts I & II," "The Moon in the Yellow River," "The Burning," "Murder in the Cathedral," "Fools and Fiends," "Readers Theatre," "Shakespearean Odyssey." Bdwy in "Roar Like a Dove" (1964), "Arsenic and Old Lace" (1986).

FRIEDMAN, PETER. Born Apr. 24, 1949 in NYC. Debut 1971 OB in "James Joyce Memorial Theatre," followed by "Big and Little," "A Soldier's Play," "Mr. and Mrs.," "And a Nightingale Sang," "Dennis," "The Common Pursuit," "Marathon '88," "The Heidi Chronicles," Bdwy in "The Visit," "Chemin de Fer," "Love for Love," "Rules of the Game," "Piaf!," "Execution of Justice," "The Heidi Chronicles," "Tenth Man."

FUGLEI, KATE. Born Aug. 13 in Omaha, NE. Graduate Coe Col. Debut OB 1989 in "Love's Labours Lost," followed by "New Anatomies."

FUJII, TIMM. Born May 26, 1952 in Detroit, MI. Attended CalStateU. Bdwy debut in "Pacific Overtures" (1976), followed by "Chu Chem," OB in "Pacific Overtures" (1984), "Chu Chem."

FULLER, PENNY. Born in 1940 in Durham, NC. Attended Northwestern U. Credits include Bdwy in "Barefoot in the Park," "Cabaret," "Richard III," "As You Like It," "Henry IV," "Applause," "Rex," OB in "The Cherry Orchard."

FURR, TERI. Born May 12, 1965 in Port Chester, NY. Graduate Syracuse U. Bdwy debut 1989 in "Gypsy."

FYFE, JIM. Born Sept. 27, 1958 in Camden, NJ. Graduate Allentown Col. Bdwy debut 1985 in "Biloxi Blues," followed by "Legs Diamond," "Artist Descending a Staircase," OB in "Remedial English," "Moonchildren," "Privates on Parade."

GABRIEL, SUSAN. Born April 29 in Denver, Co. Graduate UUtah, NYU. Debut 1984 OB in "Henry V," followed by "Nest of the Woodgrouse," "Talk Radio," "Hannah Senesh," "Hamlet" (1990), Bdwy in "Prelude to a Kiss" (1990).

GAINES, BOYD. Born May 11, 1953 in Atlanta, GA. Graduate Juilliard. Debut 1978 OB in "Spring Awakening," followed by "A Month in the Country," for which he received a Theatre World Award, BAM Theatre Co.'s "Winter's Tale," "The Barbarians," and "Johnny on a Spot," "Vikings," "Double Bass," "The Maderati," "The Heidi Chronicles," Bdwy in "The Heidi Chronicles" (1989).

GALANTICH, TOM. Born in Brooklyn, NY. Debut 1985 OB in "On the 20th Century," followed by "Mademoiselle Colombe," Bdwy in "Into the Woods" (1989), "City of Angels."

GALINDO, RAMON. Born June 3 in San Francisco, CA. Graduate U of Calif. Berkeley. Bdwy debut 1979 in "Carmelina," followed by "Merlin," "Cats," "Song and Dance," "Jerome Robbins' Broadway," OB in "Funny Feet" (1987).

GALLAGHER, COLLEEN. Born Sept. 20, 1959 in Englewood, NJ. Attended Boston Conservatory. Bdwy debut 1990 in "Zoya's Apartment," OB in "The Awakening," "Harry Black."

GALLAGHER, MEGAN. Born Feb. 6, 1960 in Reading, Pa. Graduate Juilliard. Debut 1983 OB in "Tartuffe," followed by "Miss Julie," "Come and Go," "Play," Bdwy in "A Few Good Men" (1989) for which she received a Theatre World Award.

GALLEGLY, DAVID. Born June 2, 1950 in Pampa, Tx. Attended WTexStateU. Debut 1973 OB in "Boy Meets Boy," followed by "Troubadour."

GAM, RITA. Born Apr. 2, 1928 in Pittsburgh, Pa. Attended Columbia, Actors Studio. Bdwy Debut 1946 in "A Flag Is Born," followed by "Temporary Island," "Insect Comedy" (CC), "The Young and the Fair," "Montserrat," "There's a Girl in My Soup," OB in "Hamlet," "Rasputin."

GARBER, VICTOR. Born Mar. 16, 1949 in London, Canada. Debut 1973 OB in "Ghosts," for which he received a Theatre World Award, followed by "Joe's Opera," "Cracks," "Wenceslas Square," "Love Letters," Bdwy in "Tartuffe," "Deathtrap," "Sweeney Todd," "They're Playing Our Song," "Little Me," "Noises Off," "You Never Can Tell," "Devil's Disciple," "Lend Me a Tenor."

GARRETT, BETTY. Born May 23, 1919 in St. Joseph, Mo. Credits include "Of V We Sing," "Let Freedom Ring," "Something for the Boys," "Jackpot," "Laffing Room Only," "Call Me Mister," "Bells Are Ringing," "Beg, Borrow or Steal," "Spoon River Anthology," "A Girl Could Get Lucky," "Supporting Cast," "Meet Me in St. Louis."

GARRICK, BARBARA. Born Feb. 3, 1962 in NYC. Debut 1986 OB in "Today I Am a Fountain Pen," followed by "A Midsummer Night's Dream," "Rosencrantz and Guildenstern Are Dead," "Eastern Standard," Bdwy in "Eastern Standard" (1988).

GASSELL, SYLVIA. Born July 1, 1923 in NYC. Attended Hunter Col. Bdwy debut 1952 in "The Time of the Cuckoo," followed by "Sunday Breakfast," "Fair Game for Lovers," "Inquest," OB in "U.S.A.," "Romeo and Juliet," "Electra," "A Darker Flower," "Fragments," "Gos," "God Bless You, Harold Fineberg," "Philosophy in the Boudoir," "Stag Movie," "The Old Ones," "Where Memories Are Magic," "Jesse's Land," "Under Milk Wood," "Little Lies."

GAVON, IGORS. Born Nov. 14, 1937 in Latvia. Bdwy bow 1961 in "Carnival," followed by "Hello, Dolly!" "Marat/deSade," "Billy," "Sugar," "Mack and Mabel," "Musical Jubilee," "Strider," "42 St," OB in "Your Own Thing," "Promenade," "Exchange," "Nevertheless They Laugh," "Polly," "The Boss," "Biography: A Game," "Murder in the Cathedral."

GEDRICK, JASON. Born 1965 in Chicago, IL. Graduate Drake U. Debut 1988 OB in "Mrs. Dolly," Bdwy in "Our Town" (1989).

GEFFNER, DEBORAH. Born Aug. 26, 1952 in Pittsburgh, PA. Attended Juilliard, HB Studio. Debut 1978 OB in "Tenderloin," Bdwy in "Pal Joey," "A Chorus Line."

GEHMAN, MARTHA. Born May 15, 1955 in NYC. Graduate Sarah Lawrence Col. Debut 1984 OB in "Cinders," followed by "Day Room," "Baba Goya."

GEIER, PAUL. Born Aug. 7, 1944 in NYC. Graduate Pratt Inst. Debut 1980 in "Family Business," followed by "Women in Shoes," "Johnstown Vindicator," "No Time Flat," "Marathon '90," Bdwy in "Lunch Hour" (1981).

GELB, JODY. Born March 11 in Cincinnatti, OH. Graduate Boston U. Debut 1983 OB in "Wild Life," followed by "36 Dramatic Situations," "Love Suicides," "Baal," "Past Lives," "Marathon '89."

GELFER, STEVEN. Born Feb. 21, 1949 in Brooklyn, NY. Graduate NYU, IndU. Debut 1968 OB and Bdwy in "The Best Little Whorehouse in Texas," followed by "Cats."

GELKE, BECKY. Born Feb. 17, 1953 in Ft. Knox, KY. Graduate WKyU. Bdwy debut 1978 in "The Best Little Whorehouse in Texas," followed by "A Streetcar Named Desire" (1988), OB in "Altitude Sickness," "John Brown's Body," "Chamber Music," "To Whom It May Concern," "Two Gentlemen of Verona," "Bob's Guns," "Buzzsaw Berkeley."

GENEST, EDMOND. Born Oct. 27, 1943 in Boston, Ma. Attended Suffolk U. Debut 1972 OB in "The Real Inspector Hound," followed by "Second Prize: Two Months in Leningrad," "Maneuvers," "Pantomime," "Scooncat," Bdwy in "Dirty Linen/New Found Land," "Whose Life Is It Anyway?," "A Few Good Men."

GENEVIERE, DEBORAH. Born Oct. 15, 1961 in Tokyo, Japan. Graduate SUNY/Stoneybrook. Bdwy debut 1988 in "Chess," OB in "Wonderful Town."

GENTLES, AVRIL. Born Apr. 2, 1929 in Upper Montclair, NJ. Graduate UNC. Bdwy debut 1955 in "The Great Sebastians," followed by "Nude with Violin," "Present Laughter," "My Mother, My Father and Me," "Jimmy Shine," "Grin and Bare It," "Lysistrata," "Texas Trilogy," "Show Boat" (1983), "Musical Comedy Murders of 1940," OB in "Dinny and the Witches," "The Wives," "Now Is the Time," "Man with a Load of Mischief," "Shay," "A Winter's Tale," "Johnny on a Spot," "The Barbarians," "The Wedding," "Nymph Errant," "A Little Night Music," "Doctor's Dilemma."

GEORGE, BEN. Born June 7, 1947 in Oxford, Eng. Attended Leeds Music Col. Debut 1984 OB in "Last of the Knucklemen," Bdwy in "The Best Little Whorehouse in Texas" (1985), "Grand Hotel."

GERACI, FRANK. Born Sept. 8, 1939 in Brooklyn, NY. Attended Yale. Debut 1961 OB in "Color of Darkness," followed by "Mr. Grossman," "Balm in Gilead," "The Fantasticks," "Tom Paine," "End of All Things Natural," "Union Street," "Uncle Vanya," "Success Story," "Hughie," "Merchant of Venice," "Three Zeks," "Taming of the Shrew," "The Lady from the Sea," "Rivals," "Deep Swimmer," "The Imaginary Invalid," "Candida," "Uncle Vanya," "Hedda Gabler," "Serious Co.," "Berenice," "The Philanderer," "Hedda Gabler," "All's Well That Ends Well," "Three Sisters," "A Midsummer Night's Dream," "Medea," "The Importance of Being Earnest." Bdwy in "Love Suicide at Schofield Barracks" (1972).

GERACI, PAUL. Born June 2, 1963 in Chicago, Il. Attended Webster U. Bdwy debut 1987 in "Anything Goes," followed by "Gypsy" (1989).

GERAGHTY, MARITA. Born Mar. 26, 1965 in Chicago, IL. Graduate UIll. Bdwy debut 1987 in "Coastal Disturbances," followed by "The Night of the Iguana," "The Heidi Chronicles."

GERBER, CHARLES E. Born Apr. 2, 1949 in Chicago, Il. Attended Wright Col., Juilliard. Bdwy debut 1981 in "Oh! Calcutta!," OB in "A Midsummer Night's Dream," One Act Festival.

GERDES, GEORGE. Born Feb. 23, 1948 in NYC. Carnegie Tech graduate. Debut 1979 OB in "Modigliani," followed by "The Idolmakers," "The Doctor and the Devils," "The Hit Parade," "A Country for Old Men," "Fool for Love," "To Whom It May Concern," "New Works '87," Bdwy 1989 in "A Few Good Men."

GERROLL, DANIEL. Born Oct. 16, 1951 in London, Eng. Attended Central Sch. of Speech. Debut 1980 OB in "Slab Boys," followed by "Knuckle," and "Translations," for which he received a Theatre World Award, "The Caretaker," "Scenes from La Vie de Boheme," "The Knack," "Terra Nova," "Dr. Faustus," "Second Man," "Cheapside," "Bloody Poetry," "The Common Pursuit," "Woman in Mind," "Poets' Corner," "The Film Society," "Emerald City," "Arms and the Man," Bdwy in "Plenty" (1982).

GERSHENSON, SUE ANNE. Born Feb. 18, 1953 in Chicago, Il. Attended Ind. U. Debut 1976 OB in "Panama Hattie," followed by "Carnival," "Street Scene," "The Rothschilds," Bdwy in "Sunday in the Park with George" (1984).

GERUT, ROSALIE W. Born in Boston, Ma. Debut 1989 OB in "Songs of Paradise."

GIBBS, SHEILA. Born Feb. 16, 1947 in NYC. Graduate NYU. Bdwy debut 1971 in "Two Gentlemen of Verona," followed by "Runaways," OB in "Last Days of British Honduras," "Poets from the Inside," "Once on This Island."

GIBSON, JULIA. Born June 8, 1962 in Norman, OK. Graduate UIowa. NYU. Debut 1987 OB in "A Midsummer Night's Dream," followed by "Love's Labor's Lost," "Crucible."

GIBSON, THOMAS. Born July 3, 1962 in Charleston, SC. Graduate Juilliard. Debut 1985 OB in "Map of the World," followed by "Twelfth Night," "Bloody Poetry," "Marathon '87," "Two Gentlemen of Verona," "Class 1 Acts," "Macbeth," "Marathon '88," "Positive Me." Bdwy in "Hay Fever" (1985).

GILBERT, TONY. Born March 22 in Roanoke, Va. Graduate UVa. Debut 1983 OB in "The Robber Bridegroom," followed by "Sweeney Todd," Bdwy in "Oliver!" (1984), "Sweeney Todd."

GILL, RAY. Born Aug. 1, 1950 in Bayonne, NJ. Attended Rider Col. Bdwy debut 1978 in "On the 20th Century" followed by "Pirates of Penzance," "The First," "They're Playing Our Song," "Sunday in the Park with George," "Cat on a Hot Tin Roof," OB in "A Bundle of Nerves," "Driving Miss Daisy," "Romance in Hard Times."

GILLETTE, ANITA. Born Aug. 16, 1938 in Baltimore, MD. Debut 1960 OB in "Russell Patterson's Sketchbook," for which she received a Theatre World Award, followed by "Rich and Famous," "Dead Wrong," "Road Show," "Class 1 Acts," "The Blessing," "Moving Targets," Bdwy in "Carnival," "All American," "Mr. President," "Guys and Dolls," "Don't Drink the Water," "Cabaret," "Jimmy," "Chapter Two," "They're Playing Our Song," "Brighton Beach Memoirs."

GILPIN, JACK. Born May 31, 1951 in Boyce, VA. Harvard graduate. Debut 1976 OB in "Goodbye and Keep Cold," followed by "Shay," "The Soft Touch," "Beyond Therapy," "The Lady or the Tiger," "The Middle Ages," "The Rise of Daniel Rocket," "No Happy Ending," "Strange Behavior," "The Foreigner," "Marathon '86," "The Spring Thing," "Human Nature." Bdwy in "Lunch Hour" (1980).

GIONSON, MEL DUANE. Born Feb. 23, 1954 in Honolulu, HI. Graduate UHi. Debut 1979 OB in "Richard II," followed by "Sunrise," "Monkey Music," "Behind Enemy Lines," "Station J," "Teahouse," "A Midsummer Night's Dream," "Empress of China," "Chip Shot," "Manoa Valley," "Ghashiram," "Shogun Macbeth," "Life of the Land," "Noiresque," "Three Sisters."

GIOSA, SUE. Born Nov. 23, 1958 in Connecticut. Graduate Queens Col., RADA, LAMDA. Debut OB 1988 in "Tamara."

GLAZE, SUSAN. Born Oct. 9, 1956 in Murfreesboro, Tn. Graduate UTn, AADA. Debut 1982 OB in "The Broken Heart," followed by "Le Grande Cafe," "Tribute to Jerome Kern," "Pippin," "Feast Here Tonight," Bdwy in "Big River" (1985).

GLEASON, JAMES. Born Sept. 30, 1952 in NYC. Graduate Santa Fe Col. Debut 1982 OB in "Guys in the Truck," followed by "Corkscrews!," "Patrick Pearse Motel," "Taboo in Revue," "Curse of the Starving Class," "Signal Season," "The Ambassador," Bdwy in "Guys in the Truck" (1983).

GLEASON, JOANNA. Born June 2, 1950 in Toronto, Canada. Graduate UCLA. Bdwy debut 1977 in "I Love My Wife," for which she received a Theatre World Award, followed by "The Real Thing," "Social Security," "Into the Woods," OB in "A Hell of a Town," "Joe Egg," "It's Only a Play," "Eleemosynary."

GLEASON, LAURENCE. Born Nov. 15, 1956 in Utica, NY. Graduate Utica Col. Debut 1984 OB in "Romance Language," followed by "Agamemnon," "A Country Doctor," "The Misanthrope," "The Sleepless City," "Electra," "Morning Song."

GLOVER, SAVION. Born Nov. 19, 1973 in Newark, NJ. Bdwy debut 1984 in "The Tap Dance Kid," followed by "Black and Blue."

GLUSHAK, JOANNA. Born May 27, 1958 in NYC. Attended NYU. Debut 1983 OB in "Lenny and the Heartbreakers," followed by "Lies and Legends," "Miami," Bdwy in "Sunday in the Park with George" (1984), "Rags" "Les Miserables."

GOLDBLUM, JEFF. Born Oct. 22, 1952 in Pittsburgh, Pa. Attended Neighborhood Playhouse. Debut 1971 on Bdwy in "Two Gentlemen of Verona," followed by "Moony Shapiro Songbook," OB in "El Grande de Coca Cola," "Our Late Night," "City Sugar," "Twelfth Night."

GOLDSTEIN, STEVEN. Born Oct. 22, 1963 in NYC. Graduate NYU. Debut 1987 OB in "Boys' Life," followed by "Oh, Hell," Bdwy in "Our Town" (1988).

GOODMAN, LISA. Born in Detroit, Mi. Attended UMi. Debut 1982 OB in "Talking With," followed by "The First Warning," "The Show-Off," "Escape from Riverdale," "Jesse's Land," "State of the Union," "The Wonder Years," "Girl of the Golden West," "Medea."

GOODSPEED, DON. Born Apr. 1, 1958 in Truro, NS, Can. Bdwy debut 1983 in "The Pirates of Penzance," followed by "Into the Woods," "Aspects of Love," OB in "Diamonds," "Charley's Tale."

GOOR, CAROLYN. Born Oct. 11, 1960 in Paris, Fr. Debut 1983 OB in "The Jewish Gypsy," followed by "Oy Mama, Am I in Love," "A Little Night Music," "Singin' in the Rain," Bdwy in "Jerome Robbins' Broadway."

GORDON, CARL. Born Jan. 20, 1932 in Richmond, Va. Bdwy debut 1966 in "The Great White Hope," followed by "Ain't Supposed to Die a Natural Death," "The Piano Lesson," OB in "Day of Absence," "Happy Ending," "The Strong Breed," "Trials of Brother Jero," "Kongi's Harvest," "Welcome to Black River," "Shark," "Orrin and Sugar Mouth," "A Love Play," "The Great MacDaddy," "In an Upstate Motel," "Zooman and the Sign."

Sylvia
Gassell

Igors
Gavon

Martha
Gehman

Paul
Geier

Jody
Gelb

Edmond
Genest

Ben
George

Becky
Gelke

Frank
Geraci

Marita
Geraghty

Charles E.
Gerber

Sue Anne
Gershenson

Sheila
Gibbs

Thomas
Gibson

Julia
Gibson

Tony
Gilbert

Anita
Gillette

Ray
Gill

Jack
Gilpin

Sue
Giosa

James
Gleason

Joanna
Gleason

Savion
Glover

Joanna
Glushak

Lisa
Goodman

Don
Goodspeed

Carolyn
Goor

Carl
Gordon

Ruth
Gottschall

Gordon
Gould

Christopher
Goutman

Randy
Graff

Todd
Graff

Rachel
Graham

Stewart
Granger

Judith
Granite

Faye
Grant

Sean
Grant

Helen
Greenberg

James
Greene

Lyn
Greene

Clark
Gregg

Michael Scott
Gregory

Kristin
Griffith

John
Griesemer

Tammy
Grimes

Cris
Groenendaal

Amy
Gross

Robin
Groves

Laurence
Guittard

Julie J.
Hafner

John
Hagan

Margaret
Hall

Charles Edward
Hall

George
Hall

Julie
Halston

Stephen
Hanan

Marcia Gay
Harden

Arthur
Hanket

Delphi
Harrington

GORDON, CLARKE. Born in Detroit, Mi. Graduate WayneStateU. Debut 1949 OB in "The Son," followed by "The Philistines," "The Truth," "Porch," "China Fish," "Them," Bdwy in "Night Music" (1951), "Pal Joey" (1952), "The Vamp."

GORDON-CLARK, SUSAN. Born Dec. 31, 1947 in Jackson, Ms. Graduate Purdue U. Debut 1984 OB in "The Nunsense Story," followed by "Chip Shot," "Nunsense."

GOTTSCHALL, RUTH. Born Apr. 14, 1957 in Wilmington, DE. Bdwy debut 1981 in "The Best Little Whorehouse in Texas," followed by "Cabaret" (1987), "Legs Diamond," "Prince of Central Park."

GOULD, GORDON. Born May 4, 1930 in Chicago, Il. Graduate Yale, Cambridge U. Bdwy debut 1965 in "You Can't Take It with You," followed by "War and Peace," "Right You Are," "The Wild Duck," "Pantagleize," "Exit the King," "The Show-Off," "School for Wives," "Freedom of the City," "Strider," "Amadeus," "Merchant of Venice," OB in "Man and Superman," "Scapin," "Impromptu at Versailles," "The Lower Depths," "The Tavern," "Judith," "Naked," "The Middle Ages," "On Approval," "Swan Song."

GOULD, HAROLD. Born Dec. 10, 1923 in Schenectady, NY. Graduate SUNY, Cornell. Debut 1969 OB in "The Increased Difficulty of Concentration," followed by "Amphitryon," "House of Blue Leaves," "Touching Bottom," Bdwy in "Fools" (1981), "Grownups," "Artist Descending the Stairs."

GOUTMAN, CHRISTOPHER. Born Dec. 19, 1952 in Bryn Mawr, PA. Graduate Haverford Col., Carnegie-Mellon U. Debut 1978 OB in "The Promise," for which he received a Theatre World Award, followed by "Grand Magic," "The Skirmishers," "Imaginary Lovers," "Balm in Gilead," "Love's Labour's Lost," "Tamara."

GOZ, HARRY. Born June 23, 1932 in St. Louis, MO. Attended St. Louis Inst. Bdwy debut 1957 in "Utopia Limited," followed by "Bajour," "Fiddler on the Roof," "Two by Two," "Prisoner of Second Avenue," "Chess," "Cafe Crown" (1989), OB in "To Bury a Cousin," "Ferocious Kisses," "Cafe Crown."

GRAAE, JASON. Born May 15, 1958 in Chicago, IL. Graduate Cincinnati Consv. Debut 1981 OB in "Godspell," followed by "Snoopy," "Heaven on Earth," "Promenade," "Feathertop," "Tales of Tinseltown," "Living Color," "Just So," "Olympus on My Mind," "Sitting Pretty in Concert," "Babes in Arms," "The Cat and the Fiddle," "Forever Plaid," Bdwy 1982 in "Do Black Patent Leather Shoes Really Reflect Up?," "Stardust."

GRAFF, RANDY. Born May 23, 1955 in Brooklyn, NY. Graduate Wagner Col. Debut 1978 OB in "Pins and Needles," followed by "Station Joy," "A . . . My Name Is Alice," "Once on a Summer's Day," Bdwy in "Sarava," "Grease," "Les Miserables," "City of Angels."

GRAFF, TODD. Born Oct. 22, 1959 in NYC. Attended SUNY/Purchase. Debut 1983 OB in "American Passion," followed by "Birds of Paradise," "Grandma Plays," Bdwy in "Baby" (1983) for which he received a Theatre World Award.

GRAHAM, RACHAEL. Born June 26, 1977 in Wilton, Ct. Debut 1987 in "Keeping Up with the 80's," Bdwy 1989 in "Meet Me in St. Louis."

GRANGER, STEWART. Born May 6, 1913 in London. Attended Webber-Douglas Sch. Bdwy debut 1989 in "The Circle."

GRANITE, JUDITH. Born Apr. 22, 1936 in Rochester, NY. Graduate Syracuse U. NYU. Bdwy debut 1965 in "The Devils," followed by "Criss-Crossing," "The Cemetery Club," OB in "Lovers in the Metro," "So Who's Afraid of Edward Albee," "Macbird," "The World of Gunter Grass," "The Survival of St. Joan," "Equinox," "Savings," "The Flatbush Faithful," "Special Interest."

GRANT, DAVID MARSHALL. Born June 21, 1955 in New Haven, Ct. Attended ConnCol, Yale. Debut OB 1978 in "Sganarelle," followed by "Table Settings," "The Tempest," "Making Movies," Bdwy in "Bent" (1979), "The Survivor."

GRANT, FAYE. Born July 16 in Detroit, MI. Bdwy debut 1985 in "Singin' in the Rain," for which she received a Theatre World Award, followed by "House of Blue Leaves," "Lend Me a Tenor."

GRANT, SEAN. Born July 13, 1966 in Brooklyn, NY. Attended NCSchool of Arts. Bdwy debut 1987 in "Starlight Express," followed by "Prince of Central Park."

GRAY, KEVIN. Born Feb. 25, 1958 in Westport, Ct. Graduate Duke U. Debut 1982 OB in "Lola," followed by "Pacific Overtures," "Family Snapshots," "The Baker's Wife," "The Knife," "Magdalena in Concert," Bdwy in "The Phantom of the Opera" (1989).

GREEN, DAVID. Born June 16, 1942 in Cleveland, OH. Attended KanState U. Bdwy debut 1980 in "Annie," followed by "Evita," "Teddy and Alice," "The Pajama Game" (LC), OB in "Once on a Summer's Day," "Miami," "On the 20th Century."

GREENBERG, HELEN. Born Sept. 28, 1961 on Long Island, NY. Graduate NYU. Debut 1987 OB in "Words, Words, Words," followed by "Double Blessing."

GREENBERG, MITCHELL. Born Sept. 19, 1950 in Brooklyn, NY. Graduate Harpur Col., Neighborhood Playhouse. Debut 1979 OB in "Two Grown Men," followed by "Scrambled Feet," "A Christmas Carol," "A Thurber Carnival," "Isn't It Romantic?," "Crazy Arnold," Bdwy in "A Day in Hollywood/A Night in the Ukraine" (1980), "Can-Can," "Marilyn," "Into the Light," "3 Penny Opera."

GREENE, ELLEN. Born Feb. 22 in NYC. Attended Ryder Col. Debut 1973 on Bdwy in "Rachel Lily Rosenbloom," followed by "The Little Prince and the Aviator," OB in "In the Boom Boom Room," "Threepenny Opera," "Disrobing the Bride," "The Little Shop of Horrors," "Starting Monday."

GREENE, JAMES. Born Dec. 1, 1926 in Lawrence, MA. Graduate Emerson Col. OB in "The Iceman Cometh," "American Gothic," "The King and the Duke," "The Hostage," "Plays for Bleecker Street," "Moon in the Yellow River," "Misalliance," "Government Inspector," "Baba Goya," LCRep 2 years, "You Can't Take It with You," "School for Scandal," "Wild Duck," "Right You Are," "The Show-Off," "Pantagleize," "Festival of Short Plays," "Nourish the Beast," "One Crack Out," "Artichoke," "Othello," "Salt Lake City Skyline," "Summer," "Rope Dancers," "Frugal Repast," "Bella Figura," "The Freak," "Park Your Car in the Harvard Yard," "Pigeons on the Walk," "Endgame," "Great Days," "Playboy of the Western World," "Brimstone and Treacle," Bdwy "Romeo and Juliet," "Girl on the Via Flaminia," "Compulsion," "Inherit the Wind," "Shadow of a Gunman," "Andersonville Trial," "Night Life," "School for Wives," "Ring Round the Bathtub," "Great God Brown," "Don Juan," "Foxfire," "Play Memory," "The Iceman Cometh."

GREENE, LYN. Born May 21, 1955 in Boston, Ma. Graduate NYU, Juilliard. Debut 1984 OB in "Kid Purple," followed by "Flora the Red Menace," "Prisoner of Second Avenue."

GREGG, CLARK. Born April 2, 1962 in Boston, Ma. Graduate NYU. Debut 1987 OB in "Fun," followed by "The Detective," "Boys' Life," Bdwy in "A Few Good Men" (1990).

GREGORIO, ROSE. Born in Chicago, Ill. Graduate Northwestern, Yale. Debut 1962 OB in "The Days and Nights of Beebee Fenstermaker," followed by "Kiss Mama," "The Balcony," "Bivouac at Lucca," "Journey to the Day," "Diary of Anne Frank," "Weekends Like Other People," "Curse of the Starving Class," "Dream of a Blacklisted Actor," Bdwy in "The Owl and the Pussycat," "Daphne in Cottage D," "Jimmy Shine," "The Cuban Thing," "The Shadow Box," "A View from the Bridge," "M. Butterfly."

GREGORY, MICHAEL SCOTT. Born Mar. 13, 1962 in Ft. Lauderdale, FL. Attended Atlantic Foundation. Bdwy debut 1981 in "Sophisticated Ladies," followed by "Starlight Express," "Jerome Robbins' Broadway."

GRENIER, ZACH. Born Feb. 12, 1954 in Englewood, NJ. Graduate UMi., Boston U. Debut 1982 OB in "Baal," followed by "Tomorrowland," "Water Music," "Morocco," "The Cure," "Birth of the Poet," "Talk Radio," "Marathon '90," Bdwy 1989 in "Mastergate."

GRIESEMER, JOHN. Born Dec. 5, 1947 in Elizabeth, NJ. Graduate Dickinson Col., URI. Debut 1981 OB in "Turnbuckle," followed by "Death of a Miner," "Little Victories," "Macbeth," "A Lie of the Mind," "Kate's Diary," Bdwy in "Our Town" (1989).

GRIFFITH, KRISTIN. Born Sept. 7, 1953 in Odessa, Tx, Juilliard graduate. Bdwy debut 1976 in "A Texas Trilogy," OB in "Rib Cage," "Character Lines," "3 Friends/2 Rooms," "A Month in the Country," "Fables for Friends," "The Trading Post," "Marching in Georgia," "American Garage," "A Midsummer Night's Dream," "Marathon '87," "Bunker Reveries," "On the Bench."

GRIMES, TAMMY. Born Jan. 30, 1934 in Lynn, MA. Attended Stephens Col., Neighborhood Playhouse. Debut 1956 OB in "The Littlest Revue," followed by "Clerambard," "Molly Trick," "Are You Now or Have You Ever Been," "Father's Day," "A Month in the Country," "Sunset," "Waltz of the Toreadors," "Mlle. Colombe," "Tammy Grimes in Concert," Bdwy in "Look after Lulu" (1959) for which she received a Theatre World Award, "The Unsinkable Molly Brown," "Private Lives," "High Spirits," "Rattle of a Simple Man," "The Only Game in Town," "Musical Jubilee," "California Suite," "Tartuffe," "Pal Joey in Concert," "42nd Street," "Orpheus Descending."

GRODIN, CHARLES. Born Apr. 21, 1935 in Pittsburgh, Pa. Attended UMiami, Pittsburgh Playhouse. Bdwy debut 1962 in "Tchin-Tchin," followed by "Absence of a Cello," "Same Time Next Year," OB in "Hooray! It's a Glorious Day," "Steambath," "Price of Fame" (which he wrote).

GROENENDAAL, CRIS. Born Feb. 17, 1948 in Erie, PA. Attended Allegheny Col., Exeter U., HB Studio. Bdwy debut 1979 in "Sweeney Todd," followed by "Sunday in the Park with George," "Brigadoon" (LC), "Desert Song" (LC), LC's "South Pacific," and "Sweeney Todd," "Phantom of the Opera," OB in "Francis," "Sweethearts in Concert," "Oh, Boy," "No No Nanette in Concert," "Sitting Pretty," "The Cat and the Fiddle."

GROSS, AMY. Born Oct. 1, 1978 in NYC. Bdwy debut 1990 in "Cat on a Hot Tin Roof."

GROSSMAN, HENRY. Born Oct. 11, 1938 in NYC. Attended Actors Studio. Debut 1961 OB in "The Magistrate," followed by "Galileo," Bdwy 1989 in "Grand Hotel."

GROVE, GREGORY. Born Dec. 15, 1949 in Ada, OK. Graduate SMU, HB Studio. Debut 1977 OB in "K: Impressions of Kafka's Trial," "Early One Evening at the Rainbow Bar & Grill," "Human Nature," Bdwy in "Lone Star/Private Wars" (1979).

GROVES, ROBIN. Born Nov. 24, 1951 in Neenah, Wi. Graduate Hollins Col. Bdwy debut 1976 in "Lady from the Sea," OB in "Vanities," "Starluster," "Territorial Rites," "The Carpenters," "Weekend Near Madison," "Sonata," 1 Act Festival, "Spare Parts."

GUITTARD, LAWRENCE. Born July 16, 1939 in San Francisco, Ca. Graduate Stanford U. Bdwy debut 1965 in "Baker Street," followed by "Anya," "Man of La Mancha," "A Little Night Music," for which he received a Theatre World Award, "Rodgers and Hart," "She Loves Me," "Oklahoma!" (1979), "The Sound of Music" (1990LC), OB in "Umbrellas of Cherbourg."

GUNTON, BOB. Born Nov. 15, 1945 in Santa Monica, CA. Attended UCal. Debut 1971 OB in "Who Am I?," followed by "The Kid," "Desperate Hours," "Tip-Toes," "How I Got That Story," "Hamlet," "Death of Von Richthofen," "Man Who Could See Through Time," "Phaedra Brittanica," "Sweeney Todd," Bdwy in "Happy End" (1977), "Working," "King of Hearts," "Evita," "Passion," "Big River."

HACK, STEVEN. Born Apr. 20, 1958 in St. Louis, MO. Attended CalArts, AADA, Debut 1978 OB in "The Coolest Cat in Town," followed by Bdwy in "Cats" (1982).

HADARY, JONATHAN. Born Oct. 11, 1948 in Chicago, IL. Attended Tufts U. Debut 1974 OB in "White Nights," followed by "El Grande de Coca Cola," "Songs from Pins and Needles," "God Bless You, Mr. Rosewater," "Pushing 30," "Scrambled Feet," "Coming Attractions," "Tom Foolery," "Charley Bacon and Family," "Road Show," "1-2-3-4-5," "Wenceslas Square," Bdwy in "Gemini," (1977/also OB), "Torch Song Trilogy," "As Is," "Gypsy."

HAFNER, JULIE J. Born June 4, 1952 in Dover, Oh. Graduate KentStateU. Debut 1976 OB in "The Club," followed by "Nunsense," Bdwy in "Nine."

HAGAN, JOHN. Born May 24, 1950 in NYC. Graduate NYU. Debut 1979 OB in "Disparate Acts," followed by "Chang in a Void Moon," "Two Kietzches in Love," "Deep Sleep," "Peter and Noel and Noel and Gertie," "Dark Shadows," "All That Fall."

HALL, CHARLES EDWARD. Born Nov. 12, 1951 in Frankfort, Ky. Graduate Murray State U. Debut 1977 OB in "Molly's Dream," followed by "Sheridan Square," "The Doctor in Spite of Himself," "Loudspeaker," "Action," "The Tavern," "Snow White," Radio City's Christmas Spectacular.

HALL, GEORGE. Born Nov. 19, 1916 in Toronto, Can. Attended Neighborhood Playhouse. Bdwy debut 1946 in "Call Me Mister," followed by "Lend an Ear," "Touch and Go," "Live Wire," "The Boy Friend," "There's a Girl in My Soup," "An Evening with Richard Nixon," "We Interrupt This Program," "Man and Superman," "Bent," "Noises Off," "Wild Honey," OB in "The Balcony," "Ernest in Love," "A Round with Rings," "Family Pieces," "Carousel," "The Case Against Roberta Guardino," "Marry Me!," "Arms and the Man," "The Old Glory," "Dancing for the Kaiser," "Casualties," "The Seagull," "A Stitch in Time," "Mary Stuart," "No End of Blame," "Hamlet," "Colette Collage," "The Homecoming," "And a Nightingale Sang," "The Bone Ring," "Much Ado About Nothing," "Measure for Measure," "Doctor's Dilemma," "The Crucible."

HALL, MARGARET. Born in Richmond, VA. Graduate Wm. & Mary Col. Bdwy debut 1960 in "Becket," followed by "High Spirits," "Mame," "The Leaf People," "Sunday in the Park with George," "Lettice and Lovage." OB in "The Boy Friend," "Fallout," "U.S.A.," "A Midsummer Night's Dream," "Little Mary Sunshine," "Just Say No."

HALLIDAY, ANDY. Born Mar. 31, 1953 in Orange, CT. Attended USIU/San Diego. Debut OB 1985 in "Vampire Lesbians of Sodom," followed by "Times Square Angel," "Psycho Beach Party," "The Lady in Question."

HALLIGAN, TIM. Born May 17, 1952 in Chicago, Il. Graduate UCol. Debut 1985 OB in "Responsible Parties," followed by "Rain. Some Fish. No Elephants."

HALSTON, JULIE. Born Dec. 7, 1954 in NY. Graduate Hofstra U. Debut OB 1985 in "Times Square Angel," followed by "Vampire Lesbians of Sodom," "Sleeping Beauty or Coma," "The Dubliners," "The Lady in Question."

HANAN, STEPHEN. Born Jan 7, 1947 in Washington, DC. Graduate Harvard, LAMDA. Debut 1978 OB in "All's Well That Ends Well," followed by "Taming of the Shrew," "Rabboni," Bdwy in "Pirates of Penzance" (1978),"Cats."

HANDLER, EVAN. Born Jan. 10, 1961 in NYC. Attended Juilliard. Debut 1979 OB in "Biography, A Game," followed by "Strider," "Final Orders," "Marathon '84," "Found a Peanut," "What's Wrong with This Picture?," "Bloodletters," Young Playwright Festival, "Human Nature," "Six Degrees of Separation," Bdwy in "Solomon's Child," (1982), "Biloxi Blues," "Brighton Beach Memoirs," "Broadway Bound," "Six Degrees of Separation."

HANKET, ARTHUR. Born June 23, 1934 in Virginia. Graduate UVa., FlaStateU. Debut 1979 OB in "Cuchculain Cycle," followed by "The Boys Next Door," "In Perpetuity throughout the Universe," "L'Illusion," "White Collar," "Heaven on Earth," "One Act Festival," "Kingfish."

HARAN, MARY-CLEERE. Born May 13, 1952 in San Francisco, Ca. Attended San Francisco State. Bdwy debut 1979 in "The 1940's Radio Hour," followed by OB in "Hollywood Opera."

HARDEN, MARCIA GAY. Born in La Jolla, CA. Graduate UTex. Debut 1989 OB in "The Man Who Shot Lincoln," followed by "One of the Guys."

HARMAN, PAUL. Born July 29, 1952 in Mineola, NY. Graduate Tufts U. Bdwy debut 1980 in "It's So Nice to Be Civilized," followed by "Les Miserables," "Chess," OB in "City Suite."

HARRINGTON, DELPHI. Born Aug. 26 in Chicago, Il. Graduate NorthwesternU. Debut 1960 OB in "A Country Scandal," followed by "Moon for the Misbegotten," "A Baker's Dozen," "The Zykovs," "Character Lines," "Richie," "American Garage," "After the Fall," "Rosencrantz and Guildenstern Are Dead," "Good Grief," Bdwy in "Thieves" (1974), "Everything in the Garden," "Romeo and Juliet," "Chapter Two."

HARRIS, ESTELLE. Born Apr. 22, 1932 in NYC. Debut 1984 OB in "Enter Laughing," followed by "Prisoner of Second Avenue."

HARRIS, JULIE. Born Dec. 2, 1925 in Grosse Pt., MI. Attended YaleU. Bdwy debut 1945 in "It's a Gift," followed by "Henry V," "Oedipus," "Playboy of the Western World," "Alice in Wonderland," "Macbeth," "Sundown Beach," for which she received a Theatre World Award, "The Young and the Fair," "Magnolia Alley," "Montserrat," "Member of the Wedding," "I Am a Camera," "Mlle. Colombe," "The Lark," "Country Wife," "Warm Peninsula," "Little Moon of Alban," "A Shot in the Dark," "Marathon '33," "Ready When You Are, CB.," "Hamlet" (CP), "Skyscraper," "40 Carats," "And Miss Reardon Drinks a Little," "Voices," "Last of Mrs. Lincoln," "Au Pair Man" (LC), "In Praise of Love," "Belle of Amherst" (Solo), "Break a Leg," "Driving Miss Daisy" (NTC).

HARRIS, NIKI. Born July 20, 1948 in Pittsburgh, Pa. Graduate Duquesne U. Bdwy debut 1980 in "A Day in Hollywood/A Night in the Ukraine," followed by "My One and Only," "Grand Hotel," OB in "Leave It to Jane," "No, No, Nanette," "Berkeley Square."

HARRIS, RONALD LEW. Born May 29, 1953 in Louisville, Ky. Graduate Moorehead State U, AADA. Debut 1976 OB in "Compulsion," followed by "Between Time and Timbuktu," "Going Home," "A Midsummer Night's Dream," "Mandrake," "Three Cuckolds," "Two Gentlemen of Verona," "Taming of the Shrew," "Julius Caesar," "Henry V," "Magic Time."

HARRIS, ROSALIND. Born Dec. 22 in White Plains, NY. Attended Ithaca Col. Debut 1968 OB in "Now," followed by "Do I Hear a Waltz?," "The Rise of David Levinsky," "Crazy Locomotive," "Has Anybody Here Found Love?," "It's Hard to Be a Jew," "Love Songs," "Triptych," "D," "Hollywood Opera," "Double Blessing," Bdwy in "Fiddler on the Roof" (1968).

HARRIS, TOM. Born Feb. 17, 1949 in Kingston, Pa. Graduate King's Col. Debut 1971 OB in "The Basic Training of Pavlo Hummel," followed by "Fishing," "Better People," Bdwy in "Grease" (1972).

HARRISON, REX. Born Mar. 5, 1908 in Huyten, Eng. Attended Liverpool Col. Bdwy debut 1936 in "Sweet Aloes," followed by "Anne of a Thousand Days," "Bell, Book and Candle," "Venus Observed," "Love of Four Colonels," "My Fair Lady" (1956/1981), "Fighting Cock," "Emperor Henry IV," "In Praise of Love," "Caesar and Cleopatra," "The Kingfisher," "Heartbreak House," "Aren't We All?," "The Circle."

HART, LINDA. Born Aug. 1, 1950 in Dallas, TX. Attended LACC. Debut 1982 OB in "Livin' Dolls," followed by "Sunday Serenade," "Gospel Rocks the Ballroom," "Sid Caesar & Company." Bdwy in "Bette Midler's Divine Madness" (1979), "Anything Goes" (1987) for which she received a Theatre World Award.

HART, MELISSA JOAN. Born Apr. 18, 1976 in Smithtown, NY. Debut 1989 OB in "Beside Herself," followed by "Imagining Brad."

HART, ROXANNE. Born in 1952 in Trenton, NJ. Attended Skidmore, PrincetonU. Bdwy debut 1977 in "Equus," followed by "Loose Ends," "Passion," "Devil's Disciple," OB in "Winter's Tale," "Johnny On a Spot," "The Purging," "Hedda Gabler," "Waiting for the Parade," "La Brea Tarpits," "Marathon '84," "Digby."

HAWKES, TERRI. Born Dec. 26 in Montreal, Can. Graduate UCalgary. Debut 1986 OB in "Sorrows and Sons," followed by "The Taming of the Shrew," "The Greenhouse Keeper Died," "Tamara."

HAYDEN, CYNTHIA. Born Dec. 23, 1948 in Memphis, Tn. Graduate Adelphi U. Debut 1981 OB in "The Idol Makers," followed by "Occupations," "Absent Friends," "The Crimes of Vautrin," "Abel's Sister," "In Pursuit of the Song of Hydrogen."

HAYES, LOREY. Born Oct. 12, 1956 in Wallace, NC. Graduate UNC Arts, UWisc. Debut 1975 OB in "For Colored Girls . . .," followed by "The Michigan," "Forty Deuce," "Like Them That Dream," "Special Interests," Bdwy in "Home" (1980), "Inacent Black."

HAYS, REX. Born June 17, 1946 in Hollywood, Ca. Graduate SanJoseStateU, BrandeisU. Bdwy debut 1975 in "Dance with Me," followed by "Angel," "King of Hearts," "Evita," "Onward Victoria!," "Woman of the Year," "La Cage aux Folles," "Grand Hotel," OB in "Charley's Tale."

HEALD, ANTHONY. Born Aug. 25, 1944 in New Rochelle, NY. Graduate MiStateU. Debut 1980 OB in "Glass Menagerie," followed by "Misalliance" for which he received a Theatre World Award, "The Caretaker," "The Fox," "Quartermaine's Terms," "The Philanthropist," "Henry V," "Digby," "Principia Scriptoriae," "Lisbon Traviata," "Elliot Loves," Bdwy in "Wake of Jamey Foster" (1982), "Marriage of Figaro," "Anything Goes."

HEARN, GEORGE. Born June 18, 1934 in St. Louis, MO. Graduate Southwestern Col. OB in "Macbeth," "Antony and Cleopatra," "As You Like It," "Richard III," "Merry Wives of Windsor," "Midsummer Night's Dream," "Hamlet," "Horseman, Pass By," "The Chosen," Bdwy in "A Time for Singing," "The Changing Room," "An Almost Perfect Person," "I Remember Mama," "Watch on the Rhine," "Sweeney Todd," "A Doll's Life," "Whodunnit," "La Cage aux Folles," "Ah! Wilderness!," "Ghetto," "Meet Me in St. Louis."

HECHT, PAUL. Born Aug. 16, 1941 in London, Eng. Attended McGill U. OB in "Sjt. Musgrave's Dance," "Macbird," "Phaedra," "Enrico IV," "Coriolanus," "The Cherry Orchard." Bdwy in "Rosencrantz and Guildenstern Are Dead," "1776," "The Rothschilds," "The Ride Across Lake Constance," "The Great God Brown," "Don Juan," "Emperor Henry IV," "Herzl," "Caesar and Cleopatra," "Night and Day," "Noises Off."

HECKART, EILEEN. Born Mar. 29, 1919 in Columbus, OH. Graduate Ohio StateU. Debut OB in "Tinker's Dam" (1942) followed by "Eleemosynary," Bdwy in "Our Town," "They Knew What They Wanted," "The Traitor," "Hilda Crane," "In Any Language," "Picnic" for which she received a Theatre World Award, "Bad Seed," "View from the Bridge," "Dark at the Top of the Stairs," "Invitation to a March," "Pal Joey," "Everybody Loves Opal," "And Things That Go Bump in the Night," "Barefoot in the Park," "You Know I Can't Hear You When the Water's Running," "Mother Lover," "Butterflies Are Free," "Veronica's Room," "Ladies at the Alamo," "The Cemetery Club."

HEINBERG, ALLAN. Born June 29, 1967 in New Orleans, La. Yale graduate. Debut 1990 OB in "Hannah..1939."

HEINSOHN, ELISA. Born Oct. 11, 1962 in Butler, PA. Debut 1984 OB in "Oy, Mama, Am I in Love," followed by "Scandal," Bdwy in "42nd Street" (1985), "Smile," "Phantom of the Opera."

HELLER, ADAM. Born June 8, 1960 in Englewood, NJ. Graduate NYU. Debut 1984 OB in "Kuni-Leml," followed by "The Special," "Half a World Away," Bdwy in "Les Miserables" (1989).

HELLER, ROBERT. Born Dec. 26, 1930 in Brooklyn, NY. Attended Actors Studio. Debut 1955 OB in "Terrible Swift Sword," followed by "The Cradle Will Rock," "My Prince, My King," "Waiting for Lefty," "Upside-Down on the Handlebars," "Briss," "Cabel of Hypocrites," "Common Ground," "Rasputin," Bdwy in "Marathon '33" (1963).

HENDERSON, SUZANNE. Born May 21, 1960 in New Jersey. Attended UDel. Debut 1981 OB in "City Suite," Bdwy in "Grand Hotel" (1989).

HENRITZE, BETTE. Born May 23 in Betsy Layne, KY. Graduate UTenn, OB in "Lion in Love," "Abe Lincoln in Illinois," "Othello," "Baal," "Long Christmas Dinner," "Queens of France," "Rimers of Eldritch," "Displaced Person," "Acquisition," "Crime of Passion," "Happiness Cage," "Henry VI," "Richard III," "Older People," "Lotta," "Catsplay," "A Month in the Country," "The Golem," "Daughters," "Steel Magnolias," Bdwy in "Jenny Kissed Me" (1948), "Pictures in the Hallway," "Giants, Sons of Giants," "Ballad of the Sad Cafe," "The White House," "Dr. Cook's Garden," "Here's Where I Belong," "Much Ado About Nothing," "Over Here," "Angel Street," "Man and Superman," "Macbeth" (1981), "Present Laughter," "The Octette Bridge Club," "Orpheus Descending," "Lettice and Lovage."

HENRY, BUCK. Born in 1930 in NYC. Dartmouth graduate. Bdwy debut 1952 in "Bernardine," OB in "The Premise," "Fortress of Glass," "Kingfish."

HENRY, SPRUCE. Born Apr. 14, 1962 in Covington, La. Graduate Clinch Valley Col. AADA. Debut 1989 OB in "Pericles."

HIBBERT, EDWARD. Born Sept. 9, 1955 in NYC. Attended Hurstpierpont Col., RADA. Bdwy debut 1982 in "Alice in Wonderland," followed by "Me and My Girl," OB in "Candida in Concert," "Dandy Dick," "Privates on Parade."

HICKS, LAURA. Born Nov. 17, 1956 in NYC. Juilliard graduate. Debut 1978 OB in "Spring Awakening," followed by "Talking With," "The Cradle Will Rock," "Paducah," "10 by Tennessee," "On the Verge," Bdwy in "The Heidi Chronicles" (1989).

HILER, KATHERINE. Born June 24, 1961 in Carson City, NV. Graduate Mt. Holyoke Col. Bdwy debut 1985 in "Hurlyburly," OB in "Liebelei" (1987), "The Year of the Duck," "A Shayna Maidel," "Temptation," "What a Man Weighs," "Macbeth," "Young Playwrights' Festival."

HILLIARD, RYAN. Born Jan. 20, 1945 in Ashtabula, Oh. Graduate KentStateU. Debut 1971 OB in "Godspell," followed by "The Bear," "Under Milk Wood," "The Madwoman of Chaillot," "Behind a Mask," One Act Festival.

HILLNER, NANCY. Born June 7, 1949 in Wakefield, RI. Graduate ULowell. Bdwy debut 1975 in "Dance with Me," followed by OB in "Nite Club Confidential," "Trading Places," "Nunsense," "Puppetmaster of Lodz."

HINES, GREGORY. Born Feb. 14, 1946 in NYC. Bdwy debut 1954 in "The Girl in Pink Tights," followed by "Eubie!" for which he received a Theatre World Award, "Comin' Uptown," "Black Broadway," "Sophisticated Ladies," OB in "Twelfth Night."

HODES, GLORIA. Born Aug. 20 in Norwich, Ct. Bdwy debut in "Gantry" (1969), followed by "Me and My Girl," OB in "The Club" for which she received a Theatre World Award, "Cycles of Fancy," "The Heroine," "Pearls," "Songs of Pyre."

HODGES, PATRICIA. Born in Puyallup, Wa. Graduate UWa. Debut 1985 OB in "The Normal Heart," followed by "On the Verge," "Hard Times," One Act Festival.

HOFFMAN, AVI. Born Mar. 3, 1958 in Bronx, NY. Graduate UMiami. Debut 1983 OB in "The Rise of David Levinsky," followed by "It's Hard to Be a Jew," "A Rendezvous With God," "The Golden Land," "Songs of Paradise."

HOFFMAN, DUSTIN. Born Aug. 8, 1937 in Los Angeles, Ca. Attended Santa Monica Col., Pasadena Playhouse. Bdwy debut 1963 in "A Cook for Mr. General," followed by "The Subject Was Roses," "Jimmy Shine," "Death of a Salesman" (1984), "Merchant of Venice" (1989), OB in "A View from the Bridge," "Harry, Noon and Night," "Journey of the 5th Horse," "Eh?" for which he received a Theatre World Award.

HOFFMAN, JANE. Born July 24 in Seattle, Wa. Graduate UCal. Bdwy debut 1940 in "'Tis of Thee," followed by "Crazy with the Heat," "Something for the Boys," "One Touch of Venus," "Calico Wedding," "Mermaids Singing," "Temporary Island," "Story for Strangers," "Two Blind Mice," "The Rose Tattoo," "The Crucible," "Witness for the Prosecution," "Third Best Sport," "Rhinoceros," "Mother Courage and Her Children," "Fair Game for Lovers," "A Murderer among Us," "Murder among Friends," "Some Americans Abroad," OB in "American Dream," "Sandbox," "Picnic on the Battlefield," "Theatre of the Absurd," "Child Buyer," "A Corner of the Bed," "Slow Memories," "Last Analysis," "Dear Oscar," "Hocus Pocus," "Lessons," "The Art of Dining," "Second Avenue Rag," "One Tiger to a Hill," "Isn't It Romantic," "Alto Part," "Frog Prince," "Alterations," "The Grandma Plays."

HOFMAIER, MARK. Born July 4, 1950 in Philadelphia, Pa. Graduate Az. Debut OB 1978 in "Midsummer Night's Dream," followed by "Marvelous Gray," "Modern Romance," "Relative Values," "The Racket," "Come as You Are."

HOFVENDAHL, STEVE. Born Sept. 1, 1956 in San Jose, Ca. Graduate USanta Clara, Brandeis U. Debut 1986 OB in "A Lie of the Mind," followed by "Ragged Trousered Philanthropists," "The Miser," "A Midsummer Night's Dream," Bdwy 1989 in "Mastergate."

HOLGATE, RONALD. Born May 26, 1937 in Aberdeen, SD. Attended Northwestern U. NewEng Conserv. Debut 1961 OB in "Hobo," followed by "Hooray, It's a Glorious Day," "Blue Plate Special," Bdwy "A Funny Thing Happened on the Way to the Forum," "Milk and Honey," "1776," "Saturday, Sunday, Monday," "The Grand Tour," "Musical Chairs," "42nd Street," "Lend Me a Tenor."

HOLLIDAY, POLLY. Born July 2, 1937 in Jasper, Al. Attended AlaCol., FlaStateU. Debut 1964 OB in "Orphee," followed by "Dinner on the Ground," "Wedding Band," "Girls Most Likely to Succeed," "Carnival Dreams," Bdwy in "All Over Town" (1974), "Cat on a Hot Tin Roof" (1989).

HOLLIS, TOMMY. Born Mar. 27, 1954 in Jacksonville, Tx. Attended Lon Morris Col., UHouston. Debut 1985 OB in "Diamonds," followed by "Secrets of the Lava Lamp," "Paradise," "Africanus Instructus," "The Colored Museum," Bdwy 1990 in "The Piano Lesson" for which he received a Theatre World Award.

HOLMES, PRUDENCE WRIGHT. Born in Boston, Ma. Attended Carnegie-Tech. Debut 1971 OB in "Godspell," followed by "Polly," "The Crazy Locomotive," "Dona Rosita," Bdwy in "Happy End" (1977), "Lettice and Lovage."

HOLTZMAN, MERRILL. Born Sept. 1, 1959. Bdwy debut 1989 in "Mastergate."

HONDA, CAROL A. Born Nov. 20 in Kealakekus, Hi. Graduate UHi. Debut 1983 OB in "Yellow Fever," followed by "Empress of China," "Manoa Valley," "Once Is Never Enough," "Life of the Land," "Rosie's Cafe," "And the Soul Shall Dance."

HOPKINS, LINDA. Born 1925 in New Orleans, LA. Bdwy in "Purlie," "Inner City," "Me and Bessie," "Black and Blue."

HORGAN, PATRICK. Born May 26, 1929 in Nottingham, Eng. Attended Stoneyhurst Col. Bdwy debut 1958 in "Redhead," followed by "Heartbreak House," "The Devil's Advocate," "Beyond the Fringe," "Baker Street," "Crown Matrimonial," "Sherlock Holmes," "My Fair Lady," "Deathtrap," "Noises Off," OB in "The Importance of Being Earnest," "Tamara."

HORVATH, JAN. Born Jan. 31, 1958 in Lake Forest, Il. Graduate CinConserv. Bdwy debut 1983 in "Oliver!," followed by "Sweet Charity," "Phantom of the Opera," "3 Penny Opera," OB in "Sing Me Sunshine," "Jacques Brel Is Alive and Well . . ."

HOSHKO, JOHN. Born July 28, 1959 in Bethesda, Md. Graduate USCal. Bdwy debut 1989 in "Prince of Central Park."

HOTY, DEE. Born Aug. 16, 1952 in Lakewood, Oh. Graduate Otterbein Col. Debut 1979 OB in "The Golden Apple," followed by "Ta-Dah!," "Personals," Bdwy in "The 5 O'Clock Girl" (1981), "Shakespeare Cabaret," "City of Angels."

HOTY, TONY. Born Sept. 29, 1949 in Lakewood, Oh. Attended Ithaca Col., UWVa. Debut 1974 OB in "Godspell" (also Bdwy 1976), followed by "Joseph and the Amazing Technicolor Dreamcoat," "Robin Hood," "Success and Succession," Bdwy in "Gypsy" (1989).

HOUGHTON, KATHARINE. Born Mar. 10, 1945 in Hartford, CT. Graduate Sarah Lawrence Col. Bdwy debut 1965 in "A Very Rich Woman," followed by "The Front Page" (1969), "Our Town" (1989), OB in "A Scent of Flowers," for which she received a Theatre World Award, "To Heaven in a Swing," "Madwoman of Chaillot," "Vivat! Vivat Regina!," "The Time of Your Life," "Children of the Sun," "Buddha," "On the Shady Side," "The Right Number," "The Hooded Eye."

HOWARD, CELIA. Born Aug. 23, 1937 in Oakland, Ca. Graduate Stanford U. Debut OB in "Cat and the Canary" (1965), followed by "Whitsuntide," "Last Summer at Blue Fish Cove," "After the Rain."

HOWARD, KEN. Born Mar. 28, 1944 in El Centro, CA. Graduate Yale. Bdwy debut 1968 in "Promises, Promises," followed by "1776," for which he received a Theatre World Award, "Child's Play," "Seesaw," "Little Black Sheep" (LC), "The Norman Conquests," "1600 Pennsylvania Avenue," "Rumors," "Love Letters."

HOWARD, TAYLOR. Born Dec. 31, 1957 in Mobile, AL. Graduate Auburn U. Debut 1988 OB in "Tartuffe," followed by "Dreams of Clytemnestra."

HUBER, KATHLEEN. Born Mar. 3, 1947 in NYC. Graduate UCal. Debut 1969 OB in "A Scent of Flowers," followed by "The Virgin and the Unicorn," "The Constant Wife," "Milestones," "Tamara."

HUDGINS, MARILYN. Born June 24 in Washington, DC. Graduate SBV Col., URedlands. Bdwy debut 1978 in "Hello, Dolly!," followed by "The Prince of Central Park" (1989), OB in "The Rothschilds."

HUDSON, TRAVIS. Born Feb. 2 in Amarillo, Tx. UTx graduate. Bdwy debut in "New Faces of 1962," followed by "Pousse Cafe," "Very Good Eddie," "The Grand Tour," OB in "Triad," "Tattooed Countess," "Young Abe Lincoln," "Get Thee to Canterbury," "The Golden Apple," "Annie Get Your Gun," "Nunsense."

HUFFMAN, CADY. Born Feb. 2, 1965 in Santa Barbara, CA. Debut 1983 OB in "They're Playing Our Song," followed by "Festival of 1 Acts," "Oh, Hell!," Bdwy 1985 in "La Cage aux Folles," followed by "Big Deal."

HUGHES, BARNARD. Born July 16, 1915 in Bedford Hills, NY. Attended Manhattan Col. Credits include OB's "Rosmersholm," "A Doll's House," "Hogan's Goat," "Lime," "Older People," "Hamlet," "Merry Wives of Windsor," "Pericles," "Pericles," "Three Sisters," "Translations," "Prelude to a Kiss" Bdwy in "The Ivy Green," "Dinosaur Wharf," "Teahouse of the August Moon," "A Majority of One," "Advise and Consent," "The Advocate," "Hamlet," "I Was Dancing," "Generations," "How Now Dow Jones," "Wrong Way Light Bulb," "Sheep on the Runway," "Abelard and Heloise," "Much Ado about Nothing," "Uncle Vanya," "The Good Doctor," "All over Town," "Da," "Angels Fall," "End of the World," "The Iceman Cometh," "Prelude to a Kiss."

HUGHES, LAURA. Born Jan. 28, 1959 in NYC. Graduate Neighborhood Playhouse. Debut 1980 OB in "The Diviners," followed by "A Tale Told," "Time Framed," "Fables for Friends," "Talley and Son," "Kate's Diary."

HUGHES, TRESA. Born Sept. 17, 1929 in Washington, DC. Attended Wayne U. OB in "Electra," "The Crucible," "Hogan's Goat," "Party on Greenwich Avenue," "Fragments," "Passing Through from Exotic Places," "Beggar on Horseback," "Early Morning," "The Old Ones," "Holy Places," "Awake and Sing," "Standing on My Knees," "Modern Ladies of Guanabacoa," "After the Fall," "Claptrap," "Cafe Crown," Bdwy in "The Miracle Worker," "The Devil's Advocate," "Dear Me, the Sky Is Falling," "The Last Analysis," "Spofford," "Man in the Glass Booth," "Prisoner of 2nd Avenue," "Tribute," "A View From the Bridge," "V & V Only," "Cafe Crown."

HULCE, TOM. Born Dec. 6, 1953 in Plymouth, MI. Graduate NCSchArts. Bdwy debut 1975 in "Equus," followed by "A Few Good Men," OB "A Memory of Two Mondays," "Julius Caesar," "Twelve Dreams," "The Rise and Rise of Daniel Rocket," "Haddock's Eyes."

HUMES, LINDA H. Born Oct. 19, 1955 in NYC. Graduate SUNY/Stonybrook. Debut 1978 OB in "Antigone," followed by "Spirit, Black and Female."

HURT, MARY BETH. Born Sept. 26, 1948 in Marshalltown, Ia. Attended UIowa, NYU. Debut 1972 OB in "More Than You Deserve," followed by "As You Like It," "Trelawny of the Wells," "The Cherry Orchard," "Love for Love," "A Member of the Wedding," "Boy Meets Girl," "Secret Service," "Father's Day," "Nest of the Wood Grouse," "The Day Room," "Secret Rapture," Bdwy in "Crimes of the Heart" (1981), "The Misanthrope," "Benefactors."

HURT, WILLIAM. Born Mar. 20, 1950 in Washington, DC. Graduate Tufts U., Juilliard. Debut 1976 OB in "Henry V," followed by "My Life," "Ulysses in Traction," "Lulu," "5th of July," "The Runner Stumbles," "Hamlet," "Mary Stuart," "Childe Byron," "The Diviners," "Richard II," "The Great Grandson of Jedediah Kohler," "A Midsummer Night's Dream," "Hurlyburly," "Joan of Arc at the Stake," "Beside Herself," Bdwy in "5th of July," "Hurlyburly." He received a 1978 Theatre World Award for his work that season with Circle Rep Theatre.

HUTTON, TIMOTHY. Born Aug. 16, 1960 in Malibu, Ca. Bdwy debut 1989 in "Love Letters," followed by "Prelude to a Kiss," "Remembrance," "Long Day's Journey into Night," "Sleep Beauty," "Driving Miss Daisy."

HYMAN, EARLE. Born Oct. 11, 1926 in Rocky Mount, NC. Attended New School, AmTh Wing. Bdwy debut 1943 in "Run Little Chillun," followed by "Anna Lucasta," "Climate of Eden," "Merchant of Venice," "Othello," "Julius Caesar," "The Tempest," "No Time for Sergeants," "Mr. Johnson," for which he received a Theatre World Award, "St. Joan," "Hamlet," "Waiting for Godot," "The Duchess of Malfi," "Les Blancs," "The Lady from Dubuque," "Execution of Justice," "Death of the King's Horseman," OB in "The White Rose and the Red," "Worlds of Shakespeare," "Jonah," "Life and Times of J. Walter Smintheus," "Orrin," "The Cherry Orchard," "House Party," "Carnival Dreams," "Agamemnon," "Othello," "Julius Caesar," "Coriolanus," "Remembrance," "Long Day's Journey into Night," "Sleep Beauty," "Driving Miss Daisy."

INNES, LAURA. Born Aug. 16, 1957 in Pontiac, Mi. Graduate Northwestern U. Debut 1982 OB in "Edmond," followed by "My Uncle Sam," "Life Is a Dream," "Alice and Fred," "A Country Doctor," "Vienna Lusthaus," "Stella," "Prison Made Tuxedos," "American Notes," "In Perpetuity throughout the Universe," "Paradise for the Worried."

IRVING, GEORGE S. Born Nov. 1, 1922 in Springfield, Ma. Attended Leland Powers Sch. Bdwy debut 1943 in "Oklahoma!," followed by "Call Me Mister," "Along 5th Avenue," "Two's Company," "Me and Juliet," "Can-Can," "Shinbone Alley," "Bells Are Ringing," "The Good Soup," "Tovarich," "A Murderer Among Us," "Alfie," "Anya," "Galileo," "4 on a Garden," "An Evening with Richard Nixon . . .," "Irene," "Who's Who in Hell," "All Over Town," "So Long 174th Street," "Once in a Lifetime," "I Remember Mama," "Copperfield," "Pirates of Penzance," "On Your Toes," "Me and My Girl," OB in "Rosalie in Concert," "Pal Joey in Concert," "Mexican Hayride."

IRWIN, BILL. Born Apr. 11, 1950 in California. Attended UCLA, Oberlin, Clown Col. Debut 1982 OB in "The Regard of Flight," followed by "The Courtroom," "Waiting For Godot," Bdwy in "5-6-7-8 Dance" (1983), "Accidental Death of an Anarchist," "Regard of Flight" (LC), "Largely New York."

IVEY, DANA. Born Aug. 12, in Atlanta, GA. Graduate Rollins Col., LAMDA. Bdwy debut 1981 in "Macbeth" (LC), followed by "Present Laughter," "Heartbreak House," "Sunday in the Park with George," "Pack of Lies," "Marriage of Figaro," OB in "A Call From the East," "Vivien," "Candida in Concert," "Major Barbara in Concert," "Quartermaine's Terms," "Baby with the Bathwater," "Driving Miss Daisy," "Wencelas Square," "Love Letters," "Hamlet."

JACKSON, CHELLI. Born Jan. 29, 1956 in North Hills, Pa. Graduate Elizabethtown Col. Debut 1981 OB in "Seesaw," followed by "Brush Arbor Revival."

JACKSON, DAVID. Born Dec. 4, 1948 in Philadelphia, PA. Bdwy debut 1980 in "Eubie!," followed by "My One and Only," "La Cage aux Folles," "Grand Hotel," OB in "Blackamoor."

JACOBS, MAX. Born Apr. 28, 1937 in Buffalo, NY. Graduate UAz. Bdwy debut 1965 in "The Zulu and the Zayda," OB in "Full Circle," "The Working Man," "Hallowed Halls," "The Man in the Glass Booth," "Different People, Different Rooms," "Second Avenue," "Othello."

JACOBY, MARK. Born May 21, 1947 in Johnson City, Tn. Graduate GaStateU, Fla StateU, St. John's U. Debut 1984 OB in "Bells Are Ringing," Bdwy in "Sweet Charity" for which he received a Theatre World Award, "Grand Hotel."

JAMES, KELLI. Born Mar. 18, 1959 in Council Bluffs, Iowa. Bdwy debut 1987 in "Les Miserables."

JAMROG, JOSEPH. Born Dec. 21, 1932 in Flushing, NY. Graduate CCNY. Debut 1970 OB in "Nobody Hears a Broken Drum," followed by "Tango," "And Whose Little Boy Are You?," "When You Comin' Back, Red Ryder?," "Drums at Yale," "The Boy Friend," "Love," "Death Plays," "Too Much Johnson," "A Stitch in Time," "Pantagleize," "Final Hours," "Returnings," "Brass Birds Don't Sing," "And Things That Go Bump in the Night," "Fun," "Henry Lumpur," "I Am a Winner," "Little Lies."

JAY, WILLIAM. Born May 15, 1935 in Baxter Springs, Ks. Attended Omaha U. Debut 1963 OB in "Utopia" followed by "The Blacks," "Loop the Loop," "Happy Ending," "Day of Absence," "Hamlet," "Othello," "Song of the Lusitanian Bogey," "Ceremonies in Dark Old Men," "The Harangues," "Brotherhood," "Perry's Mission," "Rosalee Pritchett," "Sister Sadie," "Coriolanus," "Getting Out," "Henrietta," "The Boys Next Door," "Burner's Frolic."

JBARA, GREGORY. Born Sept. 28, 1961 in Wayne, MI. Graduate UMi., Juilliard. Debut 1986 OB in "Have I Got a Girl for You!," "Serious Money," "Privates on Parade." Bdwy in "Serious Money" (1988), "Born Yesterday."

JENKINS, KEN. Born in Kentucky in 1940. Bdwy debut 1986 in "Big River," followed OB in "Feast Here Tonight."

JENNINGS, KEN. Born Oct. 10, 1947 in Jersey City, NJ. Graduate St. Peter's Col. Bdwy debut 1975 in "All God's Chillun Got Wings," followed by "Sweeney Todd" for which he received a Theatre World Award, "Present Laughter," "Grand Hotel," OB in "Once on a Summer's Day," "Mayor," "Rabboni," "Gifts of the Magi," "Carmilla."

JEROME, TIMOTHY. Born Dec. 29, 1943 in Los Angeles, CA. Graduate Ithaca Col. Bdwy debut 1969 in "Man of La Mancha," followed by "The Rothschilds," "Creation of the World . . .," "Moony Shapiro Songbook," "Cats," "Me and My Girl," "Grand Hotel," OB in "Beggar's Opera," "Pretzels," "Civilization and Its Discontents," "The Little Prince," "Colette Collage," "Room Service," "Romance in Hard Times."

JETER, MICHAEL. Born Aug. 26, 1952 in Lawrenceburg, TN. Graduate Memphis State U. Bdwy debut 1978 in "Once in a Lifetime," followed by "Grand Hotel," OB in "The Master and Margarita," "G.R. Point," for which he received a Theatre World Award, "Alice in Concert," "El Bravo," "Cloud 9," "Greater Tuna," "The Boys Next Door," "Only Kidding."

JOHANSON, DON. Born Oct. 19, 1952 in Rock Hill, SC. Graduate USC. Bdwy debut 1976 in "Rex," followed by "Cats," OB in "The American Dance Machine."

JOHNS, GLYNIS. Born Oct. 5, 1923 in Pretoria, S.Af. Bdwy debut 1952 in "Gertie," followed by "Major Barbara," "Too True To Be Good," "A Little Night Music," "The Circle."

JOHNS, KURT. Born Feb. 28, 1954 in Cincinnati, Oh. Graduate CinConsv. Bdwy debut 1988 in "Chess," followed by "Aspects of Love."

JOHNSON, DANIEL T. Born Aug. 13, 1947 in Cass County, Mi. Graduate WMiU, OreU. Debut 1980 OB in "Romeo and Juliet," followed by "The Scarecrow," "Meetings with Ben Franklin," "Edward II," "Two Wills," "Julius Caesar," "Porter's Brandy," "Leave It to Me," "Troubadour."

JOHNSON, PAGE. Born Aug. 25, 1930 in Welch, WV. Graduate Ithaca Col. Bdwy bow 1951 in "Romeo and Juliet," followed by "Electra," "Oedipus," "Camino Real," "In April Once," for which he received a Theatre World Award, "Red Roses for Me," "The Lovers," "Equus," "You Can't Take It With You," "Brush Arbor Revival," OB in "The Enchanted," "Guitar," "4 in 1," "Journey of the Fifth Horse," APA's "School for Scandal," "The Tavern," and "The Seagull," "Odd Couple," "Boys In The Band," "Medea," "Deathtrap," "Best Little Whorehouse in Texas," "Fool for Love."

JOHNSON, TIM. Born Apr. 6, 1956 in Cleveland, Oh. Graduate Baldwin-Wallace Col. Debut 1987 in "The Death of Bessie Smith," followed by "Porgy and Bess," "Lost in the Stars," "Zora Neale Hurston."

JONES, JAY AUBREY. Born Mar. 30, 1954 in Atlantic City, NJ. Graduate Syracuse U. Debut 1981 OB in "Sea Dream," followed by "Divine Hysteria," "Inacent Black and the Brothers," "La Belle Helene," Bdwy in "Cats" (1986).

JONES, SABRA. Born Mar. 22, 1951 in California. Debut 1982 OB in "Joan of Lorraine," followed by "Inheritors," "Paradise Lost," "Ghosts," "Clarence," "Madwoman of Chaillot," "Vivat! Vivat Regina!," "Children of the Sun," "Six Degrees of Separation."

JONES, SIMON. Born July 27, 1950 in Wiltshire, Eng. Attended Trinity Hall. NY debut 1984 OB in "Terra Nova," followed by "Magdalena in Concert," "Woman in Mind," "Privates on Parade," Bdwy in "The Real Thing" (1984), "Benefactors."

JONES, WALKER. Born Aug. 27, 1956 in Pensacola, Fl. Graduate BostonU, Yale. Debut 1989 OB in "Wonderful Town."

JOY, ROBERT. Born Aug. 17, 1951 in Montreal, Can. Graduate Oxford U. Debut 1978 OB in "The Diary of Anne Frank," followed by "Fables for Friends," "Lydie Breeze," "Sister Mary Ignatius Explains It all," "Actor's Nightmare," "What I Did Last Summer," "The Death of von Richthofen," "Lenny and the Heartbreakers," "Found a Peanut," "Field Day," "Life and Limb," "Hyde in Hollywood," Bdwy in "Hay Fever" (1985), "The Nerd."

JOYCE, HEIDI. Born Sept. 12, 1960 in Cleveland, OH. Graduate IndU. Debut 1986 OB in "Girl Crazy," followed by "The Shop on Main Street," "Have I Got a Girl For You!," "Leave It to Jane."

JOYCE, JOE. Born Nov. 22, 1957 in Pittsburgh, Pa. Graduate Boston U. Debut 1981 in "Close Enough for Jazz," followed by "Oh, Johnny!," "They Came from Planet Mirth."

JUDD, REBECCA. Born in Fresno, Ca. Graduate UNev. Debut 1988 OB in "Dutchman," followed by "Lost in the Stars," "The Golden Apple," Bdwy 1989 in "Sweeney Todd."

JULIA, RAUL. Born Mar. 9, 1940 in San Juan, PR. Graduate UPR. OB credits include "Macbeth," "Titus Andronicus," "Theatre in the Streets," "Life Is a Dream," "Blood Wedding," "Ox Cart," "No Exit," "Memorandum," "Frank Gagliano's City Scene," "Your Own Thing," "Persians," "Castro Complex," "Pinkville," "Hamlet," "King Lear," "As You Like It," "Emperor of Late Night Radio," "Threepenny Opera," "The Cherry Orchard," "Taming of the Shrew," "Othello," "The Tempest," "A Christmas Carol," "Macbeth," Bdwy in "The Cuban Thing," "Indians," "Two Gentlemen of Verona," "Via Galactica," "Where's Charley?," "Dracula," "Betrayal," "Nine," "Design for Living," "Arms and the Man."

KAGAN, DIANE. Born in Maplewood, NJ. Graduate FlaStateU. Debut 1963 OB in "Asylum," followed by "Days and Nights of Beebee Fenstermaker," "Death of a Well-Loved Boy," "Mme. de Sade," "Blue Boys," "Alive and Well in Argentina," "Little Black Sheep," "The Family," "Ladyhouse Blues," "Scenes from Everyday Life," "Marvelous Gray," "Enrico IV," Bdwy in "Chinese Prime Minister" (1964), "Never Too Late," "Any Wednesday," "Venus Is," "Tiger at the Gates," "Vieux Carre."

KAHN, GARY. Born Feb. 22, 1956 in The Bronx, NY. Graduate UMiami, UTx. Debut OB 1982 in "All of the Above," followed by Bdwy in "City of Angels" (1989).

KANDEL, PAUL. Born Feb. 15, 1951 in Queens, NYC. Graduate Harpur Col. Debut 1977 OB in "Nightclub Cantata," followed by "Two Grown Men," "Scrambled Feet," "The Taming of the Shrew," "Lucky Stiff," "20 Fingers, 20 Toes."

KANE, DONNA. Born Aug. 12, 1962 in Beacon, NY. Graduate Mt. Holyoke Col. Debut 1985 OB in "Dames at Sea," for which she received a Theatre World Award, followed by "The Vinegar Tree," "Johnny Pye and the Foolkiller," "Babes in Arms," "Young Rube," Bdwy in "Meet Me in St. Louis."

KANE, MARY. Born March 21, 1961 in Scranton, Pa. Graduate Mt. Holyoke Col. Debut 1986 OB in "Alterations," Bdwy in "Accomplice" (1990).

KARIBALIS, CURT. Born Feb. 24, 1947 in Superior, WI. Graduate UWis. Debut 1971 OB in "Woyzeck," followed by "The Taming of the Shrew," Bdwy in "The Great God Brown" (1972), "Don Juan," "The Visit," "Chemin de Fer," "Holiday," "Goodbye Fidel," "M. Butterfly."

KATARINA, ANNA. Born Feb. 25, 1956 in Bern, Switz. Attended Bern Consv. Debut 1987 OB in "Tamara."

KAUFMAN, ERIC H. Born Sept. 11, 1961 in NYC. Attended UWis., NYU. Bdwy debut 1986 in "L'Chaim to Life," followed by "Gypsy" (1989).

KAYE, JUDY. Born Oct. 11, 1948 in Phoenix, AZ. Attended UCLA, Ariz. State U. Bdwy debut 1977 in "Grease," followed by "On the 20th Century," for which she received a Theatre World Award, "Moony Shapiro Songbook," "Oh, Brother!," "Phantom of the Opera," "The Pajama Game" (LC), OB in "Eileen in Concert," "Can't Help Singing," "Four to Make Two," "Sweethearts in Concert," "Love," "No No Nanette in Concert," "Magdalena in Concert," "Babes in Arms," "Desire Under the Elms," "The Cat and the Fiddle."

KEAL, ANITA. Born in Philadelphia, PA. Graduate Syracuse U. Debut 1956 OB in "Private Life of the Master Race," followed by "Brothers Karamazov," "Hedda Gabler," "Witches Sabbath," "Six Characters in Search of an Author," "Yes, My Darling Daughter," "Speed Gets the Poppy," "You Don't Have to Tell Me," "Val Christie and Others," "Do You Still Believe the Rumor?," "Farmyard," "Merry Wives of Scarsdale," "Exiles," "Fish Riding Bikes," "Haven," "The Affair," "Mother Bickerdyke," "Made in Heaven," "Bradley & Beth," "Carbondale Dreams." Bdwy in "M. Butterfly" (1989).

KEATS, STEVEN. Born Feb. 6, 1945 in NYC. Attended MontclairStateCol., Yale U. Debut 1970 OB in "One Flew over the Cuckoo's Nest," followed by "We Bombed in New Haven," "Awake and Sing," "The Rose Tattoo," "I'm Getting My Act Together . . .," "Sunday Runners in the Rain," "Who They Are and How It Is with Them," "Other People's Money," Bdwy in "Oh! Calcutta!" (1971).

KELLY, EAMON. Born Mar. 30, 1914 in County Kerry, Ire. Graduate Ntl.Col. of Art. Bdwy debut 1966 in "Philadelphia, Here I Come," OB in "In My Father's Time," "English That for Me."

KENER, DAVID. Born May 21, 1959 in Brooklyn, NY. Graduate NYU. Debut 1987 OB in "The Rise of David Levinsky," followed by "Songs of Paradise."

KEPROS, NICHOLAS. Born Nov. 8, 1932 in Salt Lake City, UT. Graduate UUtah, RADA. Debut 1958 OB in "The Golden Six," followed by "Wars of Roses," "Julius Caesar," "Hamlet," "Henry IV," "She Stoops to Conquer," "Peer Gynt," "Octaroon," "Endicott and the Red Cross," "The Judas Applause," "Irish Hebrew Lesson," "Judgment at Havana," "The Millionairess," "Androcles and the Lion," "The Redempter," "Othello," "The Times and Appetites of Toulouse-Lautrec," "Two Fridays," "Rameau's Nephew," "Good Grief," Bdwy in "St. Joan" (1968), "Amadeus," "Execution of Justice."

KERBECK, ROBERT. Born July 30, 1963 in Philadelphia, Pa. Graduate UPa. Debut 1990 OB in "Bovver Boys," followed by "Lloyd and Lee."

KERNS, LINDA. Born June 2, 1953 in Columbus, Oh. Attended Temple U, AADA. Debut 1981 OB in "Crisp," followed by "Henry 8th at the Grand Ole Opry," "Smoke on the Mountain," Bdwy in "Nine" (1982), "Big River."

KERSHAW, WHITNEY. Born Apr. 10, 1962 in Orlando, FL. Attended Harkness/Joffrey Ballet Schools. Debut 1981 OB in "Francis," Bdwy in "Cats."

KHOURY, PAMELA. Born May 17, 1954 in Beirut, Lebanon. Graduate UTx. Bdwy debut 1980 in "West Side Story," followed by "Oh, Brother!," "Jerome Robbins' Broadway," OB in "Too Many Girls."

KIDD, WILEY. Born Dec. 11, 1960 in Portsmouth, Va. Graduate Carnegie-MellonU. Bdwy debut in "Me and My Girl" (1987) followed by "Aspects of Love," OB in "Mores."

KILTY, JEROME. Born June 24, 1922 in Pala Indian Reservation, Ca. Attended Guildhall School/London. Bdwy debut 1950 in "The Relapse," followed by "Love's Labours Lost," "Misalliance," "A Pin to See the Peepshow," "Frogs of Spring," "Quadrille," "Othello," "Henry IV," "Moon for the Misbegotten," "Mastergate," OB in "Dear Liar," "A Month in the Country," "Enter a Free Man," "The Doctor's Dilemma."

KINGSLEY-WEIHE, GRETCHEN. Born Oct. 6, 1961 in Washington, DC. Attended Tulane U. Debut 1985 OB in "Mowgli," followed by "This Could Be the Start," Bdwy in "Les Miserables" (1987), "Sweeney Todd."

KLEMPERER, WERNER. Born Mar. 20, 1920 in Cologne, Ger. Graduate Pasadena Playhouse. Bdwy debut 1947 in "Heads or Tails," followed by "Galileo," "The Insect Comedy," "20th Century," "Dear Charles," "Night of the Tribades," "Cabaret," "The Sound of Music" (LC), OB in "Master Class."

KLINE, KEVIN. Born Oct. 24, 1947 in St. Louis, MO. Graduate IndU, Juilliard. Debut 1970 OB in "War of Roses," followed by "School for Scandal," "Lower Depths," "The Hostage," "Women Beware Women," "Robber Bridegroom," "Edward II," "The Time of Your Life," "Beware the Jubjub Bird," "Dance on a Country Grave," "Richard III," "Henry V," "Hamlet," "Much Ado About Nothing," "Hamlet," Bdwy in "Three Sisters," "Measure for Measure," "Beggar's Opera," "Scapin'," "On the 20th Century," "Loose Ends," "Pirates of Penzance," "Arms and the Man."

KLUNIS, TOM. Born in San Francisco, CA. Bdwy debut 1961 in "Gideon," followed by "The Devils," "Henry V," "Romeo and Juliet," "St. Joan," "Hide and Seek," "Bacchae," "Plenty," "M. Butterfly," OB in "The Immoralist," "Hamlet," "Arms and the Man," "The Potting Shed," "Measure for Measure," "Romeo and Juliet," "The Balcony," "Our Town," "The Man Who Never Died," "God Is My Ram," "Rise Marlow," "Iphigenia in Aulis," "Still Life," "The Master and Margarita," "As You Like It," "The Winter Dancers," "When We Dead Awaken," "Vieux Carre," "The Master Builder," "Richard III," "A Map of the World."

KNAPP, SARAH. Born Jan. 20, 1959 in Kansas City, MO. Graduate AADA. Debut OB 1986 in "Gifts of the Magi," followed by "The No Frills Revue," "Nunsense."

Tim
Halligan

Estelle
Harris

Evan
Handler

Lorey
Hayes

Anthony
Heald

Eileen
Heckart

Elisa
Heinsohn

Adam
Heller

Suzanne
Henderson

Spruce
Henry

Nancy
Hillner

Gregory
Hines

Mark
Hofmaier

Jane
Hoffman

Steve
Hofvendahl

Prudence
Holmes

Merrill
Holtzman

Carol A.
Honda

Dee
Hoty

Tony
Hoty

Katharine
Houghton

Taylor
Howard

Kathleen
Huber

Earle
Hyman

Bill
Irwin

Dana
Ivey

David
Jackson

Glynis
Johns

Page
Johnson

Heidi
Joyce

205

KNELL, DANE. Born Sept. 27, 1932 in Winthrop, Ma. Bdwy debut 1952 in "See the Jaguar," followed by "Lettice and Lovage," OB in "Ulster," "Moon Dances," "Court of Miracles," "Gas Station," "Zeks," "She Stoops to Conquer."

KNIGHT, WAYNE. Born Aug. 7, 1955 in NYC. Graduate UGa. Bdwy debut 1979 in "Gemini," followed by "Mastergate," OB in "One of the Guys."

KOKA, JULIETTE. Born Apr. 4, 1930 in Finland. Attended Helsinki School of Dramatic Arts. Debut 1977 OB in "Piaf . . . A Remembrance," for which she received a Theatre World Award, followed by "Ladies and Gentlemen Jerome Kern," "Salon," "The Concert That Could Have Been," Bdwy in All Star Players Club Centennial Salute" (1989).

KOLINSKI, JOSEPH. Born June 26, 1953 in Detroit, Mi. Attended UDetroit. Bdwy debut 1980 in "Brigadoon," followed by "Dance a Little Closer," "The Three Musketeers," "Les Miserables," OB in "Hijinks!," "The Human Comedy" (also Bdwy).

KOPACHE, THOMAS. Born Oct. 17, 1945 in Manchester, NH. Graduate San Diego State U. CalInstArts. Debut 1976 OB in "The Architect and the Emperor of Assyria," followed by "Bronto-saurus Rex," "Extravagant Triumph," "Caligula," "The Tempest," "Macbeth," "Measure for Measure," "Hunting Scenes from Lower Bavaria," "The Danube," "Friends Too Numerous to Mention," "Twelfth Night," "A Winter's Tale," "Working 1 Acts," Bdwy in "Our Town" (1989), "Orpheus Descending."

KORBICH, EDDIE. Born Nov. 6, 1960 in Washington, DC. Graduate Boston Consv. Debut 1985 OB in "A Little Night Music," followed by "Flora, the Red Menace," "No Frills Revue," "The Last Musical Comedy," "Godspell," "Sweeney Todd" (also Bdwy 1989), Bdwy in "Singin' in the Rain" (1985).

KORNFELD, ERIC. Born July 6, 1956 in Reading, Pa. Attended Kent State U. Debut 1981 OB in "Catch 22," followed by "The West Street Gang," "Doesn't the Sky Look Green Today?," "The Ventriloquist," "Something Old, Something New," "Midsummer Nights."

KORTHAZE, RICHARD. Born Feb. 11 in Chicago, IL. Graduate Chicago Musical Col. Bdwy debut 1953 in "Pal Joey," followed by "Wonderful Town," "Happy Hunting," "Conquering Hero," "How to Succeed in Business . . . ," "Skyscraper," "Walking Happy," "Promises, Promises," "Pippin," "Chicago," "Dancin'," "Take Me Along" (1985), "Anything Goes," OB in "Phoenix '55" (1955), "Romance in Hard Times."

KORZEN, ANNIE. Born Nov. 8, 1938 in NYC. Graduate Bard Col. Debut 1976 OB in "Fiorello," followed by "Intermission," "I Can't Keep Running in Place," "Pearls," "The Return."

KRAG, JAMES. Born July 23, 1962 in Chicago, Il. Graduate DePaul U. Bdwy debut 1988 in "Burn This," followed by OB's "Mill Fire."

KRAKOWSKI, JANE. Born Oct. 11, 1968 in New Jersey. Debut 1984 OB in "American Passion," followed by "Miami," "A Little Night Music," Bdwy in "Starlight Express" (1987), "Grand Hotel."

KRISTIEN, DALE. Born May 18 in Washington, DC. Graduate Ithaca Col. Bdwy debut 1981 in "Camelot," followed by "Show Boat," "Radio City Music Specials" "Phantom of the Opera."

KUHN, BRUCE W. Born Dec. 7, 1955 in Davenport, IA. Graduate UWVa., UWash. Bdwy debut 1987 in "Les Miserables."

KURSHAL, RAYMOND. Born in NYC. Hunter Col. graduate. Bdwy debut 1985 in "Singin' in the Rain," OB in "Garden of Earthly Delights," "Winter's Tale," "Ghosts in the Dining Room."

KURTZ, MARCIA JEAN. Born in The Bronx, NY. Graduate Juilliard. Debut 1966 OB in "Jonah," followed by "America Hurrah," "Red Cross," "Muzeeka," "Effect of Gamma Rays . . . ," "The Year Boston Won the Pennant," "The Mirror," "The Orphan," "Action," "The Dybbuk," "Ivanov," "What's Wrong with This Picture?," "Today I Am a Fountain Pen," "The Chopin Playoffs," "Lowman Family Picnic," "Human Nature," "When She Danced," Bdwy in "The Chinese and Dr. Fish," "Thieves," "Execution of Justice."

KURTZ, SWOOSIE. Born Sept. 6 in Omaha, Ne. Attended USCal, LAMDA. Debut 1968 OB in "The Firebugs," followed by "The Effect of Gamma Rays . . . ," "Enter a Free Man," "Children," "Museum," "Uncommon Women and Others," "Wine Untouched," "Summer," "The Beach House," "Six Degrees of Separation," Bdwy in "Ah, Wilderness!" (1975), "Tartuffe," "A History of the American Film," "5th of July," " House of Blue Leaves."

LABLE, LORNA. Born June 30, 1947 in Brooklyn, NYC. Graduate Brooklyn Col. Debut 1986 OB in "Funny Girl," followed by "Ragtime Christmas," "Bleacher Bums."

LACONI, ROBERT. Born Apr. 23, 1954 in Akron, OH. Graduate Kent StateU. Debut 1978 OB in "Gulliver's Travels," followed by "A Book of Etiquette," "cummings and goings," "Let's Face It," "Julius Caesar," "Comedy of Errors," "New Girl in Town," "The Gambler," "Based on a True Story," "Picture of Dorian Gray."

LaCOY, DEBORAH. Born Oct. 20, 1963 in Worcester, Ma. Graduate Boston U. Debut 1988 OB in "What About Love," followed by "Insatiable/Temporary People."

LACY, TOM. Born Aug. 30, 1933 in NYC. Debut 1965 OB in "The Fourth Pig," followed by "The Fantasticks," "Shoemaker's Holiday," "Love and Let Love," "The Millionairess," "Crimes of Passion," "The Real Inspector Hound," "Enemies," "Flying Blind," "Abel & Bela/Architruc," Bdwy in "Last of the Red Hot Lovers."

LAGERFELT, CAROLINE. Born Sept. 23 in Paris. Graduate AADA. Bdwy debut 1971 in "The Philanthropist," followed by "4 on a Garden," "Jockey Club Stakes," "The Constant Wife," "Otherwise Engaged," "Betrayal," "The Real Thing," OB in "Look Back in Anger," "Close of Play," "Sea Anchor," "Quartermaine's Terms," "Other Places," "Phaedra Britanica," "Swim Visit."

LAHTI, CHRISTINE. Born Apr. 4, 1950 in Detroit, MI. Graduate UMich, HB Studio. Debut 1979 OB in "The Wood," for which she received a Theatre World Award, followed by "Landscape of the Body," "The Country Girl," "Little Murders," Bdwy in "Loose Ends" (1980), "Division Street," "Scenes and Revelations," "Present Laughter," "The Heidi Chronicles."

LAMB, MARY ANN. Born July 4, 1959 in Seattle, WA. Attended Neighborhood Playhouse. Bdwy debut 1985 in "Song and Dance," followed by "Starlight Express," "Jerome Robbins' Broadway."

LAMBERT, JULIET. Born Jan. 15, 1964 in Massachusetts. Graduate Middlebury Col. Debut 1989 OB in "Genesis," followed by Bdwy in "Meet Me in St. Louis" (1989).

LAMBERT, ROBERT. Born July 28, 1960 in Ypsilanti, Mi. Graduate Wayne State U. Bdwy debut 1989 in "Gypsy" for which he received a Theatre World Award.

LANDER, JOHN-MICHAEL. Born Jan. 17th in Hamilton, Oh. Attended UCal/Irvine, Wright-StateU. Debut 1989 OB in "Adam and the Experts."

LANDFIELD, TIMOTHY. Born Aug. 22, 1950 in Palo Alto, Ca. Graduate Hampshire Col. Bdwy debut 1977 in "Tartuffe," followed by "Crucifer of Blood," "Wild Honey," "Rumors," OB in "Actor's Nightmare," "Sister Mary Ignatius Explains It All . . . ," "Charlotte Sweet," "Flight of the Earls."

LANDMAN, JEFFREY. Born Apr. 5, 1978 in East Amherst, NY. Bdwy debut 1989 in "Les Miserables," OB in "Traveler in the Dark."

LANDRON, JACK. Born June 2, 1938 in San Juan, PR. Graduate Emerson Col. Debut 1970 OB in "Ododo," followed by "Mother Courage and Her Children," "If You Promise Not to Learn," "What's a Nice Country Like You . . . ," "Spell 7," "Mondongo," "Ballet Behind the Bridge," "The Garden," "Don Juan in NYC," "I Am a Winner," "The Chinese Charade," "Capitol Walk." Bdwy in "Hurry Harry" (1972), "Dr. Jazz," "Tough to Get Help," "Murderous Angels."

LANDRY, LAURI. Born Nov. 30th in Manchester, NH. Graduate UNH. Bdwy debut 1990 in "Zoya's Apartment."

LANE, EDDIE. Born May 25, 1933 in McKees Rocks, Pa. Attended UPittsburgh, Pittsburgh Playhouse. Debut 1988 OB in "The Good and Faithful Servant," followed by "Before Dawn."

LANE, NATHAN. Born Feb. 3, 1956 in Jersey City, NJ. Debut 1978 OB in "A Midsummer Night's Dream," followed by "Love," "Measure for Measure," "Claptrap," "The Common Pursuit," "In a Pig's Valise," "Uncounted Blessings," "The Film Society," "The Lisbon Traviata," "Bad Habits," Bdwy in "Present Laughter" (1982), "Merlin," "Wind in the Willows," "Some Americans Abroad."

LANG, MARK EDWARD. Born May 2nd in NYC. Graduate Vassar Col. Debut 1986 OB in "In Their Own Words," followed by "Initiation Rites," "Milestones," "A Midsummer Night's Dream," "Julius Caesar," "The Tempest," "Radical Roots," "Mary Stuart," "Dark of the Moon."

LANG, STEPHEN. Born July 11, 1952 in NYC. Graduate Swarthmore Col. Debut 1975 OB in "Hamlet," followed by "Henry V," "Shadow of a Gunman," "A Winter's Tale," "Johnny on a Spot," "Barbarians," "Ah, Men," "Clownmaker," "Hannah," "Rosencrantz and Guildenstern Are Dead," Bdwy in "St. Joan" (1977), "Death of a Salesman" (1984), "A Few Good Men."

LANGE, ANNE. Born June 24, 1953 in Pipestone, MN. Attended Carnegie-Mellon U. Debut 1979 OB in "Rat's Nest," followed by "Hunting Scenes from Lower Bavaria," "Crossfire," "Linda Her and the Fairy Garden," "Little Footsteps," Bdwy in "The Survivor" (1981), "The Heidi Chronicles."

LANGELLA, FRANK. Born Jan. 1, 1940 in Bayonne, NJ. Graduate Syracuse U. Debut 1963 OB in "The Immoralist," followed by "The Old Glory," "Good Day," "The White Devil," "Yerma," "Iphigenia in Aulis," "A Cry of Players," "Prince of Homburg," "After the Fall," "The Tempest," Bdwy in "Seascape" (1975), "Dracula," "Amadeus," "Passion," "Design for Living," "Hurlybur-ly," "Sherlock's Last Case."

LANIGAN, LORRAINE. Born Mar. 10, 1956 in Long Branch, NJ. Graduate Kean Col., RutgersU. Debut OB in "My Unknown," followed by "Insatiable/Temporary People."

LANK, ANNA BESS. Born Nov. 22 in Rochester, NY. Graduate UCLA. Debut 1989 OB in "The Witch."

LANNING, JERRY. Born May 17, 1943 in Miami, FL. Graduate USCal. Bdwy debut 1966 in "Mame," for which he received a Theatre World Award, followed by "1776," "Where's Charley?," "My Fair Lady," OB in "Memphis Store Bought Teeth," "Berlin to Broadway," "Sextet," "Isn't It Romantic?," "Paradise," "Emerald City."

LANSING, ROBERT. Born June 5, 1929 in San Diego, CA. Bdwy debut 1951 in "Stalag 17," followed by "Cyrano de Bergerac," "Richard III," "Charley's Aunt," "The Lovers," "Cue for Passion," "The Great God Brown," "Cut of the Axe," "Finishing Touches," OB in "The Father," "The Cost of Living," "The Line," "Phaedra," "Mi Vida Loca."

LARSEN, LIZ. Born Jan. 16, 1959 in Philadelphia, PA. Attended HofstraU, SUNY/Purchase. Bdwy debut 1981 in "Fiddler on the Roof," followed by "Starmites," OB in "Kuni Leml," "Hamlin," "Personals," "Starmites," "Company," "After These Messages," "One Act Festival."

LAURENCE, PAULA. Born Jan. 25 in Brooklyn, NY. Bdwy debut 1936 in "Horse Eats Hat," followed by "Dr. Faustus," "Junior Miss," "Something for the Boys," "One Touch of Venus," "Cyrano de Bergerac," "The Liar," "Season in the Sun," "Tovarich," "The Time of Your Life," "Beggar's Opera," "Hotel Paradiso," "Night of the Iguana," "Have I Got a Girl For You," "Ivanov," "Rosalie in Concert," OB in "7 Days of Mourning," "Roberta in Concert," "One Touch of Venus," "Coming of Age in SoHo," "George White's Scandals," "Sitting Pretty," "Mexican Hayride."

LAVIN, LINDA. Born Oct. 15, 1939 in Portland, Me. Graduate Wm & Mary Col. Bdwy debut 1962 in "A Family Affair," followed by "Riot Act," "The Game Is Up," "Hotel Passionata," "It's a Bird, It's Superman!," "On a Clear Day You Can See Forever," "Something Different," "Cop-Out," "Last of the Red Hot Lovers," "Story Theatre," "The Enemy Is Dead," "Broadway Bound," "Gypsy" (1990), OB in "Wet Paint" (1965) for which she received a Theatre World Award.

LAWRENCE, BURKE. Born Apr. 7, 1959 in Montreal, Can. Graduate Queen's U/Kingston. Bdwy debut 1989 in "Shenandoah."

LAWRENCE, DEA. Born Nov. 5 in Hartford, Ct. Graduate Catholic U. Debut 1988 OB in "Psycho Beach Party," followed by "Vampire Lesbians of Sodom," One Act Festival.

LAWRENCE, ELIZABETH. Born Sept. 6, 1932 in Huntington, WVa. Graduate UMi, Yeshiva U. Bdwy debut 1954 in "The Rainmaker," followed by "All the Way Home," "Look Homeward, Angel," "A Matter of Gravity," "Strange Interlude," OB in "The Misunderstanding," "Rockaway," "Children," "Beauty Marks."

LEE, KAIULANI. Born Feb. 28, 1950 in Princeton, NJ. Attended AmericanU. Bdwy debut 1975 in "Kennedy's Children," followed by "Macbeth," "Pack of Lies," OB in "Ballad of the Sad Cafe," "Museum," "Safe House," "Days to Come," "Othello," "Strange Snow," "Aristocrats," "Rimers Of Eldritch."

LEE-ARANAS, MARY. Born Sept. 23, 1959 in Taipei, Taiwan. Graduate UOttawa. Debut 1984 OB in "Empress of China," followed by "A State without Grace," "Return of the Phoenix," "Yellow Is My Favorite Color," "Man Who Turned into a Stick," "The Impostor," "Rosie's Cafe," "Three Sisters," "Noiresque," "Song of Shim Chung."

LeFEVRE, ADAM. Born Aug. 11, 1950 in Albany, NY. Graduate Williams Col., UIowa. Debut 1981 OB in "Turnbuckle," followed by "Badgers," "Goose and Tomtom," "In the Country," "Submariners," "Boys Next Door," "Doctor's Dilemma," Bdwy in "Devil's Disciple" (1988).

LEFFERT, JOEL. Born Dec. 8, 1951 in NYC. Graduate Brown U. Debut 1976 OB in "Orphee," followed by "Heroes," "The Last Burning," "Relatively Speaking," "The Bachelor," "Scaramouche," "Macbeth," "Don Juan in Hell," "Village Wooing," "The Long Smoldering," "Loveplay," "The Straw."

LEGUIZAMO, JOHN. Born July 22, 1965. Attended NYU. Debut 1987 OB in "La Puta Vida," followed by "A Midsummer Night's Dream," "Parting Gestures," "She First Met Her Parents on the Subway."

LEIBMAN, RON. Born Oct. 11, 1937 in NYC. Attended Ohio Wesleyan, Actors Studio. Bdwy debut 1963 in "Dear Me, the Sky Is Falling," followed by "Bicycle Ride to Nevada," "The Deputy," "We Bombed in New Haven" for which he received a Theatre World Award, "Cop-Out," "I Ought to Be in Pictures," "Doubles," "Rumors," OB in "The Academy," "John Brown's Body," "Scapin," "The Premise," "Legend of Lovers," "Dead End," "Poker Session," "Transfers," "Room Service," "Love Two," "Rich and Famous," "Children of Darkness," "Non Pasquale."

LEONARD, ROBERT SEAN. Born Feb. 28, 1969 in Westwood, NJ. Debut 1985 OB in "Sally's Gone, She Left Her Name," followed by "Coming of Age in Soho," "Beach House," "Young Playwrights Festival," "When She Danced," Bdwy in "Brighton Beach Memoirs" (1985), "Breaking The Code."

LESHEIM, LOLITA. Born Jan. 25, 1960 in Rocky River, Oh. Graduate Boston U., Harvard. Bdwy debut 1989 in "M. Butterfly."

LESLIE, BETHEL. Born Aug. 3, 1929 in NYC. Bdwy debut 1944 in "Snafu," followed by "Years Ago," "Wisteria Trees," "Goodbye My Fancy," "Time of the Cuckoo," "Mary Rose," "Brass Ring," "Inherit the Wind," "Catch Me if You Can," "But Seriously," "Long Day's Journey into Night." OB in "The Aunts."

LESTER, BARBARA. Born Dec. 27, 1928 in London, Eng. Columbia U. Graduate. Bdwy debut 1956 in "Protective Custody," followed by "Legend of Lizzie," "Luther," "Inadmissible Evidence," "Johnny-No-Trump," "Grin and Bare It," "Abelard and Heloise," "One in Every Marriage," "Butley," "Man and Superman," "Faith Healer," "Present Laughter," "Lettice and Lovage," OB in "Electra," "Queen after Death," "Summer of the 17th Doll," "Richard II," "Much Ado about Nothing," "One Way Pendulum," "Biography," "Heartbreak House," "Hedda Gabler."

LeSTRANGE, PHILIP. Born May 9, 1942 in The Bronx, NYC. Graduate Catholic U, Fordham U. Debut 1970 OB in "Getting Married," followed by "Erogenous Zones," "The Quilling of Prue," "The Front Page," "Six Degrees of Separation."

LEVINE, RICHARD S. Born July 16, 1954 in Boston, MA. Graduate Juilliard. Debut 1978 OB in "Family Business," followed by "Magic Time," "It's Better With a Band," "Emma," "Mistress of the Inn," Bdwy in "Dracula," "Rock n' Roll: First 5000 Years," "Rumors."

LEVINE-THOMPSON, ANNA. Born Sept. 18 in NYC. Debut 1975 OB in "Kid Champion," followed by "Uncommon Women and Others," "City Sugar," "A Winter's Tale," "Johnny-on-the-Spot," "The Wedding," "American Days," "The Singular Life of Albert Nobbs," "Cinders," "Rose Cottages," "School of Giorgione," "The Moderati," "Abingdon Square," "Poets Corner," "Heart of a Dog," "Marathon '90."

LEWIS, EDMUND. Born Feb. 12, 1959 in London, Eng. Attended Reading Blue Coat, RADA. Debut OB in "The Longboat," followed by "A Most Secret War," "Without Apologies," "Up 'n' Under," "Progress."

LEWIS, MARCIA. Born Aug. 18, 1938 in Melrose, Ma. Attended UCin. OB in "The Impudent Wolf," "Who's Who, Baby," "God Bless Coney," "Let Yourself Go," "Romance Language," "When She Danced," Bdwy in "The Time of Your Life," "Hello, Dolly!," "Annie," "Rags," "Roza," "Orpheus Descending."

LEWIS, MARK. Born Feb. 28, 1957 in Rosario, Argentina. Graduate So.MethodistU, Portland StU. Debut 1988 OB in "Julius Caesar," followed by "Midsummer Night's Dream," "Tamara."

LEWIS, MATTHEW. Born Jan. 12, 1937 in Elizabeth, NJ. Graduate HarvardU. Debut 1970 OB in "Chicago '70," followed by "Fathers and Sons," "The Freak," "Happy Days Are Here Again," "Levitation," "The Seagull" "My Papa's Wine," "Apocalyptic Butterflies," "White Collar," Bdwy in "Angels Fall" (1983).

LEWIS, VICKI. Born Mar. 17, 1960 in Cincinnati, Oh. Graduate CinConserv. Bdwy debut 1982 in "Do Black Patent Leather Shoes Really Reflect Up?," followed by "Wind in the Willows," OB in "Snoopy," "A Bundle of Nerves," "Angry Housewives," "1-2-3-4-5," "One Act Festival," "The Love Talker," "Buzzsaw Berkeley," "Marathon '90," "The Crucible."

LEYDEN, LEO. Born Jan. 28, 1929 in Dublin, Ire. Attended Abbey ThSch. Bdwy debut 1960 in "Love and Libel," followed by "Darling of the Day," "Mundy Scheme," "The Rothschilds," "Capt. Brassbound's Conversion," "The Plough and the Stars" (LC), "Habeas Corpus," "Me and My Girl," "The Merchant of Venice," OB in "The Cat and the Fiddle."

LIBIN, ANDREA CLARK. Born Sept. 18 in NYC. Graduate Sarah Lawrence Col. Bdwy debut 1989 in "Ghetto."

LIDE, MILLER. Born Aug. 10, 1935 in Columbia, SC. Graduate USC, AmThWing. Debut 1961 OB in "3 Modern Japanese Plays," followed by "The Trial at Rouen," "Street Scene," "Joan of Arc at the Stake," "The Heiress," "The Doctor's Dilemma," "School for Wives," Bdwy in "Ivanov," "Halfway Up the Tree," "Who's Who in Hell," "We Interrupt This Program," "The Royal Family," "84 Charing Cross Road."

LIGHTSTONE, MARILYN. Born June 28, 1940 in Montreal, Can. Graduate McGillU. Bdwy debut 1968 in "King Lear," followed by OB's "Tamara."

LIMA, PAUL. Born Feb. 5, 1961 in Ithaca, NY. Graduate AADA. Debut 1987 OB in "Deathmarch," followed by "Idiot's Delight," "Fanny's First Play," "The Archbishop's Ceiling," "Threepenny Opera," "The Knack," "The Three Sisters."

LINES, MARION SYBIL. Born Feb. 10th in London, Eng. Attended Central Sch. Debut 1976 OB in "The Philanderer," followed by "Claw," "The Penultimate Problem of Sherlock Holmes," "The Wit to Woo," "The Team," "Quartermaine's Terms," "Rockabye," "Crimes of Vautrain," Bdwy in "London Assurance" (1974), "Bedroom Farce," "Aren't We All," "Lettice and Lovage."

LINVILLE, LARRY. Born Sept. 29, 1939 in Ojai, CA. Attended UColo., RADA. Appeared 4 seasons with APA before Bdwy debut 1967 in "More Stately Mansions," followed by "Rumors."

LISH, JAMES. Born Oct. 28 in NYC. Graduate Ithaca Col. Debut 1984 OB in "It's Hard To Be a Jew," followed by "Male Animal," "Solitaire," "Three Sisters," "Carbondale Dreams."

LISS, RICHARD. Born Oct. 27, 1956 in Toronto, Can. Attended UToronto, AMDA. Bdwy debut 1989 in "Shenandoah."

LITTLE, DAVID. Born Mar. 21, 1937 in Wadesboro, NC. Graduate Wm & Mary Col., Catholic U. Debut 1967 OB in "Macbird," followed by "Iphigenia in Aulis," "Antony and Cleopatra," "Antigone," "An Enemy of the People," "Three Sons," "Almost in Vegas," "Six Degrees of Separation," Bdwy in "Les Blancs," "Thieves," "Zalmen, or the Madness of God."

LITTLE, JOHN. Born Aug. 12, 1956 in DeKalb, IL. Graduate Yale, NYU, Debut 1988 OB in "Moby Dick," followed by "After the Rain."

LIZZUL, ANTHONY JOHN. Born Jan. 11, in the Bronx, NYC. Graduate NYU. Debut 1977 OB in "Cherry Orchard," followed by "The Prophets," "Lady Windermere's Fan," "Revenger's Tragedy," "Twelfth Night," "Night Talk," "Butterfingers Angel," "Consulting Adults," "Hyde Park."

LOCKWOOD, LISA. Born Feb. 13, 1958 in San Francisco, CA. Bdwy debut 1988 in "Phantom of the Opera."

LOCORRIERE, DENNIS. Born June 13, 1949 in Jersey City, NJ. Debut 1989 OB in "Oh, Hell/The Devil and Billy Markham."

LOCRICCHIO, MATTHEW. Born June 3, 1947 in Detroit, Mi. Attended E.Mi.U. Debut 1983 OB in "Fool for Love," followed by "Largo Desalato," "Of Mice and Men," "Hyde in Hollywood."

LOESSER, EMILY. Born June 2, 1965 in NYC. Graduate Northwestern U. Debut 1988 OB in "The Secret Garden," followed by "Together Again for the First Time," "The Witch," Bdwy in "The Sound of Music" (LC/90).

LOGAN, JEFFERY. Born Aug. 18, 1956 in Victorville, Ca. Graduate UC/Berkeley. Bdwy debut 1986 in "Shakespeare on Broadway," followed by "Related Retreats."

LOGEN, CAROL. Born July 14 in Detroit, MI. Graduate US Int'lU. Bdwy debut 1974 in "Where's Charley," followed by "Rex," "On the 20th Century," "Evita," "Dreamgirls," "Sweeney Todd."

LOMBARD, MICHAEL. Born Aug. 8, 1934 In Brooklyn, NY. Graduate Brooklyn Col., BostonU. OB in "King Lear," "Merchant of Venice," "Cages," "Pinter Plays," "La Turista," "Elizabeth the Queen," "Room Service," "Mert and Phil," "Side Street Scenes," "Angelo's Wedding," "Friends in High Places," "What's Wrong With This Picture?," Bdwy in "Poor Bitos", (1964), "The Devils," "Gingerbread Lady," "Bad Habits," "Otherwise Engaged," "Awake and Sing."

LONDON, BECKY. Born Feb. 11, 1958 in Philadelphia, Pa. Yale graduate. Debut 1985 OB in "Isn't It Romantic," followed by "Vampire Lesbians of Sodom," "Psycho Beach Party," "Last of the Red Hot Lovers," "Othello."

LOOZE, KAREN. Born Feb. 19, 1938 in Chicago, Il. Graduate IndU. Debut 1964 OB in "Streets of New York," followed by "The Wide Open Cage," "Grace," "Marathon '90," Bdwy in "Big River" (1987).

LOPEZ, PRISCILLA. Born Feb. 26, 1948 in The Bronx, NYC. Bdwy debut 1966 in "Breakfast at Tiffany's," followed by "Henry, Sweet Henry," "Lysistrata," "Company," "Her First Roman," "Boy Friend," "Pippin," "A Chorus Line" (also OB), "Day in Hollywood/Night in the Ukraine," "Nine," OB in "What's a Nice Country Like You . . ." "Key Exchange," "Buck," "Extremites," "Non Pasquale," "Be Happy for Me," "Times and Appetites of Toulouse-Lautrec," "Marathon '88," "Other People's Money."

LOTI, ELISA. Born Aug. 26 in Guayaquil, Ecuador, Vassar graduate. Bdwy debut 1961 in "Rhinoceros," OB in "Come Share My House" for which she received a Theatre World Award (1960), followed by "The Laundry," "Lucky Rita," "A Murder Is Announced," "Enter Laughing," "Before the Dawn," "Picture Perfect."

LOUDON, DOROTHY. Born Sept. 17, 1933 in Boston, MA. Attended Emerson Col., Syracuse U. Debut 1961 OB in "World of Jules Feiffer," Bdwy 1963 in "Nowhere to Go but Up" for which she received a Theatre World Award followed by "Noel Coward's Sweet Potato," "Fig Leaves Are Falling," "Three Men on a Horse," "The Women," "Annie," "Ballroom," "West Side Waltz," "Noises Off," "Jerry's Girls."

LOVE, VICTOR. Born Aug. 4, 1967 in Camp LeJeune, NC. Attended LACC, UWis. Bdwy debut 1989 in "A Few Good Men." OB in "Richard II," "Jonin'."

LOWERY, MARCELLA. Born Apr. 27, 1945 in Jamaica, NY. Graduate Hunter Col. Debut 1967 OB in "Day of Absence," followed by "American Pastoral," "Ballet behind the Bridge," "Jamimma," "Recent Killing," "Miracle Play," "Welcome to Black River," "Anna Lucasta," "Baseball Wives," "Louis," "Bless Me, Father," "Ladies," "Sugar Hill," Bdwy in "Member of the Wedding" (1975), "Lolita."

LUCAS, ROXIE. Born Aug. 25, 1951 In Memphis, TN. Attended UHouston. Bdwy debut 1981 in "Best Little Whorehouse in Texas," followed by "Harrigan 'n' Hart," OB in "Forbidden Broadway," "Best of Forbidden Broadway," "20 Fingers, 20 Toes."

LUCAS, WILLIAM. Born Dec. 25, 1959 in Rio de Janeiro, Brazil. Graduate UGa. Debut 1981 OB in "Dreams of Flight," followed by "Will They Love Us on Broadway," "Boesman and Lena," "Topokana Martyrs Day," "The Song of Shim Chung."

LUM, ALVIN. Born May 28, 1931 in Honolulu, HI. Attended UHI. Debut 1969 OB in "In the Bar of a Tokyo Hotel," followed by "Pursuit of Happiness," "Monkey Music," "Flowers and Household Gods," "Station J," "Double Dutch," "Teahouse," "Song for a Nisei Fisherman," "Empress of China," "Manos Valley," "Hot Sake," "Chu Chem" (also Bdwy), Bdwy in "Lovely Ladies, Kind Gentlemen" (1970), "Two Gentlemen of Verona," "City of Angels."

LuPONE, ROBERT. Born July 29, 1956 in Brooklyn, NY. Juilliard graduate. Bdwy debut 1970 in "Minnie's Boys," followed by "Jesus Christ Superstar," "The Rothschilds," "Magic Show," "A Chorus Line," "St. Joan," "Late Night Comic," "Zoya's Apartment." OB in "Charlie Was Here," "Twelfth Night," "In Connecticut," "Snow Orchid," "Lennon," "Black Angel," "The Quilling of Prue," "Time Framed," "Class 1 Acts." "Remembrance," "Children of Darkness," "Kill."

LYLES, LESLIE. Born in Plainfield, NJ. Graduate Monmouth Col., RutgersU. Debut 1981 OB in "Sea Marks," followed by "Highest Standard of Living," "Vanishing Act," "I Am Who I Am," "The Arbor," "Terry by Terry," "Marathon '88," "Sleeping Dogs," "Marathon '90," Bdwy in "The Real Thing" (1985).

LYNDECK, EDMUND. Born Oct. 4, 1925 in Baton Rouge, La. Graduate Montclair State Col., Fordham U. Bdwy debut 1969 in "1776," followed by "Sweeney Todd," "A Doll's Life," "Merlin," "Into the Woods," "Artist Descending a Staircase." OB in "The King and I" (JB), "Mandragola," "A Safe Place," "Amoureuse," "Piaf, A Remembrance," "Children of Darkness," "Kill."

MACCHIO, RALPH. Born Nov. 4, 1962 in Huntington, NY. Debut 1986 Off and on Bdwy in "Cuba and His Teddy Bear," followed OB in "Only Kidding."

MacDONALD, PIRIE. Born Mar. 24, 1932 in NYC. Harvard graduate. Debut 1957 OB in "Under Milk Wood," followed by "The Zoo Story," "Innocent Pleasure," "Marathon 87," "Swim Visit," Bdwy in "Shadow and Substance," "The Golden Fleecing," "Big Fish, Little Fish," "Death of a Salesman," "But Not for Me."

MacINTOSH, JOAN E. Born Nov. 25, 1945 in NJ. Graduate Beaver Col., NYU. Debut OB 1969 in "Dionysus in '69," followed by "Macbeth," "The Beard," "Tooth of Crime," "Mother Courage," "Marilyn Project," "Seneca's Oedipus," "St. Joan of the Stockyards," "Wonderland in Concert," "Dispatches," "Endgame," "Killings on the Last Line," "Request Concert," "3 Acts of Recognition," "Consequence," "Whispers," "Cymbeline," Bdwy in "Our Town" (1989), "Orpheus Descending."

MacKAY, JOHN. Graduate CUNY. Bdwy debut 1960 in "Under the Yum Yum Tree," followed by "A Gift of Time," "A Man for All Seasons," "The Lovers," "Borstal Boy," OB in "Oedipus Cycle," "Gilles de Rais," "Marathon '89," "3 Poets."

MACKAY, LIZBETH. Born March 7th in Buffalo, NY. Graduate Adelphi U., Yale. Bdwy debut 1981 in "Crimes of the Heart" for which she received a Theatre World Award, followed by OB in "Kate's Diary," "Tales of the Lost Formicans," "Price of Fame."

MACKENZIE, PETER. Born Jan. 23rd in Chapel Hill, NC. Debut 1989 OB in "Abel & Bela," followed by "Ben-Hur."

MacMILLAN, ANN. Born Apr. 7, 1942 in Scotland. Attended RADA. Debut 1979 OB in "Merry Wives of Windsor" followed by "The Winslow Boy," "Learned Ladies," "The Housekeeper."

MacNICOL, PETER. Born April 10 in Dallas, Tx. Attended UMin. Bdwy debut 1981 in "Crimes of the Heart" for which he received a Theatre World Award, OB in "Found a Peanut," "Rum and Coke," "Twelfth Night," "Richard II," "The Spring Thing," "Human Nature."

MacPHERSON, LORI. Born July 23 in Albany, NY. Attended Skidmore Col. Bdwy debut 1988 in "The Phantom of the Opera."

MacVITTIE, BRUCE. Born Oct. 14, 1956 in Providence, RI. Graduate BostonU. Bdwy. debut 1983 in "American Buffalo," followed OB in "California Dog Fight," "The Worker's Life," "Cleveland and Half Way Back," "Marathon 87," "One of the Guys."

MACY, W. H. Born Mar. 13, 1950 in Miami, FL. Graduate Goddard Col. Debut 1980 OB in "The Man in 605," followed by "Twelfth Night," "The Beaver Coat," "A Call from the East," "Sittin'," "Sunshine," "The Dining Room," "Speakeasy," "Wild Life," "Flirtations," "Baby with the Bathwater," "Prairie/Shawl," "The Nice and the Nasty," "Bodies, Rest and Motion," "Oh, Hell!," "Marathon '90," Bdwy in "Our Town" (1989).

MAHON, KRISTEN. Born Jan. 13, 1979 in Oceanside, NY. Bdwy debut 1989 in "Gypsy."

MAILER, STEPHEN. Born Mar. 10, 1966 in NYC. Attended Middlebury Col., NYU. Debut OB 1989 in "For Dear Life," followed by "What's Wrong With This Picture?"

MALCOLM, GRAEME. Born July 31, 1951 in Dunfermline, Scot. Graduate Central School. Debut 1985 OB in "Scapin," followed by "Pantalone," "Rough Crossing," "The Return," Bdwy in "Benefactors" (1986), "Death and the King's Horsemen."

MALINA, JOEL. Born June 1, 1964 in NYC. Yale graduate. Debut 1990 OB in "The Rothschilds."

MALINA, JOSHUA. Born Jan. 17, 1966 in NYC. Yale graduate. Bdwy debut 1989 in "A Few Good Men."

MALLON, BRIAN. Born May 12, 1952 in Detroit, MI. Attended UMich. Debut 1980 OB in "Guests of the Nation," followed by "Moliere in spite of Himself," "Mr. Joyce Is Leaving Paris," "Shadow of a Gunman," "Derek," "A Doll House," "Rasputin."

MANDRACCHIA, CHARLES. Born Mar. 29, 1962 in Brooklyn, NY. Graduate Brooklyn Col. Debut OB 1987 in "Wish You Were Here," followed by "Mr. Universe," "Philoctetes," Bdwy in "South Pacific," "Kismet," "Desert Song," "Grand Hotel."

MANIS, DAVID. Born Nov. 24, 1959 in Ann Arbor, Mi. Graduate UWash. Debut 1983 in "Pericles," followed by "Pieces of Eight," "A New Way to Pay Old Debts," "As You Like It," "The Skin of Our Teeth," "And They Dance Real Slow in Jackson," "Rough Crossing," "Starting Monday."

MANN, TERRENCE. Born in 1945 in Kentucky. Graduate NCSch of Arts. Bdwy debut 1980 in "Barnum," followed by "Cats," "Rags," "Les Miserables," "Jerome Robbins' Broadway," OB in "A Night at the Fights," "The Queen's Diamond."

MANTELL, MICHAEL (formerly Mantel). Born Dec. 30, 1952 in Cleveland, Oh. Graduate Pratt Inst. Debut 1980 OB in "Success Story," followed by "Incident at Vichy," "Awake and Sing," "King John," "The Dolphin Position," "Welcome to the Moon," "Extenuating Circumstances," "Dennis," "Bad Habits," Bdwy in "The Tenth Man" (1989).

MANTELLO, JOE. Born Dec. 27, 1962 in Rockford, Il. Debut 1986 OB in "Crackwalker" followed by "Progress."

MANZI, WARREN. Born July 1, 1955 in Laurence, MA. Graduate Holy Cross, Yale. Bdwy debut 1980 in "Amadeus," OB in "Perfect Crime."

MARA, MARY. Born Sept. 21, 1960 in Syracuse, NY. Graduate Yale. Debut OB 1990 in "Moving Targets," followed by "Twelfth Night."

MARCEAU, YVONNE. Born July 13, 1950 in Chicago, Il. Graduate UUtah. Bdwy debut 1989 in "Grand Hotel."

MARCHAND, NANCY. Born June 19, 1928 in Buffalo, NY. Graduate Carnegie Tech, Debut 1951 in CC's "Taming of the Shrew," followed by "Merchant of Venice," "Much Ado About Nothing," "Three Bags Full," "After the Rain," "The Alchemist," "Yerma," "Cyrano de Bergerac," "Mary Stuart," "Enemies," "The Plough and the Stars," "40 Carats," "And Miss Reardon Drinks a Little," "Veronica's Room," "Awake and Sing," "Morning's at Seven," "The Octette Bridge Club," OB in "The Balcony," "Children," "Taken in Marriage," "Sister Mary Ignatius Explains It All," "Elecktra," "The Cocktail Hour," "Love Letters.

MARCY, HELEN. Born June 3, 1920 in Worcester, MA. Attended Yale U. Bdwy in "Twelfth Night," "In Bed We Cry," "Dream Girl," "Love and Let Love," OB in "Lady Windermere's Fan," "Relative Values," "Verdict," "Hound of the Baskervilles," "Appointment With Death," "Ladies in Retirement," "Dr. Cook's Garden," "Murder at the Vicarage," "Black Coffee," "George Washington Slept Here," "White Collar."

MARDIROSIAN, TOM. Born Dec. 14, 1947 in Buffalo, NY. Graduate UBuffalo. Debut 1976 OB in "Gemini," followed by "Grand Magic," "Losing Time," "Passione," "Success and Succession," "Ground Zero Club," "Cliffhanger," "Cap and Bells," "The Normal Heart," "Measure for Measure," "Largo Desolato," "The Good Coach," "Subfertile." Bdwy in "Happy End," "Magic Show."

MARLEY, SUSANNE. Born Sept. 25, 1947 in Cleveland, Oh. Graduate Ohio WesleyanU. Debut 1985 OB in "Fool for Love," followed by "Missouri Legend," "Dutchman," "Balm in Gilead," "Other People's Money," "White Collar."

MARSHALL, LARRY. Born Apr. 3, 1944 in Spartanburg, SC. Attended FordhamU, New Eng.Consv. Bdwy debut in "Hair," followed by "Two Gentlemen of Verona," "A Midsummer Night's Dream," "Rockabye Hamlet," "Porgy and Bess," "A Broadway Musical," "Comin' Uptown," "Oh, Brother!," "Big Deal," "3 Penny Opera," OB in "Spell #7," "Jus' Like Livin'," "The Haggadah," "Lullabye and Goodnight," "Alladin," "In the House of the Blues."

MARTEL, BILLY ARTHUR. Born Mar. 3, 1962 in Providence, RI. Graduate Emerson Col. Debut 1989 OB in "Sadie Thompson," followed by "Wonderful Town."

MARTEL, JENNY. Born Sept. 19 in Matewan, WVa. Graduate MoreheadStateU. Debut 1982 OB in "The Beckett Plays," followed by "Telemachus Clay," "Birdbath," "Final Commitment," "The Visit," "Forget Him," "Pericles."

MARTIN, CHRISTOPHER. Born May 10, 1961 in St. John's, Nfld, Can. Graduate Mt. Allison U. Bdwy debut 1989 in "Shenandoah."

MARTIN, JAMIE. Born Aug. 21, 1962 in Houston, Tx. Graduate North State Tx U., Neighborhood Playhouse. Debut 1989 OB in "Gigi," followed by "Midsummer Nights," "There Is an Angel in Las Vegas."

MARTIN, KEN. Born Nov. 18, 1959 in Newark, NJ. Graduate UFla. Debut 1989 OB in "The Visit," followed by "Jealousy," "Brunch at Trudy and Paul's"/One Act Festival.

MARTIN, LEILA. Born Aug. 22, 1932 in NYC. Bdwy debut 1944 in "Peepshow," followed by "Two on the Aisle," "Wish You Were Here," "Guys and Dolls," "Best House in Naples," "Henry, Sweet Henry," "The Wall," "Visit to a Small Planet," "The Rothschilds," "42nd Street," "The Phantom of the Opera," OB in "Ernest in Love," "Beggar's Opera," "King of the U.S.," "Philemon," "Jerry's Girls."

MARTINI, ROBERT LEE. Born July 30, 1960 in NYC. Graduate Wagner Col. Debut 1987 OB in "The Tavern," followed by "Hamlet," "Pericles."

MASTRANTONIO, MARY ELIZABETH. Born Nov. 17, 1958 in Chicago, Il. Attended UIll. Bdwy debut 1980 in "West Side Story," followed by "Copperfield," "Oh, Brother!," "The Marriage of Figaro," OB in "Henry V," "A Christmas Carol," "Measure for Measure," "The Knife," "Twelfth Night."

MASTRONE, FRANK. Born Nov. 1, 1960 in Bridgeport, CT. Graduate CentralStStateU. Bdwy debut 1988 in "The Phantom of the Opera."

MATSUSAKA, TOM. Born Aug. 8 in Wahiawa, Hi. Graduate MiStateU. Bdwy debut 1968 in "Mame," followed by "Ride the Winds," "Pacific Overtures," "South Pacific," OB in "Agamemnon," "Chu Chem," "Jungle of Cities," "Santa Anita '42," "Extenuating Circumstances," "Rohwer," "Teahouse," "Song of a Nisei Fisherman," "Empress of China," "Pacific Overtures" (1984), "Eat a Bowl of Tea," "Shogun Macbeth," "The Impostor," "Privates on Parade."

MATTHEWS, ANDERSON. Born Oct. 21, 1950 in Springfield, OH. Graduate Carnegie-Mellon U. Bdwy debut 1975 in "The Robber Bridegroom," followed by "Edward II," "The Time of Your Life," "Ten by Tennessee," "Beef," "The Sneaker Factory," "Driving Miss Daisy."

MATTHIESSEN, JOAN. Born Feb. 27, 1930 in Orange, NJ. Graduate Allegheny Col. Debut 1979 OB in "The Art of Dining," followed by "The Cocktail Party," "A Doll House."

MAUPIN, SAMUEL. Born Dec. 27, 1947 in Portsmouth, Va. Graduate VaCommonwealthU. Debut 1977 OB in "The Passion of Dracula," followed by "Death Takes a Holiday," "The Importance of Being Earnest," "The Common Pursuit," Bdwy in "Accomplice" (1990).

MAYES, SALLY. Born Aug. 3 in Livingston, Tx. Attended UHouston. Broadway debut 1989 in "Welcome to the Club" for which she received a Theatre World Award, OB in "Closer Than Ever."

MAYFIELD, KATHERINE. Born Apr. 22, 1958 in St. Louis, Mo. Attended Webster Col., Loretto Heights Col. OB in "The Jew of Malta," "The Cherry Orchard," "The War in New Jersey," "Big Al Goes Straight," "Will Kemp."

McALLEN, KATHLEEN ROWE. Born Nov. 30 in Bay Area, Ca. Attended UCB, UCLA. Debut 1981 OB in "Joseph and the Amazing Technicolor Dreamcoat," Bdwy in "Joseph and . . ." (1982), followed by "Aspects of Love" for which she received a Theatre World Award.

McBRIDE, TOM. Born Oct. 7, 1952 in Charleston, WVa. Graduate Xavier U. Debut 1980 OB in "Plain and Fancy," followed by "Fast Women," "House," "Honor Bright," "Going Down," "Hollywood Scheherazade," Bdwy in "5th of July" (1981).

McCALL, KATHLEEN. Born Jan. 11 in Denver. CO. Graduate Moorhead State U., LAMDA. Debut 1986 OB in "Thanksgiving," followed by "Acapella Hardcore," "Class 1 Acts," "Steel Magnolias," Bdwy 1989 in "M. Butterfly."

McCANN, CHRISTOPHER. Born Sept. 29, 1952 in NYC. Graduate NYU. Debut 1975 OB in "The Measures Taken," followed by "Ghosts," "Woyzeck," "St. Joan of the Stockyards," "Buried Child," "Dwelling in Milk," "Tongues," "3 Acts of Recognition," "Don Juan," "Michi's Blood," "Five of Us," "Richard III," "The Golem," "Kafka Father and Son," "Flatbush Faithful," "Black Market."

McCARTY, CONAN. Born Sept. 16, 1955 in Lubbock, TX. Attended USCal, AADA/West. Debut 1980 OB in "Star Treatment," followed by "Beyond Therapy," "Henry IV Part 1," "Titus Andronicus," "The Man Who Shot Lincoln." Bdwy in "Macbeth" (1988), "A Few Good Men."

McCARTY, MICHAEL. Born Sept. 7, 1946 in Evansville, IN. Graduate IndU., MiStateU. Debut 1976 OB in "Fiorello!," followed by "The Robber Bridegroom," "Sweeney Todd," Bdwy in "Dirty Linen," "King of Hearts," "Amadeus," "Oliver!," "Big River," "Sweeney Todd."

McCLINTOCK, JODIE LYNNE. Born Apr. 7, 1955 in Pittsburgh, Pa. Graduate Westminster Col. Debut 1983 OB in "As You Like It," followed by "1984," "The Art of Success," Bdwy in "Long Day's Journey into Night."

McCONNELL, DAVID. Born Feb. 12, 1962 in Los Alamos, NM. Graduate AADA. OB in "You Never Can Tell," "Hot l Baltimore," "Cloud 9," "Working," "The Normal Heart," "The Winter's Tale."

Gary
Kahn

Donna
Kane

Curt
Karibalis

Judy
Kaye

Steven
Keats

Pamela
Khoury

Sarah
Knapp

Dane
Knell

Juliette
Koka

Eddie
Korbich

Swoosie
Kurtz

Robert
Laconi

John-Michael
Lander

Lauri
Landry

Mark Edward
Lang

Lorraine
Lanigan

Jerry
Lanning

Elizabeth
Lawrence

Kaiulani
Lee

Joel
Leffert

Lolita
Lesheim

Philip
LeStrange

Anna
Levine

Edmund
Lewis

Paul
Lima

Sybil
Lines

James
Lish

Lisa
Lockwood

Matthew J.
Locricchio

Carol
Logen

McCORD, LISA MERRILL. Born Mar. 3, 1962 in Louisville, Ky. Graduate SyracuseU. Debut 1986 OB in "Two Gentlemen of Verona," followed by "As You Like It," "No, No Nanette," Bdwy in "Grand Hotel" (1990).

McCOWEN, ALEC. Born May 26, 1925 in Tunbridge Wells, Eng. Attended RADA. Bdwy debut 1951 in "Antony and Cleopatra," followed by "Caesar and Cleopatra," "King Lear," "Comedy of Errors," "After the Rain," "Hadrian VII," "The Philanthropist," "The Misanthrope," "Equus," "Kipling," OB in "St. Mark's Gospel."

McCRANE, PAUL. Born Jan. 19, 1961 in Philadelphia, Pa. Debut 1977 OB in "Landscape of the Body," followed by "Dispatches," "Split," "Hunting Scenes," "Crossing Niagara," "Hooters," "Fables for Friends," "Moonchildren," "Right Behind the Flag," "Human Nature," "Six Degrees of Separation," Bdwy in "Runaways" (1978), "Curse of an Aching Heart," "The Iceman Cometh" (1985).

McCULLOH, BARBARA. Born Mar. 5 in Washington, DC. Attended Col. of William & Mary, UMd. Debut 1984 OB in "Up in Central Park," followed by "Kuni-Leml," "On the 20th Century," "1-2-3-4-5," "Life Forms."

McCUTCHEON, BILL. Born May 23, 1924 in Russell, KY. Attended OhioU. Bdwy credits: "New Faces of 1956," "Dandelion Wine," "Out West of Eighth," "My Daughter, Your Son," "Over Here," "West Side Story," "The Front Page," "The Man Who Came to Dinner," "You Can't Take It with You," "Anything Goes," OB in "How to Steal an Election," "Wet Paint," "One's a Crowd," "Shoestring Revue," "Upstairs at the Downstairs," "The Little Revue," "The Marriage of Bette and Boo."

McDONNELL, MARY. Born in 1952 in Wilkes Barre, Pa. Graduate SUNY/Fredonia. Debut 1978 OB in "Buried Child," followed by "Letters Home," "Still Life," "Death of a Miner," "Black Angel," "A Weekend Near Madison," "All Night Long," "Savage in Limbo," "Three Ways Home," Bdwy in "Execution of Justice" (1986), "The Heidi Chronicles."

McDONOUGH, ANN. Born in Portland, ME. Graduate Towson State U. Debut 1975 OB in "Trelawny of the Wells," followed by "Secret Service," "Boy Meets Girl," "Scribes," "Uncommon Women," "City Sugar," "Fables for Friends," "The Dining Room," "What I Did Last Summer," "The Rise of Daniel Rocket," "The Middle Ages," "Fighting International Fat," "Room Service," "The Spring Thing," "Human Nature," Bdwy in "Mastergate."

McFARLAND, ROBERT. Born May 7, 1931 in Omaha, NE. Graduate UMi, ColumbiaU. Debut 1978 OB in "The Taming of the Shrew," followed by "When the War Was Over," "Divine Fire," "Ten Little Indians," "The Male Animal," "Comedy of Errors," "Appointment with Death," "The Education of One Miss February," "Rule of Three," "The Male Animal," "Little Lies."

McGANN, MICHAELJOHN. Born Feb. 2, 1952 in Cleveland, Oh. Graduate OhioU. Debut 1975 OB in "Three Musketeers," followed by "Panama Hattie," "A Winter's Tale," "Johnny-on-a-Spot," "Barbarians," "A Midsummer Night's Dream," "The Wild Duck," "Jungle of Cities," "The Tempest."

McGOVERN, ELIZABETH. Born July 18, 1961 in Evanston, Il. Attended Juilliard. Debut 1981 OB in "To Be Young, Gifted and Black," followed by "Hotel Play," "My Sister in This House" for which she received a Theatre World Award, "Painting Churches," "Hitch-Hikers," "Map of the World," "Two Gentlemen of Verona," "Maids of Honor." Bdwy in "Love Letters" (1989).

McGOVERN, MAUREEN. Born July 27, 1949 in Youngstown, Oh. Bdwy debut 1981 in "Pirates of Penzance," followed by "Nine," "3 Penny Opera," OB in "Brownstone."

McGREEVEY, ANNIE. Born in Brooklyn, NY. Graduate AADA. Bdwy debut 1971 in "Company," followed by "The Magic Show," "Sweeney Todd." "Annie," OB in "Booth Is Back in Town," "Tatterdemalion," "She Loves Me."

McGUINNESS, MICHAEL JOHN. Born May 13, 1961 in Corning, NY. Graduate NYU. Debut 1985 OB in "Brand," followed by "Frankenstein," "Wakefield/Chester Mystery Play Cycle," "The Real Inspector Hound," "Richard II," "Andromache," "She Stoops to Conquer," "All's Well That Ends Well," "Three Sisters," "Midsummer Night's Dream," "Medea," "Importance of Being Earnest."

McHATTIE, STEPHEN. Born Feb. 3 in Antigosh, NS, Can. Graduate Arcadia U, AADA. Bdwy debut 1969 in "The American Dream," followed by "The Misanthrope," "Heartbreak House," "You Never Can Tell," "Ghetto," OB in "Henry IV," "Richard III," "The Persians," "Pictures in the Hallway," "Now There's Just the Three of Us," "Anna K," "Twelfth Night," "Mourning Becomes Electra," "Alive and Well in Argentina," "The Iceman Cometh," "Winter Dancers," "Casualties," "Three Sisters," "Mensch Meier," "Haven," "A Perfect Diamond."

McINTYRE, GERRY. Born May 31, 1962 in Grenada, West Indies. Graduate Montclair-StateCol. Debut 1985 OB in "Joan of Arc at the Stake," followed by "Homeseekers," "Once on This Island." Bdwy in "Anything Goes" (1987).

McINTYRE, STEPHEN. Born Nov. 14, 1961 in Fairbanks, Ak. Graduate UWindsor, Can. Bdwy debut 1989 in "Shenandoah."

McKEAN, MICHAEL. Born Oct. 17, 1947 in NYC. Attended Carnegie-Mellon, NYU. Bdwy debut 1990 in "Accomplice" for which he received a Theatre World Award.

McMANUS, DON R. Born in 1960 in Sylacauga, AL. Graduate Yale U. Debut 1987 OB in "Holy Ghosts," followed by "Titus Andronicus," "One of the Guys," "Neddy," "The Art of Success."

McMARTIN, JOHN. Born in Warsaw, In. Attended ColumbiaU. Debut 1959 OB in "Little Mary Sunshine" for which he received a Theatre World Award, followed by "Too Much Johnson," "The Misanthrope," "Sung and Unsung Sondheim," "Julius Caesar," Bdwy in "Conquering Hero" (1961), "Blood, Sweat and Stanley Poole," "Children from Their Games," "A Rainy Day in Newark," "Sweet Charity," "Follies," "The Great God Brown," "Don Juan," "The Visit," "Chemin de Fer," "Love for Love," "Rules of the Game," "Happy New Year," "Solomon's Child," "A Little Family Business," "Artist Descending the Staircase."

McNABB, BARRY. Born Aug. 26, 1960 in Toronto, CAN. Graduate UOre. Bdwy debut 1986 in "Me and My Girl," followed by "The Phantom of the Opera."

McNAMARA, DERMOT. Born Aug. 24, 1925 in Dublin, Ire. Bdwy debut 1959 in "A Touch of the Poet," followed by "Philadelphia, Here I Come," "Donnybrook," "Taming of the Shrew," OB in "The Wise Have Not Spoken," "3 by Synge," "Playboy of the Western World," "Shadow and Substance," "Happy as Larry," "Sharon's Grave," "A Whistle in the Dark," "Red Roses for Me," "The Plough and the Stars," "Shadow of a Gunman," "No Exit," "Stephen D.," "Hothouse," "Home Is the Hero," "Sunday Morning Bright and Early," "Birthday Party," "All the Nice People," "Roots," "Philadelphia, Here I Come."

McNAMARA, MAUREEN. Born Mar. 17, 1957 in NYC. Studied at HB Studio. Debut 1978 OB in "Company," followed by "Festival," "The Ziegfeld Girl," "The First Time."

McNAMARA, PAT. Born July 22, 1938 in Astoria, NY. Attended Columbia U, AADA. Debut 1961 OB in "Red Roses For Me," followed by "Crystal and Fox," "Nobody Hears a Broken Drum," "The Passing Game," "Killings on the Last Line," Bdwy in "The Poison Tree" (1976), "Brothers," "The Iceman Cometh" (1985), "Sherlock's Last Case," "Legs Diamond," "Orpheus Descending."

McNEELY, ANNA. Born June 23, 1950 in Tower Hill, IL. Graduate McKendree Col. Bdwy debut 1982 in "Little Johnny Jones," followed by "Cats," "Gypsy."

McNIGHT, SHARON. Born Dec. 18 in Modesto, CA. Graduate SanFranStateCol. Debut 1987 OB in "Murder at the Rutherford House," Bdwy 1989 in "Starmites" for which she received a Theatre World Award.

McROBBIE, PETER. Born Jan. 31, 1943 in Hawick, Scotland. Graduate Yale U. Debut 1976 OB in "The Wobblies," followed by "The Devil's Disciple," "Cinders," "The Ballad of Soapy Smith," "Rosmersholm," "American Bagpipes." Bdwy in "Whose Life is it Anyway?" (1979), "Macbeth" (1981), "The Mystery of Edwin Drood."

McVETY, DREW. Born Apr. 16, 1965 in Port Huron, MI. Graduate NYU. Debut OB 1988 in "The Heidi Chronicles," Bdwy in "The Heidi Chronicles" (1989).

McWILLIAMS, RICHARD. Born June 27, 1950 in Baytown, TX. Graduate Sam Houston State U. Debut 1983 OB in "Except in My Memory," followed by "Why Marry?", "Get Any Guy," "The Night Hank Williams Died," Bdwy in "Orpheus Descending."

MEDINA, HAZEL. Born Oct. 8 in Colon, Panama. Attended LACC. Debut 1982 OB in "Brixton Recovery," followed by "Time Out of Time," "Street Sounds," "The Beautiful LaSalles," "State of the Union," "Two Can Play," "Time Out of Time," "Prince," "The Crucible."

MEISLE, KATHRYN. Born June 7 in Appleton, Wi. Graduate Smith Col., UNC/Chapel Hill. Debut 1988 OB in "Dandy Dick," followed by "Cahoots."

MEISTER, FREDERICA. Born Aug. 18, 1951 in San Francisco, CA. Graduate NYU. Debut 1978 OB in "Museum," followed by "Dolphin Position," "Waiting for the Parade," "Dream of a Blacklisted Actor," "No Damn Good," "The Magic Act," "Subfertile."

MELIUS, NANCY. Born Nov. 20, 1964 in East Meadow, NY. Attended NYU. Debut 1989 OB in "Leave It to Jane," Bdwy in "Gypsy" (1989).

MELLOR, STEPHEN. Born Oct. 17, 1954 in New Haven, CT. Graduate Boston U. Debut 1980 OB in "Paris Lights," followed by "Coming Attractions," "Plenty," "Tooth of Crime," "Shepard Sets," "A Country Doctor," "Harm's Way," "Brightness Falling," "Terminal Hip," Bdwy in "Big River."

MENDILLO, STEPHEN. Born Oct. 9, 1942 in New Haven, Ct. Graduate Colo. Col., Yale. Debut 1973 OB in "Nourish the Beast," followed by "Gorky," "Time Steps," "The Marriage," "Loot," "Subject to Fits," "Wedding Band," "As You Like It," "Fool for Love," "Twelfth Night," Bdwy in "National Health" (1974), "Ah, Wilderness," "A View from the Bridge," "Wild Honey," "Orpheus Descending."

MERKERSON, S. EPATHA. Born Nov. 28, 1952 in Saganaw, Mi. Graduate Wayne State U. Debut 1979 OB in "Spell #7," followed by "Home," "Puppetplay," "Tintypes," "Every Goodbye Ain't Gone," "Hospice," "The Harvesting," "Moms," "Lady Day at Emerson's Bar and Grill," Bdwy in "Tintypes" (1982), "The Piano Lesson."

MERRILL, KIM. Born in Philadelphia, Pa. Graduate Georgetown U. Debut 1989 OB in "Beauty Marks."

MERRITT, GEORGE. Born July 10, 1942 in Raleigh, NC. Graduate Catholic U. Bdwy debut 1976 in "Porgy and Bess," followed by its 1983 revival, "Ain't Misbehavin'," "Big River," OB in "Step Into My World," "A Midsummer Night's Dream."

MERRITT, THERESA. Born Sept. 24, 1922 in Newport News, Va. Bdwy credits include "Carmen Jones," "Golden Boy," "Tambourines to Glory," "Trumpets of the Lord," "Don't Play Us Cheap," "Division Street," "The Wiz," "Ma Rainey's Black Bottom," OB in "The Crucible," "F. Jasmine Adams," "Trouble in Mind," "God's Trombones," "Henry IV Part I."

MERRYMAN, MONICA. Born June 2, 1950 in Sao Paulo, Brazil. Graduate EMichU. Debut 1975 OB in "East Lynne," followed by "A Night at the Black Pig," "Vanities," "The Voice of the Turtle," "Rhapsody Tachiste," "Jacques and His Master."

METCALF, MARK. Born March 11 in Findlay, Oh. Attended UMi. Debut 1973 OB in "Creeps," followed by "The Tempest," "Beach Children," "Hamlet," "Patrick Henry Lake Liquors," "Streamers," "Salt Lake City Skyline," "Mr. & Mrs.," "Romeo and Juliet," "Blue Window," "A Midsummer Night's Dream," "Trinity Site," "Swim Visit," "Marathon '90."

METZEL, MICHAEL. Born Sept. 18 in Columbus, Oh. Graduate Catholic U. Debut 1989 OB in "Wonderful Town," followed by "Sweethearts," "Alice in Wonderland," "My Lord, What a Morning."

METZMAN, IRVING. Born Mar. 28, 1946 in NYC. Debut 1989 OB in "Baba Goya."

METZO, WILLIAM. Born June 21, 1937 in Wilkes-Barre, PA. Graduate King's Col. Debut 1963 OB in "The Bald Soprano," followed by "Papers," "A Moon for the Misbegotten," "Arsenic and Old Lace," "Super Spy," "Hamlet," "Cradle Song," Bdwy in "Cyrano" (1973).

MEYERS, T. J. Born July 18, 1953 in Pittsburgh, PA. Graduate Mesa Col. Bdwy debut 1984 in "Sunday in the Park with George," followed by "Metamorphosis," "Prince of Central Park."

MICHEL, CAROLYN. Born Jan. 14, 1946 in St. Louis, Mo. Graduate Boston U. Bdwy debut 1989 in "Caesar & Company."

MILLENBACH, GEORGE. Born Aug. 24, 1953 in Toronto, Can. Graduate UToronto. Debut 1982 OB in "Cinderella," followed by "As You Like It," "A Cricket on the Hearth," "Ceremony in Bohemia," "The Lion in Winter," "Little Lies."

MILLER, REBECCA. Born in 1962 in Roxbury, Ct. Attended Yale U. Debut 1988 OB in "The Cherry Orchard," followed by "The American Plan."

MILLS, DONNA. Born Dec. 11, 1943 in Chicago, Il. Attended UIll. Bdwy debut 1966 in "Don't Drink the Water," followed by "Love Letters" (1989).

MITCHELL, GREGORY. Born Dec. 9, 1951 in Brooklyn, NY. Juilliard graduate. Principal with Eliot Feld Ballet before Bdwy debut 1983 in "Merlin," followed by "Song and Dance," "Phantom of the Opera," "Dangerous Games," "Aspects of Love." OB in "One More Song, One More Dance," "Tango Apasionado."

MOFFET, SALLY. Born Apr. 21, 1931 in NYC. Attended Friends Academy. Bdwy debut 1948 in "The Young and Fair," OB in "Under Milk Wood," "A Perfect Analysis," "Rasputin."

MOHRMANN, AL. Born July 7, 1949 in Hoboken, NJ. Graduate Montclair State, U. Mich. Debut 1988 OB in "Circle on the Cross," followed by "On the Move."

MONK, DEBRA. Born Feb. 27, 1949 in Middletown, Oh. Graduate Frostburg State, S.Methodist U. Bdwy debut 1982 in "Pump Boys and Dinettes," followed by "Prelude to a Kiss," OB in Young Playwrights Festival, "A Narrow Bed," "Oil City Symphony," "Prelude to a Kiss."

MONSON, LEX. Born Mar. 11, 1926 in Grindstone, Pa. Attended DePaul U,UDetroit. Debut 1961 OB in "The Blacks," followed by "Pericles," "Macbeth," "See How They Run," "Telemachus Clay," "Keyboard," "Oh, My Mother Passed Away," "The Confession Stone," "Linty Lucy," "Burnscape," "God's Trombones," Bdwy in "Moby Dick," "Trumpets of the Lord," "Watch on the Rhine," "Grapes of Wrath."

MONTELEONE, JOHN. Born Mar. 2, 1956 in Far Rockaway, NY. Attended Dowling Col., NYU. Debut 1981 OB in "The Butler Did It," followed by "The Devil's Advocate."

MONTEVECCHI, LILIANE. Born Oct. 12, 1933 in Paris, Fr. With Roland Petit's Ballet, and Folies Bergere before her Bdwy debut in "Nine" (1982), followed by "Grand Hotel," OB in her one-woman show "On the Boulevard."

MONTVILLE, CLEA. Born June 15, 1967 in Paterson, NJ. Graduate TowsonStateU. Debut 1990 OB in "When She Danced."

MOONEY, WILLIAM. Born in Bernie, Mo. Attended UCol. Bdwy debut 1961 in "A Man for All Seasons," followed by "A Place for Polly," "Lolita," OB in "Half Horse, Half Alligator," "Strike Heaven on the Face," "Conflict of Interest," "Overnight," "The Brownsville Raid," "The Truth," "The Upper Depths," "Damn Everything but the Circus," "Manhattan Punch Line 1 Acts," "Jonquil," "Burner's Frolic."

MOOR, BILL. Born July 13, 1931 in Toledo, OH. Attended Northwestern, Denison U. Bdwy debut 1964 in "Blues for Mr. Charlie," followed by "Great God Brown," "Don Juan," "The Visit," "Chemin de Fer," "Holiday," "P.S. Your Cat Is Dead," "Night of the Tribades," "Water Engine," "Plenty," "Heartbreak House," "The Iceman Cometh," OB in "Dandy Dick," "Love Nest," "Days and Nights of Beebee Fenstermaker," "The Collection," "The Owl Answers," "Long Christmas Dinner," "Fortune and Men's Eyes," "King Lear," "Cry of Players," "Boys in the Band," "Alive and Well in Argentina," "Rosmersholm," "The Biko Inquest," "A Winter's Tale," "Johnny on a Spot," "Barbarians," "The Purging," "Potsdam Quartet," "Zones of the Spirit," "The Marriage of Bette and Boo," "Temptation," "Devil's Disciple."

MOORE, BRUCE. Born Feb. 5, 1962 in Gettysburg, Pa. Graduate CinConsv. Debut 1986 OB in "Olympus on My Mind," followed by Bdwy in "Gypsy" (1989).

MOORE, CHARLOTTE. Born July 7, 1939 in Herrin, Il. Attended Smith Col. Bdwy debut 1972 in "Great God Brown," followed by "Don Juan," "The Visit," "Chemin de Fer," "Holiday," "Love for Love," "A Member of the Wedding," "Morning's at 7," "Meet Me in St. Louis," OB in "Out of Our Father's House," "A Lovely Sunday for Creve Coeur," "Summer," "Beside the Seaside," "The Perfect Party."

MOORE, CRISTA. Born Sept. 17th in Washington, DC. Attended AmBalletTh School. Debut 1987 OB in "Birds of Paradise," followed by Bdwy in "Gypsy" (1989) for which she received a Theatre World Award.

MOORE, JUDITH. Born Feb. 12, 1944 in Princeton, WVa. Graduate UInd. Debut 1971 OB in "The Drunkard," followed by "Ten by Six," "The Boys from Syracuse," "The Evangelist," "Miracle of the Month," "Sunday in the Park with George," "Midsummer Nights," Bdwy in "Sunday in the Park with George," "Into the Woods."

MOORE, JULIANNE. Graduate Boston U. Debut 1987 OB in "Serious Money," followed by "Ice Cream with Hot Fudge."

MOORE, KIM. Born Jan. 11, 1956 in Weaton, Mn. Graduate Moorhead State U. LAMDA. Debut 1985 OB in "The Fantasticks," followed by "Frankie."

MOORE, LEE. Born Feb. 19, 1929 in Brooklyn, NY. Debut 1978 OB in "Once More with Feeling," followed by "The Caine Mutiny Court-Martial," "Christopher Blake," "Cat and Canary," "Shrunken Heads," "Raspberry Picker," "Blessed Event," "Before Dawn."

MOORE, MICHAEL. Born Sept. 15, 1942 in New Jersey. Attended UMd., Hunter Col. Debut 1967 OB in "No Exit," followed by "Vis-a-Vis."

MOREAU, JENNIE. Born Nov. 19, 1960 in Lewisburg, PA. Graduate NCSchool of Arts. Debut 1988 OB in "Tony 'n' Tina's Wedding," followed by "Rimers of Eldritch," "Eleemosynary" for which she received a Theatre World Award.

MORFOGEN, GEORGE. Born Mar. 30, 1933 in NYC. Graduate Brown U., Yale. Debut 1957 OB in "The Trial of D. Karamazov," followed by "Christmas Oratorio," "Othello," "Good Soldier Schweik," "Cave Dwellers," "Once in a Lifetime," "Total Eclipse," "Ice Age," "Prince of Homburg," "Biography: A Game," "Mrs. Warren's Profession," "Principia Scriptoriae," "Tamara," Bdwy in "The Fun Couple" (1962), "Kingdoms," "Arms and the Man."

MORGAN, RON. Born Dec. 13, 1958 in Indianapolis, In. Attended Ball State, Butler U. Bdwy debut 1987 in "Starlight Express," followed by "Meet Me in St. Louis."

MORIARTY, MICHAEL. Born Apr. 5, 1941 in Detroit, Mi. Graduate Dartmouth, LAMDA. Debut 1963 OB in "Antony and Cleopatra," followed by "Peanut Butter and Jelly," "Long Day's Journey into Night," "Henry V," "Alfred the Great," "Our Father's Failing," "G. R. Point," "Love's Labours Lost," "Dexter Creed," "A Special Providence," "Children of the Sun," Bdwy in "Trial of the Catonsville 9," "Find Your Way Home" for which he received a Theatre World Award, "Richard III," "The Caine Mutiny Court-Martial."

MORRIS, KENNY. Born Nov. 4, 1954 in Brooklyn, NY. Graduate UNC/Chapel Hill. Debut 1981 OB in "Francis," followed by "She Loves Me," "Half a World Away," "Jacques Brel Is Alive . . .," Bdwy in "Joseph and the Amazing Technicolor Dreamcoat" (1983), "The Tenth Man."

MORSE, PETER G. Born Oct. 9, 1958 in Hanover, NH. Graduate Dartmouth Col., UCal/San Diego. Debut 1983 OB in "That's It, Folks!," followed by "The Weekend," "The Merchant of Venice," "The Racket," "The Foundation."

MORSE, ROBERT. Born May 18, 1931 in Newton, Ma. Bdwy debut 1955 in "The Matchmaker," followed by "Say, Darling" for which he received a Theatre World Award, "Take Me Along," "How to Succeed in Business . . .," "Sugar," "So Long 174th Street," "Tru," OB in "More of Loesser," "Eileen in Concert."

MORSE, ROBIN. Born July 8, 1963 in NYC. Bdwy debut 1981 in "Bring Back Birdie," followed by "Brighton Beach Memoirs," OB in "Green Fields," "Dec. 7th," "Class 1 Acts," "Eleemosynary," "One Act Festival," "Six Degrees of Separation."

MOSS, KATHI. Born Oct. 22, 1945 in Dallas, Tx. Graduate Barat Col., UNewOrleans. Debut 1972 OB in "Grease," followed by "Country Cabaret," "Hot Grog," "Jack the Ripper Revue," "The Perils of Pericles," "Dr. Selavy's Magic Theatre," "Walk on the Wild Side," Bdwy in "Grease" (1972), "Nine," "Grand Hotel."

MOSTEL, JOSHUA. Born Dec. 21, 1946 in NYC. Graduate Brandeis U. Debut 1971 OB in "The Proposition," followed by "More Than You Deserve," "The Misanthrope," "Rocky Road," "The Boys Next Door," "A Perfect Diamond," Bdwy in "Unlikely Heroes" (1971), "American Millionaire," "Texas Trilogy," "3 Penny Opera."

MOZER, ELIZABETH. Born Nov. 17, 1960 in Jamaica, NY. Graduate SUNY/Brockport. Debut 1986 OB in "Funny Girl," followed by Bdwy's "Dangerous Games" (1989).

MUENZ, RICHARD. Born in 1948 in Hartford, CT. Attended Eastern Baptist Col. Bdwy debut 1976 in "1600 Pennsylvania Avenue," followed by "The Most Happy Fella," "Camelot," "Rosalie in Concert," "Chess," "The Pajama Game" (LC), OB in "Closer Than Ever."

MUIR, HOWIE. Born May 6, 1957 in Hartford, Ct. Graduate URhodesia. Debut 1990 OB in "Deep to Center."

MULLAVEY, GREG. Born Sept. 10, 1939 in Buffalo, NY. Bdwy debut 1979 in "Romantic Comedy," followed by "Rumors."

MULLER, FRANK. Born May 5, 1951 in Beverwijk, Netherlands. Attended UMin, NCSch of Arts. Debut 1980 OB in "Salt Lake City Skyline," followed by "Henry V," "King Lear," "The Taming of the Shrew," "Under Milk Wood," "Cyrano de Bergerac," "The Crucible."

MULLINS, MELINDA. Born Apr. 20, 1958 in Clanton, AL. Graduate Mt. Holyoke Col., Juilliard. Bdwy debut 1987 in "Sherlock's Last Case," followed by "Serious Money," "Mastergate," OB in "Macbeth."

MURCH, ROBERT. Born Apr. 17, 1935 in Jefferson Barracks, MO. Graduate Wash. U. Bdwy debut 1966 in "Hostile Witness," followed by "The Harangues," "Conduct Unbecoming," "The Changing Room," "Born Yesterday," OB in "Charles Abbot & Son," "She Stoops to Conquer," "Transcendental Love," "Julius Caesar," "Hamlet."

MURFITT, MARY. Born Mar. 29, 1954 in Kansas City, MO. Graduate Marymount Col. Debut 1987 OB in "Oil City Symphony" for which she received a Theatre World Award.

MURNEY, CHRISTOPHER. Born July 20, 1943 in Narragansett, RI. Graduate URI, PaStateU. Bdwy debut 1973 in "Tricks," followed by "Mack and Mabel," OB in "As You Like It," "Holeville," "The Lady or the Tiger," "Bathroom Plays," "Two Fish in the Sky," "Wild Life," "Making Movies."

MURPHY, DONNA. Born Mar. 7, 1959 in Corona, NY. Attended NYU. Bdwy debut 1979 in "They're Playing Our Song," followed by "The Human Comedy," "The Mystery of Edwin Drood," OB in "Francis," "Portable Pioneer and Prairie Show," "Little Shop of Horrors," "A . . . My Name is Alice," "Showing Off," "Privates on Parade."

MURPHY, SALLY. Born Oct. 12, 1962 in Chicago, Il. Graduate NorthwesternU. Bdwy debut 1990 in "The Grapes of Wrath."

MURRAY, BRIAN. Born Oct. 9, 1939 in Johannesburg, SA. Debut 1964 OB in "The Knack," followed by "King Lear," "Ashes," "The Jail Diary of Albie Sachs," "A Winter's Tale," "Barbarians," "The Purging," "Midsummer Night's Dream," "The Recruiting Officer," "The Arcata Promise," "Candida in Concert," "Much Ado About Nothing," "Hamlet," Bdwy in "All in Good Time," "Rosencrantz and Guildenstern Are Dead," "Sleuth," "Da," "Noises Off."

MURRAY, LELAND. Born Nov. 13, 1929 in NYC. Attended CCNY. Debut 1988 OB in "Tamara."

MURRAY, MIKE. Born Nov. 15, 1950 in Brooklyn, NY. Graduate Brooklyn Col. Debut 1982 OB in "The Country Wife," followed by "The Hostage," "The Importance of Being Earnest," "Uncle Vanya," "Arms and the Man," "Major Barbara," "Deep to Center."

MURTAUGH, JAMES. Born Oct. 28, 1942 in Chicago, IL. Debut OB in "The Firebugs," followed by "Highest Standard of Living," "Marathon '87," "Other People's Money," "Marathon '88."

MYERS, LOU. Born Sept. 26, 1938 in Charleston, WVa. Graduate WVaStateCol., NYU. Debut 1975 OB in "First Breeze of Summer," followed by "Fat Tuesday," "Do Lord Remember Me," "Paducah," Bdwy in "First Breeze of Summer," "Ma Rainey's Black Bottom," "The Piano Lesson."

NAHRWOLD, THOMAS. Born June 25, 1954 in Ft. Wayne, In. Attended USIntlU, AmConsTh. Bdwy debut 1982 in "84 Charing Cross Road," followed by OB's "A Midsummer Night's Dream," "Bigfoot Stole My Wife," "Resistance," "The Foundation."

NAKAHARA, RON. Born July 20, 1947 in Honolulu, HI. Attended UHI., Tenri U. Debut 1981 OB in "Danton's Death," followed by "Flowers and Household Gods," "A Few Good Men," "Rohwer," "A Midsummer Night's Dream," "Teahouse," "Song for Nisei Fisherman," "Eat a Bowl of Tea," "Once is Never Enough," "Noiresque," "Play Ball," "Three Sisters," "And the Soul Shall Dance."

NAUFFTS, GEOFFREY. Born in Arlington, Ma. Graduate NYU. Debut 1987 OB in "Moonchildren," followed by "Stories from Home," "Another Time, Another Place," "The Alarm," "The Jerusalem Oratorio," "The Survivor," "Spring Awakening," Bdwy in "A Few Good Men" (1989).

NAUGHTON, AMANDA. Born Nov. 23, 1965 in NYC. Attended HB Studio. Debut 1982 OB in "Life with Father," followed by "Wonderful Town," "Romance in Hard Times."

NAUGHTON, JAMES. Born Dec. 6, 1945 in Middletown, Ct. Graduate BrownU, Yale. Debut 1971 OB in "Long Day's Journey into Night" for which he received a Theatre World Award, followed by "Drinks before Dinner," "Losing Time," Bdwy in "I Love My Wife," "Whose Life Is It Anyway?," "City of Angels."

NEAR, TIMOTHY. Born Feb. 23, 1945 in Los Angeles, Ca. Graduate SanFrancisco State Col., LAMDA. Debut 1978 OB in "The Immediate Family," followed by "Still Life," "A Mom's Life."

NEENAN, MARIA. Born July 14, 1965 in Boston, MA. Bdwy debut 1989 in "Jerome Robbins' Broadway."

NEIDEN, DANIEL. Born July 9, 1958 in Lincoln, Ne. Graduate Drake U. Debut 1980 OB in "City of Life," followed by "Ratman and Wilbur," "Nuclear Follies," "Pearls," "Sophie," "The Witch."

NELLIGAN, KATE. Born Mar. 16, 1951 in London, Can. Attended York U., Central School. Debut 1982 OB in "Plenty," followed by "Virginia," "Spoils of War," (also Bdwy), "Bad Habits," Bdwy in "Plenty" (1983), "Moon for the Misbegotten," "Serious Money," "Love Letters."

NELSON, MARK. Born Sept. 26, 1955 in Hackensack, NJ. Graduate Princeton U. Debut 1977 OB in "The Dybbuk," followed by "Green Fields," "The Keymaker," "The Common Pursuit," Bdwy in "Amadeus" (1981), "Brighton Beach Memoirs," "Biloxi Blues," "Broadway Bound," "Rumors," "A Few Good Men."

NELSON, RUTH. Born Aug. 2, 1905 in Saginaw, Mi. Attended AmThLab. Bdwy debut 1931 in "House of Connelly," among other Group Theatre productions, followed by "The Grass Harp," "Solitaire," "To Grandmother's House We Go," OB in "Collette," "Scenes from the Everyday Life," "3 Acts of Recognition," "Imagination Dead Imagine," "The Crucible."

NEUBERGER, JAN. Born Jan. 21, 1953 in Amityville, NY. Attended NYU. Bdwy debut 1975 in "Gypsy," followed by "A Change in the Heir." OB in "Silk Stockings," "Chase a Rainbow," "Anything Goes," "A Little Madness," "Forbidden Broadway," "After These Messages," "Ad Hock."

NEVINS, KRISTINE. Born Oct. 9, 1951 in Champagn, Il. Graduate KanStateU. Debut 1986 OB in "Charley's Tale," followed by "Starmites," "Kiss Me Quick before the Lava Reaches the Village," "Midsummer Nights."

NEWMAN, WILLIAM. Born June 15, 1934 in Chicago, Il. Graduate UWVa, Columbia U. Debut 1972 OB in "Beggar's Opera," followed by "Are You Now . . .?," "Conflict of Interest," "Mr. Runaway," "Uncle Vanya," "1 Act Festival," "Routed," "The Great Divide," "Come Back, Little Sheba," "Hit Parade," "Women Beware Women," "Heart of a Dog," Bdwy in "Over Here" (1974), "Rocky Horror Show," "Strangers."

NICCORE, VALORIE. Born Mar. 2, 1950 in Detroit, MI. Graduate Wayne StateU. Debut OB 1985 in "Carolyn," followed by "The Gambler," "Picture of Dorian Gray."

NIVEN, KIP. Born May 27, 1945 in Kansas City, Mo. Graduate KanU. Debut 1987 OB in "Company," followed by "The Golden Apple," Bdwy in "Chess" (1988).

NIXON, CYNTHIA. Born Apr. 9, 1966 in NYC. Debut 1980 in "The Philadelphia Story" (LC) for which she received a Theatre World Award, OB in "Lydie Breeze," "Hurlyburly," "Sally's Gone, She Left Her Name," "Lemon Sky," "Cleveland and Half-Way Back," "Alterations," "Young Playwrights," "Moonchildren," "Romeo and Juliet," "The Cherry Orchard," Bdwy in "The Real Thing" (1983), "Hurlyburly," "The Heidi Chronicles."

NOCKENGUST, REX. Born Feb. 7, 1965 in Cleveland, Oh. Graduate Baldwin-Wallace Consv. Bdwy debut 1988 in "Sally in Concert," OB in "Footprints on the Moon," "Little Lies."

NOGULICH, NATALIA. Born in Chicago, Il. Graduate Lake Forest Col. Debut 1982 OB in "The Transfiguration of Benno Blimpie," followed by "Cliffhanger," Bdwy in "Hurlyburly," "The Iceman Cometh," "Accomplice."

NOLEN, TIMOTHY. Born July 9, 1941 in Rotan, TX. Graduate Trenton State Col., Manhattan School of Music. Debut in "Sweeney Todd" (1984) with NYC Opera. Bdwy in "Grind" (1985) followed by "Phantom of the Opera."

NORCIA, PATRIZIA. Born Apr. 6, 1954 in Rome, Italy. Graduate Hofstra U., Yale. Debut 1978 OB in "Sganarelle," followed by "The Master and Margarita," "The Loves of Cass McGuire," "Fanshen," "The Price of Genius," "The Taming of the Shrew," "Epic Proportions," "Oklahoma Samivar," "Rough Crossing."

NORMAN, JOHN. Born May 13, 1961 in Detroit, Mi. Graduate Cincinnati Conservatory. Bdwy debut 1987 in "Les Miserables."

NOSTRAND, MICHAEL. Born Mar. 30, 1956 in Hempstead, NY. Graduate Wagner Col., Catholic U. Bdwy debut 1983 in "The Corn Is Green," OB in "The Cherry Orchard."

NOZICK, BRUCE. Born Jan. 29, 1960 in Winchester, MA. Graduate NYU. Debut 1982 OB in "Romeo and Juliet," followed by "And That's How the Rent Gets Paid," "Too Ugly for L.A.," "Sundance," "A Shayna Maidel," "Made in Heaven," "The Return."

NUGENT, JAMES. Born June 22, 1940 in The Bronx, NY. Graduate UFla. Debut 1984 OB in "Air Rights," followed by "Merchant of Venice," "Arms and the Man," "Mme. Colombe," "Two Gentlemen of Verona," "Days to Come," "The Good Doctor," "Pericles," "The Rivals," "Lady From the Sea," "Deep Swimmer," "Macbeth," "The Imaginary Invalid," "Uncle Vanya," "All's Well That Ends Well," "Dodger Blue," "The Philanderer," "Hedda Gabler," "3 Sisters," "Midsummer Night's Dream," "School for Wives."

NUTE, DON. Born Mar. 13, in Connellsville, PA. Attended Denver U. Debut OB 1965 in "The Trojan Women" followed by "Boys in the Band," "Mad Theatre for Madmen," "The Eleventh Dynasty," "About Time," "The Urban Crisis," "Christmas Rappings," "The Life of a Man," "A Look at the Fifties," "Aunt Millie."

NYE, CARRIE. Born in Mississippi. Attended Stephens Col., Yale U. Bdwy debut 1960 in "Second String," followed by "Mary, Mary," "Half a Sixpence," "A Very Rich Woman," "Cop-Out," "The Man Who Came to Dinner," "Love Letters," OB in "Ondine," "Ghosts," "The Importance of Being Earnest," "The Trojan Women," "The Real Inspector Hound," "a/k/a Tennessee," "The Wisteria Trees," "Madwoman of Chaillot," "Without Apologies."

O'CONNELL, PATRICIA. Born May 17 in NYC. Attended AmThWing. Debut 1958 OB in "The Saintliness of Margery Kemp," followed by "Time Limit," "An Evening's Frost," "Mrs. Snow," "Electric Ice," "Survival of St. Joan," "Rain," "Rapists," "Who Killed Richard Corey?," "Misalliance," "The Singular Life of Albert Nobbs," "Come Back, Little Sheba," "Starting Monday," Bdwy in "Criss-Crossing," "Summer Brave," "Break a Leg," "The Man Who Came To Dinner."

O'CONNELL, PATRICK. Born July 7, 1957 in Westport, CT. Graduate Juilliard. Bdwy debut 1983 in "Amadeus," OB in "A Man for All Seasons" (1987), "1000 Airplanes on the Roof," "Tower of Evil."

O'CONNOR, KEVIN. Born May 7, 1939 in Honolulu, HI. Attended UHI, Neighborhood Playhouse. Debut 1964 OB in "Up to Thursday," followed by "Six from La Mama," "Rimers of Eldritch," "Tom Paine," "Boy on the Straightback Chair," "Dear Janet Rosenberg," "Eyes of Chalk," "Alive and Well in Argentina," "Duet," "Trio," "The Contractor," "Kool Aid," "The Frequency," "Chucky's Hutch," "Birdbath," "The Breakers," "Crossing the Crab Nebula," "Jane Avril," "Inserts," "3 by Beckett," "The Dicks," "A Kiss Is Just a Kiss," "Last of the Knucklemen," "Thrombo," "The Dark and Mr. Stone," "The Miser," "The Heart Outright," "By and For Havel." Bdwy in "Gloria and Esperanza," "The Morning After Optimism," "Figures in the Sand," "Devour the Snow," "The Lady From Dubuque."

ODO, CHRIS: Born Feb. 7, 1954 in Kansas City, MO. Attended SWMoStateU. Debut 1984 OB in "A Midsummer Night's Dream," followed by "Oedipus," "Sleepless City," "Summer Face Woman," Bdwy in "M. Butterfly" (1988).

O'HARA, PAIGE. Born May 10, 1956 in Ft. Lauderdale, FL. Debut 1975 OB in "The Gift of the Magi," followed by "Company," "The Great American Backstage Musical," "Oh, Boy!," "Rabboni," "Sitting Pretty," "The Cat and the Fiddle," Bdwy in "Show Boat" (1983), "The Mystery of Edwin Drood."

O'HERN, JOHN. Born Jan. 2, 1953 in Albany, NY. Graduate St. Michael's Col. Debut 1986 OB in "Out!," followed by "Deep to Center."

OLIENSIS, ADAM. Born Mar. 22, 1960 in Passaic, NJ. Graduate UWis. Debut 1985 OB in "Inside-Out," followed by "Little Blood Brother."

OLSEN, ROBERT. Born Dec. 11, 1959 in Kansas City, Kan. Graduate Emporia State U. Debut 1990 OB in "Smoke on the Mountain."

O'MARA, MOLLIE. Born Sept. 5, 1960 in Pittsburgh, Pa. Attended Catholic U. Debut 1989 OB in "Rodents and Radios," followed by "Crowbar."

O'MEARA, EVAN. Born Oct. 12, 1955 in Houston, TX. Graduate UTx,SMU. Debut 1986 OB in "One Fine Day," followed by "The Racket," "The Tempest."

O'REILLY, CIARAN. Born Mar. 13, 1959 in Ireland. Attended Carmelite Col., Juilliard. Debut 1978 OB in "Playboy of the Western World," followed by "Summer," "Freedom of the City," "Fannie," "The Interrogation of Ambrose Fogarty," "King Lear," "Shadow of a Gunman," "The Marry Month of May," "I Do Not Like Thee, Dr. Fell," "The Plough and the Stars," "Yeats: A Celebration!" "Philadelphia, Here I Come!"

ORLEANS, ILO. Born May 6, 1965 in Livingston, NJ. Graduate Syracuse U., AADA, LAMDA, RADA. Debut 1989 OB in "Body Game," followed by "Starting Monday."

O'ROURKE, KEVIN. Born Jan. 25, 1956 in Portland, OR. Graduate Williams Col. Debut 1981 OB in "Declassee," followed by "Sister Mary Ignatius . . .," "Submariners," "A Midsummer Night's Dream," "Visions of Kerouac," "Self Defense," "Spoils of War" (also Bdwy), "The Spring Thing," Bdwy in "Alone Together" (1984), "Cat on a Hot Tin Roof."

OSCAR, BRAD. Born Sept. 22, 1964 in Washington, DC. Graduate Boston U. Bdwy debut 1990 in "Aspects of Love."

O'SHEA, MILO. Born June 2, 1926 in Dublin, Ire. Bdwy debut 1968 in "Staircase," followed by "Dear World," "Mrs. Warren's Profession," "Comedians," "A Touch of the Poet," "Mass Appeal," "Corpse," "Meet Me in St. Louis," OB in "Waiting for Godot," "Mass Appeal," "The Return of Herbert Bracewell," "Educating Rita."

O'STEEN, MICHAEL. Born Jan. 28, 1962 in NYC. Graduate Carnegie-Mellon U. Bdwy debut 1988 in "Starlight Express," followed by "Meet Me in St. Louis."

OSTROW, RON. Born Dec. 9, 1960 in White Plains, NY. Graduate Ithaca Col. Bdwy debut 1989 in "A Few Good Men."

OYSTER, JIM. Born May 3, 1930 in Washington, DC. OB in "Coriolanus," "The Cretan Woman," "Man and Superman," "Fallen Angels," "The Underlings," "Traveler in the Dark," Bdwy in "Cool World" (1960), "Hostile Witness," "The Sound of Music," "The Prime of Miss Jean Brodie," "Who's Who in Hell," "Mrs. Dally Has a Lover," "Romulus."

PAIS, JOSH. Born June 21, 1958 in Princeton, NJ. Graduate Syracuse U, LAMDA. Debut 1985 OB in "Short Change," followed by "I'm Not Rappaport," "The Lower Depths," "The Survivor," "Untitled Play," "Heart of a Dog," Bdwy in "I'm Not Rappaport" (1987).

PALMIERI, JOSEPH. Born Aug. 1, 1939 in Brooklyn, NY. Attended Catholic U. OB in "Cyrano de Bergerac," "Butter and Egg Man," "Boys in the Band," "Beggar's Opera," "The Family," "The Crazy Locomotive," "Umbrellas of Cherbourg," "Amidst the Gladiolas," Bdwy in "Lysistrata," "Candide," "Zoya's Apartment."

PALMINTERI, CHAZZ. Born May 15, 1951 in The Bronx, NYC. Graduate Bronx Com. Col. Debut 1982 OB in "The Guys in the Truck," followed by "The King's Men," "22 Years," "The Flatbush Faithful," "A Bronx Tale," Bdwy in "The Guys in the Truck" (1983).

PANKOW, JOHN. Born 1955 in St. Louis, MO. Attended St. Nichols Sch. of the Arts. Debut 1980 OB in "Merton of the Movies," followed by "Slab Boys," "Forty-Deuce," "Hunting Scenes from Lower Bavaria," "Cloud 9," "Jazz Poets at the Grotto," "Henry V," "North Shore Fish," "Two Gentlemen of Verona," "Italian American Reconciliation," "Aristocrats," "Ice Cream with Hot Fudge," Bdwy in "Amadeus" (1981), "The Iceman Cometh" (1985), "Serious Money."

PAQUET, LUCINA. Born Jan. 16, 1922 in New Orleans, La. Graduate LaStateU., UIowa, UIll. Bdwy debut 1990 in "The Grapes of Wrath."

PARADY, RON. Born Mar. 12, 1940 in Columbus, OH. Graduate Ohio Wesleyan U., OH State U. Bdwy debut 1981 in "Candida," followed by "Our Town," "Prelude to a Kiss," OB in "Uncle Vanya," "The Father," "The New Man," "For Sale," "Prelude to a Kiss."

PARK, STEVE. Born May 4, 1962 in Brooklyn, NY. Graduate SUNY/Binghamton. Debut 1987 OB in "Whai Whai A Long Time Ago," followed by "Play Ball," "Three Sisters," "Shogun Macbeth," "Rosie's Cafe," "Distant Laughter," "Timon of Athens," "St. Joan," "Song of Shim Chung."

PARKER, ELLEN. Born Sept. 30, 1949 in Paris, Fr. Graduate Bard Col. Debut 1971 OB in "James Joyce Liquid Theatre," followed by "Uncommon Women and Others," "Dusa, Fish, Stas and Vi," "A Day in the Life of the Czar," "Fen," "Isn't It Romantic?," "The Winter's Tale," "Aunt Dan and Lemon," "Cold Sweat," "The Heidi Chronicles," Bdwy in "Equus," "Strangers," "Plenty."

PARKER, LEONARD. Born July 22, 1932 in Cleveland, Oh. Graduate Western Reserve U. Debut OB 1958 in "Dark of the Moon," followed by "The Apple," "The Connection," "In White America," "Capital Cakewalk," Bdwy in "Porgy and Bess," "Fly Blackbird," "The Physicists," "The Long Dream," "One Flew over the Cuckoo's Nest."

PARKER, MARY-LOUISE. Born Aug. 2, 1964 in Ft. Jackson, SC. Graduate NCSchool of Arts. Debut 1989 OB in "The Art of Success," followed by "Prelude to a Kiss," Bdwy in "Prelude to a Kiss" for which she received a 1990 Theatre World Award.

MichaelJohn
McGann

Sharon
McNight

Peter
McRobbie

Frederica
Meister

T.J.
Meyers

Donna
Mills

Sally
Moffet

Ron
Morgan

Elizabeth
Mozer

Howie
Muir

Mary
Murfitt

Mike
Murray

Geoffrey
Nauffts

Maria
Neenan

Daniel
Neiden

Ruth
Nelson

Mark
Nelson

Kristine
Nevins

Natalia
Nogulich

Don
Nute

Patricia
O'Connell

Chris
Odo

Paige
O'Hara

John
O'Hern

Robert
Olsen

Mollie
O'Mara

John
Pankow

Lucinda
Paquet

Ron
Parady

Ellen
Parker

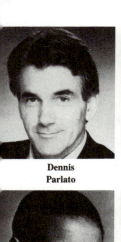

Dennis Parlato	Marilyn Pasekoff	Jay Patterson
Lucille Patton	Guy Paul	Talia Paul

Dennis
Parlato

Marilyn
Pasekoff

Jay
Patterson

Lucille
Patton

Guy
Paul

Talia
Paul

Peachena

Stephen
Pearlman

Patti
Perkins

Ron
Perlman

Lynnette
Perry

Bronson
Pinchot

Michael
Piontek

Alice
Playten

Jon
Polito

Jane
Potter

William
Preston

Amelia
Prentice

Ginger
Prince

Paul
Provenza

Colleen
Quinn

Patrick
Quinn

Careayre
Rambeau

Remak
Ramsay

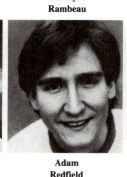

David
Rasche

Laura
Rathgeb

Jeff
Reade

Terry
Reamer

Adam
Redfield

Lynn
Redgrave

214

PARKER, NATHANIEL. Born in Reading, Eng. in 1962. Graduate LAMDA. Bdwy debut 1989 in "Merchant of Venice."

PARLATO, DENNIS. Born Mar. 30, 1947 in Los Angeles. Graduate Loyola U. Bdwy debut 1979 in "A Chorus Line," followed by "The First," "Chess," OB in Beckett," "Elizabeth and Essex," "The Fantasticks," "Moby Dick," "The Knife," "Shylock," "Have I Got a Girl For You," "Romance! Romance!," "The Lark," "Violent Peace," "Traveler in the Dark."

PARRY, WILLIAM. Born Oct. 7, 1947 in Steubenville, OH. Graduate Mt. Union Col. Bdwy debut 1971 in "Jesus Christ Superstar," followed by "Rockabye Hamlet," "The Leaf People," "Camelot" (1980), "Sunday in the Park with George," "Into the Light," OB in "Sgt. Pepper's Lonely Hearts Club Band," "The Conjurer," "Noah," "The Misanthrope," "Joseph and the Amazing Technicolor Dreamcoat," "Agamemnon," "Coolest Cat in Town," "Dispatches," "The Derby," "The Knife," "Cymbeline," "Marathon '90."

PARSONS, ESTELLE. Born Nov. 20, 1927 in Lynn, MA. Attended Boston U., Actors Studio. Bdwy debut 1956 in "Happy Hunting," followed by "Whoop Up!," "Beg, Borrow or Steal," "Mother Courage," "Ready When You Are, C.B.," "Malcolm," "Seven Descents of Myrtle," "And Miss Reardon Drinks a Little," "The Norman Conquests," "Ladies at the Alamo," "Miss Margarida's Way," "Pirates of Penzance," OB in "Demi-Dozen," "Pieces of 8," "Threepenny Opera," "Automobile Graveyard," "Mrs. Dally Has a Lover" for which she received a 1963 Theatre World Award, "Next Time I'll Sing to You," "Come to the Palace of Sin," "In the Summer House," "Monopoly," "The East Wind," "Galileo," "Peer Gynt," "Mahagonny," "People Are Living There," "Barbary Shore," "Oh Glorious Tintinnabulation," "Mert and Paul," "Elizabeth and Essex," "Dialogue for Lovers," "New Moon in Concert," "Orgasmo Adulto Escapes from the Zoo," "The Unguided Missile," "Baba Goya."

PASEKOFF, MARILYN. Born Nov. 7, 1949 in Pittsburgh, Pa. Graduate Boston U. Debut 1975 OB in "Godspell," followed by "Maybe I'm Doing It Wrong," "Professionally Speaking," "Forbidden Broadway," "Showing Off," "Forbidden Broadway 1990," Bdwy in "Godspell" (1976), "The Odd Couple" (1985).

PASSELTINER, BERNIE. Born Nov. 21, 1931 in NYC. Graduate Catholic U. OB in "Square in the Eye," "Sourball," "As Virtuously Given," "Now Is the Time for All Good Men," "Rain," "Kaddish," "Against the Sun," "End of Summer," "Yentl, the Yeshiva Boy," "Heartbreak House," "Every Place Is Newark," "Isn't It Romantic?," "Buck," "Pigeons on the Walk," "Waving Goodbye," "The Sunshine Boys," Bdwy in "The Office," "The Jar," "Yentl."

PATERSON, W. J. Born Aug. 25, 1941 in Lindenhurst, NY. Attended UWichita. Debut 1990 OB in "Price of Fame."

PATINKIN, MANDY. Born Nov. 30, 1952 in Chicago, IL. Attended Juilliard. OB in "Henry IV," followed by "Leave It to Beaver Is Dead," "Rebel Women," "Hamlet," "Trelawny of the Wells," "Savages," "The Split," "The Knife," "Winter's Tale." Bdwy in "The Shadow Box," "Evita," "Sunday in the Park with George," "Mandy Patinkin in Concert."

PATTERSON, JAY. Born Aug. 22 in Cincinnati, OH. Attended OhioU. Bdwy debut 1983 in "K-2," followed by OB's "Caligula," "The Mound Builders," "Quiet in the Land," "Of Mice and Men," "Domino," "Early One Evening," "Tempest," "A Doll House."

PATTERSON, KELLY. Born Feb. 22, 1964 in Midland, TX. Attended Southern Methodist U. Debut 1984 OB in "Up in Central Park," followed by "Manhattan Serenade," "Golden Apple," Bdwy in "Sweet Charity" (1986), "Jerome Robbins' Broadway."

PATTON, LUCILLE. Born in NYC. Attended Neighborhood Playhouse. Bdwy debut 1946 in "A Winter's Tale," followed by "Topaze," "Arms and the Man," "Joy to the World," "All You Need Is One Good Break," "Fifth Season," "Heavenly Twins," "Rhinoceros," "Marathon 33," "The Last Analysis," "Dinner at 8," "La Strada," "Unlikely Heroes," "Love Suicide at Schofield Barracks," OB in "Ulysses in Nighttown," "Failures," "Three Sisters," "Yes Yes No No," "Tango," "Mme. de Sade," "Apple Pie," "Follies," "Yesterday Is Over," "My Prince, My King," "I Am Who I Am," "Double Game," "Love in a Village," "1984," "A Little Night Music," "Cheri," "Till the Eagle Hollers."

PAUL, GUY. Born Sept. 12, 1949 in Milwaukee, Wi. Attended UMinn. Debut 1984 OB in "Flight of the Earls," followed by "Frankenstein," "The Underpants," "Oresteia," "Ever Afters," "Oh Baby, Oh Baby," Bdwy in "Arms and the Man" (1985), "Wild Honey," "Rumors."

PAUL, TALIA. Born May 12, 1967 in NYC. Attended SUNY/Purchase. Debut 1989 OB in "Crossing the Line," followed by Bdwy in "Zoya's Apartment" (1990).

PAYAN, ILKA TANYA. Born Jan. 7, 1943 in Santo Domingo, DR. Attended Peoples Col. of Law. Debut 1969 OB in "The Respectful Prostitute," followed by "Francesco Cenci," "The Effect of Gamma Rays . . .," "Blood Wedding," "Miss Margarida's Way," "The Bitter Tears of Petra Von Kant," "The Servant," "Parting Gestures."

PAYTON-WRIGHT, PAMELA. Born Nov. 1, 1941 in Pittsburgh, PA. Graduate Birmingham Southern Col., RADA. Bdwy debut 1967 in "The Show-Off," followed by "Exit the King," "The Cherry Orchard," "Jimmy Shine," "Mourning Becomes Electra," "The Glass Menagerie," "Romeo and Juliet," "Night of the Iguana," "M. Butterfly," OB in "The Effect of Gamma Rays . . .," "The Crucible," "The Seagull," "Don Juan," "In the Garden."

PEACHENA, LADY. Born May 15, 1948 in Lancaster, PA. Graduate Carnegie Tech. Bdwy debut 1961 in "Bye Bye Birdie," followed by "A Teaspoon Every Four Hours," "Oliver!," OB in "The Glorious Age," "Over Forty."

PEACOCK, CHIARA. Born Sept. 19, 1962 in Ann Arbor, MI. Graduate Sarah Lawrence Col. Debut 1985 OB in "Yours, Anne" followed by "Maggie Magalita," "One Step at a Time," "Octoberfest '87," "A Shayna Maidel," "Fantasma."

PEARLMAN, STEPHEN. Born Feb. 26, 1935 in NYC. Graduate DartmouthCol. Bdwy debut 1964 in "Barefoot in the Park," followed by "La Strada," OB in "Threepenny Opera," "Time of the Key," "Pimpernel," "In White America," "Viet Rock," "Chocolates," "Bloomers," "Richie," "Isn't It Romantic," "Bloodletters," "Light Up the Sky," "Perfect Party," "Come Blow Your Horn," "A Shayna Maidel," "Value Of Names," "Hyde in Hollywood," "Six Degrees of Separation."

PEERCE, HARRY. Born Feb. 21, 1952 in Detroit, Mi. Graduate UMich, Goodman Sch. Debut 1982 OB in "Little Murders," followed by "Anatol," "Songs of Paradise."

PELLEGRINO, SUSAN. Born June 3, 1950 in Baltimore, MD. Attended CCSan Francisco, CalStU. Debut 1982 OB in "Wisteria Trees," followed by "Steel on Steel," "Master Builder," "Equal Wrights," "Come As You Are."

PENDLETON, AUSTIN. Born Mar. 27, 1940 in Warren, OH. Attended YaleU. Debut 1962 OB in "Oh Dad, Poor Dad . . .," followed by "Last Sweet Days of Isaac," "Three Sisters," "Say Goodnight, Gracie," "Office Murders," "Up From Paradise," "The Overcoat," "Two Character Play," "Master Class," "Educating Rita," "Uncle Vanya," "Serious Company," "Philotetes," "Hamlet," "Richard III," Bdwy in "Fiddler on the Roof," "Hail Scrawdyke," "Little Foxes," "American Millionaire," "Runner Stumbles," "Doubles."

PENDLETON, DAVID. Born Nov. 5, 1937 in Pittsburgh, Pa. Graduate Lincoln U., CCNY. Bdwy debut 1971 in "No Place to Be Somebody," OB in "Screens," "Don't Bother Me, I Can't Cope," "Blueberry Mountain," "Julius Caesar," "Capitol Cakewalk."

PENDLETON, WYMAN. Born Apr. 18, 1916 in Providence, RI. Graduate Brown U. Bdwy debut 1964 in "Tiny Alice," followed by "Malcolm," "Quotations from Chairman Mao Tse-Tung," "Happy Days," "Henry V," "Othello," "There's One in Every Family," "Cat on a Hot Tin Roof," "Scenes and Revelations," "Prelude to a Kiss," OB in "Gallows Humor," "American Dream," "Zoo Story," "Corruption in the Palace of Justice," "Giant's Dance," "Child Buyer," "Happy Days," "Butter and Egg Man," "Othello," "Albee Directs Albee," "Dance for Me, Simeon," "Mary Stuart," "The Collyer Brothers," "Period Piece," "A Bold Stroke for a Wife," "Hitch-Hikers," "Waltz of the Toreadors," "Time of the Cuckoo," "Stopping the Desert."

PENN, MATT. Born Mar. 29, 1958 in Chicago, Il. Graduate Syracuse U., Debut 1986 OB in "Macbeth," followed by "The Balcony."

PEREZ, LUIS. Born July 28, 1959 in Atlanta, GA. With Joffrey Ballet before 1986 debut in "Brigadoon" (LC) followed by "Phantom of the Opera," "Jerome Robbins' Bdwy," "Dangerous Games," OB in "Wonderful Ice Cream Suit," "Tango Apasionada."

PEREZ, MIGUEL. Born Sept. 7, 1957 in San Jose, Ca. Attended NtlShakeConsv. Debut 1986 OB in "Women Beware Women," followed by "Don Juan of Seville," "Cymbeline," "Mountain Language," "The Birthday Party," "Hamlet."

PERKINS, DON. Born Oct. 23, 1928 in Boston, Ma. Emerson Col. graduate. Bdwy in "Borstal Boy" (1970), OB in "Drums under the Window," "Henry VI," "Richard III," "The Dubliners," "The Rehearsal," "Fallen Angels," "Our Lord of Lynchville," "A Touch of the Poet," "Crossing the Bar," "Two by Two."

PERKINS, PATTI. Born July 9th in New Haven, Ct. Attended AMDA. Debut 1972 OB in "The Contrast," followed by "Fashion," "Tuscaloosa's Calling Me," "Patch," "Shakespeare's Cabaret," "Maybe I'm Doing It Wrong," "Fabulous La Fontaine," "Hannah 1939," Bdwy "All Over Town," "Shakespeare's Cabaret."

PERLMAN, RON. Born Apr. 13, 1950 in NYC. Graduate Lehman Col., UMin. Debut 1976 OB in "The Architect and the Emperor of Assyria," followed by "Tartuffe," "School for Buffoons," "Measure for Measure," "Hedda Gabler," Bdwy in "Teibele and Her Demon" (1979), "A Few Good Men."

PERRY, JEFF. Born Aug. 16, 1955 in Highland Park, Il. Attended IllStateU. Debut 1984 OB in "Balm in Gilead," Bdwy in "The Caretaker" (1986), "The Grapes of Wrath."

PERRY, KEITH. Born Oct. 29, 1931 in Des Moines, Iowa. Graduate Rice U. Bdwy debut 1965 in "Pickwick," followed by "I'm Solomon," "Copperfield," "City of Angels," OB in "Epicene, the Silent Woman," "Hope and Feathers," "Ten Little Indians."

PERRY, LYNNETTE. Born Sept. 29, 1963 in Bowling Green, Oh. Graduate CinConsv. Debut 1987 OB in "The Chosen," followed by "Lucy's Lapses," Bdwy in "Grand Hotel" (1989).

PETTIT, DODIE. Born Dec. 29 in Princeton, NJ. Attended Westminster Choir Col. Bdwy debut 1984 in "Cats," followed by "The Phantom of the Opera."

PFEIFFER, MICHELLE. Born Apr. 29, 1957 in Santa Ana, Ca. Debut 1989 OB in "Twelfth Night."

PHILLIPS, MARY ELLEN. Born Apr. 17, 1963 in Providence, RI. Graduate RI Col. Debut OB 1989 in "Sweeney Todd," Bdwy in "Sweeney Todd" (1989).

PIERCE, DAVID. Born Apr. 3, 1959 in Albany, NY. Graduate Yale U. Debut 1982 on Bdwy in "Beyond Therapy," followed by "The Heidi Chronicles," OB in "Summer," "That's It, Folks!," "The Three Zeks," "Donuts," "Hamlet," "The Maderati," "Marathon 87," "The Cherry Orchard," "Zero Positive," "Much Ado about Nothing," "Elliot Loves."

PIETROPINTO, ANGELA. Born Feb. 5th in NYC. Graduate NYU. OB credits include "Henry IV," "Alice in Wonderland," "Endgame," "The Seagull," "Jinx Bridge," "The Mandrake," "Marie and Bruce," "Green Card Blues," "3 by Pirandello," "The Broken Pitcher," "Cymbeline," "Romeo and Juliet," "A Midsummer Night's Dream," "Twelve Dreams," "The Rivals," "Cap and Bells," "Thrombo," "Lies My Father Told Me," "Sorrows of Stephen," "Between the Wars," "The Hotel Play," "Rain. Some Fish. No Elephants," Bdwy in "The Suicide" (1980), "Eastern Standard."

PINCHOT, BRONSON. Born May 20, 1959 in NYC. Yale graduate. Debut 1982 OB in "Poor Little Lambs," followed by "Mr. Joyce Is Leaving Paris," Bdwy in "Zoya's Apartment" (1990).

PINKINS, TONYA. Born May 30, 1962 in Chicago, IL. Attended Carnegie-Mellon U. Bdwy debut 1981 in "Merrily We Roll Along," OB in "Five Points," "A Winter's Tale," "An Ounce of Prevention," "Just Say No," "Mexican Hayride."

PIONTEK, MICHAEL E. Born Jul. 31, 1956 in Canoga Park, CA. Graduate FSU-Asolo Conserv. Bdwy debut 1987 in "Into the Woods," followed by "3 Penny Opera." OB in "Reckless," "The Pajama Game," "Dames at Sea," "One Act Festival," "Florida Crackers."

PLAYTEN, ALICE. Born Aug. 28, 1947 in NYC. Attended NYU. Bdwy debut 1960 in "Gypsy," followed by "Oliver!," "Hello, Dolly!," "Henry, Sweet Henry," for which she received a Theatre World Award, "George M!," "Spoils of War," "Rumors," OB in "Promenade," "The Last Sweet Days of Isaac," "National Lampoon's Lemmings," "Valentine's Day," "Pirates of Penzance," "Up From Paradise," "A Visit," "Sister Mary Ignatius Explains It All," "An Actor's Nightmare," "That's It, Folks," "1-2-3-4-5," "Spoils of War," "Marathon '90."

POLITO, JON. Born Dec. 29, 1950 in Philadelphia, Pa. Graduate Villanova U. Debut 1976 OB in "The Transfiguration of Benno Blimpie," followed by "New Jerusalem," "Emigres," "A Winter's Tale," "Johnny-on-a-Spot," "Barbarians," "The Wedding," "Digby," "Other People's Money." Bdwy in "American Buffalo" (1977), "Curse of an Aching Heart," "Total Abandon," "Death of a Salesman."

POTTER, JANE. Born June 15, 1966 in Milwaukee, Wi. Graduate Syracuse U. Debut 1989 OB in "Nunsense," followed by "Smoke on the Mountain."

PRENTICE, AMELIA. Born Sept. 14 in Toronto, Can. Graduate AADA, LAMDA. Bdwy debut 1987 in "Starlight Express," OB in "Hooray for Hollywood," "Lenny Bruce Revue," "Broadway Jukebox."

PRESTON, LAWRENCE. Born Jan. 24, 1963 in North Miami, Fl. Graduate NYU. Debut 1986 OB in "The Private Ear," followed by "Othello."

PRESTON, WILLIAM. Born Aug. 26, 1921 in Columbia, PA. Graduate PaStateU. Debut 1972 OB in "We Bombed in New Haven," followed by "Hedda Gabler," "Whisper into My Good Ear," "A Nestless Bird," "Friends of Mine," "Iphigenia in Aulis," "Midsummer," "The Fantasticks," "Frozen Assets," "The Golem," "The Taming of the Shrew," "His Master's Voice," "Much Ado about Nothing," "Hamlet," "Winter Dreams," "Palpitations," Bdwy in "Our Town."

PRICE, LONNY. Born Mar. 9, 1959 in NYC. Attended Juilliard. Debut 1979 OB in "Class Enemy," for which he received a Theatre World Award, followed by "Up from Paradise," "Rommel's Garden," "Times and Appetites of Toulouse-Lautrec," "Room Service," "Come Blow Your Horn," "The Immigrant," "A Quiet End," Bdwy in "The Survivor" (1980), "Merrily We Roll Along," "Master Harold and the Boys," "The Time of Your Life," "Children of the Sun," "Rags," "Broadway," "Burn This."

PRINCE, FAITH. Born Aug. 5, 1957 in Augusta, GA. Graduate UCincinnati. Debut OB 1981 in "Scrambled Feet," followed by "Olympus on My Mind," "Groucho," "Living Color," "Bad Habits," Bdwy in "Jerome Robbins' Broadway" (1989).

PRINCE, GINGER. Born June 3, 1945 in Stuart, Fl. Attended Stephens Col. Debut 1987 OB in "Steel Magnolias," followed by Bdwy in "Gypsy" (1989).

PROVENZA, PAUL. Born July 31, 1957 in NYC. Graduate UPa., RADA. Debut OB 1988 in "Only Kidding," for which he received a Theatre World Award.

PRUNEAU, PHILLIP. Born July 10th in Chicago, Il. Attended New School. Bdwy debut 1949 in "The Cellar and the Well," followed by "Sabrina Fair," "The Winner," "The Bad Seed," "There Was a Little Girl," "Sophie," "The Last Analysis," "Arsenic and Old Lace," OB in "The Madwoman of Chaillot," "Vivat! Vivat Regina!," "Clarence," "The Time of Your Life," "Children of the Sun," "The Cherry Orchard."

PUGH, RICHARD WARREN. Born Oct. 20, 1950 in NYC. Graduate Tarkio Col. Bdwy debut 1979 in "Sweeney Todd," followed by "The Music Man," "The Five O'Clock Girl," "Copperfield," "Zorba" (1983), "Phantom of the Opera," OB in "Chase a Rainbow."

PURSLEY, DAVID. Born July 13, 1938 in Lewisburg, PA. Graduate HarvardU, BaylorU. Debut 1969 OB in "Peace," followed by "The Faggott," "Wings," "The Three Musketeers," Bdwy in "Happy End" (1977), "Snow White," "Anything Goes," "3 Penny Opera."

QUINN, COLLEEN. Born Apr. 24th in Lindenhurst, NY. Debut 1988 OB in "Borderlines," followed by "Keeping an Eye on Louie," "Octoberfest," "Dutchman," "Beauty Marks."

QUINN, PATRICK. Born Feb. 12, 1950 in Philadelphia, Pa. Graduate Temple U. Bdwy debut 1976 in "Fiddler on the Roof," followed by "A Day in Hollywood/A Night in the Ukraine," "Oh, Coward!," "Lend Me a Tenor," OB in "It's Better with a Band," "By Strouse," "Forbidden Broadway," "A Little Night Music."

RAGNO, JOSEPH. Born Mar. 11, 1936 in Brooklyn, NY. Attended Allegheny Col. Debut 1960 OB in "Worm in the Horseradish," followed by "Elizabeth the Queen," "A Country Scandal," "The Shrike," "Cymbeline," "Love Me, Love My Children," "Interrogation of Havana," "The Birds," "Armenians," "Feedlot," "Every Place Is Newark," "Modern Romance," "Hunting Cockroaches," "Just Say No," "The Return," Bdwy in "Indians" (1969), "The Iceman Cometh."

RAGSDALE, WILLIAM. Born Jan. 19, 1961 in El Dorado, Ak. Graduate Hendrix Col. Bdwy debut 1985 in "Biloxi Blues," followed by OB's "Blind Spot," "Step Lively and Watch the Closing Doors," "Briarpatch."

RAIDER-WEXLER, VICTOR. Born Dec. 31, 1943 in Toledo, OH. Attended UToledo. Debut 1976 OB in "The Prince of Homburg," followed by "The Passion of Dracula," "Ivanov," "Brandy Before Breakfast," "The Country Girl," "Dream of a Blacklisted Actor," "One Act Festival," "Loveplay," "Our Own Family," "The Boys Next Door," "L'Illusion," "Cherry Orchard," "Doctor's Dilemma," "Double Blessing." Bdwy in "Best Friend" (1976), "Ma Rainey's Black Bottom."

RAITER, FRANK. Born Jan. 17, 1932 in Cloquet, Mn. Yale graduate. Bdwy debut 1958 in "Cranks," followed by "Dark at the Top of the Stairs," "J. B.," "Camelot," OB in "Soft Core Pornographer," "The Winter's Tale," "Twelfth Night," "Tower of Evil," "Endangered Species."

RAMBEAU, CAREAYRE. Born June 23rd in Pasadena, Ca., Graduate Pasadena Col. Bdwy debut 1990 in "Zoya's Apartment."

RAMSAY, REMAK. Born Feb. 2, 1937 in Baltimore, MD. Graduate Princeton U. Debut 1964 OB in "Hang Down Your Head and Die," followed by "The Real Inspector Hound," "Landscape of the Body," "All's Well That Ends Well," "Rear Column," "The Winslow Boy," "The Dining Room," "Pygmalion in Concert," "Save Grand Central," "Quartermaine's Terms," "Woman in Mind," "Prin," Bdwy in "Half a Sixpence" (1965), "Sheep on the Runway," "Lovely Ladies, Kind Gentlemen," "On the Town," "Jumpers," "Private Lives," "Dirty Linen," "Every Good Boy Deserves Favor," "The Devil's Disciple."

RANCK, CHRISTINE. Born Dec. 8, 1951 in Columbus, Oh. Graduate URochester. Debut 1978 OB in "Company," followed by "A Night at Texas Guinan's," "Trading Places," "Mexican Hayride."

RAPHAEL, GERRIANNE. Born Feb. 23, 1935 in NYC. Attended New School, Columbia U. Bdwy debut 1941 in "Solitaire," followed by "A Guest in the House," "Violet," "Goodbye, My Fancy," "Seventh Heaven," "Li'l Abner," "Saratoga," "Man of LaMancha," "King of Hearts," OB in "Threepenny Opera," "The Boy Friend," "Ernest in Love," "Say When," "The Prime of Miss Jean Brodie," "The Butler Did It," "The Ninth Step," "An Evening with Sid Caesar."

RASCHE, DAVID. Born Aug. 7, 1944 in St. Louis, MO. Graduate Elmhurst Col, UChicago. Debut 1976 OB in "John," followed by "Snow White," "Isadora Duncan Sleeps with the Russian Navy," "End of the War," "A Sermon," "Routed," "Geniuses," "Dolphin Position," "To Gillian on Her 37th Birthday," "Custom of the Country," Bdwy in "Shadow Box" (1977), "Loose Ends," "Lunch Hour," "Speed-the-Plow," "Mastergate."

RATHGEB, LAURA. Born Sept. 5, 1962 in Burlington, VT. Graduate St. Michael's Col. Debut 1987 OB in "Deep Swimmer," followed by "The Imaginary Invalid," "Electra," "All's Well That Ends Well," "She Stoops to Conquer," "The Philanderer," "Three Sisters," "Midsummer Night's Dream" "Importance of Being Earnest," "Medea."

READE, JEFF. Born Sept. 29, 1941 in Tampa, Fl. Graduate L.A. City Col. Debut 1981 OB in "Marching to Georgia," followed by "The End of the Beginning," "Our Bettors," "Andrea Rescued," "In the Country's Night," "Louisiana Summer," "Short Eyes," "A Day for Surprises," "The Aching Heart of Samuel Kleinerman," "The Nuns," "All That Fall."

REAMER, TERRY. Born July 30, 1938 in Chicago, Il. Graduate Northwestern, Goddard Col. Debut 1989 OB in "Wonderful Town."

REAUX, ANGELINA. Born Jan. 23, 1954 in Houston, Tx. Graduate Northwestern U. Debut 1979 OB in "King of Schnorrers," followed by "My Heart Is in the East," "La Calisto," "The Cat and the Fiddle," "Sweet Song."

REAVES-PHILLIPS, SANDRA. Born Dec. 23rd in Mullins, SC. Bdwy debut 1973 in "Raisin," OB in "Li'l Bit," "Ragtime Blues," "Blues in the Night," "Basin Street," "Karma," "Sparrow in Flight," "Take Care," "American Dreams," "The Late Great Ladies," "Oh! Oh! Obesity!," "Further Mo'."

REBHORN, JAMES. Born Sept. 1, 1948 in Philadelphia, PA. Graduate Wittenberg U, Columbia U. Debut 1972 OB in "Blue Boys," followed by "Are You Now or Have You Ever Been?," "Trouble with Europe," "Othello," "Hunchback of Notre Dame," "Period of Adjustment," "The Freak," "Half a Lifetime," "Touch Black," "To Gillian on Her 37th Birthday," "Rain," "The Hasty Heart," "Husbandry," "Isn't It Romantic?," "Blind Date," "Cold Sweat," "Spoils of War," "Marathon 88," "Ice Cream with Hot Fudge." Bdwy in "I'm Not Rappaport," "Our Town" (1989).

REDFIELD, ADAM. Born Nov. 4, 1959 in NYC. Attended NYU. Debut 1977 OB in "Hamlet," followed by "Androcles and the Lion," "Twelfth Night," "Reflected Glory," "Movin' Up," "The Unicorn," "The Doctor's Dilemma," Young Playwrights Festival, "Swan Song," Bdwy (1980) in "A Life" for which he received a Theatre World Award, "Beethoven's Tenth," "Execution of Justice."

REDGRAVE, LYNN. Born Mar. 8, 1943 in London, Eng. Attended Central School. Bdwy debut 1967 in "Black Comedy," followed by "My Fat Friend," "Mrs. Warren's Profession," "Knock, Knock," "St. Joan," "Aren't We All?," "Love Letters," OB in "Sister Mary Ignatius Explains It All."

REDGRAVE, VANESSA. Born Jan. 30, 1937 in London, Eng. Attended Central School of Speech and Drama. Bdwy debut 1976 in "The Lady from the Sea," followed by "Orpheus Descending" (1989).

REDWOOD, JOHN HENRY. Born Sept. 10 in Brooklyn, NY. Graduate UKs, Fordham U, St. John's U. Debut 1971 OB in "One Flew over the Cuckoo's Nest," followed by "Black Visions," "When the Sun Gets Blue," "Mark VIII," "Walkers," "The Balcony," Bdwy in "Guys and Dolls."

REEHLING, JOYCE. Born Mar. 5, 1949 in Baltimore, MD. Graduate NCSchool of Arts. Debut 1976 OB in "The Hot l Baltimore," followed by "Who Killed Richard Cory?," "Lulu," "5th of July," "The Runner Stumbles," "Life and/or Death," "Back in the Race," "Time Framed," "Extremities," "Hands of Its Enemy," "Reckless," "Prelude to a Kiss," Bdwy in "A Matter of Gravity" (1976), "5th of July," "Prelude to a Kiss."

REISSA, ELEANOR. Born May 11 in Brooklyn, NY. Graduate Brooklyn Col. Debut 1979 OB in "Rebecca the Rabbi's Daughter," followed by "That's Not Funny, That's Sick," "The Rise of David Levinsky," "Match Made in Heaven," "Song for a Saturday," "No No Nanette," "Songs of Paradise."

REMME, JOHN. Born Nov. 21, in Fargo, ND. Attended UMn. Debut 1972 OB in "One for the Money," followed by "Anything Goes," "The Rise of David Levinsky," "Jubilee in Concert," "The Firefly in Concert," "Sweet Adeline in Concert," "George White's Scandals in Concert," "Tomfoolery," Bdwy in "The Ritz" (1975), "The Royal Family," "Can-Can," "Alice in Wonderland," "Teddy and Alice," "Gypsy."

RENDERER, SCOTT. Born in Palo Alto, CA. Graduate Whitman Col. Bdwy debut 1983 in "Teaneck Tanzi," OB in "And Things That Go Bump in the Night," "Crossfire," "Just Like the Lions," "The Dreamer Examines His Pillow," "Nasty Little Secrets."

RENFROE, REBECCA. Born Nov. 9, 1951 in Alexandria, VA. Graduate UCincinnati. Bdwy debut 1981 in "Bring Back Birdie," OB in "The Gifts of the Magi."

REY, ANTONIA. Born Oct. 12, 1927 in Havana, Cuba. Graduate Havana U. Bdwy debut 1964 in "Bajour," followed by "Mike Downstairs," "Engagement Baby," "The Ritz," OB in "Yerma," "Fiesta in Madrid," "Camino Real" (LC), "Back Bog Beast Bait," "Rain," "42 Seconds from Broadway," "Streetcar Named Desire" (LC), "Poets from the Inside," "Blood Wedding," "Missing Persons," "Crisp," "The Last Latin Lover," "New York 1937."

RHYNE, SYLVIA. Born Dec. 27 in Chicago, IL. Graduate Carleton Col. OB in "Candide," "South Pacific," "La Vie Parisienne," "Golden Apple," Bdwy in "Sweeney Todd" (1989).

RHYS, WILLIAM. Born Jan. 2, 1945 in NYC. Graduate Wesleyan U. Bdwy debut 1969 with National Theatre of the Deaf, followed by "The Changing Room," OB in "Birth," "The Balcony."

RICE, SARAH. Born Mar. 5, 1955 in Okinawa. Attended AzStateU. Debut 1974 OB in "The Fantasticks," followed by "The Enchantress," "The Music Man," "Swan Song," "The Waves," Bdwy 1979 in "Sweeney Todd" for which she received a Theatre World Award.

RICHARDS, CAROL. Born Dec. 26 in Aurora, IL. Graduate Northwestern U, Columbia U. Bdwy debut 1965 in "Half a Sixpence," followed by "Mame," "Last of the Red Hot Lovers," "Company," "Cats."

RICHARDS, JESS. Born Jan. 23, 1943 in Seattle, WA. Attended UWash. Bdwy debut 1966 in "Walking Happy," followed by "South Pacific" (LC), "Two by Two," "On the Town" for which he received a 1972 Theatre World Award, "Mack and Mabel," "Musical Chairs," "A Reel American Hero," "Barnum," "Meet Me in St. Louis," OB in "One for the Money," "Lovesong," "A Musical Evening with Josh Logan," "The Lullaby of Broadway," "All Night Strut!," "Station Joy," "Sing for Your Supper."

RICHARDSON, LEE. Born Sept. 11, 1926 in Chicago, IL. Graduate Goodman Theatre. Debut 1952 OB in "Summer and Smoke," followed by "St. Joan," "Volpone," "The American Dream," "Bartleby," "Plays for Bleecker Street," "Merchant of Venice," "King Lear," "Thieves Carnival," "Waltz of the Toreadors," "Talented Tenth," "Elliot Loves." Bdwy in "The Legend of Lizzie" (1959), "Lord Pengo," "House of Atreus," "Find Your Way Home," "Othello," "The Jockey Club Stakes," "The Devil's Disciple."

RICKETTS, JIM. Born May 11, 1948 in NYC. Attended IllWesleyanU, AMDA. Debut 1977 OB in "Peg O' My Heart," followed by "The Flatbush Faithful," "All That Fall."

John Henry
Redwood

Joyce
Reehling

John
Remme

Rebecca
Renfore

William
Rhys

Sarah
Rice

Carol
Richards

Lee
Richardson

Eden
Riegel

Sam
Riegel

Elaine
Rinehart

Roger
Rignack

Joey
Rigol

Nancy
Ringham

Manuel
Rivera

Jana
Robbins

Tony
Roberts

Laila
Robins

Caryn
Rosenthal

Howard
Ross

Stephanie
Roth

John
Rothman

Patricia
Ruck

Charles
Rule

William
Ryall

Jack
Ryland

Peter
Samuel

Jaime
Sanchez

Jay O.
Sanders

Michael
Santoro

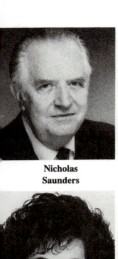    

Nicholas **Saunders**	**Sharon** **Schlarth**	**Robert** **Schlee**	**Seret** **Scott**	**Peter** **Schmitz**	**Lorraine** **Serabian**

Debbie **Shapiro**	**Edward** **Seamon**	**Nicola** **Sheara**	**Johnny** **Seaton**	**Claudia** **Shell**	**Thom** **Sesma**

Mark **Shannon**	**Sloane** **Shelton**	**Barry** **Sherman**	**Madeleine** **Sherwood**	**Timothy** **Shew**	**Betty** **Silberman**

Maureen **Silliman**	**Joseph R.** **Sicari**	**Margo** **Skinner**	**Albert** **Sinkys**	**Neva** **Small**	**Victor** **Slezak**

John **Sloman**	**Jennifer** **Smith**	**Rex** **Smith**	**Lois** **Smith**	**William** **Solo**	**J.** **Smith-Cameron**

RIEGEL, EDEN. Born Jan. 1, 1981 in Washington, DC. Bdwy debut 1989 in "Les Miserables."

RIEGEL, SAM. Born Oct. 9, 1976 in Washington, DC. Bdwy debut 1990 in "The Sound of Music."

RIEGERT, PETER. Born Apr. 11, 1947 in NYC. Graduate UBuffalo. Debut 1975 OB in "Dance with Me," followed by "Sexual Perversity in Chicago," "Sunday Runners," "Isn't It Romantic," "La Brea Tarpits," "A Hell of a Town," "Festival of One Acts," "A Rosen by Any Other Name," "The Birthday Party," "Mountain Language," Bdwy in "The Nerd" (1987).

RIEHLE, RICHARD. Born May 12, 1948 in Menomonee Falls, WI. Graduate UNotre Dame, UMn. Bdwy debut 1986 in "Execution of Justice," OB in "A Midsummer Night's Dream," "The Birthday Party," "Right Behind the Flag," "Knepp," "Just Say No," "Phaedra Britannica," "Mountain Language/The Birthday Party."

RIFKIN, ROGER. Born Dec. 29, 1954 in Brooklyn, NYC. Attended Queens Col. Debut 1989 OB in "Wonderful Town."

RIFKIN, RON. Born Oct. 31, 1939 in NYC. Graduate NYU. Bdwy debut 1960 in "Come Blow Your Horn," followed by "The Goodbye People," "The Tenth Man," OB in "Rosebloom," "The Art of Dining," "Temple."

RIGNACK, ROGER. Born Sept. 24, 1962 in NYC. Graduate Emerson Col. Debut 1985 OB in "Dead! A Love Story," followed by "Disappearing Acts," "The Red Madonna," "Our Lady of the Tortilla," "In Available Light," "Troubadour."

RIGOL, JOEY. Born Jan. 6, 1979 in Miami, Fl. Debut 1988 OB in "The Chosen," followed by "The Voyage of the Beagle," "The Music Man," "Stop the World," "Sympathy," Bdwy in "Les Miserables" (1989).

RILEY, ERIC. Born Mar. 22, 1955 in Albion, MI. Graduate UMI. Bdwy debut 1979 in "Ain't Misbehavin'," followed by "Dream Girls," "Ain't Misbehavin' " (1988), OB in "Once on This Island."

RINEHART, ELAINE. Born Aug. 16, 1958 in San Antonio, TX. Graduate NCSchArts. Debut 1975 OB in "Tenderloin," followed by "Native Son," "Joan of Lorraine," "Dumping Ground," "Fairweather Friends," "The Color of the Evening Sky," "The Best Little Whorehouse in Texas," "The Wedding of the Siamese Twins," "Festival of 1 Acts," "Up 'n' Under," "Crystal Clear," "Black Market."

RINGHAM, NANCY. Born Nov. 16, 1954 in Minneapolis, Mn. Graduate St. Olaf Col, Oxford U. Bdwy debut 1954 in "My Fair Lady," (1981), followed by "3 Penny Opera," OB in "That Jones Boy," "Bugles at Dawn," "Not-So-New Faces of 1982," "Trouble in Tahiti," "Lenny and the Heartbreakers," "Four 1-Act Musicals," "Esther. A Vaudeville Megillah."

RIVERA, MANUEL. Born Jan. 27, 1959 in NYC. Debut 1984 OB in "Cuban Swimmer/Dog Lady" followed by "She First Met Her Parents on the Subway."

RIVIN, LUCILLE. Born Mar. 25 in Brooklyn, NY. Graduate SUNY. Debut OB 1982 in "The Beggar," followed by "Golden Leg," "She First Met Her Parents on the Subway."

ROBB, R. D. Born Mar. 31, 1972 in Philadelphia, Pa. Bdwy debut 1980 in "Charlie and Algernon," followed by "Oliver!," "Les Miserables."

ROBBINS, JANA. Born Apr. 18, 1947 in Johnstown, PA. Graduate Stephens Col. Bdwy debut 1974 in "Good News," followed by "I Love My Wife," "Crimes of the Heart," "Romance/Romance," "Gypsy," OB in "Tickles by Tucholsky," "Tip-Toes," "All Night Strut," "Colette Collage," "Circus Gothic," "Ad Hock."

ROBERTS, GRACE. Born Nov. 9, 1935 in NYC. Attended New School. Debut 1956 OB in "Out of This World," followed by "Affairs of Anatol," "Beethoven/Karl," "Friends Too Numerous to Mention," "Applesauce," "A . . . My Name Is Alice," "Briss," "The Matchmaker," "Unlikely Heroes," "Come Blow Your Horn," "Green Field," "Pearls," "Made in Heaven," "The Dreams of Clytemnestra."

ROBERTS, TONY. Born Oct. 22, 1939 in NYC. Graduate Northwestern U. Bdwy debut 1962 in "Something about a Soldier," followed by "Take Her, She's Mine," "Last Analysis," "Never Too Late," "Barefoot in the Park," "Don't Drink the Water," "How Now, Dow Jomes," "Play It Again, Sam," "Promises, Promises," "Sugar," "Absurd Person Singular," "Murder at the Howard Johnson's," "They're Playing Our Song," "Doubles," "Brigadoon" (LC), "South Pacific" (LC), "Love Letters," "Jerome Robbins' Broadway," OB in "The Cradle Will Rock," "Losing Time," "The Good Parts," "Time Framed."

ROBERTSON, CLIFF. Born Sept. 9, 1925 in La Jolla, Ca. Attended Antioch Col. Bdwy debut 1953 in "Late Love," followed by "The Wisteria Trees," "Orpheus Descending" for which he received a Theatre World Award, "Rosalie in Concert," "Love Letters."

ROBINS, LAILA. Born Mar. 14, 1959 in St. Paul, MN. Graduate UWis, Yale. Bdwy debut 1984 in "The Real Thing," OB in "Bloody Poetry," "The Film Society," "For Dear Life," "Maids of Honor."

ROBINSON, HAL. Born in Bedford, In. Graduate IndU. Debut 1971 OB in "Memphis Store-Bought Teeth," followed by "From Berlin to Broadway," "The Fantasticks," "Promenade," "The Baker's Wife," "Yours, Anne," "Personals," "And a Nightingale Sang," Bdwy in "On Your Toes (1983), "Broadway," "Grand Hotel."

ROBINSON, MEGHAN. Born Aug. 11, 1955 in Wilton, CT. Graduate Bennington Col. Debut 1982 OB in "The Dubliners," followed by "The Habits of Rabbits," "Episode 26," "Macbeth," "King Lear," "Sleeping Beauty or Coma," "Vampire Lesbians of Sodom," "Psycho Beach Party," "Hunger," "3 Pieces for a Warehouse," "No One Dances," "The Lady in Question."

ROGERS, GIL. Born Feb. 4, 1934 in Lexington, Ky. Attended Harvard U. OB in "The Ivory Branch," "Vanity of Nothing," "Warrior's Husband," "Hell-Bent fer Heaven," "Gods of Lightning," "Pictures in a Hallway," "Rose," "Memory Bank," "A Recent Killing," "Birth," "Come Back, Little Sheba," "Life of Galileo," "Remembrance," "Mortally Fine," "Frankie," Bdwy in "The Great White Hope," "The Best Little Whorehouse in Texas," "The Corn Is Green" (1983).

ROGERS, MICHAEL. Born Dec. 8, 1954 in Trinidad. Attended Long Island U., Yale. Debut 1974 OB in "Elena," followed by "Chiaroscuro," "Forty Duece," "Antigone," "Julius Caesar," "Insufficient Evidence," "Othello."

ROLF, FREDERICK. Born Aug. 14, 1926 in Berlin, Ger. Bdwy debut 1951 in "St Joan," followed by "The Egg," "Time Remembered," OB in "Coriolanus," "The Strong Are Lonely," "The Smokeweaver's Daughter," "Between Two Thieves," "Hedda Gabler," "The Day the Whores Came Out to Play Tennis," "Hogan's Goat," "In the Matter of J. Robert Oppenheimer," "Dark Lady of the Sonnets," "Tamara."

ROOS, CASPER. Born Mar. 21, 1925 in The Bronx, NYC. Attended Manhattan School of Music. Bdwy debut 1959 in "First Impressions,", followed by "How to Succeed in Business . . .," "Mame," "Brigadoon," "Shenandoah" (1975/1989), "My One and Only," "Into the Light," OB in "Street Scene," "Another Part of the Forest."

ROSENTHAL, CARYN. Born July 15, 1965 in Brooklyn, NYC. Graduate UFla. Yale. Debut 1987 OB in "Power, Greed and Self-Destruction in America," followed by "At Home," "How Are Things in Costa del Fuego?"

ROSS, HOWARD. Born Aug. 21, 1934 in NYC. Attended Juilliard, NYU. Bdwy debut 1965 in "Oliver!," followed by "1600 Pennsylvania Avenue," "Carmelina," OB in "Jacques Brel Is Alive . . .," "Beggar's Opera," "Philemon," "Isadora Duncan Sleeps with the Russian Navy," "The Further Inquiry," "Frankie."

ROTH, STEPHANIE. Born in 1963 in Boston, Ma. Juilliard graduate. Bdwy debut 1987 in "Les Liaisons Dangereuses," followed by "Artist Descending a Staircase," OB in "The Cherry Orchard," "Measure for Measure."

ROTHMAN, JOHN. Born June 3, 1949 in Baltimore, MD. Graduate Wesleyan U, Yale. Debut 1978 OB in "Rats Nest," followed by "The Impossible H.L. Mencken," "The Buddy System," "Rosario and the Gypsies," "Italian Straw Hat," "Modern Ladies of Guanabacoa," "Faith Hope Charity," "Some Americans Abroad," Bdwy in "End of the World . . ." (1984), "Some Americans Abroad."

ROWE, FLORENCE. Born Mar. 12, 1931 in Minneapolis, Mn. Graduate Sarah Lawrence Col. Bdwy debut in "Zoya's Apartment" (1990).

ROWE, STEPHEN. Born June 3, 1948 in Johnstown, Pa. Graduate Emerson Col., Yale. Debut 1979 OB in "Jungle Coup," followed by "A Private View," "Cinders," "Coming of Age in Soho," "The Normal Heart," "Whispers," "Terry by Terry," "Macbeth," Bdwy in "Serious Money" (1988).

RUBINSTEIN, JOHN. Born Dec. 8, 1946 in Los Angeles. Attended UCLA. Bdwy debut 1972 in "Pippin," for which he received a Theatre World Award, followed by "Children of a Lesser God," "Fools," "The Soldier's Tale," "The Caine Mutiny Court-Martial," "Hurlyburly," "M. Butterfly," OB in "Rosencrantz and Guildenstern Are Dead," "Urban Blight," "Love Letters."

RUCK, PATRICIA. Born Sept. 11, 1963 in Washington, DC. Attended Goucher Col. Bdwy debut 1986 in "Cats."

RUIZ, ANTHONY. Born Oct. 17, 1956 in NYC. Attended NYCC. Debut 1987 OB in "The Wonderful Ice Cream Suit," followed by "Danny and the Deep Blue Sea."

RULE, CHARLES. Born Aug. 4, 1928 in Springfield, MO. Bdwy debut 1951 in "Courtin' Time," followed by "Happy Hunting," "Oh, Captain!," "The Conquering Hero," "Donnybrook," "Bye Bye Birdie," "Fiddler on the Roof," "Henry Sweet Henry," "Maggie Flynn," "1776," "Cry for Us All," "Gypsy," "Goodtime Charley," "On the 20th Century," "Phantom of the Opera," OB in "Family Portrait."

RYALL, WILLIAM. Born Sept. 18, 1954 in Binghamton, NY. Graduate AADA. Debut 1979 OB in "Canterbury Tales," followed by "Elizabeth and Essex," "He Who Gets Slapped," "The Seagull," "Tartuffe," Bdwy in "Me and My Girl" (1986), "Grand Hotel."

RYDER, RIC. Born Mar. 31 in Baltimore, MD. Graduate UMd., Peabody Conserv Bdwy debut in "Starmites" (1989), OB in "The Gifts of the Magi."

RYLAND, JACK. Born July 22, 1935 in Lancaster, PA. Attended AADA. Bdwy debut 1958 in "The World of Suzie Wong," followed by "A Very Rich Woman," "Henry V," OB in "A Palm Tree in a Rose Garden," "Lysistrata," "The White Rose and the Red," "Old Glory," "Cyrano de Bergerac," "Mourning Becomes Electra," "Beside the Seaside," "Quartermaine's Terms," "The Miracle Worker," "Enrico IV," "Good Grief."

SALATA, GREGORY. Born July 21, 1949 in NYC. Graduate Queens Col. Bdwy debut 1975 in "Dance with Me," followed by "Equus," "Bent," OB in "Piaf: A Remembrance," "Sacraments," "Measure for Measure," "Subject of Childhood," "Dance with Me," "Jacques and His Master."

SAMUEL, PETER. Born Aug. 15, 1958 in Pana, Il. Graduate E.Ill.U. Bdwy debut 1981 in "The First," followed by "Joseph and the Amazing Technicolor Dreamcoat," "Three Musketeers," "Rags," "Les Miserables," OB in "The Human Comedy," "3 Guys Naked from the Waist Down," "The Road to Hollywood," "Elizabeth and Essex," "Little Eyolf."

SAMUELSOHN, HOWARD. Born Oct. 21, 1958 in Philadelphia, PA. Graduate NYU. Debut 1985 OB in "Measure for Measure," followed by "The Job Search," "The Emperor's New Clothes," "The Racket," "Vampire Lesbians of Sodom," "A Midsummer Night's Dream," "One Act Festival."

SANCHEZ, JAIME. Born Dec. 19, 1938 in Rincon, PR. Attended Actors Studio. Bdwy debut 1957 in "West Side Story," followed by "Oh, Dad, Poor, Dad . . .," "A Midsummer Night's Dream," "Richard III," OB in "The Toilet/Conerico Was Here to Stay" for which he received a 1963 Theatre World Award, "The Ox-Cart," "The Tempest," "Merry Wives of Windsor," "Julius Caesar," "Coriolanus," "He Who Gets Slapped," "State without Grace," "The Sun Always Shines for the Cool," "Othello," "Elektra," "Domino," "The Promise."

SANDERS, FRED. Born Feb. 24, 1955 in Philadelphia, PA. Graduate Yale. Debut 1981 OB in "Coming Attractions," followed by "The Tempest," "Responsible Parties," "An Evening With Lenny Bruce," "Green Fields," "Incident at Vichy," "The Wonder Years," "Festival of One Acts," "Roots," "The Miser," "Feast Here Tonight," "Tales of the Lost Formicans."

SANDERS, JAY O. Born Apr. 16, 1953 in Austin, TX. Graduate SUNY/Purchase. Debut 1976 OB in "Henry V," followed by "Measure for Measure," "Scooping," "Buried Child," "Fables for Friends," "In Trousers," "Girls Girls Girls," "Twelfth Night," "Geniuses," "The Incredibly Famous Willy Rivers," "Rommel's Garden," "Macbeth," "Heaven on Earth," Bdwy in "Loose Ends" (1979), "The Caine Mutiny Court Martial."

SANTORIELLO, ALEX. Born Dec. 30, 1956 in Newark, NJ. Attended Ks State, Kean State. Debut 1986 OB in "La Belle Helene," followed by "A Romantic Detachment," "Passionate Extremes," Bdwy in "Les Miserables" (1987), "3 Penny Opera."

SANTORO, MICHAEL. Born Nov. 23, 1957 in Brooklyn, NYC. Attended Lee Strasberg Inst. Debut 1985 OB in "The Normal Heart," followed by "Homesick," "There Is an Angel in Las Vegas."

SAUNDERS, NICHOLAS. Born June 2, 1914 in Kiev, Russia. Bdwy debut 1942 in "Lady in the Dark," followed by "A New Life," "Highland Fling," "Happily Ever After," "The Magnificent Yankee," "Anastasia," "Take Her, She's Mine," "A Call on Kuprin," "Passion of Josef D.," OB in "An Enemy of the People," "End of All Things Natural," "The Unicorn in Captivity," "After the Rise," "All My Sons," "My Great Dead Sister," "The Investigation," "Past Tense," "Scenes and Revelations," "Zeks," "Blood Moon," "Family Comedy," "American Power Play," "Take Me Along," "The Tavern," "The Visit," "Palpitations."

SAVIN, RON LEE. Born July 20, 1947 in Norfolk, Va. Graduate Wm. & Mary Col. Debut 1981 OB in "Francis," followed by "Greater Tuna," "Road to Hollywood," "Streetheat," "One-Act Festival," "The Fantasticks," "Johnny Pye and the Fool Killer," "Gifts of the Magi."

SCHANUEL, GREG. Born Mar. 17, 1958 in Oakland, CA. Attended U Pacific, NYU. Bdwy debut 1981 in "Can-Can," followed by "Jerome Robbins' Broadway," OB in "Mozez."

SCHECHTER, DAVID. Born Apr. 12, 1956 in NYC. Graduate Bard Col., Neighborhood Playhouse. Debut 1976 OB in "Nightclub Cantata," followed by "Dispatches," "The Haggadah," "Temptation," "Balcony," Bdwy in "Runaways" (1978), "3 Penny Opera."

SCHEINE, RAYNOR. Born Nov. 10 in Emporia, Va. Graduate VaCommonwealthU. Debut 1978 OB in "Curse of the Starving Class," followed by "Blues for Mr. Charlie," "Salt Lake City Skyline," "Mother Courage," "The Lady or the Tiger," "Bathroom Plays," "Wild Life," "Re-Po," "Almost a Man," "Heaven on Earth," Bdwy in "Joe Turner's Come and Gone" (1988).

SCHLARTH, SHARON. Born Jan. 19th in Buffalo, NY. Graduate SUNY/Fredonia. Debut 1983 OB in "Full Hookup," followed by "Fool for Love," "Love's Labour's Lost," "Caligula," "The Mound Builders," "Quiet in the Land," "The Early Girl," "Borderlines," "Making Movies," Bdwy in "Sleight of Hand" (1987).

SCHLEE, ROBERT. Born June 13, 1938 in Williamsport, Pa. Graduate Lycoming Col. Debut 1972 OB in "Dr. Selavy's Magic Theatre," followed by "Hotel for Criminals," "Threepenny Opera," "Penguin Touquet," "Rasputin."

SCHMITZ, PETER. Born Aug. 20, 1962 in St. Louis, MO. Graduate Yale, NYU. Debut 1987 OB in "Henry IV Part I," followed by "We the People," "Blitzstein Project," "Imperceptible Mutabilities."

SCHOB, HANK. Born Sept. 18 in Philadelphia, Pa. Attended AADA. Debut 1969 OB in "Your Own Thing," followed by "Pirates of Penzance," "The Mikado," "Dark of the Moon," "An Evening of Adult Fairy Tales," "Dorian."

SCHOEFFLER, PAUL G. Born Nov. 21, 1958 in Montreal, Can. Graduate UC/Berkely, Carnegie-Mellon U., UBrussels. Debut 1988 OB in "Much Ado about Nothing," followed by "The Cherry Orchard."

SCHULMAN, CRAIG. Born Mar. 1, 1956 in Wiesbaden, WGer. Graduate SUNY/Oswego. Debut 1980 OB in "Pirates of Penzance," Light Opera of Manhattan, Gilbert & Sullivan Players, Bdwy in "Les Miserables" (1990).

SCHULTZ, ARMAND. Born May 17, 1959 in Rochester, NY. Graduate Niagara U, Catholic U. Debut OB 1988 in "Crystal Clear," followed by "Titus Andronicus," "Tower of Evil."

SCOTT, ERNIE. Born Mar. 20 in New Brunswick, NJ. Attended Fisk, Rutgers, Kean, Trenton State. Debut 1980 OB in "Jam," Bdwy in "Paul Robeson" (1988), followed by "The Piano Lesson."

SCOTT, SERET. Born Sept. 1, 1949 in Washington, DC. Attended NYU. Debut 1969 OB in "Slave Ship," followed by "Ceremonies in Dark Old Men," "Black Terror," "Dream," "One Last Look," "My Sister, My Sister," "Weep Not for Me," "Meetings," "The Brothers," "Eyes of the American," "Remembrances/Mojo," "Tapman," "A Burning Beach," "Human Nature," Bdwy in "For Colored Girls . . ."

SEAMON, EDWARD. Born Apr. 15, 1937 in San Diego, CA. Attended San Diego State Col. Debut 1971 OB in "The Life and Times of J. Walter Smintheous," followed by "The Contractor," "The Family," "Fishing," "Feedlot," "Cabin 12," "Rear Column," "Devour the Snow," "Buried Child," "Friends," "Extenuating Circumstances," "Confluence," "Richard II," "Great Grandson of Jedediah Kohler," "Marvelous Gray," "Time Framed," "The Master Builder," "Full Hookup," "Fool for Love," "The Harvesting," "A Country for Old Men," "Love's Labour's Lost," "Caligula," "The Mound Builders," "Quiet in the Land," "Talley and Son," "Tomorrow's Monday," "Ghosts," "Of Mice and Men," "Beside Herself," "You Can't Think of Everything," "Tales of the Lost Formicans." Bdwy in "The Trip Back Down" (1977), "Devour the Snow," "American Clock."

SEATON, JOHNNY. Born Mar. 19, 1959 in Cheveriv, Md. Debut 1984 OB in "Elvismania," followed by "Elvis: A Rockin' Remembrance."

SEIDMAN, JOHN. Born Oct. 11, 1949 in Miami, Fl. Graduate NYU. Debut 1982 on Bdwy in "Alice in Wonderland," followed by OB's "In the Troll Palace," "Adam and the Experts."

SENNETT, DAVID. Born July 7, 1954 in Champaign, Il. Attended Brandeis U., ANTA. Debut OB 1983 in "Buck," followed by "Frankenstein," "Wakefield Plays," "Room Service," "Three Sisters," "Winter's Tale," "Dorian."

SERABIAN, LORRAINE. Born June 12, 1945 in NYC. Graduate Hofstra U. OB in "Sign of Jonah," "Electra," "Othello," "Secret Life of Walter Mitty," "Bugs and Veronica," "Trojan Women," "American Gothics," "Gallows Humor," "Company," "Dorian," Bdwy in "Cabaret," "Zorba."

SERRANO, CHARLIE. Born Dec. 4, 1952 in Rio Piedras, PR. Attended Brooklyn Col. Debut 1978 OB in "Allegro," followed by "Mama, I Want to Sing," "El Bravo," "Non Pasquale," "Working," Bdwy in "Got to Go Disco" (1979), "Joseph and the Amazing Technicolor Dreamcoat."

SESMA, THOM. Born June 1, 1955 in Sasebo, Japan. Graduate UCal. Bdwy debut 1983 in "La Cage aux Folles," followed by "Chu Chem" (OB & Bdwy), OB in "In a Pig's Valise," "Baba Goya."

SHAFER, PAMELA. Born Jan. 25, 1963 in Tiffin, OH. Graduate Point PKCol. Debut 1989 OB in "Gigi," "Harriet the Spy."

SHAKAR, MARTIN. Born Jan. 1, 1940 in Detroit, Mi. Attended Wayne State U. Bdwy debut 1969 in "Our Town," followed by OB's "Lorenzaccio," "Macbeth," "The Infantry," "American Pastoral," "No Place to Be Somebody," "World of Mrs. Solomon," "And Whose Little Boy Are You?," "Investigation of Havana," "Night Watch," "Owners," "Actors," "Richard III," "Transfiguration of Benno Blimpie," "Jack Gelber's New Play," "Biko Inquest," "Second Story Sunlight," "Secret Thighs of New England," "After the Fall," "Faith Healer," "Hunting Cockroaches," "Yellow Dog Contract," "Marathon '90."

SHALHOUB, TONY. Born Oct. 9, 1953 in Green Bay, WI. Graduate YaleU. Bdwy debut 1985 in "Odd Couple," followed by "Heidi Chronicles," OB in "Richard II," "One Act Festival," "Zero Positive," "Rameau's Nephew," "For Dear Life."

SHANNON, MARK. Born Dec. 13, 1948 in Indianapolis, IN. Attended UCin. Debut 1969 OB in "Fortune and Men's Eyes," followed by "Brotherhood," "Nothing to Report," "Three Sisters," "K2."

SHAPIRO, DEBBIE. Born Sept. 29, 1954 in Los Angeles, CA. Graduate LACC. Bdwy debut 1979 in "They're Playing Our Song," followed by "Perfectly Frank," "Blues in the Night," "Zorba," "Jerome Robbin's Bdwy," OB in "They Say It's Wonderful," "New Moon in Concert."

SHEARA, NICOLA. Born May 23 in NYC. Graduate USyracuse. Debut 1975 OB in "Another Language," followed by "Sananda Sez," "All the Way Home," "Inadmissible Evidence," "Another Part of the Forest," "Working One Acts," Bdwy 1990 in "Grapes of Wrath."

SHELL, CLAUDIA. Born Sept. 11, 1959 in Passaic, NJ. Debut 1980 OB in "Jam," Bdwy in "Merlin," followed by "Cats."

SHELTON, SLOANE. Born Mar. 17, 1934 in Asheville, NC. Attended Bates Col., RADA. Bdwy debut 1967 in "The Imaginary Invalid," followed by "A Touch of the Poet," "Tonight at 8:30," "I Never Sang for My Father," "Sticks and Bones," "The Runner Stumbles," "Shadow Box," "Passione," "Open Admission," "Orpheus Descending," OB in "Androcles and the Lion," "The Maids," "Basic Training of Pavlo Hummel," "Play and Other Plays," "Julius Caesar," "Chieftans," "Passione," "The Chinese Viewing Pavilion," "Blood Relations," "The Great Divide," "Highest Standard of Living," "The Flower Palace," "April Snow."

SHERMAN, BARRY. Born Nov. 10, 1962 in Fontana, CA. Attended Col. of Marin, Nat'l Theatre Conserv. Debut 1988 OB in "Rimers of Eldritch," followed by "Kingfish."

SHERWOOD, MADELEINE. Born Nov. 13, 1926 in Montreal, Can. Attended Yale U. OB in "Brecht on Brecht," "Medea," "Hey, You Light Man," "Friends and Relations," "Older People," "O Glorious Tintinnabulation," "Getting Out," "Secret Thighs of New England Women," "Rain," "Ghosts," "Paradise Lost," "Madwoman of Chaillot," "Marathon '90," Bdwy in "The Chase" (1952), "The Crucible," "Cat on a Hot Tin Roof," "Invitation to a March," "Camelot," "Arturo Ui," "Do I Hear a Waltz?," "Inadmissible Evidence," "All Over!"

SHEW, TIMOTHY. Born Feb. 7, 1959 in Grand Forks, ND. Graduate Millikin U., UMi. Debut 1987 OB in "The Knife," Bdwy in "Les Miserables."

SHROPSHIRE, NOBLE. Born Mar. 2, 1946 in Cartersville, Ga. Graduate LaGrange Col., RADA. Debut 1976 OB in "Hound of the Baskervilles," followed by "The Misanthrope," "The Guardsman," "Oedipus Cycle," "Gilles de Rais," "Leonce and Lena," "King Lear," "Danton's Death," "Tartuffe," "The Maids," "A Midsummer Night's Dream," "Henry IV," "Richard II," "Marquis of Keith," "Wozzeck," "Peer Gynt," "The Cherry Orchard," "Ghost Sonata," "Faust," "Hamlet," "Big and Little," "Chopin in Space," "The Crucible."

SHUE, ELISABETH. Born in Delaware. Attended Wellesley Col., Harvard U. Debut 1990 off and on Broadway in "Some Americans Abroad."

SICARI, JOSEPH. Born Apr. 29, 1939 in Boston, Ma. Graduate Catholic U. Debut 1965 OB in "The Parasite," followed by "The Comedy of Errors," "Henry IV," "Love and Let Love," "Dames at Sea," "Comedy," "Loose Ends," "Price of Fame."

SIEGLER, BEN. Born Apr. 9, 1958 in Queens, NYC. Attended HBStudio. Debut 1980 OB in "Innocent Thoughts, Harmless Intentions," followed by "Threads," "Many Happy Returns," "Snow Orchid," "The Diviners," "What I Did Last Summer," "Time Framed," "Gifted Children," "Levitation," "Elm Circle," "Romance Language," "Raw Youth," "Voices in the Head," "V & V Only," "Bitter Friends," "One of the Guys." Bdwy in "Fifth of July."

SILBER, DAVID. Born Feb. 21, 1953 in New Haven, Ct. Graduate Boston U. Debut 1978 OB in "The Changeling," followed by "The Doctor's Dilemma," "The Story of the Gadsbys," Bdwy in "Zoya's Apartment" (1990).

SILBERMAN, BETTY. Born Aug. 9, 1954 in Montreal, Can. Attended Boston Consv. Debut 1984 OB in "The Golden Land," followed by "Broome Street, America," "The Imported Bride," "Songs of Paradise."

SILLIMAN, MAUREEN. Born Dec. 3 in NYC. Attended Hofstra U. Bdwy debut 1975 in "Shenandoah," followed by "I Remember Mama," "Is There Life after High School?," OB in "Umbrellas of Cherbourg," "Two Rooms," "Macbeth," "Blue Window," "Three Postcards," "Pictures in the Hall."

SIMES, DOUGLAS. Born Apr. 21, 1949 in New Salem, NY. Graduate Lehigh U., Yale. Debut 1974 OB in "The Lady's Not for Burning," followed by "The Dumbwaiter," "The Revenger's Tragedy," "The Lady from the Sea," "Between Time and Timbuktu," "A Chaste Maid and Cheapside," "Measure for Measure."

SIMMONS, J. K. (formerly Jonathan) Born Jan. 9, 1955 in Detroit, Mi. Graduate UMon. Debut 1987 OB in "Birds of Paradise," followed by "Dirty Dick," Bdwy in "A Change in the Heir" (1990).

SINKYS, ALBERT. Born July 10, 1940 in Boston, Ma. Attended Boston U, UCLA. Debut 1981 OB in "In the Matter of J. Robert Oppenheimer," followed by "The Caine Mutiny Court-Martial," "Man in the Glass Booth," "Six Candles," "Fellow Travelers," "The Balcony."

SISTO, ROCCO. Born Feb. 8, 1953 in Bari, Italy. Graduate UIl., NYU. Debut 1982 OB in "Hamlet," followed by "Country Doctor," "Times and Appetites of Toulouse-Lautrec," "Merchant of Venice," "What Did He See," "Winter's Tale," "Tempest."

SKINNER, MARGO. Born Jan. 3, 1950 in Middletown, Oh. Graduate Boston U. Debut 1980 OB in "Missing Persons," followed by "The Dining Room," "Mary Barnes," "The Perfect Party," "Spare Parts."

SLEZAK, VICTOR. Born July 7, 1957 in Youngstown, OH. Debut 1979 OB in "Electra Myth," followed by "Hasty Heart," "Ghosts," "Alice and Fred," "Widow Claire," "Miracle Worker," "Talk Radio," "Marathon '88," "One Act Festival," "Briar Patch," "Marathon '90."

SLOMAN, JOHN. Born June 23, 1954 in Rochester, NY. Graduate SUNY/Genasco. Debut 1977 OB in "Unsung Cole," followed by "Apple Tree," "Romance in Hard Times," "The Waves," Bdwy in "Whoopee," "1940's Radio Hour," "Day in Hollywood/Night in the Ukraine," "Mayor."

SMALL, NEVA. Born Nov. 17, 1952 in NYC. Bdwy debut 1964 in "Something More," followed by "The Impossible Years," "Henry, Sweet Henry," "Frank Merriwell," "Something's Afoot," OB in "Ballad for a Firing Squad," "Show Me Where the Good Times Are," "How Much, How Much," "F. Jasmine Addams," "Macbeth," "Yentl and the Yeshiva Boy," "Life Is Not a Doris Day Movie," "The Golden Land," "Half a World Away," "Hannah 1939."

Cynthia
Sophiea

Dennis
Sook

Zipora
Spaisman

Theodore
Sorel

Robin
Spielberg

Fritz
Sperberg

Howard
Spiegel

Tamara
Robin

Lewis J.
Stadlen

Mary Leigh
Stahl

Gordon
Stanley

Florence
Stanley

Jean
Stapleton

Molly
Stark

Dakota
Staton

Helen
Stenborg

Arlene
Sterne

Frances
Sternhagen

Robert
Stattel

Gwen
Stuart

Fisher
Stevens

Mary
Stout

Colin
Stinton

Kate
Stillwell

Elaine
Stritch

Eric
Stoltz

Heather
Summerhayes

Sam
Stoneburner

Jane
Summerhays

Guy
Stroman

**Kim
Sullivan**

**Jean
Tafler**

**Keith
Szarabajka**

**Zoe
Taleporos**

**Neil
Tadken**

**Ann
Talman**

**Olga
Talyn**

**Mark
Tankersley**

**Christen
Tassin**

**Scott
Taylor**

**Marianne
Tatum**

**Stephen
Temperley**

**Greg
Templeton**

**Regina
Taylor**

**Russ
Thacker**

**Mary
Testa**

**John Norman
Thomas**

**Linda
Thorson**

**Ellen
Tovatt**

**Richard
Thomas**

**Laurine
Towler**

**Evan
Thompson**

**Elizabeth Ann
Townsend**

**Alec
Timerman**

**Patrick
Tovatt**

**Betsy
True**

**Joseph
Travers**

**Pamela
Tucker-White**

**Sam
Tsoutsouvas**

**Laura
Turnbull**

SMITH, CARRIE. Born in Ga. Bdwy debut 1989 in "Black and Blue."
SMITH, DEREK D. Born Dec. 4, 1959 in Seattle, Wa. Graduate Juilliard. Debut 1986 OB in "Cruise Control," followed by "Ten by Tennessee," "Traps," "Hyde in Hollywood."
SMITH, JENNIFER. Born Mar. 9, 1956 in Lubbock, TX. Graduate TxTechU. Debut 1981 OB in "Seesaw," followed by "Suffragette," "Henry the 8th and the Grand Old Opry," "No Frills Revue," "1-2-3-4-5," "You Die at Recess," Bdwy in "La Cage aux Folles" (1983), "A Change in the Heir."
SMITH, LOIS. Born Nov. 3, 1930 in Topeka, KS. Attended UWVa. Bdwy debut 1952 in "Time Out for Ginger," followed by "Young and the Beautiful," "Wisteria Trees," "Glass Menagerie," "Orpheus Descending," "Stages," "The Grapes of Wrath," OB in "Midsummer Night's Dream," "Non Pasquale," "Promenade," "La Boheme," "Bodies, Rest and Motion," "Marathon '87," "Gus and Al," "Marathon '88," "Measure for Measure," "Spring Thing," "Beside Herself."
SMITH, MAGGIE. Born Dec. 28, 1934 in Ilford, Eng. Attended Oxford Playhouse School. Bdwy debut in "New Faces of 1956," followed by "Private Lives" (1975). "Night and Day" (1979), "Lettice and Lovage" (1990).
SMITH, REX. Born Sept. 19, 1955 in Jacksonville, Fl. Bdwy debut 1978 in "Grease," followed by "The Pirates of Pemzance" for which he received a Theatre World Award, "The Human Comedy," "Grand Hotel," OB in "Brownstone," "Common Pursuit."
SMITH-CAMERON, J. Born Sept. 7, in Louisville, KY. Attended FlStU. Bdwy debut 1982 in "Crimes of the Heart," followed by "Wild Honey," "Lend Me A Tenor," OB in "Asian Shade," "The Knack," "Second Prize: 2 Weeks in Leningrad," "Great Divid," "Voice of the Turtle," "Women of Manhattan," "Alice and Fred," "Mi Vida Loca."
SOLO, WILLIAM. Born Mar. 16, 1948 in Worcester, MA. Graduate UMa. Bdwy debut 1987 in "Les Miserables."
SOMMER, ELKE. Born Nov. 5, 1940 in Berlin, Ger. Debut 1989 OB in "Tamara."
SOMMER, JOSEF. Born June 26, 1934 in Griefswald, Ger. Graduate Carnegie Tech. Bdwy debut 1970 in "Othello," followed by "Children Children," "Trial of the Catonsville 9," "Full Circle," "Who's Who in Hell," "Shadow Box," "Spoke Song," "The 1940's Radio Show," "Whose Life Is It Anyway?," OB in "Enemies," "Merchant of Venice," "The Dog Ran Away," "Drinks before Dinner," "Lydie Breeze," "Black Angel," "The Lady and the Clarinet," "Love Letters on Blue Paper," "Largo Desolato," "Hamlet."
SOOK, DENNIS. Born Apr. 29, 1945 in Marshall, Mn. Graduate Mankato State U., S.Ill.U. Debut 1971 OB in "The Debate," followed by "The Fantasticks," "White, Brown, Black," "Stud Silo," "New Mexican Rainbow Fishing," "A Perfect Diamond."
SOPHIEA, CYNTHIA. Born Oct. 26, 1954 in Flint, Mi. Attended UMi. Bdwy debut 1981 in "My Fair Lady," followed by OB's "Lysistrata," "Suffragette," "The Golden Apple."
SOREL, THEODORE/TED. Born Nov. 14, 1936 in San Francisco, CA. Graduate Col. of Pacific. Bdwy debut 1977 in "Sly Fox," followed by "Horowitz and Mrs. Washington," "A Little Family Business," OB in "Arms and the Man," "Moon Mysteries," "A Call from the East," "Hedda Gabler," "Drinks before Dinner," "Tamara."
SPAISMAN, ZIPORA. Born Jan. 2, 1920 in Lublin, Poland. Debut 1955 OB in "Lonesome Ship," followed by "In My Father's Court," "Thousand and One Nights," "Eleventh Inheritor," "Enchanting Melody," "Fifth Commandment," "Bronx Express," "Melody Lingers On," "Yoshke Muzikant," "Stempenyu," "Generations of Green Fields," "Shop," "A Play for the Devil," "Broome St. America," "Flowering Peach," "Riverside Drive," "Big Winner," "The Land of Dreams."
SPERBERG, FRITZ. Born July 20 in Borger, Tx. Graduate Trinity U. Debut 1979 OB in "Getting Out," followed by "Battery," "The Sea Gull," Bdwy in "Loose Ends" (1979), "Macbeth" (LC), "A Few Good Men."
SPIEGEL, HOWARD. Born Mar. 30, 1954 in Brooklyn, NYC. Attended Queens Col. Debut 1989 OB in "Only Kidding," for which he received a Theatre World Award.
SPIELBERG, ROBIN. Born Nov. 20, 1962 in New Jersey. Attended MiStateU, NYU. Debut 1988 OB in "Boys' Life," followed by "Marathon '90."
SPIEWAK, TAMARA ROBIN. Born Feb. 20, 1980 in Bridgeport, Ct. Bdwy debut 1990 in "Les Miserables."
STADLEN, LEWIS J. Born Mar. 7, 1947 in Brooklyn, NY. Attended Stella Adler Studio. Bdwy debut 1970 in "Minnie's Boys," for which he received a Theatre World Award, followed by "The Sunshine Boys," "Candide," "The Odd Couple," OB in "The Happiness Cage," "Heaven on Earth," "Barb-A-Que," "Don Juan and Non Don Juan," "Olympus on My Mind," "1-2-3-4-5," "S.J. Perelman in Person."
STAHL, MARY LEIGH. Born Aug. 29, 1946 in Madison, WI. Graduate JacksonvilleStateU. Debut 1974 OB in "Circus," followed by "Dragons," "Sullivan and Gilbert," "The World of Sholem Aleichem," Bdwy in "The Phantom of the Opera" (1988).
STANLEY, FLORENCE. Born July 1 in Chicago, Ill. Graduate Northwestern U. Debut 1960 OB in "Machinal," followed by "Electra," "What's Wrong with This Picture?," "It's Only a Play," "Mexican Hayride," Bdwy in "The Glass Menagerie" (1965), "Fiddler on the Roof," "A Safe Place," "Prisoner of Second Avenue," "Secret Affairs of Mildred Wild."
STANLEY, GORDON. Born Dec. 20, 1951 in Boston, Ma. Graduate Brown U, Temple U. Debut 1977 OB in "Lyrical and Satirical," followed by "Allegro," "Elizabeth and Essex," "Red, Hot and Blue," "Two on the Isles," "Moby Dick," "Johnny Pye and the Foolkiller," "Golden Apple," Bdwy in "Onward Victoria" (1980), "Joseph and the Amazing Technicolor Dreamcoat," "Into the Light," "Teddy and Alice."
STAPLETON, JEAN. Born Jan. 19, 1923 in NYC. Attended Hunter Col., AmThWing. Bdwy debut 1953 in "In the Summer House," followed by "Damn Yankees," "Bells Are Ringing," "Juno," "Rhinoceros," "Funny Girl," "Arsenic and Old Lace," OB in "Mountain Language/The Birthday Party."
STARK, MOLLY. Born in NYC. Graduate Hunter Col. Debut 1969 OB in "Sacco-Vanzetti," followed by "Riders to the Sea," "Medea," "One Cent Plain," "Elizabeth and Essex," "Principally Pinter," "Toulouse," "Winds of Change," "The Education of Hyman Kaplan," "The Land of Dreams," Bdwy 1973 in "Molly."
STATON, DAKOTA. Born in Pittsburgh, PA. Graduate NSID. Bdwy debut 1989 in "Black and Blue."
STATTEL, ROBERT. Born Nov. 20, 1937 in Floral Park, NY. Graduate Manhattan Col. Debut 1958 OB in "Heloise," followed by "When I Was a Child," "Man and Superman," "The Storm," "Don Carlos," "Taming of the Shrew," "Titus Andronicus," "Henry IV," "Peer Gynt," "Hamlet," C Rep's, "Damon's Death," "The Country Wife," "The Caucasian Chalk Circle," and "King Lear," "Iphigenia in Aulis," "Ergo," "The Persians," "Blue Boys," "The Minister's Black Veil," "Four Friends," "Two Character Play," "The Merchant of Venice," "Cuchulain," "Oedipus Cycle," "Gilles de Rais," "Woyzeck," "King Lear," "The Fuehrer Bunker," "Learned Ladies," "Domestic Issues," "Great Days," "The Tempest," "Brand," "A Man for All Seasons," "Bunker Reveries," "Enrico IV," "Tempest," Bdwy in "Zoya's Apartment."
STENBORG, HELEN. Born Jan. 24, 1925 in Minneapolis, MN. Attended Hunter Col. OB in "A Doll's House," "A Month in the Country," "Say Nothing," "Rosmersholm," "Rimers of Eldritch," "Trial of the Catonsville 9," "The Hot l Baltimore," "Pericles," "Elephant in the House," "A Tribute to Lili Lamont," "Museum," "5th of July," "In the Recovery Lounge," "The Chisholm Trail," "Time Framed," "Levitation," "Enter a Free Man," "Talley and Son," "Tomorrow's Monday," "Niedecker," "Heaven on Earth," Bdwy in "Sheep on the Runway," (1970), "Da," "A Life."
STERNE, ARLENE. Born March 23rd in Boston, Ma. Graduate Northwestern U. Debut 1986 OB in "The First Night of Pgmalion," followed by "Final Curtain," "Papa's Violin," "Pericles."
STERNHAGEN, FRANCES. Born Jan. 13, 1932 in Washington, DC. Graduate Vassar Col. OB in "Admirable Bashful," "Thieves' Carnival," "Country Wife," "Ulysses in Nighttown," "Saintliness of Margery Kemp," "The Room," "A Slight Ache," "Displaced Person," "Playboy of the Western World," "The Prevalence of Mrs. Seal," "Summer," "Laughing Stock," "The Return of Herbert Bracewell," "Little Murders," "Driving Miss Daisy," Bdwy in "Great Day in the Morning," "The Right Honourable Gentleman," with APA in "The Cocktail Party," and "Cock-a-Doodle Dandy," "The Sign in Sidney Brustein's Window," "Enemies" (LC), "The Good Doctor," "Equus," "Angel," "On Golden Pond," "The Father," "Grownups," "You Can't Take It With You."
STEVENS, FISHER. Born Nov. 27, 1963 in Chicago, Il. Attended NYU. Bdwy debut 1982 in "Torch Song Trilogy," followed by "Brighton Beach Memoirs," OB in "Out of Gas on Lover's Leap," "Miami," "Little Murders," "Terminal Bar," "One-Act Festival," "Carrying School Children," "Twelfth Night," "Aven' U Boys."
STEWART, GWEN. Born Sept. 5 in Newark, NJ. Attended Farmingdale U. Debut 1986 OB in "Mama, I Want to Sing," followed by "God's Creation," "Suds," Bdwy in "Starmites" (1989), "Truly Blessed."
STILLMAN, ROBERT. Born Dec. 2, 1954 in NYC. Graduate Princeton U. Debut 1981 OB in "The Haggadah," followed by "Street Scene," "Lola," "No Frills Revue," Bdwy in "Grand Hotel" (1989).
STING (Gordon Matthew Sumner) born Oct. 2, 1951 in Wallsend, Eng. Bdwy debut 1989 in "3 Penny Opera."
STINTON, COLIN. Born Mar. 10, 1947 in Kansas City, Mo. Attended Northwestern U. Debut 1978 OB in "The Water Engine" (also Bdwy) for which he received a Theatre World Award, followed by "Twelfth Night," "The Beaver Coat," "Some Americans Abroad" (also Bdwy), Bdwy in "The Curse of an Aching Heart."
STOLTZ, ERIC. Born in 1961 in California. Attended USCal. Debut 1987 OB in "The Widow Claire," Bdwy 1989 in "Our Town," for which he received a Theatre World Award, OB in "The American Plan."
STONEBURNER, SAM. Born Feb. 24, 1934 in Fairfax, Va. Graduate Georgetown U., AADA. Debut 1960 OB in "Ernest in Love," followed by "Foreplay," "Anyone Can Whistle," "Twilight Cantata," "Six Degrees of Separation," Bdwy in "Different Times" (1972), "Bent," "Macbeth" (1981), "The First," "Six Degrees of Separation."
STORK, RENEE. Born Nov. 11, 1962 in St. Louis, MO. Attended NCSA, ABT. Debut 1989 on Bdwy in "Jerome Robbins' Broadway."
STORMARE, PETER. Born Aug. 27, 1953 in Arbro, Sweden. Attended Royal Dramatic Theatre. Debut OB in "Hamlet," followed by "Rasputin."
STOUT, MARY. Born Apr. 8, 1952 in Huntington, WVa. Graduate Marshall U. Debut 1980 OB in "Plain and Fancy," followed by "Sound of Music," "Crisp," "A Christmas Carol," "Song for a Saturday," "Prizes," "Golden Apple," Bdwy in "Copperfield" (1981), "A Change in the Heir."
STOUT, STEPHEN. Born May 19, 1952 in Huntington, WVa. Graduate SMU. Bdwy debut 1981 in "Kingdoms," followed by "The Heidi Chronicles," OB in "Cloud 9," "A Midsummer Night's Dream," "Loose Ends."
STRITCH, ELAINE. Born Feb. 2, 1925 in Detroit, Mi. Bdwy debut 1946 in "Loco," followed by "Made in Heaven," "Angel in the Wings," "Call Me Madam," "Pal Joey," "On Your Toes," "Bus Stop," "The Sin of Pat Muldoon," "Goldilocks," "Sail Away," "Who's Afraid of Virginia Woolf?," "Wonderful Town" (CC), "Company," "Love Letters," OB in "Private Lives."
STROMAN, GUY. Born Sept. 11, 1951 in Terrell, Tx. Graduate TxChristianU. Bdwy debut 1979 in "Peter Pan," followed by "Annie," OB in "After the Rain," "Berlin to Broadway," "Jerome Moross Revue," "Close Your Eyes," "Juno and the Paycock," "Glory Hallelujah!," "To Whom It May Concern," "Aldersgate '88," "Forever Plaid."
STUART, IAN. Born May 25, 1940 in London, Eng. Debut 1971 OB in "Misalliance," followed by "Count Dracula," "Jack the Ripper Review," "The Accrington Pals," "The Foreigner," "The Doctor's Dilemma," Bdwy in "Caesar and Cleopatra" (1977), "Run for Your Wife."
STUART, MARIE. Born Jan. 23 in Plymouth, Pa. Debut 1990 OB in "Rasputin."
SULLIVAN, BRAD. Born Nov. 18, 1931 in Chicago, Il. Graduate UMe, AmThWing. Debut 1961 OB in "Red Roses for Me," followed by "South Pacific," "Hot House," "Leavin' Cheyenne," "The Ballad of Soapy Smith," "Cold Sweat," Bdwy in "The Basic Training of Pavlo Hummel" (1977), "Working," "The Wake of Jamie Foster," "The Caine Mutiny Court-Martial," "Orpheus Descending."
SULLIVAN, KIM. Born July 21, 1952 in Philadelphia, Pa. Graduate NYU. Debut 1972 OB in "The Black Terror," followed by "Legend of the West," "Deadwood Dick," "Big Apple Messenger," "Dreams Deferred," "A Raisin in the Sun," "The Tempest," "Ground People."
SUMMERHAYES, HEATHER. Born May 23, 1952 in Brantford, Ont., Can. Attended Ryerson Col., Sheridan Col. Debut 1990 OB in "Mountain," followed by "Day Six."

SUMMERHAYS, JANE. Born Oct. 11 in Salt Lake City, UT. Graduate UUt., Catholic U. Debut 1980 OB in "Paris Lights," followed by "On Approval," "One Act Festival," Bdwy in "Sugar Babies" (1980), "A Chorus Line," "Me and My Girl," "Lend Me a Tenor."

SUMMERS, MARC-DURANTE. Born Oct. 28, 1964 in Newport News, Va. Graduate Hampton U. Debut 1990 OB in "Capitol Cakewalk."

SYMINGTON, DONALD. Born Aug. 30, 1925 in Baltimore, Md. Bdwy debut 1947 in "Galileo," followed by "Mourning Pictures," CC's "Caesar and Cleopatra," "Dream Girl" and "Lute Song," "A Girl Can Tell," OB in "Suddenly Last Summer," "Lady Windermere's Fan," "Rate of Exchange," "Shrinking Bride," "Murderous Angels," "An Evening with the Poet Senator," "The Tennis Game," "Come as You Are."

SZARABAJKA, KEITH. Born Dec. 2, 1952 in Oak Park, Il. Attended Trinity U., UChicago. Bdwy debut 1973 in "Warp!," followed by "Doonesbury," OB in "Bleacher Bums," "Class Enemy," "Digby," "Rich Relations," "Women of Manhattan," "Class 1-Acts," "Hyde in Hollywood," "Perfect Act of Contrition."

TADKEN, NEIL. Born Apr. 25, 1960 in NYC. Graduate Occidental Col., Cornell U. Debut 1989 OB in "Pericles, Prince of Tyre."

TAFLER, JEAN. Born Nov. 18, 1957 in Schenectady, NY. Graduate Hofstra U. Debut 1981 OB in "Mandragola," followed by "Lady Windermere's Fan," "Richard II," "Towards Zero," "The Cotton Web," "A Lady Named Joe," "Guadeloupe," "Brass Jackal."

TALBERTH, KENNETH. Born June 22, 1956 in Boston, Ma. Graduate NYU. Debut OB 1981 in "Total Eclipse," followed by "Henry IV Part I," "The Misanthrope," "Stray Dog Story," "A Winter's Tale," "After the Rain."

TALEPOROS, ZOE. Born Oct. 23, 1979 in NYC. Debut 1989 OB in "Rasputin," followed by "Trojan Women," Bdwy in "The Grapes of Wrath" (1990).

TALMAN, ANN. Born Sept. 13, 1957 in Welch, WVa. Graduate PaStateU. Debut 1980 OB in "What's So Beautiful about a Sunset over Prairie Avenue?," followed by "Louisiana Summer," "Winterplay," "Prairie Avenue," "Broken Eggs," "Octoberfest," "We're Home," "Yours, Anne," "Songs on a Shipwrecked Sofa," "House Arrest," "One Act Festival," "Some Americans Abroad." Bdwy in "The Little Foxes" (1981), "House of Blue Leaves," "Some Americans Abroad."

TALYN, OLGA. Born Dec. 5 in West Germany. Attended SyracuseU, UBuffalo. Debut 1973 OB in "The Proposition," followed by "Corral," "Tales of Tinseltown," "Shop on Main Street," Bdwy in "A Doll's House," "The Phantom of the Opera."

TANKERSLEY, MARK. Born Aug. 23, 1958 in Houston, Tx. Attended Houston Baptist U., Juilliard. Debut 1985 OB in "Life Is a Dream," followed by "Macbeth," "Picture of Dorian Gray."

TASSIN, CHRISTEN. Born Jan. 2, 1979 in Spartanburg, SC. Bdwy debut 1989 in "Gypsy."

TATUM, MARIANNE. Born Feb. 18, 1951 in Houston, TX. Attended Manhattan Sch. of Music. Debut 1971 OB in "Ruddigore," followed by "The Gilded Cage," "Charley's Tale," "Passionate Extremes," Bdwy in "Barnum" (1980) for which she received a Theatre World Award, "The Three Musketeers," "The Sound of Music."

TAYLOR, REGINA. Born Aug. 22, 1960 in Dallas, TX. Graduate SMU. Debut 1983 OB in "Young Playwrights Festival," followed by "As You Like It," "Macbeth," "Map of the World," "The Box," "Dr. Faustus," "L'Illusion," "New Anatomies," Bdwy in "Shakespeare on Broadway" (1987).

TAYLOR, SCOTT. Born June 29, 1962 in Milan, Tn. Attended Ms.State U. Bdwy in "Wind in the Willows" (1985), followed by "Cats."

TEMPERLEY, STEPHEN. Born July 29, 1949 in London, Eng. Attended AADA. Debut 1968 OB in "Invitation to a Beheading," followed by "Henry IV Parts I and II," "Up Against It."

TEMPLETON, GREG. Born Oct. 3, 1961 in Vancouver, Can. Graduate AMDA. Debut 1989 OB in "Wonderful Town."

TESTA, MARY. Born June 4, 1955 in Philadelphia, PA. Attended URI. Debut 1979 OB in "In Trousers," followed by "Company," "Life Is Not a Doris Day Movie," "Not-So-New Faces of '82," "American Princess," "Mandrake," "4 One Act Musicals," "Next Please!," "Daughters," "One Act Festival," "The Knife," "Young Playwrights," "Lucky Stiff," "1-2-3-4-5," "Young Playwrights Festival," Bdwy in "Barnum" (1980), "Marilyn," "The Rink."

THACKER, RUSS. Born June 23, 1946 in Washington, DC. Attended Montgomery Col. Bdwy debut 1967 in "Life with Father" followed by "Music! Music!," "The Grass Harp," "Heathen," "Home Sweet Homer," "Me Jack, You Jill," "Do Black Patent Leather Shoes Really Reflect Up?," OB in "Your Own Thing" for which he received a 1968 Theatre World Award, "Dear Oscar," "Once I Saw a Boy Laughing," "Tip-Toes," "Oh, Coward!," "New Moon in Concert," "The Firefly in Concert," "Rosalie in Concert," "Some Enchanted Evening," "Roberta in Concert," "Olio," "Genesis."

THOLE, CYNTHIA. Born Sept. 21, 1957 in Silver Spring, Md. Graduate Butler U. Debut 1982 OB in "Nymph Errant," followed by Bdwy in "42nd Street" (1985), "Me and My Girl," "Meet Me in St. Louis."

THOMAS, JOHN NORMAN. Born May 13, 1961 in Detroit, Mi. Graduate CinConsv. Bdwy debut 1987 in "Les Miserables," followed by "The Merchant of Venice."

THOMAS, RAYMOND ANTHONY. Born Dec. 19, 1956 in Kentwood, La. Graduate UTex/El Paso. Debut 1981 OB in "Escape to Freedom," followed by "The Sun Gets Blue," "Blues for Mr. Charlie," "The Hunchback of Notre Dame," "Ground People," "The Weather Outside," One-Act Festival.

THOMAS, RICHARD. Born June 13, 1951 in NYC. Bdwy debut 1958 in "Sunrise at Campobello," followed by "Member of the Wedding," "Strange Interlude," "The Playroom," "Richard III," "Everything in the Garden," "5th of July," "The Front Page" (LC), OB in "The Seagull," "Love Letters," "Square One."

THOMPSON, EVAN. Born Sept. 3, 1931 in NYC. Graduate UCal. Bdwy debut 1969 in "Jimmy," followed by "1776," "City of Angels," OB in "Mahagony," "Treasure Island," "Knitters in the Sun," "Half-Life," "Fasnacht Dau," "Importance of Being Earnest," "Under the Gaslight," "Henry V," "The Fantasticks," "Walk the Dog, Willie," "Macbeth," "1984," "Leave It to Me."

THOMPSON, OWEN. Born Sept. 16, 1962 in Los Angeles, Ca. Debut 1974 OB in "The Trojan Women," followed by "The Importance of Being Earnest," "She Loves Me," "The Browning Version," "King John," "Richard III," "Enter Laughing," "Misalliance," "Lion in Winter."

THORSON, LINDA. Born June 18, 1947 in Toronto, Can. Graduate RADA. Bdwy debut 1982 in "Steaming" for which she received a Theatre World Award, followed by "Noises Off," "Zoya's Apartment."

TIMERMAN, ALEC. Born Aug. 23, 1963 in Philadelphia, Pa. Attended Temple U. Bdwy debut 1987 in "Anything Goes," followed by "Gypsy," OB in "Oy, Mama, Am I in Love."

TOMPOS, DOUG. Born Jan. 27, 1962 in Columbus, OH. Graduate Syracuse U., LAMDA. Debut 1985 OB in "Very Warm for May," followed by "A Midsummer Night's Dream," "Mighty Fine Music," "Muzeeks," "Wish You Were Here," "Vampire Lesbians of Sodom," Bdwy in "City of Angels."

TOVATT, ELLEN. Born in NYC. Attended Antioch Col., LAMDA. Debut 1962 OB in "Taming of the Shrew," followed by "The Show-Off," "Don Juan Comes Back from the War," Bdwy in "The Great God Brown," "The Visit," "Chemin de Fer," "Holiday," "Love for Love," "Rules of the Game," "Herzl," "Sound of Music" (LC).

TOVATT, PATRICK. Born Dec. 11, 1940 in Garrett Ridge, CO. Attended Antioch, Harvard Col. Debut 1984 OB in "Husbandry," followed by "The Right Number," "Good Grief," "Feast Here Tonight." Bdwy in "Our Town" (1989).

TOWLER, LAURINE. Born Oct. 19, 1952 in Oberlin, Oh. Graduate Stanford U., UCal. Debut 1981 OB in "Godspell," followed by "The Tempest," "Something Old, Something New," Bdwy in "Lettice and Lovage" (1990).

TOWNSEND, ELIZABETH ANN. Born in Jackson, Mi. Graduate Columbia U. Debut 1989 OB in "Pericles, Prince of Tyre."

TRAVERS, JOSEPH. Born Jan. 2, 1960 in NYC. Graduate SUNY/Albany. Debut 1987 OB in "The Jew of Malta," followed by "The Witch."

TRUE, BETSY. Born Apr. 19, 1960 in Cincinnati, Oh. Graduate Boston Consv. Bdwy debut 1989 in "Les Miserables."

TSOUTSOUVAS, SAM. Born Aug. 20, 1948 in Santa Barbara, CA. Attended UCal., Juilliard. Debut 1969 OB in "Peer Gynt," followed by "Twelfth Night," "Timon of Athens," "Cymbeline," "School for Scandal," "The Hostage," "Women Beware Women," "Lower Depths," "Emigre," "Hello Dali," "The Merchant of Venice," "The Leader," "The Bald Soprano," "The Taming of the Shrew," "Gus & Al," "Tamara," "The Man Who Shot Lincoln," "Puppetmaster of Lodz." Bdwy in "Three Sisters," "Measure for Measure," "Beggar's Opera," "Scapin," "Dracula."

TUCCI, MARIA. Born June 19, 1941 in Florence, IT. Attended Actors Studio. Bdwy debut 1963 in "The Milk Train Doesn't Stop Here Anymore," followed by "The Rose Tattoo," "The Little Foxes," "The Cuban Thing," "The Great White Hope," "School for Wives," "Lesson from Aloes," "Kingdoms," "Requiem for a Heavyweight," "The Night of the Iguana," OB in "Corruption in the Palace of Justice," "Five Evenings," "Trojan Women," "White Devil," "Horseman, Pass By," "Yerma," "Shepherd of Avenue B," "The Gathering," "A Man for All Seasons," "Love Letters."

TUCKER-WHITE, PAMELA. Born Mar. 6, 1955 in Peoria, Il. Graduate UWis., Juilliard Debut 1981 OB in "How It All Began," followed by "The Dubliners," "The Country Wife," "Home Again, Kathleen," "The Rehearsal," "Believing," "Starting Monday."

TULL, PATRICK. Born July 28, 1941 in Sussex, Eng. Attended LAMDA. Bdwy debut 1967 in "The Astrakhan Coat," OB in "Ten Little Indians," "The Tamer Tamed," "Brand," "Frankenstein," "What the Butler Saw," "She Stoops to Conquer," "The Art of Success."

TURNBULL, LAURA. Born Sept. 9, 1956 in Denver, Co. Attended UDenver. Debut 1986 OB in "Sex Tips for Modern Girls," followed by "Showing Off," Bdwy in "Sid Caesar and Company" (1989).

TURNER, GLENN. Born Sept. 21, 1957 in Atlanta, GA. Bdwy debut 1984 in "My One and Only," followed by "A Chorus Line," "Grand Hotel."

TURNER, KATHLEEN. Born June 19, 1954 in Springfield, Mo. Graduate Southwest MoStateU. Bdwy debut 1978 in "Gemini," followed by "Cat on a Hot Tin Roof" (1990) for which she received a Theatre World Award.

TURNER, PATRICK. Born Dec. 2, 1952 in Seattle, WA. Attended UWash, AmCons Theatre. Debut 1984 OB in "The Merchant of Venice," followed by "Double Inconstancy," "The Taming of the Shrew," "Lady from the Sea," "Two Gentlemen of Verona," "The Contrast," "Pericles," "The Rivals," "Rosaline," "Much Ado about Nothing," "You Never Can Tell," "The Winter's Tale," "Domino Courts," "After the Rain."

TURPIN, BAHNI. Born June 4th in Pontiac, Mi. Attended Howard U., NYU. Debut 1990 OB in "Ground People."

TURTURRO, JOHN. Born Feb. 28, 1957 in Brooklyn, NY. Graduate SUNY/New Paltz, La U. Debut 1984 OB in "Danny and the Deep Blue Sea," for which he received a Theatre World Award, followed by "Men without Dates," "Chaos and Hard Times," "Steel on Steel," "Tooth of Crime," "Of Mice and Men," "Jamie's Gang," "Marathon 86," "The Bald Soprano/The Leader," "La Puta Vita Trilogy," "Italian American Reconciliation," Bdwy in "Death of a Salesman" (1984).

TUTHS, EVELYN. Born Sept. 2, 1959 in Rockville Centre, NY. Graduate Brockport StateU. Debut 1990 OB in "By and for Havel," followed by "The Dark and Mr. Stone."

TWOMEY, ANNE. Born June 7, 1951 in Boston, Ma. Graduate Temple U. Debut 1975 OB in "Overruled," followed by "The Passion of Dracula," "When We Dead Awaken," "Vieux Carre," "Vampires," Bdwy in "Nuts" (1980) for which she received a Theatre World Award, "To Grandmother's House We Go," "Orpheus Descending."

TYZACK, MARGARET. Born Sept. 9, 1931 in London, Eng. Attended RADA. Debut 1975 OB in "Summerfolk," followed by "Tom and Viv," Bdwy in "All's Well That Ends Well" (1983), "Lettice and Lovage."

URLA, JOE. Born Dec. 25, 1958 in Pontiac, Mi. Graduate UMi., Yale U. Debut 1985 OB in "Measure for Measure," followed by "Henry V," "Principia Scriptoriae" for which he received a Theatre World Award, "Our Own Family," "Return of Pinocchio," "The Boys Next Door," "Maids of Honor."

VAN DYCK, JENNIFER. Born Dec. 23, 1962 in St. Andrews, Scotland. Graduate BrownU. Debut OB 1988 in "Gus and Al," followed by "Marathon 88," "Secret Rapture," Bdwy in "Secret Rapture."

VAN FOSSEN, DIANA. Born Aug. 30 in Baltimore, Md. Graduate Goucher Col., Bristol Old Vic School. Debut 1989 OB in "Progress."

Glenn
Turner

Kathleen
Turner

Patrick
Turner

Bahni
Turpin

John
Turturro

Evelyn
Tuths

Anne
Twomey

Joe
Urla

Diana
Van Fossen

Randy
Vasquez

Joyce
Van Patten

John C.
Vennema

Steve
Vinovich

Ray
Virta

Sel
Vitella

David
Vosburgh

Scott
Waara

Adam
Wade

Ray
Walker

Jessica
Walter

Lee
Wallace

Eloise
Watt

Kenneth H.
Waller

Danyelle
Weaver

Ann
Wedgeworth

Carl
Wallnau

Donnah
Welby

Jim
Walton

Amelia
White

Douglas Turner
Ward

VAN PATTEN, JOYCE. Born Mar. 9 in Kew Gardens, NY. Bdwy debut 1941 in "Popsy," followed by "This Rock," "Tomorrow the World," "The Perfect Marriage," "The Wind Is 90," "Desk Set," "A Hole in the Head," "Murder at the Howard Johnson's," "I Ought to Be in Pictures," "Supporting Cast," "Brighton Beach Memoirs," "Rumors," OB in "Between Two Thieves," "Spoon River Anthology," "The Seagull."

VASQUEZ, RANDY. Born Oct. 16, 1961 in Escondido, Ca. Attended UCLA. Debut 1990 OB in "Each Day Dies with Sleep."

VENNEMA, JOHN C. Born Aug. 24, 1948 in Houston, TX. Graduate Princeton U., LAMDA. Bdwy debut 1976 in "The Royal Family," followed by "The Elephant Man," "Otherwise Engaged," OB in "Loot," "Statements after an Arrest," "The Biko Inquest," "No End of Blame," "In Celebration," "Custom of the Country," "The Basement," "A Slight Ache," "Young Playwrights Festival," "Dandy Dick," "Nasty Little Secrets," "Mountain."

VENNER, TRACY. Born in 1968 in Boulder, Co. Attended Stephens Col. Bdwy debut 1989 in "Gypsy."

VENORA, DIANE. Born in 1952 in Hartford, CT. Graduate Juilliard. Debut 1981 OB in "Penguin Touquet," followed by "A Midsummer Night's Dream," "Hamlet" (title role), "Uncle Vanya," "Messiah," "Tomorrow's Monday," "Largo Desolato," "A Man for All Seasons," "Winter's Tale," "Hamlet."

VINOVICH, STEPHEN. Born Jan. 22, 1945 in Peoria, Il. Graduate UIll., UCLA, Juilliard. Debut 1974 OB in "The Robber Bridegroom," followed by "King John," "Father Uxbridge Wants to Marry," "Hard Sell," "Ross," "Double Feature," "Tender Places," "A Private View," "Love," "Poker Session," "Paradise," "Secret Rapture," Bdwy in "Robber Bridegroom" (1976), "The Magic Show," "The Grand Tour," "Loose Ends," "A Midsummer Night's Dream."

VIPOND, NEIL. Born Dec. 24, 1929 in Toronto, Can. Bdwy debut 1956 in "Tamburlaine the Great," followed by "Macbeth," OB in "Three Friends," "Sunday Runners," "Hamlet," "Routed," "Mr. Joyce Is Leaving Paris," "The Time of Your Life," "Children of the Sun," "Romeo and Juliet," "The Lark," "The Crucible."

VIRTA, RAY. Born June 18, 1958 in L'Anse, MI. Debut 1982 OB in "Twelfth Night," followed by "The Country Wife," "Dubliners," "Pericles," "Tartuffe," "The Taming of the Shrew," "No One Dances," "Jacques and His Master," "Progress."

VITELLA, SEL. Born July 7, 1934 in Boston, Ma. Graduate San Francisco Inst. of Music. Debut 1975 OB in "The Merchant of Venice," followed by "Gorey Stories," "Jane Eyre," "Preppies," "Professionally Speaking," "Dazy," Bdwy in "Something's Afoot" (1976), "Gorey Stories," "Prince of Central Park."

VON BARGEN, DANIEL. Born June 5, 1950 in Cincinnati, Oh. Graduate Purdue U. Debut 1981 OB in "Missing Persons," followed by "Macbeth," Bdwy debut in "Mastergate" (1989) for which he received a Theatre World Award.

VOSBURGH, DAVID. Born Mar. 14, 1938 in Coventry, RI. Attended Boston U. Bdwy debut 1968 in "Maggie Flynn," followed by "1776," "A Little Night Music," "Evita," "A Doll's Life," "Cabaret" (1987), "Sweeney Todd" (1989), OB in "Smith," "The Rise of David Levinsky."

WAARA, SCOTT. Born June 5, 1957 in Chicago, IL. Graduate SMU. Debut 1982 OB in "The Rise of Daniel Rocket," followed by "The Dining Room," "Johnny Pye and the Foolkiller," "Gifts of the Magi," Bdwy in "The Wind in the Willows" (1985), "Welcome to the Club," "City of Angels."

WADE, ADAM. Born Mar. 17, 1935 in Pittsburgh, Pa. Attended VaStateU. Debut 1976 OB in "My Sister My Sister," followed by "Shades of Harlem," "Falling Apart," "The War Party," "Staggerlee," "Lifetimes," "Burner's Frolic."

WALKEN, CHRISTOPHER. Born Mar. 31, 1943 in Astoria, NY. Attended Hofstra U. Bdwy debut 1958 in "J.B.," followed by "High Spirits," "Baker Street," "The Lion in Winter," "Measure for Measure," "The Rose Tattoo" for which he received a Theatre World Award, "The Unknown Soldier and His Wife," "Rosencrantz and Guildenstern Are Dead," "Scenes from American Life," "Cymbeline," "Enemies," "The Plough and the Stars," "Merchant of Venice," "The Tempest," "Troilus and Cressida," "Macbeth," "Sweet Bird of Youth," OB in "Best Foot Forward" (1963), "Iphigenia in Aulis," "Lemon Sky," "Kid Champion," "The Seagull," "Cinders," "Hurlyburly," "House of Blue Leaves," "Love Letters," "Coriolanus."

WALKER, RAY. Born Aug. 13, 1963 in St. Johnsbury, VT. Graduate NYU. Debut 1985 OB in "Christmas Spectacular," followed by "Merrily We Roll Along," Bdwy 1988 in "Les Miserables."

WALLACE, LEE. Born July 15, 1930 in NYC. Attended NYU. Debut 1966 OB in "Journey of the Fifth Horse," followed by "Saturday Night," "An Evening with Garcia Lorca," "Macbeth," "Booth Is Back in Town," "Awake and Sing," "Shepherd of Avenue B," "Basic Training of Pavlo Hummel," "Curtains," "Elephants," "Goodnight, Grandpa," "Jesse's Land," "The Sunshine Boys," Bdwy in "Secret Affairs of Mildred Wild," "Molly," "Zalmen, or the Madness of God," "Some of My Best Friends," "Grind," "The Cemetery Club."

WALLER, KENNETH. Born Apr. 12, 1945 in Atlanta, Ga. Graduate Piedmont Col. Debut 1976 OB in "Boys from Syracuse," Bdwy in "Sarava" (1979), "Onward Victoria," "Me and My Girl," "Phantom of the Opera."

WALLNAU, CARL N. Born July 8, 1953 in NYC. Graduate Dickenson Col., Rutgers U. Debut 1984 OB in "The Custom of the Country," followed by "Dance with Me."

WALSH, ELIZABETH. Born Oct. 12 in Puerto Rico. Graduate UWisc, UMa. Debut 1987 OB in "Mademoiselle Colombe," followed by "She Loves Me," "Frankie."

WALTER, JESSICA. Born Jan. 31, 1944 in NYC. Attended Neighborhood Playhouse. Bdwy debut 1961 in "Advise and Consent," followed by "A Severed Head," "Night Life," "Photo Finish," "Rumors," OB in "The Murder of Me," "Fighting International Fat."

WALTON, JIM. Born July 31, 1955 in Tachikawa, Japan. Graduate UCincinnati. Debut 1979 OB in "Big Bad Burlesque," followed by "Scrambled Feet," "Stardust," "Sweeney Todd," "Closer Than Ever," Bdwy in "Perfectly Frank" (1980), "Merrily We Roll Along," "42nd Street," "Stardust," "Sweeney Todd."

WARD, DOUGLAS TURNER. Born May 5, 1930 in Burnside, La. Attended UMi. Bdwy debut 1959 in "Raisin in the Sun," followed by "One Flew over the Cuckoo's Nest," "Last Breeze of Summer," OB in "The Iceman Cometh," "The Blacks," "Pullman Car Hiawatha," "Bloodknot," "Happy Ending," "Day of Absence," "Kongi's Harvest," "Ceremonies in Dark Old Men," "The Harangues," "The Reckoning," "Frederick Douglas through His Own Words," "River Niger," "The Brownsville Raid," "The Offering," "Old Phantoms," "The Michigan," "About Heaven and Earth," "Louie and Ophelia," "Lifetimes."

WARFIELD, JOE. Born Nov. 6, 1937 in Baltimore, Md. Graduate UMd. Debut 1959 OB in "Little Mary Sunshine," followed by "O Say Can You See," "Corners," "Positive Me," Bdwy in "110 in the Shade" (1964) followed by "Jimmy Shine," "Baby."

WARREN, JOSEPH. Born June 5, 1916 in Boston, MA. Graduate UDenver. Bdwy debut 1951 in "Barefoot in Athens," followed by "One Bright Day," "Love of Four Colonels," "Hidden River," "The Advocate," "Philadelphia, Here I Come," "Borstal Boy," "Lincoln Mask," OB in "Brecht on Brecht," "Jonah," "Little Black Sheep," "Black Tuesday," "The Show-Off," "Big Apple Messenger," "The Ballad of Soapy Smith," "Her Great Match," "Measure for Measure," "Hamlet," "The Rivals," "Of Mice and Men," "Uncle Vanya," "Aristocrats," "She Stoops to Conquer," "Three Sisters."

WASHINGTON, DENZEL. Born Dec. 28, 1954 in Mt. Vernon, NY. Graduate Fordham U. Debut 1975 OB in "The Emperor Jones," followed by "Othello," "Coriolanus," "Mighty Gents," "Becket," "Spell #7," "Ceremonies in Dark Old Men," "One Tiger To a Hill," "A Soldier's Play," "Every Goodbye Ain't Gone," Bdwy 1988 in "Checkmates."

WASHINGTON, MELVIN. Born Dec. 19 in Brooklyn, NY. Attended CCNY., HB Studio. Debut 1980 OB in "Streamers," followed by "Something to Live For," Bdwy in "My One and Only" (1983), "Black and Blue."

WATT, ELOISE. Born Jan. 19th in Easton, Pa. Graduate Emerson Col. Debut 1979 OB in "The Price of Genius" followed by "The Merchant of Venice," "The Carpenters," "Summerfolk," "Cymbeline."

WEATHERS, PATRICK. Born Jan. 22, 1954 in Hattiesburg, Ms. Graduate S. M. U. Debut 1981 OB in "Daisy the Shopping Bag Lady," followed by "Elvis: A Rockin' Remembrance," Bdwy in "Rock and Roll: The First 5000 Years" (1982).

WEAVER, DANYELLE. Born Nov. 29, 1978 in New Brunswick, NJ. Debut OB in "Dangerous Games" (1989).

WEBER, JAKE. Born Mar. 12, 1963 in London, Eng. Graduate Middlebury Col., Juilliard. Debut 1988 OB in "Road," followed by "Twelfth Night," "Maids of Honor," "Richard III."

WEDGEWORTH, ANN. Born Jan. 21, 1935 in Abilene, Tx. Bdwy debut 1958 in "Make a Million," followed by "Blues for Mr. Charlie," "The Last Analysis," "Thieves," "Chapter 2," OB in "Chapparal," "The Crucible," "The Days and Nights of Beebee Fenstermaker," "Ludlow Fair," "Line," "Elba," "A Lie of the Mind," "The Debutante Ball," "The Aunts."

WEISS, JEFF. Born in 1940 in Allentown, PA. Debut 1986 OB in "Hamlet," followed by "The Front Page" (LC), Bdwy in "Macbeth" (1988), "Our Town," "Mastergate."

WELBY, DONNAH. Born May 4, 1952 in Scranton, PA. Graduate Catholic U. Debut 1981 OB in "Between Friends," followed by "Double Inconstancy," "The Taming of the Shrew," "The Contrast," "Macbeth," "Electra," "All's Well That Ends Well," "Hot l Baltimore," "The Philanderer," "Three Sisters," "The Importance of Being Earnest," "A Midsummer Night's Dream," "Between Friends."

WELDON, CHARLES. Born June 1, 1940 in Wetumka, Ok. Bdwy debut 1969 in "Big Time Buck White," followed by "River Niger," OB in "Ride a Black Horse," "Long Time Coming," "Jamimma," "In the Deepest Part of Sleep," "Brownsville Raid," "The Great MacDaddy," "The Offering," "Colored People's Time," "Raisin in the Sun," "Lifetimes," "Jonquil," "Burner's Frolic."

WELLS, CHRISTOPHER. Born June 18, 1955 in Norwalk, CT. Graduate Amherst Col. Debut 1981 OB in "Big Apple Country," followed by "Broadway Jukebox," "Savage Amusement," "Overruled," "Heart of Darkness," "Ancient History," "One Act Festival." Bdwy in "Harrigan 'n' Hart" (1985), "Broadway," "Teddy and Alice."

WELLS, CRAIG. Born July 2, 1955 in Newark, NJ. Graduate Albion Col. Debut 1985 OB in "Forbidden Broadway," "The Best of Forbidden Broadway," "Closer Than Ever." Bdwy in "Chess" (1988).

WESTENBERG, ROBERT. Born Oct. 26, 1953 in Miami Beach, FL. Graduate UCal/Fresno. Debut 1981 OB in "Henry IV Part I," followed by "Hamlet," "The Death of von Richthofen," Bdwy in "Zorba" (1983) for which he received a Theatre World Award, "Sunday in the Park with George," "Into the Woods," "Les Miserables."

WESTON, JACK. Born Aug. 21, 1915 in Cleveland, OH. Attended Cleveland Playhouse, Am.Thea.Wing. Bdwy debut 1950 in "Season in the Sun," followed by "South Pacific," "Bells Are Ringing," "California Suite," "The Ritz," "Cheaters," "Floating Light Bulb," "Tenth Man," OB in "Baker's Wife," "Measure For Measure."

WETHERALL, JACK. Born Aug. 5, 1950 in Sault Ste. Marie, Can. Graduate Glendon Col, York U. Bdwy debut 1979 in "The Elephant Man," followed by OB's "Tamara." (1987).

WHALLEY-KILMER, JOANNE. Born Aug. 25 in Manchester, Eng. Debut 1989 OB in "What the Butler Saw," for which she received a Theatre World Award.

WHITE, AMELIA. Born Sept. 14, 1954 in Nottingham, Eng. Attended London's Central School of Speech & Drama. Debut 1984 OB in "The Accrington Pals," for which she received a Theatre World Award, "American Bagpipes."

WHITE, PATRICK. Born Sept. 9, 1963 in Albany, NY. Graduate AADA. Debut 1988 OB in "Male Animal," followed by "After the Rain."

WHITE, RICHARD. Born Aug. 4, 1953 in Oak Ridge, Tn. Graduate Oberlin Col. Bdwy debut 1979 in "The Most Happy Fella," followed by "Brigadoon," "South Pacific," "The Desert Song," OB in "Elizabeth and Essex," "Frankie."

WHITEHEAD, PAXTON. Born in Kent, Eng. Attended Webber-Douglas Acad. Bdwy debut 1962 in "The Affair," followed by "Beyond the Fringe," "Candida," "Habeas Corpus," "Crucifer of Blood," "Camelot," "Noises Off," "Run For Your Wife," "Artist Descending a Staircase," "Lettice and Lovage," OB in "Gallows Humor," "One Way Pendulum," "Doll's House," "Rondelay."

WHITFIELD, DEBRA. Born July 1, 1957 in Charlotte, NC. Graduate OhStateU, Kent StateU. Debut 1983 OB in "Brandy before Breakfast," followed by "Dr. Jekyll and Mr. Hyde," "Bravo," "Appointment with Death," "Hound of the Baskervilles," "The Land Is Bright," "Black Coffee," "On the Move."

Joseph
Warren

Denzel
Washington

Patrick
Weathers

Jake
Weber

Christopher
Wells

Craig
Wells

Robert
Westenberg

Donnah
Welby

Jack
Wetherall

Debra
Whitfield

Patrick
White

Margaret
Whitton

Colm
Wilkinson

Barry
Williams

Curt
Williams

Walter
Willison

Ray
Wills

Tyrone
Wilson

Lori
Wilner

Julie
Wilson

Lee
Wilson

Beatrice
Winde

Suzi
Winson

Charlaine
Woodard

Ray
Xifo

Ronald
Yamamoto

Jo Ann
Yeoman

Stuart
Zagnit

Janet
Zarish

Kurt
Ziskie

227

WHITTON, MARGARET. (formerly Peggy) Born Nov. 30 in Philadelphia, Pa. Debut 1973 OB in "Baba Goya," followed by "Arthur," "The Wager," "Nourish the Beast," "Another Language," "Chinchilla," "Othello," "The Art of Dining," "One Tiger to a Hill," "Henry IV Parts I & II," "Don Juan," "My Uncle Sam," "Aunt Dan and Lemon," "Ice Cream with Hot Fudge," Bdwy in "Steaming" (1982).

WIDDOES, KATHLEEN. Born Mar. 21, 1939 in Wilmington, De. Attended Paris Theatre de Nations. Bdwy debut 1958 in "The Firstborn," followed by "The World of Suzy Wong," "Much Ado about Nothing," "The Importance of Being Earnest," "Brighton Beach Memoirs," OB in "The Three Sisters," "The Maids," "You Can't Take It with You," "To Clothe the Naked," "World War 2½," "Beggar's Opera," "As You Like It," "A Midsummer Night's Dream," "One-Act Festival," "Hamlet," "The Tower of Evil."

WIEST, DIANNE. Born Mar. 28, 1948 in Kansas City, Mo. Attended UMd. Debut 1976 OB in "Ashes," followed by "Leave It to Beaver Is Dead," "The Art of Dining" for which she received a Theatre World Award, "Bonjour La Bonjour," "The Three Sisters," "Serenading Louie," "Other Places," "Hunting Cockroaches," "After the Fall," "Square One," Bdwy in "Frankenstein" (1981), "Othello," "Beyond Therapy."

WILKINSON, COLM. Born June 5, 1944 in Dublin, Ire. Bdwy debut 1987 in "Les Miserables" for which he received a Theatre World Award.

WILLIAMS, BARRY. Born Sept. 30, 1954 in Santa Monica, Ca. Attended Pepperdine U. Bdwy debut 1977 in "Pippin," followed by "Romance/Romance," OB in "Slay It with Music."

WILLIAMS, CURT. Born Nov. 17, 1935 in Mt. Holly, NJ. Graduate Oberlin Col., UMiami. Debut 1964 OB in "The Fantasticks," followed by "Pinafore," "Mikado," "Night Must Fall," "The Hostage," "Macbeth," "Ice Age," "Colored People's Time," "About Heaven and Earth," "Appointment with Death," "Something Old, Something New," "Enter a Free Man," "Jonquil," Bdwy in "Purlie" (1970), "Play Memory."

WILLIAMS, TREAT. Born Dec. 1, 1951 in Rowayton, CT. Bdwy debut 1974 in "Grease," followed by "Over Here," "Once in a Lifetime," "Pirates of Penzance," "Love Letters" (also OB), OB in "Maybe I'm Doing It Wrong," "Some Men Need Help," "Oh, Hell!"

WILLIAMS, VAN. Born Apr. 10, 1925 in Pharr, TX. Attended UTx, Yale U. Bdwy debut 1951 in "Richard II," followed by "St. Joan," "Dial 'M' for Murder," "Little Moon of Alban," "No Time for Sergeants," "The Teahouse of the August Moon."

WILLISON, WALTER. Born June 24, 1947 in Monterey Park, Ca. Bdwy debut 1970 in "Norman, Is That You?," followed by "Two by Two" for which he received a Theatre World Award, "Wild and Wonderful," "A Celebration of Richard Rodgers," "Pippin," "A Tribute to Joshua Logan," "A Tribute to George Abbott," "Grand Hotel," OB in "South Pacific in Concert," "They Say It's Wonderful," "Broadway Scandals of 1928," and "Options," both of which he wrote, "Aldersgate 88."

WILLS, RAY. Born Sept. 14, 1960 in Santa Monica, CA. Graduate WichitaStU, BrandeisU. Debut 1988 OB in "Side by Side by Sondheim," followed by "Kiss Me Quick," "The Grand Tour," "The Cardigans," "The Rothschilds."

WILNER, LORI. Born July 17, 1959 in NYC. Graduate SUNY/Binghamton. OB in "I Never Told Anybody," "Poor Murderer," "Hair," "Hannah Senesh," "Cricket on the Hearth," "The Witch," "Hannah 1939."

WILSON, JULIE. Born in 1925 in Omaha, NE. Bdwy debut 1946 in "Three to Make Ready," followed by "Kiss Me Kate," "Kismet," "Pajama Game," "Jimmy," "Park," "Legs Diamond," OB in "From Weill to Sondheim," "Hannah 1939."

WILSON, LEE. Born Jan. 23, 1948 in Wilmington, De. Attended Columbia U, HB Studio. Debut 1967 in "Hello, Dolly!," followed by "Here's Where I Belong," "How Now Dow Jones," "La Strada," "Oklahoma!" (LC). "You're a Good Man, Charlie Brown," "A Chorus Line," "Meet Me in St. Louis."

WILSON, TYRONE. Born Feb. 23, 1959 in Lumberton, NC. Graduate Middlebury Col., Yale U. Debut 1988 OB in "Julius Caesar," followed by "Water Music," "The Vigil," "A Lesson from Aloes," "Macbeth," "The Country Doctor," Bdwy in "Lettice and Lovage" (1990).

WINBORN, BRENT. Born July 28, 1959 in Fayetteville, Ark. Graduate UArk, OklaCityU. Debut 1990 OB in "The Golden Apple."

WINDE, BEATRICE. Born Jan. 6, in Chicago, IL. Debut 1966 OB in "In White America," followed by "June Bug Graduates Tonight," "Strike Heaven on the Face," "Divine Comedy," "Crazy Horse," "My Mother, My Father and Me," "Steal Away," "The Actress," "Richard II," "1-2-3-4-5," "Le Bourgeois Gentilhomme," "The American Plan," Bdwy in "Ain't Supposed to Die a Natural Death" (1971) for which she received a Theatre World Award.

WINSON, SUZI. Born Feb. 28, 1962 in NYC. Bdwy debut 1980 in "Brigadoon," followed by OB in "Moondance," "Nunsense."

WINTERSTELLER, LYNNE. Born Sept. 18, 1955 in Sandusky, Oh. Graduate UMd. Bdwy debut 1982 in "Annie," followed by OB's "Gifts of the Magi" (1984), "The Rise of David Levinsky," "Nunsense," "Closer than Ever."

WISE, WILLIAM. Born May 11, in Chicago, IL. Attended BradleyU., NorthwesternU. Debut 1970 OB in "Adaptation/Next," followed by "Him," "Hot l Baltimore," "Just the Immediate Family," "36," "For the Use of the Hall," "Orphans," "Working Theatre Festival," "Copperhead," "Early One Evening at the Rainbow Bar & Grill," "Special Interests."

WISEMAN, JOSEPH. Born May 15, 1919 in Montreal, Can. Attended CCNY. Bdwy in "Journey to Jerusalem," "Abe Lincoln in Illinois," "Candle in the Wind," "The Three Sisters," "Storm Operation," "Joan of Lorraine," "Antony and Cleopatra," "Detective Story," "That Lady," "King Lear," "Golden Boy," "The Lark," "Zalmen, or the Madness of God," "Tenth Man," OB in "Marco Millions," "Incident at Vichy," "In the Matter of J. Robert Oppenheimer," "Enemies," "Duchess of Malfi," "The Last Analysis," "The Lesson," "The Golem."

WISNISKI, RON. Born Aug. 11, 1957 in Pittsburg, PA. Debut 1983 OB in "Promises, Promises," followed by "Tatterdemalion," "Most Secret War," "Frankie."

WITTENBAUER, JOHN. Born in Teaneck, NJ. Attended Ithaca Col. Debut 1989 OB in "The Tempest," followed by "Long May She Wave."

WOJDA, JOHN. Born Feb. 19, 1957 in Detroit, Mi. Attended UMi. Bdwy debut 1982 in "Macbeth" followed by "The Merchant of Venice," OB in "The Merchant of Venice," "Natural Disasters," "The Coming of Mr. Pine."

WONG, B. D. (aka Bradd). Born Oct. 24, 1962 in San Francisco, CA. Debut 1981 OB in "Androcles and the Lion," followed by "Applause," "Tempest," Bdwy in "M. Butterfly" (1988) for which he received a Theatre World Award.

WOODARD, CHARLAINE. Born Dec. 29 in Albany, NY. Graduate Goodman Theatre, SUNY. Debut 1975 OB in "Don't Bother Me, I Can't Cope," followed by "Dementos," "Under Fire," "A . . . My Name Is Alice," "Twelfth Night," "Hang on to the Good Times," "Paradise," "Twelfth Night" (CP), Bdwy in "Hair" (1977), "Ain't Misbehavin' " (1978/1988)

WOODESON, NICHOLAS. Born in England and graduate of RADA. Debut 1978 OB in "Strawberry Fields," followed by "The Taming of the Shrew," "Backers Audition," "The Art of Success," Bdwy in "Man and Superman" (1978), "Piaf," "Good."

WOODS, RICHARD. Born May 9, 1923 in Buffalo, NY. Graduate Ithaca Col. Bdwy in "Beg, Borrow or Steal," "Capt. Brassbound's Conversion," "Sail Away," "Coco," "Last of Mrs. Lincoln," "Gigi," "Sherlock Holmes," "Murder among Friends," "Royal Family," "Deathtrap," "Man and Superman," "Man Who Came to Dinner," "The Father," "Present Laughter," "Alice in Wonderland," "You Can't Take It with You," "Design For Living," "Smile," OB in "The Crucible," "Summer and Smoke," "American Gothic," "Four-in-One," "My Hearts in the Highlands," "Eastward in Eden," "Long Gallery," "Year Boston Won the Pennant," "In the Matter of J. Robert Oppenheimer," with APA in "You Can't Take It with You," "War and Peace," "School for Scandal," "Right You Are," "Wild Duck," "Pantagleize," "Exit the King," "Cherry Orchard," "Cock-a-doodle Dandy,"and "Hamlet," "Crimes and Dreams," "Marathon '84," "Much Ado about Nothing," "Sitting Pretty in Concert," "The Cat and the Fiddle."

WORKMAN, JASON. Born Oct. 9, 1962 in Omaha, Neb. Attended UKy., Goodman School. Bdwy debut 1989 in "Meet Me in St. Louis" for which he received a Theatre World Award.

WORKMAN, SHANELLE. Born Aug. 3, 1978 in Fairfax, VA. Bdwy debut 1988 in "Les Miserables."

WORLEY, JO ANNE. Born Sept. 6, 1937 in Lowell, In. Attended CCLA, Pasadena Playhouse. Bdwy debut 1961 in "The Billy Barnes People," followed by "Prince of Central Park," OB in "That Thing at the Cherry Lane," "Hotel Passionato," "The Mad Show," "The Second City Revue."

WORTH, PENNY. Born Mar. 2, 1950 in London, Eng. Attended Sorbonne/Paris. Bdwy debut 1970 in "Coco," followed by "Irene," "Annie," "Grand Hotel."

WRIGHT, AMY. Born Apr. 15, 1950 in Chicago, Il. Graduate Beloit Col. Debut 1977 OB in "The Stronger," followed by "Nightshift," "Hamlet," "Miss Julie," "Slacks and Tops," "Terrible Jim Fitch," "Village Wooing," "The Stronger," "Time Framed," "Trifles," "Words from the Moon," "Prin," Bdwy in "5th of July" (1980), "Noises Off."

WROE, CRAIG. Born Apr. 8, 1958 in Los Angeles, Ca. Graduate Loyola U., Catholic U. Debut 1989 OB in "The Tempest," followed by "Othello."

WYCHE, MIMI. Born Dec. 2, 1955 in Greenville, SC. Graduate Stanford U. Debut 1986 OB in "Once on a Summer's Day," followed by "Senor Discretion," "Juan Darien," "The Golden Apple," Bdwy in "Cats" (1988).

WYLIE, JOHN. Born Dec. 14, 1925 in Peacock, TX. Graduate No.TxStU. Debut 1987 OB in "Lucky Spot," followed by Bdwy in "Born Yesterday" (1989), "Grand Hotel."

WYMAN, NICHOLAS. Born May 18, 1950 in Portland, Me. Graduate Harvard U. Bdwy debut 1975 in "Very Good Eddie," followed by "Grease," "The Magic Show," "On the 20th Century," "Whoopee!," "My Fair Lady" (1981), "Doubles," "Musical Comedy Murders of 1940," "Phantom of the Opera," OB in "Paris Lights," "When We Dead Awaken," "Charlotte Sweet," "Kennedy at Colonus," "Once on a Summer's Day," "Angry Housewives."

WYNKOOP, CHRISTOPHER. Born Dec. 7, 1943 in Long Branch, NJ. Graduate AADA. Debut 1970 OB in "Under the Gaslight," followed by "And So to Bed," "Cartoons for a Lunch Hour," "Telecast," "Fiorello," "The Aunts," Bdwy in "Whoopee!" (1979).

XIFO, RAY. Born Sept. 3, 1942 in Newark, NJ. Graduate Don Bosco Col. Debut 1974 OB in "The Tempest," followed by "Frogs," "My Uncle Sam," "Shlemiel the First," Bdwy in "City of Angels" (1989).

YAMAMOTO, RONALD. Born Mar. 13, 1953 in Seatle, WA. Graduate QueensCol. Debut 1983 OB in "Song for a Nisei Fisherman," followed by "Pacific Overtures," "Rosie's Cafe," Bdwy in "Anything Goes" (1989), "Lettice and Lovage."

YEOMAN, JO ANN. Born Mar. 19, 1948 in Phoenix, AZ. Graduate AzStateU, PurdueU. Debut 1974 OB in "The Boy Friend," followed by "Texas Starlight," "Ba Ta Clan," "A Christmas Carol."

ZAGNIT, STUART. Born Mar. 28 in New Brunswick, NJ. Graduate MontclairStCol. Debut 1978 OB in "The Wager," followed by "Manhattan Transference," "Women in Tune," "Enter Laughing," "Kuni Leml," "Tatterdemalion," "Golden Land," "Little Shop of Horrors," "Lucky Stiff," "Grand Tour," "Majestic Kid," "Made in Heaven."

ZALOOM, JOE. Born July 30, 1944 in Utica, NY. Graduate CatholicU. Bdwy Debut 1972 in "Capt. Brassbound's Conversion," followed by "Kingdoms," OB in "Nature and the Purpose of the Universe," "Plot Counter Plot," "Midsummer Night's Dream," "Madrid, Madrid," "Much Ado about Nothing," "Cymbeline," "Tamara."

ZARISH, JANET. Born Apr. 21, 1954 in Chicago, IL. Graduate Juilliard. Debut 1981 OB in "The Villager," followed by "Playing with Fire," "Royal Bob," "Enemy of the People," "Midsummer Night's Dream," "Festival of 1-Acts," "Other People's Money," "Human Nature."

ZEMON, TOM. Born Jan. 13, 1964 in Hartford, Ct. Graduate UHartford. Bdwy debut 1988 in "Les Miserables."

ZIEN, CHIP. Born in Mar. 20, 1947 in Milwaukee, WI. Attended UPa. OB in "You're a Good Man, Charlie Brown," followed by "Kadish," "How to Succeed . . . ," "Dear Mr. G," "Tuscaloosa's Calling," "Hot l Baltimore," "El Grande de Coca Cola," "Split," "Real Life Funnies," "March of the Falsettos," "Isn't It Romantic," "Diamonds," "Falsettoland," Bdwy in "All Over Town" (1974), "The Suicide," "Into the Woods."

ZIMMERMAN, MARK. Born Apr. 19, 1952 in Harrisburg, Pa. Graduate UPa. Debut 1976 OB in "Fiorello!," followed by "Silk Stockings," "On a Clear Day You Can See Forever," "110 in the Shade," "Fellow Travelers," "Frankie," Bdwy 1981 in "Brigadoon."

ZISKIE, KURT. Born Apr. 16, 1956 in Oakland, CA. Graduate StanfordU., Neighborhood Playhouse. Debut 1985 OB in "Flash of Lightning," followed by "Ulysses in Nighttown," "Three Sisters," Bdwy in "Broadway" (1987).

Nancy
Andrews

John C.
Attle

Jim
Backus

Samuel
Beckett

Irving
Berlin

Raleigh
Bond

OBITUARIES
(June 1, 1989–May 31, 1990)

ALVIN AILEY, 58, Texas-born actor, dancer, teacher, choreographer, and founder of the internationally renowned Alvin Ailey American Dance Theater, died of dyscrasia on Dec. 1, 1989 in NYC. He made his Broadway debut in *House of Flowers,* followed by *Jamaica, Tiger Tiger Burning Bright, The Carefree Tree, Call Me by My Rightful Name.* He founded his modern dance company in 1958. Surviving are his mother, step-father and half-brother.

NANCY ANDREWS, 68, Minneapolis-born stage, screen and TV actress, died on July 29, 1989 in Queens, NY, of a heart attack. She followed her 1948 Broadway debut in *Hilarities* with *Touch and Go,* for which she received a Theatre World Award, *Gentlemen Prefer Blondes, Hazel Flagg, Plain and Fancy, Pipe Dream, Juno, Christine, Flower Drum Song, Little Me, 70 Girls 70,* and Off-Broadway appearances in *Threepenny Opera, Tiger Rag, Madame Aphrodite, Say Nothing, How Much, How Much?* She is survived by a daughter.

DON APPELL, 73, stage actor, playwright and director, died on May 4, 1990 of heart failure in New York City. On Broadway he appeared as an actor in *According to Law, Native Son, Tapestry in Gray,* and *Odyssey,* directed *Career Angel, This Too Shall Pass* (which he also wrote), *Dr. Social, A Girl Could Get Lucky* (which he also wrote), and wrote *Lullaby* and *Milk and Honey.* No reported survivors.

JOHN C. ATTLE (John Paul Padur Welker), 48, stage and TV actor-dancer, who appeared for 6 years in the original Broadway production of *Fiddler on the Roof,* died on August 29, 1989 in Austin, TX of AIDS. He also appeared Off-Broadway in *Jacques Brel is Alive and Well and Living in Paris.* He is survived by his father, a stepbrother, and two stepsisters.

JIM BACKUS, 76, born James Gilmore Backus in Cleveland, OH, became best known for his voice of *Mr. Magoo* in cartoons and for the millionaire in *Gilligan's Island.* He was an actor and or writer in theatre, radio television and film. He appeared on Broadway in *Too Many Heroes* (1937) and *Paint Your Wagon* (1951). His wife survives.

KATHERINE BALFOUR, 69, actress and writer, died of Lou Gehrig's disease in her NYC home on Apr. 3, 1990. She created the role of Alma in the original production of Tennessee Williams' *Summer and Smoke* in Dallas. She had also appeared OB and in films. A daughter and a brother survive.

ARNOLD BANKSTON III, 34, Los Angeles-born actor, died March 28, 1990 of brain cancer. He appeared on Broadway in *Shakespeare on Broadway* and worked off Broadway in *A Flash of Lightning* (debut 1985) followed by *Mirandolina* and *Journal of Albion Moonlight.* Survived by his mother, brother and sister.

FRANCES BAVIER, 86, NY born actress on stage, screen and TV, died Dec. 6, 1989 in Silver City, NC., where she had retired. She received an Emmy for her Aunt Bee on *The Andy Griffith Show.* Among her numerous Bdwy roles are *The Black Pit, The Mother, The Marching Song, Native Son, Kiss and Tell, Little A, Jenny Kissed Me, Magnolia Alley* and *Point of No Return.* No reported survivors.

SAMUEL BECKETT, 83, Irish-born writer, died of respiratory failure Dec. 22, 1989 in his adopted Paris, France. The Nobel Prize-winning poet, playwright and novelist was considered one of the greatest writers of the 20th Century, and was a great influence on modern literature. His plays include *Waiting for Godot* (translated and performed in 20 languages), *Endgame, Krapp's Last Tape, Happy Days, Play, Not I,* and *Rockaby.* He was reclusive and refused to attend the ceremony for his Nobel Prize. His wife died in July. They had no children.

IRVING BERLIN, 101, Russia-born composer who became one of the most popular and significant American songwriters of the 20th Century, died on Sept. 22, 1989 in his sleep at his New York townhouse. He began composing in 1907, publishing over 1,000 songs in the next 59 years. His music appeared in the Broadway shows *Ziegfeld Follies* (1911, 1919, 1920, 1927), *Watch Your Step, Stop! Look! Listen!, The Century Girl, The Cohan Revue of 1918, Yip, Yip, Yaphank, The Canary, Music Box Revue* (1921, 1922, 1923, 1924), *The Cocoanuts, Face the Music, As Thousands Cheer, Louisiana Purchase, This Is the Army, Annie Get Your Gun, Miss Liberty, Call Me Madam,* and *Mr. President.* In 1963 he received a special Tony Award for his "distinguished contribution to the musical theatre for many years." He is survived by three daughters.

CHRISTOPHER BERNAU, 49, California-born stage and tv actor, died June 14, 1989. He appeared in *Sweet Bird of Youth, The Jockey Club Stakes, The Boys in the Band, The Real Inspector Hound* and *The Passion of Dracula.* For 10 years he was Alan Spaulding on tv's *Guiding Light.* His mother survives.

RALEIGH BOND, 54, stage, screen, tv actor and author, died of Lymphoma Aug. 10, 1989 in Los Angeles. He had appeared in *Abe Lincoln in Illinois, The Taming of the Shrew, The Andersonville Trial, The Buttered Side* and *The Fables* both of which he authored, *Sly Fox.* He was a regular on several tv series. His widow survives.

ALAN BOWNE, 44, playwright and author died suddenly of AIDS in his home near Petaluma, CA. His produced plays include *Forty-Deuce, The Able-Bodied Seaman, The Beany and Cecil Show, Sharon and Billy,* and *Beirut.* Surviving are his parents and a sister.

RICHARD L. BOWNE, 40, Bronxville-born actor, died May 19, 1990 in NYC. He played Prince Charming in Radio City's *Snow White* in 1979, subsequently appearing in several regional companies. His father and a brother survive.

HENRY BRANDON, 77, German-born stage, film and tv actor, died of a heart attack Feb. 15, 1990 in Hollywood. He was born Heinrich von Kleinbach in Berlin and came to the U.S. as an infant. He first appeared in films as Henry Kleinbach, before changing to Brandon. He appeared in over 75 films, and on Broadway in *Boudoir, Macbeth, Medea* with Judith Anderson, *Twelfth Night,* and *The Lady's Not for Burning.* A brother and sister survive.

ERIC BROTHERSON, 78, Chicago-born actor-singer, died Oct. 21, 1989 in NYC. Bdwy debut 1937 in *Between the Devil,* followed by *Set to Music, Lady in the Dark, My Dear Public, Gentlemen Prefer Blondes, Room Service, The Hot Corner, Musical Jubilee, My Fair Lady, Make Mine Manhattan, The Fifth Season, The King and I,* and *Hello Dolly!.* Three grandchildren survive.

NORTHERN J. CALLOWAY, 41, stage and tv actor, died of undetermined causes on Jan. 9, 1990 in his native Ossining, NY. In NYC he appeared in *The Me Nobody Knows, Salvation, Pippin* (replacing Ben Vereen), *Whose Life Is It Anyway?,* and *Louis.* For 16 years he was "David" on *Sesame Street.* He is survived by his mother, a sister and a brother.

RICHARD W. CAMP, 67, Iowa-born antiques dealer and actor, died in Wainscott, NY of lung cancer on Apr. 26, 1990. After acting for 15 years he became an antiques dealer in NYC and on Long Island. He had appeared in such plays as *Junior Miss, Three's a Family, Men to the Sea, Little Women, This Too Shall Pass.* Surviving is his long time companion and partner David Murray.

MICHAEL CARMINE, 30, Brooklyn-born stage, screen and TV actor, died on Oct. 14, 1989 of heart failure at his home in New York. His theatre credits include several shows with the Puerto Rican Traveling Theatre and INTAR, as well as appearing on Broadway in *Cuba and His Teddy Bear,* and Off-Broadway in *Sarita,* and *La Puta Vida.* He is survived by his mother, two brothers, and a grandmother.

AUDREY CHRISTIE, 79, stage, screen and TV actress, died of emphysema on Dec. 20, 1989 in West Hollywood. Following a stint as a dancer on the Chicago vaudeville circuit she made her Broadway debut in 1933 in *Shady Lady,* followed by *Sailor, Beware!, Alley Cat, Geraniums in My Window, The Women* (1936), *I Married an Angel, Return Engagement, Banjo Eyes, The Voice of the Turtle* (for which she received a Donaldson Award), *The Duchess Misbehaves, Light Up the Sky, Buy Me Blue Ribbons, Holiday for Lovers, The Desk Set, Auntie Mame, Wonderful Town, Nature's Way, Forty Carats,* and *Mame.* She is survived by her son, sister and grandchildren.

PETER COOKSON, 76, Oregon-born actor, producer and writer, died of bone cancer on Jan. 7, 1990 in Southfield, MA. He appeared on Broadway in *Message for Margaret* for which he received a Theatre World Award, followed by *The Heiress, The Little Blue Light, Can-Can, the River Line, Four Winds,* and *Wonderful Town.* He is survived by his second wife, actress Beatrice Straight, 3 sons and a daughter.

ALBERT CORBIN, 63, Connecticut-born actor and puppeteer, died of prostate cancer on July 27, 1989 in NYC. He had appeared on Broadway in *The Wayward Saint, Tiger at the Gates, Cyrano de Bergerac, Henry IV Part I,* and OB in *School for Wives, White Devil, Our Town, Fashion, The Crucible, Columbe,* and *Taming of the Shrew.* Surviving is his mother.

BETTE DAVIS, 81, Massachusetts-born stage, screen, and TV actress, one of the cinema's greatest and most enduring stars, died on October 6, 1989 of breast cancer at the American Hospital in Neuilly-sur-Seine, France. She appeared in nearly 100 movies and won 2 Academy Awards for Best Actress. She made her Broadway debut in 1929 in *The Earth Between,* followed by *Broken Dishes, Solid South, Two's Company, The World of Carl Sanburg,* and *Night of the Iguana.* She is survived by her daughter and two adopted children.

Henry Brandon	Eric Brotherson	Bette Davis	Sammy Davis Jr.	Joe De Santis	Jack Fletcher
Sergio Franchi	Betty Garde	Robert Gerringer	Charles T. Harper	Jessica James	Scott Jarvis
Reed Jones	Arthur Kennedy	Claire Luce	Art Lund	Kathleen Maguire	Gary Merrill
Arnold Moss	David O'Brien	Susan Oliver	Laurence Olivier	Erik Rhodes	Gregory Rozakis
Albert Salmi	Franklyn Seales	Michael Shawn	Paul Shenar	Cornel Wilde	William Traylor

230

LEE DAVIS, 81, stage actor-singer-dancer died on Dec. 2, 1989 in Hawaii. He appeared on Broadway in *Kiss Me Kate, Follow the Girls, Anything Goes, Carousel, Brigadoon, Wish You Were Here, A Tree Grows in Brooklyn,* and *What Makes Sammy Run?* He is survived by his wife and two children.

SAMMY DAVIS, JR., 64, New York City-born stage, screen, and TV, actor, singer and dancer, who broke through racial barriers to become one of America's most beloved entertainers, died of throat cancer on May 16, 1990 at his home in Beverly Hills, CA. He appeared on Broadway in *Mr. Wonderful, Golden Boy* and the 1978 revival of *Stop the World—I Want to Get Off.* He is survived by his wife, his mother, a sister, a daughter, two sons, and two grandchildren.

PALMER DEANE, 56, Texas-born stage, screen and TV actor, died on April 23, 1990 in New York of AIDS. He appeared on the New York stage in *Babu, The Unknown Soldier and His Wife, The Blacks, Toussaint, All the King's Men, The Breakout, The War Party, The Good Ship Credit,* and as a member of the Lincoln Center Repertory Theatre in such productions as *A Midsummer Night's Dream, An Evening for Merlin Finch, The Doctor in spite of Himself,* and *The Birds.* For several years he appeared as a regular on the daytime serial *The Doctors.* He is survived by his mother and a sister.

JOSEPH DE SANTIS, 80, New York-born stage, screen and TV actor, died on Aug. 30, 1989 in Provo, UT of chronic obstructive lung disease. He made his Broadway debut in 1931 in *Sirena,* followed by *Cyrano de Bergerac, St. Helena, Journey to Jerusalem, Walk into My Parlor, Men in Shadow, Storm Operation, The Searching Wind, The Front Page* (1946), *In Any Language, The Highest Tree,* and *Daughter of Silence.* He is survived by two sons, and two grandchildren.

JOHN DEXTER, 64, British director of theatre and opera, died on March 23, 1990 of heart failure in London. His credits in England include work with the Royal Court and the National Theatre. On Broadway he directed *Saint Joan, Chips With Everything, The Royal Hunt of the Sun, Do I Hear a Waltz?, Black Comedy, The Unknown Soldier and His Wife, Hamlet* (1969), *Equus* (for which he won a Tony Award), *The Glass Menagerie* (1983), *M. Butterfly* (Tony Award), and *3 Penny Opera,* in 1989. No reported survivors.

MARK DIGNAM, 80, British stage, screen and TV actor, died on Sept. 29, 1989 in London of undisclosed causes. In addition to his extensive work on the London stage he appeared on Broadway in *Oscar Wilde* (his New York debut in 1938), *Love's Labour's Lost, Twelfth Night, The World of Sholom Aleichem, Hamlet* (1969), and *A Voyage Round My Father.* He is survived by his third wife.

FABIA DRAKE, 86, British stage, screen and TV actress died on Feb. 28, 1990 in London. She made her stage debut at age 9 in *The Fairy Doll* and had her first major role on the London stage in *Major Barbara* in 1921. She made her Broadway debut in 1926 in *The Scarlet Lady,* followed by *Loyalties, Anthony and Anna,* and *Indian Summer.* No reported survivors.

JACK FLETCHER, 68, New York-born stage, screen and TV actor died on Feb. 15, 1990 in Los Angeles of heart failure while auditioning for a commercial. He made his Broadway debut in 1947 in *Trial Honeymoon,* followed by *She Stoops to Conquer, Romeo and Juliet, Ben Franklin in Paris, Drat! The Cat!, A Joyful Noise, Lysistrata, Lorelei, Sugar Babies, Can-Can* (CC), *Cyrano,* and *Wonderful Town.* His Off-Broadway credits include *Comic Strip, Way of the World, Thieves' Carnival, The Amorous Flea, American Hamburger League, The Time of Your Life,* and *The Music Man* (JB). No reported survivors.

SERGIO FRANCHI, 64, Italian-born singer-actor died on May 1, 1990 in Stonington, CT. of brain cancer. As a vocalist he performed frequently on TV and in nightclubs and recorded 25 albums. He acted on Broadway in the musicals *Do I Hear a Waltz?* and *Nine.* He is survived by his wife, a daughter, a son and two sisters.

BETTY GARDE, 84, Philadelphia-born radio and stage actress, died in Sherman Oaks, Ca. on Dec. 25, 1989. Among her many credits are *Easy Come Easy Go, The Primrose Path, Oklahoma!* (the original Aunt Eller for many years of the run), *Agatha Sue I Love You, Stephen D.* No reported survivors.

ROBERT GERRINGER, 63, NYC-born stage, film and tv actor, died Nov. 8, 1989 of complications from a series of strokes in Damariscotta, ME. He had appeared on Broadway in *Pictures in the Hallway, A Flea in Her Ear, The Andersonville Trial, Waltz of the Toreadors, After the Fall, A Doll's House, Hedda Gabler, Hide and Seek,* and Off Bdwy in *Thieves Carnival, Home, The Birthday Party, Richard III, Henry VI, Much Ado about Nothing.* He is survived by his wife, actress Patricia Falkenhain.

JAY GORNEY, 93, Russia-born composer, best known for writing the song *"Brother Can You Spare a Dime,"* died on June 14, 1990 in New York of natural causes. The song, written with lyricist E. Y. "Yip" Harburg for the 1932 show *Americana,* became the "theme song" of the Depression. He also wrote music for the shows *Top Hole, Merry-Go-Round, Caravan, Earl Carroll's Sketch Book, Earl Carroll's Vanities, Meet the People, Heaven on Earth, Touch and Go,* and *These Are the Times.* He is survived by his wife, a daughter and two sons.

CHARLES THOMAS HARPER, 40, actor and teacher, died of AIDS July 4, 1989 in NYC. His credits include *Down by the River, Holy Ghosts, Hamlet, Mary Stuart, Twelfth Night, The Beaver Coat, Richard II, Great Grandson of Jedediah Kohler, Applause, Love's Labours Lost, Dylan,* and *Passion.* Surviving are his parents, four sisters and two brothers.

ANDY HOSTETTLER, 41, Tennessee-born actor-dancer-choreographer, died of complications from AIDS on Dec. 25, 1989. He had appeared on Broadway in *Goodtime Charley, Music Man,* and *Take Me Along,* as well as several touring musicals. He was on Equity's Council since 1979 and a founding member of Equity Fights AIDS Committee. His parents, two brothers, a sister, and two step-brothers survive.

JESSICA JAMES, 60, Los Angeles born stage, screen and TV actress, best known for playing the role of Bunny in the Broadway play *Gemini* for five years, died on May 7, 1990 in Los Angeles of cancer. After her Broadway debut in 1970 in *Company,* she appeared in *Little Me* (1982), *Nourish the Beast, Hothouse, Loss of Innocence, Rebirth, Celebration of the Human Race, Silver Bee,* and *42nd Street.* She is survived by two children and two grandchildren.

SCOTT JARVIS, 48, actor and singer, died on Feb. 26, 1990 in New York of AIDS. He made his Broadway debut in 1968 in *Here's Where I Belong* followed by *1776,* in which he sang *Mama Look Sharp.* He appeared Off-Broadway in *Leaves of Grass* and *The Harold Arlen Songbook.* No reported survivors.

REED JONES, 35, Oregon-born stage actor and choreographer died on June 19, 1989 in Sherman Oaks, CA of liver cancer. He made his Broadway debut in 1979 in *Peter Pan,* followed by appearances in *West Side Story, America, Play Me a Country Song, Cats, The Loves of Anatol* (which he also choreographed), and *As Is.* He served as choreographer on the 1983 production of *You Can't Take It With You.* He is survived by his parents and a sister.

ARTHUR KENNEDY, 75, Massachusetts-born actor on stage and screen, died of a brain tumor on Jan. 5, 1990 in Branford, CT. His 1934 Broadway debut in *Merrily We Roll Along,* was followed by *Richard II, Henry IV, Life and Death of an American, International Incident, All My Sons, Death of a Salesman* for which he received a Tony, *See the Jaguar, The Crucible, Time Limit, The Loud Red Patrick, The Price, Veronica's Room,* and *Becket* with Olivier in 1960. His wife, former actress Mary Cheffrey, died in 1975. Surviving is his daughter, actress Laurie Kennedy.

LEON LEONIDOFF, 95, Rumania-born producer of Radio City Music Hall spectacles, died July 29, 1989 in North Palm Beach, FL. From 1927 to 1932 he directed the stage shows at the Roxy Theatre before moving to Radio City and staging the show for its opening. He had presented lavish productions there for 42 years when he retired in 1974. He is survived by his widow, two daughters and one son.

JOSEPH I. LEVINE, 63, producer, attorney and business manager, died of stomach cancer on his birthday, Oct. 17, 1989 in Tarzana, CA. He produced or co-produced over 60 plays before moving to California in 1977, including the Pulitzer-Prize winner *J.B., Goldilocks, At the Drop of a Hat, Big Fish Little Fish* and *Bob and Ray—the Two and Only.* He leaves his widow and two daughters.

CLAIRE LUCE, 88, dancer and actress and Ziegfeld star, died Aug. 31, 1989 after a lengthy illness in her NYC home. After her NYC debut in *Little Jessie James* (1921), she subsequently starred in *Ziegfeld's Follies, Music Box Revue, No Foolin', Scarlet Pages, Society Girl, Gay Divorce, Vintage Wine, Love and Let Love, Follow the Sun, Of Mice and Men, Vanity Fair, Portrait in Black, With a Silk Thread, The Taming of the Shrew, Antony and Cleopatra, Much Ado about Nothing, These Are My Loves, Feast of Panthers, Mary Queen of Scots,* and *The Cave Dwellers.* She appeared both in NY and London with Fred Astaire in *The Gay Divorce.* She remained in England during WWII, and became the first U.S. actress to perform leading roles with the Shakespeare Memorial Theatre. A sister survives.

ART LUND, 75, Salt Lake City-born singer and actor, died of cancer May 31, 1990 in Holliday, UT. He was the lead singer for many years with the Benny Goodman Orchestra before he became an actor on stage, film and tv. He made his Broadway debut in *The Most Happy Fella* (1956), followed by a musical adaptation of *Of Mice and Men* (Off-Bdwy), *Destry Rides Again, Donnybrook!, Sophie,* City Center revivals of *Fiorello!,* and *Most Happy Fella, Breakfast at Tiffany's.* In addition to his widow, he leaves a son, a daughter, and a sister.

KATHLEEN MAGUIRE, 64, stage and tv actress, died of cancer on Aug. 9, 1989 in her native NYC. After her Broadway debut in *Sundown Beach* (1948), her credits include *Greatest Man Alive, Miss Isobel, The Sudden and Accidental Re-education of Horse Johnson, Ring Round the Bathtub.* She received an Obie Award for her performance in *Time of the Cuckoo.* After 20 years in tv soaps, she retired in 1984. No reported survivors.

JOHN MERIVALE, 72, Canada-born actor on stage, film and tv, died of pneumonia Feb. 2, 1990 in London. After his NYC debut in *Lorelei* (1938), he had roles in *Journey's End, Romeo and Juliet, Lady Windermere's Fan, An Inspector Calls, Anne of the Thousand Days, Day after Tomorrow, Getting Married, Venus Observed, The Deep Blue Sea, The Reluctant Debutante, Duel of Angels,* and *Ivanov.* He was twice married and divorced. No reported survivors.

GARY MERRILL, 74, Connecticut-born stage, screen and TV actor, died on March 5, 1990 in Falmouth, ME of cancer. He made his Broadway debut in 1937 in *Brother Rat,* followed by *See My Lawyer, This Is the Army, Winged Victory, Born Yesterday, At War With the Army, The World of Carl Sandburg, Step on a Crack,* and *Morning's at 7.* He appeared in many motion pictures, most notably *All About Eve,* with Bette Davis, to whom he was married for ten years. He is survived by an adopted son and daughter.

ARNOLD MOSS, 80, Brooklyn-born stage, radio, film and tv classical actor, died of lung cancer on Dec. 15, 1989 in his Manhattan home. In addition to appearing and touring with his own repertory company, The Shakespeare Festival Players, and Eva LeGallienne's Repertory Co, he appeared on Bdwy in *Fifth Column, Hold on to Your Hats, Journey to Jerusalem, Flight to the West, The Land Is Bright, The Tempest, Front Page, Twelfth Night, King Lear, Measure for Measure,* and *Follies.* Surviving are his widow, a daughter and a son.

DAVID O'BRIEN, 54, Chicago-born stage and tv actor, died in June 1989 in NYC. He had been Steve Aldrich on tv's The Doctors from 1967 to 1982. His Bdwy debut was in *Passage to India* (1962), followed by *Arturo Ui, A Time for Singing, End of the World,* and OB in *Under Milk Wood, A Month in the Country, Henry IV, The Boys in the Band, The Nice and the Nasty.* No reported survivors.

SUSAN OLIVER, 61, New York City-born stage, screen, and TV actress, died on May 10, 1990 in Woodland Hills, CA, of cancer. She made her New York debut Off-Broadway in *La Ronde* and appeared on Broadway in *Small War on Murray Hill*, "Patate" (for which she received a 1959 Theatre World Award), and *Look Back in Anger*. She is survived by three half-brothers.

LAURENCE OLIVIER, 82, one of the greatest classical actors of this century, died "peacefully in his sleep" on July 11, 1989 in his home in Steyning, West Sussex, England. His talent and virtuosity were rewarded with knighthood in 1947 and raised to life peerage in 1970, and his performances on stage, screen and television gave him artistic immortality. Although he retired from the stage in 1974 because of illness, he never stopped working. He made his Broadway debut in 1929 in *Murder on the Second Floor*, followed by *Private Lives, The Green Bay Tree, No Time for Comedy, Romeo and Juliet, Oedipus, The Critic, Uncle Vanya, Henry IV Parts I & II, Antony and Cleopatra, Caesar and Cleopatra, The Entertainer*, and *Becket*. He is survived by his third wife, actress Joan Plowright, two sons and two daughters. Interment was in Westminster Abbey in London.

ANTHONY QUAYLE, 76, England-born versatile actor and director, died of cancer Oct. 20, 1989 in his London home. He had performed on stage, film and tv, and was knighted in 1985 by Queen Elizabeth II. After his Broadway debut in *The Country Wife* (1936), he appeared in *Tambourlaine the Great, Firstborn, Galileo, Halfway up the Tree, Sleuth, Do You Turn Somersaults?*. He is survived by his second wife, former actress Dorothy Hyson, two daughters, and a son.

ERIK RHODES, 84, Oklahoma-born stage, film and tv actor, died Feb. 17, 1990 of pneumonia in Oklahoma City. His Broadway debut in 1928 in *A Most Immoral Lady* using his real name of Ernest Rhoades Sharpe, followed by *The Little Show* and *Hey Nonny Nonny!*. In 1932 he changed his name and subsequently appeared in *Gay Divorce* (also in London), *The Great Campaign, Dance Me a Song, Collector's Item, Can-Can, Shinbone Alley, Jamaica, Song of Norway, How to Make a Man, A Funny Thing Happened on the Way to the Forum, My Fair Lady* (CC), and OB in *Colette, The Sea Gull*. No immediate survivors.

TOM ROLFING, 40, Iowa-born stage, screen and TV actor and director, died on April 24, 1990 in New York of an AIDS-related illness. He appeared on Broadway in *Godspell, Equus, Working*, and *Little Johnny Jones*, and in such Off-Broadway productions as *Malone Dies*, and *On Company Time*. He is survived by his parents and five brothers and sisters.

JOHN ROOT, 85, set designer, died of heart failure on March 13, 1990 in a Doylestown, PA. hospital. He had designed sets for 53 Broadway productions, including *Harvey, Kiss the Boys Goodbye, Red Harvest*, and *George Washington Slept Here*. He also designed for television. Surviving are his widow, a daughter, and a son.

GREGORY ROZAKIS, 46, NYC-born actor and playwright, died of AIDS on Aug. 24, 1989 in Brooklyn, NY. He made his Bdwy debut in *Natural Affection* (1963), followed by *Royal Hunt of the Sun, What Did We Do Wrong?*, OB in *Pousse Cafe, Abelard and Heloise*. Two of his plays were produced Off Broadway: *Chalk Marks on a Brick Wall*, and *The Class*. His mother and a sister survive.

ALBERT SALMI, 62, New York-born stage, screen and TV actor, who played the role of Bo in the original 1955 Broadway production of *Bus Stop*, shot himself to death on April 22, 1990 at his home in Spokane, WA, after killing his wife. His other New York stage appearances include *The Scarecrow, End as a Man, The Rainmaker, The Good Woman of Setzuan, Howie, Failures, Once There Was a Russian*, and *The Price*. No reported survivors.

ISAO SATO, 40, Japanese-born stage and TV actor, died on Mar. 9, 1990 when his plane collided with another near Miami. He appeared on Broadway in the 1976 production of *Pacific Overtures*, for which he received a Tony Award nomination, and Off-Broadway in *A Bowler Hat* and several productions for the New York Shakespeare Festival. He is survived by his mother.

FRANKLYN SEALES, 37, stage, film and tv actor, died of AIDS May 21, 1990 in Brooklyn, NYC. He was born on the Carribean Island St. Vincent and studied at Juilliard with John Houseman. He worked almost steadily after graduation in regional companies as well as with the NY Shakespeare Festival, and Los Angeles legitimate theatres, including *Hamlet* at the L.A. Theatre Center. He is probably best known as Dexter Stuffins on tv's *Silver Spoons* for 4 years. Surviving are his mother, 3 sisters and 3 brothers.

ELEANOR SHALER, 89, socially prominent actress-singer in the 1920's and 1930's, died of pulmonary problems Dec. 22, 1989 in her home in Gladwyn, Pa. Among her credits are *Garrick Gaieties, The Manhatters, Murray Anderson's Almanac, How's Your Health?, The Streets of New York, The Pillars of Society, The Bride the Sun Shines On, Housewarming, Pardon My English*. She is survived by two sons and a step-daughter.

MICHAEL SHAWN, 45, stage director, choreographer and dancer, died on April 28, 1990 in New York of AIDS. He appeared as a dancer in the Broadway musicals *Golden Rainbow, Promises Promises*, and *Golden Boy*, and choreographed *Oh Brother, Onward Victoria* and worked on *Legs Diamond* prior to his death. He is survived by his wife, mother, two brothers and two sisters.

PAUL SHENAR, 53, Milwaukee-born stage, film and tv actor, died of AIDS on Oct. 11, 1989 in West Hollywood, Ca. He taught and performed at the American Conservatory Theatre in San Francisco. He made his Broadway debut in *Tiny Alice* (1969), followed by *The Three Sisters, Macbeth* (1988), and Off-Broadway productions of *Six Characters in Search of an Author, Hedda Gabler*. Surviving are his mother and three brothers.

MARTIN SHWARTZ, 66, theatre press agent for over 40 years, died of heart failure Apr. 29, 1990 in his Los Angeles home. Before moving to Los Angeles he represented more than 90 Broadway productions, including *My Fair Lady, Camelot, Funny Girl, Member of the Wedding, The Great White Hope, Kismet*, and *I Am a Camera*. A sister survives.

PAUL SHYRE, 63, New York-born playwright, stage director and actor, died on Nov. 19, 1989 of septisimia, infections linked with AIDS, at his Manhattan home. He adapted, directed and co-produced production of *Pictures in the Hallway, Drums Under the Windows, I Knock at the Door, U.S.A., The Child Buyer*, directed and co-produced *Purple Dust, Cock-a-Doodle Dandy, The Long Voyage Home* and *Creditors*, and wrote *An Evening with H. L. Mencken, A Whitman Portrait*, and others. As an actor he appeared in several of his plays and in *Absurd Person Singular* and *St. Joan*. He is survived by several cousins..

BELLA SPEWACK (Bella Cohen), 91, Transylvania-born stage and screen writer who collaborated with her husband Samuel Spewack on several Broadway plays, died on April 27, 1990 at her Manhattan home. Her Broadway credits include *Poppa, Spring Song, Clear All Wires!, Boy Meets Girl, Miss Swan Expects, Woman Bites Dog, Leave It to Me, Two Blind Mice, Kiss Me Kate, The Golden State, My Three Angels*, and *Festival*. There are no survivors; her husband died in 1971.

EARL SYDNOR, 81, stage, screen and TV actor, died on July 9, 1989 in New York of lung cancer. He appeared on Broadway in *The Trial of Dr. Beck, Two on an Island, Cabin in the Sky, The Skin of Our Teeth, Set My People Free, Shuffle Along, Sweet Bird of Youth, Detective Story, The Emperor Jones, I Never Sang for My Father*, and *First Monday in October*. He is survived by his wife and sister.

NORMA TERRIS, 87, stage and film actress, who played Magnolia in the original 1927 Broadway production of *Show Boat*, died on Nov. 15, 1989 in Lyme, CT, after a brief illness. She had her first major role in George M. Cohan's *Little Nellie Kelly*. Her other New York stage appearances include *Queen of Hearts, A Night in Paris, A Night in Spain, The Well of Romance, Smilin' Through, Radio Carnival, Be Yourself*, the 1932 revival of *Show Boat, The Climax, So Many Paths, Private Lives, Hands Across the Sea, Still Life, Fumed Oak*, and *Great Lady*. For 30 years she served on the board of directors of the Goodspeed Opera House in Conn., where she also sang occasionally. She is survived by her husband.

FRANK M. THOMAS, 100, St. Louis-born stage, screen and TV actor, died on Nov. 25, 1989. He made his Broadway debut in 1912 in *Along Came Ruth*, followed by *The House of Glass, Red Light Annie, The Girl in the Limousine, The National Anthem, Back Pay, Aloma of the South Seas, Little Spitfire, Night Hawk, Praying Curve, The House of Fear, Launcelot and Elaine, Louder Please!, The Inside Story, Carry Nation, The Tragedy of the Ages, The Gods We Make, Remember the Day, Chicken Every Sunday, The Rich Full Life, Jeb, Christopher Blake, The Hallams, End as a Man*, and *The Legend of Lizzie*. He is survived by his wife, actress Mona Burns, and son Frank Jr., also an actor.

WILLIAM TRAYLOR, 60, Missouri-born actor and drama coach, died on Sept. 23, 1989 in Los Angeles after a long illness. He made his Broadway debut in 1957 in *Nude with Violin*, followed by *Present Laughter, Show Boat* (LC), *Of Love Remembered*, and Off-Broadway's *Cry of the Raindrop*. He is survived by his mother, 2 daughters, and 2 sisters.

JIMMY VAN HEUSEN (Edward Chester Babcock), 77, Syracuse-born screen and stage composer, died on Feb. 5, 1990 at his home in Rancho Mirage, CA, after a long illness. He wrote the music for dozens of movie musicals, winning four Academy Awards for Best Song. For Broadway he wrote songs for *Swingin' the Dream, New Aquacade Revue, Nellie Bly, Carnival in Flanders, Skyscraper*, and *Walking Happy*. He is survived by his wife.

DORIS VINTON, 81, dancer, died on Sept. 10, 1989 in New York of a nervous-system disorder. She appeared in many versions of the Ziegfeld Follies during the 1920s, followed by Broadway appearances in *Artists and Models, The Manhatters, Say When, Luckee Girl, Merry Go Round*, and *Orchids Preferred*. For years she served as president of the National Ziegfeld Club, which assisted needy women in show business. No reported survivors.

L. EDMOND WESLEY, 42, stage dancer, choreographer and singer died on April 29, 1990 in St. Louis after a long illness. He appeared on Broadway in *Promises Promises, Hello Dolly!, Over There, Bubbling Brown Sugar*, and *Lena Horne: The Lady and Her Music*. He served as assistant director and choreographer for *Don't Bother Me I Can't Cope*. He is survived by his father, a sister and five brothers.

CORNEL WILDE, 74, New York born stage, screen and television actor, died on Oct. 16, 1989 of leukemia in Los Angeles. He appeared on Broadway in *Pastoral, White Plume*, and *Romeo and Juliet*, prior to beginning a long career in films in 1940, which would include an Academy Award nomination for *A Song to Remember* in 1945, and additional credits as a director and producer. He is survived by a son, daughter, and 2 stepsons.

HOPE WILLIAMS, 92, New York-born stage actress, died on May 3, 1990 of cardiac arrest at her Manhattan home. A leading Broadway star of the 1920s and '30s she had perhaps her greatest success in the 1928 Philip Barry comedy *Holiday*. Her other Broadway appearances include *What Next?, Paris Bound, Rebound, The New Yorkers, The Passing Present, Too True to Be Good, Strike Me Pink, All Good Americans, Amphitryon*, and *The Importance of Being Earnest* in 1939, after which she retired. She is survived by 2 nephews and 5 nieces.

LAVINIA WILLIAMS, 73, Philadelphia-born stage dancer, died on July 19, 1989 in Port-au-Prince, Haiti, of a heart attack. From 1940-45 she danced with the Katherine Dunham Dance Co. appearing in the chorus of *Cabin in the Sky* on Broadway, followed by appearances in *Showboat* (1946), *Finian's Rainbow*, and *My Darlin' Aida*. She is survived by 2 daughters.

ROLAND WINTERS, 84, Boston-born stage, screen and TV actor, died on Oct. 22, 1989 in Englewood, NJ, of a stroke. He appeared on Broadway in *Who Was That Lady I Saw You With?, Cook for Mr. General, The Country Girl, Calculated Risk*, and *Minnie's Boys*. He is survived by a brother.

VICTOR WOLFSON, 81 or 82, stage and TV writer, died on May 23, 1990 in a fire at his home in Wellfleet, MA. Formerly an actor he appeared on Broadway in *Street Scene* and *Counsellor-at-Law,* before turning to playwriting. His work produced on Broadway includes *Bitter Stream, Excursion, Pastoral, The Family, Pride's Crossing, American Gothic,* and *Seventh Heaven.* He served as director and producer for the 1935 production *Crime and Punishment,* directed *The Mother,* and was the author of two novels. He is survived by three sons.

WILLIAM A. WRIGHT, 46, stage actor, died on Dec. 29, 1989 in Los Angeles, CA, of AIDS. He appeared on Broadway in *Equus* and *The Merchant of Venice* (at Lincoln Center), and was a member of John Houseman's Acting Co. He is survived by his longtime companion Joe Cappelli, his mother and sister.

INDEX

A Few Good Men, 19
A'Hearn, Patrick, 108, 185
Aaron, Hank, 39
Aaron, Jack, 74, 185
Abady, Josephine R., 132
Abaldo, Joseph, 35
Abar, James, 159
Abarbanel, Noah, 175
Abatemarco, Tony, 90, 185
Abbott, Charles, 169, 171
Abbott, George, 101, 135, 167
Abbott, Kathryn, 48
Abbott, Lisa, 125
Abdessalam, Conja, 133
Abdulov, Alexander, 61
Abel, Marc, 68
Abel, Marybeth, 45
Abel, Timothy, 45, 46, 110
Abele, Jim, 132, 157
Aberbach, Jean, 50
Aberbach, Julian, 50
Aberdeen, Robert, 134
Aberger, Tom, 57, 83
Abosada, Kory, 161
Abraham, Christine, 70
Abrahao, Roberto, 27
Abramov, Fyodor, 153
Abrams, Anne, 110, 111
Abramsohn, Roy Michael, 174
Abrash, Victoria, 65
Abreu, Jorge Luis, 96
Abronski, Linda, 152
Abry, Fluffy, 93
Abs, Marina, 54
Absent Friends, 151
Abuba, Ernest, 37, 92, 185
Acabbo, Andrew, 28
Accardo, Jon R., 152
Accomplice, 34, 180
Accurso, Aron, 135
Aching Heart of Samuel Kleinerman, The, 54
Achom, John, 131
Ackerman, Loni, 40, 185
Ackerman, Robert Allan, 131
Ackermann-Blount, Joan, 120
Acosta, Elizabeth, 141
Act/A Contemporary Theatre, 118
Acting Company, The, 144, 173
Actman, John, 103
Actors Theatre of Louisville, 120
Adam and the Experts, 59
Adam, Ben, 56
Adamian, Daniel, 68
Adamian, Leo, 52
Adams, April, 155
Adams, Becky Lynn, 154
Adams, Betsy, 74, 136
Adams, Brooke, 42, 185
Adams, Jane, 160
Adams, Jonathan, 126
Adams, Mary Kay, 53
Adams, Robert, 103
Adams, Tamara, 167
Adams, Wayne, 145
Adamson, David, 56, 62, 185
Adamson, Ellen, 50
Aday, Gary, 127
Addinsell, Richard, 146
Addison, Michael, 171
Adios, Tropicana, 88
Adkins, David, 132
Adler, Jay, 15
Adler, Joanna, 62
Adler, Nancy Ann, 147
Adney, K. Aurora, 103
Adshead, Nina L., 59
Adshead, Patricia, 59, 156
Adult Fiction, 136
Adventures of Huckleberry Finn, 135
Adventures of Marco Polo, The, 119
Adzima, Nanzi, 165
Aeby, Kim, 170
Affetto, Lewis A., 138
*Afternoons at the Playhouse—*Four One Act Plays, 127
Agafonnikov, Igor, 54
Agee, Joel, 129
Agent Yellow, 167
Agnitsch, Jeffrey, 135
Aguilar, Rafael, 133
Ahearn, Daniel, 95, 142, 185
Ahrens, Lynn, 94, 145
Ahromheim, Albert, 63
Aibel, Douglas, 99
Aidem, Betsy, 122, 142, 185
Aiello, Danny, 39, 182
Ailey, Alvin, 229
Ain't Misbehavin', 127
Ain't Nobody Dead, 167
Ainsley, Paul, 110
Ainslie, Scott, 119
Airaldi, Remo, 122
Akalaitis, JoAnne, 141, 138
Akerlind, Christopher, 32, 88, 130, 144, 170
Akers, Karen, 18, 185
Akey, William, 148
Akimova, Natalya, 153
Akin, Ann Marie, 119
Akin, Charlotte, 167
Akins, Jimmy-John, 125
Akman, Andrew, 176
Ako, 154
Akune, Shuko, 168
Al-Bilali, Judyie, 134
Al-Rouf, Khaliq Abdul, 134
Alabado, Humberto, 66
Alabama Shakespeare Festival, 171
Alasa, Michael, 66, 88
Alban, Sherry, 137
Albanian Softshoe, 161
Albano, John, 73
Albee, Edward, 130, 131
Albers, Keith, 152
Albers, Kenneth, 152
Albert, Stephen J., 32, 131
Alberti, Bruno, 76
Albrecht, Beth, 160
Albrecht, J. Grant, 142
Albright, Jennifer Selby, 124
Alchourron, Rodolfo, 11
Alder, Jac, 167
Alderfer, Franz C., 141, 154
Alderfer, Julie, 97
Aldous, Brian, 65
Aldredge, Theoni V., 20, 41, 144
Aldrich, Janet, 185
Aldrin, "Buzz", Col., 39
Aleichem, Sholom, 106
Alekseyenko, Viktor, 26
Aleksidze, Giorgi, 69
Alemany, Joshua, 94
Alessan, Henry, 6
Alessandrini, Gerard, 52, 62
Alexander, Adinah, 84, 139
Alexander, C. Renee, 143
Alexander, Deborah, 52
Alexander, George, 124
Alexander, Jace, 77, 97, 185
Alexander, Jackie, 72
Alexander, Jane, 39, 131
Alexander, Jason, 34, 43, 185
Alexander, Lane Edwin, 148
Alexander, Leslie, 167
Alexander, Robert, 72
Alexander, Terry, 131
Alexandrov Red Army Song and Dance Ensemble, The, 54
Alexis, Connie L., 76
Alexis, Kim, 39
Alfano, Jorge, 11
Alfiorova, Irena, 61
Algarin, Frank, 71
Ali, Kenshaka, 95
Ali, Muhammad, 39
Ali, Tatyana, 84
All God's Dangers, 57, 171
All My Sons, 174
All That Fall, 68
All's Well That Ends Well, 129
Allard, Janet, 94
Allaway, Keith, 129
Allegrucci, Scott, 90
Allen, B. J., 102
Allen, Gregory Lamont, 52
Allen, Hank, 128
Allen, Jay Presson, 23, 122
Allen, Joan, 42, 185
Allen, Lewis, 19, 23, 122
Allen, Malcolm, 55
Allen, Penny, 60, 73
Allen, Phillip R., 131
Allen, Phillip, 74
Allen, Priscilla, 161
Allen, Ricky, 124
Allen, Tyress, 125
Allen-Jones, Augusta, 51
Aller, John, 40
Allera, Cheryl Z., 72
Allessan, Henry, 185
Allete, Joey, 167
Alley, David Brian, 131
Allgood, Anne, 141
Alliance Theatre Company, 119
Alliger, Richard, 169
Allinson, Michael, 185
Allison, George A., 56, 62
Allison, Mary Ellen, 123
Allison, Patti, 9, 185
Allore, Jonathan, 170
Allport, Christopher, 131
Allyn, Sari, 51
Alm, Geoffrey, 118
Almberg, John, 139
Almost Like Being in Love: The Magic of Alan Jay Lerner, 121
Almquist, Gregg, 97, 185
Almy, Brooks, 35, 185
Alpaugh, Robert, 126
Alper, Jonathan, 83
Alper, Steven M., 61, 137
Alpiar, Haley, 70
Alsaker, Timian, 147
Alston, Chiron, 172
Alston, Peggy, 95
Alston, Stephanie, 134
Altay, Rengin, 138
Altieri, Marcia, 91
Altman, Bruce, 170
Altman, Peter, 143
Altmeyer, Timothy, 158
Alvarez, Lynne, 161
Alyson, Eydie, 110
Amadeus, 151
Amar, 148
Amarel, David, 57
Amaro, Richard, 11, 43
Ambassador, The, 56
Ambrose, Joe, 97
Ambrosone, John, 122, 133
Amendola, Dana F. X., 23
Amendola, Tony, 131
American Bagpipes, 59
American Conservatory Theatre, 121
American Jewish Theatre, 74
American Place Theatre, 75
American Plan, The, 83
American Repertory Theatre, 122
American Stage Company, 123
Amerling, Victor, 46
Ames, Marcia Ann, 165
Ames, Paul V., 70
Amirante, Robert, 40
Amos, John, 59, 71, 87, 123, 185
Amos, Patrick, 167
Amsden, Jeffrey, 113
Amster, Peter, 29, 138
Amtzis, Alan, 50
Anania, Michael, 35, 154
Anarchestra, 88
Anastasio, Diane, 114
Anastos, Peter, 94, 103
And a Nightengale Sang, 92, 153
And Baby Makes Seven, 147
And Further Mo', 134
And One Bell Shattered, 94
And The Soul Shall Dance, 92
Andersen, Tobias, 158
Anderson, Arthur, 73
Anderson, Carole Jean, 118
Anderson, Christine, 185
Anderson, Cletus, 157
Anderson, Cynthia, 147
Anderson, D. C., 113
Anderson, Edmund, 84
Anderson, Elman R., 169
Anderson, Eric Ray, 118, 166
Anderson, Fred, 169
Anderson, Holly, 69
Anderson, Jane, 120, 121
Anderson, Joel, 185
Anderson, Keith, 15
Anderson, Kevin, 9, 185
Anderson, Lynn, 63
Anderson, Nels, 125
Anderson, Sarah Pia, 172
Anderson, Scott T., 38
Anderson, Stanley, 124
Anderson, Stephen Lee, 135
Anderson, Steven J., 177
Anderson, Sue, 40
Anderson, Thomas, 143
Anderson, Tim, 105
Anderson, Timothy, 113
Andersson, Benny, 103, 148
Andino, Eddie, 96
Andonyadis, Nephelie, 50, 170
Andre, Marion, 54
Andreas, Christine, 143, 144
Andreassi, James, 159
Andres, Barbara, 135, 154
Andrews, Bert, 52
Andrews, Brian, 40
Andrews, Dwight D., 32, 129, 130, 136, 144
Andrews, George Lee, 46, 185
Andrews, Jennifer Lee, 18
Andrews, Judy, 159
Andrews, Mark S., 45
Andrews, Meghan, 29
Andrews, Mitch, 119
Andrews, Nancy, 229
Andreyko, Helena, 50, 185, 189
Andrieux, Philipe, 53
Andrus, Arch, 173
Andrus, Dee, 136
Angel Street, 128
Angela, June, 92, 186
Angela, Sharon, 48
Anglim, Philip, 162
Animal Fair, 135
Animal Farm, 132, 135
Animal Nation, 161
Ankeny, Mark, 99, 159, 186, 189
Ann-Lewis, Victoria, 147
Anna Christie, 146
Anna and the King of Siam, 108
Annenberg, Eve, 65
Annie 2, 143, 144
Annie Get Your Gun, 119
Annis, Eric, 124
Antalosky, Charles, 159
Antaramian, Jacqueline, 135
Anthony, James, 127, 150
Anthony, Joe, 55, 69
Anthony, Peter, 114
Anthony, Richard, 160
Antoinette Perry (Tony) Award Productions, 184
Anton Himself, 120
Anton, William, 153
Antoniou, Elkin, 113
Antony and Cleopatra, 177
Anything Goes, 94
Anzalone, Frank, 169
Anzalone, Johnny, 40
Apeksemova, Irina, 88
Apfel, Mimi, 94
Apocalyptic Butterflies, 50, 51
Apolloni, Mark, 152
Appel, Libby, 174
Appel, Peter, 87
Appel, Susan, 126
Appell, Don, 229
Appelt, Joseph, 151
Applebaum, Louis, 176
Aprahamian, Steven, 64
Aquilina, Corinne, 136
Aquino, Amy, 42, 186, 189
Aquino, Kelly, 157
Arabian, Michael, 131
Aran, 65
Aranas, Raul, 92
Aranha, Ray, 135
Aranson, Jack, 120, 143
Aravena, Michelle, 27
Arcaro, Eddie, 39
Arcaro, Robert, 51, 63, 186
Arcenas, Loy, 36, 76, 77, 91, 94, 124, 134, 142
Archuleta, Oscar, 173
Ard, Ken, 11, 103
Arditti, Paul, 9, 25
Are You Lonesome Tonight?, 161
Arena Stage, 124
Arenberg, Lee "Beef", 88
Argast, Jeane, 30
Ari, Bob, 164, 168, 186, 173
Ariano, 96
Arias, Richard, 131
Arif, N. Richard, 87
Arino, Alan, 43
Aristocrats, 94, 69
Arizona Theatre Company, 126
Arkansas Repertory Theatre, 125
Arlen, Steeve, 133
Arlt, Lewis, 9, 186, 189
Arluck, Neal, 71
Armento, Tony, 78
Armitage, Calvin Lennon, 29, 186
Arms and the Man, 94
Armstrong, Alan, 171
Armstrong, April Beth, 146
Armstrong, April, 141
Armstrong, Christopher, 115, 131
Armstrong, Karen, 13, 94
Armstrong, Reed, 110
Armstrong, Valorie, 130
Armus, Sidney, 82, 186
Arnaz, Desi, Jr., 133
Arndt, Denis, 124
Arnold, Jeanne, 150
Arnold, Jennifer, 52
Arnold, John Sterling, 136, 150
Arnold, Mark, 119, 128
Arnold, Michael, 40, 74, 105
Arnold, Stephen, 111, 112
Arnone, John, 63, 141, 142
Arons, Elly, 154
Arons, Ellyn, 144
Aronson, Boris, 43, 106
Aronson, Frances, 75, 77, 94, 141, 172
Aronson, Henry, 17, 135, 139
Aronstein, Martin, 34, 130
Arrabal, Miguel, 11, 69
Arrick, Larry, 132
Arrigo, Nancy, 57, 186, 189
Arrott, H. G., 73
Arsenault, Brian, 89
Art of Success, The, 83
Art-Williams, Samm, 65
Artemieva, Ludmilla, 61
Arthur, Beatrice, 39
Arthur, Helen-Jean, 124
Arthur, Loyce, 54
Arthurs, Madeleine, 76
Artist Descending a Staircase, 22
Artistic Direction, The, 63
Arundale, Susan, 164, 165
As You Like It, 91, 120, 173
AsSwaudi, Tajj, 75
Asbury, Claudia, 144
Asbury, Cleve, 43, 144
Aschinger, Brian, 169
Aschner, Michael, 63
Asciolla, Steve, 156
Ash, Jeffrey, 49
Ashe, Jennifer, 95
Ashe-Croft, Terry, 68
Ashley, Christopher, 63, 100
Ashley, Elizabeth, 94, 186
Ashley, Mary Ellen, 123, 159
Ashwell, Ariel, 61
Askin, Peter, 55
Asner, Edward, 39, 186
Asolo Theatre Company, 126
Aspects of Love, 31, 180
Asquith, Ward, 133
Asters, Jonica, 119
Astrachan, Joshua, 50
Astredo, Humbert Allen, 143, 145, 165
Aswegan, Jared, 126
At Risk, 167
Aten, Renee, 145
Atha, Steve, 24
Athayde, Roberto, 26
Athens, Jim, 101
Atherlay, John, 127
Atkins, Eileen, 83, 186
Atkinson, Clinton J., 145
Atkinson, Jayne, 83, 186
Atkinson, Linda, 60
Atlas, Ravil, 110
Atlee, Barbara, 52
Atlee, Howard, 51, 52, 59, 64, 72, 95
Attile, Larry, 156
Attle, John C., 229
Auberjonois, Rene, 24, 186
Aubert, Florence, 82
Audience, 66
Aufiery, Joe, 169
Augeson, Roxanna, 147
August Snow, Night Dance, Better Days, 132
Augustine, John, 186, 189
Aulgur, Ronald J., 125
Aulino, Tom, 89, 138
Aulisi, Joseph G., 22, 43, 130, 153
Aunts, The, 55
Aural Fixation, 44, 67, 78, 82, 98, 100
Austin, Lee J., 169
Austin, Lyn, 61
Austin, Robert Winn, 133, 148
Austin, Robert, 157
Avan, 51, 59
Avari, Erick, 138, 141
Avedisian, Paul, 45
Averill, Timothy, 164, 165
Avery, Lovell M., Jr., 164
Avery, Patricia, 13
Avery, Suzanne, 152
Averyt, Bennet, 156
Avian, Bob, 41
Avidon, Nelson, 78, 186, 189
Avner, Jon, 134, 186
Avni, Ran, 80
Away Alone, 60
Axelrod, Dana, 131
Ayckbourn, Alan, 118, 127, 149, 151, 162, 167, 169
Ayers, Christopher, 112
Aylesworth, John, 105
Aylward, John, 160
Aylward, Peter, 138, 140
Aylward, Tony, 143
Ayvazian, Leslie, 132
Azar, Rick, 57
Azenberg, Emanuel, 22, 130
Azzara, Candice, 153
Azzard, Dale, 105
B. Beaver Animation, The, 91
Baar-Bittman, Kate, 170
Baba Goya, 98
Babatunde, Akin, 167
Babatunde, Obba, 133
Babbish, Lenny, 50
Babbitt, Rob, 18
Babcock, Craig, 173
Babcock, John, 108, 137
Babe, Thomas, 63, 94
Babel on Babylon, 51
Babes in Arms, 50
Babich, Debra, 173
Babin, Michael, 64, 109
Bach, Del-Bourree, 68
Bachelor Flats, 65
Bachman, Susan, 133, 148
Bacino, Jan, 152
Bacino, Miki, 152
Back, Maribeth, 122
Backes, Roy W., 97
Backlund, Ulla, 66
Backstrom, Kevin, 15
Backus, Jim, 229
Backus, Karl, 174
Backus, Richard, 186
Bacon, Bruce, 151
Bacon, Jenny, 138
Bacon, Kevin, 186
Bad Habits, 83
Bad Penny, 51
Badrak, James S., 55, 59
Baehr, Sonya, 61
Baer, Athena, 79
Baer, Richard, 133
Baez, Michael, 71
Baez, Rafael, 89, 94, 186
Bagden, Ron, 56
Baggesen, Bonnie J., 158
Baggot, Kate, 60
Bagneris, Vernel, 70, 134, 186
Bagwell, Marsha, 154
Bailey, Adrian, 17, 66, 186
Bailey, Alan, 71, 149
Bailey, Dennis, 120
Bailey, Kevin, 169
Bailey, Mary K, 131
Bailey, Michele, 127
Bailey, Victoria, 83
Bain, Reginald F., 127
Baird, Campbell, 59, 97
Baird, Chuck, 144
Baird, Danny, 166
Baird, David, 61
Baird, Jane Todd, 31
Baird, Peter, 78
Baitz, Jon Robin, 129, 146, 160
Baker, Allan, 131
Baker, Becky Ann, 124
Baker, Bertilla, 109, 139
Baker, Cliff Fannin, 125
Baker, David, 165
Baker, Douglas C., 23, 36
Baker, Dylan, 83, 186
Baker, Jim, 135
Baker, Joe, 84
Baker, Joseph, 139
Baker, Keith Alan, 163
Baker, Mark Linn, 39
Baker, Michael Conway, 176
Baker, Susan, 165
Baker, Word, 47
Balaban, Bob, 81, 144, 186
Balcony, The, 78
Bald Soprano, The, 122
Baldan, Bernard, 161
Baldassare, Jim, 7
Baldasso, Carl, 96
Baldridge, Charlene, 153
Baldwin, Alec, 76, 186
Baldwin, James, 114
Baldwin, Philip, 145
Balfour, Katherine, 229
Balgord, Linda, 148
Balkan, Glenda, 113
Ball, Emily, 164
Ball, Michael, 31, 186
Ball, Stephen, 175
Ball, Wilber, 50
Ballantyne, Wayne, 166, 171
Ballard, Laurence, 118
Balletta, Dominick, 92
Ballinger, June, 186, 189
Balmont, Alexandr, 39
Balmont, Nina, 39
Balsam, Talia, 153
Baltazar, Mark, 81
Bamman, Gerry, 72, 142, 186
Bancroft, Anne, 131
Bandiera, Nancy, 167
Banes, Lisa, 186
Bang-Hansen, Kjetil, 149
Bank, Marji, 138
Banks, Carl, 39

Banks, Jackie, 138
Bankston, Arnold, III, 229
Bannon, Anne Louise, 177
Baptist, Sarah, 156
Baraka, Amiri, 121, 131
Baran, Edward, 54, 135, 186
Baranski, Christine, 73, 138, 186
Barbeau, Francois, 51
Barbee, David, 145
Barber, Debi Frye, 73
Barber, Diane, 167
Barber, Mary Lou, 68
Barber, Matt, 141
Barbour, Thomas, 129, 186, 189
Barcan, Nan, 68
Barcellona, Mary Anne, 113
Barclay, William, 99, 137, 139
Barcone, Eugene, 121
Barefield, Barbara, 136
Bargains, 125
Barilla, John J., 62
Barkan, Mark, 53
Barker, Gary, 46, 110
Barker, Pat, 54
Barlow, Allan Michael, 160
Barlow, John, 44, 67, 108
Barlow, Roxane, 102
Barnes, Bill, 68
Barnes, Ethel Beatty, 84
Barnes, Gregg, 84, 100, 154
Barnes, Lloyd W. L., Jr., 167
Barnes, Peter, 118
Barnes, Robert, 92
Barnes, Scott, 169
Barnes, William Joseph, 168
Barneson, Jeff, 48
Barnett, Bob, 136
Barnett, Jeff, 110
Barnett, Patricia, 158
Barnette, M. Neema, 83
Barney, Tina, 53
Baron, Christy, 45, 110
Baron, Courtney, 167
Baron, Evalyn, 45, 139, 186, 189
Baron, Sheldon, 47
Barone, Anita, 150
Barr, Shannon, 6, 44, 59
Barr, Sharon, 60
Barranger, Milly S., 158
Barre, Gabriel, 97, 123, 139, 186
Barreca, Christopher H., 97, 129, 141, 162
Barrero, Oliver, 135
Barrett, Brent, 18, 57, 186, 189
Barrett, James Lee, 6
Barrett, Joe, 123
Barrett, Laurinda, 126, 170, 186, 189
Barrett, Mace, 20
Barrett, Vikki J., 138
Barricelli, Marco, 174
Barrie, Barbara, 83, 186, 189
Barrie, James M., 43, 112
Barrie, Jody Keith, 17
Barrier, Donna, 147
Barrile, Anthony, 142, 143
Barrish, Seth, 62, 64, 70
Barriskill, Michael, 40
Barron, David, 8, 186
Barron, Rob, 170
Barrow, Bernie, 54, 55
Barry, B. H., 11, 24, 58, 62, 87, 90, 91
Barry, Daniel, 118
Barry, Diane, 68
Barry, Ellen, 173
Barry, Paul, 173
Barry, Raymond J., 147
Barry, Shannon, 173
Barsha, Debra, 48
Barsness, Eric, 69
Bart, Roger, 89, 186, 189
Bartenieff, George, 186
Barter Theatre, 127
Bartlett, Bridget, 128
Bartlett, Charles, 170
Bartlett, D'Jamin, 182
Bartlett, Neil, 138
Bartlett, Peter, 100, 141, 186
Bartlett, Robin, 186, 189
Bartley, Robert, 169
Barton, Alexander, 139
Barton, Fred, 135
Barton, John, 59
Barton, Scott, 101
Barton, Steve, 46, 186
Barton, Todd, 135, 172, 174
Bartosik, Ed, 96
Barzee, Anastasia, 167
Barzon, Jeffrey, 77
Basch, Peter, 63
Basco, Cindy, 171
Baskin, Lyle, 133
Baskous, Christian, 170
Baslow, Ron, 128
Basoli, Anna, 74
Basom, Jonas, 118
Bass, Ann, 170
Bass, Tracey M., 139
Bassham, Cynthia, 130
Bassin, Joel, 62
Batchelder, W. Allen, 135
Bateman, Bill, 112
Bateman, Justine, 97, 186
Bates, Jerome Preston, 123, 170
Bates, Kathy, 144
Batho, Kristofer, 61
Batman, Elena Jeanne, 46
Batt, Bryan, 101, 187, 189
Battis, Emery, 172
Battle, Edwin, 84
Battle, Hinton, 144
Bauer, Beaver, 121
Bauer, Chris, 124
Bauer, Daniel Y., 149
Bauer, Kathryn, 144
Bauer, Lori Lynn, 108
Bauer, Richard, 124, 170
Bauerlein, Lori Lynn, 152
Bauerlein, Pat, 152
Bauling, Daniel J., 152
Bauling, Randy, 152
Baum, Joanne, 187, 189
Baum, Kathleen, 165
Baum, Vicki, 18
Bauman, John Elijah, 135
Bavier, Frances, 229
Baxter, Rebecca, 15, 137
Baxter, Robin, 163
Baxter, Rosemary, 167
Baxter-Birney, Meredith, 111
Bayer, Ethel, 63
Bayer, Frank, 131
Bayer, Peggy, 139, 154
Bayes, Christopher, 141
Bayes, Sammy Dallas, 106
Bayless, Beth, 161
Bayliss, John, 150
Bays, Deborah, 64
Bazan, Iris, 66
Bazarini, Ronald, 126
Bazewicz, James A., 173
Bazin, Tuka, 124
Beach, Gary, 110
Beacock, Brian, 110
Beadles, Leslie-Noriko, 113
Beaird, David, 147
Beaird, John, 167
Beal, Harrison, 43
Bealer, Mable, 125
Beamish, Stephen, 105
Bean, Douglas Bryan, 168
Bean, Neville, 59, 71, 149, 187, 189
Beard, Mark, 55, 59, 69
Beard, Robert, 176
Bearden, Jim, 6, 187, 189
Beasly, Larry Darnell, 152
Beattie, Kurt, 118, 160
Beatty, Bruce, 119
Beatty, John Lee, 38, 76, 81, 83, 87, 111, 144, 145, 146, 160
Beatty, Ned, 111
Beatty, Robert, Jr., 170
Beauchamp, Geoffrey, 150
Beauchamp, Steve, 169
Beauty Marks, 54, 55
Beauty Shop, 67
Beaver, Kathy, 156
Bechtel, Roger, 77
Beck, Jennifer Rae, 106
Beck, Judy, 169
Becker, Gerry, 138
Becker, Victor, 119, 164, 165
Beckett, Samuel, 66, 68, 79, 131, 153, 168, 173, 229
Beckett: Short Works, 129
Beckler, Steven, 44, 82
Beckman, Claire, 91, 187, 189
Beckos, Barbara, 165
Beckwith, Spencer, 144
Beckwith, William, 25
Becvar, William, 166
Bedford, Brian, 176
Bedford-Lloyd, John, 187, 189
Bednarczyk, Pat, 145
Beebe, Steve, 139
Beechman, Laurie, 45, 169, 187
Beef and Boards Dinner Theatre, 127
Beer, Arthur J., 150
Beers, Francine, 187, 189
Beery, Leigh, 99, 187
Before Dawn, 54
Begley, Ed, Jr., 111
Behrman, S. N., 154
Bekhterev, Sergei, 153
Bekins, Richard, 119
Belack, Doris, 38, 187
Belden, Mark, 131
Belden, Ursula, 67
Belfer, Glenn, 110
Belgrader, Andrei, 122, 170
Belknap, Allen R., 136
Bell, Barbara A., 93, 155
Bell, David H., 35, 133, 148, 153
Bell, Gail, 53
Bell, George Anthony, 126
Bell, Glynis, 159
Bell, Jake, 110, 114
Bell, Jan, 55, 59
Bell, Kristen, 153
Bell, Monica, 171
Bell, Neal, 135
Bellamy, Ned "Corn Dancer", 88
Bellamy, Terry, 141
Bellerose, Mary, 166
Belling, Edward, 74
Bellucci, John, 171
Belmonte, Vicki, 187
Belousov, Vladimir, 61
Belsky, Igor, 39
Belusar, Shelley, 23
Belzer, Rick, 102, 117
Ben-Ari, Neal, 25, 140, 187
Bench, The, 73
Bender, David M., 157
Bender, Jeff, 57, 187, 189
Benedict, Gail, 120
Benedict, Lisa, 158
Benedict, Paul, 83
Benefactors, 135
Benet, Stephen Vincent, 137
Bengele, Rosemary E., 125
Benham, Dorothy, 43, 187, 189
Benjamin, Karen, 113
Benjamin, P. J., 135
Benjamin, Randy, 91
Benjamin, Shawn, 52
Benkahala, Christina, 124
Benkahala, Shawn, 124
Benner, Brett, 157
Bennet, Joan, 183
Bennett, Craig, 110
Bennett, Frank, 128
Bennett, Georgia, 66
Bennett, Jeanne, 110
Bennett, Keith Robert, 139
Bennett, Lynette, 57, 187
Bennett, Mark, 51, 69, 83, 91, 142
Bennett, Matthew Eaton, 47
Bennett, Michael, 41
Bennett, Patricia, 170
Bennett, Rhona, 138
Bennett, Robert Russell, 27, 70
Bennett, Robert, 15
Bennyhoff, Eric, 169
Benson, Cindy, 40, 187
Benson, Esther, 167
Benson, Martin, 162
Benson, Mary, 150, 161
Benson, Sally, 15
Benson, Susan, 176
Benson, Wade, 119
Benstar, Bonnie, 14
Bensussen, Melia, 65, 73, 88, 96
Bent, Hannah, 142
Bentley, Mary Denise, 117
Benvictor, Paul, 160
Benzali, Daniel, 83
Bercu, Barbara, 60, 70
Berde, Gabriel, 55
Berdes, Madelyn, 113
Beresford, Teddy, 149
Berezin, Tanya, 76
Berg, Richard, 17
Berg, Tracey, 84
Bergell, Charles, 114
Bergen, Polly, 12, 187
Berger, Sidney, 173
Bergeret, Albert, 68
Berghof, Herbert, 187
Berglass, Marilyn, 52
Bergman, Alan, 39
Bergman, Marilyn, 39
Bergstein, David, 56, 65, 89, 94
Berigan, Charles, 129
Berke, Michelle, 60
Berkeley Shakespeare Festival, 171
Berkey, Daniel, 87, 90
Berky, Bob, 87
Berl, Ennalls, 147
Berlin to Broadway with Kurt Weill, 127
Berlin, Irving, 43, 119, 229
Berlin, Jeannie, 97
Berlin, Pamela, 38, 144
Berlind, Roger, 22, 24, 30, 73
Berman, David, 82, 187
Berman, Heather, 139
Berman, Irene B., 72
Bermingham, Gigi, 87
Bernardi, James, 20
Bernardo, Keith, 41
Bernau, Christopher, 229
Berney, Brig, 18, 69
Bernheim, Shirl, 157
Bernkoff, Mark, 6
Bernstein, Alisa Beth, 124
Bernstein, Jesse, 90
Bernstein, Joel, 93
Bernstein, Leonard, 43, 56, 141
Bernstein, Mark D., 159
Bernstein, Susan, 57, 187
Berquist, Guy, 124
Berresse, Michael, 106
Berridge, Elizabeth, 60, 187
Berry, Brenda, 161
Berry, Denny, 46, 113
Berry, Gabriel, 73, 77, 91, 138
Berry, Gregory Phillip, 51
Berry, James, 177
Berry, Patricia, 17, 49
Bertenshaw, Kelly, 141
Bertish, Suzanne, 83, 187
Bertone, Maxine Kraswoski, 124
Bertrand, Jacqueline, 94, 187
Berutti, Karin, 148
Beside Herself, 76
Bessette, Mimi, 151, 160
Bessoir, Robert, 68, 74
Best Friends, 53
Best of Burlesque, The, 127
Best of Seima Hazouri & Pals, The, 50
Besterman, Doug, 137, 164
Bestock, Shana, 118
Bethel, Pepsi, 70, 134
Bethel, Shari, 125
Better Days, 132
Bettis, Randy, 102
Beuf, Peter Gallatin, 169
Bevan, Alison, 187
Beverley, Trazana, 86, 124, 187
Beyond Belief, 69
Beyond Therapy, 164
Biagi, Michael D., 108
Bianca, Robert, 56
Bianco, Rich, 53
Bibb, Teri, 114, 139, 154
Bicardo, Nicholas, 121
Bicat, Nick, 13
Bichler, Randy, 133, 148
Bickell, Ross, 97, 143, 165, 187
Bieber, Cathy, 145
Biederman, Richard, 48
Biegler, Gloria, 168
Bielecki, Bob, 61
Big Hotel, 54, 55
Bigelow, Dennis, 174
Biggs, Karen, 175
Biggs, Robert, 175
Biggs, Roxann, 41
Biglin, Tom, 173
Bihm, Jerry, 62
Bilder, Maggie, 110
Bilderback, Walter, 138
Biles, Kevin, 117
Bill, Mary, 140
Billig, Etel, 145
Billig, Robert, 45
Billig, Steve S., 145
Billings, Casey, 168
Billings, Glenn, 138
Billingsley, Russ, 62
Billington, Ken, 12, 15, 23, 30, 58, 103, 106, 122, 144
Binder, Jay, 15, 43, 130
Binkley, Howell, 122
Binkley, Lane, 145
Binks, Andrew, 176
Binotto, Paul, 117
Biondi, Michael, 154
Birch, Michael, 97
Birch, Patricia, 50
Bird, Jacy, 124
Bird, Thomas, 56, 62
Birdsall, Jim, 151
Birk, Raye, 131
Birkelund, Olivia, 77, 164, 187
Birkenhead, Peter, 132, 136
Birkett, Jeremiah, 29
Birmingham, Laurie, 171
Birn, David, 60
Birnbaum, Nathan, 131, 162
Birney, Reed, 67, 99, 187
Birthday Party, The, 77
Bishins, David, 77
Bishoff, Joel, 27, 111
Bishop, Andre, 94
Bishop, Conrad, 135, 169
Bishop, David, 141
Bishop, John Martin, 173
Bishop, John, 76
Bishop, Kelly, 82, 140, 187
Bishop, Mark, 136
Bishop, T. Jane, 119
Bissonnette, Mark J., 120
Bitterman, Shem, 131, 162
Bittner, Jason, 149
Bittrich, Stephen, 65
Bizub, Jeffrey, 124
Bjornson, Maria, 31, 46
Blachly, Jamie, 61
Black 47, 60
Black Eagles, 134
Black Hat Karma, 53
Black Market, 95
Black Medea, 67
Black, Bill, 177
Black, Brent, 169
Black, David Horton, 134
Black, Don, 31
Black, Jack "Flesh", 88
Black, James, 173
Black, Judith, 140
Black, Malcolm, 169
Black, Rachel, 59
Black, William Electric, 66
Black-Eyed Susan, 62
Blackful, Karen, 145
Blackman, Harry, 59
Blackman, Robert, 121
Blackman, Sean, 70
Blackmer, Clare, 56
Blackwell, Charles, 43
Blackwell-Cook, Deborah, 86
Bladen, Sara, 65
Blair, Isla, 130
Blair, Jeffrey, 157
Blair, Kevin, 15
Blair, Pamela, 19, 187
Blair, Steven Douglas, 114
Blaisdell, Geoffrey, 110
Blaisdell, Nesbitt, 28, 187
Blake, Curtis, 120
Blake, Mervyn, 176
Blake, Paul, 121
Blake, Richard H., 17, 27
Blake, Robin, 6
Blakemore, Michael, 24, 30
Blakeslee, Suzanne, 62
Blakesley, Weston, 52, 61
Blanco, Rafael V., 133
Bland, John David, 161
Blane, Ralph, 15
Blaney, Robert, 155
Blank, Larry, 113
Blankenship, Hal, 154
Blanks, Harvy, 135
Blanks, Scott, 172
Blase, Linda, 167
Blaser, Cathy B., 10
Blau, Frances, 80
Blazer, Judith, 35, 50, 187
Bleasdale, Alan, 161
Blendick, James, 176
Blessing, Lee, 118, 119, 159, 165
Blitch, Robin, 119
Blithe Spirit, 127
Bloch, Ivan, 14
Bloch, Scotty, 49
Bloch, Sonny, 14
Bloch, Susan, 54
Block, Giles, 25
Block, Jean, 15
Block, Larry, 145, 164
Blodgette, Kristin, 114
Blommaert, Susan, 164
Blood Relations, 136
Bloodgood, William, 174
Bloom, Louise, 124
Bloom, Michael, 80, 122
Bloom, Sandra M., 96, 155
Bloom, Tom, 58
Bloomrosen, J., 67
Blossom, Roberts, 122
Blue, Adrian, 144
Blue, Elena, 144
Blue, Pete, 62, 74
Blue, Peter Scarborough, 172
Blum, Joel, 105
Blumenfeld, Robert, 66, 187
Blumenkrantz, Jeff, 16, 84, 187
Blumenthal, Hilarie, 73
Bly, Mark, 160
Bobb-Semple, Ron, 159
Bobbie, Walter, 63, 187
Bobby Gould in Hell, 81
Bobby, Anne, 78, 187
Bobo's Birthday, 75
Bobrusky, Pavel M., 135
Bock, Jerry, 43, 74, 106, 127
Bockhorn, Craig, 36, 76
Boddy, Claudia, 138
Bodge, James, 143
Bodle, Jane, 144, 187
Bodriguian, Margaret, 71
Body Builder's Book of Love, The, 69
Boesche, John, 172
Boese, Jody, 76
Boesman and Lena, 143, 168
Bogaev, Paul, 31, 103, 117
Bogardus, Stephen, 103, 187
Bogdan-Kechely, Cheri, 134
Bogetich, Marilynn, 148
Boggs, Jennifer E., 93
Bogosian, Eric, 53, 63, 122, 187
Boher, Melissa Jane, 68
Bohne, Bruce, 141
Bokhour, Ray, 122
Bokuniewicz, Erick, 141
Bolan, Charles, 65
Bolduc, Jean, 128
Boles, Robert, 135
Bolger, John, 143
Bolinger, Don, 125
Boll, Patrick, 168
Bolt, Jonathan, 145, 157
Bolton, Guy, 139
Bonasorte, Gary, 55
Bond, Christopher, 8, 106
Bond, Cynthia, 85, 95
Bond, Raleigh, 229
Bonds, Rufus, Jr., 89, 124
Boneau, Chris, 6, 9, 12, 15, 25, 44, 52, 59, 60, 71, 79, 93, 97, 108
Bonet, Wilma, 121
Bonmon, Lamont R., 67
Bonnard, Raymond, 164
Bonnell, Dan, 119
Bonnell, Mary Lynn, 150
Bonner, Frank, 125
Bonney, Jo, 63, 122
Boochie, 50, 51
Book, Bill, 127
Booker, Charlotte, 170, 187
Booker, Margaret, 132
Bookman, Kirk, 133, 136, 139, 154
Bookston, Bill, 153
Bookwalter, D Martyn, 130, 147, 161
Boone, Debby, 27, 39, 187
Boone, Michael Kelly, 63, 135, 187
Booth, Debra, 165
Booth, Randy, 107, 144
Borbón, Jimmy, 96
Boretski, Paul, 176
Borge, Ronald, 23
Borge, Victor, 23
Borges, Yamil, 133
Bormann, Ruth, 111
Born Yesterday, 151, 152
Bornstein, Daryl, 17
Borod, Robert, 16, 39
Borow, Rena Berkowicz, 58
Borrego, Jesse, 138, 141
Borror, David, 87
Borts, Joanne, 106
Borzotta, Peter, 127
Bosaipo, Wilmar, 27
Bosakowski, Phil, 50
Bosboom, David H., 92
Bosco, Philip, 44, 50, 187
Boss, Sarah, 125
Bosseau, Remi Barclay, 168
Boston, Aisha, 124
Boswell, Jo, 125
Boswell, William, 136
Bosworth, Jill, 27
Both, Andrei, 141
Bottari, Michael, 17, 55, 111
Bottitta, Ron, 79
Bottoms, Ben, 135
Bottoms, John, 141
Bottrell, David, 164
Boublil, Alain, 45
Bouchard, Bruce, 128
Bouchard, Suzanne, 135
Bouffard, Suzy, 28
Bougere, Teagle F., 124
Bourgeois, Tommy, 35
Bourne, Rob, 134
Bourneuf, Stephen, 17, 169, 187
Boushey, David, 160
Boussom, Ron, 162
Bouvy, Harry, 157, 177
Bova, Steve, 120
Bovver Boys, 95
Bowden, Jonny, 58, 103
Bowden, Richard, 127, 151
Bowe, Riddick, 39
Bowen, Bryan, 131
Bowen, John, 63
Bowers, Bill, 156
Bowers-Rheay, Kim, 119
Bowin, Monica, 62, 91
Bowman, Elizabeth, 173
Bowman, Rob, 35, 133, 148
Bowne, Alan, 229
Bowne, Richard L., 229
Box Office of the Damned, Part II, 54
Box, Diane, 120
Boxer, Amanda, 53
Boy Meets Girl, 144
Boyd, Guy, 147
Boyd, Julianne, 123, 168
Boyd, Julie, 51, 94, 170, 187
Boyd, Kirk, 174
Boyd, Leila, 62, 73
Boyer, Andrew, 140

Boyer, Lauren Noel, 152
Boyer, Vladimir, 161
Boyett, Mark, 167
Boyle, Hunter, 172
Boyle, Nick, 173
Boyle, Viki, 54, 128
Boylen, Daniel, 149, 168
Boynes, Corbiere T., 138
Boynton, Rick, 148
Boys Next Door, The, 120, 126, 133, 150, 152
Boys' Life, 147
Boys' Play, 125
Boys, Barry, 149
Bozyk, Reizl, 80, 187
Bracchitta, Jim, 20, 187
Brache, Denia, 96
Bradbury, Peter, 119
Bradbury, Stephen, 19, 144
Bradby, Melissa, 168
Braden, John, 78, 146
Bradford, Scott, 135
Bradish, Barbara, 146
Bradley and Beth, 57
Bradley, Sarah Joem, 131
Bradley, Scott, 67, 80, 122
Bradshaw, Barbara, 128
Bradshaw, Deborah, 45, 109
Bradshaw, Peter, 125, 137
Brady, Brigid, 141
Brady, Fiona, 63
Brady, James, 79
Brady, Kay, 128
Brady, Patrick Scott, 57
Brady, Thomas Adam, 131
Brady-Garvin, Kathleen, 135
Braet, James, 148
Bragg, Melvyn, 169
Braha, Judy, 143
Brainin, Risa, 141
Brakhage, Robin, 135
Bramble, Mark, 154
Bramon, Risa, 81
Branagh, Kenneth, 115, 131
Brancato, Joe, 155
Branch, Robert, 173
Brand, Gibby, 130
Brandafino, Lori-Jo, 168
Brandeberry, Jim, 20
Brandenburg, Eric, 61
Brandenburg, Larry, 138
Brandman, Michael, 22
Brandon, Henry, 229, 230
Brandt, James F., 106
Brandt, Richard, 59, 60, 64, 77
Branescu, Smaranda, 124
Bras, Stacey Lynn, 89
Brashear, Shelley, 173
Brasington, Alan, 151, 163
Brass, Stacey Lynn, 89, 187
Brassard, Gail, 74, 145, 149
Brassea, Bill, 43, 111
Brassington, Don, 82
Bratton, Brittany Nicole, 135
Braugher, Andre, 87
Braune, Brad, 144
Bravo, Anthony, 138
Braxton, Brenda, 40, 84
Braye, Brenda, 141
Breaking Legs, 153
Breaking the Code, 145, 162
Breaking the Silence, 118, 174
Breaks, 50, 51
Brechner, Stanley, 74
Brecht, Bertolt, 16, 73, 122
Brecht, Mary, 131
Breckenridge, Joy, 126
Brecker, Candace, 96
Breed, Helen Lloyd, 143
Breedlove, Gina, 134
Breen, J. Patrick, 98, 187
Brehm, Heide, 53
Breitbarth, David, 150, 156
Brendel, Crickette, 125
Brenn, Janni, 128
Brennan, Gary, 79
Brennan, James, 188
Brennan, Maureen, 188, 70
Brennan, Nora, 188, 189
Brenner, Janet, 57
Brenner, Susan, 100
Brenner, William, 135
Brera, Mario, 113
Bretz, Matthew Allen, 124
Breuer, Lee, 62, 91, 138
Breul, Garry Allan, 126
Breuler, Robert, 29
Brevoort, Gregg W., 173
Brewster, Karen, 127
Brian, Michael, 139
Briar Patch, 60
Briar, Suzanne, 188, 31
Briars, Richard, 115
Brice, Ron, 28
Brickhill, Joan, 15
Bricusse, Leslie, 133
Bridge, Andrew, 31, 46
Bridges, Beau, 111
Bridges, Calvin, 138
Bridges, Susan, 125
Briel, Joel, 68
Brielle, Jonathan, 76
Brierbeir, Barbara, 167
Briers, Richard, 115, 131
Briggs, Jody, 118
Briggs, John R., 171
Briggs, Kelly, 110
Briggs, Mark, 135
Bright, Daniel, 162
Brightman, Julian, 112
Brighton Beach Memoirs, 137, 166
Brigleb, John, 73
Brill, Fran, 94, 188
Brill, Robert, 153
Brimage, Jewel, 95
Brimm, Thomas Martell, 136
Brinkerhoff, Linda, 127
Brinkley, David Anthony, 141
Brito, Adrian, 11
Bro, Judy, 135
Broadhurst, Jeffrey Lee, 43
Broadhust, Kent, 129
Broadway Bound, 125, 137
Broadway, 167
Brochert, Park, 70
Brock, Lee, 62, 70
Brockman, C. Lance, 150
Brockman, Kevin, 27, 54, 55, 57, 61, 66, 67, 74, 77, 84
Brockway, Adrienne, 54
Brockway, Lou, 66
Broder, J. Scott, 14
Broder, Josh, 73
Broderick, William, 68, 111, 188
Brodski, Vladimir, 54
Brody, Jonathan, 111, 136, 188, 189
Brogger, Ivar, 78, 143, 154, 188
Brohn, William D., 43
Brokaw, Mark, 94, 100
Brolaski, Carol, 142
Brolin, Josh, 136
Bromberg, Conrad, 160
Bronskill, Reginald, 6
Bronson, Sylvia, 67
Bronx Tale, A, 56
Brooke, Sarah, 160
Brooking, Simon, 59, 66, 140, 188
Brooks, Alan, 153
Brooks, Avery, 159
Brooks, Carol, 58
Brooks, Colette, 129, 141
Brooks, Donald, 53, 99
Brooks, Eric, 56, 188
Brooks, Garth, 39
Brooks, Gertrude, 70
Brooks, Jeff, 44, 188
Brooks, Joe, 39
Brooks, Kimberly Ann, 67
Brooks, Tom, 144
Broom, Sharon, 158
Broome, John, 176
Brosius, Peter C., 131
Brothers and Sisters, 153
Brothers, Carla, 134
Brotherson, Eric, 229, 230
Broughton, Barbara, 157
Brouillard, Jennifer, 159
Brourman, Michele, 147
Brousseau, James, 15, 107
Browder, Ben, 25
Brown, Ann, 100, 101, 188
Brown, Anthony, 152
Brown, Arthur B., 62
Brown, Arvin, 145, 146
Brown, Barry, 20
Brown, Big Skinny, 173
Brown, Blair, 13, 188
Brown, Charles, 85, 95, 130
Brown, Claudia, 51, 63, 65, 91
Brown, Colleen, 40, 43, 46, 114
Brown, Cynthia, 95
Brown, David Brian, 43
Brown, David, 19, 22, 23, 38, 122, 176
Brown, Dean, 139
Brown, Deloss, 77
Brown, F. T., 129
Brown, Georgia, 16, 188
Brown, Gerald, 119
Brown, Graham, 83, 95, 167, 188
Brown, Jamie, 126, 135
Brown, Jason (J.J.), 108
Brown, Kermit, 165
Brown, Laura, 131
Brown, Lewis, 153, 176
Brown, Lynn, 119
Brown, Molly, 139
Brown, P. J., 29, 77, 188
Brown, Robert, 159
Brown, Robin Leslie, 93, 188
Brown, Roscoe C., 134
Brown, Ruth, 188
Brown, Shawn, 170
Brown, Spencer S., 96
Brown, Stephanie, 94
Brown, Suzanne, 113
Brown, Tener, 46
Brown, Timothy T., 173
Brown, Velina, 121
Brown, Vincent, 163
Brown, William Scott, 46, 113, 188
Brown, William, 138, 148
Browne, Gail, 110
Browne, Leslie, 39
Browne, Roscoe Lee, 157
Browning, Robert, 171
Browning, Susan, 132
Brownrigg, Tony, 167
Brownstone, Diana, 139
Brozzo, Jennifer, 127
Bruce, Andrew, 45
Bruce, Barry, 119
Bruce, Cheryl Lynn, 29
Bruce, Susan, 76, 159
Bruckner, Gisela, 52
Brugman, Willem, 58
Bruice, Ann, 147, 162
Brüll, Pamela, 34
Brunch at Trudy and Paul's, 63
Brundage, Gene, 113
Brune, Eva, 67, 69
Bruneau, Ainslie, 173
Bruner, Glenn, 164
Brunetti, Ted, 157
Brunner, Howard, 119
Brunner, Michael, 139
Brunner, Roslyn, 139
Bruns, Jean, 132
Brush Arbor Revival, 67
Brustein, Robert, 122
Brustman, Kirk, 131
Brutsman, Laura, 135
Bryan, Jennifer, 16
Bryan-Brown, Adrian, 6, 9, 12, 15, 25, 33, 36, 38, 44, 51, 52, 67, 97, 107, 108
Bryant, Celia, 159
Bryant, Damon, 161
Bryant, David, 188
Bryant, Linda, 114
Brydon, W. B., 79, 188
Bryggman, Larry, 36, 76, 90, 188
Bryne, Barbara, 142, 188
Bua, Nick, 152
Buch, Rene, 128
Buchalter, Fred, 150
Buchanan, Earl, 124
Buchanan, Linda, 56, 138
Buchner, Georg, 142
Buchsbaum, Jeffrey, 164
Buck, George, 147
Buck, John, Jr., 140
Buck, Nathaniel, 125
Buckley, Andy, 65
Buckley, Betty, 143, 144
Buckley, Candy, 122
Buckley, Melinda, 54, 188, 189
Buckley, Ralph, 168
Buckley, William J., III, 101
Bucknam, David, 91
Buckner, Clay, 159
Budbill, David, 121
Buddeke, Kate, 56
Budge, Don, 39
Budin, Rachel, 96, 168
Budries, David, 49, 142
Buell, Bill, 83, 119, 188
Buelow, Dan, 15
Buelteman, Anne, 110
Buff, Jim, 62
Buffaloe, Katherine, 46, 111
Bugbee, Charles, 144
Bukovec, John A., 149
Bulasky, David, 58, 93
Bulgakov, Mikhail, 37, 77
Bull, Roland, 129
Bullard, Thomas Allan, 83
Buller, Francesca, 25
Bullpen, 136
Bulos, Yusef, 65, 99, 172, 188
Bumbalo, Victor, 59
Bumpass, Rodger, 161
Bundries, David, 162
Bundy, Rob, 142
Bundy, Robert, 138
Bunn, Sharon, 167
Buntel, Tim, 143
Bunting, Brandi, 125
Buono, Cara, 81, 82, 188
Burbach, Matthew, 149
Burbutashvili, Lily, 69
Burdett, Patricia, 128
Burdick, David, 17
Burdick, Melissa L., 78
Burdick, Riette, 135
Burge, Gregg, 144
Burgess, Granville, 169
Burgess, Joy Faye, 124
Burgess, Patricia, 72
Burgreen, Andrew, 73
Burgreen, J. Andrew, 58
Burk, Susan, 113
Burk, Terence, 188, 189
Burke, David, 158
Burke, Deena, 174
Burke, Geneva, 133
Burke, Louis, 15
Burke, Maggie, 137
Burke, Marylouise, 50, 51, 164, 170
Burke, Robert, 63, 188
Burke, Sean, 72
Burkhartsmeier, Bruce, 174
Burland, David, 72
Burmeister, Leo, 45, 91
Burn This, 121, 128, 157
Burner's Frolic, 85, 95
Burnett, Carol, 111
Burnett, Frances Hodgson, 168
Burnett, John Hall, 127
Burnett, Robert, 188
Burnham, Margaret, 61, 188, 189
Burns, Bill, 43
Burns, Traber, 133
Burr, Raymond, 39
Burrage, Marie, 143
Burrell, Fred, 60, 73, 188
Burrell, Pamela, 145
Burrows, Abe, 125
Burrows, Allyn, 175
Burrus, Bob, 120
Burse-Mickelbury, Denise, 50, 51, 75, 179, 182, 188
Burstyn, Mike (formerly Burstein), 74, 188
Burton, Donald, 25, 97, 188
Burton, Josh, 152
Burton, Kate, 81, 188
Burton, Laura, 176
Burton, Miriam, 67
Burton, Victoria Lynn, 15, 188
Burton, Warren, 63, 188
Burwinkel, Jim, 159
Bus Stop, 123, 128
Busby, Barbara, 136
Busch, Charles, 48, 52, 188
Buschmann, Don, 165
Busfield, Timothy, 19, 188
Bush, Barbara, 80, 171, 172
Bush, Michael, 83
Busheme, Joseph, 24, 43
Bushnell, Bill, 147
Bushor, Geoffrey, 152
Business of Murder, The, 127, 145
Bussanich, Rachele, 40
Bussert, Meg, 188
Bussert, Victoria, 140
Bustle, Jonathan, 71
Buterbaugh, Keith, 114
Buteux, Julia Averett, 173
Butler, Dan, 58
Butler, David, 157
Butler, Dean, 188, 189
Butler, E. Faye, 148
Butler, Jerome, 149
Butler, Leslie, 73
Butler, Megan, 131
Butler, Paul, 19, 144
Butler, Rick, 154
Butler, Sam, Jr., 138
Butsch, Tom, 126
Butt, Jennifer, 45, 188
Butterbaugh, Keith, 46
Butterfield, Catherine, 75, 188
Butterfield, Darcy, 147
Butterfield, Richard, 121
Button, Dick, 22
Button, Jamie, 152
Button, Jeanne, 50, 87, 90, 97
Buttram, Jan, 65, 173
Butz, Norbert, 159
Buxbaum, Lisa, 144
Buzas, Jason McConnell, 63
Buzzsaw Berkeley, 100
By and For Havel, 66
Byers, Bill, 24, 41
Byers, Catherine, 145, 188
Byers, Karen L., 144
Byger, Peter, 151
Bykov, Vladislav, 61
Bykowski, Benedykt, 55
Bynoe, Christina, 175
Bynoe, Philip, 175
Bynum, Betty K., 134
Bynum, Brenda, 119
Byram, Amick, 110
Byrd, Ann Gee, 147
Byrd, Lillian, 161
Byrne, Alexandra, 81
Byrne, Dorothy, 114
Byrnes, Jim, 163
Byrnes, Peter, 71
Byron—Mad, Bad and Dangerous to Know, 130
Byron-Kirk, Keith, 29, 138
Caball, Aaron, 163
Caballero, Christophe, 43
Cabaniss, Thomas, 83
Cacaci, Joe, 64
Caccavallo, Catherine, 113
Cachianes, Ed, 73
Caddick, David, 40, 46
Cade, Christopher, 73
Cadora, Eric, 48
Caesar, Sid, 14, 50, 51, 188
Caffey, Marion J., 139
Caffrey, Stephen, 142
Cagan, John, 9
Cahill, Danny, 66, 73
Cahill, James, 24, 87, 188
Cahill, Sally, 176
Cahn, Larry, 137, 190, 191
Cahn, Sammy, 43
Cahoots, 67
Cain, Bill, 124, 142, 174
Cain, Candice, 168
Cain, Michael, 73
Cain, Michael-Demby, 117
Cain, Rebecca, 113
Cain, William, 10, 191
Cain, Wilson, III, 138
Caine, Michael, 39
Caird, John, 45
Caisley, Bill, 152
Caitlyn, Deryl, 63, 87, 191
Calabro, Rita, 160
Calamates, Andy, 51
Calder, John W., III, 111
Calderone, Michael, 53
Caldwell Theatre Company, 128
Caldwell, Charles, 171
Caldwell, Ed, 166
Caldwell, L. Scott, 147
Caldwell-Fields, Felicia, 127
Cale, David, 68
Calegari, Maria, 39
Calhoun, Vern T., 39
Caliban, Richard, 65
Caligagan, Tony, 43
Calkins, Carol, 154
Calkins, Michael, 61, 191
Call Me Ethel!, 74
Call, Ivonne, 161
Callaghan, Edward, 57
Callahan, Steven C., 81
Callas, Demetri, 20
Callen, Chris, 17, 44, 190, 191
Callender, L. Peter, 36, 76, 87, 129
Callow, Simon, 147
Calloway, Cab, 39
Calloway, David, 124
Calloway, Northern J., 229
Calman, Camille, 98
Camacho, Blanca, 66, 191
Camera, John, 160
Cameron, Bruce, 14, 144
Cameron, Clark, 71
Cameron, John, 45
Cameron, Linda, 135
Cameron, Susan, 156, 168
Cameron-Webb, Gavin, 149, 171
Camp, Bill, 87, 91, 170
Camp, Joanne, 42, 93, 146, 191
Camp, Richard W., 229
Campanella, Philip, 97
Campbell, Amelia, 153
Campbell, Bruce, 10, 56, 62, 81
Campbell, Catherine, 157
Campbell, Christine, 56
Campbell, Erma, 75, 159, 164, 179, 182, 191
Campbell, Jennifer, 127
Campbell, Neve, 113
Campbell, Robert F., 170
Campbell, Robert, 150
Campbell, Ron, 131, 147
Campbell, Sally, 32
Campora, Giancarlo, 27
Canaan, Robert, 51
Canada, Frederick Charles, 119
Canary, David, 101, 190, 191
Candelaria, La, 88
Candide, 141
Canepari, Bernard, 140
Cannarozzi, Peter, 39
Cannon, Carey, 157
Cannon, Stephanie, 149
Canova, Diana, 50, 51
Canter, Nina, 62, 70
Cantley, Kelly, 143
Cantor, Arthur, 56, 68
Cantor, David, 74
Cantor, Geoffrey P., 155
Cantrell, Christine, 114
Cantrell, James, 173
Cantrell, Roger, 113
Capenos, James, 177
Capital Repertory Company, 128
Capitol Cakewalk, 66
Capitola, Jeff, 18
Capone, Tony, 169
Capote, Truman, 23, 122
Cappelli, Joe, 16
Capps, Tom, 20
Capri, Mark, 149
Carballido, Emilio, 161
Carbondale Dreams: Bradley & Beth/Arnold, 57
Carbone, Franco, 50
Cardin, Pierre, 61
Cardona, Debra, 141
Cardwell, Sylvia, 119
Carell, Candace, 40
Carey, Helen, 142
Carey, Robert, 48, 52
Carey, William D., 152
Carey-Jones, Selena, 120
Cargle, Council, 136
Cariou, Len, 68, 137, 191
Carley, Jeff, 173
Carlile, John Douglas, 138
Carlin, Amanda, 42, 190, 191
Carlin, Chet, 177
Carlin, Clive, 125
Carlin, Joy, 121
Carlin, Nancy, 121
Carlin, Tony, 42, 99
Carlos, Aaron, 158
Carlos, Chris, 167
Carlow, Richard, 59
Carlsen, Allan, 93, 152
Carlson, Ann, 53
Carlson, Katherine, 127
Carlton, Regie, 136
Carlucci, Kim, 51
Carmello, Carolee, 24, 103, 109
Carmichael, Bill, 139
Carmichael, Marnie, 89
Carmine, Michael, 229
Carmines, Al, 129
Carnage, A Comedy, 88
Carnahan, Kirsti, 109, 139
Carneiro, Claudio, 27
Carnelia, Craig, 190, 191
Carney, Jennifer, 114
Carnival of the Animals, The, 64
Carol, Seraiah, 126
Carollo, Scott, 89
Carpenter, Adam, 150
Carpenter, Gordon, 160
Carpenter, John, 132, 143
Carpenter, Karen L., 32, 130, 144, 170
Carpenter, Larry, 97, 143, 165
Carpenter, Steve, 61
Carpenter, Terry W., 150
Carpenter, Thelma, 58
Carr, Charles, 125
Carr, David, 48
Carr, Elizabeth Katherine, 48, 52
Carr, Jennifer, 29
Carr, Mimi, 174
Carr, Scott Noflet, 72
Carr, Sharon, 125
Carrafa, John, 94, 168
Carrellas, Barbara, 15
Carrey, Mitchell, 133
Carricart, Robertson, 37, 191
Carrick, Chris, 79
Carrière, Berthold, 176
Carrigan, Ann Patrice, SSJ, 136
Carrillo, Ramiro, 145
Carroll, Barbara, 13, 87
Carroll, Bob, 106
Carroll, David (formerly David-James), 18, 191
Carroll, John W., 168
Carroll, Pat, 171, 172
Carroll, Philip, 16
Carroll, Rocky, 32, 130, 179, 182, 191
Carroll, Ronn, 20
Carson, A. D., 157
Carson, Heather, 61, 142
Carson, Jeannie, 160
Carson, Jo, 142, 147
Carson, Susan Dawn, 45, 109
Carson, Terrence A., 138
Carson, Thomas, 68, 136, 173, 191
Carter, Andrew, 135
Carter, Bob, 128
Carter, Bobby John, 20
Carter, Christopher, 152
Carter, Jimmy, 138
Carter, Lou, 66
Carter, Michael, 25
Carter, Myra, 165
Carter, Omar, 135
Carter, Ralph, 59, 191
Carter, Rosanna, 128
Carteris, Gabrielle, 137
Cartwright, Melinda, 133
Cartwright, Mindy, 43
Cartwright, Robert, 60
Caruso, Dana Lynn, 110

Carver, Marc, 127
Carver, Mary, 131
Carver, Victoria, 166
Cary, Cheri Catherine, 147
Cary, Jim, 129
Cary, Meghan, 126
Casale, Amy, 57
Casas, Myrna, 88
Casas, Sylvia, 114
Cascio, Anna Theresa, 51
Case of Harriet Grinde, The, 149
Case, Evelyn Carol, 171
Case, Ronald, 17, 55, 111
Casey, Warren, 148
Casey, James, 173
Casey, Robert E., 97
Cash, Darla, 146, 161
Cash, David, 50
Cash, Rosalind, 129
Casillo, Lisa, 48
Caskey, Marilyn, 46
Casnoff, Philip, 61, 89, 191
Cassaro, Nancy, 48
Cassel, Gwen, 73
Castaldo, Ralph, 72
Castay, Leslie, 16, 190, 191
Casteel, Karen, 65
Castellano, Dennis, 162
Castellanos, John, 147
Castelli, Victor, 43
Castellino, Bill, 90
Castilla, Sergio, 71
Castillo, E. J., 147
Castle, Diana, 156
Castleman, William, 53
Casto, Jacqui, 86, 91
Castro, Linda, 161
Castro, Vicente, 96
Castronovo, T. J., 153
Caswell, Lexi, 168
Cat and the Fiddle, The, 70
Cat on a Hot Tin Roof, 28, 171, 176
Catalano, George, 160
Catanese, Charles, 53, 60, 61
Catastrophe, 66, 129
Cates, Madelyn, 74, 190, 191
Cates, Phoebe, 82
Cates, Steven, 117
Cathcart, Sarah, 175
Cather, Willa, 143
Cathey, Reg E., 51, 63, 65, 90, 91
Catlin, Lori S., 59
Caton, Karen, 42
Cats, 40, 102
Catt, Christopher, 61
Cattaneo, Anne, 81
Cattrall, Kim, 138
Caucasian Chalk Circle, The, 122
Causey, Kevin, 60
Cavallo, Frank, 136
Cavanagh, Thomas, 6
Cavanaugh, Mary Beth, 174
Cavander, Kenneth, 168
Cave, James, 98
Cave, Lisa Dawn, 40
Cavell, Linda, 129
Cavett, Dick, 12, 39, 191
Cavey, George, 127
Cavise, Joe Antony, 191
Cawelti, Michael, 153
Cayler, Tom, 53, 147
Caza, Terrence, 126, 143
Cea, Robert, 48
Ceballos, Rene, 11
Cele, Baby, 116
Cellario, Maria, 53
Cellier, Jacques, 73
Cemetery Club, The, 38, 144
Center Stage, 129
Center Theatre Group Ahmanson Theatre, 130
Center Theatre Group Mark Taper Forum, 131
Centrella, Christopher, 170
Cepero, Roy, 145
Cernovitch, Nicholas, 143
Cerullo, Jonathan, 56, 84
Cerveris, Michael, 153
Cesaretti, Anthony, 145
Cesari, Julie, 48
Cesario, Michael J., 157
Chada, Jennifer, 148
Chadderdon, David E., 138
Chadwick, Robin, 21
Chaiken, Stephen, 27
Chaikin, Joseph, 131
Chairs, The, 122
Chalfant, Kathleen, 97, 131, 191
Chalmers, Tom, 54
Chamberlain, Douglas, 176
Chamberlin, Kevin, 71, 75, 149, 170, 190, 191
Chamberlin, Mark, 118, 160
Chambers, Craig, 67
Chambers, David, 162
Chambers, Jane, 53, 60
Chambers, Jonathan, 127
Chambers, Michael, 90
Chambers, Ray, 153, 171
Chambers, Renee Lynette, 117
Champagne, Lenora, 77
Champion, Charles, 130
Champion, Kelly, 65
Chan, Donald, 133
Chan, Mr. Kim, 119
Chandani, Sanjay, 131
Chandler, Brian Evaret, 144
Chandler, David, 120
Chandler, Jack, 168
Chandler, Jeffrey Allan, 153
Chandler, Ray, 105
Chandler, Stan, 71
Chandler, Terry, 75
Chaney, David, 8
Chang, Du-Yee, 92
Chang, Judith, 135
Chang, Roxanne, 92
Chang, Tisa, 92
Changa, Jimmy, 154
Change in the Heir, A, 35
Changeling, The, 176
Channing, Carol, 39
Channing, Stockard, 12, 82, 153, 191
Chant, Holley, 37, 190, 191
Chapin, Harry, 119
Chapman, John, 133
Chapman, Ray, 138
Chapman, Topsy, 70, 134
Chappell, Fred, 126
Chappell, Kandis, 130, 153, 191
Chargin, Tom, 63
Charlap, Moose, 43, 112
Charles, Josh, 146
Charles, Leo, 124
Charles, Walter, 31
Charleville, Randy, 154
Charlton, William, 61, 190, 191
Charney, Allison, 129
Charney, Tina, 57, 92
Charnin, Martin, 14, 144
Chase, L. Everett, 15
Chase, Lonnie, 15
Chase, Mary, 141
Chase, Tony, 144
Chasse, Maurice, 138
Chate, Kate, 53
Chausow, Lynn, 122, 170
Chavanne, Brian, 11, 100
Chayefsky, Paddy, 82
Cheadle, Don, 138
Cheatham, Jamie, 70
Check, Ed, 170
Cheeseman, Ken, 175
Cheeseman, Pat, 24
Chekhov, Anton, 93, 101, 120, 138, 141, 153, 158, 159, 160, 176
Chelini, Nicole, 114
Cheng, Maria, 141
Chenier, Leon B., Jr., 107
Chenoweth, Brian, 114
Chepulis, Kyle, 51, 65
Cheretun, Deborah, 117
Cheretun, Stephanie, 26
Chernomirdik, Vlada, 138
Cherry Orchard, The, 101, 158, 160
Cherry, Kate, 175
Cherry, Vivian, 52
Chesnutt, Judy, 127
Chess, 103, 148
Chesterman, Mary, 110
Chestnutt, Judy, 127
Chevan, Julie Abels, 173
Chew, Lee, 127
Chianese, Dominic, 80, 191
Chiang, Gar, 63
Chiasson, Gilles, 110
Chic Street Man, 91, 134
Chiclana, Margarita Lopez, 96
Chicoine, Susan, 12, 39, 41, 78, 81, 100
Chien, Chia Lin, 92
Child, Desmond, 52
Children of the Sun, 120
Childs, Casey, 95
Chinese Charade, The, 96
Chinn, Lori Tan, 190, 191
Chioran, Juan, 176
Chirgotis, Candice, 142
Chisholm, Anthony, 56, 62
Chitty, Alison, 9
Chiyoda, Tacko, 12
Chmelko-Jaffe, Mary, 150
Chmiel, Mark, 63
Cho, Irene, 43, 113
Chodorov, Jerome, 56
Chong, Marcus, 142, 143
Chonishvilli, Sergey, 61
Chorus Line, A, 41, 94
Chorus of Disapproval, A, 162
Christakos, Jerry, 110
Christen, Robert, 56, 138
Christensen, Cheryl Soper, 168
Christian, Martha, 142
Christian, Patricia, 135
Christian, William, 134
Christianson, Catherine, 120
Christie, Audrey, 229
Christmas Carol, A, 118, 120, 121, 136, 138, 140, 141, 149, 150, 151, 152, 161, 171
Christopher, Christine, 136
Christopher, Donald, 151, 157
Christopher, Rick, 136
Christopher, Thom, 190, 191
Christy, Donald, 58
Christy, James, 173
Christy, Roberta, 16
Chudy, Jennifer, 145
Chugg, Eliza, 171
Chunayev, Boris, 61
Church, Dawn Marie, 117
Church, Tony, 135
Churchill, Caryl, 60, 91
Churchill, Marcia, 163
Churchman, Shawn, 68
Chute, Lionel, 65, 191
Chute, Susan, 51
Chybowski, Michael, 164
Ciacco, Tom, 6
Cibula, Nan, 138, 144
Cibulskis, Meghan Roberts, 149
Cicchini, Robert, 141
Ciccolella, Jude, 63
Cilento, Wayne, 52, 103, 133
Cimolino, Antoni, 176
Cinnante, Kelly, 48
Cinzano, 120
Cioffi, Charles, 146
Cipriano, David, 130
Circle Repertory Theatre, 76
Cirillo, Jack, 159
Cistone, Danny, 20, 191
City of Angels, 4, 24
Ciulei, Liviu, 124
Clancy, John, 167
Clancy, Katy, 164
Clanton, Rony, 83, 159
Clara, 121
Clarence Fountain and the Five Blind Boys of Alabama, 138
Clarey, Alan, 159
Clark, Anne Halsey, 175
Clark, Bobby, 144
Clark, Brian, 147, 169
Clark, Cathy, 134
Clark, Danny Robinson, 32, 190, 191
Clark, Darren, 170
Clark, Dick, 39
Clark, G. Thomas, 32, 130, 144, 168
Clark, James A., 165
Clark, Janet, 124
Clark, John Edward, 135
Clark, John, 12, 119
Clark, Jon Roger, 74
Clark, Keith, 72
Clark, Patrick, 176
Clark, Sheandra, 149
Clark, Thais, 134
Clark, Thomas W., 170
Clark, Victoria, 109, 137, 168
Clarke, Bill, 168
Clarke, Brian, 124
Clarke, Caitlin, 131
Clarke, David, 98, 191
Clarke, Elizabeth W., 120
Clarke, Hope, 91, 134
Clarke, Michael A., 17
Clarke, Richard, 191
Clarkson, Patricia, 83
Clarvoe, Anthony, 121
Classic Stage Company/CSC, 77
Clausell, Eric, 117
Clausen, Richard, 79
Claxon, Beth, 173
Claypool, Kathleen, 145
Claypool, Veronica, 130
Clayton, Anne, 167
Clayton, Lawrence, 89
Clayton, Philip, 31, 191
Clear & Present Danger, 169
Clear, Patrick, 138
Cleary, Malachy, 67
Cleaveland, Scot B., 150
Cleghorne, Ellen, 95
Clelland, Deborah, 45
Clemence, Andrew, 144
Clemens, Elizabeth, 67
Clemente, Alex, 155
Clements, Rafeal, 170
Clemmons, David, 164
Cleveland Play House, The, 132
Cleveland, Celeste, 160
Cleveland, David, 46
Cleveland, Sally, 161
Clevenger, Joann, 70, 134
Clewell, Tom, 71, 137
Cliff, Oliver, 126
Clifton, John, 143, 165
Cline, Perry, 8, 31, 117
Clinkscales, J. T., 138
Clohessy, Robert, 83
Clonts, Jeffrey, 45
Clonts, John, 154
Clontz, Dennis, 73
Cloran, Matthew, 54
Close, Del, 138
Closer Than Ever, 57
Closer, The, 51
Cloud Nine, 60
Cloud, Darrah, 143
Clouds, The, 69
Clough, Peter H., 128
Clown's Play, 127
Clugstone, Scott, 168
Coates, Carolyn, 183
Coates, Eric, 176
Coates, George, 121
Coates, Nelson, 167
Coates, Norman, 17, 67, 114
Coates, Susan, 115, 131
Coats, Steve, 65
Cobb, 119
Cobbs, Bill, 132, 168
Coble, McKay, 158
Coburn, Rachel, 173
Coccioletti, Philip, 72, 73, 191
Cochran, Ray, 94, 191
Cochran, Shannon, 148
Cochrane, Steve, 61, 111
Cochren, Daniel, 174
Cochren, Felix E., 51, 59, 128
Cockrum, Roy, 48
Cocktail Hour, The, 119, 126, 130, 132, 144, 154
Coconut Grove Playhouse, The, 133
Coe, Robert, 103
Coe, Tracy, 159
Coffey, Peggy, 176
Coffey, Tom, 58
Coffield, Kelly, 56
Coffield, Phil, 159
Coffin, Barbara, 160
Coffin, Gregg, 174
Coffman, Kate, 143
Cohan, Blossom, 164
Cohen, Alexander H., 34, 39
Cohen, Bill, 63
Cohen, Bruce, 51, 63
Cohen, Buzz, 13
Cohen, Edward M., 80
Cohen, Geoffrey, 154
Cohen, Jamie, 43, 191
Cohen, Jason Steven, 13, 41, 87
Cohen, Jedidiah, 168
Cohen, Judith, 89
Cohen, Justine, 144
Cohen, Katharine, 77
Cohen, Larry, 99, 155
Cohen, Leo K., 6
Cohen, Lynn, 9, 190, 191
Cohen, Margery, 75, 191
Cohen, Martin, 113
Cohen, Ruth, 94
Cohen, Samuel D., 80, 191
Cohen, Scott, 97
Cohen, Sherry, 113
Cohenour, Patti, 164, 165, 164, 191
Cohn, Henoch, 80
Cohn, Ruby, 131
Colantti, Stephen, 54
Colavecchia, Franco, 97
Colavin, Charlotte, 95
Colby, Michael, 57
Cole, Darren Lee, 53, 60
Cole, Dori, 160
Cole, Nora, 164
Cole, Robert, 63
Cole, Tom, 164
Coleman, Alex, 177
Coleman, Cy, 24
Coleman, Heather, 57
Coleman, Jack, 142
Coleman, Jim, 154
Coleman, Kevin, 175
Coleman, Minnette, 66, 59
Coleman, Rahn, 153
Coleman, Rosalyn, 170
Coleman, Stephen, 177
Coleridge, Alan, 55
Coleridge, E. P., 93
Coles, Diana, 165
Coletta, Dario, 110
Colfelt, Barry M., 132
Colias, Jim, 23
Collie, Stephanie, 115, 131
Collier, Michael, 54
Collings, Nancy, 60
Collins, Bethanne, 54
Collins, Cynthia, 173
Collins, Deborah, 154
Collins, Michael, 68
Collins, Neana, 124
Collins, Pat, 42, 129, 131, 133, 138, 142, 146, 160, 164, 165
Collins, Pharra J., 136
Collins, Stephen, 87, 90, 191
Colman, Booth, 150
Coloff, Rachel, 160
Colon, Alex, 76, 161, 190, 191
Colorado, Vira, 190, 191
Colson, Kevin, 31
Colt, Alvin, 34, 39, 43
Colt, Christopher, 122
Colteaux, Andrew, 142
Colton, Jacque Lynn, 90
Columbia Artists, 117
Columbia, Susanne, 65
Colyn, Miriam, 71
Colyott, Joseph, 102
Combes, Charlie, 169
Comden, Betty, 43, 56, 112
Come As You Are, 64
Comedy Tonight, 43
Comedy of Errors, 176
Commings, Katina, 168
Commire, Anne, 100
Common Pursuit, The, 163
Compton, Forrest, 151
Comstock, David, 62
Conaway, David, 53, 190, 191
Conde, Emilia, 96
Conde, George, 152
Cone, Jeff, 119
Cone, Michael, 144
Conely, James, 171
Conery, Edward, 103, 151
Congdon, Constance, 69, 142
Conger, Eric, 146, 149
Conger, Shelly, 53
Conklin, John, 90, 138, 142
Conklin, Mark W., 94
Conley, Willy, 144
Conlon, Kathleen, 173
Connally, Mary, 61
Connaughton, Kevin, 80
Connecticut Yankee, A, 139
Connell, David, 173
Connell, Gordon, 139
Connell, Jane, 44, 190, 191
Connelly, Bruce, 80
Connelly, R. Bruce, 191
Conner, Ronald, 147
Connolly, David, 6, 192
Connor, James Michael, 135
Connor, Martin, 139
Connors, Bridget, 126, 162
Conolly, Patricia, 21, 192
Conquest of the South Pole, 124
Conrad, Jeff, 111
Conrad, Kent, 126
Conroy, Frances, 13, 81, 190, 192
Conroy, Jarlath, 124, 142, 190, 192
Considine, John, 147
Constan, Victoria, 48
Constantine, Deborah, 95
Consuming Passions of Lydia Pinkham & Rev. Sylvester Graham, The, 75
Conte, John, 145
Conti, Joe, 167
Contic, Phillip, 93, 173
Converse, Frank, 146
Converse-Roberts, William, 90, 129
Conway, Charles J., 135
Conway, Dan, 132, 145
Conway, Kevin, 49, 192
Conwell, Charles, 170
Cook, Candy, 154
Cook, Debbie Blackwell, 86
Cook, Divina, 67
Cook, Donn, 114
Cook, Dwight R. B., 134
Cook, Grace, 128
Cook, James, 47
Cook, Karen Case, 127
Cook, Peter C., 149
Cook, Pierre, 64
Cook, Roderick, 78
Cook, Victor Trent, 89, 192
Cooke, John C., 142
Cooke, Michael, 132
Cookson, Brian, 170
Cookson, Jeffrey, 151
Cookson, Peter, 229
Coombs, Amy A. C., 62
Coon, Susan J., 128
Cooney, Kevin, 146
Cooney, Ray, 133
Coonrod, Bob, 167
Cooper, Adrienne, 58
Cooper, Denise, 83
Cooper, Helmar Augustus, 134, 139
Cooper, J. Barrett, 125
Cooper, Jeremy, 112
Cooper, Marilyn, 126
Cooper, Max, 34
Cooper, Michael, 176
Cooper, Mindy, 89
Cooper, Reva, 13, 87
Copeland, Carolyn Rossi, 61, 71
Copeland, Joan, 83, 190, 192
Copeland, Marissa, 124
Corbalis, Brendan, 140
Corbett, Hilary, 169
Corbin, Albert, 229
Corbin, Demitri, 132, 168
Corbino, Maurizio, 113
Corcoran, Daniel, 48
Corcoran, Joseph, 48
Corcoran, KellyAnn, 159
Cordle, Dan, 77
Cordle, Jill, 56, 84
Cordon, Susie, 90
Cordova, Richard, 61
Cordtz, Richard, 155
Corey, Jill, 192
Corey, John, 145
Corfman, Caris, 83, 146, 192
Coriolanus, 173
Corley, Hal, 73, 165
Corley, Nick, 74, 174
Cormican, Peter, 113
Corne, Lesley, 6
Corneille, Pierre, 142, 147
Cornell, Jeffrey Blair, 155, 157
Cornish Game, 73
Cornish, Anthony, 93
Corpse!, 166
Corpus, Willy, 163
Corrado, Frank, 118, 168
Corrado, Fred, 168
Correa, Stephanie, 127
Corrigan, Liz, 151, 160
Corrin, Dean, 166
Corsetti, Dina, 72
Corti, Jim, 148
Corvinus, Dede, 158
Corzatte, Clayton, 172
Corzatte, Susan, 172
Cosell, Howard, 39
Cosgrave, Peggy, 132, 192
Cosgrove, Caprice, 53
Cosham, Ralph, 124
Cosham, Victoria, 124
Cosier, E. David, Jr., 32, 74, 130, 144
Cossa, Roberto M., 153
Costa, Joseph, 87, 90, 97, 190, 192
Costa-Greenspon, Muriel, 101
Costallos, Suzanne, 140
Costanza, Maryann, 133
Costello, Jeffrey R., 56
Costigan, Kelley, 173
Costigan, Ken, 127
Costin, James D., 151
Costin, Kevin, 122
Cothran, John, Jr., 131
Cotton Patch Version of Matthew and John, The, 119
Cotton, Misty, 110
Couch, Guy, 125
Coucill, Christopher, 143
Coughlin, Bruce, 89
Coughlin, Kaem, 64
Coughlin, Sylvia, 150
Coullet, Rhonda, 149
Coulter, Ned, 151
Council, Richard, 94, 192
Countryman, Michael, 19, 67, 69, 97, 192
Coupar, Mark, 152
Courie, Jonathan, 100, 192
Courson, Robert, 14
Courtney, Dennis, 117
Courtney, Larry, 60
Courts, Randy, 61, 137
Cousins, Brian, 22, 36, 60, 192
Cousins, Craig, 73
Cousy, Bob, 39
Cover, A. D., 136, 156
Cover, Franklin, 192
Covey, Elizabeth, 149
Cowan, Casey, 131, 147
Coward, Noel, 127, 128, 159
Cowles, Peggy, 149
Cowling, Gary, 72
Cox, Catherine, 91, 192
Cox, John Henry, 143
Cox, Laura, 51
Cox, Richard, 98, 192
Cox, Veanne, 145, 154
Cox, Walter, 171
Coy, Mary, 175
Coyle, James, 149
Coyote, Peter, 153
Cozart, Anthony, 136
Cozort, Kim, 128
Craik, Allan, 176
Crampton, Glory, 47, 120
Crane, David, 155
Cranendonk, Terence, 92

Crank, David M., 171
Cranzano, Joe, 34, 39
Craven, James, 157
Craven, Matt, 170
Cravens, Rutherford, 173
Craver, Mike, 71, 120, 149, 156
Craver, Neal, 135
Crawford, Constance, 9, 190, 192
Crawford, Dan, 22
Crawford, Ellen, 153
Crawford, Kevin, 37
Crawford, Martha Maulsby, 155
Crawford, Michael, 113, 192
Crawford, Norma, 127
Crawford, Pat, 65
Crawford, Ron, 29
Creamer, Tom, 138
Creason, Don, 126
Creatore, Luigi, 55
Creedon, Don, 60
Creelman, Patric A., 105
Creery, Don, 160
Cress, Quinn, 124
Crigler, Lynn, 139
Crimes of the Heart, 171
Criner, Mary, 155
Crist, Gloria, 73
Crist, Sheridan, 173
Cristaldi, Kevin, 142
Criswell, Kim, 16, 192
Critelli, Pam, 69
Crivello, Anthony, 192
Croft, Jeanne, 133, 148
Croft, Martin, 110
Croft, Paddy, 79, 100, 192
Crognale, Thomas, 169
Cromarty, Peter, 50, 54, 59, 60, 61, 62, 64, 66, 67, 69, 74, 84, 92
Cromwell, David, 83, 164, 192
Cromwell, Gloria, 130
Cromwell, Keith, 154
Cronauer, Gail, 167
Crone, Tom, 125
Cronin, Jane, 44
Cronin, Joseph, 174
Cronkite, Walter, 39
Cronyn, Hume, 39
Cronyn, Tandy, 133, 192
Crook, Peter, 160
Crooks, Kitty, 63, 94, 192
Croom, Gabriel, 164
Crosby, Cathy Lee, 39
Crosby, Don, 107
Crosby, Kim, 192
Crosby, Shelley, 145
Croskery, Virginia, 114
Cross, Gregory, 113
Cross, Marcia, 22
Cross, Stephen, 192
Cross, Steve, 73
Crossing Delancey, 128
Crossley, Steven, 53
Crossroads Theatre Company, 134
Crothers, Sam, 18
Crouse, Russell, 27
Crow, Laura, 67, 157
Crowbar, 65
Crowley, Bob, 159
Crowley, Dennis, 94
Crowningshield, Keith, 18, 190, 192
Crucible, The, 97, 146
Crumb, Ann, 31
Crumlish, Cynthia, 132
Crush, Kate, 131
Crutchfield, Buddy, 154
Cruttwell, Hugh, 115, 131
Cruz, Charmaine, 57
Cruz, Cinta, 96
Cruz, Frank, 102
Cruz, Gilbert, 136
Cruz, Holly, 102
Cryer, David, 44, 190, 192
Cryer, Gretchen, 192
Cryer, Jon, 147
Crystal, Raphael, 59
Cucciolo, Bob, 74, 154, 192
Cuervo, Alma, 13, 42, 192
Cull, Christopher, 151, 173
Cullen, David, 31, 40, 46, 117
Cullen, John, 57
Cullen, Kaethleen, 59
Cullen, Michael, 71
Cullen, Sean, 170
Culliver, Karen, 15, 114, 190, 192
Cullum, John, 6, 137, 192
Culman, Peter W., 129
Culpepper, Stuart, 119
Culpin, Debora Jean, 122, 159
Cuming, Danette, 107
Cummings, A. Benard, 124, 170
Cummings, Anthony, 136, 144, 157
Cummings, Blondell, 53
Cummings, Claudia, 27
Cummins, Stephen, 167
Cumpsty, Michael, 22, 91
Cunneen, Kathleen, 168
Cunningham, Jo Ann, 107
Cunningham, John, 82, 146, 192
Cunningham, Laura, 56, 76
Cunningham, Randall, 39
Curiale, Joe, 39
Curless, John, 78, 83, 190, 192
Curley, Cynthia, 135
Curnock, Richard, 176
Curran, Michael, 65
Currie, Richard, 55, 59, 69
Currier, Terrence, 124, 129, 137, 144, 170
Curry, Eddie, 127
Curry, Jack, 167
Curry, John, 97, 192
Curry, Tim, 83, 192
Curtis, Elyse, 57
Curtis, Jeff, 114, 133
Curtis, Keene, 121, 130, 144, 192
Curtis, Yvette, 139
Curtis-Brown, Robert, 87, 94, 131
Cusack, Joan, 50, 138, 190, 192
Cushing, James O'Sullivan, 28
Cushing, Maureen O'Sullivan, 28
Cusick, Russ, 52
Cutko, Valerie, 154
Cutler, R. J., 51, 94, 168
Cwikowski, Bill, 190, 192
Cybula, Robert, 19
Cygan, John, 155
Cyrano de Bergerac, 52, 174
Czechlewski, Kam, 55
Czecklewska, Zofia, 55
Czoka, Larry, 161
Czyzewska, Elzbieta, 65
d'Amboise, Charlotte, 43
D'Ambrosio, Franc, 8
D'Arcy, Mary, 113
D'Arms, Ted, 160
D'Entremont, James, 170
D'Introna, Nino, 131
D'Lugoff, Art, 51
D'Wolf, Elizabeth, 135
Da Silva, Mari Nobles, X
Dabdoub, Jack, 133
Daddona, Robert J., 154
Daigle, Kenneth M., 106
Dailey, Dannul, 50
Dailey, Dina, 103
Daily, Daniel, 82, 192
Daines, John, 78
Dainton, Scott, 139
Dakin, Kymberly, 78, 120
Dalby, Michael, 59, 192, 193
Dale, Grover, 43
Dale, James E., 105
Dale, Jim, 97, 194
Dale, Lorraine, 110
Dale, Patt, 50, 70, 112
Daley, Donna, 132
Daley, Joseph, 70
Daley, Margery, 25
Daley, R. F., 8, 194
Daley, Robert, 163
Daley, Steven Michael, 47
Dallas, L. B., 62
Dallas, Walter, 75, 170
Dalrymple, Frank, 52
Dalton, Devin, 113
Dalton, Lezlie, 190, 194
Daly, Brenda, 55
Daly, Joseph, 10, 194
Daly, Peter-Hugo, 25
Daly, Timothy, 194
Daly, Tyne, 20, 39, 144, 183, 194
Damon, Mark, 106
Dana, F. Mitchell, 49, 136, 149, 171
Dana, Nicole, 172
Dance Lesson, A, 146
Dance of Death, The, 147
Dance with Me, 93
Dancer, Stanley, 39
Dandeneau, Jacqueline, 176
Danforth, Roger T., 132
Dangerous Corner, 164, 165, 164
Dangerous Games, 11
Daniel, Tamara, 132, 143
Daniele, Graciela, 11, 94
Danielle, Marlene, 40, 193, 194
Danielle, Susan, 41
Daniels, Breelund, 33
Daniels, Danny, 144
Daniels, Duane, 161
Daniels, J. D., 54
Daniels, Kaipo, 108
Daniels, Leslie, 194
Daniels, Paul S., 94
Daniels, Tenille, 124
Daniels, Zelie, 58
Dann, Elonzo, 19
Danner, Blythe, 194
Danner, Braden, 194
Danny and the Deep Blue Sea, 66
Danshiro, Ichikawa, 54
Dansicker, Michael, 100
Danson, Randy, 63, 120, 194
Dante, Nicholas, 41
Dantuono, Michael, 193, 194
Danzer, Kathy, 128
Danzig, Adrian, 138
Dara, Olu, 131
Darcy, Pattie, 52
Dardaris, Janis, 169
Daring Bride, A, 146
Darlow, Cynthia, 36, 165, 193, 194
Darlow, David, 138
Darlow, Gillian, 120
Darnutzer, Don, 126
Darveris, George, 67
Darwall, Barbara, 9, 58
Datcher, Irene, 134
Daugherty, Matthew V., 117
Davenport, Johnna, 152
Davenport, Johnny Lee, 138, 145
David, Amelia, 73, 194
David, Hal, 39
David, John, 165
David, Keith, 87
David, Steven H., 13
Davidorf, Brad, 119
Davidson, Gordon, 32, 130, 131
Davidson, Jeannie, 174
Davidson, Philip, 174
Davidson, Ralph P., 144
Davidson, Richard M., 172
Davidson-Gorbea, Patti, 114, 148
Davies, Andrew, 83
Davies, Ann, 115, 131
Davies, Carol, 152
Davies, Geraint Wyn, 176
Davies, Howard, 28
Davies, John, 167
Davies, Katharyn, 129
Davies, Sue, 59
Davis, Anita-Ali, 37
Davis, Anthony, 53
Davis, Bette, 229, 230
Davis, Catherine Lynn, 152, 159
Davis, Chris, 145
Davis, Christopher, 168
Davis, Clifton, 39
Davis, Clinton Turner, 135
Davis, Dennis, 51
Davis, Donna, 159
Davis, Edythe, 135
Davis, Elizabeth Brady, 65
Davis, Fiona, 37
Davis, Gerald A., 48
Davis, Hal, 27
Davis, Helene, 58, 83
Davis, Jeff, 35, 151, 154
Davis, John Henry, 68, 137
Davis, Jonathan, 119
Davis, Ken, 72
Davis, Kevin, 51
Davis, Lee, 231
Davis, Lindsay W., 38, 97, 142, 143, 154
Davis, Lloyd, Jr., 75
Davis, Luther, 18
Davis, Matthew, 174
Davis, Michael, 50
Davis, Nathan, 29
Davis, Nick, 54
Davis, Paul, 87
Davis, Penny, 22
Davis, Peter, 24, 67, 69, 164
Davis, Polly K., 169
Davis, Rick, 129
Davis, Roslyn, 57
Davis, Sammy, Jr., 230, 231
Davis, Sarah, 51
Davis, Sylvia, 93, 194
Davis, Ted, 136
Davis, Vicki R., 72
Davis, Wanda, 167
Davison, Bruce, 130, 144, 193, 194
Davison, Natasha, 102
Davison, Pat, 127
Davys, Edmund, 136, 149
Dawes, Lucy Anne, 173
Dawson, David, 66, 194
Dawson, James, 25
Day, Connie, 35, 193, 194
Day, Stephen, 72
Day, Suzanne, 150
Daylight in Exile, 170
Daytrips, 142, 147
Dazidenko, Olga, 153
de Barbieri, Mary Ann, 172
de Beer, Gerrit, 18, 194
de Berry, David, 174
de Botton, Yvette, 127
de Broca, Philippe, 144
de Bruno, Tony, 161, 174
De Cordoba, Manolo, 133, 148
De Dilva, William, 55
de Ganon, Camille, 43, 194
de Guzman, Josie, 128
de Jager, Felicity, 39
de Kruyff, Nicholas, 176
de Laclos, Choderlos, 137, 157
de Lavallade, Carmen, 39, 55, 84, 194
De Mare, Anne, 72
De Niro, Robert, 20, 28, 39, 50, 82
de Oni, Christofer, 96
De Paul, Darin, 114
De Paulo, Tony, 34
de Pass, Paul, 112
De Santis, Joseph, 230, 231
De Shae, Ed, 95
de Soto, Edouard, 96
de Winter, Jo, 143
De Volder, Max, 159
De Zarn, Teresa, 16
DeAngelis, Christina Marie, 109
DeAngelis, Rosemary, 164
DeArmas, Juan, 48
DeBartolo, Valerie, 114
DeBerry, Teresa, 119
DeBiase, Gemma, 68
DeBlasio, Chris, 59
DeBonis, Marcia, 66, 70
DeBoy, Paul, 150, 159
DeBuskey, Merle, 8
DeCaro, Paula, 57
DeCormier, Robert, 23
DeCosmo, Jacqueline, 62, 193, 194
DeCristo, Al, 109
DeCristo, Sal, 109
DeFoe, Diane, 131
DeGonge, Marcy, 40, 193, 194
deKoven, Lenore, 169
DeLancey, Eric, 54
DeLaurentis, Semina, 194
DeLuise, John, 110
DeMarse, James, 67
DeMatthews, Ralph, 62, 193, 194
DeMattis, Ray, 37, 194
DeMay, Brendon, 138
DeMichele, Mark, 125
DePetris, Annette, 136
DeRaey, Daniel, 168
DeRose, Teresa, 114
DeRycke, Andrew, 166
DeShields, Andre, 193, 194
DeSoto, Edouard, 96, 170
DeVine, Sean Michael, 125
DeVito, Christine, 43
DeVito, Ron, 117
DeVries, Jon, 87
DeVries, Michael, 18, 111, 194
DeWalt, Caty, 177
DeWitt, Tim, 136
DeZarn, Teresa, 16
Deakins, Mark, 29
Deal, Dennis, 64
Dean, Allison, 94, 194
Dean, Charlotte, 176
Dean, Loren, 160, 194
Dean, Robertson, 21
Deane, Melinda, 135
Deane, Palmer, 231
Dear, Nick, 83
Dearborn, Dalton R., 126
Dearing, Judy, 86, 90, 94, 95, 139, 168
Deasy, Maria, 97
Death of a Salesman, 147
Deavers, Dorothy, 167
Debonis, Marcia, 62
Debuskey, Merle, 10, 37, 39, 41, 81
Decastro, Travis, 83
Decker, Kenneth, 128
Decker, Pat, 145
Decker, Sheldon, 170
Dedrickson, Tracy, 53, 60, 70
Dee, Ruby, 124
Deegan, John Michael, 21
Deeley, Susan, 173
Deep to Center, 62
Deer, Sandra, 119
Dein, Joel W., 70, 103, 105
Deitch, Belle M., 17
Dekker, Thomas, 176
Del Rio, Michael Philip, 52
Del Rossi, Angelo, 154
Delaine, Sheri, 61, 194
Delane, Lee, 14
Delaney, Ann, 73
Delaney, Dennis, 58
Delano, Dee, 14
Delano, Laura E., 66, 194
Delano, Lee, 14, 51, 193, 194
Delate, Brian, 72, 142
Delaware Theatre Company, 135
Delgado, Judith, 133
Delinger, Larry, 135, 149, 160
Della Piazza, Diane, 194
Della, Phyllis, 16
Dellger, Joseph, 113
Delling, Thomas, 77
Dellinger, Todd, 124
Delsener, Ron, 7
Demaline, Wayne, 128
Demattis, Ray, 136
Demers, Jacinthe, 176
Dempsey, Dru, 128
Dempsey, Jerome, 28, 194
Dempsey, Mike, 152
Dempster, Curt, 60
Denal, Alina, 161
Dene, Davina, 161
Denison, Ken, 153
Denler, Andrew, 27
Denmark, Ira, 105
Dennehy, Dennis, 57, 145
Dennehy, Elizabeth, 136
Dennett, Drew, 64
Denney, Nora, 151
Denniberg, Lori Alan, 51
Dennis, Rick, 94, 128
Dennis, Robert, 38
Denniston, Leslie, 193, 194
Denson, Cheryl, 167
Dentinger, Jane, 154
Denver Center Theatre Company, 135
Depena, Valerie, 103
Depoy, Scott, 119
Der Ring Gott Farblonjett, 69
Derbeneva, Tatiana, 61
Derecki, Noel, 69
Derlycia, Zirka, 120
Derrah, Thomas, 122
Derricks, Cleavant, 89
Dervis, Paul, 60, 73
Deshe, A., 106
Desire Under the Elms, 135
Desmond, Dan, 130, 194
Detroit Repertory Theatre, 136
Detweiler, Lowell, 165
Deutchman, Aaron, 15
Deutsch, Kurt, 19, 67, 94, 193, 194
Deutsch, Nicholas, 59
Devil and Billy Markham, The, 81
Devine, Brigette, 57
Devine, Erick, 14, 124, 194
Devine, Jilana, 12, 21, 32, 58, 78, 100
Devine, Loretta, 153
Devine, Michael, 162
Devlin, Bonnie, 67
Dewar, John, 31, 194
Dewey, Alice, 110
Dewhurst, Colleen, 12, 194
Dexter, John, 16, 135, 174, 231
Deyle, John, 124
Dezen, Alex, 45
Di Dia, Maria, 64
Di Gesu, Traci, 60, 64, 73
di Loreto, Dante, 162
Di Maggio, John, 53
Di Meo, Donna, 43
Di Noia, Mark, 114
Di Zazzo, James Gene, 2d, 93
DiBuono, Toni, 52, 89
DiCostanzo, Justine, 103
DiFalco, Tony, 148
DiFilippo, Renee, 150
DiGabriele, Linda, 126
DiGesu, Traci, 66
DiLauro, Stephen, 58
DiMaggio, Joe, 39
DiMase, Francia, 126
DiMeo, Donna, 194
DiPaolo, Elvira, 157
DiRocco, Joseph, 59
DiVita, Diane, 143
Dial M for Murder, 150
Diamini, Dumisani, 116
Diamini, Kumbuzile, 116
Diamini, Ntob'khona, 116
Diamond, Dennis, 10, 53
Diamont, Don, 39
Diaquino, John, 161
Diary of a Scoundrel, The, 150
Diaz, Bonnie, 96
Diaz, Claude, 131
Diaz-Farrar, Gabriella, 142
Dibble, Susan, 175
Dick, William, 147
Dickens, Charles, 120, 136, 138, 141, 149, 151, 161
Dickenson, Karen, 117
Dickerson, Glenda, 128
Dickey, Dale, 25
Dickson, Douglas R., 170
Diebolt, Susan, 150
Dieffenbacher, Joe, 161
Diehl, Crandall, 55
Diekmann, Nancy Kassak, 91
Dieter, Gary Marshall, 127
Dietz, Steven, 118, 147
Dietz, Susan, 111
Diggory, Lori Anne, 170
Diggs, Virginia, 166
Digioia, Michael, 194
Dignam, Mark, 231
Dignan, Pat, 66, 91
Dilkes, Katy, 170
Dillard, Bill, 70
Dillard, Harrison, 39
Dillard, Rob, 120
Dilley, Carol, 159
Dilliard, Marcus, 141
Dillon, Brent, 103
Dillon, John, 159
Dillon, Leigh, 95
Dillon, Mia, 55, 193, 194
Dillon, Rhonda, 46, 113
Dilworth, Janice, 166
Dimmick, Kathleen, 54
Dinicol, Keith, 176
Dining Room, The, 166
Dinkins, David, Mayor, 39
Dinosaurs, 170
Dirickson, Barbara, 160
Dirk, Sandy, 50
Dirty Talk, 99
Disability: A Comedy, 136
Dishy, Bob, 82, 194
Ditmas, Bruce, 72
Dividends, 80
Dix, Richard, 172
Dixon, Beth, 120
Dixon, Ed, 45
Dixon, Jerry, 94
Dixon, MacIntyre, 16, 91, 193, 194
Dixon, William Lynn, 114
Djinoria, Mourman, 69
Dmitriev, Alex, 123
Dobrowolski, Tony, 150
Dobson, Terry, 167
Doctor's Dilema, The, 97
Doctorow, E. L., 39
Dodd, Judy, 106
Dodd, Terry, 73
Dodds, William, 9
Dodge, Marcia Milgrom, 89, 91, 159
Dodin, Lev, 153
Dodrill, Marji, 140
Dodson, Colleen, 50, 51, 194
Dodson, Daryl T., 110
Doepp, John, 165
Does Anybody Know What I'm Talking About?, 14
Dog Logic, 159
Doherty, Patricia E., 132
Doherty, Paul, 60, 66, 73
Dohi, Sylvia, 102
Dokuchitz, Jonathan, 141
Dolan, Andrew, 121
Dolan, Kira, 152
Dolan, Michael, 19, 144, 194
Dolan, Tara, 60, 73
Dolas, Lura, 171
Dolce, Richard, 127
Dold, Mark, 69
Dolgoy, Sholem, 105
Dolha, Andrew, 176
Dolidze, Tatuli, 69
Doll House, A, 72, 124
Dollar, Darren, 50
Domenech, Angel, 88
Dommermuth, Paul, 52
Don Cossacks, 26
Don Juan in Hell, 127
Don, Carl, 82, 169, 195
Donaghy, Tom, 62, 63
Donahoe, Lynn, 110
Donald, Linda, 59
Donaldson, Peter, 176
Donaldson, Selena, 167
Donat, Peter, 121
Dondlinger, Mary Jo, 37, 8, 97, 101, 128
Donkin, Eric, 176
Donleavy, J. P., 168
Donley, Robert, 97, 195
Donnalley, Robert G., Jr., 68
Donnelly, Candice, 10, 98, 122, 159
Donnelly, Donal, 145, 146
Donnelly, Kyle, 143
Donohoe, Rob, 127
Donovan, 65
Donovan, Kevin, 157
Donovan, Tate, 83, 146
Doolan, Constance, 174
Dooley, Ray, 158
Dopulos, Vincent, 97
Dorbian, Iris, 127
Dorfman, Robert, 94, 129, 141, 195
Dorfman, Rodrigo, 161

Dorfman, Toni, 59
Dorian, 68
Dorn, Franchelle Stewart, 171, 172
Dorn, Kirstin, 172
Dornan, Kate, 131, 130, 144, 153, 164, 171, 172
Dorson, Tyler John, 122
Doseth, Eli, 149
Dossett, John, 10, 36, 76
Doty, Cynthia, 37
Doubleday, Kay, 135
Doucette, Adrienne, 127
Dougherty, Christine, 164
Dougherty, J. P., 57, 195
Douglas, David, 165
Douglas, Eric, 58, 195
Douglas, Illeana, 134
Douglas, James "Buster", 39
Douglas, Kelly, 171
Douglas, Mark, 124, 172
Douglas, Shirley, 176
Douglas, Suzzanne, 16
Douglas, Tim, 175
Douglass, Mary Ellen, 169
Doulin, Jack, 91
Dovel, Ken, 53
Dovey, Mark, 113
Dowaliby, Suzanne, 168
Dowd, Ann, 80, 146
Dowd, Michael, 177
Dowling, Joe, 124
Dowling, Kevin, 62
Dowling, Rachael, 131
Dowling, Sam, 72
Dowling, Vincent, 164
Downer, Herb, 25
Downey, Roma, 21, 195
Downing, Becky, 139
Downing, David, 129, 172
Downing, Rebecca, 56, 193, 195
Downing, Virginia, 68, 146, 195
Downing-Bryant, Cassidy, 122
Downs, Lulu, 119
Downs, Michael E., 90
Downs, Sarah, 68
Downside, The, 118
Doxsee, Lenore, 62
Doyle, Al, 60, 66, 73
Doyle, Arthur Conan, 169
Doyle, Jack, 159
Doyle, Jay, 149
Doyle, Julie, 63
Doyle, Lori M., 120
Doyle, Mary, 135
Doyle, Patrick, 115, 131
Doyle, Richard, 162
Dr. Jekyll & Mr. Hyde, 59
Dracula, 150
Draesel, Bert, 72
Draghici, Marina, 57, 129
Draine, Kevin, 137
Drake, David, 140
Drake, Donald C., 169
Drake, Donna A., 25
Drake, Fabia, 231
Drake, Robert, 153
Drakeford, Deborah, 176
Draper, David F., 121
Draper, Paul, 141
Draper, Polly, 111
Draughon, Rick, 65
Drawbaugh, Laura, 55
Drayton, Cisco, 64
Drayton, Denise, 134
Dreams of Clytemnestra, The, 55
Dreisbach, Bill, 81
Dreisbach, Jeffrey, 19, 144, 193, 195
Dresser, Richard, 118
Dressler, Ralph, 120
Dretsch, Curtis, 156
Drevers, Louise, 48
Dreyer, Liz, 170
Driver, John, 74
Driving Miss Daisy, 94, 104, 119, 153
Drobny, Christopher, 94
Drobot, David, 135
Droz, Ken, 160
Drum, Leonard, 139, 157
Drumgold, Yvette, 105
Drummond, David, 118
Drummond, Joseph, 138
Drummond, Robin L., 98
Drury, Kacie, 137
Drusch, Mark, 118
Druzhkin, Andrey, 61
Dry, Steven K., 117
Dtamini, Lindiwe, 116
du Bois, Raoul Pene, 43
DuBoff, Rochelle, 53
DuClos, Danielle, 31, 195
DuClos, Deanna, 31, 193, 195
DuMont, James, 63
DuPois, Starletta, 131
DuPré, Lynette G., 33
DuRae, Liliane, 48
DuSold, Robert, 109
Duarte, Derek, 121
Dubin, Al, 154
Dubin, Allison, 62
Dubose, Virginia, 67
Duchess of Malfi, The, 141
Duchin, Jason, 168
Duckworth, Stuart, 166
Dudley, Craig, 193, 195
Dudley, William, 28
Dudo, Christy, 173
Dudwitt, Kimberly, 36, 76, 193, 195
Due with Variations, 175
Duell, William, 195
Duesing, Paula, 132
Duet with Variations, 175
Duff-Griffin, William, 120
Duff-MacCormick, Cara, 129, 168, 195
Duffey, Maureen, 110
Dufour, Isabelle, 57
Duggan, Charles H., 64
Dukakis, Olympia, 50, 168
Duke, O. L., 85, 95, 144
Duke, Stuart, 78, 101
Dukes, David, 12, 195
Dulack, Tom, 144, 153
Dulaine, Pierre, 18
Dulaney, Margaret, 71
Dulcie, Greg, 167
Dullea, Keir, 39, 195
Dumakude, Thuli, 61, 134
Dumas, Alexandre, 77
Dumas, Charles, 149
Dumas, Debra, 61, 64, 69, 70, 94
Dun, Dennis, 92
Dunbar, Brian, 43
Duncan, Kirk, 48
Duncan, Morgan, 172
Dundara, David, 48
Dunfee, Nora, 65
Dunford, Christine, 71
Dunham, Christine, 39
Dunham, Clarke, 139
Dunlop, William, 176
Dunn, Eileen, 44
Dunn, Glenn, 159
Dunn, Jeffrey, 111
Dunn, Margaret Anne, 131
Dunn, Terry, 145
Dunn, Tom, 60
Dunn, Wally, 65, 84
Dunnam, William, 161
Dunne, Stuart, 164
Dunning, Philip, 167
Dunnington, Steve, 69
Duplechain, Deanna, 156
Dupont, Milly, 151
Dupree, Ava, 167
Duquesnay, Ann, 91
Duran, Michael, 144
Durang, Christopher, 94, 147, 161, 164
Durante, 105
Durante, Jimmy, 105
Durante, Margie, Mrs., 105
Durbin, Holly Poe, 159
Durfee, Duke, 16
Durham, Christopher, 154
Durling, Ronald, 72
Durnin, Michael, 15
Durning, Charles, 28, 195
Durst, Anita, 65
Dussault, Nancy, 195
Dutton, Charles, 32, 130, 195
Duval, Vicki, 136
Duvall, Susan, 150
Duyal, Funda, 157
Dwenger, Ronald, 127
Dwyer, Frank, 37
Dybek, Tom, 50
Dye, Melissa, 145, 148
Dyer, Chris, 25
Dykstra, Brian, 52
Dylan Thomas: Return Journey, 78
Dylan, Abby, 60
Dys, Deanna, 15, 193, 195
Dyson, Erika, 62
Dzneladze, Ghia, 69
Each Day Dies With Sleep, 76
Eagan, Michael, 176
Eardley, Marilyn, 115, 131
Earl, Courtney, 144
Earle, Dorothy R., 89
Earley, Dyanne, 148
Early, Michael, 170
Earnest, Mimi, 171
Easley, Richert, 150
Easterline, Mary, 148
Eastley, Keely, 193, 195
Eastman, Donald, 77, 168, 172
Easton, Edward, 193, 195
Easton, Richard, 153
Easton, Robert, 34
Eaton, Daniel, 18
Eaton, Eve, 158
Eaton, Philip, 143
Ebb, Fred, 148
Ebel, Elizabeth M., 72
Ebersole, Christine, 147
Ebert, Joyce, 146
Ebsary, Kelly, 48
Eck, Scott Hayward, 57
Eckerle, James, 55, 59
eda-Young, Barbara, 120, 132
Ede, George, 149
Edegran, Lars, 70, 134
Edelhart, Yvette, 195
Edelman, Gregg, 4, 24, 50, 195
Edelstein, Gordon, 69, 145, 146
Edgerton, Earle, 93, 158, 165
Edington, Pamela, 98, 146
Edmead, Wendy, 195
Edmiston, Scott, 156
Edmonds, Mitchell, 153
Edmondson, James, 174
Edmunds, Kate, 143
Edney, Beatie, 53
Educating Rita, 156
Education of Paul Bunyan, The, 159
Edwards, Adrianne Monique, 168
Edwards, Alison, 171
Edwards, Ben, 19, 144
Edwards, Burt, 132, 154
Edwards, Daryl, 71, 164, 165
Edwards, Dex, 119
Edwards, Gus, 95
Edwards, Jack, 141
Edwards, Kate, 23
Edwards, Kelli, 151
Edwards, Larry, 125
Edwards, Matthew, 153
Edwards, Maurice, 64
Edwards, Michael, 174
Edwards, Sarah, 23, 122
Edwards, Stephen, 9
Edwardson, David, 70
Efremoff, Andrei, 144
Egan, Donal, 168
Egan, Kate, 68, 111
Egan, Kathleen, 156
Egan, Michael, 51, 80, 193, 195
Egan, Patricia, 129
Egan, Robert, 131
Egi, Stan, 92
Egloff, Elizabeth, 83, 120
Ehlert, Matt, 54
Ehman, Don, 71, 149
Ehrenberg, Steven, 17, 49, 61, 69
Ehrenreich, Jake, 90
Ehrlich, Jon, 19
Ehrlich, Joy, 122
Eichel, Paul, 129
Eichelberger, Ethyl, 16, 100, 170, 195
Eichenberger, Rebecca, 113, 160
Eichholz, Laura, 114
Eifert, Karen, 20
Eigeman, Chris, 120
Eigen, Richard, 145
Eigenberg, David, 82, 94, 193, 195
Eigsti, Karl, 157
Einhorn, Anne, 95
Einhorn, Susan, 67
Eisen, Max, 53, 55, 57, 59, 62, 67, 86, 96, 139
Eisenberg, Avner, 145
Eisenberg, Ned, 99, 195
Eisenhouer, Peggy, 11, 50
Eisloeffel, Elizabeth, 159
Eisner, John C., 144
Eister, Karen, 122
Ekstrand, Laura, 50
Ekstrom, Peter, 120
El Coronel No Tiene Quien Le Escriba (No One Writes to the Colonel), 88
El Gran Circo E.U. Craniano (The Great U.S. Kranial Circus), 88
El Paso o Parábola del Camino (El Paso or Parable of the Path), 88
El, Myron E., 127
Elbert, Wayne, 95
Eldard, Ron, 195
Elden, Kevin, 173
Elder, Susan, 149
Eldon, Jack, 154
Eldon, Thomas, 94
Eldridge, Robin, 143
Eleanor, 157
Elftman, Kurt, 68
Elg, Taina, 143
Elich, Michael, 123
Elio, Donna Marie, 43, 193, 195
Eliot, Drew, 193, 195
Eliot, Jane, 77
Eliot, T. S., 40
Elise, Christine, 147
Elizabeth, Joan, 138
Elizabeth, Susan, 150
Eljas, Anders, 103
Elkins, Doug, 53, 141
Elledge, David, 18, 195
Ellens, Rebecca, 120
Ellenstein, Peter, 162
Ellington, Duke, 144
Ellington, John, 162
Elliot Loves, 73, 138
Elliot, Christine, 120
Elliot, Kenneth, 52
Elliot, Marc, 133
Elliot, Milton, 60, 71, 134
Elliott, Christine, 120
Elliott, James, 173
Elliott, Kenneth, 48, 89, 195
Elliott, Marianna, 147
Elliott, Robert, 151
Elliott, Scott, 109, 129, 164
Elliott, Shawn, 24
Ellis, Anthony, 167
Ellis, Chris, 163
Ellis, Fraser, 41
Ellis, James, 6, 9, 12, 33, 36, 38, 44, 50, 51, 52, 67
Ellis, Joshua, 108
Ellis, Leslie, 74, 193, 195
Ellis, May, 68
Ellis, Tracey, 142
Ellis, Vicki, 119
Ellis, William, 93
Ellison & Eden, 65
Ellison, Nancy, 16
Ellman, Bruce, 55, 66, 83, 99, 168
Elmer, George, 17, 49
Elmore, Carole B., 135
Elmore, Richard, 174
Elmore, Sharon, 167
Elmore, Steve, 135
Elrod, Susan, 8, 37
Elsperger, Bruce, 121
Elten, Gina, 147
Elvgren, Gillette A., 177
Elvis: A Rockin' Remembrance, 50, 51
Embraceable You, 133
Emerald City, 162
Emery, Lisa, 130, 195
Emi, Evelyn Kiyomi, 131
Emmes, David, 162
Emmons, Beverly, 28, 55, 77, 83, 90
Emmott, Tom, 150
Emond, Linda, 138
Emonts, Ann, 76
End of the Day, The, 160
Endwords, 79
Enemy of the People, An, 129, 149
Eney, Woody, 160
Engan, Elisabeth, 25
Engel, Christopher, 75
Engel, David, 71, 195
Engel, Georgia, 133
Engel, Jeff, 39
Engels, Randy, 164
Engle, Stephen, 168
Engler, Michael, 10, 122, 129, 142, 160
English That for Me!, 79
English, Ellia, 101
English, Martin, 151
English, Rhonda Freya, 67
Ennosuke's Kabuki, 54
Ennosuke, Ichikawa, III, 54
Eno, Mary, 24
Eno, Terry, 17
Enriquez, David, 106
Enzell, John, 140
Ephron, Kai, 131
Epic Proportions, 155
Epperson, C. Jane, 60
Epps, Christian, 51, 59
Epps, Sheldon, 123, 139
Epstein, Alvin, 16
Epstein, Jonathan, 175
Epstein, Morey, 163
Epstein, Sabin, 121
Erb, Stephanie, 157
Erbe, Kathryn, 29
Erdman, Dennis, 147
Erdy, Brent, 57, 193, 195
Ergener, Sibel, 72
Ericksen, Susan, 168
Erickson, David Michael, 121
Erickson, Megan, 152
Erickson, Mitchell, 21, 30
Erickson, Ron, 166
Ericson, Russ, 62
Ernotte, Andre, 99, 139
Ernster, Mary, 133, 148
Ernster, Sharon, 56, 76
Errico, Melissa, 109
Erté, 144
Ervin, Pam, 167
Erwin, Barbara, 20, 195
Esbjornson, David, 132
Eschelman, Drew, 109
Escher, Elsbeth House, 149
Eskew, Doug, 33
Eskolsky, Alan, 46
Esposito, Giancarlo, 195
Esposito, Larry, 50
Esposito, Mark, 43
Esposito, Vicki, 53
Essen, B. J., 136
Essene, R., 134
Essner, Stephen W., 127
Established Price, 146
Estabrook, Christine, 58, 98, 195
Esterman, Laura, 138
Estey, SuEllen, 8
Estey, Suellen, 195
Etheredge, Randall, 62, 67
Etienne, Jerry, 176
Ettinger, Cynthia, 88
Ettinger, Daniel, 127, 145, 168
Eureka, 55, 59, 69
Euripides, 93
Eustace, Robert, 135
Eustis, John, 170
Eustis, Oskar, 131
Evans, Abby, 22, 73
Evans, Albert, 154
Evans, Bill, 73
Evans, Brent, 146
Evans, Craig, 58, 100
Evans, David, 139
Evans, Dawn, 60
Evans, Dillon, 170, 195
Evans, Gary, 72
Evans, Harvey, 195
Evans, Jessica, 124
Evans, Joan V., 60
Evans, Mari, 51
Evans, Rosalynn J., 78
Evans, Scott, 84
Evans, Stephen, 115
Evans, Tony, 72
Evans-Kandel, Karen, 62, 143, 160, 193, 195
Evening of Two One Act Plays, An, 51
Evenson, Wayne A., 126
Evering, Valerie Monique, 52
Evers, Brian, 82, 195
Evers, Bruce, 119
Everson, Patricia Ann, 120
Every Goodbye Ain't Gone, 51
Everybody Knows Your Name, 73
Evett, Benjamin, 59, 151
Evigan, Greg, 39
Ewald, Mary, 118
Ewen, Malcolm, 29
Ewer, Donald, 159, 169
Ewing, Christopher C., 135
Ewing, Mac, 56
Ewing, Tim, 159
Execution of Justice, 171
Expectations, 166
Experiment at the Asylum, 72
Expiation, 175
Ezell, John, 126, 151, 159
F.O.B., 92
Faber, Ron, 98, 99, 196, 197
Fabian, Kevin, 153
Fabrique, Tina, 33
Fabris, Bill, 68
Fabulous La Fontaine, The, 64
Facciponti, Laura, 165
Face á Face, 169
Facher, Trellis, 175
Fahmie, Fred, 52
Fails, Connie, 125
Fairbanks, Douglas, Jr., 39
Fairchild, Morgan, 39
Fairy Tales of New York, 168
Faison, Donald, 52
Faith Tabernacle Voices, 138
Faith, Chrissy, 24
Falabella, John, 97, 119, 143, 165
Falcone, Jane, 167
Faletto, Lisa, 114
Falk, Willy, 45, 109, 197
Fall of the House of Usher, The, 53
Fallender, Deborah, 131
Fallon, Dan, 157
Falls, Gregory A., 118
Falls, Patrick, 59
Falls, Robert, 138
Falstein, Bruce, 114
Fanning, Michael, 175
Fanning, Tony, 170
Fanny, 154
Fantasticks, The, 47, 145, 167
Farbrother, Mindy, 130
Farer, Rhonda, 196, 197
Farina, Marilyn J., 197
Farkas, James, 156
Farkas, Suzanne, 65
Farley, Robert J., 119
Farmer, Holly Frances, 113
Farr, Michele, 143
Farrar, Albert, 153
Farrar, John, 39
Farrell, Amy, 152
Farrell, Chris, 152
Farrell, Christine, 132
Farrell, Gordon, 95
Farrell, Kevin, 106, 112
Farrell, Richard, 118, 126
Farrell, Shari, 152
Farrell, Tom, 62, 70
Farwell, Elisabeth, 31
Farwell, Susan, 60, 70
Fata, Wesley, 66, 170
Father, The, 122
Faul, Kathy J., 97
Faulkner, Cliff, 153, 162
Faulkner-Alexander, Kenneth, 57
Fauss, M. Michael, 112, 119
Faver, Cheryl, 129
Favorini, Attilio, 177
Fawkes, Michael, 113
Fay, Tom, 89
Feagan, Leslie, 154
Feagin, Hugh, 167
Fearnley, John, 58
Feast Here Tonight, 99
Feast of Fools, 64, 137, 160
Feaster, George, 129
Featherston, Joe, 125
Federation of Confederates, A, 167
Fedor, Marck A., 53
Feenan, Marj, 60, 70
Feiffer, Jules, 73, 138
Feikis, Joe, 114
Feinberg, Linda, 72, 83
Feinberg, Paul N., 164
Feiner, Harry, 60, 149, 151, 165, 171
Feingold, Michael, 16, 73, 77
Feininger, Conrad, 172
Feinstein, Michael, 39
Feist, Gene, 97
Feke, Gilbert David, 94
Feld, Kenneth, 55
Feldman, Dave, 71
Feldman, Douglas L., 67
Feldman, Ruth M., 139, 146
Feldshuh, David, 129, 131
Feldshuh, Tovah, 44, 197
Feldstein, Claudia, 170
Feldstein, Wendy, 60
Felina, Queen of Sorrows, 30
Feller Precision, 20
Feller, Pete, 17, 22, 40, 43
Feller, Peter, Sr., 44, 107
Fellow Travellers, 63
Felton, Holly, 136
Fences, 119, 124, 126, 132, 135, 136, 159, 168
Fenhagen, Jim, 136
Fenley, Molissa, 53
Fennell, Bob, 71, 79
Fenton, James, 45
Ferencz, George, 161
Fergurson, Chamblee, 167
Ferguson, Georgianna, 152
Ferguson, John, 176
Ferguson, Lou, 143
Ferguson, Lynnda, 130, 143
Ferguson, Mark, 6
Ferguson, Nancy, 176
Ferguson, Nicholas, 115
Fergusson, Honora, 62, 91
Ferlita, Ernest, 67
Ferlo, Patrick A., 128
Fernandez, Lucio, 56, 196, 197
Fernandez, Peter Jay, 90
Fernandez, Roberto, 84
Ferra, Max, 60, 67, 69
Ferrall, Gina, 110
Ferrante, Evan, 74
Ferrante, Frank, 167
Ferrari, Marianne, 137
Ferraro, John, 60, 94
Ferren, Bran, 50
Ferrer, Jose, 154
Ferrier, Nathalie, 73
Ferrigno, Gillian, 154
Ferrone, Richard, 136
Fertig, Steven, 111
Fertilization Opera, The, 63
Fervoy, Tom, 129
Fessenden, Brian, 110
Festa, John Joseph, 40
Festa, Ken, 146
Festival Latino, 88
Few Good Men, A, 144, 180
Feydeau, Georges, 143, 145, 160
Fiat, 99
Fichandler, Zelda, 124
Fiddler on the Roof, 106, 127
Fiedler, Christine, 131
Fiedler, John, 135, 197
Field, Barbara, 141, 151, 159

Field, Crystal, 63, 196, 197
Field, Jules, 47
Fielding, Henry, 173
Fields, Christopher, 120
Fields, Dorothy, 119
Fields, Edith, 147
Fields, Herbert, 119, 139
Fields, James T., 167
Fields, Johnny, 138
Fields, Joseph, 56
Fields, Tony, 162
Fierman, Daniel, 143
Fierst, Gerald, 168
Fierstein, Harvey, 127
Fife, Julie A., 128
50/60 Vision, 131
Figg, David, 167
Figg, Emily, 167
Figueroa, Anaysha, 64
Figueroa, Liza, 163
Filiaci, Larry, 62
Film Society, The, 129
Finch, John, 59, 73
Finding Donis Anne, 165
Findley, Danielle, 144
Fine and Private Place, A, 123
Fineman, Carol, 13, 87
Finer, Gayle, 65, 144
Finerty, Mara, 110
Fingerhut, Arden, 62, 104, 131, 146
Fink, Dann, 110
Finkel, Barry, 155, 169
Finkel, Elliot, 14, 51, 80
Finkel, Fyvush, 80, 196, 197
Finkel, Joshua, 110
Finlay, Melodee, 105
Finlay, William, 122
Finley, David, 64
Finn, William, 11, 89
Finnegan's Funeral Parlor and Ice Cream Shoppe, 94
Finnegan, James, 174
Fiore, Jon, 52
Firestone, Doreen, 154
Firestone, I. W., 59
First Night, 166
Fischer, Don, 128
Fischer, John, 150
Fischer, Takayo, 168
Fischetti, Michael, 128, 146
Fishburne, Larry, 170
Fisher, Anne, 47
Fisher, Douglas, 139
Fisher, Ed, 74
Fisher, Edith, 165
Fisher, Jules, 11, 18, 50, 50, 91
Fisher, Linda, 132, 141, 144, 165
Fisher, M. Anthony, 107
Fisher, Rick, 81
Fisher, Robert, 16, 136, 167
Fishman, Carol, 98
Fishman, Joan, 50
Fiske, Richard, 50, 51
Fistos, John, 59
Fitters, Stefan, 57
Fitz, Norman, 124
Fitz-Simmons, James, 94
Fitzgerald, Ed, 83
Fitzgerald, Geraldine, 196, 197
Fitzgerald, Kathy, 126
Fitzgerald, Patrick, 79
Fitzgerald, Peter, 16, 20, 24, 33, 34, 70, 112
Fitzgerald, T. Richard, 28
Fitzgibbons, Jean, 45
Fitzmaurice, Catherine, 138, 141
Fitzpatrick, Allen, 56, 74, 197
Fitzpatrick, Colleen, 43, 101
Fitzsimmons, James, 68, 137
Five Dollar Drinks, 99
Fjelde, Rolf, 149
Flackett, Jennifer, 162
Flagg, Alan, 67
Flaherty, Stephen, 94
Flaherty, Steven, 145
Flam, Shira, 59
Flanagan, Courtney, 53, 60, 61
Flanagan, Pauline, 79, 159, 197
Flanders, Kristin, 170
Flanders, Lili, 129
Flaningam, Louisa, 57, 135, 196, 197
Flannery, Kara, 120
Flate, John-Michael, 196, 197
Flatt, Ernest O., 105
Flea in Her Ear, A, 145, 146, 160
Fleck, John, 147, 153
Fleet, Ian, 68, 197
Fleischer, Stacey, 49
Fleischer, Yolanda, 136
Fleishman, Sandra, 163
Fleming, Cynthia, 41
Fleming, Joyce, 148
Fleming, Sara J., 177
Fletcher, Bill, 131
Fletcher, David, 35, 145
Fletcher, Jack, 230, 231
Fletcher, John C., 121
Fletcher, Robert, 121, 149
Fletcher, Susann, 43, 196, 197
Flight, 73
Flockhart, Calista, 76, 95
Flomenhaft, Zivia, 51
Flood, Amy, 139
Flood, F. Hallinan, 124
Floor Above the Roof, 51
Flora, Becky, 22, 23, 24
Flora, Pat A., 119
Florida Crackers, 94
Flowers, Reginald, 144
Floyd, Tony, 141
Fluger, Martin, 72
Flynn, Bori, 117
Flynn, James V., 54
Flynn, Jimmy, 54, 60, 65, 70
Flynn, Juliann, X
Flynn, Lori, 117
Flynn, Steven, 162
Flynn, Tom, 103, 131
Foard, Merwin, 45
Foeller, William, 71, 129, 146, 168
Foerder, Preston, 57
Fogarty, Mary, 129, 154
Fogarty, Sharon, 59
Foglia, Leonard, 62
Fokin, Igor, 61
Fokine, Isabelle, 197
Folden, Lewis, 135
Foley, Alison, 91
Foley, John, 71, 145, 159
Foley, Robert, 169
Folger Shakespeare Theatre, 172
Foliage Festival of Wharton Plays, A, 175
Folk, Alexander, 160
Folts, Barbara, 20
Fonda, Jane, 39
Fontaine, Joel, 121, 159, 171
Fontana, Franco, 27
Fontana, Sam, 121
Fonte, Henry, 65
Food and Shelter, 121
Foote, Horton, 126, 167
Forad, Merwin, 45
Forbes, Barbara, 25, 78, 137, 156
Forbes, John B., 153
Forbes, Roger, 171
Forbidden Broadway 1989: Summer Shock Edition, 52
Forbidden Broadway 1990, 62
Forcade, Mary, 161
Ford, Anne Kerry, 16, 137
Ford, Clebert, 123, 124, 132, 168
Ford, Faith, 39
Ford, John, 138
Ford, Karen E., 139
Ford, Paul, 7
Foreman, Karole Lynn, 147
Foreman, Richard, 142
Forest in Aden, A, 91
Forever Plaid, 71
Forgette, Katie, 160
Forgiving Typhoid Mary, 136
Forkush, Anthony, 162
Forlow, Ted, 74, 196, 197
Forman, Bob, 101
Fornadel, Jeanne, 94
Fornes, Maria Irene, 67
Forrest, Donald, 161
Forrest, George, 18, 145
Forrester, William, 118, 166
Forshey, Les, 62
Forster, John, 157
Forston, Don, 148
Forsyth, Jerold R., 144, 169
Forsyth, Nancy S., 159
Forsythe, Henderson, 81, 197
Forte, Patricia, 67
Fortenberry, Philip, 52, 62
42nd Street, 154
Foskett, Mary, 51
Fosse, Nicole, 46
Foster, Angela, 95
Foster, Apryl R., 32
Foster, Curtis, 138
Foster, Frances, 73, 75, 197
Foster, Frank, Jr., 127
Foster, Gloria, 196, 197
Foster, Herb, 30, 196, 197
Foster, Jeff "V. J.", 88
Foster, Meg, 147
Foster, Skip, 119
Foster, Tim, 139
Fowler, Beth, 8, 128, 196, 197
Fowler, Clement, 91, 145, 146
Fowler, Monique, 143, 153, 171, 172
Fowler, Scott, 43, 196, 197
Fowlkes, Deborah A., 73
Fox, Alan, 64, 73
Fox, Bernard, 24, 69, 137
Fox, Dan, 119
Fox, David, 146
Fox, Gordon, 167
Fox, Hilliary, 131
Fox, Marilyn, 162
Fox, Neal, 170
Fox, Thomas, 124
Foy, Kenneth, 20, 112, 132, 139
Fraboni, Angelo H., 43
Fracher, Drew, 137
Fraley, Michal, 117
Frampton, Todd William, 125
France, Nicholas R., 152
Francesca, Diane, 169
Franceschina, John, 136
Franchi, Sergio, 230, 231
Francis, Alan, 17
Francis, Ron, 105
Francis, Tom, 118
Francis-James, Peter, 196, 197
Francks, Lili, 105
Frank Scardino Associates, 105
Frank, Chris, 159
Frank, Dan, 68
Frank, David, 164
Frank, Elizabeth, 76
Frank, Helen, 102
Frank, Jonathan, 175
Frank, Richard, 131
Franke, Georgeanne, 127
Frankel, Kenneth, 111
Frankel, Richard, 12
Frankel, Scott, 43
Frankenstein, 101
Frankfather, William, 120
Frankie and Johnny in the Clair De Lune, 120, 136, 162, 163
Frankie, 101
Franklin, Al, 169
Franklin, Aretha, 39
Franklin, David S., 90, 147
Franklin, Joseph, 160
Franklin, Nancy, 60, 196, 197
Franklin, Roger, 96
Franz, Elizabeth, 38, 197
Franz, Gina, 141
Franz, Joy, 154, 197
Franzel, Jeff, 52
Fraser, Alexander, 31
Fraser, Alison, 89, 197
Fraser, Brian, 174
Fraser, Donald, 130
Fraser, Doug, 105
Fraser, Jenny, 105
Fraser, Kevin, 176
Fraser, Patricia, 126, 153, 162
Fratantoni, Diane, 91
Frautschy, John G., 152
Frawley, Bernard, 79
Frawley, Kathryn, 78
Frawley, Mark, 84
Frayn, Michael, 120, 125, 127, 135, 156, 171
Frazier, Cliff, 86
Frazier, David O., 132
Frazier, Grenoldo, 86
Frazier, Joe, 39
Frazier, Michael, 70
Frazier, Randy, 50, 51
Frazier, Shannette, 167
Frechette, Peter, 94, 197
Frechtman, Bernard, 78
Freda, Richard, 137
Frederick, Matt, 143
Fredric, Arthur, 52
Fredrickson, Joel, 196, 197
Freed, Donald, 146
Freed, Sharon, 172
Freedman, Gerald, 97, 140
Freedman, Glenna, 11, 16, 17, 20, 27, 28, 48, 49, 52, 62, 80
Freedom Lies, 167
Freeman, Cheryl, 84
Freeman, Geoffrey M., 53
Freeman, K. Todd, 91, 129, 131
Freeman, Morgan, 197
Freeman, Neil, 175
Freeman, Scott, 121
Freeman, Virginia, 135
Freese, Ross, 151
Freeston, Mary, 152
Freeze Tag, 51
Frehner, Harry, 176
Frei, Nicki, 9
Freidson, Boris, 153
Fremgen, Beth, 11
French, Larry D., 154
French, Martha, 62
French, Michael, 50, 89, 94
Fretts, Chris, 168
Freud, 169
Freund, Jeff, 57, 60, 65
Frewen, Ray, 133, 148
Freydberg, James B., 144
Frezza, Christine, 171, 177
Frid, Jonathan, 197
Friedman, David, 169
Friedman, Doug, 41
Friedman, Janet, 29
Friedman, Jennifer, 108
Friedman, Mark, 147
Friedman, Neil, 133, 148
Friedman, Peter, 42, 82, 197
Friedman, Steve, 161
Friedmann, Joyce, 130
Friel, Brian, 79, 131
Friend, Angela, 145
Frierson, Andrea, 94
Frimark, Merle, 26, 29, 31, 40, 42, 43, 45, 46, 56, 58, 66, 69, 110, 113, 114
Frisch, Bob, 169
Frith, Norman, 101
Fritts, David, 151
Fritz, Ken, 23
Fritz, Lana, 55, 80
Frkonja, Jeffrey, 160, 166
Frost, Sue, 139
Frotscher, Donna, 119
Frow, Ben, 146
Fry, Ray, 120
Fry, Suzanne, 118
Frye, Andrea, 73
Fudge, Diedre, 102
Fugard, Athol, 91, 135, 143, 144, 167, 168, 168
Fugard, Lisa, 91
Fuglei, Kate, 65, 164, 196, 197
Fuhrman, Debbi, 154
Fujii, Timm, 103, 196, 197
Fujima, Eiken, 12
Fulbright, Peter, 14, 31
Fuller, Charles, 95
Fuller, Cory, 173
Fuller, David, 169
Fuller, Elizabeth, 135
Fuller, James E., Jr., 52, 101
Fuller, Janice, 196
Fuller, Nathaniel, 141
Fuller, Penny, 101, 197
Fung, Margaret, 56
Funicello, Ralph, 121, 149, 153, 160
Funny Girl, 148
Funny Thing Happened on the Way to the Forum, A, 177, 167
Fuqua, Joseph, 170
Furr, Teri, 20, 196, 197
Furth, George, 124
Further Mo', 70
Fusco, Anthony, 77
Fyfe, Jim, 22, 97, 197
Fylan, Nicky, 105
Fyodorov, Viktor, 54
Gabai, Inna, 153
Gabis, Stephen, 127
Gabler, Jolie, 14
Gabler, Linda, 157
Gabriel, Ethel, 55
Gabriel, Susan, 36, 91, 196, 197
Gaffin, Artie, 16
Gaffney, Lauren, 27
Gagliardi, Leon, 30, 40, 102
Gahnz, Craig, 106
Gaines, Boyd, 42, 196, 197
Gaines, Davis, 46, 70
Gaines, Sonny Jim, 134
Gal Baby, 119
Galantich, Tom, 24, 196, 197
Galas, Diamanda, 53
Galasso, Thom, 136
Galati, Frank, 29, 138, 160
Galde, Anthony, 17
Gale, Andy, 109
Gale, Brian, 90, 131, 147, 162
Gale, James, 173
Galendeev, Valeri, 153
Galgano, Richard, 72
Galich, Alexander, 88
Galilee, Clove, 62, 91
Galileo, 164
Galindo, Eileen, 96
Galindo, Ramon, 43, 196, 197
Gallagher, Colleen, 37, 70, 196, 198
Gallagher, Dick, 100
Gallagher, Kathleen, 25, 34
Gallagher, Maureen, 138
Gallagher, Megan, 19, 129, 180, 182, 183, 198
Gallagher, Terence, 138
Gallagher, William T., 138
Gallant, Joe, 61
Gallegly, David, 196, 198
Gallenz, Stephanie, 152
Galligan, Patrick, 176
Gallin, Susan Quint, 49
Gallo, Andrea, 70
Gallo, David K., 63
Gallo, Paul, 24, 44, 73, 82, 98, 138
Galloway, David, 124
Galloway, Jane, 147
Galloway, Pat, 176
Galo, John M., 108, 112
Galuszka, Sean, 165
Galvin, Tara M., 124
Gam, Rita, 196, 198
Gamache, Laurie, 41
Gamage, Steven, 67
Gamble, Julian, 171
Gamble, Kirsten, 27
Gandy, Irene, 12, 21, 32, 67, 78, 100, 116
Gangi, Jamie Dawn, 133, 148
Ganio, Michael, 135
Ganly, Kilian, 67
Ganshaw, Robert, 53, 70
Gant, Richard, 83
Gantt, Leland, 168, 173
Ganun, John, 154
Garber, Robert S., 132
Garber, Victor, 44, 124, 196, 198
Garboriau, Linda, 51
García, Santiago, 88
García Márquez, Gabriel, 88
Garces, Michael, 65, 69
Gardali, Glen, 34
Garde, Betty, 230, 231
Gardiner, John, 128
Gardner, Ashley, 142
Gardner, Herb, 125
Gardner, Jeff, 43, 110
Gardner, Kelly, 166
Gardner, Rita, 94
Gardner, William T., 157
Gardner, Worth, 120
Gari, Angela, 44
Garland, Geoff, 169
Garner, Julian, 149
Garner, Kenneth, 108
Garnett, David, 31
Garnett, Richard, 25
Garr, Nicholas, 43
Garr, Teri, 131
Garrett, Betty, 15, 198
Garrett, Brook, 84
Garrett, Mary, 121
Garrett, Paul, 135
Garrett, Shelly, 67
Garrett, Shelly, II, 67
Garrett, Shenea Starr, 67
Garrett, Susan S., 149
Garrett-Groag, Lillian, 153
Garrick, Barbara, 196, 198
Garrick, Beulah, 133
Garrison, C. Andrew, 151
Garrison, David, 124
Garrison, Gregorey, 43
Gartner, Thia, 94
Garver, Jack, 68
Garver, Kristen, 68
Garvey, Kathleen, 165
Garza, Ronald, 117
Garza, Troy, 41
Gasbarre, Roberta, 172
Gash, Kent, 171
Gaskill, William, 71, 77
Gaspar, Francine, 53
Gaspard, Raymond L., 64
Gasperec, Joseph, 27
Gass, Kyle, 88
Gassell, Sylvia, 198, 199
Gaston, Lyd-Lyd, 43, 154
Gatchell, Paul, 113
Gatchell, R. Tyler, Jr., 40, 117
Gates, Sarah Nash, 135
Gatien, Peter, 56
Gattica, Rene, 173
Gattoni, Susan, 105
Gaudio, Kate, 39
Gaughan, Jack, 102, 114
Gault, Willie, 39
Gaumer, Stephanie, 133
Gavin, Sherry, 125
Gavon, Igors, 198, 199
Gavva, Valeri, 54
Gayle, Crystal, 39
Gayr, Sheridan, 147
Gazzara, Ben, 111
Geddes, B. Alan, 105
Geddes, Jill, 107
Gedissman, Karen, 162
Gedrick, Jason, 198
Gee, Kevin John, 58, 154
Geer, Kevin, 146
Geffen, David, 40
Geffner, Deborah, 198
Gefroh, Steven J., 164
Gehman, Martha, 98, 198, 199
Geidt, Jan, 122
Geidt, Jeremy, 122
Geier, Paul, 198, 199
Geiger, Mary Louise, 52, 77, 84, 95
Geisslinger, Bill, 174
Gelb, Jody, 132, 198, 199
Gelbart, Larry, 10, 24, 43, 167, 169, 177
Geld, Gary, 6
Gelfer, Steven, 198
Gelinas, Gratien, 50, 51
Gelke, Becky, 100, 198, 199
Gellar, Sarah Michelle, 153
Geller, Susan Denison, 162
Gelman, Alexander, 88, 169
Gemignani, Paul, 43
Gendreau, Allison, 151
Genest, Edmond, 19, 144, 198, 199
Genet, Jean, 78, 131, 141
Genet, Michael, 19, 144
Geneviere, Deborah, 56, 198
Genise, Livia, 158
Gennaro, Michael P., 137
Gennaro, Peter, 16, 84
Genovese, Mike, 153
Genovese, Nicki, 96
Gentiles, Avril, 97, 198
Gentry, Jane, 177
Geoghan, Jim, 132
Geography of Luck, The, 147
Geoly, Guy, 6, 154
George Coates Performance Works, 121
George Street Playhouse, 137
George Washington Slept Here, 157
George, Ben, 18, 198, 199
George, Jeffry, 154
George, Libby, 60
George, Phillip, 52
Georgiades, James, 48
Georgianna, Frank, 135
Geraci, Drew, 41, 71
Geraci, Frank, 93, 198, 199
Geraci, Leslie, 77
Geraci, Paul, 20, 198
Geraghty, Marita, 42, 198, 199
Gerard, Anne-Marie, 17, 133
Gerber, Charles E., 63, 78, 198, 199
Gerdes, George, 19, 119, 144, 146, 198
Gere, Richard, 39
Gerhart, Michael, 103
Germann, Greg, 50, 51
Germano, Paul, 154
Gero, Edward, 171, 172
Gerringer, Robert, 230, 231
Gerrity, Dan, 142
Gerroll, Daniel, 160, 198
Gershenson, Sue Anne, 74, 198, 199
Gershon, Gina, 146
Gershovsky, Varon, 24
Gershwin, George, 68, 139
Gershwin, Ira, 68, 139
Gersten, Alexandra, 74
Gerston, Bernard, 41, 81
Gerth, James, 111
Gerut, Rosalie, 58, 198
Gervais, Richard, 154, 169
Gesner, Clark, 135
Gessur, Samuel, 51
Gets, Malcolm, 170
Gettel, Douglas, 48, 168
Getting Married, 145
Getty, Estelle, 39
Geva Theatre, 136
Gevirtz, Molly, 159
Geyer, Charles, 10
Geyer, Rick, 112
Ghaghanidze, Djemal, 69
Ghilardi, David Mitchell, 171
Ghoghitidze, Ivan, 69
Ghost of the Chinese Elm, The, 127
Ghostman, The, 146
Giamatti, Marcus, 142
Giampa, Wade J., 167
Gianfrancesco, Edward, 58, 100
Gianono, Joe, 114
Gianopoulos, David, 165
Gibb, David, 105
Gibbons, June, 141
Gibbs, Nancy Nagel, 20, 68, 71
Gibbs, Sheila, 94, 198, 199
Giberson, Philip D., 71
Gibson, Anne, 159
Gibson, Julia, 97, 140, 164, 198, 199
Gibson, Margaret, 120
Gibson, Matt, 67
Gibson, Maureen F., 82
Gibson, Michael, 15
Gibson, Rufus C., 149
Gibson, Teri, 139, 154
Gibson, Thomas, 51, 90, 198, 199
Gibson, William, 137
Gien, Pamela, 87, 147, 162
Gierasch, Stefan, 147
Giesenschlag, Russell, 111
Gievers-Yntema, Christa, 150
Gifts of the Magi, The, 61, 120
Gigl, Aloysius, 91
Giguere, Edi, 80

Gilbert, Alan, 111
Gilbert, Alyce, 18, 41
Gilbert, Edward, 143
Gilbert, Jennifer, 57, 64
Gilbert, Tony, 8, 198, 199
Gilbert, W. S., 154
Gilburne, Jessica, 37
Gill, Jackie, 53
Gill, James, 87
Gill, Michael, 46, 57, 114
Gill, Michel R., 170
Gill, Ray, 28, 89, 198, 199
Gillan, Tony, 170
Gillen, Linda, 157
Gillette, Anita, 99, 140, 198, 199
Gilley, Mickey, 39
Gilliam, Len, 167
Gillie, Joe, 128
Gillis, Susan, 177
Gillman, Robert A., 135
Gilmore, Philip, 66
Gilpin, Jack, 146, 198, 199
Gilpin, Michael, 62
Giménez, Carlos, 88
Gimpel, Erica, 76
Gin, Ray, 110
Gingerich, Peter, 52
Ginsberg, Ned, 39
Ginsburg, Kari, 172
Ginzler, Robert, 20
Gionson, Mel Duane, 198
Giordano, Tony, 73, 80, 137, 164
Giorgio, Joanne, 27
Giosa, Sue, 153, 198, 199
Giovanni, Nikki, 65
Giovine, Heidi W., 137
Girdler, Deb G., 145
Girouard, Tina, 91
Giroux, Laurent, 144
Gisselman, Gary, 126
Gisselman, Margo, 126
Gitto, George, 150
Giunand, Louise, 157
Gjelsteen, Karen, 118
Gladden, Dean R., 132
Gladman, Kimberly A., 117
Glander, Julia, 171
Glaser, John, 89
Glaser, Milton, 23
Glass Menagerie, The, 124, 156
Glass, Philip, 53, 122, 141
Glasser, D. Scott, 118
Glasser, Isabel, 58
Glassman, A. J., 145
Glaze, Susan, 99, 198
Glazer, Peter, 151, 160
Glazier, Andrew, 147
Gleason, James, 56, 164, 165, 198, 199
Gleason, Joanna, 198, 199
Gleason, John, 55
Gleason, Laurence, 198
Gleboya, Tatiana, 37
Glenn, David M., 124
Glenn, Gregory, 95
Glines, John, 53, 60
Glockner, Eleanor, 24
Glor, Gary, 137
Glover, Frederic, 80
Glover, Richard, 125
Glover, Savion, 198, 199
Glovsky, Jeff, 72, 72
Glushak, Joanna, 139, 164, 198, 199
Gobernik, Gregory, 37
God's Country, 174
God's Trombones, 86
Godinez, Henry, 153
Godinho, Mary, 173
Godwin, Stephen, 166
Goede, Jay P., 170
Goell, Julie, 145
Goetz, Jacqueline M., 152
Goetz, Michael, 81
Goetz, Peter Michael, 120
Goff, Charles, 137, 139
Going to New England, 67
Going, John, 154
Gold, Cindy, 171
Gold, Claudia, 66
Gold, Franne, 52
Gold, Jeremy, 120
Gold, Max, 115, 131
Goldberg, Deborah, 170
Goldberg, Hal, 74
Goldberg, Jerry, 41
Goldberg, Keren, 147
Goldberg, Lawrence, 103, 177
Goldberg, Marcia, 14
Goldblum, Jeff, 198, 87
Golden Apple, The, 101
Golden, Annie, 52
Golden, Charles, 58, 64
Golden, Norman, 59
Golden, Ruth, 70
Golden, Suzanne, 36
Goldenthal, Elliot, 61
Goldfaden, Abraham, 80
Goldfaden, Harold, 93
Goldhirsch, Sheri M., 94
Goldman, David, 61
Goldman, James, 57
Goldman, Judy, 82
Goldman, Marcyanne, 132
Goldpaugh, Kathleen, 124
Goldray, Martin, 122
Goldring, Danny, 147
Goldschmidt, Kurt, 155
Goldsman, Sam, 165
Goldstein, David Ira, 118, 126
Goldstein, Jess, 49, 57, 83, 94, 97, 99, 142, 146
Goldstein, Joe, 39
Goldstein, Steven, 81, 198
Goldstone, Bob, 99
Golin, Mark, 156
Golub, Peter, 87
Gomes, Rob, 72, 73
Gomez, Chuck, 88
Goncalves, Monica, 27
González, Cordelia, 170
Gooch, Katherine, 51
Good, Elaine, 136
Good, Peter, 144
Goodall, Howard, 169
Goodin, Steve, 120
Goodman Theatre, 138
Goodman, Lisa, 93, 198, 199
Goodman, Robyn, 98
Goodson, Jeffrey, 119
Goodspeed Opera House, The, 139
Goodspeed, Don, 31, 198, 199
Goodstein, Gerry, 73
Goodwin, Philip, 91, 142, 172
Goodwin, Rick, 121
Goodyear, Sam, 57
Goor, Carolyn, 43, 198, 199
Goose! Beyond the Nursery, 84
Gordina, Irina, 88
Gordon, Adele, 127
Gordon, Carl, 32, 130, 198, 199
Gordon, Clarke, 58, 201
Gordon, David, 52, 141
Gordon, Ellen Scrimger, 97
Gordon, Geoffrey, 61
Gordon, Jonhenry, 25
Gordon, Pamela, 131
Gordon, Sam, 165
Gordon, Seth, 95
Gordon, Susie, 69
Gordon, Thomas, 170
Gordon-Clark, Susan, 201
Goree, 86
Gorenstein, Scott, 14
Gorham, George H., 35
Gorky, Maxim, 120
Gorlick, Brenda, 176
Gorman, Anne E., 164
Gorman-Oomens, Prindle, 126
Gorney, Jay, 231
Gorostiza, Rebeca, 113
Gorton, Rob, 75, 149
Gorzelnik, Chris, 53, 58
Gospel at Colonus, The, 138
Goss, Deborah, 143
Gottlieb, John, 161
Gottlieb, Jon, 131, 147
Gottlieb, Nicholas, 50
Gottlieb, Peter, 152
Gottschall, Ruth, 17, 199, 201
Gould, Ari, 169
Gould, Christopher, 36
Gould, Gordon, 25, 199, 201
Gould, Harold, 22
Gould, Morton, 43, 169, 201
Gould, Richard, 113
Gould, Stephen, 114
Gould, Tom, 51, 60, 63, 66, 95
Gounder, Jill B., 107
Goutman, Christopher, 200, 201
Gow, Brian, 6, 70
Gow, John, 173
Goz, Harry, 201
Graae, Jason, 50, 70, 71, 141, 201
Grabowski, Christopher, 91
Grace, Richard, 125
Gradl, Christine, 135
Grady, Michael, 161
Graff, Randy, 4, 24, 200, 201
Graff, Todd, 200, 201
Graham, Dion, 129
Graham, Douglas, 114, 148
Graham, Elain, 83
Graham, Rachael, 15, 200, 201
Graham, Richard, 173
Graham, Ronny, 143, 144, 146
Granata, Dona, 131
Grand Guignol, The, 72
Grand Hotel, 18
Grande, Loretta, 48
Grandma Moses: An American Primitive, 140
Granger, Stewart, 21, 200, 201
Granite, Judith, 38, 63, 200, 201
Granny, The, 153
Grant, David Marshall, 67, 147, 201
Grant, Faye, 200, 201
Grant, Kathryn, 126
Grant, Lisa Ann, 45
Grant, Mary Ellen, 169
Grant, Richard, 134
Grant, Sean, 17, 43, 200, 201
Grant, William H., III, 86, 134, 168
Grapes of Wrath, The, 29
Grassilli, John, 159
Grate, Gail, 131, 170
Gravatt, Lynda, 128
Graver, Steven, 173
Graves, Aaron, 33
Graves, Julie, 20
Graves, Kia, 27
Graves, Michael, 57, 159
Gray, Allan, 176
Gray, Bruce, 130
Gray, Chuck E., 157
Gray, Daniel, 127
Gray, David Barry, 94
Gray, Kathy C., 125
Gray, Kenneth, 142, 173
Gray, Kevin, 46, 201
Gray, Larry, 145
Gray, Malcolm, 68
Gray, Paula, 11
Gray, Spalding, 53
Gray, Steve, 154
Grays, Marvin, 141
Grayson, Bobby H., 36, 76, 84
Grease, 148
Great Lakes Theatre Festival, 140
Great Sebastians, The, 150
Great US Kranial Circus, The, 88
Greco, Jose, 39
Green, Adolph, 43, 56, 112
Green, David, 123, 201
Green, Dennis, 134
Green, Fanni, 91, 141
Green, Frank, 28
Green, George, Jr., 40, 102
Green, Jackie, 6, 9, 12, 15, 25, 33, 36, 38, 44, 67, 97, 108
Green, John Martin, 52
Green, Larry, 91, 134, 144
Green, Mary-Pat, 144
Green, Susan, 114
Green, Suzanne M., 135
Greenan, Sean, 164
Greenberg, Helen, 200, 201
Greenberg, Mitchell, 16, 154, 201
Greenberg, Richard, 83
Greenberg, Rob, 119
Greenblatt, Kenneth D., 18
Greenblatt, Sandra, 18
Greene, Arthur M., 101
Greene, Ellen, 100, 201
Greene, H. Richard, 147
Greene, James, 200, 201
Greene, Lisa Gabrielle, 167
Greene, Lyn, 51, 74, 200, 201
Greeney, James, 141
Greenfield, Daniel, 160
Greenfield, Tom, 120
Greenleaf, John, 144
Greenspan, David, 56, 89, 94
Greenspan, Muriel Costa, 101
Greenwald, Ray, 58
Greenwald, Raymond J., 78
Greenwood, Jane, 13, 21, 58, 81, 82, 83, 145, 170
Greenwood, Paul, 75
Greer, Dean, 117
Greer, Larry, 151
Greer, Michael, 134
Gregg, Bill, 171
Gregg, Clark, 19, 144, 200, 201
Gregg, Jacqueline, 53
Gregg, Susan, 159
Gregorie, Alan, 55, 59
Gregorio, Rose, 146, 201
Gregory, Allison, 135
Gregory, Andre, 175
Gregory, Cynthia, 39
Gregory, Gilliam, 115, 131
Gregory, Helen, 91
Gregory, Julia, 111
Gregory, Marina, 175
Gregory, Michael Alan, 151
Gregory, Michael Scott, 43, 144, 200, 201
Gregus, Lubitza, 14
Greiss, Terry, 73
Greist, Arjuna, 170
Grenier, Zach, 10, 201
Greve, Susan Rae, 151
Grey, Jane, 23, 175
Grey, Joel, 39
Grey, Larry, 154
Griesemer, John, 89, 94, 200, 201
Griffin, Carmen, 95
Griffin, Donald, 119
Griffin, Jennifer, 6, 125
Griffin, Julianne, 125
Griffin, Lynne, 153
Griffin, Rodney, 139
Griffin, Sean G., 132
Griffin, Tom, 120, 133
Griffin, Victor, 126
Griffing, Lois, 138
Griffis, William, 158
Griffith, Jim, 48
Griffith, John P., 145
Griffith, Kristin, 73, 129, 200, 201
Griffith, Lisa, 173
Griglak, Jeffrey, 50
Grigsby, Peter, 148
Grille, Denise, 94
Grimaldi, Dan, 48
Grimaldi, Dennis, 22, 49
Grimaldi, Stacey, 139
Grimes, Justin, 158
Grimes, Tammy, 9, 132, 182, 200, 201
Grimm, Timothy, 56
Griswold, Mary, 152
Griswold, Tracy, 95, 143
Grodin, Charles, 97, 201
Grody, Gordon, 52
Grody, Kathryn, 90
Groenendaal, Cris, 46, 70, 113, 200, 201
Groff, Nancy, 58
Grollman, Elaine, 128
Gromada, John, 19, 51, 68, 69, 83, 83, 94, 94, 144, 146
Gromkowska, Ewa, 55
Gromov, Leonid, 61
Groom, Sam, 97
Groos, Daphne, 55, 69
Grosbard, Ulu, 82
Grose, Andrew, 43
Grose, Molly Pickering, 101
Groseclose, Frank, 143
Gross, Amy, 28, 200, 201
Grossman, Bill, 40
Grossman, Henry, 18, 201
Grossman, Laurie, 51
Grothe, Judy, 102
Groucho: A Life in Revue, 136, 167
Ground People, 75, 179
Ground, Kelly, 110
Grove, Barry, 58, 83
Grove, David, 122
Grove, Gregory, 201
Groves, Robin, 63, 67, 200, 201
Gruber, Michael, 41
Grubman, Patty, 18
Gruen, Barbara, 73
Gruenewald, Thomas, 139
Grunfeld, Deborah, 34
Grunions, 63
Grupper, Adam, 50
Grusin, Richard, 141
Gualtieri, Tom, 165
Guan, Jamie H. J., 92
Guaraldi, Mary G., 151
Guare, John, 82
Gubanov, Mikhail, 39
Gubelman, Serge, 170
Gudahl, Kevin, 176
Guergue, Marquerite, 53
Guerin, Lyse, 113
Guess, Alvaleta, 127
Guest, Lance, 62
Guevara, Dedre, 52
Guidall, George, 146
Guiguet, Kristina Marie, 113
Guilbault, Cheri L., 156
Guilbert, Ann, 135
Guillaume, Robert, 113
Guillory, Bennet, 131
Guin, Mark, 153
Guinan, Francis, 29
Guinan, Patricia, 127
Guinand, Louise, 176
Guittard, Laurence, 27, 200, 201
Gulan, Barbara, 120, 154
Gulledge, Chris, 125
Gulley, John, 126, 165
Gulliksen, Lainie, 119
Gunas, Gary, 50
Guncler, Sam, 128, 156
Gunderman, H. David, 15, 35
Gunderson, Anne, 111
Gunning, Thomas, 158
Gunther, Peter, 109
Gunther, Rosemary, 149
Gunton, Bob, 8, 201
Guralnick, Judi, 169
Gurney, A. R., 12, 111, 119, 128, 130, 132, 144, 154
Gurney, A. R., Jr., 166
Guskin, Harold, 87
Gustafson, Susan, 24
Gutenberg, Nina, 37
Guthrie Theatre, The, 141
Guthrie, Clay, 110
Guthrie, James R., 114
Guthrie, Lee, 138
Guthrie, Woody, 151, 160
Gutierrez, Gerald, 94, 144
Gutkin, Benjamin, 74, 132
Gutmann, David, 72
Gutrick, Tina, 50
Guttmacher, Peter, 60
Gutzi, Mary, 45
Guy, Leslie, 154
Guy, Rosa, 94
Guys and Dolls, 125
Guzman, Alberto, 108
Gwaltney, Jack, 95
Gwin, Kelly, 132
Gypsy, 20, 144, 180, 181
Haag, Christina, 138
Haagensen, Erik, 123, 139
Haas, Barbara, 165
Haas, Karl, 72, 94
Haas, Kate, 166
Haas, Susan, 118
Haatainen, Christina, 153
Haber, John L., 159
Hack, Steven, 201
Hackady, Hal, 154
Hadary, Jonathan, 20, 144, 201
Hadeba, Congo, 116
Hadley, Jennifer, 57, 171
Hadley, Jonathan, 107
Hadley, Mark, 167
Hadley, Michael, 57, 171
Haege, Jeana, 20
Hafer, Phillip, 173
Hafner, Julie J., 200, 201
Haft, Dan, 70
Hagan, Donna, 139
Hagan, Earl, Jr., 51
Hagan, John, 68, 200, 201
Hagar, Teresa, 48
Hagen, Daniel, 63
Hagerty, Julie, 111
Haggerty, John, 70
Haggerty, Steven, 158
Hahn, Fred, 68
Hahn, Howard, 145
Hahn, Jessica, 152
Haig, Peter, 128
Haigh, Jacqueline, 105
Haile, Evans, 50
Haimes, Todd, 97
Haines, Mervyn, Jr., 87
Haj, Joseph, 141
Hajian, Chris, 63
Hakawati, El, 53
Halbert, Sally, 64
Halden, Charles, 125
Hale, Dawn Marie, 70
Hale, Mother, 39
Hale, Pamela, 127
Haley, Donna, 67
Halim, Atchudta, 126
Hall, Adrian, 153
Hall, Bonnie Brittain, 162
Hall, Carl, 33
Hall, Carol, 67
Hall, Charles Edward, 200, 201
Hall, Debbie, 72
Hall, Ed, 153
Hall, George, 97, 200, 201
Hall, John, 52
Hall, Marcie, 128
Hall, Margaret, 30, 200, 202
Hall, Margo, 124
Hall, Michael, 128
Hall, Nancy, 40
Hall, Nicholas, 115, 131
Hall, Peter, 9, 25
Hall, Phil, 154
Hall, Philip Baker, 147
Hall, Rick, 169
Hall, Robert, 171
Hall, Sara-Page, 133
Hall, Thomas, 153
Hall, William, Jr., 119
Halley's Comet, 71, 123
Halley, Ben, Jr., 129, 141
Halley, Sharon, 154
Halliday, Andy, 52, 202
Halligan, Tim, 202, 205
Hally, Martha, 52, 128, 157
Halpern, Arthur, 120
Halpern, Martin, 123
Halpern, Mortimor, 6, 33, 38
Halstead, Cara, 155
Halston, Julie, 52, 200, 202
Hamacher, Al, 119
Hambrick, General McArthur, 102
Hamburger, Anne, 51, 65
Hamer, Nigel, 6
Hamilton, Ann, 167
Hamilton, Jane, 68
Hamilton, Kim, 124, 132, 168
Hamilton, Lisa Gay, 32, 87, 130
Hamilton, Mark, 52
Hamilton, Patrick, 128, 154, 169
Hamilton, Seth, 50, 121
Hamilton, Stephen, 67
Hamilton, Tim, 76
Hamilton, Victoria, 64
Hamlet, 91, 140, 177
Hamlin, Jeff, 81, 82
Hamlisch, Marvin, 41
Hamm, Lori W., 127
Hammar, Scott L., 172
Hammer, Ben, 165
Hammer, Erich, 108
Hammer, Mark, 90, 146, 170
Hammerstein, James, 27, 111
Hammerstein, Oscar, II, 27, 43, 108
Hammon, Susan, 173
Hammond, Andrew, 154
Hammond, David, 158
Hammond, Dorothea, 124
Hammond, Jared, 52, 61
Hammond, Paul, 162
Hammond, Rixon, 119
Hammond, Wendy, 146
Hampton, Christopher, 128, 137
Hampton, Donald, 54
Hampton, Marion, 125
Hampton, Verna, 54
Hanafin, Hope, 61
Hanahan, Lindsey, 154
Hanan, Stephen, 112, 121, 200, 202
Hanayagi, Hagi, 12
Hanayagi, Yoshijiro, 12
Hancock, John, 135
Handerek, Kelly, 176
Handler, Evan, 51, 82, 160, 202, 205
Handman, Wynn, 75
Handy Dandy, 137
Handy, John, 19, 30, 53
Haney, Kevin, 23, 122
Haney, Michael, 134
Hanket, Arthur, 63, 90, 100, 200, 202
Hanley, Mickey, 161
Hanlon, Maura, 100
Hanlon-Cressler, Sandra, 102
Hanna, Christopher, 168
Hanna, Deborah, 72
Hannah . . . 1939, 99
Hannah, Don, 58
Hannah, Elleen, 128
Hannah, James, 48
Hannah, Marguerite, 119
Hannah, Michael, 114
Hannah, Ned, 20, 43
Hannemann, Jane, 152
Hannibal, Ellie, 77
Hanrahan, Michael, 176
Hanreddy, Joseph, 152
Hansen, Elizabeth, 108
Hansen, Melanie, 10
Hansen, Randy, 169
Hanson, Alan, 125
Hanson, David, 127, 176
Hanson, Fred, 46
Hanson, Kenneth, 33
Hanson, Luther, 161
Hanson, Suzan, 135
Hanway, Tom, 99
Hapgood, 121
Happenstance, 118
Happy Days, 168
Happy End, 73
"Happy" New Yorkers, 63
Harada, Ann, 154
Harada, Deborah, 108
Haran, Mary-Cleere, 202
Harbach, Otto, 70, 139
Harbour, James, 125
Harcum, Bobby, 57
Harden, Marcia Gay, 55, 200, 202
Harder, Mitzi, 30, 102
Hardin, Belynda, 52
Hardin, Faser, 171
Harding, Jan Leslie, 51, 65, 159, 161
Harding, Kimberly, 73
Hardts, Walter, 167
Hardwick, Kevin, 57
Hardwick, Mark, 71, 120, 145, 149, 156
Hardwicke, Catherine, 88
Hardy, C. W., 124, 172
Hardy, Judy, 67
Hardy, Qiana, 152
Hardy, William, 129, 159
Hare, David, 13

Hare, William, 8, 37
Harelik, Mark, 120, 162
Harger, Gary, 109
Haring, Andrea, 175
Harker, James, 36, 87, 144
Harker, Wiley, 151
Harley, Margot, 144
Harling, Robert, 133, 154
Harloff, Lisa Comeaux, 148
Harman, Paul, 40, 164, 202
Harmon, Richard, 86
Harms, James, 148
Harnagel, John, 131
Harner, Barbara, 73
Harnick, Aaron, 165
Harnick, Sheldon, 43, 74, 106, 127
Haroche, Kim, 73
Harper, Arthur, 75
Harper, Bob, 71
Harper, Charles T., 230, 231
Harper, Clyde T., 136
Harper, Wally, 18
Harpster, K. Bruce, 93
Harrell, Gordon Lawry, 24, 139
Harrelson, Helen, 120
Harrington, Cheryl Francis, 153
Harrington, Delphi, 200, 202
Harrington, Laura, 94
Harrington, Nancy, 56
Harrington, Wendall K., 42, 89, 94, 160
Harris, Albert, 73, 144
Harris, Aurand, 127
Harris, Bill, 51
Harris, Bryan, 139
Harris, C. K., 65
Harris, Christopher, 53
Harris, Deborah, 169
Harris, Doug, 167
Harris, Estelle, 74, 202, 205
Harris, Gary, 55, 58, 80, 96, 98, 133
Harris, Harriet, 90, 97, 98, 146
Harris, Jane B., 70
Harris, Jeremiah J., 6, 16, 117
Harris, John, 73, 123
Harris, Joseph, 16, 25
Harris, Joseph, Jr., 16, 25
Harris, Julie, 146, 202
Harris, Linda, 172
Harris, Lloyd, 134
Harris, Mark, 126
Harris, Niki, 18, 202
Harris, Olivia, 55
Harris, Peter Lind, 110
Harris, Richard, 127, 145
Harris, Ronald Lew, 70, 202
Harris, Rosalind, 202
Harris, Roy, 42, 94
Harris, Sabrina, 110
Harris, Steve, 34
Harris, Timmy, 58, 80, 96, 98
Harris, Todd C., 152
Harris, Tom, 202
Harrison, Dean, 122
Harrison, Fran, 122
Harrison, Gregory, 39, 111
Harrison, John, 60
Harrison, Llewellyn, 86
Harrison, Noel, 111
Harrison, Peter, 71, 159
Harrison, Rex, 21, 202
Harrison, Stanley Earl, 108
Harrison, Tom, 126, 162
Harrop, Laurie, 135
Harry, Jimmy, 91
Harsdorff, Chris, 167
Hart, Caitlin, 59
Hart, Charles, 31, 46
Hart, Earnest, 64
Hart, Ed, 97
Hart, Elizabeth, 27
Hart, Gail Land, 113
Hart, Joe, 53
Hart, Kitty Carlisle, 39
Hart, Linda, 14, 202
Hart, Lorenz, 50, 139
Hart, M. E., 124
Hart, Melissa Joan, 76, 202
Hart, Moss, 124, 132, 157, 164, 171
Hart, Paul, 106
Hart, Richard, 93
Hart, Roxanne, 144, 202
Hartdagen, Diane, 89, 94, 134
Hartenstein, Frank, 14
Hartford Stage Company, 142
Hartley, Richard, 64
Hartley, Sean, 50
Hartley, Stewart, 64
Hartman, Karen, 94
Hartman, Mary, 175
Hartman, Michael, 29, 128
Hartman, Tim, 177
Hartnett, Mickey, 164
Hartwell, Peter, 131
Hartwig, Randy Lee, 84
Harum, David, 171
Harum, Eivind, 18, 41
Harvey, 141
Harvey, Don, 87
Harvey, Donald A., 170
Harvey, Justin, 111
Harvey, K. Lee, 110
Harvey, Nate, 62, 70
Hase, Thomas C., 152
Hashimoto, Kazuakira, 12
Haskell, Don W., 126
Haskell, Kelly, 174
Haskins-Prost, Yona, 143
Haslett, Dave, 150
Hassett-Murphy, Marybeth, 128
Hastings, Edward, 121
Hastings, Ron, 132, 176
Hat, 94
Hatch, Beddow, 132
Hatch, Ray, 127
Hatcher, Jeffrey, 63, 75
Hatcher, Robyn, 121
Hatfield, Susan, 128
Hathway, Christine, 115, 131
Hatsfelt, Naomi, 167
Haun, Scott K., 126
Haunton, Carol, 173
Haupt, Paulette, 94
Hauptle, Beth, 172
Hauser, Frank, 8
Hausman, Elaine, 131
Havard, Bernard, 169
Havard, Celine, 169
Havel, Vaclav, 66
Havis, Allan, 146
Hawkanson, David, 142
Hawkes, Terri, 202
Hawking, Judith, 156
Hawkinson, Jennifer, 152
Hawley, Colette, 140
Haworth, Steven, 145
Hay Fever, 128, 159
Hay, Richard L., 135, 174
Hay, Suzanna, 142, 165
Hayama, Kiyomi, 12
Hayden, Cynthia, 60, 136, 202
Hayden, Sophie, 123
Hayden, Tamra, 110
Hayes, Helen, 39
Hayes, Joanna, 119
Hayes, Lorey, 63, 202, 205
Hayes, Mary L., 137
Hayes, Neil, 51
Hayman, Charles, 173
Haynes, Jerry, 167
Hays, David, 144
Hays, Rex, 18, 202
Hayter, Rhonda, 63
Hayward, Bridget, 31, 44
Hayward, Elizabeth, 120
Hayward-Jones, Michael, 108
Hazel, Derek, 176
Hazen, John, 105
Hazouri, Selma, 50, 51
Hazzard, Karen, 6
Heacock, Kent, 127
Headley, Sue, 166
Heald, Anthony, 58, 73, 138, 202, 205
Healy, Christine, 131
Healy, Michael, 60
Heard, Denise, 139
Heard, Lynise, 139
Hearn, George, 15, 202
Heart of a Dog, 77
Heasley, Katherine, 149
Heath, Kia, 26
Heaven on Earth, 100
Hebert, Bob, 54
Hebert, Rich, 110
Hebert-Slater, Marilee, 120
Hecht, Deborah, 129
Hecht, Jessica, 77
Hecht, Lawrence, 121
Hecht, Paul, 101, 202
Heckart, Eileen, 38, 202, 205
Hedda Gabler, 145
Hedden, Roger, 63
Hedges, Peter, 76
Hedwall, Deborah, 42
Heeley, Desmond, 21, 176
Heer, Casey, 124
Heffan, Martin, 175
Heffernan, Maureen, 156, 157
Heggie, Femi Sarah, 103
Heggie, Iain, 59
Heidenreich, V Craig, 120
Heidi Chronicles, The, 42, 160
Heifner, Jack, 125
Heim, Michael Henry, 153
Heinberg, Allan, 99, 202
Heinsohn, Elisa, 46, 202, 205
Heintz, Karl R., 146
Heintzman, Michael, 75, 165
Heitman, Patricia, 79
Helde, Annette, 19, 120
Helfinstein, Bert I., 124
Helfman, Max, 80
Helland, J. Roy, 43
Heller, Adam, 45, 110, 202, 205
Heller, Heidi, 145
Heller, Laura, 67
Heller, Marc, 27
Heller, Maris, 75
Heller, Michael, 34
Heller, Nina, 63, 80
Heller, Robert, 202
Hellesen, Richard, 162
Hellman, Jerome, 16
Helm, Tom, 154
Helms, Bob, 148
Helrig, Gretchen, 113
Hemenway, David, 30, 117
Hemesath, Brian, 125
Hemingway, Alan, 62
Henderson, Aland, 117
Henderson, David, 166
Henderson, Deborah, 144
Henderson, Judy, 49, 71
Henderson, Kevin, 164
Henderson, Mark, 28
Henderson, Stephen McKinley, 164
Henderson, Stephen, 135
Henderson, Suzanne, 18, 202, 205
Henderson, Tracey, 152
Hendren, Mark, 120
Hendricks, Michael, 148
Hendrickson, Steven, 141
Henig, Nancy, 114
Henley, Beth, 171
Henley, Susan, 176
Hennig, Kate, 176
Henrikson, Steven, 113
Henritze, Bette, 9, 30, 202
Henry IV, 135
Henry IV, Part Two, 174
Henry V, 176
Henry, Brian, 106
Henry, Buch, 90
Henry, Buck, 202
Henry, Elizabeth L., 93
Henry, J. Chris, 63
Henry, Spruce, 61, 202, 205
Henry, Stephen Anthony, 135
Hensel, Karen, 162
Hensley, Charlie, 156, 169
Hensley, Dale, 40
Hensley, Sam, Jr., 119
Hensley, Todd, 152
Henson, Basil, 25
Henzel, Edward, 52
Hepburn, Katherine, 39
Herber, Pete, 109
Herbert, Jocelyn, 16
Herbert, Larry, 176
Herbst, Jeffrey, 35
Here in My Father's House, 95
Hereford, Nancy, 131
Heretz, John, 35
Herman, Anna Ungar, 156
Herman, Jerry, 127
Hermelin, Henrietta, 136
Hernandez, Alina, 46
Hernandez, Ismael, 65
Hernandez, Philip, 103
Herndon, Dorie, 154
Herochik, John, 149
Heron, Nye, 60
Herrera, Emil, 141
Herrera, John, 103
Herrera, Pilar, 158
Herrick, Jack S., 159
Herring, Linda, 86
Herrle, Robert, 150
Herrmann, Edward, 12, 39
Herscher, David, 39
Herscher, Seymour, 34
Hersey, David, 40, 45, 117
Hershman, Dara, 77
Hertzberg, Martha, 23
Hertzler, John, 161
Herz, Andrea Lauren, 72
Herz, Shirley, 16, 35, 48, 50, 52, 55, 62, 63, 68, 69, 71, 77, 80, 94, 99
Herz, Alexia, 43
Hess, Nancy, 43
Hess, Rodger, 50
Hester, Richard, 44, 75, 77, 83
Hetler, Lou, 160
Hetmanek, Thomas, 64
Heughens, Todd, 106
Hevner, Suzanne, 165
Hewett, Peggy, 89
Hewitt, Frankie, 33
Hewitt, Kenneth R., Jr., 136
Hewitt, Paul F., 62
Hewitt, Tom, 124
Heyerdahl, Chris, 176
Heyman, Sheila, 140
Heymann, Henry, 177
Heywood, Tim, 53
Hibbard, David, 141
Hibbert, Edward, 97, 170, 202
Hibler-Kerr, Rio, 113
Hicken, Tana, 124
Hickey, John, 67, 87, 132, 145
Hickey, Louise, 43
Hicklin, Walker, 36, 76
Hicklin, Walter, 162
Hickok, John, 100, 137
Hickok, Molly, 73
Hickox, A. C., 101
Hicks, Bryan, 19, 77, 87
Hicks, D'Atra, 64
Hicks, Israel, 135
Hicks, Jim, 124
Hicks, Laura, 42, 202
Hicks, Leslie, 121
Hicks, Munson, 143
Hicks, Peter W., 150
Hicks, Shauna, 15, 100
Hickson, Kevin, 23
Hidalgo, Allen, 133
Hiegel, Adrienne, 76
Higgans, Frank, 151
Higgins, Gerri, 34
Higgins, Janet Kay, 112
Higgins, John Michael, 75, 144
Higgins, Lisa K., 156
Higginsen, Vy, 64
Higginsen-Wydro, Knoelle, 64
High Button Shoes, 43
Hilbrich, Todd, 145
Hild, Dan, 40
Hildreth, Robert, 114
Hiler, Katherine, 94, 98, 202
Hilferty, Susan, 91, 98, 103, 138, 144
Hill, Alan, 68
Hill, Brian, 105
Hill, Collette, 50
Hill, Donald David, 147
Hill, E. Bruce, 177
Hill, Erin, 165
Hill, Frances, 60, 66, 73
Hill, Gary Leon, 135
Hill, Lawrence W., 101
Hill, Melissa, 149
Hill, Thomas, 28
Hill, William, 50
Hillary, Ann, 74
Hiller, Katherine, 90
Hillgartner, Jim, 145, 158
Hilliard, Ryan, 63, 202
Hillman, Jared, 72
Hillmer, Jay, 172
Hillner, Nancy, 202, 205
Hills, Randy, 58
Hillyer, Joe, 73
Hillyer, Michael, 72
Hilsabeck, Rick, 114
Hiltebrand, Steve, 154
Hilton, Donna Cooper, 139
Hilton, Margaret, 93
Hilton, Mary, 125
Hindman, Earl, 170
Hindman, James, 24
Hine, Roy, 55
Hines, Gregory, 87, 202, 205
Hinkle, Candyce, 125
Hinkle, Wendall S., 62
Hinkley, Brent "Hink", 88
Hipkins, Billy, 48
Hired Man, The, 169
Hirschfeld, Abraham, 17, 114
Hirschfield, Jeffrey, 176
Hissom, Eric, 150
Hitchcock, Jane Stanton, 73
Hjelmervik, Paul, 144
Hladsky, Barbara, 42
Hlatywayo, Thamsanga, 116
Hlegwa, Lindiwe, 116
Hoadley, Nancy, 166
Hobart, Sebastian, 58
Hoberman, Perry, 90
Hobson, Anne Marie, 56, 61
Hobson, Michalann, 168
Hocevar, Meta, 122
Hochman, Larry, 133, 137
Hochwald, Bari, 136
Hock, Robert, 81, 127
Hocking, Leah, 99
Hodes, Gloria, 202
Hodge, Mike, 19
Hodges, Cheryl, 154
Hodges, Francis, 173
Hodges, Patricia, 63, 118, 202
Hodgin, Lizz, 127
Hodgkin-Valcy, Tracey, 133, 148
Hodson, Ed, 121
Hoebec, Mark, 43
Hoebee, Mark S., 148
Hoemke, Robert, 152
Hofflund, Mark, 153
Hoffman, Avi, 58, 155, 202
Hoffman, Bob, 119
Hoffman, Constance, 173
Hoffman, Dustin, 25, 203
Hoffman, Jane, 81, 203, 205
Hoffman, John, 164
Hoffman, Kent, 79
Hoffman, Miriam, 58
Hoffman, Phil, 168
Hoffmann, E. T. A., 158
Hoffmann, Susannah, 176
Hofmaier, Mark, 64, 203, 205
Hofmann, Isabella, 138
Hofmeier, Mark, 64
Hofstetter, Benita, 124
Hofvendahl, Steve, 10, 63, 122, 203, 205
Hogan, Adam Michael, 174
Hogan, Bosco, 164
Hogan, James, 113
Hogan, Kevin, 93, 173
Hogan, Robert, 19, 144
Hogan, Tessie, 51, 156
Hogenmiller, Rudy, 148
Hogue, Annie G., 72
Hogue, Mitch, 72
Hoisington, Eric A., 43
Hoke-Witherspoon, Kenneth, 129
Holcombe, Gary, 151
Holder, Donald, 59, 80, 83, 91, 124, 134, 137, 156
Holder, Geoffrey, 39
Holder, Laurence, 75
Holdgrive, David, 101
Holgate, Danny, 125, 153
Holgate, Ronald, 44, 203
Holladay, Cleo, 127
Holland, Jan, 68
Holland, Reece, 113
Hollander, Leslie R., 72
Hollander, Providence, 132
Holliday, David, 164
Holliday, Polly, 28, 203
Hollis, Stephen, 63
Hollis, Tommy, 32, 130, 170, 179, 183, 203
Holly, Dennis, 101
Hollywood Scheherazade, 95
Hollywood, Danielle, 69
Holm, John Cecil, 135
Holman, Terry Tittle, 167
Holmes, Bryan, 150
Holmes, Chad, 150
Holmes, Denis, 25
Holmes, Doug, 127
Holmes, George, 133
Holmes, Prudence Wright, 30, 203, 205
Holmes, Richard, 68
Holmes, Rupert, 34
Holms, John Pynchon, 51, 95
Holt, Lorri, 131
Holt, Monique, 51
Holt, Shannon "Bunny", 88
Holt, Tamara, 65
Holt, Thelma, 9, 25
Holten, Michael, 64, 137, 160
Holton, Melody, 135
Holtzman, Merrill, 10, 50, 146, 203, 205
Holtzman, Will, 51, 95
Holy Days, 162
Home Games, 78
Home and Away, 160
Homeless . . . But We Gotta Life, 167
Homesick, 66
Homewood, Charles, 6
Honda, Carol A., 92, 203, 205
Honea, Marc, 129
Honegger, Gitta, 135, 170
Honeyman, John, 159
Honeywell, Roger, 176
Hooker, Brian, 52
Hoon, Barbara, 43
Hoover, Bruce A., 116, 144
Hoover, Richard, 131
Hope, Leslie, 162
Hope, Samantha, 124
Hope, Sharon, 66
Hopkins, Anthony, 78
Hopkins, Bernard, 176
Hopkins, Billy, 81
Hopkins, Linda, 203
Hopkins, Thelma, 39
Hopper, Paul, 150
Hopson, Hollie, 153
Horan, Gerard, 115, 131
Horen, Robert L., 127
Horgan, Patrick, 169, 203
Horman, Michelle, 120, 156
Hormann, Nicholas, 165
Horn, Andrew M., 155
Horn, John, 131
Horne, Dawn, 172
Horne, J. R., 123
Horowitz, Israel, 58, 147
Horowitz, Jeffrey, 52, 77
Horrigan, Patrick, 28
Horsey, Susan Urban, 68
Horsman, Kim, 176
Horton, Brian, 127
Horton, Edward "Buddy", 107
Horton, Jamie, 135
Horvath, Jan, 16, 46, 102, 203
Horvitz, Wayne, 77
Hoschna, Karl, 139
Hoshke, John, 17, 203
Hoskins, Jim, 136
Hoskins, Sally, 115, 131
Hosmer, George, 145, 165
Hostetter, Curt, 91
Hostetter, Paula, 27
Hostettler, Andy, 231
Hot Minute, A, 52
Hotopp, Michael J., 112, 136
Hoty, Dee, 24, 203, 205
Hoty, Tony, 20, 203
Houdyshell, Jayne, 150
Houghton, Diane, 148
Houghton, Katharine, 203, 205
Hould-Ward, Ann, 94, 107, 124, 144, 160
Houlton, Loyce, 141
House of Blue Leaves, 174
House of Horrors, The, 99
House, Ron, 161
Houseman, John, 144
Houser, Christie, 147
Houston Shakespeare Festival, 173
Houston, Jessica, 127
Houston, Kipling, 43
Houston, Velina Hasu, 168
How Are Things in Costa Del Fuego?, 63
How the Other Half Loves, 169
Howard, Arliss, 147
Howard, Celia, 156, 203
Howard, Charles, 167
Howard, David S., 136, 137, 168
Howard, Ed, 144
Howard, Ken, 12, 203
Howard, M. A., 36, 76
Howard, Marcial, 28
Howard, Margaret, 120
Howard, Norman, 155, 155
Howard, Peter, 144
Howard, Richard, 174
Howard, Stuart, 20, 28, 48, 106, 108
Howard, Taylor, 55, 205
Howe, Stephen J., 149
Howell, Mary E., 129
Howland, Gerard, 121
Hoy, Linda, 153
Hoyle, Geoff, 64, 137, 160
Hoyle, Kalen, 167
Hoylen, Tony, 84
Hoyt, J. C., 173
Hoyt, Lon, 117
Hubbard, Jeffrey, 113
Hubbard, Philip, 174
Hubbard, Valorie, 97
Huber, Kathleen, 128, 203, 205
Huddleston, Harvey, 50
Hudgins, Marilyn, 17, 111, 203
Hudson Guild Theatre, 78
Hudson, Heather, 169
Hudson, Ken, 167
Hudson, Mitchell, 160
Hudson, Rodney Scott, 122
Hudson, Travis, 203
Hudson, Walter, 168
Huerta, Jorge, 161
Huessy, Raymond, 40, 102
Huffman, Cady, 137, 203
Huffman, Felicity, 81, 144, 153
Huffman, Ted, 27
Hughes, Alice S., 154
Hughes, Allen Lee, 94, 124, 159
Hughes, Annie, 56
Hughes, Barnard, 36, 76, 203
Hughes, Bonny, 168
Hughes, Douglas, 141, 160
Hughes, Julia C., 89
Hughes, Julie, 8, 18, 37
Hughes, Laura, 89, 94, 203
Hughes, Mark, 125, 171
Hughes, Phillip, 176
Hughes, Rhetta, 86
Hughes, Tracy, 161
Hughes, Tresa, 122, 203
Hugo, Victor, 45
Hugot, Marceline, 128, 133
Hui, Alyson, 66
Huisenga, Craig, 118
Hul, Wolfgang, 149
Hulce, Tom, 19, 144, 203
Hull, Bryan, 47
Hull, Mindy, 161
Hull, Rob, 169
Hull, Susan, 155
Hulsey, Robert, 125
Hulswit, Mart, 136
Hulteen, Cheryl, 63
Humana Festival of New American Plays, The, 120
Hume, Michael J., 128, 142
Hume, Nancy, 160
Humeniuk, Roman, 105
Humes, Linda H., 65, 203
Hummer, Robert, 131
Hundley, C. L., 132, 168
Huneryager, David, 114
Hunt, Helen, 111

Hunt, James, 96
Hunt, Pamela, 159
Hunt, Trey, 8
Hunt, W. M., 156, 157
Hunt, William Dennis, 156, 161
Hunter, Dawn, 72
Hunter, Edith Taylor, 159
Hunter, JoAnn M., 43
Hunter, Marc, 169
Hunter, Mary, 160
Hunter, Nakomi, 130
Hunter, Ronald, 74, 133
Hunter, Tim, 73, 116
Hunting Cockroaches, 174
Huntington Theatre Company, 143
Huntington, Burr, 136
Huntington, Crystal, 58, 67
Huntington, John, 50
Huntley, Paul, 8, 23, 40, 42, 102, 122, 144, 157
Huntsman, Laurie, 149
Hurd, Hugh, 126
Hurd, Mary L., 93
Hurd, Patricia, 114
Hurd-Sharlein, Adrienne, 11
Hurdle, James, 132
Hurlburt, Carolyn, 128
Hursey, Shirese, 127
Hurst, David, 103, 144
Hurst, Gregory S., 137
Hurst, Howard, 6, 33, 38
Hurst, Sophie, 6, 33, 38
Hurston, Zora Neale, 134
Hurt, Elisa, 119
Hurt, Mary Beth, 13, 203
Hurt, William, 76, 203
Hussey, Raymond, 117
Husted, Patrick, 153, 162
Husted, Sandra, 150
Hutcheson, Scott, 125
Hutchings, Jeannine, 151
Hutchinson, Ann, 146
Hutchison, Paul, 78
Hutchman, David F., 169
Hutton, John, 138
Hutton, Timothy, 12, 36, 203
Hwang, David Henry, 92, 122
Hwong, Lucia, 53, 92
Hyde Park, 143
Hyde in Hollywood, 94
Hydenburg, Patrick, 91
Hyland, Edward James, 165
Hyman, Earle, 203, 205
Hyman, Fracaswell, 63
Hyman, Ralph, 125
Hynd, Ghretta, 62, 138
Hyndman, Grace, 154
Hyslop, David, 144
I Am a Winner!, 96
I'm Not Rappaport, 125
ICM Artists, 12
Iacangelo, Peter, 147
Iacovelli, John, 147, 162
Ibsen, Henrik, 72, 124, 129, 145, 149
Ice Cream with Hot Fudge, 91
Ietto, Domenick, 153
Iglewski, Richard S., 141
Ikeda, Thomas, 119, 154
Iljima, Ken, 12
Illg, Roberta, 119
Illien, Phyllis Della, 107
Illinois Theatre Center, 145
Illusion, The, 142, 147
Ilo, Angelique, 41
Imaginary Invalid, The, 121
Imagining Brad, 76
Imai, Naoji, 12
Imam, Sheikh, 53
Imbody, Joel, 119
Imbrie, Peggy, 154
Immigrant, The, 120
Importance of Being Earnest, The, 93, 126, 142, 149
In Darkest Africa, 120
In Darkest America, 120
In Her Own Words: A Portrait of Jane, 53
In the Hollow, 159
Inches, Sandi, 144
Incommunicado, 144
Infidelities, 71
Infinity's House, 120
Ingalls, James, 122, 138
Inge, William, 123, 128
Ingraham, Margaret, 148
Ingram, Elizabeth, 175
Ingram, Michael, 97
Ingram, Tad, 143
Ingster, Peter, 6
Innaurato, Albert, 94
Innes, John, 176
Innes, K. Craig, 15, 43
Innes, Laura, 69, 137, 203
Inside Technocult, 121
Into the Woods, 94, 107, 144, 148
Ionesco, Eugene, 122, 131
Ireland, James, 54
Irie, Kaoru, 12
Irish Repertory Theatre, 79
Irish, Mark, 73
Irizarry, Richard V., 96
Irvine, Barbara, 56
Irving, George S., 154, 203
Irving, Janet, 58
Irwin, Bill, 203, 205
Irwin, Holly, 112
Irwin, Robin, 148
Is He Still Dead?, 146
Isaacs, Pamela, 139
Isaacson, Lyons, 58, 83
Isen, Richard, 123, 139
Ishee, Suzanne, 46
Ishida, Masaya, 12
Ishihama, Hideo, 12
Ishii, Leslie, 121
Ishioka, Eiko, 141
Istomin, Marta, 144
It's a Wonderful Life! The Musical, 127
Italian American Reconciliation, 145, 155
Iten, Terry, 17
Itzin, Gregory, 130, 162
Ives, David, 63
Ives, Donald, 169
Ivey, Dana, 91, 162, 203, 205
Ivey, Lela, 147
Ivory, 69
JQ and the Bandits, 50
Jackel, Paul, 61, 107
Jackness, Andrew, 98, 124, 168
Jacksina, Judy, 18, 69
Jackson, Andrew, 176
Jackson, B. J., 152
Jackson, Brian H., 176
Jackson, Chelli, 67, 203
Jackson, David, 18, 203, 205
Jackson, Duane, 134
Jackson, Freddie, 39
Jackson, Gary, 169
Jackson, Glenda, 130
Jackson, Julie, 138
Jackson, Kevin, 91, 134
Jackson, Kirk, 129
Jackson, Marsha A., 73
Jackson, Nagle, 121, 149
Jackson, Rosemarie, 128
Jackson, Russell, 115, 131
Jackson, Samuel L., 95, 170
Jackson, Sara, 58
Jackson, Suzanne, 170
Jackson, Trevor, 124
Jacob, Abe, 27, 41, 61, 111
Jacobi, Derek, 130
Jacobs, Ben, 52
Jacobs, Craig, 20
Jacobs, Douglas, 161
Jacobs, Ellen, 62, 73
Jacobs, George, 54
Jacobs, Jim, 148
Jacobs, Max, 77, 203
Jacobs, Peter Anthony, 147
Jacobs, Robert, 160
Jacobs, Sally J., 40
Jacobs, Sander, 18
Jacobs, Stefan, 74
Jacobson, Donna, 99
Jacobson, Jay B., 27
Jacobson, Naomi, 144
Jacoby, Gordon, 73
Jacoby, Marc, 114
Jacoby, Mark, 18, 203
Jacox, Martin, 138
Jaeck, Scott, 138
Jaffe, Daniel M., 150
Jaffe, Jill, 69
Jaffrey, Sakina, 120
Jahncke, Carter, 172
Jake's Women, 153
Jakes, John, 171
Jakiel, Richard, 77
James, Anthony, 69
James, Bob, 91
James, Brian d'Arcy, 148
James, Camille, 176
James, Di Ray, 157
James, Geraldine, 25
James, Grant, 167
James, Harold Dean, 10
James, Hilary, 153
James, Jerry, 62
James, Jessica, 230, 231
James, Karl, 115, 131
James, Kathryn Ann, 124
James, Kelli, 203
James, Lawrence, 126
James, Peter Francis, 91
James, Toni-Leslie, 66, 91, 92, 96, 134
James-Greene, Richard, 151
James-Reed, Michael, 91
Jamieson, Todd, 143
Jamison, Chris, 106
Jampolis, Neil Peter, 9, 14, 25, 27, 64, 71, 144, 160
Jamrog, Joseph, 96, 203
Janasz, Charles, 141
Janecek, Jim, 152
Janney, Allison, 156
Janzen, Melanie, 176
Jaramillo, Leticia, 135
Jarczyk, Michal, 55
Jared, Todd A., 147
Jarett, Debbie, 142
Jaroslow, Ruth, 106
Jarvis, Lucy, 61
Jarvis, Scott, 230, 231
Jarzabski, Elaine, 102
Jasien, Deborah, 137
Jasmine, 17
Jason, Jill, 70
Jason, Mitchell, 18
Jasper, Zina, 100
Javore, James, 133
Jay, Brian, 15
Jay, Mary, 154, 157
Jay, Michael, 136
Jay, William, 95, 119, 133, 204
Jay-Alexander, Richard, 45
Jayson, Jennifer, 154
Jbara, Gregory, 97, 103, 204
Jefferis, Barclay, 135
Jefferson, Paul, 135
Jeffrey, Debbie, 50
Jeffrey, Terry Mike, 50, 51
Jekyll!, 151
Jekyll and Hyde, 137
Jellis, Paula, 150
Jellison, John, 91, 137
Jemison, Eddie, 138
Jenkin, Len, 63
Jenkins, Carol Mayo, 130
Jenkins, Daniel, 99
Jenkins, David, 34, 49, 97, 164
Jenkins, Ken, 99, 204
Jenkins, Lorilyn, 167
Jenkins, Paulie, 131, 160, 162
Jenkins, Tamara, 109, 157
Jenks, Barbara, 150
Jenner, Cynthia, 75
Jenness, Morgan, 91, 94, 147
Jennings, Byron, 135, 153
Jennings, Ken, 18, 204
Jennings, Kim, 57
Jennings, Michael, 139
Jennings, Nolan, 176
Jennings, Richard, 162
Jensen, Eric, 118
Jensen, Jared, 152
Jensen, Paul, 59
Jenson, Kari, 149
Jepson, J. J., 18
Jerome Robbins' Broadway, 43
Jerome, Timothy, 18, 204
Jerry, Philip, 11
Jeter, Camille L., 144
Jeter, Michael, 18, 204
Jetton, Austin, 102
Jewesbury, Edward, 115, 131
Jewett, Bob, 161
Jewish Repertory Theatre, 80
Jiang, John Q., 92
Jiggetts, Shelby, 134
Jimenez, Robert, 53, 62
Jirak, Joan, 152
Jirovec, Susan, 65
Jo-Ann, Ebony, 134
Joanitis, Sean, 150
Jobe, Amanda, 95
Jochim, Keith, 159
Joe Turner's Come and Gone, 157, 164
Johanson, Don, 204
Johanson, Jane, 105
Johanson, Robert, 154
John F. Kennedy Center for the Performing Arts, The, 144
Johnny Pye and the Foolkiller, 137
Johns, Glynis, 21, 204, 205
Johns, Kurt, 31, 109, 204
Johns, Randy Allen, 133, 148
Johnson, Angela, 126
Johnson, Ann, 170
Johnson, Antonio, 161
Johnson, Arch, 49
Johnson, Beverly, 39
Johnson, Bjorn, 109, 135, 145
Johnson, Daniel Timothy, 52, 72, 204
Johnson, Danny, 152
Johnson, David, 93
Johnson, Denton, 39
Johnson, Diana, 135
Johnson, Doug, 119
Johnson, Eric, 31, 75, 174
Johnson, Erika, 175
Johnson, Ethan, 88
Johnson, Evans, 67
Johnson, Eve, 143
Johnson, G. Michael, 152
Johnson, Garry, 134
Johnson, Gary Neal, 151
Johnson, Geordie, 176
Johnson, Greg, 55, 63
Johnson, Gustave, 122
Johnson, Heidi Karol, 154
Johnson, James Weldon, 86
Johnson, Jay, 57
Johnson, Jennifer, 73
Johnson, JoAnn, 174
Johnson, Joy, 128
Johnson, Karl, 63
Johnson, Keith, 124, 132, 168
Johnson, Ken, 134
Johnson, Lamont, 164
Johnson, Larry, 139
Johnson, Lauren, 119
Johnson, Lea Ann, 53, 54, 55, 60
Johnson, Lori, 65
Johnson, Marjorie, 135
Johnson, Mark Whitman, 125
Johnson, Marta, 120
Johnson, Mary H., 135
Johnson, Mary Lea, 18
Johnson, Michelle, 81
Johnson, Page, 67, 204, 205
Johnson, Philip, 61
Johnson, Pookie, 84
Johnson, Reid G., 150
Johnson, Robert A., 67
Johnson, Robert, 62
Johnson, Rod, 136
Johnson, Roosevelt T., 136
Johnson, Russell W., 32, 130
Johnson, Scott, 53
Johnson, Sheri M., 135
Johnson, Shontae Olivia, 25
Johnson, Susan, 148
Johnson, Tim, 75, 204
Johnson, Toni Ann, 95
Johnson, Virgil, 138, 151
Johnson, Virginia, 39
Johnson-Liff & Zerman, 44
Johnston, Bonnie, 153
Johnston, Brian, 129
Johnston, Donald W., 139
Johnston, Jay, 125
Johnston, Nancy, 54
Johnston, Richard, 121
Johnston, Rick, 67
Jolles, Annette, 170
Jolly, Russ, 159
Jonah and the Whale, 90
Jones, Albert, 153, 157
Jones, B. J., 56
Jones, Bill T., 53
Jones, Browen, 66
Jones, Bryan C., 119
Jones, Cassie, 149
Jones, Cherry, 122
Jones, Christine, 53
Jones, David Edward, 159
Jones, David, 68
Jones, Dexter, 139
Jones, Gordon G., 159
Jones, Jane, 118, 174
Jones, Jay Aubrey, 40, 204
Jones, Jeffrey M., 51
Jones, Jennifer, 136
Jones, John Christopher, 83
Jones, Ken, 122
Jones, Kimberly, 66
Jones, LeRoy, 131
Jones, Llewellyn, 65
Jones, Ora, 138
Jones, Rachel, 15
Jones, Reed, 230, 231
Jones, Retha, 67
Jones, Robert A., 125, 166
Jones, Robert Earl, 138
Jones, Robert, 166
Jones, Russ, 111
Jones, Sabra, 204
Jones, Seth, 170
Jones, Silas, 124
Jones, Simon, 97, 204
Jones, Stephen, 100
Jones, Steven Anthony, 121
Jones, Thomas W., 2d, 73
Jones, Tom, 47, 145, 167, 173
Jones, Walker, 56, 204
Jones, Walton, 170
Jonquil, 85, 95
Jonson, Ben, 141
Joplin, Joneal, 159
Jordan, Bruce, 144
Jordan, Clarence, 119
Jordan, David, 110
Jordan, Henry J., 153
Jordan, Richard, 90
Jordan, Samantha, 110
Jory, Jon, 120
Joseph and the Amazing Technicolor Dreamcoat, 169
Joseph, Leonard, 50
Joseph, Robin Anne, 61
Joslyn, Betsy, 106, 107, 106
Jost, Ted, 154
Joubert, Joseph, 33
Jovovich, Scott, 43
Joy, James Leonard, 112, 119, 143, 151
Joy, Robert, 94, 204
Joyce, Ella, 170
Joyce, Geraldine, 161
Joyce, Heidi, 204, 205
Joyce, Joe, 157, 204
Joyce, Walker, 164
Joyner, Kimble, 94
Joyner-Kersee, Jackie, 39
Ju, Helen C., 170
Juan Darien, 61
Judd, Rebecca, 8, 204
Judevine, 121
Judge, Cynthia, 152
Judge, Diane, 78, 100, 103
Judge, Don, 22
Judge, Shawn, 141
Judy, James, 137, 143
Jue, Francis, 154
Jukes, D. E. , 177
Julia, Raul, 90, 204
Julian, Richard, 167
Jung, Philipp, 10, 57, 58, 68, 73, 95, 122, 137, 151, 160, 164
Junge, Alexa, 164
Juno and the Paycock, 124
Junon and Avos-The Hope, 61
Jurglanis, Marla, 135
Jurosko, Keith, 68
Justis, Jim, 152
Jutras, Simon, 67
Juviler, Elizabeth, 175
K2, 64
Kabel, James M., 21
Kachel, Roger, 102
Kaczmarek, Jan A. P., 138
Kaczmarek, Jane, 91
Kaczmarek, Peri, 138
Kaczorowski, Peter, 83, 89, 142, 164
Kadel, Steve, 117
Kading, Charles Stanley, 171
Kadokawa, Haruki, 16
Kadri, Ron, 35, 53
Kagan, Diane, 204
Kahl, Drew, 172
Kahn, Gary, 24, 204, 209
Kahn, Judy, 68
Kahn, Michael, 141, 172
Kahn, Tobi, 90
Kaikkonen, Gus, 52, 60, 136
Kakhiani, Marina, 69
Kaladjian, Shirleyann, 159
Kalaidjian, Robert, 80
Kalas, Janet, 76, 94, 129
Kalfin, Robert, 11, 33, 123, 139
Kall, James, 140, 148
Kallos, Stephanie, 158
Kalriess, Karen, 68
Kamal, Youssif, 73
Kamlot, Robert, 44
Kamm, Tom, 76, 77, 91, 98
Kammer, Nancy, 145
Kanai, Shunichiro, 54
Kancheli, Ghia, 69
Kandel, Paul, 100, 139, 154, 204
Kander, John, 20, 148
Kane, Andrea, 61
Kane, Cynthia, 50
Kane, Donna, 15, 50, 204, 209
Kane, Francis, 172
Kane, Mary, 204
Kanee, Stephen, 150
Kani, John, 86, 91
Kanin, Garson, 136, 151
Kantor, Mary, 11
Kantor, Mitchell, 101
Kantor, Pamela, 67
Kantrowitz, Jason, 23, 97, 108, 122
Kapen, Ben, 82
Kaplan, Barry Jay, 149
Kaplan, Claudia, 151
Kaplan, Howard Tsvi, 126
Kaplan, Paul A., 67
Kaplan, Steve, 63, 69
Kaplin, Stephen, 61
Karachentsev, Nikolai, 61
Karasiov, Denis, 61
Karbacz, Kelly, 27
Karge, Manfred, 124
Karibalis, Curt, 204, 209
Karlya, Tom, 48
Karnaushkin, Alexander, 61
Karnes, Jay, 151
Karoku, Nakamura, 54
Karol, John, 51
Karr, Elizabeth, 54
Karvonides, Chrisi, 170
Kaske, Betsy, 152
Kaslow, Susan, 59
Kass, Jon, 11
Katarina, Anna, 204
Kate's Diary, 89, 94
Kater, Peter, 76
Kathy & Mo Show, The, 94
Katigbak, Mia, 92
Katkowsky, Robert, 136
Katlin, Bruce, 169
Katona, Raissa, 46
Katsaros, Doug, 89
Katsman, A., 153
Katz, Abbie H., 122
Katz, Cindy, 170
Katz, Leon, 129
Katz, Natasha, 20, 38, 57, 112
Katz, Paul, 57
Katz, Steven, 50
Katz, Tracy, 107
Katzman, Jodi, 67
Katzman, Wendi L., 173
Kauders, Sylvia, 74
Kauffman, Thomas M., 156
Kaufman, Brian A., 7, 51
Kaufman, Dale, 43
Kaufman, Eric H., 20, 204
Kaufman, George S., 68, 124, 132, 157, 164, 170, 171
Kaufman, Kyuf, 39
Kaufman, Laurie, 39
Kaufman, Martin R., 18
Kaufmann, Phil, 170
Kaunders, Sylvia, 74
Kavilis, Diana, 41
Kawolsky, Christopher, 133, 136
Kay, Hershy, 41
Kay, Kenneth, 128
Kay, Michael, 65
Kay, Stephen T., 132
Kaye, Bradley D., 137
Kaye, Judy, 50, 70, 204, 209
Kaye, Toni, 105
Keach, Stacy, 39
Keagy, Grace, 126
Keal, Anita, 57, 74, 204
Kean, Greg, 147
Kearney, Edmund J., 171
Kearney, Karon, 126
Kearney, Kristine, 171
Kearney, Patricia, 54
Kearns, Daniel, 26
Keathley, George, 151
Keating, Brad, 114
Keating, Charles, 97
Keaton, Ronald, 133, 148
Keats, Steven, 49, 204, 209
Kebour, Farid, 37
Kechely, Gary E., 134
Keck, Michael, 60, 95
Kedzierski, Art, 167
Kee, Chung, 154
Keefe, Anne, 145, 146
Keefe, Robert, 121, 143, 145
Keegan, Jane, 165
Keegan, Ted, 8
Keeler, Brian, 160
Keeler, William, 132, 169
Keeley, David, 176
Keen, Keith, 106
Keenan, Claudia, 168
Keener, Christopher, 135
Keith, Laura, 152
Keith, Randal, 114, 148
Keith, Susan, 72
Keith, Warren, 71, 135
Kekana, Fana, 86
Keleher, Maryann, 167
Kelik, Jan, 173
Kellachan, Daniel J. P., 23
Kelleher, Susan, 60, 65
Keller, Jeff, 46
Keller, Jim, 49, 142
Keller, John-David, 162
Kelley, Kevin, 51
Kelley, Sam, 170
Kelley, Warren, 59, 145
Kellin, Orange, 70, 134
Kellogg, Marjorie Bradley, 132, 136, 146, 160
Kellogg, Robert, 18
Kelly, Alexa, 65
Kelly, Brian P., 59
Kelly, Charles, 48
Kelly, Chris A., 53, 63, 79
Kelly, Daniel Hugh, 28
Kelly, David Patrick, 142
Kelly, David, 164
Kelly, Dennis, 148
Kelly, Dona Lee, 70
Kelly, Donna, 113
Kelly, Drew, 72
Kelly, Eamon, 79, 204
Kelly, Glen, 154
Kelly, Hubert Baron, 120, 176
Kelly, Hubert, Jr., 162
Kelly, Jude, 97
Kelly, Kate, 128
Kelly, Kieran, 137
Kelly, Lisa, 166
Kelly, Maura, 169
Kelly, Michelle, 102
Kelly, Patrick, 77, 167
Kelly, Paula, 147
Kelly, Randy, 60, 65
Kelly, Thomas A., 25, 34, 144

Kelly-Young, Leonard, 151, 177
Kelvin and Co., 138
Kemp, Emme, 70
Kemp, Sally, 131, 162
Kendall, Joan, 135
Kendrick, Richard A., 93
Keneally, Thomas, 131
Kener, David, 58, 155, 204
Kenison, R. Scott, 68
Kennedy, Arthur, 230, 231
Kennedy, Ashley York, 119, 170
Kennedy, Beau, 58
Kennedy, Bryan, 115, 131
Kennedy, Craig, 52, 86
Kennedy, Dennis, 138
Kennedy, Eleanor, 173
Kennedy, Jihmi, 131
Kennedy, Karen, 59
Kennedy, Laurie, 119
Kennedy, Lorne, 176
Kennedy, Michael, 105
Kennedy, Morgan, 132
Kenner, Pat, 168
Kennon, William, 56, 89, 94
Kenny, Frances, 118, 135, 166
Kenny, Jack, 106
Kenny, Jason, 161
Kenshaka, 95
Kensington Stories, The, 15
Kent, Monroe, 127
Kent, Robert, 48
Kent, Steven, 147
Kenwright, Bill, 22
Kenyon, Neal, 67
Kenyon, Sandy, 130
Keough, Rosemary, 48
Kepros, Nicholas, 204
Kerbeck, Robert, 95, 204
Kerber, Jim, 102
Kerenyi, Mihaly, 51
Keriotis, Adrienne, 177
Kerlin, K. William, 133
Kermoyan, Michael, 108
Kern, Jerome, 70
Kernan, Peter S., 158
Kerner, Howard, 165
Kerner, Susan, 137
Kerns, Linda, 71, 110, 204
Kerr, Glen, 113
Kerr, Mary MacDonald, 152
Kerr, Patrick, 54, 135
Kerr, Robert, 94
Kerrigan, Donal, 143
Kerrigan, Maureen, 144
Kersey, Yvonne, 134
Kershaw, Whitney, 204
Kert, Larry, 133
Kerwin, Brian, 130
Kesling, Thomas Kresten, 135
Kessler, Lyle, 160
Kessler, William H., Jr., 103
Kesten, Frederika, 175
Ketcham, Ben, 153
Keudell, Devin M., 131
Kevin, Michael, 174
Kevoian, Peter, 160
Kevrick, Robin, 145, 146
Key, Tom, 119
Khalil, Amer, 53
Khan, Rick, 134
Kharshiladze, Daredjan, 69
Khidasheli, Akaki, 69
Khmelnitski, Pytor, 54
Khmelnitski, Usher, 54
Khodadad, Victor, 173
Khoury, Cynthia, 114
Khoury, Pamela, 43, 204, 209
Khovanskaya, Alyona, 88
Khumalo, Leleti, 116
Khumalo, Sibongile, 86
Khumalo, Siphiwe, 86
Khuzwayo, Mhlathi, 116
Kiamco, Rich, 53
Kiara, Dorothy, 52
Kid 'n' Play, 39
Kidd, Ron, 47
Kidd, Wiley, 31, 204
Kikuchi, Susan, 43
Kilburn, Terence, 150
Kilby, Kim, 119
Kildare, Martin, 171
Kilgarriff, Patricia, 30, 83
Kilgore, John, 89, 94
Kilik, Howard, 72
Kilkelly, Mary Beth, 77
Killen, Milton, 167
Killian, Philip, 174
Killian, Scott, 91, 129
Killmer, Ted, 51, 65
Killy, Peter, 156
Kilroy, Colette, 50, 51, 56, 65, 75
Kilty, Jerome, 10, 97, 122, 204
Kim, Jacqueline, 172
Kim, Willa, 144
Kimball, David A., 120
Kimbrough, Matthew, 61
Kimel, Janna, 175
Kincaid, Eric Scott, 40
Kincaid, John A., 97
Kincaid, Leslie, 127
Kincaid, Mark, 119
Kindl, Charles, 25, 38
Kindlon, Peter M., 128
Kinematic, 69
Kinerk, Diane, 120
Kinet, Kristina, 26, 39
King Lear, 69, 115, 131, 168
King and I, The, 108
King of Hearts, 144
King, Anne S., 122
King, Denis, 97, 146
King, Doug, 127
King, Eric, 95
King, Floyd, 172
King, Jeffrey, 131
King, Joyce P., 84
King, Kimberly, 149
King, Natalie, 167
King, Robert, 176
King, Willie, 171
King, Woodie, Jr., 59, 86
Kingdom, Bob, 78
Kingfish, 90
Kingsbury, John W., 172
Kingsley, Barbara, 141
Kingsley, Gretchen, 8
Kingsley-Weihe, Gretchen, 204
Kingston, Debora, 72, 77
Kingston, Kaye, 128
Kinney, Mary Lisa, 66
Kinney, Terry, 29
Kinsey, Richard, 110
Kinsherf, John, 143
Kinter, Alexandra, 114
Kinter, Richard, 114, 127
Kinter, Roddy, 127
Kiouses, John, 164
Kirkwood, James, 41
Kirman, John, 110, 119
Kirsch, Gary, 139
Kirsch, Hugh William, 141
Kirschner, Richard, 68
Kirwan, Larry, 60
Kisciolek, Ryszard, 55
Kismet, 145
Kiss Me Kate, 176
Kitch, Geoffrey, 127
Kittner, Harriett, 45
Kittredge, Ann, 157
Kjeldsberg, Johan Brun, 149
Kjenaas, Peter, 174
Kladitis, Manny, 108
Klain, Margery, 68
Klaisner, Kathy, 148
Klampert, Jay Philip, 93
Klappas, Pam, 127
Klapper, Stephanie, 80
Klausen, Ray, 39
Klavan, Laurence, 63
Klavan, Scott, 163
Kleban, Edward, 41
Klein, Amanda J., 84, 143
Klein, David S., 166
Klein, Jeff, 118
Klein, Jon, 119, 168
Klein, Lauren, 94
Klein, Robert, 39
Klein, Sharon, 111
Klein, Steven M., 118, 160
Klein, Will, 54
Kleinsmith, Dennis T., 150
Klementowicz, Paul, 99
Klemperer, Werner, 27, 204
Kletter, Debra J., 36, 76
Kliegel, Frank, 41
Klimovitsky, Alex, 62
Kline, Elmer, 66
Kline, Kevin, 91, 144, 204
Kline, Randall, 64, 160
Kling, Kevin, 160
Klingelhoefer, Robert, 59, 71, 92, 96, 155
Klinger, Brian, 54
Klinger, Bruce, 19
Klinger, Mary K, 131
Klotz, Florence, 24
Klug, Mary, 143
Kluga, Ray, 71
Kluger, Steven, 136
Klunis, Tom, 204
Knall, Christopher C., 173
Knapp, Bob, 143
Knapp, Jacqueline, 159
Knapp, Sarah, 144, 204, 209
Knecht, Peter J., 135
Knee, Allan, 122, 155
Kneeland, Richard, 153
Knell, Dane, 30, 206, 209
Knepper, Robert, 91
Knight, Aaron, 158
Knight, Darwin, 114
Knight, Gladys, 39
Knight, Lily, 156
Knight, Martha, 124
Knight, Michael E., 78
Knight, Shirley, 140
Knight, Susan, 50, 87, 91, 91, 94, 132
Knight, Wayne, 10, 90, 206
Knott, Frederick, 156
Knower, Rosemary, 129
Knox, John, 136
Knox, Kerro, 3, 165
Knudsen, John, 27
Knutsen, Erik, 91, 97
Kobart, Ruth, 121
Kobayashi, Kohei, 12
Kobryner, Joe, 153
Koch, Carl, 173
Koch, Danielle T., 124
Koch, David Hunter, 118
Kochergin, Eduard, 153
Kociolek, Ted, 139
Kodner, Eric, 141
Koetting, Michael, 102, 111
Koger, Jeffrey S., 73
Kohler, Laura, 145
Kohrman, Ellen, 122
Koka, Juliette, 206, 209
Kokkin, Janne, 149
Kolb, Norbert U., 132
Koletzke, Peter, 57
Kolinski, Joseph, 45, 206
Kolo, Fred, 33, 139
Kolodner, Arnie, 52
Koloskov, N., 88
Kolsby, Marian, 55
Kolyada, Nikolai, 161
Komiyama, Yuko, 92
Komolova, Valentina, 61
Kompst, Richel, 110
Kondek, Charles, 101
Kondoleon, Harry, 160
Kondrat, Michael J., 55
Konicki, Joe, 43
Konig, David, 63
Konopka, Albin, 143
Konstantin, Elise-Ann, 68
Konynenburg, Susan, 105
Kooch, Peggy, 125
Koon, Robert, 152
Kopache, Thomas, 9, 206
Kopit, Arthur, 122
Korbick, Eddie, 8, 206, 209
Korder, Howard, 147, 162
Koreto, Abigail, 67
Korey, Alix, 89
Korf, Geoff, 170
Korf, Mia, 154
Korker, Ron, 108
Korker, Russell, 108
Kormendi, Kati, 65
Kornberg, Richard, 13, 41, 87, 98
Kornfeld, Eric, 84, 206
Kornfeld, Lawrence, 129
Korobko, Vyacheslav, 54
Korotkova, Paulina, 26
Korp, Pamela, 54
Korshak, Margie, 114
Korshunov, Vadim, 54
Korthaze, Richard, 206
Korzan, Kelly, 177
Korzen, Annie, 80, 206
Kosak, Iwana, 55
Kosciolek, Elzbieta, 55
Kosek, Kenny, 99
Kosher, Alan Ross, 103, 107
Kostalik-Boussom, Linda, 162
Kotlisky, Marge, 160
Kotlowitz, Dan, 57
Kotoske, Tamar, 69
Kotto, Yaphet, 124
Koustik, Art, 162
Koutoukas, H. M., 55, 69
Kovarik, Christopher, 167
Kovcic, Zoran, 149
Kovitz, Randy, 147
Kowal, James, 11
Kowalkowski, Carl, 164
Kozeluh, John, 101
Kozlov, Gennady, 61
Kozlov, Igor, 88
Kozlov, Oleg, 153
Kozlova, Valentina, 39
Kozlowski, Matt, 120
Kraemer, Bruce A., 91
Kraft, Barry, 121
Krag, James, 56, 206
Kraii, Christian, 173
Krain, Colin, 129
Krakower, Bob, 120
Krakowski, Jane, 18, 206
Kramer, Eric, 173
Kramer, Jeff, 174
Kramer, Joel, 106
Kramer, Larry, 65
Kramer, Rob, 146
Kramer, Sherry, 98
Krane, David, 8, 105
Krank, Meghan Rose, 128, 156
Krantz, Doug, 113
Krasker, Tommy, 50, 139
Krasnansky, Jennifer, 53
Krass, Michael, 60, 91, 104
Krause, Mark, 50, 103
Krause, Neal, 39
Krausnick, Dennis, 175
Krauss, Marvin A., 11, 18, 50, 112
Krauss, Michael, 73
Kravchenko, Vladimir, 26
Kravits, Jason, 172
Kravitz, Barbara, 170
Krawic, Michael A., 140
Krebs, Eric, 53, 64, 66
Krebs, Michael, 152
Kreider, William, 156
Krell, Daniel, 158
Krementz, Steve, 13, 87
Kremer, Dan, 174
Krenz, Frank, 30
Kressin, Lianne, 132, 159
Kressyn, Miriam, 59
Kretzmer, Herbert, 45
Krieger, Barbara Zinn, 99
Krieger, Donald, 147
Kriewall, Adrianne, 150
Krim, Mathilde, Dr., 39
Krist, Andrea, 140
Kristien, Dale, 113, 206
Kristina, Lisa, 114
Krisukas, Mike, 156
Kriz, Zdenek, 58
Krizan, Robbie, 164
Krizner, Douglas, 143, 144
Kroeger, Perry Arthur, 66
Kroeze, Jan, 63
Krok, Loren, 15
Kroll, James A., 127
Kron, Ron, 70
Kronenberg, Bruce, 48
Kroner, John, 127
Krouner, Betsy, 39
Kruger, Herschel, 72
Kruger, Simcha, 59
Krugman, Ken, 141
Krupa, Olek, 77
Krupp, Jon, 80, 129
Kruschke, Gerhard, 6
Kruse, Paul James, 161
Kruskamp, Jennifer, 110
Kubala, Michael, 43
Kubota, Glenn, 50
Kuhlke, Kevin, 143
Kuhn, Bruce, 45, 206
Kuhn, Kevin, 84
Kuhns, David, 177
Kuipers, Kristen R., 171
Kulerman, Ruth, 53
Kulok, Peter T., 16, 25
Kumalo, Siboniso, 116
Kumin, Fran, 10, 22, 32
Kumin, Jeremy, 80
Kumor, Michael, 68
Kunzelman, Betsy, 129
Kuper, Yuri, 144
Kuptsova, Yadviga, 39
Kurdyumova, N., 88
Kuroda, Kati, 92, 141
Kurowski, Ron, 41
Kurowski, Susan, 54
Kurshal, Raymond, 206
Kurth, Juliette, 128
Kurtz, Ken, 114, 126
Kurtz, Marcia Jean, 94, 206
Kurtz, Normand, 34
Kurtz, Swoosie, 12, 39, 82, 111, 206, 209
Kurtzman, Katy, 133
Kuschner, Jason, 175
Kushner, Tony, 131, 142, 147
Kute, Kay E., 162
Kutsevalov, S., 88
Kux, Bill, 51, 129
Kuyk, Dirk, 168
Kuznechenko, Roman, 88
Kuznetsov, Villor, 61
Kuznetsov, Vladimir, 61
Kuznetsova, Galina, 39
Kuzuhara, Russell, 138
Kvares, Donald, 52
Kvasov, Anatoly, 26
Kvasova, Raisa, 26
Kwinn, Mark, 54
Kybart, Peter, 164, 165
L.A. Scene, The, 66
LLoyd-Evans, David, 176
La Cage Aux Folles, 127
La Chanze, 94
La Chiusa, Michael John, 66, 100
La Fosse, Robert, 43
La Ronde, 59
La Vallee, Sandra, 71
LaBelle, Patti, 39
LaBelle, Rob, 90
LaBrecque, Donna, 122
LaCoy, Deborah, 206
LaFleche, Michel, 105
LaFleur, John Robert, 131
LaGue, Michael, 173
LaGuerre, Irma-Estel, 108
LaMar, Diana, 173
LaMarque, Kimberly, 131
LaPenna, Joseph, 57
LaPierre, Robert, 75, 134
LaPorta, Robert, 153
LaRocca, Sabrina, 161
LaRon, Ken, 124
LaRonde, 127
LaTessa, Dick, 169
LaTouche, John, 141
Laakko, Wayne, 65
Labkovski, Eduard, 54
Lable, Lorna, 206
Laboissonniere, Wade, 40
Lachow, Stan, 82
Lackey, Herndon, 45
Lackner, Greg, 152
Laconi, Robert, 206, 209
Lacy, Tom, 206
Ladik, Andrea, 111
Ladman, Jeff, 153
Lady Day at Emerson's Bar & Grill, 125, 153
Lady from Maxim's, The, 143
Lady in Question, The, 52
Lady, Robb, 38
Laffer, Denise, 63
Lafferty, Sandra Ellis, 166
Lafleur, John Robert, 131
Lagerfelt, Caroline, 44, 206
Laghidze, Soso, 69
Lagioia, John, 132
Laham, Roxxane, 71
Lahey, Sara, 151
Lahti, Christine, 42, 111, 206
Lai, Gladys, 92
Laing, Alan, 176
Laird, Fiona, 69
Laird, Marvin, 144
Laird, Michael James, 150
Lakeman, Alfred, 136
Lakes, Dale Allen, 165
Lakis, Maria, 69
Lally, James, 122, 170
Lam, Zoie, 154
Lamb, Chris, 129
Lamb, Gary, 145
Lamb, James Robert, 55
Lamb, Jim, 69
Lamb, Mary Ann, 43, 143, 206
Lamb, Rebecca, 136
Lambermont, Jeannette, 176
Lambert, Greta, 171
Lambert, Juliet, 15, 206
Lambert, Mikel Sarah, 129
Lambert, Robert, 20, 144, 180, 182, 183, 206
Lambert, Sarah, 170
Lambert, Stephen, 133
Lamitola, Mike, 144
Lamoreux, Melinda, 143
Lamos, Mark, 49, 142
Lamude, Terence, 60
Lancaster, James, 153
Lancaster, Mark, 143
Lancaster, Samuel, 135
Lanchester, Brian, 149
Lanchester, Kyra, 149
Lanchester, Robert, 77, 149
Land of Dreams, The, 59
Landau, Penny, 67
Lander, John-Michael, 59, 206, 209
Landesman, Heidi, 107, 168
Landesman, Rocco, 107
Landeta, Sean, 39
Landfield, Timothy, 130, 206
Landis, Jeanette, 149, 156
Landis, Jim, 137, 156
Landis, Lynn, 81, 82
Landman, Jeffrey, 101, 206
Landon, Hal, Jr., 162
Landon, Margaret, 108
Landrine, Bryan, 40
Landron, Jack, 66, 96, 206
Landry, Lantz, 109
Landry, Lauri, 37, 206, 209
Landry, Marlo, 45
Landsburg, Valerie, 147
Landwehr, Hugh, 141, 146, 153, 160, 164
Lane, Cheryle, 95
Lane, Colin, 79
Lane, Diane, 122
Lane, Dorothy, 73
Lane, Eddie, 54, 206
Lane, Janice C., 33
Lane, Lauren, 121
Lane, Nancy, 77
Lane, Nathan, 58, 81, 83, 206
Lane, Roger, 73
Lane, Sara Beth, 139
Lane, Stewart F., 35
Lane, Timothy, 72
Lane-Plescia, Gillian, 160
Lang, Barbara, 113
Lang, Mark Edward, 206, 209
Lang, Michael, 127
Lang, Stephen, 19, 144, 206
Lang, William H., 51
Langan, William, 87, 170
Lange, Anne, 42, 206
Lange, Joanna, 164
Lange, Ted, 104
Langeder, Rob, 145
Langella, Frank, 97, 206
Langford-Thomas, Marcus, 172
Langham, Michael, 176
Langhofer, Bobbi, 107
Langhofer, Dan W., 107, 144
Langley, Jeff, 77
Langley, Joan, 174
Langone, Lauri Grace, 72
Langsdale, Keith, 19, 95
Langton, Paula, 175
Langworth, Joe, 41
Lanier, David, 43
Lanier, Rob, 120
Lanier, Robert, 69
Lanier, Thomas, 173
Lanigan, Lorraine, 206, 209
Lank, Anna Bess, 80, 206
Lankford, Raye, 171
Lanning, Jerry, 206, 209
Lansbury, David, 42, 94
Lansdale, Keith, 95
Lansing, Robert, 83, 206
Lanteri, Joe, 100
Lanuza, Fred, 161
Lanyer, Charles, 131
Lanzener, Sonja, 132
Lapchinski, Larissa, 176
Lapine, James, 107, 144, 148, 160
Large, Norman, 113
Largely/New York, 94
Larkin, Bob, 68
Larkin, James, 115, 131
Larkin, Jill, 57
Larkin, Kevin, 113
Larkin, Robert, 11, 16, 17, 20, 28
Larmett, Jill, 138
Larroquette, John, 131
Larsen, Donna Marie, 168
Larsen, Liz, 63, 154, 206
Larsen, Lori, 118
Larsen, Robert R., 103
Larsen, Susan, 161
Larson, Christa, 109
Larson, Larry, 119
Laskawy, Harris, 131
Lasley, David, 52
Lasley, Lisa, 141
Last Love, 164
Last Song of John Proffit, The, 159
Latessa, Dick, 169
Lathen, John, 157
Latimer, Chip, 128
Latin, Montana, 73
Latiolais, Lori, 167
Latouche, John, 101
Lattanzio, Angela, 114
Latuja, Nancy, 108
Latus, James, 59, 172
Laub, Sandra, 62
Laubacher, Mary Alyce, 113
Lauch, Erik, 135
Laudati, Michael, 16
Lauder, Olaf, 70
Lauderdale, Jim, 119
Laufer, Deborah, 155
Laughing Wild, 164
Laughlin, Richard, 127
Laureano, Paul, 46
Laurence, Paula, 206
Laurenson, Diana, 11
Laurents, Arthur, 20, 43, 144
Lauria, Dan, 56
Laurie Beechman in Concert, 169
Laurino, Adelaide, 40, 45, 46, 102, 110, 117
Laurino, John, 45
Lauze, Gene, 70
Laverdiere, Renee, 139
Lavey, Martha, 56, 138
Lavezzo, Giulietta, 80
Lavin, Linda, 20, 39, 131, 206
Lawder, Anne, 121
Lawless, James J., 135
Lawless, Rick, 136
Lawless, Sarah, 135
Lawless, Sue, 168
Lawn, Sand, 114
Lawrence, Burke, 6, 206
Lawrence, Dale C., 119
Lawrence, Darrie, 159
Lawrence, David H., 21, 42
Lawrence, Dea, 48, 63, 206
Lawrence, Donald, 120
Lawrence, Elizabeth, 54, 55, 206, 209
Lawrence, Howard, 47
Lawrence, Jeremy, 131
Lawrence, Kirk, 49
Lawrence, Mark Christopher, 147

Lawrence, Peter, 22, 73, 116, 130, 138, 144, 153
Lawrence, Sharon, 106
Lawrey, Mundi, 117
Lawson, David, 54, 75, 134
Lawson, Leigh, 25
Lawson, Mary-Stewart, 93
Lawson, Richard, 83
Layman, Terry, 135
Layne, Mary, 28, 142
Layton, Michael, 127
Lazar, Mark, 152
Lazar, Paul, 73
Lazarus, Paul, 137
Lazarus, Sara Louise, 50
LeBanz, Jane, 154
LeBouef, Clayton, 124
LeBrecht, James, 153
LeClerc, Jean, 39, 50
LeFevre, Adam, 97, 206
LePage, Sue, 176
LeShay, David, 21, 32, 78
LeStrange, Philip, 82, 164, 207, 209
Leach, Nancy, 56
Leach, William, 97, 140
Leachman, Cloris, 140
Leadbetter, Betsy Ann, 139
Leake, Damien, 129, 134
Leaming, Greg, 142
Leander, Mike, 133
Lear, 62
Lear, Robert N., 147
Learned, Michael, 111, 121
Leary, Champe, 127, 159
Leask, Katherine, 67
Least of These, The, 123
Leatherman, Allen, 175
Leavell, Myron, 132
Leavitt, George, 23
Lebow, Barbara, 156
Lebowsky, Stanley, 102
Lecesne, James, 133
Lecube, Graciela, 96
Lecyk, Krystyna, 55
Ledbetter, Sammy, 130
Ledbetter, William, 27
Lederberg, Sarah, 72
Lederer, Deedy, 97
Ledwich, Lisa, 26
Lee, Baayork, 41
Lee, Barry, 128
Lee, Chandra, 37
Lee, Daven, 175
Lee, Gypsy Rose, 20
Lee, Jack, 18
Lee, Janice, 58, 66
Lee, Jeff, 40, 102
Lee, Jennifer, 124, 166
Lee, Jonathan Barlow, 131
Lee, Jonathan, 92
Lee, Kaiulani, 206, 209
Lee, Kathryn, 163
Lee, Leslie, 75, 95, 134
Lee, Levi, 119
Lee, Linda, 11, 32
Lee, Liz, 119
Lee, Mark, 153
Lee, Mary, 92
Lee, Ming Cho, 170
Lee, Paul J. Q., 90
Lee, Peggy, 39
Lee, Phil, 59
Lee, Sokie, 92
Lee, Stephen, 62, 97
Lee, Susan, 163
Lee, Victoria, 74
Lee-Aranas, Mary, 206
Leeds, Andrew Harrison, 110
Leeds, Jordan, 45, 133
Leek, Marcie, 125
Leet, Brady, 125
Leffert, Joel, 59, 206, 209
Legal Tender, 123
Leggero, Natasha, 152
Leggett, Paula, 41
Leggio, John Vincent, 40
Leguillou, Lisa, 43
Leguizamo, John, 60, 71, 207
Lehane, Gregory, 95
Lehman, Helen Reed, 161
Lehman, Ross, 138, 148
Lehr, Wendy, 126
Lehrer, Scott, 36, 42, 76, 94, 160
Lehrer, Tom, 135, 159
Leiber, Jerry, 39
Leibman, Ron, 130, 207
Leigh, Carolyn, 43, 112
Leigh, Christa Cricket, 138
Leigh, Jacqui, 69
Leigh, Jennifer Jason, 76
Leigh, Richard, 39
Leigh-Smith, Andrea, 43
Leighton, Betty, 158
Leighton, John, 146
Leighton, Richard, 149
Leishman, Gina, 161
Leistner, John, 174
Lemenager, Nancy, 15
Lemsky, Mitchell, 46, 113
Lemus, Luis, 173
Len, David, 150
Lend Me a Tenor, 44, 94
Lengel, Karl, 110
Lenger, Philip, 59
Lengson, Jose, 139
Leningrad State Music Hall, 39
Lennart, Isobel, 148
Lennix, Harry J., 138
Lenoire, Rosetta, 58
Lenten Pudding, 99
Leon, Kenneth, 119
Leonard, Cathy, 63
Leonard, Linda, 102
Leonard, Robert Sean, 94, 207
Leonardo, Joe, 148
Leone, Bill, 128
Leone, Joey, 114
Leone, John, 154
Leone, Vivien, 52, 89
Leong, David, 77, 94, 138
Leonidoff, Leon, 231
Leonov, Andrey, 61
Lepor, Pauline, 150
Lerch, Stuart, 93
Lerner, Alan Jay, 111, 127
Leroux, Gaston, 46
Les Liaisons Dangereuses, 128, 137, 157, 171
Les Misérables, 45, 109, 110
Les Romanesques, 47
Lescault, John, 163
Lesheim, Lolita, 207, 209
Leshin, Philip, 51
Leslie, Bethel, 55, 132, 207
Lesser, Sally, 155
Lester, Barbara, 30, 207
Lester, Nobie Lee, 159
Lester, Todd, 117
Lettice & Lovage, 30
Levan, Martin, 31, 40, 46, 117
Levene, Ellen, 43
Levenson, Jeanine, 164
Levenson, Keith, 164
Leventhal, Max, 122
Lever, Yasmine, 175
Leverett, James, 131
Leverett, T. Doyle, 141
Leveridge, Lynn Ann, 147
Levesque, Roxann, 166
Levi, Sally, 147
Levin, Kathy, 19, 20, 22
Levine, Anna, 209
Levine, Earl Aaron, 47, 64
Levine, Joseph I., 231
Levine, Rachel S., 74
Levine, Richard S., 207
Levine-Thompson, Anna, 207
Levinson, Lee Ann, 59
Levit, David Ethan, 165
Levitow, Roberta, 76
Levo, Julia, 155
Levy, Jacques, 133
Levy, Mark, 50
Levy, Steven M., 56
Lewin, Danny, 147
Lewin, Deborah, 122
Lewin, John, 141
Lewis, Althea, 59
Lewis, Bob, 100
Lewis, Bobo, 133
Lewis, Carol Jean, 84, 128
Lewis, Edmund, 78, 146, 207, 209
Lewis, Edwina, 28, 139
Lewis, Irene, 129, 131
Lewis, Jayne, 176
Lewis, Jim, 11, 98
Lewis, Kevin P., 64
Lewis, Kimberly, 177
Lewis, Marcia, 9, 94, 133, 207
Lewis, Mark, 207
Lewis, Matthew, 50, 51, 123, 207
Lewis, Michael, 95
Lewis, Pamela, 154
Lewis, Ralph, 154
Lewis, Scott, 152
Lewis, Sharon A., 38
Lewis, Vicki, 97, 100, 207
Lewis-Evans, Kecia, 94
Lewman, David, 148
Lewton, Christopher V., 124
Leyden, Leo, 25, 70, 207
Leys, Bryan D., 84
Li, Donald, 92
Liani, Michael, 91, 136
Liars, 56
Libby, Linda, 161
Libin, Andrea Clark, 207
Libin, Claire, 8, 37
Libin, Paul, 8, 37
Libman, Lillian, 26
Lichte, Richard, 50
Lichtefeld, Michael, 8
Lichtenstein, Mitchell, 147
Lichter, Kathy, 169
Liciaga, Peter, 117
Lickteig, Regina F., 158
Lide, Miller, 93, 207
Lieberman, Donna, 100
Lieberson, Will, 54
Liebert, Andrea, 135
Liebman, Steve, 133, 145
Lien, Jennifer, 145
Lifetimes on the Streets, 95
Lifetimes, 85
Lightburn, Jessica Ann, 110
Lightstone, Marilyn, 207
Ligon, K. C., 65
Ligon, Kevin, 144
Liljestrand, Eric, 62, 65
Lillo, Tony, 133
Lilly, Anne, 62
Lilly, Randy, 149
Lima, Paul, 93, 207, 209
Lima, Rafael, 60
Lima, Vera, 27
Limbo Tales, 63
Limpet, Alexandra, 72
Lincecum, David, 137
Lincoln Center Theater Company, 81
Lind, Jean, 125
Lind, Kirsten, 154
Lindemann, Gary, 46
Linden, Amelia, 6
Linden, Hal, 39
Lindig, Jillian, 150
Lindley, Audra, 137, 164
Lindo, Delroy, 129
Linds, Brian, 176
Lindsay, Barbara, 63
Lindsay, Howard, 27
Lindsay, Kim, 103
Lines, (Marion) Sybil, 30, 162, 207, 209
Link, Ron, 142, 153
Linklater, Hamish, 175
Linklater, Kristin, 175
Linney, Romulus, 51, 120, 159
Linstrum, Jon, 115, 131
Linton, John K., 162
Lintz, Marie-Therese, 172
Linville, Larry, 207
Lion in Winter, The, 57
Lion, Margo, 16
Lipman, Maureen, 146
Lipp, Larry, 55
Lipsky, David, 60
Lipton, Elizabeth, 71
Lisbon Traviata, The, 58
Liscow, Wendy, 137
Lisell-Frank, Dawn, 174
Lisell-Frank, Robert, 174
Lish, James, 57, 64, 207, 209
Lisner, Stephen, 75
Liss, Rhonda, 113
Liss, Richard, 6, 207
Lissandrello, June, 167
Lissek, Leon, 25
Lithgow, John, 39, 130
Litkel, Ervin, 55
Little Lulu in a Tight Orange Dress, 125
Little Night Music, A, 135
Little, Brad, 106
Little, Cleavon, 57, 171
Little, David, 170, 207
Little, Iris, 85, 95
Little, John, 127, 207
Little, Rich, 39
Littleton, Percy, 138
Littleway, Lorna, 134
Littman, Jack Carter, 138
Lively, William Fleet, 63
Liveright, Josh, 120
Livesay, Marcelle, 167
Livingston, James, 92, 127
Livingston, Jennifer, 167
Livingston, Marie, 174
Livingston, Megan, 149
Livingston, Shari, 140
Lizer, Kari, 147
Lizzul, Anthony John, 207
Lloyd, Christopher, 122
Lloyd, John Bedford, 81
Lloyd, Julie, 73
Lloyd, Karen, 44
Lloyd-Evans, David, 176
Llynn, Jana, 99, 100
López, Eduardo Iván, 96
LoBianco, Robert, 55
Loar, Rosemary, 102
Lobanov, Irina, 39
Lobanov, Olga, 39
Lobenhofer, Lee, 40, 102
Lober, David, 107, 114
Locarro, Joseph, 45, 109
Locatell, Carol, 132
Locke, Robert, 52
Locker, Phillip, 150
Lockett, Jimmy, 117
Lockett, Miron, 66
Lockhart, Keith, 157
Lockhart, Robert, 25
Lockwood, Lisa, 46, 207, 209
Lockwood, Shirley, 165
Locorriere, Dennis, 81, 207
Locricchio, Matthew, 94, 207, 209
Lodahl, Mar'ia, 118
Loeb, Leslie, 94, 98
Loehle, Steven, 57
Loesser, Emily, 27, 80, 207
Loesser, Frank, 125
Loewe, Frederick, 111, 127
Loftus, Elizabeth, 157
Loftus, Mary Fran, 42
Logan, Bellina, 142
Logan, Carol, 8
Logan, Jeffery, 207
Logan, Joshua, 154
Logan, Stacy, 56
Logen, Carol, 8, 207, 209
Loggia, Joey, 114
Loggia, Robert, 39
Lohnes, Peter, 160
Lohr, Elizabeth, 126
Lois-Louise, 167
Lolashvili, Zhanri, 69
Lombard, Kirk, 99
Lombard, Michael, 132, 207
Lomotey, Juba Jubulani, 164
Loncar, Kathryn, 167
London, Amy Jane, 24
London, Becky, 77, 207
London, Carol, 182
London, Charlotte Eve, 160
London, Chuck, 73, 76
London, Mark, 84
Londre, Felicia Hardison, 151
Long Island Stage, 145
Long Wharf Theatre, 145
Long, Andrew, 174
Long, Anni, 162
Long, Christopher, 167
Long, Kathryn, 158, 164, 165, 174
Long, Quincy, 54
Long, Sue, 115, 131
Long, William Ivey, 44, 82
Longbottom, Robert, 58
Longe, Jerry, 132
Longo, Robert, 6
Longstreet, Stephen, 43
Longstreth, Lori, 148
Lonn Entertainment, 112
Looze, Karen, 207
Lopardo, James, 54
Lopez, Carlos, 41
Lopez, Priscilla, 39, 49, 207
Lopez-Morillas, Julian, 171
Lopicolo, James, 71
Loquasto, Santo, 13, 18, 26, 82
Lord, Catherine, 148
Lorentz, Eric, 135
Lorenzen, Mark, 99
Lorigo, Jim, 53
Loring, David, 46
Lortel, Lucille, 67, 68, 183
Los Angeles Theatre Center, 147
Losito, Dina, 48
Lost Art, The, 73
Lost Boys, The, 122
Lothes, Doug, 119
Loti, Elisa, 71, 207
Lotito, Mark, 84
Lotorto, Louis, 172, 174
Lott, Frank, 102
Loud, David, 168
Loudon, Dorothy, 143, 144, 207
Louganis, Greg, 39
Loughrin, Tim, 101
Loui, Lola, 67
Loui, Michael, 170
Louis, Rick, 63
Louise, Merle, 101
Love Diatribe, 160
Love Letters, 12, 111
Love's Labour's Lost, 144, 158, 176
Love, Bobby, 117
Love, Edith H., 119
Love, Victor, 19, 144, 207
Love, Wil, 129
Lovejoy, Deirdre, 99
Loveless, David, 93
Lovelle, Herb, 59, 168
Lover, The, 146
Lovett, Marcus, 31
Lovett, Rita, 167
Lovingham, Mirth, 173
Low, Betty, 137
Low, Maggie, 73
Lowe, Chad, 39
Lowe, Dan Cameron, 172
Lowe, Don, 63
Lowe, Frank, 135, 149
Lowe, Kathleen, 16
Lowell, Marguerite, 107
Lowell, Scott, 138
Lowenstein, David, 43
Lowery, Marcella, 84, 207
Lowery, Nancy Ann, 119
Lowrie, John Patrick, 160
Lowstetter, Ken, 62, 67
Lowy, Marcie, 79
LuPone, Robert, 37, 207
Lubas, Gene, 157
Lubeck, Charles H., 102
Lubeck, Jackie, 53
Lubin, Shellen, 56
Lubovitch, Lar, 107, 144
Lucas, Anthony, 136
Lucas, Craig, 36, 76, 157, 162
Lucas, Greg, 126
Lucas, Jan, 138
Lucas, Roxie, 100, 207
Lucas, William, 92, 207
Lucchi, Tony, 172
Lucci, Susan, 39
Luce, Claire, 230, 231
Luce, Meredith, 62
Luce, Tom, 120
Lucia, Vita, 128
Lucie, Doug, 78
Luckey, Judge, 119
Lucky Stiff, 145
Lucy's Lapses, 94
Ludlam, Charles, 55, 69, 125
Ludwig, Ken, 44
Ludwig, Salem, 137
Luft, Carrie, 120
Lugar, Jana, 127
Lugar, Joel, 127
Lugering, Michael, 175
Lugo, Edwin, 142, 143
Luigs, Jim, 120
Lukas, Victor, 101
Luker, Rebecca, 46
Lum, Alvin, 24, 207
Lum, Benjamin, 147
Luman, Vicki, 173
Lumbard, Dirk, 176
Lumbly, Carl, 131
Lumet, Sidney, 39
Lumpkin, Bruce, 18, 66
Luna, Tony, 95
Lund, Art, 230, 231
Lund, Clyde, 118
Lund, Kenny, 52, 108
Lund, Morgan, 132
Lundell, Kert, 6
Lundie, Ken, 156
Lundquist, Lori, 98
Lupp, Andrew J., 133, 148
Lupp, K. C., 133
Luscombe, Tim, 22, 94
Lusko, Robert A., 123
Lussier, Henry, 122
Lutken, David, 151, 160
Lutwak, Mark, 63
Lutz, John David, 132
Lutz, Renee F., 55
Luvinsky, Leonid, 61
Lyall, Susan, 76
Lyapunova, Irina, 153
Lybrand, Ben, 125
Lyles, Leslie, 63, 207
Lyman, Will, 137
Lynch, Brian, 110
Lynch, Dinah M., 150
Lynch, Jayne Ackley, 68, 108
Lynch, John Carroll, 141
Lynch, Michael S., 43, 148
Lynch, Sharon, 63
Lynch, T. Paul, 138
Lynch, Thomas, 42, 104, 160
Lynch, Victoria, 51, 63
Lyndeck, Edmund, 22, 207
Lynes, Kristi, 40
Lyng, Nora Mae, 107, 154
Lynley, Carol, 182
Lynn, Abby, 124
Lynn, Alice, 102
Lynn, Jana, 66
Lynn, Jess, 63
Lynn, Loretta, 39
Lynn, Paula, 127
Lynne, Gillian, 31, 40, 46
Lyon, Robin, 41
Lyons, Andi, 128
Lyons, Bob, 68
Lyons, Jeff, 52, 62
Lyons, Marty, 39
Lytton, Scott Jackson, 159
M. Butterfly, 94
Ma Rainey's Black Bottom, 136
Ma, Jason, 17, 154
Maaske, Dee, 174
Mabe, Matthew, 135
Mabee, Elizabeth, 113
Mabon, Paul, 56
Mac Leod, Charles, 135
MacAdam, Adam, 69
MacAller, Natasha, 46
MacBean, Andrew, 31
MacCalla, Sylvia, 162
MacCallum, Robert, 54
MacCauley, Michael, 144, 172
MacDermot, Galt, 39
MacDermott, Laura, 137, 160, 168
MacDevitt, Brian, 56, 91, 94, 128
MacDonald, Bob, 13, 87
MacDonald, Catherine, 172
MacDonald, Gordon, 137
MacDonald, Jason, 97
MacDonald, Karen, 175
MacDonald, Pirie, 143, 208
MacDonald, Robert David, 172
MacDonald, Rod, 152
MacDonald, Scott, 119, 160
Macdonald, Sharman, 162
MacDonald, T. Vincent, 176
MacDougall, Maureen, 58
MacInnis, John, 43
MacIntosh, Joane, 9, 208
MacIver, Jane, 138
MacKay, John, 208
MacKenzie, Daniel, 127
MacKenzie, Heather D., 133
MacLean, Rebecca, 138
MacMillan, Ann, 208
MacMurtry, David, 147
MacNair, Susan, 73
MacNamara, John, 105
MacNamara, Terrance, 29
MacNicol, Peter, 208
MacPherson, George, 103, 107
MacPherson, Greg, 55, 60, 63
MacPherson, Lori, 46, 208
MacVay, James, 147
MacVittie, Bruce, 90, 208
Macbeth, 90, 171
Macchio, Ralph, 208
Mace, Cynthia, 95
Macer, Sterling, Jr., 153, 162
Macfie, Jane, 52
Machado, Eduardo, 147
Machala, Mary, 118
Machiste, Candace Brecker, 96
Machray, Robert, 131, 174
Macias, Olga, 153, 161
Macintosh, Cameron, 45
Macintosh, Joan, 168
Mack, Jana, 173
Mackay, Lizbeth, 69, 89, 94, 97, 208
Mackenzie, Peter, 129, 208
Mackenzie-Wood, Barbara, 73
Mackey, Bernadette, 128
Mackey, Doug, 166
Mackintosh, Cameron, 40, 46, 135, 159
Macleod, Wendy, 50
Macoka, Magoichi, 12
Maculan, Tim, 152
Macy, W. H., 81, 208
Madame Sherry, 139
Maddalone, Trary, 135
Madden, Corey Beth, 131
Madden, Stephanie, 136
Madden, Thomas M., 145
Maddox, Diana, 153
Maddrie, Leah, 157
Made in Bangkok, 163
Made in Heaven, 74
Madeira, Marcia, 97, 119, 143, 165
Madigan, Amy, 147
Madison, Cathy, 86
Madole, Cherry, 73
Madris, Richard, 53
Madris, Susan, 53
Maeck, Gabriel, 122
Maffel, Dorothy J., 98
Maffin, Neil, 120, 124, 143
Maggio, Michael, 87, 137, 138, 160
Magic Time, 70
Magierski, Tomasz, 71
Maglich, Marko, 55
Maglione, Christine, 41
Magness, Marilyn, 112
Magnuson, Janet, 152
Mago, Patrice, 164
Magowan, Stephen, 57
Magradey, Jack, 40
Maguire, Ellen, 21
Maguire, George F., 174
Maguire, Kate, 175
Maguire, Kathleen, 230, 231
Maguire, Matthew, 51
Maguire, Michael, 121
Magwili, Dom, 162
Mahaffey, Valerie, 131
Mahard, Thomas D., 150
Maher, Sheri, 29
Mahl, Lori Ann, 20
Mahle, Marjorie, 70
Mahler, Ed, 94
Mahlmann, Jean, 154
Mahon, Judy French, 167
Mahon, Kristen, 20, 208
Mahon, Marcia, 169
Mahone, Sydné, 134
Mahoney, John, 138
Mahony-Bennett, Kathleen, 99, 132

Mahos, Paul, 50
Maier, Charlotte, 159
Maier, David, 121
Maika, Michele, 110
Mailer, Stephen, 208
Maio, Frank, 15
Maisano, Paul, 48
Maitre, Natalie, 173
Majeski, Marilyn, 72
Major Barbara, 122, 171
Major, Charles, 53
Major, Fred, 120
Makharadze, Avtandil, 69
Makhene, Motsumi, 86
Making Movies, 67
Making of Americans, The, 129
Makkena, Wendy, 44, 77, 83
Makstutis, Jeff, 54
Malamud, Marc D., 61, 66
Malcolm, Graeme, 66, 80, 208
Malebo, Annelen, 134
Maleczech, Ruth, 62, 91, 141
Maletsky, Sophie, 55, 69
Malina, Joel, 74, 208
Malina, Joshua, 19, 144, 208
Malinowski, John, 55
Malkmus, R. J., II, 108
Mallard, David E., 8
Mallon, Brian, 72, 208
Mallow, Tom, 103, 107
Malloy, Judy, 169
Malloy, Larkin, 39
Malm, Mia, 154
Maloney, Bill, 53
Maloney, Peter, 82
Malpass, Kevin, 22
Maltby, Jacquey, 24
Maltby, Richard, Jr., 57, 127
Maltsev, Anatoly, 54
Maly Drama Theatre of Leningrad, The, 153
Mama Drama, 132
Mama, I Want to Sing Part II, 64
Mamet, David, 81, 138, 144, 162, 164, 165, 168
Man Who Came to Dinner, The, 124, 132
Man Who Shot Lincoln, The, 55
Man Who Was Peter Pan, The, 155
Man and Superman, 129
Man of the Flesh, 162
Man with Connections, A, 169
Manaka, Matsemela, 86
Manaka, Nomsa, 86
Manassee, Jackie, 60, 151, 157, 168
Mancinelli, Margaret, 73
Mancuso, Nick, 147
Mancuso, Sam, 6
Mandel, Mel, 137
Mandell, Alan, 147
Mandell, Michael, 89
Mandracchia, Charles, 18, 208
Mandy Patinkin in Concert: Dress Casual, 7
Manetta, Michael, 56, 62
Manfredi, Richard, 131
Manger, Itzik, 80
Mangham, Tramekia, 119
Mangold, Kevin, 112
Manhattan Punch Line's 6th Annual Festival of One Act Comedies, 63
Manhattan Theatre Club, 83
Manheim, Ralph, 56, 122
Manim, Mannie, 116, 144
Manis, David, 66, 100, 120, 208
Mankiewicz, Joseph, 39
Mankin, Nina, 91
Manley, Donna, 143
Manley, Jim, 168
Manley, Sarah, 81, 82
Mann, Barry, 153, 163
Mann, Cecile, 59
Mann, Gloria, 131
Mann, Marjorie Anita, 108
Mann, Terrence, 43, 208
Mann, Theodore, 8, 37
Mann, Wesley, 121
Manning, Dan, 71, 149, 169
Mans, Lorenzo, 69
Manson, Alan, 82
Manson, Bevan, 58
Mantell, Michael, 82, 83, 208
Mantello, Joe, 76, 78, 136, 208
Mantovani, Claudio, 131
Manukov, Gregory, 120
Manza, Brandy, 166
Manzi, Warren, 208
Mara, Mary, 87, 99, 208
Maradudin, Peter, 135, 153, 159, 160, 162, 172, 174
Maraini, Dacia, 55
Marantz, Seth, 152
Marasek, Jan, 22
Marc, Peter, 84
Marceau, Yvonne, 18, 208
March on Russia, The, 132
March, Barbara, 141
March, Kevin Patrick, 173
Marchand, Mitchell, 95
Marchand, Nancy, 130, 144, 208
Marchande, Teal, 67
Marchionni, Margie, 30
Marciona, Anthony, 117
Marcosson, Lory, 52
Marcoux, Ted, 19, 144
Marcovicci, Andrea, 121
Marcus, Bonnie Rose, 48
Marcus, Brian H., 172
Marcus, Daniel, 140
Marcus, Leslie, 127
Marcus, Michael, 156
Marcus, Paul, 162
Marcy, Helen, 208
Mardikes, Tom, 151
Mardirosian, Tom, 94, 208
Maredi, Selaelo, 86
Margolis, Jeff, 39
Margoshes, Steven, 103, 154
Margulies, David, 160
Margulis, John, 72
Marholin, Matthew G., 52, 108
Marie, Jean, 154
Marin, Graciela, 125
Marineau, Barbara, 107
Marino, Frank, 46
Marino, James, 150
Marino, Peter Michael, 65
Marivaux, 71
Mariye, Lily, 168
Mark Twain Revealed, 169
Markell, Jodie, 63
Markham, R L, 128
Markinson, Brian, 62
Markle, Stephen, 153
Markovitz, Paula, 145, 160
Markowitz, David, 56
Markowitz, Mitch, 51
Marks, David, 124
Marks, Jack R., 123, 140
Marks, Kenneth L., 94, 164
Marland, Stuart, 108
Marlay, Andrew B., 33
Marley, Donovan, 135
Marley, Susanne, 208
Marlow, Carolyn, 64
Marlowe, Theresa, 52
Marrero, Maria, 165
Marrero, Ralph, 83
Marriage of Bette and Boo, The, 147, 161
Marriott's Lincolnshire Theatre, 148
Marrow, Queen Esther, 33
Marruz, Sergio Garcia, 71, 96
Marsden, Les, 136, 167
Marsh, Bernard J., 75
Marsh, Frazier W., 120
Marsh, Jamie, 155
Marsh, Judith, 111
Marshal, Gary, 113
Marshall, Dorothy L., 159
Marshall, E. G., 129
Marshall, Jennifer, 120
Marshall, Kathleen, 102
Marshall, Larry, 16, 208
Marshall, Maggie, 128
Marshall, Maynard, 163
Marshall, Peter Drew, 142
Marshall, Rob, 126, 157
Marsicano, Mary, 62, 96
Marson, Mary Lee, 101
Marte, Paul, 157
Martel, Bill, 56
Martel, Billy Arthur, 208
Martel, Daria, 122
Martel, Jenny, 61, 208
Martel, Joelle, 60
Martell, Ronald, 173
Martello, Mary, 149
Martells, Cynthia, 141
Martenson, Edward A., 141
Martin, Brian, 149
Martin, Christopher, 6, 208
Martin, Clay, 58, 83
Martin, Dan, 119
Martin, Dorothy, 47, 173
Martin, Elliot, 21, 182
Martin, Erin, 93
Martin, Greta, 43
Martin, Hugh, 15, 43
Martin, Jamie, 60, 84, 208
Martin, Jane, 120
Martin, Janet, 176
Martin, Jennifer, 160
Martin, John Wills, 131
Martin, John, 72
Martin, Ken, 63, 208
Martin, Leila, 46, 208
Martin, Marjorie, 21
Martin, Michael X., 135
Martin, Nan, 144, 162
Martin, Nicholas, 153
Martin, Norma L., 148
Martin, Randal, 157
Martin, Steven David, 171
Martin, T. R., 159
Martin, Terrence, 65
Martin, Tony, 176
Martinez, Alma, 156
Martinez, Eve, 62
Martinez, Margaret, 114
Martinez, Richard, 61
Martini, Lou, Jr., 48
Martini, Richard, 106
Martini, Robert Lee, 208
Martini, Robert, 61
Martinov, Lucy, 103, 107
Martins, Ricardo D., 171
Martinsen, Ronald A., 167
Martorella, Drew, 173
Maruyama, Karen, 131
Marvin's Room, 138
Marvin, Mel, 122
Marx, Ara, 83
Marx, Arthur, 136, 167
Marx, Juliana, 144
Mary, Kathleen, 53, 60
Mary Stuart, 171
Maryan, Charles, 55, 80
Marz, Charles, 122
Marzullo, John, 145
Marzullo, Steve, 94
Maschek, Karl, 138
Mascolo, Joseph, 132
Masekela, Hugh, 116
Mashkov, Vladimir, 88
Maskela, Hugh, 144
Masloff, Helen, 127
Maslon, Laurence, 124
Maso, Michael, 143
Mason, Cecelia, 152
Mason, Dan, 131
Mason, Jack, 119
Mason, Jackie, 144
Mason, Karen, 43
Mason, Marshall W., 76
Mason, Terry, 102
Masotti, Richard, 52, 53
Masque of the Red Death, 53
Massel, Paul, 113
Massey-Peters, Cheryl, 160
Massman, Margaret, 65
Mastergate, 10, 181
Masters, David, 106
Masterton, Philip, 102
Mastracola, Frank, 40
Mastrantonio, Mary Elizabeth, 87, 208
Mastrone, Frank, 46, 208
Mastrosimone, William, 76, 168
Mastrototaro, Michael, 50, 155
Matador, 133, 148
Matagrano, Francine, 173
Matalon, Vivan, 93
Match Made in Heaven, A, 73
Matchmaker, The, 159
Mather, Ada Brown, 59
Mather, Ted, 117
Mathews, Sheila, 49
Mathias, Anna, 161
Mathiesen, Gorli, 149
Mathiesen, Robin C., 39
Mathis, Cynthia, 171
Mathis, Lynn, 167
Mathis, Stanley Wayne, 139
Matias, Fiely, 144
Matinee, 73
Matlack, Deborah, 54
Matone, Rocco, 168
Matosich, Frank, Jr., 133
Matschulat, Kay, 63
Matsumura, Yoko, 66
Matsusaka, Tom, 97, 208
Matthew, George, 138
Matthews, Anderson, 208
Matthews, Dakin, 135
Matthews, Evan, 64, 72
Matthews, Jon, 131, 161
Matthews, Renee, 148
Matthews, Rodtrice Marie, 164
Matthias, Darren, 148
Matthiessen, Joan, 72, 123, 208
Mattsey, Jeff, 70
Matz, Jerry, 106
Matz, Peter, 18
Mauceri, Patricia, 146, 165
Maugans, Wayne, 128
Maugham, W. Somerset, 21
Maupin, Samuel, 149, 208
Maurel, Linda, 170
Mauro, Wilson, 27
Maury, Mya Risa, 147
Mavimbela, Thandani, 116
Mavromatis, Helen, 128
Maxey, Caty, 99
Maxman, Mimi, 59, 66, 100
Maxson, James, 52, 57
Maxwell, Jennifer, 143
Maxwell, Larry, 62
May Day, 160
May, Christopher, 50
May, Corinna, 175
May, Gary, 165
May, Linda, 102
Mayans, Nancy, 61
Mayberry, James, 119
Mayer, Max, 124
Mayerson, Frederick H., 107
Mayes, Sally, 57, 208
Mayfield, Katherine, 61, 208
Mayhew, David, 145
Maynard, Richard, 157
Mayo, Don, 140, 168
Mazer, Arnie, 73
Mazey, Duane, 51
Mazzarantani, Jane, 133
Mazzella, Neal, 19, 23, 36
Mazzello, Mary, 27
Mazzie, Narin, 124
Mbulu, Letta, 134
McAdams, Ted, 172
McAlister, Tom, 170
McAllen, Kathleen Rowe, 31, 180, 182, 208
McAnarney, Kevin P., 23, 39, 54
McAnuff, Des, 103
McArt, Jan, 17
McAssey, Michael, 58
McAuliffe, Jody, 168
McBride, Geoff, 176
McBride, Michele, 27
McBride, Tara, 39
McBride, Tom, 95, 208
McBride, Vaughn, 120
McCain, Frances Lee, 121
McCall, Kathleen, 208
McCallany, Holt, 95
McCallum, Martin, 45
McCallum, Sandy, 174
McCammond, James A., 152
McCann, Carol, 67
McCann, Christopher, 95, 208
McCann, David, 169
McCann, Elizabeth Ireland, 9
McCann, Hugh, 153
McCarren, Paul, 163
McCarter Theatre, 149
McCarthy, Jeff, 160
McCarthy, Julianna, 147
McCarthy, Sheila, 164
McCarthy, Theresa, 144
McCartney, Ellen, 95, 100, 122, 164
McCartney, Liz, 169
McCarty, Bruce, 95
McCarty, Conan, 19, 55, 143, 208
McCarty, Kevin, 132, 140
McCarty, Michael, 8, 170, 208
McCarty, Stephen W., 152
McCauley, James, 87
McClaine, Kathleen, 125
McClanahan, Rue, 39
McCleary, Dan, 143
McClellan, Maggie, 52
McClelland, Kay, 4, 24
McClendon, Afi, 94
McClendon, David, 171
McClennahan, Charles, 64, 70, 72, 75, 83, 95, 128, 134, 135, 164
McClinn, Tiffany, 95
McClintock, Jodie Lynne, 83, 165, 208
McCloskey, Steven, 128
McClure, James, 173
McClure, Spike, 132, 134
McCollister, Frier, 62, 91
McComb, Bill, 55, 56
McConnell, David, 60, 65, 70, 208
McConnell, Mary Jo, 135
McCoo, Marilyn, 39
McCord, L. A., 127
McCord, Lisa Merrill, 18, 210
McCorkle, Pat, 19, 23, 34, 97, 104
McCorkle, Steve, 114
McCormack, Eric, 176
McCormick, Carolyn, 135, 153
McCormick, Michael, 109, 152, 157, 168
McCormick, Robert R., 101, 139
McCorry, Marion, 157
McCourt, Frank, 79
McCowan, Marjorie, 171
McCowen, Alec, 68, 210
McCoy, Elizabeth A., 169
McCoy, Terri, 39
McCrane, Paul, 60, 82, 210
McCready, Kevin Neil, 41
McCready, Walter, 169
McCrum, James, 157
McCulloch, Jane, 130
McCulloh, Barbara, 135, 210
McCullough, Allen, 146
McCullough, Mark L., 170
McCurdy, Christine, 151
McCutcheon, Bill, 210
McDaniel, Brian, 63
McDaniel, James, 82
McDermid, Ed, 143
McDermott, James T., 130, 131
McDermott, Kevin, 143
McDermott, Sean, 117
McDermott, Tom, 10, 159
McDermott, Tom, Jr., 75
McDonald, Beth, 19, 137
McDonald, Casey, 58
McDonald, Christopher, 147
McDonald, David B., 52
McDonald, Tanny, 87, 143
McDonald, Thomas-David, 135
McDonnell, Diramund, 136
McDonnell, James, 94, 164, 165
McDonnell, Mary, 42, 143, 210
McDonough, Ann, 10, 210
McDonough, Elizabeth, 80
McDowall, Jennifer, 51
McDowell, Bob, 159
McDowell, Rex, 118
McDowell, W. Stuart, 141
McEldowney, Harrison, 133, 148
McElduff, Ellen, 62
McElhaney, Susan, 152
McElrath, Jonna, 125
McElvain, Richard, 143
McElwee, Theresa, 48, 63, 94
McElya, Amanda, 120
McFall, Michael, 121
McFarland, Martha, 162
McFarland, Robert, 210
McGann, MichaelJohn, 97, 210, 213
McGarity, Jerry, 118
McGarry, Mary Anne, 162
McGeachy, Martin, 125
McGee, Joanne, 136
McGhee, Susan, 148
McGill, Vince, 167
McGillis, Kelly, 171, 172
McGlinn, John, 70
McGovern, Elizabeth, 12, 162, 182, 183, 210
McGovern, Marjorie, 102
McGovern, Maureen, 16, 210
McGovern, Stacy, 175
McGowan, Nora, 150
McGowan, Tom, 120, 170
McGranaghan, Joseph, 60
McGrath, Katherine, 153
McGrath, Kay, 139
McGrath, Mark, 169
McGrath, Michael, 135
McGraw, Melinda, 131
McGreevey, Annie, 8, 210
McGrew, Don, 145
McGruder, Jasper, 123
McGuinness, Michael John, 93, 210
McGuire, Joe, 70
McGuire, Kevin, 109, 110
McGuire, Maeve, 136
McGuire, Patti, 88
McGuire, William Biff, 160
McHale, Christopher, 90, 164
McHattie, Stephen, 210
McHugh, Joanne, 15
McIntyre, Dennis, 146
McIntyre, Dianne, 86, 129, 131
McIntyre, Gerry, 94, 144, 210
McIntyre, Stephen, 6, 210
McIntyre, Therese, 55, 69
McIvery, Ulrike, 167
McKay, Gardner, 79
McKay, Johanna, 138
McKay, Roy, 6
McKayle, Donald, 144
McKean, Michael, 34, 180, 182, 210
McKechnie, Donna, 39
McKee, A. Michael, 106
McKee, Lonette, 144
McKelvey, Lori, 80
McKenna, Andrew, 105
McKenna, Seana, 176
McKennan, Jean, 169
McKenney, Ruth, 56
McKenzie, Bruce, 161
McKenzie, Kelleigh, 72
McKenzie, Richard, 141
McKenzie, Rita, 74
McKernon, John, 70
McKinley, Betty, 62
McKinley, Philip Wm., 154
McKinney, Lou Ann, 152
McKinney, Marie, 67
McKinney, Mark, 68
McKneely, Joey, 43
McKonly, Curtis J., 114
McLain, John, 172
McLain, Matt, 52
McLanahan, Matt, 48
McLane, Derek, 122, 129, 141, 172
McLane, Judy, 107
McLarty, Gwendolyn, 173
McLaughlin, Ellen, 120, 131
McLaughlin, Julia, 65, 70
McLeish, Jamie, 166
McLure, James, 149
McMahon, Eileen, 111
McMahon, John, 139
McMahon, Leslie, 58
McMahon, Mark, 89
McMahon, Terri, 174
McManus, Don R., 75, 83, 87, 90, 210
McMartin, John, 22, 183, 210
McMillan, Richard, 177
McMonagle, Susie, 148
McMullan, James, 82
McMullen, Larry, 172
McMurdo-Wallis, Cristine, 174
McMurtry, Jonathan, 153, 162
McNabb, Barry, 46, 210
McNally, Ellen, 170
McNally, Joseph, 160
McNally, Terrence, 58, 83, 120, 136, 162
McNamara, Dermot, 79, 210
McNamara, Eileen, 111
McNamara, John C., 170
McNamara, Joseph, 39
McNamara, Maureen, 210
McNamara, Pat, 9, 210
McNeal, Lawrence, III, 67
McNeeley, Gale, 161
McNeely, Anna, 20, 210
McNeill, Jane, 125
McNeill, Katlyn, 146
McNeill, Robert Duncan, 94
McNenny, Kathleen, 90
McNider, Cate, 97
McNight, Sharon, 210, 213
McNitt, David, 57
McNulty, William, 120
McOmber, Kori, 127
McOmber, Kyra, 127
McPherson, Charles, 153
McPherson, George, 103
McPherson, Scott, 138
McQuary, Chuck, 118
McQueeney, Ellen, 72
McQuiggan, John A., 67
McRobbie, Peter, 59, 210, 213
McShane, Michael, 121
McTigue, Mary, 165
McVety, Drew, 157, 210
McVey, Anne, 112
McVey, Beth, 114
McVey, Drew, 42
McVey, Mark, 109
McWilliams, Richard, 9, 136, 210
Mchunu, Linda, 116
Me and My Girl, 94
Mead, Kathy, 139
Mead, William, 41
Meade, Bill, 144
Meade, Julia, 145
Meader, Derek, 143
Meadow Brook Theatre, 150
Meadow, Lynne, 58, 83
Meadow, M. R., 53
Meadows, Audrey, 39
Meadows, Carol Lee, 15
Meadows, Jayne, 39
Meadows, PattiLynne, 169
Meara, Anne, 73
Mears, DeAnn, 119
Measure for Measure, 119, 153, 160, 171
Medalis, Joseph G., 131
Medea, 93
Medina, David, 169, 172
Medina, Hazel, 97, 210
Medina, Julio, 153
Medrano, Hugo, 163
Medsker, Kermit, 125
Meeh, Gregory, 34, 81
Meehan, Thomas, 144
Meeker, Leslie Lynn, 150
Meeker, Matthew, 174
Meeker, Michael, 174
Meeker, Roger, 143
Meesey, Chris, 167
Meet Me in St. Louis, 15, 181
Meeting, The, 138
Megara, Kelly Anne, 65
Mehle, Donna, 142
Mehrbach, Glenn, 56
Mehrten, Greg, 62, 91
Meikle, David Scott, 146
Meineck, Peter, 69
Meisle, Kathryn, 67, 210
Meissner, Don, 75
Meister, Brian, 24
Meister, Frederica, 94, 210, 213
Mekka, DeLee Lively, 18
Meksin, Robert, 132
Melancon, Corinne, 144

Melcher, Kathleen, 102
Mele, Carla, 58
Meleck, Amy, 156
Meli, James C., Jr., 150
Melia, Hector, 96
Melici, Sarah, 164
Melius, Nancy, 20, 210
Mell, Randle, 97, 143
Mellon, Christopher, 72
Mellon, James J., 169
Mellor, Stephen, 51, 210
Mellor, Steve, 63
Melnichenko, Ludmila, 26
Melvin, Ken, 128
Membreno, Alejandro, 94
Memoir, 135
Men Without Wives, 99
Menchell, Ivan, 38, 144
Mendelson, Aaron, 66
Mendelson, Gary, 89
Mendenhall, Jennifer, 163
Mendillo, Stephen, 9, 87, 210
Meng, Connie, 54, 74
Meng, Hal, 166
Mengers, Julia, 65
Menke, Rick, 164, 165
Mennen, James G., 40
Mennone, Kate, 99
Menson, Uriel, 155
Menza, Gina, 72
Meola, Tony, 73, 104, 167
Mercant, Marsha, 147
Mercer, Marian, 147
Mercer, Ray, 39
Mercer, Sally, 169
Merchant of Venice, The, 25, 176
Mercier, G. W., 52, 57, 61, 75, 99, 171
Mercurio, Jo-Dee, 71
Mercurio, Valerie, 127
Merediz, Olga, 45, 109
Merivale, John, 231
Merkerson, S. Epatha, 32, 130, 210
Merkin, Robby, 35, 50
Merkur, Jordan, 65
Merlin!, 119
Merlin, Joanna, 73, 107
Merrifield, Gail, 87
Merrill, Bob, 99
Merrill, Dina, 39
Merrill, Gary, 230, 231
Merrill, Kim, 54, 55, 210
Merrill, Robert, 39
Merrily We Roll Along, 124
Merriman, Richard, 127
Merritt, George, 84, 210
Merritt, Michael, 144
Merritt, Theresa, 86, 136, 210
Merry Wives of Windsor, Texas, The, 159
Merry Wives of Windsor, The, 143, 171, 172, 174
Merryman, Monica, 154, 210
Merton, Alice, 30
Merzon, Jill, 57
Mesney, Barbara, 166, 171
Mesney, Kathryn, 166
Mesnik, William, 170
Mess, Suzanne, 27
Messaline, Peter, 120, 135
Messenger, John, 136
Messersmith, Randolph, 70
Messinger, Blaise, 153
Metamorphosis, 94
Metcalf, Mark, 210
Metcalf, Percy, 120
Metheny, Russell, 163
Mette, Nancy, 146
Metz, Janet, 57, 164
Metzel, Michael, 56, 210
Metzger, Janet, 119
Metzman, Irving, 98, 210
Metzo, William, 210
Mexico, 53
Meyer, Andrew, 75
Meyer, Craig A., 15
Meyer, Edgar, 151, 152
Meyer, Jon, 125
Meyer, Karen, 118
Meyer, Marlane, 90, 147
Meyer, Michael, 147, 160
Meyer, Richard, 64, 175
Meyer, Ursula, 174
Meyers, D. Lynn, 101, 128
Meyers, Elliot, 56
Meyers, Larry John, 157, 177
Meyers, Lee, 152
Meyers, Patrick, 64
Meyers, Suzanne, 67
Meyers, T. J., 144, 210, 213
Mezon, Jim, 164, 165
Mi Vida Loca, 83
Miami Lights, 133
Michael, Christine, 164
Michael, Lori, 131, 162
Michaels, Christopher Lee, 15
Michaels, Daniel, 143
Michaels, J. P., 113
Michaels, Jillsyn, 147
Michaels, Kelly, 148
Michaels, Mark A., 97
Michaels, Tommy J., 29
Michaelson, Ron, 162
Michalski, John, 150, 171
Micheaux, Mirage, 67
Michel, Carolyn, 14, 51, 210
Michel, John, 57
Michell, Roger, 81
Michie, William, 52
Michuda, Marie, 145
Mickelsen, David Kay, 126
Mickey, Susan E., 119, 136
Middleton, Clark, 53, 176
Midkiff, H. D., 136
Midsummer Night's Dream, A, 93, 115, 124, 125, 131, 151, 162, 176
Midsummer Nights, 84
Mielziner, Jo, 43
Mieske, Dale, 176
Mihok, Andrew, 87
Mikado, The, 154
Mikan, George, 39
Mikelson, Ivars, 135
Mila, Lydia, 70
Milani, Linda, 154
Milazzo, Ann Marie, 90
Milbank, Stephen, 99
Milburn, Rob, 29, 56, 138, 152
Miles, Cassel H., 176
Miles, Julia, 56, 66, 69
Milgrim, Lynn, 147
Milhoan, Michael, 147
Milia, Hector, 56, 96
Milikin, Paul, 73
Milione, Lou, 83
Militello, Anne, 58, 68, 69, 83, 147, 168
Mill Fire, 56
Millan, Bruce E., 136
Millenbach, George, 57, 210
Millennium Approaches, 131
Miller, Arthur, 97, 121, 146, 147
Miller, Belinda, 76, 91
Miller, Bill, 110
Miller, Bruce, 39
Miller, Cameron, 87
Miller, Craig, 55, 139, 146, 160
Miller, Earl F., Rev., 138
Miller, Elliott, 166
Miller, Gary, 135
Miller, Jacqueline M., 167
Miller, Jerry, 173
Miller, Joanne, 176
Miller, Joel McKinnon, 89
Miller, John, 39
Miller, Jonathan Seth, 122
Miller, Kara, 173
Miller, Kenny, 131
Miller, Larch, 20
Miller, Lisa Ann, 172
Miller, Lisa Beth, 50
Miller, Lowry, 66, 124
Miller, Marilyn Suzanne, 90
Miller, Marjorie Ann, 164, 165
Miller, Mark, 167
Miller, Mary, 31, 57
Miller, Michael, 174
Miller, Nina, 88
Miller, Patrick, 161, 162
Miller, Paul, 176
Miller, Phil, 62
Miller, Rebecca, 83, 210
Miller, Robert Strong, 17
Miller, Roy, 154
Miller, Stephen, 61
Miller, Steve, 167
Miller, Thomas Jay, 119
Millholland, Woody, 105
Milligan, John, 171
Millman, Devora, 150
Millman, Howard J., 136, 150
Mills, Aurelia, 55
Mills, Dana, 37
Mills, Donna, 12, 210, 213
Milos, Shole, 145
Minahan, Greg, 40
Minami, Roger, 12
Minarovich, Christi, 73
Mine Alone, 135
Mineo, John, 11, 50
Miner, Mary Michele, 91, 130, 131
Minetor, Nic, 136
Minichiello, M. D., 70
Mink, Gary, 54, 55, 69
Minkoff, Bradford, 102
Minns, Byron Keith, 170
Minny and the James Boys, 51
Minor, Jason, 20
Minor, John Hugh, 139
Minot, Anna, 93
Minskoff, Jerome, 9, 25
Minsky, Greta, 60, 100
Mintern, Terence, 55, 59
Minton, Nina F., 72
Mintz, Cheryl, 35
Mintz, Ethan, 77
Mintz, Jonathon, 63
Mintz, Melanie, 52
Mintz, Sandra C., 75
Mirabal, Jeannette, 161
Mirkin, Jorge, 66
Mironov, Yevgeny, 88
Misanthrope, The, 138
Miser, The, 142, 174
Miss Evers' Boys, 129, 131
Miss Julie, 170
Miss Margarida's Way, 26
Missimi, Nancy, 133, 148
Missouri Repertory Theatre, 151
Mistretta, Sal, 108
Mitchell, Anne, 60, 65
Mitchell, Bill, 169
Mitchell, Camille, 157
Mitchell, David, 23, 103, 122, 144
Mitchell, Delores, 126
Mitchell, Gloria, 86
Mitchell, Gregory, 11, 31, 210
Mitchell, J. F., 151
Mitchell, James, 182
Mitchell, Jerry, 43
Mitchell, Joel, 143
Mitchell, John Cameron, 82, 131
Mitchell, Katalin, 122
Mitchell, Lauren, 144
Mitchell, LeRoy, Jr., 150
Mitchell, Ruth, 46, 106
Mitchell, Thom, 114
Mitchell-Leon, Carol, 119
Mitchelson, Bill, 51, 63
Mittelman, Arnold, 133
Mixon, Christopher, 52
Mixson, Sarah, 166
Miyake, Kiki, 16
Miyazaki, Gerrielani, 168
Mizzy, Danianne, 63
Mlaba, Pat, 116
Möhrlein, John, 138
Moberly, Phyllis, 131
Mobley, Areesah, 172
Mochel, Ned, 138
Mockus, Tony, 118
Moe, Ruth, 64
Moeller, Todd, 160
Moffat, Donald, 87
Moffet, Sally, 211, 213
Moffett, D. W., 146
Mofokeng, Jerry, 86
Mohrmann, Al, 211
Moinot, Michel, 18
Moiseiwitsch, Tanya, 176
Mokokeng, Mubi, 116
Mokone, Tsepo, 168
Molaskey, Jessica, 45
Molefe, Ray, 116, 144
Moliere, 93, 121, 135, 138, 142, 171
Molina, Arnold, 19, 144
Mollenhauer, Heidi, 139
Moller, Pamela, 73
Molloy, 129
Molnar, Ferenc, 66
Mom's Life, A, 90
Monaco, John, 11, 18, 20, 50
Monagan, Tim, 168
Monahan, Dan, 164
Monat, Phil, 78, 83, 90, 99, 136, 139, 154, 157, 165
Moncada, Raul, 71, 153
Monchek, Robin, 69
Moncure, Lisa "Sparrow", 88
Mondy, Bill, 124
Monette, Richard, 176
Mong, David, 118, 166
Monge, Julio, 43
Monich, Timothy, 129
Monison, Tim, 138
Moniz, Susan, 133, 148
Monk, Debra, 36, 76, 94, 120, 145, 156, 170, 211
Monk, Isabell, 62, 141
Monroe, Jarion, 162
Monson, Lex, 29, 86, 211
Monster Time, 58
Mont, Ira, 84, 99
Montano, Robert, 63, 71
Monteith, John, 50
Monteleone, John, 211
Monteleone, Kathleen, 173
Montevecchi, Liliane, 18, 39, 211
Montez, Paul-Felix, 146
Montgomerie, Jeffrey, 132
Montgomery, Andre, 140
Montgomery, David, 50
Montgomery, Jack, 117
Montgomery, Jean, 150
Montgomery, Reggie, 91, 72, 134
Monthertrand, Carine, 52
Montoya, Patricia, 71
Montpetit, Christopher M., 87
Montville, Clea, 94, 211
Monzione, David, 139
Moody, Michael R., 83
Moon for the Misbegotten, A, 164
Moon, Gerald, 166
Moon, Jill, 161
Moon, Marjorie, 51, 59, 71
Mooney, Debra, 146
Mooney, Robert, 52
Mooney, Roger, 168
Mooney, William, 85, 95, 211
Moor, Bill, 77, 131, 211
Moore, Benjamin, 160
Moore, Bruce, 20, 169, 211
Moore, Charlotte, 15, 79
Moore, Christina, 124
Moore, Crista, 20, 144, 181, 183, 211
Moore, Dana, 11, 41
Moore, Deidre, 79
Moore, Edward J., 128
Moore, Gregory, 170
Moore, Jane, 129, 169
Moore, John Jay, 108
Moore, Judith, 84, 129, 211
Moore, Julianne, 91, 211
Moore, Kim, 101, 120, 211
Moore, Larry, 139
Moore, Lee, 54, 211
Moore, Lorraine, 64
Moore, Maureen, 43
Moore, Melba, 182
Moore, Michael, 110, 211
Moore, Paul, 61
Moore, Richard, 149, 160
Moore, Scott, 108
Moore, Sharon, 139
Moore, Stephen E., 145
Moore, Steven Edward, 111
Moore, Tracey, 6
Moorer, Margo, 119
Moose, G. Eugene, 139
Mooy, Brad, 125
Moraes, Leda, 27
Morain, Michelle, 174
Morales, Mark, 133
Morales, William R., 88
Moran, Dan, 168
Moran, Johnny, 145
Moran, Neal, 171
Morath, Kathy, 35
Mordecai, Benjamin, 32, 130, 170
Morden, David, 172
More Sex Drugs Rock & Roll, 122
Moreau, Jennie, 211
Morehead, Rozz, 141
Morelan, Paula, 167
Moreland, Gary, 114
Morelli, Anne Marie, 173
Morer, Paul, 53
Morfogen, George, 211
Morgan, Barbara, 165
Morgan, Belinda, 120
Morgan, Carrie Beutler, 135
Morgan, Cass, 99, 145
Morgan, Dale, 133, 148
Morgan, David, 135
Morgan, Edward, 159, 172
Morgan, Elizabeth Anne, 127
Morgan, Francine, 115, 131
Morgan, James Richard, 143
Morgan, James, 8, 37, 64, 101, 123, 128
Morgan, Matthew, 135
Morgan, Michael, 131
Morgan, Monique, 177
Morgan, Robert, 121
Morgan, Roger, 157, 168
Morgan, Ron, 15, 127, 211, 213
Mori, Brian Richard, 136
Moriarty, Michael, 64, 211
Moriber, Brooke Sunny, 31
Morick, Jeanine, 157
Moritz, Marc, 132
Moritz, Susan Trapnell, 118
Moriyasu, Atsushi, 92
Morkert, Jessica Arnwine, 126
Morley, Carol, 140
Morley, Ruth, 90
Morlino, Jim, 139
Morosini, Dana, 170
Moross, Jerome, 101
Moroz, Barbara, 144
Morozov, Boris A., 37
Morreale, Chris, 70
Morrill, Ed, 66
Morris, Anita, 50
Morris, Cleveland, 135
Morris, Garrett, 147
Morris, Iona, 71
Morris, Janet, 135
Morris, Kenny, 82, 127, 211
Morris, Robert Michael, 157
Morris, Sydney, 61
Morris, Victor, 118, 160
Morris, Wendy, 7
Morrisey, Bob, 160
Morrison, John, 153, 173
Morrison, Vivian, 125
Morriss, Bruce K., 135
Morrissey, Connan, 120
Morrow, Elizabeth, 150
Morrow, Kevyn, 41
Morrow, Rob, 146
Morse, Bobbi, 145
Morse, Peter G., 211
Morse, Robert, 23, 39, 122, 182, 183, 211
Morse, Robin, 82, 211
Morse, Tom, 22, 130
Mortensen, Arthur C., 93
Mortimer, Scott, 17, 28
Morton, Carlos, 167
Morton, Neal, 167
Morze, Stacy, 84
Moseley, Robin, 73, 143
Moseley, Stacey, 168
Moser, Joseph S., 141
Moses, Gerard E., 165
Moses, Mark, 131
Mosher, Gregory, 81, 144
Mosher, Jane, 150
Moshier, Steven, 90, 147
Moskowitz, Annette, 72
Moss, Arnold, 230, 231
Moss, Barry, 8, 18, 37
Moss, Kathi, 18, 211
Moss, Peter, 51
Moss, Stephanie, 126
Mossberg, Julie, 11
Mosse, Spencer, 51, 63, 128, 168
Mostel, Josh, 16, 71, 211
Motley, Damon, 131
Motondo, Paul, 70
Mott, Jordan, 72, 73, 76
Mottola, Keith Joseph, 154
Mountain Language, 77
Mountain, 68, 137
Mountcastle, James, 32, 50, 170
Mouser, Kirk, 110
Move Over, Mrs. Markham, 133
Moving Targets, 99
Moya, Pat, 50, 103
Moye, Michell, 127
Moyer, Allen, 84, 94
Moyes, Dennis W., 155
Moynihan, David, 141
Moynihan, John G., 125
Mozer, Elizabeth, 11, 211, 213
Mozon, Nadine, 121
Mrozek, Slawomir, 56
Mshvelidze, Mirian, 69
Mtume, James, 83
Mu, Zvuki, 53
Much Ado About Nothing, 171, 174
Mueller, Hollie, 128
Mueller, Lavonne, 66
Mueller, Marie, 157
Muenz, Richard, 57, 211
Muir, Howie, 211, 213
Muir, Keri, 129
Muirhead, Jayne, 118
Mujica, Rick, 117
Mulburn, Rob, 138
Mulcahy, Patrick, 140, 169
Mulert, Carl, 42, 94
Mulgrew, Kate, 87, 131
Mulhare, Edward, 133
Mulhern, Leonard A., 48
Mulhern, Michael, 154
Mulkey, David, 127
Mull, Kathe, 79
Mullavey, Greg, 143, 153, 211
Mullen, David, 50
Muller, Frank, 52, 97, 146, 211
Muller, Herman-Jay, 15
Muller, Jennifer, 89
Mullin, Paul, 65
Mullins, Melinda, 10, 90, 211
Mulloy, Paul, 6
Mumford, Peter B., 94
Mundell, Anne, 157
Munderloh, Otts, 11, 18, 23, 43, 50, 122
Mundinger, Matthew, 24
Mundy, Meg, 160, 170
Munford, Juanita, 126
Mungioli, Arnold, 37
Munier, Leon, 61
Munkacsi, Kurt, 122
Munnell, Mandy, 133
Munoz, Ana, 157
Munoz, Elias Miguel, 66
Munro, John, 176
Munro, Leigh, 113
Munroe, Jan, 131, 147
Munson, James, 64
Muraoka, Alan, 154
Murcelo, Karmin, 131
Murch, Robert, 91, 169, 211
Murdock, Christine, 147
Murfitt, Mary, 120, 156, 211, 213
Murin, David, 35, 73, 143, 146, 157, 168
Murlin-Gardner, Michelle, 110
Murney, Christopher, 67, 211
Murphey, Mark, 174
Murphy, Austin, 54
Murphy, Bronagh, 60
Murphy, Donna, 97, 211
Murphy, Gary, 76, 91
Murphy, Harry S., 90
Murphy, Jayne, 144
Murphy, Karen, 144
Murphy, Laura, 73
Murphy, Mark David, 149
Murphy, Mary Elizabeth, 150
Murphy, Mary, 105
Murphy, Michael, 161
Murphy, Ron, 69
Murphy, Rosemary, 183
Murphy, Sally, 29, 138, 211
Murphy, Thomas, 79
Murphy-Palmer, Kathleen, 64
Murray, Abigail, 94
Murray, Art, 50
Murray, Brian, 21, 91, 211
Murray, Cora, 60
Murray, Daniel L., 135
Murray, John Horton, 46
Murray, Josette, 175
Murray, Leland, 211
Murray, Margery, 149
Murray, Mary Gordon, 107, 124
Murray, Mike, 211, 213
Murray, Peg, 53
Murray, Rick, 59
Murrell, John, 135, 169
Murrow, Jessica, 10, 67
Murtaugh, James, 49, 211
Musante, Tony, 183
Muscha, Colleen, 171
Music Fair Productions, 23
Musical Theatre Works, 84
Musselman, David, 55, 59
Musser, Tharon, 22, 41, 97, 130, 153
Mustafin, V., 39
Mutch, Helen, 171
Muzhikova, Nina, 88
Muzio, Gloria, 49, 97, 99
Muzzi, Michèle, 176
My Big Land (Sailors' Silence), 88
My Blue Heaven, 60
My Children! My Africa!, 91
My Fair Lady, 111, 127
My Love, My Love, 94
My Sister Eileen, 56
Mydlack, Danny, 53
Myers, Lou, 32, 130, 211
Myers, Mary, 72
Myers, Pamela, 119
Myers, Troy, 43
Myler, Andrew, 131
Myler, Randal, 135
Mylius, Wade, 173
Myrow, Fredric, 147
Mystery of Irma Vep, The, 125
Mystery of the Rose Bouquet, 131
Myth Project: A Festival of Competency, The, 50
Nabel, Bill, 8
Nachtmann, Rita, 132
Nackley, Elizabeth, 139
Nadeau, James, 15
Nadir, Robert, 118, 126, 174
Nagy, Ken, 154
Naharin, Ohad, 53
Nahrwold, Thomas, 149, 211
Nail, Rusty, 125
Naimo, Jennifer, 109
Nakagawa, Jon, 99
Nakagawa, Kikue, 12
Nakahara, Ron, 92, 141, 211
Nakamura, Midori, 168, 175
Nakao, Kenji, 108
Nakauchi, Paul, 154
Namath, Joe, 39
Namkoong, Diana, 92
Nance, Cortez, Jr., 151
Nanus, Susan, 144
Napier, Grace, 108
Napier, John, 40, 45, 117
Naranjo, Valerie, 61
Nardiello, Joe, 152
Nardini, James, 162
Nash, Kathryn, 150
Nash, N. Richard, 64
Nash, Neil, 47
Nash, Ollie, 153
Nash, Paul, 174
Nash, Raphael, 119, 172
Nason, Brian, 16, 80, 143, 164
Nasvytis, Julia, 55
Natel, Jean-Marc, 45
Nathan, Anne L., 110
Nathan, Fred, 29, 30, 31, 46, 56, 66, 69
Nathan, Robert, 90

Nathanson, Gary, 128
Nathanson, Roy, 68
National Folk Ballet Company of Poland/SLASK, 55
Nations, Denise, 61
Natural Shocks, 167
Nature of Things, The, 68
Nauffts, Geoffrey, 19, 144, 211, 213
Naughton, Amanda, 89, 211
Naughton, Barbara, 166
Naughton, James, 4, 24, 182, 183, 211
Naumkin, Yury, 61
Naunton, David, 138
Nause, Allen, 174
Nautiyal, Leslie, 152
Navarro, Tina Cantu, 76
Navazio, Michele, 65
Navins, Deborah, 56, 68
Nay, Gerry, 73
Naylor, Anthony, 62
Naylor, Marcus, 50, 51
Naylor, Wesley, 64
Nayyar, Harsh, 114
Ndlovu, Duma, 116, 134
Ndlovu, Nandi, 116
Neal, R. C., 134
Neals, Lawrence A., Jr., 61
Nealy, Milton Craig, 94
Near, Timothy, 90, 159, 211
Neary, Jack, 166
Nease, Byron, 113
Nebgen, Stephen W., 30
Nebozenko, Jan, 63
Neddy, 75
Nederlander, James M., 9, 11, 16, 26
Neeb, Sherri, 105
Needles, William, 176
Neel, Joanna, 119
Neely, Barbara, 73
Neenan, Maria, 43, 211, 213
Nees, Jennifer, 148
Neet, Alison Stair, 65, 144
Neff, Debra, 94
Neff, Tracey Lynn, 133
Negrini, Gualtiero, 113
Negro Ensemble Company, 95
Neiden, Daniel, 80, 212, 213
Neilson, Richard, 111
Neisler, John, 143
Nelligan, Kate, 12, 83, 212
Nels, Peter, 90
Nelson, Beth, 156
Nelson, Bruce, 161
Nelson, Connie, 167
Nelson, Diane, 39
Nelson, Mari, 82, 87, 89
Nelson, Marjorie, 160
Nelson, Mark, 19, 144, 175, 212, 213
Nelson, Novella, 146
Nelson, Rebecca, 81, 95
Nelson, Richard, 7, 13, 81, 83, 87, 90, 93, 103, 107, 144
Nelson, Ruth, 97, 212, 213
Nelson, Sara, 109
Nelson, Selena, 71
Nelson, Steve, 72
Nemeth, Sally, 56, 162
Nemrow, Clayton, 51
Neofitou, Andreane, 45
Nerd, The, 125, 166
Nesby, Ann Bennett, 120
Nesci, John, 131
Nettleton, Lois, 146
Neuberger, Jan, 35, 84, 84, 212
Neufeld, Jane, 139
Neufeld, Mary, 59, 69
Neufeld, Peter, 40, 117
Neuman, Jani, 113
Neumann, David, 91
Neumann, Frederick, 91, 142
Neville, David, 125
Neville, John, 176
Neville, Marcus, 24
Neville, Tom, 158
Nevins, Kristine, 84, 212, 213
New American Theater, 152
New Anatomies, 65
New Federal Theatre, 86
New Jersey Shakespeare Festival, 173
New Listings, 73
New Music, 132
New York 1937, 80
New York Choral Society and Orchestra, 23
New York City Opera Company, 27
New York Drama Critics Circle Awards, 184
New York Shakespeare Festival, 87, 88, 89, 90, 91
New York Theatre Workshop, 91
New, David, 176
New, Marty, 170
New, Scott Allen, 149
Newcomb, Don, 100, 145
Newcomb, James, 174
Newcott, Rosemary, 119
Newell, Alana, 159
Newell, Charles, 158
Newell, Scot A., 73
Newfield, Anthony, 128
Newhall, Anne, 97
Newley, Anthony, 133
Newman, Barry, 39
Newman, Buck, 119
Newman, Emily, 158
Newman, Holly, 154
Newman, Jim, 89
Newman, Joel, 154
Newman, Paula, 68
Newman, Thomas, 147
Newman, William, 77, 119, 159, 212
Newman, Wills, 68
Newsome, Paula, 138
Newson, Pip, 167
Newton, Jesse, 136
Newton, John, 28
Newton, Marilyn, 163
Newton, Vincent, 67
Newton-John, Olivia, 39
Neye, Adrienne, 169
Ng, Paula, 65
Ngema, Mbongeni, 116, 134, 144
Ngema, Nhlanhia, 116
Nhlanhla, Thandekile, 116
Niccore, Valorie, 212
Nichols, Jonathan, 77
Nichols, Mike, 73, 125, 138
Nichols, Nancy, 59
Nichols, Peter, 97
Nichols, Richard Alan, 151
Nicholson, Betsy, 28
Nickel, Nancy, 145
Nickol, Richard, 110
Nicola, James C., 91
Nicoletti, John, 106
Niebanck, Paul, 143
Niebuhr, Mark, 129
Niederjohn, Clark, 141
Nielsen, Kristine, 75, 146, 170
Nielsen, Leslie, 111
Nielsen, William, 174
Nieminski, Joseph, 138
Niessen, James, 73
Night With Doris, A, 94
Night of 100 Stars III, 39
Night of the Iguana, 173
Nigro, Bob, 100
Nikitushkin, Viktor, 54
Nimmo, Bob, 169
Nininger, Susan, 90
Nisbet, David, 151
Nishizaki, Mayumi, 12
Nissenson, Gloria, 17, 101
Niven, Kip, 101, 157, 212
Nixon, Cynthia, 42, 101, 130, 212
No + (No More), 88
No Exit, 145
Noah, Delores, 148
Noah, James, 29
Noble, Adrian, 83
Noble, Dorset, 133
Noble, James, 183
Noble, Janet, 60
Nockengust, Rex, 212
Noel, Craig, 153
Noel, Fred, 144, 157
Noel, Lowell V., 135
Nogulich, Natalia, 34, 212, 213
Noises Off, 125, 127, 152, 156, 171
Nokwe, Tu, 134
Nolan, Anto, 60, 146
Nolan, Robert, 117
Nolen, Timothy, 212
Noling, David, 151, 160
Nolte, Bill, 144
Nolte, Charles, 150
Noonan, John Ford, 70
Noone, James, 56, 62, 66, 83, 84, 128, 146
Norberg, Catherine, 136
Norcia, Patrizia, 66, 212
Nordli, Robin, 171
Norma Terris Theatre, The, 139
Normal Heart, The, 65
Norman, Grant, 114
Norman, John, 212
Norman, Marsha, 101, 168
Normoyle, Tracie, 54
Norris, Bruce, 138, 162
Norris, Margie, 133
Norris, William J., 138
North, Alex, 147
Norton, Cari, 131
Norton, Kristin, 54
Noseworthy, Jack, 41, 43
Nostrand, Michael, 101, 212
Not About Heroes, 174
Nothing Sacred, 167
Noto, Lore, 47
Noto, Tony, 47
Nottbusch, Kaye, 160
Novack, Ellen, 77
Novak, David Alan, 138
Novak, Delrae, 126
Novak, Mark, 129
Novin, Michael J., 154, 169
Nowitzky, Vanessa, 174
Nozick, Bruce, 74, 80, 212
Ntinga, Mshengu THemba, 86
Ntinga, Themba, 86
Nugent, James, 93, 212
Null, Panchali, 106
Nunes, Paul, 72
Nunn, Barbara, 114
Nunn, Bill, 119
Nunn, Trevor, 31, 40, 45, 117
Nureyev, Rudolf, 108
Nurradin, Ahmad, 167
Nussbaum, Bernard, 26
Nussbaum, Toby, 26
Nutcracker, The, 158
Nute, Don, 182, 212, 213
Nutt, J. R., 57
Nutt, Sandra, 85, 95
Nutu, Dan, 122
Nyberg, Pamela, 124
Nye, Carrie, 12, 212
Nyrop, Lise, 168
O Pioneers!, 143
O'Boyle, Jerry, 148
O'Brady, Mary, 130
O'Brien, Adale, 120
O'Brien, Brenda, 103
O'Brien, Dale, 47
O'Brien, David, 230, 231
O'Brien, Jack, 130, 144, 153
O'Brien, Joycelyn, 131
O'Brien, Liam, 110
O'Brien, Maria, 131
O'Brien, Marienne, 166
O'Brien, Patty, 57
O'Brien, Paul, 51, 58, 63, 71
O'Brien, Quentin, 128, 146
O'Byrne, Brian F., 79
O'Casey, Sean, 124
O'Connell, Andrea, 128
O'Connell, Caitlin, 129, 172
O'Connell, Deirdre, 69, 147
O'Connell, Elinore, 31
O'Connell, Gretchen, 118,
O'Connell, Patricia, 100, 212, 213
O'Connell, Patrick, 77, 212
O'Connell, Peggy, 160
O'Conner, Sara, 74
O'Connor, Daniel, 131
O'Connor, J. Christopher, 118
O'Connor, James, 62
O'Connor, Joyce, 13
O'Connor, Kevin, 65, 66, 212
O'Connor, Paul Vincent, 174
O'Connor, Ryan, 118
O'Connor, Sean, 60
O'Dell, Herbert H., 95
O'Dell, K. Lype, 128
O'Donovan, Gene, 19
O'Dwyer, Laurence, 167
O'Flaherty, Douglas, 65, 93
O'Grady, Dan, 102
O'Hara, John, 54
O'Hara, Paige, 70, 212, 213
O'Hara, Sandy, 127
O'Hare, Michael, 19
O'Hern, John, 212, 213
O'Horgan, Tom, 66, 69
O'Keefe, John, 53, 98
O'Keefe, Paul, 52, 90
O'Kelley, Kim, 147
O'Kelly, Aideen, 146, 170
O'Leary, Barbara Ann, 69
O'Leary, Thomas James, 103
O'Lone, Charles, 135
O'Mara, Mollie, 65, 212, 213
O'Meara, Evan, 97, 212
O'Melia, Bob, 72
O'Neal, Patrick, 111
O'Neil, Chris, 79
O'Neill, Denis, 79
O'Neill, Eugene, 59, 135, 146, 164
O'Neill, James Jaye, 146
O'Neill, Vincent, 79
O'Regan, Hannah, 151
O'Reilly, Allen, 119
O'Reilly, Ciaran, 79, 212
O'Relly, Maya, 62
O'Relly, Terry, 91
O'Rourke, Barry, 60
O'Rourke, Kevin, 28, 90, 212
O'Shea, Kathleen, 170
O'Shea, Milo, 15, 212
O'Shea, Ollie, 159
O'Slynne, Timothy, 138
O'Steen, Michael, 15, 212
O'Steen, Michelle, 144
O'Sullivan, Anne, 120
O'Sullivan, Sean, 127
O'Sullivan-Moore, Emmet, 146
O'Toole, Shawn, 63
Oates, Joyce Carol, 120
Oba Oba '90, 27
Ober, Jennifer, 39
Obrow, Susan, 130
Ochoa, Steve, 43, 103
Odenz, Leon, 135
Odishaw, Tracy, 126
Odland, Bruce, 149
Odle, Dwight Richard, 162
Odo, Chris, 212
Odom, Ben, 138
Odom, Denise, 125
Odom, Richard, 120
Odorisio, Robert T., 156
Oetken, Patricia, 136
Of Mice and Men, 151
Of Thee I Sing, 68
Offner, Deborah, 170
Offstage Voices, 127
Ogarkov, Vladimir, 54
Ogborn, Michael James, 54
Ogden, Constance, 124
Oglesby, Randy, 131
Ogurtsov, Boris, 26
Ogus, Carol, 171
Oh! Calcutta!, 94
Oh, Hell, 81
Oh, Kay!, 139
Oh, The Innocents, 136
Ohara, Hirotoshi, 12
Ohlson, Lary, 161
Oien, Tim, 29, 138
Oil City Symphony, 120, 156
Oka, Marc, 154
Okada, Kimi, 64, 160
Okamura, Koji, 26
Oken, Carol, 131
Okun, Alexander, 133
Olcott, C. Townsend, II, 149
Olcott, Nick, 124
Old Globe Theatre, 154
Old Possum's Book of Practical Cats, 40
Old Times, 158
Oldfather, Craig, 110
Olds, Gabriel, 90
Olds, Tim, 152
Oleniacz, Thomas S., 153, 161
Oleynik, Larisa, 110
Olich, Michael, 119, 160
Oliensis, Adam, 212
Oligny, Huguette, 50, 51
Olim, Dorothy, 47
Olive, David, 169
Olive, John, 119, 155
Oliver, Allen, 153
Oliver, John, 55, 127
Oliver, Jorge, 96
Oliver, LaFontaine, 124
Oliver, Natalie, 136
Oliver, Susan, 230, 231
Oliveros, Pauline, 62
Olivier, Laurence, 230, 232
Ollmann, Kurt, 70
Olsen, Robert, 71, 149, 212, 213
Olson, James, 149
Olson, Karen, 127
Olson, Marcus, 107
Olson, Stephan, 63, 149
Olster, Fredi, 121
Oman, Timothy W., 52, 60
Omilami, Afemo, 119, 138
Omilami, Elizabeth, 119
On the Bench, 73
Onate, Erik, 87
Once in Arden, 162
Once in Doubt, 147
Once on This Island, 94
One Choice, 167
One Man Band, 133
One of the Guys, 90
1000 Airplanes on the Roof, 122
Only Kidding, 94, 132
Only the Sky Was Blue!, 155
Onrubia, Cynthia, 43
Ontiveros, Bill, 166
Ooms, Richard, 141
Opening, The, 57
Oppenheimer, Alan, 131
Oppusunggu, Johannes, 51
Opsahl, Jason, 154
Orange, Gerald, 80
Orchard, Robert J., 122
Orear, Cheryl, 152
Oregon Shakespeare Festival, 174
Oreskes, Daniel, 138, 151
Orgy in the Air-Traffic Control Tower, 72
Oriel, Ray, 142, 143
Orient Beach, 52
Orinoco!, 161
Orion, Janice, 143
Orlandi, Janice, 73
Orleans, Ilo, 100, 212
Orman, Richard, 152
Orner, Fredric H., 82
Ornston, David E., 133
Oropeza, Luis, 121
Orpheus Descending, 9
Orser, Leland, 135
Ortega, Richard, 153, 161
Orth-Pallavicini, Nicole, 136
Orton, Joe, 89, 146
Orwell, George, 132
Osborn, Tricia, 167
Osborne, Douglas M., 150
Osborne, Georga L., 15
Osborne, Will, 156, 157
Osbun, Eric, 94
Osburn, Alan, 110
Oscar, Brad, 31, 212
Oser, Harriet, 128
Osgood, Kimberly, 138
Osgood, Steve, 73
Osman, Daniel, 175
Osorio, Raul, 88
Osterman, Georg, 59
Ostrenko, Kim, 114
Ostrow, Ron, 19, 144, 212
Othello, 72, 77, 145
Other People's Money, 49
Ottavino, John, 130
Otter, Karl, 129
Ottiwell, Frank, 121
Ottley, Rachelle, 15
Otto, Victoria, 174
Our Country's Good, 131
Our Town, 152
Ousley, Robert, 16
Ouzounian, Richard, 176
Ovchinnikov, Rady, 61
Over by the Corner of Claredon and Hampton, on the Edge of Nowhere, 167
Overmire, Laurence, 48, 150
Overmyer, Eric, 83, 129
Owen, Marianne, 160
Owen, Paul, 120
Owen, Rusty, 58
Owens, Albert, 128
Owens, Edwin C., 128, 144, 145
Owens, Elizabeth, 159
Owens, Gordon, 41
Owens, Louise, 183
Oyewole, Abiodun, 65
Oyster, Jim, 101, 212
Pace, Atkin, 55, 80, 137
Pace, Michael, 135
Packard, Carl, 112
Packer, Tina, 175
Padgett, Billy, 154
Padilla, Louis, 168
Padron, Aurelio, 139
Page, Cindi, 110
Page, Elizabeth, 67
Pagliotti, Douglas, 130, 153
Pagnol, Marcel, 154
Painted Rain, 94
Painter, Walter, 24
Pais, Josh, 77, 212
Pajer, Jeff, 127
Pakledinaz, Martin, 91, 141, 142, 168, 172
Palazzo, Larry, 45
Palazzo, Paul, 59
Paley, Petronia, 124
Palisin, Robert, 128
Palma, Michael, 67, 69
Palmas, Joseph, 80
Palmer, Mack, 136
Palmieri, Joe, 37, 159, 212
Palminteri, Chazz, 56, 212
Pan Asian Repertory Theatre, 92
Panaro, Hugh, 45, 109
Pang, Andrew, 163
Pankow, John, 91, 212, 213
Pannell, Glen, 101, 139
Panson, Bonnie, 117
Paoletti, John, 148, 152
Papava, Vickie, 176
Paper Mill Playhouse, 154
Papp, Joseph, 7, 13, 41, 87
Pappas, Evan, 105
Papuashvili, David, 69
Paquet, Lucina, 29, 212, 213
Paradise for the Worried, 69
Paradiso, Tina, 160
Parady, Ron, 36, 170, 212, 213
Pardee, Steve, 96
Pardess, Yael, 131, 142
Pareja, Ramon, 88
Parente, Teresa, 80
Parenti, Christopher, 68
Parfitt, David, 115, 131
Parichy, Dennis, 12, 67, 68, 73, 76, 82, 91, 97, 98, 111, 132, 144
Paris '31, 58
Paris, Myrna, 177
Paris, Nancy, 163
Paris, Patrick, 27, 69
Parise, Tony, 154
Parish, Mitchell, 144
Parish, Scot A., 60
Park, Claudia, 175
Park, Stephanie, 141
Park, Steve, 92, 212
Parker, Alecia, 20, 28
Parker, Blaine, 113
Parker, Candace, 159
Parker, Ellen, 42, 212, 213
Parker, Herbert Mark, 52, 136
Parker, Jean, 79
Parker, Leonard, 66, 170, 212
Parker, Mary-Louise, 36, 76, 83, 142, 181, 183, 212
Parker, Nathaniel, 25, 215
Parker, Shanga, 161
Parker, Wayne David, 150
Parkman, Russell, 145
Parks, Brian, 119
Parks, Hildy, 34, 39
Parks, Julia, 70
Parks, Monica, 53, 128
Parlato, Dennis, 66, 101, 214, 215
Parnell, Peter, 94
Parnes, Joey, 11, 18, 50
Parone, Edward, 131
Parr, Katherine, 173
Parrinello, Richard, 27, 111
Parrish, Jack, 171
Parry, Chris, 153, 162
Parry, William, 157, 215
Parson, Annie B., 73
Parsons, Estelle, 26, 98, 215
Parsons, Jennifer, 133
Parsons, Robert, 174
Parting Gestures, 60
Partington, Dixie, 127
Partington, Rex, 127
Partington, Tony, 127
Partlan, William, 57, 171
Pascal, Gabriel, 111
Pasekoff, Marilyn, 62, 214, 215
Pashalinski, Lola, 62, 141
Passarella, Lynn, 158
Passaro, Michael J., 31
Passeltiner, Bernie, 215
Passion of Narcisse Mondoux, The, 50, 51
Past Is the Past, The, 59
Patch, Jerry, 162
Paterson, David S., 154
Paterson, W. J., 97, 215
Paterson, William, 121
Patinkin, Mandy, 7, 215
Paton, Angela, 131, 147
Patrello, Shawn, 167
Patricio, Ann, 166
Patten, Michael, Jr., 171
Patterson, Anne C., 51, 63
Patterson, Jackie, 144
Patterson, Jay, 72, 97, 214, 215
Patterson, Kelly, 43, 101, 215
Patterson, Neil J., 150
Patterson, Zelda, 95
Patti, Sandi, 39
Pattison, Liann, 123, 126
Patton, Eva, 71, 79, 93
Patton, Lucille, 38, 135, 214, 215
Patton, Pat, 174
Patton, Shirley, 174
Paul, Frank, 40
Paul, Guy, 130, 214, 215
Paul, Stephanie, 169
Paul, Talia, 37, 214, 215
Paul, Tina, 11, 99
Pauley, Wilbur, 25
Paull, John H., III, 45, 46, 110
Paulsen, Jeanne, 118, 162, 174
Paulsen, Larry, 118, 166, 174
Paulsen, Rick, 118, 160, 174
Pavlich, Frank, 142
Pawl, Christina, 15
Paxton, Marie, 111
Payan, Ilka Tanya, 60, 215
Paynter, Lynn, 127
Payton, Key, 169
Payton-Wright, Pamela, 142, 215
Peabody, Sam, 119
Peaboy, Steve, 91
Peachena, Lady, 214, 215
Peacock, Chiara, 215
Peacock, Lucy, 176
Peak, Danny, 135
Pearce, Bobby, 51, 62
Pearl Theatre Company, The, 93
Pearl, Deborah, 153
Pearl, Minnie, 39
Pearlman, Stephen, 82, 94, 214, 215
Pearlstein, Julia, 122
Pearson, Robert, 141
Pearthree, Pippa, 146
Peaslee, Richard, 147

Pecaro, Christopher, 110
Peccadillo, 136
Pechenkina, E., 88
Peck, James J., 174
Peck, Jonathan, 124, 132, 168
Peck, M. Susan, 153
Pedala, Maureen, 173
Peden, Margaret Sayers, 161
Pedernera, Alfredo, 69
Pedersen, Matt, 41
Pederson, Rose, 118, 160
Peek, Jenny, 87
Peer Gynt, 174
Peerce, Harry, 58, 215
Peggy and Jackson, 88
Peipers, David H., 67
Pekar, Gregory, 57
Peldon, Courtney, 15
Pelinski, Stephen, 141
Pell, Stephen, 55, 69
Pellegrini, Larry, 48
Pellegrino, Susan, 52, 64, 142, 215
Pellicciaro, Elena, 73
Peltoniemi, Eric Bain, 118, 147
Pelzig, Daniel, 97, 143
Pen, Polly, 135
Pendleton, Austin, 60, 168, 215
Pendleton, David, 215
Pendleton, Wyman, 36, 215
Penguin Repertory Company, 155
Penn, Arthur, 90
Penn, Joan, 58
Penn, Matt, 78, 215
Pennell, Nicholas, 176
Pennington, Mark, 88
Pennsylvania Stage Company, 156
Penrod, Shannon, 135
Pentecost, James, 20
People Who Could Fly, The, 53
Peoples, Jamal, 119
Peppe, Michael, 53
Pepper, Allan, 52
Pepper, Melissa, 120
Peppiatt, Caroline, 105
Peppiatt, Frank, 105
Perantoni, Martha, 153
Percassi, Don, 144
Pere, Dana, 153
Pereiras, Manuel, 96
Perera, Fia, 51
Perez, Joseph, 133
Perez, Josie, 88
Perez, Luis, 11, 43, 215
Perez, Mercedes, 169
Perez, Miguel, 77, 91, 142, 215
Perez, Tim, 80, 141
Perez, Tony, 147
Perfect Diamond, A, 71
Perfect Party, The, 128
Pericles, Prince of Tyre, 61, 173, 174
Perkins, Don, 173, 215
Perkins, Patti, 64, 99, 150, 214, 215
Perkins, Phineas, 50
Perkovich, David, 145
Perl, Arnold, 106
Perl, Joshua, 87
Perla, Gene, 69
Perley, William, 155
Perlman, Bonnie, 17
Perlman, Laura, 133
Perlman, Ron, 19, 214, 215
Perlmatt, Bonnie, 17
Perloff, Carey, 77, 131
Perman, Dennis, 80
Perone, Paul, 128
Perreca, Michael, 71
Perren, Dennis, 67
Perrineau, Harold, Jr., 84
Perrotta, Laura, 144
Perry, Alvin, 83, 135
Perry, Doug, 171
Perry, Ernest, Jr., 138
Perry, Gwenna, 84
Perry, Jeff, 29, 215
Perry, Keith, 24, 215
Perry, Louis, 27
Perry, Lynnette, 18, 94, 214, 215
Perry, Navarre T., 153
Perry, Steven, 37, 58, 64, 133, 145, 155
Perryman, Dwayne B., III, 73, 86
Persons, Fern, 138
Peter Breaks Through, 94
Peter Pan, 112
Peter, Paul & Mary, 23
Peterman, Robyn, 148
Peters, Bernadette, 182
Peters, Charlie, 95
Peters, Sarah E., 120
Petersen, William L., 144
Peterson, Candice, 114
Peterson, Lenka, 49
Peterson, Lisa, 60, 91, 94
Peterson, Melinda, 161
Peterson, Patricia Ben, 120
Peterson, Peggy, 40
Peterson, Peter R., 149
Peterson, Robert, 153, 174
Peterson, Robina, 127
Peterson, Sarah, 146
Peterson, Wally, 21
Petit, Christopher, 53
Petit, Lenard, 61
Petition, The, 169
Petito, Robert, 68
Petlock, Martin, 126
Petrarca, David, 56, 138
Petrilli, Stephen, 93, 173, 177
Petrino, Debbie, 58
Petronio, Stephen, 53
Petrov, Yuri, 54
Petrovich, Victoria, 69, 161
Petrushevskaya, Liudmila, 120
Pettengill, Richard, 138
Pettiford, Valarie, 78, 170
Pettit, Dodie, 46, 215
Petway, Brandi Royale, 147
Pevsner, David, 106
Peyser, Lynne, 133
Pfeiffer, Michelle, 87, 215
Pfisterer, Sarah, 114
Pfluger, Len, 139
Phalen, Robert, 153
Phantom Tollbooth, The, 144
Phantom of the Opera, The, 46, 113, 114
Phelan, Kate, 143
Philadelphia, Here I Come!, 79
Philip Glass Buys a Loaf of Bread, 63
Philip Glass Ensemble, 122
Philip, Tania, 46
Phillip, Jessica, 152
Phillip, Joseph, 56
Phillip, Vince, 167
Phillip, William R., 152
Phillippi, Michael S., 152
Phillips, Andy, 16, 67
Phillips, Arlene, 117
Phillips, Barbara-Mae, 38
Phillips, Bob, 60
Phillips, Burr Cochran, 70
Phillips, Cristina, 183
Phillips, Eddie, 51
Phillips, Edward, 98, 99
Phillips, Ethan, 129
Phillips, J. P., 174
Phillips, J. T., 54
Phillips, Joseph, 39
Phillips, Ken, 48
Phillips, Lloyd, 16
Phillips, Mary Ellen, 215
Phillips, Mary, 8, 101
Phillips, Patricia, 141
Phillips, Romy, 54
Phillips, Susan, 128
Phillips, Tim, 73
Philpot, Mark, 172
Phippin, Jackson, 129
Phipps, Jim, 153
Piacenti, Valerie, 160
Piano Lesson, The, 32, 130, 144, 179
Piano, 147
Piasecki, Gregory S., 150
Piazza, Joseph, 73
Piazzolla, Astor, 11
Picard, Nicole, 117
Piccione, Nancy, 13
Pichette, David, 118, 160
Pichette, Joe, 73
Pick Up Ax, 121
Pickering, Patrice, 46, 113
Pickering, Steve, 87, 138
Picture Perfect, 71
Piech, Jennifer, 169
Pielmeier, John, 120
Pierce, David, 42, 73, 138, 215
Pierce, J'Von, 158
Pierce, Ray, 127
Pierce, Russell, 167
Pierce, Scott, 167
Pierre, Christopher, 66
Pietraszek, Rita, 143
Pietropinto, Angela, 215
Piggee, Timothy McCuen, 135
Piggot, Patricia, 101
Pigliavento, Michele, 20
Pill Hill, 170
Pillitteri, Paul, 60
Pinchot, Bronson, 37, 214, 215
Pincus, Joy, 65
Pincus, Warren, 139
Pinhasik, Howard, 101
Pini, Robert, 14
Pink Studio, The, 120
Pinkard, Fred, 130
Pinkins, Tonya, 157, 215
Pinkney, Mikell, 51
Pinkney, Scott, 135
Pinkston, Jerry, 166
Pinkston, Socorro, 166
Pinsley, Michelle, 143
Pintauro, Joe, 76, 99
Pinter, Harold, 77, 131, 146, 158
Piontek, Michael, 16, 214, 215
Piper, Wendy, 154
Pippin, Don, 41, 108
Piretti, Ron, 60
Piro, Jacquelyn, 45, 110
Pirri, Jim, 162
Pistone, Charles, 109
Pistone, Martino N., 121
Pitoniak, Anne, 170, 183
Pittman, Demetra, 174
Pitts, Christopher, 136
Pitts, William, 124, 136
Pittsburgh Public Theater, 157
Pittu, David, 82
Pixie Led, The, 53
Pizzi, Joey, 102
Plachy, William J., 71
Plaisant, Dominique, 164
Plaisted, Joy, 47
Plass, Sally, 95
Platt, Martin, 158
Platt, Oliver, 73, 138
Play, 129
Playboy of the Western World, The, 160
Playfair, David, 176
Playmaker, The, 131
Playmakers Repertory Company, 158
Plays in the Park, 51
Playten, Alice, 214, 215
Playwrights Horizons, 94
Pleasants, Philip, 171
Plimpton, Martha, 160
Plotch, Adam Paul, 74
Plotnick, Ellen-Stuart, 80
Plotnick, Jack, 177
Plumpis, John, 95, 177
Plunkett, Mary Ann, 146
Plunkett, Terence, 138
Plymale, Trip, 127, 145
Pocaro, Michael A., 174
Poddubiuk, Christina, 105
Podlozny, Cathy, 103
Pody, Donna, 135
Poe, Gregory, 147
Poe, Richard, 142
Poggi, Jack, 166
Poindexter, Jay, 40
Poindexter, Karen, 17, 114
Poiner, Alex, 92
Polantz, David, 125
Polcsa, Juliet, 99
Polenz, Robert, 156
Polese, Daniel, 153
Poletick, Robert, 58
Poliakoff, Stephen, 118
Policella, Catherine, 100
Polischuk, Geoffrey, 114
Polito, Jon, 49, 214, 215
Polk, Andrew, 120, 137
Pollard, Karen, 174
Pollitt, Barbara, 91
Pollitt, Linda, 172
Pollock, Patti, 167
Pollock, Sharon, 136
Pomahac, Bruce, 15
Pompei, Donna M., 41
Pomranz, Craig, 67
Ponceti, Tony, 167
Ponte, Wendy, 56
Pontini, Antony, 155
Ponzo, Rosemary, 65
Poole, Richard, 110
Poole, Stan H., 171
Pooler, Chuck, 72
Pope, Deborah J., 66
Pope, John, 53
Pope, Peggy, 130, 141, 160
Pope, Sabrynaah, 86
Popkhadze, L., 69
Popkin, Meera, 117
Popova, Tatyana, 153
Porgina, Ludmilla, 61
Porreta, Greg, 120
Porretta, Matthew, 110
Port, Debra, 172
Port, Sharon, 65
Porter, Adina, 123
Porter, Catherine, 65
Porter, Cathy, 90
Porter, Cole, 58, 176
Porter, Edward, 175
Porter, Jessica, 51
Porter, Tom, 41
Porteus, Cameron, 105
Portfolio, 63
Portillo, Rose, 153
Portner, Paul, 144
Poser, Linda, 154
Posey, Molly, 125
Posner, Kenneth, 64
Post, Douglas, 139
Postel, Suzan, 108
Poster, Kim, 18
Pothier, Kevin, 128
Potter, Don, 112
Potter, Jane, 71, 139, 149, 214, 215
Potter, Madeleine, 79
Potter, Nicole, 73
Potter, Sam, 158
Pottinger, Alan, 120
Potts, Albert, 148
Potts, David, 67, 76, 93, 119, 132, 165
Pounders, Steven, 158
Powel, Marilyn, 137
Powell, Anthony, 30, 135, 140
Powell, Denisha V., 138
Powell, John, 110
Powell, Linda, 53
Powell, Mary Ann, 164
Powell, Michael Warren, 36, 62, 76
Powell, Nanci, 117
Powell, W. Tony, 13
Powell-Parker, Maryanne, 101
Powers, David, 19, 104
Powers, Dennis, 121
Powers, Marilyn, 125
Powers, Neva Rae, 127
Powers, Stefanie, 39
Powers, Susan, 40
Powers, Winifred H., 54
Powich, Christopher, 74
Poyer, Lisa M., 44
Poyner, Margaret, 25
Poynter, David, 162
Prada, Rick, 167
Prager, Benjamin, 118, 160
Pratt, Wendy, 146
Precious Memories, 152, 159
Prelude to a Kiss, 36, 76, 181
Premo, Joelle, 150
Prendergast, Marge, 168
Prendergast, Shirley, 75, 128, 134, 145
Prenevost, William, 143
Prentice, Amelia, 136, 214, 216
Prentice, Jeffrey, 176
Prescott, Jennifer, 106
Prescott, Ken, 100
Presley, Elvis, 50
Presnell, Harve, 144
Press, Warren, 167
Pressley, Brenda, 139
Pressner, Stan, 57
Presti, Jackie, 24
Preston, Corliss, 101, 151
Preston, Lawrence, 72, 216
Preston, Travis, 129
Preston, William, 146, 169, 214, 216
Previn, André, 66
Pribyl, John, 174
Price of Fame, 97
Price, Eddie, 167
Price, Faye M., 164
Price, Gene Raye, 167
Price, Harvey, 135
Price, Iona, 115, 131
Price, Karen, 120, 137
Price, Lonny, 72, 73, 74, 105, 182, 216
Price, Michael P., 139
Price, Molly, 146
Price, Peggity, 120
Price, Phillip, 68
Price, Reynolds, 132
Prichard, Dianne M., 121
Pridgen, Angela, 119
Pridgen, Rodney, 139
Priestley, J. B., 165
Primary Stages, 95
Prin, 83
Prince of Central Park, 17
Prince, Daisy, 74
Prince, Faith, 43, 83, 216
Prince, Ginger, 20, 214, 216
Prince, Harold, 46
Principia Scriptoriae, 163
Prinz, Rosemary, 69, 104
Prisoner of Second Avenue, The, 74
Pritchard, Timothy, 59
Pritchett, James, 123
Private Lives, 128
Privates on Parade, 97
Procaccino, John, 160
Profile in Faith, 167
Progress, 78
Prosky, Andrew, 87
Prosser, Peter, 107
Protko, José, 141
Provenza, Paul, 214, 216
Provenza, Rosario, 90
Pruet, Kris, 113
Pruett, Glen Allen, 150
Pruitt, Richard, 127
Pruneau, Phillip, 101, 173, 216
Prymus, Ken, 100
Pryor, Deborah, 60
Pryor, Kaye, 50
Pshenichny, Leonid, 54
Public Relations and Marketing, 125
Puchalski, John W., 136
Puddle of Hot Way, A, 167
Puerto Rican Traveling Theatre, 96
Pugh, Caroline, 125
Pugh, Richard Warren, 46, 216
Puhich, Jeanette, 166
Puig, Manuel, 131
Pulio, Laura, 135
Pulitzer Prize Productions, 184
Pulliam, Darcy, 59, 111
Pullinsi, William, 148
Pump Boys & Dinettes, 145
Pupello, Angela, 117
Puppetmaster of Lodz, The, 74
Purcell, John, 119
Purdham, David, 87
Purdy, Claude, 126, 136, 157
Purdy, Marshall B., 55, 57
Pursley, David, 16, 129, 145, 216
Pursuit of the Song of Hydrogen, In, 60
Pvt. Wars, 149
Pyant, Paul, 9
Pygmalion, 111, 170
Pyle, Julie, 157
Pyle, Russell, 74
Quackenbush, Karyn, 145, 157
Quandt, Stephen, 67
Quarles, Aaron F., 13
Quarry, 126
Quayle, Anthony, 232
Quezada, Alba, 46
Quick, Theresa, 125
Quiet End, A, 72, 73, 94
Quigley, Chip, 62
Quigley, Erin, 29
Quillin, Mimi, 78
Quilters, 126
Quinby, Priscilla, 80
Quinn, Brian, 58
Quinn, Colleen, 54, 55, 214, 216
Quinn, Deborah Baer, 169
Quinn, Margaret Adair, 170
Quinn, Nancy, 94
Quinn, Patrick, 44, 214, 216
Quint, Stephen M., 68
Quintard, Scott, 135
Quintessential Image, The, 53
Quinton, Everett, 54, 55, 59, 69
R, Essene, 67, 134
Rabbitt, Eddie, 39
Raben, Larry, 71
Rabenau, Alison, 87
Rabinowitz, Robert, 50
Rabinowitz, Scott, 143
Rabold, Rex, 174
Racheff, James, 139
Rackleff, Owen S., 64
Racolin, Alexander E., 54, 68, 72
Racolin, Dina, 54
Rader, Mason, 88
Rae, Charlotte, 131
Raether, Richard, 152
Rafter, Michael, 20, 84
Ragaway, Jill, 131
Ragland, Jim, 118, 153
Ragno, Joseph, 80, 216
Ragsdale, Robert C., 176
Ragsdale, William, 60, 216
Rahn, Rob, 148
Rahn, Rosalyn, 109
Raider-Wexler, Victor, 97, 101, 216
Raiman, Paul, 148
Rain. Some Fish. No Elephants., 159
Rainer, John, 137
Raines, Lee, 50
Rainey, David, 134, 141, 144
Rainey, Ford, 131
Rainwater, John, 71
Raiter, Frank, 77, 87, 168, 216
Raitt, James, 15, 71, 144
Raitt, Kathleen, 18
Rak, Rachelle, 117
Rakestraw, Fred, 125
Rakhlin, Ilya, 39
Rakov, Victor, 61
Raley, Wade, 168
Ralph, Alee, 48
Ralstin, Monte, 58, 154
Ramach, Michael, 60
Ramage, Edmond, 52, 60
Ramay, Steven, 78
Rambeau, Careayre, 37, 214, 216
Ramblin', Lute, 62
Rameau, Patrick, 87
Ramicova, Dunya, 122, 162
Ramin, Sid, 20, 43
Ramirez, Jillian M., 72, 93
Ramirez, Louie, 133
Ramirez, Tom, 174
Ramone, Phil, 50
Ramont, Mark, 76
Ramos, Bridget, 27
Ramos, Luis, 124
Ramos, Richard, 126, 143
Ramos, Sixto, 142
Ramp, The, 162
Rampino, Lewis D., 87, 120
Ramsay, Matthew S., 129
Ramsay, Remak, 83, 214, 216
Ramsey, Dale, 93
Ramsey, David L., 132
Ramsey, Steve, 29
Ranbom, Jeff, 145
Ranck, Christine, 216
Rand, Ian, 26, 40, 42, 43, 45, 46, 100, 110, 114
Randall, Ginni, 128
Randall, Juliet, 150
Randall, Lisa, 73
Randall, Tony, 39
Randell, Ron, 140
Randle, Robert, 111
Randolph, Beverly, 43
Randolph, Christopher, 95
Randolph, Jim, 22, 23, 24, 73
Randolph, Larry, 167
Ranelli, J, 144
Rankin, Claire, 176
Ransom, Kenny, 175
Raper, Lyle, 135
Raphael, Gerrianne, 51, 216
Raphael, Marc, 65
Raphael-Schirmer, Nanalee, 173
Raphel, David, 60, 79
Rapp, Amy J., 128
Rapp, Anthony, 82
Rapport, Michael, 151
Rardin, Brian K., 127
Rasche, David, 214, 216
Rascoff, Joseph, 50
Rashid, Beatrix, 138
Rashovich, Gordana, 142, 169
Rasmuson, Judy, 144, 146
Rasmussen, Kathleen, 160
Rasmussen, Rick, 128
Rathgeb, Laura, 93, 214, 216
Ratnikoff, Lara, 144
Rattigan, Terence, 54
Raven-Symone, 39
Ravicchio, Giacomo, 131
Rawcliffe, Susan, 61
Rawlins, Theodore, 123
Rawn, Debbie, 125
Ray, Connie, 60, 71, 149
Ray, Max, 141
Ray, Miles, 60
Ray, Robin, 135, 159
Ray, Tim, 6, 9, 12, 15, 25, 33, 36, 38, 44, 97, 108
Rayman, Melinda, 152
Raymond, Bill, 62, 63, 77, 132
Raymond, Devon, 162
Raymond, Duncan, 62
Raymond, Guy, 135
Raymond, William Joseph, 132
Rayppy, Gary, 25
Re, Tommy, 41
Re:Joyce!, 146
Réaux, Angelina, 70
Reade, Jeff, 54, 68, 214, 216
Ready for the River, 135
Real Family, 50
Real Life Story of Johnny De Facto, The, 139
Ream, James, 163
Reamer, Terry, 56, 214, 216
Reams, Lee Roy, 154
Reap, J. J., 72
Reap, Jessica Leigh, 173
Reardon, Peter, 15
Reardon, Richard L., 114
Rearwin, Laura, 153
Reas, Leann, 125
Reaux, Angelina, 216
Reaux, Roumel, 124
Reaves-Phillips, Sandra, 70, 134, 216
Rebel Armies Deep Into Chad, 153
Rebhorn, James, 91, 216
Rebich, Cissy, 45
Recht, Ray, 80, 116, 156, 157
Reckless, 157
Red Noses, 118
Red Shoes, The, 52
Red Sneaks, The, 52
Reddick, Danielle, 51
Reddin, Keith, 100
Reddin, Naomi, 15
Reddy, Brian, 77, 119
Redfield, Adam, 97, 214, 216
Redford, Paul, 118
Redgrave, Lynn, 12, 214, 216
Redgrave, Vanessa, 9, 216
Redman, John, 161

Redmond, Barbara, 136
Redmond, Kathi Lee, 163
Redmond, Lawrence, 124, 163
Redmond, Markus, 147
Redmond, Siobhan, 115, 131
Redway, Kate, 156
Redwood, John Henry, 78, 119, 157, 216, 217
Redwood, Manning, 9
Reece, Keith, 151
Reed, Bobby, 55, 69
Reed, Janet, 95
Reed, Jason Roland, 172
Reed, Joseph, 150
Reed, Penelope, 149
Reed, Rex, 39
Reed, Rondi, 29, 148
Reed, Stephen, 43
Reed, T. Michael, 102
Reed, Vivian, 133
Reeder, Joi, 67
Reeger, John, 148
Reehling, Joyce, 76, 216, 217
Rees, Linda, 127
Reese, Georgia, 74
Reeve, Christopher, 39, 111
Reeves, Keanu, 175
Reeves, Raymond, 134
Reeves, Sabrina, 157
Reeves, Susan F., 149
Regal, David, 150
Regan, Bette, 142
Regan, Mick, 135
Regan, Molly, 168
Rehberg, Stephen, 53
Reich, Robert, 166
Reichert, Daniel, 121
Reichert, Whit, 159
Reichler, Alexandra, 96
Reid, Barbara, 141
Reid, Jeffery, 135
Reid, Valency, 164
Reider, Joel, 158
Reilly, Albertina, 154
Reilly, Charles Nelson, 104, 146
Reilly, Chris, 159
Reilly, Don, 91
Reilly, Jacqueline, 102
Reilly, Michael, 77
Reilly, Philip, 68
Reilly, Robert, 41
Reilly, William, 148
Reineke, Gary, 143
Reinglas, Fred, 67, 76
Reingold, Jackie, 51
Reinheimer, Cathy, 72
Reinking, Ann, 39
Reisch, Michele, 57
Reischerl, Karl C., 165
Reisman, Jane, 71, 149
Reiss, Jody, 73
Reissa, Eleanor, 58, 216
Reiter, Amy, 87
Reiter, Josef, 139
Relapse, The, 176
Remington, Letha, 172
Remme, John, 20, 216, 217
Rempel, Nicholas, 174
Remsberg, Calvin, 113
Renaissance Theatre Company, 115
Renderer, Scott, 63, 216
Rene, Nikki, 94
René, Norman, 36, 76
Reneau, Russ, 148
Renee, Dawn, 152
Renfore, Rebecca, 217
Renfroe, Molly, 132
Renfroe, Rebecca, 61, 216
Renick, Kyle, 52, 100
Renino, Robert D., 57
Renn, Daniel, 139
Reno, Phil, 57
Rensenhouse, John, 159
Renzi, Marta, 53
Reo, Barbara, 142
Repertory Theatre of St. Louis, 159
Repicci, Albert, 70
Repicci, Bill, 70
Repole, Charles, 50, 57
Resendez, Sonya, 167
Resident Acting Company, 173
Resnik, Hollis, 109, 148
Rethgeb, Laura, 93
Return, The, 80
Rex, 99
Rey, Antonia, 80, 216
Rey, Jose, 96
Reynal, Max, 56
Reynolds, James E., 58, 119
Reynolds, Louise, 124
Reynolds, William J., 170
Reyvler, Steve, 54
Rhalse, Foster, 57
Rhodes, Erik, 230, 232
Rhodes, Evan H., 17
Rhodes, Tran Wm., 57
Rhoze, Tim, 136
Rhyne, Sylvia, 8, 101, 216
Rhys, Will, 78, 128, 156, 216, 217
Rhythm Ranch, 154
Ribblett, Beth A., 75, 134
Ribnikov, Alexis, 61
Ribot, Marc, 68
Ricard, Russell, 154
Ricci, Rosemary, 169
Ricciardi, Gene, 87
Riccucci, John, 139
Rice, James Goodwin, 128
Rice, Jerry, 39
Rice, John Patrick, 129, 140
Rice, Linda, 37, 82
Rice, Misty, 125
Rice, Reva, 117
Rice, Sarah, 91, 216, 217
Rice, Sean Michael, 62
Rice, Tim, 103, 148, 169
Rice, Wesley, 166
Rich, Royce, 80
Richard III, 60, 175
Richard, Ellen, 97
Richard, Mark, 111
Richard, Raquel, 52
Richards, Arleigh, 127
Richards, Carol, 216, 217
Richards, Cordelia, 65, 136
Richards, Doug, 126
Richards, Gary, 80
Richards, Gerald, 136
Richards, Jeffrey, 32, 58, 67, 100, 132
Richards, Jess, 15, 216
Richards, Julian, 53
Richards, Kathy, 150
Richards, Lloyd, 32, 119, 130, 144, 170
Richards, Martin, 18
Richards, Reve, 147
Richards, Rob, 94
Richardson, Edward D., 138
Richardson, Julie A., 119
Richardson, Kathy E., 119
Richardson, Kevin M., 165
Richardson, Latanya, 73, 83, 138
Richardson, Lee, 216, 217
Richardson, Ron, 75, 139
Richardson, Sally, 118
Richardson, Stanley, 175
Richardson, Tammy, 62
Riche, G. B., 167
Richert, William, 149
Richey, Mary Lee, 150
Richie, Brooke, 143
Richin, Laura, 168
Richmond, Doyle, 9
Richmond, Marnice, 127
Richter, Charles, 156
Richter, Mary, 69
Rickenbacher, Anne, 107
Rickert, Nannette, 124
Ricketts, Jeffery A., 167
Ricketts, Jim, 68, 216
Rico, Sylvia, 113
Riddell, Bob, 105
Riddell, Richard, 122
Riddle, George, 151
Riddle, Kate, 94
Riddle, Steven J., 119
Rider, Cynthia, 143
Rider, Stuart, 72
Riebling, Tia, 106
Riegel, Eden, 45, 110, 217, 219
Riegel, Sam, 27, 109, 110, 217, 219
Riegert, Peter, 77, 219
Riegl, Eden, 45
Riehle, Richard, 77, 219
Rifkin, Don, 53, 71
Rifkin, Roger, 56, 219
Rifkin, Ron, 82, 146, 219
Rigby, Cathy, 112
Rigdon, Kevin, 29, 81, 131, 144
Riggins, Cheryl, 129
Riggs, Sally, 125
Right Mind, 121
Rignack, Roger, 217, 219
Rigol, Joey, 45, 217, 219
Rigotti, Rio, 152
Riley, Colleen E., 133
Riley, Eric, 94, 219
Rinaldi, Philip, 42, 61, 63, 67, 94
Rinehart, Elaine, 95, 217, 219
Rinehart, Susanna, 158
Ringham, Nancy, 16, 217, 219
Risberg, Del W., 129
Rising, David, 56
Ritchie, Chuck, 132
Ritchie, Lynn, 101
Ritchie, Margaret, 79
Ritchie, Michael F., 81
Ritchie, William, 160
Ritman, William, 130
Rivals, The, 158
Rivamonte, Lia, 141
Rivas, Fernando, 133
Rivas, Geoffrey, 162
Rivera, Chita, 39
Rivera, Geraldo, 39
Rivera, James, 43
Rivera, Jose M., 76, 154
Rivera, Manuel, 71, 217, 219
Rivera, Rene, 67, 90, 91
Riverman, 72
Rivers, Gwynne, 77
Rivers, Voza, 116
Rivin, Lucille, 71, 219
Rivkin, Gigi, 65
Rizk, Joumana, 54
Rizzo, Victor, 167
Roach, Bruce, 151
Roach, Dan, 136
Road to Mecca, The, 126, 135, 144, 167, 168, 174
Road to Nirvana, 122
Road, 125
Roar of the Greasepaint—The Smell of the Crowd, The, 133
Roark, Jonathan, 145
Robards, Jason, 12, 39, 146
Robb, R. D., 219
Robbers, 160
Robbins, Carrie, 84
Robbins, David, 88
Robbins, Erin, 43
Robbins, Jana, 20, 217, 219
Robbins, Janine, 63
Robbins, Jerome, 43, 106
Robbins, Kerri Lea, 101
Robbins, Mark, 151
Robbins, Rex, 107, 119, 146
Robbins, Tim, 88
Robbins, Tom, 16, 43, 109, 137, 137
Robert, Susan, 128
Roberts, Eric, 39
Roberts, Eve, 119
Roberts, Grace, 73, 74, 219
Roberts, Jamey, 135
Roberts, Kenneth, 177
Roberts, Louise, 101
Roberts, Mason, 56
Roberts, Michael T., 53
Roberts, Norman, 113
Roberts, Sarah, 116, 144
Roberts, Simon, 115, 131
Roberts, Tony, 43, 217, 219
Roberts-Frost, Gwendolyn, 50, 51, 128
Robertson, Alene, 148
Robertson, Barbara E., 138
Robertson, Cliff, 12, 219
Robertson, Dennis, 162
Robertson, Jenny, 66
Robertson, Joel, 45
Robertson, Karen L., 160
Robertson, Lanie, 125, 153
Robertson, Liz, 108
Robertson, Oscar, 39
Robertson, Ray, 62
Robertson, Rudy, 164
Robertson, Scott C., 170
Robertson, Scott, 144
Robertson, Will, 153
Robin Goodfellow, 127
Robin, Tamara, 221
Robins, Laila, 170, 217, 219
Robinson & Crusoe, 131
Robinson, André, Jr., 134
Robinson, Andrew, 131
Robinson, Anne, 54
Robinson, Bernita, 56
Robinson, Catherine Gilk, 160
Robinson, Charles Shaw, 132, 171
Robinson, Cindy, 112
Robinson, Dean "D-No", 88
Robinson, Eddie Tyclus, 172
Robinson, Eddie, 124
Robinson, Hal, 18, 219
Robinson, Jo-Anne, 40
Robinson, Kathy, 133
Robinson, Lewis, 52
Robinson, Mary B., 94, 162
Robinson, Meghan, 52, 219
Robinson, Michael, 33
Robinson, Robin, 20, 119
Robinson, Wendy, 124
Robinson-Clark, Danny, 130
Robison, Blake, 158
Robison, Matthew J., 138
Roblin, Jennifer, 129
Rocco, James, 154
Rocco, Jean, 55
Rocco, Tom, 103
Roccoberton, Bart P., Jr., 57
Rochon, Valerie Jerusha, 134
Rock 'n' Roles from William Shakespeare, 120
Rockaby, 129
Rockett, Jennifer, 176
Rockettes, The, 39
Rocklin, Barry, 122
Rockne, Ellen, 110
Rodabaugh, Scott, 98
Rodd, Marcia, 106
Roddy, Ethna, 115, 131
Roderick, Ray, 40
Rodgers, Richard, 27, 43, 50, 108, 139
Rodrigo, Al, 80
Rodrigues, Lisabeth, 165
Rodriguez, Agustin, 66
Rodriguez, E. J., 68
Rodriguez, Marco, 156
Rodriguez, Robynn, 174
Rodriguez, Steven, 100
Rodriguez, Valente, 131, 147
Roe, Don, 132
Roe, Jim, 6
Roe, Patrick, 169
Roeder, Peggy, 138
Rogers, Anne, 133
Rogers, David, 113, 155
Rogers, Diana, 110
Rogers, Douglas R., 167
Rogers, Duncan M., 143
Rogers, Erica, 153
Rogers, Gil, 101, 219
Rogers, Irma, 106
Rogers, Ken Leigh, 139
Rogers, Michael Elting, 160
Rogers, Michael, 77, 219
Rogers, Paul, 120
Rogers, Poli, 96
Rogers, Willie, 138
Rogers-Adler, Candace, 113
Rogerson, Anita, 63
Rogerson, Bob, 62
Rogerson, Gus, 63, 82, 155
Roggensack, David, 19, 50
Rogow, David, 59
Rohn, Jennifer, 143
Rohrbacher, Jacquiline, 127
Roine, Eva, 149
Roitz, Janet, 59
Rolf, Frederick, 219
Rolfing, Tom, 232
Romaine, Katherine, 162
Roman Fever, 175
Roman, Carmen, 138
Roman, Pedro, 133
Romance in Hard Times, 89
Romanello, Paul, 72
Romano, David, 46
Romans, Bruce Marshall, 120
Rome, Harold, 154
Romeo and Juliet, 153, 171
Romero, Constanza, 32, 126, 130, 136, 144, 170
Romero, Evan, 183
Romick, James, 46
Ronan, Brian, 55
Ronn, Susan, 166
Rooney, Deborah, 56, 71
Roos, Casper, 6, 101, 129, 219
Roose-Evans, James, 146
Root, Frank, 154
Root, John, 232
Root, Melina, 50, 170
Ropes, Bradford, 154
Rorstelmann, Jim, 43
Rorvik, Alice, 135
Rosa, Dennis, 151
Rosado, Pedro, 62
Rosado, Pedro, Jr., 55
Rosati, Frank, Jr., 72
Rosato, Jeffrey, 108
Rosato, Mary Lou, 141
Rose Tattoo, The, 165
Rose, Charles, 76, 160
Rose, Cristine, 141
Rose, Hugh A., 21
Rose, Ian, 52, 168
Rose, Patrick, 169
Rose, Philip, 6, 33, 38
Rose, Richard, 78, 173
Rose, Tiffany, 124
Roseman, Ralph, 21, 24, 144
Rosen's Son, 99
Rosen, Lawrence, 114
Rosen, Louis, 87
Rosenberg, D. C., 80
Rosenberg, Jan, 8, 117
Rosenberg, Natalie, 164
Rosenblum, Joshua, 81
Rosenblum, M. Edgar, 145
Rosenfels, Joan, 156
Rosengarten, Theodore, 57, 171
Rosenstock, Milton, 15
Rosentel, Robert W., 142
Rosenthal, Caryn, 63, 217, 219
Rosenthal, Mark, 138
Rosenwinkel, Mark, 141
Rosette, Scott, 48
Roshe, Deborah, 133
Roslevich, John, Jr., 159
Rosmarin, Seth, 175
Rosqui, Tom, 147
Ross, Bertram, 55
Ross, Blair, 56
Ross, Carolyn Leslie, 135, 159
Ross, Clarinda, 171
Ross, Howard, 217, 219
Ross, J. Michael, 161
Ross, Jamie, 94, 137
Ross, Leon, 119
Ross, Mark, 145
Ross, Michael, 142
Ross, Ryan, 173
Ross, Sandra, 95
Ross, Stephen, 6
Ross, Stuart, 71
Ross, Tavis, 161
Ross, Tom, 89
Rosser, Kip, 149
Rosson, Doug, 135, 160
Rostand, Edmund, 47, 52
Roston, Karen, 14
Rotella, Mary T., 111
Rotello, Zachery, 152
Roth, Ann, 73, 98, 138, 143
Roth, Ari, 136
Roth, Daryl, 57
Roth, Dena, 169
Roth, Janet, 156
Roth, Lynn, 169
Roth, Mark, 173
Roth, Michael, 51, 161, 162, 170
Roth, Stephanie, 22, 217, 219
Roth, Stewart, 164
Roth, Tisha, 140, 164
Rothchild, Ken, 73
Rothenberg, David, 59, 64, 66, 68, 75
Rothman, Carole, 98
Rothman, Jane, 157
Rothman, John, 81, 146, 217, 219
Rothman, Malcolm, 152
Rothman, Stephen, 136, 156, 161
Rothschilds, The, 74
Rough Crossings, 66
Roundabout Theatre, 97
Rounds, Danny, 102
Rourke, Michael, 171
Routh, Marc, 12
Routman, Steve, 140
Routolo, Robert, 130, 131
Routt, Jean M., 145
Rouzan, Wanda, 70
Rovain, Leo, 74
Roven, Glen, 10, 39
Roveta, Sandy, 24
Rowe, Florence, 37, 219
Rowe, Russell G., 167
Rowe, Stephen, 81, 90, 219
Rowe, Tonia, 124, 172
Rowell, David, 158
Rowell, Jody, 146
Rowen, Glenn, 27
Rowlands, Gena, 111
Rowley, Bill, 154, 176
Roy, Richard, 60
Roy, William, 58
Royal, Reginald, 33
Royce, Andreas, 154
Rozakis, Gregory, 230, 232
Rubell, Irene, 68
Rubell, Michael, 68
Rubens, Herbert, 74, 94, 95
Rubenstein, Jay, 74
Rubiecki, Jerzy, 55
Rubin, Arthur, 11
Rubin, Bruce, 73
Rubin, Donna, 113
Rubin, John Gould, 71
Rubin, Judith, 54
Rubin, Steven, 94, 130, 144, 153
Rubinstein, David, 113
Rubinstein, John, 12, 182, 183, 219
Rubinstein, Murray, 51, 137
Rubsam, Scott, 95
Ruck, Patricia, 217, 219
Rudel, Julius, 16
Rudetsky, Seth, 84
Rudko, Michael, 171
Rudman, Bill, 140
Ruduk, Oleg, 61
Rudy, Bradley C., 176
Rudy, Sam, 11, 16, 17, 20, 28, 35, 48, 49, 50, 52, 68, 80, 94, 99
Ruebel, Joyce Volker, 159
Rueda, Manuel, 88
Ruehl, Mercedes, 49
Ruess, John, 109, 148
Ruffian on the Stair, The, 146
Ruffin, Robert, 72
Ruffo, Mario, 27
Ruginis, Vyto, 90
Ruivivar, Francis, 102
Ruiz, Anthony, 66, 219
Rule, Charles, 46, 217, 219
Rumbaugh, Gretchen, 174
Rumors, 94, 130
Rumpf, Robin, 15
Rundgren, Todd, 89
Runion, Tim, 73
Runnels, Terry, 165
Runnette, Sean, 122
Runnfeldt, Tait, 114
Runolfsson, Anne Marie, 31
Ruoti, Helena, 157
Rupich, Thomas, 72
Rupnik, Kevin, 133, 150, 159
Rupp, Debra Jo, 28
Rupp, Tom, 129
Ruptash, Troy, 52, 53
Rush, Maggie, 55, 123
Rusich, Stellina, 176
Rusk, Pat, 148
Ruskin, Jeanne, 146
Russell, Brian, 143
Russell, George, 43
Russell, Jack L., 127
Russell, Kelly A., 148
Russell, Kim, 71
Russell, Monte, 36, 157, 159
Russell, Stephen, 176
Russell, Willy, 156
Russo, Larry, 148
Russo, Rita, 70
Russotto, Michael, 163
Rust and Ruin, 170
Ruta, Ken, 121, 153
Ruth, Anita, 126
Rutigliano, James, 80
Rutkowski, Eddie, 171
Ruybe, Raymond J. S., 60
Ruzika, Donna, 162
Ruzika, Tom, 162
Ryall, William, 18, 217, 219
Ryan, Amy, 132
Ryan, Matthew, 158
Ryan, Michael Scott, 121
Ryan, Mitchell, 147
Ryan, Thomas M., 133, 148
Ryan, Vera, 96
Ryane, Melody, 171
Ryba, Ellen, 35, 67
Rybak, Karen A., 164
Rybolt, Peter, 138
Rydberg, Steven, 172
Ryder, Amy, 164
Ryder, Craig, 135, 160
Ryder, Ric, 61, 219
Rye, Melissa, 159
Ryecart, Patrick, 168
Ryland, Jack, 97, 217, 219
Rymer, Jennifer, 111
Ryskind, Morrie, 68
S. J. Perelman in Person, 94
Saarmann, Mary, 173
Sabellico, Richard, 20
Sabin, David, 137, 169, 172
Sablow, Jane, 58
Sabourin, Marie-Claude, 113
Sachs, Ann, 132
Sachs, Norman, 137
Sachs, Sharon, 148
Sackmann, Jennifer, 163
Saddler, Donald, 101, 176
Sadler, Nick, 63
Sado, Alexander, 61
Sadusk, Maureen, 129, 139
Saffran, Christina, 144
Sager, Jeri, 106
Sagharadze, Guram, 69
Saint Joan, 135
Saint, David, 84, 147
Saint-Saens, Camille, 64
Saito, Dawn A., 92
Saka, Haruhiko, 12
Sakata, Jeanne, 90
Sakow, Hayden Reed, 142
Saks, Gene, 130
Sala, John, 183
Salancy, Fred, 133
Salas, Nicolette, 99
Salata, Gregory, 93, 219
Salazar, Angel, 96
Salce, Tim, 101
Sale, James, 174
Sale, Jim, 119
Salem, Francois Abu, 53
Salem, Kario, 122
Salinas, Pablo, 71
Salinger, Diane, 70
Salinger, Ross, 122
Salisbury, D. J., 111, 154
Salisbury, Kim, 141
Salmi, Albert, 230, 232
Salsbury, Lynda L., 128
Saltz, Amy, 75, 170
Saltzman, Avery, 80
Salvadore, J. Kelly, 72
Salzberg, Marc, 10
Samal, Michele, 128
Sametz, Laura, 90
Sammler, Bronislaw J., 170
Sampliner, Susan, 13, 87
Sams, Blair, 167
Sams, Jeremy, 81
Sams, Lekeisha, 153
Samson, Mary, 120

Samuel, Peter, 45, 110, 217, 219
Samuels, Steven, 57
Samuelsohn, Howard, 48, 63, 83, 84, 97, 219
Samuelson, Sam, 148
San Diego Repertory Theatre, 161
Sanchez, Alba, 71
Sanchez, David, 71
Sanchez, George Emilio, 50
Sanchez, Jaime, 161, 183, 217, 219
Sanchez-Franklin, Elizabeth, 169
Sand Mountain Matchmaking, 51
Sandbox, The, 131
Sande, Michael, 118
Sandefur, James D., 66, 96, 136, 157
Sanders, Abigael, 80
Sanders, Ann Marie, 164
Sanders, Cam, 50
Sanders, Charles, 173
Sanders, Cynthena, 118
Sanders, Fred, 69, 104, 219
Sanders, James, 65
Sanders, Jay O., 100, 217, 219
Sanders, Linda Sue, 125
Sanders, Pete, 11, 16, 17, 20, 28, 48, 49, 57, 80
Sanders, Scott, 62
Sanderson, Austin, 173
Sandifur, Virginia, 57
Sandish, Dale, 157
Sandler, Susan, 128
Sandoval, Trini, 153
Sandri, Remi, 174
Sandri, Thomas, 46
Sandwall, Peter, 165
Sandy, J. Craig, 176
Sanet, Brian, 155
Sanfilippo, Michael, 110
Sanford, Tim, 94
Sankowich, Lee, 157
Santacroce, Mary Nell, 119
Santaniello, Eric, 97
Santiago, Glen, 65
Santillano, Sherry, 127
Santo, Michael, 118, 160
Santopietro, Thomas P., 23
Santore, Regina B., 100
Santoriello, Alex, 16, 219
Santoro, Michael, 60, 66, 73, 217, 219
Santoro, Susan, 41
Santos, Fernando, 6
Santos, SallyAnne, 65
Santos, Steve, 39
Sanz, Carlos, 138
Saporta, Joan, 55
Sapp, Tony, 127
Sappington, Margo, 133
Sara, Kenneth, 70
Sarafina!, 94, 116, 144
Sardi, Adelle, 66, 73
Sargeant, Angela, 78
Sargent, Peter E., 159
Sarno, Janet, 120, 173
Sartre, Jean Paul, 145
Sasson, Richard, 168
Sassoon, Vidal, 108
Sater, Steven, 57
Sateren, Terry, 160
Saternow, Tim, 35, 154
Sato, Isao, 232
Satterwhite, Catherine, 137
Saukiavicus, Tim, 175
Saunders, Donald, 6
Saunders, Nicholas, 37, 218, 220
Savadove, Lane, 62
Savage in Limbo, 73
Savage, Keith, 139, 169
Savage, Melodee, 89, 124
Savidge, David, 149
Savin, Ron Lee, 61, 137, 220
Savino, Frank, 159
Sawaishi, Ryoko, 108
Sawyer, Frank, 72
Sawyer, Ken, 65, 144
Sawyer, Timothy, 143
Sawyer-Dailey, Mark, 120
Sawyer-Young, Kat, 161
Saxon, Carolyn, 164
Saxon, Ingrid, 67
Sayre, April, 167
Scandalous Adventures of Sir Toby Trollope, The, 161
Scanlan, John, 142
Scanlan, Robert, 122
Scarcella, Kim, 105
Scardino, Don, 19, 67, 144
Scassellati, Vincent, 151
Scattergood, A. Ronald, 152
Schachter, Ellen, 111, 113
Schader, Lizanne, 118
Schaefer, Michael, 66
Schaefer, Nancy, 15
Schaefer, Richard, 50
Schaeffer, Eric, 135
Schaeffer, Joan, 145
Schaeffer, Ron, 151
Schaffer, Stephen J., 93
Schaffert, Greg, 35
Schall, Thomas, 143
Schanda, Christine, 51
Schanker, Larry, 138
Schanuel, Greg, 43, 220
Scharbrough, Dan, 127
Scharer, Jonathan, 52, 62
Schatz, Ken, 51, 65
Schechter, Ben, 59
Schechter, David, 16, 78, 84, 220
Schechter, Howard, 147
Schechter, Joel, 170
Schecter, Amy, 28, 106, 108
Scheeder, Louis, 63
Scheeler, Bob, 170
Scheib, Rachael, 35
Scheine, Raynor, 100, 220
Schelble, William, 26, 29, 30, 40, 42, 43, 45, 46, 58, 110, 114
Schenck, Ann G., 135
Schenkkan, Robert, 100
Scher, Judith, 59
Scherer, John, 154, 159
Schermer, Phil, 118, 166
Schermer, Shelley Henze, 118, 166
Schertler, Nancy, 94, 124, 168, 172
Schierhorn, Paul, 114
Schifini, George, 48
Schiller, Adrian, 69
Schiller, Caroline, 113
Schilling, Sandra, 165
Schilling, Thom, 9, 45
Schimmel, John, 145
Schindler, George, 81
Schirle, Joan, 161
Schirman, David, 70
Schirmer, Gus, 39
Schissler, Jeffrey, 56
Schjelderup, Gerdi, 149
Schlarth, Sharon, 67, 218, 220
Schlee, Robert, 218, 220
Schliessmann, Lucia, 129
Schlosser, Robert J., 130, 131
Schmalz, Michael, 84
Schmidt, Douglas W., 50
Schmidt, Harvey, 47, 145, 167
Schmidt, Henry J., 142
Schmidt, Jake, 161
Schmidt, Lisa, 167
Schmidt, Lynna, 171
Schmidt, Paul, 141
Schmidtke, Ned, 138
Schmit, Sheryl, 166
Schmitz, Peter, 164, 218, 220
Schneider, Carol, 81
Schneider, Dan, 152
Schneider, Gary, 48
Schneider, M. Leah, 59
Schnirman, David, 64
Schnitzler, Arthur, 59, 127
Schob, Hank, 68, 220
Schoeffler, Paul, 101, 110, 220
Schoen, Kelly, 163
Schoen, Walter, 161
Schofield, Barbara, 72
Schomacher, Michelle, 40
Schonberg, Claude-Michel, 45
School for Scandal, The, 153
School for Wives, The, 93
Schramm, David, 162
Schreiber, Gillian, 62, 64, 70
Schreier, Daniel, 77, 82, 90
Schuberg, Carol, 15
Schubert, Alan E., 20
Schuette, James A., 170
Schulberg, Carol, 15
Schulfer, Roche, 138
Schulman, Craig, 45, 109, 220
Schulman, Susan H., 8
Schultz, Armand, 13, 77, 87, 129, 220
Schultz, Carol, 136
Schultz, Steven M., 117
Schulz, Theodore, 29
Schumacher, Michelle, 40
Schurkamp, Richard, 9
Schurr, Carl, 159
Schurr, Wendy, 164
Schutzman, Steve, 129
Schwartz, Clifford, 44
Schwartz, Gary, 106
Schwartz, Larry, 39
Schwartz, Robert Joel, 93
Schwarz, Joe, 18
Schwarz, Robert, 68
Schwarz, William, 29
Schwarz, Willy, 138
Schweid, Carole, 73
Schweiger, Scott, 157
Schweizer, David, 90, 147
Sciafani, Sal, 14, 21, 27
Scilla, Maryellen, 154
Scimeca, Jane, 137
Scioscia, Marie Elena, 59
Sclar, Deborah, 135
Scofield, Pamela, 71, 78, 119, 136, 149, 165
Scogin, Robert, 138, 152
Scorese, Angela, 155
Scotellano, Christopher, 55
Scott, Brad, 113
Scott, Camilla, 6
Scott, Campbell, 69
Scott, Christopher, 15, 139
Scott, Daniel, 152
Scott, David, 59
Scott, Deborah, 70, 95, 101
Scott, Dennis, 170
Scott, Douglas, 68, 137
Scott, Ernie, 32, 134, 220
Scott, Frances, 67
Scott, Gayton, 129
Scott, Harold, 159
Scott, Jacqueline, 133
Scott, James, 99
Scott, John David, 110
Scott, Kimberly, 62
Scott, Matt, 51
Scott, Pamela, 66
Scott, Seret, 123, 129, 218, 220
Scott, Steve, 138
Scovill, Jay, 119
Scrapbooks, 145
Screens, The, 141
Scribner, Amy, 54
Scruggs, Sharon, 168
Scullin, Kevin, 155
Scully, Patrick J., 78
Sea Horse, The, 128
Sea Marks, 79
Seabrooke, Christopher, 15
Seacrist, Lisa, 156
Seago, Edward, 133
Seagull, The, 120, 140
Seales, Franklyn, 230, 232
Seals, Shari A., 138
Seamon, Edward, 69, 76, 142, 218, 220
Search and Destroy, 162
Sears, Joe, 144
Seasongood, Eda, 143
Seaton, Johnny, 50, 51, 218, 220
Seattle Repertory Theatre, 160
Sebastian, Denys, 84
Sebesky, Don, 17
Second Man, The, 174
Second Stage, 98
Secor, Jonathan Dimock, 14, 170
Secret Garden, The, 168
Secret Rapture, The, 13
Sedgwick, Robert, 52
See, Joan, 73
Seery, Florie, 42
Seff, Richard, 146
Segal, Cindy Storm, 95
Segal, David F., 153
Segal, Giles, 74
Segal, Kathrin King, 63
Seger, Richard, 160
Segura, Enrique, 102
Seidman, John, 59, 220
Seifried, Amy, 177
Seinfeld, Barbara, 35
Seinfeld, Jerry, 39
Sekacz, Ilona, 28
Sekiya, Toshiaki, 12
Selbie, Christopher, 135
Seldes, Marian, 144
Selig, John, 102
Seliverstov, A., 88
Selke, Ron, 71
Sellers, Barbara E., 135
Sellon, Andrew W., 93
Sellon, Kim, 12
Selman, Jim, 6
Seltz, Charlie, 108
Selverstone, Katy, 129
Semak, Pyotr, 153
Semenova, Nina, 153
Semmelman, Jim, 15
Semple, Goldie, 176
Sempliner, Woody, 60
Sendak, Maurice, 129
Sennett, David, 70, 220
Senske, Rebecca, 101, 128
Serabian, Lorraine, 68, 218, 220
Serbagi, Roger, 38
Serban, Andrei, 122
Sereda, Susan, 113
Serious Fun!: Third Season, 53
Serko, David, 35
Serling, Rod, 62
Serrano, Charlie, 220
Sesma, Thom, 98, 124, 218, 220
Setrakian, Mary, 99
Setzer, Dawn, 147
70, Girls, 70, 126, 148
Sevier, Jack, 127, 169
Sevy, Bruce K., 135, 166
Sex, Drugs, Rock & Roll, 63
Sexton, Michael, 10, 63
Seykell, Rohn, 45, 110
Seymour in the Very Heart of Winter, 99
Shabaka [Barry Henley], 131, 171
Shabba-Doo, 142, 143
Shaddock, Pamela, 58
Shafer, Pamela, 220
Shaffer, Janece, 119
Shaffer, Malinda, 11, 103
Shaffer, Peter, 30, 151
Shah, Sharon, 71
Shaheen, Nancy, 72
Shahn, Judith, 118
Shakar, Martin, 220
Shakes, David, 136
Shakespeare & Company, 175
Shakespeare, William, 25, 60, 61, 62, 69, 70, 72, 77, 87, 88, 90, 91, 93, 97, 119, 120, 121, 122, 124, 125, 128, 129, 131, 135, 138, 143, 144, 145, 151, 153, 158, 159, 160, 162, 165, 168, 170, 171, 172, 173, 175, 176, 177
Shakin' the Mess Outta Misery, 128
Shaler, Eleanor, 232
Shalhoub, Tony, 42, 220
Shallo, Karen, 154
Shamash, Beba, 8, 101
Shampain, Robert, 70, 159
Shanahan, Donna, 136
Shange, Ntozake, 65
Shangraw, Howard, 162
Shanina, Yelena, 61
Shanks, Priscilla C., 10, 120
Shanley, John Patrick, 66, 73, 145, 155
Shannon, Mark, 64, 218, 220
Shannon, Peggy, 147, 171
Shapiro, Anne, 53
Shapiro, Debbie, 43, 218, 220
Shapiro, Mel, 157
Shapli, Omar, 65
Sharaff, Irene, 43
Sharek, William, 177
Sharon, Yvette, 65
Sharp, Alex, 154
Sharp, Andy, 166
Sharp, Chad Jared, 165
Sharp, Mahlon, 125
Sharp, Michael, 68, 155
Sharp, Monti, 124
Sharpe, Ascanio, 65, 123
Shavitz, Peter, 60
Shaw, Bernard, 145
Shaw, Christopher, 94
Shaw, Deborah, 69, 132, 160
Shaw, George Bernard, 97, 111, 122, 127, 129, 135, 170, 171
Shaw, Harold, 130
Shaw, James D., 127
Shaw, Joseph, 176
Shaw, Kobi, 154
Shaw, Steven, 9
Shaw, Wenna, 176
Shawn, Michael, 111, 230, 232
Shawn, Peter, 14
Shawn, Steven, 119
Shayna Maidel, A, 156
Shayne, Tracy, 45
She First Met Her Parents on the Subway, 71
Shea, Tim, 67
Shea, Wendy, 164
Shear Madness, 144
Sheara, Nicola, 29, 218, 220
Shearer, Jack, 171
Shearer, Lori, 120
Sheaves, Lisa, 105
Sheehan, Matthew, 122
Sheehan, Maurice, 79
Sheeler, Sheila M., 133
Sheets, J. C., 45
Sheffer, Geordie, 20
Sheffield, Allen T., 136
Sheffield-Dewees, James, 52
Sheide, Evgeni, 153
Sheila's Day, 134
Sheintsiss, Oleg, 61
Shelby, James, 151
Sheldon, Anne, 171
Shell, Claudia, 40, 218, 220
Shelle, Michael, 64
Shelley, Mary, 101
Shelton, Sloane, 9, 218, 220
Shen, Freda Foh, 78
Shenandoah, 6
Shenar, Paul, 230, 232
Shentalinsky, Sergei, 88
Shepard, Kelvin R., 126
Shepard, Sam, 131, 158
Shepard, Suzanne, 168
Shepherd, Elizabeth, 132
Shepherd, Ruth, 125
Shepski, Ken, 15
Sherer, Joshua, 65
Sherer, Werner, 18
Sheridan, Jessica, 154
Sheridan, Jim, 60
Sheridan, Kent, 105
Sheridan, Richard Brinsley, 153, 158
Sherlock Holmes and the Speckled Band, 169
Sherlock, George H., 150
Sherman, Alan, 161
Sherman, Barry, 90, 218, 220
Sherman, Daniel J., 57
Sherman, Geoffrey, 78
Sherman, Howard, 142
Sherman, James, 70
Sherman, Kate M., 70
Sherman, Keith, 14, 64, 101
Sherman, Kim D., 129, 141, 143
Sherman, Liz, 65
Sherman, Loren, 60, 90, 97, 144
Sherman, Lori, 100
Sherman, Martin, 94
Sherman, Stuart, 53
Sherman, Terrence, 169
Sherrard, Nancy, 173
Sherrill, Angela, 97, 165
Sherrill, Brad, 119
Sherry, Karen, 39
Sherwood, Madeleine, 120, 218, 220
Sherwood, Tony, 130
Shevelove, Burt, 43, 167, 177
Shew, Timothy, 218, 220
Shick, Caryn, 130
Shields, Aaron, 144
Shields, Brooke, 39
Shields, Elizabeth, 137
Shields, Timothy J., 149
Shiflett, Melissa, 69
Shigeko, 92
Shimabuku, Norris M., 92
Shimizu, Sachi, 41
Shimizu, Tsuyu, 92
Shimmer, 98
Shimrock, John, 37
Shine, Stephanie, 174
Shinn, P. Hamilton, 119
Shinner, Sandy, 138
Shipley, Sandra, 143
Shire, David, 57
Shirkey, Clay, 54, 129
Shirley Valentine, 94
Shirley, James, 143
Shiroma, Glenn, 117
Shirvis, Barbara, 27
Shiryayev, Vladimir, 61
Shoemakers' Holiday, 176
Shook, Warner, 162, 174
Shore, Rosie, 20
Short, John, 79
Short, Martin, 39
Shorts, Barbara, 70
Shotwell, Judith, 129
Shoukoufeh-Azari, 52
Show Must Go On, The, 63
Showing Off, 94
Showstoppers, 128
Shpitko, Evgeny, 39
Shropshire, Anne, 145
Shropshire, Jennifer, 169
Shropshire, Noble, 97, 159, 220
Shtefutsa, Vasili, 54
Shubart, Suzanne, 59
Shue, Elisabeth, 81, 220
Shue, Larry, 125, 166
Shugart, Paula, 39
Shultz, Mary, 56
Shulz, Karen, 132
Shusharin, Nikolai, 61
Shwartz, Martin, 232
Shyer, Christopher, 176
Shyre, Paul, 232
Sibanda, Seth, 86, 168
Siberry, Michael, 25
Sicangco, Eduardo, 139
Sicari, Joseph R., 97, 218, 220
Siccardi, Arthur, 17, 20, 22, 28, 30, 40, 43, 44
Sichel, Jeff, 51
Sicular, Robert, 162, 172
Sid Caesar & Company, 51
Siders, Irving, 112
Sidner, Sydney, 81
Sidney, Sylvia, 39
Siebert, Jeff, 46, 139
Siegel, Betty, 124
Siegel, David, 133, 157
Sieger, Steve, 53
Siegfried & Roy, 55
Siegler, Ben, 90, 132, 220
Sigerson, Joe, 169
Sigvardt, Mary K., 118
Silber, David, 37, 220
Silberman, Betty, 218, 220
Silberman, Joel, 17, 137
Silbert, Peter, 118
Silliman, Maureen, 139, 218, 220
Sills, Douglas, 107
Silver, Ron, 39
Silverman, Ethan, 131
Silverman, Jonathan, 147
Silverman, Stanley, 69, 176
Silversher, Michael, 131
Silverstein, Shel, 81
Simek, Vasek, 66
Simes, Douglas, 127, 220
Simmons, Bill, 66, 95, 96
Simmons, Bonnie, 40
Simmons, Gregory, 82
Simmons, J. K., 35, 140, 144, 220
Simmons, Ken, 55
Simmons, Nancy, 25
Simmons, Stanley, 108
Simms, Stephen, 6
Simo, Ana Maria, 67
Simon, Adam, 88
Simon, Annie, 68
Simon, Avivah, 60
Simon, Deborah, 133
Simon, John, 155
Simon, Lucy, 168
Simon, Meg, 10, 22, 32
Simon, Neil, 74, 125, 130, 137, 153, 166
Simone, Natalie, 172
Simons, Hal, 48, 101
Simonson, Eric, 29
Simotes, Tony, 161
Simper, Walden, 136
Simpson, Bland, 159
Simpson, James, 170
Simpson, Jim, 51
Simpson, Maggie, 143
Simpson, Shari, 121
Sinclair, Didi, 93
Sinclair, Madge, 147
Sing Hallelujah!, 120
Singer, Connie, 65
Singer, Geraldine, 173
Singer, James R., 123
Singer, Pamela, 43, 58
Singer, Stephen, 55
Sinise, Gary, 29
Sinkonnen, Eric, 171
Sinkys, Albert, 78, 218, 220
Siravo, Joseph, 168
Siretta, Dan, 139
Sirlin, Jerome, 122
Sirois, Richard L., 93
Sisters, 73
Sisto, Rocco, 97, 175, 220
Six Degrees of Separation, 82
Six, David, 145
Sizemore, Jim, 129
Skala, Lawson, 114
Skatual, Kathryn, 119
Skelton, Thomas R., 19, 144
Skinker, Sherry, 145, 159
Skinner, Kate, 136, 172
Skinner, Margo, 67, 218, 220
Sklepinski, Jan, 55
Sklepinski, Zofia, 55
Skoulaxenos, Nick, 128
Skriloff, Nina, 18
Skujins, Yuri, 156
Skura, Stephanie, 53
Skweyiya, Kipizane, 116
Skybell, Steven, 122
Skye, Robin, 110
Slade, Catherine, 138
Slaff, Jonathan, 53
Slagle, Susan, 147
Slaiman, Marjorie, 124
Slask: The National Folk Ballet of Poland, 55
Slate, Rex, 72
Slattery, John, 58, 83
Slavin, L. J., 29
Slay It With Music, 57
Slezak, Victor, 60, 142, 218, 220
Slezak, Vivi, 142
Slingshot, 161
Sloan, Gary, 143
Sloman, John, 89, 91, 218, 220
Sloman, P. K., 15
Sly Fox, 169
Small, Cathy, 72
Small, Larry, 40
Small, Liz, 91, 100
Small, Neva, 99, 218, 220
Small, Peg, 9, 157
Small, Ralph, 105
Smallwood, Tucker, 62
Smaltz, Mark Kenneth, 50, 51, 139, 159
Smanko, Michael, 111

Smarr, Sara M., 135
Smart, Annie, 77, 91
Smiar, Brian, 169
Smiley, Terry L., 110
Smirnov, Roman, 153
Smit, Michael, 55
Smith, Alice Eliott, 121
Smith, Andrea-Michelle, 164
Smith, Anna Deavere, 147
Smith, Archie, 135
Smith, Bobby, 68
Smith, Britta, 164
Smith, Buddy, 154
Smith, Calvin, 112
Smith, Carol Denise, 50, 103
Smith, Caroline, 162
Smith, Carrie, 152, 223
Smith, Chuck, 138
Smith, Connor, 169
Smith, David Rae, 27
Smith, Denise, 103
Smith, Derek D., 94, 129, 223
Smith, Diane, 170
Smith, Donald U., III, 169
Smith, Douglas D., 147
Smith, Dugg, 65, 93
Smith, E. E., 175
Smith, Edward G., 164
Smith, Elizabeth, 141, 172
Smith, Ellen Jane, 140, 143
Smith, Ennis, 65
Smith, Frank, 60
Smith, Geddeth, 173
Smith, Gerard L. A., 136
Smith, Hazel, 64
Smith, Jack, 97
Smith, Janet E., 97
Smith, Jeanne, 110
Smith, Jeffrey, 66
Smith, Jennifer, 35, 54, 218, 223
Smith, Julia, 176
Smith, Kelly, 124, 136, 167
Smith, Ken, 84
Smith, Kendall A., 72
Smith, Kiki, 175
Smith, Leslie Carroll, 135
Smith, Libby, 125
Smith, Liz, 39
Smith, Lois, 7, 29, 76, 218, 223
Smith, Maggie, 30, 223
Smith, Marlynn, 121
Smith, MaryAnn D., 155
Smith, Meagan, 72
Smith, Michael C., 61
Smith, Michael James, 166
Smith, Michael, 29
Smith, Nancy Jo, 161, 171
Smith, Nicholas, 69
Smith, Oliver, 43
Smith, Patrick, 48
Smith, Paul J., 57, 64
Smith, Regina Byrd, 161
Smith, Rex, 18, 218, 223
Smith, Robert Vincent, 47
Smith, Sean, 113
Smith, Steven Scott, 57
Smith, Sydney, 108
Smith, T. Ryder, 173
Smith, Tammy, 128
Smith, Toukie, 39
Smith, Vicki, 126, 135, 174
Smith-Cameron, J., 44, 83, 218, 223
Smithgall, Jill, 136
Smithwick, Jane, 119
Smoke on the Mountain, 71, 149
Smolens, Jean C., 103
Smurr, Katherine M., 160
Smythe, Louise, 134
Smythe, Sally, 166
Snadowsky, Stanley, 52
Snead, Lawrence E., 119
Sneed, Terry, 125
Snider, Lee, 68
Snow, Clarence, 120
Snow, Donna, 169
Snow, Norman, 140
Snowden, William, 170
Snyder, Rick, 29
Snyder, Roger, 21
Snyder, Ron, 174
Sobel, Lloyd, 68
Sobel, Sharon, 126
Sobel, Shepard, 93
Soble, Stanley, 131
Sockwell, Sally, 125
Soddu, Antonio, 98
Soeder, Fran, 112, 119
Soft Dude, 99
Sohmers, Barbara, 131
Sokol, Marilyn, 51, 172
Sokol-Hessner, Peter, 143
Sokoloff, Michael, 29, 143
Sokolsky, Yosi, 59
Soldo, Sally, 167
Sole-Robertson, Seth, 143
Solid Gold Cadillac, The, 170
Solis, Jeffrey, 58
Solis, Octavio, 162
Solo, William, 45, 218, 223
Solomon, Alisa, 62
Solomon, Madelon Rosen, 53, 57, 86, 96
Soloway, Leonard, 22, 43, 116, 144
Solowitz, Larry, 103
Solters/Roskin/Friedman, 14, 117
Some Americans Abroad, 81
Somerville, Barbara, 170
Somerville, Phyllis, 145
Somewhere Foreign, 73
Somkin, Steven, 93
Somma, Maria, 26, 42, 45, 78, 100
Sommer, Elke, 223
Sommer, Josef, 91, 223
Sommer, Kathy, 24
Sommers, Allison, 87
Sommers, Michael, 118
Somsen, Pennell, 129
Sondheim, Stephen, 8, 20, 43, 107, 124, 135, 141, 144, 148, 160, 167, 177
Song of Shim Chung, The, 92
Songs of Paradise, 58
Sook, Dennis, 71, 221, 223
Soon, Terence Tam, 121
Soper, Tony, 160, 166
Sophiea, Cynthia, 101, 221, 223
Sophisticated Ladies, 144
Sorce, Tom, 73, 116, 144
Sordelet, Rick, 134
Sorel, Edward, 81
Sorel, Theodore, 221, 223
Sorenson, Bob, 125
Sorenson, Cheri, 118, 166
Sorkin, Aaron, 19, 67, 144, 183
Sorkin, Naomi, 46
Soroka, John, 169
Sorvino, Paul, 39, 123
Sosnow, Pat, 10, 63
Sostek, Judith, 93
Soto, Richard, 153, 161
Sottile, Michael S., 55, 90
Souhrada, Tom, 111
Soul Stirrers, 138
Sound of Music, The, 27
Soundbite, 135
South Coast Repertory, 162
Southern Cross, 119
Southern, Daniel, 141
Souza, Alan, 101
Sowa, Larry, 50
Sowers, Scott, 51, 120
Spackman, Tom, 150
Spahn, Karen S., 171
Spahr, Scott, 43
Spain, Robert, 149
Spaisman, Zipora, 59, 221, 223
Spalding, Don, 120, 128
Spangenberg, Saul, 96
Spanish Eyes, 96
Spano, Joe, 162
Sparber, Herschel, 24
Spare Parts, 67
Sparks, Rick, 109, 161
Spaulding, Dave, 97
Spear, Cary, 60, 124
Spears, Louie, 147
Special Interests, 63
Special Providence, A, 64
Specter, Amy, 20
Speechley, Julie, 69
Speed-the-Plow, 144, 162, 164, 165, 168
Speer, Alexander, 120
Spellman, Gina, 162
Spellman, Larry, 14, 51
Spencer, Alex, 124
Spencer, Robert, 150
Spencer, Sally, 162
Spencer, Vernon, 103
Sperberg, Fritz, 19, 144, 221, 223
Sperling, Ted, 39, 69, 89
Sperow, Janelle, 58
Spewack, Bella, 144, 176, 232
Spewack, Sam, 144, 176
Spiegel, Howard, 221, 223
Spielberg, Robin, 221, 223
Spiewak, Tamara Robin, 45, 223
Spiller, Tom, 118, 174
Spina, Anthony, 52
Spinella, Stephen, 131
Spirit, Black & Female: A Tribute to Black Womanhood, 65
Spisak, Neil, 88
Spittle, James P., 150
Spivack, Marcia B., 135
Spivey, Brian K., 138
Splaine, Kate, 120
Split, 70
Spock, Benjamin, Dr., 39
Spooner, Lydia, 173
Spooner, Paul, 145
Spore, Richard, 146, 170
Spradling, Valerie, 29
Sprague, Peter, 56
Sprague, Sharon, 59
Sprecher, Ben, 58
Sprigge, Elizabeth, 170
Spriggs, Rachel, 69
Spring, Barnaby, 132
Springer, Gary, 34
Springer, John, 34, 39
Sproul, George, 128
Spunk, 134
Spunk: Three Tales by Zora Neale Hurston, 91, 134
Spurck, Peter, 150
Square One, 98
Squier, William, 72
Sririn, Alexander, 61
St. George, Kathy, 106
St. Germain, Mark, 61, 123, 136, 137
St. John, Janice, 151
St. John, Marco, 142, 177
St. Louis, Louis, 84
St. Mark's Gospel, 68
St. Paule, Irma, 57
Stabile, Bill, 155
Stack, Terry, 156
Stacklin, Andy, 131
Stadelman, John, 171
Stadlen, Lewis J., 140, 221, 223
Stadt, Judy, 155
Stafford, Kate, 59
Stafford, Richard, 31, 40, 102
Stafford, Ronald, 41
Stafford-Clark, Max, 131
Stahl, Mary Leigh, 46, 221, 223
Stahl, Steven, 142
Staines, Kent, 176
Staller, David, 114
Stallings, Heidi, 40
Stallins, Luke, 154
Stallone, Sylvester, 39
Stametz, Lee, 135
Stand-Up Tragedy, 124, 142, 143
Staniak, Ewa, 55
Stanley, Dorothy, 43, 144
Stanley, Florence, 221, 223
Stanley, Gordon, 15, 101, 137, 221, 223
Stanley, Mark, 154
Stanton, Alice Regan, 173
Stanton, David, 150
Stanton, Robert, 122
Staples, Roebuck Pops, 138
Stapleton, Jean, 77, 221, 223
Stardust, 143, 144
Starger, Martin, 44
Stark, Amy Jo, 127
Stark, Douglas E., 127
Stark, Fred, 154
Stark, Molly, 59, 221, 223
Stark, Suzanne, 127
Starlight Express, 117
Starmites, 94
Starobin, Michael, 94, 135, 144
Starr, Mike, 170
Starting Monday, 100
State Academic Ensemble of Rostov, USSR, 26
State Theatre, New Brunswick, NJ, 50
States, Garrett, 114
Staton, Dakota, 221, 223
Stattel, John R., 64
Stattel, Robert, 37, 97, 221, 223
Stauffer, Michael, 119
Staunton, Kim, 32, 130
Stauter, Susan, 121
Stead, Chuck, 155
Steber, John, 67
Stechschulte, Tom, 28, 119
Stecko, Robert, 169
Steel Magnolias, 94, 133, 154
Steele, Ed, 171
Steele, J. D., 138
Steele, Philip, 46
Steele, Suzanne, 65
Steenburgen, Mary, 125
Stefanowicz, Janus, 173
Stehl, Eric, 150
Stein, Debra, 71
Stein, Douglas, 94, 124, 129, 131, 141
Stein, Gertrude, 129
Stein, J. Michael, 90
Stein, James J., Jr., 164
Stein, Joan, 111
Stein, Joseph, 43, 106
Stein, Julian, 47
Stein, Leonard, 26
Stein, Lorian, 46
Stein, Michael, 35
Stein, Navida, 57
Stein, Saul, 69, 170
Steinbeck, John, 29, 151
Steinberg, David J., 141
Steinberg, Lori, 82
Steiner, Rick, 107
Steitzer, Jeff, 118, 174
Stell, W. Joseph, 149
Stem of a Briar, 132
Stenborg, Helen, 100, 142, 221, 223
Stennett, Myra, 165
Stenson, Eric, 119
Stephanson, Kimme, 153
Stephen Rehberg: Cynnrctfctldglllllhw or the Secret of True Happiness, 53
Stephen Wade on the Way Home, 124
Stephens, Christopher J., 159
Stephens, Claudia, 56, 95
Stephens, Lannyl, 140
Stephens, Linda, 148
Stephenson, Albert, 39
Stepper, Davyd, 149
Steppling, John, 131
Stepter, Stacy, 175
Steriopoulos, Alkiviades "Alki", 139
Sterling, Clark, 110
Sterling, Lynn, 139
Stern, David, 173
Stern, Deborah, 169
Stern, Edward, 159
Stern, Eric, 20
Stern, Hilaury, 54
Stern, Jamie, 68
Stern, Kate, 147
Stern, Leo, 8, 37, 81
Stern, Marcus, 50
Stern, Noel, 113
Stern, Reva, 133
Stern, Ricki, 158
Sternberg, Jennifer, 80
Sternberg, Ruth E., 142
Sterne, Arlene, 61, 221, 223
Sterner, Jerry, 49
Sterner, Steve, 155
Sternhagen, Frances, 221, 223
Steshoel, Peter, 141
Stetler, Steve, 66
Stetson, Jeff, 138
Stettler, Steve, 66, 135
Steuber, Michael, 140
Stevenor, Joel, 68, 154
Stevens, Allan, 157
Stevens, Byam, 57
Stevens, Fisher, 87, 221, 223
Stevens, Katrina, 10
Stevens, Roger, 19, 22, 45
Stevens, Steve, 73
Stevens, Susan Riley, 120
Stevenson, Dwayne, 176
Stevenson, Mark Philip, 177
Stevenson, Paula, 67
Stevenson-Whitney, Ann, 148
Stevie Wants to Play the Blues, 147
Stewart, Adrian, 161
Stewart, Anita, 122, 170
Stewart, Benjamin, 126, 142
Stewart, Charles, 64
Stewart, Colin, 164
Stewart, George, 135
Stewart, Gwen, 33, 223
Stewart, James, 39
Stewart, Maggie, 161
Stewart, Michael, 154
Stewart, Pamela, 120
Stewart, Parry, 150
Stewart, Ray, 61
Stewart, Tara, 143
Sticco, Dan, 35, 148
Stickler, Sam, 45, 110
Stieb, Alan, 15, 107
Stiehm, Roberta, 172
Stiles, Jed, 50
Stilgoe, Richard, 40, 46, 117
Still, Chuck, 168
Still, Peter A., 144
Stiller, Amy, 60
Stillman, Bob, 18
Stillman, Robert, 223
Stillwell, Kate, 221
Stilwell, Barry, 113
Stimac, Anthony J., 84
Sting, 16, 223
Stinton, Colin, 81, 221, 223
Stirrings Still, 129
Stites, Kevin, 114, 148
Stives, Jeanne M., 149
Stoccardo, Buddy, 97
Stocker, Gary, 103, 108
Stockley, Travis, 148
Stockman, Ed, 127
Stocks, Joey, 125
Stodola, Jana, 125
Stoeckle, Robert, 120
Stoker, Sue Jane, 92
Stokes, Nelle, 137
Stokes, Ronald, 111
Stokes, Simon, 162
Stolbtsov, Dmitri, 88
Stoller, Amy, 157
Stoller, Michael, 39
Stoltz, Eric, 83, 221, 223
Stone Carver, A, 168
Stone, Brett, 117
Stone, David, 136
Stone, Dawn Leigh, 46
Stone, Fredric, 152
Stoneback, Ric, 147
Stoneburner, Sam, 82, 145, 221, 223
Stookey, Noel Paul, 23
Stopoulos, Susan, 125
Stoppard, Tom, 22, 66, 121
Storch, Arthur, 108, 165
Storey, David, 132
Stork, Renee, 43, 223
Stormare, Peter, 223
Story of Kufur Shamma, The, 53
Story, Kim, 145
Story, N. Patricia, 111
Stotts, Michael, 83
Stout, Mary, 35, 101, 221, 223
Stout, Stephen, 42, 75, 223
Stoutenburg, Robyn, 126
Stovall, Eugene, 157
Stovall, James, 84, 89
Stover, Ty, 127
Strachan, Alan, 146
Straiges, Tony, 11, 22, 107, 130, 144, 153
Strand, Christopher, 162
Strane, Robert, 136, 173
Strang, David A., 135
Strang, Deborah, 137
Strange, Melanie, 170
Strassler, Abbie M., 108
Stratford Festival, 176
Strathairn, David, 77
Stratton, Charlie, 147
Straus, Robert V., 61
Strauss, Edward, 44
Strauss, Kim, 148
Straw, The, 59
Strawbridge, Stephen, 10, 91, 122, 129, 141
Strayhorn, Danny, 18
Streeper, Chuck, 51
Streetcar Named Desire, A, 136
Streeter, Wendy, 124
Strelich, Thomas, 159
Stretch, Patrick, 121
Strevey, Jay, 146
Striglos, Bill, 168
Strike, The, 62
Strindberg, August, 122, 147, 170
Stringer, Elisabeth, 113
Stritch, Elaine, 12, 221, 223
Stroman, Guy, 71, 221, 223
Stroman, Susan, 154
Strong Man's Weak Child, 147
Strong, Kee, 119
Strong, Rider, 110
Stronin, Mikhail, 153
Stroop, Dean, 154
Strother, Frederick, 163
Strotter, Patricia Lee, 57
Strouse, Charles, 39, 144
Strozier, Henry, 124
Struckman, Jeff, 171
Struppmann, Chaz, 144
Struth, Sandy, 142
Stuart, Barbara, 177
Stuart, Brian Paul, 175
Stuart, Gwen, 221
Stuart, Ian, 97, 145, 223
Stuart, Marie, 223
Stuart, Mary Ellen, 43
Studio Arena Theatre, 164
Studio Theatre, The, 163
Studwell, David, 148
Sturchio, Malcolm, 67, 98
Sturiale, Grant, 74, 105
Sturm, Jason, 26, 59
Sturm, Miriam, 29, 138
Sturmer, Carl, 125
Sturn, Suzanne, 173
Sturua, R., 69
Stutchkoff, Nahum, 59
Styne, Jule, 20, 39, 43, 112, 144, 148
Suarez, Cynthia, 145
Suber, Kate, 47, 135
Subfertile, 94
Substance of Fire, The, 146
Suda, Thomas M., 150
Sudduth, Skipp, 29, 138
Suêno de Una Noche de Verano (Midsummer Night's Dream), 88
Suenkel, Michael, 137
Sueoka-Matos, Sandy, 108
Sugar Hill, 84
Sugarman, Leah, 137
Sugarman, Merri, 110
Sugawara, Hiroshi, 16
Sulanowski, James Stephen, 169
Sullivan, Arthur, 154
Sullivan, Bernadette, 141
Sullivan, Billy L., 28
Sullivan, Brad, 9, 223
Sullivan, Christopher, 173
Sullivan, Daniel, 42, 160
Sullivan, J. R., 152
Sullivan, John Carver, 132, 159
Sullivan, John, 121
Sullivan, K. T., 16, 151
Sullivan, Kim, 75, 123, 222, 223
Sullivan, Matt Bradford, 90, 172
Sullivan, Sean Frank, 15
Sullo, Teresina, 52
Sumbatsivily, Josef, 37
Summer and Smoke, 170
Summerhayes, Heather, 68, 137, 221, 223
Summerhays, Jane, 44, 221, 224
Summers, Fred, 158
Summers, Marc D., 66, 224
Sumner, Bart, 54
Sunday in the Park with George, 160
Sunde, Karen, 120
Sunderlin, Steven, 128
Sunshine, 76
Supple, Kelly, 45
Suria, Leo, 163
Surratt, Harold, 121
Survival, 86
Susa, Conrad, 153
Suskin, Steven, 10, 71
Suso, Foday Musa, 141
Sussel, Deborah, 121
Susser, Harry, 129
Sussman, Bette, 52
Suter, William, 63
Sutherland, Brian, 35, 139
Sutherland, Elaine, 150
Suto, Kinga, 149
Sutton, Greg, 57
Sutton, Joe, 63, 95
Suzanna, P., 142
Svastics, Mark, 131
Swackhamer, Ten Eyck, 118
Swados, Elizabeth, 52, 77, 90
Swados, Robin, 73
Swain, Howard, 121
Swallows, Wayne, 173
Swan, The, 120
Swanson, Eric, 143
Swanson, Lanitta, 120
Swarm, Sally Ann, 68
Swearingnen, Beth, 40
Swedlund, Kristina, 53
Swee, Daniel, 42, 94
Sweeney Todd, 8
Sweeney, Kevin, 132
Sweeney, Pepper, 128
Sweeney, Will, 15
Sweeney-Samuelson, Emily, 160
Sweet By and By, The, 151
Sweet, Sam, 172
Swenson, Christian, 53
Swenson, Julie, 73
Swenson, Paula, 166
Swerling, Jo, 125
Swetland, Dudley, 169
Swift, Allen, 164
Swift, Julia, 25
Swoboda, Seth, 133
Swonger, James, 129
Sword, David L., 170
Sword, Gretchen Liddell, 149
Sydnor, Earl, 232
Syer, Fontaine, 119, 152
Sykes, Diane, 70
Sylvester, Harold, 147
Sylvester, Mark D., 133
Sylvester, Tani Rasheen, 126
Symington, Donald, 64, 224
Symons, Kevin, 147
Synge, John Millington, 160
Synodinos, Jean, 48
Syracuse Stage, 165
Szarabajka, Keith, 94, 222, 224
Szentgyorgyi, Tom, 83
T Bone N Weasel, 168
Tabachnik, Robin, 27
Tabakov, Oleg P., 88
Taber, Min, 152
Taccone, Anthony, 64, 137, 160
Tack, Dianne, 125
Tackaberry, Celia, 137
Tacoma Actors Guild, 166

Tadken, Neil, 61, 222, 224
Tafler, Jean, 222, 224
Tagg, Alan, 30
Takano, Kenichi, 12
Takarazuka, 12
Takayama, Akira, 37
Takazauckas, Albert, 121
Takazawa, Marie, 108
Taking Steps, 127
Takita, Kyoko, 108
Talberth, Kenneth, 70, 224
Talcott, Linda, 43
Tale of Two Cities, A, 121, 149
Talented Tenth, The, 83
Taleporos, Zoe, 29, 222, 224
Tales of the Lost Formicans, 69
Talking Pictures, 126
Talking Things Over with Chekhov, 70
Tallaksen, Fred, 117
Talley's Folly, 156
Talman, Ann, 81, 222, 224
Talso, Liisa, 166
Talyn, Olga, 46, 70, 114, 222, 224
Tamagawa, Emiko, 175
Tamara, 94
Tambella, Mark, 73
Taming of the Shrew, The, 164,, 165, 171
Tammi, Tom, 60
Tan, Victor En Yu, 66, 92, 134, 168
Tandy, Jessica, 39
Tango, 11
Tani, Masazumi, 12
Tanji, Lydia, 131
Tankersley, Mark, 222, 224
Tanner, Betsy, 83
Tanner, Jill, 149
Tanner, Tony, 17
Tapley, Gloria, 171
Taranto, 50
Tarrant, Gage, 173
Tarson, Geoffrey, 155
Tartuffe, 135, 171
Tasker, Jill, 94, 170
Tassin, Christen, 20, 222, 224
Tassinaro, Gregory, 17
Tate, Judy, 53, 60
Tate, Kamella, 162
Tate, Robin, 149
Tatge, Pamela, 145
Tatum, Marianne, 27, 222, 224
Tauji, Anne M., 92
Tavares, Eric, 150
Taylor, Andy, 141
Taylor, Bernadette, 105
Taylor, C. P., 153
Taylor, Clark, 119
Taylor, Clifton, 53, 61
Taylor, David, 67, 102
Taylor, Dendrie, 162
Taylor, E. Oliver, 152
Taylor, Helyn, 56
Taylor, Holland, 130, 144
Taylor, Jeffrey, 54
Taylor, John Wendes, 145
Taylor, Kathy, 109
Taylor, Lili, 50
Taylor, Lynne Faljian, 78
Taylor, Myra, 120
Taylor, Noel, 146, 169
Taylor, Paul, 135
Taylor, Regina, 65, 129, 168, 222, 224
Taylor, Robin, 154
Taylor, Robyn Karen, 29
Taylor, Scott, 40, 222, 224
Taylor, Todd, 114
Taylor, Ty, 157
Taylor, Wally, 124
Taylor-Corbett, Lynne, 137
Taylor-Morris, Maxine, 165
Taymor, Julie, 61
Tazewell, Paul, 59, 124
Tcharkviani, C., 69
Tchkhaidze, Revaz, 69
Tchkhikvadze, Ramaz, 69
Tea, 168
Teachout, Dan, 173
Tecce, Justin, 149
Techman, Charles, 169
Tecson, David, 91
Tegtmeier, Treva, 138
Teichmann, Howard, 170
Teirstein, Alice, 93
Tejero, Lisa, 138
Tekampe, Robert, 136, 167
Telson, Bob, 138
Temperate Zone, The, 175
Temperley, Stephen, 89, 93, 222, 224
Tempest, The, 97, 171, 172, 173, 175
Templeton, Greg, 56, 222, 224
Ten November, 147
Tenney, Jon, 153
Tenny, Hal, 120
Tenth Man, The, 82
Tenuta, Judy, 39
Teplay, Wayne, 51
Tepper, Eileen, 169
Terada, Takio, 12
Terpis, James, 54
Terra Nova, 174
Terrace Theatre, 144
Terrell, Jheri, 33
Terris, Norma, 232
Terriss, Elaine, 68
Terrors of Pleasure-The Uncut Version, The, 53
Terry, Elizabeth, 153
Terry, Jon, 60, 155
Terry, Jonathan, 68
Terry, Keith, 64, 160
Terry, Marjorie, 127
Terry, Matt, 117
Terry, Michael, 120
Terry, W. Benson, 134
Terzi, Al, 170
Tesich, Steve, 98
Tessier, Claude R., 110
Testa, Elizabeth, 165
Testa, Mary, 94, 222, 224
Tezla, Michael, 141
Thacker, Russ, 222, 224
Thall, Christopher, 57
Tharpe, Ouida, 23
Thatch, Robert L., 151
Thau, Harold, 14
Thaxter, Phyllis, 154
Thayer, Joel O., 119
The Circle, 21
The Immigrant: A Hamilton County Album, 150
Theatre Three, 167
Theatre World Award Recipients, 179
Thebus, Mary Ann, 56
Them That's Got, 121
Them, 58
There's an Angel in Las Vegas, 60
Therriault, Daniel, 51
Thibodeau, Joe, 125
Thibodeau, Marc, 26, 29, 40, 42, 43, 45, 46, 110, 113, 114
Thicke, Alan, 39
Thiel, Nancy, 149
Thiergaard, Judith, 74
Thies, Howard, 66
Thin Air: Tales from a Revolution, 161
Thoemke, Peter, 140, 141
Thole, Cynthia, 15, 224
Thomas, B. J., 39
Thomas, Carlo, 113
Thomas, Carmen, 165
Thomas, Colby, 64
Thomas, Dylan, 78
Thomas, Eberle, 136
Thomas, Frank M., 232
Thomas, Frozine, 70
Thomas, G. Valmont, 118, 160
Thomas, Isa, 140, 142
Thomas, Jody, 45
Thomas, John C., 61
Thomas, John Norman, 25, 222, 224
Thomas, Leonard, 95
Thomas, Marie, 83
Thomas, Megan, 154
Thomas, Raymond Anthony, 62, 75, 134, 224
Thomas, Richard, 12, 98, 111, 222, 224
Thomas, Robert, 41
Thomas, Rohn, 132
Thomas, Sheriden, 158
Thomas, Traci Lyn, 84
Thomas-Grant, Cathy, 121
Thomasson, Peter, 119
Thompson, Adrienne, 51
Thompson, Beth, 106
Thompson, Brian, 135
Thompson, Courtney, 156
Thompson, David, 174
Thompson, Don, 47
Thompson, Emma, 115, 131
Thompson, Evan, 24, 222, 224
Thompson, Gil, 163
Thompson, Jeffrey V., 124, 142
Thompson, John Leonard, 124
Thompson, Julie, 129
Thompson, Kent, 171
Thompson, Kerry, 124
Thompson, Lauren, 112
Thompson, Lea, 147
Thompson, Martha, 123, 144
Thompson, Owen, 57, 224
Thompson, Paul Henry, 138
Thompson, Peter, 115
Thompson, Richard, 128, 163
Thompson, Sada, 153
Thompson, Stuart, 19
Thompson, Susan, 62
Thompson, Sylvia M'Lafi, 161
Thompson, Tazewell, 124, 132, 143, 168
Thompson, Tommy, 159
Thompson, Trinity, 159
Thomsen, Richard, 57, 99, 132
Thomson, Anna Levine, 77
Thomson, Jeff, 125
Thomson, Tommy, 43
Thoresen, Howard, 60, 65, 70
Thorne, Creon, 133
Thorne, Raymond, 139, 144
Thornton, Cheryl, 57
Thornton, Greg, 159, 171
Thoron, Elise, 153
Thorp, Peggy, 150
Thorpe, Bud, 59
Thorson, Linda, 37, 182, 183, 224
Threats, Aurora L., 67
Three Men on a Horse, 135
Three Rivers Shakespeare Festival, 177
Three Sisters, The, 93, 176
Threepenny Opera, The, 16, 140
Thrill, The, 131
Thropp, Randall, 48
Thun, Nancy, 168
Thuna, Leonora, 137
Thunhurst, William, 157
Thurber, Robert, 69, 78
Thurman, Annette, 148
Thurston, Philip, 70, 103, 105
Tichenor, Austin, 84
Tichler, Rosemarie, 13, 87
Tichman, Nomi, 72
Ticotin, Nancy, 43
Tidwell, Byron, 165
Tidwell, Mike, 125
Tierney, Thomas, 157
Tiesi, William S., 165
Tiggeloven, John, 105
Tighe, Kevin, 160
Tighe, Susanne, 6, 9, 12, 15, 25, 33, 36, 38, 44, 97, 108
Tilchin, Marcia, 144
Tilden, Leif, 131
Tilford, Joe, 101, 128
Tillinger, John, 12, 58, 83, 145, 146
Tillman, Ellis, 133
Tillman, Judith, 151
Tillotson, John, 144
Tilney, Thom, 93
Tilton, James, 133
Timerman, Alec, 20, 222, 224
Timm, Faye Bailey, 168
Timms, Cindy, 154
Timms, Rebecca, 40
Tinapp, Barton, 141
Tindel, James, 167
Tindle, Jon, 163
Tinsley, James K., 136
Tipton, Jennifer, 43, 87, 138, 141, 170
Tirabassi, Maria, 147
Tiramani, Jenny, 115, 131
'Tis Pity She's a Whore, 138
Titterton, Patricia, 128
Titus Andronicus, 87, 173, 176
Titus, Donald W., 170
Titus, Hiram, 141
Tkachenko, Valentin, 39
Tkachuk, Dave, 23
Tkatch, Peter Jack, 49
Tobie, Ellen, 137
Tobolowsky, Stephen, 147
Tod, the Boy, Tod, 134
Toda, Chiaki, 108
Todaro, Paul, 72
Todd, Gina, 101
Toggenburger, Joan, 147
Toho International, 12
Tokar, Michael, 15
Tokarski, Stanislaw, 55
Tokoro, Harumi, 12
Tokuda, Marilyn, 168
Tolan, Kathleen, 89, 94
Tolan, Peter, 63
Tollkuhn, Richard, 159
Tom Jones, 173
Tom Sawyer, 127
Tom, Lauren, 138, 141
Tomasino, Matt, 62
Tomasovic, Tom, 72
Tombrello, Drew, 161
Tomczak, Art, 164
Tomfoolery, 135, 159
Tomkins, Steve, 118
Tomlin, Cathy, 63
Tomlinson, Carol, 57
Tomlinson, Libby, 139
Tompkins, Michael, 118
Tompos, Doug, 24, 224
Tompson, Marian, 39
Tondo, Jerry, 131
Tony 'n' Tina's Wedding, 48
Took, Don, 162
Toole, James E., 165
Toombs, Robert, 173
Toon, Tami, 130, 131
Toon, Terpsie, 61
Topol, 106
Topol, Richard, 94, 149
Toporek, Mark Ethan, 59
Toppin, Dwight, 117
Torme, Mel, 39
Toro, Natalie, 45
Torpey, Erin, 28
Torres, Gina, 134
Torres, Rafael, Jr., 67
Torrey, Michael, 138
Tost, William, 47
Tostevin, Cynthia J., 137
Toth, Helen, 29
Touda, Ikuei, 12
Tourtillotte, Paul, 158
Toussaint, Lorraine, 83
Tovatt, Ellen, 27, 222, 224
Tovatt, Patrick, 99, 222, 224
Tower of Evil, The, 77
Towers, Charles, 168
Towler, Laurine, 30, 222, 224
Townsend, Elizabeth Ann, 61, 222, 224
Toy, Christine, 154
Tracy, Jeanie, 121
Tracy, Jim, 62
Tracy, Magen, 146
Trade, Les, 169
Traina, Joseph, 117
Trainor, Saxon, 147
Traister, Andrew J., 153
Tramon, Dan, 34
Tran, Lannhi, 167
Trapp Family Singers, The, 27
Trapp, Maria Augusta, 27
Travanti, Daniel J., 132
Traveler in the Dark, 101
Traveling Lady, The, 167
Travers, Joseph, 80, 222, 224
Travers, Mary, 23
Travis, Mark X., 56
Travis, Warren, 121, 171
Trawick, Tiffany Brandy, 135
Traxler, Mark, 127
Trayer, Leslie, 43
Traylor, William, 230, 232
Treadway, Teman, 163
Treadwell, Tom, 164
Treat, Martin, 67
Treatment of Dr. Love, The, 72
Tree, Brian, 176
Tremblay, Ernest, 169
Tremblay, Kay, 176
Trevens, Francine L., 53, 54, 55, 56, 57, 60, 73
Trevino, Frankie, 118
Trevino, Vic, 162
Treyz, Russell M., 119
Trigger, Ian, 169
Trisilla, Craig, 152
Trofimov, Gennady, 61
Troilus and Cressida, 170, 173
Troob, Danny, 39, 103, 139, 164
Troubadour, 72
Troublefield, Michael, 33
Troupe, Tom, 133
Troutman, Darrell, 171
Troy, Doris, 64
Troy, Ellen, 43
Tru, 23, 122
True West, 158
True, Betsy, 45, 109, 222, 224
True, Jim, 29
Trujillo, Sergio, 43
Trulock, Dianne, 19
Truly Blessed, 33
Trumbull, Robert, 57
Tschetter, Dean, 147
Tsoutsouvas, Sam, 55, 74, 131, 222, 224
Tsu, Susan, 114
Tsuji, Ann M., 92
Tsuji, Yukio, 92
Tsypin, George, 138, 141
Tubb, Dan, 89
Tubert, Marcelo, 153
Tubert, Myriam, 153
Tubert, Susana, 71, 96
Tucci, Maria, 224
Tucker, Dianne, 167
Tucker, R. Christian, 173
Tucker, Regina, 119
Tucker, Robert, 6
Tucker-White, Pamela, 100, 157, 222, 224
Tukish, Anatoly, 39
Tuleja, Cynthia, 169
Tulin, Michael, 131
Tull, Eric, 55
Tull, Patrick, 83, 224
Tumanyan, Barseg, 54
Tuna Christmas, A, 144
Tune, Tommy, 18
Tunick, Jonathan, 41, 107
Tupikin, Igor, 153
Turai, Terrie, 105
Turchetta, Tamara, 152
Turco-Lyon, Kathleen, 174
Turenne, Louis, 21
Turich, Sam, 177
Turnbull, Horace, 139
Turnbull, Laura, 14, 222, 224
Turner Entertainment Co., 18
Turner, Aimee, 154
Turner, Ann, 152
Turner, Cedric H., 136
Turner, Charles, 53
Turner, Craig, 158
Turner, Glenn, 18, 224, 225
Turner, Jake, 95
Turner, Jenny, 169
Turner, Jerry, 174
Turner, Jill, 169
Turner, Kathleen, 28, 182, 183, 224, 225
Turner, Keith, 44
Turner, Lily, 68
Turner, Patrick, 70, 224, 225
Turner, Richard V., 95
Turner, Susan Watson, 95
Turner, Suzanne, 22
Turner, Tyne, 150
Turns, Ali, 86, 95
Turpin, Bahni, 75, 224, 225
Turrin, Joseph, 101
Turturro, Aida, 48
Turturro, John, 170, 224, 225
Tussey, Julie, 41
Tuths, Evelyn, 66, 224, 225
Tutor, Rick, 160
Tuttle, Michael, 118
Twain, Mark, 135
Twedt, Mary, 125
Twelfth Night, 87, 121, 122, 128, 171, 172
Twelfth Night, Or What You Will, 87
Twenty Fingers, Twenty Toes, 100
Twice Shy, 94
Twitty, Conway, 39
Two Acts of Passion: Dutchman, 121
Two Gentleman of Verona, 174
Two Good Boys, 149
2 Plays, 120
2 Samuel 11, Etc., 56
Two Trains Running, 170
Twomey, Anne, 9, 224, 225
Tyler, Andi, 43
Tyler, Bonnie, 39
Tyler, Chad, 136
Tyler, Pete, 76
Tynan, Mark, 108
Tyrrell, Lyn, 166
Tyrrell, Susan, 147
Tyson, Fred, 9
Tyson, Pamala, 123
Tyzack, Margaret, 30, 224
Udell, Peter, 6
Ueda, Shinju, 12
Uhry, Alfred, 104, 119, 153
Ukena, Paul, Jr., 159
Ulissev, Catherine, 46
Ullmann, Liv, 39
Ullrick, Sharon, 135
Ulmer, Joan, 171
Ulmer, John, 126, 150
Ulrich, Mark, 152
Ultz, 83
Ulvaeus, Bjorn, 103, 148
Uncle Vanya, 138, 141, 153
Understanding, The, 155
Ungar, Steven, 68
Unkovski, Slobodan, 122
Untitled, 167
Up Against It, 89
Upchurch, Reenie, 59
Upton, Carey, 125
Urbano, Maryann, 157
Uribe, Pilar, 71
Urich, Tom, 154
Urla, Joe, 224, 225
Utech, Greg, 150
Utley, Byron, 164
Utterances, 121
Vador, Ella, 154
Vajtay, Nicolette, 122
Vaky, Matthew, 141
Valdes, Ching, 65
Valdez, Albert, 153
Valdez, Dino A., 136
Valdez, Reggie, 127
Valdez, Thaddeus, 119
Valentine, James, 152
Valentine, Karen, 73
Valentino, Eileen, 169
Valenzuela, Jose Luis, 147
Valle, Fred, 96
Valle, Miriam Colon, 96
Valsing, Elizabeth, 62
Vampire Lesbians of Sodom, 48, 94
Van Ark, Joan, 39
van Betten, Melanie, 160
Van Dyck, Jennifer, 13, 224
Van Dyke, Dick, 39
Van Dyke, Elizabeth, 75, 128
Van Dyke, Peter, 153
Van Fossen, Diana, 78, 224, 225
van Griethuysen, Ted, 142, 171, 172
Van Heusen, Jimmy, 232
Van Itallie, Jean-Claude, 101, 160
Van Keuren, Carol, 54
Van Keyser, William, 127
van Maanen, James, 93
Van Nostrand, Amy, 93
Van Patten, Joyce, 153, 225, 226
Van Shelton, Ricky, 39
Van Tieghem, David, 65
Van Zandt, Karen, 121
Vanbiesbrouck, John, 39
Vanbrugh, John, 176
Vance, Courtney B., 82, 91
Vance, Courtney, 91
Vance, Danitra, 91, 134
VanderHeyden, Tina, 113
Vandergriff, Robert, 52, 111
Vandertholen, Jon, 137
Vandivort, Terry, 167
Vandross, Luther, 39
vanLeer, Robert, 136
Vanoff, Nick, 24
Vanti, Cecelia, 173
Vardasheva, Olga, 39
Varga, Joseph A., 68, 136, 171
Vargas, Angel, 117
Vargas, Leonard, 154
Vargas, Ovidio, 56, 68
Vargyas, Carmel, 45
Vasconcellos, Anthony, 62, 91
Vasnick, Andy, 144
Vasquez, Alden, 138
Vasquez, Randy, 76, 225, 226
Vasseux, Jean-Claude, 69
Vassiliev, Vladimir, 61
Vaubel, Alexis, 141
Vaughan, Melanie, 168
Vaughn, Jack, 174
Vaughn, Robert, 12
Vaux, Lyn, 61
Vawter, Ron, 62
Veatch, Greg, 166
Veazey, Jeff, 48
Vega, Laura P., 153
Vehicle, 167
Velez, Anita, 96
Venard, Shirley, 141
Venberg, Lorraine, 177
Veneziale, Renee, 109
Vennema, John C., 68, 137, 225, 226
Venner, Tracy, 20, 226
Venora, Diane, 91, 226
Venton, Harley, 21
Ventriss, Jennie, 81
Venus and Adonis, 62
Verderber, William, 142
Verdon, Gwen, 111
Verges, Chrisann, 50
Verhein, Midge, 167
Verheyan, Mariann, 112, 119, 143
Verini, Bob, 70
Verlaque, Robert, 58, 95
Verleny, Christine, 77
Vern-Harris, Pat, 148
Vernace, Kim, 101
Vernan, Ron, 161
Vernon, Jack, 163
Versenyi, Adam, 158
Vesenka, Hannah, 120
Vesper, Karen, 153
Vevera, Trish, 50
Viade, Michael, 183
Viator, Alma, 116
Vic, Cliff, 69
Vichi, Gerry, 170
Vickerman, Linda, 161
Vickers, Larry, 33
Vickery, John, 131
Vickery, K. Edward, 119
Victor Borge Holiday Show, The, 23
Victor, Neil, 52
Vidal, Marta, 96
Vidal, Whitney, 152
Vigoda, Abe, 39
Viktyuk, Roman, 161
Villa, Christopher, 174
Villa, Marc, 11, 43
Villaire, Holly, 177
Villamor, Christen, 92
Villari, Libby, 167
Villella, Donna, 48
Vineyard Theatre, 99
Vinkler, Greg, 145
Vinovich, Stephen, 13, 225, 226
Vinton, Doris, 232

Violent Peace, 66
Vipond, Neil, 97, 140, 146, 226
Viracola, Fiddle, 16
Virginia Stage Company, 168
Virostek, Linda, 166
Virta, Ray, 78, 225, 226
Viselli, Nicholas, 173
Vital Signs, 120
Vitella, Sel, 17, 225, 226
Viverito, Sam, 164
Viverito, Suzanne, 40
Viverta, Joanna, 49
Vivian, Dean, 151
Viviano, Sal, 169
Vivino, Jimmy, 52
Vlasak, Christine, 54
Vlasova, Evgeniya, 39
Vodde, Michael, 110
Vode, Timothy, 55
Vogel, Elfin Frederick, 125
Vogel, Paula, 147
Voice in the Well, A, 65
Voice of the Prairie, The, 119, 127, 155, 174
Voices Unsilenced: A Multicultural Awakening, 167
Volkmann, Julie, 145
Vollack, Lia, 132
Volpone, 141
Voltaire, 141
Volz, Jim, 171
von Bargen, Daniel, 10, 90, 181, 183, 226
Von Bayer, Christopher, 175
Von Berg, Peter, 64
von Mayrhauser, Darwall, 14, 68
von Mayrhauser, Jennifer, 42, 60, 165
von Mayrhauser, Peter, 58
von Rosenchilde, Natasha, 58
von Schiller, Friedrich, 172
VonNessen, Doug, 138
Vosburgh, David, 8, 225, 226
Vose, Holland, 90
Voulgaris, John, 53
Voznesensky, Andrey, 61
Vroman, Lisa, 31, 110
Vrtol, Stephen F., III, 152
WPA Theatre, 100
Waara, Scott, 24, 225, 226
Waddell, Jack, 66
Wade, Adam, 85, 95, 225, 226
Wade, Jeree Palmer, 84
Wade, Melinda, 52
Wade, Stephen, 124
Wadsworth, Don, 177
Wager, Douglas C., 124, 170
Wages, Brad, 119
Waggenhurst, Mark, 55
Wagget, David, 59
Wagner, Chuck, 107
Wagner, Daniel MacLean, 163
Wagner, George, 24, 44
Wagner, Guy S., 87
Wagner, Katherine, 173
Wagner, Kathryn, 58, 61, 66
Wagner, Robin, 24, 41, 43, 91, 154
Wagrowski, Gregory, 147
Wahl, David, 145
Wait until Dark, 156
Waite, John Thomas, 47, 172
Waiting for Godot, 131, 153, 173
Waiting for the Parade, 169
Wakefield, Colin, 115, 131
Wakefield, Scott, 151, 160
Walbye, Kay, 133
Walch, James, 131
Walck, Erick, 114
Walcutt, John, 135
Walden, Stanley, 133
Walden, William, 159
Waldheim, Julianne, 18
Waldman, Julie, 106
Waldman, Risa, 105
Waldman, Robert, 94, 104, 153
Waldo, Terry, 66
Waldron, Michael, 44
Waletzko, Craig, 20
Walinski, Cliff, 141
Walk in the Woods, A, 118, 150, 159, 165
Walken, Christopher, 39, 226
Walker, Bonnie, 20
Walker, Chris, 170
Walker, Dana, 40
Walker, Don, 106
Walker, George F., 167
Walker, Janet Hayes, 8, 101
Walker, Jonathan, 94
Walker, Kary M., 148
Walker, Margaret, 65
Walker, Mary, 137
Walker, Natalie, 79
Walker, Paul, 124
Walker, Randolph, 149
Walker, Ray, 45, 225, 226
Walker, Seth Jerome, 28
Walker, Sullivan, 170
Walker, Sydney, 121
Walker, Toni-Ann, 153
Walker-Lichtig, Jody, 107
Wall, John, 61
Wall, Susie, 159
Wallace, Basil, 164
Wallace, Bradford, 136, 150
Wallace, Claudine, 118
Wallace, Gregory, 141, 144, 168
Wallace, Jack, 98
Wallace, Jenny, 173
Wallace, Kevin, 128
Wallace, Lee, 38, 225, 226
Wallace, Marian, 126
Wallace, Mike, 39
Wallace, Ronald, 146
Wallem, Linda, 63
Waller, Brad, 124
Waller, Fats, 127
Waller, Kenneth, 46, 225, 226
Walling, Hayden, 143
Walling, Jessica, 143
Walling, Stratton, 151
Wallnau, Carl, 93, 225, 226
Wallner, Robert H., 28
Waln, Kathleen, 131
Walnut Street Theatre, The, 169
Walnut, Dawn, 36
Walsh, Barbara, 103
Walsh, Elizabeth, 101, 114, 226
Walsh, James, 42
Walsh, Susie, 131
Walsh, Tony, 84
Walsh, Winifred, 132
Walstedt, Eric, 93
Walston, Dee Dee, 152
Walter, Jessica, 130, 225, 226
Walters, Barbara, 39
Walters, Kelly, 168
Walters, W. Francis, 161, 174
Walton, Dereck R., 177
Walton, Jim, 8, 50, 57, 225, 226
Walton, Kathy, 128
Walton, Tony, 18, 43, 43, 44, 73, 82, 98, 138
Walworth, Mary, 135
Wanamaker, Mary, 154
Wandrey, Donna, 133
Wann, Jim, 145, 159
Ward, Adolphus, 126
Ward, Bethany, 160
Ward, Bethe, 46
Ward, Buzz, 170
Ward, Diane, 83
Ward, Douglas Turner, 65, 85, 95, 225, 226
Ward, Elizabeth, 110
Ward, Elsa, 67, 89, 94
Ward, Grace, 150
Ward, Ken, 129
Ward, Michael, 97
Ward, Patricia, 114
Ward, Patrick, 74
Ward, Tracy, 110
Ward, William P., 150
Ware, Jeffrey, 164
Ware, Tom, 111
Waren, Mark G., 52
Waren, Stanley A., 52
Wares, Kyle, 153
Warfel, William B., 170
Warfield, Joe, 226
Wargo, Steven, 152
Warik, Joe, 127
Warmen, Tim, 101
Warner, David Strong, 7, 36
Warner, Lee H., 126
Warner, Russell, 139
Warner, Stacey, 167
Warrack, David, 6
Warren, BriJuin, 136
Warren, David, 83, 89, 94, 146
Warren, Diane, 39, 127, 145
Warren, Harry, 154
Warren, Jennifer Leigh, 84
Warren, Joseph, 93, 226, 227
Warren, Lesley Ann, 111
Warren, Mary Mease, 157
Warren, Robert, 101
Warshofsky, David, 159
Washabaugh, Chip, 131
Washington, Alicia Rene, 149
Washington, Cheryle, 167
Washington, Denzel, 226, 227
Washington, Don Corey, 86
Washington, Kenneth, 160
Washington, Melvin, 226
Washington, Sharon, 78, 129
Washington, Steve, 124
Washington-Nance, Vickie, 167
Waskow, Darryl S., 149
Wasser, Alan, 45, 46, 110, 113, 114
Wasser, Scott, 53
Wassermann, Ross, 103, 164
Wasserstein, Wendy, 42, 160
Wasylik, Kerri Lynn, 105
Waterhouse, Jane, 154
Waters, Amanda, 124
Waters, Harry, Jr., 131
Waters, Kyle, 68
Waters, Les, 91, 131
Waterston, Sam, 39
Watkins, Jeffrey, 119
Watkins, Steve, 102
Watson, Donald, 122
Watson, Ian, 176
Watson, Janet, 119
Watson, Joe, 138
Watson, Lisa L., 95
Watson, Michael, 169
Watt, Billie Lou, 128, 154
Watt, Douglas, 182
Watt, Eloise, 225, 226
Waugh, Ann, 173
Waugh, Sandra, 73
Waves, The, 91
Waxman, Jeff, 99, 160
Way, Wendy, 55
Weather Outside, The, 62
Weatherly, Michael M., 103
Weathers, Patrick, 50, 226, 227
Weatherstone, James, 107
Weaver, Danyelle, 11, 225, 226
Weaver, Margie, 141
Weaver, Rose, 153
Weaver, Sara, 66
Weaver, Sylvester A., Jr., 95
Webb, Alexander, 159
Webb, Christian, 132
Webb, John R., 152
Webb, Mitch, 9
Webber, Andrew Lloyd, 31, 40, 44, 46, 117
Webber, Julian, 59
Webber, Lloyd, 31, 169
Webber, Melanie, 55
Weber, Debbie, 125
Weber, Holly, 174
Weber, Jake, 87, 226, 227
Weber, Kym, 108
Weber, Patricia, 108
Weber, Robert, 133
Webster, Bryan, 55, 69
Webster, Douglas, 110
Webster, John, 141
Webster, Karen, 102
Webster, Leigh, 40
Webster, Peter, 157, 171, 172
Wedgeworth, Ann, 55, 225, 226
Weeden, Derrick Lee, 174
Weeks, Todd Bryant, 140
Wehle, Brenda, 141
Wehner, Pam, 154
Weidmann, Ginnie, 47
Weidner, Paul, 79
Weihs, Stephen, 74
Weil, Melissa, 164, 165
Weill, Kurt, 16, 73
Weimerskirch, Lorraine K. M., 127
Weinberg, Hazel, 169
Weinberg, Helene, 140
Weindling, Craig, 118
Weinstein, Connie, 106
Weinstein, Irv, 164
Weinstein, Robert J., 70
Weir, Dan, 51, 65
Weir, Jonathan, 148
Weir, Scott, 60, 73
Weiss, Adrienne, 50, 56
Weiss, Christine, 55, 69
Weiss, Eric Radford, 165
Weiss, Greg, 95
Weiss, Gregory Linus, 52
Weiss, Jeff, 10, 65, 226
Weiss, Julie, 131, 164
Weiss, Marc B., 23, 132, 145, 146, 165
Weiss, Mitchell A., 29
Weiss, Norman, 98
Weissler, Barry, 20, 28, 106
Weissler, Fran, 20, 28, 106
Weissman, Neile, 53
Weitzman, Ira, 94
Welborn, Cathy, 169
Welby, Donnah, 93, 225, 226, 227
Welch, David, 88
Welch, Jane, 64
Welch, Raquel, 39
Welch, Stephen, 172
Weldin, Scott, 64, 118, 137, 160
Weldon, Charles, 85, 95, 226
Weldon, Duncan C., 9, 25
Weldon, Kevin, 139
Wellborn, Michael, 166
Weller, Michael, 70
Wellman, Mac, 51, 65, 161
Wells, Alexander, 173
Wells, Christopher, 63, 120, 226, 227
Wells, Craig, 57, 110, 226, 227
Wells, Deanna, 43, 124
Wells, James R., 137
Wells, Laura, 167
Wells, Tico, 119, 134
Wells-Ruhl, Pamela, 125
Welsh, Sarah, 160
Wenceslas Square, 152
Wenderlich, Mark, 136
Wendland, Mark, 131, 147
Wentworth, Scott, 129
Weppner, Christina, 69
Werkheiser, Ian, 110
Werner, Howard, 29
Werner, Lori, 43
Werner, Stewart, 76
Wernick, Adam, 144
Wertenbaker, Timberlake, 65, 131
Wesler, Ken, 169
Wesley, John, 136
Wesley, L. Edmond, 232
Wesley, Richard, 59, 83
Wessler, Frederick, 94
West Memphis Mojo, 163
West, Britt, 112
West, Caryn, 126
West, Dennis, 171
West, Jeffery, 158
West, Joyce, 56
West, Kevin S., 56
West, Margo L., 172
West, Peter, 122
West, Steven Major, 16
Westcott, Kimberly, 65
Westenberg, Robert, 45, 226, 227
Westerland, Jim, 166
Westlake, Chappell, 167
Weston, Jack, 82, 226
Wetherall, Jack, 157, 226, 227
Wetzel, Harry, 136
Whalen, David, 133, 165
Whalley-Kilmer, Joanne, 226
What a Man Weighs, 98
Wheel and Deal, 50
Wheeler, Bronia Stefan, 122
Wheeler, Ed, 95
Wheeler, Harold, 144
Wheeler, Hugh, 8, 15
Wheeler, Jedediah, 122
Wheeler, William, 87
Whelan, Denise, 169
Whelan, Susan, 17
When I Was a Girl I Used to Scream and Shout, 162
When She Danced, 94
Whistle in the Dark, A, 79
Whitaker, Julian, 50, 51
Whitcomb, Mary, 173
White, Al, 170
White, Alton F., 148
White, Amelia, 59, 128, 225, 226
White, Betty, 39
White, Boysie, 64
White, Brad, 138, 146
White, Carolyn Johnson, 138
White, Charlene M., 135
White, Cynthia, 174
White, David, 118, 147
White, Doug, 135
White, Harrison, 116
White, Ian, 176
White, Jane, 170
White, Jesse, 39
White, Julie, 42, 160
White, K. Dale, 175
White, Lillias, 89
White, Miles, 43
White, Pat, 22
White, Patrick, 226, 227
White, Richard E. T., 153, 171, 172
White, Richard, 101, 226
White, Susan A., 74
White, Susan R., 124
White, Thea Ruth, 173
Whitehead, Beauris, 67
Whitehead, David P., 118
Whitehead, Michael, 105
Whitehead, Paxton, 22, 30, 153, 226
Whitehead, Robert, 19, 22
Whitehead, William M., 167
Whitehill, B. T., 52, 89
Whitehurst, Scott, 134
Whiteley, Ben, 108
Whitelock, Patricia Ann, 135
Whiteman, Bart, 124
Whitemore, Hugh, 145, 162
Whitescarver, Randall, 117
Whitfield, Debra, 226, 227
Whitfield, Michael J., 176
Whitford, Bradley, 19, 77
Whitley, Kym, 67
Whitley, Maria, 173
Whitlock, Isiah, Jr., 10, 25
Whitmore, James, 137, 164
Whitner, Daniel, 156
Whitney, Ann, 138, 148
Whitney, Gregg, 15
Whittaker, Julie, 113
Whitted, Earl, 71
Whittemore, Cari Dean, 88
Whitton, Margaret, 91, 227, 228
Who's Afraid of Virginia Woolf?, 130
Whole Theatre, 168
Whyte, Kyle, 15
Whyte, Ron, 136
Wibbin, Dale, 74
Wickham, William, 151
Widdall, Russ, 173
Widdoes, Kathleen, 77, 228
Widdowson-Reynolds, Rosina, 161
Widow's Blind Date, The, 58
Wiedt, Sara, 154
Wielkotz, Linda, 63
Wierzel, Robert, 76, 88, 90, 122, 129, 158
Wiesel, Elie, 39
Wiest, Dianne, 98, 228
Wiger, Merete, 149
Wiggall, David, 128
Wiggins, Pamela, 100
Wilborn, Kip, 70
Wilbur, John, 105
Wilbur, Richard, 135, 141
Wilcher, James "Red", 70, 134
Wilchinski, Jim, 20
Wilcox, Charlotte, 6, 27, 28, 33, 38
Wild Rose, 39
Wilde, Cornel, 230, 232
Wilde, Julie, 74
Wilde, Oscar, 93, 142, 149
Wilder, Andrew, 166
Wilder, Baakari Askia, 172
Wilder, Eva, 151
Wilder, Jessica, 29
Wilder, Thornton, 159
Wildern, Steven H., 77
Wildhorn, Frank, 122
Wildman, James, 165
Wildman, Robert, 170
Wiley, Irene, 61
Wiley, J. Heather, 95
Wilkens, Claudia, 141
Wilker, Lawrence J., 36
Wilkerson, Edward, 138
Wilkerson, Steve, 125
Wilkins, Janet, 152
Wilkinson, Colm, 113, 227, 228
Wilkinson, Kate, 122
Wilks, Talvin, 134
Will, Ethyl, 40
Will, John, 93
William, David, 176
Williams, Adrian, 70
Williams, Allan, 45, 46, 110, 114
Williams, Alon, 112
Williams, Barry, 57, 227, 228
Williams, Beth, 110
Williams, Bruce, 121
Williams, Cheryl, 173
Williams, Curt, 85, 95, 227, 228
Williams, Cynthia, 167
Williams, Diane Ferry, 133, 148
Williams, Edwyn, 129
Williams, Elizabeth, 111
Williams, Ellis E., 94
Williams, Hope, 232
Williams, Jacqueline, 56, 138
Williams, Jaston, 144
Williams, Jeff, 50
Williams, Jonathan, 69
Williams, K. R., 70, 100
Williams, Kathleen, 27
Williams, LB, 135
Williams, Lavinia, 232
Williams, Marshall, 64
Williams, Michael, 143
Williams, Olivia, 157
Williams, Ralph, 168
Williams, Robert N., 77, 91
Williams, Robin, 144
Williams, Sandra Lea, 168
Williams, Sarah McCord, 150
Williams, Tennessee, 9, 28, 124, 127, 136, 156, 165, 170, 171, 173, 176
Williams, Tom, 65, 70
Williams, Treat, 12, 81, 111, 228
Williams, Van, 228
Williamson, David, 162
Williamson, Laird, 121, 135, 160
Williamson, Nance, 153
Williamson, Ruth, 124, 154
Williford, Lou, 137
Williford, Steven, 166
Willis, Aileen, 183
Willis, Connie, 152
Willis, Gay, 107
Willis, John, 182
Willis, Jonathan, 53
Willis, Ray, 74
Willis, Sheila, 152
Willison, Walter, 18, 127, 227, 228
Wills, Ray, 227, 228
Willson, John, 167
Wilner, Lori, 80, 99, 227, 228
Wilson, Aileen, 105
Wilson, Andrea, 133
Wilson, August, 32, 119, 124, 130, 132, 135, 136, 144, 157, 159, 164, 168, 170
Wilson, Bernadette, 171
Wilson, Charlotte, 169
Wilson, Darlene, 40
Wilson, Erin Cressida, 76
Wilson, Gregory, 150
Wilson, James, 131
Wilson, John, 130
Wilson, Julie, 99, 227, 228
Wilson, K. C., 154
Wilson, Lanford, 121, 128, 156, 157
Wilson, Laurel Ann, 26, 32
Wilson, Lee, 15, 227, 228
Wilson, Mark, 129, 159
Wilson, Mary Louise, 90
Wilson, Mary, 39
Wilson, Michael, 151
Wilson, Rainn, 87
Wilson, Steve, 135
Wilson, Tena, 66
Wilson, Tristan, 167
Wilson, Tyrone, 30, 135, 227, 228
Wiltse, David, 146
Wimmer, Nephi Jay, 103
Winant, Bruce, 110, 160
Winborn, Brent, 101, 228
Wincott, Michael, 13
Wind Beneath My Wings, The, 61
Winde, Beatrice, 83, 227, 228
Winder, Julia, 176
Windsor, Edward, 31
Wineman, J. Christopher, 120
Wines, Halo, 124
Wing, Douglas, 159, 169
Wingert, Sally, 141
Winker, James R., 153, 162
Winkler, Henry, 170
Winkler, Mel, 131
Winkler, Richard, 132, 144
Winn, David, 53
Winn, Krystyna, 53
Winn-Austin, Robert, 148
Winsett, Betty, 58
Winslow, Pamela, 135
Winslow, Pippa, 121
Winson, Suzi, 227, 228
Winsor, William J., 177
Winston, Hattie, 84
Wint, Leslie, 60, 66
Winter's Tale, The, 70, 138
Winters, Andrew, 54
Winters, Michael, 118, 121
Winters, Roland, 232
Wintersteller, Lynne, 57, 228
Winther, Michael, 22, 165
Winton, Graham, 87, 97
Wipf, Alex, 169
Wise, John, 74
Wise, Scott, 43
Wise, Steve, 120
Wise, William, 63, 146, 228
Wiseman, Joseph, 82, 228
Wishengrad, Nina, 166
Wisnet, Charles, 57
Wisniski, Ron, 101, 177, 228
Wison, Nat, 144
Witch B, The, 80
Witherby, Eryka Hope, 152
Witherspoon, Dane, 135
Withey, Bruce H., 170
Witkowski, Marek, 55
Witt, Howard, 138
Wittenbauer, John, 97, 228
Witter, Terrence J., 35
Wittmaack, Kevin, 76
Wittrock, Peter, 175
Wittstein, Ed, 47
Wlcek, James, 56
Wodehouse, P. G., 139
Woelzl, Susan, 27
Woffington, Matthew, 157
Wofford, Darrell, 167
Wohl, David, 147
Wojcik, Jamie, 40
Wojcik, Randy, 40, 102
Wojda, John, 25, 228
Wojewodski, Robert, 153
Wojewodski, Stan, Jr., 129, 141

Wolf, Barbara, 55
Wolf, Catherine, 38
Wolf, Jeffrey, 73
Wolf, Jerry, 110
Wolf, Michael F., 147
Wolf, Peter, 102
Wolf, Teresa, 126
Wolf-Man, 83
Wolfe, George C., 91, 134
Wolfe, Holly, 147
Wolfe, Mindy, 29
Wolff, Art, 34
Wolfson, Victor, 232
Wolhandler, Joe, 84
Wolk, James, 57, 74, 152
Wolos-Fonteno, David, 50, 51
Wolpert, Harold E., 76
Wolshonak, Derek, 135
Wolsk, Gene, 71
Wolsky, Albert, 130
Womack, Cornell Charles, 172
Woman in Mind, 118, 149, 167
Womble, Terence, 48
Wonderful Life, 127
Wonderful Town, 56
Wondisford, Diane, 61, 69
Wondsel, Jeff, 6
Wondsei, Ted, 16
Wong, B. D., 97, 228
Wong, Carey, 174
Wong, Don, 92
Wong, Lily-Lee, 40
Wonsek, Paul, 78, 169
Wood, Bernice A., 169
Wood, Chris, 174
Wood, Donna, 144
Wood, Greg, 169
Wood, James, 127
Wood, Jody, 54
Wood, John, 176
Wood, Karen S., 131
Wood, Sally Ann, 137
Wood, Susan, 103
Wood, Tom, 142
Woodall, Oliver, 144, 154
Woodall, Ron, 70
Woodall, Sandra, 121
Woodard, Charlaine, 87, 227, 228
Woodbury, Richard, 138
Woodeson, Nicholas, 83, 146, 228
Woodhouse, Sam, 161
Woodman, Jeff, 119

Woodruff, Pamela, 54
Woods, Allie, Jr., 129, 135
Woods, Les, 152
Woods, Richard, 70, 170, 228
Woodson, John, 146
Woodward, Jeffrey, 142
Woodward, Neil, 160
Woodworth, E. Kevin, 9
Woody Guthrie's American Song, 151, 160
Woolard, David C., 19, 68, 83, 89, 94, 141, 144
Wooley, Jim, 73
Woolf, Steven, 159
Woolf, Virginia, 91
Wooliver, Jeffrey, 174
Woolsey, Wysandria, 31
Worcell, Michael, 127
Working One Acts '89, 51
Workman, Jacque, 127
Workman, Jason, 15, 181, 182, 183, 228
Workman, Shanelle, 228
World According to Me, The, 144
Worley, Jo Anne, 17, 228
Woronicz, Henry, 174
Woronoff, Rob, 141
Woronov, Mary, 147
Worth, Penny, 18, 228
Worthington, Conwell S., II, 108
Wortman, Bryna, 59, 66
Wowk, Michael, 157
Woyzeck, 142
Wrenn-Meleck, Peter, 156
Wright, Amy, 83, 228
Wright, Anne, 176
Wright, Anne-Marie, 22, 64
Wright, Christopher James, 127
Wright, Daniel, 102
Wright, David, 160
Wright, Doug, 100, 170
Wright, Elaine, 43
Wright, Garland, 141
Wright, Gary Landon, 169
Wright, Hamilton R., 118
Wright, Harland, 167
Wright, Jeffrey, 123, 124, 170
Wright, Kevin R., 107
Wright, Linda, 12
Wright, Margaret, 129
Wright, Mark, 130

Wright, Melissa Bess, 130
Wright, Miller, 16, 17, 20, 48, 49, 52, 53, 55, 62, 63, 69, 71, 77, 80, 95
Wright, R. Hamilton, 118, 160
Wright, Richard, 165
Wright, Robert, 18, 145
Wright, Samuel E., 170
Wright, Stephen, 106
Wright, Travis L., 114
Wright, Wendell, 160
Wright, William A., 232
Wright, Z., 6
Wrightson, Ann G., 119
Wrigley, Ben, 111
Wroe, Craig, 77, 97, 228
Wulf, Mary Kay, 153
Wulp, John, 143
Wuthrich, Terry, 56, 62
Wyche, Mimi, 61, 101, 135, 140, 228
Wyche, Ronald, 70
Wydner, Cathy, 154
Wydro, Ken, 64
Wyeth, Zoya, 37
Wyler, Gretchen, 121
Wylie, John, 18, 53, 228
Wylie, Teressa, 169
Wyman, Nicholas, 46, 228
Wyman, Stacey, 73
Wyn, Courtney, 112
Wynkoop, Christopher, 55, 168, 228
Wynters, Gail, 155
Xavier, Sherian, 60
Xenos, George, 68, 91
Xifo, Ray, 24, 227, 228
Xrossley, Steven, 53
Yabuku, Reuben, 136
Yacko, Robert, 119
Yaji, Shigeru, 136, 153, 162
Yajuro, Bando, 54
Yakim, Mina, 37
Yale Repertory Theatre, 170
Yamada, Sylvia, 108
Yamada, Taku, 12
Yamaguchi, Eiko, 92
Yamamoto, Ronald, 30, 227, 228
Yamauchi, Wakako, 92
Yanes, Dorothy, 124
Yaney, Denise, 76
Yankee Dawg You Die, 94
Yankee, Luke, 101

Yankovsky, Filip, 88
Yankowitz, Susan, 121
Yannon, Angela, 151
Yarborough, Michael, 47
Yarrow, Peter, 23
Yates, Lauren P., 95
Yawn, Gary, 167
Yeager, Barbara, 43
Year of the Baby, The, 54
Yeargan, Michael, 142, 146, 170
Yearsley, Alice, 17, 43
Yee, Kelvin Han, 121
Yee, Nelson, 117
Yekimov, Yuri, 88
Yellen, Sherman, 74
Yelshevskaya, Liya, 88
Yelusich, Andrew V., 135, 160
Yeoman, Jo Ann, 227, 228
Yergan, David, 128
Yerxa, Alison, 138
Yesso, Don, 147
Yesterdays: Billie Holiday Remembered, 59
Yeston, Maury, 18
Yezzi, David D., 72
Yglesias, Jose, 80
Yi, Harold, 108
Yionoulis, Evan, 83
Yoakam, Stephen, 141
Yohe, Christopher, 135
Yonekawa, Toshiko, 12
York Theatre Company, 101
York, David, 149
York, Mark, 74
York, Rachel, 24
York, Will, 171
York, Y, 159
Yorke, Steve, 176
Yoshii, Sumio, 54
Yoshizaki, Kenji, 12
You Can't Take It With You, 164, 171
You Die at Recess, 54
Youmans, James, 69, 83, 89, 90, 94
Youmans, William, 120, 168
Young Playwrights Festival 1989, 94
Young, Billy Joe, 48
Young, Bruce A., 73, 138
Young, Cavan, 176
Young, Connie Paraskevin, 39
Young, Linda Carol, 66
Young, Norma, 167

Young, Pamela J., 110
Young, Rex, 174
Young, Robert L., 63
Young, Susan, 55, 59, 67, 69
Young, Taylor, 25
Young, Victor A., 176
Young, William, 122, 125
Young-Lowe, Karyn, 148
Youngblood, Shay, 128
Younger, Amy, 64
Youngman, Henny, 39
Youngs, Hazel, 119
Yudman, Gary, 63
Yuill, Jimmy, 115, 131
Yulin, Harris, 98
Yushkevich, Michellee, 139
Yutaka Fresh J, 142
Yvon, Bernie, 133, 148
Yzraely, Yossi, 177
Zabinski, Gary M., 78
Zaccaro, Zeke, 65, 70
Zachos, Ellen, 58
Zadora, Pia, 39
Zadravec, Stefanie, 124
Zafer, Jerry, 132
Zager, Jim, 133, 148
Zagnit, Stuart, 74, 107, 227, 228
Zaguirre, Susan, 114
Zahn, Steven, 122
Zaitsev, Slava, 144
Zakharenko, Yevgeni, 54
Zakharov, Mark, 61
Zakharova, Alexandra, 61
Zakow, Andrew, 173
Zakowska, Donna, 69
Zaks, Jerry, 44, 81, 82, 98
Zale, Alexander, 129
Zalkind, Robert, 172
Zaloom, Joe, 228
Zaloom, Paul, 53, 99
Zambri, Catherine, 165
Zammit, Eddie, 153
Zamsky, Stuart, 169
Zandarski, Grace, 174
Zane, Arnie, 53
Zane, Lisa, 160
Zara Spook and Other Lures, 120
Zarish, Janet, 49, 227, 228
Zavani, Franco, 131
Zehr, Peggy, 127
Zehr, Robert D., 127
Zeidman, Dale, 27

Zeisler, Ellen, 39, 54
Zeisler, Mark, 120, 122
Zelenin, Yury, 61
Zeller, Mark, 106, 107
Zemach, Amielle, 80
Zemach, Benjamin, 80
Zemisov, Sergei, 120
Zemon, Tom, 45, 228
Zerbe, Anthony, 136
Zerkle, Greg, 110
Zhaivoronok, Boris, 54
Zheltkov, Oleg, 39
Ziawinski, Rupert, 128
Ziegler, Tom, 78
Ziel, Lloyd, 129
Zielinski, Scott, 50, 170
Ziemann, August, 145
Ziemba, Karen, 143, 144
Zien, Chip, 18, 228
Ziman, Richard, 143
Zimbler, Jason, 6
Zimmer, Frederick, 72
Zimmerman, Lee, 133
Zimmerman, Mark, 101, 228
Zimmerman, Zoey, 170
Zingales, Rosi, 57
Zinoman, Joy, 163
Zippel, David, 24
Zipper, Allen, 133
Zipprodt, Patricia, 11, 28, 43, 106, 107
Ziskie, Kurt, 93, 227, 228
Zito, Christine, 72
Zito, Ralph, 172
Zizka, Blanka, 144
Zolli, Robert, 164
Zollo, Frederick, 63
Zolotovitski, Igor, 120
Zommer, Ken, 172
Zoo of Tranquility, 145
Zooda, Benjamin, 68
Zora Neale Hurston, 75
Zorich, Louis, 168
Zoya's Apartment, 37
Zuber, Catherine, 122, 129, 131, 141, 142, 172
Zubiena, Jim, 110
Zucker, Grover, 52, 60
Zuckerman, Charlie, 11, 18
Zuckerman, Robert, 73, 77
Zulu, Thandi, 116
Zuse, Ted, 145
Zwahlen, Christian, 136
Zweifler, Liz, 150
Zweigbaum, Steven, 24